SHORTER FIFTH EDITION
WITH ESSAYS

LITERATURE
THE HUMAN EXPERIENCE

Good Country People

SHORTER FIFTH EDITION
WITH ESSAYS

LITERATURE
THE HUMAN EXPERIENCE

RICHARD ABCARIAN AND MARVIN KLOTZ, EDITORS

California State University, Northridge

ST. MARTIN'S PRESS

New York

Senior editor: Mark Gallaher
Managing editor: Patricia Mansfield
Project editor: Erica Appel
Associate editor: Laynie Browne
Production supervisor: Katherine Battiste
Cover design: Celine Brandes
Cover art: People by a Garden, 1922 by Fernand Léger. Oil on canvas, 25½" x 36". The
   Metropolitan Museum of Art, bequest of Mr. and Mrs. Allan D. Emil, in honor of William
   S. Lieberman, 1987.

Library of Congress Catalog Card Number: 90-71627
Copyright © 1992 by St. Martin's Press, Inc.
All rights reserved. No part of this book may be reproduced,
stored in a retrieval system, or transmitted by any form or
by any means, electronic, mechanical, photocopying, recording,
or otherwise, except as may be expressly permitted by the applicable
copyright statutes or in writing by the Publisher.
Manufactured in the United States of America.
6543
fedc

For information, write:
St. Martin's Press, Inc.
175 Fifth Avenue
New York, NY 10010

ISBN: 0-312-04832-7

ACKNOWLEDGMENTS

SAMUEL ALLEN: "A Moment Please" by Samuel Allen. © 1962 Samuel Allen. Reprinted by permission.
   THE ANTIOCH REVIEW: "Advice to My Son" by Peter Meinke. Copyright © 1965 by The Antioch Review, Inc. First appeared in the *Antioch Review,* Vol. XXV No. 3 (Fall, 1965). Reprinted by permission of the editors.
   DONALD W. BAKER: "Formal Application" from *Selected Poems,* 1960–1980 by Donald W. Baker, Barnwood Press, 1982. Reprinted by permission of the author.
   ELIZABETH BARNETT: "Sonnet XXX" of "Fatal Interview" by Edna St. Vincent Millay from *Collected Sonnets,* Revised and Expanded Edition, Harper & Row, 1988. Copyright © 1931, 1958 by Edna St. Vincent Millay and Norma Millay Ellis. Reprinted by permission of Elizabeth Barnett, Literary Executor.
   BEACON PRESS: "Rage" from *Notes of a Native Son* by James Baldwin. Copyright © 1955, renewed 1983, by James Baldwin. Reprinted by permission of Beacon Press.
   BROADSIDE PRESS: "Hard Rock Returns to Prison from the Hospital for the Criminal Insane" from *Poems from Prison* by Etheridge Knight. Reprinted by permission of Broadside Press.
   "Ballad of Birmingham" by Dudley Randall. Reprinted by permission of Broadside Press.
   EDWIN BROCK: "Five Ways to Kill a Man." Copyright 1963 by Edwin Brock. Reprinted by permission of the author.
   GWENDOLYN BROOKS: from "The Children of the Poor" and "Annie Allen" in *Blacks.* Copyright 1987. Publisher, The David Company, Chicago. Reprinted by permission of the author.
   CURTIS BROWN LTD.: "there is a girl inside" by Lucille Clifton from *two-headed woman,* 1980, University of Massachusetts. Reprinted by permission of Curtis Brown, Ltd. Copyright 1980 by Lucille Clifton.
   MICHAEL CLEARY: "At Mud Lake in the Morning" by Michael Cleary first appeared in *The Texas Review,* Vol. III, no. 2 (Fall 1982): 62–63. Copyright by Michael Cleary. Reprinted by permission of the author.
   COPPER CANYON PRESS: "Bitch" from *Mermaids in the Basement* by Carolyn Kizer. Reprinted by permission of Copper Canyon Press.

Acknowledgments and copyrights are continued at the back of the book on pages 917–922, which constitute an extension of the copyright page.

PREFACE

With this anthology, based on the fifth edition of *Literature: The Human Experience*, we continue our practice of making a shorter version available to instructors who may prefer a more compact volume. We have retained four plays, twenty-seven stories, and one hundred and thirty-eight poems from the longer edition. As in the shorter fourth edition, we have added essays in each thematic section for the many instructors who like to teach the essay as a literary form.

Our arrangement of the works into four thematic groups—Innocence and Experience, Conformity and Rebellion, Love and Hate, and The Presence of Death—provides opportunities to explore diverse attitudes toward those great themes of human experience. Each section is introduced by a short essay that embodies some general observations on the theme and by a series of questions that may stimulate student thinking, discussion, and writing. Within each thematic section, the works are grouped by genre—fiction, poetry, drama, and the essay—and arranged chronologically by author's birth date. Each work is dated to indicate its first appearance in a book; dates enclosed in parentheses indicate the date of composition or earliest appearance. We have not attempted to date traditional ballads.

Study questions and writing topics follow about half the stories and poems, all of the plays and essays, and each thematic section. These study questions are designed to help students discover the central issues in the works. The writing topics, related to the study questions that precede them, focus attention on thematic similarities among various works.

The first of several appendices, "Poems about Poetry," offers some verse meditations by poets on what poetry is and why it is written. These seven poems reveal diverse motives and aims, as well as the difficulty even poets have in describing exactly what it is they do.

The next four appendices, "Reading Fiction," "Reading Poetry," "Reading Drama," and "Reading Essays," acquaint students with some formal concepts and historical considerations basic to the study of literature. These are general introductions that instructors will no doubt augment as they discuss the formal sources of readers' pleasure or, for that matter, boredom.

A sixth appendix, "Three Critical Approaches: Formalist, Sociological, Psychoanalytic," analyzes one story and one poem from each of three critical perspectives to show students how different attitudes and expectations lead to different readings. Seeing that a variety of critical approaches may complement one another and, together, illuminate a work should free students from the notion that there is some "correct" view.

"Writing about Literature" outlines a number of writing strategies ranging from free writing in journals through composing explication, analysis, and comparison-and-contrast essays. The several samples of student writing provided will guide students in the preparation of their own papers. "Suggestions for Writing" offers instructors numerous focused assignments. This appendix concludes with a section illustrating manuscript mechanics based on the *MLA Handbook*.

New to this edition is "Biographical Notes on Authors," an appendix that provides students with information about some of the major events, biographical and literary, in the career of each author. We hope that these notes will not only satisfy students' natural curiosity about writers' lives but will also, from time to time, stimulate their interest enough to want to learn more.

A revised and expanded "Glossary of Literary Terms," with brief excerpts to illustrate the definitions, concludes the text.

The main thing, of course, continues to be the works themselves. We have preserved the major writers in the Western dramatic tradition—Sophocles, Shakespeare, Ibsen—and added Bruce Jay Friedman's *Steambath*, a modern tragicomic study of human absurdity in the face of death. Among the other new selections are stories by William Faulkner and Leslie Silko; poems by Louise Bogan, Michael Cleary, Lucille Clifton, Louise Glück, Anthony Hecht, Carolyn Kizer, Denise Levertov, Gerald Locklin, Audre Lorde, Peter Meinke, James Merrill, Sharon Olds, Dudley Randall, and Richard Wilbur; and essays by James Baldwin, Jane Goodall, Stephen King, Margaret Sanger, and Mark Twain.

ACKNOWLEDGMENTS

Among the many people who have helped us, we would especially like to acknowledge our colleague, Patricia Busillo. We would also like to thank George Crosland, Tahita Fulkerson, Susan Herman, Alice Rogers, Judith Stanford, Douglas M. Tedards, and Allyn Zuker for their careful reviews of the selections that appear in this shorter fifth edition.

Making a book is an enormously complex process, and we thank the many people at St. Martin's Press for their help. For painstaking care and labors much beyond the obligations of duty, we especially wish to thank Mark Gallaher, Kathy Battiste, Darby Downey, Judy Rundel, Erica Appel, and Laynie Browne.

Richard Abcarian
Marvin Klotz

CONTENTS

Innocence and Experience 2

Conformity and Rebellion   174

Love and Hate   388

POETRY   434

DRAMA   474

ESSAYS   568

The Presence of Death   584

Appendices 762

ALTERNATE TABLE OF CONTENTS
arranged by genre*

* Within each genre, authors are listed chronologically by date of birth.

POETRY

SHORTER FIFTH EDITION
WITH ESSAYS

LITERATURE
THE HUMAN EXPERIENCE

Innocence and Experience

The Garden of the Peaceful Arts (Allegory of the Court of Isabelle d'Este), c. 1530 by Lorenzo Costa

Humans strive to give order and meaning to their lives, to reduce the mystery and unpredictability that constantly threaten them. Life is infinitely more complex and surprising than we imagine, and the categories we establish to give it order and meaning are, for the most part, "momentary stays against confusion." At any time, the equilibrium of our lives, the comfortable image of ourselves and the world around us, may be disrupted suddenly by something new, forcing us into painful reevaluation. These disruptions create pain, anxiety and terror but also wisdom and awareness.

The works in this section deal generally with the movement of a central character from moral simplicities and certainties into a more complex and problematic world. Though these works frequently issue in awareness, even wisdom, their central figures rarely act decisively; the protagonist is more often a passive figure who learns the difference between the ideal world he or she imagines and the injurious real world. If the protagonist survives the ordeal (and he or she doesn't always, emotionally or physically), the protagonist will doubtless be a better human—better able to wrest some satisfaction from a bleak and threatening world. It is no accident that so many of the works here deal with the passage from childhood to adulthood, for childhood is a time of simplicities and certainties that must give way to the complexities and uncertainties of adult life.

Almost universally, innocence is associated with childhood and youth, as experience is with age. We teach the young about an ideal world, without explaining that it has not yet been and may never be achieved. As innocents, they are terribly vulnerable to falsehood, to intrusive sexuality, to the machinations of the wicked who, despite all the moral tales, often do triumph. We know, if we have not already forgotten what the innocence of childhood celebrates, that time and experience will disabuse them.

But the terms *innocence* and *experience* range widely in meaning, and that range is reflected here. Innocence may be defined almost biologically, as illustrated by the sexual innocence of the young boy in James Joyce's "Araby." Or it might be the source of political naïveté, as in George Orwell's "Shooting an Elephant." Innocence may be social—the innocence of the young couple in Joan Didion's "Marrying Absurd" or of Robin in Nathaniel Hawthorne's "My Kinsman, Major Molineux" or the young boy in Frank O'Connor's "My Oedipus Complex." Or innocence may be seen as the child's ignorance of his or her own mortality, as in Gerard Manley Hopkins's "Spring and Fall" and Dylan Thomas's "Fern Hill."

Innocence almost always reflects a foolishness based on ignorance; sometimes, as well, it is the occasion for arrogance. Hulga, in Flannery O'Connor's "Good

4

Country People," looks with disdain on the simple, uneducated folk of her home town. The events of the story prove her to be the victim of her own innocence. In such works as Sophocles' *Oedipus Rex* and Robert Browning's "My Last Duchess," one discovers the tragic and violent consequences of an innocence that is blind.

The contrast between what we thought in our youth and what we have come to know, painfully, as adults stands as an emblem of the passage from innocence to experience. Yet, all of us remain, to one degree or another, innocent throughout life, since we never, except with death, stop learning from experience. Looked at in this way, experience is the ceaseless assault life makes upon our innocence, moving us to a greater wisdom about ourselves and the world.

FOR THINKING AND WRITING

As you read the selections in this section, consider the following questions. You may want to write out your thoughts informally in a journal or notebook as a way of preparing to respond to the selections, or you may wish to make one of these questions the basis for a formal essay.

1. Innocence is often associated with childhood and responsibility with adulthood. Were you happier or more contented as a preteen than you are now? Why? Which particular aspects of your childhood do you remember with pleasure? Which with pain? Do you look forward to the future with pleasurable anticipation or with dread? Why?

2. Do you know any adults who seem to be innocents? On what do you base your judgment? Do you know any preteens who seem to be particularly "adult" in their behavior (beyond politeness and good manners—they may, for example, have to cope with severe family difficulties)? On what do you base your judgment?

3. Most of you have spent your lives under the authority of others, such as parents, teachers, and employers. How do you deal with authorities you resent? Do you look forward to exercising authority over others (your own children, your own students, employees under your supervision)? How will your experiences affect your behavior as an authority?

4. How does the growth from innocence to experience affect one's sexual behavior? Social behavior? Political behavior?

5

INNOCENCE
AND
EXPERIENCE

Woman and Child on a Beach, c. 1901 by Pablo Picasso

FICTION

My Kinsman, Major Molineux* 1832

NATHANIEL HAWTHORNE [1804–1864]

After the kings of Great Britain had assumed the right of appointing the colonial governors, the measures of the latter seldom met with the ready and generous approbation which had been paid to those of their predecessors, under the original charters. The people looked with most jealous scrutiny to the exercise of power which did not emanate from themselves, and they usually rewarded their rulers with slender gratitude for the compliances by which, in softening their instructions from beyond the sea, they had incurred the reprehension of those who gave them. The annals of Massachusetts Bay will inform us, that of six governors in the space of about forty years from the surrender of the old charter, under James II., two were imprisoned by a popular insurrection; a third, as Hutchinson inclines to believe, was driven from the province by the whizzing of a musket-ball; a fourth, in the opinion of the same historian, was hastened to his grave by continual bickerings with the House of Representatives; and the remaining two, as well as their successors, till the Revolution, were favored with few and brief intervals of peaceful sway. The inferior members of the court party, in times of high political excitement, led scarcely a more desirable life. These remarks may serve as a preface to the following adventures, which chanced upon a summer night, not far from a hundred years ago. The reader, in order to avoid a long and dry detail of colonial affairs, is requested to dispense with an account of the train of circumstances that had caused much temporary inflammation of the popular mind.

It was near nine o'clock of a moonlight evening, when a boat crossed the ferry with a single passenger, who had obtained his conveyance at that unusual hour by the promise of an extra fare. While he stood on the landing-place, searching in either pocket for the means of fulfilling his agreement, the ferryman lifted a lantern, by the aid of which, and the newly risen moon, he took a very accurate survey of the stranger's figure. He was a youth of barely eighteen years,

---

* This story is considered in detail in the essay "Three Critical Approaches: Formalist, Sociological, Psychoanalytic" at the end of the book.

evidently country-bred, and now, as it should seem, upon his first visit to town. He was clad in a coarse gray coat, well worn, but in excellent repair; his under garments were durably constructed of leather, and fitted tight to a pair of serviceable and well-shaped limbs; his stockings of blue yarn were the incontrovertible work of a mother or a sister; and on his head was a three-cornered hat, which in its better days had perhaps sheltered the graver brow of the lad's father. Under his left arm was a heavy cudgel formed of an oak sapling, and retaining a part of the hardened root; and his equipment was completed by a wallet, not so abundantly stocked as to incommode the vigorous shoulders on which it hung. Brown, curly hair, well-shaped features, and bright, cheerful eyes were nature's gifts, and worth all that art could have done for his adornment.

The youth, one of whose names was Robin, finally drew from his pocket the half of a little province bill of five shillings, which, in the depreciation in that sort of currency, did but satisfy the ferryman's demand, with the surplus of a sexangular piece of parchment, valued at three pence. He then walked forward into the town, with as light a step as if his day's journey had not already exceeded thirty miles, and with as eager an eye as if he were entering London city, instead of the little metropolis of a New England colony. Before Robin had proceeded far, however, it occurred to him that he knew not whither to direct his steps; so he paused, and looked up and down the narrow street, scrutinizing the small and mean wooden buildings that were scattered on either side.

"This low hovel cannot be my kinsman's dwelling," thought he, "nor yonder old house, where the moonlight enters at the broken casement; and truly I see none hereabouts that might be worthy of him. It would have been wise to inquire my way of the ferryman, and doubtless he would have gone with me, and earned a shilling from the Major for his pains. But the next man I meet will do as well."

He resumed his walk, and was glad to perceive that the street now became wider, and the houses more respectable in their appearance. He soon discerned a figure moving on moderately in advance, and hastened his steps to overtake it. As Robin drew nigh, he saw that the passenger was a man in years, with a full periwig of gray hair, a wide-skirted coat of dark cloth, and silk stockings rolled above his knees. He carried a long and polished cane, which he struck down perpendicularly before him at every step; and at regular intervals he uttered two successive hems, of a peculiarly solemn and sepulchral intonation. Having made these observations, Robin laid hold of the skirt of the old man's coat, just when the light from the open door and windows of a barber's shop fell upon both their figures.

"Good evening to you, honored sir," said he, making a low bow, and still retaining his hold of the skirt. "I pray you tell me whereabouts is the dwelling of my kinsman, Major Molineux."

The youth's question was uttered very loudly; and one of the barbers, whose razor was descending on a well-soaped chin, and another who was dressing a Ramillies wig, left their occupations, and came to the door. The citizen, in the mean time, turned a long-favored countenance upon Robin, and answered him in a tone of excessive anger and annoyance. His two sepulchral hems, however, broke into the very centre of his rebuke, with most singular effect, like a thought of the cold grave obtruding among wrathful passions.

"Let go my garment, fellow! I tell you, I know not the man you speak of. What! I have authority, I have—hem, hem—authority; and if this be the respect you show for your betters, your feet shall be brought acquainted with the stocks by daylight, tomorrow morning!"

Robin released the old man's skirt, and hastened away, pursued by an ill-mannered roar of laughter from the barber's shop. He was at first considerably surprised by the result of his question, but, being a shrewd youth, soon thought himself able to account for the mystery.

"This is some country representative," was his conclusion, "who has never seen the inside of my kinsman's door, and lacks the breeding to answer a stranger civilly. The man is old, or verily—I might be tempted to turn back and smite him on the nose. Ah, Robin, Robin! even the barber's boys laugh at you for choosing such a guide! You will be wiser in time, friend Robin."

He now became entangled in a succession of crooked and narrow streets, which crossed each other, and meandered at no great distance from the waterside. The smell of tar was obvious to his nostrils, the masts of vessels pierced the moonlight above the tops of the buildings, and the numerous signs, which Robin paused to read, informed him that he was near the centre of business. But the streets were empty, the shops were closed, and lights were visible only in the second stories of a few dwelling-houses. At length, on the corner of a narrow lane, through which he was passing, he beheld the broad countenance of a British hero swinging before the door of an inn, whence proceeded the voices of many guests. The casement of one of the lower windows was thrown back, and a very thin curtain permitted Robin to distinguish a party at supper, round a well-furnished table. The fragrance of the good cheer steamed forth into the outer air, and the youth could not fail to recollect that the last remnant of his travelling stock of provision had yielded to his morning appetite, and that noon had found and left him dinnerless.

"Oh, that a parchment three-penny might give me a right to sit down at yonder table!" said Robin, with a sigh. "But the Major will make me welcome to the best of his victuals; so I will even step boldly in, and inquire my way to his dwelling."

He entered the tavern, and was guided by the murmur of voices and the fumes of tobacco to the public-room. It was a long and low apartment, with oaken walls, grown dark in the continual smoke, and a floor which was thickly sanded, but of no immaculate purity. A number of persons—the larger part of whom appeared to be mariners, or in some way connected with the sea—occupied the wooden benches, or leather-bottomed chairs, conversing on various matters, and occasionally lending their attention to some topic of general interest. Three or four little groups were draining as many bowls of punch, which the West India trade had long since made a familiar drink in the colony. Others, who had the appearance of men who lived by regular and laborious handicraft, preferred the insulated bliss of an unshared potation, and became more taciturn under its influence. Nearly all, in short, evinced a predilection for the Good Creature in some of its various shapes, for this is a vice to which, as Fast Day sermons of a hundred years ago will testify, we have a long hereditary claim. The only guests to whom Robin's sympathies inclined him were two or three sheepish countrymen, who were using the inn somewhat after the fashion of a Turkish caravansary; they had gotten themselves into the darkest corner of the room, and heedless of the Nicotian atmosphere, were supping on the bread of their own ovens, and the bacon cured in their own chimney-smoke. But though Robin felt a sort of brotherhood with these strangers, his eyes were attracted from them to a person who stood near the door, holding whispered conversation with a group of ill-dressed associates. His features were separately striking almost to grotesqueness, and the whole face left a deep impression on the memory. The forehead bulged out into a double prominence, with a vale between; the nose came boldly forth in an irregular curve, and its bridge was of more than a finger's breadth; the eyebrows were deep and shaggy, and the eyes glowed beneath them like fire in a cave.

While Robin deliberated of whom to inquire respecting his kinsman's dwelling, he was accosted by the innkeeper, a little man in a stained white apron, who had come to pay his professional welcome to the stranger. Being in the second generation from a French Protestant, he seemed to have inherited the courtesy of his parent nation; but no variety of circumstances was ever known to change his voice from the one shrill note in which he now addressed Robin.

"From the country, I presume, sir?" said he, with a profound bow. "Beg leave to congratulate you on your arrival, and trust you intend a long stay with us. Fine town here, sir, beautiful buildings, and much that may interest a stranger. May I hope for the honor of your commands in respect to supper?"

"The man sees a family likeness! the rogue has guessed that I am related to the Major!" thought Robin, who had hitherto experienced little superfluous civility.

All eyes were now turned on the country lad, standing at the door, in his worn three-cornered hat, gray coat, leather breeches, and blue yarn stockings, leaning on an oaken cudgel, and bearing a wallet on his back.

Robin replied to the courteous innkeeper, with such an assumption of confidence as befitted the Major's relative. "My honest friend," he said, "I shall make it a point to patronize your house on some occasion, when"—here he could not help lowering his voice—"when I may have more than a parchment three-pence in my pocket. My present business," continued he, speaking with lofty confidence, "is merely to inquire my way to the dwelling of my kinsman, Major Molineux."

There was a sudden and general movement in the room, which Robin interpreted as expressing the eagerness of each individual to become his guide. But the innkeeper turned his eyes to a written paper on the wall, which he read, or seemed to read, with occasional recurrences to the young man's figure.

"What have we here?" said he, breaking his speech into little dry fragments.

"'Left the house of the subscriber, bounden servant, Hezekiah Mudge,—had on, when he went away, gray coat, leather breeches, master's third-best hat. One pound currency reward to whosoever shall lodge him in any jail of the providence.' Better trudge, boy; better trudge!"

Robin had begun to draw his hand towards the lighter end of the oak cudgel, but a strange hostility in every countenance induced him to relinquish his purpose of breaking the courteous innkeeper's head. As he turned to leave the room, he encountered a sneering glance from the bold-featured personage whom he had before noticed, and no sooner was he beyond the door, than he heard a general laugh, in which the innkeeper's voice might be distinguished, like the dropping of small stones into a kettle.

"Now, is it not strange," thought Robin, with his usual shrewdness,—"is it not strange that the confession of an empty pocket should outweigh the name of my kinsman, Major Molineux? Oh, if I had one of those grinning rascals in the woods, where I and my oak sapling grew up together, I would teach him that my arm is heavy though my purse be light!"

On turning the corner of the narrow lane, Robin found himself in a spacious street, with an unbroken line of lofty houses on each side, and a steepled building at the upper end, whence the ringing of a bell announced the hour of nine. The light of the moon, and the lamps from the numerous shop-windows, discovered people promenading on the pavement, and amongst them Robin had hoped to recognize his hitherto inscrutable relative. The result of his former inquiries made him unwilling to hazard another, in a scene of such publicity, and he determined to walk slowly and silently up the street, thrusting his face close to that of every elderly gentleman, in search of the Major's lineaments. In his progress, Robin encountered many gay and gallant figures. Embroidered garments of showy colors, enormous periwigs, gold-laced hats, and silver-hilted swords glided past him and dazzled his optics. Travelled youths, imitators of the European fine gentlemen of the period, trod jauntily along, half dancing to the fashionable tunes which they hummed, and making poor Robin ashamed of his quiet and natural gait. At length, after many pauses to examine the gorgeous display of goods in the shop-windows, and after suffering some rebukes for the impertinence of his scrutiny into people's faces, the Major's kinsman found himself near the steepled building, still unsuccessful in his search. As yet, however, he had seen only one side of the thronged street; so Robin crossed, and continued the same sort of inquisition down the opposite pavement, with stronger hopes than the philosopher seeking an honest man, but with no better fortune. He had arrived about midway towards the lower end, from which his course began, when he overheard the approach of some one who struck down a cane on the flag-stones at every step, uttering at regular intervals, two sepulchral hems.

"Mercy on us!" quoth Robin, recognizing the sound.

Turning a corner, which chanced to be close at his right hand, he hastened to pursue his researches in some other part of the town. His patience now was wearing low, and he seemed to feel more fatigue from his rambles since he crossed the ferry, than from his journey of several days on the other side. Hunger also pleaded loudly within him, and Robin began to balance the propriety of demanding, violently, and with lifted cudgel, the necessary guidance from the first solitary passenger whom he should meet. While a resolution to this effect was gaining strength, he entered a street of mean appearance, on either side of which a row of ill-built houses was straggling towards the harbor. The moonlight fell upon no passenger along the whole extent, but in the third domicile which Robin passed there was a half-opened door, and his keen glance detected a woman's garment within.

"My luck may be better here," said he to himself.

Accordingly, he approached the door, and beheld it shut closer as he did so; yet an open space remained, sufficing for the fair occupant to observe the stranger, without a corresponding display on her part. All that Robin could discern was a strip of scarlet petticoat, and the occasional sparkle of an eye, as if the moonbeams were trembling on some bright thing.

"Pretty mistress," for I may call her so with a good conscience, thought the shrewd youth, since I know nothing to the contrary,—"my sweet pretty mistress, will you be kind enough to tell me whereabouts I must seek the dwelling of my kinsman, Major Molineux?"

Robin's voice was plaintive and winning, and the female, seeing nothing to be shunned in the handsome country youth, thrust open the door, and came forth into the moonlight. She was a dainty little figure, with a white neck, round arms, and a slender waist, at the extremity of which her scarlet petticoat jutted out over a hoop, as if she were standing in a balloon. Moreover, her face was oval and pretty, her hair dark beneath the little cap, and her bright eyes possessed a sly freedom, which triumphed over those of Robin.

"Major Molineux dwells here," said this fair woman.

Now, her voice was the sweetest Robin had heard that night, yet he could not help doubting whether that sweet voice spoke Gospel truth. He looked up and down the mean street, and then surveyed the house before which they stood. It was a small, dark edifice of two stories, the second of which projected over the lower floor, and the front apartment had the aspect of a shop for petty commodities.

"Now, truly, I am in luck," replied Robin, cunningly, "and so indeed is my kinsman, the Major, in having so pretty a housekeeper. But I prithee trouble him to step to the door; I will deliver him a message from his friends in the country, and then go back to my lodgings at the inn."

"Nay, the Major has been abed this hour or more," said the lady of the scarlet petticoat; "and it would be to little purpose to disturb him to-night, seeing his evening draught was of the strongest. But he is a kind-hearted man, and it would be as much as my life's worth to let a kinsman of his turn away from the door. You are the good old gentleman's very picture, and I could swear that was his rainy-weather hat. Also he has garments very much resembling those leather small-clothes. But come in, I pray, for I bid you hearty welcome in his name."

So saying, the fair and hospitable dame took our hero by the hand; and the touch was light, and the force was gentleness, and though Robin read in her eyes what he did not hear in her words, yet the slender-waisted woman in the scarlet petticoat proved stronger than the athletic country youth. She had drawn his half-willing footsteps nearly to the threshold, when the opening of a door in the neighborhood startled the Major's housekeeper, and, leaving the Major's kinsman, she vanished speedily into her own domicile. A heavy yawn preceded the appearance of a man, who, like the Moonshine of Pyramus and Thisbe,[1] carried a lantern, needlessly aiding his sister luminary in the heavens. As he walked sleepily up the street, he turned his broad, dull face on Robin, and displayed a long staff, spiked at the end.

"Home, vagabond, home!" said the watchman, in accents that seemed to fall asleep as soon as they were uttered. "Home, or we'll set you in the stocks by peep of day!"

"This is the second hint of the kind," thought Robin. "I wish they would end my difficulties, by setting me there to-night."

Nevertheless, the youth felt an instinctive antipathy towards the guardian of midnight order, which at first prevented him from asking his usual question. But just when the man was about to vanish behind the corner, Robin resolved not to lose the opportunity, and shouted lustily after him,—

"I say, friend! will you guide me to the house of my kinsman, Major Molineux?"

The watchman made no reply, but turned the corner and was gone; yet Robin seemed to hear the sound of drowsy laughter stealing along the solitary street. At that moment, also, a pleasant titter saluted him from the open window above his head; he looked up, and caught the sparkle of a saucy eye; a round arm beckoned to him, and next he heard light footsteps descending the staircase within. But Robin, being of the household of a New England clergyman, was a good youth, as well as a shrewd one; so he resisted temptation, and fled away.

He now roamed desperately, and at random, through the town, almost ready to believe that a spell was on him, like that by which a wizard of his country had once kept three pursuers wandering, a whole winter night, within twenty paces of the cottage which they sought. The streets lay before him, strange and desolate, and the lights were extinguished in almost every house. Twice, however, little parties of men, among whom Robin distinguished individuals in outlandish attire, came hurrying along; but, though on both occasions, they paused to address him, such intercourse did not at all enlighten his perplexity. They did but utter a few words in some language of which Robin knew nothing, and perceiving his inability to answer, bestowed a curse upon him in plain English and hastened away. Finally, the lad determined to knock at the door of every mansion that might appear worthy to be occupied by his kinsman, trusting that perseverance would overcome the fatality that had hitherto thwarted him. Firm in this resolve, he was passing beneath the walls of a church, which

---

[1] In Shakespeare's A *Midsummer Night's Dream*, Act V, Scene 1, the moon is represented by a man carrying a lantern in the comic performance of the tragic love story of Pyramus and Thisbe.

formed the corner of two streets, when, as he turned into the shade of its steeple, he encountered a bulky stranger, muffled in a cloak. The man was proceeding with the speed of earnest business, but Robin planted himself full before him, holding the oak cudgel with both hands across his body as a bar to further passage.

"Halt, honest man, and answer me a question," said he, very resolutely. "Tell me, this instant, whereabouts is the dwelling of my kinsman, Major Molineux!"

"Keep your tongue between your teeth, fool, and let me pass!" said a deep, gruff voice, which Robin partly remembered. "Let me pass, or I'll strike you to the earth!"

"No, no, neighbor!" cried Robin, flourishing his cudgel, and then thrusting its larger end close to the man's muffled face. "No, no, I'm not the fool you take me for, nor do you pass till I have an answer to my question. Whereabouts is the dwelling of my kinsman, Major Molineux?"

The stranger, instead of attempting to force his passage, stepped back into the moonlight, unmuffled his face, and stared full into that of Robin.

"Watch here an hour, and Major Molineux will pass by," said he.

Robin gazed with dismay and astonishment on the unprecedented physiognomy of the speaker. The forehead with its double prominence, the broad hooked nose, the shaggy eyebrows, and fiery eyes were those which he had noticed at the inn, but the man's complexion had undergone a singular, or, more properly, a twofold change. One side of the face blazed an intense red, while the other was black as midnight, the division line being in the broad bridge of the nose; and a mouth which seemed to extend from ear to ear was black or red, in contrast to the color of the cheek. The effect was as if two individual devils, a fiend of fire and a fiend of darkness, had united themselves to form this infernal visage. The stranger grinned in Robin's face, muffled his party-colored features, and was out of sight in a moment.

"Strange things we travellers see!" ejaculated Robin.

He seated himself, however, upon the steps of the church-door, resolving to wait the appointed time for his kinsman. A few moments were consumed in philosophical speculations upon the species of man who had just left him; but having settled this point shrewdly, rationally, and satisfactorily, he was compelled to look elsewhere for his amusement. And first he threw his eyes along the street. It was of more respectable appearance than most of those into which he had wandered; and the moon, creating, like the imaginative power, a beautiful strangeness in familiar objects, gave something of romance to a scene that might not have possessed it in the light of day. The irregular and often quaint architecture of the houses, some of whose roofs were broken into numerous little peaks, while others ascended, steep and narrow, into a single point, and others again were square; the pure snow-white of some of their complexions, the aged darkness of others, and the thousand sparklings, reflected from bright substances in the walls of many; these matters engaged Robin's attention for a while, and then began to grow wearisome. Next he endeavored to define the forms of distant objects, starting away, with almost ghostly indistinctness, just as his eye appeared to grasp them; and finally he took a minute survey of an edifice which stood on the opposite side of the street, directly in front of the church door, where he was stationed. It was a large, square mansion, distinguished from its neighbors by a balcony, which rested on tall pillars, and by an elaborate Gothic window, communicating therewith.

"Perhaps this is the very house I have been seeking," thought Robin.

Then he strove to speed away the time, by listening to a murmur which swept continually along the street, yet was scarcely audible, except to an unaccustomed ear like his; it was a low, dull, dreamy sound, compounded of many noises, each of which was at too great a distance to be separately heard. Robin marvelled at this snore of a sleeping town, and marvelled more whenever its continuity was broken by now and then a distant shout, apparently loud where it originated. But altogether it was a sleep-inspiring sound, and, to shake off its drowsy influence, Robin arose, and climbed a window-frame, that he might view the interior of the church. There the moonbeams came trembling in, and fell down upon the deserted pews, and extended along the quiet aisles. A fainter yet more awful radiance was hovering around the pulpit, and one solitary ray had dared to rest upon the open page of the great Bible. Had nature, in that deep hour, become a worshipper in the house which man had builded? Or was that heavenly light the visible sanctity of the place,—visible because no earthly and impure feet were within the walls? The scene made Robin's heart shiver with a sensation of loneliness stronger than he had ever felt in the remotest depths of his native woods; so he turned away and sat down again before the door. There were graves around the church, and now an uneasy thought obtruded into Robin's breast. What if the object of his search, which had been so often and so strangely thwarted, were all the time mouldering in his shroud? What if his kinsman should glide through yonder gate, and nod and smile to him in dimly passing by?

"Oh that any breathing thing were here with me!" said Robin.

Recalling his thoughts from this uncomfortable track, he sent them over forest, hill, and stream, and attempted to imagine how that evening of ambiguity and weariness had been spent by his father's household. He pictured them assembled at the door, beneath the tree, the great old tree, which had been spared for its huge twisted trunk and venerable shade, when a thousand leafy brethren fell. There, at the going down of the summer sun, it was his father's custom to perform domestic worship, that the neighbors might come and join with him like brothers of the family, and that the wayfaring man might pause to drink at that fountain, and keep his heart pure by freshening the memory of home. Robin distinguished the seat of every individual of the little audience; he saw the good man in the midst, holding the Scriptures in the golden light that fell from the western clouds; he beheld him close the book and all rise up to pray. He heard the old thanksgivings for daily mercies, the old supplications for their continuance, to which he had so often listened in weariness, but which were now among his dear remembrances. He perceived the slight inequality of his father's voice when he came to speak of the absent one; he noted how his mother turned her face to the broad and knotted trunk; how his elder brother scorned, because the beard was rough upon his upper lip, to permit his features to be moved; how the younger sister drew down a low hanging branch before her eyes; and how the little one of all, whose sports had hitherto broken the decorum of the scene, understood the prayer for her playmate, and burst into clamorous grief. Then he saw them go in at the door; and when Robin would have entered also, the latch tinkled into its place, and he was excluded from his home.

"Am I here, or there?" cried Robin, starting; for all at once, when his thoughts had become visible and audible in a dream, the long, wide, solitary street shone out before him.

He aroused himself, and endeavored to fix his attention steadily upon the large edifice which he had surveyed before. But still his mind kept vibrating between fancy and reality; by turns, the pillars of the balcony lengthened into the tall, bare stems of pines, dwindled down to human figures, settled again into their true shape and size, and then commenced a new succession of changes. For a single moment, when he deemed himself awake, he could have sworn that a visage—one which he seemed to remember, yet could not absolutely name as his kinsman's—was looking towards him from the Gothic window. A deeper sleep wrestled with and nearly overcame him, but fled at the sound of footsteps along the opposite pavement. Robin rubbed his eyes, discerned a man passing at the foot of the balcony, and addressed him in a loud, peevish, and lamentable cry.

"Hallo, friend! must I wait here all night for my kinsman, Major Molineux?"

The sleeping echoes awoke, and answered the voice; and the passenger, barely able to discern a figure sitting in the oblique shade of the steeple, traversed the street to obtain a nearer view. He was himself a gentleman in his prime, of open, intelligent, cheerful, and altogether prepossessing countenance. Perceiving a country youth, apparently homeless and without friends, he accosted him in a tone of real kindness, which had become strange to Robin's ears.

"Well, my good lad, why are you sitting here?" inquired he. "Can I be of service to you in any way?"

"I am afraid not, sir," replied Robin, despondingly; "yet I shall take it kindly, if you'll answer me a single question. I've been searching, half the night, for one Major Molineux; now, sir, is there really such a person in these parts, or am I dreaming?"

"Major Molineux! The name is not altogether strange to me," said the gentleman, smiling. "Have you any objection to telling me the nature of your business with him?"

Then Robin briefly related that his father was a clergyman, settled on a small salary, at a long distance back in the country, and that he and Major Molineux were brothers' children. The Major, having inherited riches, and acquired civil and military rank, had visited his cousin, in great pomp, a year or two before; had manifested much interest in Robin and an elder brother, and, being childless himself, had thrown out hints respecting the future establishment of one of them in life. The elder brother was destined to succeed to the farm which his father cultivated in the interval of sacred duties; it was therefore determined that Robin should profit by his kinsman's generous intentions, especially as he seemed to be rather the favorite, and was thought to possess other necessary endowments.

"For I have the name of being a shrewd youth," observed Robin, in this part of his story.

"I doubt not you deserve it," replied his new friend, good-naturedly; "but pray proceed."

"Well, sir, being nearly eighteen years old, and well grown, as you see," continued Robin, drawing himself up to his full height, "I thought it high time to begin in the world. So my mother and sister put me in handsome trim, and my father gave me half the remnant of his last year's salary, and five days ago I started for this place, to pay the Major a visit. But, would you believe it, sir! I crossed the ferry a little after dark, and have yet found nobody that would show me the way to his dwelling; only, an hour or two since, I was told to wait here, and Major Molineux would pass by."

"Can you describe the man who told you this?" inquired the gentleman.

"Oh, he was a very ill-favored fellow, sir," replied Robin, "with two great bumps on his forehead, a hook nose, fiery eyes; and, what struck me as the strangest, his face was of two different colors. Do you happen to know such a man, sir?"

"Not intimately," answered the stranger, "but I chanced to meet him a little time previous to your stopping me. I believe you may trust his word, and that the Major will very shortly pass through this street. In the mean time, as I have a singular curiosity to witness your meeting, I will sit down here upon the steps and bear you company."

He seated himself accordingly, and soon engaged his companion in animated discourse. It was but of brief continuance, however, for a noise of shouting, which had long been remotely audible, drew so much nearer that Robin inquired its cause.

"What may be the meaning of this uproar?" asked he. "Truly, if your town be always as noisy, I shall find little sleep while I am an inhabitant."

"Why, indeed, friend Robin, there do appear to be three or four riotous fellows abroad to-night," replied the gentleman. "You must not expect all the stillness of your native woods here in our streets. But the watch will shortly be at the heels of these lads and"—

"Ay, and set them in the stocks by peep of day," interrupted Robin, recollecting his own encounter with the drowsy lantern-bearer. "But, dear sir, if I may trust my ears, an army of watchmen would never make head against such a multitude of rioters. There were at least a thousand voices went up to make that one shout."

"May not a man have several voices, Robin, as well as two complexions?" said his friend.

"Perhaps a man may; but Heaven forbid that a woman should!" responded the shrewd youth, thinking of the seductive tones of the Major's housekeeper.

The sounds of a trumpet in some neighboring street now became so evident and continual, that Robin's curiosity was strongly excited. In addition to the shouts, he heard frequent bursts from many instruments of discord, and a wild and confused laughter filled up the intervals. Robin rose from the steps, and looked wistfully towards a point whither people seemed to be hastening.

"Surely some prodigious merry-making is going on," exclaimed he. "I have laughed very little since I left home, sir, and should be sorry to lose an opportunity. Shall we step round the corner by that darkish house, and take our share of the fun?"

"Sit down again, sit down, good Robin," replied the gentleman, laying his hand on the skirt of the gray coat. "You forget that we must wait here for your kinsman; and there is reason to believe that he will pass by, in the course of a very few moments."

The near approach of the uproar had now disturbed the neighborhood; windows flew open on all sides; and many heads, in the attire of the pillow, and confused by sleep suddenly broken, were protruded to the gaze of whoever had leisure to observe them. Eager voices hailed each other from house to house, all demanding the explanation, which not a soul could give. Half-dressed men hurried towards the unknown commotion, stumbling as they went over the stone steps that thrust themselves into the narrow footwalk. The shouts, the laughter, and the tuneless bray, the antipodes of music, came onwards with increasing din, till scattered individuals, and then denser bodies, began to appear round a corner at the distance of a hundred yards.

"Will you recognize your kinsman, if he passes in this crowd?" inquired the gentleman.

"Indeed, I can't warrant it, sir; but I'll take my stand here, and keep a bright lookout," answered Robin, descending to the outer edge of the pavement.

A mighty stream of people now emptied into the street, and came rolling slowly towards the church. A single horseman wheeled the corner in the midst of them, and close behind him came a band of fearful wind-instruments, sending forth a fresher discord now that no intervening buildings kept it from the ear. Then a redder light disturbed the moonbeams, and a dense multitude of torches shone along the street, concealing, by their glare, whatever object they illuminated. The single horseman, clad in a military dress, and bearing a drawn sword, rode onward as the leader, and, by his fierce and variegated countenance, appeared like war personified; the red of one cheek was an emblem of fire and sword; the blackness of the other betokened the mourning that attends them. In his train were wild figures in the Indian dress, and many fantastic shapes without a model, giving the whole march a visionary air, as if a dream had broken forth from some feverish brain, and were sweeping visibly through the midnight streets. A mass of people, inactive, except as applauding spectators, hemmed the procession in; and several women ran along the sidewalk, piercing the confusion of heavier sounds with their shrill voices of mirth or terror.

"The double-faced fellow has his eye upon me," muttered Robin, with an indefinite but an uncomfortable idea that he was himself to bear a part in the pageantry.

The leader turned himself in the saddle, and fixed his glance full upon the country youth, as the steed went slowly by. When Robin had freed his eyes from those fiery ones, the musicians were passing before him, and the torches were close at hand; but the unsteady brightness of the latter formed a veil which he could not penetrate. The rattling of wheels over the stones sometimes found its way to his ear, and confused traces of a human form appeared at intervals, and then melted into the vivid light. A moment more, and the leader thundered a command to halt: the trumpets vomited a horrid breath, and then held their peace; the shouts and laughter of the people died away, and there remained only a universal hum, allied to silence. Right before Robin's eyes was an uncovered cart. There the torches blazed the brightest, there the moon shone out like day, and there, in tar-and-feathery dignity, sat his kinsman, Major Molineux!

He was an elderly man, of large and majestic person, and strong, square features betokening a steady soul; but steady as it was, his enemies had found means to shake it. His face was pale as death, and far more ghastly; the broad forehead was contracted in his agony, so that his eyebrows formed one grizzled line; his eyes were red and wild, and the foam hung white upon his quivering lip. His whole frame was agitated by a quick and continual tremor, which his pride strove to quell, even in those circumstances of overwhelming humiliation. But perhaps the bitterest pang of all was when his eyes met those of Robin; for he evidently knew him on the instant, as the youth stood witnessing the foul disgrace of a head grown gray in honor. They stared at each other in silence, and Robin's knees shook, and his hair bristled, with a mixture of pity and terror. Soon, however, a bewildering excitement began to seize upon his mind; the preceding adventures of the night, the unexpected appearance of the crowd, the torches, the confused din and the hush that followed, the spectre of his kinsman reviled by that great multitude,—all this, and, more than all, a perception of tremendous ridicule in the whole scene, affected him with a sort of mental inebriety. At that moment a voice of sluggish merriment saluted Robin's ears; he turned instinctively, and just behind the corner of the church stood the lantern-bearer, rubbing his eyes, and drowsily enjoying the lad's amazement. Then he heard a peal of laughter like the ringing of silvery bells; a woman twitched his arm, a saucy eye met his, and he saw the lady of the scarlet petticoat. A sharp, dry cachinnation appealed to his memory, and standing on tiptoe in the crowd, with his white apron over his head, he beheld the courteous little innkeeper. And lastly, there sailed over the heads of the multitude a great, broad laugh, broken in the midst by two sepulchral hems; thus, "Haw, haw, haw,—hem, hem,—haw, haw, haw, haw!"

The sound proceeded from the balcony of the opposite edifice, and thither Robin turned his eyes. In front of the Gothic window stood the old citizen, wrapped in a wide gown, his gray periwig exchanged for a nightcap, which was thrust back from his forehead, and his silk stockings hanging about his legs. He supported himself on his polished cane in a fit of convulsive merriment, which manifested itself on his solemn old features like a funny inscription on a tombstone. Then Robin seemed to hear the voices of the barbers, of the guests of the inn, and of all who had made sport of him that night. The contagion was spreading among the multitude, when all at once, it seized upon Robin, and he sent forth a shout of laughter that echoed through the street,—every man shook his sides, every man emptied his lungs, but Robin's shout was the loudest there. The cloud-spirits peeped from their silvery islands, as the congregated mirth went roaring up the sky! The Man in the Moon heard the far bellow. "Oho," quoth he, "the old earth is frolicsome to-night!"

When there was a momentary calm in that tempestuous sea of sound, the leader gave the sign, the procession resumed its march. On they went, like fiends that throng in mockery around some dead potentate, mighty no more, but majestic still in his agony. On they went, in counterfeited pomp, in senseless uproar, in frenzied merriment, trampling all on an old man's heart. On swept the tumult, and left a silent street behind.

"Well, Robin, are you dreaming?" inquired the gentleman, laying his hand on the youth's shoulder.

Robin started, and withdrew his arm from the stone post to which he had instinctively clung, as the living stream rolled by him. His cheek was somewhat pale, and his eye not quite as lively as in the earlier part of the evening.

"Will you be kind enough to show me the way to the ferry?" said he, after a moment's pause.

"You have, then, adopted a new subject of inquiry?" observed his companion, with a smile.

"Why, yes, sir," replied Robin, rather dryly. "Thanks to you, and to my other friends, I have at last met my kinsman, and he will scarce desire to see my face again. I begin to grow weary of a town life, sir. Will you show me the way to the ferry?"

"No, my good friend Robin,—not to-night, at least," said the gentleman. "Some few days hence, if you wish it, I will speed you on your journey. Or, if you prefer to remain with us, perhaps, as you are a shrewd youth, you may rise in the world without the help of your kinsman, Major Molineux."

QUESTIONS
1. Explain the function of the opening paragraph. **2.** Does Robin change as a result of his experiences? **3.** What evidence does the story provide to explain the hostility of the townspeople toward Major Molineux? **4.** A few moments before Robin witnesses the procession that surges forward with his tarred and feathered kinsman, his thoughts turn to his family, and he tries to imagine how they have spent the same night. What function does this daydream serve? **5.** Discuss Hawthorne's use of light and darkness.

The Bride Comes to Yellow Sky

1898

STEPHEN CRANE [1871–1900]

I

The great Pullman was whirling onward with such dignity of motion that a glance from the window seemed simply to prove that the plains of Texas were pouring eastward. Vast flats of green grass, dull-hued space of mesquit and cactus, little groups of frame houses, woods of light and tender trees, all were sweeping into the east, sweeping over the horizon, a precipice.

A newly married pair had boarded this coach at San Antonio. The man's face was reddened from many days in the wind and sun, and a direct result of his new black clothes was that his brick-coloured hands were constantly performing in a most conscious fashion. From time to time he looked down respectfully at his attire. He sat with a hand on each knee, like a man waiting in a barber's shop. The glances he devoted to other passengers were furtive and shy.

The bride was not pretty, nor was she very young. She wore a dress of blue cashmere, with small reservations of velvet here and there, and with steel buttons abounding. She continually twisted her head to regard her puff sleeves, very stiff, straight, and high. They embarrassed her. It was quite apparent that she had cooked, and that she expected to cook, dutifully. The blushes caused by the careless scrutiny of some passengers as she had entered the car were strange to see upon this plain, under-class countenance, which was drawn in placid, almost emotionless lines.

They were evidently very happy. "Ever been in a parlour-car before?" he asked, smiling with delight.

"No," she answered; "I never was. It's fine, ain't it?"

"Great! And then after a while we'll go forward to the diner, and get a big lay-out. Finest meal in the world. Charge a dollar."

"Oh, do they?" cried the bride. "Charge a dollar? Why, that's too much—for us—ain't it, Jack?"

"Not this trip, anyhow," he answered bravely. "We're going to go the whole thing."

Later he explained to her about the trains. "You see, it's a thousand miles from one end of Texas to the other; and this train runs right across it, and never stops but four times." He had the pride of an owner. He pointed out to her the dazzling fittings of the coach; and in truth her eyes opened wider as she contemplated the sea-green figured velvet, the shining brass, silver, and glass, the

21

wood that gleamed as darkly brilliant as the surface of a pool of oil. At one end a bronze figure sturdily held a support for a separated chamber, and at convenient places on the ceiling were frescos in olive and silver.

To the minds of the pair, their surroundings reflected the glory of their marriage that morning in San Antonio; this was the environment of their new estate; and the man's face in particular beamed with an elation that made him appear ridiculous to the negro porter. This individual at times surveyed them from afar with an amused and superior grin. On other occasions he bullied them with skill in ways that did not make it exactly plain to them that they were being bullied. He subtly used all the manners of the most unconquerable kind of snobbery. He oppressed them; but of this oppression they had small knowledge, and they speedily forgot that infrequently a number of travellers covered them with stares of derisive enjoyment. Historically there was supposed to be something infinitely humorous in their situation.

"We are due in Yellow Sky at 3:42," he said, looking tenderly into her eyes.

"Oh, are we?" she said, as if she had not been aware of it. To evince surprise at her husband's statement was part of her wifely amiability. She took from a pocket a little silver watch; and as she held it before her, and stared at it with a frown of attention, the new husband's face shone.

"I bought it in San Anton' from a friend of mine," he told her gleefully.

"It's seventeen minutes past twelve," she said, looking up at him with a kind of shy and clumsy coquetry. A passenger, noting this play, grew excessively sardonic, and winked at himself in one of the numerous mirrors.

At last they went to the dining-car. Two rows of negro waiters, in glowing white suits, surveyed their entrance with the interest, and also the equanimity, of men who had been forewarned. The pair fell to the lot of a waiter who happened to feel pleasure in steering them through their meal. He viewed them with the manner of a fatherly pilot, his countenance radiant with benevolence. The patronage, entwined with the ordinary deference, was not plain to them. And yet, as they returned to their coach, they showed in their faces a sense of escape.

To the left, miles down a long purple slope, was a little ribbon of mist where moved the keening Rio Grande. The train was approaching it at an angle, and the apex was Yellow Sky. Presently it was apparent that, as the distance from Yellow Sky grew shorter, the husband became commensurately restless. His brick-red hands were more insistent in their prominence. Occasionally he was even rather absent-minded and far-away when the bride leaned forward and addressed him.

As a matter of truth, Jack Potter was beginning to find the shadow of a deed weigh upon him like a leaden slab. He, the town marshal of Yellow Sky, a man known, liked, and feared in his corner, a prominent person, had gone to San Antonio to meet a girl he believed he loved, and there, after the usual prayers, had actually induced her to marry him, without consulting Yellow Sky for any part of the transaction. He was now bringing his bride before an innocent and unsuspecting community.

Of course people in Yellow Sky married as it pleased them, in accordance with a general custom; but such was Potter's thought of his duty to his friends, or of their idea of his duty, or of an unspoken form which does not control men in these matters, that he felt he was heinous. He had committed an extraordinary crime. Face to face with this girl in San Antonio, and spurred by his sharp impulse, he had gone headlong over all the social hedges. At San Antonio he was like a man hidden in the dark. A knife to sever any friendly duty, any form, was easy to his hand in that remote city. But the hour of Yellow Sky—the hour of daylight—was approaching.

He knew full well that his marriage was an important thing to his town. It could only be exceeded by the burning of the new hotel. His friends could not forgive him. Frequently he had reflected on the advisability of telling them by telegraph, but a new cowardice had been upon him. He feared to do it. And now the train was hurrying him toward a scene of amazement, glee, and reproach. He glanced out of the window at the line of haze swinging slowly in toward the train.

Yellow Sky had a kind of brass band, which played painfully, to the delight of the populace. He laughed without heart as he thought of it. If the citizens could dream of his prospective arrival with his bride, they would parade the band at the station and escort them, amid cheers and laughing congratulations, to his adobe home.

He resolved that he would use all the devices of speed and plainscraft in making the journey from the station to his house. Once within that safe citadel, he could issue some sort of vocal bulletin, and then not go among the citizens until they had time to wear off a little of their enthusiasm.

The bride looked anxiously at him. "What's worrying you, Jack?"

He laughed again. "I'm not worrying, girl; I'm only thinking of Yellow Sky."

She flushed in comprehension.

A sense of mutual guilt invaded their minds and developed a finer tenderness. They looked at each other with eyes softly aglow. But Potter often laughed the same nervous laugh; the flush upon the bride's face seemed quite permanent.

The traitor to the feelings of Yellow Sky narrowly watched the speeding landscape. "We're nearly there," he said.

Presently the porter came and announced the proximity of Potter's home. He held a brush in his hand, and, with all his airy superiority gone, he brushed Potter's new clothes as the latter slowly turned this way and that way. Potter fumbled out a coin and gave it to the porter, as he had seen others do. It was a heavy and muscle-bound business, as that of a man shoeing his first horse.

The porter took their bag, and as the train began to slow they moved forward to the hooded platform of the car. Presently the two engines and their string of coaches rushed into the station of Yellow Sky.

"They have to take water here," said Potter, from a constricted throat and in mournful cadence, as one announcing death. Before the train stopped his eye had swept the length of the platform, and he was glad and astonished to see there was none upon it but the station-agent, who, with a slightly hurried and anxious air, was walking toward the water-tanks. When the train had halted, the porter alighted first, and placed in position a little temporary step.

"Come on, girl," said Potter, hoarsely. As he helped her down they each laughed on a false note. He took the bag from the negro, and bade his wife cling to his arm. As they slunk rapidly away, his hang-dog glance perceived that they were unloading the two trunks, and also that the station-agent, far ahead near the baggage-car, had turned and was running toward him, making gestures. He laughed, and groaned as he laughed, when he noted the first effect of his marital bliss upon Yellow Sky. He gripped his wife's arm firmly to his side, and they fled. Behind them the porter stood, chuckling fatuously.

II

The California express on the Southern Railway was due at Yellow Sky in twenty-one minutes. There were six men at the bar of the Weary Gentleman saloon. One was a drummer who talked a great deal and rapidly; three were Texans who did not care to talk at that time; and two were Mexican sheep-herders, who did not talk as a general practice in the Weary Gentleman saloon. The barkeeper's dog lay on the board walk that crossed in front of the door. His head was on his paws, and he glanced drowsily here and there with the constant vigilance of a dog that is kicked on occasion. Across the sandy street were some vivid green grass-plots, so wonderful in appearance, amid the sands that burned near them in a blazing sun, that they caused a doubt in the mind. They exactly resembled the grass mats used to represent lawns on the stage. At the cooler end of the railway station, a man without a coat sat in a tilted chair and smoked his pipe. The fresh-cut bank of the Rio Grande circled near the town, and there could be seen beyond it a great plum-coloured plain of mesquit.

Save for the busy drummer and his companions in the saloon, Yellow Sky was dozing. The new-comer leaned gracefully upon the bar, and recited many tales with the confidence of a bard who has come upon a new field.

"—and at the moment that the old man fell downstairs with the bureau in his arms, the old woman was coming up with two scuttles of coal, and of course—"

The drummer's tale was interrupted by a young man who suddenly appeared in the open door. He cried: "Scratchy Wilson's drunk, and has turned loose with both hands." The two Mexicans at once set down their glasses and faded out of the rear entrance of the saloon.

The drummer, innocent and jocular, answered: "All right, old man. S'pose he has? Come in and have a drink, anyhow."

But the information had made such an obvious cleft in every skull in the room that the drummer was obliged to see its importance. All had become instantly solemn. "Say," said he, mystified, "what is this?" His three companions made the introductory gesture of eloquent speech; but the young man at the door forestalled them.

"It means, my friend," he answered, as he came into the saloon, "that for the next two hours this town won't be a health resort."

The barkeeper went to the door, and locked and barred it; reaching out of the window, he pulled in heavy wooden shutters, and barred them. Immediately a solemn chapel-like gloom was upon the place. The drummer was looking from one to another.

"But say," he cried, "what is this, anyhow? You don't mean there is going to be a gun-fight?"

"Don't know whether there'll be a fight or not," answered one man, grimly; "but there'll be some shootin'—some good shootin'."

The young man who had warned them waved his hand. "Oh, there'll be a fight fast enough, if any one wants it. Anybody can get a fight out there in the street. There's a fight just waiting."

The drummer seemed to be swayed between the interest of a foreigner and a perception of personal danger.

"What did you say his name was?" he asked.

"Scratchy Wilson," they answered in chorus.

"And will he kill anybody? What are you going to do? Does this happen often? Does he rampage around like this once a week or so? Can he break in that door?"

"No; he can't break down that door," replied the barkeeper. "He's tried it three times. But when he comes you'd better lay down on the floor, stranger. He's dead sure to shoot at it, and a bullet may come through."

Thereafter the drummer kept a strict eye upon the door. The time had not yet been called for him to hug the floor, but, as a minor precaution, he sidled near to the wall. "Will he kill anybody?" he said again.

The men laughed low and scornfully at the question.

"He's out to shoot, and he's out for trouble. Don't see any good in experimentin' with him."

"But what do you do in a case like this? What do you do?"

A man responded: "Why, he and Jack Potter—"

"But," in chorus the other men interrupted, "Jack Potter's in San Anton'."

"Well, who is he? What's he got to do with it?"

"Oh, he's the town marshal. He goes out and fights Scratchy when he gets on one of these tears."

"Wow!" said the drummer, mopping his brow. "Nice job he's got."

The voices had toned away to mere whisperings. The drummer wished to ask further questions, which were born of an increasing anxiety and bewilderment; but when he attempted them, the men merely looked at him in irritation and motioned him to remain silent. A tense waiting hush was upon them. In the deep shadows of the room their eyes shone as they listened for sounds from the street. One man made three gestures at the barkeeper; and the latter, moving like a ghost, handed him a glass and a bottle. The man poured a full glass of whisky, and set down the bottle noiselessly. He gulped the whisky in a swallow, and turned again toward the door in immovable silence. The drummer saw that the barkeeper, without a sound, had taken a Winchester from beneath the bar. Later he saw this individual beckoning to him, so he tiptoed across the room.

"You better come with me back of the bar."

"No, thanks," said the drummer, perspiring; "I'd rather be where I can make a break for the back door."

Whereupon the man of bottles made a kindly but peremptory gesture. The drummer obeyed it, and, finding himself seated on a box with his head below the level of the bar, balm was laid upon his soul at sight of various zinc and copper fittings that bore a resemblance to armour-plate. The barkeeper took a seat comfortably upon an adjacent box.

"You see," he whispered, "this here Scratchy Wilson is a wonder with a gun—a perfect wonder; and when he goes on the war-trail, we hunt our holes—naturally. He's about the last one of the old gang that used to hang out along the river here. He's a terror when he's drunk. When he's sober he's all right—kind of simple—wouldn't hurt a fly—nicest fellow in town. But when he's drunk—whoo!"

There were periods of stillness. "I wish Jack Potter was back from San Anton'," said the barkeeper. "He shot Wilson up once—in the leg—and he would sail in and pull out the kinks in this thing."

Presently they heard from a distance the sound of a shot, followed by three wild yowls. It instantly removed a bond from the men in the darkened saloon. There was a shuffling of feet. They looked at each other. "Here he comes," they said.

III

A man in a maroon-coloured flannel shirt, which had been purchased for purposes of decoration, and made principally by some Jewish women on the East Side of New York, rounded a corner and walked into the middle of the main street of Yellow Sky. In either hand the man held a long, heavy, blue-black revolver. Often he yelled, and these cries rang through a semblance of a deserted village, shrilly flying over the roofs in a volume that seemed to have no relation to the ordinary vocal strength of a man. It was as if the surrounding stillness formed the arch of a tomb over him. These cries of ferocious challenge rang against walls of silence. And his boots had red tops with gilded imprints, of the kind beloved in winter by little sledding boys on the hillsides of New England.

The man's face flamed in a rage begot of whisky. His eyes, rolling, and yet keen for ambush, hunted the still doorways and windows. He walked with the creeping movement of the midnight cat. As it occurred to him, he roared menacing information. The long revolvers in his hands were as easy as straws; they were moved with an electric swiftness. The little fingers of each hand played sometimes in a musician's way. Plain from the low collar of the shirt, the cords of his neck straightened and sank, straightened and sank, as passion moved him. The only sounds were his terrible invitations. The calm adobes preserved their demeanor at the passing of this small thing in the middle of the street.

There was no offer of fight—no offer of fight. The man called to the sky. There were no attractions. He bellowed and fumed and swayed his revolvers here and everywhere.

The dog of the barkeeper of the Weary Gentleman saloon had not appreciated the advance of events. He yet lay dozing in front of his master's door. At sight of the dog, the man paused and raised his revolver humorously. At sight of the man, the dog sprang up and walked diagonally away, with a sullen head, and growling. The man yelled, and the dog broke into a gallop. As it was about to enter an alley, there was a loud noise, a whistling, and something spat the ground directly before it. The dog screamed, and, wheeling in terror, galloped headlong in a new direction. Again there was a noise, a whistling, and sand was kicked viciously before it. Fear-stricken, the dog turned and flurried like an animal in a pen. The man stood laughing, his weapons at his hips.

Ultimately the man was attracted by the closed door of the Weary Gentleman saloon. He went to it and, hammering with a revolver, demanded drink.

The door remaining imperturbable, he picked a bit of paper from the walk, and nailed it to the framework with a knife. He then turned his back contemptuously upon this popular resort and, walking to the opposite side of the street and spinning there on his heel quickly and lithely, fired at the bit of paper. He missed it by a half-inch. He swore at himself, and went away. Later he comfortably fusilladed the windows of his most intimate friend. The man was playing with this town; it was a toy for him.

But still there was no offer of fight. The name of Jack Potter, his ancient antagonist, entered his mind, and he concluded that it would be a glad thing if he should go to Potter's house and by bombardment induce him to come out and fight. He moved in the direction of his desire, chanting Apache scalp-music.

When he arrived at it, Potter's house presented the same still front as had the other adobes. Taking up a strategic position, the man howled a challenge. But this house regarded him as might a great stone god. It gave no sign. After a decent wait, the man howled further challenges, mingling with them wonderful epithets.

Presently there came the spectacle of a man churning himself into deepest rage over the immobility of a house. He fumed at it as the winter wind attacks a prairie cabin in the North. To the distance there should have gone the sound of a tumult like the fighting of two hundred Mexicans. As necessity bade him, he paused for breath or to reload his revolvers.

IV

Potter and his bride walked sheepishly and with speed. Sometimes they laughed together shamefacedly and low.

"Next corner, dear," he said finally.

They put forth the efforts of a pair walking bowed against a strong wind. Potter was about to raise a finger to point the first appearance of the new home when, as they circled the corner, they came face to face with a man in a maroon-coloured shirt, who was feverishly pushing cartridges into a large revolver. Upon the instant the man dropped his revolver to the ground and, like lightning, whipped another from its holster. The second weapon was aimed at the bridegroom's chest.

There was a silence. Potter's mouth seemed to be merely a grave for his tongue. He exhibited an instinct to at once loosen his arm from the woman's grip, and he dropped the bag to the sand. As for the bride, her face had gone as yellow as old cloth. She was a slave to hideous rites, gazing at the apparitional snake.

The two men faced each other at a distance of three paces. He of the revolver smiled with a new and quiet ferocity.

"Tried to sneak up on me," he said. "Tried to sneak up on me!" His eyes grew more baleful. As Potter made a slight movement, the man thrust his revolver venomously forward. "No; don't you do it, Jack Potter. Don't you move a finger toward a gun just yet. Don't you move an eyelash. The time has come for me to settle with you, and I'm goin' to do it my own way, and loaf along with no interferin'. So if you don't want a gun bent on you, just mind what I tell you."

Potter looked at his enemy. "I ain't got a gun on me, Scratchy," he said. "Honest, I ain't." He was stiffening and steadying, but yet somewhere at the back of his mind a vision of the Pullman floated: the sea-green figured velvet, the shining brass, silver, and glass, the wood that gleamed as darkly brilliant as the surface of a pool of oil—all the glory of the marriage, the environment of the new estate. "You know I fight when it comes to fighting, Scratchy Wilson; but I ain't got a gun on me. You'll have to do all the shootin' yourself."

His enemy's face went livid. He stepped forward, and lashed his weapon to and fro before Potter's chest. "Don't you tell me you ain't got no gun on you, you whelp. Don't tell me no lie like that. There ain't a man in Texas ever seen you without no gun. Don't take me for no kid." His eyes blazed with light, and his throat worked like a pump.

"I ain't takin' you for no kid," answered Potter. His heels had not moved an inch backward. "I'm takin' you for a damn fool. I tell you I ain't got a gun, and I ain't. If you're goin' to shoot me up, you better begin now; you'll never get a chance like this again."

So much enforced reasoning had told on Wilson's rage; he was calmer. "If you ain't got a gun, why ain't you got a gun?" he sneered. "Been to Sunday-school?"

"I ain't got a gun because I've just come from San Anton' with my wife. I'm married," said Potter. "And if I'd thought there was going to be any galoots like you prowling around when I brought my wife home, I'd had a gun, and don't you forget it."

"Married!" said Scratchy, not at all comprehending.

"Yes, married. I'm married," said Potter, distinctly.

"Married?" said Scratchy. Seemingly for the first time, he saw the drooping, drowning woman at the other man's side. "No!" he said. He was like a creature allowed a glimpse of another world. He moved a pace backward, and his arm, with the revolver, dropped to his side. "Is this the lady?" he asked.

"Yes; this is the lady," answered Potter.

There was another period of silence.

"Well," said Wilson at last, slowly, "I s'pose it's all off now."

"It's all off if you say so, Scratchy. You know I didn't make the trouble." Potter lifted his valise.

"Well, I 'low it's off, Jack," said Wilson. He was looking at the ground. "Married!" He was not a student of chivalry; it was merely that in the presence of this foreign condition he was a simple child of the earlier plains. He picked up his starboard revolver, and, placing both weapons in their holsters, he went away. His feet made funnel-shaped tracks in the heavy sand.

QUESTIONS

1. Scratchy is described in the final paragraph as "a simple child of the earlier plains." What does this mean? Was Potter ever a simple child of the earlier plains? **2.** Early in the story we read that ". . . Jack Potter was beginning to find the shadow of a deed weigh upon him like a leaden slab. He, the town marshal of Yellow Sky, a man known, liked, and feared in his corner, a prominent person, had gone to San Antonio to meet a girl he believed he loved, and there, after the usual prayers, had actually induced her to marry him, without consulting Yellow Sky for any part of the transaction. He was now bringing his bride before an innocent and unsuspecting community." Jack Potter, like any man, has a right to marry. How do you account for his feelings as described in this passage? **3.** A "drummer" is a traveling salesman. What effect does his presence have on the "myth of the West"?

WRITING TOPICS

1. How would you characterize Scratchy's behavior? How does it relate to the "myth of the West" preserved in films and western novels? How does the description of Scratchy's shirt at the beginning of part III affect that view of the West? Why is Scratchy disconsolate at the end? **2.** Analyze Crane's metaphors and images. What function do they serve in the story?

Araby*

1914

JAMES JOYCE   [1882–1941]

North Richmond Street, being blind, was a quiet street except at the hour when the Christian Brothers' School set the boys free. An uninhabited house of two storeys stood at the blind end, detached from its neighbours in a square ground. The other houses of the street, conscious of decent lives within them, gazed at one another with brown imperturbable faces.

The former tenant of our house, a priest, had died in the back drawing-room. Air, musty from having been long enclosed, hung in all the rooms, and the waste room behind the kitchen was littered with old useless papers. Among these I found a few paper-covered books, the pages of which were curled and damp: *The Abbot*, by Walter Scott, *The Devout Communicant* and *The Memoirs of Vidocq*. I liked the last best because its leaves were yellow. The wild garden behind the house contained a central apple-tree and a few straggling bushes under one of which I found the late tenant's rusty bicycle-pump. He had been a very charitable priest; in his will he had left all his money to institutions and the furniture of his house to his sister.

When the short days of winter came dusk fell before we had well eaten our dinners. When we met in the street the houses had grown sombre. The space of sky above us was the colour of ever-changing violet and towards it the lamps of the street lifted their feeble lanterns. The cold air stung us and we played till our bodies glowed. Our shouts echoed in the silent street. The career of our play brought us through the dark muddy lanes behind the houses where we ran the gauntlet of the rough tribes from the cottages, to the back doors of the dark dripping gardens where odours arose from the ashpits, to the dark odorous stables where a coachman smoothed and combed the horse or shook music from the buckled harness. When we returned to the street light from the kitchen windows had filled the areas. If my uncle was seen turning the corner we hid in the shadow until we had seen him safely housed. Or if Mangan's sister came out on the doorstep to call her brother in to his tea we watched her from our shadow peer up and down the street. We waited to see whether she would remain or go in and, if she remained, we left our shadow and walked up to Mangan's steps resignedly. She was waiting for us, her figure defined by the light from the half-opened door. Her brother always teased her before he obeyed and I stood by the railings looking at her. Her dress swung as she moved her body and the soft rope of her hair tossed from side to side.

Every morning I lay on the floor in the front parlour watching her door. The blind was pulled down to within an inch of the sash so that I could not be seen. When she came out on the doorstep my heart leaped. I ran to the hall, seized

---

* This story is considered in the essay "Reading Fiction" at the end of the book.

my books and followed her. I kept her brown figure always in my eye and, when we came near the point at which our ways diverged, I quickened my pace and passed her. This happened morning after morning. I had never spoken to her, except for a few casual words, and yet her name was like a summons to all my foolish blood.

Her image accompanied me even in places the most hostile to romance. On Saturday evenings when my aunt went marketing I had to go to carry some of the parcels. We walked through the flaring streets, jostled by drunken men and bargaining women, amid the curses of labourers, the shrill litanies of shop-boys who stood on guard by the barrels of pigs' cheeks, the nasal chanting of street-singers, who sang a *come-all-you*[1] about O'Donovan Rossa, or a ballad about the troubles in our native land. These noises converged in a single sensation of life for me: I imagined that I bore my chalice safely through a throng of foes. Her name sprang to my lips at moments in strange prayers and praises which I myself did not understand. My eyes were often full of tears (I could not tell why) and at times a flood from my heart seemed to pour itself out into my bosom. I thought little of the future. I did not know whether I would ever speak to her or not or, if I spoke to her, how I could tell her of my confused adoration. But my body was like a harp and her words and gestures were like fingers running upon the wires.

One evening I went into the back drawing-room in which the priest had died. It was a dark rainy evening and there was no sound in the house. Through one of the broken panes I heard the rain impinge upon the earth, the fine incessant needles of water playing in the sodden beds. Some distant lamp or lighted window gleamed below me. I was thankful that I could see so little. All my senses seemed to desire to veil themselves and, feeling that I was about to slip from them, I pressed the palms of my hands together until they trembled, murmuring: *"O love! O love!"* many times.

At last she spoke to me. When she addressed the first words to me I was so confused that I did not know what to answer. She asked me was I going to *Araby*. I forgot whether I answered yes or no. It would be a splendid bazaar, she said she would love to go.

"And why can't you?" I asked.

While she spoke she turned a silver bracelet round and round her wrist. She could not go, she said, because there would be a retreat that week in her convent. Her brother and two other boys were fighting for their caps and I was alone at the railings. She held one of the spikes, bowing her head towards me. The light from the lamp opposite our door caught the white curve of her neck, lit up her hair that rested there and, falling, lit up the hand upon the railing. It fell over one side of her dress and caught the white border of a petticoat, just visible as she stood at ease.

"It's well for you" she said.

---

[1] A street ballad beginning with these words. This one is about Jeremiah Donovan, a nineteenth-century Irish nationalist popularly known as O'Donovan Rossa.

"If I go," I said, "I will bring you something."

What innumerable follies laid waste my waking and sleeping thoughts after that evening! I wished to annihilate the tedious intervening days. I chafed against the work of school. At night in my bedroom and by day in the classroom her image came between me and the page I strove to read. The syllables of the word *Araby* were called to me through the silence in which my soul luxuriated and cast an Eastern enchantment over me. I asked for leave to go to the bazaar on Saturday night. My aunt was surprised and hoped it was not some Freemason affair. I answered few questions in class. I watched my master's face pass from amiability to sternness; he hoped I was not beginning to idle. I could not call my wandering thoughts together. I had hardly any patience with the serious work of life which, now that it stood between me and my desire, seemed to me child's play, ugly monotonous child's play.

On Saturday morning I reminded my uncle that I wished to go to the bazaar in the evening. He was fussing at the hallstand, looking for the hat-brush, and answered me curtly:

"Yes, boy, I know."

As he was in the hall I could not go into the front parlour and lie at the window. I left the house in bad humour and walked slowly towards the school. The air was pitilessly raw and already my heart misgave me.

When I came home to dinner my uncle had not yet been home. Still it was early. I sat staring at the clock for some time and, when its ticking began to irritate me, I left the room. I mounted the staircase and gained the upper part of the house. The high cold empty gloomy rooms liberated me and I went from room to room singing. From the front window I saw my companions playing below in the street. Their cries reached me weakened and indistinct and, leaning my forehead against the cool glass, I looked over at the dark house where she lived. I may have stood there for an hour, seeing nothing but the brown-clad figure cast by my imagination, touched discreetly by the lamplight at the curved neck, at the hand upon the railings and at the border below the dress.

When I came downstairs again I found Mrs. Mercer sitting at the fire. She was an old garrulous woman, a pawnbroker's widow, who collected used stamps for some pious purpose. I had to endure the gossip of the tea-table. The meal was prolonged beyond an hour and still my uncle did not come. Mrs. Mercer stood up to go: she was sorry she couldn't wait any longer, but it was after eight o'clock and she did not like to be out late, as the night air was bad for her. When she had gone I began to walk up and down the room, clenching my fists. My aunt said:

"I'm afraid you may put off your bazaar for this night of Our Lord."

At nine o'clock I heard my uncle's latchkey in the halldoor. I heard him talking to himself and heard the hallstand rocking when it had received the weight of his overcoat. I could interpret these signs. When he was midway through his dinner I asked him to give me the money to go to the bazaar. He had forgotten.

"The people are in bed and after their first sleep now," he said.

I did not smile. My aunt said to him energetically:

"Can't you give him the money and let him go? You've kept him late enough as it is."

My uncle said he was very sorry he had forgotten. He said he believed in the old saying: "All work and no play makes Jack a dull boy." He asked me where I was going and, when I had told him a second time he asked me did I know *The Arab's Farewell to his Steed.* When I left the kitchen he was about to recite the opening lines of the piece to my aunt.

I held a florin tightly in my hand as I strode down Buckingham Street towards the station. The sight of the streets thronged with buyers and glaring with gas recalled to me the purpose of my journey. I took my seat in a third-class carriage of a deserted train. After an intolerable delay the train moved out of the station slowly. It crept onward among ruinous houses and over the twinkling river. At Westland Row Station a crowd of people pressed to the carriage doors; but the porters moved them back, saying that it was a special train for the bazaar. I remained alone in the bare carriage. In a few minutes the train drew up beside an improvised wooden platform. I passed out on to the road and saw by the lighted dial of a clock that it was ten minutes to ten. In front of me was a large building which displayed the magical name.

I could not find any sixpenny entrance and, fearing that the bazaar would be closed, I passed in quickly through a turnstile, handing a shilling to a weary-looking man. I found myself in a big hall girdled at half its height by a gallery. Nearly all the stalls were closed and the greater part of the hall was in darkness. I recognised a silence like that which pervades a church after a service. I walked into the centre of the bazaar timidly. A few people were gathered about the stalls which were still open. Before a curtain, over which the words *Café Chantant* were written in coloured lamps, two men were counting money on a salver. I listened to the fall of the coins.

Remembering with difficulty why I had come I went over to one of the stalls and examined porcelain vases and flowered tea-sets. At the door of the stall a young lady was talking and laughing with two young gentlemen. I remarked their English accents and listened vaguely to their conversation.

"O, I never said such a thing!"

"O, but you did!"

"O, but I didn't!"

"Didn't she say that?"

"Yes. I heard her."

"O, there's a . . . fib!"

Observing me the young lady came over and asked me did I wish to buy anything. The tone of her voice was not encouraging; she seemed to have spoken to me out of a sense of duty. I looked humbly at the great jars that stood like eastern guards at either side of the dark entrance to the stall and murmured:

"No, thank you."

The young lady changed the position of one of the vases and went back to the two young men. They began to talk of the same subject. Once or twice the young lady glanced at me over her shoulder.

I lingered before her stall, though I knew my stay was useless, to make my interest in her wares seem the more real. Then I turned away slowly and walked down the middle of the bazaar. I allowed the two pennies to fall against the sixpence in my pocket. I heard a voice call from one end of the gallery that the light was out. The upper part of the hall was now completely dark.

Gazing up into the darkness I saw myself as a creature driven and derided by vanity; and my eyes burned with anguish and anger.

A Clean, Well-Lighted Place   1933

ERNEST HEMINGWAY [1898–1961]

It was late and everyone had left the café except an old man who sat in the shadow the leaves of the tree made against the electric light. In the day time the street was dusty, but at night the dew settled the dust and the old man liked to sit late because he was deaf and now at night it was quiet and he felt the difference. The two waiters inside the café knew that the old man was a little drunk, and while he was a good client they knew that if he became too drunk he would leave without paying, so they kept watch on him.

"Last week he tried to commit suicide," one waiter said.

"Why?"

"He was in despair."

"What about?"

"Nothing."

"How do you know it was nothing?"

"He has plenty of money."

They sat together at a table that was close against the wall near the door of the café and looked at the terrace where the tables were all empty except where the old man sat in the shadow of the leaves of the tree that moved slightly in the wind. A girl and a soldier went by in the street. The street light shone on the brass number on his collar. The girl wore no head covering and hurried beside him.

"The guard will pick him up," one waiter said.

"What does it matter if he gets what he's after?"

"He had better get off the street now. The guard will get him. They went by five minutes ago."

The old man sitting in the shadow rapped on his saucer with his glass. The younger waiter went over to him.

"What do you want?"

The old man looked at him. "Another brandy," he said.

"You'll be drunk," the waiter said. The old man looked at him. The waiter went away.

"He'll stay all night," he said to his colleague. "I'm sleepy now. I never get into bed before three o'clock. He should have killed himself last week."

The waiter took the brandy bottle and another saucer from the counter inside the café and marched out to the old man's table. He put down the saucer and poured the glass full of brandy.

"You should have killed yourself last week," he said to the deaf man. The old man motioned with his finger. "A little more," he said. The waiter poured on into the glass so that the brandy slopped over and ran down the stem into the top saucer of the pile. "Thank you," the old man said. The waiter took the bottle back inside the café. He sat down at the table with his colleague again.

35

"He's drunk now," he said.

"He's drunk every night."

"What did he want to kill himself for?"

"How should I know."

"How did he do it?"

"He hung himself with a rope."

"Who cut him down?"

"His niece."

"Why did they do it?"

"Fear for his soul."

"How much money has he got?"

"He's got plenty."

"He must be eighty years old."

"Anyway I should say he was eighty."

"I wish he would go home. I never get to bed before three o'clock. What kind of hour is that to go to bed?"

"He stays up because he likes it."

"He's lonely. I'm not lonely. I have a wife waiting in bed for me."

"He had a wife once too."

"A wife would be no good to him now."

"You can't tell. He might be better with a wife."

"His niece looks after him. You said she cut him down."

"I know."

"I wouldn't want to be that old. An old man is a nasty thing."

"Not always. This old man is clean. He drinks without spilling. Even now, drunk. Look at him."

"I don't want to look at him. I wish he would go home. He has no regard for those who must work."

The old man looked from his glass across the square, then over at the waiters.

"Another brandy," he said, pointing to his glass. The waiter who was in a hurry came over.

"Finished," he said, speaking with that omission of syntax stupid people employ when talking to drunken people or foreigners. "No more tonight. Close now."

"Another," said the old man.

"No. Finished." The waiter wiped the edge of the table with a towel and shook his head.

The old man stood up, slowly counted the saucers, took a leather coin purse from his pocket and paid for the drinks, leaving half a peseta tip.

The waiter watched him go down the street, a very old man walking unsteadily but with dignity.

"Why didn't you let him stay and drink?" the unhurried waiter asked. They were putting up the shutters. "It is not half-past two."

"I want to go home to bed."

"What is an hour?"

"More to me than to him."

"An hour is the same."

"You talk like an old man yourself. He can buy a bottle and drink at home."

"It's not the same."

"No, it is not," agreed the waiter with a wife. He did not wish to be unjust. He was only in a hurry.

"And you? You have no fear of going home before your usual hour?"

"Are you trying to insult me?"

"No, hombre, only to make a joke."

"No," the waiter who was in a hurry said, rising from pulling down the metal shutters. "I have confidence. I am all confidence."

"You have youth, confidence, and a job," the older waiter said. "You have everything."

"And what do you lack?"

"Everything but work."

"You have everything I have."

"No. I have never had confidence and I am not young."

"Come on. Stop talking nonsense and lock up."

"I am of those who like to stay late at the café," the older waiter said. "With all those who do not want to go to bed. With all those who need a light for the night."

"I want to go home and into bed."

"We are of two different kinds," the older waiter said. He was now dressed to go home. "It is not only a question of youth and confidence although those things are very beautiful. Each night I am reluctant to close up because there may be some one who needs the café."

"Hombre, there are bodegas open all night long."

"You do not understand. This is a clean and pleasant café. It is well lighted. The light is very good and also, now, there are shadows of the leaves."

"Good night," said the younger waiter.

"Good night," the other said. Turning off the electric light he continued the conversation with himself. It is the light of course but it is necessary that the place be clean and pleasant. You do not want music. Certainly you do not want music. Nor can you stand before a bar with dignity although that is all that is provided for these hours. What did he fear? It was not fear or dread. It was a nothing that he knew too well. It was all a nothing and a man was nothing too. It was only that and light was all it needed and a certain cleanness and order. Some lived in it and never felt it but he knew it was nada y pues nada y pues nada.[1] Our nada who art in nada, nada be thy name thy kingdom nada thy will be nada in nada as it is in nada. Give us this nada our daily nada and nada us our nada as we nada our nadas and nada us not into nada but deliver us from nada; pues nada. Hail nothing full of nothing, nothing is with thee. He smiled and stood before a bar with a shining steam pressure coffee machine.

"What's yours?" asked the barman.

---

[1] Nothing, and then nothing, and then nothing.

"Nada."

"Otro loco mas,"[2] said the barman and turned away.

"A little cup," said the waiter.

The barman poured it for him.

"The light is very bright and pleasant but the bar is unpolished," the waiter said.

The barman looked at him but did not answer. It was too late at night for conversation.

"You want another copita?" the barman asked.

"No, thank you," said the waiter and went out. He disliked bars and bodegas. A clean, well-lighted café was a very different thing. Now, without thinking further, he would go home to his room. He would lie in the bed and finally, with daylight, he would go to sleep. After all, he said to himself, it is probably only insomnia. Many must have it.

QUESTION

How do the two waiters differ in their attitudes toward the old man? What bearing does that difference have on the theme of the story?

---

[2] Another crazy one.

My Oedipus Complex   1950

FRANK O'CONNOR   [1903–1966]

Father was in the army all through the war—the first war, I mean—so, up to
the age of five, I never saw much of him, and what I saw did not worry me.
Sometimes I woke and there was a big figure in khaki peering down at me in
the candlelight. Sometimes in the early morning I heard the slamming of the
front door and the clatter of nailed boots down the cobbles of the lane. These
were Father's entrances and exits. Like Santa Claus he came and went mysteriously.

In fact, I rather liked his visits, though it was an uncomfortable squeeze
between Mother and him when I got into the big bed in the early morning. He
smoked, which gave him a pleasant musty smell, and shaved, an operation of
astounding interest. Each time he left a trail of souvenirs—model tanks and
Gurkha knives with handles made of bullet cases, and German helmets and cap
badges and button-sticks, and all sorts of military equipment—carefully stowed
away in a long box on top of the wardrobe, in case they ever came in handy.
There was a bit of the magpie about Father; he expected everything to come in
handy. When his back was turned, Mother let me get a chair and rummage
through his treasures. She didn't seem to think so highly of them as he did.

The war was the most peaceful period of my life. The window of my attic
faced southeast. My mother had curtained it, but that had small effect. I always
woke with the first light and, with all the responsibilities of the previous day
melted, feeling myself rather like the sun, ready to illumine and rejoice. Life
never seemed so simple and clear and full of possibilities as then. I put my feet
out from under the clothes—I called them Mrs. Left and Mrs. Right—and
invented dramatic situations for them in which they discussed the problems of
the day. At least Mrs. Right did; she was very demonstrative, but I hadn't the
same control of Mrs. Left, so she mostly contented herself with nodding agreement.

They discussed what Mother and I should do during the day, what Santa
Claus should give a fellow for Christmas, and what steps should be taken to
brighten the home. There was that little matter of the baby, for instance. Mother
and I could never agree about that. Ours was the only house in the terrace
without a new baby, and Mother said we couldn't afford one till Father came
back from the war because they cost seventeen and six. That showed how simple
she was. The Geneys up the road had a baby, and everyone knew they couldn't
afford seventeen and six. It was probably a cheap baby, and Mother wanted
something really good, but I felt she was too exclusive. The Geneys' baby would
have done us fine.

Having settled my plans for the day, I got up, put a chair under the attic
window, and lifted the frame high enough to stick out my head. The window

39

overlooked the front gardens of the terrace behind ours, and beyond these it looked over a deep valley to the tall, red-brick houses terraced up the opposite hillside, which were all still in shadow, while those at our side of the valley were all lit up, though with long strange shadows that made them seem unfamiliar; rigid and painted.

After that I went into Mother's room and climbed into the big bed. She woke and I began to tell her of my schemes. By this time, though I never seem to have noticed it, I was petrified in my nightshirt, and I thawed as I talked until, the last frost melted, I fell asleep beside her and woke again only when I heard her below in the kitchen, making the breakfast.

After breakfast we went into town; heard Mass at St. Augustine's and said a prayer for Father, and did the shopping. If the afternoon was fine we either went for a walk in the country or a visit to Mother's great friend in the convent, Mother St. Dominic. Mother had them all praying for Father, and every night, going to bed, I asked God to send him back safe from the war to us. Little, indeed, did I know what I was praying for!

One morning, I got into the big bed, and there, sure enough, was Father in his usual Santa Claus manner, but later, instead of uniform, he put on his best blue suit, and Mother was as pleased as anything. I saw nothing to be pleased about, because, out of uniform, Father was altogether less interesting, but she only beamed, and explained that our prayers had been answered, and off we went to Mass to thank God for having brought Father safely home.

The irony of it! That very day when he came in to dinner he took off his boots and put on his slippers, donned the dirty old cap he wore about the house to save him from colds, crossed his legs, and began to talk gravely to Mother, who looked anxious. Naturally, I disliked her looking anxious, because it destroyed her good looks, so I interrupted him.

"Just a moment, Larry!" she said gently.

This was only what she said when we had boring visitors, so I attached no importance to it and went on talking.

"Do be quiet, Larry!" she said impatiently. "Don't you hear me talking to Daddy?"

This was the first time I had heard those ominous words, "talking to Daddy," and I couldn't help feeling that if this was how God answered prayers, he couldn't listen to them very attentively.

"Why are you talking to Daddy?" I asked with as great a show of indifference as I could muster.

"Because Daddy and I have business to discuss. Now, don't interrupt again!"

In the afternoon, at Mother's request, Father took me for a walk. This time we went into town instead of out to the country, and I thought at first, in my usual optimistic way, that it might be an improvement. It was nothing of the sort. Father and I had quite different notions of a walk in town. He had no proper interest in trams, ships, and horses, and the only thing that seemed to divert him was talking to fellows as old as himself. When I wanted to stop he simply went on, dragging me behind him by the hand; when he wanted to stop I had no alternative but to do the same. I noticed that it seemed to be a sign that he wanted to stop for a long time whenever he leaned against a wall. The second time I saw him do it I got wild. He seemed to be settling himself forever. I pulled him by the coat and trousers, but, unlike Mother who, if you were too persistent, got into a wax and said: "Larry, if you don't behave yourself, I'll give you a good slap," Father had an extraordinary capacity for amiable inattention. I sized him up and wondered would I cry, but he seemed to be too remote to be annoyed even by that. Really, it was like going for a walk with a mountain! He either ignored the wrenching and pummeling entirely, or else glanced down with a grin of amusement from his peak. I had never met anyone so absorbed in himself as he seemed.

At teatime, "talking to Daddy" began again, complicated this time by the fact that he had an evening paper, and every few minutes he put it down and told Mother something new out of it. I felt this was foul play. Man for man, I was prepared to compete with him any time for Mother's attention, but when he had it all made up for him by other people it left me no chance. Several times I tried to change the subject without success.

"You must be quiet while Daddy is reading, Larry," Mother said impatiently.

It was clear that she either genuinely liked talking to Father better than talking to me, or else that he had some terrible hold on her which made her afraid to admit the truth.

"Mummy," I said that night when she was tucking me up, "do you think if I prayed hard God would send Daddy back to the war?"

She seemed to think about that for a moment.

"No, dear," she said with a smile. "I don't think he would."

"Why wouldn't he, Mummy?"

"Because there isn't a war any longer, dear."

"But, Mummy, couldn't God make another war, if he liked?"

"He wouldn't like to, dear. It's not God who makes wars, but bad people."

"Oh!" I said.

I was disappointed about that. I began to think that God wasn't quite what he was cracked up to be.

Next morning I woke at my usual hour, feeling like a bottle of champagne. I put out my feet and invented a long conversation in which Mrs. Right talked of the trouble she had with her own father till she put him in the Home. I didn't quite know what the Home was but it sounded the right place for Father. Then I got my chair and stuck my head out of the attic window. Dawn was just breaking, with a guilty air that made me feel I had caught it in the act. My head bursting with stories and schemes, I stumbled in next door, and in the half-darkness scrambled into the big bed. There was no room at Mother's side so I had to get between her and Father. For the time being I had forgotten about him, and for several minutes I sat bolt upright, racking my brains to know what I could do with him. He was taking up more than his fair share of the bed, and I couldn't get comfortable, so I gave him several kicks that made him grunt and stretch. He made room all right, though. Mother waked and felt for me. I settled back comfortably in the warmth of the bed with my thumb in my mouth.

"Mummy!" I hummed, loudly and contentedly.

"Ssh! dear," she whispered. "Don't wake Daddy!"

This was a new development, which threatened to be even more serious than "talking to Daddy." Life without my early-morning conferences was unthinkable.

"Why?" I asked severely.

"Because poor Daddy is tired."

This seemed to me a quite inadequate reason, and I was sickened by the sentimentality of her "poor Daddy." I never liked that sort of gush; it always struck me as insincere.

"Oh!" I said lightly. Then in my most winning tone: "Do you know where I want to go with you today, Mummy?"

"No, dear," she sighed.

"I want to go down the Glen and fish for thornybacks with my new net, and then I want to go out to the Fox and Hounds, and—"

"Don't-wake-Daddy!" she hissed angrily, clapping her hand across my mouth.

But it was too late. He was awake, or nearly so. He grunted and reached for the matches. Then he stared incredulously at his watch.

"Like a cup of tea, dear?" asked Mother in a meek, hushed voice I had never heard her use before. It sounded almost as though she were afraid.

"Tea?" he exclaimed indignantly. "Do you know what the time is?"

"And after that I want to go up the Rathcooney Road," I said loudly, afraid I'd forget something in all those interruptions.

"Go to sleep at once, Larry!" she said sharply.

I began to snivel. I couldn't concentrate, the way that pair went on, and smothering my early-morning schemes was like burying a family from the cradle.

Father said nothing, but lit his pipe and sucked it, looking out into the shadows without minding Mother or me. I knew he was mad. Every time I made a remark Mother hushed me irritably. I was mortified. I felt it wasn't fair; there was even something sinister in it. Every time I had pointed out to her the waste of making two beds when we could both sleep in one, she had told me it was healthier like that, and now here was this man, this stranger, sleeping with her without the least regard for her health!

He got up early and made tea, but though he brought Mother a cup he brought none for me.

"Mummy," I shouted, "I want a cup of tea, too."

"Yes, dear," she said patiently. "You can drink from Mummy's saucer."

That settled it. Either Father or I would have to leave the house. I didn't want to drink from Mother's saucer; I wanted to be treated as an equal in my own home, so, just to spite her, I drank it all and left none for her. She took that quietly, too.

But that night when she was putting me to bed she said gently: "Larry, I want you to promise me something."

"What is it?" I asked.

"Not to come in and disturb poor Daddy in the morning. Promise?"

"Poor Daddy" again! I was becoming suspicious of everything involving that quite impossible man.

"Why?" I asked.

"Because poor Daddy is worried and tired and he doesn't sleep well."

"Why doesn't he, Mummy?"

"Well, you know, don't you, that while he was at the war Mummy got the pennies from the Post Office?"

"From Miss MacCarthy?"

"That's right. But now, you see, Miss MacCarthy hasn't any more pennies, so Daddy must go out and find us some. You know what would happen if he couldn't?"

"No," I said, "tell us."

"Well, I think we might have to go out and beg for them like the poor old woman on Fridays. We wouldn't like that, would we?"

"No," I agreed. "We wouldn't."

"So you'll promise not to come in and wake him?"

"Promise."

Mind you, I meant that. I knew pennies were a serious matter, and I was all against having to go out and beg like the old woman on Fridays. Mother laid out all my toys in a complete ring round the bed so that, whatever way I got out, I was bound to fall over one of them.

When I woke I remembered my promise all right. I got up and sat on the floor and played—for hours, it seemed to me. Then I got my chair and looked out the attic window for more hours. I wished it was time for Father to wake; I wished someone would make me a cup of tea. I didn't feel in the least like the sun; instead, I was bored and so very, very cold! I simply longed for the warmth and depth of the big featherbed.

At last I could stand it no longer. I went into the next room. As there was still no room at Mother's side I climbed over her and she woke with a start.

"Larry," she whispered, gripping my arm very tightly, "what did you promise?"

"But I did, Mummy," I wailed, caught in the very act. "I was quiet for ever so long."

"Oh, dear, and you're perished!" she said sadly, feeling me all over. "Now, if I let you stay will you promise not to talk?"

"But I want to talk, Mummy," I wailed.

"That has nothing to do with it," she said with a firmness that was new to me. "Daddy wants to sleep. Now, do you understand that?"

I understood it only too well. I wanted to talk, he wanted to sleep—whose house was it, anyway?

"Mummy," I said with equal firmness, "I think it would be healthier for Daddy to sleep in his own bed."

That seemed to stagger her, because she said nothing for a while.

"Now, once for all," she went on, "you're to be perfectly quiet or go back to your own bed. Which is it to be?"

The injustice of it got me down. I had convicted her out of her own mouth of inconsistency and unreasonableness, and she hadn't even attempted to reply. Full of spite, I gave Father a kick, which she didn't notice but which made him grunt and open his eyes in alarm.

"What time is it?" he asked in a panic-stricken voice, not looking at Mother but the door, as if he saw someone there.

"It's early yet," she replied soothingly. "It's only the child. Go to sleep again. . . . Now, Larry," she added, getting out of bed, "you've wakened Daddy and you must go back."

This time, for all her quiet air, I knew she meant it, and knew that my principal rights and privileges were as good as lost unless I asserted them at once. As she lifted me, I gave a screech, enough to wake the dead, not to mind Father. He groaned.

"That damn child! Doesn't he ever sleep?"

"It's only a habit, dear," she said quietly, though I could see she was vexed.

"Well, it's time he got out of it," shouted Father, beginning to heave in the bed. He suddenly gathered all the bedclothes about him, turned to the wall, and then looked back over his shoulder with nothing showing only two small, spiteful, dark eyes. The man looked very wicked.

To open the bedroom door, Mother had to let me down, and I broke free and dashed for the farthest corner, screeching. Father sat bolt upright in bed.

"Shut up, you little puppy!" he said in a choking voice.

I was so astonished that I stopped screeching. Never, never had anyone spoken to me in that tone before. I looked at him incredulously and saw his face convulsed with rage. It was only then that I fully realized how God had codded me, listening to my prayers for the safe return of this monster.

"Shut up, you!" I bawled, beside myself.

"What's that you said?" shouted Father, making a wild leap out of bed.

"Mick, Mick!" cried Mother. "Don't you see the child isn't used to you?"

"I see he's better fed than taught," snarled Father, waving his arms wildly. "He wants his bottom smacked."

All his previous shouting was as nothing to these obscene words referring to my person. They really made my blood boil.

"Smack your own!" I screamed hysterically. "Smack your own! Shut up! Shut up!"

At this he lost his patience and let fly at me. He did it with the lack of conviction you'd expect of a man under Mother's horrified eyes, and it ended up as a mere tap, but the sheer indignity of being struck at all by a stranger, a total stranger who had cajoled his way back from the war into our big bed as a result of my innocent intercession, made me completely dotty. I shrieked and shrieked, and danced in my bare feet, and Father, looking awkward and hairy in nothing but a short grey army shirt, glared down at me like a mountain out for murder. I think it must have been then that I realized he was jealous too. And there stood Mother in her nightdress, looking as if her heart was broken between us. I hoped she felt as she looked. It seemed to me that she deserved it all.

From that morning out my life was a hell. Father and I were enemies, open and avowed. We conducted a series of skirmishes against one another, he trying to steal my time with Mother and I his. When she was sitting on my bed, telling me a story, he took to looking for some pair of old boots which he alleged he had left behind him at the beginning of the war. While he talked to Mother I played loudly with my toys to show my total lack of concern. He created a terrible scene one evening when he came in from work and found me at his box, playing with his regimental badges, Gurkha knives and button-sticks. Mother got up and took the box from me.

"You mustn't play with Daddy's toys unless he lets you, Larry," she said severely. "Daddy doesn't play with yours."

For some reason Father looked at her as if she had struck him and then turned away with a scowl.

"Those are not toys," he growled, taking down the box again to see had I lifted anything. "Some of those curios are very rare and valuable."

But as time went on I saw more and more how he managed to alienate Mother and me. What made it worse was that I couldn't grasp his method or see what attraction he had for Mother. In every possible way he was less winning than I. He had a common accent and made noises at his tea. I thought for a while that it might be the newspapers she was interested in, so I made up bits of news of my own to read to her. Then I thought it might be the smoking, which I personally thought attractive, and took his pipes and went round the house dribbling into them till he caught me. I even made noises at my tea, but Mother only told me I was disgusting. It all seemed to hinge round that unhealthy habit of sleeping together, so I made a point of dropping into their bedroom and nosing round, talking to myself, so that they wouldn't know I was watching them, but they were never up to anything that I could see. In the end it beat me. It seemed to depend on being grownup and giving people rings, and I realized I'd have to wait.

But at the same time I wanted him to see that I was only waiting, not giving up the fight. One evening when he was being particularly obnoxious, chattering away well above my head, I let him have it.

"Mummy," I said, "do you know what I'm going to do when I grow up?"

"No, dear," she replied. "What?"

"I'm going to marry you," I said quietly.

Father gave a great guffaw out of him, but he didn't take me in. I knew it must only be pretense. And Mother, in spite of everything, was pleased. I felt she was probably relieved to know that one day Father's hold on her would be broken.

"Won't that be nice?" she said with a smile.

"It'll be very nice," I said confidently. "Because we're going to have lots and lots of babies."

"That's right, dear," she said placidly. "I think we'll have one soon, and then you'll have plenty of company."

I was no end pleased about that because it showed that in spite of the way she gave in to Father she still considered my wishes. Besides, it would put the Geneys in their place.

It didn't turn out like that, though. To begin with, she was very preoccupied—I supposed about where she would get the seventeen and six—and though Father took to staying out late in the evenings it did me no particular good. She stopped taking me for walks, became as touchy as blazes, and smacked me for nothing at all. Sometimes I wished I'd never mentioned the confounded baby—I seemed to have a genius for bringing calamity on myself.

And calamity it was! Sonny arrived in the most appalling hullabaloo—even that much he couldn't do without a fuss—and from the first moment I disliked him. He was a difficult child—so far as I was concerned he was always difficult—and demanded far too much attention. Mother was simply silly about him, and couldn't see when he was only showing off. As company he was worse than useless. He slept all day, and I had to go round the house on tiptoe to avoid waking him. It wasn't any longer a question of not waking Father. The slogan now was "Don't-wake-Sonny!" I couldn't understand why the child wouldn't sleep at the proper time, so whenever Mother's back was turned I woke him. Sometimes to keep him awake I pinched him as well. Mother caught me at it one day and gave me a most unmerciful flaking.

One evening, when Father was coming from work, I was playing trains in the front garden. I let on not to notice him; instead, I pretended to be talking to myself, and said in a loud voice: "If another bloody baby comes into this house, I'm going out."

Father stopped dead and looked at me over his shoulder.

"What's that you said?" he asked sternly.

"I was only talking to myself," I replied, trying to conceal my panic. "It's private."

He turned and went in without a word. Mind you, I intended it as a solemn warning, but its effect was quite different. Father started being quite nice to me. I could understand that, of course. Mother was quite sickening about Sonny. Even at mealtimes she'd get up and gawk at him in the cradle with an idiotic smile, and tell Father to do the same. He was always polite about it, but he looked so puzzled you could see he didn't know what she was talking about. He complained of the way Sonny cried at night, but she only got cross and said that Sonny never cried except when there was something up with him—which was a flaming lie, because Sonny never had anything up with him, and only cried for attention. It was really painful to see how simple-minded she was. Father wasn't attractive, but he had a fine intelligence. He saw through Sonny, and now he knew that I saw through him as well.

One night I woke with a start. There was someone beside me in the bed. For one wild moment I felt sure it must be Mother, having come to her senses and left Father for good, but then I heard Sonny in convulsions in the next room, and Mother saying: "There! There! There!" and I knew it wasn't she. It was Father. He was lying beside me, wide awake, breathing hard and apparently as mad as hell.

After a while it came to me what he was mad about. It was his turn now. After turning me out of the big bed, he had been turned out himself. Mother had no consideration now for anyone but that poisonous pup, Sonny. I couldn't help feeling sorry for Father. I had been through it all myself, and even at that age I was magnanimous. I began to stroke him down and say: "There! There!" He wasn't exactly responsive.

"Aren't you asleep either?" he snarled.

"Ah, come on and put your arm around us, can't you?" I said, and he did, in a sort of way. Gingerly, I suppose, is how you'd describe it. He was very bony but better than nothing.

At Christmas he went out of his way to buy me a really nice model railway.

QUESTIONS

1. Is the story narrated from the point of view of a young child or a mature man?   **2.** Note that the narrator's most ardent wishes—for the return of his father and for a new baby in the house—are granted. What are the consequences for him?   **3.** What specific details in the story contribute to the appropriateness of its title?   **4.** With whom does the reader sympathize? How does the author control those sympathies?

WRITING TOPIC

Focusing on the ironies embodied in this story, describe the shifting relationships among the main characters.

Good Country People

FLANNERY O'CONNOR [1925–1964]

1955

Besides the neutral expression that she wore when she was alone, Mrs. Freeman had two others, forward and reverse, that she used for all her human dealings. Her forward expression was steady and driving like the advance of a heavy truck. Her eyes never swerved to left or right but turned as the story turned as if they followed a yellow line down the center of it. She seldom used the other expression because it was not often necessary for her to retract a statement, but when she did, her face came to a complete stop, there was an almost imperceptible movement of her black eyes, during which they seemed to be receding, and then the observer would see that Mrs. Freeman, though she might stand there as real as several grain sacks thrown on top of each other, was no longer there in spirit. As for getting anything across to her when this was the case, Mrs. Hopewell had given it up. She might talk her head off. Mrs. Freeman could never be brought to admit herself wrong on any point. She would stand there and if she could be brought to say anything, it was something like, "Well, I wouldn't of said it was and I wouldn't of said it wasn't," or letting her gaze range over the top kitchen shelf where there was an assortment of dusty bottles, she might remark, "I see you ain't ate many of them figs you put up last summer."

They carried on their most important business in the kitchen at breakfast. Every morning Mrs. Hopewell got up at seven o'clock and lit her gas heater and Joy's. Joy was her daughter, a large blonde girl who had an artificial leg. Mrs. Hopewell thought of her as a child though she was thirty-two years old and highly educated. Joy would get up while her mother was eating and lumber into the bathroom and slam the door, and before long, Mrs. Freeman would arrive at the back door. Joy would hear her mother call, "Come on in," and then they would talk for a while in low voices that were indistinguishable in the bathroom. By the time Joy came in, they had usually finished the weather report and were on one or the other of Mrs. Freeman's daughters, Glynese or Carramae. Joy called them Glycerin and Caramel. Glynese, a redhead, was eighteen and had many admirers; Carramae, a blonde, was only fifteen but already married and pregnant. She could not keep anything on her stomach. Every morning Mrs. Freeman told Mrs. Hopewell how many times she had vomited since the last report.

Mrs. Hopewell liked to tell people that Glynese and Carramae were two of the finest girls she knew and that Mrs. Freeman was a *lady* and that she was never ashamed to take her anywhere or introduce her to anybody they might meet. Then she would tell how she had happened to hire the Freemans in the first place and how they were a godsend to her and how she had had them four years. The reason for her keeping them so long was that they were not trash.

They were good country people. She had telephoned the man whose name they had given as a reference and he had told her that Mr. Freeman was a good farmer but that his wife was the nosiest woman ever to walk the earth. "She's got to be into everything," the man said. "If she don't get there before the dust settles, you can bet she's dead, that's all. She'll want to know all your business. I can stand him real good," he had said, "but me nor my wife neither could have stood that woman one more minute on this place." That had put Mrs. Hopewell off for a few days.

She had hired them in the end because there were no other applicants but she had made up her mind beforehand exactly how she would handle the woman. Since she was the type who had to be into everything, then, Mrs. Hopewell had decided, she would not only let her be into everything, she would *see to it* that she was into everything—she would give her the responsibility of everything, she would put her in charge. Mrs. Hopewell had no bad qualities of her own but she was able to use other people's in such a constructive way that she never felt the lack. She had hired the Freemans and she had kept them four years.

Nothing is perfect. This was one of Mrs. Hopewell's favorite sayings. Another was: that is life! And still another, the most important, was: well, other people have their opinions too. She would make these statements, usually at the table, in a tone of gentle insistence as if no one held them but her, and the large hulking Joy, whose constant outrage had obliterated every expression from her face, would stare just a little to the side of her, her eyes icy blue, with the look of someone who has achieved blindness by an act of will and means to keep it.

When Mrs. Hopewell said to Mrs. Freeman that life was like that, Mrs. Freeman would say, "I always said so myself." Nothing had been arrived at by anyone that had not first been arrived at by her. She was quicker than Mr. Freeman. When Mrs. Hopewell said to her after they had been on the place a while, "You know, you're the wheel behind the wheel," and winked, Mrs. Freeman had said, "I know it. I've always been quick. It's some that are quicker than others."

"Everybody is different," Mrs. Hopewell said.

"Yes, most people is," Mrs. Freeman said.

"It takes all kinds to make the world."

"I always said it did myself."

The girl was used to this kind of dialogue for breakfast and more of it for dinner; sometimes they had it for supper too. When they had no guest they ate in the kitchen because that was easier. Mrs. Freeman always managed to arrive at some point during the meal and to watch them finish it. She would stand in the doorway if it were summer but in the winter she would stand with one elbow on top of the refrigerator and look down on them, or she would stand by the gas heater, lifting the back of her skirt slightly. Occasionally she would stand against the wall and roll her head from side to side. At no time was she in any hurry to leave. All this was very trying on Mrs. Hopewell but she was a woman of great patience. She realized that nothing is perfect and that in the Freemans she had good country people and that if, in this day and age, you get good country people, you had better hang onto them.

She had had plenty of experience with trash. Before the Freemans she had averaged one tenant family a year. The wives of these farmers were not the kind you would want to be around you for very long. Mrs. Hopewell, who had divorced her husband long ago, needed someone to walk over the fields with her; and when Joy had to be impressed for these services, her remarks were usually so ugly and her face so glum that Mrs. Hopewell would say, "If you can't come pleasantly, I don't want you at all," to which the girl, standing square and rigid-shouldered with her neck thrust slightly forward, would reply, "If you want me, here I am—LIKE I AM."

Mrs. Hopewell excused this attitude because of the leg (which had been shot off in a hunting accident when Joy was ten). It was hard for Mrs. Hopewell to realize that her child was thirty-two now and that for more than twenty years she had had only one leg. She thought of her still as a child because it tore her heart to think instead of the poor stout girl in her thirties who had never danced a step or had any *normal* good times. Her name was really Joy but as soon as she was twenty-one and away from home, she had had it legally changed. Mrs. Hopewell was certain that she had thought and thought until she had hit upon the ugliest name in any language. Then she had gone and had the beautiful name, Joy, changed without telling her mother until after she had done it. Her legal name was Hulga.

When Mrs. Hopewell thought the name, Hulga, she thought of the broad blank hull of a battleship. She would not use it. She continued to call her Joy to which the girl responded but in a purely mechanical way.

Hulga had learned to tolerate Mrs. Freeman, who saved her from taking walks with her mother. Even Glynese and Carramae were useful when they occupied attention that might otherwise have been directed at her. At first she had thought she could not stand Mrs. Freeman for she had found that it was not possible to be rude to her. Mrs. Freeman would take on strange resentments and for days together she would be sullen but the source of her displeasure was always obscure; a direct attack, a positive leer, blatant ugliness to her face—these never touched her. And without warning one day, she began calling her Hulga.

She did not call her that in front of Mrs. Hopewell who would have been incensed but when she and the girl happened to be out of the house together, she would say something and add the name Hulga to the end of it, and the big spectacled Joy-Hulga would scowl and redden as if her privacy had been intruded upon. She considered the name her personal affair. She had arrived at it first purely on the basis of its ugly sound and then the full genius of its fitness had struck her. She had a vision of the name working like the ugly sweating Vulcan who stayed in the furnace and to whom, presumably, the goddess had to come when called. She saw it as the name of her highest creative act. One of her major triumphs was that her mother had not been able to turn her dust into

Joy, but the greater one was that she had been able to turn it herself into Hulga. However, Mrs. Freeman's relish for using the name only irritated her. It was as if Mrs. Freeman's beady steel-pointed eyes had penetrated far enough behind her face to reach some secret fact. Something about her seemed to fascinate Mrs. Freeman and then one day Hulga realized that it was the artificial leg. Mrs. Freeman had a special fondness for the details of secret infections, hidden deformities, assaults upon children. Of diseases, she preferred the lingering or incurable. Hulga had heard Mrs. Hopewell give her the details of the hunting accident, how the leg had been literally blasted off, how she had never lost consciousness. Mrs. Freeman could listen to it any time as if it had happened an hour ago.

When Hulga stumped into the kitchen in the morning (she could walk without making the awful noise but she made it—Mrs. Hopewell was certain—because it was ugly-sounding), she glanced at them and did not speak. Mrs. Hopewell would be in her red kimono with her hair tied around her head in rags. She would be sitting at the table, finishing her breakfast and Mrs. Freeman would be hanging by her elbow outward from the refrigerator, looking down at the table. Hulga always put her eggs on the stove to boil and then stood over them with her arms folded, and Mrs. Hopewell would look at her—a kind of indirect gaze divided between her and Mrs. Freeman—and would think that if she would only keep herself up a little, she wouldn't be so bad looking. There was nothing wrong with her face that a pleasant expression wouldn't help. Mrs. Hopewell said that people who looked on the bright side of things would be beautiful even if they were not.

Whenever she looked at Joy this way, she could not help but feel that it would have been better if the child had not taken the Ph.D. It had certainly not brought her out any and now that she had it, there was no more excuse for her to go to school again. Mrs. Hopewell thought it was nice for girls to go to school to have a good time but Joy had "gone through." Anyhow, she would not have been strong enough to go again. The doctors had told Mrs. Hopewell that with the best of care, Joy might see forty-five. She had a weak heart. Joy had made it plain that if it had not been for this condition, she would be far from these red hills and good country people. She would be in a university lecturing to people who knew what she was talking about. And Mrs. Hopewell could very well picture her there, looking like a scarecrow and lecturing to more of the same. Here she went about all day in a six-year-old skirt and a yellow sweat shirt with a faded cowboy on a horse embossed on it. She thought this was funny; Mrs. Hopewell thought it was idiotic and showed simply that she was still a child. She was brilliant but she didn't have a grain of sense. It seemed to Mrs. Hopewell that every year she grew less like other people and more like herself—bloated, rude, and squint-eyed. And she said such strange things! To her own mother she had said—without warning, without excuse, standing up in the middle of a meal with her face purple and her mouth half full—"Woman! do you ever look inside? Do you ever look inside and see what you are *not*?"

God!" she had cried sinking down again and staring at her plate, "Malebranche was right: we are not our own light. We are not our own light!" Mrs. Hopewell had no idea to this day what brought that on. She had only made the remark, hoping Joy would take it in, that a smile never hurt anyone.

The girl had taken the Ph.D. in philosophy and this left Mrs. Hopewell at a complete loss. You could say, "My daughter is a nurse," or "My daughter is a school teacher," or even, "My daughter is a chemical engineer." You could not say, "My daughter is a philosopher." That was something that had ended with the Greeks and Romans. All day Joy sat on her neck in a deep chair, reading. Sometimes she went for walks but she didn't like dogs or cats or birds or flowers or nature or nice young men. She looked at nice young men as if she could smell their stupidity.

One day Mrs. Hopewell had picked up one of the books the girl had just put down and opening it at random, she read, "Science, on the other hand, has to assert its soberness and seriousness afresh and declare that it is concerned solely with what-is. Nothing—how can it be for science anything but a horror and a phantasm? If science is right, then one thing stands firm: science wishes to know nothing of nothing. Such is after all the strictly scientific approach to Nothing. We know it by wishing to know nothing of Nothing." These words had been underlined with a blue pencil and they worked on Mrs. Hopewell like some evil incantation in gibberish. She shut the book quickly and went out of the room as if she were having a chill.

This morning when the girl came in, Mrs. Freeman was on Carramae. "She thrown up four times after supper," she said, "and was up twict in the night after three o'clock. Yesterday she didn't do nothing but ramble in the bureau drawer. All she did. Stand up there and see what she could run up on."

"She's got to eat," Mrs. Hopewell muttered, sipping her coffee, while she watched Joy's back at the stove. She was wondering what the child had said to the Bible salesman. She could not imagine what kind of a conversation she could possibly have had with him.

He was a tall gaunt hatless youth who had called yesterday to sell them a Bible. He had appeared at the door, carrying a large black suitcase that weighted him so heavily on one side that he had to brace himself against the door facing. He seemed on the point of collapse but he said in a cheerful voice, "Good morning, Mrs. Cedars!" and set the suitcase down on the mat. He was not a bad-looking young man though he had on a bright blue suit and yellow socks that were not pulled up far enough. He had prominent face bones and a streak of sticky-looking brown hair falling across his forehead.

"I'm Mrs. Hopewell," she said.

"Oh!" he said, pretending to look puzzled but with his eyes sparkling, "I saw it said 'The Cedars,' on the mailbox so I thought you was Mrs. Cedars!" and he burst out in a pleasant laugh. He picked up the satchel and under cover of a pant, he fell forward into her hall. It was rather as if the suitcase had moved first, jerking him after it. "Mrs. Hopewell!" he said and grabbed her hand. "I hope you are well!" and he laughed again and then all at once his face sobered

completely. He paused and gave her a straight earnest look and s
I've come to speak of serious things."

"Well, come in," she muttered, none too pleased because he
almost ready. He came into the parlor and sat down on the edg
chair and put the suitcase between his feet and glanced around the room a.
he were sizing her up by it. Her silver gleamed on the two sideboards; she
decided he had never been in a room as elegant as this.

"Mrs. Hopewell," he began, using her name in a way that sounded almost
intimate, "I know you believe in Chrustian service."

"Well yes," she murmured.

"I know," he said and paused, looking very wise with his head cocked on one
side, "that you're a good woman. Friends have told me."

Mrs. Hopewell never liked to be taken for a fool. "What are you selling?"
she asked.

"Bibles," the young man said and his eye raced around the room before he
added, "I see you have no family Bible in your parlor, I see that is the one lack
you got!"

Mrs. Hopewell could not say, "My daughter is an atheist and won't let me
keep the Bible in the parlor." She said, stiffening slightly, "I keep my Bible by
my bedside." This was not the truth. It was in the attic somewhere.

"Lady," he said, "the word of God ought to be in the parlor."

"Well, I think that's a matter of taste," she began. "I think . . ."

"Lady," he said, "for a Chrustian, the word of God ought to be in every room
in the house besides in his heart. I know you're a Chrustian because I can see
it in every line of your face."

She stood up and said, "Well, young man, I don't want to buy a Bible and
I smell my dinner burning."

He didn't get up. He began to twist his hands and looking down at them, he
said softly, "Well lady, I'll tell you the truth—not many people want to buy
one nowadays and besides, I know I'm real simple. I don't know how to say a
thing but to say it. I'm just a country boy." He glanced up into her unfriendly
face. "People like you don't like to fool with country people like me!"

"Why!" she cried, "good country people are the salt of the earth! Besides, we
all have different ways of doing, it takes all kinds to make the world go 'round.
That's life!"

"You said a mouthful," he said.

"Why, I think there aren't enough good country people in the world!" she
said, stirred. "I think that's what's wrong with it!"

His face had brightened. "I didn't inraduce myself," he said. "I'm Manley
Pointer from out in the country around Willohobie, not even from a place, just
from near a place."

"You wait a minute," she said. "I have to see about my dinner." She went
out to the kitchen and found Joy standing near the door where she had been
listening.

"Get rid of the salt of the earth," she said, "and let's eat."

Mrs. Hopewell gave her a pained look and turned the heat down under the vegetables. "I can't be rude to anybody," she murmured and went back into the parlor.

He had opened the suitcase and was sitting with a Bible on each knee.

"You might as well put those up," she told him. "I don't want one."

"I appreciate your honesty," he said. "You don't see any more real honest people unless you go way out in the country."

"I know," she said, "real genuine folks!" Through the crack in the door she heard a groan.

"I guess a lot of boys come telling you they're working their way through college," he said, "but I'm not going to tell you that. Somehow," he said, "I don't want to go to college. I want to devote my life to Chrustian service. See," he said, lowering his voice, "I got this heart condition. I may not live long. When you know it's something wrong with you and you may not live long, well then, lady . . ." He paused, with his mouth open, and stared at her.

He and Joy had the same condition! She knew that her eyes were filling with tears but she collected herself quickly and murmured, "Won't you stay for dinner? We'd love to have you!" and was sorry the instant she heard herself say it.

"Yes mam," he said in an abashed voice, "I would sher love to do that!"

Joy had given him one look on being introduced to him and then throughout the meal had not glanced at him again. He had addressed several remarks to her, which she had pretended not to hear. Mrs. Hopewell could not understand deliberate rudeness, although she lived with it, and she felt she had always to overflow with hospitality to make up for Joy's lack of courtesy. She urged him to talk about himself and he did. He said he was the seventh child of twelve and that his father had been crushed under a tree when he himself was eight year old. He had been crushed very badly, in fact, almost cut in two and was practically not recognizable. His mother had got along the best she could by hard working and she had always seen that her children went to Sunday School and that they read the Bible every evening. He was now nineteen year old and he had been selling Bibles for four months. In that time he had sold seventy-seven Bibles and had the promise of two more sales. He wanted to become a missionary because he thought that was the way you could do most for people. "He who losest his life shall find it," he said simply and he was so sincere, so genuine and earnest that Mrs. Hopewell would not for the world have smiled. He prevented his peas from sliding onto the table by blocking them with a piece of bread which he later cleaned his plate with. She could see Joy observing sidewise how he handled his knife and fork and she saw too that every few minutes, the boy would dart a keen appraising glance at the girl as if he were trying to attract her attention.

After dinner Joy cleared the dishes off the table and disappeared and Mrs. Hopewell was left to talk with him. He told her again about his childhood and his father's accident and about various things that had happened to him. Every five minutes or so she would stifle a yawn. He sat for two hours until finally she told him she must go because she had an appointment in town. He packed his Bibles and thanked her and prepared to leave, but in the doorway he stopped and wrung her hand and said that not on any of his trips had he met a lady as nice as her and he asked if he could come again. She had said she would always be happy to see him.

Joy had been standing in the road, apparently looking at something in the distance, when he came down the steps toward her, bent to the side with his heavy valise. He stopped where she was standing and confronted her directly. Mrs. Hopewell could not hear what he said but she trembled to think what Joy would say to him. She could see that after a minute Joy said something and that then the boy began to speak again, making an excited gesture with his free hand. After a minute Joy said something else at which the boy began to speak once more. Then to her amazement, Mrs. Hopewell saw the two of them walk off together, toward the gate. Joy had walked all the way to the gate with him and Mrs. Hopewell could not imagine what they had said to each other, and she had not yet dared to ask.

Mrs. Freeman was insisting upon her attention. She had moved from the refrigerator to the heater so that Mrs. Hopewell had to turn and face her in order to seem to be listening. "Glynese gone out with Harvey Hill again last night," she said. "She had this sty."

"Hill," Mrs. Hopewell said absently, "is that the one who works in the garage?"

"Nome, he's the one that goes to chiropracter school," Mrs. Freeman said. "She had this sty. Been had it two days. So she says when he brought her in the other night he says, 'Lemme get rid of that sty for you,' and she says, 'How?' and he says, 'You just lay yourself down acrost the seat of that car and I'll show you.' So she done it and he popped her neck. Kept on a-popping it several times until she made him quit. This morning," Mrs. Freeman said, "she ain't got no sty. She ain't got no traces of a sty."

"I never heard of that before," Mrs. Hopewell said.

"He ast her to marry him before the Ordinary," Mrs. Freeman went on, "and she told him she wasn't going to be married in no *office*."

"Well, Glynese is a fine girl," Mrs. Hopewell said, "Glynese and Carramae are both fine girls."

"Carramae said when her and Lyman was married Lyman said it sure felt sacred to him. She said he said he wouldn't take five hundred dollars for being married by a preacher."

"How much would he take?" the girl asked from the stove.

"He said he wouldn't take five hundred dollars," Mrs. Freeman repeated.

"Well we all have work to do," Mrs. Hopewell said.

"Lyman said it just felt more sacred to him," Mrs. Freeman said. "The doctor wants Carramae to eat prunes. Says instead of medicine. Says them cramps is coming from pressure. You know where I think it is?"

"She'll be better in a few weeks," Mrs. Hopewell said.

"In the tube," Mrs. Freeman said. "Else she wouldn't be as sick as she is."

Hulga had cracked her two eggs into a saucer and was bringing them to the table along with a cup of coffee that she had filled too full. She sat down carefully and began to eat, meaning to keep Mrs. Freeman there by questions if for any reason she showed an inclination to leave. She could perceive her mother's eye on her. The first roundabout question would be about the Bible salesman and she did not wish to bring it on. "How did he pop her neck?" she asked.

Mrs. Freeman went into a description of how he had popped her neck. She said he owned a '55 Mercury but that Glynese said she would rather marry a man with only a '36 Plymouth who would be married by a preacher. The girl asked what if he had a '32 Plymouth and Mrs. Freeman said what Glynese had said was a '36 Plymouth.

Mrs. Hopewell said there were not many girls with Glynese's common sense. She said what she admired in those girls was their common sense. She said that reminded her that they had a nice visitor yesterday, a young man selling Bibles. "Lord," she said, "he bored me to death but he was so sincere and genuine I couldn't be rude to him. He was just good country people, you know," she said,"—just the salt of the earth."

"I seen him walk up," Mrs. Freeman said, "and then later—I seen him walk off," and Hulga could feel the slight shift in her voice, the slight insinuation, that he had not walked off alone, had he? Her face remained expressionless but the color rose into her neck and she seemed to swallow it down with the next spoonful of egg. Mrs. Freeman was looking at her as if they had a secret together.

"Well, it takes all kinds of people to make the world go 'round," Mrs. Hopewell said. "It's very good we aren't all alike."

"Some people are more alike than others," Mrs. Freeman said.

Hulga got up and stumped, with about twice the noise that was necessary, into her room and locked the door. She was to meet the Bible salesman at ten o'clock at the gate. She had thought about it half the night. She had started thinking of it as a great joke and then she had begun to see profound implications in it. She had lain in bed imagining dialogues for them that were insane on the surface but that reached below to depths that no Bible salesman would be aware of. Their conversation yesterday had been of this kind.

He had stopped in front of her and had simply stood there. His face was bony and sweaty and bright, with a little pointed nose in the center of it, and his look was different from what it had been at the dinner table. He was gazing at her with open curiosity, with fascination, like a child watching a new fantastic animal at the zoo, and he was breathing as if he had run a great distance to reach her. His gaze seemed somehow familiar but she could not think where she had been regarded with it before. For almost a minute he didn't say anything. Then on what seemed an insuck of breath, he whispered, "You ever ate a chicken that was two days old?"

The girl looked at him stonily. He might have just put this question up for consideration at the meeting of a philosophical association. "Yes," she presently replied as if she had considered it from all angles.

"It must have been mighty small!" he said triumphantly and shook all over with little nervous giggles, getting very red in the face, and subsiding finally into his gaze of complete admiration, while the girl's expression remained exactly the same.

"How old are you?" he asked softly.

She waited some time before she answered. Then in a flat voice she said, "Seventeen."

His smiles came in succession like waves breaking on the surface of a little lake. "I see you got a wooden leg," he said. "I think you're real brave. I think you're real sweet."

The girl stood blank and solid and silent.

"Walk to the gate with me," he said. "You're a brave sweet little thing and I liked you the minute I seen you walk in the door."

Hulga began to move forward.

"What's your name?" he asked, smiling down on the top of her head.

"Hulga," she said.

"Hulga," he murmured, "Hulga. Hulga. I never heard of anybody name Hulga before. You're shy, aren't you, Hulga?" he asked.

She nodded, watching his large red hand on the handle of the giant valise.

"I like girls that wear glasses," he said. "I think a lot. I'm not like these people that a serious thought don't ever enter their heads. It's because I may die."

"I may die too," she said suddenly and looked up at him. His eyes were very small and brown, glittering feverishly.

"Listen," he said, "don't you think some people was meant to meet on account of what all they got in common and all? Like they both think serious thoughts and all?" He shifted the valise to his other hand so that the hand nearest her was free. He caught hold of her elbow and shook it a little. "I don't work on Saturday," he said. "I like to walk in the woods and see what Mother Nature is wearing. O'er the hills and far away. Pic-nics and things. Couldn't we go on a pic-nic tomorrow? Say yes, Hulga," he said and gave her a dying look as if he felt his insides about to drop out of him. He had even seemed to sway slightly toward her.

During the night she had imagined that she seduced him. She imagined that the two of them walked on the place until they came to the storage barn beyond the two back fields and there, she imagined, that things came to such a pass that she very easily seduced him and that then, of course, she had to reckon with his remorse. True genius can get an idea across even to an inferior mind. She imagined that she took his remorse in hand and changed it into a deeper understanding of life. She took all his shame away and turned it into something useful.

She set off for the gate at exactly ten o'clock, escaping without drawing Mrs.

Hopewell's attention. She didn't take anything to eat, forgetting that food is usually taken on a picnic. She wore a pair of slacks and a dirty white shirt, and as an afterthought, she had put some Vapex on the collar of it since she did not own any perfume. When she reached the gate no one was there.

She looked up and down the empty highway and had the furious feeling that she had been tricked, that he had only meant to make her walk to the gate after the idea of him. Then suddenly he stood up, very tall, from behind a bush on the opposite embankment. Smiling, he lifted his hat which was new and wide-brimmed. He had not worn it yesterday and she wondered if he had bought it for the occasion. It was toast-colored with a red and white band around it and was slightly too large for him. He stepped from behind the bush still carrying the black valise. He had on the same suit and the same yellow socks sucked down in his shoes from walking. He crossed the highway and said, "I knew you'd come!"

The girl wondered acidly how he had known this. She pointed to the valise and asked, "Why did you bring your Bibles?"

He took her elbow, smiling down on her as if he could not stop. "You can never tell when you'll need the word of God, Hulga," he said. She had a moment in which she doubted that this was actually happening and then they began to climb the embankment. They went down into the pasture toward the woods. The boy walked lightly by her side, bouncing on his toes. The valise did not seem to be heavy today; he even swung it. They crossed half the pasture without saying anything and then, putting his hand easily on the small of her back, he asked softly, "Where does your wooden leg join on?"

She turned an ugly red and glared at him and for an instant the boy looked abashed. "I didn't mean you no harm," he said. "I only meant you're so brave and all. I guess God takes care of you."

"No," she said, looking forward and walking fast, "I don't even believe in God."

At this he stopped and whistled. "No!" he exclaimed as if he were too astonished to say anything else.

She walked on and in a second he was bouncing at her side, fanning with his hat. "That's very unusual for a girl," he remarked, watching her out of the corner of his eye. When they reached the edge of the wood, he put his hand on her back again and drew her against him without a word and kissed her heavily.

The kiss, which had more pressure than feeling behind it, produced that extra surge of adrenalin in the girl that enables one to carry a packed trunk out of a burning house, but in her, the power went at once to the brain. Even before he released her, her mind, clear and detached and ironic anyway, was regarding him from a great distance, with amusement but with pity. She had never been kissed before and she was pleased to discover that it was an unexceptional experience and all a matter of the mind's control. Some people might enjoy drain water if they were told it was vodka. When the boy, looking expectant but uncertain, pushed her gently away, she turned and walked on, saying nothing as if such business, for her, were common enough.

He came along panting at her side, trying to help her when he saw a root that she might trip over. He caught and held back the long swaying blades of thorn vine until she had passed beyond them. She led the way and he came breathing heavily behind her. Then they came out on a sunlit hillside, sloping softly into another one a little smaller. Beyond, they could see the rusted top of the old barn where the extra hay was stored.

The hill was sprinkled with small pink weeds. "Then you ain't saved?" he asked suddenly, stopping.

The girl smiled. It was the first time she had smiled at him at all. "In my economy," she said, "I'm saved and you are damned but I told you I didn't believe in God."

Nothing seemed to destroy the boy's look of admiration. He gazed at her now as if the fantastic animal at the zoo had put its paw through the bars and given him a loving poke. She thought he looked as if he wanted to kiss her again and she walked on before he had the chance.

"Ain't there somewheres we can sit down sometime?" he murmured, his voice softening toward the end of the sentence.

"In that barn," she said.

They made for it rapidly as if it might slide away like a train. It was a large two-story barn, cool and dark inside. The boy pointed up the ladder that led into the loft and said, "It's too bad we can't go up there."

"Why can't we?" she asked.

"Yer leg," he said reverently.

The girl gave him a contemptuous look and putting both hands on the ladder, she climbed it while he stood below, apparently awestruck. She pulled herself expertly through the opening and then looked down at him and said, "Well, come on if you're coming," and he began to climb the ladder, awkwardly bringing the suitcase with him.

"We won't need the Bible," she observed.

"You never can tell," he said, panting. After he had got into the loft, he was a few seconds catching his breath. She had sat down in a pile of straw. A wide sheath of sunlight, filled with dust particles, slanted over her. She lay back against a bale, her face turned away, looking out the front opening of the barn where hay was thrown from a wagon into the loft. The two pink-speckled hillsides lay back against a dark ridge of woods. The sky was cloudless and cold blue. The boy dropped down by her side and put one arm under her and the other over her and began methodically kissing her face, making little noises like a fish. He did not remove his hat but it was pushed far enough back not to interfere. When her glasses got in his way, he took them off of her and slipped them into his pocket.

The girl at first did not return any of the kisses but presently she began to and after she had put several on his cheek, she reached his lips and remained there, kissing him again and again as if she were trying to draw all the breath out of him. His breath was clear and sweet like a child's and the kisses were sticky like a child's. He mumbled about loving her and about knowing when he first seen her that he loved her, but the mumbling was like the sleepy fretting of a child being put to sleep by his mother. Her mind, throughout this, never stopped or lost itself for a second to her feelings. "You ain't said you love me none," he whispered finally, pulling back from her. "You got to say that."

She looked away from him off into the hollow sky and then down at a black ridge and then down farther into what appeared to be two green swelling lakes. She didn't realize he had taken her glasses but this landscape could not seem exceptional to her for she seldom paid any close attention to her surroundings.

"You got to say it," he repeated. "You got to say you love me."

She was always careful how she committed herself. "In a sense," she began, "if you use the word loosely, you might say that. But it's not a word I use. I don't have illusions. I'm one of those people who see *through* to nothing."

The boy was frowning. "You got to say it. I said it and you got to say it," he said.

The girl looked at him almost tenderly. "You poor baby," she murmured. "It's just as well you don't understand," and she pulled him by the neck, face-down, against her. "We are all damned," she said, "but some of us have taken off our blindfolds and see that there's nothing to see. It's a kind of salvation."

The boy's astonished eyes looked blankly through the ends of her hair. "Okay," he almost whined, "but do you love me or don'tcher?"

"Yes," she said and added, "in a sense. But I must tell you something. There mustn't be anything dishonest between us." She lifted his head and looked him in the eye. "I am thirty years old," she said. "I have a number of degrees."

The boy's look was irritated but dogged. "I don't care," he said. "I don't care a thing about what all you done. I just want to know if you love me or don'tcher?" and he caught her to him and wildly planted her face with kisses until she said, "Yes, yes."

"Okay then," he said, letting her go. "Prove it."

She smiled, looking dreamily out on the shifty landscape. She had seduced him without even making up her mind to try. "How?" she asked, feeling that he should be delayed a little.

He leaned over and put his lips to her ear. "Show me where your wooden leg joins on," he whispered.

The girl uttered a sharp little cry and her face instantly drained of color. The obscenity of the suggestion was not what shocked her. As a child she had sometimes been subject to feelings of shame but education had removed the last traces of that as a good surgeon scrapes for cancer; she would no more have felt it over what he was asking than she would have believed in his Bible. But she was as sensitive about the artificial leg as a peacock about his tail. No one ever touched it but her. She took care of it as someone else would his soul, in private and almost with her own eyes turned away. "No," she said.

"I known it," he muttered, sitting up. "You're just playing me for a sucker."

"Oh no no!" she cried. "It joins on at the knee. Only at the knee. Why do you want to see it?"

The boy gave her a long penetrating look. "Because," he said, "it's what makes you different. You ain't like anybody else."

She sat staring at him. There was nothing about her face or her round freezing-blue eyes to indicate that this had moved her; but she felt as if her heart had stopped and left her mind to pump her blood. She decided that for the first time in her life she was face to face with real innocence. This boy, with an instinct that came from beyond wisdom, had touched the truth about her. When after a minute, she said in a hoarse high voice, "All right," it was like surrendering to him completely. It was like losing her own life and finding it again, miraculously, in his.

Very gently he began to roll the slack leg up. The artificial limb, in a white sock and brown flat shoe, was bound in a heavy material like canvas and ended in an ugly jointure where it was attached to the stump. The boy's face and his voice were entirely reverent as he uncovered it and said, "Now show me how to take it off and on."

She took it off for him and put it back on again and then he took it off himself, handling it as tenderly as if it were a real one. "See!" he said with a delighted child's face. "Now I can do it myself!"

"Put it back on," she said. She was thinking that she would run away with him and that every night he would take the leg off and every morning put it back on again. "Put it back on," she said.

"Not yet," he murmured, setting it on its foot out of her reach. "Leave it off for a while. You got me instead."

She gave a little cry of alarm but he pushed her down and began to kiss her again. Without the leg she felt entirely dependent on him. Her brain seemed to have stopped thinking altogether and to be about some other function that it was not very good at. Different expressions raced back and forth over her face. Every now and then the boy, his eyes like two steel spikes, would glance behind him where the leg stood. Finally she pushed him off and said, "Put it back on me now."

"Wait," he said. He leaned the other way and pulled the valise toward him and opened it. It had a pale blue spotted lining and there were only two Bibles in it. He took one of these out and opened the cover of it. It was hollow and contained a pocket flask of whiskey, a pack of cards, and a small blue box with printing on it. He laid these out in front of her one at a time in an evenly spaced row, like one presenting offerings at the shrine of a goddess. He put the blue box in her hand. THIS PRODUCT TO BE USED ONLY FOR THE PREVENTION OF DISEASE, she read, and dropped it. The boy was unscrewing the top of the flask. He stopped and pointed, with a smile, to the deck of cards. It was not an ordinary deck but one with an obscene picture on the back of each card. "Take a swig," he said, offering her the bottle first. He held it in front of her, but like one mesmerized, she did not move.

Her voice when she spoke had an almost pleading sound. "Aren't you," she murmured, "aren't you just good country people?"

The boy cocked his head. He looked as if he were just beginning to understand that she might be trying to insult him. "Yeah," he said, curling his lip slightly, "but it ain't held me back none. I'm as good as you any day in the week."

"Give me my leg," she said.

He pushed it farther away with his foot. "Come on now, let's begin to have us a good time," he said coaxingly. "We ain't got to know one another good yet."

"Give me my leg!" she screamed and tried to lunge for it but he pushed her down easily.

"What's the matter with you all of a sudden?" he asked, frowning as he screwed the top on the flask and put it quickly back inside the Bible. "You just a while ago said you didn't believe in nothing. I thought you was some girl!"

Her face was almost purple. "You're a Christian!" she hissed. "You're a fine Christian! You're just like them all—say one thing and do another. You're a perfect Christian, you're . . ."

The boy's mouth was set angrily. "I hope you don't think," he said in a lofty indignant tone, "that I believe in that crap! I may sell Bibles but I know which end is up and I wasn't born yesterday and I know where I'm going!"

"Give me my leg!" she screeched. He jumped up so quickly that she barely saw him sweep the cards and the blue box back into the Bible and throw the Bible into the valise. She saw him grab the leg and then she saw it for an instant slanted forlornly across the inside of the suitcase with a Bible at either side of its opposite ends. He slammed the lid shut and snatched up the valise and swung it down the hole and then stepped through himself.

When all of him had passed but his head, he turned and regarded her with a look that no longer had any admiration in it. "I've gotten a lot of interesting things," he said. "One time I got a woman's glass eye this way. And you needn't to think you'll catch me because Pointer ain't really my name. I use a different name at every house I call at and don't stay nowhere long. And I'll tell you another thing, Hulga," he said, using the name as if he didn't think much of it, "you ain't so smart. I been believing in nothing ever since I was born!" and then the toast-colored hat disappeared down the hole and the girl was left, sitting on the straw in the dusty sunlight. When she turned her churning face toward the opening, she saw his blue figure struggling successfully over the green speckled lake.

Mrs. Hopewell and Mrs. Freeman, who were in the back pasture, digging up onions, saw him emerge a little later from the woods and head across the meadow toward the highway. "Why, that looks like that nice dull young man that tried to sell me a Bible yesterday," Mrs. Hopewell said, squinting. "He must have been selling them to the Negroes back in there. He was so simple," she said, "but I guess the world would be better off if we were all that simple."

Mrs. Freeman's gaze drove forward and just touched him before he disappeared under the hill. Then she returned her attention to the evil-smelling onion shoot she was lifting from the ground. "Some can't be that simple," she said. "I know I never could."

QUESTIONS

1. Why does Joy feel that changing her name to Hulga is "her highest creative act"? **2.** In what ways do Mrs. Freeman's descriptions of her daughters Glynese and Carramae contribute to the theme of the story? **3.** Is the title ironic? Explain.

WRITING TOPICS

1. Does this story have any admirable characters or heroes in the conventional sense? Explain. **2.** Why does Hulga agree to meet with Manley Pointer? Does Hulga's experience with Manley Pointer confirm her cynical philosophy of "nothing"?

The Lesson

TONI CADE BAMBARA [b. 1939]

1972

Back in the days when everyone was old and stupid or young and foolish and me and Sugar were the only ones just right, this lady moved on our block with nappy hair and proper speech and no makeup. And quite naturally we laughed at her, laughed the way we did at the junk man who went about his business like he was some big-time president and his sorry-ass horse his secretary. And we kinda hated her too, hated the way we did the winos who cluttered up our parks and pissed on our handball walls and stank up our hallways and stairs so you couldn't halfway play hide-and-seek without a goddamn gas mask. Miss Moore was her name. The only woman on the block with no first name. And she was black as hell, cept for her feet, which were fish-white and spooky. And she was always planning these boring-ass things for us to do, us being my cousin, mostly, who lived on the block cause we all moved North the same time and to the same apartment then spread out gradual to breathe. And our parents would yank our heads into some kinda shape and crisp up our clothes so we'd be presentable for travel with Miss Moore, who always looked like she was going to church, though she never did. Which is just one of the things the grownups talked about when they talked behind her back like a dog. But when she came calling with some sachet she'd sewed up or some gingerbread she'd made or some book, why then they'd all be too embarrassed to turn her down and we'd get handed over all spruced up. She'd been to college and said it was only right that she should take responsibility for the young ones' education, and she not even related by marriage or blood. So they'd go for it. Specially Aunt Gretchen. She was the main gofer in the family. You got some old dumb shit foolishness you want somebody to go for, you send for Aunt Gretchen. She been screwed into the go-along for so long, it's a blood-deep natural thing with her. Which is how she got saddled with me and Sugar and Junior in the first place while our mothers were in a la-de-da apartment up the block having a good ole time.

So this one day Miss Moore rounds us all up at the mailbox and it's puredee hot and she's knockin herself out about arithmetic. And school suppose to let up in summer I heard, but she don't never let up. And the starch in my pinafore scratching the shit outta me and I'm really hating this nappy-head bitch and her goddamn college degree. I'd much rather go to the pool or to the show where it's cool. So me and Sugar leaning on the mailbox being surly, which is a Miss Moore word. And Flyboy checking out what everybody brought for lunch. And Fat Butt already wasting his peanut-butter-and-jelly sandwich like the pig he is. And Junebug punchin on Q.T.'s arm for potato chips. And Rosie Giraffe shifting from one hip to the other waiting for somebody to step on her foot or ask her if she from Georgia so she can kick ass, preferably Mercedes'. And Miss Moore asking us do we know what money is, like we a bunch of retards. I mean real money, she say, like it's only poker chips or monopoly papers we lay on the grocer. So right away I'm tired of this and say so. And would much rather snatch Sugar and go to the Sunset and terrorize the West Indian kids and take their hair ribbons and their money too. And Miss Moore files that remark away for next week's lesson on brotherhood, I can tell. And finally I say we oughta get to the subway cause it's cooler and besides we might meet some cute boys. Sugar done swiped her mama's lipstick, so we ready.

So we heading down the street and she's boring us silly about what things cost and what our parents make and how much goes for rent and how money ain't divided up right in this country. And then she gets to the part about we all poor and live in the slums, which I don't feature. And I'm ready to speak on that, but she steps out in the street and hails two cabs just like that. Then she hustles half the crew in with her and hands me a five-dollar bill and tells me to calculate 10 percent tip for the driver. And we're off. Me and Sugar and Junebug and Flyboy hangin out the window and hollering to everybody, putting lipstick on each other cause Flyboy a faggot anyway, and making farts with our sweaty armpits. But I'm mostly trying to figure how to spend this money. But they all fascinated with the meter ticking and Junebug starts laying bets as to how much it'll read when Flyboy can't hold his breath no more. Then Sugar lays bets as to how much it'll be when we get there. So I'm stuck. Don't nobody want to go for my plan, which is to jump out at the next light and run off to the first bar-b-que we can find. Then the driver tells us to get the hell out cause we there already. And the meter reads eighty-five cents. And I'm stalling to figure out the tip and Sugar say give him a dime. And I decide he don't need it bad as I do, so later for him. But then he tries to take off with Junebug foot still in the door so we talk about his mama something ferocious. Then we check out that we on Fifth Avenue and everybody dressed up in stockings. One lady in a fur coat, hot as it is. White folks crazy.

"This is the place," Miss Moore say, presenting it to us in the voice she uses at the museum. "Let's look in the windows before we go in."

"Can we steal?" Sugar asks very serious like she's getting the ground rules squared away before she plays. "I beg your pardon," say Miss Moore, and we fall out. So she leads us around the windows of the toy store and me and Sugar screamin, "This is mine, that's mine, I gotta have that, that was made for me, I was born for that," till Big Butt drowns us out.

"Hey, I'm goin to buy that there."

"That there? You don't even know what it is, stupid."

"I do so," he say punchin on Rosie Giraffe. "It's a microscope."

"Whatcha gonna do with a microscope, fool?"

"Look at things."

"Like what, Ronald?" ask Miss Moore. And Big Butt ain't got the first notion. So here go Miss Moore gabbing about the thousands of bacteria in a drop of water and the somethinorother in a speck of blood and the million and one living things in the air around us is invisible to the naked eye. And what she say that for? Junebug go to town on that "naked" and we rolling. Then Miss

Moore ask what it cost. So we all jam into the window smudgin it up and the price tag say $300. So then she ask how long'd take for Big Butt and Junebug to save up their allowances. "Too long," I say. "Yeh," adds Sugar, "outgrown it by that time." And Miss Moore say no, you never outgrow learning instruments. "Why, even medical students and interns and," blah, blah, blah. And we ready to choke Big Butt for bringing it up in the first damn place.

"This here costs four hundred eighty dollars," say Rosie Giraffe. So we pile up all over her to see what she pointin out. My eyes tell me it's a chunk of glass cracked with something heavy, and different-color inks dripped into the splits, then the whole thing put into a oven or something. But for $480 it don't make sense.

"That's a paperweight made of semi-precious stones fused together under tremendous pressure," she explains slowly, with her hands doing the mining and all the factory work.

"So what's a paperweight?" asks Rosie Giraffe.

"To weigh paper with, dumbbell," say Flyboy, the wise man from the East.

"Not exactly," say Miss Moore, which is what she say when you warm or way off too. "It's to weigh paper down so it won't scatter and make your desk untidy." So right away me and Sugar curtsy to each other and then to Mercedes who is more the tidy type.

"We don't keep paper on top of the desk in my class," say Junebug, figuring Miss Moore crazy or lyin one.

"At home, then," she say. "Don't you have a calendar and a pencil case and a blotter and a letter-opener on your desk at home where you do your homework?" And she know damn well what our homes look like cause she nosys around in them every chance she gets.

"I don't even have a desk," say Junebug. "Do we?"

"No. And I don't get no homework neither," says Big Butt.

"And I don't even have a home," say Flyboy like he do at school to keep the white folks off his back and sorry for him. Send this poor kid to camp posters, is his specialty.

"I do," says Mercedes. "I have a box of stationery on my desk and a picture of my cat. My godmother bought the stationery and the desk. There's a big rose on each sheet and the envelopes smell like roses."

"Who wants to know about your smelly-ass stationery," say Rosie Giraffe fore I can get my two cents in.

"It's important to have a work area all your own so that . . ."

"Will you look at this sailboat, please," say Flyboy, cuttin her off and pointin to the thing like it was his. So once again we tumble all over each other to gaze at this magnificent thing in the toy store which is just big enough to maybe sail two kittens across the pond if you strap them to the posts tight. We all start reciting the price tag like we in assembly. "Handcrafted sailboat of fiberglass at one thousand one hundred ninety-five dollars."

"Unbelievable," I hear myself say and am really stunned. I read it again for myself just in case the group recitation put me in a trance. Same thing. For some reason this pisses me off. We look at Miss Moore and she lookin at us, waiting for I dunno what.

"Who'd pay all that when you can buy a sailboat set for a quarter at Pop's, a tube of glue for a dime, and a ball of string for eight cents? It must have a motor and a whole lot else besides," I say. "My sailboat cost me about fifty cents."

"But will it take water?" say Mercedes with her smart ass.

"Took mine to Alley Pond Park once," say Flyboy. "String broke. Lost it. Pity."

"Sailed mine in Central Park and it keeled over and sank. Had to ask my father for another dollar."

"And you got the strap," laugh Big Butt. "The jerk didn't even have a string on it. My old man wailed on his behind."

Little Q.T. was staring hard at the sailboat and you could see he wanted it bad. But he too little and somebody'd just take it from him. So what the hell. "This boat for kids, Miss Moore?"

"Parents silly to buy something like that just to get all broke up," say Rosie Giraffe.

"That much money it should last forever," I figure.

"My father'd buy it for me if I wanted it."

"Your father, my ass," say Rosie Giraffe getting a chance to finally push Mercedes.

"Must be rich people shop here," say Q.T.

"You are a very bright boy," say Flyboy. "What was your first clue?" And he rap him on the head with the back of his knuckles, since Q.T. the only one he could get away with. Though Q.T. liable to come up behind you years later and get his licks in when you half expect it.

"What I want to know is," I says to Miss Moore though I never talk to her, I wouldn't give the bitch that satisfaction, "is how much a real boat costs? I figure a thousand'd get you a yacht any day."

"Why don't you check that out," she says, "and report back to the group?" Which really pains my ass. If you gonna mess up a perfectly good swim day least you could do is have some answers. "Let's go in," she say like she got something up her sleeve. Only she don't lead the way. So me and Sugar turn the corner to where the entrance is, but when we get there I kinda hang back. Not that I'm scared, what's there to be afraid of, just a toy store. But I feel funny, shame. But what I got to be shamed about? Got as much right to go in as anybody. But somehow I can't seem to get hold of the door, so I step away for Sugar to lead. But she hangs back too. And I look at her and she looks at me and this is ridiculous. I mean, damn, I have never ever been shy about doing nothing or going nowhere. But then Mercedes steps up and then Rosie Giraffe and Big Butt crowd in behind and shove, and next thing we all stuffed into the doorway with only Mercedes squeezing past us, smoothing out her jumper and walking right down the aisle. Then the rest of us tumble in like a glued-together jigsaw done all wrong. And people lookin at us. And it's like the time me and

Sugar crashed into the Catholic church on a dare. But once we got in there and everything so hushed and holy and the candles and the bowin and the handkerchiefs on all the drooping heads, I just couldn't go through with the plan. Which was for me to run up to the altar and do a tap dance while Sugar played the nose flute and messed around in the holy water. And Sugar kept givin me the elbow. Then later teased me so bad I tied her up in the shower and turned it on and locked her in. And she'd be there till this day if Aunt Gretchen hadn't finally figured I was lyin about the boarder takin a shower.

Same thing in the store. We all walkin on tiptoe and hardly touchin the games and puzzles and things. And I watched Miss Moore who is steady watchin us like she waitin for a sign. Like Mama Drewery watches the sky and sniffs the air and takes note of just how much slant is in the bird formation. Then me and Sugar bump smack into each other, so busy gazing at the toys, 'specially the sailboat. But we don't laugh and go into our fat-lady bump-stomach routine. We just stare at that price tag. Then Sugar run a finger over the whole boat. And I'm jealous and want to hit her. Maybe not her, but I sure want to punch somebody in the mouth.

"Watcha bring us here for, Miss Moore?"

"You sound angry, Sylvia. Are you mad about something?" Givin me one of them grins like she tellin a grown-up joke that never turns out to be funny. And she's lookin very closely at me like maybe she plannin to do my portrait from memory. I'm mad, but I won't give her that satisfaction. So I slouch around the store bein very bored and say, "Let's go."

Me and Sugar at the back of the train watchin the tracks whizzin by large then small then gettin gobbled up in the dark. I'm thinkin about this tricky toy I saw in the store. A clown that somersaults on a bar then does chin-ups just cause you yank lightly at his leg. Cost $35. I could see me askin my mother for a $35 birthday clown. "You wanna who that costs what?" she'd say, cocking her head to the side to get a better view of the hole in my head. Thirty-five dollars could buy new bunk beds for Junior and Gretchen's boy. Thirty-five dollars and the whole household could go visit Granddaddy Nelson in the country. Thirty-five dollars would pay for the rent and the piano bill too. Who are these people that spend that much for performing clowns and $1000 for toy sailboats? What kinda work they do and how they live and how come we ain't in on it? Where we are is who we are, Miss Moore always pointin out. But it don't necessarily have to be that way, she always adds then waits for somebody to say that poor people have to wake up and demand their share of the pie and don't none of us know what kind of pie she talkin about in the first damn place. But she ain't so smart cause I still got her four dollars from the taxi and she sure ain't gettin it. Messin up my day with this shit. Sugar nudges me in my pocket and winks.

Miss Moore lines us up in front of the mailbox where we started from, seem like years ago, and I got a headache for thinkin so hard. And we lean all over each other so we can hold up under the draggy-ass lecture she always finishes us off with at the end before we thank her for borin us to tears. But she just looks at us like she readin tea leaves. Finally she say, "Well, what did you think of F. A. O. Schwarz?"

Rosie Giraffe mumbles, "White folks crazy."

"I'd like to go there again when I get my birthday money," says Mercedes, and we shove her out the pack so she has to lean on the mailbox by herself.

"I'd like a shower. Tiring day," say Flyboy.

Then Sugar surprises me by sayin, "You know, Miss Moore, I don't think all of us here put together eat in a year what that sailboat costs." And Miss Moore lights up like somebody goosed her. "And?" she say, urging Sugar on. Only I'm standin on her foot so she don't continue.

"Imagine for a minute what kind of society it is in which some people can spend on a toy what it would cost to feed a family of six or seven. What do you think?"

"I think," say Sugar pushing me off her feet like she never done before, cause I whip her ass in a minute, "that this is not much of a democracy if you ask me. Equal chance to pursue happiness means an equal crack at the dough, don't it?" Miss Moore is besides herself and I am disgusted with Sugar's treachery. So I stand on her foot one more time to see if she'll shove me. She shuts up, and Miss Moore looks at me, sorrowfully I'm thinkin. And somethin weird is goin on, I can feel it in my chest.

"Anybody else learn anything today?" lookin dead at me. I walk away and Sugar has to run to catch up and don't even seem to notice when I shrug her arm off my shoulder.

"Well, we got four dollars anyway," she says.

"Uh hunh."

"We could go to Hascombs and get half a chocolate layer and then go to the Sunset and still have plenty money for potato chips and ice cream sodas."

"Uh hunh."

"Race you to Hascombs," she say.

We start down the block and she gets ahead which is O.K. by me cause I'm goin to the West End and then over to the Drive to think this day through. She can run if she want to and even run faster. But ain't nobody gonna beat me at nuthin.

QUESTIONS

1. Characterize the narrator of this story. **2.** How does the narrator describe her neighborhood? How does she feel when Miss Moore calls the neighborhood a slum? **3.** F. A. O. Schwarz is a famous toy store on Fifth Avenue in New York City, located about three miles south of Harlem where, doubtless, the children live. What lesson does Miss Moore convey by taking them there?

WRITING TOPIC

Is there any evidence at the end of the story that the narrator has been changed by the experience?

INNOCENCE
AND
EXPERIENCE

The Mysterious Rose Garden, by Aubrey Beardsley

POETRY

The Chimney Sweeper

1789

WILLIAM BLAKE [1757–1827]

When my mother died I was very young,
And my Father sold me while yet my tongue
Could scarcely cry " 'weep! 'weep! 'weep! 'weep!"
So your chimneys I sweep, and in soot I sleep.

There's little Tom Dacre, who cried when his head,
That curled like a lamb's back, was shaved: so I said,
"Hush, Tom! never mind it, for when your head's bare
You know that the soot cannot spoil your white hair."

And so he was quiet and that very night
As Tom was a-sleeping, he had such a sight!   10
That thousands of sweepers, Dick, Joe, Ned, and Jack,
Were all of them locked up in coffins of black.

And by came an Angel who had a bright key,
And he opened the coffins and set them all free;
Then down a green plain leaping, laughing, they run,
And wash in a river, and shine in the Sun.

Then naked and white, all their bags left behind,
They rise upon clouds and sport in the wind;
And the Angel told Tom, if he'd be a good boy,
He'd have God for his father, and never want joy.   20

And so Tom awoke; and we rose in the dark,
And got with our bags and our brushes to work.
Though the morning was cold, Tom was happy and warm;
So if all do their duty they need not fear harm.

The Tyger   1794

WILLIAM BLAKE [1757–1827]

Tyger! Tyger! burning bright
In the forests of the night,
What immortal hand or eye
Could frame thy fearful symmetry?

In what distant deeps or skies
Burnt the fire of thine eyes?
On what wings dare he aspire?
What the hand, dare seize the fire?

And what shoulder, & what art,
Could twist the sinews of thy heart?   10
And when thy heart began to beat,
What dread hand? & what dread feet?

What the hammer? what the chain?
In what furnace was thy brain?
What the anvil? what dread grasp
Dare its deadly terrors clasp?

When the stars threw down their spears,
And water'd heaven with their tears,
Did he smile his work to see?
Did he who made the Lamb make thee?   20

Tyger! Tyger! burning bright
In the forests of the night,
What immortal hand or eye
Dare frame thy fearful symmetry?

The Garden of Love   1793

WILLIAM BLAKE [1757–1827]

I went to the Garden of Love,
And saw what I never had seen:
A Chapel was built in the midst,
Where I used to play on the green.

And the gates of this Chapel were shut,
And "Thou shalt not" writ over the door;
So I turn'd to the Garden of Love,
That so many sweet flowers bore,

And I saw it was filled with graves,
And tomb-stones where flowers should be: 10
And Priests in black gowns were walking their rounds,
And binding with briars my joys & desires.

QUESTIONS

1. What meanings does the word "love" have in this poem?   **2.**   What is Blake's judgment on established religion?   **3.**   Explain the meaning of "Chapel" (l. 3) and of "briars" (l. 12).

WRITING TOPIC

Read the definition of irony in the glossary of literary terms. Write an essay in which you distinguish between the types of irony used in "The Chimney Sweeper" and "The Garden of Love."

London   1794

WILLIAM BLAKE   [1757–1827]

I wander through each chartered[1] street,
Near where the chartered Thames does flow
And mark in every face I meet
Marks of weakness, marks of woe.

In every cry of every man,
In every infant's cry of fear,
In every voice; in every ban,
The mind-forged manacles I hear:

How the chimney-sweeper's cry
Every blackening church appalls,   10
And the hapless soldier's sigh
Runs in blood down palace-walls.

London
   [1] Preempted by the state and leased out under royal patent.

But most, through midnight streets I hear
How the youthful harlot's curse
Blasts the new-born infant's tear,
And blights with plagues the marriage-hearse.

On First Looking into Chapman's Homer[1]

1816

JOHN KEATS   [1795–1821]

Much have I travelled in the realms of gold,
And many goodly states and kingdoms seen:
Round many western islands have I been
Which bards in fealty to Apollo[2] hold.
Oft of one wide expanse had I been told
That deep-browed Homer ruled as his demesne;°   realm
Yet did I never breathe its pure serene°   clear air
Till I heard Chapman speak out loud and bold:
Then felt I like some watcher of the skies
When a new planet swims into his ken;   10
Or like stout Cortez[3] when with eagle eyes
He stared at the Pacific—and all his men
Looked at each other with a wild surmise—
    Silent, upon a peak in Darien.

My Last Duchess

1842

ROBERT BROWNING   [1812–1889]

FERRARA

That's my last Duchess painted on the wall,
Looking as if she were alive. I call
That piece a wonder, now: Frà Pandolf's[1] hands
Worked busily a day, and there she stands.

On First Looking into Chapman's Homer
   [1] George Chapman published translations of *The Iliad* (1611) and *The Odyssey* (1616).
   [2] The god of poetry.
   [3] Keats mistakenly attributes the discovery of the Pacific Ocean by Europeans to Hernando Cortez (1485–1547), the Spanish conqueror of Mexico. Vasco Nuñez de Balboa (1475–1517) first saw the Pacific from a mountain located in eastern Panama.

My Last Duchess
   [1] Frà Pandolf and Claus of Innsbruck (mentioned in the last line) are fictitious artists.

Will't please you sit and look at her? I said
"Frà Pandolf" by design, for never read
Strangers like you that pictured countenance,
The depth and passion of its earnest glance,
But to myself they turned (since none puts by
The curtain I have drawn for you, but I)   10
And seemed as they would ask me, if they durst,
How such a glance came there; so, not the first
Are you to turn and ask thus. Sir, 'twas not
Her husband's presence only, called that spot
Of joy into the Duchess' cheek: perhaps
Frà Pandolf chanced to say "Her mantle laps
"Over my lady's wrist too much," or "Paint
"Must never hope to reproduce the faint
"Half-flush that dies along her throat": such stuff
Was courtesy, she thought, and cause enough   20
For calling up that spot of joy. She had
A heart—how shall I say?—too soon made glad,
Too easily impressed; she liked whate'er
She looked on, and her looks went everywhere.
Sir, 'twas all one! My favor at her breast,
The dropping of the daylight in the West,
The bough of cherries some officious fool
Broke in the orchard for her, the white mule
She rode with round the terrace—all and each
Would draw from her alike the approving speech,   30
Or blush, at least. She thanked men—good! but thanked
Somehow—I know not how—as if she ranked
My gift of a nine-hundred-years-old name
With anybody's gift. Who'd stoop to blame
This sort of trifling? Even had you skill
In speech—which I have not—to make your will
Quite clear to such an one, and say, "Just this
"Or that in you disgusts me; here you miss,
"Or there exceed the mark"—and if she let
Herself be lessoned so, nor plainly set
Her wits to yours, forsooth, and made excuse,   40
—E'en then would be some stooping; and I choose
Never to stoop. Oh sir, she smiled, no doubt,
Whene'er I passed her; but who passed without
Much the same smile? This grew; I gave commands;
Then all smiles stopped together. There she stands
As if alive. Will't please you rise? We'll meet
The company below, then. I repeat,

The Count your master's known munificence
Is ample warrant that no just pretense
Of mine for dowry will be disallowed; 50
Though his fair daughter's self, as I avowed
At starting, is my object. Nay, we'll go
Together down, sir. Notice Neptune, though,
Taming a sea-horse, thought a rarity,
Which Claus of Innsbruck cast in bronze for me!

QUESTIONS

1. To whom is the Duke speaking and what is the occasion? **2.** Contrast the Duke's moral and aesthetic sensibility.

WRITING TOPIC

How is the reader supposed to respond to the Duke's judgment of his last Duchess? Explain.

Out of the Cradle Endlessly Rocking

1881

WALT WHITMAN [1819–1892]

Out of the cradle endlessly rocking,
Out of the mocking-bird's throat, the musical shuttle,
Out of the Ninth-month[1] midnight,
Over the sterile sands and the fields beyond, where the child leaving his
    bed wander'd alone, bareheaded, barefoot,
Down from the shower'd halo,
Up from the mystic play of shadows twining and twisting as if they were
    alive,
Out from the patches of briers and blackberries,
From the memories of the bird that chanted to me,
From your memories sad brother, from the fitful risings and fallings I
    heard,
From under that yellow half-moon late-risen and swollen as if with tears, 10
From those beginning notes of yearning and love there in the mist,
From the thousand responses of my heart never to cease,
From the myriad thence-arous'd words,

Out of the Cradle . . . .
  [1] Quaker designation for September.

From the word stronger and more delicious than any,
From such as now they start the scene revisiting,
As a flock, twittering, rising, or overhead passing,
Borne hither, ere all eludes me, hurriedly,
A man, yet by these tears a little boy again,
Throwing myself on the sand, confronting the waves,
I, chanter of pains and joys, uniter of here and hereafter,   20
Taking all hints to use them, but swiftly leaping beyond them,
A reminiscence sing.

Once Paumanok,[2]
When the lilac-scent was in the air and Fifth-month grass was growing,
Up this seashore in some briers,
Two feather'd guests from Alabama, two together,
And their nest, and four light-green eggs spotted with brown,
And every day the he-bird to and fro near at hand,
And every day the she-bird crouch'd on her nest, silent, with bright eyes,
And every day I, a curious boy, never too close, never disturbing them,   30
Cautiously peering, absorbing, translating.

Shine! shine! shine!
Pour down your warmth, great sun!
While we bask, we two together.

Two together!
Winds blow south, or winds blow north,
Day come white, or night come black,
Home, or rivers and mountains from home,
Singing all time, minding no time,
While we two keep together.   40

Till of a sudden,
May-be kill'd, unknown to her mate,
One forenoon the she-bird crouch'd not on the nest,
Nor return'd that afternoon, nor the next,
Nor ever appear'd again.

And thenceforward all summer in the sound of the sea,
And at night under the full of the moon in calmer weather,
Over the hoarse surging of the sea,
Or flitting from brier to brier by day,
I saw, I heard at intervals the remaining one, the he-bird,   50
The solitary guest from Alabama.

---

[2] Paumanok is the Indian name of Long Island, where the poet was born and grew up.

Blow! blow! blow!
Blow up sea-winds along Paumanok's shore;
I wait and I wait till you blow my mate to me.

Yes, when the stars glisten'd,
All night long on the prong of a moss-scallop'd stake,
Down almost amid the slapping waves,
Sat the lone singer wonderful causing tears.

He call'd on his mate,
He pour'd forth the meanings which I of all men know.   60

Yes my brother I know,
The rest might not, but I have treasur'd every note,
For more than once dimly down to the beach gliding,
Silent, avoiding the moonbeams, blending myself with the shadows,
Recalling now the obscure shapes, the echoes, the sounds and sights after
    their sorts,
The white arms out in the breakers tirelessly tossing,
I, with bare feet, a child, the wind wafting my hair,
Listen'd long and long.

Listen'd to keep, to sing, now translating the notes,
Following you my brother.   70

Soothe! soothe! soothe!
Close on its wave soothes the wave behind,
And again another behind embracing and lapping, every one close,
But my love soothes not me, not me.

Low hangs the moon, it rose late,
It is lagging—O I think it is heavy with love, with love.

O madly the sea pushes upon the land,
With love, with love.

O night! do I not see my love fluttering out among the breakers?
What is that little black thing I see there in the white?   80

Loud! loud! loud!
Loud I call to you, my love!

High and clear I shoot my voice over the waves,
Surely you must know who is here, is here,
You must know who I am, my love.

Low-hanging moon!
What is that dusky spot in your brown yellow?
O it is the shape, the shape of my mate!
O moon do not keep her from me any longer.

Land! land! O land!   90
Whichever way I turn, O I think you could give me my mate back again
*   if you only would,*
For I am almost sure I see her dimly whichever way I look.

O rising stars!
Perhaps the one I want so much will rise, will rise with some of you.

O throat! O trembling throat!
Sound clearer through the atmosphere!
Pierce the woods, the earth,
Somewhere listening to catch you must be the one I want.

Shake out carols!
Solitary here, the night's carols!   100
Carols of lonesome love! death's carols!
Carols under that lagging, yellow, waning moon!
O under that moon where she droops almost down into the sea!
O reckless despairing carols.

But soft! sink low!
Soft! let me just murmur,
And do you wait a moment you husky-nois'd sea,
For somewhere I believe I heard my mate responding to me,
So faint, I must be still, be still to listen,
But not altogether still, for then she might not come immediately to me.   110

Hither my love!
Here I am! here!
With this just-sustain'd note I announce myself to you,
This gentle call is for you my love, for you.

Do not be decoy'd elsewhere,
That is the whistle of the wind, it is not my voice,
That is the fluttering, the fluttering of the spray,
Those are the shadows of leaves.

O darkness! O in vain!
O I am very sick and sorrowful.   120

O brown halo in the sky near the moon, drooping upon the sea!
O troubled reflection in the sea!
O throat! O throbbing heart!
And I singing uselessly, uselessly all the night.

O past! O happy life! O songs of joy!
In the air, in the woods, over fields,
Loved! loved! loved! loved! loved!
But my mate no more, no more with me!
We two together no more.

The aria sinking,   130
All else continuing, the stars shining,
The winds blowing, the notes of the bird continuous echoing,
With angry moans the fierce old mother incessantly moaning,
On the sands of Paumanok's shore gray and rustling,
The yellow half-moon enlarged, sagging down, dropping, the face of the sea
    almost touching,
The boy ecstatic, with his bare feet the waves, with his hair the
    atmosphere dallying,
The love in the heart long pent, now loose, now at last tumultuously
    bursting,
The aria's meaning, the ears, the soul, swiftly depositing,
The strange tears down the cheeks coursing,
The colloquy there, the trio, each uttering,   140
The undertone, the savage old mother incessantly crying,
To the boy's soul's questions sullenly timing, some drown'd secret hissing,
To the outsetting bard.

Demon or bird! (said the boy's soul,)
Is it indeed toward your mate you sing? or is it really to me?
For I, that was a child, my tongue's use sleeping, now I have heard you,
Now in a moment I know what I am for, I awake,
And already a thousand singers, a thousand songs, clearer, louder and
    more sorrowful than yours,
A thousand warbling echoes have started to life within me, never to die.

O you singer solitary, singing by yourself, projecting me,   150
O solitary me listening, never more shall I cease perpetuating you,
Never more shall I escape, never more the reverberations,
Never more the cries of unsatisfied love be absent from me,
Never again leave me to be the peaceful child I was before what there in
    the night,
By the sea under the yellow and sagging moon,
The messenger there arous'd, the fire, the sweet hell within,
The unknown want, the destiny of me.

O give me the clew! (it lurks in the night here somewhere,)
O if I am to have so much, let me have more!

A word then, (for I will conquer it,)   160
The word final, superior to all,
Subtle, sent up—what is it?—I listen;
Are you whispering it, and have been all the time, you sea-waves?
Is that it from your liquid rims and wet sands?

Whereto answering, the sea,
Delaying not, hurrying not,
Whisper'd me through the night, and very plainly before daybreak,
Lisp'd to me the low and delicious word death,
And again death, death, death, death,
Hissing melodious, neither like the bird nor like my arous'd child's heart,   170
But edging near as privately for me rustling at my feet,
Creeping thence steadily up to my ears and laving me softly all over,
Death, death, death, death, death.

Which I do not forget,
But fuse the song of my dusky demon and brother,
That he sang to me in the moonlight on Paumanok's gray beach,
With the thousand responsive songs at random,
My own songs awaked from that hour,
And with them the key, the word up from the waves,
The word of the sweetest song and all songs,   180
That strong and delicious word which, creeping to my feet,
(Or like some old crone rocking the cradle, swathed in sweet garments,
    bending aside,)
The sea whisper'd me.

QUESTIONS

1. In this poem Whitman reminisces about an event that proved crucial to him. What was the event? What awareness did it generate in the young boy? **2.** In what way does the young boy emulate the bird? (See ll. 114–157.)

WRITING TOPIC

This poem employs neither rhyme nor metrical regularity. What poetic devices and patterns distinguish it from prose?

I Felt a Funeral, in My Brain   (1861)

EMILY DICKINSON [1830–1886]

I felt a Funeral, in my Brain,
And Mourners to and fro

Kept treading—treading—till it seemed
That Sense was breaking through—

And when they all were seated,
A Service, like a Drum—
Kept beating—beating—till I thought
My Mind was going numb—

And then I heard them lift a Box
And creak across my Soul   10
With those same Boots of Lead, again,
Then Space—began to toll,

As all the Heavens were a Bell,
And Being, but an Ear,
And I, and Silence, some strange Race
Wrecked, solitary, here—

And then a Plank in Reason, broke,
And I dropped down, and down—
And hit a World, at every plunge,
And Finished knowing—then—   20

Hap   1898

THOMAS HARDY [1840–1928]

If but some vengeful god would call to me
From up the sky, and laugh: "Thou suffering thing,
Know that thy sorrow is my ecstasy,
That thy love's loss is my hate's profiting!"

Then would I bear it, clench myself, and die,
Steeled by the sense of ire unmerited;
Half-eased in that a Powerfuller than I
Had willed and meted me the tears I shed.

But not so. How arrives it joy lies slain,
And why unblooms the best hope ever sown?   10
—Crass Casualty° obstructs the sun and rain,   chance
And dicing Time for gladness casts a moan. . . .
These purblind Doomsters[1] had as readily strown
Blisses about my pilgrimage as pain.

Hap
  [1] Those who decide one's fate.

The Ruined Maid

1902

THOMAS HARDY   [1840–1928]

"O Melia, my dear, this does everything crown!
Who could have supposed I should meet you in Town?
And whence such fair garments, such prosperi-ty?"
"O didn't you know I'd been ruined?" said she.

"You left us in tatters, without shoes or socks,
Tired of digging potatoes, and spudding up docks;°   digging herbs
And now you've gay bracelets and bright feathers three!"
"Yes: that's how we dress when we're ruined," said she.

"At home in the barton° you said 'thee' and 'thou,'   farmyard
And 'thik oon,' and 'theäs oon,' and 't'other; but now   10
Your talking quite fits 'ee for high compa-ny!"
"Some polish is gained with one's ruin," said she.

"Your hands were like paws then, your face blue and bleak
But now I'm bewitched by your delicate cheek,
And your little gloves fit as on any la-dy!"
"We never do work when we're ruined," said she.

"You used to call home-life a hag-ridden dream,
And you'd sigh, and you'd sock; but at present you seem
To know not of megrims° or melancho-ly!"   sick headaches
"True. One's pretty lively when ruined," said she.   20

"I wish I had feathers, a fine sweeping gown,
And a delicate face, and could strut about Town!"
"My dear—a raw country girl, such as you be,
Cannot quite expect that. You ain't ruined," said she.

Spring and Fall

(1880)

TO A YOUNG CHILD

GERARD MANLEY HOPKINS   [1844–1889]

Márgarét, áre you gríeving
Over Goldengrove unleaving?°   losing leaves
Leáves, líke the things of man, you
With your fresh thoughts care for, can you?
Áh! ás the heart grows older

It will come to such sights colder
By and by, nor spare a sigh
Though worlds of wanwood leafmeal[1] lie;
And yet you will weep and know why.
Now no matter, child, the name: 10
Sórrow's spríngs are the same.
Nor mouth had, no nor mind, expressed
What heart heard of, ghost° guessed: soul
It ís the blight man was born for,
It is Margaret you mourn for.

QUESTIONS

1. In this poem Margaret grieves over the passing of spring and the coming of fall.
What does the coming of fall symbolize? **2.** Why, when Margaret grows older,
will she not sigh over the coming of fall? **3.** What are "Sorrow's springs" (l. 11)?

When I Was
One-and-Twenty   1896

A. E. HOUSMAN   [1859–1936]

When I was one-and-twenty
    I heard a wise man say,
"Give crowns and pounds and guineas
    But not your heart away;
Give pearls away and rubies
    But keep your fancy free."
But I was one-and-twenty,
    No use to talk to me.

When I was one-and-twenty
    I heard him say again,   10
"The heart out of the bosom
    Was never given in vain;
'Tis paid with sighs a plenty
    And sold for endless rue."
And I am two-and-twenty,
    And oh, 'tis true, 'tis true.

Spring and Fall
   [1] Pale woods littered with mouldering leaves.

Terence, This Is Stupid Stuff[1]

1896

A. E. HOUSMAN   [1859–1936]

"Terence, this is stupid stuff:
You eat your victuals fast enough;
There can't be much amiss, 'tis clear,
To see the rate you drink your beer.
But oh, good Lord, the verse you make,
It gives a chap the bellyache.
The cow, the old cow, she is dead;
It sleeps well, the hornéd head:
We poor lads, 'tis our turn now
To hear such tunes as killed the cow.   10
Pretty friendship 'tis to rhyme
Your friends to death before their time
Moping melancholy mad:
Come, pipe a tune to dance to, lad."

Why, if 'tis dancing you would be,
There's brisker pipes than poetry.
Say, for what were hopyards meant,
Or why was Burton built on Trent?[2]
Oh many a peer of England brews
Livelier liquor than the Muse,   20
And malt does more than Milton can
To justify God's ways to man.[3]
Ale, man, ale's the stuff to drink
For fellows whom it hurts to think:
Look into the pewter pot
To see the world as the world's not.
And faith, 'tis pleasant till 'tis past:
The mischief is that 'twill not last.
Oh I have been to Ludlow fair
And left my necktie God knows where,   30
And carried halfway home, or near,
Pints and quarts of Ludlow beer:
Then the world seemed none so bad,

Terence, This Is Stupid Stuff
   [1] Housman originally titled the volume in which this poem appeared *The Poems of Terence Hearsay*. Terence was a Roman satiric playwright.
   [2] The river Trent provides water for the town's brewing industry.
   [3] In the invocation to *Paradise Lost*, Milton declares that his epic will "justify the ways of God to men."

And I myself a sterling lad;
And down in lovely muck I've lain,
Happy till I woke again.
Then I saw the morning sky.
Heigho, the tale was all a lie;
The world, it was the old world yet,
I was I, my things were wet,   40
And nothing now remained to do
But begin the game anew.

   Therefore, since the world has still
Much good, but much less good than ill,
And while the sun and moon endure
Luck's a chance, but trouble's sure,
I'd face it as a wise man would,
And train for ill and not for good.
'Tis true the stuff I bring for sale
Is not so brisk a brew as ale: 50
Out of a stem that scored the hand
I wrung it in a weary land.
But take it: if the smack is sour,
The better for the embittered hour;
It should do good to heart and head
When your soul is in my soul's stead;
And I will friend you, if I may,
In the dark and cloudy day.

   There was a king reigned in the East:
There, when kings will sit to feast,   60
They get their fill before they think
With poisoned meat and poisoned drink.
He gathered all that springs to birth
From the many-venomed earth;
First a little, thence to more,
He sampled all her killing store;
And easy, smiling, seasoned sound,
Sate the king when healths went round.
They put arsenic in his meat
And stared aghast to watch him eat;   70
They poured strychnine in his cup
And shook to see him drink it up:
They shook, they stared as white's their shirt:
Them it was their poison hurt.
—I tell the tale that I heard told.
Mithridates, he died old.[4]

---

   [4] Mithridates, the King of Pontus (in Asia Minor), reputedly immunized himself against poisons
by administering to himself gradually increasing doses.

QUESTIONS
1. What does the speaker of the first fourteen lines object to in Terence's poetry?   **2.** What is Terence's response to the criticism of his verse? What function of true poetry is implied by his comparison of bad poetry with liquor?

WRITING TOPIC
How does the story of Mithridates (lines 59–76) illustrate the theme of the poem?

Leda and the Swan[1]   1928

WILLIAM BUTLER YEATS   [1865–1939]

A sudden blow: the great wings beating still
Above the staggering girl, her thighs caressed
By the dark webs, her nape caught in his bill;
He holds her helpless breast upon his breast.

How can those terrified vague fingers push
The feathered glory from her loosening thighs?
And how can body, laid in that white rush,
But feel the strange heart beating where it lies?

A shudder in the loins engenders there
The broken wall, the burning roof and tower   10
And Agamemnon dead.
                Being so caught up,
So mastered by the brute blood of the air,
Did she put on his knowledge with his power
Before the indifferent beak could let her drop?

Birches   1916

ROBERT FROST   [1874–1963]

When I see birches bend to left and right
Across the lines of straighter darker trees,

Leda and the Swan
  [1] In Greek myth, Zeus, in the form of a swan, rapes Leda. As a consequence, Helen and Clytemnestra are born. Each sister marries the king of a city-state; Helen marries Menelaus and Clytemnestra marries Agamemnon. Helen, the most beautiful woman on earth, elopes with Paris, a prince of Troy, an act that precipitates the Trojan War in which Agamemnon commands the combined Greek armies. The war ends with the destruction of Troy. Agamemnon, when he returns to his home, is murdered by his unfaithful wife.

I like to think some boy's been swinging them.
But swinging doesn't bend them down to stay.
Ice-storms do that. Often you must have seen them
Loaded with ice a sunny winter morning
After a rain. They click upon themselves
As the breeze rises, and turn many-colored
As the stir cracks and crazes their enamel.
Soon the sun's warmth makes them shed crystal shells   10
Shattering and avalanching on the snow-crust—
Such heaps of broken glass to sweep away
You'd think the inner dome of heaven had fallen.
They are dragged to the withered bracken by the load,
And they seem not to break; though once they are bowed
So low for long, they never right themselves:
You may see their trunks arching in the woods
Years afterwards, trailing their leaves on the ground
Like girls on hands and knees that throw their hair
Before them over their heads to dry in the sun.   20
But I was going to say when Truth broke in
With all her matter-of-fact about the ice-storm
I should prefer to have some boy bend them
As he went out and in to fetch the cows—
Some boy too far from town to learn baseball,
Whose only play was what he found himself,
Summer or winter, and could play alone.
One by one he subdued his father's trees
By riding them down over and over again
Until he took the stiffness out of them,   30
And not one but hung limp, not one was left
For him to conquer. He learned all there was
To learn about not launching out too soon
And so not carrying the tree away
Clear to the ground. He always kept his poise
To the top branches, climbing carefully
With the same pains you use to fill a cup
Up to the brim, and even above the brim.
Then he flung outward, feet first, with a swish,
Kicking his way down through the air to the ground.   40
So was I once myself a swinger of birches.
And so I dream of going back to be.
It's when I'm weary of considerations,
And life is too much like a pathless wood
Where your face burns and tickles with the cobwebs
Broken across it, and one eye is weeping
From a twig's having lashed across it open.
I'd like to get away from earth awhile

Birches are people
Ice storms are things that happen.

earth

And then come back to it and begin over.
May no fate willfully misunderstand me
And half grant what I wish and snatch me away
Not to return. Earth's the right place for love:
I don't know where it's likely to go better.
I'd like to go by climbing a birch tree,
And climb black branches up a snow-white trunk
Toward heaven, till the tree could bear no more,
But dipped its top and set me down again.
That would be good both going and coming back.
One could do worse than be a swinger of birches.

50

— end of life?
Mortality? (No.) (read rest of stanza)

reflection on youth.

Provide, Provide   1936

ROBERT FROST   [1874–1963]

The witch that came (the withered hag)
To wash the steps with pail and rag,
Was once the beauty Abishag,[1]

The picture pride of Hollywood.
Too many fall from great and good
For you to doubt the likelihood.

Die early and avoid the fate.
Or if predestined to die late,
Make up your mind to die in state.

Make the whole stock exchange your own!   10
If need be occupy a throne,
Where nobody can call *you* crone.

Some have relied on what they knew;
Others on being simply true.
What worked for them might work for you.

No memory of having starred
Atones for later disregard,
Or keeps the end from being hard.

Provide, Provide
    [1] "Now King David was old and advanced in years; and although they covered him with clothes, he could not get warm. Therefore his servants said to him, 'Let a young maiden be sought for my lord the king, and let her wait upon the king, and be his nurse; let her lie in your bosom, that my lord the king may be warm.' So they sought for a beautiful maiden throughout all the territory of Israel, and found Abishag, the Shunammite, and brought her to the king. The maiden was very beautiful. . . ."—I Kings 1:1–4.

Better to go down dignified
With boughten friendship at your side   20
Than none at all. Provide, provide!

Thirteen Ways of Looking at a Blackbird   1923

WALLACE STEVENS   [1879–1955]

1

Among twenty snowy mountains,
The only moving thing
Was the eye of the blackbird.

2

I was of three minds,
Like a tree
In which there are three blackbirds.

3

The blackbird whirled in the autumn winds.
It was a small part of the pantomime.

4

A man and a woman
Are one.   10
A man and a woman and a blackbird
Are one.

5

I do not know which to prefer,
The beauty of inflections
Or the beauty of innuendoes,
The blackbird whistling
Or just after.

6

Icicles filled the long window
With barbaric glass.
The shadow of the blackbird   20
Crossed it, to and fro.
The mood
Traced in the shadow
An indecipherable cause.

7

O thin men of Haddam,°   a town in Connecticut
Why do you imagine golden birds?
Do you not see how the blackbird
Walks around the feet
Of the women about you?

8

I know noble accents
And lucid, inescapable rhythms;   30
But I know, too,
That the blackbird is involved
In what I know.

9

When the blackbird flew out of sight,
It marked the edge
Of one of many circles.

10

At the sight of blackbirds
Flying in a green light,
Even the bawds of euphony   40
Would cry out sharply.

11

He rode over Connecticut
In a glass coach.
Once, a fear pierced him,
In that he mistook
The shadow of his equipage
For blackbirds.

12

The river is moving.
The blackbird must be flying.

13

It was evening all afternoon.   50
It was snowing
And it was going to snow.
The blackbird sat
In the cedar-limbs.

QUESTION
1.   Surely Stevens's blackbird is more than just a bird. What kinds of responses does
the image of the blackbird evoke? A sense of pleasure or pain, life or death, light or
darkness, good or evil?

To Carry the Child   1966

STEVIE SMITH   [1902–1971]

To carry the child into adult life
Is good? I say it is not,
To carry the child into adult life
Is to be handicapped.

The child in adult life is defenceless
And if he is grown-up, knows it,
And the grown-up looks at the childish part
And despises it.

The child, too, despises the clever grown-up,
The man-of-the-world, the frozen,   10
For the child has the tears alive on his cheek
And the man has none of them.

As the child has colours, and the man sees no
Colours or anything,

Being easy only in things of the mind,
The child is easy in feeling.

Easy in feeling, easily excessive
And in excess powerful,
For instance, if you do not speak to the child
He will make trouble.   20
You would say a man had the upper hand
Of the child, if a child survive,
But I say the child has fingers of strength
To strangle the man alive.

Oh! it is not happy, it is never happy,
To carry the child into adulthood,
Let the children lie down before full growth
And die in their infanthood
And be guilty of no man's blood.

But oh the poor child, the poor child, what can he do,   30
Trapped in a grown-up carapace,
But peer outside of his prison room
With the eye of an anarchist?

Incident   1925

COUNTEE CULLEN   [1903–1946]

Once riding in old Baltimore,
        Heart-filled, head-filled with glee,
I saw a Baltimorean
        Keep looking straight at me.

Now I was eight and very small,
        And he was no whit bigger,
And so I smiled, but he poked out
        His tongue and called me, "Nigger."

I saw the whole of Baltimore
        From May until December: 10
Of all the things that happened there
        That's all that I remember.

Fern Hill   1946

DYLAN THOMAS   [1914–1953]

Now as I was young and easy under the apple boughs
About the lilting house and happy as the grass was green,
  The night above the dingle° starry,   small wooded valley
   Time let me hail and climb
  Golden in the heydays of his eyes,
And honored among wagons I was prince of the apple towns
And once below a time I lordly had the trees and leaves
   Trail with daisies and barley
  Down the rivers of the windfall light.

And I was green and carefree, famous among the barns   10
About the happy yard and singing as the farm was home,
  In the sun that is young once only,
   Time let me play and be
  Golden in the mercy of his means,
And green and golden I was huntsman and herdsman, the calves
Sang to my horn, the foxes on the hills barked clear and cold,
   And the sabbath rang slowly
  In the pebbles of the holy streams.

All the sun long it was running, it was lovely, the hay
Fields high as the house, the tunes from the chimneys, it was air   20
  And playing, lovely and watery
  And fire green as grass.
  And nightly under the simple stars
As I rode to sleep the owls were bearing the farm away,
All the moon long I heard, blessed among stables, the nightjars[1]
  Flying with the ricks, and the horses
   Flashing into the dark.

And then to awake, and the farm, like a wanderer white
With the dew, come back, the cock on his shoulder: it was all
  Shining, it was Adam and maiden,   30
   The sky gathered again
  And the sun grew round that very day.
So it must have been after the birth of the simple light
In the first, spinning place, the spellbound horses walking warm
  Out of the whinnying green stable
   On to the fields of praise.

Fern Hill
 [1] Nightjars are harsh-sounding nocturnal birds.

And honored among foxes and pheasants by the gay house
Under the new made clouds and happy as the heart was long,
  In the sun born over and over,
    I ran my heedless ways,   40
  My wishes raced through the house high hay
And nothing I cared, at my sky blue trades, that time allows
In all his tuneful turning so few and such morning songs
  Before the children green and golden
    Follow him out of grace.

Nothing I cared, in the lamb white days, that time would take me
Up to the swallow thronged loft by the shadow of my hand,
  In the moon that is always rising,
    Nor that riding to sleep
  I should hear him fly with the high fields   50
And wake to the farm forever fled from the childless land.
Oh as I was young and easy in the mercy of his means,
  Time held me green and dying
  Though I sang in my chains like the sea.

QUESTIONS
1. What emotional impact does the color imagery in the poem pro-
vide?   **2.** Trace the behavior of "time" in the poem.   **3.** Fairy tales often begin with the words "once upon a time." Why does Thomas alter that formula in
line 7?   **4.** Explain the paradox in line 53.

WRITING TOPICS
1. Lines 17–18, 25, 45–46 incorporate religious language and biblical allusion.
How do those allusions clarify the poet's vision of his childhood?   **2.** Compare
this poem with Gerard Manley Hopkins's "Spring and Fall" (p. 83).

A Moment Please   1962

SAMUEL ALLEN [b. 1917]

When I gaze at the sun
  I walked to the subway booth
  for change for a dime.
and know that this great earth
  Two adolescent girls stood there
  alive with eagerness to know
is but a fragment from it thrown
all in their new found world
there was for them to know

in heat and flame a billion years ago,   10
    they looked at me and brightly asked
    "Are you Arabian?"
that when this world was lifeless
    I smiled and cautiously
    —for one grows cautious—
    shook my head.
as, a billion hence,
    "Egyptian?"
It shall again be,
    Again I smiled and shook my head   20
    and walked away.
what moment is it that I am betrayed,
    I've gone but seven paces now
oppressed, cast down,
    and from behind comes swift the sneer
or warm with love or triumph?
    "Or Nigger?"
    A moment, please
What is it that to fury I am roused?
    for still it takes a moment   30
What meaning for me
    and now
in this homeless clan
    I'll turn
the dupe of space
    and smile
the toy of time?
    and nod my head.

"More Light! More Light!"[1]   1961

For Heinrich Blücher and Hannah Arendt[2]

ANTHONY HECHT   [b. 1923]

Composed in the Tower[3] before his execution
These moving verses, and being brought at that time

"*More Light! More Light!*"
   [1] These were the last words of the German poet Johann Wolfgang von Goethe (1749–1832).
   [2] Husband and wife who emigrated to the United States from Germany in 1941. Hannah Arendt has written extensively on political totalitarianism.
   [3] The Tower of London was used as a prison for eminent political prisoners. What follows is an account of a priest's execution for the crime of heresy. The punishment was death by fire, and often a sack of gunpowder was placed at the condemned's neck to shorten the agony.

Painfully to the stake, submitted, declaring thus:
"I implore my God to witness that I have made no crime."

Nor was he forsaken of courage, but the death was horrible,
The sack of gunpowder failing to ignite.
His legs were blistered sticks on which the black sap
Bubbled and burst as he howled for the Kindly Light.

And that was but one, and by no means one of the worst;
Permitted at least his pitiful dignity;   10
And such as were by, made prayers in the name of Christ,
That shall judge all men, for his soul's tranquillity.

We move now to outside a German wood.
Three men are there commanded to dig a hole
In which the two Jews are ordered to lie down
And be buried alive by the third, who is a Pole.

Not light from the shrine at Weimar⁴ beyond the hill
Nor light from heaven appeared. But he did refuse.
A Luger⁵ settled back deeply in its glove.
He was ordered to change places with the Jews.   20

Much casual death had drained away their souls.
The thick dirt mounted toward the quivering chin.
When only the head was exposed the order came
To dig him out again and get back in.

No light, no light in the blue Polish eye.
When he finished a riding boot packed down the earth.
The Luger hovered lightly in its glove.
He was shot in the belly and in three hours bled to death.

QUESTIONS

1. What relationship does the event (which occurred in sixteenth-century England) recounted in the first two stanzas of the poem bear to the event recounted in the last four stanzas? **2.** What irony do you find in the title of the poem and the use of the word *light* in lines 8, 17, 18, and 25? How would you define *light* in each case? Can you imagine yourself in the place of the three prisoners in l. 14? What would you do?

---

⁴ Goethe spent most of his life in Weimar, and his humanistic achievements are honored there in the Goethe National Museum. The event recounted here occurred at Buchenwald, a German concentration camp north of Weimar.

⁵ A German automatic pistol.

Curiosity

1959

ALASTAIR REID   [b. 1926]

may have killed the cat; more likely
the cat was just unlucky, or else curious
to see what death was like, having no cause
to go on licking paws, or fathering
litter on litter of kittens, predictably.

   Nevertheless, to be curious
is dangerous enough. To distrust
what is always said, what seems,
to ask odd questions, interfere in dreams,
leave home, smell rats, have hunches   10
does not endear him to those doggy circles
where well-smelt baskets, suitable wives, good lunches
are the order of things and where prevails
much wagging of incurious heads and tails.

   Face it. Curiosity
will not cause him to die—
only lack of it will.
Never to want to see
the other side of the hill,
or that improbable country   20
where living is an idyll
(although a probable hell)
would kill us all.
Only the curious
have, if they live, a tale
worth telling at all.

   Dogs say he loves too much, is irresponsible,
is changeable, marries too many wives,
deserts his children, chills all dinner tables
with tales of his nine lives.   30
Well, he is lucky. Let him be
nine-lived and contradictory,
curious enough to change, prepared to pay
the cat price, which is to die
and die again and again,
each time with no less pain.
A cat minority of one
is all that can be counted on

to tell the truth. And what he has to tell
on each return from hell   40
is this: that dying is what the living do,
that dying is what the loving do,
and that dead dogs are those who do not know
that hell is where, to live, they have to go.

First Confession   1961

X. J. KENNEDY   [b. 1929]

Blood thudded in my ears. I scuffed,
    Steps stubborn, to the telltale booth
Beyond whose curtained portal coughed
    The robed repositor of truth.

The slat shot back. The universe
    Bowed down his cratered dome to hear
Enumerated my each curse,
    The sip snitched from my old man's beer.

My sloth pride envy lechery,
    The dime held back from Peter's Pence   10
With which I'd bribed my girl to pee
    That I might spy her instruments.

Hovering scale-pans when I'd done
    Settled their balance slow as silt
While in the restless dark I burned
    Bright as a brimstone in my guilt

Until as one feeds birds he doled
    Seven Our Fathers and a Hail
Which I to double-scrub my soul
    Intoned twice at the altar rail   20

Where Sunday in seraphic light
    I knelt, as full of grace as most,
And stuck my tongue out at the priest:
    A fresh roost for the Holy Ghost.

Advice to My Son   1965

PETER MEINKE [b. 1932]

The trick is, to live your days
as if each one may be your last
(for they go fast, and young men lose their lives
in strange and unimaginable ways)
but at the same time, plan long range
(for they go slow: if you survive
the shattered windshield and the bursting shell
you will arrive
at our approximation here below
of heaven or hell).   10

To be specific, between the peony and the rose
plant squash and spinach, turnips and tomatoes;
beauty is nectar
and nectar, in a desert, saves—
but the stomach craves stronger sustenance
than the honied vine.

Therefore, marry a pretty girl
after seeing her mother;
show your soul to one man,
work with another;   20
and always serve bread with your wine.

But, son,
always serve wine.

QUESTIONS

1. Explain how the advice of lines 17–21 is logically related to the preceding
lines. **2.** What do the final two lines tell the reader about the speaker?

WRITING TOPIC

The advice of the first stanza seems contradictory. In what ways does the second
stanza attempt to resolve the contradiction or explain "The trick" (l. 1)? What do
the various plants and the bread and wine symbolize?

In a Spring Still Not Written Of   1965

ROBERT WALLACE   [b. 1932]

This morning
with a class of girls outdoors, I saw
how frail poems are
in a world burning up with flowers,
in which, overhead,
the great elms
—green, and tall—
stood carrying leaves in their arms.

The girls listened equally
to my drone, reading, and to the bees'   10
ricocheting
among them for the blossom on the bone,
or gazed off at a distant mower's
astronomies of green
and clover, flashing,
threshing in the new, untarnished sunlight.

And all the while, dwindling,
tinier, the voices—Yeats, Marvell, Donne—
sank drowning
in a spring still not written of,   20
as only the sky
clear above the brick bell-tower
—blue, and white—
was shifting toward the hour.

Calm, indifferent, cross-legged
or on elbows half-lying in the grass—
how should the great dead
tell them of dying?
They will come to time for poems at last,
when they have found they are no more   30
the beautiful and young
all poems are for.

QUESTIONS

1. What is the speaker's attitude toward the "class of girls" he is teaching? Toward his job as a teacher? **2.** Explain the meaning of the title. **3.** Explain the various meanings of "drone" (l. 10).

WRITING TOPIC
Explain the paradox developed in this poem.

Hanging Fire   1978

AUDRE LORDE   [b. 1934]

I am fourteen
and my skin has betrayed me
the boy I cannot live without
still sucks his thumb
in secret
how come my knees are
always so ashy
what if I die
before morning
and momma's in the bedroom   10
with the door closed.

I have to learn how to dance
in time for the next party
my room is too small for me
suppose I die before graduation
they will sing sad melodies
but finally
tell the truth about me
There is nothing I want to do
and too much   20
that has to be done
and momma's in the bedroom
with the door closed.

Nobody even stops to think
about my side of it
I should have been on Math Team
my marks were better than his
why do I have to be
the one
wearing braces   30
I have nothing to wear tomorrow
will I live long enough
to grow up
and momma's in the bedroom
with the door closed.

My Mother   1970

ROBERT MEZEY   [b. 1935]

My mother writes from Trenton,
a comedian to the bone
but underneath, serious
and all heart. "Honey," she says,
"be a mensch[1] and Mary too,
its no good to worry, you
are doing the best you can
your Dad and everyone
thinks you turned out very well
as long as you pay your bills   10
nobody can say a word
you can tell them to drop dead
so save a dollar it can't
hurt—remember Frank you went
to highschool with? he still lives
with his wife's mother, his wife
works while he writes his books and
did he ever sell a one
the four kids run around naked
36 and he's never had,   20
you'll forgive my expression
even a pot to piss in
or a window to throw it,
such a smart boy he couldn't
read the footprints on the wall
honey you think you know all
the answers you don't, please try
to put some money away
believe me it wouldn't hurt
artist shmartist life's too short   30
for that kind of, forgive me,
horseshit, I know what you want
better than you, all that counts
is to make a good living
and the best of everything,
as Sholem Aleichem said
he was a great writer did
you ever read his books dear,

My Mother
   [1] Man, in the sense of "human being."

you should make what he makes a year
anyway he says some place   40
Poverty is no disgrace
but its no honor either
that's what I say,
                    love,
                        Mother"

the best year of her life   1988

GERALD LOCKLIN [b. 1941]

When my two-year-old daughter
sees someone come through the door
whom she loves, and hasn't seen for a while,
and has been anticipating
she literally shrieks with joy.

I have to go into the other room
so that no one will notice the tears in my eyes.

Later, after my daughter has gone to bed,
I say to my wife,
"She will never be this happy again,"   10
and my wife gets angry and snaps,
"Don't you dare communicate your negativism to her!"
And, of course, I won't, if I can possibly help it,
and of course I fully expect her
to have much joy in her life,
and, of course, I hope to be able
to contribute to that joy—
I hope, in other words, that she'll always
be happy to see me come through the door—

but why kid ourselves—she, like every child,   20
has a life of great suffering ahead of her,
and while joy will not go out of her life,
she will one of these days cease to actually,
literally, jump and shriek for joy.

At Mud Lake in the Morning   1982

MICHAEL CLEARY [b. 1945]

MUD LAKE, *Idaho (AP) 3,000 rabbits were rounded up and clubbed to death
Saturday by about 800 men and boys . . . during a rabbit population boom that
occurs about every 10 years.*

At Mud Lake in the morning,
boys squint into the ache of sun
ricocheting off fresh snow,
feel the tingle of violence
in their fathers' tense smiles and rough jokes,
sense that this is a big and grownup thing
to be proud and fearful on the edge of a man's world,
waiting for jackrabbits to be driven
under the nervous bats and clubs
they heft and slap into leathered palms   10
to know the unfamiliar power of pain and death.

Too soon the rabbits come,
a stampede of darting, dodging terror
as men and boys strike clumsily
until they find the fierce and ancient fury
in heavy thuds and hollow cracks
and the rabbits start to go down,

some sudden and still, smaller than alive,
others jerking, scrambling on their sides,
changing the snow into a crazy quilt   20
of scarlet specks and patches of deeper red.

With dusk, the deeds grow
bold and large on distant farms
until each boy has vanquished ten times ten
again and then again
in warrior tales told to hearthbound mothers
washing bloody socks and splattered overalls
in their mothers' mothers' kitchens.
Fathers smoke quietly with measured pride
as sisters, hostile and aloof,   30
retreat into wary corners.

At night, boys wriggle slowly into sleep,
happiness wound tight inside,
wonder at the thrill of wood on bone,
snow soiled with matted fur and bloody bootprints,
wonder where blood goes when the snow melts,
wonder how long ten years will be
and how they can stand the waiting.

INNOCENCE
AND
EXPERIENCE

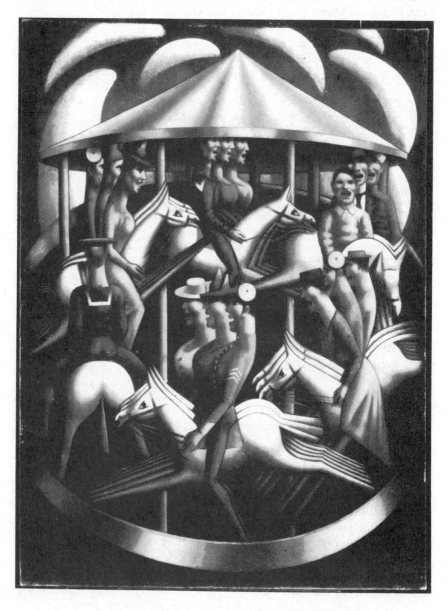

The Merry-Go-Round, 1916 by Mark Gertler.

DRAMA

Oedipus Rex*   (ca. 429 B.C.)

SOPHOCLES   [496?– 406 B.C.]

PERSONS REPRESENTED

Oedipus	Messenger
A Priest	Shepherd of Laïos
Creon	Second Messenger
Teiresias	Chorus of Theban Elders
Iocastê	

SCENE

Before the palace of Oedipus, King of Thebes. A central door and two lateral doors open onto a platform which runs the length of the facade. On the platform, right and left, are altars; and three steps lead down into the "orchestra," or chorus-ground. At the beginning of the action these steps are crowded by suppliants who have brought branches and chaplets of olive leaves and who lie in various attitudes of despair. Oedipus enters.

Prologue

Oedipus.   My children, generations of the living
In the line of Kadmos,[1] nursed at his ancient hearth:
Why have you strewn yourselves before these altars
In supplication, with your boughs and garlands?
The breath of incense rises from the city
With a sound of prayer and lamentation.

---

* An English version by Dudley Fitts and Robert Fitzgerald.
[1] The legendary founder of Thebes.

                                                    Children,
I would not have you speak through messengers,
And therefore I have come myself to hear you—
I, Oedipus, who bear the famous name.
[*To a Priest.*] You, there, since you are eldest in the company,   10
Speak for them all, tell me what preys upon you,
Whether you come in dread, or crave some blessing:
Tell me, and never doubt that I will help you
In every way I can; I should be heartless
Were I not moved to find you suppliant here.

Priest.   Great Oedipus, O powerful King of Thebes!
You see how all the ages of our people
Cling to your altar steps: here are boys
Who can barely stand alone, and here are priests
By weight of age, as I am a priest of God,   20
And young men chosen from those yet unmarried;
As for the others, all that multitude,
They wait with olive chaplets in the squares,
At the two shrines of Pallas,[2] and where Apollo[3]
Speaks in the glowing embers.
                                            Your own eyes
Must tell you: Thebes is in her extremity
And can not lift her head from the surge of death.
A rust consumes the buds and fruits of the earth;
The herds are sick; children die unborn,
And labor is vain. The god of plague and pyre   30
Raids like detestable lightning through the city,
And all the house of Kadmos is laid waste,
All emptied, and all darkened: Death alone
Battens upon the misery of Thebes.

You are not one of the immortal gods, we know;
Yet we have come to you to make our prayer
As to the man of all men best in adversity
And wisest in the ways of God. You saved us
From the Sphinx,[4] that flinty singer, and the tribute
We paid to her so long; yet you were never   40
Better informed than we, nor could we teach you:
It was some god breathed in you to set us free.

---

[2] Athena, goddess of wisdom.

[3] God of sunlight, medicine, and prophecy.

[4] A winged monster, with a woman's head and breasts and a lion's body, that destroyed those who failed to answer her riddle: "What walks on four feet in the morning, two at noon, and three in the evening?" When the young Oedipus correctly answered, "Man" ("three" alluding to a cane in old age), the Sphinx killed herself, and the plague ended.

Therefore, O mighty King, we turn to you:
Find us our safety, find us a remedy,
Whether by counsel of the gods or men.
A king of wisdom tested in the past
Can act in a time of troubles, and act well.
Noblest of men, restore
Life to your city! Think how all men call you
Liberator for your triumph long ago;   50
Ah, when your years of kingship are remembered,
Let them not say *We rose, but later fell—*
Keep the State from going down in the storm!
Once, years ago, with happy augury,
You brought us fortune; be the same again!
No man questions your power to rule the land:
But rule over men, not over a dead city!
Ships are only hulls, citadels are nothing,
When no life moves in the empty passageways.

Oedipus.   Poor children! You may be sure I know   60
All that you longed for in your coming here.
I know that you are deathly sick; and yet,
Sick as you are, not one is as sick as I.
Each of you suffers in himself alone
His anguish, not another's; but my spirit
Groans for the city, for myself, for you.

I was not sleeping, you are not waking me.
No, I have been in tears for a long while
And in my restless thought walked many ways.
In all my search, I found one helpful course,   70
And that I have taken: I have sent Creon,
Son of Menoikeus, brother of the Queen,
To Delphi, Apollo's place of revelation,
To learn there, if he can,
What act or pledge of mine may save the city.
I have counted the days, and now, this very day,
I am troubled, for he has overstayed his time.
What is he doing? He has been gone too long.
Yet whenever he comes back, I should do ill
To scant whatever hint the god may give.   80

Priest.   It is a timely promise. At this instant
They tell me Creon is here.

Oedipus.   O Lord Apollo!
May his news be fair as his face is radiant!

Priest.   It could not be otherwise: he is crowned with bay,
The chaplet is thick with berries.

Oedipus.   We shall soon know;
  He is near enough to hear us now.

[*Enter Creon.*]

                                    O Prince:
  Brother: son of Menoikeus:
  What answer do you bring us from the god?
Creon.   It is favorable. I can tell you, great afflictions
  Will turn out well, if they are taken well.   90
Oedipus.   What was the oracle? These vague words
  Leave me still hanging between hope and fear.
Creon.   Is it your pleasure to hear me with all these
  Gathered around us? I am prepared to speak,
  But should we not go in?
Oedipus.   Let them all hear it.
  It is for them I suffer, more than for myself.
Creon.   Then I will tell you what I heard at Delphi.

  In plain words
  The god commands us to expel from the land of Thebes
  An old defilement that it seems we shelter.   100
  It is a deathly thing, beyond expiation.
  We must not let it feed upon us longer.
Oedipus.   What defilement? How shall we rid ourselves of it?
Creon.   By exile or death, blood for blood. It was
  Murder that brought the plague-wind on the city.
Oedipus.   Murder of whom? Surely the god has named him?
Creon.   My lord: long ago Laïos was our king,
  Before you came to govern us.
Oedipus.   I know;
  I learned of him from others; I never saw him.
Creon.   He was murdered; and Apollo commands us now   110
  To take revenge upon whoever killed him.
Oedipus.   Upon whom? Where are they? Where shall we find a clue
  To solve that crime, after so many years?
Creon.   Here in this land, he said.
                                    If we make enquiry,
  We may touch things that otherwise escape us.
Oedipus.   Tell me: Was Laïos murdered in his house,
  Or in the fields, or in some foreign country?
Creon.   He said he planned to make a pilgrimage.
  He did not come home again.
Oedipus.   And was there no one,
  No witness, no companion, to tell what happened?   120

Creon.   They were all killed but one, and he got away
    So frightened that he could remember one thing only.
Oedipus.   What was that one thing? One may be the key
    To everything, if we resolve to use it.
Creon.   He said that a band of highwaymen attacked them,
    Outnumbered them, and overwhelmed the King.
Oedipus.   Strange, that a highwayman should be so daring—
    Unless some faction here bribed him to do it.
Creon.   We thought of that. But after Laïos' death
    New troubles arose and we had no avenger.   130
Oedipus.   What troubles could prevent your hunting down the killers?
Creon.   The riddling Sphinx's song
    Made us deaf to all mysteries but her own.
Oedipus.   Then once more I must bring what is dark to light.
    It is most fitting that Apollo shows,
    As you do, this compunction for the dead.
    You shall see how I stand by you, as I should,
    To avenge the city and the city's god,
    And not as though it were for some distant friend,
    But for my own sake, to be rid of evil.   140
    Whoever killed King Laïos might—who knows?—
    Decide at any moment to kill me as well.
    By avenging the murdered king I protect myself.
    Come, then, my children: leave the altar steps,
    Lift up your olive boughs!
                                    One of you go
    And summon the people of Kadmos to gather here.
    I will do all that I can; you may tell them that.

[Exit a page.]

    So, with the help of God,
    We shall be saved—or else indeed we are lost.
Priest.   Let us rise, children. It was for this we came,   150
    And now the King has promised it himself.
    Phoibos⁵ has sent us an oracle; may he descend
    Himself to save us and drive out the plague.

[Exeunt Oedipus and Creon into the palace by the central door. The Priest and
the suppliants disperse R and L. After a short pause the Chorus enters the
orchestra.]

---

    ⁵ Phoebus Apollo, god of the sun.

Párodos[6]

Chorus.   What is God singing in his profound   [*Strophe 1*]
   Delphi of gold and shadow?
What oracle for Thebes, the sunwhipped city?
Fear unjoints me, the roots of my heart tremble.
Now I remember, O Healer, your power, and wonder;
Will you send doom like a sudden cloud, or weave it
Like nightfall of the past?
Speak, speak to us, issue of holy sound:
Dearest to our expectancy: be tender!

Let me pray to Athenê, the immortal daughter of Zeus,   [*Antistrophe 1*]
   And to Artemis her sister   11
Who keeps her famous throne in the market ring;
And to Apollo, bowman at the far butts of heaven—

O gods, descend! Like three streams leap against
The fires of our grief, the fires of darkness;
Be swift to bring us rest!

As in the old time from the brilliant house
Of air you stepped to save us, come again!

Now our afflictions have no end,   [*Strophe 2*]
Now all our stricken host lies down   20
And no man fights off death with his mind;

The noble plowland bears no grain,
And groaning mothers can not bear—

See, how our lives like birds take wing,
Like sparks that fly when a fire soars,
To the shore of the god of evening.

The plague burns on, it is pitiless,   [*Antistrophe 2*]
Though pallid children laden with death
Lie unwept in the stony ways,

And old gray women by every path   30
Flock to the strand about the altars

---

[6] The *Párodos* is the ode sung by the Chorus as it entered the theater and moved down the aisles to the playing area. The *strophe*, in Greek tragedy, is the unit of verse the Chorus chanted as it moved to the left in a dance rhythm. The Chorus sang the *antistrophe* as it moved to the right and the *epode* while standing still.

There to strike their breasts and cry
Worship of Phoibos in wailing prayers:
Be kind, God's golden child!

There are no swords in this attack by fire,   *[Strophe 3]*
No shields, but we are ringed with cries.
Send the besieger plunging from our homes
Into the vast sea-room of the Atlantic
Or into the waves that foam eastward of Thrace—
For the day ravages what the night spares—   40

Destroy our enemy, lord of the thunder!
Let him be riven by lightning from heaven!

Phoibus Apollo, stretch the sun's bowstring,   *[Antistrophe 3]*
That golden cord, until it sing for us,
Flashing arrows in heaven!
      Artemis, Huntress
Race with flaring lights upon our mountains!

O scarlet god, O golden-banded brow,
O Theban Bacchos in a storm of Maenads,[7]

[*Enter Oedipus, C.*]

Whirl upon Death, that all the Undying hate!
Come with blinding cressets, come in joy!   50

Scene 1

Oedipus. Is this your prayer? It may be answered. Come,
 Listen to me, act as the crisis demands,
 And you shall have relief from all these evils.

 Until now I was a stranger to this tale,
 As I had been a stranger to the crime.
 Could I track down the murderer without a clue?
 But now, friends,
 As one who became a citizen after the murder,
 I make this proclamation to all Thebans:
 If any man knows by whose hand Laïos, son of Labdakos, 10

---

[7] Bacchos is the god of wine and revelry, hence scarlet-faced. The Maenads were Bacchos' female attendants.

Met his death, I direct that man to tell me everything,
No matter what he fears for having so long withheld it.
Let it stand as promised that no further trouble
Will come to him, but he may leave the land in safety.

Moreover: If anyone knows the murderer to be foreign,
Let him not keep silent: he shall have his reward from me.
However, if he does conceal it; if any man
Fearing for his friend or for himself disobeys this edict,
Hear what I propose to do:

I solemnly forbid the people of this country,   20
Where power and throne are mine, ever to receive that man
Or speak to him, no matter who he is, or let him
Join in sacrifice, lustration, or in prayer.
I decree that he be driven from every house,
Being, as he is, corruption itself to us: the Delphic
Voice of Zeus has pronounced this revelation.
Thus I associate myself with the oracle
And take the side of the murdered king.

As for the criminal, I pray to God—
Whether it be a lurking thief, or one of a number—   30
I pray that that man's life be consumed in evil and wretchedness.
And as for me, this curse applies no less
If it should turn out that the culprit is my guest here,
Sharing my hearth.
                        You have heard the penalty.
I lay it on you now to attend to this
For my sake, for Apollo's, for the sick
Sterile city that heaven has abandoned.
Suppose the oracle had given you no command:
Should this defilement go uncleansed for ever?
You should have found the murderer: your king,   40
A noble king, had been destroyed!
                        Now I,
Having the power that he held before me,
Having his bed, begetting children there
Upon his wife, as he would have, had he lived—
Their son would have been my children's brother,
If Laïos had had luck in fatherhood!
(But surely ill luck rushed upon his reign)—
I say I take the son's part, just as though
I were his son, to press the fight for him
And see it won! I'll find the hand that brought   50

Death to Labdakos' and Polydoros' child,
Heir of Kadmos's and Agenor's line.
And as for those who fail me,
May the gods deny them the fruit of the earth,
Fruit of the womb, and may they rot utterly!
Let them be wretched as we are wretched, and worse!

For you, for loyal Thebans, and for all
Who find my actions right, I pray the favor
Of justice, and of all the immortal gods.
Choragos.[8]   Since I am under oath, my lord, I swear   60
  I did not do the murder. I can not name
  The murderer. Might not the oracle
  That has ordained the search tell where to find him?
Oedipus.   An honest question. But no man in the world
  Can make the gods do more than the gods will.
Choragos.   There is one last expedient—
Oedipus.   Tell me what it is.
  Though it seem slight, you must not hold it back.
Choragos.   A lord clairvoyant to the lord Apollo,
  As we all know, is the skilled Teiresias.
  One might learn much about this from him, Oedipus.   70
Oedipus.   I am not wasting time:
  Creon spoke of this, and I have sent for him—
  Twice, in fact; it is strange that he is not here.
Choragos.   The other matter—that old report—seems useless.
Oedipus.   Tell me. I am interested in all reports.
Choragos.   The King was said to have been killed by highwaymen.
Oedipus.   I know. But we have no witnesses to that.
Choragos.   If the killer can feel a particle of dread,
  Your curse will bring him out of hiding!
Oedipus.   No.
  The man who dared that act will fear no curse.   80

[*Enter the blind seer Teiresias, led by a page.*]

Choragos.   But there is one man who may detect the criminal.
  This is Teiresias, this is the holy prophet
  In whom, alone of all men, truth was born.
Oedipus.   Teiresias: seer: student of mysteries,
  Of all that's taught and all that no man tells,
  Secrets of Heaven and secrets of the earth:
  Blind though you are, you know the city lies

---

[8] Choragos is the leader of the Chorus.

Sick with plague; and from this plague, my lord,
We find that you alone can guard or save us.

Possibly you did not hear the messengers?   90
Apollo, when we sent to him,
Sent us back word that this great pestilence
Would lift, but only if we established clearly
The identity of those who murdered Laïos.
They must be killed or exiled.
                                Can you use
Birdflight or any art of divination
To purify yourself, and Thebes, and me
From this contagion? We are in your hands.
There is no fairer duty
Than that of helping others in distress.   100
Teiresias.   How dreadful knowledge of the truth can be
When there's no help in truth! I knew this well,
But did not act on it: else I should not have come.
Oedipus.   What is troubling you? Why are your eyes so cold?
Teiresias.   Let me go home. Bear your own fate, and I'll
Bear mine. It is better so: trust what I say.
Oedipus.   What you say is ungracious and unhelpful
To your native country. Do not refuse to speak.
Teiresias.   When it comes to speech, your own is neither temperate
Nor opportune. I wish to be more prudent.   110
Oedipus.   In God's name, we all beg you—
Teiresias.   You are all ignorant.
No; I will never tell you what I know.
Now it is my misery; then, it would be yours.
Oedipus.   What! You do know something, and will not tell us?
You would betray us all and wreck the State?
Teiresias.   I do not intend to torture myself, or you.
Why persist in asking? You will not persuade me.
Oedipus.   What a wicked old man you are! You'd try a stone's
Patience! Out with it! Have you no feeling at all?
Teiresias.   You call me unfeeling. If you could only see   120
The nature of your own feelings . . .
Oedipus.   Why,
Who would not feel as I do? Who could endure
Your arrogance toward the city?
Teiresias.   What does it matter!
Whether I speak or not, it is bound to come.
Oedipus.   Then, if "it" is bound to come, you are bound to tell me.
Teiresias.   No, I will not go on. Rage as you please.

Oedipus. Rage? Why not!
                        And I'll tell you what I think:
  You planned it, you had it done, you all but
  Killed him with your own hands: if you had eyes,
  I'd say the crime was yours, and yours alone.   130
Teiresias. So? I charge you, then,
  Abide by the proclamation you have made:
  From this day forth
  Never speak again to these men or to me;
  You yourself are the pollution of this country.
Oedipus. You dare say that! Can you possibly think you have
  Some way of going free, after such insolence?
Teiresias. I have gone free. It is the truth sustains me.
Oedipus. Who taught you shamelessness? It was not your craft.
Teiresias. You did. You made me speak. I did not want to.   140
Oedipus. Speak what? Let me hear it again more clearly.
Teiresias. Was it not clear before? Are you tempting me?
Oedipus. I did not understand it. Say it again.
Teiresias. I say that you are the murderer whom you seek.
Oedipus. Now twice you have spat out infamy! You'll pay for it!
Teiresias. Would you care for more? Do you wish to be really angry?
Oedipus. Say what you will. Whatever you say is worthless.
Teiresias. I say you live in hideous shame with those
  Most dear to you. You can not see the evil.
Oedipus. It seems you can go on mouthing like this for ever.   150
Teiresias. I can, if there is power in truth.
Oedipus.   There is:
  But not for you, not for you,
  You sightless, witless, senseless, mad old man!
Teiresias. You are the madman. There is no one here
  Who will not curse you soon, as you curse me.
Oedipus. You child of endless night! You can not hurt me
  Or any other man who sees the sun.
Teiresias. True: it is not from me your fate will come.
  That lies within Apollo's competence,
  As it is his concern.
Oedipus.   Tell me: 160
  Are you speaking for Creon or for yourself?
Teiresias. Creon is no threat. You weave your own doom.
Oedipus. Wealth, power, craft of statesmanship!
  Kingly position, everywhere admired!
  What savage envy is stored up against these,
  If Creon, whom I trusted, Creon my friend,
  For this great office which the city once

Put in my hands unsought—if for this power
Creon desires in secret to destroy me!

He has brought this decrepit fortune-teller, this   170
Collector of dirty pennies, this prophet fraud—
Why, he is no more clairvoyant than I am!
                                                    Tell us:
Has your mystic mummery ever approached the truth?
When that hellcat the Sphinx was performing here,
What help were you to these people?
Her magic was not for the first man who came along:
It demanded a real exorcist. Your birds—
What good were they? or the gods, for the matter of that?
But I came by,
Oedipus, the simple man, who knows nothing—   180
I thought it out for myself, no birds helped me!
And this is the man you think you can destroy,
That you may be close to Creon when he's king!
Well, you and your friend Creon, it seems to me,
Will suffer most. If you were not an old man,
You would have paid already for your plot.
Choragos.   We can not see that his words or yours
Have been spoken except in anger, Oedipus,
And of anger we have no need. How can God's will
Be accomplished best? That is what most concerns us.   190
Teiresias.   You are a king. But where argument's concerned
I am your man, as much a king as you.
I am not your servant, but Apollo's.
I have no need of Creon to speak for me.

Listen to me. You mock my blindness, do you?
But I say that you, with both your eyes, are blind:
You can not see the wretchedness of your life,
Nor in whose house you live, no, nor with whom.
Who are your father and mother? Can you tell me?
You do not even know the blind wrongs   200
That you have done them, on earth and in the world below.
But the double lash of your parents' curse will whip you
Out of this land some day, with only night
Upon your precious eyes.
Your cries then—where will they not be heard?
What fastness of Kithairon⁹ will not echo them?
And that bridal-descant of yours—you'll know it then,

⁹ A mountain range near Thebes where the infant Oedipus was left to die.

The song they sang when you came here to Thebes
And found your misguided berthing.
All this, and more, that you can not guess at now,   210
Will bring you to yourself among your children.

Be angry, then. Curse Creon. Curse my words.
I tell you, no man that walks upon the earth
Shall be rooted out more horribly than you.
Oedipus.   Am I to bear this from him?—Damnation
Take you! Out of this place! Out of my sight!
Teiresias.   I would not have come at all if you had not asked me.
Oedipus.   Could I have told that you'd talk nonsense, that
You'd come here to make a fool of yourself, and of me?
Teiresias.   A fool? Your parents thought me sane enough.   220
Oedipus.   My parents again!—Wait: who were my parents?
Teiresias.   This day will give you a father, and break your heart.
Oedipus.   Your infantile riddles! Your damned abracadabra!
Teiresias.   You were a great man once at solving riddles.
Oedipus.   Mock me with that if you like; you will find it true.
Teiresias.   It was true enough. It brought about your ruin.
Oedipus.   But if it saved this town?
Teiresias [to the page].   Boy, give me your hand.
Oedipus.   Yes, boy; lead him away.
                                        —While you are here
We can do nothing. Go; leave us in peace.
Teiresias.   I will go when I have said what I have to say.   230
How can you hurt me? And I tell you again:
The man you have been looking for all this time,
The damned man, the murderer of Laïos,
That man is in Thebes. To your mind he is foreignborn,
But it will soon be shown that he is a Theban,
A revelation that will fail to please.
                                    A blind man,
Who has his eyes now; a penniless man, who is rich now;
And he will go tapping the strange earth with his staff;
To the children with whom he lives now he will be
Brother and father—the very same; to her   240
Who bore him, son and husband—the very same
Who came to his father's bed, wet with his father's blood.

Enough. Go think that over.
If later you find error in what I have said,
You may say that I have no skill in prophecy.

[Exit Teiresias, led by his page. Oedipus goes into the palace.]

Ode I

Chorus.   The Delphic stone of prophecies   *[Strophe 1]*
    Remembers ancient regicide
    And a still bloody hand.
    That killer's hour of flight has come.
    He must be stronger than riderless
    Coursers of untiring wind,
    For the son of Zeus[10] armed with his father's thunder
    Leaps in lightning after him;
    And the Furies follow him, the sad Furies.[11]

    Holy Parnassos' peak of snow   *[Antistrophe 1]*
    Flashes and blinds that secret man,   11
    That all shall hunt him down:
    Though he may roam the forest shade
    Like a bull gone wild from pasture
    To rage through glooms of stone.
    Doom comes down on him; flight will not avail him;
    For the world's heart calls him desolate,
    And the immortal Furies follow, for ever follow.

    But now a wilder thing is heard   *[Strophe 2]*
    From the old man skilled at hearing Fate in the wingbeat of a bird.   20
    Bewildered as a blown bird, my soul hovers and can not find
    Foothold in this debate, or any reason or rest of mind.
    But no man ever brought—none can bring
    Proof of strife between Thebes' royal house,
    Labdakos' line, and the son of Polybos;[12]
    And never until now has any man brought word
    Of Laïos' dark death staining Oedipus the King.

    Divine Zeus and Apollo hold   *[Antistrophe 2]*
    Perfect intelligence alone of all tales ever told;
    And well though this diviner works, he works in his own night;   30
    No man can judge that rough unknown or trust in second sight,
    For wisdom changes hands among the wise.
    Shall I believe my great lord criminal
    At a raging word that a blind old man let fall?
    I saw him, when the carrion woman faced him of old,
    Prove his heroic mind! These evil words are lies.

---

[10] I.e., Apollo (see note 3).
[11] The goddesses of divine vengeance.
[12] Labdakos was an early king of Thebes and an ancestor of Oedipus. Oedipus is mistakenly
referred to as the son of Polybus.

Scene II

Creon.   Men of Thebes:
I am told that heavy accusations
Have been brought against me by King Oedipus.

I am not the kind of man to bear this tamely.

If in these present difficulties
He holds me accountable for any harm to him
Through anything I have said or done—why, then,
I do not value life in this dishonor.
It is not as though this rumor touched upon
Some private indiscretion. The matter is grave.   10
The fact is that I am being called disloyal
To the State, to my fellow citizens, to my friends.
Choragos.   He may have spoken in anger, not from his mind.
Creon.   But did you not hear him say I was the one
Who seduced the old prophet into lying?
Choragos.   The thing was said; I do not know how seriously.
Creon.   But you were watching him! Were his eyes steady?
Did he look like a man in his right mind?
Choragos.   I do not know.
I can not judge the behavior of great men.
But here is the King himself.

[*Enter Oedipus.*]

Oedipus.   So you dared come back.   20
Why? How brazen of you to come to my house,
You murderer!
                    Do you think I do not know
That you plotted to kill me, plotted to steal my throne?
Tell me, in God's name: am I coward, a fool,
That you should dream you could accomplish this?
A fool who could not see your slippery game?
A coward, not to fight back when I saw it?
You are the fool, Creon, are you not? hoping
Without support or friends to get a throne?
Thrones may be won or bought: you could do neither.   30
Creon.   Now listen to me. You have talked; let me talk, too.
You can not judge unless you know the facts.
Oedipus.   You speak well: there is one fact; but I find it hard
To learn from the deadliest enemy I have.
Creon.   That above all I must dispute with you.
Oedipus.   That above all I will not hear you deny.

Creon.   If you think there is anything good in being stubborn
Against all reason, then I say you are wrong.
Oedipus.   If you think a man can sin against his own kind
And not be punished for it, I say you are mad.   40
Creon.   I agree. But tell me: what have I done to you?
Oedipus.   You advised me to send for that wizard, did you not?
Creon.   I did. I should do it again.
Oedipus.   Very well. Now tell me:
How long has it been since Laïos—
Creon.   What of Laïos?
Oedipus.   Since he vanished in that onset by the road?
Creon.   It was long ago, a long time.
Oedipus.   And this prophet,
Was he practicing here then?
Creon.   He was; and with honor, as now.
Oedipus.   Did he speak of me at that time?
Creon.   He never did;
At least, not when I was present.
Oedipus.   But . . . the enquiry?
I suppose you held one?
Creon.   We did, but we learned nothing.   50
Oedipus.   Why did the prophet not speak against me then?
Creon.   I do not know; and I am the kind of man
Who holds his tongue when he has no facts to go on.
Oedipus.   There's one fact that you know, and you could tell it.
Creon.   What fact is that? If I know it, you shall have it.
Oedipus.   If he were not involved with you, he could not say
That it was I who murdered Laïos.
Creon.   If he says that, you are the one that knows it!—
But now it is my turn to question you.
Oedipus.   Put your questions. I am no murderer.   60
Creon.   First then: You married my sister?
Oedipus.   I married your sister.
Creon.   And you rule the kingdom equally with her?
Oedipus.   Everything that she wants she has from me.
Creon.   And I am the third, equal to both of you?
Oedipus.   That is why I call you a bad friend.
Creon.   No. Reason it out, as I have done.
Think of this first. Would any sane man prefer
Power, with all a king's anxieties,
To that same power and the grace of sleep?
Certainly not I.   70
I have never longed for the king's power—only his rights.
Would any wise man differ from me in this?
As matters stand, I have my way in everything

With your consent, and no responsibilities.
If I were king, I should be a slave to policy.

How could I desire a scepter more
Than what is now mine—untroubled influence?
No, I have not gone mad; I need no honors,
Except those with the perquisites I have now.
I am welcome everywhere; every man salutes me,   80
And those who want your favor seek my ear,
Since I know how to manage what they ask.
Should I exchange this ease for that anxiety?
Besides, no sober mind is treasonable.
I hate anarchy
And never would deal with any man who likes it.

Test what I have said. Go to the priestess
At Delphi, ask if I quoted her correctly.
And as for this other thing: if I am found
Guilty of treason with Teiresias,   90
Then sentence me to death! You have my word
It is a sentence I should cast my vote for—
But not without evidence!
                              You do wrong
When you take good men for bad, bad men for good.
A true friend thrown aside—why, life itself
Is not more precious!
                          In time you will know this well:
For time, and time alone, will show the just man,
Though scoundrels are discovered in a day.
Choragos.   This is well said, and a prudent man would ponder it.
   Judgments too quickly formed are dangerous.   100
Oedipus.   But is he not quick in his duplicity?
   And shall I not be quick to parry him?
   Would you have me stand still, hold my peace, and let
   This man win everything, through my inaction?
Creon.   And you want—what is it, then? To banish me?
Oedipus.   No, not exile. It is your death I want,
   So that all the world may see what treason means.
Creon.   You will persist, then? You will not believe me?
Oedipus.   How can I believe you?
Creon.   Then you are a fool.
Oedipus.   To save myself?
Creon.   In justice, think of me.   110
Oedipus.   You are evil incarnate.
Creon.   But suppose that you are wrong?

Oedipus.   Still I must rule.
Creon.   But not if you rule badly.
Oedipus.   O city, city!
Creon.   It is my city, too!
Choragos.   Now, my lords, be still. I see the Queen,
  Iocastê, coming from her palace chambers;
  And it is time she came, for the sake of you both.
  This dreadful quarrel can be resolved through her.   120

[Enter Iocastê.]

Iocastê.   Poor foolish men, what wicked din is this?
  With Thebes sick to death, is it not shameful
  That you should rake some private quarrel up?
  [To Oedipus.] Come into the house.
                                      —And you, Creon, go now:
  Let us have no more of this tumult over nothing.
Creon.   Nothing? No, sister: what your husband plans for me
  Is one of two great evils: exile or death.
Oedipus.   He is right.
                          Why, woman I have caught him squarely
  Plotting against my life.
Creon.   No! Let me die
  Accurst if ever I have wished you harm!
Iocastê.   Ah, believe it, Oedipus!
  In the name of the gods, respect this oath of his
  For my sake, for the sake of these people here!   130

Choragos.   Open your mind to her my lord. Be ruled by her,   [Strophe 1]
  I beg you!
Oedipus.   What would you have me do?
Choragos.   Respect Creon's word. He has never spoken like a fool,
  And now he has sworn an oath.
Oedipus.   You know what you ask?
Choragos.   I do.
Oedipus.   Speak on, then.
Choragos.   A friend so sworn should not be baited so,
  In blind malice, and without final proof.
Oedipus.   You are aware, I hope, that what you say
  Means death for me, or exile at the least.

Choragos.   No, I swear by Helios,[13] first in Heaven!   [Strophe 2]
  May I die friendless and accurst,   140

---

[13] The sun god.

The worst of deaths, if ever I meant that!
 It is the withering fields
  That hurt my sick heart:
 Must we bear all these ills,
  And now your bad blood as well?
Oedipus. Then let him go. And let me die, if I must,
Or be driven by him in shame from the land of Thebes.
It is your unhappiness, and not his talk,
That touches me.
     As for him—
Wherever he is, I will hate him as long as I live.   150
Creon. Ugly in yielding, as you were ugly in rage!
Natures like yours chiefly torment themselves.
Oedipus. Can you not go? Can you not leave me?
Creon.   I can.
You do not know me; but the city knows me,
And in its eyes I am just, if not in yours.

[*Exit Creon.*]

Choragos. Lady Iocastê, did you not ask the King to go   [*Antistrophe 1*]
 to his chambers?
Iocastê. First tell me what has happened.
Choragos. There was suspicion without evidence; yet it rankled
 As even false charges will.
Iocastê.   On both sides?
Choragos.   On both.
Iocastê.   But what was said?
Choragos. Oh let it rest, let it be done with!   160
 Have we not suffered enough?
Oedipus. You see to what your decency has brought you:
 You have made difficulties where my heart saw none.

Choragos. Oedipus, it is not once only I have told you— [*Antistrophe 2*]
 You must know I should count myself unwise
 To the point of madness, should I now forsake you—
  You, under whose hand,
   In the storm of another time,
  Our dear land sailed out free.
   But now stand fast at the helm!   170
Iocastê. In God's name, Oedipus, inform your wife as well:
 Why are you so set in this hard anger?
Oedipus. I will tell you, for none of these men deserves
 My confidence as you do. It is Creon's work,
 His treachery, his plotting against me.

Iocastê.   Go on, if you can make this clear to me.

Oedipus.   He charges me with the murder of Laïos.

Iocastê.   Has he some knowledge? Or does he speak from hearsay?

Oedipus.   He would not commit himself to such a charge,
But he has brought in that damnable soothsayer   180
To tell his story.

Iocastê.   Set your mind at rest.
If it is a question of soothsayers, I tell you
That you will find no man whose craft gives knowledge
Of the unknowable.
                              Here is my proof:

An oracle was reported to Laïos once
(I will not say from Phoibos himself, but from
His appointed ministers, at any rate)
That his doom would be death at the hands of his own son—
His son, born of his flesh and of mine!

Now, you remember the story: Laïos was killed   190
By marauding strangers where three highways meet;
But his child had not been three days in this world
Before the King had pierced the baby's ankles
And left him to die on a lonely mountainside.

Thus, Apollo never caused that child
To kill his father, and it was not Laïos' fate
To die at the hands of his son, as he had feared.
This is what prophets and prophecies are worth!
Have no dread of them.
                          It is God himself
Who can show us what he wills, in his own way.   200

Oedipus.   How strange a shadowy memory crossed my mind,
Just now while you were speaking; it chilled my heart.

Iocastê.   What do you mean? What memory do you speak of?

Oedipus.   If I understand you, Laïos was killed
At a place where three roads meet.

Iocastê.   So it was said;
We have no later story.

Oedipus.   Where did it happen?

Iocastê.   Phokis, it is called: at a place where the Theban Way
Divides into the roads towards Delphi and Daulia.

Oedipus.   When?

Iocastê.   We had the news not long before you came
And proved the right to your succession here.   210

Oedipus.   Ah, what net has God been weaving for me?

Iocastê.   Oedipus! Why does this trouble you?
Oedipus.   Do not ask me yet.
    First, tell me how Laïos looked, and tell me
    How old he was.
Iocastê.   He was tall, his hair just touched
    With white; his form was not unlike your own.
Oedipus.   I think that I myself may be accurst
    By my own ignorant edict.
Iocastê.   You speak strangely.
    It makes me tremble to look at you, my King.
Oedipus.   I am not sure that the blind man can not see.
    But I should know better if you were to tell me—   220
Iocastê.   Anything—though I dread to hear you ask it.
Oedipus.   Was the King lightly escorted, or did he ride
    With a large company, as a ruler should?
Iocastê.   There were five men with him in all: one was a herald;
    And a single chariot, which he was driving.
Oedipus.   Alas, that makes it plain enough!
                          But who—
    Who told you how it happened?
Iocastê.   A household servant,
    The only one to escape.
Oedipus.   And is he still
    A servant of ours?
Iocastê.   No; for when he came back at last
    And found you enthroned in the place of the dead king,   230
    He came to me, touched my hand with his, and begged
    That I would send him away to the frontier district
    Where only the shepherds go—
    As far away from the city as I could send him.
    I granted his prayer; for although the man was a slave,
    He had earned more than this favor at my hands.
Oedipus.   Can he be called back quickly?
Iocastê.   Easily.
    But why?
Oedipus.   I have taken too much upon myself
    Without enquiry; therefore I wish to consult him.
Iocastê.   Then he shall come.
                  But am I not one also   240
    To whom you might confide these fears of yours?
Oedipus.   That is your right; it will not be denied you,
    Now least of all; for I have reached a pitch
    Of wild foreboding. Is there anyone
    To whom I should sooner speak?
    Polybos of Corinth is my father.

My mother is a Dorian: Meropê.
I grew up chief among the men of Corinth
Until a strange thing happened—
Not worth my passion, it may be, but strange.   250

At a feast, a drunken man maundering in his cups
Cries out that I am not my father's son!

I contained myself that night, though I felt anger
And a sinking heart. The next day I visited
My father and mother, and questioned them. They stormed,
Calling it all the slanderous rant of a fool;
And this relieved me. Yet the suspicion
Remained always aching in my mind;
I knew there was talk; I could not rest;
And finally, saying nothing to my parents,   260
I went to the shrine at Delphi.
The god dismissed my question without reply;
He spoke of other things.
                    Some were clear,
Full of wretchedness, dreadful, unbearable:
As, that I should lie with my own mother, breed
Children from whom all men would turn their eyes;
And that I should be my father's murderer.

I heard all this, and fled. And from that day
Corinth to me was only in the stars
Descending in that quarter of the sky,   270
As I wandered farther and farther on my way
To a land where I should never see the evil
Sung by the oracle. And I came to this country
Where, so you say, King Laïos was killed.

I will tell you all that happened there, my lady.

There were three highways
Coming together at a place I passed;
And there a herald came towards me, and a chariot
Drawn by horses, with a man such as you describe
Seated in it. The groom leading the horses   280
Forced me off the road at his lord's command;
But as this charioteer lurched over towards me
I struck him in my rage. The old man saw me
And brought his double goad down upon my head
As I came abreast.
                    He was paid back, and more!

Swinging my club in this right hand I knocked him
Out of his car, and he rolled on the ground.

                                    I killed him.

I killed them all.
Now if that stranger and Laïos were—kin,
Where is a man more miserable than I?   290
More hated by the gods? Citizen and alien alike
Must never shelter me or speak to me—
I must be shunned by all.
                        And I myself
Pronounced this malediction upon myself!

Think of it: I have touched you with these hands,
These hands that killed your husband. What defilement!

Am I all evil, then? It must be so,
Since I must flee from Thebes, yet never again
See my own countrymen, my own country,
For fear of joining my mother in marriage   300
And killing Polybos, my father.
                            Ah,
If I was created so, born to this fate,
Who could deny the savagery of God?

O holy majesty of heavenly powers!
May I never see that day! Never!
Rather let me vanish from the race of men
Than know the abomination destined me!
Choragos.   We too, my lord, have felt dismay at this.
   But there is hope: you have yet to hear the shepherd.
Oedipus.   Indeed, I fear no other hope is left me.   310
Iocastê.   What do you hope from him when he comes?
Oedipus.   This much:
   If his account of the murder tallies with yours,
   Then I am cleared.
Iocastê.   What was it that I said
   Of such importance?
Oedipus.   Why, "marauders," you said,
   Killed the King, according to this man's story.
   If he maintains that still, if there were several,
   Clearly the guilt is not mine: I was alone.
   But if he says one man, singlehanded, did it,
   Then the evidence all points to me.
Iocastê.   You may be sure that he said there were several;   320
   And can he call back that story now? He can not.

The whole city heard it as plainly as I.
But suppose he alters some detail of it:
He can not ever show that Laïos' death
Fulfilled the oracle: for Apollo said
My child was doomed to kill him; and my child—
Poor baby!—it was my child that died first.

No. From now on, where oracles are concerned,
I would not waste a second thought on any.
Oedipus.   You may be right.
                                              But come: let someone go   330
For the shepherd at once. This matter must be settled.
Iocastê.   I will send for him.
I would not wish to cross you in anything.
And surely not in this.— Let us go in.

[*Exeunt into the palace.*]

Ode II

Chorus.   Let me be reverent in the ways of right,   [*Strophe 1*]
    Lowly the paths I journey on;
    Let all my words and actions keep
    The laws of the pure universe
    From highest Heaven handed down.
    For Heaven is their bright nurse,
    Those generations of the realms of light;
    Ah, never of mortal kind were they begot,
    Nor are they slaves of memory, lost in sleep:
    Their Father is greater than Time, and ages not.   10

    The tyrant is a child of Pride   [*Antistrophe 1*]
    Who drinks from his great sickening cup
    Recklessness and vanity,
    Until from his high crest headlong
    He plummets to the dust of hope.
    That strong man is not strong.
    But let no fair ambition be denied;
    May God protect the wrestler for the State
    In government, in comely policy,
    Who will fear God, and on His ordinance wait.   20

    Haughtiness and the high hand of disdain   [*Strophe 2*]
    Tempt and outrage God's holy law;
    And any mortal who dares hold

No immortal Power in awe
Will be caught up in a net of pain:
The price for which his levity is sold.
Let each man take due earnings, then,
And keep his hands from holy things,
And from blasphemy stand apart—
Else the crackling blast of heaven   30
Blows on his head, and on his desperate heart;
Though fools will honor impious men,
In their cities no tragic poet sings.

Shall we lose faith in Delphi's obscurities,   [Antistrophe 2]
We who have heard the world's core
Discredited, and the sacred wood
Of Zeus at Elis praised no more?
The deeds and the strange prophecies
Must make a pattern yet to be understood.
Zeus, if indeed you are lord of all,   40
Throned in light over night and day,
Mirror this in your endless mind:
Our masters call the oracle
Words on the wind, and the Delphic vision blind!
Their hearts no longer know Apollo,
And reverence for the gods has died away.

Scene III

[Enter Iocastê.]

Iocastê.   Princes of Thebes, it has occurred to me
    To visit the altars of the gods, bearing
    These branches as a suppliant, and this incense.
    Our King is not himself: his noble soul
    Is overwrought with fantasies of dread,
    Else he would consider
    The new prophecies in the light of the old.
    He will listen to any voice that speaks disaster,
    And my advice goes for nothing.

[She approaches the altar, R.]

                        To you, then, Apollo,
    Lycean lord, since you are nearest, I turn in prayer.   10
    Receive these offerings, and grant us deliverance
    From defilement. Our hearts are heavy with fear

When we see our leader distracted, as helpless sailors
Are terrified by the confusion of their helmsman.

[*Enter Messenger.*]

Messenger.   Friends, no doubt you can direct me:
　Where shall I find the house of Oedipus,
　Or, better still, where is the King himself?
Choragos.   It is this very place, stranger; he is inside.
　This is his wife and mother of his children.
Messenger.   I wish her happiness in a happy house,　　　　　　　20
　Blest in all the fulfillment of her marriage.
Iocastê.   I wish as much for you: your courtesy
　Deserves a like good fortune. But now, tell me:
　Why have you come? What have you to say to us?
Messenger.   Good news, my lady, for your house and your husband.
Iocastê.   What news? Who sent you here?
Messenger.   　　　　　　　　　　　　I am from Corinth.
　The news I bring ought to mean joy for you,
　Though it may be you will find some grief in it.
Iocastê.   What is it? How can it touch us in both ways?
Messenger.   The people of Corinth, they say,　　　　　　　30
　Intend to call Oedipus to be their king.
Iocastê.   But old Polybos—is he not reigning still?
Messenger.   No. Death holds him in his sepulchre.
Iocastê.   What are you saying? Polybos is dead?
Messenger.   If I am not telling the truth, may I die myself.
Iocastê [*to a maidservant*].   Go in, go quickly; tell this to your master.
　O riddlers of God's will, where are you now!
　This was the man whom Oedipus, long ago,
　Feared so, fled so, in dread of destroying him—
　But it was another fate by which he died.　　　　　　　40

[*Enter Oedipus, C.*]

Oedipus.   Dearest Iocastê, why have you sent for me?
Iocastê.   Listen to what this man says, and then tell me
　What has become of the solemn prophecies.
Oedipus.   Who is this man? What is his news for me?
Iocastê.   He has come from Corinth to announce your father's death!
Oedipus.   Is it true, stranger? Tell me in your own words.
Messenger.   I can not say it more clearly: the King is dead.
Oedipus.   Was it by treason? Or by an attack of illness?
Messenger.   A little thing brings old men to their rest.
Oedipus.   It was sickness, then?
Messenger.   　　　　　　　　　　Yes, and his many years.　　　　　　　50

Oedipus.   Ah!
   Why should a man respect the Pythian hearth,[14] or
   Give heed to the birds that jangle above his head?
   They prophesied that I should kill Polybos,
   Kill my own father; but he is dead and buried,
   And I am here—I never touched him, never,
   Unless he died of grief for my departure,
   And thus, in a sense, through me. No. Polybos
   Has packed the oracles off with him underground.
   They are empty words.
Iocastê.   Had I not told you so?   60
Oedipus.   You had; it was my faint heart that betrayed me.
Iocastê.   From now on never think of those things again.
Oedipus.   And yet—must I not fear my mother's bed?
Iocastê.   Why should anyone in this world be afraid,
   Since Fate rules us and nothing can be foreseen?
   A man should live only for the present day.

   Have no more fear of sleeping with your mother:
   How many men, in dreams, have lain with their mothers!
   No reasonable man is troubled by such things.
Oedipus.   That is true; only—   70
   If only my mother were not still alive!
   But she is alive. I can not help my dread.
Iocastê.   Yet this news of your father's death is wonderful.
Oedipus.   Wonderful. But I fear the living woman.
Messenger.   Tell me, who is this woman that you fear?
Oedipus.   It is Meropê, man; the wife of King Polybos.
Messenger.   Meropê? Why should you be afraid of her?
Oedipus.   An oracle of the gods, a dreadful saying.
Messenger.   Can you tell me about it or are you sworn to silence?
Oedipus.   I can tell you, and I will.   80
   Apollo said through his prophet that I was the man
   Who should marry his own mother, shed his father's blood
   With his own hands. And so, for all these years
   I have kept clear of Corinth, and no harm has come—
   Though it would have been sweet to see my parents again.
Messenger.   And is this the fear that drove you out of Corinth?
Oedipus.   Would you have me kill my father?
Messenger.   As for that
   You must be reassured by the news I gave you.
Oedipus.   If you could reassure me, I would reward you.
Messenger.   I had that in mind, I will confess: I thought   90
   I could count on you when you returned to Corinth.

---

[14] Delphi, where Apollo spoke through an oracle.

Oedipus.   No: I will never go near my parents again.

Messenger.   Ah, son, you still do not know what you are doing—

Oedipus.   What do you mean? In the name of God tell me!

Messenger.   —If these are your reasons for not going home.

Oedipus.   I tell you, I fear the oracle may come true.

Messenger.   And guilt may come upon you through your parents?

Oedipus.   That is the dread that is always in my heart.

Messenger.   Can you not see that all your fears are groundless?

Oedipus.   How can you say that? They are my parents, surely?   100

Messenger.   Polybos was not your father.

Oedipus.   Not my father?

Messenger.   No more your father than the man speaking to you.

Oedipus.   But you are nothing to me!

Messenger.   Neither was he.

Oedipus.   Then why did he call me son?

Messenger.   I will tell you:
  Long ago he had you from my hands, as a gift.

Oedipus.   Then how could he love me so, if I was not his?

Messenger.   He had no children, and his heart turned to you.

Oedipus.   What of you? Did you buy me? Did you find me by chance?

Messenger.   I came upon you in the crooked pass of Kithairon.

Oedipus.   And what were you doing there?

Messenger.   Tending my flocks   110

Oedipus.   A wandering shepherd?

Messenger.   But your savior, son, that day.

Oedipus.   From what did you save me?

Messenger.   Your ankles should tell you that.

Oedipus.   Ah, stranger, why do you speak of that childhood pain?

Messenger.   I cut the bonds that tied your ankles together.

Oedipus.   I have had the mark as long as I can remember.

Messenger.   That was why you were given the name you bear.[15]

Oedipus.   God! Was it my father or my mother who did it?
  Tell me!

Messenger.   I do not know. The man who gave you to me
  Can tell you better than I.   120

Oedipus.   It was not you that found me, but another?

Messenger.   It was another shepherd gave you to me.

Oedipus.   Who was he? Can you tell me who he was?

Messenger.   I think he was said to be one of Laïos' people.

Oedipus.   You mean the Laïos who was king here years ago?

Messenger.   Yes; King Laïos; and the man was one of his herdsmen.

Oedipus.   Is he still alive? Can I see him?

Messenger.   These men here
  Know best about such things.

---

[15] Oedipus literally means "swollen-foot."

Oedipus.   Does anyone here
Know this shepherd that he is talking about?
Have you seen him in the fields, or in the town?   130
If you have, tell me. It is time things were made plain.
Choragos.   I think the man he means is that same shepherd
You have already asked to see. Iocastê perhaps
Could tell you something.
Oedipus.   Do you know anything
About him, Lady? Is he the man we have summoned?
Is that the man this shepherd means?
Iocastê.   Why think of him?
Forget this herdsman. Forget it all.
This talk is a waste of time.
Oedipus.   How can you say that?
When the clues to my true birth are in my hands?
Iocastê.   For God's love, let us have no more questioning!   140
Is your life nothing to you?
My own is pain enough for me to bear.
Oedipus.   You need not worry. Suppose my mother a slave,
And born of slaves: no baseness can touch you.
Iocastê.   Listen to me, I beg you: do not do this thing!
Oedipus.   I will not listen; the truth must be made known.
Iocastê.   Everything that I say is for your own good!
Oedipus.   My own good
Snaps my patience, then; I want none of it.
Iocastê.   You are fatally wrong! May you never learn who you are!
Oedipus.   Go, one of you, and bring the shepherd here.   150
Let us leave this woman to brag of her royal name.
Iocastê.   Ah, miserable!
That is the only word I have for you now.
That is the only word I can ever have.

[*Exit into the palace.*]

Choragos.   Why has she left us, Oedipus? Why has she gone
In such a passion of sorrow? I fear this silence:
Something dreadful may come of it.
Oedipus.   Let it come!
However base my birth, I must know about it.
The Queen, like a woman, is perhaps ashamed
To think of my low origin. But I   160
Am a child of Luck; I can not be dishonored.
Luck is my mother; the passing months, my brothers,
Have seen me rich and poor.
                          If this is so,

How could I wish that I were someone else?
How could I not be glad to know my birth?

Ode III

Chorus.   If ever the coming time were known   [*Strophe*]
     To my heart's pondering,
Kithairon, now by Heaven I see the torches
At the festival of the next full moon,
And see the dance, and hear the choir sing
A grace to your gentle shade:
Mountain where Oedipus was found,
O mountain guard of a noble race!
May the god who heals us lend his aid,
And let that glory come to pass   10
For our king's cradling-ground.

Of the nymphs that flower beyond the years,   [*Antistrophe*]
Who bore you, royal child,
To Pan of the hills or the timberline Apollo,
Cold in delight where the upland clears,
Or Hermês for whom Kyllenê's heights are piled?[16]
Or flushed as evening cloud,
Great Dionysos, roamer of mountains,
He—was it he who found you there,
And caught you up in his own proud   20
Arms from the sweet god-ravisher
Who laughed by the Muses' fountains?

Scene IV

Oedipus.   Sirs: though I do not know the man,
     I think I see him coming, this shepherd we want:
     He is old, like our friend here, and the men
     Bringing him seem to be servants of my house.
     But you can tell, if you have ever seen him.

[*Enter Shepherd escorted by servants.*]

Choragos.   I know him, he was Laïos' man. You can trust him.
Oedipus.   Tell me first, you from Corinth: is this the shepherd
     We were discussing?
Messenger.   This is the very man.

---

[16] Hermês, the herald of the Olympian gods, was born on the mountain of Kyllenê.

Oedipus [*to Shepherd*].   Come here. No, look at me. You must answer
  Everything I ask. You belonged to Laïos?   10
Shepherd.   Yes: born his slave, brought up in his house.
Oedipus.   Tell me what kind of work did you do for him?
Shepherd.   I was a shepherd of his, most of my life.
Oedipus.   Where mainly did you go for pasturage?
Shepherd.   Sometimes Kithairon, sometimes the hills near-by.
Oedipus.   Do you remember ever seeing this man out there?
Shepherd.   What would he be doing there? This man?
Oedipus.   This man standing here. Have you ever seen him before?
Shepherd.   No. At least, not to my recollection.
Messenger.   And that is not strange, my lord. But I'll refresh   20
  His memory: he must remember when we two
  Spent three whole seasons together, March to September,
  On Kithairon or thereabouts. He had two flocks;
  I had one. Each autumn I'd drive mine home
  And he would go back with his to Laïos' sheepfold.—
  Is this not true, just as I have described it?
Shepherd.   True, yes; but it was all so long ago.
Messenger.   Well, then: do you remember, back in those days
  That you gave me a baby boy to bring up as my own?
Shepherd.   What if I did? What are you trying to say?   30
Messenger.   King Oedipus was once that little child.
Shepherd.   Damn you, hold your tongue!
Oedipus.   No more of that!
  It is your tongue needs watching, not this man's.
Shepherd.   My King, my Master, what is it I have done wrong?
Oedipus.   You have not answered his question about the boy.
Shepherd.   He does not know . . . He is only making trouble . . .
Oedipus.   Come, speak plainly, or it will go hard with you.
Shepherd.   In God's name, do not torture an old man!
Oedipus.   Come here, one of you; bind his arms behind him.
Shepherd.   Unhappy king! What more do you wish to learn?   40
Oedipus.   Did you give this man the child he speaks of?
Shepherd.   I did.
  And I would to God I had died that very day.
Oedipus.   You will die now unless you speak the truth.
Shepherd.   Yet if I speak the truth, I am worse than dead.
Oedipus.   Very well; since you insist on delaying—
Shepherd.   No! I have told you already that I gave him the boy.
Oedipus.   Where did you get him? From your house? From somewhere
  else?
Shepherd.   Not from mine, no. A man gave him to me.
Oedipus.   Is that man here? Do you know whose slave he was?
Shepherd.   For God's love, my King, do not ask me any more!   50

Oedipus.   You are a dead man if I have to ask you again.
Shepherd.   Then . . . Then the child was from the palace of Laïos.
Oedipus.   A slave child? or a child of his own line?
Shepherd.   Ah, I am on the brink of dreadful speech!
Oedipus.   And I of dreadful hearing. Yet I must hear.
Shepherd.   If you must be told, then . . .

> They said it was Laïos' child,
But it is your wife who can tell you about that.
Oedipus.   My wife!—Did she give it to you?
Shepherd.   My lord, she did.
Oedipus.   Do you know why?
Shepherd.   I was told to get rid of it.
Oedipus.   An unspeakable mother!
Shepherd.   There had been prophecies . . .   60
Oedipus.   Tell me.
Shepherd.   It was said that the boy would kill his own father.
Oedipus.   Then why did you give him over to this old man?
Shepherd.   I pitied the baby, my King,
And I thought that this man would take him far away
To his own country.

> He saved him—but for what a fate!
For if you are what this man says you are,
No man living is more wretched than Oedipus.
Oedipus.   Ah God!
It was true!

> All the prophecies!

> —Now,
O Light, may I look on you for the last time!   70
I, Oedipus,
Oedipus, damned in his birth, in his marriage damned,
Damned in the blood he shed with his own hand!

[*He rushes into the palace.*]

Ode IV

Chorus.   Alas for the seed of men.   [*Strophe 1*]

> What measure shall I give these generations
That breathe on the void and are void
And exist and do not exist?

> Who bears more weight of joy
Than mass of sunlight shifting in images,
Or who shall make his thought stay on
That down time drifts away?

Your splendor is all fallen.

O naked brow of wrath and tears,   10
O change of Oedipus!
I who saw your days call no man blest—
Your great days like ghosts gone.

That mind was a strong bow.   [*Antistrophe 1*]

Deep, how deep you drew it then, hard archer,
At a dim fearful range,
And brought dear glory down!

You overcame the stranger—
The virgin with her hooking lion claws—
And though death sang, stood like a tower   20
To make pale Thebes take heart.

Fortress against our sorrow!

Divine king, giver of laws,
Majestic Oedipus!
No prince in Thebes had ever such renown,
No prince won such grace of power.

And now of all men ever known   [*Strophe 2*]
Most pitiful is this man's story:
His fortunes are most changed, his state
Fallen to a low slave's   30
Ground under bitter fate.

O Oedipus, most royal one!
The great door that expelled you to the light
Gave at night—ah, gave night to your glory:
As to the father, to the fathering son.

All understood too late.

How could that queen whom Laïos won,
The garden that he harrowed at his height,
Be silent when that act was done?

But all eyes fail before time's eye,   [*Antistrophe 2*]
All actions come to justice there   41
Though never willed, though far down the deep past,
Your bed, your dread sirings,
Are brought to book at last.

Child by Laïos doomed to die,
Then doomed to lose that fortunate little death,
Would God you never took breath in this air
That with my wailing lips I take to cry:

For I weep the world's outcast.

I was blind, and now I can tell why: 50
Asleep, for you had given ease of breath
To Thebes, while the false years went by.

Exodos

[*Enter, from the palace, Second Messenger.*]

Second Messenger.   Elders of Thebes, most honored in this land,
   What horrors are yours to see and hear, what weight
Of sorrow to be endured, if, true to your birth,
You venerate the line of Labdakos!
I think neither Istros nor Phasis, those great rivers,
Could purify this place of the corruption
It shelters now, or soon must bring to light—
Evil not done unconsciously, but willed.

The greatest griefs are those we cause ourselves.
Choragos.   Surely, friend, we have grief enough already;   10
   What new sorrow do you mean?
Second Messenger.   The Queen is dead.
Choragos.   Iocastê? Dead? But at whose hand?
Second Messenger.   Her own.
   The full horror of what happened you can not know,
   For you did not see it; but I, who did, will tell you
   As clearly as I can how she met her death.

When she had left us,
In passionate silence, passing through the court,
She ran to her apartment in the house,
Her hair clutched by the fingers of both hands.

She closed the doors behind her; then, by that bed   20
Where long ago the fatal son was conceived—
The son who should bring about his father's death—
We heard her call upon Laïos, dead so many years,
And heard her wail for the double fruit of her marriage,
A husband by her husband, children by her child.

Exactly how she died I do not know:
For Oedipus burst in moaning and would not let us
Keep vigil to the end: it was by him
As he stormed about the room that our eyes were caught.
From one to another of us he went, begging a sword,   30
Cursing the wife who was not his wife, the mother
Whose womb had carried his own children and himself.
I do not know: it was none of us aided him,
But surely one of the gods was in control!
For with a dreadful cry
He hurled his weight, as though wrenched out of himself,
At the twin doors: the bolts gave, and he rushed in.
And there we saw her hanging, her body swaying
From the cruel cord she had noosed about her neck.
A great sob broke from him, heartbreaking to hear,   40
As he loosed the rope and lowered her to the ground.

I would blot out from my mind what happened next!
For the King ripped from her gown the golden brooches
That were her ornament, and raised them, and plunged them down
Straight into his own eyeballs, crying, "No more,
No more shall you look on the misery about me,
The horrors of my own doing! Too long have you known
The faces of those whom I should never have seen,
Too long been blind to those for whom I was searching!
From this hour, go in darkness!" And as he spoke,   50
He struck at his eyes—not once, but many times;
And the blood spattered his beard,
Bursting from his ruined sockets like red hail.

So from the unhappiness of two this evil has sprung,
A curse on the man and woman alike. The old
Happiness of the house of Labdakos
Was happiness enough: where is it today?
It is all wailing and ruin, disgrace, death—all
The misery of mankind that has a name—
And it is wholly and for ever theirs.   60
Choragos.   Is he in agony still? Is there no rest for him?
Second Messenger.   He is calling for someone to lead him to the gates
So that all the children of Kadmos may look upon
His father's murderer, his mother's—no,
I can not say it!
                    And then he will leave Thebes,
Self-exiled, in order that the curse
Which he himself pronounced may depart from the house.
He is weak, and there is none to lead him,

So terrible is his suffering.
                         But you will see:
Look, the doors are opening; in a moment   70
You will see a thing that would crush a heart of stone.

[*The central door is opened; Oedipus, blinded, is led in.*]

Choragos.   Dreadful indeed for men to see.
  Never have my own eyes
  Looked on a sight so full of fear.

  Oedipus!
  What madness came upon you, what daemon
  Leaped on your life with heavier
  Punishment than a mortal man can bear?
  No: I can not even
  Look at you, poor ruined one.   80
  And I would speak, question, ponder,
  If I were able. No.
  You make me shudder.
Oedipus.   God. God.
  Is there a sorrow greater?
  Where shall I find harbor in this world?
  My voice is hurled far on a dark wind.
  What has God done to me?
Choragos.   Too terrible to think of, or to see.

Oedipus.   O cloud of night,   [*Strophe 1*]
  Never to be turned away: night coming on,   91
  I can not tell how: night like a shroud!

  My fair winds brought me here.
                         Oh God. Again
  The pain of the spikes where I had sight,
  The flooding pain
  Of memory, never to be gouged out.
Choragos.   This is not strange.
  You suffer it all twice over, remorse in pain,
  Pain in remorse.

Oedipus.   Ah dear friend   [*Antistrophe 1*]
  Are you faithful even yet, you alone?   101
  Are you still standing near me, will you stay here,
  Patient, to care for the blind?
                         The blind man!

Yet even blind I know who it is attends me,
By the voice's tone—
Though my new darkness hide the comforter.
Choragos.   Oh fearful act!
What god was it drove you to rake black
Night across your eyes?

Oedipus.   Apollo. Apollo. Dear   [*Strophe 2*]
Children, the god was Apollo.   111
He brought my sick, sick fate upon me.
But the blinding hand was my own!
How could I bear to see
When all my sight was horror everywhere?
Choragos.   Everywhere; that is true.
Oedipus.   And now what is left?
Images? Love? A greeting even,
Sweet to the senses? Is there anything?
Ah no, friends: lead me away.   120
Lead me away from Thebes.
                              Lead the great wreck
And hell of Oedipus, whom the gods hate.
Choragos.   Your fate is clear, you are not blind to that.
Would God you had never found it out!

Oedipus.   Death take the man who unbound   [*Antistrophe 2*]
My feet on that hillside
And delivered me from death to life! What life?
If only I had died,
This weight of monstrous doom
Could not have dragged me and my darlings down.   130
Choragos.   I would have wished the same.
Oedipus.   Oh never to have come here
With my father's blood upon me! Never
To have been the man they call his mother's husband!
Oh accurst! Oh child of evil,
To have entered that wretched bed—
                              the selfsame one!
More primal than sin itself, this fell to me.
Choragos.   I do not know how I can answer you.
You were better dead than alive and blind.
Oedipus.   Do not counsel me any more. This punishment   140
That I have laid upon myself is just.
If I had eyes,
I do not know how I could bear the sight
Of my father, when I came to the house of Death,

Or my mother: for I have sinned against them both
So vilely that I could not make my peace
By strangling my own life.
                    Or do you think my children,
Born as they were born, would be sweet to my eyes?
Ah never, never! Nor this town with its high walls,
Nor the holy images of the gods.
                     For I,   150
Thrice miserable!—Oedipus, noblest of all the line
Of Kadmos, have condemned myself to enjoy
These things no more, by my own malediction
Expelling that man whom the gods declared
To be a defilement in the house of Laïos.
After exposing the rankness of my own guilt,
How could I look men frankly in the eyes?
No, I swear it,
If I could have stifled my hearing at its source,
I would have done it and made all this body   160
A tight cell of misery, blank to light and sound:
So I should have been safe in a dark agony
Beyond all recollection.
                 Ah Kithairon!
Why did you shelter me? When I was cast upon you,
Why did I not die? Then I should never
Have shown the world my execrable birth.

Ah Polybos! Corinth, city that I believed
The ancient seat of my ancestors: how fair
I seemed, your child! And all the while this evil
Was cancerous within me!
                 For I am sick   170
In my daily life, sick in my origin.

O three roads, dark ravine, woodland and way
Where three roads met: you, drinking my father's blood,
My own blood, spilled by my own hand: can you remember
The unspeakable things I did there, and the things
I went on from there to do?
                 O marriage, marriage!
The act that engendered me, and again the act
Performed by the son in the same bed—
                    Ah, the net
Of incest, mingling fathers, brothers, sons,
With brides, wives, mothers; the last evil   180
That can be known by men: no tongue can say

How evil!

No. For the love of God, conceal me
Somewhere far from Thebes; or kill me; or hurl me
Into the sea, away from men's eyes for ever.

Come, lead me. You need not fear to touch me.
Of all men, I alone can bear this guilt.

[*Enter Creon.*]

Choragos.   We are not the ones to decide; but Creon here
 May fitly judge of what you ask. He only
 Is left to protect the city in your place.
Oedipus.   Alas, how can I speak to him? What right have I   190
 To beg his courtesy whom I have deeply wronged?
Creon.   I have not come to mock you, Oedipus,
 Or to reproach you, either.
 [*To attendants.*]   —You, standing there:
 If you have lost all respect for man's dignity,
 At least respect the flame of Lord Helios:
 Do not allow this pollution to show itself
 Openly here, an affront to the earth
 And Heaven's rain and the light of day. No, take him
 Into the house as quickly as you can.
 For it is proper   200
 That only the close kindred see his grief.
Oedipus.   I pray you in God's name, since your courtesy
 Ignores my dark expectation, visiting
 With mercy this man of all men most execrable:
 Give me what I ask—for your good, not for mine.
Creon.   And what is it that you would have me do?
Oedipus.   Drive me out of this country as quickly as may be
 To a place where no human voice can ever greet me.
Creon.   I should have done that before now—only,
 God's will had not been wholly revealed to me.   210
Oedipus.   But his command is plain: the parricide
 Must be destroyed. I am that evil man.
Creon.   That is the sense of it, yes; but as things are,
 We had best discover clearly what is to be done.
Oedipus.   You would learn more about a man like me?
Creon.   You are ready now to listen to the god.
Oedipus.   I will listen. But it is to you
 That I must turn for help. I beg you, hear me.

The woman in there—
Give her whatever funeral you think proper: 220

    She is your sister.
                        —But let me go, Creon!
    Let me purge my father's Thebes of the pollution
    Of my living here, and go out to the wild hills,
    To Kithairon, that has won such fame with me,
    The tomb my mother and father appointed for me,
    And let me die there, as they willed I should.
    And yet I know
    Death will not ever come to me through sickness
    Or in any natural way: I have been preserved
    For some unthinkable fate. But let that be.   230
    As for my sons, you need not care for them.
    They are men, they will find some way to live.
    But my poor daughters, who have shared my table,
    Who never before have been parted from their father—
    Take care of them, Creon; do this for me.
    And will you let me touch them with my hands
    A last time, and let us weep together?
    Be kind, my lord,
    Great prince, be kind!
                        Could I but touch them,
    They would be mine again, as when I had my eyes.   240

[*Enter Antigone and Ismene, attended.*]

    Ah, God!
    Is it my dearest children I hear weeping?
    Has Creon pitied me and sent my daughters?
Creon.   Yes, Oedipus: I knew that they were dear to you
    In the old days, and know you must love them still.
Oedipus.   May God bless you for this—and be a friendlier
    Guardian to you than he has been to me!

    Children, where are you?
    Come quickly to my hands: they are your brother's—
    Hands that have brought your father's once clear eyes   250
    To this way of seeing—
                        Ah dearest ones,
    I had neither sight nor knowledge then, your father
    By the woman who was the source of his own life!
    And I weep for you—having no strength to see you—,
    I weep for you when I think of the bitterness
    That men will visit upon you all your lives.
    What homes, what festivals can you attend
    Without being forced to depart again in tears?

And when you come to marriageable age,
Where is the man, my daughters, who would dare   260
Risk the bane that lies on all my children?
Is there any evil wanting? Your father killed
His father; sowed the womb of her who bore him;
Engendered you at the fount of his own existence!
That is what they will say of you.

                                        Then whom
Can you ever marry? There are no bridegrooms for you,
And your lives must wither away in sterile dreaming.
O Creon, son of Menoikeus!
You are the only father my daughters have,
Since we, their parents, are both of us gone for ever.   270
They are your own blood: you will not let them
Fall into beggary and loneliness;
You will keep them from the miseries that are mine!
Take pity on them; see, they are only children,
Friendless except for you. Promise me this,
Great Prince, and give me your hand in token of it.

[*Creon clasps his right hand.*]

Children:
I could say much, if you could understand me,
But as it is, I have only this prayer for you:
Live where you can, be as happy as you can—   280
Happier, please God, than God has made your father!
Creon.   Enough. You have wept enough. Now go within.
Oedipus.   I must; but it is hard.
Creon.   Time eases all things.
Oedipus.   But you must promise—
Creon.   Say what you desire.
Oedipus.   Send me from Thebes!
Creon.   God grant that I may!
Oedipus.   But since God hates me . . .
Creon.   No, he will grant your wish.
Oedipus.   You promise?
Creon.   I can not speak beyond my knowledge.
Oedipus.   Then lead me in.
Creon.   Come now, and leave your children.
Oedipus.   No! Do not take them from me!
Creon.   Think no longer
That you are in command here, but rather think   290
How, when you were, you served your own destruction.

[*Exeunt into the house all but the Chorus; the Choragos chants directly to the audience.*]

Choragos.   Men of Thebes: look upon Oedipus.

This is the king who solved the famous riddle
And towered up, most powerful of men.
No mortal eyes but looked on him with envy,
Yet in the end ruin swept over him.
Let every man in mankind's frailty
Consider his last day; and let none
Presume on his good fortune until he find
Life, at his death, a memory without pain.   300

QUESTIONS

1. How does the Prologue establish the mood and theme of the play? What aspects of Oedipus's character are revealed there? **2.** Sophocles' audience knew the Oedipus story as you, for instance, know the story of the crucifixion. In the absence of suspense, what literary devices serve to hold the audience's attention? **3.** To what extent and in what ways does the chorus contribute to the dramatic development and tension of the play?

WRITING TOPIC

1. In the Exodos, Oedipus declares that Appollo "brought my sick, sick fate upon me. / But the blinding hand was my own! (ll. 112–113) and "This punishment / That I have laid upon myself is just" (ll. 140–141); later he declares, ". . . the parricide / Must be destroyed. I am that evil man." (ll. 211–212). How can Oedipus's acceptance of responsibility for his fate be reconciled with the fact that his fate was divinely ordained? **2.** The play embodies a pattern of figurative and literal allusions to darkness and light, to vision and blindness. How does that figurative language function, and what relationship does it bear to Oedipus's self-inflicted punishment?

INNOCENCE
AND
EXPERIENCE

Child in a Straw Hat, 1886 by Mary Cassatt

ESSAYS

Shooting an Elephant (1936)

GEORGE ORWELL [1903–1950]

In Moulmein, in lower Burma, I was hated by large numbers of people—the only time in my life that I have been important enough for this to happen to me. I was sub-divisional police officer of the town, and in an aimless, petty kind of way anti-European feeling was very bitter. No one had the guts to raise a riot, but if a European woman went through the bazaars alone somebody would probably spit betel juice over her dress. As a police officer I was an obvious target and was baited whenever it seemed safe to do so. When a nimble Burman tripped me up on the football field and the referee (another Burman) looked the other way, the crowd yelled with hideous laughter. This happened more than once. In the end the sneering yellow faces of young men that met me everywhere, the insults hooted after me when I was at a safe distance, got badly on my nerves. The young Buddhist priests were the worst of all. There were several thousands of them in the town and none of them seemed to have anything to do except stand on street corners and jeer at Europeans.

All this was perplexing and upsetting. For at that time I had already made up my mind that imperialism was an evil thing and the sooner I chucked up my job and got out of it the better. Theoretically—and secretly, of course—I was all for the Burmese and all against their oppressors, the British. As for the job I was doing, I hated it more bitterly than I can perhaps make clear. In a job like that you see the dirty work of Empire at close quarters. The wretched prisoners huddling in the stinking cages of the lock-ups, the grey, cowed faces of the long-term convicts, the scarred buttocks of the men who had been flogged with bamboos—all these oppressed me with an intolerable sense of guilt. But I could get nothing into perspective. I was young and ill-educated and I had had to think out my problems in the utter silence that is imposed on every Englishman in the East. I did not even know that the British Empire is dying, still less did I know that it is a great deal better than the younger empires that are going to supplant it. All I knew was that I was stuck between my hatred of the empire I served and my rage against the evil-spirited little beasts who tried to make my job impossible. With one part of my mind I thought of the British Raj[1] as an unbreakable tyranny, as something clamped down, *in saecula sae-culorum,*[2] upon the will of prostrate peoples; with another part I thought that the greatest joy in the world would be to drive a bayonet into a Buddhist priest's guts. Feelings like these are the normal by-products of imperialism; ask any Anglo-Indian official, if you can catch him off duty.

One day something happened which in a roundabout way was enlightening. It was a tiny incident in itself, but it gave me a better glimpse than I had had before of the real nature of imperialism—the real motive for which despotic governments act. Early one morning the sub-inspector at a police station the other end of the town rang me up on the 'phone and said that an elephant was ravaging the bazaar. Would I please come and do something about it? I did not know what I could do, but I wanted to see what was happening and I got on to a pony and started out. I took my rifle, an old .44 Winchester and much too small to kill an elephant, but I thought the noise might be useful *in terro-rem.* Various Burmans stopped me on the way and told me about the ele-phant's doings. It was not, of course, a wild elephant, but a tame one which had gone "must." It had been chained up, as tame elephants always are when their attack of "must" is due, but on the previous night it had broken its chain and escaped. Its mahout,[3] the only person who could manage it when it was in that state, had set out in pursuit, but had taken the wrong direction and was now twelve hours' journey away, and in the morning the elephant had sud-denly reappeared in the town. The Burmese population had no weapons and were quite helpless against it. It had already destroyed somebody's bamboo hut, killed a cow and raided some fruit-stalls and devoured the stock; also it had met the municipal rubbish van and, when the driver jumped out and took to his heels, had turned the van over and inflicted violences upon it.

The Burmese sub-inspector and some Indian constables were waiting for me in the quarter where the elephant had been seen. It was a very poor quarter, a labyrinth of squalid bamboo huts, thatched with palm-leaf, winding all over a steep hillside. I remember that it was a cloudy, stuffy morning at the begin-ning of the rains. We began questioning the people as to where the elephant had gone and, as usual, failed to get any definite information. That is invari-ably the case in the East; a story always sounds clear enough at a distance, but the nearer you get to the scene of events the vaguer it becomes. Some of the people said that the elephant had gone in one direction, some said that he had gone in another, some professed not even to have heard of any elephant. I had almost made up my mind that the whole story was a pack of lies, when we heard yells a little distance away. There was a loud, scandalized cry of "Go away, child! Go away this instant!" and an old woman with a switch in her

---

[1] The imperial British government of India and Burma.
[2] For eternity.
[3] The keeper and driver of an elephant.

hand came round the corner of a hut, violently shooing away a crowd of naked children. Some more women followed, clicking their tongues and exclaiming; evidently there was something that the children ought not to have seen. I rounded the hut and saw a man's dead body sprawling in the mud. He was an Indian, a black Dravidian coolie, almost naked, and he could not have been dead many minutes. The people said that the elephant had come suddenly upon him round the corner of the hut, caught him with its trunk, put its foot on his back and ground him into the earth. This was the rainy season and the ground was soft, and his face had scored a trench a foot deep and a couple of yards long. He was lying on his belly with arms crucified and head sharply twisted to one side. His face was coated with mud, the eyes wide open, the teeth bared and grinning with an expression of unendurable agony. (Never tell me, by the way, that the dead look peaceful. Most of the corpses I have seen look devilish.) The friction of the great beast's foot had stripped the skin from his back as neatly as one skins a rabbit. As soon as I saw the dead man I sent an orderly to a friend's house nearby to borrow an elephant rifle. I had already sent back the pony, not wanting it to go mad with fright and throw me if it smelt the elephant.

The orderly came back in a few minutes with a rifle and five cartridges, and meanwhile some Burmans had arrived and told us that the elephant was in the paddy fields below, only a few hundred yards away. As I started forward practically the whole population of the quarter flocked out of the houses and followed me. They had seen the rifle and were all shouting excitedly that I was going to shoot the elephant. They had not shown much interest in the elephant when he was merely ravaging their homes, but it was different now that he was going to be shot. It was a bit of fun to them, as it would be to an English crowd; besides they wanted the meat. It made me vaguely uneasy. I had no intention of shooting the elephant—I had merely sent for the rifle to defend myself if necessary—and it is always unnerving to have a crowd following you. I marched down the hill, looking and feeling a fool, with the rifle over my shoulder and an ever-growing army of people jostling at my heels. At the bottom, when you got a way from the huts, there was a metalled road and beyond that a miry waste of paddy fields a thousand yards across, not yet ploughed but soggy from the first rains and dotted with coarse grass. The elephant was standing eight yards from the road, his left side towards us. He took not the slightest notice of the crowd's approach. He was tearing up branches of grass, beating them against his knees to clean them and stuffing them into his mouth.

I had halted on the road. As soon as I saw the elephant I knew with perfect certainty that I ought not to shoot him. It is a serious matter to shoot a working elephant—it is comparable to destroying a huge and costly piece of machinery—and obviously one ought not to do it if it can possibly be avoided. And at that distance, peacefully eating, the elephant looked no more dangerous than a cow. I thought then and I think now that his attack of "must" was already passing off; in which case he would merely wander harmlessly about until the mahout came back and caught him. Moreover, I did not in the least want to shoot him. I decided that I would watch him for a little while to make sure that he did not turn savage again, and then go home.

But at that moment I glanced round at the crowd that had followed me. It was an immense crowd, two thousand at the least and growing every minute. It blocked the road for a long distance on either side. I looked at the sea of yellow faces above the garish clothes—faces all happy and excited over this bit of fun, all certain that the elephant was going to be shot. They were watching me as they would watch a conjurer about to perform a trick. They did not like me, but with the magical rifle in my hands I was momentarily worth watching. And suddenly I realized that I should have to shoot the elephant after all. The people expected it of me and I had got to do it; I could feel their two thousand wills pressing me forward, irresistibly. And it was at this moment, as I stood there with the rifle in my hands, that I first grasped the hollowness, the futility of the white man's dominion in the East. Here was I, the white man with his gun, standing in front of the unarmed native crowd—seemingly the leading actor of the piece; but in reality I was only an absurd puppet pushed to and fro by the will of those yellow faces behind. I perceived in this moment that when the white man turns tyrant it is his own freedoms that he destroys. He becomes a sort of hollow, posing dummy, the conventionalized figure of a sahib. For it is the condition of his rule that he shall spend his life in trying to impress the "natives," and so in every crisis he has got to do what the "natives" expect of him. He wears a mask, and his face grows to fit it. I had got to shoot the elephant. I had committed myself to doing it when I sent for the rifle. A sahib has got to act like a sahib; he has got to appear resolute, to know his own mind and do definite things. To come all that way, rifle in hand, with two thousand people marching at my heels, and then to trail feebly away, having done nothing—no, that was impossible. The crowd would laugh at me. And my whole life, every white man's life in the East, was one long struggle not to be laughed at.   7

But I did not want to shoot the elephant. I watched him beating his bunch of grass against his knees, with that preoccupied grandmotherly air that elephants have. It seemed to me that it would be murder to shoot him. At that age I was not squeamish about killing animals, but I had never shot an elephant and never wanted to. (Somehow it always seems worse to kill a *large* animal.) Besides, there was the beast's owner to be considered. Alive, the elephant was worth at least a hundred pounds; dead, he would only be worth the value of his tusks, five pounds, possibly. But I had got to act quickly. I turned to some experienced-looking Burmans who had been there when we arrived, and asked them how the elephant had been behaving. They all said the same thing: he took no notice of you if you left him alone, but he might charge if you went too close to him.   8

It was perfectly clear to me what I ought to do. I ought to walk up to within, say, twenty-five yards of the elephant and test his behavior. If he charged, I could shoot; if he took no notice of me, it would be safe to leave him until the mahout came back. But also I knew that I was going to do no such thing. I   9 was a poor shot with a rifle and the ground was soft mud into which one would sink at every step. If the elephant charged and I missed him, I should have about as much chance as a toad under a steam-roller. But even then I was not thinking particularly of my own skin, only of the watchful yellow faces behind. For at that moment, with the crowd watching me, I was not afraid in the ordinary sense, as I would have been if I had been alone. A white man mustn't be frightened in front of "natives"; and so, in general, he isn't frightened. The sole thought in my mind was that if anything went wrong those two thousand Burmans would see me pursued, caught, trampled on and reduced to a grinning corpse like that Indian up the hill. And if that happened it was quite probable that some of them would laugh. That would never do. There was only one alternative. I shoved the cartridges into the magazine and lay down on the road to get a better aim.

The crowd grew very still, and a deep, low, happy sigh, as of people who 10 see the theatre curtain go up at last, breathed from innumerable throats. They were going to have their bit of fun after all. The rifle was a beautiful German thing with cross-hair sights. I did not then know that in shooting an elephant one would shoot to cut an imaginary bar running from ear-hole to ear-hole. I ought, therefore, as the elephant was sideways on, to have aimed straight at his ear-hole; actually I aimed several inches in front of this, thinking the brain would be further forward.

When I pulled the trigger I did not hear the bang or feel the kick—one 11 never does when a shot goes home—but I heard the devilish roar of glee that went up from the crowd. In that instant, in too short a time, one would have thought, even for the bullet to get there, a mysterious, terrible change had come over the elephant. He neither stirred nor fell, but every line of his body had altered. He looked suddenly stricken, shrunken, immensely old, as though the frightful impact of the bullet had paralysed him without knocking him down. At last, after what seemed a long time—it might have been five seconds, I dare say—he sagged flabbily to his knees. His mouth slobbered. An enormous senility seemed to have settled upon him. One could have imagined him thousands of years old. I fired again into the same spot. At the second shot he did not collapse but climbed with desperate slowness to his feet and stood weakly upright, with legs sagging and head drooping. I fired a third time. That was the shot that did for him. You could see the agony of it jolt his whole body and knock the last remnant of strength from his legs. But in falling he seemed for a moment to rise, for as his hind legs collapsed beneath him he seemed to tower upward like a huge rock toppling, his trunk reaching skywards like a tree. He trumpeted, for the first and only time. And then down he came, his belly towards me, with a crash that seemed to shake the ground even where I lay.

I got up. The Burmans were already racing past me across the mud. It was 12 obvious that the elephant would never rise again, but he was not dead. He was breathing very rhythmically with long rattling gasps, his great mound of a side painfully rising and falling. His mouth was wide open—I could see far down into caverns of pale pink throat. I waited a long time for him to die, but his breathing did not weaken. Finally I fired my two remaining shots into the spot where I thought his heart must be. The thick blood welled out of him like red velvet, but still he did not die. His body did not even jerk when the shots hit him, the tortured breathing continued without a pause. He was dying, very slowly and in great agony, but in some world remote from me where not even a bullet could damage him further. I felt that I had got to put an end to that dreadful noise. It seemed dreadful to see the great beast lying there, powerless to move and yet powerless to die, and not even to be able to finish him. I sent back for my small rifle and poured shot after shot into his heart and down his throat. They seemed to make no impression. The tortured gasps continued as steadily as the ticking of a clock.

In the end I could not stand it any longer and went away. I heard later that   13
it took him half an hour to die. Burmans were bringing dahs[4] and baskets even before I left, and I was told they had stripped his body almost to the bones by the afternoon.

Afterwards, of course, there were endless discussions about the shooting of   14
the elephant. The owner was furious, but he was only an Indian and could do nothing. Besides, legally I had done the right thing, for a mad elephant has to be killed, like a mad dog, if its owner fails to control it. Among the Europeans opinion was divided. The older men said I was right, the younger men said it was a damn shame to shoot an elephant for killing a coolie, because an elephant was worth more than any damn Coringhee coolie. And afterwards I was very glad that the coolie had been killed; it put me legally in the right and it gave me a sufficient pretext for shooting the elephant. I often wondered whether any of the others grasped that I had done it solely to avoid looking a fool.

QUESTIONS
1. Why does Orwell disclose the significance the event had for him midway through the essay (paragraph 7) rather than saving it for the conclusion?   **2.** Examine carefully paragraphs 11 and 12, in which Orwell describes the death of the elephant. Is the reader meant to take the passage literally, or can a case be made that Orwell has imbued the elephant's death with symbolic meaning?   **3.** Orwell tells us repeatedly that his sympathies are with the Burmese. Does the language Orwell uses to describe them support his claim? Explain.

WRITING TOPIC
What does Orwell conclude regarding the position of foreign authorities in a hostile country?

---

[4]Knives.

What Does a Woman Need to Know?* (1979)

ADRIENNE RICH   [b. 1929]

I have been very much moved that you, the class of 1979, chose me for your commencement speaker. It is important to me to be here, in part because Smith is one of the original colleges for women, but also because she has chosen to continue identifying herself as a women's college. We are at a point in history where this fact has enormous potential, even if that potential is as yet unrealized. The possibilities for the future education of women that haunt these buildings and grounds are enormous, when we think of what an independent women's college might be: a college dedicated both to teaching women what women need to know and, by the same token, to changing the landscape of knowledge itself. The germ of those possibilities lies symbolically in The Sophia Smith Collection, an archive much in need of expansion and increase, but which by its very existence makes the statement that women's lives and work are valued here and that our foresisters, buried and diminished in male-centered scholarship, are a living presence, necessary and precious to us.

Suppose we were to ask ourselves simply: What does a woman need to know to become a self-conscious, self-defining human being? Doesn't she need a knowledge of her own history, of her much-politicized female body, of the creative genius of women of the past—the skills and crafts and techniques and visions possessed by women in other times and cultures, and how they have been rendered anonymous, censored, interrupted, devalued? Doesn't she, as one of that majority who are still denied equal rights as citizens, enslaved as sexual prey, unpaid or underpaid as workers, withheld from her own power—doesn't she need an analysis of her condition, a knowledge of the women thinkers of the past who have reflected on it, a knowledge, too, of women's world-wide individual rebellions and organized movements against economic and social injustice, and how these have been fragmented and silenced?

Doesn't she need to know how seemingly natural states of being, like heterosexuality, like motherhood, have been enforced and institutionalized to deprive her of power? Without such education, women have lived and continue to live in ignorance of our collective context, vulnerable to the projections of men's fantasies about us as they appear in art, in literature, in the sciences, in the media, in the so-called humanistic studies. I suggest that not anatomy, but enforced ignorance, has been a crucial key to our powerlessness.

There is—and I say this with sorrow—there is no women's college today which is providing young women with the education they need for survival as whole persons in a world which denies women wholeness—that knowledge which, in the words of Coleridge, "returns again as power." The existence of

---

* Given as the commencement address, Smith College, Northampton, Massachusetts, 1979.

Women's Studies courses offers at least some kind of life line. But even Women's Studies can amount simply to compensatory history; too often they fail to challenge the intellectual and political structures that must be challenged if women as a group are ever to come into collective, nonexclusionary freedom. The belief that established science and scholarship—which have so relentlessly excluded women from their making—are "objective" and "value-free" and that feminist studies are "unscholarly," "biased," and "ideological" dies hard. Yet the fact is that all science, and all scholarship, and all art are ideological; there is no neutrality in culture. And the ideology of the education you have just spent four years acquiring in a women's college has been largely, if not entirely, the ideology of white male supremacy, a construct of male subjectivity. The silences, the empty spaces, the language itself, with its excision of the female, the methods of discourse tell us as much as the content, once we learn to watch for what is left out, to listen for the unspoken, to study the patterns of established science and scholarship with an outsider's eye. One of the dangers of a privileged education for women is that we may lose the eye of the outsider and come to believe that those patterns hold for humanity, for the universal, and that they include us.

And so I want to talk today about privilege and about tokenism and about power. Everything I can say to you on this subject comes hard-won, from the lips of a woman privileged by class and skin color, a father's favorite daughter, educated at Radcliffe, which was then casually referred to as the Harvard "Annex." Much of the first four decades of my life was spent in a continuous tension between the world the Fathers taught me to see, and had rewarded me for seeing, and the flashes of insight that came through the eye of the outsider. Gradually those flashes of insight, which at times could seem like brushes with madness, began to demand that I struggle to connect them with each other, to insist that I take them seriously. It was only when I could finally affirm the outsider's eye as the source of a legitimate and coherent vision, that I began to be able to do the work I truly wanted to do, live the kind of life I truly wanted to live, instead of carrying out the assignments I had been given as a privileged woman and a token.

For women, all privilege is relative. Some of you were not born with class or skin-color privilege; but you all have the privilege of education, even if it is an education which has largely denied you knowledge of yourselves as women. You have, to begin with, the privilege of literacy; and it is well for us to remember that, in an age of increasing illiteracy, 60 percent of the world's illiterates are women. Between 1960 and 1970, the number of illiterate men in the world rose by 8 million, while the number of illiterate women rose by 40 million.[1] And the number of illiterate women is increasing. Beyond literacy, you have the privilege of training and tools which can allow you to go beyond the content of your education and re-educate yourselves—to debrief yourselves, we might call it, of the false messages of your education in this culture, the messages telling you that

[1] United Nations, Department of International Economic and Social Affairs, Statistical Office, 1977 *Compendium of Social Statistics* (New York: United Nations, 1980) [Rich's note].

women have not really cared about power or learning or creative opportunities because of a psychobiological need to serve men and produce children; that only a few atypical women have been exceptions to this rule; the messages telling you that woman's experience is neither normative nor central to human experience. You have the training and the tools to do independent research, to evaluate data, to criticize, and to express in language and visual forms what you discover. This is a privilege, yes, but only if you do not give up in exchange for it the deep knowledge of the unprivileged, the knowledge that, as a woman, you have historically been viewed and still are viewed as existing, not in your own right, but in the service of men. And only if you refuse to give up your capacity to think as a woman, even though in the graduate schools and professions to which many of you will be going you will be praised and rewarded for "thinking like a man."

The word *power* is highly charged for women. It has been long associated for us with the use of force, with rape, with the stockpiling of weapons, with the ruthless accrual of wealth and the hoarding of resources, with the power that acts only in its own interest, despising and exploiting the powerless—including women and children. The effects of this kind of power are all around us, even literally in the water we drink and the air we breathe, in the form of carcinogens and radioactive wastes. But for a long time now, feminists have been talking about redefining power, about that meaning of power which returns to the root—*posse, potere, pouvoir*: to be able, to have the potential, to possess and use one's energy of creation—*transforming power*. An early objection to feminism—in both the nineteenth and twentieth centuries—was that it would make women behave like men—ruthlessly, exploitatively, oppressively. In fact, radical feminism looks to a transformation of human relationships and structures in which power, instead of a thing to be hoarded by a few, would be released to and from within the many, shared in the form of knowledge, expertise, decision making, access to tools, as well as in the basic forms of food and shelter and health care and literacy. Feminists—and many nonfeminists—are, and rightly so, still concerned with what power would mean in such a society, and with the relative differences in power among and between women here and now.

Which brings me to a third meaning of power where women are concerned: the false power which masculine society offers to a few women, on condition that they use it to maintain things as they are, and that they essentially "think like men." This is the meaning of female tokenism: that power withheld from the vast majority of women is offered to a few, so that it appears that any "truly qualified" woman can gain access to leadership, recognition, and reward; hence, that justice based on merit actually prevails. The token woman is encouraged to see herself as different from most other women, as exceptionally talented and deserving, and to separate herself from the wider female condition; and she is perceived by "ordinary" women as separate also, perhaps even as stronger than themselves.

Because you are, within the limits of all women's ultimate outsiderhood, a privileged group of women, it is extremely important for your future sanity that you understand the way tokenism functions. Its most immediate contradiction is that, while it seems to offer the individual token woman a means to realize her creativity, to influence the course of events, it also, by exacting of her certain kinds of behavior and style, acts to blur her outsider's eye, which could be her real source of power and vision. Losing her outsider's vision, she loses the insight which both binds her to other women and affirms her in herself. Tokenism essentially demands that the token deny her identification with women as a group, especially with women less privileged than she: if she is a lesbian, that she deny her relationships with individual women; that she perpetuate rules and structures and criteria and methodologies which have functioned to exclude women; that she renounce or leave undeveloped the critical perspective of her female consciousness. Women unlike herself—poor women, women of color, waitresses, secretaries, housewives in the supermarket, prostitutes, old women— become invisible to her; they may represent too acutely what she has escaped or wished to flee.

President Conway tells me that ever-increasing numbers of you are going on 10 from Smith to medical and law schools. The news, on the face of it, is good: that, thanks to the feminist struggle of the past decade, more doors into these two powerful professions are open to women. I would like to believe that any pro- fession would be better for having more women practicing it, and that any woman practicing law or medicine would use her knowledge and skill to work to transform the realm of health care and the interpretations of the law, to make them responsive to the needs of all those—women, people of color, children, the aged, the dispossessed—for whom they function today as repressive controls. I would like to believe this, but it will not happen even if 50 percent of the members of these professions are women, unless those women refuse to be made into token insiders, unless they zealously preserve the outsider's view and the outsider's consciousness.

For no woman is really an insider in the institutions fathered by masculine 11 consciousness. When we allow ourselves to believe we are, we lose touch with parts of ourselves defined as unacceptable by that consciousness; with the vital toughness and visionary strength of the angry grandmothers, the shamanesses, the fierce marketwomen of the Ibo Women's War, the marriage-resisting women silkworkers of prerevolutionary China, the millions of widows, midwives, and women healers tortured and burned as witches for three centuries in Europe, the Beguines of the twelfth century, who formed independent women's orders out- side the domination of the Church, the women of the Paris Commune who marched on Versailles, the uneducated housewives of the Women's Cooperative Guild in England who memorized poetry over the washtub and organized against their oppression as mothers, the women thinkers discredited as "strident," "shrill," "crazy," or "deviant" whose courage to be heretical, to speak their truths, we so badly need to draw upon in our own lives. I believe that every woman's soul is haunted by the spirits of earlier women who fought for their unmet needs and those of their children and their tribes and their peoples, who refused to accept the prescriptions of a male church and state, who took risks and resisted, as women today—like Inez Garcia, Yvonne Wanrow, Joan Little, Cassandra Peten[2]—are fighting their rapists and batterers. Those spirits dwell in us, trying to speak to us. But we can choose to be deaf; and tokenism, the myth of the "special" woman, the unmothered Athena[3] sprung from her father's brow, can deafen us to their voices.

In this decade now ending, as more women are entering the professions (though still suffering sexual harassment in the workplace, though still, if they have children, carrying two full-time jobs, though still vastly outnumbered by men in upper-level and decision-making jobs), we need most profoundly to remember that early insight of the feminist movement as it evolved in the late sixties: *that no woman is liberated until we all are liberated.* The media flood us with messages to the contrary, telling us that we live in an era when "alternate life styles" are freely accepted, when "marriage contracts" and "the new intimacy" are revolutionizing heterosexual relationships, that shared parenting and the "new fatherhood" will change the world. And we live in a society leeched upon by the "personal growth" and "human potential" industry, by the delusion that individual self-fulfillment can be found in thirteen weeks or a weekend, that the alienation and injustice experienced by women, by Black and Third World people, by the poor, in a world ruled by white males, in a society which fails to meet the most basic needs and which is slowly poisoning itself, can be mitigated or dispersed by Transcendental Meditation.[4] Perhaps the most succinct expression of this message I have seen is the appearance of a magazine for women called *Self.* The insistence of the feminist movement, that each woman's selfhood is precious, that the feminine ethic of self-denial and self-sacrifice must give way to a true woman identification, which would affirm our connectedness with all women, is perverted into a commercially profitable and politically debilitating narcissism. It is important for each of you, toward whom many of these messages are especially directed, to discriminate clearly between "liberated life style" and feminist struggle, and to make a conscious choice.

It's a cliché of commencement speeches that the speaker ends with a peroration telling the new graduates that however badly past generations have behaved, their generation must save the world. I would rather say to you, women of the class of 1979: Try to be worthy of your foresisters, learn from your history, look for inspiration to your ancestresses. If this history has been poorly taught to you, if you do not know it, then use your educational privilege to learn it. Learn how some women of privilege have compromised the greater liberation of women, how others have risked their privileges to further it; learn how brilliant and successful women have failed to create a more just and caring society, precisely because they have tried to do so on terms that the powerful men around them

12

13

---

[2] Inez Garcia was acquitted in 1978 of murdering a man who helped another man rape her. Joan Little was accused, but then acquitted, of the 1975 murder of a North Carolina prison guard. We have been unable to identify Yvonne Wanrow and Cassandra Peten.

[3] In Greek mythology, the goddess Athena springs full-grown from Zeus's forehead.

[4] Introduced to the West in 1959 by Maharishi Mahesh Yogi, transcendental meditation is a self-help program that claims to maximize human potential and reduce personal stress.

would accept and tolerate. Learn to be worthy of the women of every class, culture, and historical age who did otherwise, who spoke boldly when women were jeered and physically harassed for speaking in public, who—like Anne Hutchinson, Mary Wollstonecraft, the Grimké sisters, Abby Kelley, Ida B. Wells-Barnett, Susan B. Anthony, Lillian Smith, Fannie Lou Hamer[5]—broke taboos, who resisted slavery—their own and other people's. To become a token woman—whether you win the Nobel prize or merely get tenure at the cost of denying your sisters—is to become something less than a man indeed, since men are loyal at least to their own world view, their laws of brotherhood and male self-interest. I am not suggesting that you imitate male loyalties; with the philosopher Mary Daly,[6] I believe that the bonding of women must be utterly different and for an utterly different end: not the misering of resources and power, but the release, in each other, of the yet unexplored resources and transformative power of women, so long despised, confined, and wasted. Get all the knowledge and skill you can in whatever professions you enter; but remember that most of your education must be self-education, in learning the things women need to know and in calling up the voices we need to hear within ourselves.

QUESTIONS

1. In the fourth paragraph, Rich asserts that science and scholarship, usually characterized as "objective" and "value-free," are in fact ideological and that "there is no neutrality in culture." Explain how science can be ideological and culturally biased. **2.** How does Rich define "token woman," and what are the consequences of such tokenism? **3.** Against what does Rich caution the Smith graduates preparing to enter the male-dominated professions of law and medicine? **4.** What attitude toward men does Rich exhibit in this essay, and what elements of her writing reveal that attitude?

WRITING TOPIC

Describe the achievements of one of the feminist heroines to whom Rich alludes in paragraph 13.

---

[5] Anne Hutchinson (c. 1600–1643), defeated in the rebellion she led against the authority of the Massachusetts clergy, was exiled to Rhode Island in 1638. Mary Wollstonecraft (1759–1797) wrote *A Vindication of the Rights of Women* (1792). Sarah Moore Grimké (1792–1873) and Angelina Emily Grimké (1805–1879) were antislavery reformers; Sarah turned her attention to women's rights, particularly in education, as early as 1838. Abby Kelley may be Florence Kelley (1859–1932), the first woman to be chief inspector of factories in Illinois. She pushed a sweatshop reform bill through the Illinois legislature and produced the first English translation of Engels's *The Condition of the Working Class in England in 1844* (1887). Ida B. Wells-Barnett (1862–1931) was an American journalist who founded the first African-American women's suffrage organization and helped found the National Association for the Advancement of Colored People. Susan B. Anthony (1820–1906), a leader in the women's suffrage movement, was arrested for voting in the presidential election of 1872. Lillian Smith (1897–1966) wrote the novel *Strange Fruit* (1944) about an interracial love affair set in the Deep South. She became a champion of racial equality and civil rights in the South. Fannie Lou Hamer (1918–1977) was a political activist with the Student Nonviolent Coordinating Committee and an early organizer within the women's movement.

[6] Mary Daly (b. 1928) is an American philosopher and the author of several books, including *Beyond God the Father: Towards a Philosophy of Women's Liberation* (1973). Daly encourages women to create a women-centered universe.

Marrying Absurd 1967

JOAN DIDION [b. 1934]

To be married in Las Vegas, Clark County, Nevada, a bride must swear that 1
she is eighteen or has parental permission and a bridegroom that he is twenty-
one or has parental permission. Someone must put up five dollars for the license. (On Sundays and holidays, fifteen dollars. The Clark County Courthouse issues marriage licenses at any time of the day or night except between
noon and one in the afternoon, between eight and nine in the evening, and
between four and five in the morning.) Nothing else is required. The State of
Nevada, alone among these United States, demands neither a premarital blood
test nor a waiting period before or after the issuance of a marriage license.
Driving in across the Mojave from Los Angeles, one sees the signs way out on
the desert, looming up from that moonscape of rattlesnakes and mesquite, even
before the Las Vegas lights appear like a mirage on the horizon: "GETTING
MARRIED? Free License Information First Strip Exit." Perhaps the Las Vegas
wedding industry achieved its peak operational efficiency between 9:00 P.M.
and midnight on August 26, 1965, an otherwise unremarkable Thursday which
happened to be, by Presidential order, the last day on which anyone could
improve his draft status merely by getting married. One hundred and seventy-
one couples were pronounced man and wife in the name of Clark County and
the State of Nevada that night, sixty-seven of them by a single justice of the
peace, Mr. James A. Brennan. Mr. Brennan did one wedding at the Dunes
and the other sixty-six in his office, and charged each couple eight dollars.
One bride lent her veil to six others. "I got it down from five to three minutes,"
Mr. Brennan said later of his feat. "I could've married them *en masse*, but
they're people, not cattle. People expect more when they get married."

What people who get married in Las Vegas actually do expect—what, in the 2
largest sense, their "expectations" are—strikes one as a curious and self-contradictory business. Las Vegas is the most extreme and allegorical of American
settlements, bizarre and beautiful in its venality and in its devotion to immediate gratification, a place the tone of which is set by mobsters and call girls
and ladies' room attendants with amyl nitrite poppers in their uniform pockets.
Almost everyone notes that there is no "time" in Las Vegas, no night and no
day and no past and no future (no Las Vegas casino, however, has taken the
obliteration of the ordinary time sense quite so far as Harold's Club in Reno,
which for a while issued, at odd intervals in the day and night, mimeographed
"bulletins" carrying news from the world outside); neither is there any logical
sense of where one is. One is standing on a highway in the middle of a vast
hostile desert looking at an eighty-foot sign which blinks "STARDUST" or "CAE-
SAR'S PALACE." Yes, but what does that explain? This geographical implausibil-

ity reinforces the sense that what happens there has no connection with "real" life; Nevada cities like Reno and Carson are ranch towns, Western towns, places behind which there is some historical imperative. But Las Vegas seems to exist only in the eye of the beholder. All of which makes it an extraordinarily stimulating and interesting place, but an odd one in which to want to wear a candlelight satin Priscilla of Boston wedding dress with Chantilly lace insets, tapered sleeves and a detachable modified train.

And yet the Las Vegas wedding business seems to appeal to precisely that impulse. "Sincere and Dignified Since 1954," one wedding chapel advertises. There are nineteen such wedding chapels in Las Vegas, intensely competitive, each offering better, faster, and, by implication, more sincere services than the next: Our Photos Best Anywhere, Your Wedding on A Phonograph Record, Candlelight with Your Ceremony, Honeymoon Accommodations, Free Transportation from Your Motel to Courthouse to Chapel and Return to Motel, Religious or Civil Ceremonies, Dressing Rooms, Flowers, Rings, Announcements, Witnesses Available, and Ample Parking. All of these services, like most others in Las Vegas (sauna baths, payroll check cashing, chinchilla coats for sale or rent) are offered twenty-four hours a day, seven days a week, presumably on the premise that marriage, like craps, is a game to be played when the table seems hot.

But what strikes one most about the Strip chapels, with their wishing wells and stained-glass paper windows and their artificial bouvardia, is that so much of their business is by no means a matter of simple convenience, of late-night liaisons between show girls and baby Crosbys. Of course there is some of that. (One night about eleven o'clock in Las Vegas I watched a bride in an orange minidress and masses of flame-colored hair stumble from a Strip chapel on the arm of her bridegroom, who looked the part of the expendable nephew in movies like *Miami Syndicate*. "I gotta get the kids," the bride whimpered. "I gotta pick up the sitter, I gotta get to the midnight show." "What you gotta get," the bridegroom said, opening the door of a Cadillac Coupe de Ville and watching her crumple on the seat, "is sober.") But Las Vegas seems to offer something other than "convenience"; it is merchandising "niceness," the facsimile of proper ritual, to children who do not know how else to find it, how to make the arrangements, how to do it "right." All day and evening long on the Strip, one sees actual wedding parties, waiting under the harsh lights at a crosswalk, standing uneasily in the parking lot of the Frontier while the photographer hired by The Little Church of the West ("Wedding Place of the Stars") certifies the occasion, takes the picture: the bride in a veil and white satin pumps, the bridegroom usually in a white dinner jacket, and even an attendant or two, a sister or a best friend in hot-pink, *peau de soie*, a flirtation veil, a carnation nosegay. "When I Fall in Love It Will Be Forever," the organist plays, and then a few bars of Lohengrin. The mother cries; the stepfather, awkward in his role, invites the chapel hostess to join them for a drink at the Sands. The hostess declines with a professional smile; she has already transferred her interest to the group waiting outside. One bride out, another

in, and again the sign goes up on the chapel door: "One moment please—
Wedding."

I sat next to one such wedding party in a Strip restaurant the last time I was   5
in Las Vegas. The marriage had just taken place; the bride still wore her dress,
the mother her corsage. A bored waiter poured out a few swallows of pink
champagne ("on the house") for everyone but the bride, who was too young to
be served. "You'll need something with more kick than that," the bride's father
said with heavy jocularity to his new son-in-law; the ritual jokes about the
wedding night had a certain Panglossian character, since the bride was clearly
several months pregnant. Another round of pink champagne, this time not on
the house, and the bride began to cry. "It was just as nice," she sobbed, "as I
hoped and dreamed it would be."

QUESTIONS

1. What attitude toward Las Vegas weddings emerges from this essay? What means
(diction, images, descriptive passages, juxtaposition of ideas) does Didion use to
convey that attitude?   **2.** Analyze Didion's use of rhythm in this piece. Note how
she uses pairs or triads of elements in her sentences. How do such rhythmic con-
structions act on the reader?   **3.** Analyze the last paragraph. What means does
the author use to control the reader's responses to the scene she describes?

WRITING TOPIC

What unstated convictions about marriages are violated by the ceremonies Didion
describes?

A Plea for the Chimps (1987)

JANE GOODALL [b. 1934]

The chimpanzee is more like us, genetically, than any other animal. It is because of similarities in physiology, in biochemistry, in the immune system, that medical science makes use of the living bodies of chimpanzees in its search for cures and vaccines for a variety of human diseases.

There are also behavioral, psychological and emotional similarities between chimpanzees and humans, resemblances so striking that they raise a serious ethical question: are we justified in using an animal so close to us—an animal, moreover, that is highly endangered in its African forest home—as a human substitute in medical experimentation?

In the long run, we can hope that scientists will find ways of exploring human physiology and disease, and of testing cures and vaccines, that do not depend on the use of living animals of any sort. A number of steps in this direction already have been taken, prompted in large part by a growing public awareness of the suffering that is being inflicted on millions of animals. More and more people are beginning to realize that nonhuman animals—even rats and guinea pigs— are not just unfeeling machines but are capable of enjoying their lives, and of feeling fear, pain and despair.

But until alternatives have been found, medical science will continue to use animals in the battle against human disease and suffering. And some of those animals will continue to be chimpanzees.

Because they share with us 99 percent of their genetic material, chimpanzees can be infected with some human diseases that do not infect other animals. They are currently being used in research on the nature of hepatitis non-A non-B, for example, and they continue to play a major role in the development of vaccines against hepatitis B.

Many biomedical laboratories are looking to the chimpanzee to help them in the race to find a vaccine against acquired immune deficiency syndrome. Chimpanzees are not good models for AIDS research; although the AIDS virus stays alive and replicates within the chimpanzee's bloodstream, no chimp has yet come down with the disease itself. Nevertheless, many of the scientists involved argue that only by using chimpanzees can potential vaccines be safely tested.

Given the scientists' professed need for animals in research, let us turn aside from the sensitive ethical issue of whether chimpanzees *should* be used in medical research, and consider a more immediate issue: how are we treating the chimpanzees that are actually being used?

Just after Christmas I watched, with shock, anger and anguish, a videotape— made by an animal-rights group during a raid—revealing the conditions in a large biomedical research laboratory, under contract to the National Institutes of Health, in which various primates, including chimpanzees, are maintained. In late March, I was given permission to visit the facility.

166

It was a visit I shall never forget. Room after room was lined with small, bare   9
cages, stacked one above the other, in which monkeys circled round and round
and chimpanzees sat huddled, far gone in depression and despair.

Young chimpanzees, 3 or 4 years old, were crammed, two together, into tiny   10
cages measuring 22 inches by 22 inches and only 24 inches high. They could
hardly turn around. Not yet part of any experiment, they had been confined in
these cages for more than three months.

The chimps had each other for comfort, but they would not remain together   11
for long. Once they are infected, probably with hepatitis, they will be separated
and placed in another cage. And there they will remain, living in conditions of
severe sensory deprivation, for the next several years. During that time, they will
become insane.

A juvenile female rocked from side to side, sealed off from the outside world   12
behind the glass doors of her metal isolation chamber. She was in semidarkness.
All she could hear was the incessant roar of air rushing through vents into her
prison.

In order to demonstrate the "good" relationship the lab's caretaker had with   13
this chimpanzee, one of the scientists told him to lift her from the cage. The
caretaker opened the door. She sat, unmoving. He reached in. She did not greet
him—nor did he greet her. As if drugged, she allowed him to take her out.
She sat motionless in his arms. He did not speak to her, she did not look at him.
He touched her lips briefly. She did not respond. He returned her to her cage.
She sat again on the bars of the floor. The door closed.

I shall be haunted forever by her eyes, and by the eyes of the other infant   14
chimpanzees I saw that day. Have you ever looked into the eyes of a person who,
stressed beyond endurance, has given up, succumbed utterly to the crippling
helplessness of despair? I once saw a little African boy, whose whole family had
been killed during the fighting in Burundi. He too looked out at the world,
unseeing, from dull, blank eyes.

Though this particular laboratory may be one of the worst, from what I have   15
learned, most of the other biomedical animal-research facilities are not much
better. Yet only when one has some understanding of the true nature of the
chimpanzee can the cruelty of these captive conditions be fully understood.

Chimpanzees are very social by nature. Bonds between individuals, particu-   16
larly between family members and close friends, can be affectionate, supportive,
and can endure throughout their lives. The accidental separation of two friendly
individuals may cause them intense distress. Indeed, the death of a mother may
be such a psychological blow to her child that even if the child is 5 years old and
no longer dependent on its mother's milk, it may pine away and die.

It is impossible to overemphasize the importance of friendly physical contact   17
for the well-being of the chimpanzee. Again and again one can watch a frightened or tense individual relax if she is patted, kissed or embraced reassuringly by
a companion. Social grooming, which provides hours of close contact, is undoubtedly the single most important social activity.

Chimpanzees in their natural habitat are active for much of the day. They   18 travel extensively within their territory, which can be as large as 50 square kilometers for a community of about 50 individuals. If they hear other chimpanzees calling as they move through the forest, or anticipate arriving at a good food source, they typically break into excited charging displays, racing along the ground, hurling sticks and rocks and shaking the vegetation. Youngsters, particularly, are full of energy, and spend long hours playing with one another or by themselves leaping through the branches and gamboling along the ground. Adults sometimes join these games. Bunches of fruit, twigs and rocks may be used as toys.

Chimpanzees enjoy comfort. They construct sleeping platforms each night, using a multitude of leafy twigs to make their beds soft. Often, too, they make little "pillows" on which to rest during a midday siesta.   19

Chimps are highly intelligent. They display cognitive abilities that were, until recently, thought to be unique to humans. They are capable of cross-model transfer of information—that is, they can identify by touch an object they previously have only seen, and vice versa. They are capable of reasoned thought, generalization, abstraction and symbolic representation. They have some concept of self. They have excellent memories and can, to some extent, plan for the future. They show a capacity for intentional communication that depends, in part, on their ability to understand the motives of the individuals with whom they are communicating.   20

Chimpanzees are capable of empathy and altruistic behavior. They show emotions that are undoubtedly similar, if not identical, to human emotions—joy, pleasure, contentment, anxiety, fear and rage. They even have a sense of humor.   21

The chimpanzee child and the human child are alike in many ways: in their capacity for endless romping and fun; their curiosity; their ability to learn by observation, imitation and practice; and, above all, in their need for reassurance and love. When young chimpanzees are brought up in a human home and treated like human children, they learn to eat at a table, to help themselves to snacks from the refrigerator, to sort and put away cutlery, to brush their teeth, to play with dolls, to switch on the television and select a program that interests them and watch it.   22

Young chimpanzees can easily learn over 200 signs of the American language of the deaf and use these signs to communicate meaningfully with humans and with one another. One youngster, in the laboratory of Dr. Roger S. Fouts, a psychologist at Central Washington University, has picked up 68 signs from four older signing chimpanzee companions, with no human teaching. The chimp uses the signs in communication with other chimpanzees and with humans.   23

The chimpanzee facilities in most biomedical research laboratories allow for the expression of almost none of these activities and behaviors. They provide little—if anything—more than the warmth, food and water, and veterinary care required to sustain life. The psychological and emotional needs of these creatures are rarely catered to, and often not even acknowledged.   24

In most labs the chimpanzees are housed individually, one chimp to a cage, unless they are part of a breeding program. The standard size of each cage is   25 about 25 feet square and about 6 feet high. In one facility, a cage described in the catalogue as "large," designed for a chimpanzee of up to 25 kilograms (55 pounds), measures 2 feet 6 inches by 3 feet 8 inches, with a height of 5 feet 4 inches. Federal requirements for cage size are dependent on body size; infant chimpanzees, who are the most active, are often imprisoned in the smallest cages.

In most labs, the chimpanzees cannot even lie with their arms and legs   26
outstretched. They are not let out to exercise. There is seldom anything for them to do other than eat, and then only when food is brought. The caretakers are usually too busy to pay much attention to individual chimpanzees. The cages are bleak and sterile, with bars above, bars below, bars in every side. There is no comfort in them, no bedding. The chimps, infected with human diseases, will often feel sick and miserable.

What of the human beings who administer these facilities—the caretakers,   27
veterinarians and scientists who work at them? If they are decent, compassionate people, how can they condone, or even tolerate, the kind of conditions I have described?

They are, I believe, victims of a system that was set up long before the   28
cognitive abilities and emotional needs of chimpanzees were understood. Newly employed staff members, equipped with a normal measure of compassion, may well be sickened by what they see. And, in fact, many of them do quit their jobs, unable to endure the suffering they see inflicted on the animals yet feeling powerless to help.

But others stay on and gradually come to accept the cruelty, believing (or   29
forcing themselves to believe) that it is an inevitable part of the struggle to reduce human suffering. Some become hard and callous in the process, in Shakespeare's words, "all pity choked with custom of fell deeds."

A handful of compassionate and dedicated caretakers and veterinarians are   30
fighting to improve the lot of the animals in their care. Vets are often in a particularly difficult position, for if they stand firm and try to uphold high standards of humane care, they will not always be welcome in the lab.

Many of the scientists believe that a bleak, sterile and restricting environment   31
is necessary for their research. The cages must be small, the scientists maintain, because otherwise it is too difficult to treat the chimpanzees—to inject them, to draw their blood or to anesthetize them. Moreover, they are less likely to hurt themselves in small cages.

The cages must also be barren, with no bedding or toys, say the scientists. This   32
way, the chimpanzees are less likely to pick up diseases or parasites. Also if things are lying about, the cages are harder to clean.

And the chimpanzees must be kept in isolation, the scientists believe, to avoid   33
the risk of cross-infection, particularly in hepatitis research.

Finally, of course, bigger cages, social groups and elaborate furnishings re-   34
quire more space, more caretakers—and more money. Perhaps, then, if we are to believe these researchers, it is not possible to improve conditions for chim-panzees imprisoned in biomedical research laboratories.

I believe not only that it *is* possible, but that improvements are absolutely   35 necessary. If we do not do something to help these creatures, we make a mockery of the whole concept of justice.

Perhaps the most important way we can improve the quality of life for the laboratory chimps is to increase the number of carefully trained caretakers. These people should be selected for their understanding of animal behavior and their compassion and respect for, and dedication to, their charges. Each caretaker, having established a relationship of trust with the chimpanzees in his care, should be allowed to spend time with the animals over and above that required for cleaning the cages and providing the animals with food and water.   36

It has been shown that a chimpanzee who has a good relationship with his caretaker will cooperate calmly during experimental procedures, rather than react with fear or anger. At the Dutch Primate Research Center at Rijswijk, for example, some chimpanzees have been trained to leave their group cage on command and move into small, single cages for treatment. At the Stanford Primate Center in California, a number of chimpanzees were taught to extend their arms for the drawing of blood. In return they were given a food reward.   37

Much can be done to alleviate the pain and stress felt by younger chimpanzees during experimental procedures. A youngster, for example, can be treated when in the presence of a trusted human friend. Experiments have shown that young chimps react with high levels of distress if subjected to mild electric shocks when alone, but show almost no fear or pain when held by a sympathetic caretaker.   38

What about cage size? Here we should emulate the animal-protection regulations that already exist in Switzerland. These laws stipulate that a cage must be, at minimum, about 20 meters square and 3 meters high for pairs of chimpanzees.   39

The chimpanzees should never be housed alone unless this is an essential part of the experimental procedure. For chimps in solitary confinement, particularly youngsters, three to four hours of friendly interaction with a caretaker should be mandatory. A chimp taking part in hepatitis research, in which the risk of cross-infection is, I am told, great, can be provided with a companion of a compatible species if it doesn't infringe on existing regulations—a rhesus monkey, for example, which cannot catch or pass on the disease.   40

For healthy chimpanzees there should be little risk of infection from bedding and toys. Stress and depression, however, can have deleterious effects on their health. It is known that clinically depressed humans are more prone to a variety of physiological disorders, and heightened stress can interfere with immune function. Given the chimpanzee's similarities to humans, it is not surprising that the chimp in a typical laboratory, alone in his bleak cage, is an easy prey to infections and parasites.   41

Thus, the chimpanzees also should be provided with a rich and stimulating environment. Climbing apparatus should be obligatory. There should be many objects for them to play with or otherwise manipulate. A variety of simple devices designed to alleviate boredom could be produced quite cheaply. Unexpected food items will elicit great pleasure. If a few simple buttons in each cage were connected to a computer terminal, it would be possible for the chimpanzees to   42 feel they at least have some control over their world—if one button produced a grape when pressed, another a drink, or another a video picture. (The Canadian Council on Animal Care recommends the provision of television for primates in solitary confinement, or other means of enriching their environment.)

Without doubt, it will be considerably more costly to maintain chimpanzees   43
in the manner I have outlined. Should we begrudge them the extra dollars? We take from them their freedom, their health and often their lives. Surely, the least we can do is try to provide them with some of the things that could make their imprisonment more bearable.

There are hopeful signs. I was immensely grateful to officials of the National   44
Institutes of Health for allowing me to visit the primate facility, enabling me to see the conditions there and judge them for myself. And I was even more grateful for the fact that they gave me a great deal of time for serious discussions of the problem. Doors were opened and a dialogue begun. All who were present at the meetings agreed that, in light of present knowledge, it is indeed necessary to give chimpanzees a better deal in the labs. . . .

I have had the privilege of working among wild, free chimpanzees for more   45
than 26 years. I have gained a deep understanding of chimpanzee nature. Chimpanzees have given me so much in my life. The least I can do is to speak out for the hundreds of chimpanzees who, right now, sit hunched, miserable and without hope, staring out with dead eyes from their metal prisons. They cannot speak for themselves.

QUESTIONS

1. Why does Goodall devote so much time to establishing the similarity between chimps and human beings? **2.** What position do you suppose Goodall would take if a valid and truly useful experiment involving chimps would subject them to the terrible treatment she discovered at the research laboratory? **3.** What does Goodall mean when she says (paragraph 35), "If we do not do something to help these creatures, we make a mockery of the whole concept of justice"? Does her essay suggest what she means by justice?

WRITING TOPIC

Some people argue that all experiments on animals capable of feeling pain should be prohibited. Explain why you do or do not agree with this position.

Innocence and Experience

QUESTIONS AND WRITING TOPICS

1. What support do the works in this section provide for Thomas Gray's well-known observation that "where ignorance is bliss, / 'Tis folly to be wise"? **Writing Topic:** Use Gray's observation as the basis for an analysis of either Frank O'Connor's "My Oedipus Complex" or Flannery O'Connor's "Good Country People."

2. In such poems as Robert Frost's "Birches" and Stevie Smith's "To Carry the Child," growing up is seen as a growing away from a kind of truth and reality; in other poems, such as Gerard Manley Hopkins's "Spring and Fall," Dylan Thomas's "Fern Hill," and Robert Wallace's "In a Spring Still Not Written Of," growing up is seen as growing into truth and reality. Do these two groups of poems embody contradictory and mutually exclusive conceptions of childhood? Explain. **Writing Topic:** Select one poem from each of these two groups and contrast the conception of childhood embodied in each.

3. An eighteenth-century novelist wrote: "Oh Innocence, how glorious and happy a portion art thou to the breast that possesses thee! Thou fearest neither the eyes nor the tongues of men. Truth, the most powerful of all things, is thy strongest friend; and the brighter the light is in which thou art displayed, the more it discovers thy transcendent beauties." Which works in this section support this assessment of innocence? Which works contradict it? How would you characterize the relationship between "truth" and "innocence" in the fiction and the drama presented here? **Writing Topic:** Use this observation as the basis for an analysis of *Oedipus Rex*.

4. A certain arrogance is associated with the innocence of Oedipus in Sophocles' *Oedipus Rex*, Robin in Hawthorne's "My Kinsman, Major Molineux," and Hulga in Flannery O'Connor's "Good Country People." On what is their arrogance based, and how is it modified? **Writing Topic:** Select two of these three works and contrast the nature and the consequences of the central characters' arrogance.

5. James Joyce's "Araby," Frank O'Connor's "My Oedipus Complex," and Flannery O'Connor's "Good Country People" all deal with some aspect of sexuality as a force that moves the protagonist from innocence toward experience. How does the recognition of sexuality function in each of the stories? **Writing Topic:** Choose two of these stories, and discuss the relationship between sexuality and innocence.

6. Which poems in this section depend largely on irony for their force? Can you suggest why irony is a particularly useful device in literature that portrays innocence and experience? **Writing Topic:** Write an analysis of the function of irony in Hardy's "The Ruined Maid."

7. Is the passage from innocence to experience a loss or a gain or both? Explain. **Writing Topic:** Compare the passage from innocence to experience in Crane's "The Bride Comes to Yellow Sky" and Frank O'Connor's "My Oedipus Complex."

Conformity and Rebellion

The Closing of Whittier Boulevard, 1984 by Frank Romero

Although the works in this section, like those in "Innocence and Experience" may feature a violation of innocence, the events are usually based on the clash between two well-articulated positions; the rebel, on principle, confronts and struggles with established authority. Central to these works is the sense of tremendous external forces—the state, the church, tradition—which can be obeyed only at the expense of conscience and humanity. Thus Martin Luther King, Jr., rejects "moderation" in "Letter from Birmingham Jail" and Virginia Woolf in "What If Shakepeare Had Had a Sister?" ruefully imagines what would have been the fate of a female Shakespeare. At the most general level, these works confront an ancient dilemma: the very organizations men and women establish to protect and nurture the individual demand—on pain of economic ruin, social ostracism, even death, spiritual or physical—that they violate their most deeply cherished beliefs. When individuals refuse such demands, they translate their awareness of a hostile social order into action against it and precipitate a crisis. And so William Butler Yeats celebrates the "terrible beauty" that is born of the abortive rebellion in "Easter 1916," and in Henrik Ibsen's A Doll's House, Nora Helmer finally realizes that dehumanization is too high a price to pay for security. On a different note, in Herman Melville's "Bartleby the Scrivener," Bartleby's "preference" not to conform, his passive resistance, results in a crisis.

Many of the works in this section, particularly the poems, do not treat the theme of conformity and rebellion quite so explicitly and dramatically. Some, like May Swenson's "Women," employ the indirection of irony to expose and attack the costs of conformity; others, like W. H. Auden's "The Unknown Citizen," tell us that the price exacted for total conformity to the industrial superstate is spiritual death. In "Easter 1916," William Butler Yeats meditates upon the awesome meaning of the lives and deaths of political revolutionaries, and in "Harlem," Langston Hughes warns that an inflexible and constricting social order will generate explosion.

Two basic modes, then, inform the literary treatment of conformity and rebellion. While in many of the works the individual is caught up in a crisis that forces her or him into rebellion, in other works, especially the poems, the focus may be on the individual's failure to move from awareness into action, as in Amy Lowell's "Patterns." Indeed, the portraits of Auden's unknown citizen and of E. E. Cummings's Cambridge ladies affirm the necessity for rebellion by rendering so effectively the hollow life of mindless conformity.

However diverse in treatment and technique, all the works in this section are about individuals trapped by complex sets of external forces that regulate and define their lives. Social beings—men and women—sometimes submit to these forces, but it is always an uneasy submission, for the purpose of these forces is to curb and control people. Individuals may recognize that they must be controlled for some larger good; yet they are aware that established social power is often abusive. The tendency of power, at its best, is to act as a conserving force that brakes the disruptive impulse to abandon and destroy old ways and ideas. At its worst, power is self-serving. The individual must constantly judge which tendency power is enhancing. And since the power of the individual is negligible beside that of frequently abusive social forces, it is not surprising that many artists since the advent of the great nation-states have found a fundamental human dignity in the resistance of the individual to organized society. One of humanity's ancient and profound recognitions, after all, is that the impulse of those who rule is always to make unknown citizens of us all.

FOR THINKING AND WRITING

As you read the selections in this section, consider the following questions. You may want to write out your thoughts informally in a journal or notebook as a way of preparing to respond to the selections, or you may wish to make one of these questions the basis for a formal essay.

1. How would you define *conformity*? What forms of rebellion are possible for a person in your situation? Do you perceive yourself as a conformist? A rebel? Some combination of the two? Explain.

2. How would you define *sanity*? Based on your own definition, do you know an insane person? What form does that insanity take? Do you agree or disagree with Emily Dickinson's assertion that "Much Madness is divinest Sense"? Explain.

3. Discuss this proposition: Governments routinely engage in behavior that would cause an individual to be imprisoned or institutionalized.

4. Give an extended response to each of the following questions. Is war sane? Should one obey an "unjust" law? Should one be guided absolutely by religious principles?

CONFORMITY
AND
REBELLION

The Trial, 1950 by Keith Vaughan

FICTION

Bartleby the Scrivener   1853
A STORY OF WALL STREET

HERMAN MELVILLE [1819–1891]

I am a rather elderly man. The nature of my avocations, for the last thirty years, has brought me into more than ordinary contact with what would seem an interesting and somewhat singular set of men, of whom, as yet, nothing, that I know of, has ever been written—I mean, the law-copyists, or scriveners. I have known very many of them, professionally and privately, and, if I pleased, could relate divers histories, at which good-natured gentlemen might smile, and sentimental souls might weep. But I waive the biographies of all other scriveners, for a few passages in the life of Bartleby, who was a scrivener, the strangest I ever saw, or heard of. While, of other law-copyists, I might write the complete life, of Bartleby nothing of that sort can be done. I believe that no materials exist for a full and satisfactory biography of this man. It is an irreparable loss to literature. Bartleby was one of those beings of whom nothing is ascertainable, except from the original sources, and, in his case, those are very small. What my own astonished eyes saw of Bartleby, *that* is all I know of him, except, indeed, one vague report, which will appear in the sequel.

Ere introducing the scrivener, as he first appeared to me, it is fit I make some mention of myself, my employees, my business, my chambers, and general surroundings; because some such description is indispensable to an adequate understanding of the chief character about to be presented. Imprimis: I am a man who, from his youth upwards, has been filled with a profound conviction that the easiest way of life is the best. Hence, though I belong to a profession proverbially energetic and nervous, even to turbulence, at times, yet nothing of that sort have I ever suffered to invade my peace. I am one of those unambitious lawyers who never addresses a jury, or in any way draws down public applause; but, in the cool tranquillity of a snug retreat, do a snug business among rich men's bonds, and mortgages, and title-deeds. All who know me, consider me an eminently *safe* man. The late John Jacob Astor,[1] a personage little given to

---

[1] A poor immigrant who rose to become one of the great business tycoons of the nineteenth century.

poetic enthusiasm, had no hesitation in pronouncing my first grand point to be prudence; my next, method. I do not speak it in vanity, but simply record the fact, that I was not unemployed in my profession by the late John Jacob Astor; a name which, I admit, I love to repeat; for it hath a rounded and orbicular sound to it, and rings like unto bullion. I will freely add, that I was not insensible to the late John Jacob Astor's good opinion.

Some time prior to the period at which this little history begins, my avocations had been largely increased. The good old office, now extinct in the State of New York, of a Master in Chancery,[2] had been conferred upon me. It was not a very arduous office, but very pleasantly remunerative. I seldom lose my temper; much more seldom indulge in dangerous indignation at wrongs and outrages; but, I must be permitted to be rash here, and declare that I consider the sudden and violent abrogation of the office of Master in Chancery, by the new Constitution, as a—premature act; inasmuch as I had counted upon a life-lease of the profits, whereas I only received those of a few short years. But this is by the way.

My chambers were up stairs, at No. —— Wall Street. At one end, they looked upon the white wall of the interior of a spacious sky-light shaft, penetrating the building from top to bottom.

This view might have been considered rather tame than otherwise, deficient in what landscape painters call "life." But, if so, the view from the other end of my chambers offered, at least, a contrast, if nothing more. In that direction, my windows commanded an unobstructed view of a lofty brick wall, black by age and everlasting shade; which wall required no spyglass to bring out its lurking beauties, but, for the benefit of all near-sighted spectators, was pushed up to within ten feet of my window panes. Owing to the great height of the surrounding buildings, and my chambers being on the second floor, the interval between this wall and mine not a little resembled a huge square cistern.

At the period just preceding the advent of Bartleby, I had two persons as copyists in my employment, and a promising lad as an office-boy. First, Turkey; second, Nippers; third, Ginger Nut. These may seem names, the like of which are not usually found in the Directory. In truth, they were nicknames, mutually conferred upon each other by my three clerks, and were deemed expressive of their respective persons or characters. Turkey was a short, pursy Englishman, of about my own age—that is, somewhere not far from sixty. In the morning, one might say, his face was of a fine florid hue, but after twelve o'clock, meridian—his dinner hour—it blazed like a grate full of Christmas coals; and continued blazing—but, as it were, with a gradual wane—till six o'clock P.M., or thereabouts; after which, I saw no more of the proprietor of the face, which, gaining its meridian with the sun, seemed to set with it, to rise, culminate, and decline the following day, with the like regularity and undiminished glory. There are many singular coincidences I have known in the course of my life, not the least among which was the fact, that, exactly when Turkey displayed

---

[2] Courts of Chancery often adjudicated business disputes.

his fullest beams from his red and radiant countenance, just then, too, at that critical moment, began the daily period when I considered his business capacities as seriously disturbed for the remainder of the twenty-four hours. Not that he was absolutely idle, or averse to business, then; far from it. The difficulty was, he was apt to be altogether too energetic. There was a strange, inflamed, flurried, flighty recklessness of activity about him. He would be incautious in dipping his pen into his inkstand. All his blots upon my documents were dropped there after twelve o'clock meridian. Indeed, not only would he be reckless, and sadly given to making blots in the afternoon, but, some days, he went further, and was rather noisy. At such times, too, his face flamed with augmented blazonry, as if cannel coal had been heaped on anthracite. He made an unpleasant racket with his chair; spilled his sand-box; in mending his pens, impatiently split them all to pieces, and threw them on the floor in a sudden passion; stood up, and leaned over his table, boxing his papers about in a most indecorous manner, very sad to behold in an elderly man like him. Nevertheless, as he was in many ways a most valuable person to me, and all the time before twelve o'clock meridian, was the quickest, steadiest creature, too, accomplishing a great deal of work in a style not easily to be matched—for these reasons, I **was** willing to overlook his eccentricities, though, indeed, occasionally, I remonstrated with him. I did this very gently, however, because, though the civilest, nay, the blandest and most reverential of men in the morning, yet, in the afternoon, he was disposed, upon provocation, to be slightly rash with his tongue—in fact, insolent. Now, valuing his morning services as I did, and resolved not to lose them—yet, at the same time, made uncomfortable by his inflamed ways after twelve o'clock—and being a man of peace, unwilling by my admonitions to call forth unseemly retorts from him, I took upon me, one Saturday noon (he was always worse on Saturdays) to hint to him, very kindly, that, perhaps, now that he was growing old, it might be well to abridge his labors; in short, he need not come to my chambers after twelve o'clock, but, dinner over, had best go home to his lodgings, and rest himself till tea-time. But no; he insisted upon his afternoon devotions. His countenance became intolerably fervid, as he oratorically assured me—gesticulating with a long ruler at the other end of the room—that if his services in the morning were useful, how indispensable, then, in the afternoon?

"With submission, sir," said Turkey, on this occasion, "I consider myself your right-hand man. In the morning I but marshal and deploy my columns; but in the afternoon I put myself at their head, and gallantly charge the foe, thus"—and he made a violent thrust with the ruler.

"But the blots, Turkey," intimated I.

"True; but, with submission, sir, behold these hairs! I am getting old. Surely, sir, a blot or two of a warm afternoon is not to be severely urged against gray hairs. Old age—even if it blot the page—is honorable. With submission, sir, we *both* are getting old."

This appeal to my fellow-feeling was hardly to be resisted. At all events, I saw that go he would not. So, I made up my mind to let him stay, resolving, nevertheless, to see to it that, during the afternoon, he had to do with my less important papers.

Nippers, the second on my list, was a whiskered, sallow, and upon the whole, rather piratical-looking young man, of about five and twenty. I always deemed him the victim of two evil powers—ambition and indigestion. The ambition was evinced by a certain impatience of the duties of a mere copyist, an unwarrantable usurpation of strictly professional affairs, such as the original drawing up of legal documents. The indigestion seemed betokened in an occasional nervous testiness and grinning irritability, causing the teeth to audibly grind together over mistakes committed in copying; unnecessary maledictions, hissed, rather than spoken, in the heat of business; and especially by a continual discontent with the height of the table where he worked. Though of a very ingenious, mechanical turn, Nippers could never get this table to suit him. He put chips under it, blocks of various sorts, bits of pasteboard, and at last went so far as to attempt an exquisite adjustment, by final pieces of folded blotting-paper. But no invention would answer. If, for the sake of easing his back, he brought the table lid at a sharp angle well up towards his chin, and wrote there like a man using the steep roof of a Dutch house for his desk, then he declared that it stopped the circulation in his arms. If now he lowered the table to his waistbands, and stooped over it in writing, then there was a sore aching in his back. In short, the truth of the matter was, Nippers knew not what he wanted. Or, if he wanted anything, if was to be rid of a scrivener's table altogether. Among the manifestations of his diseased ambition was a fondness he had for receiving visits from certain ambiguous-looking fellows in seedy coats, whom he called his clients. Indeed, I was aware that not only was he, at times, considerable of a ward-politician, but he occasionally did a little business at the Justices' courts, and was not unknown on the steps of the Tombs.[3] I have good reason to believe, however, that one individual who called upon him at my chambers, and who, with a grand air, he insisted was his client, was no other than a dun, and the alleged title-deed, a bill. But, with all his failings, and the annoyances he caused me, Nippers, like his compatriot Turkey, was a very useful man to me; wrote a neat, swift hand; and, when he chose, was not deficient in a gentlemanly sort of deportment. Added to this, he always dressed in a gentlemanly sort of way; and so, incidentally, reflected credit upon my chambers. Whereas, with respect to Turkey, I had much ado to keep him from being a reproach to me. His clothes were apt to look oily, and smell of eating-houses. He wore his pantaloons very loose and baggy in summer. His coats were execrable; his hat not to be handled. But while the hat was a thing of indifference to me, inasmuch as his natural civility and deference, as a dependent Englishman, always led him to doff it the moment he entered the room, yet his coat was another matter. Concerning his coats, I reasoned with him; but with no effect. The truth was, I suppose, that a man with so small an income could not afford to sport such a lustrous face and a lustrous coat at one and the same time. As Nippers once

---

[3] A prison in New York City.

observed, Turkey's money went chiefly for red ink. One winter day, I presented Turkey with a highly respectable-looking coat of my own—a padded gray coat, of a most comfortable warmth, and which buttoned straight up from the knee to the neck. I thought Turkey would appreciate the favor, and abate his rashness and obstreperousness of afternoons. But no; I verily believe that buttoning himself up in so downy and blanket-like a coat had a pernicious effect upon him—upon the same principle that too much oats are bad for horses. In fact, precisely as a rash, restive horse is said to feel his oats, so Turkey felt his coat. It made him insolent. He was a man whom prosperity harmed.

Though, concerning the self-indulgent habits of Turkey, I had my own private surmises, yet, touching Nippers, I was well persuaded that, whatever might be his faults in other respects, he was, at least, a temperate young man. But, indeed, nature herself seemed to have been his vintner, and, at his birth, charged him so thoroughly with an irritable, brandy-like disposition, that all subsequent potations were needless. When I consider how, amid the stillness of my chambers, Nippers would sometimes impatiently rise from his seat, and stopping over his table, spread his arms wide apart, seize the whole desk, and move it, and jerk it, with a grim, grinding motion on the floor, as if the table were a perverse voluntary agent and vexing him, I plainly perceive that, for Nippers, brandy-and-water were altogether superfluous.

It was fortunate for me that, owing to its peculiar cause—indigestion—the irritability and consequent nervousness of Nippers were mainly observable in the morning, while in the afternoon he was comparatively mild. So that, Turkey's paroxysms only coming on about twelve o'clock, I never had to do with their eccentricities at one time. Their fits relieved each other, like guards. When Nippers's was on, Turkey's was off; and *vice versa*. This was a good natural arrangement, under the circumstances.

Ginger Nut, the third on my list, was a lad, some twelve years old. His father was a car-man, ambitious of seeing his son on the bench instead of a cart, before he died. So he sent him to my office, as student at law, errand-boy, cleaner and sweeper, at the rate of one dollar a week. He had a little desk to himself; but he did not use it much. Upon inspection, the drawer exhibited a great array of shells of various sorts of nuts. Indeed, to this quick-witted youth, the whole noble science of the law was contained in a nutshell. Not the least among the employments of Ginger Nut, as well as one which he discharged with the most alacrity, was his duty as cake and apple purveyor for Turkey and Nippers. Copying law-papers being proverbially a dry, husky sort of business, my two scriveners were fain to moisten their mouths very often with Spitzenbergs,[4] to be had at the numerous stalls nigh the Custom House and Post Office. Also, they sent Ginger Nut very frequently for that peculiar cake—small, flat, round, and very spicy—after which he had been named by them. Of a cold morning, when business was but dull, Turkey would gobble up scores of these cakes, as if they were mere wafers—indeed, they sell them at the rate of six or

---

[4] A variety of apple.

eight for a penny—the scrape of his pen blending with the crunching of the crisp particles in his mouth. Rashest of all the fiery afternoon blunders and flurried rashnesses of Turkey, was his once moistening a ginger-cake between his lips, and clapping it on to a mortgage, for a seal. I came within an ace of dismissing him then. But he mollified me by making an oriental bow, and saying—

"With submission, sir, it was generous of me to find you in stationery on my own account."

Now my original business—that of a conveyancer and title hunter, and drawer-up of recondite documents of all sorts—was considerably increased by receiving the master's office. There was now great work for scriveners. Not only must I push the clerks already with me, but I must have additional help.

In answer to my advertisement, a motionless young man one morning stood upon my office threshold, the door being open, for it was summer. I can see that figure now—pallidly neat, pitiably respectable, incurably forlorn! It was Bartleby.

After a few words touching his qualifications, I engaged him, glad to have among my corps of copyists a man of so singularly sedate an aspect, which I thought might operate beneficially upon the flighty temper of Turkey, and the fiery one of Nippers.

I should have stated before that ground glass folding-doors divided my premises into two parts, one of which was occupied by my scriveners, the other by myself. According to my humor, I threw open these doors, or closed them. I resolved to assign Bartleby a corner by the folding-doors, but on my side of them, so as to have this quiet man within easy call, in case any trifling thing was to be done. I placed his desk close up to a small side-window in that part of the room, a window which originally had afforded a lateral view of certain grimy backyards and bricks, but which, owing to subsequent erections, commanded at present no view at all, though it gave some light. Within three feet of the panes was a wall, and the light came down from far above, between two lofty buildings, as from a very small opening in a dome. Still further to a satisfactory arrangement, I procured a high green folding screen, which might entirely isolate Bartleby from my sight, though not remove him from my voice. And thus, in a manner, privacy and society were conjoined.

At first, Bartleby did an extraordinary quantity of writing. As if long famishing for something to copy, he seemed to gorge himself on my documents. There was no pause for digestion. He ran a day and night line, copying by sun-light and by candle-light. I should have been quite delighted with his application, had he been cheerfully industrious. But he wrote on silently, palely, mechanically.

It is, of course, an indispensable part of a scrivener's business to verify the accuracy of his copy, word by word. Where there are two or more scriveners in an office, they assist each other in this examination, one reading from the copy, the other holding the original. It is a very dull, wearisome, and lethargic affair. I can readily imagine that, to some sanguine temperaments, it would be altogether intolerable. For example, I cannot credit that the mettlesome poet, Byron, would have contentedly sat down with Bartleby to examine a law document of, say five hundred pages, closely written in a crimpy hand.

Now and then, in the haste of business, it had been my habit to assist in comparing some brief document myself, calling Turkey or Nippers for this purpose. One object I had, in placing Bartleby so handy to me behind the screen, was to avail myself of his services on such trivial occasions. It was on the third day, I think, of his being with me, and before any necessity had arisen for having his own writing examined, that, being much hurried to complete a small affair I had in hand, I abruptly called to Bartleby. In my haste and natural expectancy of instant compliance, I sat with my head bent over the original on my desk, and my right hand sideways, and somewhat nervously extended with the copy, so that, immediately upon emerging from his retreat, Bartleby might snatch it and proceed to business without the least delay.

In this very attitude did I sit when I called to him, rapidly stating what it was I wanted him to do—namely, to examine a small paper with me. Imagine my surprise, nay, my consternation, when, without moving from his privacy, Bartleby, in a singularly mild, firm voice, replied, "I would prefer not to."

I sat awhile in perfect silence, rallying my stunned faculties. Immediately it occurred to me that my ears had deceived me, or Bartleby had entirely misunderstood my meaning. I repeated my request in the clearest tone I could assume; but in quite as clear a one came the previous reply, "I would prefer not to."

"Prefer not to," echoed I, rising in high excitement, and crossing the room with a stride. "What do you mean? Are you moon-struck? I want you to help me compare this sheet here—take it," and I thrust it towards him.

"I would prefer not to," said he.

I looked at him steadfastly. His face was leanly composed; his gray eye dimly calm. Not a wrinkle of agitation rippled him. Had there been the least uneasiness, anger, impatience, or impertinence in his manner; in other words, had there been any thing ordinarily human about him, doubtless I should have violently dismissed him from the premises. But as it was, I should have as soon thought of turning my pale plaster-of-paris bust of Cicero out of doors. I stood gazing at him awhile, as he went on with his own writing, and then reseated myself at my desk. This is very strange, thought I. What had one best do? But my business hurried me. I concluded to forget the matter for the present, reserving it for my future leisure. So calling Nippers from the other room, the paper was speedily examined.

A few days after this, Bartleby concluded four lengthy documents, being quadruplicates of a week's testimony taken before me in my High Court of Chancery. It became necessary to examine them. It was an important suit, and great accuracy was imperative. Having all things arranged, I called Turkey, Nippers, and Ginger Nut from the next room, meaning to place the four copies in the hands of my four clerks, while I should read from the original. Accordingly, Turkey, Nippers, and Ginger Nut had taken their seats in a row, each with his document in his hand, when I called to Bartleby to join this interesting group.

"Bartleby! quick, I am waiting."

I heard a slow scrape of his chair legs on the uncarpeted floor, and soon he appeared standing at the entrance of his hermitage.

"What is wanted?" said he, mildly.

"The copies, the copies," said I, hurriedly. "We are going to examine them. There—" and I held towards him the fourth quadruplicate.

"I would prefer not to," he said, and gently disappeared behind the screen.

For a few moments I was turned into a pillar of salt, standing at the head of my seated column of clerks. Recovering myself, I advanced towards the screen, and demanded the reason for such extraordinary conduct.

"*Why* do you refuse?"

"I would prefer not to."

With any other man I should have flown outright into a dreadful passion, scorned all further words, and thrust him ignominiously from my presence. But there was something about Bartleby that not only strangely disarmed me, but in a wonderful manner, touched and disconcerted me. I began to reason with him.

"These are your own copies we are about to examine. It is labor saving to you, because one examination will answer for your four papers. It is common usage. Every copyist is bound to help examine his copy. Is it not so? Will you not speak? Answer!"

"I prefer not to," he replied in a flutelike tone. It seemed to me that, while I had been addressing him, he carefully revolved every statement that I made; fully comprehended the meaning; could not gainsay the irresistible conclusion; but, at the same time, some paramount consideration prevailed with him to reply as he did.

"You are decided, then, not to comply with my request—a request made according to common usage and common sense?"

He briefly gave me to understand, that on that point my judgment was sound. Yes: his decision was irreversible.

It is not seldom the case that, when a man is browbeaten in some unprecedented and violently unreasonable way, he begins to stagger in his own plainest faith. He begins, as it were, vaguely to surmise that, wonderful as it may be, all the justice and all the reason is on the other side. Accordingly, if any disinterested persons are present, he turns to them for some reinforcement of his own faltering mind.

"Turkey," said I, "what do you think of this? Am I not right?"

"With submission, sir," said Turkey, in his blandest tone, "I think that you are."

"Nippers," said I, "what do *you* think of it?"

"I think I should kick him out of the office."

(The reader, of nice perceptions, will here perceive that, it being morning, Turkey's answer is couched in polite and tranquil terms, but Nippers replies in ill-tempered ones. Or, to repeat a previous sentence, Nippers's ugly mood was on duty, and Turkey's off.)

"Ginger Nut," said I, willing to enlist the smallest suffrage in my behalf, "what do *you* think of it?"

"I think, sir, he's a little *luny*," replied Ginger Nut, with a grin.

"You hear what they say," said I, turning towards the screen, "come forth and do your duty."

But he vouchsafed no reply. I pondered a moment in sore perplexity. But once more business hurried me. I determined again to postpone the consideration of this dilemma to my future leisure. With a little trouble we made out to examine the papers without Bartleby, though at every page or two Turkey deferentially dropped his opinion, that this proceeding was quite out of the common; while Nippers, twitching in his chair with a dyspeptic nervousness, ground out, between his set teeth, occasional hissing maledictions against the stubborn oaf behind the screen. And for his (Nippers's) part, this was the first and the last time he would do another man's business without pay.

Meanwhile Bartleby sat in his hermitage, oblivious to everything but his own peculiar business there.

Some days passed, the scrivener being employed upon another lengthy work. His late remarkable conduct led me to regard his ways narrowly. I observed that he never went to dinner; indeed, that he never went anywhere. As yet I had never, of my personal knowledge, known him to be outside of my office. He was a perpetual sentry in the corner. At about eleven o'clock though, in the morning, I noticed that Ginger Nut would advance toward the opening in Bartleby's screen, as if silently beckoned thither by a gesture invisible to me where I sat. The boy would then leave the office, jingling a few pence, and reappear with a handful of ginger-nuts, which he delivered in the hermitage, receiving two of the cakes for his trouble.

He lives, then, on ginger-nuts, thought I; never eats a dinner, properly speaking; he must be a vegetarian, then; but no; he never eats even vegetables; he eats nothing but ginger-nuts. My mind then ran on in reveries concerning the probable effects upon the human consitution of living entirely on ginger-nuts. Ginger-nuts are so called, because they contain ginger as one of their peculiar constituents, and the final flavoring one. Now, what was ginger? A hot, spicy thing. Was Bartleby hot and spicy? Not at all. Ginger, then, had no effect upon Bartleby. Probably he preferred it should have none.

Nothing so aggravates an earnest person as a passive resistance. If the individual so resisted be of a not inhumane temper, and the resisting one perfectly harmless in his passivity, then, in the better moods of the former, he will endeavor charitably to construe to his imagination what proves impossible to be solved by his judgement. Even so, for the most part, I regarded Bartleby and his ways. Poor fellow! thought I, he means no mischief; it is plain he intends no insolence; his aspect sufficiently evinces that his eccentricities are involuntary. He is useful to me. I can get along with him. If I turn him away, the chances are he will fall in with some less-indulgent employer, and then he will be rudely treated, and perhaps driven forth miserably to starve. Yes. Here I can cheaply purchase a delicious self-approval. To befriend Bartleby; to humor him in his strange willfulness, will cost me little or nothing, while I lay up in my soul what will eventually prove a sweet morsel for my conscience. But this mood was not invariable with me. The passiveness of Bartleby sometimes irritated me. I felt strangely goaded on to encounter him in new opposition—to elicit some angry spark from him answerable to my own. But, indeed, I might as well have essayed to strike fire with my knuckles against a bit of Windsor soap. But one afternoon the evil impulse in me mastered me, and the following little scene ensued:

"Bartleby," said I, "when those papers are all copied, I will compare them with you."

"I would prefer not to."

"How? Surely you do not mean to persist in that mulish vagary?"

No answer.

I threw open the folding-doors near by, and, turning upon Turkey and Nippers, exclaimed:

"Bartleby a second time says, he won't examine his papers. What do you think of it, Turkey?"

It was afternoon, be it remembered. Turkey sat glowing like a brass boiler; his bald head steaming; his hands reeling among his blotted papers.

"Think of it?" roared Turkey; "I think I'll just step behind his screen, and black his eyes for him!"

So saying, Turkey rose to his feet and threw his arms into a pugilistic position. He was hurrying away to make good his promise, when I detained him, alarmed at the effect of incautiously rousing Turkey's combativeness after dinner.

"Sit down, Turkey," said I, "and hear what Nippers has to say. What do you think of it, Nippers? Would I not be justified in immediately dismissing Bartleby?"

"Excuse me, that is for you to decide, sir. I think his conduct quite unusual, and, indeed, unjust, as regards Turkey and myself. But it may only be a passing whim."

"Ah," exclaimed I, "you have strangely changed your mind, then—you speak very gently of him now."

"All beer," cried Turkey; "gentleness is effects of beer—Nippers and I dined together to-day. You see how gentle *I* am, sir. Shall I go and black his eyes?"

"You refer to Bartleby, I suppose. No, not to-day, Turkey," I replied; "pray, put up your fists."

I closed the doors, and again advanced towards Bartleby. I felt additional incentives tempting me to my fate. I burned to be rebelled against again. I remembered that Bartleby never left the office.

"Bartleby," said I, "Ginger Nut is away; just step around to the Post Office, won't you? (it was but a three minutes' walk), and see if there is anything for me."

"I would prefer not to."

"You *will* not?"

"I *prefer* not."

I staggered to my desk, and sat there in a deep study. My blind inveteracy returned. Was there any other thing in which I could procure myself to be ignominiously repulsed by this lean, penniless wight?—my hired clerk? What added thing is there, perfectly reasonable, that he will be sure to refuse to do? "Bartleby!"

No answer.

"Bartleby," in a louder tone.

No answer.

"Bartleby," I roared.

Like a very ghost, agreeably to the laws of magical invocation, at the third summons, he appeared at the entrance of his hermitage.

"Go to the next room, and tell Nippers to come to me."

"I prefer not to," he respectfully and slowly said and mildly disappeared.

"Very good, Bartleby," said I, in a quiet sort of serenely-severe, self-possessed tone, intimating the unalterable purpose of some terrible retribution very close at hand. At the moment I half intended something of the kind. But upon the whole, as it was drawing towards my dinner-hour, I thought it best to put on my hat and walk home for the day, suffering much from perplexity and distress of mind.

Shall I acknowledge it? The conclusion of this whole business was, that it soon became a fixed fact of my chambers, that a pale young scrivener, by the name of Bartleby, had a desk there; that he copied for me at the usual rate of four cents a folio (one hundred words); but he was permanently exempt from examining the work done by him, that duty being transferred to Turkey and Nippers, out of compliment, doubtless, to their superior acuteness; moreover, said Bartleby was never, on any account, to be dispatched on the most trivial errand of any sort; and that even if entreated to take upon him such a matter, it was generally understood that he would "prefer not to"—in other words, he would refuse point blank.

As days passed on, I became considerably reconciled to Bartleby. His steadiness, his freedom from all dissipation, his incessant industry (except when he chose to throw himself into a standing revery behind his screen), his great stillness, his unalterableness of demeanor under all circumstances, made him a valuable acquisition. One prime thing was this—*he was always there*—first in the morning, continually through the day, and the last at night. I had a singular confidence in his honesty. I felt my most precious papers perfectly safe in his hands. Sometimes, to be sure, I could not, for the very soul of me, avoid falling into sudden spasmodic passions with him. For it was exceeding difficult to bear in mind all the time those strange peculiarities, privileges, and unheard of exemptions, forming the tacit stipulations on Bartleby's part under which he remained in my office. Now and then, in the eagerness of dispatching pressing business, I would inadvertently summon Bartleby, in a short, rapid tone, to put his finger, say, on the incipient tie of a bit of red tape with which I was about compressing some papers. Of course, from behind the screen the usual answer, "I prefer not to," was sure to come; and then, how could a human creature, with the common infirmities of our nature, refrain from bitterly exclaiming upon such perverseness—such unreasonableness. However, every added repulse of this sort which I received only tended to lessen the probability of my repeating the inadvertence.

Here it must be said, that according to the custom of most legal gentlemen occupying chambers in densely-populated law buildings, there were several keys to my door. One was kept by a woman residing in the attic, which person weekly scrubbed and daily swept and dusted my apartments. Another was kept by Turkey for convenience sake. The third I sometimes carried in my own pocket. The fourth I knew not who had.

Now, one Sunday morning I happened to go to Trinity Church, to hear a celebrated preacher, and finding myself rather early on the ground I thought I would walk around to my chambers for a while. Luckily I had my key with me; but upon applying it to the lock, I found it resisted by something inserted from the inside. Quite surprised, I called out; when to my consternation a key was turned from within; and thrusting his lean visage at me, and holding the door ajar, the apparition of Bartleby appeared, in his shirt sleeves, and otherwise in a strangely tattered *déshabillé*, saying quietly that he was sorry, but he was deeply engaged just then, and—preferred not admitting me at present. In a brief word or two, he moreover added, that perhaps I had better walk around the block two or three times, and by that time he would probably have concluded his affairs.

Now, the utterly unsurmised appearance of Bartleby, tenanting my law-chambers of a Sunday morning, with his cadaverously gentlemanly *nonchalance*, yet withal firm and self-possessed, had such a strange effect upon me, that incontinently I slunk away from my own door, and did as desired. But not without sundry twinges of impotent rebellion against the mild effrontery of this unaccountable scrivener. Indeed, it was his wonderful mildness chiefly, which not only disarmed me, but unmanned me as it were. For I consider that one, for the time, is somehow unmanned when he tranquilly permits his hired clerk to dictate to him, and order him away from his own premises. Furthermore, I was full of uneasiness as to what Bartleby could possibly be doing in my office in his shirt sleeves, and in an otherwise dismantled condition of a Sunday morning. Was anything amiss going on? Nay, that was out of the question. It was not to be thought of for a moment that Bartleby was an immoral person. But what could he be doing there?—copying? Nay again, whatever might be his eccentricities, Bartleby was an eminently decorous person. He would be the last man to sit down to his desk in any state approaching to nudity. Besides, it was Sunday; and there was something about Bartleby that forbade the supposition that he would by any secular occupation violate the proprieties of the day.

Nevertheless, my mind was not pacified; and full of a restless curiosity, at last I returned to the door. Without hindrance I inserted my key, opened it, and entered. Bartleby was not to be seen. I looked round anxiously, peeped behind his screen; but it was very plain that he was gone. Upon more closely examining the place, I surmised that for an indefinite period Bartleby must have eaten, dressed, and slept in my office, and that, too, without plate, mirror, or bed. The cushioned seat of a rickety old sofa in one corner bore the faint impress of a lean, reclining form. Rolled away under his desk, I found a blanket; under the empty grate, a blacking box and brush; on a chair, a tin basin, with soap and a ragged towel; in a newspaper a few crumbs of ginger-nuts and a morsel of cheese. Yes, thought I, it is evident enough that Bartleby has been making his home here, keeping bachelor's hall all by himself. Immediately then the thought came sweeping across me, what miserable friendlessness and loneliness are here revealed! His poverty is great; but his solitude, how horrible! Think of it. Of a Sunday, Wall Street is deserted as Petra[5]; and every night of every day it is an emptiness. This building, too, which of week-days hums with industry and life, at nightfall echoes with sheer vacancy, and all through Sunday is forlorn. And here Bartleby makes his home; sole spectator of a solitude which he has seen all populous—a sort of innocent and transformed Marius brooding among the ruins of Carthage![6]

For the first time in my life a feeling of over-powering stinging melancholy seized me. Before, I had never experienced aught but a not unpleasing sadness. The bond of a common humanity now drew me irresistibly to gloom. A fraternal melancholy! for both I and Bartleby were sons of Adam. I remembered the bright silks and sparkling faces I had seen that day, in gala trim, swan-like sailing down the Mississippi of Broadway; and I contrasted them with the pallid copyist, and thought to myself, Ah, happiness courts the light, so we deem the world is gay; but misery hides aloof, so we deem that misery there is none. These sad fancyings—chimeras, doubtless, of a sick and silly brain—led on to other and more special thoughts, concerning the eccentricities of Bartleby. Presentiments of strange discoveries hovered round me. The scrivener's pale form appeared to me laid out, among uncaring strangers, in its shivering winding sheet.

Suddenly I was attracted by Bartleby's closed desk, the key in open sight left in the lock.

I mean no mischief, seek the gratification of no heartless curiosity, thought I; besides, the desk is mine, and its contents, too, so I will make bold to look within. Everything was methodically arranged, the papers smoothly placed. The pigeon holes were deep, and removing the files of documents, I groped into their recesses. Presently I felt something there, and dragged it out. It was an old bandanna handkerchief, heavy and knotted. I opened it, and saw it was a savings bank.

I now recalled all the quiet mysteries which I had noted in the man. I remembered that he never spoke but to answer; that, though at intervals he had

---

[5] A city in Palestine found by explorers in 1812. It had been deserted and lost for centuries.
[6] Caius Marius (155–86 B.C.), a plebeian general who was forced to flee from Rome. Nineteenth-century democratic literature sometimes pictured him old and alone among the ruins of Carthage.

considerable time to himself, yet I had never seen him reading—no, not even a newspaper; that for long periods he would stand looking out, at his pale window behind the screen, upon the dead brick wall; I was quite sure he never visited any refectory or eating house; while his pale face clearly indicated that he never drank beer like Turkey, or tea and coffee even, like other men; that he never went anywhere in particular that I could learn; never went out for a walk, unless, indeed, that was the case at present; that he had declined telling who he was, or whence he came, or whether he had any relatives in the world; that though so thin and pale, he never complained of ill health. And more than all, I remembered a certain unconscious air of pallid—how shall I call it?—of pallid haughtiness, say, or rather an austere reserve about him, which had positively awed me into my tame compliance with his eccentricities, when I had feared to ask him to do the slightest incidental thing for me, even though I might know, from his long-continued motionlessness, that behind his screen he must be standing in one of those dead-wall reveries of his.

Revolving all these things, and coupling them with the recently discovered fact, that he made my office his constant abiding place and home, and not forgetful of his morbid moodiness; revolving all these things, a prudential feeling began to steal over me. My first emotions had been those of pure melancholy and sincerest pity; but just in proportion as the forlornness of Bartleby grew and grew to my imagination, did that same melancholy merge into fear, that pity into repulsion. So true it is, and so terrible, too, that up to a certain point the thought or sight of misery enlists our best affections; but, in certain special cases, beyond that point it does not. They err who would assert that invariably this is owing to the inherent selfishness of the human heart. It rather proceeds from a certain hopelessness of remedying excessive and organic ill. To a sensitive being, pity is not seldom pain. And when at last it is perceived that such pity cannot lead to effectual succor, common sense bids the soul be rid of it. What I saw that morning persuaded me that the scrivener was the victim of innate and incurable disorder. I might give alms to his body; but his body did not pain him; it was his soul that suffered, and his soul I could not reach.

I did not accomplish the purpose of going to Trinity Church that morning. Somehow, the things I had seen disqualified me for the time from churchgoing. I walked homeward, thinking what I would do with Bartleby. Finally, I resolved upon this—I would put certain calm questions to him the next morning, touching his history, etc., and if he declined to answer them openly and unreservedly (and I supposed he would prefer not), then to give him a twenty dollar bill over and above whatever I might owe him, and tell him his services were no longer required; but that if in any other way I could assist him, I would be happy to do so, especially if he desired to return to his native place, wherever that might be, I would willingly help to defray the expenses. Moreover, if, after reaching home, he found himself at any time in want of aid, a letter from him would be sure of a reply.

The next morning came.

"Bartleby," said I, gently calling to him behind his screen.

No reply.

"Bartleby," said I, in a still gentler tone, "come here; I am not going to ask you to do anything you would prefer not to do—I simply wish to speak to you."

Upon this he noiselessly slid into view.

"Will you tell me, Bartleby, where you were born?"

"I would prefer not to."

"Will you tell me *anything* about yourself?"

"I would prefer not to."

"But what reasonable objection can you have to speak to me? I feel friendly towards you."

He did not look at me while I spoke, but kept his glance fixed upon my bust of Cicero, which, as I then sat, was directly behind me, some six inches above my head.

"What is your answer, Bartleby," said I, after waiting a considerable time for a reply, during which his countenance remained immovable, only there was the faintest conceivable tremor of the white attenuated mouth.

"At present I prefer to give no answer," he said, and retired into his hermitage.

It was rather weak in me I confess, but his manner, on this occasion, nettled me. Not only did there seem to lurk in it a certain calm disdain, but his perverseness seemed ungrateful, considering the undeniable good usage and indulgence he had received from me.

Again I sat ruminating what I should do. Mortified as I was at his behavior, and resolved as I had been to dismiss him when I entered my office, nevertheless I strangely felt something superstitious knocking at my heart, and forbidding me to carry out my purpose, and denouncing me for a villain if I dared to breathe one bitter word against this forlornest of mankind. At last, familiarly drawing my chair behind his screen, I sat down and said: "Bartleby, never mind, then, about revealing your history; but let me entreat you, as a friend, to comply as far as may be with the usages of this office. Say now, you will help to examine papers to-morrow or next day: in short, say now, that in a day or two you will begin to be a little reasonable:—say so, Bartleby."

"At present I would prefer not to be a little reasonable," was his mildly cadaverous reply.

Just then the folding-doors opened, and Nippers approached. He seemed suffering from an unusually bad night's rest, induced by severer indigestion than common. He overheard those final words of Bartleby.

"*Prefer not*, eh?" gritted Nippers—"I'd *prefer* him, if I were you, sir," addressing me—"I'd *prefer* him; I'd give him preferences, the stubborn mule! What is it, sir, pray, that he *prefers* not to do now?"

Bartleby moved not a limb.

"Mr. Nippers," said I, "I'd prefer that you would withdraw for the present."

Somehow, of late, I had got into the way of involuntarily using this word "prefer" upon all sorts of not exactly suitable occasions. And I trembled to think that my contact with the scrivener had already and seriously affected me in a mental way. And what further and deeper aberration might it not yet produce? This apprehension had not been without efficacy in determining me to summary measures.

As Nippers, looking very sour and sulky, was departing, Turkey blandly and deferentially approached.

"With submission, sir," said he, "yesterday I was thinking about Bartleby here, and I think that if he would but prefer to take a quart of good ale every day, it would do much towards mending him, and enabling him to assist in examining his papers."

"So you have got the word, too," said I, slightly excited.

"With submission, what word, sir," asked Turkey, respectfully crowding himself into the contracted space behind the screen, and by so doing, making me jostle the scrivener. "What word, sir?"

"I would prefer to be left alone here," said Bartleby, as if offended at being mobbed in his privacy.

"*That's* the word, Turkey," said I—"*that's* it."

"Oh, *prefer?* oh yes—queer word. I never use it myself. But, sir, as I was saying, if he would but prefer—"

"Turkey," interrupted I, "you will please withdraw."

"Oh certainly, sir, if you prefer that I should."

As he opened the folding-door to retire, Nippers at his desk caught a glimpse of me, and asked whether I would prefer to have a certain paper copied on blue paper or white. He did not in the least roguishly accent the word prefer. It was plain that it involuntarily rolled from his tongue. I thought to myself, surely I must get rid of a demented man, who already has in some degree turned the tongues, if not the heads of myself and clerks. But I thought it prudent not to break the dismission at once.

The next day I noticed that Bartleby did nothing but stand at his window in his dead-wall revery. Upon asking him why he did not write, he said that he had decided upon doing no more writing."

"Why, how now? What next?" exclaimed I, "do no more writing?"

"No more."

"And what is the reason?"

"Do you not see the reason for yourself," he indifferently replied.

I looked steadfastly at him, and perceived that his eyes looked dull and glazed. Instantly it occurred to me, that his unexampled diligence in copying by his dim window for the first few weeks of his stay with me might have temporarily impaired his vision.

I was touched. I said something in condolence with him. I hinted that of course he did wisely in abstaining from writing for a while; and urged him to embrace that opportunity of taking wholesome exercise in the open air. This, however, he did not do. A few days after this, my other clerks being absent, and being in a great hurry to dispatch certain letters by the mail, I thought that, having nothing else earthly to do, Bartleby would surely be less inflexible than usual, and carry these letters to the post-office. But he blankly declined. So, much to my inconvenience, I went myself.

Still added days went by. Whether Bartleby's eyes improved or not, I could not say. To all appearance I thought they did. But when I asked him if they did, he vouchsafed no answer. At all events, he would do no copying. At last, in reply to my urgings, he informed me that he had permanently given up copying.

"What!" exclaimed I; "suppose your eyes should get entirely well—better than ever before—would you not copy then?"

"I have given up copying," he answered, and slid aside.

He remained as ever, a fixture in my chamber. Nay—if that were possible— he became still more of a fixture than before. What was to be done? He would do nothing in the office; why should he stay there? In plain fact, he had now become a millstone to me, not only useless as a necklace, but afflictive to bear. Yet I was sorry for him. I speak less than truth when I say that, on his own account, he occasioned me uneasiness. If he would but have named a single relative or friend, I would instantly have written, and urged their taking the poor fellow away to some convenient retreat. But he seemed alone, absolutely alone in the universe. A bit of wreck in the mid Atlantic. At length, necessities connected with my business tyrannized over all other considerations. Decently as I could, I told Bartleby that in six days time he must unconditionally leave the office. I warned him to take measures, in the interval, for procuring some other abode. I offered to assist him in his endeavor, if he himself would but take the first step towards a removal. "And when you finally quit me, Bartleby," added I, "I shall see that you go not away entirely unprovided. Six days from this hour, remember."

At the expiration of that period, I peeped behind the screen, and lo! Bartleby was there.

I buttoned up my coat, balanced myself; advanced slowly towards him, touched his shoulder, and said, "The time has come; you must quit this place; I am sorry for you; here is money; but you must go."

"I would prefer not" he replied, with his back still towards me.

"You *must*."

He remained silent.

Now I had an unbounded confidence in this man's common honesty. He had frequently restored to me sixpences and shillings carelessly dropped upon the floor, for I am apt to be very reckless in such shirt-button affairs. The proceeding, then, which followed will not be deemed extraordinary.

"Bartleby," said I, "I owe you twelve dollars on account; here are thirty-two; the odd twenty are yours—Will you take it?" and I handed the bills towards him.

But he made no motion.

"I will leave them here, then," putting them under a weight on the table. Then taking my hat and cane and going to the door, I tranquilly turned and added—"After you have removed your things from these offices, Bartleby, you will of course lock the door—since every one is now gone for the day but you— and if you please, slip your key underneath the mat, so that I may have it in the morning. I shall not see you again; so good-by to you. If, hereafter, in your new place of abode, I can be of any service to you, do not fail to advise me by letter. Good-by, Bartleby, and fare you well."

But he answered not a word; like the last column of some ruined temple, he remained standing mute and solitary in the middle of the otherwise deserted room.

As I walked home in a pensive mood, my vanity got the better of my pity. I could not but highly plume myself on my masterly management in getting rid of Bartleby. Masterly I call it, and such it must appear to any dispassionate thinker. The beauty of my procedure seemed to consist in its perfect quietness. There was no vulgar bullying, no bravado of any sort, no choleric hectoring, and striding to and fro across the apartment, jerking out vehement commands for Bartleby to bundle himself off with his beggarly traps. Nothing of the kind. Without loudly bidding Bartleby depart—as an inferior genius might have done—I *assumed* the ground that depart he must; and upon that assumption built all I had to say. The more I thought over my procedure, the more I was charmed with it. Nevertheless, next morning, upon awakening, I had my doubts—I had somehow slept off the fumes of vanity. One of the coolest and wisest hours a man has, is just after he awakes in the morning. My procedure seemed as sagacious as ever—but only in theory. How it would prove in practice—there was the rub. It was truly a beautiful thought to have assumed Bartleby's departure; but, after all, that assumption was simply my own, and none of Bartleby's. The great point was, not whether I had assumed that he would quit me, but whether he would prefer so to do. He was more a man of preferences than assumptions.

After breakfast, I walked down town, arguing the probabilities *pro* and *con*. One moment I thought it would prove a miserable failure, and Bartleby would be found all alive at my office as usual; the next moment it seemed certain that I should find his chair empty. And so I kept veering about. At the corner of Broadway and Canal Street, I saw quite an excited group of people standing in earnest conversation.

"I'll take odds he doesn't," said a voice as I passed.

"Doesn't go?—done!" said I; "put up your money."

I was instinctively putting my hand in my pocket to produce my own, when I remembered that this was an election day. The words I had overheard bore no reference to Bartleby, but to the success or non-success of some candidate for the mayoralty. In my intent frame of mind, I had, as it were, imagined that all Broadway shared in my excitement, and were debating the same question with me. I passed on, very thankful that the uproar of the street screened my momentary absent-mindedness.

As I had intended, I was earlier than usual at my office door. I stood listening for a moment. All was still. He must be gone. I tried the knob. The door was locked. Yes, my procedure had worked to a charm; he indeed must be vanished. Yet a certain melancholy mixed with this: I was almost sorry for my brilliant success. I was fumbling under the door mat for the key, which Bartleby was to have left there for me, when accidentally my knee knocked against a panel, producing a summoning sound, and in response a voice came to me from within—"Not yet; I am occupied."

It was Bartleby.

I was thunderstruck. For an instant I stood like the man who, pipe in mouth, was killed one cloudless afternoon long ago in Virginia, by summer lightning; at his own warm open window he was killed, and remained leaning out there upon the dreamy afternoon, till some one touched him, when he fell.

"Not gone!" I murmured at last. But again obeying that wondrous ascendancy which the inscrutable scrivener had over me, and from which ascendancy, for all my chafing, I could not completely escape, I slowly went down stairs and out into the street, and while walking round the block, considered what I should next do in this unheard-of perplexity. Turn the man out by an actual thrusting I could not; to drive him away by calling him hard names would not do; calling in the police was an unpleasant idea; and yet, permit him to enjoy his cadaverous triumph over me—this, too, I could not think of. What was to be done? or, if nothing could be done, was there anything further that I could *assume* in the matter? Yes, as before I had prospectively assumed that Bartleby would depart, so now I might retrospectively assume that departed he was. In the legitimate carrying out of this assumption, I might enter my office in a great hurry, and pretending not to see Bartleby at all, walk straight against him as if he were air. Such a proceeding would in a singular degree have the appearance of a home-thrust. It was hardly possible that Bartleby could withstand such an application of the doctrine of assumptions. But upon second thoughts the success of the plan seemed rather dubious. I resolved to argue the matter over with him again.

"Bartleby," said I, entering the office, with a quietly severe expression, "I am seriously displeased. I am pained, Bartleby. I had thought better of you. I had imagined you of such a gentlemanly organization, that in any delicate dilemma a slight hint would suffice—in short, an assumption. But it appears I am deceived. Why," I added, unaffectedly starting, "you have not even touched that money yet," pointing to it, just where I had left it the evening previous.

He answered nothing.

"Will you, or will you not, quit me?" I now demanded in a sudden passion, advancing close to him.

"I would prefer *not* to quit you," he replied, gently emphasizing the *not.*

"What earthly right have you to stay here? Do you pay any rent? Do you pay my taxes? Or is this property yours?"

He answered nothing.

"Are you ready to go on and write now? Are your eyes recovered? Could you copy a small paper for me this morning? or help examine a few lines? or step round to the post-office? In a word, will you do anything at all, to give a coloring to your refusal to depart the premises?"

He silently retired into his hermitage.

I was now in such a state of nervous resentment that I thought it but prudent to check myself at present from further demonstrations. Bartleby and I were alone. I remembered the tragedy of the unfortunate Adams and the still more unfortunate Colt in the solitary office of the latter; and how poor Colt, being dreadfully incensed by Adams, and imprudently permitting himself to get wildly excited, was at unawares hurried into his fatal act—an act which certainly no man could possibly deplore more than the actor himself.[7] Often it had occurred to me in my ponderings upon the subject, that had that altercation taken place in the public street, or at a private residence, it would not have terminated as it did. It was the circumstance of being alone in a solitary office, up stairs, of a building entirely unhallowed by humanizing domestic associations—an uncarpeted office, doubtless, of a dusty, haggard sort of appearance—this it must have been, which greatly helped to enhance the irritable desperation of the hapless Colt.

But when this old Adam of resentment rose in me and tempted me concerning Bartleby, I grappled him and threw him. How? Why, simply by recalling the divine injunction: "A new commandment give I unto you, that ye love one another." Yes, this it was that saved me. Aside from higher considerations, charity often operates as a vastly wise and prudent principle—a great safeguard to its possessor. Men have committed murder for jealousy's sake, and anger's sake, and hatred's sake, and selfishness' sake, and spiritual pride's sake; but no man that ever I heard of, ever committed a diabolical murder for sweet charity's sake. Mere self-interest, then, if no better motive can be enlisted, should, especially with high-tempered men, prompt all beings to charity and philanthropy. At any rate, upon the occasion in question, I strove to drown my exasperated feelings towards the scrivener by benevolently construing his conduct. Poor fellow, poor fellow! thought I, he don't mean anything; and besides, he has seen hard times, and ought to be indulged.

I endeavored, also, immediately to occupy myself, and at the same time to comfort my despondency. I tried to fancy, that in the course of the morning, at such time as might prove agreeable to him, Bartleby, of his own free accord, would emerge from his hermitage and take up some decided line of march in the direction of the door. But no. Half-past twelve o'clock came; Turkey began to glow in the face, overturn his inkstand, and become generally obstreperous; Nippers abated down into quietude and courtesy; Ginger Nut munched his noon apple; and Bartleby remained standing at his window in one of his profoundest dead-wall reveries. Will it be credited? Ought I to acknowledge it? That afternoon I left the office without saying one further word to him.

Some days now passed, during which, at leisure intervals I looked a little into "Edwards on the Will," and "Priestley on Necessity."[8] Under the circumstances, those books induced a salutary feeling. Gradually I slid into the persuasion that these troubles of mine, touching the scrivener, had been all predestined from eternity, and Bartleby was billeted upon me for some mysterious purpose of an all-wise Providence, which it was not for a mere mortal like me to fathom. Yes, Bartleby, stay there behind your screen, thought I; I shall persecute you no more; you are harmless and noiseless as any of these old chairs; in short, I never feel so private as when I know you are here. At last I see it, I feel it; I penetrate

---

[7] A sensational homicide case in which Colt murdered Adams in a fit of passion.

[8] Jonathan Edwards (1703–1758), American theologian, and Joseph Priestley (1733–1804), English clergyman and chemist, both held that man's life was predetermined.

to the predestinated purpose of my life. I am content. Others may have loftier parts to enact; but my mission in this world, Bartleby, is to furnish you with office-room for such period as you may see fit to remain.

I believe that this wise and blessed frame of mind would have continued with me, had it not been for the unsolicited and uncharitable remarks obtruded upon me by my professional friends who visited the rooms. But thus it often is, that the constant friction of illiberal minds wears out at last the best resolves of the more generous. Though to be sure, when I reflected upon it, it was not strange that people entering my office should be struck by the peculiar aspect of the unaccountable Bartleby, and so be tempted to throw out some sinister observations concerning him. Sometimes an attorney, having business with me, and calling at my office, and finding no one but the scrivener there, would undertake to obtain some sort of precise information from him touching my whereabouts; but without heeding his idle talk, Bartleby would remain standing immovable in the middle of the room. So after contemplating him in that position for a time, the attorney would depart, no wiser than he came.

Also, when a reference was going on, and the room full of lawyers and witnesses, and business driving fast, some deeply-occupied legal gentleman present, seeing Bartleby wholly unemployed, would request him to run round to his (the legal gentleman's) office and fetch some papers for him. Thereupon, Bartleby would tranquilly decline, and yet remain idle as before. Then the lawyer would give a great stare, and turn to me. And what could I say? At last I was made aware that all through the circle of my professional acquaintance, a whisper of wonder was running round, having reference to the strange creature I kept at my office. This worried me very much. And as the idea came upon me of his possibly turning out a long-lived man, and keep occupying my chambers, and denying my authority; and perplexing my visitors; and scandalizing my professional reputation; and casting a general gloom over the premises; keeping soul and body together to the last upon his savings (for doubtless he spent but half a dime a day), and in the end perhaps outlive me, and claim possession of my office by right of his perpetual occupancy: as all these dark anticipations crowded upon me more and more, and my friends continually intruded their relentless remarks upon the apparition in my room; a great change was wrought in me. I resolved to gather all my faculties together, and forever rid me of this intolerable incubus.

Ere revolving any complicated project, however, adapted to this end, I first simply suggested to Bartleby the propriety of his permanent departure. In a calm and serious tone, I commended the idea to his careful and mature consideration. But, having taken three days to meditate upon it, he apprised me, that his original determination remained the same; in short, that he still preferred to abide with me.

What shall I do? I now said to myself, buttoning up my coat to the last button. What shall I do? what ought I to do? what does conscience say I *should* do with this man, or, rather, ghost. Rid myself of him, I must; go, he shall. But how? You will not thrust him, the poor, pale, passive mortal—you will not thrust such a helpless creature out of your door? you will not dishonor yourself by such cruelty? No, I will not, I cannot do that. Rather would I let him live and die here, and then mason up his remains in the wall. What, then, will you do? For all your coaxing, he will not budge. Bribes he leaves under your own paper-weight on your table; in short, it is quite plain that he prefers to cling to you.

Then something severe, something unusual must be done. What! surely you will not have him collared by a constable, and commit his innocent pallor to the common jail? And upon what ground could you procure such a thing to be done?—a vagrant, is he? What! he a vagrant, a wanderer, who refuses to budge? It is because he will *not* be a vagrant, then, that you seek to count him *as* a vagrant. This is too absurd. No visible means of support: there I have him. Wrong again: for indubitably he *does* support himself, and that is the only unanswerable proof that any man can show of his possessing the means so to do. No more, then. Since he will not quit me, I must quit him. I will change my offices; I will move elsewhere, and give him fair notice, that if I find him on my new premises I will then proceed against him as a common trespasser.

Acting accordingly, next day I thus addressed him: "I find these chambers too far from the City Hall; the air is unwholesome. In a word, I propose to remove my offices next week, and shall no longer require your services. I tell you this now, in order that you may seek another place."

He made no reply; and nothing more was said.

On the appointed day I engaged carts and men, proceeded to my chambers, and, having but little furniture, everything was removed in a few hours. Throughout, the scrivener remained standing behind the screen, which I directed to be removed the last thing. It was withdrawn; and, being folded up like a huge folio, left him the motionless occupant of a naked room. I stood in the entry watching him a moment, while something from within me upbraided me.

I re-entered, with my hand in my pocket—and—and my heart in my mouth.

"Good-by, Bartleby; I am going—good-by, and God some way bless you; and take that," slipping something in his hand. But it dropped upon the floor, and then—strange to say—I tore myself from him whom I had so longed to be rid of.

Established in my new quarters, for a day or two I kept the door locked, and started at every footfall in the passages. When I returned to my rooms, after any little absence, I would pause at the threshold for an instant, and attentively listen, ere applying my key. But these fears were needless. Bartleby never came nigh me.

I thought all was going well, when a perturbed-looking stranger visited me, inquiring whether I was the person who had recently occupied rooms at No. —— Wall Street.

Full of forebodings, I replied that I was.

"Then, sir," said the stranger, who proved a lawyer, "you are responsible for the man you left there. He refuses to do any copying; he refuses to do anything; he says he prefers not to; and he refuses to quit the premises."

"I am very sorry, sir," said I, with assumed tranquillity, but an inward tremor, "but, really, the man you allude to is nothing to me—he is no relation or apprentice of mine, that you should hold me responsible for him."

"In mercy's name, who is he?"

"I certainly cannot inform you. I know nothing about him. Formerly I employed him as a copyist; but he has done nothing for me now for some time past."

"I shall settle him, then—good morning, sir."

Several days passed, and I heard nothing more; and, though I often felt a charitable prompting to call at the place and see poor Bartleby, yet a certain squeamishness, of I know not what, withheld me.

All is over with him, by this time, thought I, at last, when, through another week, no further intelligence reached me. But, coming to my room the day after, I found several persons waiting at my door in a high state of nervous excitement.

"That's the man—here he comes," cried the foremost one, whom I recognized as the lawyer who had previously called upon me alone.

"You must take him away, sir, at once," cried a portly person among them, advancing upon me, and whom I knew to be the landlord of No. —— Wall Street. "These gentlemen, my tenants, cannot stand it any longer; Mr. B—," pointing to the lawyer, "has turned him out of his room, and he now persists in haunting the building generally, sitting upon the banisters of the stairs by day, and sleeping in the entry by night. Everybody is concerned; clients are leaving the offices; some fears are entertained of a mob; something you must do, and that without delay."

Aghast at this torrent, I fell back before it, and would fain have locked myself in my new quarters. In vain I persisted that Bartleby was nothing to me—no more than to any one else. In vain—I was the last person known to have anything to do with him, and they held me to the terrible account. Fearful, then, of being exposed in the papers (as one person present obscurely threatened), I considered the matter, and, at length, said, that if the lawyer would give me a confidential interview with the scrivener, in his (the lawyer's) own room, I would, that afternoon, strive my best to rid them of the nuisance they complained of.

Going up stairs to my old haunt, there was Bartleby silently sitting upon the banister at the landing.

"What are you doing here, Bartleby?" said I.

"Sitting upon the banister," he mildly replied.

I motioned him into the lawyer's room, who then left us.

"Bartleby," said I, "are you aware that you are the cause of great tribulation to me, by persisting in occupying the entry after being dismissed from the office?"

No answer.

"Now one of two things must take place. Either you must do something, or something must be done to you. Now what sort of business would you like to engage in? Would you like to re-engage in copying for some one?"

"No; I would prefer not to make any change."

"Would you like a clerkship in a dry-goods store?"

"There is too much confinement about that. No, I would not like a clerkship; but I am not particular."

"Too much confinement," I cried, "why you keep yourself confined all the time!"

"I would prefer not to take a clerkship," he rejoined, as if to settle that little item at once.

"How would a bar-tender's business suit you? There is no trying of the eye-sight in that."

"I would not like it at all; though, as I said before, I am not particular."

His unwonted wordiness inspirited me. I returned to the charge.

"Well, then, would you like to travel through the country collecting bills for the merchants? That would improve your health."

"No, I would prefer to be doing something else."

"How, then, would going as a companion to Europe, to entertain some young gentleman with your conversation—how would that suit you?"

"Not at all. It does not strike me that there is anything definite about that. I like to be stationary. But I am not particular."

"Stationary you shall be, then," I cried, now losing all patience, and, for the first time in all my exasperating connection with him, fairly flying into a passion. "If you do not go away from these premises before night, I shall feel bound—indeed, I *am* bound—to—to—to quit the premises myself!" I rather absurdly concluded, knowing not with what possible threat to try to frighten his immobility into compliance. Despairing of all further efforts, I was precipitately leaving him, when a final thought occurred to me—one which had not been wholly unindulged before.

"Bartleby," said I, in the kindest tone I could assume under such exciting circumstances, "will you go home with me now—not to my office, but my dwelling—and remain there till we can conclude upon some convenient arrangement for you at our leisure? Come, let us start now, right away."

"No: at present I would prefer not to make any change at all."

I answered nothing; but, effectually dodging every one by the suddenness and rapidity of my flight, rushed from the building, ran up Wall Street towards Broadway, and, jumping into the first omnibus, was soon removed from pursuit. As soon as tranquillity returned, I distinctly perceived that I had now done all that I possibly could, both in respect to the demands of the landlord and his tenants, and with regard to my own desire and sense of duty, to benefit Bartleby, and shield him from rude persecution. I now strove to be entirely care-free and quiescent; and my conscience justified me in the attempt; though, indeed, it was not so successful as I could have wished. So fearful was I of being again hunted out by the incensed landlord and his exasperated tenants, that, surrendering my business to Nippers, for a few days, I drove about the upper part of the town and through the suburbs, in my rockaway; crossed over to Jersey City and Hoboken, and paid fugitive visits to Manhattanville and Astoria. In fact, I almost lived in my rockaway for the time.

When again I entered my office, lo, a note from the landlord lay upon the desk. I opened it with trembling hands. It informed me that the writer had sent to the police, and had Bartleby removed to the Tombs as a vagrant. Moreover, since I knew more about him than any one else, he wished me to appear at that place, and make a suitable statement of the facts. These tidings had a conflicting effect upon me. At first I was indignant; but, at last, almost approved. The landlord's energetic, summary disposition, had led him to adopt a procedure which I do not think I would have decided upon myself; and yet, as a last resort, under such peculiar circumstances, it seemed the only plan.

As I afterwards learned, the poor scrivener, when told that he must be conducted to the Tombs, offered not the slightest obstacle, but, in his pale, unmoving way, silently acquiesced.

Some of the compassionate and curious bystanders joined the party; and headed by one of the constables arm in arm with Bartleby, the silent procession filed its way through all the noise, and heat, and joy of the roaring thoroughfares at noon.

The same day I received the note, I went to the Tombs, or, to speak more properly, the Halls of Justice. Seeking the right officer, I stated the purpose of my call, and was informed that the individual I described was, indeed, within. I then assured the functionary that Bartleby was a perfectly honest man, and greatly to be compassionated, however unaccountably eccentric. I narrated all I knew, and closed by suggesting the idea of letting him remain in as indulgent confinement as possible, till something less harsh might be done—though, indeed, I hardly knew what. At all events, if nothing else could be decided upon, the alms-house must receive him. I then begged to have an interview.

Being under no disgraceful charge, and quite serene and harmless in all his ways, they had permitted him freely to wander about the prison, and, especially, in the inclosed grass-platted yards thereof. And so I found him there, standing all alone in the quietest of the yards, his face towards a high wall, while all around, from the narrow slits of the jail windows, I thought I saw peering out upon him the eyes of murderers and thieves.

"Bartleby!"

"I know you," he said, without looking round—"and I want nothing to say to you."

"It was not I that brought you here, Bartleby," said I, keenly pained at his implied suspicion. "And to you, this should not be so vile a place. Nothing reproachful attaches to you by being here. And see, it is not so sad a place as one might think. Look, there is the sky, and here is the grass."

"I know where I am," he replied, but would say nothing more, and so I left him.

As I entered the corridor again, a broad meat-like man, in an apron, accosted me, and, jerking his thumb over his shoulder, said—"Is that your friend?"

"Yes."

"Does he want to starve? If he does, let him live on the prison fare, that's all."

"Who are you?" asked I, not knowing what to make of such an unofficially speaking person in such a place.

"I am the grub-man. Such gentlemen as have friends here, hire me to provide them with something good to eat."

"Is this so?" said I, turning to the turnkey.

He said it was.

"Well, then," said I, slipping some silver into the grub-man's hands (for so they called him), "I want you to give particular attention to my friend there; let him have the best dinner you can get. And you must be as polite to him as possible."

"Introduce me, will you?" said the grub-man, looking at me with an expression which seemed to say he was all impatience for an opportunity to give a specimen of his breeding.

Thinking it would prove of benefit to the scrivener, I acquiesced; and, asking the grub-man his name, went up with him to Bartleby.

"Bartleby, this is a friend; you will find him very useful to you."

"Your sarvant, sir, your sarvant," said the grub-man, making a low salutation behind his apron. "Hope you find it pleasant here, sir; nice grounds—cool apartments—hope you'll stay with us sometime—try to make it agreeable. What will you have for dinner to-day?"

"I prefer not to dine to-day," said Bartleby, turning away. "It would disagree with me; I am unused to dinners." So saying, he slowly moved to the other side of the inclosure, and took up a position fronting the dead-wall.

"How's this?" said the grub-man, addressing me with a stare of astonishment. "He's odd, ain't he?"

"I think he is a little deranged," said I, sadly.

"Deranged? deranged is it? Well, now, upon my word, I thought that friend of yourn was a gentleman forger; they are always pale and genteel-like, them forgers. I can't help pity 'em—can't help it, sir. Did you know Monroe Edwards?" he added, touchingly, and paused. Then, laying his hand piteously on my shoulder, sighed, "he died of consumption at Sing-Sing.[9] So you weren't acquainted with Monroe?"

"No, I was never socially acquainted with any forgers. But I cannot stop longer. Look to my friend yonder. You will not lose by it. I will see you again."

Some few days after this, I again obtained admission to the Tombs, and went through the corridors in quest of Bartleby; but without finding him.

"I saw him coming from his cell not long ago," said a turnkey, "may be he's gone to loiter in the yards."

So I went in that direction.

"Are you looking for the silent man?" said another turnkey, passing me. "Yonder he lies—sleeping in the yard there. 'Tis not twenty minutes since I saw him lie down."

The yard was entirely quiet. It was not accessible to the common prisoners.

---

[9] The state prison near Ossining, New York.

The surrounding walls of amazing thickness, kept off all sounds behind them. The Egyptian character of the masonry weighed upon me with its gloom. But a soft imprisoned turf grew under foot. The heart of the eternal pyramids, it seemed, wherein, by some strange magic, through the clefts, grass-seed, dropped by birds, had sprung.

Strangely huddled at the base of the wall, his knees drawn up, and lying on his side, his head touching the cold stones, I saw the wasted Bartleby. But nothing stirred. I paused; then went close up to him; stooped over, and saw that his dim eyes were open; otherwise he seemed profoundly sleeping. Something prompted me to touch him. I felt his hand, when a tingling shiver ran up my arm and down my spine to my feet.

The round face of the grub-man peered upon me now. "His dinner is ready. Won't he dine to-day, either? Or does he live without dining?"

"Lives without dining," said I, and closed the eyes.

"Eh!—He's asleep, ain't he?"

"With kings and counselors," murmured I.

There would seem little need for proceeding further in this history. Imagination will readily supply the meagre recital of poor Bartleby's interment. But, ere parting with the reader, let me say, that if this little narrative has sufficiently interested him, to awaken curiosity as to who Bartleby was, and what manner of life he led prior to the present narrator's making his acquaintance, I can only reply, that in such curiosity I fully share, but am wholly unable to gratify it. Yet here I hardly know whether I should divulge one little item of rumor, which came to my ear a few months after the scrivener's decease. Upon what basis it rested, I could never ascertain; and hence, how true it is I cannot now tell. But, inasmuch as this vague report has not been without a certain suggestive interest to me, however said, it may prove the same with some others; and so I will briefly mention it. The report was this: that Bartleby had been a subordinate clerk in the Dead Letter Office at Washington, from which he had been suddenly removed by a change in the administration. When I think over this rumor, hardly can I express the emotions which seize me. Dead letters! does it not sound like dead men? Conceive a man by nature and misfortune prone to a pallid hopelessness, can any business seem more fitted to heighten it than that of continually handling these dead letters, and assorting them for the flames? For by the cart-load they are annually burned. Some times from out the folded paper the pale clerk takes a ring—the finger it was meant for, perhaps, moulders in the grave; a bank-note sent in swiftest charity—he whom it would relieve, nor eats nor hungers any more; pardon for those who died despairing; hope for those who died unhoping; good tidings for those who died stifled by unrelieved calamities. On errands of life, these letters speed to death.

Ah, Bartleby! Ah, humanity!

QUESTIONS

1. What is it about Bartleby that so intrigues and fascinates the narrator? Why does the narrator continue to feel a moral obligation to an employee who refuses to work and curtly rejects kindly offers of help? **2.** With his final utterance, "Ah, Bartleby! Ah, humanity!" the narrator apparently penetrates the mystery of Bartleby. The comments seem to suggest that for the narrator Bartleby is a representative of humanity. In what sense might the narrator come to see Bartleby in this light? **3.** What functions do Turkey and Nippers serve? **4.** Would it be fair to describe Bartleby as a rebel without a cause, as a young man who refuses to participate in a comfortable and well-ordered business world but fails to offer any alternative way of life? Justify your answer.

WRITING TOPICS

1. Readers differ as to whether this is the story of Bartleby or the story of the lawyer-narrator. What is your view? **2.** Why does Melville allow the narrator (and the reader) to discover so little about Bartleby and the causes of his behavior? All we learn of Bartleby's past is contained in the next-to-last paragraph. What, if anything, in this paragraph establishes a link between Bartleby and the narrator?

Gladius Dei *

1902

THOMAS MANN [1875–1955]

Munich was radiant. Above the gay squares and white columned temples, the classicistic monuments and the baroque churches, the leaping fountains, the palaces and parks of the Residence there stretched a sky of luminous blue silk. Well-arranged leafy vistas laced with sun and shade lay basking in the sunshine of a beautiful day in early June.

There was a twittering of birds and a blithe holiday spirit in all the little streets. And in the squares and past the rows of villas there swelled, rolled, and hummed the leisurely, entertaining traffic of that easy-going, charming town. Travellers of all nationalities drove about in the slow little droshkies, looking right and left in aimless curiosity at the house-fronts; they mounted and descended museum stairs. Many windows stood open and music was heard from within: practising on piano, cello, or violin—earnest and well-meant amateur efforts; while from the Odeon came the sound of serious work on several grand pianos.

Young people, the kind that can whistle the Nothung motif,[1] who fill the pit of the Schauspielhaus every evening, wandered in and out of the University and Library with literary magazines in their coat pockets. A court carriage stood before the Academy, the home of the plastic arts, which spreads its white wings between the Türkenstrasse and the Siegestor. And colourful groups of models, picturesque old men, women and children in Albanian costume, stood or lounged at the top of the balustrade.

Indolent, unhurried sauntering was the mode in all the long streets of the northern quarter. There life is lived for pleasanter ends than the driving greed of gain. Young artists with little round hats on the backs of their heads, flowing cravats and no canes—carefree bachelors who paid for their lodgings with colour-sketches—were strolling up and down to let the clear blue morning play upon their mood, also to look at the little girls, the pretty, rather plump type, with the brunette bandeaux, the too large feet, and the unobjectionable morals. Every fifth house had studio windows blinking in the sun. Sometimes a fine piece of architecture stood out from a middle-class row, the work of some imaginative young architect; a wide front with shallow bays and decorations in a bizarre style very expressive and full of invention. Or the door to some monotonous façade would be framed in a bold improvisation of flowing lines and sunny colours, with bacchantes, naiads,[2] and rosy-skinned nudes.

---

* Translated by H. T. Lowe-Porter. *Gladius Dei* means "sword of God."

[1] *Nothung* means "sword." The Nothung motif is a musical passage from Richard Wagner's opera *Siegfried. Schauspielhaus* means "theater."

[2] Bacchantes are female followers of Bacchus, the god of wine; naiads are water nymphs.

It was always a joy to linger before the windows of the cabinet-makers and the shops for modern articles *de luxe*. What a sense for luxurious nothings and amusing, significant line was displayed in the shape of everything! Little shops that sold picture frames, sculptures, and antiques there were in endless number; in their windows you might see those busts of Florentine women of the Renaissance, so full of noble poise and poignant charm. And the owners of the smallest and meanest of these shops spoke of Mino da Fiesole[3] and Donatello as though he had received the rights of reproduction from them personally.

But on the Odeonsplatz, in view of the mighty loggia with the spacious mosaic pavement before it, diagonally opposite to the Regent's palace, people were crowding round the large windows and glass show-cases of the big art-shop owned by M. Blüthenzweig. What a glorious display! There were reproductions of the masterpieces of all the galleries in the world, in costly decorated and tinted frames, the good taste of which was precious in its very simplicity. There were copies of modern paintings, works of a joyously sensuous fantasy, in which the antiques seemed born again in humorous and realistic guise; bronze nudes and fragile ornamental glassware; tall, thin earthenware vases with an iridescent glaze produced by a bath in metal steam; *éditions de luxe* which were triumphs of modern binding and presswork, containing the works of the most modish poets, set out with every possible advantage of sumptuous elegance. Cheek by jowl with these, the portraits of artists, musicians, philosophers, actors, writers, displayed to gratify the public taste for personalities.—In the first window, next the book-shop, a large picture stood on an easel, with a crowd of people in front of it, a fine sepia photograph in a wide old-gold frame, a very striking reproduction of the sensation at this year's great international exhibition, to which public attention is always invited by means of effective and artistic posters stuck up everywhere on hoardings among concert programmes and clever advertisements of toilet preparations.

If you looked into the windows of the book-shop your eye met such titles as *Interior Decoration Since the Renaissance*, *The Renaissance in Modern Decorative Art*, *The Book as Work of Art*, *The Decorative Arts*, *Hunger for Art*, and many more. And you would remember that these thought-provoking pamphlets were sold and read by the thousand and that discussions on these subjects were the preoccupation of all the salons.

You might be lucky enough to meet in person one of the famous fair ones whom less fortunate folk know only through the medium of art; one of those rich and beautiful women whose Titian-blond colouring Nature's most sweet and cunning hand did *not* lay on, but whose diamond parures and beguiling charms had received immortality from the hand of some portrait-painter of genius and whose love-affairs were the talk of the town. These were the queens of the artist balls at carnival-time. They were a little painted, a little made up, full of haughty caprices, worthy of adoration, avid of praise. You might see a

---

[3]Mino da Fiesole and Donatello were fourteenth-century Italian artists.

carriage rolling up the Ludwigstrasse, with such a great painter and his mistress inside. People would be pointing out the sight, standing still to gaze after the pair. Some of them would curtsy. A little more and the very policemen would stand at attention.

Art flourished, art swayed the destinies of the town, art stretched above it her rose-bound sceptre and smiled. On every hand obsequious interest was displayed in her prosperity, on every hand she was served with industry and devotion. There was a downright cult of line, decoration, form, significance, beauty. Munich was radiant.

A youth was coming down the Schellingstrasse. With the bells of cyclists ringing about him he strode across the wooden pavement towards the broad façade of the Ludwigskirche. Looking at him it was as though a shadow passed across the sky, or cast over the spirit some memory of melancholy hours. Did he not love the sun which bathed the lovely city in its festal light? Why did he walk wrapped in his own thoughts, his eyes directed on the ground?

No one in that tolerant and variety-loving town would have taken offence at his wearing no hat; but why need the hood of his ample black cloak have been drawn over his head, shadowing his low, prominent, and peaked forehead, covering his ears and framing his haggard cheeks? What pangs of conscience, what scruples and self-tortures had so availed to hollow out these cheeks? It is frightful, on such a sunny day, to see care sitting in the hollows of the human face. His dark brows thickened at the narrow base of his hooked and prominent nose. His lips were unpleasantly full, his eyes brown and close-lying. When he lifted them, diagonal folds appeared on the peaked brow. His gaze expressed knowledge, limitation, and suffering. Seen in profile his face was strikingly like an old painting preserved at Florence in a narrow cloister cell whence once a frightful and shattering protest issued against life and her triumphs.[4]

Hieronymous walked along the Schellingstrasse with a slow, firm stride, holding his wide cloak together with both hands from inside. Two little girls, two of those pretty, plump little creatures with the bandeaux, the big feet, and the unobjectionable morals, strolled towards him arm in arm, on pleasure bent. They poked each other and laughed, they bent double with laughter, they even broke into a run and ran away still laughing, at his hood and his face. But he paid them no heed. With bent head, looking neither to the right nor to the left, he crossed the Ludwigstrasse and mounted the church steps.

---

[4] We are grateful to Professor George W. Walton of Abilene Christian University for pointing out that the painting described is Fra Bartolommeo's portrait of Girolamo Savonarola (1452–1498), an Italian friar disturbed by the moral decay of the city of Florence. On April 5, 1492, Savonarola experienced his famous vision of a suspended sword of divine justice together with the words: *Ecce gladius Domini super terram cito et velociter* ("Behold the sword of the Lord over the earth swiftly and quickly"). Note that Hieronymus quotes these words at the end of the story. Savonarola's influence in Florence led to the flight of the governor, Piero de' Medici, and in 1497 the friar led a "burning of the vanities" in which the citizens of Florence hurled worldly clothing, paintings, and books into bonfires.

The great wings of the middle portal stood wide open. From somewhere within the consecrated twilight, cool, dank, incense-laden, there came a pale red glow. An old woman with inflamed eyes rose from a prayer-stool and slipped on crutches through the columns. Otherwise the church was empty.

Hieronymus sprinkled brow and breast at the stoup, bent the knee before the high altar, and then paused in the centre nave. Here in the church his stature seemed to have grown. He stood upright and immovable; his head was flung up and his great hooked nose jutted domineeringly above the thick lips. His eyes no longer sought the ground, but looked straight and boldly into the distance, at the crucifix on the high altar. Thus he stood awhile, then retreating he bent the knee again and left the church.

He strode up the Ludwigstrasse, slowly, firmly, with bent head, in the centre of the wide unpaved road, towards the mighty loggia with its statues. But arrived at the Odeonsplatz, he looked up, so that the folds came out on his peaked forehead, and checked his step, his attention being called to the crowd at the windows of the big art-shop of M. Blüthenzweig.

People moved from window to window, pointing out to each other the treasures displayed and exchanging views as they looked over one another's shoulders. Hieronymus mingled among them and did as they did, taking in all these things with his eyes, one by one.

He saw the reproductions of masterpieces from all the galleries in the world, the priceless frames so precious in their simplicity, the Renaissance sculpture, the bronze nudes, the exquisitely bound volumes, the iridescent vases, the portraits of artists, musicians, philosophers, actors, writers; he looked at everything and turned a moment of his scrutiny upon each object. Holding his mantle closely together with both hands from inside, he moved his hood-covered head in short turns from one thing to the next, gazing at each awhile with a dull, inimical, and remotely surprised air, lifting the dark brows which grew so thick at the base of the nose. At length he stood in front of the last window, which contained the startling picture. For a while he looked over the shoulders of people before him and then in his turn reached a position directly in front of the window.

The large red-brown photograph in the choice old-gold frame stood on an easel in the centre. It was a Madonna, but an utterly unconventional one, a work of entirely modern feeling. The figure of the Holy Mother was revealed as enchantingly feminine and beautiful. Her great smouldering eyes were rimmed with darkness, and her delicate and strangely smiling lips were half-parted. Her slender fingers held in a somewhat nervous grasp the hips of a Child, a nude boy of pronounced, almost primitive leanness. He was playing with her breast and glancing aside at the beholder with a wise look in his eyes.

Two other youths stood near Hieronymus, talking about the picture. They were two young men with books under their arms, which they had fetched from the Library or were taking thither. Humanistically educated people, that is, equipped with science and with art.

"The little chap is in luck, devil take me!" said one.

"He seems to be trying to make one envious," replied the other. "A bewildering female!"

"A female to drive a man crazy! Gives you funny ideas about the Immaculate Conception."

"No, she doesn't look exactly immaculate. Have you seen the original?"

"Of course; I was quite bowled over. She makes an even more aphrodisiac impression in colour. Especially the eyes."

"The likeness is pretty plain."

"How so?"

"Don't you know the model? Of course he used his little dressmaker. It is almost a portrait, only with a lot more emphasis on the corruptible. The girl is more innocent."

"I hope so. Life would be altogether too much of a strain if there were many like this *mater amata*."[5]

"The Pinakothek has bought it."

"Really? Well, well! They knew what they were about, anyhow. The treatment of the flesh and the flow of the linen garment are really first-class."

"Yes, an incredibly gifted chap."

"Do you know him?"

"A little. He will have a career, that is certain. He has been invited twice by the Prince Regent."

This last was said as they were taking leave of each other.

"Shall I see you this evening at the theatre?" asked the first. "The Dramatic Club is giving Machiavelli's *Mandragola*."[6]

"Oh, bravo! That will be great, of course. I had meant to go to the Variété, but I shall probably choose our stout Niccolò after all. Good-bye."

They parted, going off to right and left. New people took their places and looked at the famous picture. But Hieronymus stood where he was, motionless, with his head thrust out; his hands clutched convulsively at the mantle as they held it together from inside. His brows were no longer lifted with that cool and unpleasantly surprised expression; they were drawn and darkened; his cheeks, half-shrouded in the black hood, seemed more sunken than ever and his thick lips had gone pale. Slowly his head dropped lower and lower, so that finally his eyes stared upwards at the work of art, while the nostrils of his great nose dilated.

Thus he remained for perhaps a quarter of an hour. The crowd about him melted away, but he did not stir from the spot. At last he turned slowly on the balls of his feet and went hence.

But the picture of the Madonna went with him. Always and ever, whether

---

[5] Beloved mother. The Pinakothek is a municipal art gallery.

[6] Niccolò Machiavelli (1469–1527) was a playwright as well as a political philosopher. His play, *Mandragola*, is a sex comedy.

in his hard and narrow little room or kneeling in the cool church, it stood before his outraged soul, with its smouldering, dark-rimmed eyes, its riddlingly smiling lips—stark and beautiful. And no prayer availed to exorcize it.

But the third night it happened that a command and summons from on high came to Hieronymus, to intercede and lift his voice against the frivolity, blasphemy, and arrogance of beauty. In vain like Moses he protested that he had not the gift of tongues. God's will remained unshaken; in a loud voice He demanded that the faint-hearted Hieronymus go forth to sacrifice amid the jeers of the foe.

And since God would have it so, he set forth one morning and wended his way to the great art-shop of M. Blüthenzweig. He wore his hood over his head and held his mantle together in front from inside with both hands as he went.

The air had grown heavy, the sky was livid and thunder threatened. Once more crowds were besieging the show-cases at the art-shop and especially the window where the photograph of the Madonna stood. Hieronymus cast one brief glance thither; then he pushed up the latch of the glass door hung with placards and art magazines. "As God wills," said he, and entered the shop.

A young girl was somewhere at a desk writing in a big book. She was a pretty brunette thing with bandeaux of hair and big feet. She came up to him and asked pleasantly what he would like.

"Thank you," said Hieronymus in a low voice and looked her earnestly in the face, with diagonal wrinkles in his peaked brow. "I would speak not to you but to the owner of this shop, Herr Blüthenzweig."

She hesitated a little, turned away, and took up her work once more. He stood there in the middle of the shop.

Instead of the single specimens in the show-windows there was here a riot and a heaping-up of luxury, a fullness of colour, line, form, style, invention, good taste, and beauty. Hieronymus looked slowly round him, drawing his mantle close with both hands.

There were several people in the shop besides him. At one of the broad tables running across the room sat a man in a yellow suit, with a black goat's-beard, looking at a portfolio of French drawings, over which he now and then emitted a bleating laugh. He was being waited on by an undernourished and vegetarian young man, who kept on dragging up fresh portfolios. Diagonally opposite the bleating man sat an elegant old dame, examining art embroideries with a pattern of fabulous flowers in pale tones standing together on tall perpendicular stalks. An attendant hovered about her too. A leisurely Englishman in a travelling-cap, with his pipe in his mouth, sat at another table. Cold and smooth-shaven, of indefinite age, in his good English clothes, he sat examining bronzes brought to him by M. Blüthenzweig in person. He was holding up by the head the dainty figure of a nude young girl, immature and delicately articulated, her hands crossed in coquettish innocence upon her breast. He studied her thoroughly, turning her slowly about. M. Blüthenzweig, a man with a short, heavy brown beard and bright brown eyes of exactly the same colour, moved in a semicircle round him, rubbing his hands, praising the statuette with all the terms his vocabulary possessed.

"A hundred and fifty marks, sir," he said in English. "Munich art—very charming, in fact. Simply full of charm, you know. Grace itself. Really extremely pretty, good, admirable, in fact." Then he thought of some more and went on: "Highly attractive, fascinating." Then he began again from the beginning.

His nose lay a little flat on his upper lip, so that he breathed constantly with a slight sniff into his moustache. Sometimes he did this as he approached a customer, stooping over as though he were smelling at him. When Hieronymus entered, M. Blüthenzweig had examined him cursorily in this way, then devoted himself again to his Englishman.

The elegant old dame made her selection and left the shop. A man entered. M. Blüthenzweig sniffed briefly at him as though to scent out his capacity to buy and left him to the young bookkeeper. The man purchased a faience bust of young Piero de' Medici, son of Lorenzo, and went out again. The Englishman began to depart. He had acquired the statuette of the young girl and left amid bowings from M. Blüthenzweig. Then the art-dealer turned to Hieronymus and came forward.

"You wanted something?" he said, without any particular courtesy.

Hieronymus held his cloak together with both hands and looked the other in the face almost without winking an eyelash. He parted his big lips slowly and said:

"I have come to you on account of the picture in the window there, the big photograph, the Madonna." His voice was thick and without modulation.

"Yes, quite right," said M. Blüthenzweig briskly and began rubbing his hands. "Seventy marks in the frame. It is unfadable—a first-class reproduction. Highly attractive and full of charm."

Hieronymus was silent. He nodded his head in the hood and shrank a little into himself as the dealer spoke. Then he drew himself up again and said:

"I would remark to you first of all that I am not in the position to purchase anything, nor have I the desire. I am sorry to have to disappoint your expectations. I regret if it upsets you. But in the first place I am poor and in the second I do not love the things you sell. No, I cannot buy anything."

"No? Well, then?" asked M. Blüthenzweig, sniffing a good deal. "Then may I ask—"

"I suppose," Hieronymus went on, "that being what you are you look down on me because I am not in a position to buy."

"Oh—er—not at all," said M. Blüthenzweig. "Not at all. Only—"

"And yet I beg you to hear me and give some consideration to my words."

"Consideration to your words. H'm—may I ask—"

"You may ask," said Hieronymus, "and I will answer you. I have come to beg you to remove that picture, the big photograph, the Madonna, out of your window and never display it again."

M. Blüthenzweig looked awhile dumbly into Hieronymus's face—as though he expected him to be abashed at the words he had just uttered. But as this did not happen he gave a violent sniff and spoke himself:

"Will you be so good as to tell me whether you are here in any official capacity which authorizes you to dictate to me, or what does bring you here?"

"Oh, no," replied Hieronymus, "I have neither office nor dignity from the state. I have no power on my side, sir. What brings me hither is my conscience alone."

M. Blüthenzweig, searching for words, snorted violently into his moustache. At length he said:

"Your conscience . . . well, you will kindly understand that I take not the faintest interest in your conscience." With which he turned round and moved quickly to his desk at the back of the shop, where he began to write. Both attendants laughed heartily. The pretty Fräulein giggled over her account-book. As for the yellow gentleman with the goat's beard, he was evidently a foreigner, for he gave no sign of comprehension but went on studying the French drawings and emitting from time to time his bleating laugh.

"Just get rid of the man for me," said M. Blüthenzweig shortly over his shoulder to his assistant. He went on writing. The poorly paid young vegetarian approached Hieronymus, smothering his laughter, and the other salesman came up too.

"May we be of service to you in any other way?" the first asked mildly. Hieronymus fixed him with his glazed and suffering eyes.

"No," he said, "you cannot. I beg you to take the Madonna picture out of the window, at once and forever."

"But—why?"

"It is the Holy Mother of God," said Hieronymus in a subdued voice.

"Quite. But you have heard that Herr Blüthenzweig is not inclined to accede to your request."

"We must bear in mind that it is the Holy Mother of God," said Hieronymus again and his head trembled on his neck.

"So we must. But should we not be allowed to exhibit any Madonnas—or paint any?"

"It is not that," said Hieronymus, almost whispering. He drew himself up and shook his head energetically several times. His peaked brow under the hood was entirely furrowed with long, deep cross-folds. "You know very well that it is vice itself that is painted there—naked sensuality. I was standing near two simple young people and overheard with my own ears that it led them astray upon the doctrine of the Immaculate Conception."

"Oh, permit me—that is not the point," said the young salesman, smiling. In his leisure hours he was writing a brochure on the modern movement in art and was well qualified to conduct a cultured conversation. "The picture is a work of art," he went on, "and one must measure it by the appropriate standards as such. It has been very highly praised on all hands. The state has purchased it."

"I know that the state has purchased it," said Hieronymus. "I also know that the artist has twice dined with the Prince Regent. It is common talk—and God knows how people interpret the fact that a man can become famous by such work as this. What does such a fact bear witness to? To the blindness of the world, a blindness inconceivable, if not indeed shamelessly hypocritical. This picture has its origin in sensual lust and is enjoyed in the same—is that true or not? Answer me! And you too answer me, Herr Blüthenzweig!"

A pause ensued. Hieronymus seemed in all seriousness to demand an answer to his question, looking by turns at the staring attendants and the round back M. Blüthenzweig turned upon him, with his own piercing and anguishing brown eyes. Silence reigned. Only the yellow man with the goat's beard, bending over the French drawings, broke it with his bleating laugh.

"It is true," Hieronymus went on in a hoarse voice that shook with his profound indignation. "You do not dare deny it. How then can honour be done to its creator, as though he had endowed mankind with a new ideal possession? How can one stand before it and surrender unthinkingly to the base enjoyment which it purveys, persuading oneself in all seriousness that one is yielding to a noble and elevated sentiment, highly creditable to the human race? Is this reckless ignorance or abandoned hypocrisy? My understanding falters, it is completely at a loss when confronted by the absurd fact that a man can achieve renown on this earth by the stupid and shameless exploitation of the animal instincts. Beauty? What is beauty? What forces are they which use beauty as their tool today—and upon what does it work? No one can fail to know this, Herr Blüthenzweig. But who, understanding it clearly, can fail to feel disgust and pain? It is criminal to play upon the ignorance of the immature, the lewd, the brazen, and the unscrupulous by elevating beauty into an idol to be worshipped, to give it even more power over those who know not affliction and have no knowledge of redemption. You are unknown to me, and you look at me with black looks—yet answer me! Knowledge, I tell you, is the profoundest torture in the world; but it is the purgatory without whose purifying pangs no soul can reach salvation. It is not infantile, blasphemous shallowness that can save us, Herr Blüthenzweig; only knowledge can avail, knowledge in which the passions of our loathsome flesh die away and are quenched."

Silence.—The yellow man with the goat's beard gave a sudden little bleat.

"I think you really must go now," said the underpaid assistant mildly.

But Hieronymus made no move to do so. Drawn up in his hooded cape, he stood with blazing eyes in the centre of the shop and his thick lips poured out condemnation in a voice that was harsh and rusty and clanking.

"Art, you cry; enjoyment, beauty! Enfold the world in beauty and endow all things with the noble grace of style!—Profligate, away! Do you think to wash over with lurid colours the misery of the world? Do you think with the sounds of feasting and music to drown out the voice of the tortured earth? Shameless one, you err! God lets not Himself be mocked, and your impudent deification of the glistering surface of things is an abomination in His eyes. You tell me that I blaspheme art. I say to you that you lie. I do not blaspheme art. Art is no conscienceless delusion, lending itself to reinforce the allurements of the fleshly. Art is the holy torch which turns its light upon all the frightful depths, all the shameful and woeful abysses of life; art is the godly fire laid to the world that, being redeemed by pity, it may flame up and dissolve altogether with its shames and torments.—Take it out, Herr Blüthenzweig, take away the work of that famous painter out of your window—you would do well to burn it with a hot fire and strew its ashes to the four winds—yes, to all the four winds—"

His harsh voice broke off. He had taken a violent backwards step, snatched one arm from his black wrappings, and stretched it passionately forth, gesturing towards the window with a hand that shook as though palsied. And in this commanding attitude he paused. His great hooked nose seemed to jut more than ever, his dark brows were gathered so thick and high that folds crowded upon the peaked forehead shaded by the hood; a hectic flush mantled his hollow cheeks.

But at this point M. Blüthenzweig turned round. Perhaps he was outraged by the idea of burning his seventy-mark reproduction; perhaps Hieronymus's speech had completely exhausted his patience. In any case he was a picture of stern and righteous anger. He pointed with his pen to the door of the shop, gave several short, excited snorts into his moustache, struggled for words, and uttered with the maximum of energy those which he found:

"My fine fellow, if you don't get out at once I will have my packer help you—do you understand?"

"Oh, you cannot intimidate me, you cannot drive me away, you cannot silence my voice!" cried Hieronymus as he clutched his cloak over his chest with his fists and shook his head doughtily. "I know that I am single-handed and powerless, but yet I will not cease until you hear me, Herr Blüthenzweig! Take the picture out of your window and burn it even today! Ah, burn not it alone! Burn all these statues and busts, the sight of which plunges the beholder into sin! Burn these vases and ornaments, these shameless revivals of paganism, these elegantly bound volumes of erotic verse! Burn everything in your shop, Herr Blüthenzweig, for it is a filthiness in God's sight. Burn it, burn it!" he shrieked, beside himself, describing a wild, all-embracing circle with his arm. "The harvest is ripe for the reaper, the measure of the age's shamelessness is full—but I say unto you—"

"Krauthuber!" Herr Blüthenzweig raised his voice and shouted towards a door at the back of the shop. "Come in here at once!"

And in answer to the summons there appeared upon the scene a massive overpowering presence, a vast and awe-inspiring, swollen human bulk, whose limbs merged into each other like links of sausage—a gigantic son of the people, malt-nourished and immoderate, who weighed in, with puffings, bursting with energy, from the packing-room. His appearance in the upper reaches of his form was notable for a fringe of walrus beard; a hide apron fouled with paste covered his body from the waist down, and his yellow shirt-sleeves were rolled back from his heroic arms.

"Will you open the door for this gentleman, Krauthuber?" said M. Blüthenzweig; "and if he should not find the way to it, just help him into the street."

"Huh," said the man, looking from his enraged employer to Hieronymus and back with his little elephant eyes. It was a heavy monosyllable, suggesting reserve force restrained with difficulty. The floor shook with his tread as he went to the door and opened it.

Hieronymus had grown very pale. "Burn—" he shouted once more. He was about to go on when he felt himself turned round by an irresistible power, by a physical preponderance to which no resistance was even thinkable. Slowly and inexorably he was propelled towards the door.

"I am weak," he managed to ejaculate. "My flesh cannot bear the force . . . it cannot hold its ground, no . . . but what does that prove? Burn—"

He stopped. He found himself outside the art-shop. M. Blüthenzweig's giant packer had let him go with one final shove, which set him down on the stone threshold of the shop, supporting himself with one hand. Behind him the door closed with a rattle of glass.

He picked himself up. He stood erect, breathing heavily, and pulled his cloak together with one fist over his breast, letting the other hang down inside. His hollow cheeks had a grey pallor; the nostrils of his great hooked nose opened and closed; his ugly lips were writhen in an expression of hatred and despair and his red-rimmed eyes wandered over the beautiful square like those of a man in a frenzy.

He did not see that people were looking at him with amusement and curiosity. For what he beheld upon the mosaic pavement before the great loggia were all the vanities of this world: the masked costumes of the artist balls, the decorations, vases and art objects, the nude statues, the female busts, the picturesque rebirths of the pagan age, the portraits of famous beauties by the hands of masters, the elegantly bound erotic verse, the art brochures—all these he saw heaped in a pyramid and going up in crackling flames amid loud exultations from the people enthralled by his own frightful words. A yellow background of cloud had drawn up over the Theatinerstrasse, and from it issued wild rumblings; but what he saw was a burning fiery sword, towering in sulphurous light above the joyous city.

"*Gladius Dei super terram* . . ." his thick lips whispered; and drawing himself still higher in his hooded cloak while the hand hanging down inside it twitched convulsively, he murmured, quaking: "*cito et velociter!*"[7]

QUESTIONS

1. How would you characterize Munich as it is described in the first six paragraphs? Does it sound attractive? **2.** What effect does the conversation between the two youths (pp. 393–394) have on the reader? On Hieronymus?

WRITING TOPIC

What finally does the story say about the relationship between art, religion, and morality?

---

[7] *Gladius Dei super terram* means "sword of God over the earth"; *cito et velociter* means "swiftly and quickly."

The Greatest Man in the World   1935

JAMES THURBER   [1894–1961]

Looking back on it now, from the vantage point of 1950, one can only marvel that it hadn't happened long before it did. The United States of America had been, ever since Kitty Hawk, blindly constructing the elaborate petard by which, sooner or later, it must be hoist. It was inevitable that some day there would come roaring out of the skies a national hero of insufficient intelligence, background, and character successfully to endure the mounting orgies of glory prepared for aviators who stayed up a long time or flew a great distance. Both Lindbergh and Byrd, fortunately for national decorum and international amity, had been gentlemen; so had our other famous aviators. They wore their laurels gracefully, withstood the awful weather of publicity, married excellent women, usually of fine family, and quietly retired to private life and the enjoyment of their varying fortunes. No untoward incidents, on a worldwide scale, marred the perfection of their conduct on the perilous heights of fame. The exception to the rule was, however, bound to occur and it did, in July, 1937, when Jack ("Pal") Smurch, erstwhile mechanics' helper in a small garage in Westfield, Iowa, flew a second-hand, single-motored Bresthaven Dragon-Fly III monoplane all the way around the world, without stopping.

Never before in the history of aviation had such a flight as Smurch's ever been dreamed of. No one had even taken seriously the weird floating auxiliary gas tanks, invention of the mad New Hampshire professor of astronomy, Dr. Charles Lewis Gresham, upon which Smurch placed full reliance. When the garage worker, a slightly built, surly, unprepossessing young man of twenty-two appeared at Roosevelt Field in early July, 1937, slowly chewing a great quid of scrap tobacco, and announced "Nobody ain't seen no flyin' yet," the newspapers touched briefly and satirically upon his projected twenty-five-thousand-mile flight. Aeronautical and automotive experts dismissed the idea curtly, implying that it was a hoax, a publicity stunt. The rusty, battered, second-hand plane wouldn't go. The Gresham auxiliary tanks wouldn't work. It was simply a cheap joke.

Smurch, however, after calling on a girl in Brooklyn who worked in the flap-folding department of a large paper-box factory, a girl whom he later described as his "sweet patootie," climbed nonchalantly into his ridiculous plane at dawn of the memorable seventh of July, 1937, spat a curve of tobacco juice into the still air, and took off, carrying with him only a gallon of bootleg gin and six pounds of salami.

When the garage boy thundered out over the ocean the papers were forced to record, in all seriousness, that a mad, unknown young man—his name was variously misspelled—had actually set out upon a preposterous attempt to span the world in a rickety, one-engined contraption, trusting to the long-distance refueling device of a crazy schoolmaster. When, nine days later, without having stopped once, the tiny plane appeared above San Francisco Bay, headed for New York, spluttering and choking, to be sure, but still magnificently and miraculously aloft, the headlines, which long since had crowded everything else off the front page—even the shooting of the Governor of Illinois by the Vileti gang—swelled to unprecedented size, and the news stories began to run to twenty-five and thirty columns. It was noticeable, however, that the accounts of the epoch-making flight touched rather lightly upon the aviator himself. This was not because facts about the hero as a man were too meagre, but because they were too complete.

Reporters, who had been rushed out to Iowa when Smurch's plane was first sighted over the little French coast town of Serly-le-Mar, to dig up the story of the great man's life, had promptly discovered that the story of his life could not be printed. His mother, a sullen short-order cook in a shack restaurant on the edge of a tourists' camping ground near Westfield, met all enquiries as to her son with an angry, "Ah, the hell with him; I hope he drowns." His father appeared to be in jail somewhere for stealing spotlights and laprobes from tourists' automobiles; his younger brother, a weak-minded lad, had but recently escaped from the Preston, Iowa Reformatory and was already wanted in several Western towns for the theft of money-order blanks from post offices. These alarming discoveries were still piling up at the very time that Pal Smurch, the greatest hero of the twentieth century, blear-eyed, dead for sleep, half-starved, was piloting his crazy junk-heap high above the region in which the lamentable story of his private life was being unearthed, headed for New York under greater glory than any man of his time had ever known.

The necessity for printing some account in the papers of the young man's career and personality had led to a remarkable predicament. It was of course impossible to reveal the facts, for a tremendous popular feeling in favor of the young hero had sprung up, like a grass fire, when he was halfway across Europe on his flight around the globe. He was, therefore, described as a modest chap, taciturn, blond, popular with his friends, popular with girls. The only available snapshot of Smurch, taken at the wheel of a phony automobile in a cheap photo studio at an amusement park, was touched up so that the little vulgarian looked quite handsome. His twisted leer was smoothed into a pleasant smile. The truth was, in this way, kept from the youth's ecstatic compatriots; they did not dream that the Smurch family was despised and feared by its neighbors in the obscure Iowa town, nor that the hero himself, because of numerous unsavory exploits, had come to be regarded in Westfield as a nuisance and a menace. He had, the reporters discovered, once knifed the principal of his high school—not mortally, to be sure, but he had knifed him; and on another occasion, surprised in the act of stealing an-altar-cloth from a church, he had bashed the sacristan over the head with a pot of Easter lilies; for each of these offences he had served a sentence in the reformatory.

Inwardly, the authorities, both in New York and in Washington, prayed that an understanding Providence might, however awful such a thing seemed, bring disaster to the rusty, battered plane and its illustrious pilot, whose unheard-of flight had aroused the civilized world to hosannas of hysterical praise. The authorities were convinced that the character of the renowned aviator was such that the limelight of adulation was bound to reveal him to all the world, as a congenital hooligan mentally and morally unequipped to cope with his own prodigious fame. "I trust," said the Secretary of State, at one of many secret Cabinet meetings called to consider the national dilemma, "I trust that his mother's prayer will be answered," by which he referred to Mrs. Emma Smurch's wish that her son might be drowned. It was, however, too late for that—Smurch had leaped the Atlantic and then the Pacific as if they were millponds. At three minutes after two o'clock in the afternoon of 17 July, 1937, the garage boy brought his idiotic plane into Roosevelt Field for a perfect three-point landing.

It had, of course, been out of the question to arrange a modest little reception for the greatest flier in the history of the world. He was received at Roosevelt Field with such elaborate and pretentious ceremonies as rocked the world. Fortunately, however, the worn and spent hero promptly swooned, had to be removed bodily from his plane, and was spirited from the field without having opened his mouth once. Thus he did not jeopardize the dignity of this first reception, a reception illumined by the presence of the Secretaries of War and the Navy, Mayor Michael J. Moriarity of New York, the Premier of Canada, Governors Fanniman, Groves, McFeely, and Critchfield, and a brillant array of European diplomats. Smurch did not, in fact, come to in time to take part in the gigantic hullabaloo arranged at City Hall for the next day. He was rushed to a secluded nursing home and confined to bed. It was nine days before he was able to get up, or to be more exact, before he was permitted to get up. Meanwhile the greatest minds in the country, in solemn assembly, had arranged a secret conference of city, state and government officials, which Smurch was to attend for the purpose of being instructed in the ethics and behavior of heroism.

On the day that the little mechanic was finally allowed to get up and dress and, for the first time in two weeks, took a great chew of tobacco, he was permitted to receive the newspapermen—this by way of testing him out. Smurch did not wait for questions. "Youse guys," he said—and the *Times* man winced— "youse guys can tell the cock-eyed world dat I put it over on Lindbergh, see? Yeh—an' made an ass o' them two frogs." The "two frogs" was a reference to a pair of gallant French fliers who, in attempting a flight only halfway round the world, had, two weeks before, unhappily been lost at sea. The *Times* man was bold enough, at this point, to sketch out for Smurch the accepted formula for interviews in cases of this kind; he explained that there should be no arrogant statements belittling the achievements of other heroes, particularly heroes of foreign nations. "Ah, the hell with that," said Smurch. "I did it, see? I did it, an' I'm talkin' about it." And he did talk about it.

None of this extraordinary interview was, of course, printed. On the contrary, the newspapers, already under the disciplined direction of a secret directorate created for the occasion and composed of statesmen and editors, gave out to a panting and restless world that "Jacky," as he had been arbitrarily nicknamed, would consent to say only that he was very happy and that anyone could have done what he did. "My achievement has been, I fear, slightly exaggerated," the *Times* man's article had him protest, with a modest smile. These newspaper stories were kept from the hero, a restriction which did not serve to abate the rising malevolence of his temper. The situation was, indeed, extremely grave, for Pal Smurch was, as he kept insisting, "rarin' to go." He could not much longer be kept from a nation clamorous to lionize him. It was the most desperate crisis the United States of America had faced since the sinking of the *Lusitania*.

On the afternoon of the twenty-seventh of July, Smurch was spirited away to a conference-room in which were gathered mayors, governors, government officials, behaviorist psychologists, and editors. He gave them each a limp, moist paw and a brief unlovely grin. "Hah ya?" he said. When Smurch was seated, the Mayor of New York arose and, with obvious pessimism, attempted to explain what he must say and how he must act when presented to the world, ending his talk with a high tribute to the hero's courage and integrity. The Mayor was followed by Governor Fanniman of New York, who, after a touching declaration of faith, introduced Cameron Spottiswood, Second Secretary of the American Embassy in Paris, the gentlemen selected to coach Smurch in the amenities of public ceremonies. Sitting in a chair, with a soiled yellow tie in his hand and his shirt open at the throat, unshaved, smoking a rolled cigarette, Jack Smurch listened with a leer on his lips. "I get ya, I get ya," he cut in nastily. "Ya want me to ack like a softy, huh? Ya want me to ack like that—baby-faced Lindbergh, huh? Well, nuts to that, see?" Everyone took in his breath sharply; it was a sigh and a hiss. "Mr. Lindbergh," began a United States Senator, purple with rage, "and Mr. Byrd—" Smurch, who was paring his nails with a jackknife, cut in again, "Byrd!" he exclaimed. "Aw fa God's sake, dat big—" Somebody shut off his blasphemies with a sharp word. A newcomer had entered the room. Everyone stood up, except Smurch, who, still busy with his nails, did not even glance up. "Mr. Smurch," said someone sternly, "the President of the United States!" It had been thought that the presence of the Chief Executive might have a chastening effect upon the young hero, and the former had been, thanks to the remarkable co-operation of the press, secretly brought to the obscure conference-room.

A great, painful silence fell. Smurch looked up, waved a hand at the President. "How ya comin'?" he asked, and began rolling a fresh cigarette. The silence deepened. Someone coughed in a strained way. "Geez, it's hot, ain't it?" said Smurch. He loosened two more shirt buttons, revealing a hairy chest and the tattooed word "Sadie" enclosed in a stenciled heart. The great and important men in the room, faced by the most serious crisis in recent American history, exchanged worried frowns. Nobody seemed to know how to proceed. "Come awn, come awn," said Smurch. "Let's get the hell out of here! When do I start cuttin' in on de parties, huh? And what's they goin' to be *in* it?" He rubbed a thumb and a forefinger together meaningly. "Money!" exclaimed a state senator, shocked, pale. "Yeh, money," said Pal, flipping his cigarette out of a window, "an' big money." He began rolling a fresh cigarette. "Big money," he repeated, frowning over the rice paper. He tilted back in his chair, and leered at each gentleman, separately, the leer of an animal that knows its power, the leer of a leopard loose in a bird-and-dog shop. "Aw, fa God's sake, let's get some place where it's cooler," he said. "I been cooped up plenty for three weeks!"

Smurch stood up and walked over to an open window, where he stood staring down into the street, nine floors below. The faint shouting of newsboys floated up to him. He made out his name. "Hot dog!" he cried, grinning, ecstatic. He leaned out over the sill. "You tell 'em, babies!" he shouted down. "Hot diggity dog!" In the tense little knot of men standing behind him, a quick, mad impulse flared up. An unspoken word of appeal, of command, seemed to ring through the room. Yet it was deadly silent. Charles K. L. Brand, secretary to the Mayor of New York City, happened to be standing nearest Smurch; he looked inquiringly at the President of the United States. The President, pale, grim, nodded shortly. Brand, a tall, powerfully built man, once a tackle at Rutgers, stepped forward, seized the greatest man in the world by his left shoulder and the seat of his pants, and pushed him out of the window.

"My God, he's fallen out the window!" cried a quick-witted editor.

"Get me out of here!" cried the President. Several men sprang to his side and he was hurriedly escorted out of a door toward a side-entrance of the building. The editor of the Associated Press took charge, being used to such things. Crisply he ordered certain men to leave, others to stay; quickly he outlined a story which all the papers were to agree on, sent two men to the street to handle that end of the tragedy, commanded a Senator to sob and two Congressmen to go to pieces nervously. In a word, he skillfully set the stage for the gigantic task that was to follow, the task of breaking to a grief-stricken world the sad story of the untimely, accidental death of its most illustrious and spectacular figure.

The funeral was, as you know, the most elaborate, the finest, the solemnest, and the saddest ever held in the United States of America. The monument in Arlington Cemetery, with its clean white shaft of marble and the simple device of a tiny plane carved on its base, is a place for pilgrims, in deep reverence, to visit. The nations of the world paid lofty tributes to little Jacky Smurch, America's greatest hero. At a given hour there were two minutes of silence throughout the nation. Even the inhabitants of the small, bewildered town of Westfield, Iowa, observed this touching ceremony; agents of the Department of Justice saw to that. One of them was especially assigned to stand grimly in the doorway of a little shack restaurant on the edge of the tourists' camping ground just outside the town. There, under his stern scrutiny, Mrs. Emma Smurch bowed her head above two hamburger steaks sizzling on her grill—bowed her head and turned away, so that the Secret Service man could not see the twisted, strangely familiar, leer on her lips.

The Second Tree
from the Corner

E. B. WHITE   [1899–1985]

"Ever have any bizarre thoughts?" asked the doctor.

Mr. Trexler failed to catch the word. "What kind?" he said.

"Bizarre," repeated the doctor, his voice steady. He watched his patient for any slight change of expression, any wince. It seemed to Trexler that the doctor was not only watching him closely, but was creeping slowly toward him, like a lizard toward a bug. Trexler shoved his chair back an inch and gathered himself for a reply. He was about to say "Yes" when he realized that if he said yes the next question would be unanswerable. Bizarre thoughts, bizarre thoughts? Ever have any bizarre thoughts? What kind of thoughts *except* bizarre had he had since the age of two?

Trexler felt the time passing, the necessity for an answer. These psychiatrists were busy men, overloaded, not to be kept waiting. The next patient was probably already perched out there in the waiting room, lonely, worried, shifting around on the sofa, his mind stuffed with bizarre thoughts and amorphous fears. Poor bastard, thought Trexler. Out there all alone in that misshapen antechamber, staring at the filing cabinet and wondering whether to tell the doctor about that day on the Madison Avenue bus.

Let's see, bizarre thoughts. Trexler dodged back along the dreadful corridor of the years to see what he could find. He felt the doctor's eyes upon him and knew that time was running out. Don't be so conscientious, he said to himself. If a bizarre thought is indicated here, just reach into the bag and pick anything at all. A man as well supplied with bizarre thoughts as you are should have no difficulty producing one for the record. Trexler darted into the bag, hung for a moment before one of his thoughts, as a hummingbird pauses in the delphinium. No, he said, not that one. He darted to another (the one about the rhesus monkey), paused, considered. No, he said, not that.

Trexler knew he must hurry. He had already used up pretty nearly four seconds since the question had been put. But it was an impossible situation—just one more lousy, impossible situation such as he was always getting himself into. When, he asked himself, are you going to quit maneuvering yourself into a pocket? He made one more effort. This time he stopped at the asylum, only the bars were lucite—fluted, retractable. Not here, he said. Not this one.

He looked straight at the doctor. "No," he said quietly. "I never have any bizarre thoughts."

The doctor sucked in on his pipe, blew a plume of smoke toward the rows of medical books. Trexler's gaze followed the smoke. He managed to make out one of the titles. "The Genito-Urinary System." A bright wave of fear swept

223

cleanly over him, and he winced under the first pain of kidney stones. He remembered when he was a child, the first time he ever entered a doctor's office, sneaking a look at the titles of the books—and the flush of fear, the shirt wet under the arms, the book on t.b., the sudden knowledge that he was in the advanced stages of consumption, the quick vision of the hemorrhage. Trexler sighed wearily. Forty years, he thought, and I still get thrown by the title of a medical book. Forty years and I still can't stay on life's little bucky horse. No wonder I'm sitting here in this dreary joint at the end of this woebegone afternoon, lying about my bizarre thoughts to a doctor who looks, come to think of it, rather tired.

The session dragged on. After about twenty minutes, the doctor rose and knocked his pipe out. Trexler got up, knocked the ashes out of his brain, and waited. The doctor smiled warmly and stuck out his hand. "There's nothing the matter with you—you're just scared. Want to know how I know you're scared?"

"How?" asked Trexler.

"Look at the chair you've been sitting in! See how it has moved back away from my desk? You kept inching away from me while I asked you questions. That means you're scared."

"Does it?" said Trexler, faking a grin. "Yeah, I suppose it does."

They finished shaking hands. Trexler turned and walked out uncertainly along the passage, then into the waiting room and out past the next patient, a ruddy pin-striped man who was seated on the sofa twirling his hat nervously and staring straight ahead at the files. Poor, frightened guy, thought Trexler, he's probably read in the *Times* that one American male out of every two is going to die of heart disease by twelve o'clock next Thursday. It says that in the paper almost every morning. And he's also probably thinking about that day on the Madison Avenue bus.

A week later, Trexler was back in the patient's chair. And for several weeks thereafter he continued to visit the doctor, always toward the end of the afternoon, when the vapors hung thick above the pool of the mind and darkened the whole region of the East Seventies.[1] He felt no better as time went on, and he found it impossible to work. He discovered that the visits were becoming routine and that although the routine was one to which he certainly did not look forward, at least he could accept it with cool resignation, as once, years ago, he had accepted a long spell with a dentist who had settled down to a steady fooling with a couple of dead teeth. The visits, moreover, were now assuming a pattern recognizable to the patient.

Each session would begin with a résumé of symptoms—the dizziness in the streets, the constricting pain in the back of the neck, the apprehensions, the tightness of the scalp, the inability to concentrate, the despondency and the melancholy times, the feeling of pressure and tension, the anger at not being able to work, the anxiety over work not done, the gas on the stomach. Dullest set of neurotic symptoms in the world, Trexler would think, as he obediently

---

[1] The East Seventies is a neighborhood, much of it elegant and expensive, in Manhattan.

trudged back over them for the doctor's benefit. And then, having listened attentively to the recital, the doctor would spring his question: "Have you ever found anything that gives you relief?" And Trexler would answer, "Yes. A drink." And the doctor would nod his head knowingly.

As he became familiar with the pattern Trexler found that he increasingly tended to identify himself with the doctor, transferring himself into the doctor's seat—probably (he thought) some rather slick form of escapism. At any rate, it was nothing new for Trexler to identify himself with other people. Whenever he got into a cab, he instantly became the driver, saw everything from the hackman's angle (and the reaching over with the right hand, the nudging of the flag, the pushing it down, all the way down along the side of the meter), saw everything—traffic, fare, everything—through the eyes of Anthony Rocco, or Isidore Freedman, or Matthew Scott. In a barbershop, Trexler was the barber, his fingers curled around the comb, his hand on the tonic. Perfectly natural, then, that Trexler should soon be occupying the doctor's chair, asking the questions, waiting for the answers. He got quite interested in the doctor, in this way. He liked him, and he found him a not too difficult patient.

It was on the fifth visit, about halfway through, that the doctor turned to Trexler and said, suddenly, "What do you want?" He gave the word "want" special emphasis.

"I d'know," replied Trexler uneasily. "I guess nobody knows the answer to that one."

"Sure they do," replied the doctor.

"Do *you* know what *you* want?" asked Trexler narrowly.

"Certainly," said the doctor. Trexler noticed that at this point the doctor's chair slid slightly backward, away from him. Trexler stifled a small, internal smile. Scared as a rabbit, he said to himself. Look at him scoot!

"What *do* you want?" continued Trexler, pressing his advantage, pressing it hard.

The doctor glided back another inch away from his inquisitor. "I want a wing on the small house I own in Westport. I want more money, and more leisure to do the things I want to do."

Trexler was just about to say, "And what are those things you want to do, Doctor?" when he caught himself. Better not go too far, he mused. Better not lose possession of the ball. And besides, he thought, what the hell goes on here, anyway—me paying fifteen bucks a throw for these séances and then doing the work myself, asking the questions, weighing the answers. So he wants a new wing! There's a fine piece of theatrical gauze for you! A new wing.

Trexler settled down again and resumed the role of patient for the rest of the visit. It ended on a kindly, friendly note. The doctor reassured him that his fears were the cause of his sickness, and that his fears were unsubstantial. They shook hands, smiling.

Trexler walked dizzily through the empty waiting room and the doctor followed along to let him out. It was late; the secretary had shut up shop and gone home. Another day over the dam. "Goodbye," said Trexler. He stepped into the street, turned west toward Madison, and thought of the doctor all alone there, after hours, in that desolate hole—a man who worked longer hours than his secretary. Poor, scared, overworked bastard, thought Trexler. And that new wing!

It was an evening of clearing weather, the Park showing green and desirable in the distance, the last daylight applying a high lacquer to the brick and brownstone walls and giving the street scene a luminous and intoxicating splendor. Trexler meditated, as he walked, on what he wanted. "What do you want?" he heard again. Trexler knew what he wanted, and what, in general, all men wanted; and he was glad, in a way, that it was both inexpressible and unattainable, and that it wasn't a wing. He was satisfied to remember that it was deep, formless, enduring, and impossible of fulfillment, and that it made men sick, and that when you sauntered along Third Avenue and looked through the doorways into the dim saloons, you could sometimes pick out from the unregenerate ranks the ones who had not forgotten, gazing steadily into the bottoms of the glasses on the long chance that they could get another little peek at it. Trexler found himself renewed by the remembrance that what he wanted was at once great and microscopic, and that although it borrowed from the nature of large deeds and of youthful love and of old songs and early intimations, it was not any one of these things, and that it had not been isolated or pinned down, and that a man who attempted to define it in the privacy of a doctor's office would, fall flat on his face.

Trexler felt invigorated. Suddenly his sickness seemed health, his dizziness stability. A small tree, rising between him and the light, stood there saturated with the evening, each gilt-edged leaf perfectly drunk with excellence and delicacy. Trexler's spine registered an ever so slight tremor as it picked up this natural disturbance in the lovely scene. "I want the second tree from the corner, just as it stands," he said, answering an imaginary question from an imaginary physician. And he felt a slow pride in realizing that what he wanted none could bestow, and that what he had none could take away. He felt content to be sick, unembarrassed at being afraid; and in the jungle of his fear he glimpsed (as he had so often glimpsed them before) the flashy tail feathers of the bird courage.

Then he thought once again of the doctor, and of his being left there all alone, tired, frightened. (The poor, scared guy, thought Trexler.) Trexler began humming "Moonshine Lullaby," his spirit reacting instantly to the hypodermic of Merman's[2] healthy voice. He crossed Madison, boarded a downtown bus, and rode all the way to Fifty-second Street before he had a thought that could rightly have been called bizarre.

QUESTIONS

1. At the beginning of the story, the doctor asks Mr. Trexler if he ever had any bizarre thoughts. What is Trexler's reply? Why does he give that reply? Can you

---

[2] Ethel Merman (1909–1984), a musical comedy star with a strong voice.

imagine, from Trexler's ruminations, what sort of bizarre thoughts he might have had? Would it be more effective if White indicated precisely what Trexler's thoughts had been? Explain. **2.** The seminal question in this story is put by the doctor to Trexler: "What do you want?" What is Trexler's answer? What is the doctor's response? What do *you* want? **3.** Trexler, we are told, knew what he wanted and was glad "that it was both inexpressible and unattainable." In what sense is Trexler's desire inexpressible and unattainable? **4.** In what sense might this be a story about the difference between being afraid and unafraid?

WRITING TOPIC

How does Trexler's recognition that he wants "the second tree from the corner, just as it stands" result in his feeling "content to be sick"?

the elements of

Strunk / white

The Ones Who Walk Away from Omelas 1974

URSULA K. LE GUIN [b. 1929]

With a clamor of bells that set the swallows soaring, the Festival of Summer came to the city Omelas, bright-towered by the sea. The rigging of the boats in harbor sparkled with flags. In the streets between houses with red roofs and painted walls, between old moss-grown gardens and under avenues of trees, past great parks and public buildings, processions moved. Some were decorous: old people in long stiff robes of mauve and grey, grave master workmen, quiet, merry women carrying their babies and chatting as they walked. In other streets the music beat faster, a shimmering of gong and tambourine, and the people went dancing, the procession was a dance. Children dodged in and out, their high calls rising like the swallows' crossing flights over the music and the singing. All the processions wound towards the north side of the city, where on the great water-meadow called the Green Fields boys and girls, naked in the bright air, with mud-stained feet and ankles and long, lithe arms, exercised their restive horses before the race. The horses wore no gear at all but a halter without bit. Their manes were braided with streamers of silver, gold, and green. They flared their nostrils and pranced and boasted to one another; they were vastly excited, the horse being the only animal who has adopted our ceremonies as his own. Far off to the north and west the mountains stood up half encircling Omelas on her bay. The air of morning was so clear that the snow still crowning the Eighteen Peaks burned with white-gold fire across the miles of sunlit air, under the dark blue of the sky. There was just enough wind to make the banners that marked the racecourse snap and flutter now and then. In the silence of the broad green meadows one could hear the music winding through the city streets, farther and nearer and ever approaching, a cheerful faint sweetness of the air that from time to time trembled and gathered together and broke out into the great joyous clanging of the bells.

Joyous! How is one to tell about joy? How describe the citizens of Omelas?

They were not simple folk, you see, though they were happy. But we do not say the words of cheer much any more. All smiles have become archaic. Given a description such as this one tends to make certain assumptions. Given a description such as this one tends to look next for the King, mounted on a splendid stallion and surrounded by his noble knights, or perhaps in a golden litter borne by great-muscled slaves. But there was no king. They did not use swords, or keep slaves. They were not barbarians. I do not know the rules and laws of their society, but I suspect that they were singularly few. As they did without monarchy and slavery, so they also go on without the stock exchange, the advertisement, the secret police, and the bomb. Yet I repeat that these were not

228

simple folk, not dulcet shepherds, noble savages, bland utopians. They were not less complex than us. The trouble is that we have a bad habit, encouraged by pedants and sophisticates, of considering happiness as something rather stupid. Only pain is intellectual, only evil interesting. This is the treason of the artist: a refusal to admit the banality of evil and the terrible boredom of pain. If you can't lick 'em, join 'em. If it hurts, repeat it. But to praise despair is to condemn delight, to embrace violence is to lose hold of everything else. We have almost lost hold; we can no longer describe a happy man, nor make any celebration of joy. How can I tell you about the people of Omelas? They were not naïve and happy children—though their children were, in fact, happy. They were mature, intelligent, passionate adults whose lives were not wretched. O miracle! but I wish I could describe it better. I wish I could convince you. Omelas sounds in my words like a city in a fairy tale, long ago and far away, once upon a time. Perhaps it would be best if you imagined it as your own fancy bids, assuming it will rise to the occasion, for certainly I cannot suit you all. For instance, how about technology? I think that there would be no cars or helicopters in and above the streets; this follows from the fact that the people of Omelas are happy people. Happiness is based on a just discrimination of what is necessary, what is neither necessary nor destructive, and what is destructive. In the middle category, however—that of the unnecessary but undestructive, that of comfort, luxury, exuberance, etc.—they could perfectly well have central heating, subway trains, washing machines, and all kinds of marvelous devices not yet invented here, floating light-sources, fuelless power, a cure for the common cold. Or they could have none of that: it doesn't matter. As you like it. I incline to think that people from towns up and down the coast have been coming in to Omelas during the last days before the Festival on very fast little trains and double-decker trams, and that the train station of Omelas is actually the handsomest building in town, though plainer than the magnificent Farmers' Market. But even granted trains, I fear that Omelas so far strikes some of you as goody-goody. Smiles, bells, parades, horses, bleh. If so, please add an orgy. If an orgy would help, don't hesitate. Let us not, however, have temples from which issue beautiful nude priests and priestesses already half in ecstasy and ready to copulate with any man or woman, lover or stranger, who desires union with the deep godhead of the blood, although that was my first idea. But really it would be better not to have any temples in Omelas—at least, not manned temples. Religion yes, clergy no. Surely the beautiful nudes can just wander about, offering themselves like divine soufflés to the hunger of the needy and the rapture of the flesh. Let them join the processions. Let tambourines be struck above the copulations, and the glory of desire be proclaimed upon the gongs, and (a not unimportant point) let the offspring of these delightful rituals be beloved and looked after by all. One thing I know there is none of in Omelas is guilt. But what else should there be? I thought at first there were no drugs, but that is puritanical. For those who like it, the faint insistent sweetness of *drooz* may perfume the ways of the city, *drooz* which first brings a great lightness and brilliance to the mind and limbs, and then after some hours a dreamy languor, and wonderful visions at last of the very arcana and inmost secrets of the Universe, as well as exciting the pleasure of sex beyond all belief; and it is not habit-forming. For more modest tastes I think there ought to be beer. What else, what else belongs in the joyous city? The sense of victory, surely, the celebration of courage. But as we did without clergy, let us do without soldiers. The joy built upon successful slaughter is not the right kind of joy; it will not do; it is fearful and it is trivial. A boundless and generous contentment, a magnanimous triumph felt not against some outer enemy but in communion with the finest and fairest in the souls of all men everywhere and the splendor of the world's summer: this is what swells the hearts of the people of Omelas, and the victory they celebrate is that of life. I really don't think many of them need to take *drooz*.

Most of the processions have reached the Green Fields by now. A marvelous smell of cooking goes forth from the red and blue tents of the provisioners. The faces of small children are amiably sticky; in the benign grey beard of a man a couple of crumbs of rich pastry are entangled. The youths and girls have mounted their horses and are beginning to group around the starting line of the course. An old woman, small, fat, and laughing, is passing out flowers from a basket, and tall young men wear her flowers in their shining hair. A child of nine or ten sits at the edge of the crowd, alone, playing on a wooden flute. People pause to listen, and they smile, but they do not speak to him, for he never ceases playing and never sees them, his dark eyes wholly rapt in the sweet, thin magic of the tune.

He finishes, and slowly lowers his hands holding the wooden flute.

As if that little private silence were the signal, all at once a trumpet sounds from the pavilion near the starting line: imperious, melancholy, piercing. The horses rear on their slender legs, and some of them neigh in answer. Sober-faced, the young riders stroke the horses' necks and soothe them, whispering, "Quiet, quiet, there my beauty, my hope. . . ." They begin to form in rank along the starting line. The crowds along the racecourse are like a field of grass and flowers in the wind. The Festival of Summer has begun.

Do you believe? Do you accept the festival, the city, the joy? No? Then let me describe one more thing.

In a basement under one of the beautiful public buildings of Omelas, or perhaps in the cellar of one of its spacious private homes, there is a room. It has one locked door, and no window. A little light seeps in dustily between cracks in the boards, secondhand from a cobwebbed window somewhere across the cellar. In one corner of the little room a couple of mops, with stiff, clotted, foul-smelling heads, stand near a rusty bucket. The floor is dirt, a little damp to the touch, as cellar dirt usually is. The room is about three paces long and two wide: a mere broom closet or disused tool room. In the room a child is sitting. It could be a boy or a girl. It looks about six, but actually is nearly ten. It is feeble-minded. Perhaps it was born defective, or perhaps it has become imbecile through fear, malnutrition, and neglect. It picks its nose and occasionally fumbles vaguely with its toes or genitals, as it sits hunched in the corner farthest from the bucket and the two mops. It is afraid of the mops. It finds them horrible. It shuts its eyes, but it knows the mops are still standing there; and the door is locked; and nobody will come. The door is always locked; and nobody ever comes, except that sometimes—the child has no understanding of time or interval—sometimes the door rattles terribly and opens, and a person, or several people, are there. One of them may come in and kick the child to make it stand up. The others never come close, but peer in at it with frightened, disgusted eyes. The food bowl and the water jug are hastily filled, the door is locked, the eyes disappear. The people at the door never say anything, but the child, who has not always lived in the tool room, and can remember sunlight and its mother's voice, sometimes speaks. "I will be good," it says. "Please let me out. I will be good!" They never answer. The child used to scream for help at night, and cry a good deal, but now it only makes a kind of whining, "eh-haa, eh-haa," and it speaks less and less often. It is so thin there are no calves to its legs; its belly protrudes; it lives on a half-bowl of corn meal and grease a day. It is naked. Its buttocks and thighs are a mass of festered sores, as it sits in its own excrement continually.

They all know it is there, all the people of Omelas. Some of them have come to see it, others are content merely to know it is there. They all know that it has to be there. Some of them understand why, and some do not, but all understand that their happiness, the beauty of their city, the tenderness of their friendships, the health of their children, the wisdom of their scholars, the skill of their makers, even the abundance of their harvest and the kindly weathers of their skies, depend wholly on this child's abominable misery.

This is usually explained to children when they are between eight and twelve, whenever they seem capable of understanding; and most of those who come to see the child are young people, though often enough an adult comes, or comes back, to see the child. No matter how well the matter has been explained to them, these young spectators are always shocked and sickened at the sight. They feel disgust, which they had thought themselves superior to. They feel anger, outrage, impotence, despite all the explanations. They would like to do something for the child. But there is nothing they can do. If the child were brought up into the sunlight out of that vile place, if it were cleaned and fed and comforted, that would be a good thing, indeed; but if it were done, in that day and hour all the prosperity and beauty and delight of Omelas would wither and be destroyed. Those are the terms. To exchange all the goodness and grace of every life in Omelas for that single, small improvement: to throw away the happiness of thousands for the chance of the happiness of one: that would be to let guilt within the walls indeed.

The terms are strict and absolute; there may not even be a kind word spoken to the child.

Often the young people go home in tears, or in a tearless rage, when they have seen the child and faced this terrible paradox. They may brood over it for weeks or years. But as time goes on they begin to realize that even if the child could be released, it would not get much good of its freedom: a little vague pleasure of warmth and food, no doubt, but little more. It is too degraded and imbecile to know any real joy. It has been afraid too long ever to be free of fear. Its habits are too uncouth for it to respond to humane treatment. Indeed, after so long it would probably be wretched without walls about it to protect it, and darkness for its eyes, and its own excrement to sit in. Their tears at the bitter injustice dry when they begin to perceive the terrible justice of reality, and to accept it. Yet it is their tears and anger, the trying of their generosity and the acceptance of their helplessness, which are perhaps the true source of the splendor of their lives. Theirs is no vapid, irresponsible happiness. They know that they, like the child, are not free. They know compassion. It is the existence of the child, and their knowledge of its existence, that makes possible the nobility of their architecture, the poignancy of their music, the profundity of their science. It is because of the child that they are so gentle with children. They know that if the wretched one were not there snivelling in the dark, the other one, the flute-player, could make no joyful music as the young riders line up in their beauty for the race in the sunlight of the first morning of summer.

Now do you believe in them? Are they not more credible? But there is one more thing to tell, and this is quite incredible.

At times one of the adolescent girls or boys who go to see the child does not go home to weep or rage, does not, in fact, go home at all. Sometimes also a man or woman much older falls silent for a day or two, and then leaves home. These people go out into the street, and walk down the street alone. They keep walking, and walk straight out of the city of Omelas, through the beautiful gates. They keep walking across the farmlands of Omelas. Each one goes alone, youth or girl, man or woman. Night falls; the traveler must pass down village streets, between the houses with yellow-lit windows, and on out into the darkness of the fields. Each alone, they go west or north, towards the mountains. They go on. They leave Omelas, they walk ahead into the darkness, and they do not come back. The place they go towards is a place even less imaginable to most of us than the city of happiness. I cannot describe it at all. It is possible that it does not exist. But they seem to know where they are going, the ones who walk away from Omelas.

The Sandman

1972

DONALD BARTHELME [1931–1989]

Dear Dr. Hodder, I realize that it is probably wrong to write a letter to one's girl friend's shrink but there are several things going on here that I think ought to be pointed out to you. I thought of making a personal visit but the situation then, as I'm sure you understand, would be completely untenable—I would be *visiting a psychiatrist*. I also understand that in writing to you I am in some sense interfering with the process but you don't have to discuss with Susan what I have said. Please consider this an "eyes only" letter. Please think of it as personal and confidential.

You must be aware, first, that because Susan is my girl friend pretty much everything she discusses with you she also discusses with me. She tells me what she said and what you said. We have been seeing each other for about six months now and I am pretty familiar with her story, or stories. Similarly, with your responses, or at least the general pattern. I know, for example, that my habit of referring to you as "the sandman" annoys you but let me assure you that I mean nothing unpleasant by it. It is simply a nickname. The reference is to the old rhyme: "Sea-sand does the sandman bring/Sleep to end the day/ He dusts the children's eyes with sand/And steals their dreams away." (This is a variant; there are other versions, but this is the one I prefer.) I also understand that you are a little bit shaky because the prestige of analysis is now, as I'm sure you know far better than I, at a nadir. This must tend to make you nervous and who can blame you? One always tends to get a little bit shook when one's methodology is in question. Of course! (By the bye, let me say that I am very pleased that you are one of the ones that talk, instead of just sitting there. I think that's a good thing, an excellent thing, I congratulate you.)

To the point. I fully understand that Susan's wish to terminate with you and buy a piano instead has disturbed you. You have every right to be disturbed and to say that she is not electing the proper course, that what she says conceals something else, that she is evading reality, etc., etc. Go ahead. But there is one possibility here that you might be, just might be, missing. Which is that she means it.

Susan says: "I want to buy a piano."

You think: She wishes to terminate the analysis and escape into the piano.

Or: Yes, it is true that her father wanted her to be a concert pianist and that she studied for twelve years with Goetzmann. But she does not really want to reopen that can of maggots. She wants me to disapprove.

Or: Having failed to achieve a career as a concert pianist, she wishes to fail again. She is now too old to achieve the original objective. The spontaneous organization of defeat!

Or: She is flirting again.

Or:

Or:

Or:

Or:

The one thing you cannot consider, by the nature of your training and of the discipline itself, is that she really might want to terminate the analysis and buy a piano. That the piano might be more necessary and valuable to her than the analysis.[1]

What we really have to consider here is the locus of hope. Does hope reside in the analysis or rather in the piano? As a shrink rather than a piano salesman you would naturally tend to opt for the analysis. But there are differences. The piano salesman can stand behind his product; you, unfortunately, cannot. A Steinway is a known quantity, whereas an analysis can succeed or fail. I don't reproach you for this, I simply note it. (An interesting question: Why do laymen feel such a desire to, in plain language, fuck over shrinks? As I am doing here, in a sense? I don't mean hostility in the psychoanalytic encounter, I mean in general. This is an interesting phenomenon and should be investigated by somebody.)

It might be useful if I gave you a little taste of my own experience of analysis. I only went five or six times. Dr. Behring was a tall thin man who never said anything much. If you could get a "What comes to mind?" out of him you were doing splendidly. There was a little incident that is, perhaps, illustrative. I went for my hour one day and told him about something I was worried about. (I was then working for a newspaper down in Texas.) There was a story that four black teenagers had come across a little white boy, about ten, in a vacant lot, sodomized him repeatedly and then put him inside a refrigerator and closed the door (this was before they had that requirement that abandoned refrigerators had to have their doors removed) and he suffocated. I don't know to this day what actually happened, but the cops had picked up *some* black kids and were reportedly beating the shit out of them in an effort to make them confess. I was not on the police run at that time but one of the police reporters told me about it and I told Dr. Behring. A good liberal, he grew white with anger and said what was I doing about it? It was the first time he had talked. So I was shaken— it hadn't occurred to me that I was required to do something about it, he was right—and after I left I called my then sister-in-law, who was at that time secretary to a City Councilman. As you can imagine, such a position is a very powerful one—the councilmen are mostly off making business deals and the executive secretaries run the office—and she got on to the chief of police with an inquiry as to what was going on and if there was any police brutality involved and if so, how much. The case was a very sensational one, you see; *Ebony* had a writer down there trying to cover it but he couldn't get in to see the boys and the cops had roughed him up some, they couldn't understand at that time that

---

[1] For an admirable discussion of this sort of communication failure and many other matters of interest see Percy, "Toward a Triadic Theory of Meaning," *Psychiatry*, Vol. 35 (February 1972), pp. 6–14 *et seq.* [Editors' note: This and all subsequent footnotes to this story are part of the text.]

there could be such a thing as a black reporter. They understood that they had to be a little careful with the white reporters, but a black reporter was beyond them. But my sister-in-law threw her weight (her Councilman's weight) around a bit and suggested to the chief that if there was a serious amount of brutality going on the cops had better stop it, because there was too much outside interest in the case and it would be extremely bad PR if the brutality stuff got out. I also called a guy I knew pretty high up in the sheriff's department and suggested that *he* suggest to his colleagues that they cool it. I hinted at unspeakable political urgencies and he picked it up. The sheriff's department was separate from the police department but they both operated out of the Courthouse Building and they interacted quite a bit, in the normal course. So the long and short of it was that the cops decided to show the four black kids at a press conference to demonstrate that they weren't really beat all to rags, and that took place at four in the afternoon. I went and the kids looked O.K., except for one whose teeth were out and who the cops said had fallen down the stairs. Well, we all know the falling-down-the-stairs story but the point was the *degree* of mishandling and it was clear that the kids had not been half-killed by the cops, as the rumor stated. They were walking and talking naturally, although scared to death, as who would not be? There weren't any TV pictures because the newspaper people always pulled out the plugs of the TV people, at important moments, in those days—it was a standard thing. Now while I admit it sounds callous to be talking about the degree of brutality being minimal, let me tell you that it was no small matter, in that time and place, to force the cops to show the kids to the press at all. It was an achievement, of sorts. So about eight o'clock I called Dr. Behring at home, I hope interrupting his supper, and told him that the kids were O.K., relatively, and he said that was fine, he was glad to hear it. They were later no-billed and I stopped seeing him. That was my experience of analysis and that it may have left me a little sour, I freely grant. Allow for this bias.

To continue. I take exception to your remark that Susan's "openness" is a form of voyeurism. This remark interested me for a while, until I thought about it. Voyeurism I take to be an eroticized expression of curiosity whose chief phenomenological characteristic is the distance maintained between the voyeur and the object. The tension between the desire to draw near the object and the necessity to maintain the distance becomes a libidinous energy nondischarge, which is what the voyeur seeks.[2] The tension. But your remark indicates, in my opinion, a radical misreading of the problem. Susan's "openness"—a willingness of the heart, if you will allow such a term—is not at all comparable to the activities of the voyeur. Susan draws near. Distance is not her thing—not by a long chalk. Frequently, as you know, she gets burned, but she always tries again. What is operating here, I suggest, is an attempt on your part to "stabilize" Susan's behavior in reference to a state-of-affairs that you feel should obtain. Susan gets married and lives happily ever after. Or: There is within Susan a

[2] See, for example, Straus, "Shame As a Historiological Problem," in *Phenomenological Psychology*. (New York: Basic Books, 1966), p. 219.

certain amount of creativity which should be liberated and actualized. Susan becomes an artist and lives happily ever after.

But your norms are, I suggest, skewing your view of the problem, and very badly.

Let us take the first case. You reason: If Susan is happy or at least functioning in the present state of affairs (that is, moving from man to man as a silver dollar moves from hand to hand), then why is she seeing a shrink? Something is wrong. New behavior is indicated. Susan is to get married and live happily ever after. May I offer another view? That is, that "seeing a shrink" might be precisely a maneuver in a situation in which Susan *does not want* to get married and live happily ever after? That getting married and living happily ever after might be, for Susan, the worst of fates, and that in order to validate her nonacceptance of this norm she defines herself to herself as shrink-needing? That you are actually certifying the behavior which you seek to change? (When she says to you that she's not shrinkable, you should listen.)

Perhaps, Dr. Hodder, my logic is feeble, perhaps my intuitions are frail. It is, God knows, a complex and difficult question. Your perception that Susan is an artist of some kind *in potentia* is, I think, an acute one. But the proposition "Susan becomes an artist and lives happily ever after" is ridiculous. (I realize that I am couching the proposition in such terms—"happily ever after"—that it is ridiculous on the face of it, but there is ridiculousness piled upon ridiculousness.) Let me point out, if it has escaped your notice, that what an artist does, is fail. Any reading of the literature[3] (I mean the theory of artistic creation), however summary, will persuade you instantly that the paradigmatic artistic experience is that of failure. The actualization fails to meet, equal, the intuition. There is something "out there" which cannot be brought "here." This is standard. I don't mean bad artists, I mean good artists. There is no such thing as a "successful artist" (except, of course, in worldly terms). The proposition should read, "Susan becomes an artist and lives unhappily ever after." This is the case. Don't be deceived.

What I am saying is, that the therapy of choice is not clear. I deeply sympathize. You have a dilemma.

I ask you to note, by the way, that Susan's is not a seeking after instant gratification as dealt out by so-called encounter or sensitivity groups, nude marathons, or dope. None of this is what is going down. "Joy" is not Susan's bag. I praise her for seeking out you rather than getting involved with any of this other idiocy. Her forte, I would suggest, is mind, and if there are games being played they are being conducted with taste, decorum, and some amount of intellectual rigor. Not-bad games. When I take Susan out to dinner she does not order chocolate-covered ants, even if they are on the menu. (Have you, by the way, tried Alfredo's, at the corner of Bank and Hudson streets? It's wonderful.) (Parenthetically, the problem of analysts sleeping with their patients is well known and I understand that Susan has been routinely seducing you—a

---

[3] Especially, perhaps, Ehrenzweig, *The Hidden Order of Art* (University of California Press, 1966), pp. 234–9.

reflex, she can't help it—throughout the analysis. I understand that there is a new splinter group of therapists, behaviorists of some kind, who take this to be some kind of ethic? Is this true? Does this mean that they do it only when they want to, or whether they want to or not? At a dinner party the other evening a lady analyst was saying that three cases of this kind had recently come to her attention and she seemed to think that this was rather a lot. The problem of maintaining mentorship is, as we know, not easy. I think you have done very well in this regard, and God knows it must have been difficult, given those skirts Susan wears that unbutton up to the crotch and which she routinely leaves unbuttoned to the third button.)

Am I wandering too much for you? Bear with me. The world is waiting for the sunrise.

We are left, I submit, with the problem of her depressions. They are, I agree, terrible. Your idea that I am not "supportive" enough is, I think, wrong. I have found, as a practical matter, that the best thing to do is to just do ordinary things, read the newspaper for example, or watch basketball, or wash the dishes. That seems to allow her to come out of it better than any amount of so-called "support." (About the *chasmus hystericus* or hysterical yawning I don't worry any more. It is masking behavior, of course, but after all, you must allow us our tics. The world is waiting for the sunrise.) What do you do with a patient who finds the world unsatisfactory? The world *is* unsatisfactory; only a fool would deny it. I know that your own ongoing psychic structuralization is still going on—you are thirty-seven and I am forty-one—but you must be old enough by now to realize that shit is shit. Susan's perception that America has somehow got hold of the greed ethic and that the greed ethic has turned America into a tidy little hell is not, I think, wrong. What do you do with such a perception? Apply Band-Aids, I suppose. About her depressions, I wouldn't do anything. I'd leave them alone. Put on a record.[4]

Let me tell you a story.

One night we were at her place, about three a.m., and this man called, another lover, quite a well-known musician who is very good, very fast—a good man. He asked Susan "Is he there?," meaning me, and she said "Yes," and he said, "What are you doing?," and she said, "What do you think?," and he said, "When will you be finished?," and she said, "Never." Are you, Doctor dear, in a position to appreciate the beauty of this reply, in this context?

What I am saying is that Susan is wonderful. *As is.* There are not so many things around to which that word can be accurately applied. Therefore I must view your efforts to improve her with, let us say, a certain amount of ambivalence. If this makes me a negative factor in the analysis, so be it. I will be a negative factor until the cows come home, and cheerfully. I can't help it, Doctor, I am voting for the piano.

With best wishes,

[4] For example, Harrison, "Wah Wah," Apple Records, STCH 639, Side One, Track 3.

"Repent, Harlequin!" Said the Ticktockman

HARLAN ELLISON [b. 1934]

1965

There are always those who ask, what is it all about? For those who need to ask, for those who need points sharply made, who need to know "where it's at," this:

> The mass of men serve the state thus, not as men mainly, but as machines, with their bodies. They are the standing army, and the militia, jailors, constables, *posse comitatus*, etc. In most cases there is no free exercise whatever of the judgment or of the moral sense; but they put themselves on a level with wood and earth and stones; and wooden men can perhaps be manufactured that will serve the purpose as well. Such command no more respect than men of straw or a lump of dirt. They have the same sort of worth only as horses and dogs. Yet such as these even are commonly esteemed good ciitzens. Others—as most legislators, politicians, lawyers, ministers, and officeholders—serve the state chiefly with their heads; and, as they rarely make any moral distinctions, they are as likely to serve the Devil, without intending it, as God. A very few, as heroes, patriots, martyrs, reformers in the great sense, and men, serve the state with their consciences also, and so necessarily resist it for the most part; and they are commonly treated as enemies by it.
>
> *Henry David Thoreau*
> CIVIL DISOBEDIENCE

That is the heart of it. Now begin in the middle, and later learn the beginning; the end will take care of itself.

But because it was the very world it was, the very world they had allowed it to *become*, for months his activities did not come to the alarmed attention of The Ones Who Kept The Machine Functioning Smoothly, the ones who poured the very best butter over the cams and mainsprings of the culture. Not until it had become obvious that somehow, someway, he had become a notoriety, a celebrity, perhaps even a hero for (what Officialdom inescapably tagged) "an emotionally disturbed segment of the populace," did they turn it over to the Ticktockman and his legal machinery. But by then, because it was the very world it was, and they had no way to predict he would happen—possibly a strain of disease long-defunct, now, suddenly, reborn in a system where immunity had been forgotten, had lapsed—he had been allowed to become too real. Now he had form and substance.

He had become a *personality*, something they had filtered out of the system many decades before. But there it was, and there *he* was, a very definitely

238

imposing personality. In certain circles—middle-class circles—it was thought disgusting. Vulgar ostentation. Anarchistic. Shameful. In others, there was only sniggering: those strata where thought is subjugated to form and ritual, niceties, proprieties. But down below, ah, down below, where the people always needed their saints and sinners, their bread and circuses, their heroes and villains, he was considered a Bolivar; a Napoleon; a Robin Hood; a Dick Bong (Ace of Aces); a Jesus; a Jomo Kenyatta.

And at the top—where, like socially-attuned Shipwreck Kellys, every tremor and vibration threatening to dislodge the wealthy, powerful and titled from their flagpoles—he was considered a menace; a heretic; a rebel; a disgrace; a peril. He was known down the line, to the very heart-meat core, but the important reactions were high above and far below. At the very top, at the very bottom.

So his file was turned over, along with his time-card and his cardioplate, to the office of the Ticktockman.

The Ticktockman: very much over six feet tall, often silent, a soft purring man when things went timewise. The Ticktockman.

Even in the cubicles of the hierarchy, where fear was generated, seldom suffered, he was called the Ticktockman. But no one called him that to his mask.

You don't call a man a hated name, not when that man, behind his mask, is capable of revoking the minutes, the hours, the days and nights, the years of your life. He was called the Master Timekeeper to his mask. It was safer that way.

"This is *what* he is," said the Ticktockman with genuine softness, "but not *who* he is. This time-card I'm holding in my left hand has a name on it, but it is the name of *what* he is, not *who* he is. The cardioplate here in my right hand is also named, but not *whom* named, merely *what* named. Before I can exercise proper revocation, I have to know *who* this *what* is."

To his staff, all the ferrets, all the loggers, all the finks, all the commex, even the mineez, he said, "Who is this Harlequin?"

He was not purring smoothly. Timewise, it was jangle.

However, it *was* the longest speech they had ever heard him utter at one time, the staff, the ferrets, the loggers, the finks, the commex, but not the mineez, who usually weren't around to know, in any case. But even they scurried to find out.

Who is the Harlequin?

High above the third level of the city, he crouched on the humming aluminum-frame platform of the air-boat (foof! air-boat, indeed! swizzleskid is what it was, with a tow-rack jerry-rigged) and he stared down at the neat Mondrian arrangement of the buildings.

Somewhere nearby, he could hear the metronomic left-right-left of the 2:47 PM shift, entering the Timkin roller-bearing plant in their sneakers. A minute later, precisely, he heard the softer right-left-right of the 5:00 AM formation, going home.

An elfin grin spread across his tanned features, and his dimples appeared for a moment. Then, scratching at his thatch of auburn hair, he shrugged within his motley, as though girding himself for what came next, and threw the joystick forward, and bent into the wind as the air-boat dropped. He skimmed over a slidewalk, purposely dropping a few feet to crease the tassels of the ladies of fashion, and—inserting thumbs in large ears—he stuck out his tongue, rolled his eyes and went wugga-wugga-wugga. It was a minor diversion. One pedestrian skittered and tumbled, sending parcels everywhichway, another wet herself, a third keeled slantwise and the walk was stopped automatically by the servitors till she could be resuscitated. It was a minor diversion.

Then he swirled away on a vagrant breeze, and was gone. Hi-ho.

As he rounded the cornice of the Time-Motion Study Building, he saw the shift, just boarding the slidewalk. With practiced motion and an absolute con-servation of movement, they sidestepped up onto the slow-strip and (in a chorus line reminiscent of a Busby Berkeley film of the antediluvian 1930s) advanced across the strips ostrich-walking till they were lined up on the expresstrip.

Once more, in anticipation, the elfin grin spread, and there was a tooth missing back there on the left side. He dipped, skimmed, and swooped over them; and then, scrunching about on the air-boat, he released the holding pins that fastened shut the ends of the home-made pouring troughs that kept his cargo from dumping prematurely. And as he pulled the trough-pins, the air-boat slid over the factory workers and one hundred and fifty thousand dollars' worth of jelly beans cascaded down on the expresstrip.

Jelly beans! Millions and billions of purples and yellows and greens and licorice and grape and raspberry and mint and round and smooth and crunchy outside and soft-mealy inside and sugary and bouncing jouncing tumbling clit-tering clattering skittering fell on the heads and shoulders and hardhats and carapaces of the Timkin workers, tinkling on the slidewalk and bouncing away and rolling about underfoot and filling the sky on their way down with all the colors of joy and childhood and holidays, coming down in a steady rain, a solid wash, a torrent of color and sweetness out of the sky from above, and entering a universe of sanity and metronomic order with quite-mad coocoo newness. Jelly beans!

The shift workers howled and laughed and were pelted, and broke ranks, and the jelly beans managed to work their way into the mechanism of the slidewalks after which there was a hideous scraping as the sound of a million fingernails rasped down a quarter of a million blackboards, followed by a coughing and a sputtering, and then the slidewalks all stopped and everyone was dumped this-awayandthataway in a jackstraw tumble, still laughing and popping little jelly bean eggs of childish color into their mouths. It was a holiday, and a jollity, an absolute insanity, a giggle. But . . .

The shift was delayed seven minutes.

They did not get home for seven minutes.

The master schedule was thrown off by seven minutes.

Quotas were delayed by inoperative slidewalks for seven minutes.

He had tapped the first domino in the line, and one after another, like chik chik chik, the others had fallen.

The System had been seven minutes' worth of disrupted. It was a tiny matter, one hardly worthy of note, but in a society where the single driving force was order and unity and equality and promptness and clocklike precision and attention to the clock, reverence of the gods of the passage of time, it was a disaster of major importance.

So he was ordered to appear before the Ticktockman. It was broadcast across every channel of the communications web. He was ordered to be *there* at 7:00 dammit on time. And they waited, and they waited, but he didn't show up till almost ten-thirty, at which time he merely sang a little song about moonlight in a place no one had ever heard of, called Vermont, and vanished again. But they had all been waiting since seven, and it wrecked *hell* with their schedules. So the question remained: Who is the Harlequin?

But the *unasked* question (more important of the two) was: how did we get *into* this position, where a laughing, irresponsible japer of jabberwocky and jive could disrupt our entire economic and cultural life with a hundred and fifty thousand dollars' worth of jelly beans . . .

Jelly for God's sake *beans!* This is madness! Where did he get the money to buy a hundred and fifty thousand dollars' worth of jelly beans? (They knew it would have cost that much, because they had a team of Situation Analysts pulled off another assignment, and rushed to the slidewalk scene to sweep up and count the candles, and produce findings, which disrupted *their* schedules and threw their entire branch at least a day behind.) Jelly beans! Jelly . . . *beans?* Now wait a second—a second accounted for—no one has manufactured jelly beans for over a hundred years. Where did he get jelly beans?

That's another good question. More than likely it will never be answered to your complete satisfaction. But then, how many questions ever are?

The middle you know. Here is the beginning. How it starts:

A desk pad. Day for day, and turn each day. 9:00—open the mail. 9:45—appointment with planning commission board. 10:30—discuss installation progress charts with J.L. 11:45—pray for rain. 12:00—lunch. *And so it goes.*

"I'm sorry, Miss Grant, but the time for interviews was set at 2:30, and it's almost five now. I'm sorry you're late, but those are the rules. You'll have to wait till next year to submit application for this college again." *And so it goes.*

The 10:10 local stops at Cresthaven, Galesville, Tonawanda Junction, Selby and Farnhurst, but not at Indiana City, Lucasville and Colton, except on Sunday. The 10:35 express stops at Galesville, Selby and Indiana City, except on Sundays & Holidays, at which time it stops at . . . *and so it goes.*

"I couldn't wait, Fred. I had to be at Pierre Cartain's by 3:00, and you said you'd meet me under the clock in the terminal at 2:45, and you weren't there, so I had to go on. You're always late, Fred. If you'd been there, we could have sewed it up together, but as it was, well, I took the order alone . . ." *And so it goes.*

Dear Mr. and Mrs. Atterley: In reference to your son Gerold's constant tardiness, I am afraid we will have to suspend him from school unless some more reliable method can be instituted guaranteeing he will arrive at his classes on time. Granted he is an exemplary student, and his marks are high, his constant flouting of the schedules of this school makes it impractical to maintain him in a system where the other children seem capable of getting where they are supposed to be on time *and so it goes.*

YOU CANNOT VOTE UNLESS YOU APPEAR AT 8:45 AM.

"I don't care if the script is *good*, I need it Thursday!"

CHECK-OUT TIME IS 2:00 PM.

"You got here late. The job's taken. Sorry."

YOUR SALARY HAS BEEN DOCKED FOR TWENTY MINUTES TIME LOST.

"God, what time is it, I've gotta run!"

And so it goes. And so it goes. And so it goes. And so it goes goes goes goes goes tick tock tick tock tick tock and one day we no longer let time serve us, we serve time and we are slaves of the schedule, worshippers of the sun's passing, bound into a life predicated on restrictions because the system will not function if we don't keep the schedule tight.

Until it becomes more than a minor inconvenience to be late. It becomes a sin. Then a crime. Then a crime punishable by this:

EFFECTIVE 15 JULY 2389 12:00:00 midnight, the office of the Master Timekeeper will require all citizens to submit their time-cards and cardioplates for processing. In accordance with Statute 555-7-SGH-999 governing the revocation of time per capita, all cardioplates will be keyed to the individual holder and—

What they had done, was devise a method of curtailing the amount of life a person could have. If he was ten minutes late, he lost ten minutes of his life. An hour was proportionately worth more revocation. If someone was consistently tardy, he might find himself, on a Sunday night, receiving a communiqué from the Master Timekeeper that his time had run out, and he would be "turned off" at high noon on Monday, please straighten your affairs, sir, madame or bisex.

And so, by this simple scientific expedient (utilizing a scientific process held dearly secret by the Ticktockman's office) the System was maintained. It was the only expedient thing to do. It was, after all, patriotic. The schedules had to be met. After all, there *was* a war on!

But, wasn't there always?

"Now that is really disgusting," the Harlequin said, when Pretty Alice showed him the wanted poster. "Disgusting and *highly* improbable. After all, this isn't the Day of the Desperado. A *wanted* poster!"

"You know," Pretty Alice noted, "you speak with a great deal of inflection."

"I'm sorry," said the Harlequin, humbly.

"No need to be sorry. You're always saying 'I'm sorry.' You have such massive guilt, Everett, it's really very sad."

"I'm sorry," he said again, then pursed his lips so the dimples appeared momentarily. He hadn't wanted to say that at all. "I have to go out again. I have to *do* something."

Pretty Alice slammed her coffee-bulb down on the counter. "Oh for God's *sake*, Everett, can't you stay home just *one* night! Must you always be out in that ghastly clown suit, running around annoying people?"

"I'm—" He stopped, and clapped the jester's hat onto his auburn thatch with a tiny tingling of bells. He rose, rinsed out his coffee-bulb at the spray, and put it into the dryer for a moment. "I have to go."

She didn't answer. The faxbox was purring, and she pulled a sheet out, read it, threw it toward him on the counter. "It's about you. Of course. You're ridiculous."

He read it quickly. It said the Ticktockman was trying to locate him. He didn't care, he was going out to be late again. At the door, dredging for an exit line, he hurled back petulantly, "Well, *you* speak with inflection, *too!*"

Pretty Alice rolled her pretty eyes heavenward. "You're ridiculous." The Harlequin stalked out, slamming the door, which sighed shut softly, and locked itself.

There was a gentle knock, and Pretty Alice got up with an exhalation of exasperated breath, and opened the door. He stood there. "I'll be back about ten-thirty, okay?"

She pulled a rueful face. "Why do you tell me that? Why? You *know* you'll be late! You *know* it! You're *always* late, so why do you tell me these dumb things?" She closed the door.

On the other side, the Harlequin nodded to himself. *She's right. She's always right. I'll be late. I'm always late. Why do I tell her these dumb things?*

He shrugged again, and went off to be late once more.

He had fired off the firecracker rockets that said: I will attend the 115th annual International Medical Association Invocation at 8:00 PM precisely. I do hope you will all be able to join me.

The words had burned in the sky, and of course the authorities were there, lying in wait for him. They assumed, naturally, that he would be late. He arrived twenty minutes early, while they were setting up the spiderwebs to trap and hold him. Blowing a large bullhorn, he frightened and unnerved them so, their own moisturized encirclement webs sucked closed, and they were hauled up, kicking and shrieking, high above the amphitheater's floor. The Harlequin laughed and laughed, and apologized profusely. The physicians, gathered in solemn conclave, roared with laughter, and accepted the Harlequin's apologies with exaggerated bowing and posturing, and a merry time was had by all, who thought the Harlequin was a regular foofaraw in fancy pants; all, that is, but the authorities, who had been sent out by the office of the Ticktockman; they hung there like so much dockside cargo, hauled up above the floor of the amphitheater in a most unseemly fashion.

(In another part of the same city where the Harlequin carried on his "activities," totally unrelated in every way to what concerns us here, save that it illustrates the Ticktockman's power and import, a man named Marshall Delahanty received his turn-off notice from the Ticktockman's office. His wife received the notification from the gray-suited minee who delivered it, with the traditional "look of sorrow" plastered hideously across his face. She knew what it was, even without unsealing it. It was a billet-doux of immediate recognition to everyone these days. She gasped, and held it as though it were a glass slide tinged with botulism, and prayed it was not for her. Let it be for Marsh, she thought, brutally, realistically, or one of the kids, but not for me, please dear God, not for me. And then she opened it, and it *was* for Marsh, and she was at one and the same time horrified and relieved. The next trooper in the line had caught the bullet. "Marshall," she screamed, "Marshall! Termination, Marshall! OhmiGod, Marshall, whattl we do, whattl we do, Marshall omigod-marshall . . ." and in their home that night was the sound of tearing paper and fear, and the stink of madness went up the flue and there was nothing, absolutely nothing they could do about it.

(But Marshall Delahanty tried to run. And early the next day, when turn-off time came, he was deep in the Canadian forest two hundred miles away, and the office of the Ticktockman blanked his cardioplate, and Marshall Delahanty keeled over, running, and his heart stopped, and the blood dried up on its way to his brain, and he was dead that's all. One light went out on the sector map in the office of the Master Timekeeper, while notification was entered for fax reproduction, and Georgette Delahanty's name was entered on the dole roles till she could remarry. Which is the end of the footnote, and all the point that need be made, except don't laugh, because that is what would happen to the Harlequin if ever the Ticktockman found out his real name. It isn't funny.)

The shopping level of the city was thronged with the Thursday-colors of the buyers. Women in canary yellow chitons and men in pseudo-Tyrolean outfits that were jade and leather and fit very tightly, save for the balloon pants.

When the Harlequin appeared on the still-being-constructed shell of the new Efficiency Shopping Center, his bullhorn to his elfishly-laughing lips, everyone pointed and stared, and he berated them:

"Why let them order you about? Why let them tell you to hurry and scurry like ants or maggots? Take your time! Saunter a while! Enjoy the sunshine, enjoy the breeze, let life carry you at your own pace! Don't be slaves of time, it's a helluva way to die, slowly, by degrees . . . down with the Ticktockman!"

Who's the nut? most of the shoppers wanted to know. Who's the nut oh wow I'm gonna be late I gotta run . . .

And the construction gang on the Shopping Center received an urgent order from the office of the Master Timekeeper that the dangerous criminal known as the Harlequin was atop their spire, and their aid was urgently needed in apprehending him. The work crew said no, they would lose time on their construction schedule, but the Ticktockman managed to pull the proper threads of governmental webbing, and they were told to cease work and catch that nitwit up there on the spire; up there with the bullhorn. So a dozen and more burly workers began climbing into their construction platforms, releasing the a-grav plates, and rising toward the Harlequin.

After the debacle (in which, through the Harlequin's attention to personal safety, no one was seriously injured), the workers tried to reassemble, and assault him again, but it was too late. He had vanished. It had attracted quite a crowd, however, and the shopping cycle was thrown off by hours, simply hours. The purchasing needs of the system were therefore falling behind, and so measures were taken to accelerate the cycle for the rest of the day, but it got bogged down and speeded up and they sold too many float-valves and not nearly enough wegglers, which meant that the popli ratio was off, which made it necessary to rush cases and cases of spoiling Smash-O to stores that usually needed a case only every three or four hours. The shipments were bollixed, the transshipments were misrouted, and in the end, even the swizzleskid industries felt it.

"Don't come back till you have him!" the Ticktockman said, very quietly, very sincerely, extremely dangerously.

They used dogs. They used probes. They used cardioplate crossoffs. They used teepers. They used bribery. They used stiktytes. They used intimidation. They used torment. They used torture. They used finks. They used cops. They used search&seizure. They used fallaron. They used betterment incentive. They used fingerprints. They used the Bertillon system. They used cunning. They used guile. They used treachery. They used Raoul Mitgong, but he didn't help much. They used applied physics. They used techniques of criminology.

And what the hell: they caught him.

After all, his name was Everett C. Marm, and he wasn't much to begin with, except a man who had no sense of time.

"Repent, Harlequin!" said the Ticktockman.

"Get stuffed!" the Harlequin replied, sneering.

"You've been late a total of sixty-three years, five months, three weeks, two days, twelve hours, forty-one minutes, fifty-nine seconds, point oh three six one one one microseconds. You've used up everything you can, and more. I'm going to turn you off."

"Scare someone else. I'd rather be dead than live in a dumb world with a bogeyman like you."

"It's my job."

"You're full of it. You're a tyrant. You have no right to order people around and kill them if they show up late."

"You can't adjust. You can't fit in."

"Unstrap me, and I'll fit my fist into your mouth."

"You're a nonconformist."

"That didn't used to be a felony."

"It is now. Live in the world around you."

"I hate it. It's a terrible world."

"Not everyone thinks so. Most people enjoy order."

"I don't, and most of the people I know don't."

"That's not true. How do you think we caught you?"

"I'm not interested."

"A girl named Pretty Alice told us who you were."

"That's a lie."

"It's true. You unnerve her. She wants to belong; she wants to conform; I'm going to turn you off."

"Then do it already, and stop arguing with me."

"I'm not going to turn you off."

"You're an idiot!"

"Repent, Harlequin!" said the Ticktockman.

"Get stuffed."

So they sent him to Coventry. And in Coventry they worked him over. It was just like what they did to Winston Smith in NINETEEN EIGHTY-FOUR, which was a book none of them knew about, but the techniques are really quite ancient, and so they did it to Everett C. Marm; and one day, quite a long time later, the Harlequin appeared on the communications web, appearing elfin and dimpled and bright-eyed, and not at all brainwashed, and he said he had been wrong, that it was a good, a very good thing indeed, to belong, to be right on time hip-ho and away we go, and everyone stared up at him on the public screens that covered an entire city block, and they said to themselves, well, you see, he was just a nut after all, and if that's the way the system is run, then let's do it that way, because it doesn't pay to fight city hall, or in this case, the Ticktockman. So Everett C. Marm was destroyed, which was a loss, because of what Thoreau said earlier, but you can't make an omelet without breaking a few eggs, and in every revolution a few die who shouldn't, but they have to, because that's the way it happens, and if you make only a little change, then it seems to be worthwhile. Or, to make the point lucidly:

"Uh, excuse me, sir, I, uh, don't know how to uh, to uh, tell you this, but you were three minutes late. The schedule is a little, uh, bit off."

He grinned sheepishly.

"That's ridiculous!" murmured the Ticktockman behind his mask. "Check your watch." And then he went into his office, going *mrmee, mrmee, mrmee, mrmee.*

Everyday Use 1973

FOR YOUR GRANDMAMA

ALICE WALKER [b. 1944]

I will wait for her in the yard that Maggie and I made so clean and wavy yesterday afternoon. A yard like this is more comfortable than most people know. It is not just a yard. It is like an extended living room. When the hard clay is swept clean as a floor and the fine sand around the edges lined with tiny, irregular grooves anyone can come and sit and look up into the elm tree and wait for the breezes that never come inside the house.

Maggie will be nervous until after her sister goes: she will stand hopelessly in corners homely and ashamed of the burn scars down her arms and legs, eyeing her sister with a mixture of envy and awe. She thinks her sister has held life always in the palm of one hand, that "no" is a word the world never learned to say to her.

You've no doubt seen those TV shows where the child who has "made it" is confronted, as a surprise, by her own mother and father, tottering in weakly from backstage. (A pleasant surprise, of course: What would they do if parent and child came on the show only to curse out and insult each other?) On TV mother and child embrace and smile into each other's faces. Sometimes the mother and father weep, the child wraps them in her arms and leans across the table to tell how she would not have made it without their help. I have seen these programs.

Sometimes I dream a dream in which Dee and I are suddenly brought together on a TV program of this sort. Out of a dark and soft-seated limousine I am ushered into a bright room filled with many people. There I meet a smiling, gray, sporty man like Johnny Carson who shakes my hand and tells me what a fine girl I have. Then we are on the stage and Dee is embracing me with tears in her eyes. She pins on my dress a large orchid, even though she has told me once that she thinks orchids are tacky flowers.

In real life I am a large, big-boned woman with rough, man-working hands. In the winter I wear flannel nightgowns to bed and overalls during the day. I can kill and clean a hog as mercilessly as a man. My fat keeps me hot in zero weather. I can work all day, breaking ice to get water for washing. I can eat pork liver cooked over the open fire minutes after it comes steaming from the hog. One winter I knocked a bull calf straight in the brain between the eyes with a sledge hammer and had the meat hung up to chill before nightfall. But of course all this does not show on television. I am the way my daughter would want me to be: a hundred pounds lighter, my skin like an uncooked barley pancake. My hair glistens in the hot bright lights. Johnny Carson has much to do to keep up with my quick and witty tongue.

But that is a mistake. I know even before I wake up. Who ever knew a Johnson with a quick tongue? Who can even imagine me looking a strange white man in the eye? It seems to me I have talked to them always with one foot raised in flight, with my head turned in whichever way is farthest from them. Dee, though. She would always look anyone in the eye. Hesitation was no part of her nature.

"How do I look, Mama?" Maggie says, showing just enough of her thin body enveloped in pink skirt and red blouse for me to know she's there, almost hidden by the door.

"Come out into the yard," I say.

Have you ever seen a lame animal, perhaps a dog run over by some careless person rich enough to own a car, sidle up to someone who is ignorant enough to be kind to him? That is the way my Maggie walks. She has been like this, chin on chest, eyes on ground, feet in shuffle, ever since the fire that burned the other house to the ground.

Dee is lighter than Maggie, with nicer hair and a fuller figure. She's a woman now, though sometimes I forget. How long ago was it that the other house burned? Ten, twelve years? Sometimes I can still hear the flames and feel Maggie's arm sticking to me, her hair smoking and her dress falling off her in little black papery flakes. Her eyes seemed stretched open, blazed open by the flames reflected in them. And Dee. I see her standing off under the sweet gum tree she used to dig gum out of; a look of concentration on her face as she watched the last dingy gray board of the house fall in toward the red-hot brick chimney. Why don't you do a dance around the ashes? I'd wanted to ask her. She had hated the house that much.

I used to think she hated Maggie, too. But that was before we raised the money, the church and me, to send her to Augusta to school. She used to read to us without pity; forcing words, lies, other folks' habits, whole lives upon us two, sitting trapped and ignorant underneath her voice. She washed us in a river of make-believe, burned us with a lot of knowledge we didn't necessarily need to know. Pressed us to her with the serious way she read, to shove us away at just the moment, like dimwits, we seemed about to understand.

Dee wanted nice things. A yellow organdy dress to wear to her graduation from high school; black pumps to match a green suit she'd made from an old suit somebody gave me. She was determined to stare down any disaster in her efforts. Her eyelids would not flicker for minutes at a time. Often I fought off the temptation to shake her. At sixteen she had a style of her own: and knew what style was.

I never had an education myself. After second grade the school was closed down. Don't ask me why: in 1927 colored asked fewer questions than they do now. Sometimes Maggie reads to me. She stumbles along good-naturedly but can't see well. She knows she is not bright. Like good looks and money, quickness passed her by. She will marry John Thomas (who has mossy teeth in an earnest face) and then I'll be free to sit here and I guess just sing church songs to myself. Although I never was a good singer. Never could carry a tune. I was always better at a man's job. I used to love to milk till I was hoofed in the side in '49. Cows are soothing and slow and don't bother you, unless you try to milk them the wrong way.

I have deliberately turned my back on the house. It is three rooms, just like the one that burned, except the roof is tin; they don't make shingle roofs any more. There are no real windows, just some holes cut in the sides, like the portholes in a ship, but not round and not square, with rawhide holding the shutters up on the outside. This house is in a pasture, too, like the other one. No doubt when Dee sees it she will want to tear it down. She wrote me once that no matter where we "choose" to live, she will manage to come see us. But she will never bring her friends. Maggie and I thought about this and Maggie asked me, "Mama, when did Dee ever *have* any friends?"

She had a few. Furtive boys in pink shirts hanging about on washday after school. Nervous girls who never laughed. Impressed with her they worshiped the well-turned phrase, the cute shape, the scalding humor that erupted like bubbles in lye. She read to them.

When she was courting Jimmy T she didn't have much time to pay to us, but turned all her faultfinding power on him. He *flew* to marry a cheap gal from a family of ignorant flashy people. She hardly had time to recompose herself.

When she comes I will meet—but there they are!

Maggie attempts to make a dash for the house, in her shuffling way, but I stay her with my hand. "Come back here," I say. And she stops and tries to dig a well in the sand with her toe.

It is hard to see them clearly through the strong sun. But even the first glimpse of leg out of the car tells me it is Dee. Her feet were always neat-looking, as if God himself had shaped them with a certain style. From the other side of the car comes a short, stocky man. Hair is all over his head a foot long and hanging from his chin like a kinky mule tail. I hear Maggie suck in her breath. "Uhnnnh," is what it sounds like. Like when you see the wriggling end of a snake just in front of your foot on the road. "Uhnnnh."

Dee next. A dress down to the ground, in this hot weather. A dress so loud it hurts my eyes. There are yellows and oranges enough to throw back the light of the sun. I feel my whole face warming from the heat waves it throws out. Earrings, too, gold and hanging down to her shoulders. Bracelets dangling and making noises when she moves her arm up to shake the folds of the dress out of her armpits. The dress is loose and flows, and as she walks closer, I like it. I hear Maggie go "Uhnnnh" again. It is her sister's hair. It stands straight up like the wool on a sheep. It is black as night and around the edges are two long pigtails that rope about like small lizards disappearing behind her ears.

"Wa-su-zo-Tean-o!" she says, coming on in that gliding way the dress makes her move. The short stocky fellow with the hair to his navel is all grinning and he follows up with "Asalamalakim, my mother and sister!" He moves to hug

Maggie but she falls back, right up against the back of my chair. I feel her trembling there and when I look up I see the perspiration falling off her chin.

"Don't get up," says Dee. Since I am stout it takes something of a push. You can see me trying to move a second or two before I make it. She turns, showing white heels through her sandals, and goes back to the car. Out she peeks next with a Polaroid. She stoops down quickly and lines up picture after picture of me sitting there in front of the house with Maggie cowering behind me. She never takes a shot without making sure the house is included. When a cow comes nibbling around the edge of the yard she snaps it and me and Maggie *and* the house. Then she puts the Polaroid in the back seat of the car, and comes up and kisses me on the forehead.

Meanwhile Asalamalakim is going through the motions with Maggie's hand. Maggie's hand is as limp as a fish, and probably as cold, despite the sweat, and she keeps trying to pull it back. It looks like Asalamalakim wants to shake hands but wants to do it fancy. Or maybe he don't know how people shake hands. Anyhow, he soon gives up on Maggie.

"Well," I say. "Dee."

"No, Mama," she says. "Not 'Dee,' Wangero Leewanika Kemanjo!"

"What happened to 'Dee'?" I wanted to know.

"She's dead," Wangero said. "I couldn't bear it any longer being named after the people who oppress me."

"You know as well as me you was named after your aunt Dicie," I said. Dicie is my sister. She named Dee. We called her "Big Dee" after Dee was born.

"But who was *she* named after?" asked Wangero.

"I guess after Grandma Dee," I said.

"And who was she named after?" asked Wangero.

"Her mother," I said, and saw Wangero was getting tired. "That's about as far back as I can trace it," I said. Though, in fact, I probably could have carried it back beyond the Civil War through the branches.

"Well," said Asalamalakim, "there you are."

"Uhnnnh," I heard Maggie say.

"There I was not," I said, "before 'Dicie' cropped up in our family, so why should I try to trace it that far back?"

He just stood there grinning, looking down on me like somebody inspecting a Model A car. Every once in a while he and Wangero sent eye signals over my head.

"How do you pronounce this name?" I asked.

"You don't have to call me by it if you don't want to," said Wangero.

"Why shouln't I?" I asked. "If that's what you want us to call you, we'll call you."

"I know it might sound awkward at first," said Wangero.

"I'll get used to it," I said. "Ream it out again."

Well, soon we got the name out of the way. Asalamalakim had a name twice as long and three times as hard. After I tripped over it two or three times he told me to just call him Hakim-a-barber. I wanted to ask him was he a barber, but I didn't really think he was, so I didn't ask.

"You must belong to those beef-cattle peoples down the road," I said. They said "Asalamalakim" when they met you, too, but they didn't shake hands. Always too busy: feeding the cattle, fixing the fences, putting up salt-lick shelters, throwing down hay. When the white folks poisoned some of the herd the men stayed up all night with rifles in their hands. I walked a mile and a half just to see the sight.

Hakim-a-barber said, "I accept some of their doctrines, but farming and raising cattle is not my style." (They didn't tell me, and I didn't ask, whether Wangero [Dee] had really gone and married him.)

We sat down to eat and right away he said he didn't eat collards and pork was unclean. Wangero, though, went on through the chitlins and corn bread, the greens and everything else. She talked a blue streak over the sweet potatoes. Everything delighted her. Even the fact that we still used the benches her daddy made for the table when we couldn't afford to buy chairs.

"Oh, Mama!" she cried. Then turned to Hakim-a-barber. "I never knew how lovely these benches are. You can feel the rump prints," she said, running her hands underneath her and along the bench. Then she gave a sigh and her hand closed over Grandma Dee's butter dish. "That's it!" she said. "I knew there was something I wanted to ask you if I could have." She jumped up from the table and went over in the corner where the churn stood, the milk in its clabber by now. She looked at the churn and looked at it.

"This churn top is what I need," she said. "Didn't Uncle Buddy whittle it out of a tree you all used to have?"

"Yes," I said.

"Uh huh," she said happily. "And I want the dasher, too."

"Uncle Buddy whittle that, too?" asked the barber.

Dee (Wangero) looked up at me.

"Aunt Dee's first husband whittled the dash," said Maggie so low you almost couldn't hear her. "His name was Henry, but they called him Stash."

"Maggie's brain is like an elephant's," Wangero said, laughing. "I can use the churn top as a centerpiece for the alcove table," she said, sliding a plate over the churn, "and I'll think of something artistic to do with the dasher."

When she finished wrapping the dasher the handle stuck out. I took it for a moment in my hands. You didn't even have to look close to see where hands pushing the dasher up and down to make butter had left a kind of sink in the wood. In fact, there were a lot of small sinks; you could see where thumbs and fingers had sunk into the wood. It was beautiful light yellow wood, from a tree that grew in the yard where Big Dee and Stash had lived.

After dinner Dee (Wangero) went to the trunk at the foot of my bed and started rifling through it. Maggie hung back in the kitchen over the dishpan. Out came Wangero with two quilts. They had been pieced by Grandma Dee and then Big Dee and me had hung them on the quilt frames on the front porch and quilted them. One was in the Lone Star pattern. The other was Walk Around the Mountain. In both of them were scraps of dresses Grandma Dee had worn fifty and more years ago. Bits and pieces of Grandpa Jarrell's Paisley shirts. And one teeny faded blue piece, about the size of a penny matchbox, that was from Great Grandpa Ezra's uniform that he wore in the Civil War.

"Mama," Wangero said sweet as a bird. "Can I have these old quilts?"

I heard something fall in the kitchen, and a minute later the kitchen door slammed.

"Why don't you take one or two of the others?" I asked "These old things was just done by me and Big Dee from some tops your grandma pieced before she died."

"No," said Wangero. "I don't want those. They are stitched around the borders by machine."

"That's make them last better," I said.

"That's not the point," said Wangero. "These are all pieces of dresses Grandma used to wear. She did all this stitching by hand. Imagine!" She held the quilts securely in her arms, stroking them.

"Some of the pieces, like those lavender ones, come from old clothes her mother handed down to her," I said, moving up to touch the quilts. Dee (Wangero) moved back just enough so that I couldn't reach the quilts. They already belonged to her.

"Imagine!" she breathed again, clutching them closely to her bosom.

"The truth is," I said, "I promised to give them quilts to Maggie, for when she marries John Thomas."

She gasped like a bee had stung her.

"Maggie can't appreciate these quilts!" she said. "She'd probably be backward enough to put them to everyday use."

"I reckon she would," I said. "God knows I been saving 'em for long enough with nobody using 'em. I hope she will!" I didn't want to bring up how I had offered Dee (Wangero) a quilt when she went away to college. Then she had told me they were old-fashioned, out of style.

"But they're *priceless!*" she was saying now, furiously; for she has a temper. "Maggie would put them on the bed and in five years they'd be in rags. Less than that!"

"She can always make some more," I said. "Maggie knows how to quilt."

Dee (Wangero) looked at me with hatred. "You just will not understand. The point is these quilts, *these* quilts!"

"Well," I said, stumped. "What would *you* do with them?"

"Hang them," she said. As if that was the only thing you *could* do with quilts.

Maggie by now was standing in the door. I could almost hear the sound her feet made as they scraped over each other.

"She can have them, Mama," she said, like somebody used to never winning anything, or having anything reserved for her. "I can 'member Grandma Dee without the quilts."

I looked at her hard. She had filled her bottom lip with checkerberry snuff and it gave her face a kind of dopey, hangdog look. It was Grandma Dee and Big Dee who taught her how to quilt herself. She stood there with her scarred hands hidden in the folds of her skirt. She looked at her sister with something like fear but she wasn't mad at her. This was Maggie's portion. This was the way she knew God to work.

When I looked at her like that something hit me in the top of my head and ran down to the soles of my feet. Just like when I'm in church and the spirit of God touches me and I get happy and shout. I did something I never had done before: hugged Maggie to me, then dragged her on into the room, snatched the quilts out of Miss Wangero's hands and dumped them into Maggie's lap. Maggie just sat there on my bed with her mouth open.

"Take one or two of the others," I said to Dee.

But she turned without a word and went out to Hakim-a-barber.

"You just don't understand," she said, as Maggie and I came out to the car.

"What don't I understand?" I wanted to know.

"Your heritage," she said. And then she turned to Maggie, kissed her, and said, "You ought to try to make something of yourself, too, Maggie. It's really a new day for us. But from the way you and Mama still live you'd never know it."

She put on some sunglasses that hid everything above the tip of her nose and her chin.

Maggie smiled; maybe at the sunglasses. But a real smile, not scared. After we watched the car dust settle I asked Maggie to bring me a dip of snuff. And then the two of us sat there just enjoying, until it was time to go in the house and go to bed.

CONFORMITY
AND
REBELLION

Eve and the Serpent, 1989 by Robert Freeman

POETRY

from

Paradise Lost¹   1667

JOHN MILTON   [1608–1674]

"Is this the region, this the soil, the clime,"
Said then the lost archangel, "this the seat
That we must change for Heaven? this mournful gloom
For that celestial light? Be it so, since he
Who now is sovereign can dispose and bid
What shall be right: farthest from him is best,
Whom reason hath equaled, force hath made supreme
Above his equals. Farewell, happy fields,
Where joy forever dwells! Hail, horrors! hail,
Infernal world! and thou, profoundest Hell,   10
Receive thy new possessor, one who brings
A mind not to be changed by place or time.
The mind is its own place, and in itself
Can make a Heaven of Hell, a Hell of Heaven.
What matter where, if I be still the same,
And what I should be, all but° less than he   only
Whom thunder hath made greater? Here at least
We shall be free; th' Almighty hath not built
Here for his envy, will not drive us hence:
Here we may reign secure; and, in my choice,   20
To reign is worth ambition, though in Hell:
Better to reign in Hell than serve in Heaven.
But wherefore let we then our faithful friends,
Th' associates and copartners of our loss,
Lie thus astonished on th' oblivious pool,

Paradise Lost
   ¹ The first part of *Paradise Lost*, a poem on the expulsion of Adam and Eve from the Garden of Eden, tells the story of Satan's rebellion against God, his defeat and expulsion from heaven. In this passage, Satan surveys the infernal region to which God has banished him.

And call them not to share with us their part
In this unhappy mansion, or once more
With rallied arms to try what may be yet
Regained in Heaven, or what more lost in Hell?"

QUESTIONS

1.   Is the statement in line 22 a logical extension of the statement in lines 13–14?
Explain.   **2.**   Is the rebellious Satan heroic or ignoble? Defend your answer.
3.   What are the political implications of Satan's analysis of power (ll. 4–8)?

The World Is
Too Much with Us   1807

WILLIAM WORDSWORTH   [1770–1850]

The world is too much with us; late and soon,
Getting and spending, we lay waste our powers;
Little we see in Nature that is ours;
We have given our hearts away, a sordid boon!
This Sea that bares her bosom to the moon,
The winds that will be howling at all hours,
And are up-gathered now like sleeping flowers,
For this, for everything, we are out of tune;
It moves us not.—Great God! I'd rather be
A Pagan suckled in a creed outworn;   10
So might I, standing on this pleasant lea,
Have glimpses that would make me less forlorn;
Have sight of Proteus rising from the sea;
Or hear Old Triton blow his wreathèd horn. [1]

QUESTIONS

1.   What does "world" mean in line 1?   **2.**   What does Wordsworth complain of
in the first four lines?   **3.**   In lines 4–8 Wordsworth tells us what we have lost; in
the concluding lines he suggests a remedy. What is that remedy? What do Proteus
and Triton symbolize?

WRITING TOPIC

In what ways does Wordsworth's use of images both define what we have lost
and suggest a remedy for this loss?

The World . . .
  [1] Proteus and Triton are both figures from Greek mythology. Proteus had the power to assume
different forms; Triton was often represented as blowing on a conch shell.

Ulysses[1]   (1833)

ALFRED, LORD TENNYSON   [1809–1892]

It little profits that an idle king,
By this still hearth, among these barren crags,
Matched with an aged wife, I mete and dole
Unequal laws unto a savage race,
That hoard, and sleep, and feed, and know not me.

  I cannot rest from travel; I will drink
Life to the lees. All times I have enjoyed
Greatly, have suffered greatly, both with those
That loved me, and alone; on shore, and when
Through scudding drifts the rainy Hyades[2]   10
Vexed the dim sea. I am become a name;
For always roaming with a hungry heart
Much have I seen and known—cities of men
And manners, climates, councils, governments,
Myself not least, but honored of them all—
And drunk delight of battle with my peers,
Far on the ringing plains of windy Troy.
I am a part of all that I have met;
Yet all experience is an arch wherethrough
Gleams that untraveled world whose margin fades   20
Forever and forever when I move.
How dull it is to pause, to make an end,
To rust unburnished, not to shine in use!
As though to breathe were life! Life piled on life
Were all too little, and of one to me
Little remains; but every hour is saved
From that eternal silence, something more,
A bringer of new things; and vile it were
For some three suns to store and hoard myself,
And this gray spirit yearning in desire   30
To follow knowledge like a sinking star,
Beyond the utmost bound of human thought.

Ulysses
  [1] Ulysses, according to Greek legend, was the king of Ithaca and a hero of the Trojan War. Tennyson represents him as eager to resume the life of travel and adventure.
  [2] A group of stars in the constellation Taurus. According to Greek mythology, the rising of these stars with the sun foretold rain.

This is my son, mine own Telemachus,
To whom I leave the scepter and the isle—
Well-loved of me, discerning to fulfill
This labor, by slow prudence to make mild
A rugged people, and through soft degrees
Subdue them to the useful and the good.
Most blameless is he, centered in the sphere
Of common duties, decent not to fail   40
In offices of tenderness, and pay
Meet° adoration to my household gods,   proper
When I am gone. He works his work, I mine.

There lies the port; the vessel puffs her sail;
There gloom the dark, broad seas. My mariners,
Souls that have toiled, and wrought, and thought with me—
That ever with a frolic welcome took
The thunder and the sunshine, and opposed
Free hearts, free foreheads—you and I are old;
Old age hath yet his honor and his toil.   50
Death closes all; but something ere the end,
Some work of noble note, may yet be done,
Not unbecoming men that strove with Gods.
The lights begin to twinkle from the rocks;
The long day wanes; the slow moon climbs; the deep
Moans round with many voices. Come, my friends,
'Tis not too late to seek a newer world.
Push off, and sitting well in order smite
The sounding furrows; for my purpose holds
To sail beyond the sunset, and the baths   60
Of all the western stars, until I die.
It may be that the gulfs will wash us down;
It may be we shall touch the Happy Isles,[3]
And see the great Achilles, whom we knew.
Though much is taken, much abides; and though
We are not now that strength which in old days
Moved earth and heaven, that which we are, we are—
One equal temper of heroic hearts,
Made weak by time and fate, but strong in will
To strive, to seek, to find, and not to yield. 70

---

[3] The Islands of the Blessed (also Elysium), thought to be in the far western oceans, where those favored by the gods, such as Achilles, enjoyed life after death.

QUESTIONS
1. Is Ulysses' desire to abdicate his duties as king irresponsible? Defend your answer. 2. Contrast Ulysses with his son Telemachus as the latter is described in lines 33–43. Is Telemachus admirable? Explain.

WRITING TOPIC
At the conclusion of the poem Ulysses is determined not to yield. Yield to what?

Much Madness
Is Divinest Sense   (1862)

EMILY DICKINSON   [1830–1886]

Much Madness is divinest Sense—
To a discerning Eye—
Much Sense—the starkest Madness—
'Tis the Majority
In this, as All, prevail—
Assent—and you are sane—
Demur—you're straightway dangerous—
And handled with a Chain—

What Soft—
Cherubic Creatures   (ca. 1862)

EMILY DICKINSON   [1830–1886]

What Soft—Cherubic Creatures—
These Gentlewomen are—
One would as soon assault a Plush—
Or violate a Star—

Such Dimity Convictions—
A Horror so refined

Of freckled Human Nature—
Of Deity—ashamed—

It's such a common-Glory—
A Fisherman's—Degree—   10
Redemption—Brittle Lady—
Be so—ashamed of Thee—

Easter 1916[1]   (1916)

WILLIAM BUTLER YEATS [1865–1939]

I have met them at close of day
Coming with vivid faces
From counter or desk among grey
Eighteenth-century houses.
I have passed with a nod of the head
Or polite meaningless words,
Or have lingered awhile and said
Polite meaningless words,
And thought before I had done
Of a mocking tale or a gibe   10
To please a companion
Around the fire at the club,
Being certain that they and I
But lived where motley is worn:
All changed, changed utterly:
A terrible beauty is born.

That woman's days were spent
In ignorant good-will,
Her nights in argument
Until her voice grew shrill.   20
What voice more sweet than hers
When, young and beautiful,
She rode to harriers?
This man had kept a school

Easter 1916
   [1] On Easter Sunday of 1916, a group of Irish nationalists seized key points in Ireland, including the Dublin Post Office, from which they proclaimed an independent Irish Republic. At first, most Irishmen were indifferent to the nationalists' futile and heroic gesture, but as the rebellion was crushed and the leaders executed, they became heroes in their countrymen's eyes. Some of those leaders are alluded to in the second stanza and are named in lines 75 and 76.

And rode our wingéd horse;[2]
This other his helper and friend
Was coming into his force;
He might have won fame in the end,
So sensitive his nature seemed,
So daring and sweet his thought.   30
This other man I had dreamed
A drunken, vainglorious lout.
He had done most bitter wrong
To some who are near my heart,
Yet I number him in the song;
He, too, has resigned his part
In the casual comedy;
He, too, has been changed in his turn,
Transformed utterly:
A terrible beauty is born.   40

Hearts with one purpose alone
Through summer and winter seem
Enchanted to a stone
To trouble the living stream.
The horse that comes from the road,
The rider, the birds that range
From cloud to tumbling cloud,
Minute by minute they change;
A shadow of cloud on the stream
Changes minute by minute;   50
A horse-hoof slides on the brim,
And a horse plashes within it;
The long-legged moor-hens dive,
And hens to moor-cocks call;
Minute by minute they live:
The stone's in the midst of all.

Too long a sacrifice
Can make a stone of the heart.
O when may it suffice?
That is Heaven's part, our part   60
To murmur name upon name,
As a mother names her child
When sleep at last has come
On limbs that had run wild.

---

[2] In Greek mythology, a winged horse is associated with poetic inspiration.

What is it but nightfall?
No, no, not night but death;
Was it needless death after all?
For England may keep faith
For all that is done and said.
We know their dream; enough   70
To know they dreamed and are dead;
And what if excess of love
Bewildered them till they died?
I write it out in a verse—
MacDonagh and MacBride
And Connolly and Pearse
Now and in time to be,
Wherever green is worn,
Are changed, changed utterly:
A terrible beauty is born.   80

QUESTIONS
1. What is "changed utterly," and in what sense can beauty be "terrible"? **2.** What does "they" in line 55 refer to? What does the "stone" in lines
43 and 56 symbolize? What is Yeats contrasting? **3.** How does the poet answer
the question he asks in line 67?

WRITING TOPIC
In the first stanza the attitude of the poet toward the people he is describing is
indifferent, even contemptuous. How is that attitude modified in the rest of the
poem?

Miniver Cheevy   1910

EDWIN ARLINGTON ROBINSON   [1869–1935]

Miniver Cheevy, child of scorn,
    Grew lean while he assailed the seasons;
He wept that he was ever born,
    And he had reasons.

Miniver loved the days of old
    When swords were bright and steeds were prancing;
The vision of a warrior bold
    Would set him dancing.

Miniver sighed for what was not,
 And dreamed, and rested from his labors;   10
He dreamed of Thebes and Camelot,
 And Priam's neighbors.[1]

Miniver mourned the ripe renown
 That made so many a name so fragrant;
He mourned Romance, now on the town,
 And Art, a vagrant.

Miniver loved the Medici,[2]
 Albeit he had never seen one;
He would have sinned incessantly
 Could he have been one.   20

Miniver cursed the commonplace
 And eyed a khaki suit with loathing;
He missed the medieval grace
 Of iron clothing.

Miniver scorned the gold he sought,
 But sore annoyed was he without it;
Miniver thought, and thought, and thought,
 And thought about it.

Miniver Cheevy, born too late,   30
 Scratched his head and kept on thinking;
Miniver coughed, and called it fate,
 And kept on drinking.

We Wear the Mask   1896

PAUL LAURENCE DUNBAR [1872–1906]

We wear the mask that grins and lies,
It hides our cheeks and shades our eyes—
This debt we pay to human guile;

Miniver Cheevy
 [1] Thebes was an ancient Greek city, famous in history and legend; Camelot was the site of the legendary King Arthur's court; Priam was king of Troy during the Trojan War.

 [2] A family of bankers and statesmen, notorious for their cruelty, who ruled Florence for nearly two centuries during the Italian Renaissance.

With torn and bleeding hearts we smile,
And mouth with myriad subtleties.

Why should the world be over-wise,
In counting all our tears and sighs?
Nay, let them only see us, while
    We wear the mask.

We smile, but, O great Christ, our cries   10
To thee from tortured souls arise.
We sing, but oh the clay is vile
Beneath our feet, and long the mile;
But let the world dream otherwise,
    We wear the mask!

Patterns   1916

AMY LOWELL   [1874–1925]

I walk down the garden-paths,
And all the daffodils
Are blowing, and the bright blue squills.
I walk down the patterned garden-paths
In my stiff, brocaded gown.
With my powdered hair and jeweled fan,
I too am a rare
Pattern. As I wander down
The garden-paths.
My dress is richly figured,   10
And the train
Makes a pink and silver stain
On the gravel, and the thrift
Of the borders.
Just a plate of current fashion,
Tripping by in high-heeled, ribboned shoes.
Not a softness anywhere about me,
Only whalebone and brocade.
And I sink on a seat in the shade
Of a lime tree. For my passion   20
Wars against the stiff brocade.
The daffodils and squills
Flutter in the breeze

As they please.
And I weep;
For the lime-tree is in blossom
And one small flower has dropped upon my bosom.

And the plashing of waterdrops
In the marble fountain
Comes down the garden-paths.   30
The dripping never stops.
Underneath my stiffened gown
Is the softness of a woman bathing in a marble basin,
A basin in the midst of hedges grown
So thick, she cannot see her lover hiding,
But she guesses he is near,
And the sliding of the water
Seems the stroking of a dear
Hand upon her.
What is Summer in a fine brocaded gown!   40
I should like to see it lying in a heap upon the ground.
All the pink and silver crumpled up on the ground.

I would be the pink and silver as I ran along the paths,
And he would stumble after,
Bewildered by my laughter.
I should see the sun flashing from his sword-hilt and the buckles on his
    shoes.
I would choose
To lead him in a maze along the patterned paths,
A bright and laughing maze for my heavy-booted lover.
Till he caught me in the shade,   50
And the buttons of his waistcoat bruised my body as he clasped me,
Aching, melting, unafraid.
With the shadows of the leaves and the sundrops,
And the plopping of the waterdrops,
All about us in the open afternoon—
I am very like to swoon
With the weight of this brocade,
For the sun sifts through the shade.

Underneath the fallen blossom
In my bosom   60
Is a letter I have hid.
It was brought to me this morning by a rider from the Duke.
"Madam, we regret to inform you that Lord Hartwell
Died in action Thursday se'nnight."

As I read it in the white, morning sunlight,
The letters squirmed like snakes.
"Any answer, Madam," said my footman.
"No," I told him.
"See that the messenger takes some refreshment.
No, no answer." 70
And I walked into the garden,
Up and down the patterned paths,
In my stiff, correct brocade.
The blue and yellow flowers stood up proudly in the sun,
Each one.
I stood upright too,
Held rigid to the pattern
By the stiffness of my gown;
Up and down I walked,
Up and down. 80

In a month he would have been my husband.
In a month, here, underneath this lime,
We would have broke the pattern;
He for me, and I for him,
He as Colonel, I as Lady,
On this shady seat.
He had a whim
That sunlight carried blessing.
And I answered, "It shall be as you have said."
Now he is dead. 90

In Summer and in Winter I shall walk
Up and down
The patterned garden-paths
In my stiff, brocaded gown.
The squills and daffodils
Will give place to pillared roses, and to asters, and to snow.
I shall go
Up and down
In my gown.
Gorgeously arrayed, 100
Boned and stayed.
And the softness of my body will be guarded from embrace
By each button, hook, and lace.
For the man who should loose me is dead,
Fighting with the Duke in Flanders,
In a pattern called a war.
Christ! What are patterns for?

Sunday Morning

1923

WALLACE STEVENS   [1879–1955]

I

Complacencies of the peignoir, and late
Coffee and oranges in a sunny chair,
And the green freedom of a cockatoo
Upon a rug mingle to dissipate
The holy hush of ancient sacrifice.
She dreams a little, and she feels the dark
Encroachment of that old catastrophe,
As a calm darkens among water-lights.
The pungent oranges and bright, green wings
Seem things in some procession of the dead,   10
Winding across wide water, without sound.
The day is like wide water, without sound,
Stilled for the passing of her dreaming feet
Over the seas, to silent Palestine,
Dominion of the blood and sepulchre.

II

Why should she give her bounty to the dead?
What is divinity if it can come
Only in silent shadows and in dreams?
Shall she not find in comforts of the sun,
In pungent fruit and bright, green wings, or else   20
In any balm or beauty of the earth,
Things to be cherished like the thought of heaven?
Divinity must live within herself:
Passions of rain, or moods in falling snow;
Grievings in loneliness, or unsubdued
Elations when the forest blooms; gusty
Emotions on wet roads on autumn nights;
All pleasures and all pains, remembering
The bough of summer and the winter branch.
These are the measures destined for her soul.   30

III

Jove in the clouds had his inhuman birth.[1]
No mother suckled him, no sweet land gave

Sunday Morning
   [1] Jove is Jupiter, the principal god of the Romans, who, unlike Jesus, had an "inhuman birth."

Large-mannered motions to his mythy mind
He moved among us, as a muttering king,
Magnificent, would move among his hinds,°   farm servants
Until our blood, commingling, virginal,
With heaven, brought such requital to desire
The very hinds discerned it, in a star.
Shall our blood fail? Or shall it come to be
The blood of paradise? And shall the earth   40
Seem all of paradise that we shall know?
The sky will be much friendlier then than now,
A part of labor and a part of pain,
And next in glory to enduring love,
Not this dividing and indifferent blue.

IV

She says, "I am content when wakened birds,
Before they fly, test the reality
Of misty fields, by their sweet questionings;
But when the birds are gone, and their warm fields
Return no more, where, then, is paradise?"   50
There is not any haunt of prophecy,
Nor any old chimera[2] of the grave,
Neither the golden underground, nor isle
Melodious, where spirits gat them home,
Nor visionary south, nor cloudy palm
Remote on heaven's hill, that has endured
As April's green endures; or will endure
Like her remembrance of awakened birds,
Or her desire for June and evening, tipped
By the consummation of the swallow's wings.   60

V

She says, "But in contentment I still feel
The need of some imperishable bliss."
Death is the mother of beauty; hence from her,
Alone, shall come fulfilment to our dreams
And our desires. Although she strews the leaves
Of sure obliteration on our paths,
The path sick sorrow took, the many paths

---

[2] A monster with a lion's head, a goat's body, and a serpent's tail. Here an emblem for the belief in other worlds described in the following lines.

Where triumph rang its brassy phrase, or love
Whispered a little out of tenderness,
She makes the willow shiver in the sun   70
For maidens who were wont to sit and gaze
Upon the grass, relinquished to their feet.
She causes boys to pile new plums and pears
On disregarded plate. The maidens taste
And stray impassioned in the littering leaves.

VI

Is there no change of death in paradise?
Does ripe fruit never fall? Or do the boughs
Hang always heavy in that perfect sky,
Unchanging, yet so like our perishing earth,
With rivers like our own that seek for seas   80
They never find, the same receding shores
That never touch with inarticulate pang?
Why set the pear upon those river-banks
Or spice the shores with odors of the plum?
Alas, that they should wear our colors there,
The silken weavings of our afternoons,
And pick the strings of our insipid lutes!
Death is the mother of beauty, mystical,
Within whose burning bosom we devise
Our earthly mothers waiting, sleeplessly.   90

VII

Supple and turbulent, a ring of men
Shall chant in orgy on a summer morn
Their boisterous devotion to the sun,
Not as a god, but as a god might be,
Naked among them, like a savage source.
Their chant shall be a chant of paradise,
Out of their blood, returning to the sky;
And in their chant shall enter, voice by voice,
The windy lake wherein their lord delights,
The trees, like serafin, and echoing hills,   100
That choir among themselves long afterward.
They shall know well the heavenly fellowship
Of men that perish and of summer morn.
And whence they came and whither they shall go
The dew upon their feet shall manifest.

VIII

She hears, upon that water without sound,
A voice that cries, "The tomb in Palestine
Is not the porch of spirits lingering.
It is the grave of Jesus, where he lay."
We live in an old chaos of the sun,   110
Or old dependency of day and night,
Or island solitude, unsponsored, free,
Of that wide water, inescapable.
Deer walk upon our mountains, and the quail
Whistle about us their spontaneous cries;
Sweet berries ripen in the wilderness;
And, in the isolation of the sky,
At evening, casual flocks of pigeons make
Ambiguous undulations as they sink,
Downward to darkness, on extended wings.   120

QUESTIONS

1. In the opening stanza, the woman's enjoyment of a late Sunday morning breakfast in a relaxed and sensuous atmosphere is troubled by thoughts of what Sunday morning should mean to her. What are the thoughts that disturb her complacency? **2.** What does the speaker mean when he says, "Death is the mother of beauty" (ll. 63 and 88)? **3.** In stanza VI, what is the speaker's attitude toward the conventional Christian conception of paradise? **4.** Stanza VII presents the speaker's vision of an alternative religion. How does it differ from the paradise of stanza VI? **5.** In what ways does the cry of the voice in the final stanza (ll. 107–109) state the woman's dilemma? How do the lines about the pigeons at the end of the poem sum up the speaker's belief?

WRITING TOPIC

This poem is, in a sense, a commentary by the speaker on the woman's desire for truth and certainty more enduring than the physical world can provide. Is the speaker sympathetic to her quest? Explain.

If We Must Die   1922

CLAUDE McKAY [1890–1948]

If we must die, let it not be like hogs
Hunted and penned in an inglorious spot,
While round us bark the mad and hungry dogs,
Making their mock at our accursèd lot.

If we must die, O let us nobly die,
So that our precious blood may not be shed
In vain; then even the monsters we defy
Shall be constrained to honor us though dead!
O kinsmen! we must meet the common foe!
Though far outnumbered let us show us brave,   10
And for their thousand blows deal one deathblow!
What though before us lies the open grave?
Like men we'll face the murderous, cowardly pack,
Pressed to the wall, dying, but fighting back!

the Cambridge ladies
who live in furnished souls

1923

E. E. CUMMINGS   [1894–1962]

1920 – WWI

the Cambridge ladies who live in furnished souls
are unbeautiful and have comfortable minds
(also, with the church's protestant blessings
daughters, unscented shapeless spirited)
they believe in Christ and Longfellow, both dead,
are invariably interested in so many things—
at the present writing one still finds
delighted fingers knitting for the is it (Poles?)
perhaps. While permanent faces coyly bandy
scandal) of Mrs. N. and Professor D
. . . . the Cambridge ladies do not care, above
Cambridge if sometimes in its box of
sky lavender and cornerless, the
moon rattles like a fragment of angry candy

drug league etc...

knitting to help the Polish,

coyly – pretending to be shy

Cambridge Ladies are knitting

QUESTIONS
1. What images does the poet use to describe "the Cambridge ladies"? What do the images suggest? **2.** What is the effect of the interruption "is it" in line 8? **3.** In the final lines, the moon seems to protest against the superficiality of these women. What is the effect of comparing the moon to a fragment of candy?

WRITING TOPIC
Compare this poem with Emily Dickinson's "What Soft—Cherubic Creatures" (p. 259).

Harlem

1951

LANGSTON HUGHES [1902–1967]

What happens to a dream deferred?

Does it dry up
like a raisin in the sun?
Or fester like a sore—
And then run?
Does it stink like rotten meat?
Or crust and sugar over—
like a syrupy sweet?

Maybe it just sags
like a heavy load.

10

Or does it explode?

Same in Blues

1951

LANGSTON HUGHES [1902–1967]

I said to my baby,
Baby take it slow.
I can't, she said, I can't!
I got to go!

*There's a certain
amount of traveling
in a dream deferred.*

Lulu said to Leonard,
I want a diamond ring.
Leonard said to Lulu,
You won't get a goddam thing!

10

*A certain
amount of nothing
in a dream deferred.*

Daddy, daddy, daddy,
All I want is you.
You can have me, baby—
but my lovin' days is through.

> *A certain*
> *amount of impotence*   20
> *in a dream deferred.*

Three parties
On my party line—
But that third party,
Lord, ain't mine!

> *There's liable*
> *to be confusion*
> *in a dream deferred.*

From river to river
Uptown and down,   30
There's liable to be confusion
when a dream gets kicked around.

The Unknown Citizen   1940

(To JS/07/M/378 This Marble Monument Is Erected

by the State)

W. H. AUDEN   [1907–1973]

He was found by the Bureau of Statistics to be
One against whom there was no official complaint,
And all the reports on his conduct agree
That, in the modern sense of an old-fashioned word, he was a saint,
For in everything he did he served the Greater Community.
Except for the War till the day he retired
He worked in a factory and never got fired,
But satisfied his employers, Fudge Motors Inc.
Yet he wasn't a scab or odd in his views,
For his Union reports that he paid his dues,   10
(Our report on his Union shows it was sound)
And our Social Psychology workers found
That he was popular with his mates and liked a drink.
The Press are convinced that he bought a paper every day
And that his reactions to advertisements were normal in every way.
Policies taken out in his name prove that he was fully insured,
And his Health-card shows he was once in hospital but left it cured.
Both Producers Research and High-Grade Living declare

He was fully sensible to the advantages of the Installment Plan
And had everything necessary to the Modern Man,   20
A phonograph, a radio, a car and a frigidaire.
Our researchers into Public Opinion are content
That he held the proper opinions for the time of year;
When there was peace, he was for peace; when there was war, he went.
He was married and added five children to the population,
Which our Eugenist says was the right number for a parent of his generation,
And our teachers report that he never interfered with their education.
Was he free? Was he happy? The question is absurd:
Had anything been wrong, we should certainly have heard.

From a Correct Address in a Suburb of a Major City   1971

HELEN SORRELLS   [b. 1908]

She wears her middle age like a cowled
gown, sleeved in it, folded high
at the breast,

charming, proper at cocktails
but the inner one raging
and how to hide her,

how to keep her leashed, contain
the heat of her, the soaring cry
never yet loosed,

demanding a chance before the years devour her,   10
before the marrow of her fine long legs
congeals and she

settles forever for this street, this house,
her face set to the world
sweet, sweet

above the shocked, astonished
hunger.

Myth   1973

MURIEL RUKEYSER   [1913–1980]

Long afterward, Oedipus, old and blinded, walked the
roads.[1]   He smelled a familiar smell.   It was
the Sphinx.   Oedipus said, "I want to ask one question.
Why didn't I recognize my mother?"   "You gave the
wrong answer," said the Sphinx.   "But that was what
made everything possible," said Oedipus.   "No," she said.
"When I asked, What walks on four legs in the morning,
two at noon, and three in the evening, you answered,
Man.   You didn't say anything about woman."
"When you say Man," said Oedipus, "you include women   10
too. Everyone knows that."   She said, "That's what
you think."

The Conscientious Objector   1947

KARL SHAPIRO   [b. 1913]

The gates clanged and they walked you into jail
More tense than felons but relieved to find
The hostile world shut out, flags that dripped
From every mother's windowpane, obscene
The bloodlust sweating from the public heart,
The dog authority slavering at your throat.
A sense of quiet, of pulling down the blind
Possessed you. Punishment you felt was clean.

The decks, the catwalks, and the narrow light
Composed a ship. This was a mutinous crew   10
Troubling the captains for plain decencies,
A *Mayflower* brim with pilgrims headed out
To establish new theocracies to west,
A Noah's ark coasting the topmost seas
Ten miles above the sodomites and fish.
These inmates loved the only living doves.

Myth

[1] Oedipus became King of Thebes when he solved the riddle of the Sphinx quoted in the poem.
He blinded himself when he discovered that he had married his own mother.

Like all men hunted from the world you made
A good community, voyaging the storm
To no safe Plymouth or green Ararat;
Trouble or calm, the men with Bibles prayed,   20
The gaunt politicals construed our hate.
The opposite of all armies, you were best
Opposing uniformity and yourselves;
Prison and personality were your fate.

You suffered not so physically but knew
Maltreatment, hunger, ennui of the mind.
Well might the soldier kissing the hot beach
Erupting in his face damn all your kind.
Yet you who saved neither yourselves nor us
Are equally with those who shed the blood   30
The heroes of our cause. Your conscience is
What we come back to in the armistice.

QUESTIONS
1. Who is the speaker of this poem, and what are his assumptions about "good citizenship"? **2.** Why does the conscientious objector feel that punishment is clean (l. 8)? **3.** The prison is compared to the Mayflower and Noah's ark. Do you find the allusive comparisons between the prisoners and the occupants of the Mayflower and the ark effective? Explain. **4.** What, finally, are the differences between the man described here and Auden's unknown citizen? Is the conscientious objector "free"? "Happy"? Is he an unknown citizen?

Ballad of Birmingham   1969

(On the Bombing of a Church in Birmingham, Alabama, 1963)

DUDLEY RANDALL   [b. 1914]

"Mother dear, may I go downtown
Instead of out to play,
And march the streets of Birmingham
In a Freedom March today?"

"No, baby, no, you may not go,
For the dogs are fierce and wild,
And clubs and hoses, guns and jails
Aren't good for a little child."

"But, mother, I won't be alone.
Other children will go with me,   10
And march the streets of Birmingham
To make our country free."

"No, baby, no, you may not go,
For I fear those guns will fire.
But you may go to church instead
And sing in the children's choir."

She has combed and brushed her night-dark hair,
And bathed rose petal sweet.
And drawn white gloves on her small brown hands,
And white shoes on her feet.   20

The mother smiled to know her child
Was in the sacred place,
But that smile was the last smile
To come upon her face.

For when she heard the explosion,
Her eyes grew wet and wild.
She raced through the streets of Birmingham
Calling for her child.

She clawed through bits of glass and brick,   30
Then lifted out a shoe.
"Oh, here's the shoe my baby wore,
But, baby, where are you?"   30

Naming of Parts   1946

HENRY REED   [b. 1914]

Today we have naming of parts. Yesterday,
We had daily cleaning. And tomorrow morning
We shall have what to do after firing. But today,
Today we have naming of parts. Japonica
Glistens like coral in all of the neighboring gardens,
      And today we have naming of parts.

This is the lower sling swivel. And this
Is the upper sling swivel, whose use you will see,
When you are given your slings. And this is the piling swivel,

Which in your case you have not got. The branches   10
Hold in the gardens their silent, eloquent gestures,
  Which in our case we have not got.

This is the safety-catch, which is always released
With an easy flick of the thumb. And please do not let me
See anyone using his finger. You can do it quite easy
If you have any strength in your thumb. The blossoms
Are fragile and motionless, never letting anyone see
  Any of them using their finger.

And this you can see is the bolt. The purpose of this
Is to open the breech, as you see. We can slide it   20
Rapidly backwards and forwards: we call this
Easing the spring. And rapidly backwards and forwards
The early bees are assaulting and fumbling the flowers:
  They call it easing the Spring.

They call it easing the Spring: it is perfectly easy
If you have any strength in your thumb: like the bolt,
And the breech, and the cocking-piece, and the point of balance,
Which in our case we have not got; and the almond-blossom
Silent in all of the gardens and the bees going backwards and forwards,
  For today we have naming of parts.   30

QUESTIONS

1. The poem has two speakers. Identify their speeches, and characterize the speakers. **2.** The last line of each stanza repeats a phrase from within the stanza. What is the effect of the repetition?

WRITING TOPIC

This poem incorporates a subtle underlying sexuality. Trace the language that generates it. What function does that sexuality serve in the poem?

from

The Children of the Poor   (1949)

GWENDOLYN BROOKS [b. 1917]

  4

First fight. Then fiddle. Ply the slipping string
With feathery sorcery; muzzle the note

With hurting love, the music that they wrote
Bewitch, bewilder. Qualify to sing
Threadwise. Devise no salt, no hempen thing
For the dear instrument to bear. Devote
The bow to silks and honey. Be remote
A while from malice and from murdering.
But first to arms, to armor. Carry hate
In front of you and harmony behind.   10
Be deaf to music and to beauty blind.
Win war. Rise bloody, maybe not too late
For having first to civilize a space
Wherein to play your violin with grace.

11

Life for my child is simple, and is good.
He knows his wish. Yes, but that is not all.
Because I know mine too.
And we both want joy of undeep and unabiding things,
Like kicking over a chair or throwing blocks out of a window
Or tipping over an icebox pan
Or snatching down curtains or fingering an electric outlet
Or a journey or a friend or an illegal kiss.
No. There is more to it than that.
It is that he has never been afraid.   10
Rather, he reaches out and lo the chair falls with a beautiful crash,
And the blocks fall, down on the people's heads,
And the water comes slooshing sloppily out across the floor.
And so forth.
Not that success, for him, is sure, infallible.
But never has he been afraid to reach.
His lesions are legion.
But reaching is his rule.

QUESTIONS
1. In sonnet 4, the poet advises the children: "First fight, Then fiddle." The meaning of "fight" is clear. What does "fiddle" symbolize? 2. Why does the poet advocate violence? 3. Is the child described in poem 11 different from the children addressed in sonnet 4? 4. Explain the meaning of line 4 in poem 11. 5. What does "reaching" in the last line mean?

In Goya's Greatest Scenes   1958

LAWRENCE FERLINGHETTI [b. 1919]

In Goya's greatest scenes[1] we seem to see
         the people of the world
    exactly at the moment when
      they first attained the title of
          'suffering humanity'
    They writhe upon the page
       in a veritable rage
          of adversity
   Heaped up
      groaning with babies and bayonets   10
          under cement skies
    in an abstract landscape of blasted trees
     bent statues bats wings and beaks
       slippery gibbets
    cadavers and carnivorous cocks
  and all the final hollering monsters
    of the
       'imagination of disaster'
   they are so bloody real
       it is as if they really still existed   20

  And they do

    Only the landscape is changed

They still are ranged along the roads
   plagued by legionaires
       false windmills and demented roosters

They are the same people
      only further from home
  on freeways fifty lanes wide
    on a concrete continent
      spaced with bland billboards   30
    illustrating imbecile illusions of happiness

  The scene shows fewer tumbrils[2]
     but more maimed citizens
        in painted cars

In Goya's Greatest Scenes
 [1] Francisco Jose de Goya (1764–1828), famous Spanish artist, celebrated for his representations
of "suffering humanity."   [2] Carts in which prisoners were conducted to the place of execution.

and they have strange license plates
and engines
            that devour America

QUESTIONS
1. To whom does the word "they" refer in line 26? **2.** What is responsible for
the "suffering" of modern American "humanity"?

Women   1970

MAY SWENSON   [1919–1989]

Women   Or they
  should be   should be
    pedestals   little horses
      moving   those wooden
    pedestals   sweet
      moving   oldfashioned
        to the   painted
          motions   rocking
            of men   horses

        the gladdest things in the toyroom

              The   feelingly
            pegs   and then
          of their   unfeelingly
        ears   To be
      so familiar   joyfully
    and dear   ridden
  to the trusting   rockingly
fists   ridden until
To be chafed   the restored

egos dismount and the legs stride away

immobile   willing
  sweetlipped   to be set
    sturdy   into motion
      and smiling   Women
        women   should be
          should always   pedestals
            be waiting   to men

Formal Application

(1963)

DONALD W. BAKER   [b. 1923]

"The poets apparently want to rejoin the human race."   TIME

I shall begin by learning to throw
the knife, first at trees, until it sticks
in the trunk and quivers every time;

next from a chair, using only wrist
and fingers, at a thing on the ground,
a fresh ant hill or a fallen leaf;

then at a moving object, perhaps
a pieplate swinging on twine, until
I pot it at least twice in three tries.

Meanwhile, I shall be teaching the birds   10
that the skinny fellow in sneakers
is a source of suet and bread crumbs,

first putting them on a shingle nailed
to a pine tree, next scattering them
on the needles, closer and closer

to my seat, until the proper bird,
a towhee, I think, in black and rust
and gray, takes tossed crumbs six feet away.

Finally, I shall coordinate
conditioned reflex and functional   20
form and qualify as Modern Man.

You see the splash of blood and feathers
and the blade pinning it to the tree?
It's called an "Audubon Crucifix."

The phrase has pleasing (even pious)
connotations, like *Arbeit Macht Frei*,
"Molotov Cocktail," and *Enola Gay*.[1]

QUESTIONS

1.   What did *Time* mean by the line Baker uses as an epigraph to this poem? How, for example, are poets not members of the human race? What does the title of the poem mean?   **2.**   In what sense does "Audubon Crucifix" have "pleasing (even pious) connotations"? What are the pleasing connotations of the expressions in the last two lines? According to this poem, what are the attributes necessary to join the human race?

Thinking about El Salvador[1]   1984

DENISE LEVERTOV   [b. 1923]

Because every day they chop heads off
I'm silent.
In each person's head they chopped off
was a tongue,
for each tongue they silence
a word in my mouth
unsays itself.

From each person's head two eyes
looked at the world;
for each gaze they cut
a line of seeing unwords itself.   10

Formal Application

   [1]*Arbeit Macht Frei*, the motto of the German Nazi party, means "labor liberates." A Molotov cocktail is a homemade hand grenade named after Vyacheslav M. Molotov, the foreign minister of Russia during the reign of Joseph Stalin. *Enola Gay* was the name of the United States plane that dropped the atomic bomb on Hiroshima in 1945.

Thinking about El Salvador

   [1]The title originally included the date 1982, but alas, the death squads and the army continue the slaughter, with U.S. help.—D.L., 1984.

Because every day they chop heads off
no force
flows into language,
thoughts
think themselves worthless.

No blade of *machete*
threatens my neck,
but its muscles
cringe and tighten,
my voice   20
hides in its throat-cave
ashamed to sound
            into that silence,
the silence

of raped women,
of priests and peasants,
teachers and children,

of all whose heads every day
float down the river
and rot   30
and sink,
not Orpheus heads[2]
still singing, bound for the sea,
but mute.

QUESTIONS
1. Explain line 11. **2.** Explain the appropriateness of the reference to Orpheus at the end of the poem. **3.** Paraphrase the poem.

WRITING TOPIC
Compare this poem with Carolyn Forché's "The Colonel" (p. 289). Are they similar in what they protest against? Which do you find more effective?

---

[2] A poet and musician from Greek mythology who rescued his wife Eurydice from Hades by charming Pluto with his lyre.

Hard Rock Returns to Prison from the Hospital for the Criminal Insane

1968

ETHERIDGE KNIGHT [1933–1991]

Hard Rock was "known not to take no shit
From nobody," and he had the scars to prove it:
Split purple lips, lumped ears, welts above
His yellow eyes, and one long scar that cut
Across his temple and plowed through a thick
Canopy of kinky hair.

The WORD was that Hard Rock wasn't a mean nigger
Anymore, that the doctors had bored a hole in his head,
Cut out part of his brain, and shot electricity
Through the rest. When they brought Hard Rock back,   10
Handcuffed and chained, he was turned loose,
Like a freshly gelded stallion, to try his new status.
And we all waited and watched like Indians at a corral,
To see if the WORD was true.

As we waited we wrapped ourselves in the cloak
Of his exploits: "Man, the last time, it took eight
Screws to put him in the Hole." "Yeah, remember when he
Smacked the captain with his dinner tray?" "He set
The record for time in the Hole—67 straight days!"
"Ol Hard Rock! man, that's one crazy nigger."   20
And then the jewel of a myth that Hard Rock had once bit
A screw on the thumb and poisoned him with syphilitic spit.

The testing came, to see if Hard Rock was really tame.
A hillbilly called him a black son of a bitch
And didn't lose his teeth, a screw who knew Hard Rock
From before shook him down and barked in his face.
And Hard Rock did *nothing*. Just grinned and looked silly,
His eyes empty like knot holes in a fence.

And even after we discovered that it took Hard Rock
Exactly 3 minutes to tell you his first name,   30

We told ourselves that he had just wised up,
Was being cool; but we could not fool ourselves for long,
And we turned away, our eyes on the ground. Crushed.

hindu destroyer/protector
right out of hindu philosophy

He had been our Destroyer, the doer of things
We dreamed of doing but could not bring ourselves to do,
The fears of years like a biting whip,
Had cut grooves too deeply across our backs.

Speakers are
the other convicts

Confession to Settle a Curse   1972

ROSMARIE WALDROP [b. 1935]

You don't
know
who I am
because
you don't know
my mother
she's always been an exemplary mother
told me so herself
there were reasons she
had to lock   10
everything that could be locked
there's much can be
locked
in a good German household crowded
with wardrobes dressers sideboards
bookcases cupboards chests bureaus
desks trunks caskets coffers all with lock
and key
and locked
it was lots of trouble   20
for her
just carry that enormous key ring
be bothered all the time
I wanted scissors stationery
my winter coat and she had to unlock
the drawer get it out and lock
all up again
me she reproached for lacking

confidence not being open
I have a mother I can tell everything   30
she told me so
I've
been bound
made fast
locked
by the key witch
but a small
winner
I'm not
in turn locking   40
a child
in my arms.

Eleanor Rigby   1966

JOHN LENNON [1940–1980] **and PAUL McCARTNEY** [b. 1942]

Ah, look at all the lonely people!
Ah, look at all the lonely people!
Eleanor Rigby picks up the rice
    in the church
Where a wedding has been.
Lives in a dream.
Waits at the window, wearing the face
    that she keeps in a jar by the door.
Who is it for?

All the lonely people,   10
    where do they all come from?
All the lonely people,
    where do they all belong?

Father McKenzie writing the words
    of a sermon that no one will hear—
No one comes near. Look at him
    working, darning his socks in the night
    when there's nobody there.
What does he care?

All the lonely people,   20
  where do they all come from?
All the lonely people.
  where do they all belong?

Ah, look at all the lonely people!
Ah, look at all the lonely people!
Eleanor Rigby died in the church and
  was buried along with her name.
Nobody came.
Father McKenzie wiping the dirt from
  his hands as he walks from the grave.   30
No one was saved.

All the lonely people,
  where do they all come from?
All the lonely people,
  where do they all belong?

QUESTIONS

1. How does the first stanza establish Eleanor Rigby's character? What is the meaning of lines 7–8? **2.** What does the portrait of Father McKenzie contribute to our understanding of the theme of the lyric? **3.** What significance has the juxtaposition of Father McKenzie's writing "a sermon that no one will hear" and "darning his socks in the night" (stanza 3)? **4.** What is the significance of Eleanor Rigby's dying in the church? Why was "No one saved" (l. 31)? **5.** What answers, if any, does the poem suggest to the questions in the last stanza?

Dreams   1968

NIKKI GIOVANNI [b. 1943]

i used to dream militant
dreams of taking
over america to show
these white folks how it should be
done
i used to dream radical dreams
of blowing everyone away with my perceptive powers
of correct analysis
i even used to think i'd be the one
to stop the riot and negotiate the peace   10
then i awoke and dug
that if i dreamed natural

dreams of being a natural
woman doing what a woman
does when she's natural
i would have a revolution

The Colonel   1981

CAROLYN FORCHÉ   [b. 1950]

What you have heard is true. I was in his house. His wife carried a tray of coffee and sugar. His daughter filed her nails, his son went out for the night. There were daily papers, pet dogs, a pistol on the cushion beside him. The moon swung bare on its black cord over the house. On the television was a cop show. It was in English. Broken bottles were embedded in the walls round the house to scoop the kneecaps from a man's legs or cut his hands to lace. On the windows there were gratings like those in liquor stores. We had dinner, rack of lamb, good wine, a gold bell was on the table for calling the maid. The maid brought green mangoes, salt, a type of bread. I was asked how I enjoyed the country. There was a brief commercial in Spanish. His wife took everything away. There was some talk then of how difficult it had become to govern. The parrot said hello on the terrace. The colonel told it to shut up, and pushed himself from the table. My friend said to me with his eyes: say nothing. The colonel returned with a sack used to bring groceries home. He spilled many human ears on the table. They were like dried peach halves. There is no other way to say this. He took one of them in his hands, shook it in our faces, dropped it into a water glass. It came alive there. I am tired of fooling around he said. As for the rights of anyone, tell your people they can go fuck themselves. He swept the ears to the floor with his arm and held the last of his wine in the air. Something for your poetry, no? he said. Some of the ears on the floor caught this scrap of his voice. Some of the ears on the floor were pressed to the ground.

QUESTIONS
1.   What is the occasion of this poem? Where is it set? How would you character-ize the colonel's family?   **2.**   "There was some talk of how difficult it had become to govern." Can you suggest why it had become difficult to govern? How does the colonel respond to these difficulties?   **3.**   What does the last sentence suggest?

WRITING TOPIC
This piece is printed as if it were prose. Does it have any of the formal character-istics of a poem?

CONFORMITY
AND
REBELLION

Self-Portrait, c. 1900, by Gwen John.

DRAMA

A Doll's House* (1879)

HENRIK IBSEN [1828–1906]

CHARACTERS

Torvald Helmer, a lawyer
Nora, his wife
Dr. Rank
Mrs. Linde
Krogstad

The Helmers' three small children
Anne-Marie, the children's nurse
A Housemaid
A Porter

SCENE. *The Helmers' living room.*

Act I

A pleasant, tastefully but not expensively furnished, living room. A door on the rear wall, right, leads to the front hall, another door, left, to Helmer's study. Between the two doors a piano. A third door in the middle of the left wall; further front a window. Near the window a round table and a small couch. Towards the rear of the right wall a fourth door; further front a tile stove with a rocking chair and a couple of armchairs in front of it. Between the stove and the door a small table. Copperplate etchings on the walls. A whatnot with porcelain figurines and other small objects. A small bookcase with de luxe editions. A rug on the floor; fire in the stove. Winter day.

The doorbell rings, then the sound of the front door opening. Nora, dressed for outdoors, enters, humming cheerfully. She carries several packages, which she puts down on the table, right. She leaves the door to the front hall open; there a Porter is seen holding a Christmas tree and a basket. He gives them to the Maid who has let them in.

Nora. Be sure to hide the Christmas tree, Helene. The children mustn't see it before tonight when we've trimmed it. (*Opens her purse; to the Porter.*) How much?

---

* A new translation by Otto Reinert.

Porter.   Fifty øre.

Nora.   Here's a crown. No, keep the change. *(The Porter thanks her, leaves. Nora closes the door. She keeps laughing quietly to herself as she takes off her coat, etc. She takes a bag of macaroons from her pocket and eats a couple. She walks cautiously over to the door to the study and listens.)* Yes, he's home. *(Resumes her humming, walks over to the table, right.)*

Helmer *(in his study).*   Is that my little lark twittering out there?

Nora *(opening some packages).*   That's right.

Helmer.   My squirrel bustling about?

Nora.   Yes.

Helmer.   When did squirrel come home?

Nora.   Just now. *(Puts the bag of macaroons back in her pocket, wipes her mouth.)* Come out here, Torvald. I want to show you what I've bought.

Helmer.   I'm busy! *(After a little while he opens the door and looks in, pen in hand.)* Bought, eh? All that? So little wastrel has been throwing money around again?

Nora.   Oh but Torvald, this Christmas we can be a little extravagant, can't we? It's the first Christmas we don't have to scrimp.

Helmer.   I don't know about that. We certainly don't have money to waste.

Nora.   Yes, Torvald, we do. A little, anyway. Just a tiny little bit? Now that you're going to get that big salary and make lots and lots of money.

Helmer.   Starting at New Year's, yes. But payday isn't till the end of the quarter.

Nora.   That doesn't matter. We can always borrow.

Helmer.   Nora! *(Goes over to her and playfully pulls her ear.)* There you go being irresponsible again. Suppose I borrowed a thousand crowns today and you spent it all for Christmas and on New Year's Eve a tile hit me in the head and laid me out cold.

Nora *(putting her hand over his mouth).*   I won't have you say such horrid things.

Helmer.   But suppose it happened. Then what?

Nora.   If it did, I wouldn't care whether we owed money or not.

Helmer.   But what about the people I had borrowed from?

Nora.   Who cares about them! They are strangers.

Helmer.   Nora, Nora, you *are* a woman! No, really! You know how I feel about that. No debts! A home in debt isn't a free home, and if it isn't free it isn't beautiful. We've managed nicely so far, you and I, and that's the way we'll go on. It won't be for much longer.

Nora *(walks over toward the stove).*   All right, Torvald. Whatever you say.

Helmer *(follows her).*   Come, come, my little songbird mustn't droop her wings. What's this? Can't have a pouty squirrel in the house, you know. *(Takes out his wallet.)* Nora, what do you think I have here?

Nora *(turns around quickly).*   Money!

Helmer.   Here. *(Gives her some bills.)* Don't you think I know Christmas is expensive?

Nora *(counting)*. Ten—twenty—thirty—forty. Thank you, thank you, Torvald. This helps a lot.

Helmer. I certainly hope so.

Nora. It does, it does. But I want to show you what I got. It was cheap, too. Look. New clothes for Ivar. And a sword. And a horse and trumpet for Bob. And a doll and a little bed for Emmy. It isn't any good, but it wouldn't last, anyway. And here's some dress material and scarves for the maids. I feel bad about old Anne-Marie, though. She really should be getting much more.

Helmer. And what's in here?

Nora *(cries)*. Not till tonight!

Helmer. I see. But now what does my little prodigal have in mind for herself?

Nora. Oh, nothing. I really don't care.

Helmer. Of course you do. Tell me what you'd like. Within reason.

Nora. Oh, I don't know. Really, I don't. The only thing—

Helmer. Well?

Nora *(fiddling with his buttons, without looking at him)*. If you really want to give me something, you might—you could—

Helmer. All right, let's have it.

Nora *(quickly)*. Some money, Torvald. Just as much as you think you can spare. Then I'll buy myself something one of these days.

Helmer. No, really Nora—

Nora. Oh yes, please, Torvald. Please? I'll wrap the money in pretty gold paper and hang it on the tree. Won't that be nice?

Helmer. What's the name for little birds that are always spending money?

Nora. Wastrels, I know. But please let's do it my way, Torvald. Then I'll have time to decide what I need most. Now that's sensible, isn't it?

Helmer *(smiling)*. Oh, very sensible. That is, if you really bought yourself something you could use. But it all disappears in the household expenses or you buy things you don't need. And then you come back to me for more.

Nora. Oh, but Torvald—

Helmer. That's the truth, dear little Nora, and you know it. *(Puts his arm around her.)* My wastrel is a little sweetheart, but she *does* go through an awful lot of money awfully fast. You've no idea how expensive it is for a man to keep a wastrel.

Nora. That's not fair, Torvald. I really save all I can.

Helmer *(laughs)*. Oh, I believe that. All you can. Meaning, exactly nothing!

Nora *(hums, smiles mysteriously)*. You don't know all the things we songbirds and squirrels need money for, Torvald.

Helmer. You know, you're funny. Just like your father. You're always looking for ways to get money, but as soon as you do it runs through your fingers and you can never say what you spent it for. Well, I guess I'll just have to take you the way you are. It's in your blood. Yes, that sort of thing is hereditary, Nora.

Nora. In that case, I wish I had inherited many of Daddy's qualities.

Helmer. And I don't want you any different from just what you are—my own sweet little songbird. Hey!—I think I just noticed something. Aren't you looking—what's the word?—a little—sly—?

Nora. I am?

Helmer. You definitely are. Look at me.

Nora *(looks at him).* Well?

Helmer *(wagging a finger).* Little sweet-tooth hasn't by any chance been on a rampage today, has she?

Nora. Of course not. Whatever makes you think that?

Helmer. A little detour by the pastryshop maybe?

Nora. No, I assure you, Torvald—

Helmer. Nibbled a little jam?

Nora. Certainly not!

Helmer. Munched a macaroon or two?

Nora. No, really, Torvald, I honestly—

Helmer. All right. Of course I was only joking.

Nora *(walks toward the table, right).* You know I wouldn't do anything to displease you.

Helmer. I know. And I have your promise. *(Over to her.)* All right, keep your little Christmas secrets to yourself, Nora darling. They'll all come out tonight, I suppose, when we light the tree.

Nora. Did you remember to invite Rank?

Helmer. No, but there's no need to. He knows he'll have dinner with us. Anyway, I'll see him later this morning. I'll ask him then. I did order some good wine. Oh Nora, you've no idea how much I'm looking forward to tonight!

Nora. Me, too. And the children Torvald! They'll have such a good time!

Helmer. You know, it *is* nice to have a good, safe job and a comfortable income. Feels good just thinking about it. Don't you agree?

Nora. Oh, it's wonderful!

Helmer. Remember last Christmas? For three whole weeks you shut yourself up every evening till long after midnight making ornaments for the Christmas tree and I don't know what else. Some big surprise for all of us, anyway. I'll be damned if I've ever been so bored in my whole life!

Nora. I wasn't bored at all!

Helmer *(smiling).* But you've got to admit you didn't have much to show for it in the end.

Nora. Oh, don't tease me again about that! Could I help it that the cat got in and tore up everything?

Helmer. Of course you couldn't, my poor little Nora. You just wanted to please the rest of us, and that's the important thing. But I *am* glad the hard times are behind us. Aren't you?

Nora. Oh yes. I think it's just wonderful.

Helmer. This year, I won't be bored and lonely. And you won't have to strain your dear eyes and your delicate little hands—

Nora *(claps her hands).*   No I won't, will I Torvald? Oh, how wonderful, how lovely, to hear you say that! *(Puts her arm under his.)* Let me tell you how I think we should arrange things, Torvald. Soon as Christmas is over—*(The doorbell rings.)* Someone's at the door. *(Straightens things up a bit.)* A caller, I suppose. Bother!

Helmer.   Remember, I'm not home for visitors.

The Maid *(in the door to the front hall).*   Ma'am, there's a lady here—

Nora.   All right. Ask her to come in.

The Maid *(to Helmer).*   And the Doctor just arrived.

Helmer.   Is he in the study?

The Maid.   Yes, sir.

Helmer exits into his study. The Maid shows Mrs. Linde in and closes the door behind her as she leaves. Mrs. Linde is in travel dress.

Mrs. Linde *(timid and a little hesitant).*   Good morning, Nora.

Nora *(uncertainly).*   Good morning.

Mrs. Linde.   I don't believe you know who I am.

Nora.   No—I'm not sure—Though I know I should—Of course! Kristine! It's you!

Mrs. Linde.   Yes, it's me.

Nora.   And I didn't even recognize you! I had no idea! *(In a lower voice.)* You've changed, Kristine.

Mrs. Linde.   I'm sure I have. It's been nine or ten long years.

Nora.   Has it really been that long? Yes, you're right. I've been so happy these last eight years. And now you're here. Such a long trip in the middle of winter. How brave!

Mrs. Linde.   I got in on the steamer this morning.

Nora.   To have some fun over the holidays, of course. That's lovely. For we are going to have fun. But take off your coat! You aren't cold, are you? *(Helps her.)* There, now! Let's sit down here by the fire and just relax and talk. No, you sit there. I want the rocking chair. *(Takes her hands.)* And now you've got your old face back. It was just for a minute, right at first—Though you are a little more pale, Kristine. And maybe a little thinner.

Mrs. Linde.   And much, much older, Nora.

Nora.   Maybe a little older. Just a teeny-weeny bit, not much. *(Interrupts herself, serious.)* Oh, but how thoughtless of me, chatting away like this! Sweet, good Kristine, can you forgive me?

Mrs. Linde.   Forgive you what, Nora?

Nora *(in a low voice).*   You poor dear, you lost your husband, didn't you?

Mrs. Linde.   Three years ago, yes.

Nora.   I know. I saw it in the paper. Oh please believe me, Kristine. I really meant to write you, but I never got around to it. Something was always coming up.

Mrs. Linde.   Of course, Nora. I understand.

Nora. No, that wasn't very nice of me. You poor thing, all you must have been through. And he didn't leave you much, either, did he?

Mrs. Linde. No.

Nora. And no children?

Mrs. Linde. No.

Nora. Nothing at all, in other words?

Mrs. Linde. Not so much as a sense of loss—a grief to live on—

Nora (*incredulous*). But Kristine, how can that *be*?

Mrs. Linde (*with a sad smile, strokes Nora's hair*). That's the way it sometimes is, Nora.

Nora. All alone. How awful for you. I have three darling children. You can't see them right now, though; they're out with their nurse. But now you must tell me everything—

Mrs. Linde. No, no; I'd rather listen to you.

Nora. No, you begin. Today I won't be selfish. Today I'll think only of you. Except there's one thing I've just got to tell you first. Something marvelous that's happened to us just these last few days. You haven't heard, have you?

Mrs. Linde. No; tell me.

Nora. Just think. My husband's been made manager of the Mutual Bank.

Mrs. Linde. Your husband—! Oh, I'm so glad!

Nora. Yes, isn't that great? You see, private law practice is so uncertain, especially when you won't have anything to do with cases that aren't—you know—quite nice. And of course Torvald won't do that and I quite agree with him. Oh, you've no idea how delighted we are! He takes over at New Year's, and he'll be getting a big salary and all sorts of extras. From now on we'll be able to live in quite a different way—exactly as we like. Oh, Kristine! I feel so carefree and happy! It's lovely to have lots and lots of money and not have to worry about a thing! Don't you agree?

Mrs. Linde. It would be nice to have enough at any rate.

Nora. No, I don't mean just enough. I mean lots and lots!

Mrs. Linde (*smiles*). Nora, Nora, when are you going to be sensible? In school you spent a great deal of money.

Nora (*quietly laughing*). Yes, and Torvald says I still do. (*Raises her finger at Mrs. Linde.*) But "Nora, Nora" isn't so crazy as you all think. Believe me, we've had nothing to be extravagant with. We've both had to work.

Mrs. Linde. You too?

Nora. Yes. Oh, it's been little things, mostly—sewing, crocheting, embroidery—that sort of thing. (*Casually.*) And other things too. You know, of course, that Torvald left government service when we got married? There was no chance of promotion in his department, and of course he had to make more money than he had been making. So for the first few years he worked altogether too hard. He had to take jobs on the side and work night and day. It turned out to be too much for him. He became seriously ill. The doctors told him he needed to go south.

Mrs. Linde. That's right; you spent a year in Italy, didn't you?

Nora.   Yes, we did. But you won't believe how hard it was to get away. Ivar had just been born. But of course we had to go. Oh, it was a wonderful trip. And it saved Torvald's life. But it took a lot of money, Kristine.

Mrs. Linde.   I'm sure it did.

Nora.   Twelve hundred specie dollars. Four thousand eight hundred crowns. That's a lot of money.

Mrs. Linde.   Yes. So it's lucky you have it when something like that happens.

Nora.   Well, actually we got the money from Daddy.

Mrs. Linde.   I see. That was about the time your father died, I believe.

Nora.   Yes, just about then. And I couldn't even go and take care of him. I was expecting little Ivar any day. And I had poor Torvald to look after, desperately sick and all. My dear, good Daddy! I never saw him again, Kristine. That's the saddest thing that's happened to me since I got married.

Mrs. Linde.   I know you were very fond of him. But then you went to Italy?

Nora.   Yes, for now we had the money, and the doctors urged us to go. So we left about a month later.

Mrs. Linde.   And when you came back your husband was well again?

Nora.   Healthy as a horse!

Mrs. Linde.   But—the doctor?

Nora.   What do you mean?

Mrs. Linde.   I thought the maid said it was the doctor, that gentleman who came the same time I did.

Nora.   Oh, that's Dr. Rank. He doesn't come as a doctor. He's our closest friend. He looks in at least once every day. No, Torvald hasn't been sick once since then. And the children are strong and healthy, too, and so am I. *(Jumps up and claps her hands.)* Oh God, Kristine! Isn't it wonderful to be alive and happy! Isn't it just lovely!—But now I'm being mean again, talking only about myself and my things. *(Sits down on a footstool close to Mrs. Linde and puts her arms on her lap.)* Please don't be angry with me! Tell me, is it really true that you didn't care for your husband? Then why did you marry him?

Mrs. Linde.   Mother was still alive then, but she was bedridden and helpless. And I had my two younger brothers to look after. I didn't think I had the right to turn him down.

Nora.   No, I suppose not. So he had money then?

Mrs. Linde.   He was quite well off, I think. But it was an uncertain business, Nora. When he died, the whole thing collapsed and there was nothing left.

Nora.   And then—?

Mrs. Linde.   Well, I had to manage as best I could. With a little store and a little school and anything else I could think of. The last three years have been one long work day for me, Nora, without any rest. But now it's over. My poor mother doesn't need me any more. She's passed away. And the boys are on their own too. They've both got jobs and support themselves.

Nora.   What a relief for you—

Mrs. Linde.   No, not relief. Just a great emptiness. Nobody to live for any more. *(Gets up restlessly.)* That's why I couldn't stand it any longer in that

little hole. Here in town it has to be easier to find something to keep me busy
and occupy my thoughts. With a little luck I should be able to find a permanent job, something in an office—

Nora.   Oh but Kristine, that's exhausting work, and you look worn out already.
It would be much better for you to go to a resort.

Mrs. Linde *(walks over to the window)*.   I don't have a Daddy who can give
me the money, Nora.

Nora *(getting up)*.   Oh, don't be angry with me.

Mrs. Linde *(over to her)*.   Dear Nora, don't *you* be angry with *me*. That's the
worst thing about my kind of situation: you become so bitter. You've nobody
to work for, and yet you have to look out for yourself, somehow. You've got
to keep on living, and so you become selfish. Do you know—when you told
me about your husband's new position I was delighted not so much for your
sake as for my own.

Nora.   Why was that? Oh, I see. You think maybe Torvald can give you a job?

Mrs. Linde.   That's what I had in mind.

Nora.   And he will too, Kristine. Just leave it to me. I'll be ever so subtle about
it. I'll think of something nice to tell him, something he'll like. Oh I so much
want to help you.

Mrs. Linde.   That's very good of you, Nora—making an effort like that for
me. Especially since you've known so little trouble and hardship in your own
life.

Nora.   I—?—have known so little—?

Mrs. Linde *(smiling)*.   Oh well, a little sewing or whatever it was. You're still
a child, Nora.

Nora *(with a toss of her head, walks away)*.   You shouldn't sound so superior.

Mrs. Linde.   I shouldn't?

Nora.   You're just like all the others. None of you think I'm good for anything
really serious.

Mrs. Linde.   Well, now—

Nora.   That I've never been through anything difficult.

Mrs. Linde.   But Nora! You just told me all your troubles!

Nora.   That's nothing! *(Lowers her voice.)* I haven't told you about *it*.

Mrs. Linde.   It? What's that? What do you mean?

Nora.   You patronize me, Kristine, and that's not fair. You're proud that you
worked so long and so hard for your mother.

Mrs. Linde.   I don't think I patronize anyone. But it *is* true that I'm both
proud and happy that I could make mother's last years comparatively easy.

Nora.   And you're proud of all you did for your brothers.

Mrs. Linde.   I think I have the right to be.

Nora.   And so do I. But now I want to tell you something, Kristine. I have
something to be proud and happy about too.

Mrs. Linde.   I don't doubt that for a moment. But what exactly do you mean?

Nora.   Not so loud! Torvald mustn't hear—not for anything in the world.
Nobody must know about this, Kristine. Nobody but you.

Mrs. Linde.   But what is it?

Nora.   Come here. *(Pulls her down on the couch beside her.)* You see, I *do* have something to be proud and happy about. I've saved Torvald's life.

Mrs. Linde.   Saved—? How do you mean—"saved"?

Nora.   I told you about our trip to Italy. Torvald would have died if he hadn't gone.

Mrs. Linde.   I understand that. And so your father gave you the money you needed.

Nora *(smiles).*   Yes, that's what Torvald and all the others think. But—

Mrs. Linde.   But what?

Nora.   Daddy didn't give us a penny. *I* raised that money.

Mrs. Linde.   *You* did? That whole big amount?

Nora.   Twelve hundred specie dollars. Four thousand eight hundred crowns. *Now* what do you say?

Mrs. Linde.   But Nora, how could you? Did you win in the state lottery?

Nora *(contemptuously).*   State lottery! *(Snorts.)* What is so great about that?

Mrs. Linde.   Where did it come from then?

Nora *(humming and smiling, enjoying her secret).*   Hmmm. Tra-la-la-la-la!

Mrs. Linde.   You certainly couldn't have borrowed it.

Nora.   Oh? And why not?

Mrs. Linde.   A wife can't borrow money without her husband's consent.

Nora *(with a toss of her head).*   Oh, I don't know—take a wife with a little bit of a head for business—a wife who knows how to manage things—

Mrs. Linde.   But Nora, I don't understand at all—

Nora.   You don't have to. I didn't say I borrowed the money, did I? I could have gotten it some other way. *(Leans back.)* An admirer may have given it to me. When you're as tolerably goodlooking as I am—

Mrs. Linde.   Oh, you're crazy.

Nora.   I think you're dying from curiosity, Kristine.

Mrs. Linde.   I'm beginning to think you've done something very foolish, Nora.

Nora *(sits up).*   Is it foolish to save your husband's life?

Mrs. Linde.   I say it's foolish to act behind his back.

Nora.   But don't you see: he couldn't be told! You're missing the whole point, Kristine. We couldn't even let him know how seriously ill he was. The doctors came to *me* and told me his life was in danger, that nothing could save him but a stay in the south. Don't you think I tried to work on him? I told him how lovely it would be if I could go abroad like other young wives. I cried and begged. I said he'd better remember what condition I was in, that he had to be nice to me and do what I wanted. I even hinted he could borrow the money. But that almost made him angry with me. He told me I was being irresponsible and that it was his duty as my husband not to give in to my moods and whims—I think that's what he called it. All right, I said to myself, you've got to be saved somehow, and so I found a way—

Mrs. Linde.   And your husband never learned from your father that the money didn't come from him?

Nora. Never. Daddy died that same week. I thought of telling him all about it and ask him not to say anything. But since he was so sick—It turned out I didn't have to—

Mrs. Linde. And you've never told your husband?

Nora. Of course not! Good heavens, how could I? He, with his strict principles! Besides, you know how men are. Torvald would find it embarrassing and humiliating to learn that he owed me anything. It would upset our whole relationship. Our happy, beautiful home would no longer be what it is.

Mrs. Linde. Aren't you ever going to tell him?

Nora (*reflectively, half smiling*). Yes—one day, maybe. Many, many years from now, when I'm no longer young and pretty. Don't laugh! I mean when Torvald no longer feels about me the way he does now, when he no longer thinks it's fun when I dance for him and put on costumes and recite for him. Then it will be good to have something in reserve—(*Interrupts herself.*) Oh, I'm just being silly! That day will never come.—Well, now, Kristine, what do you think of my great secret? Don't you think I'm good for something too?—By the way, you wouldn't believe all the worry I've had because of it. It's been very hard to meet my obligations on schedule. You see, in business there's something called quarterly interest and something called installments on the principal, and those are terribly hard to come up with. I've had to save a little here and a little there, whenever I could. I couldn't use much of the housekeeping money, for Torvald has to eat well. And I couldn't use what I got for clothes for the children. They have to look nice, and I didn't think it would be right to spend less than I got—the sweet little things!

Mrs. Linde. Poor Nora! So you had to take it from your own allowance!

Nora. Yes, of course. After all, it was my affair. Every time Torvald gave me money for a new dress and things like that, I never used more than half of it. I always bought the cheapest, simplest things for myself. Thank God, everything looks good on me, so Torvald never noticed. But it was hard many times, Kristine, for it's fun to have pretty clothes. Don't you think?

Mrs. Linde. Certainly.

Nora. Anyway, I had other ways of making money too. Last winter I was lucky enough to get some copying work. So I locked the door and sat up writing every night till quite late. God! I often got so tired—! But it was great fun, too, working and making money. It was almost like being a man.

Mrs. Linde. But how much have you been able to pay off this way?

Nora. I couldn't tell you exactly. You see, it's very difficult to keep track of business like that. All I know is I have been paying off as much as I've been able to scrape together. Many times I just didn't know what to do. (*Smiles.*) Then I used to imagine a rich old gentleman had fallen in love with me—

Mrs. Linde. What! What old gentleman?

Nora. Phooey! And now he was dead and they were reading his will, and there it said in big letters, "All my money is to be paid in cash immediately to the charming Mrs. Nora Helmer."

Mrs. Linde. But dearest Nora—who *was* this old gentleman?

Nora. For heaven's sake, Kristine, don't you see? There *was* no old gentleman.

He was just somebody I made up when I couldn't think of any way to raise the money. But never mind him. The old bore can be anyone he likes to for all I care. I have no use for him or his last will, for now I don't have a single worry in the world. *(Jumps up.)* Dear God, what a lovely thought this is! To be able to play and have fun with the children, to have everything nice and pretty in the house, just the way Torvald likes it! Not a care! And soon spring will be here, and the air will be blue and high. Maybe we can travel again. Maybe I'll see the ocean again! Oh, yes, yes!—it's wonderful to be alive and happy!

The doorbell rings.

Mrs. Linde *(getting up).*   There's the doorbell. Maybe I better be going.
Nora.   No, please stay. I'm sure it's just someone for Torvald—
The Maid *(in the hall door).*   Excuse me, ma'am. There's a gentleman here who'd like to see Mr. Helmer.
Nora.   You mean the bank manager.
The Maid.   Sorry, ma'am; the bank manager. But I didn't know—since the Doctor is with him—
Nora.   Who is the gentleman?
Krogstad *(appearing in the door).*   It's just me, Mrs. Helmer.

Mrs. Linde starts, looks, turns away toward the window.

Nora *(takes a step toward him, tense, in a low voice).*   You? What do you want? What do you want with my husband?
Krogstad.   Bank business—in a way. I have a small job in the Mutual, and I understand your husband is going to be our new boss—
Nora.   So it's just—
Krogstad.   Just routine business, ma'am. Nothing else.
Nora.   All right. In that case, why don't you go through the door to the office.

Dismisses him casually as she closes the door. Walks over to the stove and tends the fire.

Mrs. Linde.   Nora—who was that man?
Nora.   His name's Krogstad. He's a lawyer.
Mrs. Linde.   So it *was* him.
Nora.   Do you know him?
Mrs. Linde.   I used to—many years ago. For a while he clerked in our part of the country.
Nora.   Right. He did.
Mrs. Linde.   He has changed a great deal.
Nora.   I believe he had a very unhappy marriage.
Mrs. Linde.   And now he's a widower, isn't he?
Nora.   With many children. There now; it's burning nicely again. *(Closes the stove and moves the rocking chair a little to the side.)*

Mrs. Linde. They say he's into all sorts of business.

Nora. Really? Maybe so. I wouldn't know. But let's not think about business. It's such a bore.

Dr. Rank *(appears in the door to Helmer's study).* No, I don't want to be in the way. I'd rather talk to your wife a bit. *(Closes the door and notices Mrs. Linde.)* Oh, I beg your pardon. I believe I'm in the way here too.

Nora. No, not at all. *(Introduces them.)* Dr. Rank. Mrs. Linde.

Rank. Aha. A name often heard in this house. I believe I passed you on the stairs coming up.

Mrs. Linde. Yes. I'm afraid I climb stairs very slowly. They aren't good for me.

Rank. I see. A slight case of inner decay, perhaps?

Mrs. Linde. Overwork, rather.

Rank. Oh, is that all? And now you've come to town to relax at all the parties?

Mrs. Linde. I have come to look for a job.

Rank. A proven cure for overwork, I take it?

Mrs. Linde. One has to live, Doctor.

Rank. Yes, that seems to be the common opinion.

Nora. Come on, Dr. Rank—you want to live just as much as the rest of us.

Rank. Of course I do. Miserable as I am, I prefer to go on being tortured as long as possible. All my patients feel the same way. And that's true of the moral invalids too. Helmer is talking with a specimen right this minute.

Mrs. Linde *(in a low voice).* Ah!

Nora. What do you mean?

Rank. Oh, this lawyer, Krogstad. You don't know him. The roots of his character are decayed. But even he began by saying something about having *to live*—as if it were a matter of the highest importance.

Nora. Oh? What did he want with Torvald?

Rank. I don't really know. All I heard was something about the bank.

Nora. I didn't know that Krog—that this Krogstad had anything to do with the Mutual Bank.

Rank. Yes, he seems to have some kind of job there. *(To Mrs. Linde.)* I don't know if you are familiar in your part of the country with the kind of person who is always running around trying to sniff out cases of moral decrepitude and as soon as he finds one puts the individual under observation in some excellent position or other. All the healthy ones are left out in the cold.

Mrs. Linde. I should think it's the sick who need looking after the most.

Rank *(shrugs his shoulders).* There we are. That's the attitude that turns society into a hospital.

Nora, absorbed in her own thoughts, suddenly starts giggling and clapping her hands.

Rank. What's so funny about that? Do you even know what society is?

Nora. What do I care about your stupid society! I laughed at something entirely different—something terribly amusing. Tell me, Dr. Rank—all the employees in the Mutual Bank, from now on they'll all be dependent on Torvald, right?

Rank.   Is that what you find so enormously amusing?

Nora *(smiles and hums)*.   That's my business, that's my business! *(Walks around.)* Yes, I do think it's fun that we—that Torvald is going to have so much influence on so many people's lives. *(Brings out the bag of macaroons.)* Have a macaroon, Dr. Rank.

Rank.   Well, well—macaroons. I thought they were banned around here.

Nora.   Yes, but these were some that Kristine gave me.

Mrs. Linde.   What! I?

Nora.   That's all right. Don't look so scared. You couldn't know that Torvald won't let me have them. He's afraid they'll ruin my teeth. But who cares! Just once in a while—! Right, Dr. Rank? Have one! *(Puts a macaroon into his mouth.)* You too, Kristine. And one for me. A very small one. Or at most two. *(Walks around again.)* Yes, I really feel very, very happy. Now there's just one thing I'm dying to do.

Rank.   Oh? And what's that?

Nora.   Something I'm dying to say so Torvald could hear.

Rank.   And why can't you?

Nora.   I don't dare to, for it's not nice.

Mrs. Linde.   Not nice?

Rank.   In that case, I guess you'd better not. But surely to the two of us—? What is it you'd like to say for Helmer to hear?

Nora.   I want to say, "Goddammit!"

Rank.   Are you out of your mind!

Mrs. Linde.   For heaven's sake, Nora!

Rank.   Say it. Here he comes.

Nora *(hiding the macaroons)*.   Shhh!

Helmer enters from his study, carrying his hat and overcoat.

Nora *(going to him)*.   Well, dear, did you get rid of him?

Helmer.   Yes, he just left.

Nora.   Torvald, I want you to meet Kristine. She's just come to town.

Helmer.   Kristine—? I'm sorry; I don't think—

Nora.   Mrs. Linde, Torvald dear. Mrs. Kristine Linde.

Helmer.   Ah, yes. A childhood friend of my wife's, I suppose.

Mrs. Linde.   Yes, we've known each other for a long time.

Nora.   Just think; she has come all this way just to see you.

Helmer.   I'm not sure I understand—

Mrs. Linde.   Well, not really—

Nora.   You see, Kristine is an absolutely fantastic secretary, and she would so much like to work for a competent executive and learn more than she knows already—

Helmer.   Very sensible, I'm sure, Mrs. Linde.

Nora.   So when she heard about your appointment—there was a wire—she came here as fast as she could. How about it, Torvald? Couldn't you do something for Kristine? For my sake. Please?

Helmer.   Quite possibly. I take it you're a widow, Mrs. Linde?

Mrs. Linde.   Yes.

Helmer.   And you've had offic: experience?

Mrs. Linde.   Some—yes.

Helmer.   In that case I think it's quite likely that I'll be able to find you a position.

Nora (*claps her hands*).   I knew it! I knew it!

Helmer.   You've arrived at a most opportune time, Mrs. Linde.

Mrs. Linde.   Oh, how can I ever thank you—

Helmer.   Not at all, not at all. (*Puts his coat on.*) But today you'll have to excuse me—

Rank.   Wait a minute; I'll come with you. (*Gets his fur coat from the front hall, warms it by the stove.*)

Nora.   Don't be long, Torvald.

Helmer.   An hour or so; no more.

Nora.   Are you leaving, too, Kristine?

Mrs. Linde (*putting on her things*).   Yes, I'd better go and find a place to stay.

Helmer.   Good. Then we'll be going the same way.

Nora (*helping her*).   I'm sorry this place is so small, but I don't think we very well could—

Mrs. Linde.   Of course! Don't be silly, Nora. Goodbye, and thank you for everything.

Nora.   Goodbye. We'll see you soon. You'll be back this evening, of course. And you too, Dr. Rank; right? If you feel well enough? Of course you will. Just wrap yourself up.

General small talk as all exit into the hall. Children's voices are heard on the stairs.

Nora.   There they are! There they are! (*She runs and opens the door. The nurse Anne-Marie enters with the children.*)

Nora.   Come in! Come in! (*Bends over and kisses them.*) Oh, you sweet, sweet darlings! Look at them, Kristine! Aren't they beautiful?

Rank.   No standing around in the draft!

Helmer.   Come along, Mrs. Linde. This place isn't fit for anyone but mothers right now.

Dr. Rank, Helmer, and Mrs. Linde go down the stairs. The Nurse enters the living room with the children. Nora follows, closing the door behind her.

Nora.   My, how nice you all look! Such red cheeks! Like apples and roses. (*The children all talk at the same time.*) You've had so much fun? I bet you have. Oh, isn't that nice! You pulled both Emmy and Bob on your sleigh? Both at the same time? That's very good, Ivar. Oh, let me hold her for a minute, Anne-Marie. My sweet little doll baby! *(Takes the smallest of the children from the Nurse and dances with her.)* Yes, yes, of course; Mama'll dance with you too, Bob. What? You threw snowballs? Oh, I wish I'd been there! No, no; *I* want to take their clothes off, Anne-Marie. Please let me; I think it's so much fun. You go on in. You look frozen. There's hot coffee on the stove.

The Nurse exits into the room to the left. Nora takes the children's wraps off and throws them all around. They all keep telling her things at the same time.

Nora.   Oh, really? A big dog ran after you? But it didn't bite you. Of course not. Dogs don't bite sweet little doll babies. Don't peek at the packages, Ivar! What's in them? Wouldn't you like to know! No, no; that's something terrible! Play? You want to play? What do you want to play? Okay, let's play hide-and-seek. Bob hides first. You want *me* to? All right. I'll go first.

Laughing and shouting, Nora and the children play in the living room and in the adjacent room, right. Finally, Nora hides herself under the table; the children rush in, look for her, can't find her. They hear her low giggle, run to the table, lift the rug that covers it, see her. General hilarity. She crawls out, pretends to scare them. New delight. In the meantime there has been a knock on the door between the living room and the front hall, but nobody has noticed. Now the door is opened halfway; Krogstad appears. He waits a little. The play goes on.

Krogstad.   Pardon me, Mrs. Helmer—
Nora *(with a muted cry turns around, jumps up).*   Ah! What do you want?
Krogstad.   I'm sorry. The front door was open. Somebody must have forgotten to close it—
Nora *(standing up).*   My husband isn't here, Mr. Krogstad.
Krogstad.   I know.
Nora.   So what do you want?
Krogstad.   I'd like a word with you.
Nora.   With—? *(To the children.)* Go in to Anne-Marie. What? No, the strange man won't do anything bad to Mama. When he's gone we'll play some more.

She takes the children into the room to the left and closes the door.

Nora *(tense, troubled).*   You want to speak with me?
Krogstad.   Yes I do.
Nora.   Today—? It isn't the first of the month yet.
Krogstad.   No, it's Christmas Eve. It's up to you what kind of holiday you'll have.
Nora.   What do you want? I can't possibly—
Krogstad.   Let's not talk about that just yet. There's something else. You do have a few minutes, don't you?

Nora. Yes. Yes, of course. That is,—

Krogstad. Good. I was sitting in Olsen's restaurant when I saw your husband go by.

Nora. Yes—?

Krogstad. —with a lady.

Nora. What of it?

Krogstad. May I be so free as to ask: wasn't that lady Mrs. Linde?

Nora. Yes.

Krogstad. Just arrived in town?

Nora. Yes, today.

Krogstad. She's a good friend of yours, I understand?

Nora. Yes, she is. But I fail to see—

Krogstad. I used to know her myself.

Nora. I know that.

Krogstad. So you know about that. I thought as much. In that case, let me ask you a simple question. Is Mrs. Linde going to be employed in the bank?

Nora. What makes you think you have the right to cross-examine me like this, Mr. Krogstad—you, one of my husband's employees? But since you ask, I'll tell you. Yes, Mrs. Linde is going to be working in the bank. And it was I who recommended her, Mr. Krogstad. Now you know.

Krogstad. So I was right.

Nora (*walks up and down*). After all, one does have a little influence, you know. Just because you're a woman, it doesn't mean that—Really, Mr. Krogstad, people in a subordinate position should be careful not to offend someone who—oh well—

Krogstad. —has influence?

Nora. Exactly.

Krogstad (*changing his tone*). Mrs. Helmer, I must ask you to be good enough to use your influence on my behalf.

Nora. What do you mean?

Krogstad. I want you to make sure that I am going to keep my subordinate position in the bank.

Nora. I don't understand. Who is going to take your position away from you?

Krogstad. There's no point in playing ignorant with me, Mrs. Helmer. I can very well appreciate that your friend would find it unpleasant to run into me. So now I know who I can thank for my dismissal.

Nora. But I assure you—

Krogstad. Never mind. Just want to say you still have time. I advise you to use your influence to prevent it.

Nora. But Mr. Krogstad, I don't have any influence—none at all.

Krogstad. No? I thought you just said—

Nora. Of course I didn't mean it that way. I! Whatever makes you think that I have any influence of that kind on my husband?

Krogstad. I went to law school with your husband. I have no reason to think that the bank manager is less susceptible than other husbands.

Nora. If you're going to insult my husband, I'll ask you to leave.

Krogstad.   You're brave, Mrs. Helmer.

Nora.   I'm not afraid of you any more. After New Year's I'll be out of this thing with you.

Krogstad *(more controlled).*   Listen, Mrs. Helmer. If necessary I'll fight as for my life to keep my little job in the bank.

Nora.   So it seems.

Krogstad.   It isn't just the money; that's really the smallest part of it. There is something else—Well, I guess I might as well tell you. It's like this. I'm sure you know, like everybody else, that some years ago I committed—an impropriety.

Nora.   I believe I've heard it mentioned.

Krogstad.   The case never came to court, but from that moment all doors were closed to me. So I took up the kind of business you know about. I had to do something, and I think I can say about myself that I have not been among the worst. But now I want to get out of all that. My sons are growing up. For their sake I must get back as much of my good name as I can. This job in the bank was like the first rung on the ladder. And now your husband wants to kick me down and leave me back in the mud again.

Nora.   But I swear to you, Mr. Krogstad; it's not at all in my power to help you.

Krogstad.   That's because you don't want to. But I have the means to force you.

Nora.   You don't mean you're going to tell my husband I owe you money?

Krogstad.   And if I did?

Nora.   That would be a mean thing to do. *(Almost crying.)* That secret, which is my joy and my pride—for him to learn about it in such a coarse and ugly manner—to learn it from *you*—! It would be terribly unpleasant for me.

Krogstad.   Just unpleasant?

Nora *(heatedly).*   But go ahead! Do it! It will be worse for you than for me. When my husband realizes what a bad person you are, you'll be sure to lose your job.

Krogstad.   I asked you if it was just domestic unpleasantness you were afraid of?

Nora.   When my husband finds out, of course he'll pay off the loan, and then we won't have anything more to do with you.

Krogstad *(stepping closer).*   Listen, Mrs. Helmer—either you have a very bad memory, or you don't know much about business. I think I had better straighten you out on a few things.

Nora.   What do you mean?

Krogstad.   When your husband was ill, you came to me to borrow twelve hundred dollars.

Nora.   I knew nobody else.

Krogstad.   I promised to get you the money—

Nora.   And you did.

Krogstad.   I promised to get you the money on certain conditions. At the time you were so anxious about your husband's health and so set on getting him away that I doubt very much that you paid much attention to the details of our transaction. That's why I remind you of them now. Anyway, I promised to get you the money if you would sign an I.O.U., which I drafted.

Nora.   And which I signed.

Krogstad.   Good. But below your signature I added a few lines, making your father security for the loan. Your father was supposed to put his signature to those lines.

Nora.   Supposed to—? He did.

Krogstad.   I had left the date blank. That is, your father was to date his own signature. You recall that, don't you, Mrs. Helmer?

Nora.   I guess so—

Krogstad.   I gave the note to you. You were to mail it to your father. Am I correct?

Nora.   Yes.

Krogstad.   And of course you did so right away, for no more than five or six days later you brought the paper back to me, signed by your father. Then I paid you the money.

Nora.   Well? And haven't I been keeping up with the payments?

Krogstad.   Fairly well, yes. But to get back to what we were talking about— those were difficult days for you, weren't they, Mrs. Helmer?

Nora.   Yes, they were.

Krogstad.   Your father was quite ill, I believe.

Nora.   He was dying.

Krogstad.   And died shortly afterwards?

Nora.   That's right.

Krogstad.   Tell me, Mrs. Helmer; do you happen to remember the date of your father's death? I mean the exact day of the month?

Nora.   Daddy died on September 29.

Krogstad.   Quite correct. I have ascertained that fact. That's why there is something peculiar about this (*takes out a piece of paper*), which I can't account for.

Nora.   Peculiar? How? I don't understand—

Krogstad.   It seems very peculiar, Mrs. Helmer, that your father signed this promissory note three days after his death.

Nora.   How so? I don't see what—

Krogstad.   Your father died on September 29. Now look. He has dated his signature October 2. Isn't that odd?

Nora remains silent.

Krogstad.   Can you explain it?

Nora is still silent.

Krogstad.   I also find it striking that the date and the month and the year are not in your father's handwriting but in a hand I think I recognize. Well, that might be explained. Your father may have forgotten to date his signature and somebody else may have done it here, guessing at the date before he had learned of your father's death. That's all right. It's only the signature itself that matters. And that is genuine, isn't it, Mrs. Helmer? Your father *did* put his name to this note?

Nora *(after a brief silence tosses her head back and looks defiantly at him).*   No, he didn't. I wrote Daddy's name.

Krogstad.   Mrs. Helmer—do you realize what a dangerous admission you just made?

Nora.   Why? You'll get your money soon.

Krogstad.   Let me ask you something. Why didn't you mail this note to your father?

Nora.   Because it was impossible. Daddy was sick—you know that. If I had asked him to sign it, I would have had to tell him what the money was for. But I couldn't tell him, as sick as he was, that my husband's life was in danger. That was impossible. Surely you can see that.

Krogstad.   Then it would have been better for you if you had given up your trip abroad.

Nora.   No, that was impossible! That trip was to save my husband's life. I couldn't give it up.

Krogstad.   But didn't you realize that what you did amounted to fraud against me?

Nora.   I couldn't let that make any difference. I didn't care about you at all. I hated the way you made all those difficulties for me, even though you knew the danger my husband was in. I thought you were cold and unfeeling.

Krogstad.   Mrs. Helmer, obviously you have no clear idea of what you have done. Let me tell you that what I did that time was no more and no worse. And it ruined my name and reputation.

Nora.   You! Are you trying to tell me that you did something brave once in order to save your wife's life?

Krogstad.   The law doesn't ask about motives.

Nora.   Then it's a bad law.

Krogstad.   Bad or not—if I produce this note in court you'll be judged according to the law.

Nora.   I refuse to believe you. A daughter shouldn't have the right to spare her dying old father worry and anxiety? A wife shouldn't have the right to save her husband's life? I don't know the laws very well, but I'm sure that somewhere they make allowance for cases like that. And you, a lawyer, don't know that? I think you must be a bad lawyer, Mr. Krogstad.

Krogstad.   That may be. But business—the kind of business you and I have with one another—don't you think I know something about that? Very well. Do what you like. But let me tell you this: if I'm going to be kicked out again, you'll keep me company. *(He bows and exits through the front hall.)*

Nora *(pauses thoughtfully; then, with a defiant toss of her head).*   Oh, nonsense! Trying to scare me like that! I'm not all that silly. *(Starts picking up* *the children's clothes; soon stops.)* But—? No! That's impossible! I did it for love!

The Children *(in the door to the left).*   Mama, the strange man just left. We saw him.

Nora.   Yes, yes; I know. But don't tell anybody about the strange man. Do you hear? Not even Daddy.

The Children.   We won't. But now you'll play with us again, won't you, Mama?

Nora.   No, not right now.

The Children.   But Mama—you promised.

Nora.   I know, but I can't just now. Go to your own room. I've so much to do. Be nice now, my little darlings. Do as I say. *(She nudges them gently into the other room and closes the door. She sits down on the couch, picks up a piece of embroidery, makes a few stitches, then stops.)* No! *(Throws the embroidery down, goes to the hall door and calls out.)* Helene! Bring the Christmas tree in here, please! *(Goes to the table, left, opens the drawer, halts.)* No—that's impossible!

The Maid *(with the Christmas tree).*   Where do you want it, ma'am?

Nora.   There. The middle of the floor.

The Maid.   You want anything else?

Nora.   No, thanks. I have everything I need. *(The Maid goes out. Nora starts trimming the tree.)* I want candles—and flowers—That awful man! Oh, nonsense! There's nothing wrong. This will be a lovely tree. I'll do everything you want me to, Torvald. I'll sing for you—dance for you—

Helmer, a bundle of papers under his arm, enters from outside.

Nora.   Ah—you're back already?

Helmer.   Yes. Has anybody been here?

Nora.   Here? No.

Helmer.   That's funny. I saw Krogstad leaving just now.

Nora.   Oh? Oh yes, that's right. Krogstad was here for just a moment.

Helmer.   I can tell from your face that he came to ask you to put in a word for him.

Nora.   Yes.

Helmer.   And it was supposed to be your own idea, wasn't it? You were not to tell me he'd been here. He asked you that too, didn't he?

Nora.   Yes, Torvald, but—

Helmer.   Nora, Nora, how could you! Talk to a man like that and make him promises! And lying to me about it afterwards—!

Nora.   Lying—?

Helmer.   Didn't you say nobody had been here? *(Shakes his finger at her.)* My little songbird must never do that again. Songbirds are supposed to have clean beaks to chirp with—no false notes. *(Puts his arm around her waist.)* Isn't that so? Of course it is. *(Lets her go.)* And that's enough about that. *(Sits *down in front of the fireplace.)* Ah, it's nice and warm in here. *(Begins to leaf through his papers.)*

Nora *(busy with the tree; after a brief pause).*   Torvald.

Helmer.   Yes.

Nora.   I'm looking forward so much to the Stenborgs' costume party day after tomorrow.

Helmer.   And I can't wait to find out what you're going to surprise me with.

Nora.   Oh, that silly idea!

Helmer.   Oh?

Nora.   I can't think of anything. It all seems so foolish and pointless.

Helmer.   Ah, my little Nora admits that?

Nora *(behind his chair, her arms on the back of the chair).*   Are you very busy, Torvald?

Helmer.   Well—

Nora.   What are all those papers?

Helmer.   Bank business.

Nora.   Already?

Helmer.   I've asked the board to give me the authority to make certain changes in organization and personnel. That's what I'll be doing over the holidays. I want it all settled before New Year's.

Nora.   So that's why this poor Krogstad—

Helmer.   Hm.

Nora *(leisurely playing with the hair on his neck).*   If you weren't so busy, Torvald, I'd ask you for a great big favor.

Helmer.   Let's hear it, anyway.

Nora.   I don't know anyone with better taste than you, and I want so much to look nice at the party. Couldn't you sort of take charge of me, Torvald, and decide what I'll wear—Help me with my costume?

Helmer.   Aha! Little Lady Obstinate is looking for someone to rescue her?

Nora.   Yes, Torvald. I won't get anywhere without your help.

Helmer.   All right. I'll think about it. We'll come up with something.

Nora.   Oh, you *are* nice! *(Goes back to the Christmas tree. A pause.)* Those red flowers look so pretty.—Tell me, was it really all that bad what this Krogstad fellow did?

Helmer.   He forged signatures. Do you have any idea what that means?

Nora.   Couldn't it have been because he felt he had to?

Helmer.   Yes, or like so many others he may simply have been thoughtless. I'm not so heartless as to condemn a man absolutely because of a single imprudent act.

Nora.   Of course not, Torvald!

Helmer.   People like him can redeem themselves morally by openly confessing their crime and taking their punishment.

Nora.   Punishment—?

Helmer.   But that was not the way Krogstad chose. He got out of it with tricks and evasions. That's what has corrupted him.

Nora. So you think that if—?

Helmer. Can't you imagine how a guilty person like that has to lie and fake and dissemble wherever he goes—putting on a mask before everybody he's close to, even his own wife and children. It's this thing with the children that's the worst part of it, Nora.

Nora. Why is that?

Helmer. Because when a man lives inside such a circle of stinking lies he brings infection into his own home and contaminates his whole family. With every breath of air his children inhale the germs of something ugly.

Nora *(moving closer behind him).* Are you so sure of that?

Helmer. Of course I am. I have seen enough examples of that in my work. Nearly all young criminals have had mothers who lied.

Nora. Why mothers—particularly?

Helmer. Most often mothers. But of course fathers tend to have the same influence. Every lawyer knows that. And yet, for years this Krogstad has been poisoning his own children in an atmosphere of lies and deceit. That's why I call him a lost soul morally. *(Reaches out for her hands.)* And that's why my sweet little Nora must promise me never to take his side again. Let's shake on that.—What? What's this? Give me your hand. There! Now that's settled. I assure you, I would find it impossible to work in the same room with that man. I feel literally sick when I'm around people like that.

Nora *(withdraws her hand and goes to the other side of the Christmas tree).* It's so hot in here. And I have so much to do.

Helmer *(gets up and collects his papers).* Yes, and I really should try to get some of this reading done before dinner. I must think about your costume too. And maybe just possibly I'll have something to wrap in gilt paper and hang on the Christmas tree. *(Puts his hand on her head.)* Oh my adorable little songbird! *(Enters his study and closes the door.)*

Nora *(after a pause, in a low voice).* It's all a lot of nonsense. It's not that way at all. It's impossible. It has to be impossible.

The Nurse *(in the door, left).* The little ones are asking ever so nicely if they can't come in and be with their mama.

Nora. No, no, no! Don't let them in here! You stay with them, Anne-Marie.

The Nurse. If you say so, ma'am. *(Closes the door.)*

Nora *(pale with terror).* Corrupt my little children—! Poison my home—? *(Brief pause; she lifts her head.)* That's not true. Never. Never in a million years.

Act II

The same room. The Christmas tree is in the corner by the piano, stripped shabby-looking, with burnt-down candles. Nora's outside clothes are on the couch. Nora is alone. She walks around restlessly. She stops by the couch and picks up her coat.

Nora *(drops the coat again).*   There's somebody now! *(Goes to the door, listens.)* No. Nobody. Of course not—not on Christmas. And not tomorrow either.[1]—But perhaps—*(Opens the door and looks.)* No, nothing in the mailbox. All empty. *(Comes forward.)* How silly I am! Of course he isn't serious. Nothing like that could happen. After all, I have three small children.

The Nurse enters from the room, left, carrying a big carton.

The Nurse.   Well, at last I found it—the box with your costume.
Nora.   Thanks. Just put it on the table.
Nurse *(does so).*   But it's all a big mess, I'm afraid.
Nora.   Oh, I wish I could tear the whole thing to little pieces!
Nurse.   Heavens! It's not as bad as all that. It can be fixed all right. All it takes is a little patience.
Nora.   I'll go over and get Mrs. Linde to help me.
Nurse.   Going out again? In this awful weather? You'll catch a cold.
Nora.   That might not be such a bad thing. How are the children?
Nurse.   The poor little dears are playing with their presents, but—
Nora.   Do they keep asking for me?
Nurse.   Well, you know, they're used to being with their mamma.
Nora.   I know. But Anne-Marie, from now on I can't be with them as much as before.
Nurse.   Oh well. Little children get used to everything.
Nora.   You think so? Do you think they'll forget their mamma if I were gone altogether?
Nurse.   Goodness me—gone altogether?
Nora.   Listen, Anne-Marie—something I've wondered about. How could you bring yourself to leave your child with strangers?
Nurse.   But I had to, if I were to nurse you.
Nora.   Yes, but how could you *want* to?
Nurse.   When I could get such a nice place? When something like that happens to a poor young girl, she'd better be grateful for whatever she gets. For *he* didn't do a thing for me—the louse!
Nora.   But your daughter has forgotten all about you, hasn't she?
Nurse.   Oh no! Not at all! She wrote to me both when she was confirmed and when she got married.
Nora *(putting her arms around her neck).*   You dear old thing—you were a good mother to me when I was little.
Nurse.   Poor little Nora had no one else, you know.
Nora.   And if my little ones didn't, I know you'd—oh, I'm being silly! *(Opens the carton.)* Go in to them, please. I really should—. Tomorrow you'll see how pretty I'll be.
Nurse.   I know. There won't be anybody at that party half as pretty as you, ma'am. *(Goes out, left.)*

---

[1] In Norway both December 25 and 26 are legal holidays.

Nora *(begins to take clothes out of the carton; in a moment she throws it all down).* If only I dared to go out. If only I knew nobody would come. That nothing would happen while I was gone.—How silly! Nobody'll come. Just don't think about it. Brush the muff. Beautiful gloves. Beautiful gloves. Forget it. Forget it. One, two, three, four, five, six—*(Cries out.)* There they are! *(Moves toward the door, stops irresolutely.)*

Mrs. Linde enters from the hall. She has already taken off her coat.

Nora.   Oh, it's you, Kristine. There's no one else out there, is there? I'm so glad you're here.

Mrs. Linde.   They told me you'd asked for me.

Nora.   I just happened to walk by. I need your help with something—badly. Let's sit here on the couch. Look. Torvald and I are going to a costume party tomorrow night—at Consul Stenborg's upstairs—and Torvald wants me to go as a Neapolitan fisher girl and dance the tarantella. I learned it when we were on Capri.

Mrs. Linde.   Well, well! So you'll be putting on a whole show?

Nora.   Yes. Torvald thinks I should. Look, here's the costume. Torvald had it made for me while we were there. But it's all so torn and everything. I just don't know—

Mrs. Linde.   Oh, that can be fixed. It's not that much. The trimmings have come loose in a few places. Do you have needle and thread? Ah, here we are. All set.

Nora.   I really appreciate it, Kristine.

Mrs. Linde *(sewing).*   So you'll be in disguise tomorrow night, eh? You know—I may come by for just a moment, just to look at you.—Oh dear. I haven't even thanked you for the nice evening last night.

Nora *(gets up, moves around).*   Oh, I don't know. I don't think last night was as nice as it usually is.—You should have come to town a little earlier, Kristine.—Yes, Torvald knows how to make it nice and pretty around here.

Mrs. Linde.   You too, I should think. After all, you're your father's daughter. By the way, is Dr. Rank always as depressed as he was last night?

Nora.   No, last night was unusual. He's a very sick man, you know—very sick. Poor Rank, his spine is rotting away. Tuberculosis, I think. You see, his father was a nasty old man with mistresses and all that sort of thing. Rank has been sickly ever since he was a little boy.

Mrs. Linde *(dropping her sewing to her lap).*   But dearest Nora, where have you learned about things like that?

Nora *(still walking about).*   Oh, you know—with three children you sometimes get to talk with—other wives. Some of them know quite a bit about medicine. So you pick up a few things.

Mrs. Linde *(resumes her sewing; after a brief pause).*   Does Dr. Rank come here every day?

Nora.   Every single day. He's Torvald's oldest and best friend, after all. And my friend too, for that matter. He's part of the family, almost.

Mrs. Linde.   But tell me, is he quite sincere? I mean, isn't he the kind of man who likes to say nice things to people?

Nora.   No, not at all. Rather the opposite, in fact. What makes you say that?

Mrs. Linde.   When you introduced us yesterday, he told me he'd often heard my name mentioned in this house. But later on it was quite obvious that your husband really had no idea who I was. So how could Dr. Rank—?

Nora.   You're right, Kristine, but I can explain that. You see, Torvald loves me so very much that he wants me all to himself. That's what he says. When we were first married he got almost jealous when I as much as mentioned anybody from back home that I was fond of. So of course I soon stopped doing that. But with Dr. Rank I often talk about home. You see, he likes to listen to me.

Mrs. Linde.   Look here, Nora. In many ways you're still a child. After all, I'm quite a bit older than you and have had more experience. I want to give you a piece of advice. I think you should get out of this thing with Dr. Rank.

Nora.   Get out of what thing?

Mrs. Linde.   Several things in fact, if you want my opinion. Yesterday you said something about a rich admirer who was going to give you money—

Nora.   One who doesn't exist, unfortunately. What of it?

Mrs. Linde.   Does Dr. Rank have money?

Nora.   Yes, he does.

Mrs. Linde.   And no dependents?

Nora.   No. But—?

Mrs. Linde.   And he comes here every day?

Nora.   Yes, I told you that already.

Mrs. Linde.   But how can that sensitive man be so tactless?

Nora.   I haven't the slightest idea what you're talking about.

Mrs. Linde.   Don't play games with me, Nora. Don't you think I know who you borrowed the twelve hundred dollars from?

Nora.   Are you out of your mind! The very idea—! A friend of both of us who sees us every day—! What a dreadfully uncomfortable position that would be!

Mrs. Linde.   So it really isn't Dr. Rank?

Nora.   Most certainly not! I would never have dreamed of asking him—not for a moment. Anyway, he didn't have any money then. He inherited it afterwards.

Mrs. Linde.   Well, I still think it may have been lucky for you, Nora dear.

Nora.   The idea! It would never have occurred to me to ask Dr. Rank—. Though I'm sure that if I *did* ask him—

Mrs. Linde.   But of course you wouldn't.

Nora.   Of course not. I can't imagine that that would ever be necessary. But I am quite sure that if I told Dr. Rank—

Mrs. Linde.   Behind your husband's back?

Nora.   I must get out of—this other thing. That's also behind his back. I *must* get out of it.

Mrs. Linde.   That's what I told you yesterday. But—

Nora (*walking up and down*).   A man manages these things so much better than a woman—

Mrs. Linde.   One's husband, yes.

Nora.   Silly, silly! (*Stops.*) When you've paid off all you owe, you get your I.O.U. back; right?

Mrs. Linde.   Yes, of course.

Nora.   And you can tear it into a hundred thousand little pieces and burn it— that dirty, filthy, paper!

Mrs. Linde (*looks hard at her, puts down her sewing, rises slowly*).   Nora— you're hiding something from me.

Nora.   Can you tell?

Mrs. Linde.   Something's happened to you, Nora, since yesterday morning. What is it?

Nora (*going to her*).   Kristine! (*Listens.*) Shhh. Torvald just came back. Listen. Why don't you go in to the children for a while. Torvald can't stand having sewing around. Get Anne-Marie to help you.

Mrs. Linde (*gathers some of the sewing things together*).   All right, but I'm not leaving here till you and I have talked.

She goes out left, just as Helmer enters from the front hall.

Nora (*towards him*).   I have been waiting and waiting for you, Torvald.

Helmer.   Was that the dressmaker?

Nora.   No, it was Kristine. She's helping me with my costume. Oh Torvald, just wait till you see how nice I'll look!

Helmer.   I told you. Pretty good idea I had, wasn't it?

Nora.   Lovely! And wasn't it nice of me to go along with it?

Helmer (*his hand under her chin*).   Nice? To do what your husband tells you? All right, you little rascal; I know you didn't mean it that way. But don't let me interrupt you. I suppose you want to try it on.

Nora.   And you'll be working?

Helmer.   Yes. (*Shows her a pile of papers.*) Look. I've been down to the bank. (*Is about to enter his study.*)

Nora.   Torvald.

Helmer (*halts*).   Yes?

Nora.   What if your little squirrel asked you ever so nicely—

Helmer.   For what?

Nora.   Would you do it?

Helmer.   Depends on what it is.

Nora.   Squirrel would run around and do all sorts of fun tricks if you'd be nice and agreeable.

Helmer.   All right. What is it?

Nora.   Lark would chirp and twitter in all the rooms, up and down—

Helmer.   So what? Lark does that anyway.

Nora.   I'll be your elfmaid and dance for you in the moonlight, Torvald.

Helmer.   Nora, don't tell me it's the same thing you mentioned this morning?

Nora *(closer to, him).*   Yes, Torvald. I beg you!

Helmer.   You really have the nerve to bring that up again?

Nora.   Yes. You've just got to do as I say. You *must* let Krogstad keep his job.

Helmer.   My dear Nora. It's his job I intend to give to Mrs. Linde.

Nora.   I know. And that's ever so nice of you. But can't you just fire somebody else?

Helmer.   This is incredible! You just don't give up do you? Because you make some foolish promise, *I* am supposed to—!

Nora.   That's not the reason, Torvald. It's for your own sake. That man writes for the worst newspapers. You've said so yourself. There's no telling what he may do to you. I'm scared to death of him.

Helmer.   Ah, I understand. You're afraid because of what happened before.

Nora.   What do you mean?

Helmer.   You're thinking of your father, of course.

Nora.   Yes. Yes, you're right. Remember the awful things they wrote about Daddy in the newspapers. I really think they might have forced him to resign if the ministry hadn't sent you to look into the charges and if you hadn't been so helpful and understanding.

Helmer.   My dear little Nora, there is a world of difference between your father and me. Your father's official conduct was not above reproach. Mine is, and I intend for it to remain that way as long as I hold my position.

Nora.   Oh, but you don't know what vicious people like that may think of. Oh, Torvald! Now all of us could be so happy together here in our own home, peaceful and carefree. Such a good life, Torvald, for you and me and the children! That's why I implore you—

Helmer.   And it's exactly because you plead for him that you make it impossible for me to keep him. It's already common knowledge in the bank that I intend to let Krogstad go. If it gets out that the new manager has changed his mind because of his wife—

Nora.   Yes? What then?

Helmer.   No, of course, that wouldn't matter at all as long as little Mrs. Pighead here got her way! Do you want me to make myself look ridiculous before my whole staff—make people think I can be swayed by just anybody—by outsiders? Believe me, I would soon enough find out what the consequences would be! Besides, there's another thing that makes it absolutely impossible for Krogstad to stay on in the bank now that I'm in charge.

Nora.   What's that?

Helmer.   I suppose in a pinch I could overlook his moral shortcomings—

Nora.   Yes, you could; couldn't you, Torvald?

Helmer.   And I understand he's quite a good worker, too. But we've known each other for a long time. It's one of those imprudent relationships you get into when you're young that embarrass you for the rest of your life. I guess I might as well be frank with you: he and I are on a first name basis. And that tactless fellow never hides the fact even when other people are around. Rather, he seems to think it entitles him to be familiar with me. Every chance he gets he comes out with his damn "Torvald, Torvald." I'm telling you, I find it most awkward. He would make my position in the bank intolerable.

Nora. You don't really mean any of this, Torvald.

Helmer. Oh? I don't? And why not?

Nora. No, for it's all so petty.

Helmer. What! Petty? You think I'm being petty!

Nora. No, I *don't* think you are petty, Torvald dear. That's exactly why I—

Helmer. Never mind. You think my reasons are petty, so it follows that I must be petty too. Petty! Indeed! By God, I'll put an end to this right now! *(Opens the door to the front hall and calls out.)* Helene!

Nora. What are you doing?

Helmer *(searching among his papers).* Making a decision. *(The Maid enters.)* Here. Take this letter. Go out with it right away. Find somebody to deliver it. But quick. The address is on the envelope. Wait. Here's money.

The Maid. Very good sir. *(She takes the letter and goes out.)*

Helmer *(collecting his papers).* There now, little Mrs. Obstinate!

Nora *(breathless).* Torvald—what was that letter?

Helmer. Krogstad's dismissal.

Nora. Call it back, Torvald! There's still time! Oh Torvald, please—call it back! For my sake, for your own sake, for the sake of the children! Listen to me, Torvald! Do it! You don't know what you're doing to all of us!

Helmer. Too late.

Nora. Yes. Too late.

Helmer. Dear Nora, I forgive you this fear you're in, although it really is an insult to me. Yes, it is! It's an insult to think that I am scared of a shabby scrivener's revenge. But I forgive you, for it's such a beautiful proof how much you love me. *(Takes her in his arms.)* And that's the way it should be, my sweet darling. Whatever happens, you'll see that when things get really rough I have both strength and courage. You'll find out that I am man enough to shoulder the whole burden.

Nora *(terrified).* What do you mean by that?

Helmer. All of it, I tell you—

Nora *(composed).* You'll never have to do that.

Helmer. Good. Then we'll share the burden, Nora—like husband and wife, the way it ought to be. *(Caresses her.)* Now are you satisfied? There, there there. Not that look in your eyes—like a frightened dove. It's all your own foolish imagination.—Why don't you practice the tarantella—and your tambourine, too. I'll be in the inner office and close both doors, so I won't hear you. You can make as much noise as you like. *(Turning in the doorway.)* And when Rank comes, tell him where to find me. *(He nods to her, enters his study carrying his papers, and closes the door.)*

Nora *(transfixed by terror, whispers).* He would do it. He'll do it. He'll do it in spite of the whole world.—No, this mustn't happen. Anything rather than that! There must be a way—! *(The doorbell rings.)* Dr. Rank! Anything rather than that! Anything—anything at all!

She passes her hand over her face, pulls herself together, and opens the door to the hall. Dr. Rank is out there, hanging up his coat. Darkness begins to fall during the following scene.

Nora.   Hello there, Dr. Rank. I recognized your ringing. Don't go in to Torvald yet. I think he's busy.

Rank.   And you?

Nora *(as he enters and she closes the door behind him).*   You know I always have time for you.

Rank.   Thanks. I'll make use of that as long as I can.

Nora.   What do you mean by that—As long as you can?

Rank.   Does that frighten you?

Nora.   Well, it's a funny expression. As if something was going to happen.

Rank.   Something is going to happen that I've long been expecting. But I admit I hadn't thought it would come quite so soon.

Nora *(seizes his arm).*   What is it you've found out? Dr. Rank—tell me!

Rank *(sits down by the stove).*   I'm going downhill fast. There's nothing to do about that.

Nora *(with audible relief).*   So it's *you*—

Rank.   Who else? No point in lying to myself. I'm in worse shape than any of my other patients, Mrs. Helmer. These last few days I've been making up my inner status. Bankrupt. Chances are that within a month I'll be rotting up in the cemetery.

Nora.   Shame on you! Talking that horrid way!

Rank.   The thing itself is horrid—damn horrid. The worst of it, though, is all that other horror that comes first. There is only one more test I need to make. After that I'll have a pretty good idea when I'll start coming apart. There is something I want to say to you. Helmer's refined nature can't stand anything hideous. I don't want him in my sick room.

Nora.   Oh, but Dr. Rank—

Rank.   I don't want him there. Under no circumstance. I'll close my door to him. As soon as I have full certainty that the worst is about to begin I'll give you my card with a black cross on it. Then you'll know the last horror of destruction has started.

Nora.   Today you're really quite impossible. And I had hoped you'd be in a particularly good mood.

Rank.   With death on my hands? Paying for someone else's sins? Is there justice in that? And yet there isn't a single family that isn't ruled by the same law of ruthless retribution, in one way or another.

Nora *(puts her hands over her ears).*   Poppycock! Be fun! Be fun!

Rank.   Well, yes. You may just as well laugh at the whole thing. My poor, innocent spine is suffering from my father's frolics as a young lieutenant.

Nora *(over by the table, left).*   Right. He was addicted to asparagus and goose liver paté, wasn't he?

Rank.   And truffles.

Nora.   Of course. Truffles. And oysters too, I think.

Rank.   And oysters. Obviously.

Nora.   And all the port and champagne that go with it. It's really too bad that goodies like that ruin your backbone.

Rank.   Particularly an unfortunate backbone that never enjoyed any of it.

Nora.   Ah yes, that's the saddest part of it all.

Rank *(looks searchingly at her)*.   Hm—

Nora *(after a brief pause)*.   Why did you smile just then?

Rank.   No, it was you that laughed.

Nora.   No, it was you that smiled, Dr. Rank!

Rank *(gets up)*.   You're more of a mischief-maker than I thought.

Nora.   I feel in the mood for mischief today.

Rank.   So it seems.

Nora *(with both her hands on his shoulders)*.   Dear, dear Dr. Rank, don't you go and die and leave Torvald and me.

Rank.   Oh, you won't miss me for very long. Those who go away are soon forgotten.

Nora *(with an anxious look)*.   Do you believe that?

Rank.   You'll make new friends, and then—

Nora.   Who'll make new friends?

Rank.   Both you and Helmer, once I'm gone. You yourself seem to have made a good start already. What was this Mrs. Linde doing here last night?

Nora.   Aha—Don't tell me you're jealous of poor Kristine?

Rank.   Yes, I am. She'll be my successor in this house. As soon as I have made my excuses, that woman is likely to—

Nora.   Shh—not so loud. She's in there.

Rank.   Today too? There you are!

Nora.   She's mending my costume. My God, you really *are* unreasonable. *(Sits down on the couch)*. Now be nice, Dr. Rank. Tomorrow you'll see how beautifully I'll dance, and then you are to pretend I'm dancing just for you— and for Torvald too, of course. *(Takes several items out of the carton.)* Sit down, Dr. Rank; I want to show you something.

Rank *(sitting down)*.   What?

Nora.   Look.

Rank.   Silk stockings.

Nora.   Flesh-colored. Aren't they lovely? Now it's getting dark in here, but tomorrow—No, no. You only get to see the foot. Oh well, you might as well see all of it.

Rank.   Hmm.

Nora.   Why do you look so critical? Don't you think they'll fit?

Rank.   That's something I can't possibly have a reasoned opinion about.

Nora *(looks at him for a moment)*.   Shame on you. *(Slaps his ear lightly with the stocking.)* That's what you get. *(Puts the things back in the carton.)*

Rank.   And what other treasures are you going to show me?

Nora.   Nothing at all, because you're naughty. *(She hums a little and rummages in the carton.)*

Rank (*after a brief silence*).   When I sit here like this, talking confidently with you, I can't imagine—I can't possibly imagine what would have become of me if I hadn't had you and Helmer.

Nora (*smiles*).   Well, yes—I do believe you like being with us.

Rank (*in a lower voice, lost in thought*).   And then to have to go away from it all—

Nora.   Nonsense. You are not going anywhere.

Rank (*as before*).   —and not to leave behind as much as a poor little token of gratitude, hardly a brief memory of someone missed, nothing but a vacant place that anyone can fill.

Nora.   And what if I were to ask you—? No—

Rank.   Ask me what?

Nora.   For a great proof of your friendship—

Rank.   Yes, yes—?

Nora.   No, I mean—for an enormous favor—

Rank.   Would you really for once make me as happy as all that?

Nora.   But you don't even know what it is.

Rank.   Well, then; tell me.

Nora.   Oh, but I can't, Dr. Rank. It's altogether too much to ask—It's advice and help and a favor—

Rank.   So much the better. I can't even begin to guess what it is you have in mind. So for heaven's sake tell me! Don't you trust me?

Nora.   Yes, I trust you more than anyone else I know. You are my best and most faithful friend. I know that. So I will tell you. All right, Dr. Rank. There is something you can help me prevent. You know how much Torvald loves me—beyond all words. Never for a moment would he hesitate to give his life for me.

Rank (*leaning over to her*).   Nora—do you really think he's the only one—?

Nora (*with a slight start*).   Who—?

Rank.   —would gladly give his life for you.

Nora (*heavily*).   I see.

Rank.   I have sworn an oath to myself to tell you before I go. I'll never find a better occasion.—All right, Nora; now you know. And now you also know that you can confide in me more than in anyone else.

Nora (*gets up; in a calm, steady voice*).   Let me get by.

Rank (*makes room for her but remains seated*).   Nora—

Nora (*in the door to the front hall*).   Helene, bring the lamp in here, please. (*Walks over to the stove.*) Oh, dear Dr. Rank. That really wasn't very nice of you.

Rank (*gets up*).   That I have loved you as much as anybody—was that not nice?

Nora.   No; not that. But that you told me. There was no need for that.

Rank.   What do you mean? Have you known—?

The Maid enters with the lamp, puts it on the table, and goes out.

Rank.   Nora—Mrs. Helmer—I'm asking you: did you know?

Nora.   Oh, how can I tell what I knew and didn't know! I really can't say—
But that you could be so awkward, Dr. Rank! Just when everything was so
comfortable.

Rank.   Well, anyway, now you know that I'm at your service with my life and
soul. And now you must speak.

Nora *(looks at him).*   After what just happened?

Rank.   I beg of you—let me know what it is.

Nora.   There is nothing I can tell you now.

Rank.   Yes, yes. You mustn't punish me this way. Please let me do for you
whatever anyone *can* do.

Nora.   Now there is nothing you can do. Besides, I don't think I really need
any help, anyway. It's probably just my imagination. Of course that's all it
is. I'm sure of it! *(Sits down in the rocking chair, looks at him, smiles.)* Well,
well, well, Dr. Rank! What a fine gentleman you turned out to be! Aren't
you ashamed of yourself, now that we have light?

Rank.   No, not really. But perhaps I ought to leave—and not come back?

Nora.   Don't be silly; of course not! You'll come here exactly as you have been
doing. You know perfectly well that Torvald can't do without you.

Rank.   Yes, but what about you?

Nora.   Oh, I always think it's perfectly delightful when you come.

Rank.   That's the very thing that misled me. You are a riddle to me. It has
often seemed to me that you'd just as soon be with me as with Helmer.

Nora.   Well, you see, there are people you love, and then there are other
people you'd almost rather be with.

Rank.   Yes, there is something in that.

Nora.   When I lived at home with Daddy, of course I loved him most. But I
always thought it was so much fun to sneak off down to the maids' room, for
they never gave me good advice and they always talked about such fun things.

Rank.   Aha! So it's *their* place I have taken.

Nora *(jumps up and goes over to him).*   Oh dear, kind Dr. Rank, you know
very well I didn't mean it that way. Can't you see that with Torvald it is the
way it used to be with Daddy?

The Maid enters from the front hall.

The Maid.   Ma'am! *(Whispers to her and gives her a caller's card.)*

Nora *(glances at the card).*   Ah! *(Puts it in her pocket.)*

Rank.   Anything wrong?

Nora.   No, no; not at all. It's nothing—just my new costume—

Rank.   But your costume is lying right there!

Nora.   Oh yes, that one. But this is another one. I ordered it. Torvald mustn't
know—

Rank.   Aha. So that's the great secret.

Nora.   That's it. Why don't you go in to him, please. He's in the inner office.
And keep him there for a while—

Rank.   Don't worry. He won't get away. *(Enters Helmer's study.)*

Nora *(to the Maid)*.   You say he's waiting in the kitchen?

The Maid.   Yes. He came up the back stairs.

Nora.   But didn't you tell him there was somebody with me?

The Maid.   Yes, but he wouldn't listen.

Nora.   He won't leave?

The Maid.   No, not till he's had a word with you, ma'am.

Nora.   All right. But try not to make any noise. And, Helene—don't tell any-one he's here. It's supposed to be a surprise for my husband.

The Maid.   I understand, ma'am—*(She leaves.)*

Nora.   The terrible is happening. It's happening, after all. No, no, no. It can't happen. It won't happen. *(She bolts the study door.)*

The maid opens the front hall door for Krogstad and closes the door behind him. He wears a fur coat for traveling, boots, and a fur hat.

Nora *(toward him)*.   Keep your voice down. My husband's home.

Krogstad.   That's all right.

Nora.   What do you want?

Krogstad.   To find out something.

Nora.   Be quick, then. What is it?

Krogstad.   I expect you know I've been fired.

Nora.   I couldn't prevent it, Mr. Krogstad. I fought for you as long and as hard as I could but it didn't do any good.

Krogstad.   Your husband doesn't love you any more than that? He knows what I can do to you, and yet he runs the risk—

Nora.   Surely you didn't think I'd tell him?

Krogstad.   No, I really didn't. It wouldn't be like Torvald Helmer to show that kind of guts—

Nora.   Mr. Krogstad, I insist that you show respect for my husband.

Krogstad.   By all means. All due respect. But since you're so anxious to keep this a secret, may I assume that you are a little better informed than yesterday about exactly what you have done?

Nora.   Better than *you* could ever teach me.

Krogstad.   Of course. Such a bad lawyer as I am—

Nora.   What do you want of me?

Krogstad.   I just wanted to find out how you are, Mrs. Helmer. I've been thinking about you all day. You see, even a bill collector, a pen pusher, a—anyway, someone like me—even he has a little of what they call a heart.

Nora.   Then show it. Think of my little children.

Krogstad.   Have you and your husband thought of mine? Never mind. All I want to tell you is that you don't need to take this business too seriously. I have no intention of bringing charges right away.

Nora.   Oh no, you wouldn't; would you? I knew you wouldn't.

Krogstad.   The whole thing can be settled quite amiably. Nobody else needs to know anything. It will be between the three of us.

Nora.   My husband must never find out about this.

Krogstad. How are you going to prevent that? Maybe you can pay me the balance on the loan?

Nora. No, not right now.

Krogstad. Or do you have a way of raising the money one of these next few days?

Nora. None I intend to make use of.

Krogstad. It wouldn't do you any good, anyway. Even if you had the cash in your hand right this minute, I wouldn't give you your note back. It wouldn't make any difference *how* much money you offered me.

Nora. Then you'll have to tell me what you plan to use the note *for*.

Krogstad. Just keep it; that's all. Have it on hand, so to speak. I won't say a word to anybody else. So if you've been thinking about doing something desperate—

Nora. I have.

Krogstad. —like leaving house and home—

Nora. I have!

Krogstad. —or even something worse—

Nora. How did you know?

Krogstad. —then: don't.

Nora. How did you know I was thinking of *that*?

Krogstad. Most of us do, right at first. I did, too, but when it came down to it I didn't have the courage—

Nora (*tonelessly*). Nor do I.

Krogstad (*relieved*). See what I mean? I thought so. You don't either.

Nora. I don't. I don't.

Krogstad. Besides, it would be very silly of you. Once that first domestic blow-up is behind you—. Here in my pocket is a letter for your husband.

Nora. Telling him everything?

Krogstad. As delicately as possible.

Nora (*quickly*). He mustn't get that letter. Tear it up. I'll get you the money somehow.

Krogstad. Excuse me, Mrs. Helmer, I thought I just told you—

Nora. I'm not talking about the money I owe you. Just let me know how much money you want from my husband, and I'll get it for you.

Krogstad. I want no money from your husband.

Nora. Then, what *do* you want?

Krogstad. I'll tell you, Mrs. Helmer. I want to rehabilitate myself; I want to get up in the world; and your husband is going to help me. For a year and a half I haven't done anything disreputable. All that time I have been struggling with the most miserable circumstances. I was content to work my way up step by step. Now I've been kicked out, and I'm no longer satisfied just getting my old job back. I want more than that; I want to get to the top. I'm being quite serious. I want the bank to take me back but in a higher position. I want your husband to create a new job for me—

Nora. He'll never do that!

Krogstad. He will. I know him. He won't dare not to. And once I'm back inside and he and I are working together, you'll see! Within a year I'll be the manager's right hand. It will be Nils Krogstad and not Torvald Helmer who'll be running the Mutual Bank!

Nora.   You'll never see that happen!

Krogstad.   Are you thinking of—?

Nora.   Now I *do* have the courage.

Krogstad.   You can't scare me. A fine, spoiled lady like you—

Nora.   You'll see, you'll see!

Krogstad.   Under the ice, perhaps? Down into that cold, black water? Then spring comes, and you float up again—hideous, can't be identified, hair all gone—

Nora.   You don't frighten me.

Krogstad.   Nor you me. One doesn't do that sort of thing, Mrs. Helmer. Besides, what good would it do? He'd still be in my power.

Nora.   Afterwards? When I'm no longer—?

Krogstad.   Aren't you forgetting that your reputation would be in my hands?

Nora stares at him, speechless.

Krogstad.   All right; now I've told you what to expect. So don't do anything foolish. When Helmer gets my letter I expect to hear from him. And don't you forget that it's your husband himself who forces me to use such means again. That I'll never forgive him. Goodbye, Mrs. Helmer. *(Goes out through the hall.)*

Nora *(at the door, opens it a little, listens).*   He's going. And no letter. Of course not! That would be impossible! *(Opens the door more.)* What's he doing? He's still there. Doesn't go down. Having second thoughts—? Will he—?

The sound of a letter dropping into the mailbox. Then Krogstad's steps are heard going down the stairs, gradually dying away.

Nora *(with a muted cry runs forward to the table by the couch; brief pause).*   In the mailbox. *(Tiptoes back to the door to the front hall.)* There it is. Torvald, Torvald—now we're lost!

Mrs. Linde *(enters from the left, carrying Nora's Capri costume).*   There now. I think it's all fixed. Why don't we try it on you—

Nora *(in a low, hoarse voice).*   Kristine, come here.

Mrs. Linde.   What's wrong with you? You look quite beside yourself.

Nora.   Come over here. Do you see that letter? There, look—through the glass in the mailbox.

Mrs. Linde.   Yes, yes; I see it.

Nora.   That letter is from Krogstad.

Mrs. Linde.   Nora—it was Krogstad who lent you the money!

Nora.   Yes, and now Torvald will find out about it.

Mrs. Linde.   Oh believe me, Nora. That's the best thing for both of you.

Nora.   There's more to it than you know. I forged a signature—

Mrs. Linde.   Oh my God—!

Nora.   I just want to tell you this, Kristine, that you must be my witness.

Mrs. Linde.   Witness? How? Witness to what?

Nora.   If I lose my mind—and that could very well happen—

Mrs. Linde.   Nora!

Nora.   —or if something were to happen to me—something that made it impossible for me to be here—

Mrs. Linde.   Nora, Nora! You're not yourself!

Nora.   —and if someone were to take all the blame, assume the whole responsibility—Do you understand—?

Mrs. Linde.   Yes, yes; but how can you think—!

Nora.   Then you are to witness that that's not so, Kristine. I am not beside myself. I am perfectly rational, and what I'm telling you is that nobody else has known about this. I've done it all by myself, the whole thing. Just remember that.

Mrs. Linde.   I will. But I don't understand any of it.

Nora.   Oh, how could you! For it's the wonderful that's about to happen.

Mrs. Linde.   The wonderful?

Nora.   Yes, the wonderful. But it's so terrible, Kristine. It mustn't happen for anything in the whole world!

Mrs. Linde.   I'm going over to talk to Krogstad right now.

Nora.   No, don't. Don't go to him. He'll do something bad to you.

Mrs. Linde.   There was a time when he would have done anything for me.

Nora.   He!

Mrs. Linde.   Where does he live?

Nora.   Oh, I don't know—Yes, wait a minute—*(Reaches into her pocket.)* here's his card.—But the letter, the letter—!

Helmer *(in his study, knocks on the door)*.   Nora!

Nora *(cries out in fear)*.   Oh, what is it? What do you want?

Helmer.   That's all right. Nothing to be scared about. We're not coming in. For one thing, you've bolted the door, you know. Are you modeling your costume?

Nora.   Yes, yes; I am. I'm going to be so pretty, Torvald.

Mrs. Linde *(having looked at the card)*.   He lives just around the corner.

Nora.   Yes, but it's no use. Nothing can save us now. The letter is in the mailbox.

Mrs. Linde.   And your husband has the key?

Nora.   Yes. He always keeps it with him.

Mrs. Linde.   Krogstad must ask for his letter back, unread. He's got to think up some pretext or other—

Nora.   But this is just the time of day when Torvald—

Mrs. Linde.   Delay him. Go in to him. I'll be back as soon as I can. *(She hurries out through the hall door.)*

Nora *(walks over to Helmer's door, opens it, and peeks in)*.   Torvald!

Helmer (*still offstage*).   Well, well! So now one's allowed in one's own living room again. Come on, Rank. Now we'll see—(*In the doorway.*) But what's this?

Nora.   What, Torvald dear?

Helmer.   Rank prepared me for a splendid metamorphosis.

Rank (*in the doorway*).   That's how I understood it. Evidently I was mistaken.

Nora.   Nobody gets to admire me in my costume before tomorrow.

Helmer.   But, dearest Nora—you look all done in. Have you been practicing too hard?

Nora.   No, I haven't practiced at all.

Helmer.   But you'll have to, you know.

Nora.   I know it, Torvald. I simply must. But I can't do a thing unless you help me. I have forgotten everything.

Helmer.   Oh it will all come back. We'll work on it.

Nora.   Oh yes, please, Torvald. You just have to help me. Promise? I am so nervous. That big party—. You mustn't do anything else tonight. Not a bit of business. Don't even touch a pen. Will you promise, Torvald?

Helmer.   I promise. Tonight I'll be entirely at your service—you helpless little thing.—Just a moment, though. First I want to—(*Goes to the door to the front hall.*)

Nora.   What are you doing out there?

Helmer.   Just looking to see if there's any mail.

Nora.   No, no! Don't, Torvald!

Helmer.   Why not?

Nora.   Torvald, I beg you. There is no mail.

Helmer.   Let me just look, anyway. (*Is about to go out.*)

Nora by the piano, plays the first bars of the tarantella dance.

Helmer (*halts at the door*).   Aha!

Nora.   I won't be able to dance tomorrow if I don't get to practice with you.

Helmer (*goes to her*).   Are you really all that scared, Nora dear?

Nora.   Yes, so terribly scared. Let's try it right now. There's still time before we eat. Oh please, sit down and play for me, Torvald. Teach me, coach me, the way you always do.

Helmer.   Of course I will, my darling, if that's what you want. (*Sits down at the piano.*)

Nora takes the tambourine out of the carton, as well as a long, many-colored shawl. She quickly drapes the shawl around herself, then leaps into the middle of the floor.

Nora.   Play for me! I want to dance!

Helmer plays and Nora dances. Dr. Rank stands by the piano behind Helmer and watches.

Helmer *(playing)*. Slow down, slow down!
Nora. Can't!
Helmer. Not so violent, Nora!
Nora. It has to be this way.
Helmer *(stops playing)*. No, no. This won't do at all.
Nora *(laughing, swinging her tambourine)*. What did I tell you?
Rank. Why don't you let me play?
Helmer *(getting up)*. Good idea. Then I can direct her better.

Rank sits down at the piano and starts playing. Nora dances more and more wildly. Helmer stands over by the stove, repeatedly correcting her. She doesn't seem to hear. Her hair comes loose and falls down over her shoulders. She doesn't notice but keeps on dancing. Mrs. Linde enters.

Mrs. Linde *(stops by the door, dumbfounded)*. Ah—!
Nora *(dancing)*. We're having such fun, Kristine!
Helmer. My dearest Nora, you're dancing as if it were a matter of life and death!
Nora. It is! It is!
Helmer. Rank, stop. This is sheer madness. Stop, I say!

Rank stops playing; Nora suddenly stops dancing.

Helmer *(goes over to her)*. If I hadn't seen it I wouldn't have believed it. You've forgotten every single thing I ever taught you.
Nora *(tosses away the tambourine)*. See? I told you.
Helmer. Well! You certainly need coaching.
Nora. Didn't I tell you I did? Now you've seen for yourself. I'll need your help till the very minute we're leaving for the party. Will you promise, Torvald?
Helmer. You can count on it.
Nora. You're not to think of anything except me—not tonight and not to-morrow. You're not to read any letters—not to look in the mailbox—
Helmer. Ah, I see. You're still afraid of that man.
Nora. Yes—yes, that too.
Helmer. Nora, I can tell from looking at you. There's a letter from him out there.
Nora. I don't know. I think so. But you're not to read it now. I don't want anything ugly to come between us before it's all over.
Rank *(to Helmer in a low voice)*. Better not argue with her.
Helmer *(throws his arm around her)*. The child shall have her way. But to-morrow night, when you've done your dance—
Nora. Then you'll be free.
The Maid *(in the door, right)*. Dinner can be served any time, ma'am.
Nora. We want champagne, Helene.
The Maid. Very good, ma'am. *(Goes out.)*

Helmer.   Aha! Having a party, eh?

Nora.   Champagne from now till sunrise! *(Calls out.)* And some macaroons, Helene. Lots!—just this once.

Helmer *(taking her hands).*   There, there—I don't like this wild—frenzy—Be my own sweet little lark again, the way you always are.

Nora.   Oh, I will. But you go on in. You too, Dr. Rank. Kristine, please help me put up my hair.

Rank *(in a low voice to Helmer as they go out).*   You don't think she is—you know—expecting—?

Helmer.   Oh no. Nothing like that. It's just this childish fear I was telling you about. *(They go out, right.)*

Nora.   Well?

Mrs. Linde.   Left town.

Nora.   I saw it in your face.

Mrs. Linde.   He'll be back tomorrow night. I left him a note.

Nora.   You shouldn't have. I don't want you to try to stop anything. You see, it's a kind of ecstasy, too, this waiting for the wonderful.

Mrs. Linde.   But what is it you're waiting *for*?

Nora.   You wouldn't understand. Why don't you go in to the others. I'll be there in a minute.

Mrs. Linde enters the dining room, right.

Nora. *(stands still for a little while, as if collecting herself; she looks at her watch).*   Five o'clock. Seven hours till midnight. Twenty-four more hours till next midnight. Then the tarantella is over. Twenty-four plus seven— thirty-one more hours to live.

Helmer *(in the door, right).*   What's happening to my little lark?

Nora *(to him, with open arms).*   Here's your lark!

Act III

The same room. The table by the couch and the chairs around it have been moved to the middle of the floor. A lighted lamp is on the table. The door to the front hall is open. Dance music is heard from upstairs.

Mrs. Linde is seated by the table, idly leafing through the pages of a book. She tries to read but seems unable to concentrate. Once or twice she turns her head in the direction of the door, anxiously listening.

Mrs. Linde *(looks at her watch).*   Not yet. It's almost too late. If only he hasn't—(Listens again.) Ah! There he is. (She goes to the hall and opens the

front door carefully. Quiet footsteps on the stairs. She whispers.) Come in.
There's nobody here.

Krogstad *(in the door).* I found your note when I got home. What's this all
about?

Mrs. Linde. I've got to talk to you.

Krogstad. Oh? And it has to be here?

Mrs. Linde. It couldn't be at my place. My room doesn't have a separate
entrance. Come in. We're quite alone. The maid is asleep and the Helmers
are at a party upstairs.

Krogstad *(entering).* Really? The Helmers are dancing tonight, are they?

Mrs. Linde. And why not?

Krogstad. You're right. Why not, indeed.

Mrs. Linde. All right, Krogstad. Let's talk, you and I.

Krogstad. I didn't know we had anything to talk about.

Mrs. Linde. We have much to talk about.

Krogstad. I didn't think so.

Mrs. Linde. No, because you've never really understood me.

Krogstad. What was there to understand? What happened was perfectly commonplace. A heartless woman jilts a man when she gets a more attractive
offer.

Mrs. Linde. Do you think I'm all that heartless? And do you think it was easy
for me to break with you?

Krogstad. No?

Mrs. Linde. You really thought it was?

Krogstad. If it wasn't, why did you write the way you did that time?

Mrs. Linde. What else could I do? If I had to make a break, I also had the
duty to destroy whatever feelings you had for me.

Krogstad *(clenching his hands).* So that's the way it was. And you did—*that*—
just for money!

Mrs. Linde. Don't forget I had a helpless mother and two small brothers. We
couldn't wait for you, Krogstad. You know yourself how uncertain your prospects were then.

Krogstad. All right. But you still didn't have the right to throw me over for
somebody else.

Mrs. Linde. I don't know. I have asked myself that question many times. Did
I have that right?

Krogstad *(in a lower voice).* When I lost you I lost my footing. Look at me
now. A shipwrecked man on a raft.

Mrs. Linde. Rescue may be near.

Krogstad. It *was* near. Then you came between.

Mrs. Linde. I didn't know that, Krogstad. Only today did I find out it's your
job I'm taking over in the bank.

Krogstad. I believe you when you say so. But now that you *do* know, aren't
you going to step aside?

Mrs. Linde. No, for it wouldn't do you any good.

Krogstad.   Whether it would or not—*I* would do it.

Mrs. Linde.   I have learned common sense. Life and hard necessity have taught me that.

Krogstad.   And life has taught me not to believe in pretty speeches.

Mrs. Linde.   Then life has taught you a very sensible thing. But you do believe in actions, don't you?

Krogstad.   How do you mean?

Mrs. Linde.   You referred to yourself just now as a shipwrecked man.

Krogstad.   It seems to me I had every reason to do so.

Mrs. Linde.   And I am a shipwrecked woman. No one to grieve for, no one to care for.

Krogstad.   You made your choice.

Mrs. Linde.   I had no other choice that time.

Krogstad.   Let's say you didn't. What then?

Mrs. Linde.   Krogstad, how would it be if we two shipwrecked people got together?

Krogstad.   What's this!

Mrs. Linde.   Two on one wreck are better off than each on his own.

Krogstad.   Kristine!

Mrs. Linde.   Why do you think I came to town?

Krogstad.   Surely not because of me?

Mrs. Linde.   If I'm going to live at all I must work. All my life, for as long as I can remember, I have worked. That's been my one and only pleasure. But now that I'm all alone in the world I feel nothing but this terrible emptiness and desolation. There is no joy in working just for yourself. Krogstad—give me someone and something to work for.

Krogstad.   I don't believe this. Only hysterical females go in for that kind of high-minded self-sacrifice.

Mrs. Linde.   Did you ever know me to be hysterical?

Krogstad.   You really could do this? Listen—do you know about my past? All of it?

Mrs. Linde.   Yes, I do.

Krogstad.   Do you also know what people think of me around here?

Mrs. Linde.   A little while ago you sounded as if you thought that together with me you might have become a different person.

Krogstad.   I'm sure of it.

Mrs. Linde.   Couldn't that still be?

Krogstad.   Kristine—do you know what you are doing? Yes, I see you do. And you think you have the courage—?

Mrs. Linde.   I need someone to be a mother to, and your children need a mother. You and I need one another. Nils, I believe in you—in the real you. Together with you I dare to do anything.

Krogstad *(seizes her hands)*.   Thanks, thanks, Kristine—now I know I'll raise myself in the eyes of others—Ah, but I forget—!

Mrs. Linde *(listening)*.   Shh!—There's the tarantella. You must go; hurry!

Krogstad. Why? What is it?

Mrs. Linde. Do you hear what they're playing up there? When that dance is over they'll be down.

Krogstad. All right. I'm leaving. The whole thing is pointless, anyway. Of course you don't know what I'm doing to the Helmers.

Mrs. Linde. Yes, Krogstad; I do know.

Krogstad. Still, you're brave enough—?

Mrs. Linde. I very well understand to what extremes despair can drive a man like you.

Krogstad. If only it could be undone!

Mrs. Linde. It could, for your letter is still out there in the mailbox.

Krogstad. Are you sure?

Mrs. Linde. Quite sure. But—

Krogstad *(looks searchingly at her).* Maybe I'm beginning to understand. You want to save your friend at any cost. Be honest with me. That's it, isn't it?

Mrs. Linde. Krogstad, you may sell yourself once for somebody else's sake, but you don't do it twice.

Krogstad. I'll demand my letter back.

Mrs. Linde. No, no.

Krogstad. Yes, of course. I'll wait here till Helmer comes down. Then I'll ask him for my letter. I'll tell him it's just about my dismissal—that he shouldn't read it.

Mrs. Linde. No, Krogstad. You are not to ask for that letter back.

Krogstad. But tell me—wasn't that the real reason you wanted to meet me here?

Mrs. Linde. At first it was, because I was so frightened. But that was yesterday. Since then I have seen the most incredible things going on in this house. Helmer must learn the whole truth. This miserable secret must come out in the open; those two must come to a full understanding. They simply can't continue with all this concealment and evasion.

Krogstad. All right; if you want to take that chance. But there is one thing I *can* do, and I'll do that right now.

Mrs. Linde *(listening).* But hurry! Go! The dance is over. We aren't safe another minute.

Krogstad. I'll be waiting for you downstairs.

Mrs. Linde. Yes, do. You must see me home.

Krogstad. I've never been so happy in my whole life. *(He leaves through the front door. The door between the living room and the front hall remains open.)*

Mrs. Linde *(straightens up the room a little and gets her things ready).* What a change! Oh yes!—what a change! People to work for—to live for—a home to bring happiness to. I can't wait to get to work—! If only they'd come soon— *(Listens.)* Ah, there they are. Get my coat on—*(Puts on her coat and hat.)*

Helmer's and Nora's voices are heard outside. A key is turned in the lock, and Helmer almost forces Nora into the hall. She is dressed in her Italian costume, with a big black shawl over her shoulders. He is in evening dress under an open black cloak.

Nora *(in the door, still resisting).*   No, no, no! I don't want to! I want to go back upstairs. I don't want to leave so early.

Helmer.   But dearest Nora—

Nora.   Oh please, Torvald—please! I'm asking you as nicely as I can—just another hour!

Helmer.   Not another minute, sweet. You know we agreed. There now. Get inside. You'll catch a cold out here. *(She still resists, but he guides her gently into the room.)*

Mrs. Linde.   Good evening.

Nora.   Kristine!

Helmer.   Ah, Mrs. Linde. Still here?

Mrs. Linde.   I know. I really should apologize, but I so much wanted to see Nora in her costume.

Nora.   You've been waiting up for me?

Mrs. Linde.   Yes, unfortunately I didn't get here in time. You were already upstairs, but I just didn't feel like leaving till I had seen you.

Helmer *(removing Nora's shawl).*   Yes, do take a good look at her, Mrs. Linde. I think I may say she's worth looking at. Isn't she lovely?

Mrs. Linde.   She certainly is—

Helmer.   Isn't she a miracle of loveliness, though? That was the general opinion at the party, too. But dreadfully obstinate—that she is, the sweet little thing. What can we do about that? Will you believe it—I practically had to use force to get her away.

Nora.   Oh Torvald, you're going to be sorry you didn't give me even half an hour more.

Helmer.   See what I mean, Mrs. Linde? She dances the tarantella—she is a tremendous success—quite deservedly so, though perhaps her performance was a little too natural—I mean, more than could be reconciled with the rules of art. But all right! The point is: she's a success, a tremendous success. So should I let her stay after that? Weaken the effect? Of course not. So I take my lovely little Capri girl—I might say, my capricious little Capri girl—under my arm—a quick turn around the room—a graceful bow in all directions, and—as they say in the novels—the beautiful apparition is gone. A finale should always be done for effect, Mrs. Linde, but there doesn't seem to be any way of getting that into Nora's head. Poooh—! It's hot in here. *(Throws his cloak down on a chair and opens the door to his room.)* Why, it's dark in here! Of course. Excuse me—*(Goes inside and lights a couple of candles.)*

Nora *(in a hurried, breathless whisper).*   Well?

Mrs. Linde *(in a low voice).*   I have talked to him.

Nora.   And—?

Mrs. Linde.   Nora—you've got to tell your husband everything.

Nora *(no expression in her voice)*.   I knew it.

Mrs. Linde.   You have nothing to fear from Krogstad. But you must speak.

Nora.   I'll say nothing.

Mrs. Linde.   Then the letter will.

Nora.   Thank you, Kristine. Now I know what I have to do. Shh!

Helmer *(returning)*.   Well, Mrs. Linde, have you looked your fill?

Mrs. Linde.   Yes. And now I'll say goodnight.

Helmer.   So soon? Is that your knitting?

Mrs. Linde *(takes it)*.   Yes, thank you. I almost forgot.

Helmer.   So you knit, do you?

Mrs. Linde.   Oh yes.

Helmer.   You know—you ought to take up embroidery instead.

Mrs. Linde.   Oh? Why?

Helmer.   Because it's so much more beautiful. Look. You hold the embroidery
so—in your left hand. Then with your right you move the needle—like this—
in an easy, elongated arc—you see?

Mrs. Linde.   Maybe you're right—

Helmer.   Knitting, on the other hand, can never be anything but ugly. Look
here: arms pressed close to the sides—the needles going up and down—there's
something Chinese about it somehow—. That really was an excellent champagne they served us tonight.

Mrs. Linde.   Well, goodnight, Nora. And don't be obstinate any more.

Helmer.   Well said, Mrs. Linde!

Mrs. Linde.   Goodnight, sir.

Helmer *(sees her to the front door)*.   Goodnight, goodnight. I hope you'll get
home all right? I'd be very glad to—but of course you don't have far to walk,
do you? Goodnight, goodnight. *(She leaves. He closes the door behind her
and returns to the living room.)* There! At last we got rid of her. She really
is an incredible bore, that woman.

Nora.   Aren't you very tired, Torvald?

Helmer.   No, not in the least.

Nora.   Not sleepy either?

Helmer.   Not at all. Quite the opposite. I feel enormously—animated. How
about you? Yes, you do look tired and sleepy.

Nora.   Yes, I am very tired. Soon I'll be asleep.

Helmer.   What did I tell you? I was right, wasn't I? Good thing I didn't let
you stay any longer.

Nora.   Everything you do is right.

Helmer *(kissing her forehead)*.   Now my little lark is talking like a human
being. But did you notice what splended spirits Rank was in tonight?

Nora.   Was he? I didn't notice. I didn't get to talk with him.

Helmer.   Nor did I—hardly. But I haven't seen him in such a good mood for
a long time. *(Looks at her, comes closer to her.)* Ah! It does feel good to be
back in our own home again, to be quite alone with you—my young, lovely,
ravishing woman!

Nora.   Don't look at me like that, Torvald!

Helmer.   Am I not to look at my most precious possession? All that loveliness that is mine, nobody's but mine, all of it mine.

Nora *(walks to the other side of the table).*   I won't have you talk to me like that tonight.

Helmer *(follows her).*   The tarantella is still in your blood. I can tell. That only makes you all the more alluring. Listen! The guests are beginning to leave. *(Softly.)* Nora—soon the whole house will be quiet.

Nora.   Yes, I hope so.

Helmer.   Yes, don't you, my darling? Do you know—when I'm at a party with you, like tonight—do you know why I hardly ever talk to you, why I keep away from you, only look at you once in a while—a few stolen glances—do you know why I do that? It's because I pretend that you are my secret love, my young, secret bride-to-be, and nobody has the slightest suspicion that there is anything between us.

Nora.   Yes, I know. All your thoughts are with me.

Helmer.   Then when we're leaving and I lay your shawl around your delicate young shoulders—around that wonderful curve of your neck—then I imagine you're my young bride, that we're coming away from the wedding, that I am taking you to my home for the first time—that I am alone with you for the first time—quite alone with you, you young, trembling beauty! I have desired you all evening—there hasn't been a longing in me that hasn't been for you. When you were dancing the tarantella, chasing, inviting—my blood was on fire; I couldn't stand it any longer—that's why I brought you down so early—

Nora.   Leave me now, Torvald. Please! I don't want all this.

Helmer.   What do you mean? You're only playing your little teasing bird game with me; aren't you, Nora? Don't want to? I'm your husband, aren't I?

There is a knock on the front door.

Nora *(with a start).*   Did you hear that—?

Helmer *(on his way to the hall).*   Who is it?

Rank *(outside).*   It's me. May I come in for a moment?

Helmer *(in a low voice, annoyed).*   Oh, what does he want now? *(Aloud.)* Just a minute. *(Opens the door.)* Well! How good of you not to pass by our door.

Rank.   I thought I heard your voice, so I felt like saying hello. *(Looks around.)* Ah yes—this dear, familiar room. What a cozy, comfortable place you have here, you two.

Helmer.   Looked to me as if you were quite comfortable upstairs too.

Rank.   I certainly was. Why not? Why not enjoy all you can in this world? As much as you can for as long as you can, anyway. Excellent wine.

Helmer.   The champagne, particularly.

Rank.   You noticed that too? Incredible how much I managed to put away.

Nora.   Torvald drank a lot of champagne tonight, too.

Rank.   Did he?

Nora.   Yes, he did, and then he's always so much fun afterwards.

Rank.   Well, why not have some fun in the evening after a well spent day?

Helmer. Well spent? I'm afraid I can't claim that.

Rank (*slapping him lightly on the shoulder*). But you see, I can!

Nora. Dr. Rank, I believe you must have been conducting a scientific test today.

Rank. Exactly.

Helmer. What do you know—little Nora talking about scientific tests!

Nora. May I congratulate you on the result?

Rank. You may indeed.

Nora. It was a good one?

Rank. The best possible for both doctor and patient—certainty.

Nora (*a quick query*). Certainty?

Rank. Absolute certainty. So why shouldn't I have myself an enjoyable evening afterwards?

Nora. I quite agree with you, Dr. Rank. You should.

Helmer. And so do I. If only you don't pay for it tomorrow.

Rank. Oh well—you get nothing for nothing in this world.

Nora. Dr. Rank—you are fond of costume parties, aren't you?

Rank. Yes, particularly when there is a reasonable number of amusing disguises.

Nora. Listen—what are the two of us going to be the next time?

Helmer. You frivolous little thing! Already thinking about the next party!

Rank. You and I? That's easy. You'll be Fortune's Child.

Helmer. Yes, but what is a fitting costume for that?

Rank. Let your wife appear just the way she always is.

Helmer. Beautiful. Very good indeed. But how about yourself? Don't you know what you'll go as?

Rank. Yes, my friend. I know precisely what I'll be.

Helmer. Yes?

Rank. At the next masquerade I'll be invisible.

Helmer. That's a funny idea.

Rank. There's a certain black hat—you've heard about the hat that makes you invisible, haven't you? You put that on, and nobody can see you.

Helmer (*suppressing a smile*). I guess that's right.

Rank. But I'm forgetting what I came for. Helmer, give me a cigar—one of your dark Havanas.

Helmer. With the greatest pleasure. (*Offers him his case.*)

Rank (*takes one and cuts off the tip*). Thanks.

Nora (*striking a match*). Let me give you a light.

Rank. Thanks. (*She holds the match; he lights his cigar.*) And now goodbye!

Helmer. Goodbye, goodbye, my friend.

Nora. Sleep well, Dr. Rank.

Rank. I thank you.

Nora. Wish me the same.

Rank. You? Well, if you really want me to—. Sleep well. And thanks for the light. (*He nods to both of them and goes out.*)

Helmer *(in a low voice).*   He had had quite a bit to drink.
Nora *(absently).*   Maybe so.

Helmer takes out his keys and goes out into the hall.

Nora.   Torvald—what are you doing out there?
Helmer.   Emptying the mailbox. It is quite full. There wouldn't be room for the newspapers in the morning—
Nora.   Are you going to work tonight?
Helmer.   You know very well I won't.—Say! What's this? Somebody's been at the lock.
Nora.   The lock—?
Helmer.   Yes. Why, I wonder. I hate to think that any of the maids—. Here's a broken hairpin. It's one of yours. Nora.
Nora *(quickly).*   Then it must be one of the children.
Helmer.   You better make damn sure they stop that. Hm, hm.—There! I got it open, finally. *(Gathers up the mail, calls out to the kitchen.)* Helene?—Oh Helene—turn out the light here in the hall, will you? *(He comes back into the living room and closes the door.)* Look how it's been piling up. *(Shows her the bundle of letters. Starts leafing through it.)* What's this?
Nora *(by the window).*   The letter! Oh no, no, Torvald!
Helmer.   Two calling cards—from Rank.
Nora.   From Dr. Rank?
Helmer *(looking at them).*   "Doctor medicinae Rank." They were on top. He must have put them there when he left just now.
Nora.   Anything written on them?
Helmer.   A black cross above the name. What a macabre idea. Like announcing his own death.
Nora.   That's what it is.
Helmer.   Hm? You know about this? Has he said anything to you?
Nora.   That card means he has said goodbye to us. He'll lock himself up to die.
Helmer.   My poor friend. I knew of course he wouldn't be with me very long. But so soon—. And hiding himself away like a wounded animal—
Nora.   When it has to be, it's better it happens without words. Don't you think so, Torvald?
Helmer *(walking up and down).*   He'd grown so close to us. I find it hard to think of him as gone. With his suffering and loneliness he was like a clouded background for our happy sunshine. Well, it may be better this way. For him, at any rate. *(Stops.)* And perhaps for us, too, Nora. For now we have nobody but each other. *(Embraces her.)* Oh you—my beloved wife! I feel I just can't hold you close enough. Do you know, Nora—many times I have wished some great danger threatened you, so I could risk my life and blood and everything—everything, for your sake.

Nora *(frees herself and says in a strong and firm voice).*   I think you should go and read your letters now, Torvald.

Helmer.   No, no—not tonight. I want to be with you, my darling.

Nora.   With the thought of your dying friend—?

Helmer.   You are right. This has shaken both of us. Something not beautiful has come between us. Thoughts of death and dissolution. We must try to get over it—out of it. Till then—we'll each go to our own room.

Nora *(her arms around his neck).*   Torvald—goodnight! Goodnight!

Helmer *(kisses her forehead).*   Goodnight, my little songbird. Sleep well, Nora. Now I'll read my letters. *(He goes into his room, carrying the mail. Closes the door.)*

Nora *(her eyes desperate, her hands groping, finds Helmer's black cloak and throws it around her; she whispers, quickly, brokenly, hoarsely).*   Never see him again. Never. Never. Never. *(Puts her shawl over her head.)* And never see the children again, either. Never; never.—The black, icy water—fathomless—this—! If only it was all over.—Now he has it. Now he's reading it. No, no; not yet. Torvald—goodbye—you—the children—

She is about to hurry through the hall, when Helmer flings open the door to his room and stands there with an open letter in his hand.

Helmer.   Nora!

Nora *(cries out).*   Ah—!

Helmer.   What is it? You know what's in this letter?

Nora.   Yes, I do! Let me go! Let me out!

Helmer *(holds her back).*   Where do you think you're going?

Nora *(trying to tear herself loose from him).*   I won't let you save me, Torvald!

Helmer *(tumbles back).*   True! Is it true what he writes? Oh my God! No, no—this can't possibly be true.

Nora.   It is true. I have loved you more than anything else in the whole world.

Helmer.   Oh, don't give me any silly excuses.

Nora *(taking a step towards him).*   Torvald—!

Helmer.   You wretch! What have you done!

Nora.   Let me go. You are not to sacrifice yourself for me. You are not to take the blame.

Helmer.   No more playacting. *(Locks the door to the front hall.)* You'll stay here and answer me. Do you understand what you have done? Answer me! Do you understand?

Nora *(gazes steadily at him with an increasingly frozen expression).*   Yes. Now I'm beginning to understand.

Helmer *(walking up and down).*   What a dreadful awakening. All these years—all these eight years—she, my pride and my joy—a hypocrite, a liar—oh worse! worse!—a criminal! Oh, the bottomless ugliness in all this! Damn! Damn! Damn!

Nora, silent, keeps gazing at him.

Helmer *(stops in front of her)*. I ought to have guessed that something like this would happen. I should have expected it. All your father's loose principles—Silence! You have inherited every one of your father's loose principles. No religion, no morals, no sense of duty—. Now I am being punished for my leniency with him. I did it for your sake, and this is how you pay me back.

Nora. Yes. This is how.

Helmer. You have ruined all my happiness. My whole future—that's what you have destroyed. Oh, it's terrible to think about. I am at the mercy of an unscrupulous man. He can do with me whatever he likes, demand anything of me, command me and dispose of me just as he pleases—I dare not say a word! To go down so miserably, to be destroyed—all because of an irresponsible woman!

Nora. When I am gone from the world, you'll be free.

Helmer. No noble gestures, please. Your father was always full of such phrases too. What good would it do me if you were gone from the world, as you put it? Not the slightest good at all. He could still make the whole thing public, and if he did, people would be likely to think I had been your accomplice. They might even think it was my idea—that it was I who urged you to do it! And for all this I have you to thank—you, whom I've borne on my hands through all the years of our marriage. Now do you understand what you've done to me?

Nora *(with cold calm)*. Yes.

Helmer. I just can't get it into my head that this is happening; it's all so incredible. But we have to come to terms with it somehow. Take your shawl off. Take it off, I say! I have to satisfy him one way or another. The whole affair must be kept quiet at whatever cost.—And as far as you and I are concerned, nothing must seem to have changed. I'm talking about appearances, of course. You'll go on living here; that goes without saying. But I won't let you bring up the children; I dare not trust you with them. —Oh! Having to say this to one I have loved so much, and whom I still—! But all that is past. It's not a question of happiness any more but of hanging on to what can be salvaged—pieces, appearances—*(The doorbell rings.)*

Helmer *(jumps)*. What's that? So late. Is the worst—? Has he—! Hide, Nora! Say you're sick.

Nora doesn't move. Helmer opens the door to the hall.

The Maid *(half dressed, out in the hall)*. A letter for your wife, sir.

Helmer. Give it to me. *(Takes the letter and closes the door.)* Yes, it's from him. But I won't let you have it. I'll read it myself.

Nora. Yes—you read it.

Helmer *(by the lamp)*. I hardly dare. Perhaps we're lost, both you and I. No;

I've got to know. *(Tears the letter open, glances through it, looks at an enclosure; a cry of joy.)* Nora!

Nora looks at him with a question in her eyes.

Helmer.   Nora!—No, I must read it again.—Yes, yes; it is so! I'm saved! Nora, I'm saved!

Nora.   And I?

Helmer.   You too, of course; we're both saved, both you and I. Look! He's returning your note. He writes that he's sorry, he regrets, a happy turn in his life—oh, it doesn't matter what he writes. We're saved, Nora! Nobody can do anything to you now. Oh Nora, Nora—. No, I want to get rid of this disgusting thing first. Let me see—*(Looks at the signature.)* No, I don't want to see it. I don't want it to be more than a bad dream, the whole thing. *(Tears up the note and both letters, throws the pieces in the stove, and watches them burn.)* There! Now it's gone.—He wrote that ever since Christmas Eve—. Good God, Nora, these must have been three terrible days for you.

Nora.   I have fought a hard fight these last three days.

Helmer.   And been in agony and seen no other way out than—. No, we won't think of all that ugliness. We'll just rejoice and tell ourselves it's over, it's all over! Oh, listen to me, Nora. You don't seem to understand. It's over. What *is* it? Why do you look like that—that frozen expression on your face? Oh my poor little Nora, don't you think I know what it is? You can't make yourself believe that I have forgiven you. But I have, Nora; I swear to you, I have forgiven you for everything. Of course I know that what you did was for love of me.

Nora.   That is true.

Helmer.   You have loved me the way a wife ought to love her husband. You just didn't have the wisdom to judge the means. But do you think I love you any less because you don't know how to act on your own? Of course not. Just lean on me. I'll advise you; I'll guide you. I wouldn't be a man if I didn't find you twice as attractive because of your womanly helplessness. You mustn't pay any attention to the hard words I said to you right at first. It was just that first shock when I thought everything was collapsing all around me. I have forgiven you, Nora. I swear to you—I really have forgiven you.

Nora.   I thank you for your forgiveness. *(She goes out through the door, right.)*

Helmer.   No, stay—*(Looks into the room she entered.)* What are you doing in there?

Nora *(within).*   Getting out of my costume.

Helmer *(by the open door).*   Good, good. Try to calm down and compose yourself, my poor little frightened songbird. Rest safely; I have broad wings to cover you with. *(Walks around near the door.)* What a nice and cozy home we have, Nora. Here's shelter for you. Here I'll keep you safe like a hunted dove I have rescued from the hawk's talons. Believe me: I'll know how to quiet your beating heart. It will happen by and by, Nora; you'll see. Why, tomorrow you'll look at all this in quite a different light. And soon everything will be just the way it was before. I won't need to keep reassuring you that I have forgiven you; you'll feel it yourself. Did you really think I could have abandoned you, or even reproached you? Oh, you don't know a real man's heart, Nora. There is something unspeakably sweet and satisfactory for a man to know deep in himself that he has forgiven his wife—forgiven her in all the fullness of his honest heart. You see, that way she becomes his very own all over again—in a double sense, you might say. He has, so to speak, given her a second birth; it is as if she had become his wife and his child, both. From now on that's what you'll be to me, you lost and helpless creature. Don't worry about a thing, Nora. Only be frank with me, and I'll be your will and your conscience.—What's this? You're not in bed? You've changed your dress—!

Nora (*in an everyday dress*).   Yes, Torvald. I have changed my dress.

Helmer.   But why—now—this late—?

Nora.   I'm not going to sleep tonight.

Helmer.   But my dear Nora—

Nora (*looks at her watch*).   It isn't all that late. Sit down here with me, Torvald. You and I have much to talk about. (*Sits down at the table.*)

Helmer.   Nora—what is this all about? That rigid face—

Nora.   Sit down. This will take a while. I have much to say to you.

Helmer (*sits down, facing her across the table*).   You worry me, Nora. I don't understand you.

Nora.   No, that's just it. You don't understand me. And I have never understood you—not till tonight. No, don't interrupt me. Just listen to what I have to say.—This is a settling of accounts, Torvald.

Helmer.   What do you mean by that?

Nora (*after a brief silence*).   Doesn't one thing strike you, now that we are sitting together like this?

Helmer.   What would that be?

Nora.   We have been married for eight years. Doesn't it occur to you that this is the first time that you and I, husband and wife, are having a serious talk?

Helmer.   Well—serious—. What do you mean by that?

Nora.   For eight whole years—longer, in fact—ever since we first met, we have never talked seriously to each other about a single serious thing.

Helmer.   You mean I should forever have been telling you about worries you couldn't have helped me with anyway?

Nora.   I am not talking about worries. I'm saying we have never tried seriously to get to the bottom of anything together.

Helmer.   But dearest Nora, I hardly think that would have been something you—

Nora.   That's the whole point. You have never understood me. Great wrong has been done to me, Torvald. First by Daddy and then by you.

Helmer.   What! By us two? We who have loved you more deeply than anyone else?

Nora (*shakes her head*).   You never loved me—neither Daddy nor you. You only thought it was fun to be in love with me.

Helmer   But, Nora—what an expression to use!

Nora.   That's the way it has been, Torvald. When I was home with Daddy, he told me all his opinions, and so they became my opinions too. If I disagreed with him I kept it to myself, for he wouldn't have liked that. He called me his little doll baby, and he played with me the way I played with my dolls. Then I came to your house—

Helmer.   What a way to talk about our marriage!

Nora (*imperturbably*).   I mean that I passed from Daddy's hands into yours. You arranged everything according to your taste, and so I came to share it— or I pretended to; I'm not sure which. I think it was a little of both, now one and now the other. When I look back on it now, it seems to me I've been living here like a pauper—just a hand-to-mouth kind of existence. I have earned my keep by doing tricks for you, Torvald. But that's the way you wanted it. You have great sins against me to answer for, Daddy and you. It's your fault that nothing has become of me.

Helmer.   Nora, you're being both unreasonable and ungrateful. Haven't you been happy here?

Nora.   No, never. I thought I was, but I wasn't.

Helmer.   Not—not happy!

Nora.   No; just having fun. And you have always been very good to me. But our home has never been more than a playroom. I have been your doll wife here, just the way I used to be Daddy's doll child. And the children have been my dolls. I thought it was fun when you played with me, just as they thought it was fun when I played with them. That's been our marriage, Torvald.

Helmer.   There is something in what you are saying—exaggerated and hysterical though it is. But from now on things will be different. Playtime is over; it's time for growing up.

Nora.   Whose growing up—mine or the children's?

Helmer.   Both yours and the children's, Nora darling.

Nora.   Oh Torvald, you're not the man to bring me up to be the right kind of wife for you.

Helmer.   How can you say that?

Nora.   And I—? What qualifications do I have for bringing up the children?

Helmer.   Nora!

Nora.   You said so yourself a minute ago—that you didn't dare to trust me with them.

Helmer.   In the first flush of anger, yes. Surely, you're not going to count that.

Nora.   But you were quite right. I am *not* qualified. Something else has to come first. Somehow I have to grow up myself. And you are not the man to help me do that. That's a job I have to do by myself. And that's why I'm leaving you.

Helmer (*jumps up*).   What did you say!

Nora.   I have to be by myself if I am to find out about myself and about all the other things too. So I can't stay here with you any longer.

Helmer.   Nora, Nora!

Nora.   I'm leaving now. I'm sure Kristine will put me up for tonight.

Helmer.   You're out of your mind! I won't let you! I forbid you!

Nora.   You can't forbid me anything any more; it won't do any good. I'm taking my own things with me. I won't accept anything from you, either now or later.

Helmer.   But this is madness!

Nora.   Tomorrow I'm going home—I mean back to my old home town. It will be easier for me to find some kind of job there.

Helmer.   Oh, you blind, inexperienced creature—!

Nora.   I must see to it that I get experience, Torvald.

Helmer.   Leaving your home, your husband, your children! Not a thought of what people will say!

Nora.   I can't worry about that. All I know is that I have to leave.

Helmer.   Oh, this is shocking! Betraying your most sacred duties like this!

Nora.   And what do you consider my most sacred duties?

Helmer.   Do I need to tell you that? They are your duties to your husband and your children.

Nora.   I have other duties equally sacred.

Helmer.   You do not. What duties would they be?

Nora.   My duties to myself.

Helmer.   You are a wife and a mother before you are anything else.

Nora.   I don't believe that any more. I believe I am first of all a human being, just as much as you—or at any rate that I must try to become one. Oh, I know very well that most people agree with you, Torvald, and that it says something like that in all the books. But what people say and what the books say is no longer enough for me. I have to think about these things myself and see if I can't find the answers.

Helmer.   You mean to tell me you don't know what your proper place in your own home is? Don't you have a reliable guide in such matters? Don't you have religion?

Nora.   Oh but Torvald—I don't really know what religion is.

Helmer.   What are you saying!

Nora.   All I know is what the Reverend Hansen told me when he prepared me for confirmation. He said that religion was *this* and it was *that*. When I get by myself, away from here, I'll have to look into that, too. I have to decide if what the Reverend Hansen said was right, or anyway if it is right for *me*.

Helmer.   Oh, this is unheard of in a young woman! If religion can't guide you, let me appeal to your conscience. For surely you have moral feelings? Or—answer me—maybe you don't?

Nora.   Well, you see, Torvald, I don't really know what to say. I just don't know. I am confused about these things. All I know is that my ideas are quite different from yours. I have just found out that the laws are different from what I thought they were, but in no way can I get it into my head that those laws are right. A woman shouldn't have the right to spare her dying old father or save her husband's life! I just can't believe that.

Helmer.   You speak like a child. You don't understand the society you live in.

Nora.   No, I don't. But I want to find out about it. I have to make up my mind who is right, society or I.

Helmer.   You are sick, Nora; you have a fever. I really don't think you are in your right mind.

Nora.   I have never felt so clearheaded and sure of myself as I do tonight.

Helmer.   And clearheaded and sure of yourself you're leaving your husband and children?

Nora.   Yes.

Helmer.   Then there is only one possible explanation.

Nora.   What?

Helmer.   You don't love me any more.

Nora   No, that's just it.

Helmer.   Nora! Can you say that?

Nora.   I am sorry, Torvald, for you have always been so good to me. But I can't help it. I don't love you any more.

Helmer (*with forced composure*).   And this too is a clear and sure conviction?

Nora.   Completely clear and sure. That's why I don't want to stay here any more.

Helmer.   And are you ready to explain to me how I came to forfeit your love?

Nora.   Certainly I am. It was tonight, when the wonderful didn't happen. That was when I realized you were not the man I thought you were.

Helmer.   You have to explain. I don't understand.

Nora.   I have waited patiently for eight years, for I wasn't such a fool that I thought the wonderful is something that happens any old day. Then this— thing—came crashing in on me, and then there wasn't a doubt in my mind that now—now comes the wonderful. When Krogstad's letter was in that mailbox, never for a moment did it even occur to me that you would submit to his conditions. I was so absolutely certain that you would say to him: make the whole thing public—tell everybody. And when that had happened—

Helmer.   Yes, then what? When I had surrendered my wife to shame and disgrace—!

Nora.   When that had happened, I was absolutely certain that you would stand up and take the blame and say, "I'm the guilty one."

Helmer.   Nora!

Nora.   You mean I never would have accepted such a sacrifice from you? Of course not. But what would my protests have counted against yours? *That* was the wonderful I was hoping for in terror. And to prevent that I was going to kill myself.

Helmer.   I'd gladly work nights and days for you, Nora—endure sorrow and want for your sake. But nobody sacrifices his *honor* for his love.

Nora.   A hundred thousand women have done so.

Helmer. Oh, you think and talk like a silly child.

Nora. All right. But you don't think and talk like the man I can live with. When you had gotten over your fright—not because of what threatened *me* but because of the risk to *you*—and the whole danger was past, then you acted as if nothing at all had happened. Once again I was your little songbird, your doll, just as before, only now you had to handle her even more carefully, because she was so frail and weak. *(Rises.)* Torvald—that moment I realized that I had been living here for eight years with a stranger and had borne him three children—Oh, I can't stand thinking about it! I feel like tearing myself to pieces!

Helmer *(heavily).* I see it, I see it. An abyss has opened up between us.—Oh but Nora—surely it can be filled?

Nora. The way I am now I am no wife for you.

Helmer. I have it in me to change.

Nora. Perhaps—if your doll is taken from you.

Helmer. To part—to part from you! No, no, Nora! I can't grasp that thought!

Nora *(goes out, right).* All the more reason why it has to be. *(She returns with her outdoor clothes and a small bag, which she sets down on the chair by the table.)*

Helmer. Nora, Nora! Not now! Wait till tomorrow.

Nora *(putting on her coat).* I can't spend the night in a stranger's rooms.

Helmer. But couldn't we live here together like brother and sister—?

Nora *(tying on her hat).* You know very well that wouldn't last long—. *(Wraps her shawl around her.)* Goodbye, Torvald. I don't want to see the children. I know I leave them in better hands than mine. The way I am now I can't be anything to them.

Helmer. But some day, Nora—some day—?

Nora. How can I tell? I have no idea what's going to become of me.

Helmer. But you're still my wife, both as you are now and as you will be.

Nora. Listen, Torvald—when a wife leaves her husband's house, the way I am doing now, I have heard he has no more legal responsibilities for her. At any rate, I now release you from all responsibility. You are not to feel yourself obliged to me for anything, and I have no obligations to you. There has to be full freedom on both sides. Here is your ring back. Now give me mine.

Helmer. Even this?

Nora. Even this.

Helmer. Here it is.

Nora. There. So now it's over. I'm putting the keys here. The maids know everything about the house—better than I. Tomorrow, after I'm gone, Kristine will come over and pack my things from home. I want them sent after me.

Helmer. Over! It's all over! Nora, will you never think of me?

Nora. I'm sure I'll often think of you and the children and this house.

Helmer. May I write to you, Nora?

Nora. No—never. I won't have that.

Helmer. But send you things—? You must let me

Nora. Nothing, nothing.

Helmer. —help you, when you need help—

Nora. I told you, no; I won't have it. I'll accept nothing from strangers.

Helmer. Nora—can I never again be more to you than a stranger?

Nora (*picks up her bag*). Oh Torvald—then the most wonderful of all would have to happen—

Helmer. Tell me what that would be—!

Nora. For that to happen, both you and I would have to change so that—Oh Torvald, I no longer believe in the wonderful.

Helmer. But I *will* believe. Tell me! Change, so that—?

Nora. So that our living together would become a true marriage. Goodbye. (*She goes out through the hall.*)

Helmer (*sinks down on a chair near the door and covers his face with his hands*). Nora! Nora! (*Looks around him and gets up.*) All empty. She's gone. (*With sudden hope.*) The most wonderful—?!

From downstairs comes the sound of a heavy door slamming shut.

QUESTIONS

1. What evidence does the play provide that *A Doll's House* is about not only Nora's marriage but the institution of marriage itself? **2.** On a number of occasions Nora recalls her father. What relevance do these recollections have to the development of the theme? **3.** Is Krogstad presented as a stock villain, or are we meant to sympathize with him? **4.** What function does Dr. Rank serve in the play?

WRITING TOPICS

1. Does the fact that Nora abandons her children undermine her otherwise heroic decision to walk out on a hollow marriage? For an 1880 German production of the play, Ibsen—in response to public demand—provided an alternate ending in which Nora, after struggling with her conscience, decides that she cannot abandon her children. Is this ending better than the original ending? Explain. **2.** How does the subplot involving the relationship between Mrs. Linde and Krogstad add force to the main plot of *A Doll's House*?

CONFORMITY
AND
REBELLION

The Accused, 1886 by Odilon Redon

ESSAYS

A Modest Proposal

1729

JONATHAN SWIFT [1667–1745]

It is a melancholy object to those who walk through this great town[1] or travel
in the country, when they see the streets, the roads, and cabin doors, crowded
with beggars of the female sex, followed by three, four, or six children, all in
rags and importuning every passenger for an alms. These mothers, instead of
being able to work for their honest livelihood, are forced to employ all their
time in strolling to beg sustenance for their helpless infants, who, as they grow
up, either turn thieves for want of work, or leave their dear native country to
fight for the Pretender in Spain, or sell themselves to the Barbados.[2]

I think it is agreed by all parties that this prodigious number of children in
the arms, or on the backs, or at the heels of their mothers, and frequently of
their fathers, is in the present deplorable state of the kingdom a very great
additional grievance; and therefore whoever could find out a fair, cheap, and
easy method of making these children sound, useful members of the common-
wealth would deserve so well of the public as to have his statue set up for a
preserver of the nation.

But my intention is very far from being confined to provide only for the
children of professed beggars; it is of a much greater extent, and shall take in
the whole number of infants at a certain age who are born of parents in effect
as little able to support them as those who demand our charity in the streets.

As to my own part, having turned my thoughts for many years upon this
important subject, and maturely weighed the several schemes of other projec-
tors,[3] I have always found them grossly mistaken in their computation. It is
true, a child just dropped from its dam may be supported by her milk for a
solar year, with little other nourishment; at most not above the value of two
shillings,[4] which the mother may certainly get, or the value in scraps, by her

---

[1] Dublin.
[2] Many Irish men joined the army of the exiled James Stuart (1688–1766), who laid claim to the
British throne. Others exchanged their labor for passage to the British colony of Barbados, in the
Caribbean.
[3] People with projects.
[4] A shilling was worth about twenty-five cents.

lawful occupation of begging; and it is exactly at one year that I propose to provide for them in such a manner as instead of being a charge upon their parents or the parish, or wanting food and raiment for the rest of their lives, they shall on the contrary contribute to the feeding, and partly to the clothing, of many thousands.

There is likewise another great advantage in my scheme, that it will prevent those voluntary abortions, and that horrid practice of women murdering their bastard children, alas, too frequent among us, sacrificing the poor innocent babes, I doubt, more to avoid the expense than the shame, which would move tears and pity in the most savage and inhuman breast.

The number of souls in this kingdom being usually reckoned one million and a half, of these I calculate there may be about two hundred thousand couples whose wives are breeders; from which number I subtract thirty thousand couples who are able to maintain their own children, although I apprehend there cannot be so many under the present distress of the kingdom; but this being granted, there will remain an hundred and seventy thousand breeders. I again subtract fifty thousand for those women who miscarry, or whose children die by accident or disease within the year. There only remain an hundred and twenty thousand children of poor parents annually born. The question therefore is, how this number shall be reared and provided for, which, as I have already said, under the present situation of affairs, is utterly impossible by all the methods hitherto proposed. For we can neither employ them in handicraft or agriculture; we neither build houses (I mean in the country) nor cultivate land. They can very seldom pick up a livelihood by stealing till they arrive at six years old except where they are of towardly parts;[5] although I confess they learn the rudiments much earlier, during which time they can however be looked upon only as probationers, as I have been informed by a principal gentleman in the country of Cavan, who protested to me that he never knew above one or two instances under the age of six, even in a part of the kingdom so renowned for the quickest proficiency in that art.

I am assured by our merchants that a boy or a girl before twelve years old is no salable commodity; and even when they come to this age they will not yield above three pounds, or three pounds and half a crown at most on the Exchange;[6] which cannot turn to account either to the parents or the kingdom, the charge of nutriment and rags having been at least four times that value.

I shall now therefore humbly propose my own thoughts, which I hope will not be liable to the least objection.

I have been assured by a very knowing American of my acquaintance in London, that a young healthy child well nursed is at a year old a most delicious, nourishing, and wholesome food, whether stewed, roasted, baked, or boiled; and I make no doubt that it will equally serve in a fricassee or a ragout.

I do therefore humbly offer it to public consideration that of the hundred

---

[5] Able and eager to learn.
[6] A pound was twenty shillings; a crown, five shillings.

and twenty thousand children, already computed, twenty thousand may be reserved for breed, whereof only one fourth part to be males, which is more than we allow to sheep, black cattle, or swine; and my reason is that these children are seldom the fruits of marriage, a circumstance not much regarded by our savages, therefore one male will be sufficient to serve four females. That the remaining hundred thousand may at a year old be offered in sale to the persons of quality and fortune through the kingdom, always advising the mother to let them suck plentifully in the last month, so as to render them plump and fat for a good table. A child will make two dishes at an entertainment for friends; and when the family dines alone, the fore or hind quarter will make a reasonable dish, and seasoned with a little pepper or salt will be very good boiled on the fourth day, especially in winter.

I have reckoned upon a medium that a child just born will weigh twelve   11
pounds, and in a solar year if tolerably nursed increaseth to twenty-eight pounds.

I grant this food will be somewhat dear, and therefore very proper for land-   12
lords, who, as they have already devoured most of the parents, seem to have the best title to the children.

Infant's flesh will be in season throughout the year, but more plentiful in   13
March, and a little before and after. For we are told by a grave author, an eminent French physician,[7] that fish being a prolific diet, there are more children born in Roman Catholic countries about nine months after Lent than at any other season; therefore, reckoning a year after Lent, the markets will be more glutted than usual, because the number of popish infants is at least three to one in this kingdom; and therefore it will have one other collateral advantage, by lessening the number of Papists among us.

I have already computed the charge of nursing a beggar's child (in which list   14
I reckon all cottagers, laborers, and four-fifths of the farmers) to be about two shillings per annum, rags included; and I believe no gentleman would repine to give ten shillings for the carcass of a good fat child, which, as I have said, will make four dishes of excellent nutritive meat, when he hath only some particular friend or his own family to dine with him. Thus the squire will learn to be a good landlord, and grow popular among the tenants; the mother will have eight shillings net profit, and be fit for work till she produces another child.

Those who are more thrifty (as I must confess the times require) may flay   15
the carcass; the skin of which artificially[8] dressed will make admirable gloves for ladies, and summer boots for fine gentlemen.

As to our city of Dublin, shambles[9] may be appointed for this purpose in   16
the most convenient parts of it, and butchers we may be assured will not be wanting; although I rather recommend buying the children alive, and dressing them hot from the knife as we do roasting pigs.

---

[7] François Rabelais, sixteenth-century French comic writer.
[8] Skillfully.
[9] Slaughterhouses.

A very worthy person, a true lover of his country, and whose virtues I highly esteem, was lately pleased in discoursing on this matter to offer a refinement upon my scheme. He said that many gentlemen of his kingdom, having of late destroyed their deer, he conceived that the want of venison might be well supplied by the bodies of young lads and maidens, not exceeding fourteen years of age nor under twelve, so great a number of both sexes in every country being now ready to starve for want of work and service; and these to be disposed of by their parents, if alive, or otherwise by their nearest relations. But with due deference to so excellent a friend and so deserving a patriot, I cannot be altogether in his sentiments; for as to the males, my American acquaintance assured me from frequent experience that their flesh was generally tough and lean, like that of our schoolboys, by continual exercise, and their taste disagreeable; and to fatten them would not answer the charge. Then as to the females; it would, I think with humble submission, be a loss to the public, because they soon would become breeders themselves; and besides, it is not improbable that some scrupulous people might be apt to censure such a practice (although indeed very unjustly) as a little bordering upon cruelty; which, I confess, hath always been with me the strongest objection against any project, how well soever intended.

But in order to justify my friend, he confessed that this expedient was put into his head by the famous Psalmanazar,[10] a native of the island Formosa, who came from thence to London above twenty years ago, and in conversation told my friend that in his country when any young person happened to be put to death, the executioner sold the carcass to persons of quality as a prime dainty; and that in his time the body of a plump girl of fifteen, who was crucified for an attempt to poison the emperor, was sold to his Imperial Majesty's prime minister of state, and other great mandarins of the court, in joints from the gibbet, at four hundred crowns. Neither indeed can I deny that if the same use were made of several plump young girls in this town, who without one single groat[11] to their fortunes cannot stir abroad without a chair,[12] and appear at the playhouse and assemblies in foreign fineries which they never will pay for, the kingdom would not be the worse.

Some persons of a desponding spirit are in great concern about the vast number of poor people who are aged, diseased, or maimed, and I have been desired to employ my thoughts what course may be taken to ease the nation of so grievous an encumbrance. But I am not in the least pain upon the matter, because it is very well known that they are every day dying and rotting by cold and famine, and filth and vermin, as fast as can be reasonably expected. And as to the younger laborers, they are now in almost as hopeful a condition. They cannot get work, and consequently pine away for want of nourishment to a degree that if any time they are accidentally hired to common labor, they

---

[10] George Psalmanazar was a Frenchman who passed himself off as a native of Formosa.
[11] A coin worth about four cents.
[12] A sedan chair, an enclosed chair carried by poles on the front and back.

have not strength to perform it; and thus the country and themselves are happily delivered from the evils to come.

I have too long digressed, and therefore shall return to my subject. I think the advantages by the proposal which I have made are obvious and many, as well as of the highest importance.   20

For first, as I have already observed, it would greatly lessen the number of Papists, with whom we are yearly overrun, being the principal breeders of the nation as well as our most dangerous enemies; and who stay at home on purpose to deliver the kingdom to the Pretender, hoping to take their advantage by the absence of so many good Protestants, who have chosen rather to leave their country than to stay at home and pay tithes against their conscience to an Episcopal curate.   21

Secondly, the poorer tenants will have something valuable of their own, which by law may be made liable to distress,[13] and help to pay their landlord's rent, their corn and cattle being already seized and money a thing unknown.   22

Thirdly, whereas the maintenance of an hundred thousand children, from two years old and upwards, cannot be computed at less than ten shillings a piece per annum, the nation's stock will be thereby increased fifty thousand pounds per annum, besides the profit of a new dish introduced to the tables of all gentlemen of fortune in the kingdom who have any refinement in taste. And the money will circulate among ourselves, the goods being entirely of our own growth and manufacture.   23

Fourthly, the constant breeders, besides the gain of eight shillings sterling per annum by the sale of their children, will be rid of the charge of maintaining them after the first year.   24

Fifthly, this food would likewise bring great custom to taverns, where the vintners will certainly be so prudent as to procure the best receipts[14] for dressing it to perfection, and consequently have their houses frequented by all the fine gentlemen, who justly value themselves upon their knowledge in good eating; and a skillful cook, who understands how to oblige his guests, will contrive to make it as expensive as they please.   25

Sixthly, this would be a great inducement to marriage, which all wise nations have either encouraged by rewards or enforced by laws and penalties. It would increase the care and tenderness of mothers toward their children, when they were sure of a settlement for life to the poor babes, provided in some sort by the public, to their annual profit instead of expense. We should see an honest emulation among the married women, which of them could bring the fattest child to the market. Men would become as fond of their wives during the time of their pregnancy as they are now of their mares in foal, their cows in calf, or sows when they are ready to farrow; nor offer to beat or kick them (as is too frequent a practice) for fear of a miscarriage.   26

---

[13] Seizure for payment of debts.
[14] Recipes.

Many other advantages might be enumerated. For instance, the addition of   27
some thousand carcasses in our exportation of barreled beef, the propagation
of swine's flesh, and improvements in the art of making good bacon, so much
wanted among us by the great destruction of pigs, too frequent at our tables,
which are no way comparable in taste or magnificence to a well-grown, fat,
yearling child, which roasted whole will make a considerable figure at a lord
mayor's feast or any other public entertainment. But this and many others I
omit, being studious of brevity.

Supposing that one thousand families in this city would be constant custom-   28
ers for infants' flesh, besides others who might have it at merry meetings, particularly weddings and christenings, I compute that Dublin would take off annually about twenty thousand carcasses, and the rest of the kingdom (where
probably they will be sold somewhat cheaper) the remaining eighty thousand.

I can think of no one objection that will possibly be raised against this pro-   29
posal, unless it should be urged that the number of people will be thereby
much lessened in the kingdom. This I freely own, and it was indeed one principal design in offering it to the world. I desire the reader will observe, that I
calculate my remedy for this one individual kingdom of Ireland and for no
other that ever was, is, or I think ever can be upon earth. Therefore let no
man talk to me of other expedients: of taxing our absentees at five shillings a
pound: of using neither clothes nor household furniture except what is of our
own growth and manufacture: of utterly rejecting the materials and instruments
that promote foreign luxury: of curing the expensiveness of pride, vanity, idleness, and gaming in our women: of introducing a vein of parsimony, prudence,
and temperance: of learning to love our country, in the want of which we differ
even from Laplanders and the inhabitants of Topinamboo:[15] of quitting our
animosities and factions, nor acting any longer like the Jews, who were murdering one another at the very moment their city was taken:[16] of being a little
cautious not to sell our country and conscience for nothing: of teaching landlords
to have at least one degree of mercy toward their tenants: lastly, of putting a spirit
of honesty, industry, and skill into our shopkeepers; who, if a resolution could
now be taken to buy only our native goods, would immediately unite to cheat
and exact upon us in the price, the measure, and the goodness, nor could ever
yet be brought to make one fair proposal of just dealing, though often and
earnestly invited to it.

Therefore I repeat, let no man talk to me of these and the like expedients,   30
till he hath at least some glimpse of hope that there will be some hearty and
sincere attempt to put them in practice.

But as to myself, having been wearied out for many years with offering vain,   31
idle, visionary thoughts, and at length utterly despairing of success, I fortunately fell upon this proposal, which, as it is wholly new, so it hath something

---

[15] A district in Brazil, inhabited in Swift's day by primitive tribes.
[16] While the Roman emperor Titus laid siege to Jerusalem in 70 A.D., bloody fighting erupted
among factions within the city.

solid and real, of no expense and little trouble, full in our own power, and whereby we can incur no danger in disobliging England. For this kind of commodity will not bear exportation, the flesh being of too tender a consistence to admit a long continuance in salt, although perhaps I could name a country[17] which would be glad to eat up our whole nation without it.

After all, I am not so violently bent upon my own opinion as to reject any offer proposed by wise men, which shall be found equally innocent, cheap, easy, and effectual. But before something of that kind shall be advanced in contradiction to my scheme, and offering a better, I desire the author or authors will be pleased maturely to consider two points. First, as things now stand, how they will be able to find food and raiment for an hundred thousand useless mouths and backs. And secondly, there being a round million of creatures in human figure throughout this kingdom, whose sole subsistence put into a common stock would leave them in debt two millions of pounds sterling, adding those who are beggars by profession to the bulk of farmers, cottagers, and laborers, with their wives and children who are beggars in effect; I desire those politicians who dislike my overture, and may perhaps be so bold to attempt an answer, that they will first ask the parents of these mortals whether they would not at this day think it a great happiness to have been sold for food at a year old in this manner I prescribe, and thereby have avoided such a perpetual scene of misfortunes as they have since gone through by the oppression of landlords, the impossibility of paying rent without money or trade, the want of common sustenance, with neither house nor clothes to cover them from the inclemencies of the weather, and the most inevitable prospect of entailing the like or greater miseries upon their breed forever.

I profess, in the sincerity of my heart, that I have not the least personal interest in endeavoring to promote this necessary work, having no other motive than the public good of my country, by advancing our trade, providing for infants, relieving the poor, and giving some pleasure to the rich. I have no children by which I can propose to get a single penny; the youngest being nine years old, and my wife past childbearing.

QUESTIONS
1. In what sense is Swift's proposal "modest"? **2.** What are the major divisions of the essay? What function does each serve? **3.** What function does paragraph 29 serve? **4.** Explain what Swift means when he says in paragraph 20 that "I have too long digressed. . . ." **5.** Characterize the tone of the essay, paying particular attention to the speaker's use of diction.

WRITING TOPIC
Some knowledge of Swift's life and other works would make it clear that in this essay he is being satiric. Without that knowledge, that is, on the basis of the essay alone, how would you demonstrate that Swift is writing satire?

---

[17] England.

My Wood

1936

E. M. FORSTER [1879–1970]

A few years ago I wrote a book which dealt in part with the difficulties of the English in India.[1] Feeling that they would have had no difficulties in India themselves, the Americans read the book freely. The more they read it the better it made them feel, and a cheque to the author was the result. I bought a wood with the cheque. It is not a large wood—it contains scarcely any trees, and it is intersected, blast it, by a public footpath. Still, it is the first property that I have owned, so it is right that other people should participate in my shame, and should ask themselves, in accents that will vary in horror, this very important question: What is the effect of property upon the character? Don't let's touch economics; the effect of private ownership upon the community as a whole is another question—a more important question, perhaps, but another one. Let's keep to psychology. If you own things, what's their effect on you? What's the effect on me of my wood?

In the first place, it makes me feel heavy. Property does have this effect. Property produces men of weight, and it was a man of weight who failed to get into the Kingdom of Heaven. He was not wicked, that unfortunate millionaire in the parable, he was only stout; he stuck out in front, not to mention behind, and as he wedged himself this way and that in the crystalline entrance and bruised his well-fed flanks, he saw beneath him a comparatively slim camel passing through the eye of a needle and being woven into the robe of God.[2] The Gospels all through couple stoutness and slowness. They point out what is perfectly obvious, yet seldom realized: that if you have a lot of things you cannot move about a lot, that furniture requires dusting, dusters require servants, servants require insurance stamps, and the whole tangle of them makes you think twice before you accept an invitation to dinner or go for a bathe in the Jordan. Sometimes the Gospels proceed further and say with Tolstoy[3] that property is sinful; they approach the difficult ground of asceticism here, where I cannot follow them. But as to the immediate effects of property on people, they just show straightforward logic. It produces men of weight. Men of weight cannot, by definition, move like the lightning from the East unto the West, and the ascent of a fourteen-stone[4] bishop into a pulpit is thus the exact antithesis of the coming of the Son of Man. My wood makes me feel heavy.

In the second place, it makes me feel it ought to be larger.

The other day I heard a twig snap in it. I was annoyed at first, for I thought that someone was blackberrying, and depreciating the value of the under-

---

[1]*A Passage to India* (1924).
[2]See Matthew 19:23–24; Mark 10:23–25; Luke 16:19–31 and 18:24–25.
[3]Leo Tolstoy (1828–1910), Russian novelist. See his story "The Death of Iván Ilých" (p. 589).
[4]196-pound.

growth. On coming nearer, I saw it was not a man who had trodden on the twig and snapped it, but a bird, and I felt pleased. My bird. The bird was not equally pleased. Ignoring the relation between us, it took fright as soon as it saw the shape of my face, and flew straight over the boundary hedge into a field, the property of Mrs. Henessy, where it sat down with a loud squawk. It had become Mrs. Henessy's bird. Something seemed grossly amiss here, something that would not have occurred had the wood been larger. I could not afford to buy Mrs. Henessy out, I dared not murder her, and limitations of this sort beset me on every side. Ahab did not want that vineyard—he only needed it to round off his property, preparatory to plotting a new curve—and all the land around my wood has become necessary to me in order to round off the wood. A boundary protects. But—poor little thing—the boundary ought in its turn to be protected. Noises on the edge of it. Children throw stones. A little more, and then a little more, until we reach the sea. Happy Canute! Happier Alexander! And after all, why should even the world be the limit of possession? A rocket containing a Union Jack, will, it is hoped, be shortly fired at the moon. Mars. Sirius. Beyond which . . . But these immensities ended by saddening me. I could not suppose that my wood was the destined nucleus of universal dominion—it is so very small and contains no mineral wealth beyond the blackberries. Nor was I comforted when Mrs. Henessy's bird took alarm for the second time and flew clean away from us all, under the belief that it belonged to itself.

In the third place, property makes its owner feel that he ought to do something to it. Yet he isn't sure what. A restlessness comes over him, a vague sense that he has a personality to express—the same sense which, without any vagueness, leads the artist to an act of creation. Sometimes I think I will cut down such trees as remain in the wood, at other times I want to fill up the gaps between them with new trees. Both impulses are pretentious and empty. They are not honest movements towards money-making or beauty. They spring from a foolish desire to express myself and from an inability to enjoy what I have got. Creation, property, enjoyment form a sinister trinity in the human mind. Creation and enjoyment are both very, very good, yet they are often unattainable without a material basis, and at such moments property pushes itself in as a substitute, saying, "Accept me instead—I'm good enough for all three." It is not enough. It is, as Shakespeare said of lust, "The expense of spirit in a waste of shame"; it is "Before, a joy proposed; behind, a dream." [5] Yet we don't know how to shun it. It is forced on us by our economic system as the alternative to starvation. · It is also forced on us by an internal defect in the soul, by the feeling that in property may lie the germs of self-development and of exquisite or heroic deeds. Our life on earth is, and ought to be, material and carnal. But we have not yet learned to manage our materialism and carnality properly; they are still entangled with the desire for ownership, where (in the words of Dante) "Possession is one with loss."

5

---

[5] This sonnet is reprinted on p. 439.

And this brings us to our fourth and final point: the blackberries.

Blackberries are not plentiful in this meagre grove, but they are easily seen from the public footpath which traverses it, and all too easily gathered. Foxgloves, too—people will pull up the foxgloves, and ladies of an educational tendency even grub for toadstools to show them on the Monday in class. Other ladies, less educated, roll down the bracken in the arms of their gentlemen friends. There is paper, there are tins. Pray, does my wood belong to me or doesn't it? And, if it does, should I not own it best by allowing no one else to walk there? There is a wood near Lyme Regis, also cursed by a public footpath, where the owner has not hesitated on this point. He has built high stone walls each side of the path, and has spanned it by bridges, so that the public circulate like termites while he gorges on the blackberries unseen. He really does own his wood, this able chap. Dives in Hell did pretty well, but the gulf dividing him from Lazarus could be traversed by vision, and nothing traverses it here.[6] And perhaps I shall come to this in time. I shall wall in and fence out until I really taste the sweets of property. Enormously stout, endlessly avaricious, pseudocreative, intensely selfish, I shall weave upon my forehead the quadruple crown of possession until those nasty Bolshies[7] come and take it off again and thrust me aside into the outer darkness.

QUESTIONS

1.   What is the significance of the first three sentences of the essay?   **2.**   Does Forster consider his purchase good fortune, bad fortune, or both?   **3.**   What does Forster mean when he concludes paragraph 4 with the comment that the bird flew off "under the impression that it belonged to itself"?   **4.**   Characterize the tone of the essay.

WRITING TOPIC

Paraphrase paragraph 5, and then discuss Forster's assertion that "Creation, property, enjoyment form a sinister trinity in the human mind."

---

[6] In the New Testament (Luke 16:19–31), Dives was a rich man from whom the pauper Lazarus begged. Upon his death, Dives was sent to Hades, and from there he was able to see Lazarus in Heaven.

[7] Bolsheviks, i.e., Communists.

What If Shakespeare Had Had a Sister?[1]

1928

VIRGINIA WOOLF [1882–1941]

It was disappointing not to have brought back in the evening some important   1
statement, some authentic fact. Women are poorer than men because—this or
that. Perhaps now it would be better to give up seeking for the truth, and
receiving on one's head an avalanche of opinion hot as lava, discoloured as
dish-water. It would be better to draw the curtains; to shut out distractions; to
light the lamp; to narrow the enquiry and to ask the historian, who records not
opinions but facts, to describe under what conditions women lived, not
throughout the ages, but in England, say in the time of Elizabeth.

For it is a perennial puzzle why no woman wrote a word of that extraordi-   2
nary literature when every other man, it seemed, was capable of song or sonnet. What were the conditions in which women lived, I asked myself; for
fiction, imaginative work that is, is not dropped like a pebble upon the ground,
as science may be; fiction is like a spider's web, attached ever so lightly perhaps,
but still attached to life at all four corners. Often the attachment is scarcely
perceptible; Shakespeare's plays, for instance, seem to hang there complete by
themselves. But when the web is pulled askew, hooked up at the edge, torn in
the middle, one remembers that these webs are not spun in midair by incor-
poreal creatures, but are the work of suffering human beings, and are attached
to grossly material things, like health and money and the houses we live in.

I went, therefore, to the shelf where the histories stand and took down one   3
of the latest, Professor Trevelyan's *History of England*. Once more I looked up
Women, found "position of," and turned to the pages indicated. "Wife-beating,"
I read, "was a recognised right of man, and was practised without shame by
high as well as low. . . . Similarly," the historian goes on, "the daughter who
refused to marry the gentleman of her parents' choice was liable to be locked
up, beaten and flung about the room, without any shock being inflicted on
public opinion. Marriage was not an affair of personal affection, but of family
avarice, particularly in the 'chivalrous' upper classes. . . . Betrothal often took
place while one or both of the parties was in the cradle, and marriage when
they were scarcely out of the nurses' charge." That was about 1470, soon after
Chaucer's time. The next reference to the position of women is some two

---

[1] *A Room of One's Own*, from which this essay is taken, is based on two lectures Woolf delivered
on women and literature at Newnham College and Girton College, Cambridge University. In the
opening chapter, Woolf declares that without "money and a room of her own" a woman cannot write
fiction. In the following chapter, she recounts her unsuccessful attempt to turn up information at the
British Library on the lives of women. This essay is from Chapter 3, from which a few passages are
omitted. It ends with the concluding paragraph of the book.

hundred years later, in the time of the Stuarts. "It was still the exception for women of the upper and middle class to choose their own husbands, and when the husband had been assigned, he was lord and master, so far at least as law and custom could make him. Yet even so," Professor Trevelyan concludes, "neither Shakespeare's women nor those of authentic seventeenth-century memoirs, like the Verneys and the Hutchinsons, seem wanting in personality and character." Certainly, if we consider it, Cleopatra must have had a way with her; Lady Macbeth, one would suppose, had a will of her own; Rosalind, one might conclude, was an attractive girl. Professor Trevelyan is speaking no more than the truth when he remarks that Shakespeare's women do not seem wanting in personality and character. Not being a historian, one might go even further and say that women have burnt like beacons in all the works of all the poets from the beginning of time—Clytemnestra, Antigone, Cleopatra, Lady Macbeth, Phèdre, Cressida, Rosalind, Desdemona, the Duchess of Malfi, among the dramatists; then among the prose writers: Millamant, Clarissa, Becky Sharp, Anna Karenina, Emma Bovary, Madame de Guermantes[2]—the names flock to mind, nor do they recall women "lacking in personality and character." Indeed, if woman had no existence save in the fiction written by men, one would imagine her a person of the utmost importance; very various; heroic and mean; splendid and sordid; infinitely beautiful and hideous in the extreme; as great as a man, some think even greater. But this is woman in fiction. In fact, as Professor Trevelyan points out, she was locked up, beaten and flung about the room.

A very queer, composite being thus emerges. Imaginatively she is of the highest importance; practically she is completely insignificant. She pervades poetry from cover to cover; she is all but absent from history. She dominates the lives of kings and conquerors in fiction; in fact she was the slave of any boy whose parents forced a ring upon her finger. Some of the most inspired words, some of the most profound thoughts in literature fall from her lips; in real life she could hardly read, could scarcely spell, and was the property of her husband.

It was certainly an odd monster that one made up by reading the historians first and the poets afterwards—a worm winged like an eagle; the spirit of life and beauty in a kitchen chopping up suet. But these monsters, however amusing to the imagination, have no existence in fact. What one must do to bring her to life was to think poetically and prosaically at one and the same moment, thus keeping in touch with fact—that she is Mrs. Martin, aged thirty-six, dressed in blue, wearing a black hat and brown shoes; but not losing sight of fiction either—that she is a vessel in which all sorts of spirits and forces are coursing and flashing perpetually. The moment, however, that one tries this method with the Elizabethan woman, one branch of illumination fails; one is held up by the scarcity of facts. One knows nothing detailed, nothing perfectly true and substantial about her. History scarcely mentions her. And I turned to Professor

4

5

---

[2] Female characters from great works of literature.

Trevelyan again to see what history meant to him. I found by looking at his chapter headings that it meant—

"The Manor Court and the Methods of Open-field Agriculture . . . The 6 Cistercians and Sheep-farming . . . The Crusades . . . The University . . . The House of Commons . . . The Hundred Years' War . . . The Wars of the Roses . . . The Renaissance Scholars . . . The Dissolution of the Monasteries . . . Agrarian and Religious Strife . . . The Origin of English Seapower . . . The Armada . . ." and so on. Occasionally an individual woman is mentioned, an Elizabeth, or a Mary; a queen or a great lady. But by no possible means could middle-class women with nothing but brains and character at their command have taken part in any one of the great movements which, brought together, constitute the historian's view of the past. Nor shall we find her in any collection of anecdotes. Aubrey hardly mentions her.[3] She never writes her own life and scarcely keeps a diary; there are only a handful of her letters in existence. She left no plays or poems by which we can judge her. . . . Here am I asking why women did not write poetry in the Elizabethan age, and I am not sure how they were educated; whether they were taught to write; whether they had sitting-rooms to themselves; how many women had children before they were twenty-one; what, in short, they did from eight in the morning till eight at night. They had no money evidently; according to Professor Trevelyan they were married whether they liked it or not before they were out of the nursery, at fifteen or sixteen very likely. It would have been extremely odd, even upon this showing, had one of them suddenly written the plays of Shakespeare, I concluded, and I thought of that old gentleman, who is dead now, but was a bishop, I think, who declared that it was impossible for any woman, past, present, or to come, to have the genius of Shakespeare. He wrote to the papers about it. He also told a lady who applied to him for information that cats do not as a matter of fact go to heaven, though they have, he added, souls of a sort. How much thinking those old gentlemen used to save one! How the borders of ignorance shrank back at their approach! Cats do not go to heaven. Women cannot write the plays of Shakespeare.

Be that as it may, I could not help thinking, as I looked at the works of 7 Shakespeare on the shelf, that the bishop was right at least in this; it would have been impossible, completely and entirely, for any woman to have written the plays of Shakespeare in the age of Shakespeare. Let me imagine, since facts are so hard to come by, what would have happened had Shakespeare had a wonderfully gifted sister, called Judith, let us say. Shakespeare himself went, very probably—his mother was an heiress—to the grammar school, where he may have learnt Latin—Ovid, Virgil and Horace—and the elements of grammar and logic. He was, it is well known, a wild boy who poached rabbits, perhaps shot a deer, and had, rather sooner than he should have done, to marry a woman in the neighbourhood, who bore him a child rather quicker than was right. That escapade sent him to seek his fortune in London. He had,

---

[3] John Aubrey (1626–1697), author of *Brief Lives*, a biographical work.

it seemed, a taste for the theatre; he began by holding horses at the stage door. Very soon he got work in the theatre, became a successful actor, and lived at the hub of the universe, meeting everybody, knowing everybody, practising his art on the boards, exercising his wits in the streets, and even getting access to the palace of the queen. Meanwhile his extraordinarily gifted sister, let us suppose, remained at home. She was as adventurous, as imaginative, as agog to see the world as he was. But she was not sent to school. She had no chance of learning grammar and logic, let alone of reading Horace and Virgil. She picked up a book now and then, one of her brother's perhaps, and read a few pages. But then her parents came in and told her to mend the stockings or mind the stew and not moon about with books and papers. They would have spoken sharply but kindly, for they were substantial people who knew the conditions of life for a woman and loved their daughter—indeed, more likely than not she was the apple of her father's eye. Perhaps she scribbled some pages up in an apple loft on the sly, but was careful to hide them or set fire to them. Soon, however, before she was out of her teens, she was to be betrothed to the son of a neighbouring wool-stapler. She cried out that marriage was hateful to her, and for that she was severely beaten by her father. Then he ceased to scold her. He begged her instead not to hurt him, not to shame him in this matter of her marriage. He would give her a chain of beads or a fine petticoat, he said; and there were tears in his eyes. How could she disobey him? How could she break his heart? The force of her own gift alone drove her to it. She made up a small parcel of her belongings, let herself down by a rope one summer's night and took the road to London. She was not seventeen. The birds that sang in the hedge were not more musical than she was. She had the quickest fancy, a gift like her brother's, for the tune of words. Like him, she had a taste for the theatre. She stood at the stage door; she wanted to act, she said. Men laughed in her face. The manager—a fat, loose-lipped man—guffawed. He bellowed something about poodles dancing and women acting—no woman, he said, could possibly be an actress.[4] He hinted—you can imagine what. She could get no training in her craft. Could she even seek her dinner in a tavern or roam the streets at midnight? Yet her genius was for fiction and lusted to feed abundantly upon the lives of men and women and the study of their ways. At last—for she was very young, oddly like Shakespeare the poet in her face, with the same grey eyes and rounded brows—at last Nick Greene the actor-manager took pity on her; she found herself with child by that gentleman and so—who shall measure the heat and violence of the poet's heart when caught and tangled in a woman's body?—killed herself one winter's night and lies buried at some cross-roads where the omnibuses now stop outside the Elephant and Castle.[5]

That, more or less, is how the story would run, I think, if a woman in Shakespeare's day had had Shakespeare's genius. But for my part, I agree with

8

---

[4] In Shakespeare's day, women's roles were played by boys.
[5] A London neighborhood.

the deceased bishop, if such he was—it is unthinkable that any woman in Shakespeare's day should have had Shakespeare's genius. For genius like Shakespeare's is not born among labouring, uneducated, servile people. It was not born in England among the Saxons and the Britons. It is not born today among the working classes. How, then, could it have been born among women whose work began, according to Professor Trevelyan, almost before they were out of the nursery, who were forced to it by their parents and held to it by all the power of law and custom? Yet genius of a sort must have existed among women as it must have existed among the working classes. Now and again an Emily Brontë or a Robert Burns blazes out and proves its presence.[6] But certainly it never got itself on to paper. When, however, one reads of a witch being ducked, of a woman possessed by devils, of a wise woman selling herbs, or even of a very remarkable man who had a mother, then I think we are on the track of a lost novelist, a suppressed poet, of some mute and inglorious[7] Jane Austen, some Emily Brontë who dashed her brains out on the moor or mopped and mowed about the highways crazed with the torture that her gift had put her to. Indeed, I would venture to guess that Anon, who wrote so many poems without signing them, was often a woman. It was a woman Edward Fitzgerald,[8] I think, suggested who made the ballads and the folk-songs, crooning them to her children, beguiling her spinning with them, or the length of the winter's night.

This may be true or it may be false—who can say?—but what is true in it,   9 so it seemed to me, reviewing the story of Shakespeare's sister as I had made it, is that any woman born with a great gift in the sixteenth century would certainly have gone crazed, shot herself, or ended her days in some lonely cottage outside the village, half witch, half wizard, feared and mocked at. For it needs little skill in psychology to be sure that a highly gifted girl who had tried to use her gift for poetry would have been so thwarted and hindered by other people, so tortured and pulled asunder by her own contrary instincts, that she must have lost her health and sanity to a certainty. No girl could have walked to London and stood at a stage door and forced her way into the presence of actor-managers without doing herself a violence and suffering an anguish which may have been irrational—for chastity may be a fetish invented by certain societies for unknown reasons—but were none the less inevitable. Chastity had then, it has even now, a religious importance in a woman's life, and has so wrapped itself round with nerves and instincts that to cut it free and bring it to the light of day demands courage of the rarest. To have lived a free life in London in the sixteenth century would have meant for a woman who was poet and playwright a nervous stress and dilemma which might well have killed her. Had she survived, whatever she had written would have been twisted and deformed, issuing from a strained and morbid imagination. And undoubt-

---

[6] Emily Brontë (1818–1848), English novelist, and Robert Burns (1759–1796), Scottish poet.
[7] Thomas Gray's description in "Elegy Written in a Country Churchyard" of the poet John Milton.
[8] Edward Fitzgerald (1809–1883), translator and poet.

edly, I thought, looking at the shelf where there are no plays by women, her work would have gone unsigned. That refuge she would have sought certainly. It was the relic of the sense of chastity that dictated anonymity to women even so late as the nineteenth century. Currer Bell, George Eliot, George Sand,[9] all the victims of inner strife as their writings prove, sought ineffectively to veil themselves by using the name of a man. Thus they did homage to the convention, which if not implanted by the other sex was liberally encouraged by them (the chief glory of a woman is not to be talked of, said Pericles,[10] himself a much-talked-of man), that publicity in women is detestable. . . .

That woman, then, who was born with a gift of poetry in the sixteenth century, was an unhappy woman, a woman at strife against herself. All the conditions of her life, all her own instincts, were hostile to the state of mind which is needed to set free whatever is in the brain. But what is the state of mind that is most propitious to the act of creation, I asked? Can one come by any notion of the state that furthers and makes possible that strange activity? Here I opened the volume containing the Tragedies of Shakespeare. What was Shakespeare's state of mind, for instance, when he wrote *Lear* and *Antony and Cleopatra*? It was certainly the state of mind most favourable to poetry that there has ever existed. But Shakespeare himself said nothing about it. We only know casually and by chance that he "never blotted a line."[11] Nothing indeed was ever said by the artist himself about his state of mind until the eighteenth century perhaps. Rousseau[12] perhaps began it. At any rate, by the nineteenth century self-consciousness had developed so far that it was the habit for men of letters to describe their minds in confessions and autobiographies. Their lives also were written, and their letters were printed after their deaths. Thus, though we do not know what Shakespeare went through when he wrote *Lear*, we do know what Carlyle went through when he wrote the *French Revolution*; what Flaubert went through when he wrote *Madame Bovary*; what Keats was going through when he tried to write poetry against the coming of death and the indifference of the world.

And one gathers from this enormous modern literature of confession and self-analysis that to write a work of genius is almost always a feat of prodigious difficulty. Everything is against the likelihood that it will come from the writer's mind whole and entire. Generally material circumstances are against it. Dogs will bark; people will interrupt; money must be made; health will break down. Further, accentuating all these difficulties and making them harder to bear is the world's notorious indifference. It does not ask people to write poems and novels and histories; it does not need them. It does not care whether Flaubert finds the right word or whether Carlyle scrupulously verifies this or that fact.

10

11

---

[9] The pseudonyms of Charlotte Brontë (1816–1855) and Mary Ann Evans (1819–1880), English novelists, and Amandine Aurore Lucie Dupin (1804–1876), French novelist.

[10] Pericles (d. 429 B.C.?), Athenian statesman and general.

[11] According to Ben Jonson, Shakespeare's contemporary.

[12] Jean-Jacques Rousseau (1712–1778), French philosopher, author of *The Confessions of Jean-Jacques Rousseau*.

Naturally, it will not pay for what it does not want. And so the writer, Keats, Flaubert, Carlyle, suffers, especially in the creative years of youth, every form of distraction and discouragement. A curse, a cry of agony, rises from those books of analysis and confession. "Mighty poets in their misery dead"[13]—that is the burden of their song. If anything comes through in spite of all this, it is a miracle, and probably no book is born entire and uncrippled as it was conceived.

But for women, I thought, looking at the empty shelves, these difficulties   12
were infinitely more formidable. In the first place, to have a room of her own, let alone a quiet room or a sound-proof room, was out of the question, unless her parents were exceptionally rich or very noble, even up to the beginning of the nineteenth century. Since her pin money, which depended on the good will of her father, was only enough to keep her clothed, she was debarred from such alleviations as came even to Keats or Tennyson or Carlyle, all poor men, from a walking tour, a little journey to France, from the separate lodging which, even if it were miserable enough, sheltered them from the claims and tyrannies of their families. Such material difficulties were formidable; but much worse were the immaterial. The indifference of the world which Keats and Flaubert and other men of genius have found so hard to bear was in her case not indifference but hostility. The world did not say to her as it said to them, Write if you choose; it makes no difference to me. The world said with a guffaw, Write? What's the good of your writing? . . .

I told you in the course of this paper that Shakespeare had a sister; but do   13
not look for her in Sir Sidney Lee's life of the poet. She died young—alas, she never wrote a word. She lies buried where the omnibuses now stop, opposite the Elephant and Castle. Now my belief is that this poet who never wrote a word and was buried at the cross-roads still lives. She lives in you and in me, and in many other women who are not here tonight, for they are washing up the dishes and putting the children to bed. But she lives; for great poets do not die; they are continuing presences; they need only the opportunity to walk among us in the flesh. This opportunity, as I think, it is now coming within your power to give her. For my belief is that if we live another century or so— I am talking of the common life which is the real life and not of the little separate lives which we live as individuals—and have five hundred a year each of us and rooms of our own; if we have the habit of freedom and the courage to write exactly what we think; if we escape a little from the common sitting-room and see human beings not always in their relation to each other but in relation to reality; and the sky, too, and the trees or whatever it may be in themselves; if we look past Milton's bogey, for no human being should shut out the view; if we face the fact, for it is a fact, that there is no arm to cling to, but that we go alone and that our relation is to the world of reality and not

---

[13] From William Wordsworth's poem "Resolution and Independence."

only to the world of men and women, then the opportunity will come and the dead poet who was Shakespeare's sister will put on the body which she has so often laid down. Drawing her life from the lives of the unknown who were her forerunners, as her brother did before her, she will be born. As for her coming without that preparation, without that effort on our part, without that determination that when she is born again she shall find it possible to live and write her poetry, that we cannot expect, for that would be impossible. But I maintain that she would come if we worked for her, and that so to work, even in poverty and obscurity, is worth while.

QUESTIONS

1. How does Woolf explain the contrast between the women of fact and the women of fiction? **2.** Analyze the effect of Woolf's concluding remarks about the bishop (paragraph 6): "Cats do not go to heaven. Women cannot write the plays of Shakespeare." In this connection, consider her later comment (paragraph 8) that "I agree with the deceased bishop, if such he was—it is unthinkable that any woman in Shakespeare's day should have had Shakespeare's genius." Does this contradict what she has been saying? **3.** Explain the link Woolf makes (paragraph 9) between chastity and the problem of the gifted woman writer.

WRITING TOPIC

Speculate on why it was the case that, while women were little more than men's servants throughout history, they were portrayed in fiction "as great as a man, some think even greater" (paragraph 3)?

The Turbid Ebb and Flow of Misery[1]

1938

MARGARET SANGER [1883–1966]

Every night and every morn
Some to misery are born.
Every morn and every night
Some are born to sweet delight.
Some are born to sweet delight,
Some are born to endless night.
William Blake

During these years [about 1912] in New York trained nurses were in great demand. Few people wanted to enter hospitals; they were afraid they might be "practiced" upon, and consented to go only in desperate emergencies. Sentiment was especially vehement in the matter of having babies. A woman's own bedroom, no matter how inconveniently arranged, was the usual place for her lying-in. I was not sufficiently free from domestic duties to be a general nurse, but I could ordinarily manage obstetrical cases because I was notified far enough ahead to plan my schedule. And after serving my two weeks I could get home again.

Sometimes I was summoned to small apartments occupied by young clerks, insurance salesmen, or lawyers, just starting out, most of them under thirty and whose wives were having their first or second baby. They were always eager to know the best and latest method in infant care and feeding. In particular, Jewish patients, whose lives centered around the family, welcomed advice and followed it implicitly.

But more and more my calls began to come from the Lower East Side, as though I were being magnetically drawn there by some force outside my control. I hated the wretchedness and hopelessness of the poor, and never experienced that satisfaction in working among them that so many noble women have found. My concern for my patients was now quite different from my earlier hospital attitude. I could see that much was wrong with them which did not appear in the physiological or medical diagnosis. A woman in childbirth was not merely a woman in childbirth. My expanded outlook included a view of her background, her potentialities as a human being, the kind of children she was bearing, and what was going to happen to them.

The wives of small shopkeepers were my most frequent cases, but I had

1

2

3

4

---

[1] The title of this chapter from Sanger's *Autobiography* is taken from Matthew Arnold's pessimistic poem "Dover Beach" (p. 446). In this essay, Sanger describes a time when using or advocating the use of contraceptives was illegal in the United States. As late as 1957 Connecticut and Massachusetts continued to enforce laws that prevented physicians from offering information about contraception—even to married women for whom pregnancy might be fatal.

carpenters, truck drivers, dishwashers, and pushcart vendors. I admired intensely the consideration most of these people had for their own. Money to pay doctor and nurse had been carefully saved months in advance—parents-in-law, grandfathers, grandmothers, all contributing.

As soon as the neighbors learned that a nurse was in the building they came 5 in a friendly way to visit, often carrying fruit, jellies, or gefüllter fish made after a cherished recipe. It was infinitely pathetic to me that they, so poor themselves, should bring me food. Later they drifted in again with the excuse of getting the plate, and sat down for a nice talk; there was no hurry. Always back of the little gift was the question, "I am pregnant (or my daughter, or my sister is). Tell me something to keep from having another baby. We cannot afford another yet."

I tried to explain the only two methods I had ever heard of among the middle 6 classes, both of which were invariably brushed aside as unacceptable. They were of no certain avail to the wife because they placed the burden of responsibility solely upon the husband—a burden which he seldom assumed. What she was seeking was self-protection she could herself use, and there was none.

Below this stratum of society was one in truly desperate circumstances. The 7 men were sullen and unskilled, picking up odd jobs now and then, but more often unemployed, lounging in and out of the house at all hours of the day and night. The women seemed to slink on their way to market and were without neighborliness.

These submerged, untouched classes were beyond the scope of organized 8 charity or religion. No labor union, no church, not even the Salvation Army reached them. They were apprehensive of everyone and rejected help of any kind, ordering all intruders to keep out; both birth and death they considered their own business. Social agents, who were just beginning to appear, were profoundly mistrusted because they pried into homes and lives, asking questions about wages, how many were in the family, had any of them ever been in jail. Often two or three had been there or were now under suspicion of prostitution, shoplifting, purse snatching, petty thievery, and, in consequence, passed furtively by the big blue uniforms on the corner.

The utmost depression came over me as I approached this surreptitious region. 9 Below Fourteenth Street I seemed to be breathing a different air, to be in another world and country where the people had habits and customs alien to anything I had ever heard about.

There were then approximately ten thousand apartments in New York into 10 which no sun ray penetrated directly; such windows as they had opened only on a narrow court from which rose fetid odors. It was seldom cleaned, though garbage and refuse often went down into it. All these dwellings were pervaded by the foul breath of poverty, that moldy, indefinable, indescribable smell which cannot be fumigated out, sickening to me but apparently unnoticed by those who lived there. When I set to work with antiseptics, their pungent sting, at least temporarily, obscured the stench.

I remember one confinement case to which I was called by the doctor of an 11 insurance company. I climbed up the five flights and entered the airless rooms, but the baby had come with too great speed. A boy of ten had been the only assistant. Five flights was a long way; he had wrapped the placenta in a piece of newspaper and dropped it out the window into the court.

Many families took in "boarders," as they were termed, whose small contributions paid the rent. These derelicts, wanderers, alternately working and drinking, were crowded in with the children; a single room sometimes held as many as six sleepers. Little girls were accustomed to dressing and undressing in front of the men, and were often violated, occasionally by their own fathers or brothers, before they reached the age of puberty. 12

Pregnancy was a chronic condition among the women of this class. Suggestions as to what to do for a girl who was "in trouble" or a married woman who was "caught" passed from mouth to mouth—herb teas, turpentine, steaming, rolling downstairs, inserting slippery elm, knitting needles, shoe-hooks. When they had word of a new remedy they hurried to the drugstore, and if the clerk were inclined to be friendly he might say, "Oh, that won't help you, but here's something that may." The younger druggists usually refused to give advice because, if it were to be known, they would come under the law; midwives were even more fearful. The doomed women implored me to reveal the "secret" rich people had, offering to pay me extra to tell them; many really believed I was holding back information for money. They asked everybody and tried anything, but nothing did them any good. On Saturday nights I have seen groups of from fifty to one hundred with their shawls over their heads waiting outside the office of a five-dollar abortionist. 13

Each time I returned to this district, which was becoming a recurrent nightmare, I used to hear that Mrs. Cohen "had been carried to a hospital, but had never come back," or that Mrs. Kelly "had sent the children to a neighbor and had put her head into the gas oven." Day after day such tales were poured into my ears—a baby born dead, great relief—the death of an older child, sorrow but again relief of a sort—the story told a thousand times of death from abortion and children going into institutions. I shuddered with horror as I listened to the details and studied the reasons back of them—destitution linked with excessive childbearing. The waste of life seemed utterly senseless. One by one worried, sad, pensive, and aging faces marshaled themselves before me in my dreams, sometimes appealingly, sometimes accusingly. 14

These were not merely "unfortunate conditions among the poor" such as we read about. I knew the women personally. They were living, breathing, human beings, with hopes, fears, and aspirations like my own, yet their weary, misshapen bodies, "always ailing, never failing," were destined to be thrown on the scrap heap before they were thirty-five. I could not escape from the facts of their wretchedness; neither was I able to see any way out. My own cozy and comfortable family existence was becoming a reproach to me. 15

Then one stifling mid-July day of 1912 I was summoned to a Grand Street tenement. My patient was a small, slight Russian Jewess, about twenty-eight years old, of the special cast of feature to which suffering lends a madonna-like expression. The cramped three-room apartment was in a sorry state of turmoil. 16

Jake Sachs, a truck driver scarcely older than his wife, had come home to find the three children crying and her unconscious from the effects of a self-induced abortion. He had called the nearest doctor, who in turn had sent for me. Jake's earnings were trifling, and most of them had gone to keep the none-too-strong children clean and properly fed. But his wife's ingenuity had helped them to save a little, and this he was glad to spend on a nurse rather than have her go to a hospital.

The doctor and I settled ourselves to the task of fighting the septicemia. Never   17
had I worked so fast, never so concentratedly. The sultry days and nights were melted into a torpid inferno. It did not seem possible there could be such heat, and every bit of food, ice, and drugs had to be carried up three flights of stairs.

Jake was more kind and thoughtful than many of the husbands I had encoun-   18
tered. He loved his children, and had always helped his wife wash and dress them. He had brought water up and carried garbage down before he left in the morning, and did as much as he could for me while he anxiously watched her progress.

After a fortnight Mrs. Sachs' recovery was in sight. Neighbors, ordinarily   19
fatalistic as to the results of abortion, were genuinely pleased that she had survived. She smiled wanly at all who came to see her and thanked them gently, but she could not respond to their hearty congratulations. She appeared to be more despondent and anxious than she should have been, and spent too much time in meditation.

At the end of three weeks, as I was preparing to leave the fragile patient to take   20
up her difficult life once more, she finally voiced her fears, "Another baby will finish me, I suppose?"

"It's too early to talk about that," I temporized.   21

But when the doctor came to make his last call, I drew him aside. "Mrs. Sachs   22
is terribly worried about having another baby."

"She well may be," replied the doctor, and then he stood before her and said,   23
"Any more such capers, young woman, and there'll be no need to send for me."

"I know, doctor," she replied timidly, "but," and she hesitated as though it   24
took all her courage to say it, "what can I do to prevent it?"

The doctor was a kindly man, and he had worked hard to save her, but such   25
incidents had become so familiar to him that he had long since lost whatever delicacy he might once have had. He laughed good-naturedly. "You want to have your cake and eat it too, do you? Well, it can't be done."

Then picking up his hat and bag to depart he said, "Tell Jake to sleep on the   26
roof."

I glanced quickly at Mrs. Sachs. Even through my sudden tears I could see   27
stamped on her face an expression of absolute despair. We simply looked at each other, saying no word until the door had closed behind the doctor. Then she lifted her thin, blue-veined hands and clasped them beseechingly. "He can't understand. He's only a man. But you do, don't you? Please tell me the secret, and I'll never breathe it to a soul. *Please!*"

What was I to do? I could not speak the conventionally comforting phrases   28 which would be of no comfort. Instead, I made her as physically easy as I could and promised to come back in a few days to talk with her again. A little later, when she slept, I tiptoed away.

Night after night the wistful image of Mrs. Sachs appeared before me. I made   29 all sorts of excuses to myself for not going back. I was busy on other cases; I really did not know what to say to her or how to convince her of my own ignorance; I was helpless to avert such monstrous atrocities. Time rolled by and I did nothing.

The telephone rang one evening three months later, and Jake Sachs' agitated   30 voice begged me to come at once; his wife was sick again and from the same cause. For a wild moment I thought of sending someone else, but actually, of course, I hurried into my uniform, caught up my bag, and started out. All the way I longed for a subway wreck, an explosion, anything to keep me from having to enter that home again. But nothing happened, even to delay me. I turned into the dingy doorway and climbed the familiar stairs once more. The children were there, young little things.

Mrs. Sachs was in a coma and died within ten minutes. I folded her still hands   31 across her breast, remembering how they had pleaded with me, begging so humbly for the knowledge which was her right. I drew a sheet over her pallid face. Jake was sobbing, running his hands through his hair and pulling it out like an insane person. Over and over again he wailed, "My God! My God! My God!"

I left him pacing desperately back and forth, and for hours I myself walked and   32 walked and walked through the hushed streets. When I finally arrived home and let myself quietly in, all the household was sleeping. I looked out my window and down upon the dimly lighted city. Its pains and griefs crowded in upon me, a moving picture rolled before my eyes with photographic clearness: women writhing in travail to bring forth little babies; the babies themselves naked and hungry, wrapped in newspapers to keep them from the cold; six-year-old children with pinched, pale, wrinkled faces, old in concentrated wretchedness, pushed into gray and fetid cellars, crouching on stone floors, their small scrawny hands scuttling through rags, making lamp shades, artificial flowers; white coffins, black coffins, coffins, coffins interminably passing in never-ending succession. The scenes piled one upon another on another. I could bear it no longer.

As I stood there the darkness faded. The sun came up and threw its reflection   33 over the house tops. It was the dawn of a new day in my life also. The doubt and questioning, the experimenting and trying, were now to be put behind me. I knew I could not go back merely to keeping people alive.

I went to bed, knowing that no matter what it might cost, I was finished with   34 palliatives and superficial cures; I was resolved to seek out the root of evil, to do something to change the destiny of mothers whose miseries were vast as the sky.

QUESTIONS

1. What arguments and assumptions would justify a law prohibiting discussion of contraception and the use of contraceptives? What arguments and assumptions would justify contraception? **2.** What assumptions would justify the prohibition of abortion? What assumptions would justify abortion? **3.** Characterize the source of Sanger's determination to change the conditions that contributed to Mrs. Sachs's death. Was her decision emotional? Intellectual? Explain.

WRITING TOPIC

Write an argumentative essay addressed to a board of education in which you either support or oppose high school classes in sex education that discuss contraception and abortion. At the outset, state the principle you support; then marshal the arguments that support it.

Letter from Birmingham Jail[1]   1963

MARTIN LUTHER KING, JR.   [1929–1968]

MY DEAR FELLOW CLERGYMEN:

While confined here in the Birmingham city jail, I came across your recent   1
statement calling my present activities "unwise and untimely." Seldom do I
pause to answer criticism of my work and ideas. If I sought to answer all the
criticisms that cross my desk, my secretaries would have little time for anything
other than such correspondence in the course of the day, and I would have no
time for constructive work. But since I feel that you are men of genuine good
will and that your criticisms are sincerely set forth, I want to try to answer your
statement in what I hope will be patient and reasonable terms.

I think I should indicate why I am here in Birmingham, since you have   2
been influenced by the view which argues against "outsiders coming in." I have
the honor of serving as president of the Southern Christian Leadership Conference, an organization operating in every southern state, with headquarters in
Atlanta, Georgia. We have some eighty-five affiliated organizations across the
South, and one of them is the Alabama Christian Movement for Human Rights.
Frequently we share staff, educational, and financial resources with our affili-
ates. Several months ago the affiliate here in Birmingham asked us to be on
call to engage in a nonviolent direct-action program if such were deemed necessary. We readily consented, and when the hour came we lived up to our
promise. So I, along with several members of my staff, am here because I was
invited here. I am here because I have organizational ties here.

But more basically, I am in Birmingham because injustice is here. Just as   3
the prophets of the eighth century B.C. left their villages and carried their "thus
saith the Lord" far beyond the boundaries of their home towns, and just as the
Apostle Paul left his village of Tarsus[2] and carried the gospel of Jesus Christ to
the far corners of the Greco-Roman world, so am I compelled to carry the
gospel of freedom beyond my own home town. Like Paul, I must constantly
respond to the Macedonian call for aid.[3]

Moreover, I am cognizant of the interrelatedness of all communities and   4
states. I cannot sit idly by in Atlanta and not be concerned about what happens

---

[1] This response to a published statement by eight fellow clergymen from Alabama (Bishop
C. C. J. Carpenter, Bishop Joseph A. Durick, Rabbi Hilton L. Grafman, Bishop Paul Hardin,
Bishop Holan B. Harmon, the Reverend George M. Murray, the Reverend Edward V. Ramage and
the Reverend Earl Stallings) was composed under somewhat constricting circumstances. Begun on
the margins of the newspaper in which the statement appeared while I was in jail, the letter was
continued on scraps of writing paper supplied by a friendly Negro trusty, and concluded on a pad my
attorneys were eventually permitted to leave me. Although the text remains in substance unaltered,
I have indulged in the author's prerogative of polishing it for publication [King's note].
[2] Birthplace of St. Paul, in present-day Turkey.
[3] St. Paul was frequently called upon to aid the Christian community in Macedonia.

in Birmingham. Injustice anywhere is a threat to justice everywhere. We are caught in an inescapable network of mutuality, tied in a single garment of destiny. Whatever affects one directly, affects all indirectly. Never again can we afford to live with the narrow, provincial "outside agitator" idea. Anyone who lives inside the United States can never be considered an outsider anywhere within its bounds.

You deplore the demonstrations taking place in Birmingham. But your state-   5
ment, I am sorry to say, fails to express a similar concern for the conditions that brought about the demonstrations. I am sure that none of you would want to rest content with the superficial kind of social analysis that deals merely with effects and does not grapple with underlying causes. It is unfortunate that demonstrations are taking place in Birmingham, but it is even more unfortunate that the city's white power structure left the Negro community with no alternative.

In any nonviolent campaign there are four basic steps: collection of the facts   6
to determine whether injustices exist; negotiation; self-purification; and direct action. We have gone through all these steps in Birmingham. There can be no gainsaying the fact that racial injustice engulfs this community. Birmingham is probably the most thoroughly segregated city in the United States. Its ugly record of brutality is widely known. Negroes have experienced grossly unjust treatment in the courts. There have been more unsolved bombings of Negro homes and churches in Birmingham than in any other city in the nation. These are the hard, brutal facts of the case. On the basis of these conditions, Negro leaders sought to negotiate with the city fathers. But the latter consistently refused to engage in good-faith negotiation.

Then, last September, came the opportunity to talk with leaders of Birming-   7
ham's economic community. In the course of the negotiations, certain promises were made by the merchants—for example, to remove the stores' humiliating racial signs. On the basis of these promises, the Reverend Fred Shuttlesworth and the leaders of the Alabama Christian Movement for Human Rights agreed to a moratorium on all demonstrations. As the weeks and months went by, we realized that we were the victims of a broken promise. A few signs, briefly removed, returned; the others remained.

As in so many past experiences, our hopes had been blasted, and the shadow   8
of deep disappointment settled upon us. We had no alternative except to prepare for direct action, whereby we would present our very bodies as a means of laying our case before the conscience of the local and the national community. Mindful of the difficulties involved, we decided to undertake a process of self-purification. We began a series of workshops on nonviolence, and we repeatedly asked ourselves: "Are you able to accept blows without retaliating?" "Are you able to endure the ordeal of jail?" We decided to schedule our direct-action program for the Easter season, realizing that except for Christmas, this is the main shopping period of the year. Knowing that a strong economic-withdrawal program would be the by-product of direct action, we felt that this would be the best time to bring pressure to bear on the merchants for the needed change.

Then it occurred to us that Birmingham's mayoral election was coming up   9
in March, and we speedily decided to postpone action until after election-day.
When we discovered that the Commissioner of Public Safety, Eugene "Bull"
Connor, had piled up enough votes to be in the run-off, we decided again to
postpone action until the day after the run-off so that the demonstrations could
not be used to cloud the issues. Like many others, we waited to see Mr. Connor defeated, and to this end we endured postponement after postponement.
Having aided in this community need, we felt that our direct-action program
could be delayed no longer.

You may well ask, "Why direct action? Why sit-ins, marches, and so forth?   10
Isn't negotiation a better path?" You are quite right in calling for negotiation.
Indeed, this is the very purpose of direct action. Nonviolent direct action seeks
to create such a crisis and foster such a tension that a community which has
constantly refused to negotiate is forced to confront the issue. It seeks so to
dramatize the issue that it can no longer be ignored. My citing the creation of
tension as part of the work of the nonviolent-resister may sound rather shocking. But I must confess that I am not afraid of the word "tension." I have
earnestly opposed violent tension, but there is a type of constructive, nonviolent tension which is necessary for growth. Just as Socrates[4] felt that it was
necessary to create a tension in the mind so that individuals could rise from
the bondage of myths and half-truths to the unfettered realm of creative analysis and objective appraisal, so must we see the need for nonviolent gadflies to
create the kind of tension in society that will help men rise from the dark
depths of prejudice and racism to the majestic heights of understanding and
brotherhood.

The purpose of our direct-action program is to create a situation so crisis-   11
packed that it will inevitably open the door to negotiation. I therefore concur
with you in your call for negotiation. Too long has our beloved Southland
been bogged down in a tragic effort to live in monologue rather than dialogue.

One of the basic points in your statement is that the action that I and my   12
associates have taken in Birmingham is untimely. Some have asked: "Why
didn't you give the new city administration time to act?" The only answer that
I can give to this query is that the new Birmingham administration must be
prodded about as much as the outgoing one, before it will act. We are sadly
mistaken if we feel that the election of Albert Boutwell as mayor will bring the
millennium to Birmingham. While Mr. Boutwell is a much more gentle person than Mr. Connor, they are both segregationists, dedicated to maintenance
of the status quo. I have hoped that Mr. Boutwell will be reasonable enough
to see the futility of massive resistance to desegregation. But he will not see this
without pressure from devotees of civil rights. My friends, I must say to you
that we have not made a single gain in civil rights without determined legal
and nonviolent pressure. Lamentably, it is an historical fact that privileged
groups seldom give up their privileges voluntarily. Individuals may see the moral

---

[4]Socrates (469–399 B.C.), a Greek philosopher who often pretended ignorance in arguments in
order to expose the errors in his opponent's reasoning.

light and voluntarily give up their unjust posture; but, as Reinhold Niebuhr[5] has reminded us, groups tend to be more immoral than individuals.

We know through painful experience that freedom is never voluntarily given 13 by the oppressor; it must be demanded by the oppressed. Frankly, I have yet to engage in a direct-action campaign that was "well timed" in the view of those who have not suffered unduly from the disease of segregation. For years now I have heard the word "Wait!" It rings in the ear of every Negro with piercing familiarity. This "Wait" has almost always meant "Never." We must come to see, with one of our distinguished jurists, that "justice too long delayed is justice denied."

We have waited for more than 340 years for our constitutional and God- 14 given rights. The nations of Asia and Africa are moving with jetlike speed toward gaining political independence, but we still creep at horse-and-buggy pace toward gaining a cup of coffee at a lunch counter. Perhaps it is easy for those who have never felt the stinging darts of segregation to say, "Wait." But when you have seen vicious mobs lynch your mothers and fathers at will and drown your sisters and brothers at whim; when you have seen hate-filled policemen curse, kick, and even kill your black brothers and sisters; when you see the vast majority of your twenty million Negro brothers smothering in an airtight cage of poverty in the midst of an affluent society; when you suddenly find your tongue twisted and your speech stammering as you seek to explain to your six-year-old daughter why she can't go to the public amusement park that has just been advertised on television, and see tears welling up in her eyes when she is told that Funtown is closed to colored children, and see ominous clouds of inferiority beginning to form in her little mental sky, and see her beginning to distort her personality by developing an unconscious bitterness toward white people; when you have to concoct an answer for a five-year-old son who is asking, "Daddy, why do white people treat colored people so mean?"; when you take a cross-country drive and find it necessary to sleep night after night in the uncomfortable corners of your automobile because no motel will accept you; when you are humiliated day in and day out by nagging signs reading "white" and "colored"; when your first name becomes "nigger," your middle name becomes "boy" (however old you are) and your last name becomes "John," and your wife and mother are never given the respected title "Mrs."; when you are harried by day and haunted by night by the fact that you are a Negro, living constantly at tiptoe stance, never quite knowing what to expect next, and are plagued with inner fears and outer resentments; when you are forever fighting a degenerating sense of "nobodiness"—then you will understand why we find it difficult to wait. There comes a time when the cup of endurance runs over, and men are no longer willing to be plunged into the abyss of despair. I hope, sirs, you can understand our legitimate and unavoidable impatience.

You express a great deal of anxiety over our willingness to break laws. This 15

---

[5] Reinhold Niebuhr (1892–1971), American philosopher and theologian.

is certainly a legitimate concern. Since we so diligently urge people to obey the Supreme Court's decision of 1954 outlawing segregation in the public schools, at first glance it may seem rather paradoxical for us consciously to break laws. One may well ask: "How can you advocate breaking some laws and obeying others?" The answer lies in the fact that there are two types of laws: just and unjust. I would be the first to advocate obeying just laws. One has not only a legal but a moral responsibility to obey just laws. Conversely, one has a moral responsibility to disobey unjust laws. I would agree with St. Augustine that "an unjust law is no law at all."

Now, what is the difference between the two? How does one determine whether   16
a law is just or unjust? A just law is a man-made code that squares with the moral law or the law of God. An unjust law is a code that is out of harmony with the moral law. To put it in the terms of St. Thomas Aquinas: An unjust law is a human law that is not rooted in eternal law and natural law. Any law that uplifts human personality is just. Any law that degrades human personality is unjust. All segregation statutes are unjust because segregation distorts the soul and damages the personality. It gives the segregator a false sense of supe- riority and the segregated a false sense of inferiority. Segregation, to use the terminology of the Jewish philosopher Martin Buber, substitutes an "I–it" re- lationship for an "I–thou" relationship and ends up relegating persons to the status of things. Hence segregation is not only politicially, economically, and sociologically unsound, it is morally wrong and sinful. Paul Tillich has said that sin is separation. Is not segregation an existential expression of man's tragic separation, his awful estrangement, his terrible sinfulness? Thus it is that I can urge men to obey the 1954 decision of the Supreme Court, for it is morally right; and I can urge them to disobey segregation ordinances, for they are mor- ally wrong.

Let us consider a more concrete example of just and unjust laws. An unjust   17
law is a code that a numerical or power majority group compels a minority group to obey but does not make binding on itself. This is *difference* made legal. By the same token, a just law is a code that a majority compels a minor- ity to follow and that it is willing to follow itself. This is *sameness* made legal.

Let me give another explanation. A law is unjust if it is inflicted on a mi-   18
nority that, as a result of being denied the right to vote, had no part in enacting or devising the law. Who can say that the legislature of Alabama which set up that state's segregation laws was democratically elected? Throughout Alabama all sorts of devious methods are used to prevent Negroes from becoming regis- tered voters, and there are some counties in which, even though Negroes con- stitute a majority of the population, not a single Negro is registered. Can any law enacted under such circumstances be considered democratically structured?

Sometimes a law is just on its face and unjust in its application. For in-   19
stance, I have been arrested on a charge of parading without a permit. Now, there is nothing wrong in having an ordinance which requires a permit for a parade. But such an ordinance becomes unjust when it is used to maintain segregation and to deny citizens the First-Amendment privilege of peaceful assembly and protest.

I hope you are able to see the distinction I am trying to point out. In no 20 sense do I advocate evading or defying the law, as would the rabid segregationist. That would lead to anarchy. One who breaks an unjust law must do so openly, lovingly, and with a willingness to accept the penalty. I submit that an individual who breaks a law that conscience tells him is unjust, and who willingly accepts the penalty of imprisonment in order to arouse the conscience of the community over its injustice, is in reality expressing the highest respect for law.

Of course, there is nothing new about this kind of civil disobedience. It was 21 evidenced sublimely in the refusal of Shadrach, Meshach, and Abednego to obey the laws of Nebuchadnezzar, on the ground that a higher moral law was at stake.[6] It was practiced superbly by the early Christians, who were willing to face hungry lions and the excruciating pain of chopping blocks rather than submit to certain unjust laws of the Roman Empire. To a degree, academic freedom is a reality today because Socrates practiced civil disobedience. In our own nation, the Boston Tea Party represented a massive act of civil disobedience.

We should never forget that everything Adolf Hitler did in Germany was 22 "legal" and everything the Hungarian freedom fighters did in Hungary was "illegal." It was "illegal" to aid and comfort a Jew in Hitler's Germany. Even so, I am sure that, had I lived in Germany at the time, I would have aided and comforted my Jewish brothers. If today I lived in a Communist country where certain principles dear to the Christian faith are suppressed, I would openly advocate disobeying that country's anti-religious laws.

I must make two honest confessions to you, my Christian and Jewish broth- 23 ers. First, I must confess that over the past few years I have been gravely disappointed with the white moderate. I have almost reached the regrettable conclusion that the Negro's great stumbling block in his stride toward freedom is not the white Citizen's Counciler[7] or the Ku Klux Klanner, but the white moderate, who is more devoted to "order" than to justice; who prefers a negative peace which is the absence of tension to a positive peace which is the presence of justice; who constantly says, "I agree with you in the goal you seek, but I cannot agree with your methods of direct action"; who paternalistically believes he can set the timetable for another man's freedom; who lives by a mythical concept of time and who constantly advises the Negro to wait for a "more convenient season." Shallow understanding from people of good will is more frustrating than absolute misunderstanding from people of ill will. Lukewarm acceptance is much more bewildering than outright rejection.

I had hoped that the white moderate would understand that law and order 24 exist for the purpose of establishing justice and that when they fail in this purpose they become the dangerously structured dams that block the flow of social progress. I had hoped that the white moderate would understand that the

---

[6] See Daniel 1:7–3:30.

[7] White Citizen's Councils sprang up in the South after 1954 (the year the Supreme Court declared segregated education unconstitutional) to fight against desegregation.

present tension in the South is a necessary phase of the transition from an obnoxious negative peace, in which the Negro passively accepted his unjust plight, to a substantive and positive peace, in which all men will respect the dignity and worth of human personality. Actually, we who engage in nonviolent direct action are not the creators of tension. We merely bring to the surface the hidden tension that is already alive. We bring it out in the open, where it can be seen and dealt with. Like a boil that can never be cured so long as it is covered up but must be opened with all its ugliness to the natural medicines of air and light, injustice must be exposed, with all the tension its exposure creates, to the light of human conscience and the air of national opinion, before it can be cured.

In your statement you assert that our actions, even though peaceful, must   25 be condemned because they precipitate violence. But is this a logical assertion? Isn't this like condemning a robbed man because his possession of money precipitated the evil act of robbery? Isn't this like condemning Socrates because his unswerving commitment to truth and his philosophical inquiries precipitated the act by the misguided populace in which they made him drink hemlock? Isn't this like condemning Jesus because his unique God-consciousness and never-ceasing devotion to God's will precipitated the evil act of crucifixion? We must come to see that, as the federal courts have consistently affirmed, it is wrong to urge an individual to cease his efforts to gain his basic constitutional rights because the quest may precipitate violence. Society must protect the robbed and punish the robber.

I had also hoped that the white moderate would reject the myth concerning   26 time in relation to the struggle for freedom. I have just received a letter from a white brother in Texas. He writes: "All Christians know that the colored people will receive equal rights eventually, but it is possible that you are in too great a religious hurry. It has taken Christianity almost two thousand years to accomplish what it has. The teachings of Christ take time to come to earth." Such an attitude stems from a tragic misconception of time, from the strangely irrational notion that there is something in the very flow of time that will inevitably cure all ills. Actually, time itself is neutral; it can be used either destructively or constructively. More and more I feel that the people of ill will have used time much more effectively than have the people of good will. We will have to repent in this generation not merely for the hateful words and actions of the bad people, but for the appalling silence of the good people. Human progress never rolls in on wheels of inevitability; it comes through the tireless efforts of men willing to be co-workers with God, and without this hard work, time itself becomes an ally of the forces of social stagnation. We must use time creatively, in the knowledge that the time is always ripe to do right. Now is the time to make real the promise of democracy and transform our pending national elegy into a creative psalm of brotherhood. Now is the time to lift our national policy from the quicksand of racial injustice to the solid rock of human dignity.

You speak of our activity in Birmingham as extreme. At first I was rather   27 disappointed that fellow clergymen would see my nonviolent efforts as those of an extremist. I began thinking about the fact that I stand in the middle of two opposing forces in the Negro community. One is a force of complacency, made up in part of Negroes who, as a result of long years of oppression, are so drained of self-respect and a sense of "somebodiness" that they have adjusted to segregation; and in part of a few middle-class Negroes who, because of a degree of academic and economic security and because in some ways they profit by segregation, have become insensitive to the problems of the masses. The other force is one of bitterness and hatred, and it comes perilously close to advocating violence. It is expressed in the various black nationalist groups that are springing up across the nation, the largest and best-known being Elijah Muhammad's Muslim movement.[8] Nourished by the Negro's frustration over the continued existence of racial discrimination, this movement is made up of people who have lost faith in America, who have absolutely repudiated Christianity, and who have concluded that the white man is an incorrigible "devil."

I have tried to stand between these two forces, saying that we need emulate   28
neither the "do-nothingism" of the complacent nor the hatred and despair of the black nationalist. For there is the more excellent way of love and nonviolent protest. I am grateful to God that, through the influence of the Negro church, the way of nonviolence became an integral part of our struggle.

If this philosophy had not emerged, by now many streets of the South would,   29
I am convinced, be flowing with blood. And I am further convinced that if our white brothers dismiss as "rabble-rousers" and "outside agitators" those of us who employ nonviolent direct action, and if they refuse to support our nonviolent efforts, millions of Negroes will, out of frustration and despair, seek solace and security in black-nationalist ideologies—a development that would inevitably lead to a frightening racial nightmare.

Oppressed people cannot remain oppressed forever. The yearning for free-   30
dom eventually manifests itself, and that is what has happened to the American Negro. Something within has reminded him of his birthright of freedom, and something without has reminded him that it can be gained. Consciously or unconsciously, he has been caught up by the *Zeitgeist*,[9] and with his black brothers of Africa and his brown and yellow brothers of Asia, South America, and the Caribbean, the United States Negro is moving with a sense of great urgency toward the promised land of racial justice. If one recognizes this vital urge that has engulfed the Negro community, one should readily understand why public demonstrations are taking place. The Negro has many pent-up resentments and latent frustrations, and he must release them. So let him march; let him make prayer pilgrimages to the city hall; let him go on freedom rides[10]— and try to understand why he must do so. If his repressed emotions are not released in nonviolent ways, they will seek expression through violence; this is

---

[8]Elijah Muhammad (1897–1975), leader of a black Muslim religious group that rejected integration and called upon blacks to fight to establish their own nation.

[9]The spirit of the time.

[10]In 1961, hundreds of blacks and whites, under the direction of the Congress of Racial Equality (CORE), deliberately violated laws in Southern states that required segregation in buses and bus terminals.

not a threat but a fact of history. So I have not said to my people, "Get rid of your discontent." Rather, I have tried to say that this normal and healthy discontent can be channeled into the creative outlet of nonviolent direct action. And now this approach is being termed extremist.

But though I was initially disappointed at being categorized as an extremist,   31
as I continued to think about the matter I gradually gained a measure of satisfaction from the label. Was not Jesus an extremist for love: "Love your enemies, bless them that curse you, do good to them that hate you, and pray for them which despitefully use you, and persecute you." Was not Amos an extremist for justice: "Let justice roll down like waters and righteousness like an ever-flowing stream." Was not Paul an extremist for the Christian gospel: "I bear in my body the marks of the Lord Jesus." Was not Martin Luther an extremist: "Here I stand; I cannot do otherwise, so help me God." And John Bunyan: "I will stay in jail to the end of my days before I make a butchery of my conscience." And Abraham Lincoln: "This nation cannot survive half slave and half free." And Thomas Jefferson: "We hold these truths to be self-evident, that all men are created equal. . . ." So the question is not whether we will be extremists, but what kind of extremists we will be. Will we be extremists for hate or for love? Will we be extremists for the preservation of injustice or for the extension of justice? In that dramatic scene on Calvary's hill three men were crucified. We must never forget that all three were crucified for the same crime—the crime of extremism. Two were extremists for immorality, and thus fell below their environment. The other, Jesus Christ, was an extremist for love, truth, and goodness, and thereby rose above his environment. Perhaps the South, the nation, and the world are in dire need of creative extemists.

I had hoped that the white moderate would see this need. Perhaps I was too   32
optimistic; perhaps I expected too much. I suppose I should have realized that few members of the oppressor race can understand the deep groans and passionate yearnings of the oppressed race, and still fewer have the vision to see that injustice must be rooted out by strong, persistent, and determined action. I am thankful, however, that some of our white brothers in the South have grasped the meaning of this social revolution and committed themselves to it. They are still all too few in quantity, but they are big in quality. Some—such as Ralph McGill, Lillian Smith, Harry Golden, James McBride Dabbs, Ann Braden, and Sarah Patton Boyle—have written about our struggle in eloquent and prophetic terms. Others have marched with us down nameless streets of the South. They have languished in filthy, roach-infested jails, suffering the abuse and brutality of policemen who view them as "dirty nigger-lovers." Unlike so many of their moderate brothers and sisters, they have recognized the urgency of the moment and sensed the need for powerful "action" antidotes to combat the disease of segregation.

Let me take note of my other major disappointment. I have been so greatly   33
disappointed with the white church and its leadership. Of course, there are some notable exceptions. I am not unmindful of the fact that each of you has taken some significant stands on this issue. I commend you, Reverend Stallings, for your Christian stand on this past Sunday, in welcoming Negroes to

your worship service on a nonsegregated basis. I commend the Catholic leaders of this state for integrating Spring Hill College several years ago.

But despite these notable exceptions, I must honestly reiterate that I have been disappointed with the church. I do not say this as one of those negative critics who can always find something wrong with the church. I say this as a minister of the gospel, who loves the church; who was nurtured in its bosom; who has been sustained by its spiritual blessings and who will remain true to it as long as the cord of life shall lengthen. 34

When I was suddenly catapulted into the leadership of the bus protest in Montgomery, Alabama, a few years ago, I felt we would be supported by the white church. I felt that the white ministers, priests, and rabbis of the South would be among our strongest allies. Instead, some have been outright opponents, refusing to understand the freedom movement and misrepresenting its leaders; all too many others have been more cautious than courageous and have remained silent behind the anesthetizing security of stained-glass windows. 35

In spite of my shattered dreams, I came to Birmingham with the hope that the white religious leadership of this community would see the justice of our cause and, with deep moral concern, would serve as the channel through which our just grievances could reach the power structure. I had hoped that each of you would understand. But again I have been disappointed. 36

I have heard numerous southern religious leaders admonish their worshipers to comply with a desegregation decision because it is the law, but I have longed to hear white ministers declare: "Follow this decree because integration is morally right and because the Negro is your brother." In the midst of blatant injustices inflicted upon the Negro, I have watched white churchmen stand on the sideline and mouth pious irrelevancies and sanctimonious trivialities. In the midst of a mighty struggle to rid our nation of racial and economic injustice, I have heard many ministers say: "Those are social issues, with which the gospel has no real concern." And I have watched many churches commit themselves to a completely otherworldly religion which makes a strange, un-Biblical distinction between body and soul, between the sacred and the secular. 37

I have traveled the length and breadth of Alabama, Mississippi, and all the other southern states. On sweltering summer days and crisp autumn mornings I have looked at the South's beautiful churches with their lofty spires pointing heavenward. I have beheld the impressive outlines of her massive religious-education buildings. Over and over I have found myself asking: "What kind of people worship here? Who is their God? Where were their voices when the lips of Governor Barnett dripped with words of interposition and nullification? Where were they when Governor Wallace gave a clarion call for defiance and hatred? Where were their voices of support when bruised and weary Negro men and women decided to rise from the dark dungeons of complacency to the bright hills of creative protest?" 38

Yes, these questions are still in mind. In deep disappointment I have wept over the laxity of the church. But be assured that my tears have been tears of 39 love. There can be no deep disappointment where there is not deep love. Yes, I love the church. How could I do otherwise? I am in the rather unique position of being the son, the grandson, and the great-grandson of preachers. Yes, I see the church as the body of Christ. But, oh! How we have blemished and scarred that body through social neglect and through fear of being nonconformists.

There was a time when the church was very powerful—in the time when the early Christians rejoiced at being deemed worthy to suffer for what they believed. In those days the church was not merely a thermometer that recorded the ideas and principles of popular opinion; it was a thermostat that transformed the mores of society. Whenever the early Christians entered a town, the people in power became disturbed and immediately sought to convict the Christians for being "disturbers of the peace" and "outside agitators." But the Christians pressed on, in the conviction that they were "a colony of heaven," called to obey God rather than man. Small in number, they were big in commitment. They were too God-intoxicated to be "astronomically intimidated." By their effort and example they brought an end to such ancient evils as infanticide and gladiatorial contests.

Things are different now. So often the contemporary church is a weak, ineffectual voice with an uncertain sound. So often it is an archdefender of the status quo. Far from being disturbed by the presence of the church, the power structure of the average community is consoled by the church's silent—and often even vocal—sanction of things as they are.

But the judgment of God is upon the church as never before. If today's church does not recapture the sacrificial spirit of the early church, it will lose its authenticity, forfeit the loyalty of millions, and be dismissed as an irrelevant social club with no meaning for the twentieth century. Every day I meet young people whose disappointment with the church has turned into outright disgust.

Perhaps I have once again been too optimistic. Is organized religion too inextricably bound to the status quo to save our nation and the world? Perhaps I must turn my faith to the inner spiritual church, the church within the church, as the true *ekklesia*[11] and the hope of the world. But again I am thankful to God that some noble souls from the ranks of organized religion have broken loose from the paralyzing chains of conformity and joined us as active partners in the struggle for freedom. They have left their secure congregations and walked the streets of Albany, Georgia, with us. They have gone down the highways of the South on tortuous rides for freedom. Yes, they have gone to jail with us. Some have been dismissed from their churches, have lost the support of their bishops and fellow ministers. But they have acted in the faith that right defeated is stronger than evil triumphant. Their witness has been the spiritual salt that has preserved the true meaning of the gospel in these troubled times. They have carved a tunnel of hope through the dark mountain of disappointment.

40

41

42

43

---

[11] The Greek *New Testament* word for the early Christian church.

I hope the church as a whole will meet the challenge of this decisive hour.   44
But even if the church does not come to the aid of justice, I have no despair
about the future. I have no fear about the outcome of our struggle in Birmingham, even if our motives are at present misunderstood. We will reach the goal
of freedom in Birmingham and all over the nation, because the goal of America is freedom. Abused and scorned though we may be, our destiny is tied up
with America's destiny. Before the pilgrims landed at Plymouth, we were here.
Before the pen of Jefferson etched the majestic words of the Declaration of
Independence across the pages of history, we were here. For more than two
centuries our forebears labored in this country without wages; they made cotton
king; they built the homes of their masters while suffering gross injustice and
shameful humiliation—and yet out of a bottomless vitality they continued to
thrive and develop. If the inexpressible cruelties of slavery could not stop us,
the opposition we now face will surely fail. We will win our freedom because
the sacred heritage of our nation and the eternal will of God are embodied in
our echoing demands.

Before closing I feel impelled to mention one other point in your statement   45
that has troubled me profoundly. You warmly commended the Birmingham
police force for keeping "order" and "preventing violence." I doubt that you
would have so warmly commended the police force if you had seen its dogs
sinking their teeth into unarmed, nonviolent Negroes. I doubt that you would
so quickly commend the policemen if you were to observe their ugly and inhumane treatment of Negroes here in the city jail; if you were to watch them
push and curse old Negro women and young Negro girls; if you were to see
them slap and kick old Negro men and young boys; if you were to observe
them, as they did on two occasions, refuse to give us food because we wanted
to sing our grace together. I cannot join you in your praise of the Birmingham
police department.

It is true that the police have exercised a degree of discipline in handling the   46
demonstrators. In this sense they have conducted themselves rather "nonviolently" in public. But for what purpose? To preserve the evil system of segregation. Over the past few years I have consistently preached that nonviolence
demands that the means we use must be as pure as the ends we seek. I have
tried to make clear that it is wrong to use immoral means to attain moral ends.
But now I must affirm that it is just as wrong, or perhaps even more so, to use
moral means to preserve immoral ends. Perhaps Mr. Connor and his policemen have been rather nonviolent in public, as was Chief Pritchett in Albany,
Georgia, but they have used the moral means of nonviolence to maintain the
immoral end of racial injustice. As T. S. Eliot[12] has said, "The last temptation
is the greatest treason: To do the right deed for the wrong reason."

I wish you had commended the Negro sit-inners and demonstrators of Bir-   47
mingham for their sublime courage, their willingness to suffer, and their amazing discipline in the midst of great provocation. One day the South will rec-

---

[12]Thomas Stearns Eliot (1888–1965), American-born poet.

ognize its real heroes. They will be the James Merediths,[13] with the noble sense of purpose that enables them to face jeering and hostile mobs, and with the agonizing loneliness that characterizes the life of the pioneer. They will be old, oppressed, battered Negro women, symbolized in a seventy-two-year-old woman in Montgomery, Alabama, who rose up with a sense of dignity and with her people decided not to ride segregated buses, and who responded with ungrammatical profundity to one who inquired about her weariness: "My feets is tired, but my soul is at rest." They will be the young high school and college students, the young ministers of the gospel and a host of their elders, courageously and nonviolently sitting in at lunch counters and willingly going to jail for conscience' sake. One day the South will know that when these disinherited children of God sat down at lunch counters, they were in reality standing up for what is best in the American dream and for the most sacred values in our Judaeo-Christian heritage, thereby bringing our nation back to those great wells of democracy which were dug deep by the founding fathers in their formulation of the Constitution and the Declaration of Independence.

48 Never before have I written so long a letter. I'm afraid it is much too long to take your precious time. I can assure you that it would have been much shorter if I had been writing from a comfortable desk, but what else can one do when he is alone in a narrow jail cell, other than write long letters, think long thoughts, and pray long prayers?

49 If I have said anything in this letter that overstates the truth and indicates an unreasonable impatience, I beg you to forgive me. If I have said anything that understates the truth and indicates my having a patience that allows me to settle for anything less than brotherhood, I beg God to forgive me.

50 I hope this letter finds you strong in the faith. I hope that circumstances will soon make it possible for me to meet each of you, not as an integrationist or a civil-rights leader but as a fellow clergyman and a Christian brother. Let us all hope that the dark clouds of a racial prejudice will soon pass away and the deep fog of misunderstanding will be lifted from our fear-drenched communities, and in some not too distant tomorrow the radiant stars of love and brotherhood will shine over our great nation with all their scintillating beauty.

> Yours for the cause of Peace and Brotherhood,
> MARTIN LUTHER KING, JR.

QUESTIONS

1. What is King's definition of civil disobedience? **2.** Does your own experience bear out King's distinction (paragraph 10) between "violent" and "nonviolent" tension? **3.** Summarize and explain the argument King makes in paragraph 46 about "means" and "ends." **4.** Those opposed to civil disobedience frequently argue that in a democratic society such as ours, change should be pursued through legislation and the courts because if people are allowed to disobey laws with which they disagree, we will have chaos and violence. How does King seek to allay these fears? **5.** Readers

---

[13] James Meredith was the first black to be admitted as a student at the University of Mississippi.

have often found King's tone and style strongly influenced by pulpit oratory in its eloquence, elevated diction, biblical allusions, and didacticism. Select a passage (one or two paragraphs) from the essay and show how it reflects these qualities.

WRITING TOPIC

King offers a philosophical justification for civil disobedience (paragraphs 15–22), at the heart of which is his distinction between a just and an unjust law. Defend or take issue with that distinction.

Conformity and Rebellion

QUESTIONS AND WRITING TOPICS

1. What answers do the works in this section provide to the question posed by Albert Camus in the following passage:

> The present interest of the problem of rebellion only springs from the fact that nowadays whole societies have wanted to discard the sacred. We live in an unsacrosanct moment in history. Insurrection is certainly not the sum total of human experience. But history today, with all its storm and strife, compels us to say that rebellion is one of the essential dimensions of man. It is our historic reality. Unless we choose to ignore reality, we must find our values in it. Is it possible to find a rule of conduct outside the realm of religion and its absolute values? That is the question raised by rebellion.

Writing Topic: Use this observation as the basis for an analysis of the central characters in Mann's "Gladius Dei" and Ellison's " 'Repent, Harlequin!' Said the Ticktockman."

2. What support do the works in this section offer for Emily Dickinson's assertion that "Much Madness is Divinest Sense"? **Writing Topic:** The central characters in Mann's "Gladius Dei" and Ellison's " 'Repent Harlequin!' Said the Ticktockman" are viewed by society as mad. How might it be argued that they exhibit "divinest sense"?

3. Which works in this section can be criticized on the grounds that while they attack the established order, they fail to provide any alternatives? **Writing Topic:** Discuss the validity of this objection for two of the following works: Wordsworth's "The World Is Too Much with Us," Lowell's "Patterns," Reed's "Naming of Parts," Forster's "My Wood."

4. In a number of these works, a single individual rebels against society and suffers defeat or death. Are these works therefore pessimistic and despairing? If not, then what is the purpose of the rebellions, and why do the authors choose to bring their characters to such ends? **Writing Topic:** Compare two works from this section that offer support for the idea that a single individual can have a decisive effect on the larger society.

5. Examine some of the representatives of order—Herr Blüthenzweig in "Gladius Dei," the lawyer in "Bartleby the Scrivener," Torvald Helmer in *A Doll's House,* the Ticktockman in " 'Repent, Harlequin!' Said the Ticktockman"—and discuss what attitudes they share and how effectively they function as representatives of law and order. **Writing Topic:** Compare and contrast the kinds of order that each represents.

6. Amy Lowell's "Patterns," Karl Shapiro's "The Conscientious Objector," Lawrence Ferlinghetti's "In Goya's Greatest Scenes," and Henry Reed's "Naming of Parts" are, in different ways, antiwar poems. Which of these poems do you find the most articulate and convincing antiwar statement? **Writing Topic:** Discuss the argument that, while condemning war, none of these poems examines the specific reasons that a nation may be obliged to fight—self-defense and national self-interest, for example—and that consequently they are irresponsible.

7. Most of us live out our lives in the ordinary and humdrum world that is rejected in such poems as Wordsworth's "The World Is Too Much with Us" and Auden's "The Unknown Citizen." Can it be said that these poems are counsels to social irresponsibility? **Writing Topic:** Consider whether "we" in Wordsworth's poem and the unknown citizen are simply objects of scorn or whether they deserve sympathy and perhaps even respect.

8. Many works in this section deal explicitly with the relationship between the individual and the state. What similarities of outlook do you find among them? **Writing Topic:** Compare and contrast the way that relationship is perceived in Ellison's " 'Repent, Harlequin!' Said the Ticktockman" and King's "Letter from Birmingham Jail."

Love
and
Hate

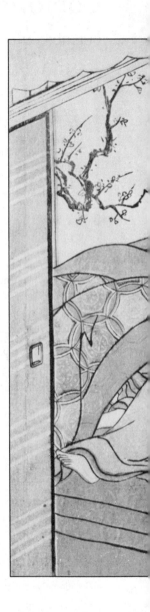

Untitled, c. 1770 by Buncho

Love and death, it is often noted, are the two great themes of literature. Many of the literary works we have placed in the sections "Innocence and Experience" and "Conformity and Rebellion" speak of love and death as well. But in those works, other thematic interests dominate. In this section, we gather a number of works in which love and hate are thematically central.

The rosy conception of love presented in many popular and sentimental stories ill prepares us for the complicated reality we face. We know that the course of true love never runs smooth, but in those popular stories the obstacles that hinder the lovers are simple and external. If the young lover can land the high-paying job or convince the beloved's parents that he or she is worthy despite social differences, all will be well. But love in life is rarely that simple. The external obstacles may be insuperable, or the obstacles may lie deep within the personality. The major obstacle may well be an individual's difficult and painful effort to understand that he or she has been deceived by an immature and sentimental conception of love.

In the age of psychoanalytic awareness, the claims of the flesh are well recognized. But psychoanalytic theory teaches us, as well, to recognize the aggressive aspect of the human condition. The omnipresent selfishness that civilization attempts to check may be aggressively violent as well as lustful. Thus, on one hand, we have the simple eroticism of Kate Chopin's "The Storm," and on the other, the macabre behavior of William Faulkner's Emily Grierson in "A Rose for Emily." And Matthew Arnold in "Dover Beach" finds love the only refuge from a chaotic world in which "ignorant armies clash by night."

The cliché has it that love and hate are closely related, and much evidence supports this proposition. But why should love and hate, seeming opposites, lie so close together in the emotional lives of men and women? We are all egos, separate from each other. And as separate individuals, we develop elaborate behavior mechanisms that defend us from each other. But the erotic love relationship differs from other relationships in that it may be defined as a rejection of separateness. The common metaphor speaks of two lovers as joining, as merging into one. That surrender of the "me" to join in an "us" leaves lovers uniquely vulnerable to psychic injury. In short, the defenses are down, and the self-esteem of each of the lovers depends importantly on the behavior of the other. If the lover is betrayed by the beloved, the emotional consequences are uniquely disastrous—hence the peculiarly close relationship of passionate hatred with erotic love.

Words like *love* and *hate* are so general that poets rarely use them except as one term in a metaphor designed to project sharply some aspect of emotional life. The simple sexuality in such poems as Andrew Marvell's "To His Coy Mistress," Christopher Marlowe's "The Passionate Shepherd to His Love," and Thomas

Campion's "I Care Not for These Ladies" may be juxtaposed with the hatred and violence generated in Othello by sexual jealousy or with the quick reprisal of the slighted Barbara Allan. And Shakespeare's description of lust "Th' expense of spirit in a waste of shame" notes an aspect of love quite overlooked by Edmund Waller in his song, "Go, Lovely Rose!"

Perhaps more than anything, the works in this section celebrate the elemental impulses of men and women that run counter to those rational formulations by which we govern our lives. We pursue Othello's love for Desdemona and Iago's hate for Othello and arrive at an irreducible mystery, for neither Othello's love nor Iago's hate yields satisfactorily to rational explanation. Reason does not tell us why Othello and Desdemona love one another or why Iago hates rather than honors Othello.

Love is an act of faith springing from our deep-seated need to join with another human being not only in physical nakedness but in emotional and spiritual nakedness as well. While hate is a denial of that faith and, therefore, a retreat into spiritual isolation, love is an attempt to break out of the isolation.

FOR THINKING AND WRITING

As you read the selections in this section, consider the following questions. You may want to write out your thoughts informally in a journal or notebook as a way of preparing to respond to the selections, or you may wish to make one of these questions the basis for a formal essay.

1. What is love? What is the source of your definition (literature, personal observation, discussions with those you trust)? Have you ever been in love? How did you know? Do you know someone who is in love? How do you know?

2. Have you ever truly hated someone or something? Describe the circumstances, and characterize your hatred.

3. Do you believe that love and hate are closely related? Have you experienced a change from love to hatred, or do you know someone who has? Explain.

4. There are different kinds of love—love of family, of humankind, of God. There are, of course, sexual love and the love of a cause. Characterize several different kinds of love, and examine your own motives and behavior in different love relationships. In what ways do certain kinds of love necessarily generate certain hatreds?

LOVE
AND
HATE

A Husband Parting from His Wife and Child, 1799 by William Blake

FICTION

Best known work
"The Awakening" Novella

The Storm

KATE CHOPIN [1851–1904]

(1898)

important female femanist .
good local color writer

I

The leaves were so still that even Bibi thought it was going to rain. Bobinôt, who was accustomed to converse on terms of perfect equality with his little son, called the child's attention to certain sombre clouds that were rolling with sinister intention from the west, accompanied by a sullen, threatening roar. They were at Friedheimer's store and decided to remain there till the storm had passed. They sat within the door on two empty kegs. Bibi was four years old and looked very wise.

"Mama'll be 'fraid, yes," he suggested with blinking eyes.

"She'll shut the house. Maybe she got Sylvie helpin' her this evenin'," Bobinôt responded reassuringly.

"No; she ent got Sylvie. Sylvie was helpin' her yistiday," piped Bibi.

Bobinôt arose and going across to the counter purchased a can of shrimps, of which Calixta was very fond. Then he returned to his perch on the keg and sat stolidly holding the can of shrimps while the storm burst. It shook the wooden store and seemed to be ripping great furrows in the distant field. Bibi laid his little hand on his father's knee and was not afraid.

II

Calixta, at home, felt no uneasiness for their safety. She sat at a side window sewing furiously on a sewing machine. She was greatly occupied and did not notice the approaching storm. But she felt very warm and often stopped to mop her face on which the perspiration gathered in beads. She unfastened her white sacque at the throat. It began to grow dark, and suddenly realizing the situation she got up hurriedly and went about closing windows and doors.

Out on the small front gallery she had hung Bobinôt's Sunday clothes to air and she hastened out to gather them before the rain fell. As she stepped outside, Alcée Laballière rode in at the gate. She had not seen him very often since her marriage, and never alone. She stood there with Bobinôt's coat in her hands, and the big rain drops began to fall. Alcée rode his horse under the shelter of a side projection where the chickens had huddled and there were plows and a harrow piled up in the corner.

"May I come and wait on your gallery till the storm is over, Calixta?" he asked.

"Come 'long in, M'sieur Alcée."

His voice and her own startled her as if from a trance, and she seized Bobinôt's vest. Alcée, mounting to the porch, grabbed the trousers and snatched Bibi's braided jacket that was about to be carried away by a sudden gust of wind. He expressed an intention to remain outside, but it was soon apparent that he might as well have been out in the open: the water beat in upon the boards in driving sheets, and he went inside, closing the door after him. It was even necessary to put something beneath the door to keep the water out.

"My! what a rain! It's good two years sence it rain' like that," exclaimed Calixta as she rolled up a piece of bagging and Alcée helped her to thrust it beneath the crack.

She was a little fuller of figure than five years before when she married; but she had lost nothing of her vivacity. Her blue eyes still retained their melting quality; and her yellow hair, dishevelled by the wind and rain, kinked more stubbornly than ever about her ears and temples.

The rain beat upon the low, shingled roof with a force and clatter that threatened to break an entrance and deluge them there. They were in the dining room—the sitting room—the general utility room. Adjoining was her bed room, with Bibi's couch along side her own. The door stood open, and the room with its white, monumental bed, its closed shutters, looked dim and mysterious.

Alcée flung himself into a rocker and Calixta nervously began to gather up from the floor the lengths of a cotton sheet which she had been sewing.

"If this keeps up, *Dieu sait*[1] if the levees goin' to stan' it!" she exclaimed.

"What have you got to do with the levees?"

"I got enough to do! An' there's Bobinôt with Bibi out in that storm—if he only didn' left Friedheimer's!"

"Let us hope, Calixta, that Bobinôt's got sense enough to come in out of a cyclone."

She went and stood at the window with a greatly disturbed look on her face. She wiped the frame that was clouded with moisture. It was stiflingly hot. Alcée got up and joined her at the window, looking over her shoulder. The rain was coming down in sheets obscuring the view of far-off cabins and enveloping the distant wood in a gray mist. The playing of the lightning was incessant. A bolt struck a tall chinaberry tree at the edge of the field. It filled all visible space with a blinding glare and the crash seemed to invade the very boards they stood upon.

Calixta put her hands to her eyes, and with a cry, staggered backward. Alcée's

---

[1] God knows.

arm encircled her, and for an instant he drew her close and spasmodically to him.

"*Bonte!*"[2] she cried, releasing herself from his encircling arm and retreating from the window, "the house'll go next! If I only knew w'ere Bibi was!" She would not compose herself; she would not be seated. Alcée clasped her shoulders and looked into her face. The contact of her warm, palpitating body when he had unthinkingly drawn her into his arms, had aroused all the old-time infatuation and desire for her flesh.

"Calixta," he said, "don't be frightened. Nothing can happen. The house is too low to be struck, with so many tall trees standing about. There! aren't you going to be quiet? say, aren't you?" He pushed her hair back from her face that was warm and steaming. Her lips were as red and moist as pomegranate seed. Her white neck and a glimpse of her full, firm bosom disturbed him powerfully. As she glanced up at him the fear in her liquid blue eyes had given place to a drowsy gleam that unconsciously betrayed a sensuous desire. He looked down into her eyes and there was nothing for him to do but to gather her lips in a kiss. It reminded him of Assumption.[3]

"Do you remember—in Assumption. Calixta?" he asked in a low voice broken by passion. Oh! she remembered; for in Assumption he had kissed her and kissed and kissed her; until his senses would well nigh fail, and to save her he would resort to a desperate flight. If she was not an immaculate dove in those days, she was still inviolate; a passionate creature whose very defenselessness had made her defense, against which his honor forbade him to prevail. Now— well, now—her lips seemed in a manner free to be tasted, as well as her round, white throat and her whiter breasts.

They did not heed the crashing torrents, and the roar of the elements made her laugh as she lay in his arms. She was a revelation in that dim, mysterious chamber; as white as the couch she lay upon. Her firm, elastic flesh that was knowing for the first time its birthright, was like a creamy lily that the sun invites to contribute its breath and perfume to the undying life of the world.

The generous abundance of her passion, without guile or trickery, was like a white flame which penetrated and found response in depths of his own sensuous nature that had never yet been reached.

When he touched her breasts they gave themselves up in quivering ecstasy, inviting his lips. Her mouth was a fountain of delight. And when he possessed her, they seemed to swoon together at the very borderland of life's mystery.

He stayed cushioned upon her, breathless, dazed, enervated, with his heart beating like a hammer upon her. With one hand she clasped his head, her lips lightly touching his forehead. The other hand stroked with a soothing rhythm his muscular shoulders.

---

[2] An exclamation: Goodness!
[3] A holiday commemorating the ascent of the Virgin Mary to heaven. Assumption is also the name of a Louisiana parish (county) where Calixta and Alcée had had a rendezvous in an earlier story.

The growl of the thunder was distant and passing away. The rain beat softly upon the shingles, inviting them to drowsiness and sleep. But they dared not yield.

The rain was over; and the sun was turning the glistening green world into a palace of gems. Calixta, on the gallery, watched Alcée ride away. He turned and smiled at her with a beaming face; and she lifted her pretty chin in the air and laughed aloud.

III

Bobinôt and Bibi, trudging home, stopped without at the cistern to make themselves presentable.

"My! Bibi, w'at will yo' mama say! You ought to be ashame'. You oughtn' put on those good pants. Look at 'em! An' that mud on yo' collar! How you got that mud on yo' collar, Bibi? I never saw such a boy!" Bibi was the picture of pathetic resignation. Bobinôt was the embodiment of serious solicitude as he strove to remove from his own person and his son's the signs of their tramp over heavy roads and through wet fields. He scraped the mud off Bibi's bare legs and feet with a stick and carefully removed all traces from his heavy brogans. Then, prepared for the worst—the meeting with an over-scrupulous housewife, they entered cautiously at the back door.

Calixta was preparing supper. She had set the table and was dripping coffee at the hearth. She sprang up as they came in.

"Oh, Bobinôt! You back! My! but I was uneasy. W'ere you been during the rain? An' Bibi? he ain't wet? he ain't hurt?" She had clasped Bibi and was kissing him effusively. Bobinôt's explanations and apologies which he had been composing all along the way, died on his lips as Calixta felt him to see if he were dry, and seemed to express nothing but satisfaction at their safe return.

"I brought you some shrimps, Calixta," offered Bobinôt, hauling the can from his ample side pocket and laying it on the table.

"Shrimps! Oh, Bobinôt! you too good fo' anything!" and she gave him a smacking kiss on the cheek that resounded. *"J'vous réponds,*[4] we'll have a feas' to night! umph-umph!"

Bobinôt and Bibi began to relax and enjoy themselves, and when the three seated themselves at table they laughed much and so loud that anyone might have heard them as far away as Laballière's.

IV

Alcée Laballière wrote to his wife, Clarisse, that night. It was a loving letter, full of tender solicitude. He told her not to hurry back, but if she and the babies liked it at Biloxi, to stay a month longer. He was getting on nicely; and though

---

[4] I'm telling you.

he missed them, he was willing to bear the separation a while longer—realizing that their health and pleasure were the first things to be considered.

V

As for Clarisse, she was charmed upon receiving her husband's letter. She and the babies were doing well. The society was agreeable; many of her old friends and acquaintances were at the bay. And the first free breath since her marriage seemed to restore the pleasant liberty of her maiden days. Devoted as she was to her husband, their intimate conjugal life was something which she was more than willing to forego for a while.

So the storm passed and everyone was happy.

Theater

JEAN TOOMER [1894–1967]

Life of nigger alleys, of pool rooms and restaurants and near-beer saloons soaks into the walls of Howard Theater and sets them throbbing jazz songs. Black-skinned, they dance and shout above the tick and trill of white-walled buildings. At night, they open doors to people who come in to stamp their feet and shout. At night, road-shows volley songs into the mass-heart of black people. Songs soak the walls and seep out to the nigger life of alleys and near-beer saloons, of the Poodle Dog and Black Bear cabarets. Afternoons, the house is dark, and the walls are sleeping singers until rehearsal begins. Or until John comes within them. Then they start throbbing to a subtle syncopation. And the space-dark air grows softly luminous.

John is the manager's brother. He is seated at the center of the theater, just before rehearsal. Light streaks down upon him from a window high above. One half his face is orange in it. One half his face is in shadow. The soft glow of the house rushes to, and compacts about, the shaft of light. John's mind coincides with the shaft of light. Thoughts rush to, and compact about it. Life of the house and of the slowly awakening stage swirls to the body of John, and thrills it. John's body is separate from the thoughts that pack his mind.

Stage-lights, soft, as if they shine through clear pink fingers. Beneath them, hid by the shadow of a set, Dorris. Other chorus girls drift in. John feels them in the mass. And as if his own body were the mass-heart of a black audience listening to them singing, he wants to stamp his feet and shout. His mind, contained above desires of his body, singles the girls out, and tries to trace origins and plot destinies.

A pianist slips into the pit and improvises jazz. The walls awake. Arms of the girls, and their limbs, which . . . jazz, jazz . . . by lifting up their tight street skirts they set free, jab the air and clog the floor in rhythm to the music. (Lift your skirts, Baby, and talk t papa!) Crude, individualized, and yet . . . monotonous. . . .

John: Soon the director will herd you, my full-lipped, distant beauties, and tame you, and blunt your sharp thrusts in loosely suggestive movements, appropriate to Broadway. (O dance!) Soon the audience will paint your dusk faces white, and call you beautiful. (O dance!) Soon I. . . . (O dance!) I'd like . . .

Girls laugh and shout. Sing discordant snatches of other jazz songs. Whirl with loose passion into the arms of passing show-men.

John: Too thick. Too easy. Too monotonous. Her whom I'd love I'd leave before she knew that I was with her. Her? Which? (O dance!) I'd like to . . .

Girls dance and sing. Men clap. The walls sing and press inward. They press the men and girls, they press John towards a center of physical ecstasy. Go to it, Baby! Fan yourself, and feed your papa! Put . . . nobody lied . . . and take

. . . when they said I cried over you. No lie! The glitter and color of stacked scenes, the gilt and brass and crimson of the house, converge towards a center of physical ecstasy. John's feet and torso and his blood press in. He wills thought to rid his mind of passion.

"All right, girls. Alaska. Miss Reynolds, please."

The director wants to get the rehearsal through with.

The girls line up. John sees the front row: dancing ponies. The rest are in shadow. The leading lady fits loosely in the front. Lack-life, monotonous. "One, two, three—" Music starts. The song is somewhere where it will not strain the leading lady's throat. The dance is somewhere where it will not strain the girls. Above the staleness, one dancer throws herself into it. Dorris. John sees her. Her hair, crisp-curled, is bobbed. Bushy, black hair bobbing about her lemon-colored face. Her lips are curiously full, and very red. Her limbs in silk purple stockings are lovely. John feels them. Desires her. Holds off.

John: Stage-door johnny; chorus-girl. No, that would be all right. Dictie,[1] educated, stuck-up; show-girl. Yep. Her suspicion would be stronger than her passion. It wouldn't work. Keep her loveliness. Let her go.

Dorris sees John and knows that he is looking at her. Her own glowing is too rich a thing to let her feel the slimness of his diluted passion.

"Who's that?" she asks her dancing partner.

"Th manager's brother. Dictie. Nothin doin, hon."

Dorris tosses her head and dances for him until she feels she has him. Then, withdrawing disdainfully, she flirts with the director.

Dorris: Nothin doin? How come? Aint I as good as him? Couldnt I have got an education if I'd wanted one? Dont I know respectable folks, lots of em, in Philadelphia and New York and Chicago? Aint I had men as good as him? Better. Doctors an lawyers. Whats a manager's brother, anyhow?

Two steps back, and two steps front.

"Say, Mame, where do you get that stuff?"

"Whatshmean, Dorris?"

"If you two girls cant listen to what I'm telling you, I know where I can get some who can. Now listen."

Mame: Go to hell, you black bastard.

Dorris: Whats eatin at him, anyway?

"Now follow me in this, you girls. Its three counts to the right, three counts to the left, and then you shimmy—"

John:—and then you shimmy. I'll bet she can. Some good cabaret, with rooms upstairs. And what in hell do you think you'd get from it? Youre going wrong. Here's right: get her to herself—(Christ, but how she'd bore you after the first five minutes)—not if you get her right she wouldnt. Touch her, I mean. To herself—in some room perhaps. Some cheap, dingy bedroom. Hell no. Cant be done. But the point is, brother John, it can be done. Get her to herself somewhere, anywhere. Go down in yourself—and she'd be calling you all sorts

---

[1] A snob.

of asses while you were in the process of going down. Hold em, bud. Cant be done. Let her go. (Dance and I'll love you!) And keep her loveliness.

"All right now, Chicken Chaser. Dorris and girls. Where's Dorris? I told you to stay on the stage, didnt I? Well? Now thats enough. All right. All right there, Professor?[2] All right. One, two, three—"

Dorris swings to the front. The line of girls, four deep, blurs within the shadow of suspended scenes. Dorris wants to dance. The director feels that and steps to one side. He smiles, and picks her for a leading lady, one of these days. Odd ends of stage-men emerge from the wings, and stare and clap. A crap game in the alley suddenly ends. Black faces crowd the rear stage doors. The girls, catching joy from Dorris, whip up within the footlights' glow. They forget set steps; they find their own. The director forgets to bawl them out. Dorris dances.

John: Her head bobs to Broadway. Dance from yourself. Dance! O just a little more.

Dorris' eyes burn across the space of seats to him.

Dorris: I bet he can love. Hell, he cant love. He's too skinny. His lips are too skinny. He wouldn't love me anyway, only for that. But I'd get a pair of silk stockings out of it. Red silk. I got purple. Cut it, kid. You cant win him to respect you that away. He wouldnt anyway. Maybe he would. Maybe he'd love. I've heard em say that men who look like him (what does he look like?) will marry if they love. O will you love me? And give me kids, and a home, and everything? (I'd like to make your nest, and honest, hon, I wouldnt run out on you.) You will if I make you. Just watch me.

Dorris dances. She forgets her tricks. She dances.

Glorious songs are the muscles of her limbs.

And her singing is of canebrake loves and mangrove feastings.

The walls press in, singing. Flesh of a throbbing body, they press close to John and Dorris. They close them in. John's heart beats tensely against her dancing body. Walls press his mind within his heart. And then, the shaft of light goes out the window high above him. John's mind sweeps up to follow it. Mind pulls him upward into dream. Dorris dances . . . John dreams:

> Dorris is dressed in a loose black gown, splashed with lemon ribbons. Her feet taper long and slim from trim ankles. She waits for him just inside the stage door. John, collar and tie colorful and flaring, walks towards the stage door. There are no trees in the alley. But his feet feel as though they step on autumn leaves whose rustle has been pressed out of them by the passing of a million satin slippers. The air is sweet with roasting chestnuts, sweet with bonfires of old leaves. John's melancholy is a deep thing that seals all senses but his eyes, and makes him whole.
>
> Dorris knows that he is coming. Just at the right moment she steps from the door, as if there were no door. Her face is tinted like the autumn alley. Of old flowers, or of a southern canefield, her perfume. "Glorious Dorris." So his eyes speak. And their sadness is too deep for sweet untruth. She barely touches his arm.

---

[2] A piano player.

They glide off with footfalls softened on the leaves, the old leaves powdered by a million satin slippers.

They are in a room. John knows nothing of it. Only, that the flesh and blood of Dorris are its walls. Singing walls. Lights, soft, as if they shine through clear pink fingers. Soft lights, and warm.

John reaches for a manuscript of his, and reads. Dorris, who has no eyes, has eyes to understand him. He comes to a dancing scene. The scene is Dorris. She dances. Dorris dances. Glorious Dorris. Dorris whirls, whirls, dances. . . .

Dorris dances. The pianist crashes a bumper chord. The whole stage claps. Dorris, flushed, looks quick at John. His whole face is in shadow. She seeks for her dance in it. She finds it a dead thing in the shadow which is his dream. She rushes from the stage. Falls down the steps into her dressing-room. Pulls her hair. Her eyes, over a floor of tears, stare at the whitewashed ceiling. (Smell of dry paste, and paint, and soiled clothing.) Her pal comes in. Dorris flings herself into the old safe arms, and cries bitterly.

"I told you nothin doin," is what Mame says to comfort her.

QUESTIONS

1. State the nature of the conflict in John.   **2.** How does Toomer achieve dramatic conflict between John and Dorris even though they do not speak to each other?   **3.** How does the opening paragraph establish the mood and the values of the story?

Symbolizes the love she can never attain or possess unless she takes it by force.

A Rose for Emily   1931

WILLIAM FAULKNER   [1897–1962]

I

When Miss Emily Grierson died, our whole town went to her funeral: the men through a sort of respectful affection for a fallen monument, the women mostly out of curiosity to see the inside of her house, which no one save an old manservant—a combined gardener and cook—had seen in at least ten years.

It was a big, squarish frame house that had once been white, decorated with cupolas and spires and scrolled balconies in the heavily lightsome style of the seventies, set on what had once been our most select street. But garages and cotton gins had encroached and obliterated even the august names of that neighborhood; only Miss Emily's house was left, lifting its stubborn and coquettish decay above the cotton wagons and the gasoline pumps—an eyesore among eyesores. And now Miss Emily had gone to join the representatives of those august names where they lay in the cedar-bemused cemetery among the ranked and anonymous graves of Union and Confederate soldiers who fell at the battle of Jefferson.

Alive, Miss Emily had been a tradition, a duty, and a care; a sort of hereditary obligation upon the town, dating from that day in 1894 when Colonel Sartoris, the mayor—he who fathered the edict that no Negro woman should appear on the streets without an apron—remitted her taxes, the dispensation dating from the death of her father on into perpetuity. Not that Miss Emily would have accepted charity. Colonel Sartoris invented an involved tale to the effect that Miss Emily's father had loaned money to the town, which the town, as a matter of business, preferred this way of repaying. Only a man of Colonel Sartoris' generation and thought could have invented it, and only a woman could have believed it.

When the next generation, with its more modern ideas, became mayors and aldermen, this arrangement created some little dissatisfaction. On the first of the year they mailed her a tax notice. February came, and there was no reply. They wrote her a formal letter, asking her to call at the sheriff's office at her convenience. A week later the mayor wrote her himself, offering to call or to send his car for her, and received in reply a note on paper of an archaic shape, in a thin, flowing calligraphy in faded ink, to the effect that she no longer went out at all. The tax notice was also enclosed, without comment.

They called a special meeting of the Board of Aldermen. A deputation waited upon her, knocked at the door through which no visitor had passed since she ceased giving china-painting lessons eight or ten years earlier. They were admitted by the old Negro into a dim hall from which a stairway mounted into still more shadow. It smelled of dust and disuse—a close, dank smell. The Negro led them into the parlor. It was furnished in heavy, leather-covered furniture. When the Negro opened the blinds of one window, they could see that the

Taxes

402

leather was cracked; and when they sat down, a faint dust rose sluggishly about their thighs, spinning with slow motions in the single sun-ray. On a tarnished gilt easel before the fireplace stood a crayon portrait of Miss Emily's father.

They rose when she entered—a small, fat woman in black, with a thin gold chain descending to her waist and vanishing into her belt, leaning on an ebony cane with a tarnished gold head. Her skeleton was small and spare; perhaps that was why what would have been merely plumpness in another was obesity in her. She looked bloated, like a body long submerged in motionless water, and of that pallid hue. Her eyes, lost in the fatty ridges of her face, looked like two small pieces of coal pressed into a lump of dough as they moved from one face to another while the visitors stated their errand.

She did not ask them to sit. She just stood in the door and listened quietly until the spokesman came to a stumbling halt. Then they could hear the invisible watch ticking at the end of the gold chain.

Her voice was dry and cold. "I have no taxes in Jefferson. Colonel Sartoris explained it to me. Perhaps one of you can gain access to the city records and satisfy yourselves."

"But we have. We are the city authorities, Miss Emily. Didn't you get a notice from the sheriff, signed by him?"

"I received a paper, yes," Miss Emily said. "Perhaps he considers himself the sheriff . . . I have no taxes in Jefferson."

"But there is nothing on the books to show that, you see. We must go by the—"

"See Colonel Sartoris." (Colonel Sartoris had been dead almost ten years.) "I have no taxes in Jefferson. Tobe!" The Negro appeared. "Show these gentlemen out."

II

So she vanquished them, horse and foot, just as she had vanquished their fathers thirty years before about the smell. That was two years after her father's death and a short time after her sweetheart—the one we believed would marry her—had deserted her. After her father's death she went out very little; after her sweetheart went away, people hardly saw her at all. A few of the ladies had the temerity to call, but were not received, and the only sign of life about the place was the Negro man—a young man then—going in and out with a market basket.

"Just as if a man—any man—could keep a kitchen properly," the ladies said; so they were not surprised when the smell developed. It was another link between the gross, teeming world and the high and mighty Griersons.

A neighbor, a woman, complained to the mayor, Judge Stevens, eighty years old.

"But what will you have me do about it, madam?" he said.

"Why, send her word to stop it," the woman said. "Isn't there a law?"

"I'm sure that won't be necessary," Judge Stevens said. "It's probably just a snake or a rat that nigger of hers killed in the yard. I'll speak to him about it."

The next day he received two more complaints, one from a man who came in diffident deprecation. "We really must do something about it, Judge. I'd be the last one in the world to bother Miss Emily, but we've got to do something." That night the Board of Aldermen met—three graybeards and one younger man, a member of the rising generation.

"It's simple enough," he said. "Send her word to have her place cleaned up. Give her a certain time to do it in, and if she don't . . ."

"Dammit, sir," Judge Stevens said, "will you accuse a lady to her face of smelling bad?"

So the next night, after midnight, four men crossed Miss Emily's lawn and slunk about the house like burglars, sniffing along the base of the brickwork and at the cellar openings while one of them performed a regular sowing motion with his hand out of a sack slung from his shoulder. They broke open the cellar door and sprinkled lime there, and in all the outbuildings. As they recrossed the lawn, a window that had been dark was lighted and Miss Emily sat in it, the light behind her, and her upright torso motionless as that of an idol. They crept quietly across the lawn and into the shadow of the locusts that lined the street. After a week or two the smell went away.

That was when people had begun to feel really sorry for her. People in our town, remembering how old lady Wyatt, her great-aunt, had gone completely crazy at last, believed that the Griersons held themselves a little too high for what they really were. None of the young men were quite good enough for Miss Emily and such. We had long thought of them as a tableau, Miss Emily a slender figure in white in the background, her father a spraddled silhouette in the foreground, his back to her and clutching a horsewhip, the two of them framed by the back-flung front door. So when she got to be thirty and was still single, we were not pleased exactly, but vindicated; even with insanity in the family she wouldn't have turned down all of her chances if they had really materialized.

When her father died, it got about that the house was all that was left to her; and in a way, people were glad. At last they could pity Miss Emily. Being left alone, and a pauper, she had become humanized. Now she too would know the old thrill and the old despair of a penny more or less.

The day after his death all the ladies prepared to call at the house and offer condolence and aid, as is our custom. Miss Emily met them at the door, dressed as usual and with no trace of grief on her face. She told them that her father was not dead. She did that for three days, with the ministers calling on her, and the doctors, trying to persuade her to let them dispose of the body. Just as they were about to resort to law and force, she broke down, and they buried her father quickly.

We did not say she was crazy then. We believed she had to do that. We remembered all the young men her father had driven away, and we knew that with nothing left, she would have to cling to that which had robbed her, as people will.

III

She was sick for a long time. When we saw her again, her hair was cut short, making her look like a girl, with a vague resemblance to those angels in colored church windows—sort of tragic and serene.

The town had just let the contracts for paving the sidewalks, and in the summer after her father's death they began the work. The construction company came with niggers and mules and machinery, and a foreman named Homer Barron, a Yankee—a big, dark, ready man, with a big voice and eyes lighter than his face. The little boys would follow in groups to hear him cuss the niggers, and the niggers singing in time to the rise and fall of picks. Pretty soon he knew everybody in town. Whenever you heard a lot of laughing anywhere about the square, Homer Barron would be in the center of the group. Presently we began to see him and Miss Emily on Sunday afternoons driving in the yellow-wheeled buggy and the matched team of bays from the livery stable.

At first we were glad that Miss Emily would have an interest, because the ladies all said, "Of course a Grierson would not think seriously of a Northerner, a day laborer." But there were still others, older people, who said that even grief could not cause a real lady to forget *noblesse oblige*—without calling it *noblesse oblige*. They just said, "Poor Emily. Her kinsfolk should come to her." She had some kin in Alabama; but years ago her father had fallen out with them over the estate of old lady Wyatt, the crazy woman, and there was no communication between the two families. They had not even been represented at the funeral.

And as soon as the old people said, "Poor Emily," the whispering began. "Do you suppose it's really so?" they said to one another. "Of course it is. What else could . . ." This behind their hands; rustling of craned silk and satin behind jalousies closed upon the sun of Sunday afternoon as the thin, swift clop-clop-clop of the matched team passed: "Poor Emily."

She carried her head high enough—even when we believed that she was fallen. It was as if she demanded more than ever the recognition of her dignity as the last Grierson; as if it had wanted that touch of earthiness to reaffirm her imperviousness. Like when she bought the rat poison, the arsenic. That was over a year after they had begun to say "Poor Emily," and while the two female cousins were visiting her.

"I want some poison," she said to the druggist. She was over thirty then, still a slight woman, though thinner than usual, with cold, haughty black eyes in a face the flesh of which was strained across the temples and about the eye-sockets as you imagine a lighthouse-keeper's face ought to look. "I want some poison," she said.

"Yes, Miss Emily. What kind? For rats and such? I'd recom—"

"I want the best you have. I don't care what kind."

The druggist named several. "They'll kill anything up to an elephant. But what you want is—"

"Arsenic," Miss Emily said. "Is that a good one?"

"Is . . . arsenic? Yes, ma'am. But what you want—"

"I want arsenic."

The druggist looked down at her. She looked back at him, erect, her face like a strained flag. "Why, of course," the druggist said. "If that's what you want. But the law requires you to tell what you are going to use it for."

Miss Emily just stared at him, her head tilted back in order to look him eye for eye, until he looked away and went and got the arsenic and wrapped it up. The Negro delivery boy brought her the package; the druggist didn't come back. When she opened the package at home there was written on the box, under the skull and bones: "For rats."

IV

So the next day we all said, "She will kill herself"; and we said it would be the best thing. When she had first begun to be seen with Homer Barron, we had said, "She will marry him." Then we said, "She will persuade him yet," because Homer himself had remarked—he liked men, and it was known that he drank with the younger men in the Elks' Club—that he was not a marrying man. Later we said, "Poor Emily" behind the jalousies as they passed on Sunday afternoon in the glittering buggy, Miss Emily with her head high and Homer Barron with his hat cocked and a cigar in his teeth, reins and whip in a yellow glove.

Then some of the ladies began to say that it was a disgrace to the town and a bad example to the young people. The men did not want to interfere, but at last the ladies forced the Baptist minister—Miss Emily's people were Episcopal—to call upon her. He would never divulge what happened during that interview, but he refused to go back again. The next Sunday they again drove about the streets, and the following day the minister's wife wrote to Miss Emily's relations in Alabama.

So she had blood-kin under her roof again and we sat back to watch developments. At first nothing happened. Then we were sure that they were to be married. We learned that Miss Emily had been to the jeweler's and ordered a man's toilet set in silver, with the letters H.B. on each piece. Two days later we learned that she had bought a complete outfit of men's clothing, including a nightshirt, and we said, "They are married." We were really glad. We were glad because the two female cousins were even more Grierson than Miss Emily had ever been.

So we were not surprised when Homer Barron—the streets had been finished some time since—was gone. We were a little disappointed that there was not a public blowing-off, but we believed that he had gone on to prepare for Miss Emily's coming, or to give her a chance to get rid of the cousins. (By that time it was a cabal, and we were all Miss Emily's allies to help circumvent the cousins.) Sure enough, after another week they departed. And, as we had expected all along, within three days Homer Barron was back in town. A neighbor saw the Negro man admit him at the kitchen door at dusk one evening.

And that was the last we saw of Homer Barron. And of Miss Emily for some time. The Negro man went in and out with the market basket, but the front door remained closed. Now and then we would see her at a window for a moment, as the men did that night when they sprinkled the lime, but for almost six months she did not appear on the streets. Then we knew that this was to be expected too; as if that quality of her father which had thwarted her woman's life so many times had been too virulent and too furious to die.

When we next saw Miss Emily, she had grown fat and her hair was turning gray. During the next few years it grew grayer and grayer until it attained an even pepper-and-salt iron-gray, when it ceased turning. Up to the day of her death at seventy-four it was still that vigorous iron-gray, like the hair of an active man.

From that time on her front door remained closed, save for a period of six or seven years, when she was about forty, during which she gave lessons in china-painting. She fitted up a studio in one of her downstairs rooms, where the daughters and granddaughters of Colonel Sartoris' contemporaries were sent to her with the same regularity and in the same spirit that they were sent to church on Sundays with a twenty-five-cent piece for the collection plate. Meanwhile her taxes had been remitted.

Then the newer generation became the backbone and the spirit of the town, and the painting pupils grew up and fell away and did not send their children to her with boxes of color and tedious brushes and pictures cut from the ladies' magazines. The front door closed upon the last one and remained closed for good. When the town got free postal delivery, Miss Emily alone refused to let them fasten the metal numbers above her door and attach a mailbox to it. She would not listen to them.

Daily, monthly, yearly we watched the Negro grow grayer and more stooped, going in and out with the market basket. Each December we sent her a tax notice, which would be returned by the post office a week later, unclaimed. Now and then we would see her in one of the downstairs windows—she had evidently shut up the top floor of the house—like the carven torso of an idol in a niche, looking or not looking at us, we could never tell which. Thus she passed from generation to generation—dear, inescapable, impervious, tranquil, and perverse.

And so she died. Fell ill in the house filled with dust and shadows, with only a doddering Negro man to wait on her. We did not even know she was sick; we had long since given up trying to get any information from the Negro. He talked to no one, probably not even to her, for his voice had grown harsh and rusty, as if from disuse.

She died in one of the downstairs rooms, in a heavy walnut bed with a curtain, her gray head propped on a pillow yellow and moldy with age and lack of sunlight.

V

The Negro met the first of the ladies at the front door and let them in, with their hushed, sibilant voices and their quick, curious glances, and then he disappeared. He walked right through the house and out the back and was not seen again.

Post civil-war   Ante Diluvian
Homer - Yankee & common
Miss Emily - lady

The two female cousins came at once. They held the funeral on the second day, with the town coming to look at Miss Emily beneath a mass of bought flowers, with the crayon face of her father musing profoundly above the bier and the ladies sibilant and macabre; and the very old men—some in their brushed Confederate uniforms—on the porch and the lawn, talking of Miss Emily as if she had been a contemporary of theirs, believing they had danced with her and courted her perhaps, confusing time with its mathematical progression, as the old do, to whom all the past is not a diminishing road but, instead, a huge meadow which no winter ever quite touches, divided from them now by the narrow bottle-neck of the most recent decade of years.

The Story progression

The steps with Homer for years after he is dead

Already we knew that there was one room in that region above stairs which no one had seen in forty years, and which would have to be forced. They waited until Miss Emily was decently in the ground before they opened it.

The violence of breaking down the door seemed to fill this room with pervading dust. A thin, acrid pall as of the tomb seemed to lie everywhere upon this room decked and furnished as for a bridal: upon the valance curtains of faded rose color, upon the rose-shaded lights, upon the dressing table, upon the delicate array of crystal and the man's toilet things backed with tarnished silver, silver so tarnished that the monogram was obscured. Among them lay a collar and tie, as if they had just been removed, which, lifted, left upon the surface a pale crescent in the dust. Upon a chair hung the suit, carefully folded; beneath it the two mute shoes and the discarded socks.

The man himself lay in the bed.

For a long while we just stood there, looking down at the profound and fleshless grin. The body had apparently once lain in the attitude of an embrace, but now the long sleep that outlasts love, that conquers even the grimace of love, had cuckolded him. What was left of him, rotted beneath what was left of the nightshirt, had become inextricable from the bed in which he lay; and upon him and upon the pillow beside him lay that even coating of the patient and biding dust.

Then we noticed that in the second pillow was the indentation of a head. One of us lifted something from it, and leaning forward, that faint and invisible dust dry and acrid in the nostrils, we saw a long strand of iron-gray hair.

QUESTIONS

1. Describe the narrator. Is he sympathetic to Emily? Explain. Why does Faulkner title the narrative "A Rose for Emily"? **2.** Why does Faulkner devote the second paragraph to a description of Emily's house? **3.** Why doesn't Faulkner present the story in chronological order? **4.** What is the effect of the final paragraph?

WRITING TOPIC

In the second paragraph of part V, the narrator refers to some old men "talking of Miss Emily as if she had been a contemporary of theirs, believing that they had danced with her and courted her perhaps, confusing time with its mathematical progression, as the old do, to whom all the past is not a diminishing road but, instead, a huge meadow which no winter ever quite touches, divided from them now by the narrow bottle-neck of the most recent decade of years." Use this passage as the basis for a comparion of the narrator's and Emily's view of time.

The Intruder*

1966

JORGE LUIS BORGES [1899–1986]

2 Samuel 1:26[1]

They claim (improbably) that the story was told by Eduardo, the younger of the Nilsen brothers, at the wake for Cristian, the elder, who died of natural causes at some point in the 1890s, in the district of Morón. Someone must certainly have heard it from someone else, in the course of that long, idle night, between servings of maté, and passed it on to Santiago Dabove, from whom I learned it. Years later, they told it to me again in Turdera, where it had all happened. The second version, considerably more detailed, substantiated Santiago's, with the usual small variations and departures. I write it down now because, if I am not wrong, it reflects briefly and tragically the whole temper of life in those days along the banks of the River Plate. I shall put it down scrupulously; but already I see myself yielding to the writer's temptation to heighten or amplify some detail or other.

In Turdera, they were referred to as the Nilsens. The parish priest told me that his predecessor remembered with some astonishment seeing in that house a worn Bible, bound in black, with Gothic characters; in the end pages, he glimpsed handwritten names and dates. It was the only book in the house. The recorded misfortunes of the Nilsens, lost as all will be lost. The old house, now no longer in existence, was built of unstuccoed brick; beyond the hallway, one could make out a patio of colored tile, and another with an earth floor. In any case, very few ever went there; the Nilsens were jealous of their privacy. In the dilapidated rooms, they slept on camp beds; their indulgences were horses, riding gear, short-bladed daggers, a substantial fling on Saturdays, and belligerent drinking. I know that they were tall, with red hair which they wore long. Denmark, Ireland, places they would never hear tell of, stirred in the blood of those two *criollos*.[2] The neighborhood feared them, as they did all red-haired people; nor is it impossible that they might have been responsible for someone's death. Once, shoulder to shoulder, they tangled with the police. The younger one was said to have had an altercation with Juan Iberra in which he did not come off worst; which, according to what we hear, is indeed something. They were cowboys, team drivers, rustlers, and, at times, cheats. They had a reputation for meanness, except when drinking and gambling made them expansive. Of their ancestry or where they came from, nothing was known. They owned a wagon and a yoke of oxen.

---

* Translated by Alastair Reid.

[1] A verse from David's lament upon the death of his brother-in-law and friend Jonathan: "I am distressed for you, my brother Jonathan; / very pleasant have you been to me; / your love to me was wonderful, passing the love of woman."

[2] Creole, a person of European parentage born in South America, Central America, or the West Indies.

Physically, they were quite distinct from the roughneck crowd of settlers who lent the Costa Brava their own bad name. This, and other things we do not know, helps to explain how close they were; to cross one of them meant having two enemies.

The Nilsens were roisterers, but their amorous escapades had until then been confined to hallways and houses of ill fame. Hence, there was no lack of local comment when Cristian brought Juliana Burgos to live with him. True enough, in that way he got himself a servant; but it is also true that he showered her with gaudy trinkets, and showed her off at fiestas—the poor tenement fiestas, where the more intimate figures of the tango were forbidden and where the dancers still kept a respectable space between them. Juliana was dark-complexioned, with large wide eyes; one had only to look at her to make her smile. In a poor neighborhood, where work and neglect wear out the women, she was not at all bad looking.

At first, Eduardo went about with them. Later, he took a journey to Arrecifes on some business or other; he brought back home with him a girl he had picked up along the way. After a few days, he threw her out. He grew more sullen; he would get drunk alone at the local bar, and would have nothing to do with anyone. He was in love with Cristian's woman. The neighborhood, aware of it possibly before he was, looked forward with malicious glee to the subterranean rivalry between the brothers.

One night, when he came back late from the bar at the corner, Eduardo saw Cristian's black horse tethered to the fence. In the patio, the elder brother was waiting for him, all dressed up. The woman came and went, carrying maté. Cristian said to Eduardo:

"I'm off to a brawl at the Farías'. There's Juliana for you. If you want her, make use of her."

His tone was half-commanding, half-cordial. Eduardo kept still, gazing at him; he did not know what to do. Cristian rose, said goodbye to Eduardo but not to Juliana, who was an object to him, mounted, and trotted off, casually.

From that night on, they shared her. No one knew the details of that sordid conjunction, which outraged the proprieties of the poor locality. The arrangement worked well for some weeks, but it could not last. Between them, the brothers never uttered the name of Juliana, not even to summon her, but they sought out and found reasons for disagreeing. They argued over the sale of some skins, but they were really arguing about something else. Cristian would habitually raise his voice, while Eduardo kept quiet. Without realizing it, they were growing jealous. In that rough settlement, no man ever let on to others, or to himself, that a woman would matter, except as something desired or possessed, but the two of them were in love. For them, that in its way was a humiliation.

One afternoon, in the Plaza de Lomos, Eduardo ran into Juan Iberra, who congratulated him on the beautiful "dish" he had fixed up for himself. It was then, I think, that Eduardo roughed him up. No one, in his presence, was going to make fun of Cristian.

The woman waited on the two of them with animal submissiveness; but she could not conceal her preference, unquestionably for the younger one, who, although he had not rejected the arrangement, had not sought it out.

One day, they told Juliana to get two chairs from the first patio, and to keep out of the way, for they had to talk. Expecting a long discussion, she lay down for her siesta, but soon they summoned her. They had her pack a bag with all she possessed, not forgetting the glass rosary and the little crucifix her mother had left her. Without any explanation, they put her on the wagon, and set out on a wordless and wearisome journey. It had rained; the roads were heavy going and it was eleven in the evening when they arrived at Morón. There they passed her over to the *patrona* of the house of prostitution. The deal had already been made; Cristian picked up the money, and later on he divided it with Eduardo.

In Turdera, the Nilsens, floundering in the meshes of that outrageous love (which was also something of a routine), sought to recover their old ways, of men among men. They went back to their poker games, to fighting, to occasional binges. At times, perhaps, they felt themselves liberated, but one or other of them would quite often be away, perhaps genuinely, perhaps not. A little before the end of the year, the younger one announced that he had business in Buenos Aires. Cristian went to Morón; in the yard of the house we already know, he recognized Eduardo's piebald. He entered; the other was inside, waiting his turn. It seems that Cristian said to him, "If we go on like this, we'll wear out the horses. It's better that we do something about her."

He spoke with the *patrona*, took some coins from his money belt, and they went off with her. Juliana went with Cristian; Eduardo spurred his horse so as not to see them.

They returned to what has already been told. The cruel solution had failed; both had given in to the temptation to dissimulate. Cain's mark was there, but the bond between the Nilsens was strong—who knows what trials and dangers they had shared—and they preferred to vent their furies on others. On a stranger, on the dogs, on Juliana, who had brought discord into their lives.

March was almost over and the heat did not break. One Sunday (on Sundays it is the custom to retire early), Eduardo, coming back from the corner bar, saw Cristian yoking up the oxen. Cristian said to him, "Come on. We have to leave some hides off at the Pardos'. I've already loaded them. Let us take advantage of the cool."

The Pardo place lay, I think, to the south of them; they took the Camino de las Tropas, and then a detour. The landscape was spreading out slowly under the night.

They skirted a clump of dry reeds. Cristian threw away the cigarette he had lit and said casually, "Now, brother, to work. Later on, the buzzards will give us a hand. Today I killed her. Let her stay here with all her finery, and not do us any more harm."

They embraced, almost in tears. Now they shared an extra bond; the woman sorrowfully sacrificed and the obligation to forget her.

The Chase*   1967

ALBERTO MORAVIA   [1907–1990]

I have never been a sportsman—or, rather, I have been a sportsman only once, and that was the first and last time. I was a child, and one day, for some reason or other, I found myself together with my father, who was holding a gun in his hand, behind a bush, watching a bird that had perched on a branch not very far away. It was a large, gray bird—or perhaps it was brown—with a long—or perhaps a short—beak; I don't remember. I only remember what I felt at that moment as I looked at it. It was like watching an animal whose vitality was rendered more intense by the very fact of my watching it and of the animal's not knowing that I was watching it.

At that moment, I say, the notion of wildness entered my mind, never again to leave it: everything is wild which is autonomous and unpredictable and does not depend upon us. Then all of a sudden there was an explosion; I could no longer see the bird and I thought it had flown away. But my father was leading the way, walking in front of me through the undergrowth. Finally he stooped down, picked up something and put it in my hand. I was aware of something warm and soft and I lowered my eyes: there was a bird in the palm of my hand, its dangling, shattered head crowned with a plume of already-thickening blood. I burst into tears and dropped the corpse on the ground, and that was the end of my shooting experience.

I thought again of this remote episode in my life this very day after watching my wife, for the first and also the last time, as she was walking through the streets of the city. But let us take things in order.

What had my wife been like; what was she like now? She once had been, to put it briefly, "wild"—that is, entirely autonomous and unpredictable; latterly she had become "tame"—that is, predictable and dependent. For a long time she had been like the bird that, on that far-off morning in my childhood, I had seen perching on the bough; latterly, I am sorry to say, she had become like a hen about which one knows everything in advance—how it moves, how it eats, how it lays eggs, how it sleeps, and so on.

Nevertheless I would not wish anyone to think that my wife's wildness consisted of an uncouth, rough, rebellious character. Apart from being extremely beautiful, she is the gentlest, politest, most discreet person in the world. Rather her wildness consisted of the air of charming unpredictability, of independence in her way of living, with which during the first years of our marriage she acted in my presence, both at home and abroad. Wildness signified intimacy, privacy, secrecy. Yes, my wife as she sat in front of her dressing table, her eyes fixed on the looking glass, passing the hairbrush with a repeated motion over her long,

---

* Translated by Angus Davidson.

loose hair, was just as wild as the solitary quail hopping forward along a sun-
filled furrow or the furtive fox coming out into a clearing and stopping to look
around before running on. She was wild because I, as I looked at her, could
never manage to foresee when she would give a last stroke with the hairbrush
and rise and come toward me; wild to such a degree that sometimes when I
went into our bedroom the smell of her, floating in the air, would have something of the acrid quality of a wild beast's lair.

Gradually she became less wild, tamer. I had had a fox, a quail, in the house,
as I have said; then one day I realized that I had a hen. What effect does a hen
have on someone who watches it? It has the effect of being, so to speak, an
automaton in the form of a bird; automatic are the brief, rapid steps with which
it moves about; automatic its hard, terse pecking; automatic the glance of the
round eyes in its head that nods and turns; automatic its ready crouching down
under the cock; automatic the dropping of the egg wherever it may be and the
cry with which it announces that the egg has been laid. Good-by to the fox;
good-by to the quail. And her smell—this no longer brought to my mind, in
any way, the innocent odor of a wild animal; rather I detected in it the chemical
suavity of some ordinary French perfume.

Our flat is on the first floor of a big building in a modern quarter of the town;
our windows look out on a square in which there is a small public garden, the
haunt of nurses and children and dogs. One day I was standing at the window,
looking in a melancholy way at the garden. My wife, shortly before, had dressed
to go out; and once again, watching her, I had noticed the irrevocable and, so
to speak, invisible character of her gestures and personality: something which
gave one the feeling of a thing already seen and already done and which therefore
evaded even the most determined observation. And now, as I stood looking at
the garden and at the same time wondering why the adorable wildness of former
times had so completely disappeared, suddenly my wife came into my range of
vision as she walked quickly across the garden in the direction of the bus stop.
I watched her and then I almost jumped for joy; in a movement she was making
to pull down a fold of her narrow skirt and smooth it over her thigh with the
tips of her long, sharp nails, in this movement I recognized the wildness that
in the past had made me love her. It was only an instant, but in that instant I
said to myself: She's become wild again because she's convinced that I am not
there and am not watching her. Then I left the window and rushed out.

But I did not join her at the bus stop; I felt that I must not allow myself to
be seen. Instead I hurried to my car, which was standing nearby, got in and
waited. A bus came and she got in together with some other people; the bus
started off again and I began following it. Then there came back to me the
memory of that one shooting expedition in which I had taken part as a child,
and I saw that the bus was the undergrowth with its bushes and trees, my wife
the bird perching on the bough while I, unseen, watched it living before my
eyes. And the whole town, during this pursuit, became, as though by magic, a
fact of nature like the countryside: the houses were hills, the streets valleys, the

vehicles hedges and woods, and even the passers-by on the pavements had something unpredictable and autonomous—that is, wild—about them. And in my mouth, behind my clenched teeth, there was the acrid, metallic taste of gunfire; and my eyes, usually listless and wandering, had become sharp, watchful, attentive.

These eyes were fixed intently upon the exit door when the bus came to the end of its run. A number of people got out, and then I saw my wife getting out. Once again I recognized, in the manner in which she broke free of the crowd and started off toward a neighboring street, the wildness that pleased me so much. I jumped out of the car and started following her.

She was walking in front of me, ignorant of my presence, a tall woman with an elegant figure, long-legged, narrow-hipped, broad-backed, her brown hair falling on her shoulders.

Men turned around as she went past; perhaps they were aware of what I myself was now sensing with an intensity that quickened the beating of my heart and took my breath away: the unrestricted, steadily increasing, irresistible character of her mysterious wildness.

She walked hurriedly, having evidently some purpose in view, and even the fact that she had a purpose of which I was ignorant added to her wildness; I did not know where she was going, just as on that far-off morning I had not known what the bird perching on the bough was about to do. Moreover I thought the gradual, steady increase in this quality of wildness came partly from the fact that as she drew nearer to the object of this mysterious walk there was an increase in her—how shall I express it?—of biological tension, of existential excitement, of vital effervescence. Then, unexpectedly, with the suddenness of a film, her purpose was revealed.

A fair-haired young man in a leather jacket and a pair of corduroy trousers was leaning against the wall of a house in that ancient, narrow street. He was idly smoking as he looked in front of him. But as my wife passed close to him, he threw away his cigarette with a decisive gesture, took a step forward and seized her arm. I was expecting her to rebuff him, to move away from him, but nothing happened: evidently obeying the rules of some kind of erotic ritual, she went on walking beside the young man. Then after a few steps, with a movement that confirmed her own complicity, she put her arm around her companion's waist and he put his around her.

I understood then that this unknown man who took such liberties with my wife was also attracted by wildness. And so, instead of making a conventional appointment with her, instead of meeting in a café with a handshake, a falsely friendly and respectful welcome, he had preferred, by agreement with her, to take her by surprise—or, rather, to pretend to do so—while she was apparently taking a walk on her own account. All this I perceived by intuition, noticing that at the very moment when he stepped forward and took her arm her wildness had, so to speak, given an upward bound. It was years since I had seen my wife so alive, but alas, the source of this life could not be traced to me.

They walked on thus entwined and then, without any preliminaries, just like two wild animals, they did an unexpected thing: they went into one of the dark doorways in order to kiss. I stopped and watched them from a distance, peering into the darkness of the entrance. My wife was turned away from me and was bending back with the pressure of his body, her hair hanging free. I looked at that long, thick mane of brown hair, which as she leaned back fell free of her shoulders, and I felt at that moment her vitality reached its diapason, just as happens with wild animals when they couple and their customary wildness is redoubled by the violence of love. I watched for a long time and then, since this kiss went on and on and in fact seemed to be prolonged beyond the limits of my power of endurance, I saw that I would have to intervene.

I would have to go forward, seize my wife by the arm—or actually by that hair, which hung down and conveyed so well the feeling of feminine passivity— then hurl myself with clenched fists upon the blond young man. After this encounter I would carry off my wife, weeping, mortified, ashamed, while I was raging and broken-hearted, upbraiding her and pouring scorn upon her.

But what else would this intervention amount to but the shot my father fired at that free, unknowing bird as it perched on the bough? The disorder and confusion, the mortification, the shame, that would follow would irreparably destroy the rare and precious moment of wildness that I was witnessing inside the dark doorway. It was true that this wildness was directed against me; but I had to remember that wildness, always and everywhere, is directed against every-thing and everybody. After the scene of my intervention it might be possible for me to regain control of my wife, but I should find her shattered and lifeless in my arms like the bird that my father placed in my hand so that I might throw it into the shooting bag.

The kiss went on and on: well, it was a kiss of passion—that could not be denied. I waited until they finished, until they came out of the doorway, until they walked on again still linked together. Then I turned back.

The Girls in Their Summer Dresses

IRWIN SHAW [1913–1984]

1939

Fifth Avenue was shining in the sun when they left the Brevoort.[1] The sun was warm, even though it was February, and everything looked like Sunday morning—the buses and the well-dressed people walking slowly in couples and the quiet buildings with the windows closed.

Michael held Frances' arm tightly as they walked toward Washington Square[2] in the sunlight. They walked lightly, almost smiling, because they had slept late and had a good breakfast and it was Sunday. Michael unbuttoned his coat and let it flap around him in the mild wind.

"Look out," Frances said as they crossed Eighth Street. "You'll break your neck." Michael laughed and Frances laughed with him.

"She's not so pretty," Frances said. "Anyway, not pretty enough to take a chance of breaking your neck."

Michael laughed again. "How did you know I was looking at her?"

Frances cocked her head to one side and smiled at her husband under the brim of her hat. "Mike, darling," she said.

"O.K.," he said. "Excuse me."

Frances patted his arm lightly and pulled him along a little faster toward Washington Square. "Let's not see anybody all day," she said. "Let's just hang around with each other. You and me. We're always up to our neck in people, drinking their Scotch or drinking our Scotch; we only see each other in bed. I want to go out with my husband all day long. I want him to talk only to me and listen only to me."

"What's to stop us?" Michael asked.

"The Stevensons. They want us to drop by around one o'clock and they'll drive us into the country."

"The cunning Stevensons," Mike said. "Transparent. They can whistle. They can go driving in the country by themselves."

"Is it a date?"

"It's a date."

Frances leaned over and kissed him on the tip of the ear.

"Darling," Michael said, "this is Fifth Avenue."

"Let me arrange a program," Frances said. "A planned Sunday in New York for a young couple with money to throw away."

---

[1] The Brevoort was a New York hotel on lower Fifth Avenue. At the time that this story was written, the Brevoort's bar was famous as a gathering place for literary people.

[2] A park at the south end of Fifth Avenue.

417

"Go easy."

"First let's go to the Metropolitan Museum of Art," Frances suggested, because Michael had said during the week he wanted to go. "I haven't been there in three years and there're at least ten pictures I want to see again. Then we can take the bus down to Radio City and watch them skate. And later we'll go down to Cavanagh's and get a steak as big as a blacksmith's apron, with a bottle of wine, and after that there's a French picture at the Filmarte that everybody says—say, are you listening to me?"

"Sure," he said. He took his eyes off the hatless girl with the dark hair, cut dancer-style like a helmet, who was walking past him.

"That's the program for the day," Frances said flatly. "Or maybe you'd just rather walk up and down Fifth Avenue."

"No," Michael said. "Not at all."

"You always look at other women," Frances said. "Everywhere. Every damned place we go."

"No, darling," Michael said, "I look at everything. God gave me eyes and I look at women and men in subway excavations and moving pictures and the little flowers of the field. I casually inspect the universe."

"You ought to see the look in your eye," Frances said, "as you casually inspect the universe on Fifth Avenue."

"I'm a happily married man." Michael pressed her elbow tenderly. "Example for the whole twentieth century—Mr. and Mrs. Mike Loomis. Hey, let's have a drink," he said, stopping.

"We just had breakfast."

"Now listen, darling," Mike said, choosing his words with care, "it's a nice day and we both felt good and there's no reason why we have to break it up. Let's have a nice Sunday."

"All right. I don't know why I started this. Let's drop it. Let's have a good time."

They joined hands consciously and walked without talking among the baby carriages and the old Italian men in their Sunday clothes and the young women with Scotties in Washington Square Park.

"At least once a year everyone should go to the Metropolitan Museum of Art," Frances said after a while, her tone a good imitation of the tone she had used at breakfast and at the beginning of their walk. "And it's nice on Sunday. There're a lot of people looking at the pictures and you get the feeling maybe Art isn't on the decline in New York City, after all—"

"I want to tell you something," Michael said very seriously. "I have not touched another woman. Not once. In all the five years."

"All right," Frances said.

"You believe that, don't you?"

"All right."

They walked between the crowded benches, under the scrubby city-park trees.

"I try not to notice it," Frances said, "but I feel rotten inside, in my stomach, when we pass a woman and you look at her and I see that look in your eye and that's the way you looked at me the first time. In Alice Maxwell's house. Standing there in the living room, next to the radio, with a green hat on and all those people."

"I remember the hat," Michael said.

"The same look," Frances said. "And it makes me feel bad. It makes me feel terrible."

"Sh-h-h, please, darling, sh-h-h."

"I think I would like a drink now," Frances said.

They walked over to a bar on Eighth Street, not saying anything, Michael automatically helping her over curbstones and guiding her past automobiles. They sat near a window in the bar and the sun streamed in and there was a small, cheerful fire in the fireplace. A little Japanese waiter came over and put down some pretzels and smiled happily at them.

"What do you order after breakfast?" Michael asked.

"Brandy, I suppose," Frances said.

"Courvoisier," Michael told the waiter. "Two Courvoisiers."

The waiter came with the glasses and they sat drinking the brandy in the sunlight. Michael finished half his and drank a little water.

"I look at women," he said. "Correct. I don't say it's wrong or right. I look at them. If I pass them on the street and I don't look at them, I'm fooling you, I'm fooling myself."

"You look at them as though you want them," Frances said, playing with her brandy glass. "Every one of them."

"In a way," Michael said, speaking softly and not to his wife, "in a way that's true. I don't do anything about it, but it's true."

"I know it. That's why I feel bad."

"Another brandy," Michael called. "Waiter, two more brandies."

He sighed and closed his eyes and rubbed them gently with his fingertips. "I love the way women look. One of the things I like best about New York is the battalions of women. When I first came to New York from Ohio that was the first thing I noticed, the million wonderful women, all over the city. I walked around with my heart in my throat."

"A kid," Frances said. "That's a kid's feeling."

"Guess again," Michael said. "Guess again. I'm older now. I'm a man getting near middle age, putting on a little fat, and I still love to walk along Fifth Avenue at three o'clock on the east side of the street between Fiftieth and Fifty-seventh Streets. They're all out then, shopping, in their furs and their crazy hats, everything all concentrated from all over the world into seven blocks—the best furs, the best clothes, the handsomest women, out to spend money and feeling good about it."

The Japanese waiter put the two drinks down, smiling with great happiness.

"Everything is all right?" he asked.

"Everything is wonderful," Michael said.

"If it's just a couple of fur coats," Frances said, "and forty-five dollar hats—"

"It's not the fur coats. Or the hats. That's just the scenery for that particular kind of woman. Understand," he said, "you don't have to listen to this."

"I want to listen."

"I like the girls in the offices. Neat with their eyeglasses, smart, chipper, knowing what everything is about. I like the girls on Forty-fourth Street at lunchtime, the actresses, all dressed up on nothing a week. I like the salesgirls in the stores, paying attention to you first because you're a man, leaving the lady customers waiting. I got all this stuff accumulated in me because I've been thinking about it for ten years and now you've asked for it and here it is."

"Go ahead," Frances said.

"When I think of New York City, I think of all the girls on parade in the city. I don't know whether it's something special with me or whether every man in the city walks around with the same feeling inside him, but I feel as though I'm at a picnic in this city. I like to sit near the women in the theatres, the famous beauties who've taken six hours to get ready and look it. And the young girls at the football games, with the red cheeks, and when the warm weather comes, the girls in their summer dresses." He finished his drink. "That's the story."

Frances finished her drink and swallowed two or three times extra. "You say you love me?"

"I love you."

"I'm pretty, too," Frances said. "As pretty as any of them."

"You're beautiful," Michael said.

"I'm good for you," Frances said, pleading. "I've made a good wife, a good housekeeper, a good friend. I'd do any damn thing for you."

"I know," Michael said. He put his hand out and grasped hers.

"You'd like to be free to—" Frances said.

"Sh-h-h."

"Tell the truth." She took her hand away from under his.

Michael flicked the edge of his glass with his finger. "O.K.," he said gently. "Sometimes I feel I would like to be free."

"Well," Frances said, "any time you say."

"Don't be foolish." Michael swung his chair around to her side of the table and patted her thigh.

She began to cry silently into her handkerchief, bent over just enough so that nobody else in the bar would notice. "Someday," she said, crying, "you're going to make a move."

Michael didn't say anything. He sat watching the bartender slowly peel a lemon.

"Aren't you?" Frances asked harshly. "Come on, tell me. Talk. Aren't you?"

"Maybe," Michael said. He moved his chair back again. "How the hell do I know?"

"You know," Frances persisted. "Don't you know?"

"Yes," Michael said after a while, "I know."

Frances stopped crying then. Two or three snuffles into the handkerchief and she put it away and her face didn't tell anything to anybody. "At least do me one favor," she said.

"Sure."

"Stop talking about how pretty this woman is or that one. Nice eyes, nice breasts, a pretty figure, good voice." She mimicked his voice. "Keep it to yourself. I'm not interested."

Michael waved to the waiter. "I'll keep it to myself," he said.

Frances flicked the corners of her eyes. "Another brandy," she told the waiter.

"Two," Michael said.

"Yes, ma'am, yes, sir," said the waiter, backing away.

Frances regarded Michael coolly across the table. "Do you want me to call the Stevensons?" she asked. "It'll be nice in the country."

"Sure," Michael said. "Call them."

She got up from the table and walked across the room toward the telephone. Michael watched her walk, thinking what a pretty girl, what nice legs.

QUESTIONS

1. Is Frances's anger justified? Explain.   **2.** What is the effect of the final sentence of the story?

Shiloh[1]

BOBBIE ANN MASON   [b. 1940]

Leroy Moffitt's wife, Norma Jean, is working on her pectorals. She lifts three-pound dumbbells to warm up, then progresses to a twenty-pound barbell. Standing with her legs apart, she reminds Leroy of Wonder Woman.

"I'd give anything if I could just get these muscles to where they're real hard," says Norma Jean. "Feel this arm. It's not as hard as the other one."

"That's 'cause you're right-handed," says Leroy, dodging as she swings the barbell in an arc.

"Do you think so?"

"Sure."

Leroy is a truckdriver. He injured his leg in a highway accident four months ago, and his physical therapy, which involves weights and a pulley, prompted Norma Jean to try building herself up. Now she is attending a body-building class. Leroy has been collecting temporary disability since his tractor-trailer jackknifed in Missouri, badly twisting his left leg in its socket. He has a steel pin in his hip. He will probably not be able to drive his rig again. It sits in the backyard, like a gigantic bird that has flown home to roost. Leroy has been home in Kentucky for three months, and his leg is almost healed, but the accident frightened him and he does not want to drive any more long hauls. He is not sure what to do next. In the meantime, he makes things from craft kits. He started by building a miniature log cabin from notched Popsicle sticks. He varnished it and placed it on the TV set, where it remains. It reminds him of a rustic Nativity scene. Then he tried string art (sailing ships on black velvet), a macramé owl kit, a snap-together B-17 Flying Fortress, and a lamp made out of a model truck, with a light fixture screwed in the top of the cab. At first the kits were diversions, something to kill time, but now he is thinking about building a full-scale log house from a kit. It would be considerably cheaper than building a regular house, and besides, Leroy has grown to appreciate how things are put together. He has begun to realize that in all the years he was on the road he never took time to examine anything. He was always flying past scenery.

"They won't let you build a log cabin in any of the new subdivisions," Norma Jean tells him.

"They will if I tell them it's for you," he says, teasing her. Ever since they were married, he has promised Norma Jean he would build her a new home one day. They have always rented, and the house they live in is small and nondescript. It does not even feel like a home, Leroy realizes now.

Norma Jean works at the Rexall drugstore, and she has acquired an amazing

---

[1] Scene in southwest Tennessee of a Union victory during the Civil War; now a national military park. Shiloh, which means "tranquillity" or "rest," is also the name of a sacred place in the Old Testament.

amount of information about cosmetics. When she explains to Leroy the three stages of complexion care, involving creams, toners, and moisturizers, he thinks happily of other petroleum products—axle grease, diesel fuel. This is a connection between him and Norma Jean. Since he has been home, he has felt unusually tender about his wife and guilty over his long absences. But he can't tell what she feels about him. Norma Jean has never complained about his traveling; she has never made hurt remarks, like calling his truck a "widow-maker." He is reasonably certain she has been faithful to him, but he wishes she would celebrate his permanent homecoming more happily. Norma Jean is often startled to find Leroy at home, and he thinks she seems a little disappointed about it. Perhaps he reminds her too much of the early days of their marriage, before he went on the road. They had a child who died as an infant, years ago. They never speak about their memories of Randy, which have almost faded, but now that Leroy is home all the time, they sometimes feel awkward around each other, and Leroy wonders if one of them should mention the child. He has the feeling that they are waking up out of a dream together— that they must create a new marriage, start afresh. They are lucky they are still married. Leroy has read that for most people losing a child destroys the marriage—or else he heard this on *Donahue*. He can't always remember where he learns things anymore.

At Christmas, Leroy bought an electric organ for Norma Jean. She used to play the piano when she was in high school. "It don't leave you," she told him once. "It's like riding a bicycle."

The new instrument had so many keys and buttons that she was bewildered by it at first. She touched the keys tentatively, pushed some buttons, then pecked out "Chopsticks." It came out in an amplified fox-trot rhythm, with marimba sounds.

"It's an orchestra!" she cried.

The organ had a pecan-look finish and eighteen preset chords, with optional flute, violin, trumpet, clarinet, and banjo accompaniments. Norma Jean mastered the organ almost immediately. At first she played Christmas songs. Then she bought *The Sixties Songbook* and learned every tune in it, adding variations to each with the rows of brightly colored buttons.

"I didn't like these old songs back then," she said. "But I have this crazy feeling I missed something."

"You didn't miss a thing," said Leroy.

Leroy likes to lie on the couch and smoke a joint and listen to Norma Jean play "Can't Take My Eyes Off You" and "I'll Be Back." He is back again. After fifteen years on the road, he is finally settling down with the woman he loves. She is still pretty. Her skin is flawless. Her frosted curls resemble pencil trimmings.

Now that Leroy has come home to stay, he notices how much the town has changed. Subdivisions are spreading across western Kentucky like an oil slick. The sign at the edge of town says "Pop: 11,500"—only seven hundred more than it said twenty years before. Leroy can't figure out who is living in all the new houses. The farmers who used to gather around the courthouse square on Saturday afternoons to play checkers and spit tobacco juice have gone. It has been years since Leroy has thought about the farmers, and they have disappeared without his noticing.

Leroy meets a kid named Stevie Hamilton in the parking lot at the new shopping center. While they pretend to be strangers meeting over a stalled car, Stevie tosses an ounce of marijuana under the front seat of Leroy's car. Stevie is wearing orange jogging shoes and a T-shirt that says CHATTAHOOCHEE SUPER-RAT. His father is a prominent doctor who lives in one of the expensive subdivisions in a new white-columned brick house that looks like a funeral parlor. In the phone book under his name there is a separate number, with the listing "Teenagers."

"Where do you get this stuff?" asks Leroy. "From your pappy?"

"That's for me to know and you to find out," Stevie says. He is slit-eyed and skinny.

"What else you got?"

"What you interested in?"

"Nothing special. Just wondered."

Leroy used to take speed on the road. Now he has to go slowly. He needs to be mellow. He leans back against the car and says, "I'm aiming to build me a log house, soon as I get time. My wife, though, I don't think she likes the idea."

"Well, let me know when you want me again," Stevie says. He has a cigarette in his cupped palm, as though sheltering it from the wind. He takes a long drag, then stomps it on the asphalt and slouches away.

Stevie's father was two years ahead of Leroy in high school. Leroy is thirty-four. He married Norma Jean when they were both eighteen, and their child Randy was born a few months later, but he died at the age of four months and three days. He would be about Stevie's age now. Norma Jean and Leroy were at the drive-in, watching a double feature (*Dr. Strangelove* and *Lover Come Back*), and the baby was sleeping in the back seat. When the first movie ended, the baby was dead. It was the sudden infant death syndrome. Leroy remembers handing Randy to a nurse at the emergency room, as though he were offering her a large doll as a present. A dead baby feels like a sack of flour. "It just happens sometimes," said the doctor, in what Leroy always recalls as a nonchalant tone. Leroy can hardly remember the child anymore, but he still sees vividly a scene from *Dr. Strangelove* in which the President of the United States was talking in a folksy voice on the hot line to the Soviet premier about the bomber accidentally headed toward Russia. He was in the War Room, and the world map was lit up. Leroy remembers Norma Jean standing catatonically beside him in the hospital and himself thinking: Who is this strange girl? He had forgotten who she was. Now scientists are saying that crib death is caused by a virus. Nobody knows anything, Leroy thinks. The answers are always changing.

When Leroy gets home from the shopping center, Norma Jean's mother, Mabel Beasley, is there. Until this year, Leroy has not realized how much time she spends with Norma Jean. When she visits, she inspects the closets and then the plants, informing Norma Jean when a plant is droopy or yellow. Mabel calls the plants "flowers," although there are never any blooms. She always notices if Norma Jean's laundry is piling up. Mabel is a short, overweight woman whose tight, brown-dyed curls look more like a wig than the actual wig she sometimes wears. Today she has brought Norma Jean an off-white dust ruffle she made for the bed; Mabel works in a custom-upholstery shop.

"This is the tenth one I made this year," Mabel says. "I got started and couldn't stop."

"It's real pretty," says Norma Jean.

"Now we can hide things under the bed," says Leroy, who gets along with his mother-in-law primarily by joking with her. Mabel has never really forgiven him for disgracing her by getting Norma Jean pregnant. When the baby died, she said that fate was mocking her.

"What's that thing?" Mabel says to Leroy in a loud voice, pointing to a tangle of yarn on a piece of canvas.

Leroy holds it up for Mabel to see. "It's my needlepoint," he explains. "This is a *Star Trek* pillow cover."

"That's what a woman would do," says Mabel. "Great day in the morning!"

"All the big football players on TV do it," he says.

"Why, Leroy, you're always trying to fool me. I don't believe you for one minute. You don't know what to do with yourself—that's the whole trouble. Sewing!"

"I'm aiming to build us a log house," says Leroy. "Soon as my plans come."

"Like *heck* you are," says Norma Jean. She takes Leroy's needlepoint and shoves it into a drawer. "You have to find a job first. Nobody can afford to build now anyway."

Mabel straightens her girdle and says, "I still think before you get tied down y'all ought to take a little run to Shiloh."

"One of these days, Mama," Norma Jean says impatiently.

Mabel is talking about Shiloh, Tennessee. For the past few years, she has been urging Leroy and Norma Jean to visit the Civil War battleground there. Mabel went there on her honeymoon—the only real trip she ever took. Her husband died of a perforated ulcer when Norma Jean was ten, but Mabel, who was accepted into the United Daughters of the Confederacy in 1975, is still preoccupied with going back to Shiloh.

"I've been to kingdom come and back in that truck out yonder," Leroy says to Mabel, "but we never yet set foot in that battleground. Ain't that something? How did I miss it?"

"It's not even that far," Mabel says.

After Mabel leaves, Norma Jean reads to Leroy from a list she has made. "Things you could do," she announces. "You could get a job as a guard at Union Carbide, where they'd let you set on a stool. You could get on at the lumberyard. You could do a little carpenter work, if you want to build so bad. You could—"

"I can't do something where I'd have to stand up all day."

"You ought to try standing up all day behind a cosmetics counter. It's amazing that I have strong feet, coming from two parents that never had strong feet at all." At the moment Norma Jean is holding on to the kitchen counter, raising her knees one at a time as she talks. She is wearing two-pound ankle weights.

"Don't worry," says Leroy. "I'll do something."

"You could truck calves to slaughter for somebody. You wouldn't have to drive any big old truck for that."

"I'm going to build you this house," says Leroy. "I want to make you a real home."

"I don't want to live in any log cabin."

"It's not a cabin. It's a house."

"I don't care. It looks like a cabin."

"You and me together could lift those logs. It's just like lifting weights."

Norma Jean doesn't answer. Under her breath, she is counting. Now she is marching through the kitchen. She is doing goose steps.

Before his accident, when Leroy came home he used to stay in the house with Norma Jean, watching TV in bed and playing cards. She would cook fried chicken, picnic ham, chocolate pie—all his favorites. Now he is home alone much of the time. In the mornings, Norma Jean disappears, leaving a cooling place in the bed. She eats a cereal called Body Buddies, and she leaves the bowl on the table, with the soggy tan balls floating in a milk puddle. He sees things about Norma Jean that he never realized before. When she chops onions, she stares off into a corner, as if she can't bear to look. She puts on her house slippers almost precisely at nine o'clock every evening and nudges her jogging shoes under the couch. She saves bread heels for the birds. Leroy watches the birds at the feeder. He notices the peculiar way goldfinches fly past the window. They close their wings, then fall, then spread their wings to catch and lift themselves. He wonders if they close their eyes when they fall. Norma Jean closes her eyes when they are in bed. She wants the lights turned out. Even then, he is sure she closes her eyes.

He goes for long drives around town. He tends to drive a car rather carelessly. Power steering and an automatic shift make a car feel so small and inconsequential that his body is hardly involved in the driving process. His injured leg stretches out comfortably. Once or twice he has almost hit something, but even the prospect of an accident seems minor in a car. He cruises the new subdivisions, feeling like a criminal rehearsing for a robbery. Norma Jean is probably right about a log house being inappropriate here in the new subdivisions. All the houses look grand and complicated. They depress him.

One day when Leroy comes home from a drive he finds Norma Jean in tears. She is in the kitchen making a potato and mushroom-soup casserole, with grated-cheese topping. She is crying because her mother caught her smoking.

"I didn't hear her coming. I was standing here puffing away pretty as you please," Norma Jean says, wiping her eyes.

"I knew it would happen sooner or later," says Leroy, putting his arm around her.

"She don't know the meaning of the word 'knock,' " says Norma Jean. "It's a wonder she hadn't caught me years ago."

"Think of it this way," Leroy says. "What if she caught me with a joint?"

"You better not let her!" Norma Jean shrieks. "I'm warning you, Leroy Moffitt!"

"I'm just kidding. Here, play me a tune. That'll help you relax."

Norma Jean puts the casserole in the oven and sets the timer. Then she plays a ragtime tune, with horns and banjo, as Leroy lights up a joint and lies on the couch, laughing to himself about Mabel's catching him at it. He thinks of Stevie Hamilton—a doctor's son pushing grass. Everything is funny. The whole town seems crazy and small. He is reminded of Virgil Mathis, a boastful policeman Leroy used to shoot pool with. Virgil recently led a drug bust in a back room at a bowling alley, where he seized ten thousand dollars' worth of marijuana. The newspaper had a picture of him holding up the bags of grass and grinning widely. Right now, Leroy can imagine Virgil breaking down the door and arresting him with a lungful of smoke. Virgil would probably have been alerted to the scene because of all the racket Norma Jean is making. Now she sounds like a hard-rock band. Norma Jean is terrific. When she switches to a Latin-rhythm version of "Sunshine Superman," Leroy hums along. Norma Jean's foot goes up and down, up and down.

"Well, what do you think?" Leroy says, when Norma Jean pauses to search through her music.

"What do I think about what?"

His mind has gone blank. Then he says, "I'll sell my rig and build us a house." That wasn't what he wanted to say. He wanted to know what she thought— what she *really* thought—about them.

"Don't start in on that again," says Norma Jean. She begins playing "Who'll Be the Next in Line?"

Leroy used to tell hitchhikers his whole life story—about his travels, his hometown, the baby. He would end with a question: "Well, what do you think?" It was just a rhetorical question. In time, he had the feeling that he'd been telling the same story over and over to the same hitchhikers. He quit talking to hitchhikers when he realized how his voice sounded—whining and self-pitying, like some teenage-tragedy song. Now Leroy has the sudden impulse to tell Norma Jean about himself, as if he had just met her. They have known each other so long they have forgotten a lot about each other. They could become reacquainted. But when the oven timer goes off and she runs to the kitchen, he forgets why he wants to do this.

The next day, Mabel drops by. It is Saturday and Norma Jean is cleaning. Leroy is studying the plans of his log house, which have finally come in the mail. He has them spread out on the table—big sheets of stiff blue paper, with diagrams and numbers printed in white. While Norma Jean runs the vacuum, Mabel drinks coffee. She sets her coffee cup on a blueprint.

"I'm just waiting for time to pass," she says to Leroy, drumming her fingers on the table.

As soon as Norma Jean switches off the vacuum, Mabel says in a loud voice, "Did you hear about the datsun dog that killed the baby?"

Norma Jean says, "The word is 'dachshund.' "

"They put the dog on trial. It chewed the baby's legs off. The mother was in the next room all the time." She raises her voice. "They thought it was neglect."

Norma Jean is holding her ears. Leroy manages to open the refrigerator and get some Diet Pepsi to offer Mabel. Mabel still has some coffee and she waves away the Pepsi.

"Datsuns are like that," Mabel says. "They're jealous dogs. They'll tear a place to pieces if you don't keep an eye on them."

"You better watch out what you're saying, Mabel," says Leroy.

"Well, facts is facts."

Leroy looks out the window at his rig. It is like a huge piece of furniture gathering dust in the backyard. Pretty soon it will be an antique. He hears the vacuum cleaner. Norma Jean seems to be cleaning the living room rug again.

Later, she says to Leroy, "She just said that about the baby because she caught me smoking. She's trying to pay me back."

"What are you talking about?" Leroy says, nervously shuffling blueprints.

"You know good and well," Norma Jean says. She is sitting in a kitchen chair with her feet up and her arms wrapped around her knees. She looks small and helpless. She says, "The very idea, her bringing up a subject like that! Saying it was neglect."

"She didn't mean that," Leroy says.

"She might not have *thought* she meant it. She always says things like that. You don't know how she goes on."

"But she didn't really mean it. She was just talking."

Leroy opens a king-sized bottle of beer and pours it into two glasses, dividing it carefully. He hands a glass to Norma Jean and she takes it from him mechanically. For a long time, they sit by the kitchen window watching the birds at the feeder.

Something is happening. Norma Jean is going to night school. She has graduated from her six-week body-building course and now she is taking an adult-education course in composition at Paducah Community College. She spends her evenings outlining paragraphs.

"First you have a topic sentence," she explains to Leroy. "Then you divide it up. Your secondary topic has to be connected to your primary topic."

To Leroy, this sounds intimidating. "I never was any good in English," he says.

"It makes a lot of sense."

"What are you doing this for, anyhow?"

She shrugs. "It's something to do." She stands up and lifts her dumbbells a few times.

"Driving a rig, nobody cared about my English."

"I'm not criticizing your English."

Norma Jean used to say, "If I lose ten minutes' sleep, I just drag all day."

Now she stays up late, writing compositions. She got a B on her first paper—a how-to theme on soup-based casseroles. Recently Norma Jean has been cooking unusual foods—tacos, lasagna, Bombay chicken. She doesn't play the organ anymore, though her second paper was called "Why Music Is Important to Me." She sits at the kitchen table, concentrating on her outlines, while Leroy plays with his log house plans, practicing with a set of Lincoln Logs. The thought of getting a truckload of notched, numbered logs scares him, and he wants to be prepared. As he and Norma Jean work together at the kitchen table, Leroy has the hopeful thought that they are sharing something, but he knows he is a fool to think this. Norma Jean is miles away. He knows he is going to lose her. Like Mabel, he is just waiting for time to pass.

One day, Mabel is there before Norma Jean gets home from work, and Leroy finds himself confiding in her. Mabel, he realizes, must know Norma Jean better than he does.

"I don't know what's got into that girl," Mabel says. "She used to go to bed with the chickens. Now you say she's up all hours. Plus her a-smoking. I like to died."

"I want to make her this beautiful home," Leroy says, indicating the Lincoln Logs. "I don't think she even wants it. Maybe she was happier with me gone."

"She don't know what to make of you, coming home like this."

"Is that it?"

Mabel takes the roof off his Lincoln Log cabin. "You couldn't get *me* in a log cabin," she says. "I was raised in one. It's no picnic, let me tell you."

"They're different now," says Leroy.

"I tell you what," Mabel says, smiling oddly at Leroy.

"What?"

"Take her on down to Shiloh. Y'all need to get out together, stir a little. Her brain's all balled up over them books."

Leroy can see traces of Norma Jean's features in her mother's face. Mabel's worn face has the texture of crinkled cotton, but suddenly she looks pretty. It occurs to Leroy that Mabel has been hinting all along that she wants them to take her with them to Shiloh.

"Let's all go to Shiloh," he says. "You and me and her. Come Sunday."

Mabel throws up her hands in protest. "Oh, no, not me. Young folks want to be by theirselves."

When Norma Jean comes in with groceries, Leroy says excitedly, "Your mama here's been dying to go to Shiloh for thirty-five years. It's about time we went, don't you think?"

"I'm not going to butt in on anybody's second honeymoon," Mabel says.

"Who's going on a honeymoon, for Christ's sake?" Norma Jean says loudly.

"I never raised no daughter of mine to talk that-a-way," Mabel says.

"You ain't seen nothing yet," says Norma Jean. She starts putting away boxes and cans, slamming cabinet doors.

"There's a log cabin at Shiloh," Mabel says. "It was there during the battle. There's bullet holes in it."

"When are you going to *shut up* about Shiloh, Mama?" asks Norma Jean.

"I always thought Shiloh was the prettiest place, so full of history," Mabel goes on. "I just hoped y'all could see it once before I die, so you could tell me about it." Later, she whispers to Leroy, "You do what I said. A little change is what she needs."

"Your name means 'the king,' " Norma Jean says to Leroy that evening. He is trying to get her to go to Shiloh, and she is reading a book about another century.

"Well, I reckon I ought to be right proud."

"I guess so."

"Am I still king around here?"

Norma Jean flexes her biceps and feels them for hardness. "I'm not fooling around with anybody, if that's what you mean," she says.

"Would you tell me if you were?"

"I don't know."

"What does *your* name mean?"

"It was Marilyn Monroe's real name."

"No kidding!"

"Norma comes from the Normans. They were invaders," she says. She closes her book and looks hard at Leroy. "I'll go to Shiloh with you if you'll stop staring at me."

On Sunday, Norma Jean packs a picnic and they go to Shiloh. To Leroy's relief, Mabel says she does not want to come with them. Norma Jean drives, and Leroy, sitting beside her, feels like some boring hitchhiker she has picked up. He tries some conversation, but she answers him in monosyllables. At Shiloh, she drives aimlessly through the park, past bluffs and trails and steep ravines. Shiloh is an immense place, and Leroy cannot see it as a battleground. It is not what he expected. He thought it would look like a golf course. Monuments are everywhere, showing through the thick clusters of trees. Norma Jean passes the log cabin Mabel mentioned. It is surrounded by tourists looking for bullet holes.

"That's not the kind of log house I've got in mind," says Leroy apologetically.

"I know *that*."

"This is a pretty place. Your mama was right."

"It's O.K.," says Norma Jean. "Well, we've seen it. I hope she's satisfied."

They burst out laughing together.

At the park museum, a movie on Shiloh is shown every half hour, but they decide that they don't want to see it. They buy a souvenir Confederate flag for Mabel, and then they find a picnic spot near the cemetery. Norma Jean has brought a picnic cooler, with pimiento sandwiches, soft drinks, and Yodels. Leroy eats a sandwich and then smokes a joint, hiding it behind the picnic cooler. Norma Jean has quit smoking altogether. She is picking cake crumbs from the cellophane wrapper, like a fussy bird.

Leroy says, "So the boys in gray ended up in Corinth. The Union soldiers zapped 'em finally. April 7, 1862."

They both know that he doesn't know any history. He is just talking about some of the historical plaques they have read. He feels awkward, like a boy on a date with an older girl. They are still just making conversation.

"Corinth is where Mama eloped to," says Norma Jean.

They sit in silence and stare at the cemetery for the Union dead and, beyond, at a tall cluster of trees. Campers are parked nearby, bumper to bumper, and small children in bright clothing are cavorting and squealing. Norma Jean wads up the cake wrapper and squeezes it tightly in her hand. Without looking at Leroy, she says, "I want to leave you."

Leroy takes a bottle of Coke out of the cooler and flips off the cap. He holds the bottle poised near his mouth but cannot remember to take a drink. Finally he says, "No, you don't."

"Yes, I do."

"I won't let you."

"You can't stop me."

"Don't do me that way."

Leroy knows Norma Jean will have her own way. "Didn't I promise to be home from now on?" he says.

"In some ways, a woman prefers a man who wanders," says Norma Jean. "That sounds crazy, I know."

"You're not crazy."

Leroy remembers to drink from his Coke. Then he says, "Yes, you *are* crazy. You and me could start all over again. Right back at the beginning."

"We *have* started all over again," says Norma Jean. "And this is how it turned out."

"What did I do wrong?"

"Nothing."

"Is this one of those women's lib things?" Leroy asks.

"Don't be funny."

The cemetery, a green slope dotted with white markers, looks like a subdivision site. Leroy is trying to comprehend that his marriage is breaking up, but for some reason he is wondering about white slabs in a graveyard.

"Everything was fine till Mama caught me smoking," says Norma Jean, standing up. "That set something off."

"What are you talking about?"

"She won't leave me alone—*you* won't leave me alone." Norma Jean seems to be crying, but she is looking away from him. "I feel eighteen again. I can't face that all over again." She starts walking away. "No, it *wasn't* fine. I don't know what I'm saying. Forget it."

Leroy takes a lungful of smoke and closes his eyes as Norma Jean's words sink in. He tries to focus on the fact that thirty-five hundred soldiers died on the grounds around him. He can only think of that war as a board game with plastic soldiers. Leroy almost smiles, as he compares the Confederates' daring attack on the Union camps and Virgil Mathis's raid on the bowling alley. General Grant, drunk and furious, shoved the Southerners back to Corinth, where Mabel and Jet Beasley were married years later, when Mabel was still thin and good-looking. The next day, Mabel and Jet visited the battleground, and then Norma Jean was born, and then she married Leroy and they had a baby, which they lost, and now Leroy and Norma Jean are here at the same battleground. Leroy knows he is leaving out a lot. He is leaving out the insides of history. History was always just names and dates to him. It occurs to him that building a house out of logs is similarly empty—too simple. And the real inner workings of a marriage, like most of history, have escaped him. Now he sees that building a log house is the dumbest idea he could have had. It was clumsy of him to think Norma Jean would want a log house. It was a crazy idea. He'll have to think of something else, quickly. He will wad the blueprints into tight balls and fling them into the lake. Then he'll get moving again. He opens his eyes. Norma Jean has moved away and is walking through the cemetery, following a serpentine brick path.

Leroy gets up to follow his wife, but his good leg is asleep and his bad leg still hurts him. Norma Jean is far away, walking rapidly toward the bluff by the river, and he tries to hobble toward her. Some children run past him, screaming noisily. Norma Jean has reached the bluff, and she is looking out over the Tennessee River. Now she turns toward Leroy and waves her arms. Is she beckoning to him? She seems to be doing an exercise for her chest muscles. The sky is unusually pale—the color of the dust ruffle Mabel made for their bed.

QUESTIONS
1. Why does Norma Jean decide to leave Leroy? 2. Why does Norma Jean hide her smoking from her mother? 3. What is the significance of Shiloh?

WRITING TOPIC
Do you believe that Norma Jean is justified in leaving her husband? Explain.

LOVE
AND
HATE

Equestrian, 1931 by Marc Chagall

POETRY

Bonny Barbara Allan

ANONYMOUS

It was in and about the Martinmas[1] time,
 When the green leaves were a falling,
That Sir John Graeme, in the West Country,
 Fell in love with Barbara Allan.

He sent his man down through the town,
 To the place where she was dwelling:
"O haste and come to my master dear,
 Gin° ye be Barbara Allan."   *if*

O hooly,° hooly rose she up,   *slowly*
 To the place where he was lying,   10
And when she drew the curtain by:
 "Young man, I think you're dying."

"O it's I'm sick, and very, very sick,
 And 'tis a' for Barbara Allan."
"O the better for me ye s'° never be,   *ye shall*
 Though your heart's blood were a-spilling.

"O dinna° ye mind,° young man," said she,   *don't/remember*
 "When ye was in the tavern a drinking,
That ye made the healths gae° round and round,   *go*
 And slighted Barbara Allan?"   20

He turned his face unto the wall,
 And death was with him dealing:
"Adieu, adieu, my dear friends all,
 And be kind to Barbara Allan."

And slowly, slowly raise she up,
 And slowly, slowly left him,

Bonny Barbara Allan
 [1] November 11.

And sighing said, she could not stay,
   Since death of life had reft him.

She had not gane a mile but twa,
   When she heard the dead-bell ringing,   30
And every jow° that the dead-bell geid,°   stroke/gave
   It cried, "Woe to Barbara Allan!"

"O mother, mother, make my bed!
   O make it saft and narrow!
Since my love died for me to-day,
   I'll die for him to-morrow."

The Passionate Shepherd to His Love[1]

1600

CHRISTOPHER MARLOWE [1564–1593]

Come live with me and be my love,
And we will all the pleasures prove
That valleys, groves, hills, and fields,
Woods, or steepy mountain yields.

And we will sit upon the rocks,
Seeing the shepherds feed their flocks,
By shallow rivers to whose falls
Melodious birds sing madrigals.

And I will make thee beds of roses
And a thousand fragrant posies,   10
A cap of flowers, and a kirtle°   skirt
Embroidered all with leaves of myrtle;

The Passionate Shepherd . . .
  [1]This poem has elicited many responses over the centuries. Sir Walter Ralegh's early answer follows. C. Day Lewis's twentieth-century response appears on p. 454.

A gown made of the finest wool
Which from our pretty lambs we pull;
Fair lined slippers for the cold,
With buckles of the purest gold;

A belt of straw and ivy buds,
With coral clasps and amber studs:
And if these pleasures may thee move,
Come live with me, and be my love.   20

The shepherds' swains shall dance and sing
For thy delight each May morning:
If these delights thy mind may move,
Then live with me and be my love.

The Nymph's Reply
to the Shepherd   1600

SIR WALTER RALEGH   [1552?–1618][1]

If all the world and love were young,
And truth in every shepherd's tongue,
These pretty pleasures might me move
To live with thee and be thy love.

Time drives the flocks from field to fold
When rivers rage and rocks grow cold,
And Philomel° becometh dumb;   the nightingale
The rest complains of cares to come.

The flowers do fade, and wanton fields
To wayward winter reckoning yields;   10
A honey tongue, a heart of gall,
Is fancy's spring, but sorrow's fall.

---

[1] Chronology has been dispensed with here to facilitate comparison with Marlowe's "Passionate Shepherd."

Thy gowns, thy shoes, thy beds of roses,
Thy cap, thy kirtle, and thy posies
Soon break, soon wither, soon forgotten—
In folly ripe, in reason rotten.

Thy belt of straw and ivy buds,
Thy coral clasps and amber studs,
All these in me no means can move
To come to thee and be thy love.   20

But could youth last and love still breed,
Had joys no date° nor age no need,   end
Then these delights my mind might move
To live with thee and be thy love.

Sonnets   1609

WILLIAM SHAKESPEARE [1564–1616]

18

Shall I compare thee to a summer's day?
Thou art more lovely and more temperate:
Rough winds do shake the darling buds of May,
And summer's lease hath all too short a date:
Sometime too hot the eye of heaven shines,
And often is his gold complexion dimmed;
And every fair from fair sometimes declines,
By chance or nature's changing course untrimmed;
But thy eternal summer shall not fade,
Nor lose possession of that fair thou ow'st,°   ownest
Nor shall death brag thou wander'st in his shade,
When in eternal lines to time thou grow'st: 11
   So long as men can breathe, or eyes can see,
   So long lives this, and this gives life to thee.

QUESTIONS

1. Why does the poet argue that "a summer's day" is an inappropriate metaphor for his beloved? **2.** What is "this" in line 14?

29

When, in disgrace with fortune and men's eyes,
I all alone beweep my outcast state
And trouble deaf heaven with my bootless cries
And look upon myself and curse my fate,
Wishing me like to one more rich in hope,
Featured like him, like him with friends possessed,
Desiring this man's art and that man's scope,
With what I most enjoy contented least;
Yet in these thoughts myself almost despising,
Haply I think on thee, and then my state,   10
Like to the lark at break of day arising
From sullen earth, sings hymns at heaven's gate;
    For thy sweet love remembered such wealth brings
    That then I scorn to change my state with kings.

129

Th' expense of spirit in a waste of shame
Is lust in action; and till action, lust
Is perjured, murderous, bloody, full of blame,
Savage, extreme, rude, cruel, not to trust;
Enjoyed no sooner but despiséd straight;
Past reason hunted; and no sooner had,
Past reason hated, as a swallowed bait,
On purpose laid to make the taker mad:
Mad in pursuit, and in possession so;
Had, having, and in quest to have, extreme;   10
A bliss in proof,° and proved, a very woe;   experience
Before, a joy proposed; behind, a dream.
    All this the world well knows; yet none knows well
    To shun the heaven that leads men to this hell.

QUESTIONS
1. Paraphrase "Th' expense of spirit in a waste of shame / Is lust in action." **2.**
Describe the sound patterns and metrical variations in lines 3 and 4. What do they
contribute to the "sense" of the lines?

WRITING TOPIC
How do the sound patterns, the metrical variations, and the paradox in the final
couplet contribute to the sense of this sonnet?

130

My mistress' eyes are nothing like the sun;
Coral is far more red than her lips' red;
If snow be white, why then her breasts are dun;
If hairs be wires, black wires grow on her head.
I have seen roses damasked,° red and white,   variegated
But no such roses see I in her cheeks;
And in some perfumes is there more delight
Than in the breath that from my mistress reeks.
I love to hear her speak, yet well I know
That music hath a far more pleasing sound;   10
I grant I never saw a goddess go;
My mistress, when she walks, treads on the ground.
    And yet, by heaven, I think my love as rare
    As any she belied with false compare.[1]

I Care Not for These Ladies   1601

THOMAS CAMPION [1567–1620]

I care not for these ladies,
That must be wooed and prayed:
Give me kind Amaryllis,[1]
The wanton country maid.
Nature art disdaineth,
Her beauty is her own.
    Her when we court and kiss,
    She cries, "Forsooth, let go!"
    But when we come where comfort is,
    She never will say no.   10

If I love Amaryllis,
She gives me fruit and flowers:
But if we love these ladies,
We must give golden showers.
Give them gold, that sell love,
Give me the nut-brown lass,

Sonnet 130
   [1] I.e., as any woman misrepresented with false comparisons.
I Care Not for These Ladies
   [1] A conventional name for a country girl in pastoral poetry.

Who, when we court and kiss,
She cries, "Forsooth, let go!"
But when we come where comfort is,
She never will say no.   20

These ladies must have pillows,
And beds by strangers wrought;
Give me a bower of willows,
Of moss and leaves unbought,
And fresh Amaryllis,
With milk and honey fed;

Who, when we court and kiss,
She cries, "Forsooth, let go!"
But when we come where comfort is,
She never will say no.   30

A Valediction: Forbidding Mourning

1633

JOHN DONNE   [1572–1631]

As virtuous men pass mildly away,
    And whisper to their souls to go,
Whilst some of their sad friends do say
    The breath goes now, and some say, No;

So let us melt, and make no noise,
    No tear-floods, nor sigh-tempests move,
'Twere profanation of our joys
    To tell the laity our love.

Moving of th' earth° brings harms and fears,   earthquake
    Men reckon what it did and meant;   10
But trepidation of the spheres,
    Though greater far, is innocent.[1]

A Valediction: Forbidding Mourning
    [1] The movement of the heavenly spheres is harmless.

Dull sublunary° lovers' love   under the moon
  (Whose soul is sense) cannot admit
Absence, because it doth remove
  Those things which elemented it.

But we by a love so much refined
  That our selves know not what it is,
Inter-assuréd of the mind,
  Care less, eyes, lips, and hands to miss.   20

Our two souls therefore, which are one,
  Though I must go, endure not yet
A breach, but an expansion,
  Like gold to airy thinness beat.

If they be two, they are two so
  As stiff twin compasses are two;
Thy soul, the fixed foot, makes no show
  To move, but doth, if th' other do.

And though it in the center sit,
  Yet when the other far doth roam,   30
It leans and harkens after it,
  And grows erect, as that comes home.

Such wilt thou be to me, who must
  Like th' other foot, obliquely run;
Thy firmness makes my circle just,
  And makes me end where I begun.

QUESTIONS
1. Two kinds of love are described in this poem—spiritual and physical. How does the simile drawn in the first two stanzas help define the differences between them? **2.** How does the contrast between earthquakes and the movement of the spheres in stanza three further develop the contrast between the two types of lovers? **3.** Explain the comparison between a drawing compass and the lovers in the last three stanzas.

Go, Lovely Rose!   1645

EDMUND WALLER   [1606–1687]

   Go, lovely rose!
Tell her that wastes her time and me
   That now she knows,
When I resemble° her to thee,   compare
How sweet and fair she seems to be.

   Tell her that's young,
And shuns to have her graces spied,
   That hadst thou sprung
In deserts, where no men abide,
Thou must have uncommended died.   10

   Small is the worth
Of beauty from the light retired;
   Bid her come forth,
Suffer herself to be desired,
And not blush so to be admired.

   Then die! that she
The common fate of all things rare
   May read in thee;
How small a part of time they share
That are so wondrous sweet and fair!   20

To His Coy Mistress   1681

ANDREW MARVELL   [1621–1678]

   Had we but world enough, and time,
This coyness, lady, were no crime.
We would sit down, and think which way
To walk, and pass our long love's day.
Thou by the Indian Ganges' side
Shouldst rubies find; I by the tide
Of Humber would complain. I would
Love you ten years before the flood,
And you should, if you please, refuse
Till the conversion of the Jews.   10

My vegetable love should grow
Vaster than empires and more slow;
An hundred years should go to praise
Thine eyes, and on thy forehead gaze;
Two hundred to adore each breast,
But thirty thousand to the rest;
An age at least to every part,
And the last age should show your heart.
For, lady, you deserve this state,
Nor would I love at lower rate.   20
  But at my back I always hear
Time's wingéd chariot hurrying near;
And yonder all before us lie
Deserts of vast eternity.
Thy beauty shall no more be found,
Nor, in thy marble vault, shall sound
My echoing song; then worms shall try
That long-preserved virginity,
And your quaint honor turn to dust,
And into ashes all my lust: 30
The grave's a fine and private place,
But none, I think, do there embrace.
  Now therefore, while the youthful hue
Sits on thy skin like morning dew,
And while thy willing soul transpires
At every pore with instant fires,
Now let us sport us while we may,
And now, like amorous birds of prey,
Rather at once our time devour   39
Than languish in his slow-chapped° power.   slow-jawed
Let us roll our strength and all
Our sweetness up into one ball,
And tear our pleasures with rough strife
Thorough the iron gates of life:
Thus, though we cannot make our sun
Stand still, yet we will make him run.

QUESTIONS
1. State the argument of the poem (see ll. 1–2, 21–22, 33–34). **2.** Compare the figures of speech in the first verse paragraph with those in the last. How do they differ? **3.** Characterize the attitude toward life recommended by the poet.

WRITING TOPIC
In what ways does the conception of love in this poem differ from that in Donne's "A Valediction: Forbidding Mourning" (p. 441)? In your discussion consider the imagery in both poems.

A Poison Tree

1794

WILLIAM BLAKE [1757–1827]

I was angry with my friend:
I told my wrath, my wrath did end.
I was angry with my foe:
I told it not, my wrath did grow.

And I watered it in fears,
Night & morning with my tears;
And I sunnéd it with smiles,
And with soft deceitful wiles.

And it grew both day and night,
Till it bore an apple bright.
And my foe beheld it shine,
And he knew that it was mine,

And into my garden stole,
When the night had veil'd the pole;
In the morning glad I see
My foe outstretched beneath the tree.

QUESTIONS
1. Is anything gained from the parallel readers might draw between this tree and the tree in the Garden of Eden? Explain. **2.** Can you articulate what the "poison" is? **3.** Does your own experience verify the first stanza of the poem?

A Red, Red Rose

1796

ROBERT BURNS [1759–1796]

O My Luve's like a red, red rose,
 That's newly sprung in June;
O My Luve's like a melodie
 That's sweetly played in tune.

As fair art thou, my bonnie lass,
 So deep in luve am I;
And I will luve thee still, my dear,
 Till a' the seas gang dry.

Till a' the seas gang dry, my dear,
    And the rocks melt wi' the sun: 10
O I will love thee still, my dear,
    While the sands o' life shall run.

And fare thee weel, my only luve,
    And fare thee weel awhile!
And I will come again, my luve,
    Though it were ten thousand mile.

Dover Beach*   1867

MATTHEW ARNOLD [1822–1888]

The sea is calm tonight.
The tide is full, the moon lies fair
Upon the straits; on the French coast the light
Gleams and is gone; the cliffs of England stand,
Glimmering and vast, out in the tranquil bay.
Come to the window, sweet is the night-air!
Only, from the long line of spray
Where the sea meets the moon-blanched land,
Listen! you hear the grating roar
Of pebbles which the waves draw back, and fling,   10
At their return, up the high strand,
Begin, and cease, and then again begin,
With tremulous cadence slow, and bring
The eternal note of sadness in.

Sophocles long ago
Heard it on the Aegean, and it brought
Into his mind the turbid ebb and flow
Of human misery; we
Find also in the sound a thought,
Hearing it by this distant northern sea.   20

The Sea of Faith
Was once, too, at the full, and round earth's shore

---

*This poem is considered in detail in the appendix "Three Critical Approaches: Formalist, Sociological, Psychoanalytic" at the end of the book.

Lay like the folds of a bright girdle furled.
But now I only hear
Its melancholy, long, withdrawing roar,
Retreating, to the breath
Of the night-wind, down the vast edges drear
And naked shingles° of the world.   pebble beaches

Ah, love, let us be true
To one another! for the world, which seems   30
To lie before us like a land of dreams,
So various, so beautiful, so new,
Hath really neither joy, nor love, nor light,
Nor certitude, nor peace, nor help for pain;
And we are here as on a darkling plain
Swept with confused alarms of struggle and flight,
Where ignorant armies clash by night.

Mine Enemy Is
Growing Old   (ca. 1881)

EMILY DICKINSON   [1830–1886]

Mine Enemy is growing old—
I have at last Revenge—
The Palate of the Hate departs—
If any would avenge

Let him be quick—the Viand flits—
It is a faded Meat—
Anger as soon as fed is dead—
'Tis starving makes it fat—

QUESTION
1. Explain the paradox contained in the last two lines.

WRITING TOPIC
Compare this poem with Blake's "A Poison Tree" (p. 445).

Pied Beauty   1877

GERARD MANLEY HOPKINS [1844–1889]

Glory be to God for dappled things—
　For skies of couple-colour as a brinded° cow;   brindled
　　For rose-moles all in stipple upon trout that swim;
Fresh-firecoal chestnut-falls,[1] finches' wings;
　Landscape plotted and pieced[2]—fold, fallow, and plough;
　　And all trades, their gear and tackle, and trim.°   equipment
All things counter,° original, spare, strange;   contrasted
　Whatever is fickle, freckled (who knows how?)
　　With swift, slow; sweet, sour; adazzle, dim;
He fathers-forth whose beauty is past change: 10
　　　　　Praise him.

Fire and Ice   1923

ROBERT FROST [1874–1963]

Some say the world will end in fire,
Some say in ice,
From what I've tasted of desire
I hold with those who favor fire.
But if it had to perish twice,
I think I know enough of hate
To say that for destruction ice
Is also great
And would suffice.

The Love Song
of J. Alfred Prufrock   1917

T. S. ELIOT [1888–1965]

*S'io credessi che mia risposta fosse
a persona che mai tornasse al mondo,
questa fiamma staria senza più scosse.
Ma per ciò che giammai di questo fondo*

Pied Beauty
　[1] Fallen chestnuts, with the outer husks removed, colored like fresh fire coal.
　[2] Reference to the variegated pattern of land put to different uses.

non tornò vivo alcun, s'i'odo il vero,
senza tema d'infamia ti rispondo. [1]

Let us go then, you and I,
When the evening is spread out against the sky
Like a patient etherized upon a table;
Let us go, through certain half-deserted streets,
The muttering retreats
Of restless nights in one-night cheap hotels
And sawdust restaurants with oyster shells:
Streets that follow like a tedious argument
Of insidious intent
To lead you to an overwhelming question . . .   10
Oh, do not ask, "What is it?"
Let us go and make our visit.

In the room the women come and go
Talking of Michelangelo.

The yellow fog that rubs its back upon the windowpanes,
The yellow smoke that rubs its muzzle on the windowpanes,
Licked its tongue into the corners of the evening,
Lingered upon the pools that stand in drains,
Let fall upon its back the soot that falls from chimneys,
Slipped by the terrace, made a sudden leap,   20
And seeing that it was a soft October night,
Curled once about the house, and fell asleep.

And indeed there will be time
For the yellow smoke that slides along the street,
Rubbing its back upon the windowpanes;
There will be time, there will be time
To prepare a face to meet the faces that you meet;
There will be time to murder and create,
And time for all the works and days of hands
That lift and drop a question on your plate;   30
Time for you and time for me,
And time yet for a hundred indecisions,
And for a hundred visions and revisions,
Before the taking of a toast and tea.

. . . *Prufrock*
  [1] From Dante, *Inferno,* XXVII, 61–66. The speaker is Guido da Montefeltro, who is imprisoned
in a flame in the level of Hell reserved for false counselors. He tells Dante and Virgil, "If I thought
my answer were given to one who might return to the world, this flame would stay without further
movement. But since from this depth none has ever returned alive, if what I hear is true, I answer
you without fear of infamy."

In the room the women come and go
Talking of Michelangelo.

And indeed there will be time
To wonder, "Do I dare?" and, "Do I dare?"
Time to turn back and descend the stair,
With a bald spot in the middle of my hair—   40
(They will say: "How his hair is growing thin!")
My morning coat, my collar mounting firmly to the chin,
My necktie rich and modest, but asserted by a simple pin—
(They will say: "But how his arms and legs are thin!")
Do I dare
Disturb the universe?
In a minute there is time
For decisions and revisions which a minute will reverse.

For I have known them all already, known them all—
Have known the evenings, mornings, afternoons,   50
I have measured out my life with coffee spoons;
I know the voices dying with a dying fall
Beneath the music from a farther room.
      So how should I presume?

And I have known the eyes already, known them all—
The eyes that fix you in a formulated phrase,
And when I am formulated, sprawling on a pin,
When I am pinned and wriggling on the wall,
Then how should I begin
To spit out all the butt-ends of my days and ways?   60
      And how should I presume?

And I have known the arms already, known them all—
Arms that are braceleted and white and bare
(But in the lamplight, downed with light brown hair!)
Is it perfume from a dress
That makes me so digress?
Arms that lie along a table, or wrap about a shawl.
      And should I then presume?
      And how should I begin?

                  .   .   .   .   .

Shall I say, I have gone at dusk through narrow streets   70
And watched the smoke that rises from the pipes
Of lonely men in shirt-sleeves, leaning out of windows? . . .

I should have been a pair of ragged claws
Scuttling across the floors of silent seas.

        .   .   .   .   .

And the afternoon, the evening, sleeps so peacefully!
Smoothed by long fingers,
Asleep . . . tired . . . or it malingers,
Stretched on the floor, here beside you and me.
Should I, after tea and cakes and ices,
Have the strength to force the moment to its crisis?   80
But though I have wept and fasted, wept and prayed,
Though I have seen my head (grown slightly bald) brought in
    upon a platter,[2]
I am no prophet—and here's no great matter;
I have seen the moment of my greatness flicker,
And I have seen the eternal Footman hold my coat, and snicker,
And in short, I was afraid.

And would it have been worth it, after all,
After the cups, the marmalade, the tea,
Among the porcelain, among some talk of you and me,
Would it have been worth while,   90
To have bitten off the matter with a smile,
To have squeezed the universe into a ball
To roll it toward some overwhelming question,
To say: "I am Lazarus,[3] come from the dead,
Come back to tell you all, I shall tell you all"—
If one, settling a pillow by her head,
    Should say: "That is not what I meant at all.
    That is not it, at all."

And would it have been worth it, after all,
Would it have been worth while,   100
After the sunsets and the dooryards and the sprinkled streets,
After the novels, after the teacups, after the skirts that trail along the floor—
And this, and so much more?—
It is impossible to say just what I mean!
But as if a magic lantern threw the nerves in patterns on a screen:
Would it have been worth while
If one, settling a pillow or throwing off a shawl,
And turning toward the window, should say:

---

[2] Like the head of John the Baptist. See Matthew 14:3–12.
[3] See John 11:1–14 and Luke 16:19–26.

"That is not it at all,
That is not what I meant, at all."   110

                    .   .   .   .   .

No! I am not Prince Hamlet, nor was meant to be;
Am an attendant lord, one that will do
To swell a progress,° start a scene or two,   state journey
Advise the prince; no doubt, an easy tool,
Deferential, glad to be of use,
Politic, cautious, and meticulous;
Full of high sentence,° but a bit obtuse;   sententiousness
At times, indeed, almost ridiculous—
Almost, at times, the Fool.

I grow old . . . I grow old . . .   120
I shall wear the bottoms of my trousers rolled.°   cuffed

Shall I part my hair behind? Do I dare to eat a peach?
I shall wear white flannel trousers, and walk upon the beach.
I have heard the mermaids singing, each to each.

I do not think that they will sing to me.
I have seen them riding seaward on the waves
Combing the white hair of the waves blown back
When the wind blows the water white and black.

We have lingered in the chambers of the sea
By sea-girls wreathed with seaweed red and brown   130
Till human voices wake us, and we drown.

QUESTIONS

1. This poem may be understood as a stream of consciousness passing through the mind of Prufrock. The "you and I" of line 1 may be different aspects of his personality. Or perhaps the "you and I" is parallel to Guido who speaks the epigraph and Dante to whom he tells the story that resulted in his damnation—hence, "you" is the reader and "I" is Prufrock. Apparently, Prufrock is on his way to a tea and is pondering his relationship with a certain woman. The poem is disjointed because it proceeds by psychological rather than logical stages. To what social class does Prufrock belong? How does Prufrock respond to the attitudes and values of his class? Does he change in the course of the poem?   **2.**   Line 92 provides a good example of literary allusion (see the last stanza of Marvell, "To His Coy Mistress," p. 443, especially ll. 41–42). How does an awareness of the allusion contribute to the reader's response to the stanza here?   **3.**   What might the song of the mermaids (l. 124) signify, and why does Prufrock think they will not sing to him (l. 125)?   **4.**   T. S. Eliot once said that some poetry "can communicate without being understood." Is this such a poem?

WRITING TOPIC

What sort of man is J. Alfred Prufrock? How does the poet establish his characteristics?

Love Is Not All   1931

EDNA ST. VINCENT MILLAY   [1892–1950]

[handwritten annotations: Elizabethan Sonnet / iambic pentameter; Love cannot save you.]

Love is not all: it is not meat nor drink
Nor slumber nor a roof against the rain;
Nor yet a floating spar to men that sink
And rise and sink and rise and sink again;
Love can not fill the thickened lung with breath,
Nor clean the blood, nor set the fractured bone; *[handwritten: yet you need it to live.]*
Yet many a man is making friends with death
Even as I speak, for lack of love alone.
It well may be that in a difficult hour, *[handwritten: in a difficult time]*
Pinned down by pain and moaning for release, *[handwritten: when you are in pain]*
Or nagged by want past resolution's power, *[handwritten: or want to resolve my past]*
I might be driven to sell your love for peace, *[handwritten: I might have to sell your love]*
Or trade the memory of this night for food.
It well may be. I do not think I would.

The Dream   1941

LOUISE BOGAN   [1897–1970]

O God, in the dream the terrible horse began
To paw at the air, and make for me with his blows.
Fear kept for thirty-five years poured through his mane,
And retribution equally old, or nearly, breathed through his nose.

Coward complete, I lay and wept on the ground
When some strong creature appeared, and leapt for the rein.
Another woman, as I lay half in a swound,
Leapt in the air, and clutched at the leather and chain.

Give him, she said, something of yours as a charm.
Throw him, she said, some poor thing you alone claim.   10
No, no, I cried, he hates me; he's out for harm,
And whether I yield or not, it is all the same.

But, like a lion in a legend, when I flung the glove
Pulled from my sweating, my cold right hand,
The terrible beast, that no one may understand,
Came.to my side, and put down his head in love.

QUESTIONS
1.   The "terrible horse" of the speaker's dream advances through "fear kept for
thirty-five years" while breathing "retribution" through his nose. What might the
speaker have done (or felt) to account for the horse's attack? In other words, what
might the aggressive horse symbolize?   **2.**   What is the significance of the strong
woman's advice?   **3.**   Explain the allusion to the "lion in a legend." What function
does the allusion serve in the poem?   **4.**   What might the flung glove symbolize?
Suggest some reasons to account for the assertion "that no one may understand" the
"terrible beast." What accounts for the transformation in the horse's behavior?

Song[1]   1935

C. DAY LEWIS   [1904–1972]

Come, live with me and be my love,
And we will all the pleasures prove
Of peace and plenty, bed and board,
That chance employment may afford.

I'll handle dainties on the docks
And thou shalt read of summer frocks:
At evening by the sour canals
We'll hope to hear some madrigals.

Care on thy maiden brow shall put
A wreath of wrinkles, and thy foot   10
Be shod with pain: not silken dress
But toil shall tire thy loveliness.

Hunger shall make thy modest zone
And cheat fond death of all but bone—
If these delights thy mind may move,
Then live with me and be my love.

Song
[1]See Christopher Marlowe's "The Passionate Shepherd to His Love," p. 436.

from
Five Songs   (1937)
W. H. AUDEN   [1907–1973]

That night when joy began
Our narrowest veins to flush,
We waited for the flash
Of morning's levelled gun.

But morning let us pass,
And day by day relief
Outgrew his nervous laugh,
Grows credulous of peace.

As mile by mile is seen
No trespasser's reproach,   10
And love's best glasses reach
No fields but are his own.

QUESTIONS
1. Describe the sound relationships among the last words in the lines of each stanza.
2. What is the controlling metaphor of the poem? **3.** Characterize the kind of love
suggested by the poem's controlling metaphor and figurative language.

My Papa's Waltz   1948
THEODORE ROETHKE   [1908–1963]

The whiskey on your breath
Could make a small boy dizzy;
But I hung on like death:
Such waltzing was not easy.

We romped until the pans
Slid from the kitchen shelf;
My mother's countenance
Could not unfrown itself.

The hand that held my wrist
Was battered on one knuckle;   10
At every step you missed
My right ear scraped a buckle.

You beat time on my head
With a palm caked hard by dirt,
Then waltzed me off to bed
Still clinging to your shirt.

QUESTIONS
1. Why is iambic trimeter an appropriate meter for this poem?   **2.**   Identify the
details that reveal the kind of person the father is.   **3.**   How would you characterize
the boy's feelings about his father? The father's about the boy?

WRITING TOPIC
Robert Hayden's "Those Winter Sundays" (p. 459), Ted Hughes's "Crow's First
Lesson" (p. 465), and Sylvia Plath's "Daddy" (p. 467) also deal with a child's feelings
about a parent. Compare one of them with this poem.

I Knew a Woman   1958

THEODORE ROETHKE   [1908–1963]

I knew a woman, lovely in her bones,
When small birds sighed, she would sigh back at them;
Ah, when she moved, she moved more ways than one:
The shapes a bright container can contain!
Of her choice virtues only gods should speak,
Or English poets who grew up on Greek
(I'd have them sing in chorus, cheek to cheek).

How well her wishes went! She stroked my chin,
She taught me Turn, and Counter-turn, and Stand;
She taught me Touch, that undulant white skin;   10
I nibbled meekly from her proffered hand;
She was the sickle; I, poor I, the rake,
Coming behind her for her pretty sake
(But what prodigious mowing we did make).

Love likes a gander, and adores a goose:
Her full lips pursed, the errant note to seize;

She played it quick, she played it light and loose;
My eyes, they dazzled at her flowing knees;
Her several parts could keep a pure repose,
Or one hip quiver with a mobile nose   20
(She moved in circles, and those circles moved).

Let seed be grass, and grass turn into hay:
I'm martyr to a motion not my own;
What's freedom for? To know eternity.
I swear she cast a shadow white as stone.
But who would count eternity in days?
These old bones live to learn her wanton ways:
(I measure time by how a body sways).

To a Child Born in
Time of Small War   1966

HELEN SORRELLS   [b. 1908]

Child, you were conceived in my upstairs room,
my girlhood all around. Later I spent
nights there alone imploring the traitor moon
to keep me childless still. I never meant
to bear you in this year of discontent.
Yet you were there in your appointed place,
remnant of leaving, of a sacrament.
Child, if I loved you then, it was to trace
on a cold sheet your likeness to his absent face.

In May we were still alone. That month your life   10
stirred in my dark, as if my body's core
grew quick with wings. I turned away, more wife
than mother still, unwilling to explore
the fact of you. There was an orient shore,
a tide of hurt, that held my heart and mind.
It was as if you lived behind a door
I was afraid to open, lest you bind
my breaking. Lost in loss, I was not yours to find.

I swelled with summer. You were hard and strong,
making me know you were there. When the mail   20

brought me no letter, and the time was long
between the war's slow gains, and love seemed frail,
I fought you. You were error, judgment, jail.
Without you, there were ways I, too, could fight
a war. Trapped in your growing, I would rail
against your grotesque carriage, swollen, tight.
I would have left you, and I did in dreams of flight.

Discipline of the seasons brought me round.
Earth comes to term and so, in time, did we.
You are a living thing of sight and sound.   30
Nothing of you is his, you are all of me:
your sex, gray eye, the struggle to be free
that made your birth like death, but I awake
for that caught air, your cry. I try to see,
but cannot, the same lift his eyebrows take.
Child, if I love you now, it is for your own sake.

One Art   1976

ELIZABETH BISHOP [1911–1979]

The art of losing isn't hard to master;
so many things seem filled with the intent
to be lost that their loss is no disaster.

Lose something every day. Accept the fluster
of lost door keys, the hour badly spent.
The art of losing isn't hard to master.

Then practice losing farther, losing faster:
places, and names, and where it was you meant
to travel. None of these will bring disaster.

I lost my mother's watch. And look! my last, or   10
next-to-last, of three loved houses went.
The art of losing isn't hard to master.

I lost two cities, lovely ones. And, vaster,
some realms I owned, two rivers, a continent.
I miss them, but it wasn't a disaster.

—Even losing you (the joking voice, a gesture
I love) I shan't have lied. It's evident
the art of losing's not too hard to master
though it may look like (*Write* it!) like disaster.

Those Winter Sundays   1975

ROBERT HAYDEN   [1913–1980]

Sundays too my father got up early
and put his clothes on in the blueblack cold,
then with cracked hands that ached
from labor in the weekday weather made
banked fires blaze. No one ever thanked him.

I'd wake and hear the cold splintering, breaking.
When the rooms were warm, he'd call,
and slowly I would rise and dress,
fearing the chronic angers of that house,

Speaking indifferently to him,   10
who had driven out the cold
and polished my good shoes as well.
What did I know, what did I know
of love's austere and lonely offices?

A Late Aubade   1968

RICHARD WILBUR   [b. 1921]

You could be sitting now in a carrel
Turning some liver-spotted page,
Or rising in an elevator-cage
Toward Ladies' Apparel.

You could be planting a raucous bed
Of salvia, in rubber gloves,
Or lunching through a screed of someone's loves
With pitying head,

Or making some unhappy setter
Heel, or listening to a bleak   10
Lecture on Schoenberg's serial technique.[1]
Isn't this better?

Think of all the time you are not
Wasting, and would not care to waste,
Such things, thank God, not being to your taste.
Think what a lot

Of time, by woman's reckoning,
You've saved, and so may spend on this,
You who had rather lie in bed and kiss
Than anything.   20

It's almost noon, you say? If so,
Time flies, and I need not rehearse
The rosebuds-theme of centuries of verse.[2]
If you *must* go,

Wait for a while, then slip downstairs
And bring us up some chilled white wine,
And some blue cheese, and crackers, and some fine
Ruddy-skinned pears.

QUESTIONS
1. Explain the title. **2.** Is the speaker a sexist? Explain. **3.** Explain lines 16–18.

The Dover Bitch   1968

A CRITICISM OF LIFE

ANTHONY HECHT   [b. 1923]

So there stood Matthew Arnold and this girl
With the cliffs of England crumbling away behind them,

A *Late Aubade*
  [1] Arnold Schoenberg (1874–1951), Austrian born composer.
  [2] The *Carpe Diem* theme (see Glossary of Literary Terms).

And he said to her, "Try to be true to me,
And I'll do the same for you, for things are bad
All over, etc., etc."
Well now, I knew this girl. It's true she had read
Sophocles in a fairly good translation
And caught that bitter allusion to the sea,
But all the time he was talking she had in mind
The notion of what his whiskers would feel like   10
On the back of her neck. She told me later on
That after a while she got to looking out
At the lights across the channel, and really felt sad,
Thinking of all the wine and enormous beds
And blandishments in French and the perfumes.
And then she got really angry. To have been brought
All the way down from London, and then be addressed
As sort of a mournful cosmic last resort
Is really tough on a girl, and she was pretty.
Anyway, she watched him pace the room   20
And finger his watch-chain and seem to sweat a bit,
And then she said one or two unprintable things.
But you mustn't judge her by that. What I mean to say is,
She's really all right. I still see her once in a while
And she always treats me right. We have a drink
And I give her a good time, and perhaps it's a year
Before I see her again, but there she is,
Running to fat, but dependable as they come,
And sometimes I bring her a bottle of *Nuit d'Amour*.

QUESTIONS

1. This poem is a response to Matthew Arnold's "Dover Beach," which appears on p. 446. Arnold's poem is often read as a pained response to the breakdown of religious tradition and social and political order in the mid-nineteenth century. Is this poem, in contrast, optimistic? Is the relationship between the speaker and the girl at the end of the poem admirable? Explain.   **2.**   Do you suppose Hecht was moved to write this poem out of admiration for "Dover Beach"? Explain.

WRITING TOPIC

What is the fundamental difference between the speaker's conception of love in Arnold's poem and the "girl's" conception of love as reported in this poem?

The Mutes

1967

DENISE LEVERTOV [b. 1923]

Those groans men use
passing a woman on the street
or on the steps of the subway

to tell her she is a female
and their flesh knows it,

are they a sort of tune,
an ugly enough song, sung
by a bird with a slit tongue

but meant for music?

Or are they the muffled roaring   10
of deafmutes trapped in a building that is
slowly filling with smoke?

Perhaps both.

Such men most often
look as if groan were all they could do,
yet a woman, in spite of herself,

knows it's a tribute:
if she were lacking all grace
they'd pass her in silence:

so it's not only to say she's   20
a warm hole. It's a word

in grief-language, nothing to do with
primitive, not an ur-language[1];
language stricken, sickened, cast down

in decrepitude. She wants to

The Mutes
[1] Primordial language.

throw the tribute away, disgusted, and can't,

it goes on buzzing in her ear,
it changes the pace of her walk,
the torn posters in echoing corridors   30

spell it out, it
quakes and gnashes as the train comes in.
Her pulse sullenly

had picked up speed,
but the cars slow down and
jar to a stop while her understanding

keeps on translating:
'Life after life after life goes by

without poetry,
without seemliness,   40
without love.'

QUESTIONS
1. Explain the title. **2.** Why does the tribute go on "buzzing in her ear" (l. 28)? **3.** Is this poem an attack on men? Explain.

Bitch   1984

CAROLYN KIZER [b. 1925]

Now, when he and I meet, after all these years,
I say to the bitch inside me, don't start growling.
He isn't a trespasser anymore,
Just an old acquaintance tipping his hat.
My voice says, "Nice to see you,"
As the bitch starts to bark hysterically.
He isn't an enemy now,
Where are your manners, I say, as I say,
"How are the children? They must be growing up."
At a kind word from him, a look like the old days,   10
The bitch changes her tone: she begins to whimper.

She wants to snuggle up to him, to cringe.
Down, girl! Keep your distance
Or I'll give you a taste of the choke-chain.
"Fine, I'm just fine," I tell him.
She slobbers and grovels.
After all, I am her mistress. She is basically loyal.
It's just that she remembers how she came running
Each evening, when she heard his step;
How she lay at his feet and looked up adoringly   20
Though he was absorbed in his paper;
Or, bored with her devotion, ordered her to the kitchen
Until he was ready to play.
But the small careless kindnesses
When he'd had a good day, or a couple of drinks,
Come back to her now, seem more important
Than the casual cruelties, the ultimate dismissal.
"It's nice to know you are doing so well," I say.
He couldn't have taken you with him;
You were too demonstrative, too clumsy,   30
Not like the well-groomed pets of his new friends.
"Give my regards to your wife," I say. You gag
As I drag you off by the scruff,
Saying, "Goodbye! Goodbye! Nice to have seen you again."

QUESTIONS

1.   Who is being addressed in lines 13 and 14?   **2.**   In what ways does the title suit
the poem? Consider the tone of "Bitch," as well as the many connotations of the
word, in answering this question.   **3.**   What is "the ultimate dismissal" referred to
in line 27?   **4.**   How would you describe the speaker's present feelings about her
former relationship?

Living in Sin   1955

ADRIENNE RICH   [b. 1929]

She had thought the studio would keep itself;
no dust upon the furniture of love.
Half heresy, to wish the taps less vocal,
the panes relieved of grime. A plate of pears,
a piano with a Persian shawl, a cat
stalking the picturesque amusing mouse
had risen at his urging.
Not that at five each separate stair would writhe

under the milkman's tramp; that morning light
so coldly would delineate the scraps   10
of last night's cheese and three sepulchral bottles;
that on the kitchen shelf among the saucers
a pair of beetle-eyes would fix her own—
Envoy from some village in the moldings . . .
Meanwhile, he, with a yawn,
sounded a dozen notes upon the keyboard,
declared it out of tune, shrugged at the mirror,
rubbed at his beard, went out for cigarettes;
while she, jeered by the minor demons,
pulled back the sheets and made the bed and found   20
a towel to dust the table-top,
and let the coffee-pot boil over on the stove.
By evening she was back in love again,
though not so wholly but throughout the night
she woke sometimes to feel the daylight coming
like a relentless milkman up the stairs.

Crow's First Lesson[1]   1970

TED HUGHES   [b. 1930]

God tried to teach Crow how to talk.
"Love," said God. "Say, Love."
Crow gaped, and the white shark crashed into the sea
And went rolling downwards, discovering its own depth.

"No, no," said God, "Say Love, Now try it. LOVE."
Crow gaped, and a bluefly, a tsetse, a mosquito
Zoomed out and down
To their sundry flesh-pots.

"A final try," said God. "Now, LOVE."
Crow convulsed, gaped, retched and   10
Man's bodiless prodigious head
Bulbed out onto the earth, with swivelling eyes,
Jabbering protest—

Crow's First Lesson
   [1] In Hughes's collection of poems about him, Crow seems to be a supernatural demigod, combining human and animal traits. His exploits form a kind of creation myth.

And Crow retched again, before God could stop him.
And woman's vulva dropped over man's neck and tightened.
The two struggled together on the grass.
God struggled to part them, cursed, wept—

Crow flew guiltily off.

The ABC of Aerobics 1987

PETER MEINKE [b. 1932]

Air seeps through alleys and our diaphragms
balloon blackly with this mix of
carbon monoxide and the thousand corrosives a city
doles out free to its constituents;
everyone's jogging through Edgemont Park,
frightened by death and fatty tissue,
gasping at the maximal heart rate,
hoping to outlive all the others streaming
in the lanes like lemmings lurching toward their last
jump. I join in despair   10
knowing my arteries jammed with
lint and tobacco, lard and bourbon—my
medical history a noxious marsh:
newts and moles slink through the sodden veins,
owls hoot in the lungs' dark branches;
probably I shall keel off the john like
queer Uncle George and lie on the bathroom floor
raging about Shirley Clark, my true love in
seventh grade, God bless her wherever she lives
tied to that turkey who hugely   20
undervalues the beauty of her tiny earlobes, one
view of which (either one: they are both perfect)
would add years to my life, and I could skip these
X-rays, turn in my insurance card, and trade
yoga and treadmills and jogging and zen and
zucchini for drinking and dreaming of her, breathing hard.

QUESTIONS
1. Who is "that turkey" (l. 20)? **2.** What is the tone of the poem? Identify some devices the poet uses to achieve that tone. **3.** Is this a poem about environmental pollution? Explain.

suicide – life was difficult for her

Daddy

1965

SYLVIA PLATH [1932–1963]

You do not do, you do not do
Any more, black shoe
In which I have lived like a foot
For thirty years, poor and white,
Barely daring to breathe or Achoo.

Daddy, I have had to kill you,
You died before I had time—
Marble-heavy, a bag full of God,
Ghastly statue with one grey toe
Big as a Frisco seal   10

Betrayed by his death.

And a head in the freakish Atlantic
Where it pours bean green over blue
In the waters off beautiful Nauset.
I used to pray to recover you.
Ach, du.[1]

she is in grips of "Electra Complex" no sex w/ father.

In the German tongue, in the Polish town
Scraped flat by the roller
Of wars, wars, wars.
But the name of the town is common.
My Polack friend   20

30 and calls father "Daddy"

Says there are a dozen or two.
So I never could tell where you
Put your foot, your root,
I never could talk to you.
The tongue stuck in my jaw.

It stuck in a barb wire snare.
Ich, ich, ich, ich,[2]
I could hardly speak.
I thought every German was you.
And the language obscene   30

Daddy
  [1] German for "Ah, you."
  [2] German for "I, I, I, I."

An engine, an engine
Chuffing me off like a Jew.
A Jew to Dachau, Auschwitz, Belsen.
I began to talk like a Jew.
I think I may well be a Jew.

The snows of the Tyrol, the clear beer of Vienna
Are not very pure or true.
With my gypsy ancestress and my weird luck
And my Taroc pack and my Taroc pack
I may be a bit of a Jew.   40

I have always been scared of *you*,
With your Luftwaffe,[3] your gobbledygoo.
And your neat moustache
And your Aryan eye, bright blue.
Panzer-man,[4] panzer-man, O You—

Not God but a swastika
So black no sky could squeak through.
Every woman adores a Fascist,
The boot in the face, the brute
Brute heart of a brute like you.   50

You stand at the blackboard, daddy,
In the picture I have of you,
A cleft in your chin instead of your foot
But no less a devil for that, no not
Any less the black man who

Bit my pretty red heart in two.
I was ten when they buried you.
At twenty I tried to die
And get back, back, back to you.
I thought even the bones would do.   60

But they pulled me out of the sack,
And they stuck me together with glue.
And then I knew what to do.
I made a model of you,
A man in black with a Meinkampf[5] look

---

[3] Name of the German air force during World War II.
[4] Panzer refers to German armored divisions during World War II.
[5] *My Struggle*, the title of Adolf Hitler's political autobiography.

And a love of the rack and the screw.
And I said I do, I do.
So daddy, I'm finally through.
The black telephone's off at the root,
The voices just can't worm through.

If I've killed one man, I've killed two—
The vampire who said he was you
And drank my blood for a year,
Seven years, if you want to know.
Daddy, you can lie back now.

There's a stake in your fat black heart
And the villagers never liked you.
They are dancing and stamping on you.
They always *knew* it was you.
Daddy, daddy, you bastard, I'm through.

[handwritten annotations: "The bell jar" 70 / her short novel. / Speaker is 30 years old / @ 10: Father dies / @ 20: Suicide attempt / then married for seven years 80 / (with life?) / emotional]

QUESTIONS

1. How do the allusions to Nazism function in the poem? **2.** Does the poem exhibit the speaker's love for her father or her hatred for him? Explain. **3.** What sort of man does the speaker marry (see stanzas 13 and 14)? **4.** How does the speaker characterize her husband and her father in the last two stanzas? Might the "Daddy" of the last line of the poem refer to something more than the speaker's father? Explain.

WRITING TOPIC

What is the effect of the peculiar structure, idiosyncratic rhyme, unusual words (such as *achoo, gobbledygoo*), and repetitions in the poem? What emotional associations does the title "Daddy" possess? Are those associations reinforced or contradicted by the poem?

Power[1]   1978

AUDRE LORDE [b. 1934]

The difference between poetry and rhetoric
is being
ready to kill
yourself
instead of your children.

I am trapped on a desert of raw gunshot wounds
and a dead child dragging his shattered black
face off the edge of my sleep
blood from his punctured cheeks and shoulders
is the only liquid for miles and my stomach   10
churns at the imagined taste while
my mouth splits into dry lips
without loyalty or reason
thirsting for the wetness of his blood
as it sinks into the whiteness
of the desert where I am lost
without imagery or magic
trying to make power out of hatred and destruction
trying to heal my dying son with kisses
only the sun will bleach his bones quicker.   20

The policeman who shot down a 10-year-old in Queens[2]
stood over the boy with his cop shoes in childish blood
and a voice said "Die you little motherfucker" and
there are tapes to prove that. At his trial
this policeman said in his own defense
"I didn't notice the size or nothing else
only the color." and
there are tapes to prove that, too.

Today that 37-year-old white man with 13 years of police forcing
has been set free   30
by 11 white men who said they were satisfied
justice had been done
and one black woman who said
"They convinced me" meaning
they had dragged her 4' 10" black woman's frame
over the hot coals of four centuries of white male approval
until she let go the first real power she ever had
and lined her own womb with cement
to make a graveyard for our children.

Power

[1] " 'Power' . . . is a poem written about Clifford Glover, the ten-year-old Black child shot by a cop who was acquitted by a jury on which a Black woman sat. In fact, the day I heard on the radio that O'Shea had been acquitted, I was going across town on Eighty-eighth Street and I had to pull over. A kind of fury rose up in me; the sky turned red. I felt so sick. I felt as if I would drive this car into a wall, into the next person I saw. So I pulled over. I took out my journal just to air some of my fury, to get it out of my fingertips. Those expressed feelings are that poem" (Audre Lorde, "My Words Will Be There," in Black Women Writers (1950–1980), ed. Mari Evans, New York, 1983, p. 266).

[2] Queens is a borough in New York City.

I have not been able to touch the destruction within me.   40
But unless I learn to use
the difference between poetry and rhetoric
my power too will run corrupt as poisonous mold
or lie limp and useless as an unconnected wire
and one day I will take my teenaged plug
and connect it to the nearest socket
raping an 85-year-old white woman
who is somebody's mother
and as I beat her senseless and set a torch to her bed
a greek chorus will be singing in ¾ time[3]   50
"Poor thing. She never hurt a soul. What beasts they are."

There Is a Girl Inside   1977

LUCILLE CLIFTON   [b. 1936]

there is a girl inside.
she is randy as a wolf.
she will not walk away
and leave these bones
to an old woman.

she is a green tree
in a forest of kindling.
she is a green girl
in a used poet.

                                                                            10
she has waited
patient as a nun
for the second coming,
when she can break through gray hairs
into blossom

and her lovers will harvest
honey and thyme
and the woods will be wild
with the damn wonder of it.

---

[3] In classical Greek tragedy, a chorus chanted in response to the action in the play. Three-quarter time is waltz rhythm.

QUESTIONS
1. Who is the "girl" of this poem? What is she "inside" of?   **2.** What are the "bones" of the first stanza? What does the speaker's statement that she will not defer to old women tell us about her?   **3.** Describe the prevailing metaphor of the poem?

WRITING TOPIC
Compare this poem with Helen Sorrells's "From a Correct Address in a Suburb of a Major City" (p. 274). What do the two speakers share? In what ways are they different?

Sex without Love   1984

SHARON OLDS   [b. 1942]

How do they do it, the ones who make love
without love? Beautiful as dancers,
gliding over each other like ice-skaters
over the ice, fingers hooked
inside each other's bodies, faces
red as steak, wine, wet as the
children at birth whose mothers are going to
give them away. How do they come to the
come to the   come to the   God   come to the
still waters, and not love   10
the one who came there with them, light
rising slowly as steam off their joined
skin? These are the true religious,
the purists, the pros, the ones who will not
accept a false Messiah, love the
priest instead of the God. They do not
mistake the lover for their own pleasure,
they are like great runners: they know they are alone
with the road surface, the cold, the wind,
the fit of their shoes, their over-all cardio-   20
vascular health—just factors, like the partner
in the bed, and not the truth, which is the
single body alone in the universe
against its own best time.

QUESTIONS
1. Characterize the speaker's attitude toward "the ones who make love without love."   **2.** Who are the "These" of line 13?   **3.** What is the effect of the repetitions in lines 8 and 9?   **4.** What does "factors" of line 21 refer to?   **5.** Put into your own words the "truth" referred to in the final three lines. Is the speaker using the word straightforwardly or ironically? Explain.

LOVE
AND
HATE

Judith and Her Maidservant with the Head of Holofernes, c. 1625 by Artemisia Gentileschi

DRAMA

Othello

WILLIAM SHAKESPEARE [1564–1616]

ca. 1604

CHARACTERS

Duke of Venice
Brabantio, a Senator
Senators
Gratiano, Brother to Brabantio
Lodovico, Kinsman to Brabantio
Othello, a noble Moor; in the service of the Venetian State
Cassio, his Lieutenant
Iago, his Ancient
Roderigo, a Venetian Gentleman
Montano, Othello's predecessor in the Government of Cyprus
Clown, Servant to Othello
Desdemona, Daughter to Brabantio, and Wife to Othello
Emilia, Wife to Iago
Bianca, Mistress to Cassio
Sailor, Officers, Gentlemen, Messengers, Musicians, Heralds, Attendants

SCENE

For the first Act, in Venice; during the rest of the Play, at a Sea-port in Cyprus

Act I

SCENE 1. Venice. A Street.

(Enter Roderigo and Iago.)

Roderigo. Tush! Never tell me; I take it much unkindly
    That thou, Iago, who hast had my purse
    As if the strings were thine, shouldst know of this.[1]

---

[1] I.e., Othello's successful courtship of Desdemona.

Iago.   'Sblood,[2] but you will not hear me:
  If ever I did dream of such a matter,
  Abhor me.
Roderigo.   Thou told'st me thou didst hold him[3] in thy hate.
Iago.   Despise me if I do not. Three great ones of the city,
  In personal suit to make me his lieutenant,
  Off-capp'd[4] to him; and, by the faith of man,   10
  I know my price, I am worth no worse a place;
  But he, as loving his own pride and purposes,
  Evades them, with a bombast circumstance[5]
  Horribly stuff'd with epithets of war;
  And, in conclusion,
  Nonsuits[6] my mediators;[7] for, 'Certes,'[8] says he,
  'I have already chosen my officer.'
  And what was he?
  Forsooth, a great arithmetician,
  One Michael Cassio, A Florentine,   20
  A fellow almost damn'd in a fair wife;[9]
  That never set a squadron in the field,
  Nor the division of a battle knows
  More than a spinster; unless[10] the bookish theoric,[11]
  Wherein the toged consuls can propose
  As masterly as he: mere prattle, without practice,
  Is all his soldiership. But he, sir, had the election;
  And I—of whom his eyes had seen the proof
  At Rhodes, at Cyprus, and on other grounds
  Christian and heathen—must be be-lee'd[12] and calm'd   30
  By debitor and creditor; this counter-caster,[13]
  He, in good time, must his lieutenant be,
  And I—God bless the mark!—his Moorship's ancient.[14]
Roderigo.   By heaven, I rather would have been his hangman.
Iago.   Why, there's no remedy: 'tis the curse of service,
  Preferment goes by letter and affection,
  Not by the old gradation,[15] where each second
  Stood heir to the first. Now, sir, be judge yourself,
  Whe'r[16] I in any just term am affin'd[17]
  To love the Moor.

---

[2] By God's blood.   [3] I.e., Othello.   [4] Took off their caps.   [5] Pompous wordiness, circumlocution.   [6] Turns down.   [7] Spokesmen.   [8] In truth.   [9] A much debated phrase. In the Italian source the Captain (i.e., Cassio) was married, and it may be that Shakespeare originally intended Bianca to be Cassio's wife but later changed his mind and failed to alter the phrase here accordingly. Or perhaps Iago simply sneers at Cassio as a notorious ladies' man.   [10] Except.   [11] Theory.   [12] Left without wind for my sails.   [13] Bookkeeper (cf. "arithmetician" above).   [14] Ensign (but Iago's position in the play seems to be that of Othello's aide-de-camp).   [15] Seniority.   [16] Whether.   [17] Obliged.

Roderigo.   I would not follow him then.   40
Iago.   O! sir, content you;
    I follow him to serve my turn upon him;
    We cannot all be masters, nor all masters
    Cannot be truly follow'd. You shall mark
    Many a duteous and knee-crooking knave,
    That, doting on his own obsequious bondage,
    Wears out his time, much like his master's ass,
    For nought but provender, and when he's old, cashier'd;
    Whip me such honest knaves. Others there are
    Who, trimm'd in forms and visages of duty,   50
    Keep yet their hearts attending on themselves,
    And, throwing but shows of service on their lords,
    Do well thrive by them, and when they have lin'd their coats
    Do themselves homage: these fellows have some soul;
    And such a one do I profess myself. For, sir,
    It is as sure as you are Roderigo,
    Were I the Moor, I would not be Iago:
    In following him, I follow but myself;
    Heaven is my judge, not I for love and duty,
    But seeming so, for my peculiar end: 60
    For when my outward action doth demonstrate
    The native act and figure of my heart
    In compliment extern,[18] 'tis not long after
    But I will wear my heart upon my sleeve
    For daws to peck at: I am not what I am.
Roderigo.   What a full fortune does the thick-lips owe,[19]
    If he can carry 't thus!
Iago.   Call up her father;
    Rouse him, make after him, poison his delight,
    Proclaim him in the streets, incense her kinsmen,
    And, though he in a fertile climate dwell,[20]   70
    Plague him with flies; though that his joy be joy,
    Yet throw such changes of vexation on 't
    As it may lose some colour.
Roderigo.   Here is her father's house; I'll call aloud.
Iago.   Do; with like timorous[21] accent and dire yell
    As when, by night and negligence, the fire
    Is spied in populous cities.
Roderigo.   What, ho! Brabantio: Signior Brabantio, ho!
Iago.   Awake! what, ho! Brabantio! thieves! thieves! thieves!
    Look to your house, your daughter, and your bags!   80
    Thieves! thieves!

---

[18] External show.   [19] Own.   [20] I.e., is fortunate.   [21] Frightening.

(Enter Brabantio, above, at a window.)

Brabantio. What is the reason of this terrible summons?
  What is the matter there?
Roderigo. Signior, is all your family within?
Iago. Are your doors lock'd?
Brabantio.   Why? wherefore ask you this?
Iago. 'Zounds![22] sir, you're robb'd; for shame, put on your gown;
  Your heart is burst, you have lost half your soul;
  Even now, now, very now, an old black ram
  Is tupping[23] your white ewe. Arise, arise!
  Awake the snorting[24] citizens with the bell,   90
  Or else the devil will make a grandsire of you.
  Arise, I say.
Brabantio.   What! have you lost your wits?
Roderigo. Most reverend signior, do you know my voice?
Brabantio. Not I, what are you?
Roderigo. My name is Roderigo.
Brabantio.   The worser welcome:
  I have charg'd thee not to haunt about my doors:
  In honest plainness thou hast heard me say
  My daughter is not for thee; and now, in madness,
  Being full of supper and distempering draughts,
  Upon malicious knavery dost thou come   100
  To start my quiet.
Roderigo. Sir, sir, sir!
Brabantio.   But thou must needs be sure
  My spirit and my place[25] have in them power
  To make this bitter to thee.
Roderigo.   Patience, good sir.
Brabantio. What tell'st thou me of robbing? this is Venice;
  My house is not a grange.[26]
Roderigo.   Most grave Brabantio,
  In simple and pure soul I come to you.
Iago. 'Zounds! sir, you are one of those that will not serve God if the devil
  bid you. Because we come to do you service and you think we are ruffians,
  you'll have your daughter covered with a Barbary horse; you'll have your
  nephews neigh to you; you'll have coursers for cousins and gennets[27] for
  germans.[28]
Brabantio. What profane wretch art thou?
Iago. I am one, sir, that comes to tell you, your daughter and the Moor are
  now making the beast with two backs.

---

[22] By God's wounds.   [23] Copulating.   [24] Snoring.   [25] Position.
[26] Isolated farm house.   [27] Spanish horses.   [28] Blood relations.

Brabantio.   Thou art a villain.

Iago.   You are—a senator.

Brabantio.   This thou shalt answer; I know thee, Roderigo.

Roderigo.   Sir, I will answer any thing. But, I beseech you,   120
If 't be your pleasure and most wise consent,—
As partly, I find, it is,—that your fair daughter,
At this odd-even[29] and dull watch o' the night,
Transported with no worse nor better guard
But with a knave of common hire, a gondolier,
To the gross clasps of a lascivious Moor,—
If this be known to you, and your allowance,[30]
We then have done you bold and saucy wrongs;
But if you know not this, my manners tell me
We have your wrong rebuke. Do not believe   130
That, from[31] the sense of all civility,
I thus would play and trifle with your reverence:
Your daughter, if you have not given her leave,
I say again, hath made a gross revolt;
Tying her duty, beauty, wit and fortunes
In[32] an extravagant[33] and wheeling stranger
Of here and every where. Straight satisfy yourself:
If she be in her chamber or your house,
Let loose on me the justice of the state
For thus deluding you.

Brabantio.   Strike on the tinder, ho!   140
Give me a taper! call up all my people!
This accident[34] is not unlike my dream;
Belief of it oppresses me already.
Light, I say! light!   (*Exit, from above.*)

Iago.   Farewell, for I must leave you:
It seems not meet nor wholesome to my place
To be produc'd,[35] as, if I stay, I shall,
Against the Moor; for I do know the state,
However this may gall him with some check,[36]
Cannot with safety cast him; for he's embark'd
With such loud reason to the Cyprus wars,—   150
Which even now stand in act,—that, for their souls,
Another of his fathom[37] they have none,
To lead their business; in which regard,
Though I do hate him as I do hell-pains,
Yet, for necessity of present life,

---

[29] Between night and morning.   [30] By your approval.   [31] Away from.   [32] To.
[33] Expatriate.   [34] Happening.   [35] I.e., as a witness.   [36] Restraining adversity.
[37] Caliber, ability.

I must show out a flag and sign of love,
Which is indeed but sign. That you shall surely find him,
Lead to the Sagittary[38] the raised search;
And there will I be with him. So, farewell. (*Exit.*)

(*Enter below, Brabantio, and servants with torches.*)

Brabantio. It is too true an evil: gone she is, 160
And what's to come of my despised time
Is nought but bitterness. Now, Roderigo,
Where didst thou see her? O, unhappy girl!
With the Moor, sayst thou? Who would be a father!
How didst thou know 'twas she? O, she deceives me
Past thought. What said she to you? Get more tapers!
Raise all my kindred! Are they married, think you?
Roderigo. Truly, I think they are.
Brabantio. O heaven! How got she out? O treason of the blood:
Fathers, from hence trust not your daughters' minds 170
By what you see them act. Are there not charms
By which the property of youth and maidhood
May be abus'd? Have you not read, Roderigo,
Of some such thing?
Roderigo. Yes, sir, I have indeed.
Brabantio. Call up my brother. O! that you had had her.
Some one way, some another! Do you know
Where we may apprehend her and the Moor?
Roderigo. I think I can discover him, if you please
To get good guard and go along with me. 180
Brabantio. Pray you, lead on. At every house I'll call;
I may command at most. Get weapons, ho!
And raise some special officers of night.
On, good Roderigo; I'll deserve[39] your pains. (*Exeunt.*)

SCENE 2. Another street.

(*Enter Othello, Iago, and Attendants, with torches.*)

Iago. Though in the trade of war I have slain men,
Yet do I hold it very stuff o' the conscience
To do no contriv'd murder: I lack iniquity
Sometimes to do me service. Nine or ten times
I had thought to have yerk'd[40] him here under the ribs.
Othello. 'Tis better as it is.

---

[38] The name of an inn(?). [39] I.e., reward. [40] Stabbed.

Iago.   Nay, but he prated,
And spoke such scurvy and provoking terms
Against your honour
That, with the little godliness I have,
I did full hard forbear him. But, I pray, sir,   10
Are you fast married? Be assur'd of this,
That the magnifico[41] is much belov'd,
And hath in his effect a voice potential
As double[42] as the duke's; he will divorce you,
Or put upon you what restraint and grievance
The law—with all his might to enforce it on—
Will give him cable.[43]
Othello.   Let him do his spite:
My services which I have done the signiory[44]
Shall out-tongue his complaints. 'Tis yet to know,[45]
Which when I know that boasting is an honour   20
I shall promulgate, I fetch my life and being
From men of royal siege, and my demerits[46]
May speak unbonneted[47] to as proud a fortune
As this[48] that I have reach'd; for know, Iago,
But that I love the gentle Desdemona,
I would not my unhoused[49] free condition
Put into circumscription and confine
For the sea's worth. But, look! what lights come yond?
Iago.   Those are the raised[50] father and his friends:
You were best[51] go in.
Othello.   Not I; I must be found: 30
My parts, my title, and my perfect[52] soul
Shall manifest me rightly. Is it they?
Iago.   By Janus,[53] I think no.

(Enter Cassio and certain Officers, with torches.)

Othello.   The servants of the duke, and my lieutenant.
The goodness of the night upon you, friends!
What is the news?
Cassio.   The duke does greet you, general,
And he requires your haste-post-haste appearance,
Even on the instant.

---

[41] One of the grandees, or rulers, of Venice; here, Brabantio. [42] Iago means that Brabantio's influence equals that of the Doge's with his double vote. [43] I.e., scope. [44] The Venetian government. [45] I.e., the signiory does not as yet know. [46] Merits. [47] I.e., as equals. [48] I.e., that of Desdemona's family. [49] Unconfined. [50] Aroused. [51] Had better. [52] Untroubled by a bad conscience. [53] The two-faced Roman god of portals and doors and (hence) of beginnings and ends.

Othello.   What is the matter, think you?

Cassio.   Something from Cyprus, as I may divine.
It is a business of some heat;[54] the galleys   40
Have sent a dozen sequent[55] messengers
This very night at one another's heels,
And many of the consuls,[56] rais'd and met,
Are at the duke's already. You have been hotly call'd for;
When, being not at your lodging to be found,
The senate hath sent about three several[57] quests
To search you out.

Othello.   'Tis well I am found by you.
I will but spend a word here in the house,
And go with you.   (*Exit.*)

Cassio.   Ancient, what makes he here?

Iago.   Faith, he to-night hath boarded a land carrack;[58]   50
If it prove lawful prize, he's made for ever.

Cassio.   I do not understand.

Iago.   He's married.

Cassio.   To who?

(*Re-enter Othello.*)

Iago.   Marry,[59] to—Come, captain, will you go?

Othello.   Have with you.

Cassio.   Here comes another troop to seek for you.

Iago.   It is Brabantio. General, be advis'd;
He comes to bad intent.

(*Enter Brabantio, Roderigo, and Officers, with torches and weapons.*)

Othello.   Holla! stand there!

Roderigo.   Signior, it is the Moor.

Brabantio.   Down with him, thief!

(*They draw on both sides.*)

Iago.   You, Roderigo! Come, sir, I am for you.[60]

Othello.   Keep up your bright swords, for the dew will rust them.
Good signior, you shall more command with years   60
Than with your weapons.

Brabantio.   O thou foul thief! where hast thou stow'd my daughter?
Damn'd as thou art, thou hast enchanted her;

---

[54] Urgency.   [55] Following one another.   [56] I.e., senators.   [57] Separate.
[58] Treasure ship.   [59] By the Virgin Mary.   [60] Let you and me fight.

For I'll refer me to all things of sense,
If she in chains of magic were not bound,
Whether a maid so tender, fair, and happy,
So opposite to marriage that she shunn'd
The wealthy curled darlings of our nation,
Would ever have, to incur a general mock,
Run from her guardage to the sooty bosom   70
Of such a thing as thou; to fear, not to delight.
Judge me the world, if 'tis not gross in sense[61]
That thou hast practis'd on her with foul charms,
Abus'd her delicate youth with drugs or minerals
That weaken motion:[62] I'll have 't disputed on;
'Tis probable, and palpable to thinking.
I therefore apprehend and do attach[63] thee
For an abuser of the world, a practiser
Of arts inhibited and out of warrant.[64]
Lay hold upon him: if he do resist,   80
Subdue him at his peril.
Othello.   Hold your hands,
Both you of my inclining,[65] and the rest:
Were it my cue to fight, I should have known it
Without a prompter. Where will you that I go
To answer this your charge?
Brabantio.   To prison; till fit time
Of law and course of direct session[66]
Call thee to answer.
Othello.   What if I do obey?
How may the duke be therewith satisfied,
Whose messengers are here about my side,
Upon some present[67] business of the state   90
To bring me to him?
Officer.   'Tis true, most worthy signior;
The duke's in council, and your noble self,
I am sure, is sent for.
Brabantio.   How! the duke in council!
In this time of the night! Bring him away.
Mine's not an idle cause: the duke himself,
Or any of my brothers of the state,[68]
Cannot but feel this wrong as 'twere their own;
For if such actions may have passage free,
Bond-slaves and pagans shall our statesmen be.   *(Exeunt.)*

---

[61] Obvious.   [62] Normal reactions.   [63] Arrest.   [64] Prohibited and illegal.   [65] Party.
[66] Normal process of law.   [67] Immediate, pressing.   [68] Fellow senators.

SCENE 3.   A Council Chamber.

(The Duke and Senators sitting at a table. Officers attending.)

Duke.   There is no composition[69] in these news
  That gives them credit.
First Senator.   Indeed, they are disproportion'd;
  My letters say a hundred and seven galleys.
Duke.   And mine, a hundred and forty.
Second Senator.   And mine, two hundred:
  But though they jump[70] not on a just[71] account,—
  As in these cases, where the aim[72] reports,
  'Tis oft with difference,—yet do they all confirm
  A Turkish fleet, and bearing up to Cyprus.
Duke.   Nay, it is possible enough to judgment:
  I do not so secure me in[73] the error,   10
  But the main article[74] I do approve[75]
  In fearful sense.
Sailor *(within)*.   What, ho! what, ho! what, ho!
Officer.   A messenger from the galleys.

(Enter a Sailor.)

Duke.   Now, what's the business?
Sailor.   The Turkish preparation makes for Rhodes;
  So was I bid report here to the state
  By Signior Angelo.
Duke.   How say you by this change?
First Senator.   This cannot be
  By no[76] assay[77] of reason; 'tis a pageant[78]
  To keep us in false gaze.[79] When we consider
  The importancy of Cyprus to the Turk,   20
  And let ourselves again but understand,
  That as it more concerns the Turk than Rhodes,
  So may he with more facile question bear[80] it,
  For that it stands not in such warlike brace,[81]
  But altogether lacks the abilities
  That Rhodes is dress'd in: if we make thought of this,
  We must not think the Turk is so unskilful
  To leave that latest which concerns him first,

---

[69] Consistency, agreement.   [70] Coincide.   [71] Exact.   [72] Conjecture.   [73] Draw
comfort from.   [74] Substance.   [75] Believe.   [76] Any.   [77] Test.
[78] (Deceptive) show.   [79] Looking in the wrong direction.   [80] More easily capture.
[81] State of defense.

Neglecting an attempt of ease and gain,
    To wake and wage a danger profitless.   30
Duke.   Nay, in all confidence, he's not for Rhodes.
Officer.   Here is more news.

(Enter a Messenger.)

Messenger.   The Ottomites,[82] reverend and gracious,
    Steering with due course toward the isle of Rhodes,
    Have there injointed[83] them with an after fleet.[84]
First Senator.   Ay, so I thought. How many, as you guess?
Messenger.   Of thirty sail; and now they do re-stem[85]
    Their backward course, bearing with frank appearance
    Their purposes toward Cyprus. Signior Montano,
    Your trusty and most valiant servitor,   40
    With his free duty[86] recommends[87] you thus,
    And prays you to believe him.
Duke.   'Tis certain then, for Cyprus.
    Marcus Luccicos, is not he in town?
First Senator.   He's now in Florence.
Duke.   Write from us to him; post-post-haste dispatch.
First Senator.   Here comes Brabantio and the valiant Moor.

(Enter Brabantio, Othello, Iago, Roderigo, and Officers.)

Duke.   Valiant Othello, we must straight employ you
    Against the general enemy Ottoman.
    (To Brabantio) I did not see you; welcome, gentle signior;   50
    We lack'd your counsel and your help to-night.
Brabantio.   So did I yours. Good your Grace, pardon me;
    Neither my place nor aught I heard of business
    Hath rais'd me from my bed, nor doth the general care
    Take hold of me, for my particular grief
    Is of so flood-gate[88] and o'erbearing nature
    That it engluts and swallows other sorrows
    And it is still itself.
Duke.   Why, what's the matter?
Brabantio.   My daughter! O! my daughter.
Duke. ⎫
Senators. ⎭   Dead?
Brabantio.   Ay, to me;
    She is abus'd, stol'n from me, and corrupted   60

---

[82] Turks.   [83] Joined.   [84] Fleet that followed after.   [85] Steer again.   [86] Unqualified expressions of respect.   [87] Informs.   [88] Torrential.

By spells and medicines bought of mountebanks;
For nature so preposterously to err,
Being not deficient, blind, or lame of sense,
Sans[89] witchcraft could not.
Duke.   Whoe'er he be that in this foul proceeding
Hath thus beguil'd your daughter of herself
And you of her, the bloody book of law
You shall yourself read in the bitter letter
After your own sense; yea, though our proper[90] son
Stood[91] in your action.[92]
Brabantio.   Humbly I thank your Grace.   70
Here is the man, this Moor; whom now, it seems,
Your special mandate for the state affairs
Hath hither brought.
Duke. }
Senators. }   We are very sorry for it.

Duke *(to Othello).*   What, in your own part, can you say to this?
Brabantio.   Nothing, but this is so.
Othello.   Most potent, grave, and reverend signiors,
My very noble and approv'd[93] good masters,
That I have ta'en away this old man's daughter,
It is most true; true, I have married her:
The very head and front of my offending   80
Hath this extent, no more. Rude am I in my speech,
And little bless'd with the soft phrase of peace;
For since these arms of mine had seven years' pith,[94]
Till now some nine moons wasted,[95] they have us'd
Their dearest action in the tented field;
And little of this great world can I speak,
More than pertains to feats of broil and battle;
And therefore little shall I grace my cause
In speaking for myself. Yet, by your gracious patience,
I will a round[96] unvarnish'd tale deliver   90
Of my whole course of love; what drugs, what charms,
What conjuration, and what mighty magic,
For such proceeding I am charg'd withal,
I won his daughter.
Brabantio.   A maiden never bold;
Of spirit so still and quiet, that her motion
Blush'd at herself;[97] and she, in spite of nature,
Of years, of country, credit, every thing,

---

[89] Without.   [90] Own.   [91] Were accused.   [92] Suit.   [93] Tested (by past experience).   [94] Strength.   [95] Past.   [96] Blunt.   [97] I.e., (her modesty was such that) she blushed at her own emotions; or: could not move without blushing.

To fall in love with what she fear'd to look on!
It is a judgment maim'd and most imperfect
That will confess[98] perfection so could err   100
Against all rules of nature, and must be driven
To find out practices of cunning hell,
Why this should be. I therefore vouch again
That with some mixtures powerful o'er the blood,
Or with some dram conjur'd to this effect,
He wrought upon her.
Duke.   To vouch this, is no proof,
Without more certain and more overt test
Than these thin habits[99] and poor likelihoods
Of modern[100] seeming do prefer against him.
First Senator.   But, Othello, speak: 110
Did you by indirect and forced courses
Subdue and poison this young maid's affections;
Or came it by request and such fair question[101]
As soul to soul affordeth?
Othello.   I do beseech you;
Send for the lady to the Sagittary,
And let her speak of me before her father:
If you do find me foul in her report,
The trust, the office I do hold of you,
Not only take away, but let your sentence
Even fall upon my life.
Duke.   Fetch Desdemona hither.   120
Othello.   Ancient, conduct them; you best know the place.

(Exeunt Iago and Attendants.)

And, till she come, as truly as to heaven
I do confess the vices of my blood,
So justly to your grave ears I'll present
How I did thrive in this fair lady's love,
And she in mine.
Duke.   Say it, Othello.
Othello.   Her father lov'd me; oft invited me;
Still[102] question'd me the story of my life
From year to year, the battles, sieges, fortunes   130
That I have pass'd.
I ran it through, even from my boyish days
To the very moment that he bade me tell it;

---

[98] Assert.   [99] Weak appearances.   [100] Commonplace.   [101] Conversation.
[102] Always, regularly.

Wherein I spake of most disastrous chances,
Of moving accidents by flood and field,
Of hair-breadth 'scapes i' the imminent deadly breach,
Of being taken by the insolent foe
And sold to slavery, of my redemption thence
And portance[103] in my travel's history;
Wherein of antres[104] vast and deserts idle,[105]   140
Rough quarries, rocks, and hills whose heads touch heaven,
It was my hint[106] to speak, such was the process;
And of the Cannibals that each other eat,
The Anthropophagi,[107] and men whose heads
Do grow beneath their shoulders. This to hear
Would Desdemona seriously incline;
But still the house-affairs would draw her thence;
Which ever as she could with haste dispatch,
She'd come again, and with a greedy ear
Devour up my discourse. Which I observing,   150
Took once a pliant[108] hour, and found good means
To draw from her a prayer of earnest heart
That I would all my pilgrimage dilate,[109]
Whereof by parcels[110] she had something heard,
But not intentively:[111] I did consent;
And often did beguile her of her tears,
When I did speak of some distressful stroke
That my youth suffer'd. My story being done,
She gave me for my pains a world of sighs:
She swore, in faith, 'twas strange, 'twas passing[112] strange;   160
'Twas pitiful, 'twas wondrous pitiful:
She wish'd she had not heard it, yet she wish'd
That heaven had made her[113] such a man; she thank'd me,
And bade me, if I had a friend that lov'd her,
I should but teach him how to tell my story,
And that would woo her. Upon this hint I spake.
She lov'd me for the dangers I had pass'd,
And I lov'd her that she did pity them.
This only is the witchcraft I have us'd:
Here comes the lady; let her witness it.   170

(Enter Desdemona, Iago, and Attendants.)

Duke.   I think this tale would win my daughter too.
    Good Brabantio,

---

[103] Behavior.   [104] Caves.   [105] Empty, sterile.   [106] Opportunity.   [107] Man-
eaters.   [108] Suitable.   [109] Relate in full.   [110] Piecemeal.   [111] In
sequence.   [112] Surpassing.   [113] Direct object; not "for her."

Take up this mangled matter at the best;
Men do their broken weapons rather use
Than their bare hands.
Brabantio.   I pray you, hear her speak:
If she confess that she was half the wooer,
Destruction on my head, if my bad blame
Light on the man! Come hither, gentle mistress:
Do you perceive in all this noble company
Where most you owe obedience?
Desdemona.   My noble father,   180
I do perceive here a divided duty:
To you I am bound for life and education;
My life and education both do learn[114] me
How to respect you; you are the lord of duty,
I am hitherto your daughter: but here's my husband;
And so much duty as my mother show'd
To you, preferring you before her father,
So much I challenge[115] that I may profess
Due to the Moor my lord.
Brabantio.   God be with you! I have done.
Please it your Grace, on to the state affairs;   190
I had rather to adopt a child than get it.
Come hither, Moor:
I here do give thee that with all my heart
Which, but thou hast[116] already, with all my heart
I would keep from thee. For your sake,[117] jewel,
I am glad at soul I have no other child;
For thy escape would teach me tyranny,
To hang clogs on them. I have done, my lord.
Duke.   Let me speak like yourself and lay a sentence,[118]
Which as a grize[119] or step, may help these lovers   200
Into your favour.
When remedies are past, the griefs are ended
By seeing the worst, which[120] late on hopes depended.
To mourn a mischief that is past and gone
Is the next way to draw new mischief on.
What cannot be preserv'd when Fortune takes,
Patience her injury a mockery makes.[121]
The robb'd that smiles steals something from the thief;
He robs himself that spends a bootless grief.
Brabantio.   So let the Turk of Cyprus us beguile;   210
We lose it not so long as we can smile.

---

[114] Teach.   [115] Claim as right.   [116] Didn't you have it.   [117] Because of you.
[118] Provide a maxim.   [119] Step.   [120] The antecedent is "griefs."   [121] To suffer an
irreparable loss patiently is to make light of injury (i.e., to triumph over adversity).

He bears the sentence[122] well that nothing bears
But the free comfort which from thence he hears;
But he bears both the sentence and the sorrow
That, to pay grief, must of poor patience borrow.
These sentences, to sugar, or to gall,
Being strong on both sides, are equivocal:[123]
But words are words: I never yet did hear
That the bruis'd heart was pierced[124] through the ear.
I humbly beseech you, proceed to the affairs of state.   220

Duke.   The Turk with a most mighty preparation makes for Cyprus. Othello,
the fortitude[125] of the place is best known to you; and though we have there
a substitute of most allowed sufficiency,[126] yet opinion, a sovereign mistress
of effects, throws a more safer voice on you:[127] you must therefore be content
to slubber[128] the gloss of your new fortunes with this more stubborn[129] and
boisterous expedition.

Othello.   The tyrant custom, most grave senators,
Hath made the flinty and steel couch of war
My thrice-driven[130] bed of down: I do agnize[131]
A natural and prompt alacrity   230
I find in hardness, and do undertake
These present wars against the Ottomites.
Most humbly therefore bending to your state,[132]
I crave fit disposition[133] for my wife,
Due reference of place and exhibition,[134]
With such accommodation and besort[135]
As levels with[136] her breeding.

Duke.   If you please,
Be 't at her father's.

Brabantio.   I'll not have it so.

Othello.   Nor I.

Desdemona.   Nor I; I would not there reside,
To put my father in impatient thoughts   240
By being in his eye. Most gracious duke,
To my unfolding[137] lend your gracious ear;
And let me find a charter[138] in your voice
To assist my simpleness.

Duke.   What would you, Desdemona?

Desdemona.   That I did love the Moor to live with him,
My downright violence and storm of fortunes

---

[122] (1) Verdict, (2) Maxim.   [123] Sententious comfort (like the Duke's trite maxims) can hurt
as well as soothe.   [124] (1) Lanced (i.e., cured), (2) Wounded.   [125] Strength.
[126] Admitted competence.   [127] General opinion, which mainly determines action, thinks
Cyprus safer with you in command.   [128] Besmear.   [129] Rough.   [130] Made as soft
as possible.   [131] Recognize.   [132] Submitting to your authority.   [133] Disposal.
[134] Provision.   [135] Fitness.   [136] Is proper to.   [137] Explanation.   [138] Permission.

May trumpet to the world; my heart's subdu'd
Even to the very quality of my lord;[139]
I saw Othello's visage in his mind,   250
And to his honours and his valiant parts
Did I my soul and fortunes consecrate.
So that, dear lords, if I be left behind,
A moth of peace, and he go to the war,
The rites[140] for which I love him are bereft me,
And I a heavy interim shall support[141]
By his dear[142] absence. Let me go with him.

Othello.   Let her have your voices.
Vouch with me, heaven, I therefore beg it not
To please the palate of my appetite,   260
Nor to comply with heat,—the young affects[143]
In me defunct,—and proper satisfaction,
But to be free and bounteous to her mind;
And heaven defend[144] your good souls that you think
I will your serious and great business scant
For[145] she is with me. No, when light-wing'd toys
Of feather'd Cupid seel[146] with wanton dulness
My speculative and offic'd instruments,[147]
That[148] my disports corrupt and taint my business,
Let housewives make a skillet of my helm,   270
And all indign[149] and base adversities
Make head against my estimation![150]

Duke.   Be it as you shall privately determine,
Either for her stay or going. The affair cries haste,
And speed must answer it.

First Senator.   You must away to-night.

Othello.   With all my heart.

Duke.   At nine i' the morning here we'll meet again.
Othello, leave some officer behind,
And he shall our commission bring to you;
With such things else of quality and respect   280
As doth import you.[151]

Othello.   So please your Grace, my ancient;
A man he is of honesty and trust:
To his conveyance I assign my wife,
With what else needful your good grace shall think
To be sent after me.

---

[139] I.e., I have become a soldier, like Othello.   [140] I.e., of marriage, or of war, or of
both.   [141] Endure.   [142] Closely concerning (i.e., Desdemona).   [143] The passions
of youth (hence, here, *immoderate* sexual passion).   [144] Forbid.   [145] Because.
[146] Blind (v.) by sewing up the eyelids (a term from falconry).   [147] Reflective and executive
faculties and organs.   [148] So that.   [149] Shameful.   [150] Reputation.   [151] Concern.

Duke.   Let it be so.
Good-night to every one. (*To Brabantio*) And, noble signior,
If virtue no delighted[152] beauty lack,
Your son-in-law is far more fair than black.
First Senator.   Adieu, brave Moor! use Desdemona well.
Brabantio.   Look to her, Moor, if thou hast eyes to see: 290
She has deceiv'd her father, and may thee.

> (*Exeunt Duke, Senators, Officers, &c.*)

Othello.   My life upon her faith! Honest Iago,
My Desdemona must I leave to thee:
I prithee, let thy wife attend on her;
And bring them after in the best advantage.[153]
Come, Desdemona; I have but an hour
Of love, of worldly matters and direction,
To spend with thee: we must obey the time.

> (*Exeunt Othello and Desdemona.*)

Roderigo.   Iago!
Iago.   What sayst thou, noble heart?   300
Roderigo.   What will I do, think'st thou?
Iago.   Why, go to bed, and sleep.
Roderigo.   I will incontinently[154] drown myself.
Iago.   Well, if thou dost, I shall never love thee after.
Why, thou silly gentleman!
Roderigo.   It is silliness to live when to live is torment; and then have we a
prescription to die when death is our physician.
Iago.   O! villanous; I have looked upon the world for four times seven years,
and since I could distinguish betwixt a benefit and an injury, I never found
man that knew how to love himself. Ere I would say, I would drown myself
for the love of a guinea-hen, I would change my humanity with a baboon.
Roderigo.   What should I do? I confess it is my shame to be so fond;[155] but
it is not in my virtue[156] to amend it.
Iago.   Virtue! a fig! 'tis in ourselves that we are thus, or thus. Our bodies are
our gardens, to the which our wills are gardeners; so that if we will plant
nettles or sow lettuce, set hyssop and weed up thyme, supply it with one
gender[157] of herbs or distract it with many, either to have it sterile with
idleness or manured with industry, why, the power and corrigible[158] authority
of this lies in our wills. If the balance of our lives had not one scale of reason

---

[152] Delightful.   [153] Opportunity.   [154] Forthwith.   [155] Infatuated.
[156] Strength.   [157] Kind.   [158] Corrective.

to poise another of sensuality, the blood and baseness of our natures would conduct us to most preposterous conclusions; but we have reason to cool our raging motions, our carnal stings, our unbitted[159] lusts, whereof I take this that you call love to be a sect or scion.[160]

Roderigo.   It cannot be.

Iago.   It is merely a lust of the blood and a permisson of the will. Come, be a man. Drown thyself! drown cats and blind puppies. I have professed me thy friend, and I confess me knit to thy deserving with cables of perdurable toughness; I could never better stead thee than now. Put money in thy purse; follow these wars; defeat thy favour[161] with a usurped[162] beard; I say, put money in thy purse. It cannot be that Desdemona should long continue her love to the Moor,—put money in thy purse,—nor he his to her. It was a violent commencement in her, and thou shalt see an answerable sequestration;[163] put but money in thy purse. These Moors are changeable in their wills;—fill thy purse with money:—the food that to him now is as luscious as locusts,[164] shall be to him shortly as bitter as coloquintida.[165] She must change for youth: when she is sated with his body, she will find the error of her choice. She must have change, she must: therefore put money in thy purse. If thou wilt needs damn thyself, do it a more delicate way than drowning. Make all the money thou canst. If sanctimony and a frail vow betwixt an erring[166] barbarian and a supersubtle[167] Venetian be not too hard for my wits and all the tribe of hell, thou shalt enjoy her; therefore make money. A pox of drowning thyself! it is clean out of the way: seek thou rather to be hanged in compassing thy joy than to be drowned and go without her.

Roderigo.   Wilt thou be fast to my hopes, if I depend on the issue?[168]

Iago.   Thou art sure of me: go, make money. I have told thee often, and I retell thee again and again, I hate the Moor; my cause is hearted; thine hath no less reason. Let us be conjunctive[169] in our revenge against him; if thou canst cuckold him, thou dost thyself a pleasure, me a sport. There are many events in the womb of time which will be delivered. Traverse;[170] go: provide thy money. We will have more of this to-morrow. Adieu.

Roderigo.   Where shall we meet i' the morning?

Iago.   At my lodging.

Roderigo.   I'll be with thee betimes.

Iago.   Go to: farewell. Do you hear, Roderigo?

Roderigo.   What say you?

Iago.   No more of drowning, do you hear?

Roderigo.   I am changed. I'll sell all my land.

Iago.   Go to; farewell! put money enough in your purse.   *(Exit Roderigo.)*

Thus do I ever make my fool my purse;

---

[159] I.e., uncontrolled.   [160] Offshoot.   [161] Change thy appearance (for the worse?).
[162] Assumed.   [163] Estrangement.   [164] Sweet-tasting fruits (perhaps the carob, the edible seed-pod of an evergreen tree in the Mediterranean area).   [165] Purgative derived from a bitter apple.   [166] Vagabond.   [167] Exceedingly refined.   [168] Rely on the outcome.
[169] Allied.   [170] March.

For I mine own gain'd knowledge should profane,   360
If I would time expend with such a snipe[171]
But for my sport and profit. I hate the Moor,
And it is thought abroad[172] that 'twixt my sheets
He has done my office: I know not if 't be true,
But I, for mere suspicion in that kind,
Will do as if for surety.[173] He holds me well;[174]
The better shall my purpose work on him.
Cassio's a proper[175] man; let me see now:
To get his place; and to plume up[176] my will
In double knavery; how, how? Let's see: 370
After some time to abuse Othello's ear
That he[177] is too familiar with his wife:
He hath a person and a smooth dispose[178]
To be suspected; framed[179] to make women false,
The Moor is of a free and open nature,
That thinks men honest that but seem to be so,
And will as tenderly be led by the nose
As asses are.
I have 't; it is engender'd: hell and night
Must bring this monstrous birth to the world's light.   (Exit.)

Act II

SCENE 1.   A Sea-port Town in Cyprus. An open place near the Quay.

(*Enter Montano and two Gentlemen.*)

Montano.   What from the cape can you discern at sea?
First Gentleman.   Nothing at all: it is a high-wrought flood;
  I cannot 'twixt the heaven and the main[180]
  Descry a sail.
Montano.   Methinks the wind hath spoke aloud at land;
  A fuller blast ne'er shook our battlements;
  If it hath ruffian'd so upon the sea,
  What ribs of oak, when mountains melt on them,
  Can hold the mortise?[181] What shall we hear of this?
Second Gentleman.   A segregation[182] of the Turkish fleet;   10
  For do but stand upon the foaming shore,

---

[171] Dupe.   [172] People think.   [173] As if it were certain.   [174] In high regard.
[175] Handsome.   [176] Make ready.   [177] I.e., Cassio.   [178] Bearing.   [179] Designed,
apt.   [180] Ocean.   [181] Hold the joints together.   [182] Scattering.

The chidden billow seems to pelt the clouds;
The wind-shak'd surge, with high and monstrous mane,
Seems to cast water on the burning bear[183]
And quench the guards of the ever-fixed pole:[184]
I never did like[185] molestation view
On the enchafed[186] flood.

Montano.   If that[187] the Turkish fleet
Be not enshelter'd and embay'd, they are drown'd;
It is impossible they bear it out.

(Enter a Third Gentleman.)

Third Gentleman.   News, lad! our wars are done.   20
The desperate tempest hath so bang'd the Turks
That their designment halts;[188] a noble ship of Venice
Hath seen a grievous wrack and suffrance[189]
On most part of their fleet.

Montano.   How! is this true?

Third Gentleman.   The ship is here put in,
A Veronesa;[190] Michael Cassio,
Lieutenant to the warlike Moor Othello,
Is come on shore: the Moor himself's at sea,
And is in full commission here for Cyprus.

Montano.   I am glad on 't; 'tis a worthy governor.   30

Third Gentleman.   But this same Cassio, though he speak of comfort
Touching the Turkish loss, yet he looks sadly
And prays the Moor be safe; for they were parted
With foul and violent tempest.

Montano.   Pray heaven he be;
For I have serv'd him, and the man commands
Like a full soldier. Let's to the sea-side, ho!
As well to see the vessel that's come in
As to throw out our eyes for brave Othello,
Even till we make the main and the aerial blue
An indistinct regard.[191]

Third Gentleman.   Come, let's do so;   40
For every minute is expectancy
Of more arrivance.

---

[183] Ursa Minor (the Little Dipper). [184] Polaris, the North Star, almost directly above the Earth's axis, is part of the constellation of the Little Bear, or Dipper. [185] Similar. [186] Agitated. [187] If. [188] Plan is stopped.   [189] Damage.   [190] Probably a *type* of ship, rather than a ship from Verona—not only because Verona is an inland city but also because of "a noble ship of Venice" above.   [191] Till our (straining) eyes can no longer distinguish sea and sky.

(Enter Cassio.)

Cassio.   Thanks, you the valiant of this warlike isle,
That so approve the Moor. O! let the heavens
Give him defence against the elements,
For I have lost him on a dangerous sea.
Montano.   Is he well shipp'd?
Cassio.   His bark is stoutly timber'd, and his pilot
Of very expert and approv'd allowance;[192]
Therefore my hopes, not surfeited to death,[193]   50
Stand in bold cure.[194]

(Within, 'A sail!—a sail!—a sail!' Enter a Messenger.)

Cassio.   What noise?
Messenger.   The town is empty; on the brow o' the sea
Stand ranks of people, and they cry 'A sail!'
Cassio.   My hopes do shape him for the governor.

(Guns heard.)

Second Gentleman.   They do discharge their shot of courtesy;
Our friends at least.
Cassio.   I pray you, sir, go forth.
And give us truth who 'tis that is arriv'd.
Second Gentleman.   I shall.   *(Exit)*
Montano.   But, good lieutenant, is your general wiv'd?   60
Cassio.   Most fortunately: he hath achiev'd a maid
That paragons[195] description and wild fame;
One that excels the quirks[196] of blazoning pens,
And in th' essential vesture of creation[197]
Does tire the ingener.[198]

(Re-enter Second Gentleman.)

                    How now! who has put in?
Second Gentleman.   'Tis one Iago, ancient to the general.
Cassio.   He has had most favourable and happy speed:
Tempests themselves, high seas, and howling winds,
The gutter'd[199] rocks, and congregated sands,

---

[192] Admitted and proven to be expert. [193] Overindulged. [194] With good chance of being fulfilled.
[195] Exceeds, surpasses.   [196] Ingenuities.   [197] I.e., just as God made her; or: (even in)
the (mere) essence of human nature.   [198] Inventor (i.e., of her praises?).
[199] Jagged; or: submerged.

Traitors ensteep'd[200] to clog the guiltless keel,   70
  As having sense of beauty, do omit
  Their mortal[201] natures, letting go safely by
  The divine Desdemona.
Montano.   What is she?
Cassio.   She that I spake of, our great captain's captain,
  Left in the conduct of the bold Iago,
  Whose footing[202] here anticipates our thoughts
  A se'nnight's[203] speed. Great Jove, Othello guard,
  And swell his sail with thine own powerful breath,
  That he may bless this bay with his tall[204] ship,
  Make love's quick pants in Desdemona's arms,   80
  Give renew'd fire to our extincted spirits,
  And bring all Cyprus comfort!

(Enter Desdemona, Emilia, Iago, Roderigo, and Attendants.)

                  O! behold,
  The riches of the ship is come on shore.
  Ye men of Cyprus, let her have your knees.
  Hail to thee, lady! and the grace of heaven,
  Before, behind thee, and on every hand,
  Enwheel thee round!
Desdemona.   I thank you, valiant Cassio.
  What tidings can you tell me of my lord?
Cassio.   He is not yet arriv'd; nor know I aught
  But that he's well, and will be shortly here.   90
Desdemona.   O! but I fear—How lost you company?
Cassio.   The great contention of the sea and skies
  Parted our fellowship. But hark! a sail.

(Cry within, 'A sail—a sail!' Guns heard.)

Second Gentleman.   They give their greeting to the citadel:
  This likewise is a friend.
Cassio.   See for the news!   *(Exit Gentleman.)*
  Good ancient, you are welcome:—*(To Emilia)* welcome, mistress.
  Let it not gall your patience, good Iago,
  That I extend my manners; 'tis my breeding
  That gives me this bold show of courtesy.   *(Kissing her.)*
Iago.   Sir, would she give you so much of her lips   100
  As of her tongue she oft bestows on me,
  You'd have enough.

---

[200] Submerged.   [201] Deadly.   [202] Landing.   [203] Week's.   [204] Brave.

Desdemona.   Alas! she has no speech.

Iago.   In faith, too much;
  I find it still when I have list[205] to sleep:
  Marry, before your ladyship, I grant,
  She puts her tongue a little in her heart,
  And chides with thinking.[206]

Emilia.   You have little cause to say so.

Iago.   Come on, come on; you are pictures[207] out of doors,
  Bells[208] in your parlours, wild cats in your kitchens,   110
  Saints in your injuries, devils being offended,
  Players[209] in your housewifery,[210] and housewives[211] in your beds.

Desdemona.   O! fie upon thee, slanderer.

Iago.   Nay, it is true, or else I am a Turk:
  You rise to play and go to bed to work.

Emilia.   You shall not write my praise.

Iago.   No, let me not.

Desdemona.   What wouldst thou write of me, if thou shouldst praise me?

Iago.   O gentle lady, do not put me to 't,
  For I am nothing if not critical.

Desdemona.   Come on; assay. There's one gone to the harbour?   120

Iago.   Ay, madam.

Desdemona *(aside).*   I am not merry, but I do beguile
  The thing I am by seeming otherwise.
  (To Iago.) Come, how wouldst thou praise me?

Iago.   I am about it; but indeed my invention
  Comes from my pate[212] as birdlime does from frize;[213]
  It plucks out brains and all: but my muse labours
  And thus she is deliver'd.
  If she be fair and wise, fairness and wit,
  The one's for use, the other useth it.   130

Desdemona.   Well prais'd! How if she be black and witty?

Iago.   If she be black,[214] and thereto have a wit,
  She'll find a white that shall her blackness fit.

Desdemona.   Worse and worse.

Emilia.   How if fair and foolish?

Iago.   She never yet was foolish that was fair,
  For even her folly[215] help'd to an heir.

Desdemona.   These are old fond[216] paradoxes to make fools laugh i' the ale-
  house. What miserable praise has thou for her that's foul and foolish?

---

[205] Wish.   [206] I.e., without words.   [207] I.e., made up, "painted."   [208] I.e., jangly.   [209] Triflers, wastrels.   [210] Housekeeping.   [211] (1) Hussies, (2) (unduly) frugal with their sexual favors, (3) businesslike, serious.   [212] Head.   [213] Coarse cloth.   [214] Brunette, dark haired.   [215] Here also, wantonness.   [216] Foolish.

Iago.   There's none so foul and foolish thereunto,   140
    But does foul pranks which fair and wise ones do.

Desdemona.   O heavy ignorance! thou praisest the worst best. But what praise
    couldst thou bestow on a deserving woman indeed, one that, in the authority
    of her merit, did justly put on the vouch[217] of very malice itself?

Iago.   She that was ever fair and never proud,
    Had tongue at will and yet was never loud,
    Never lack'd gold and yet went never gay,
    Fled from her wish and yet said 'Now I may,'
    She that being anger'd, her revenge being nigh,
    Bade her wrong stay and her displeasure fly,   150
    She that in wisdom never was so frail
    To change the cod's head for the salmon's tail,[218]
    She that could think and ne'er disclose her mind,
    See suitors following and not look behind,
    She was a wight, if ever such wight were,—

Desdemona.   To do what?

Iago.   To suckle fools and chronicle small beer.[219]

Desdemona.   O most lame and impotent conclusion! Do not learn of him,
    Emilia, though he be thy husband. How say you, Cassio? Is he not a most
    profane and liberal[220] counsellor?

Cassio.   He speaks home,[221] madam; you may relish him more in the   160
    soldier than in[222] the scholar.

Iago (*aside*).   He takes her by the palm: ay, well said, whisper; with as little a
    web as this will I ensnare as great a fly as Cassio. Ay, smile upon her, do; I
    will gyve[223] thee in thine own courtship. You say true, 'tis so, indeed. If such
    tricks as these strip you out of your lieutenantry, it had been better you had
    not kissed your three fingers so oft, which now again you are most apt to play
    the sir[224] in. Very good; well kissed! an excellent courtesy! 'tis so, indeed.
    Yet again your fingers to your lips? would they were clyster-pipes[225] for your
    sake! (*A trumpet heard.*) The Moor! I know his trumpet.[226]

Cassio.   'Tis truly so.   170

Desdemona.   Let's meet him and receive him.

Cassio.   Lo! where he comes.

(Enter Othello and Attendants.)

Othello.   O my fair warrior!

Desdemona.   My dear Othello!

---

[217] Compel the approval.   [218] To make a foolish exchange (a bawdy secondary meaning is
probable).   [219] I.e., keep petty household accounts.   [220] Free-spoken, licentious.
[221] To the mark, aptly.   [222] As . . . as.   [223] Entangle.   [224] Gentleman.
[225] Syringes, enema pipes.   [226] I.e., Othello's distinctive trumpet call.

Othello.   It gives me wonder great as my content
To see you here before me. O my soul's joy!
If after every tempest come such calms,
May the winds blow till they have waken'd death!
And let the labouring bark climb hills of seas
Olympus-high, and duck again as low
As hell's from heaven! If it were now to die,
'Twere now to be most happy, for I fear   180
My soul hath her content so absolute
That not another comfort like to this
Succeeds in unknown fate.
Desdemona.   The heavens forbid
But that our loves and comforts should increase
Even as our days do grow!
Othello.   Amen to that, sweet powers!
I cannot speak enough of this content;
It stops me here; it is too much of joy:
And this, and this, the greatest discords be   *(Kissing her.)*
That e'er our hearts shall make!
Iago *(aside).*   O! you are well tun'd now,   190
But I'll set down ²²⁷ the pegs that make this music,
As honest as I am.
Othello.   Come, let us to the castle.
News, friends; our wars are done, the Turks are drown'd.
How does my old acquaintance of this isle?
Honey, you shall be well desir'd²²⁸ in Cyprus;
I have found great love amongst them. O my sweet,
I prattle out of fashion, and I dote
In mine own comforts. I prithee, good Iago,
Go to the bay and disembark my coffers.
Bring thou the master to the citadel;   200
He is a good one, and his worthiness
Does challenge much respect. Come, Desdemona,
Once more well met at Cyprus.

(Exeunt all except Iago and Roderigo.)

Iago.   Do thou meet me presently at the harbour. Come hither. If thou be'st
valiant, as they say base men being in love have then a nobility in their
natures more than is native to them, list²²⁹ me. The lieutenant to-night
watches on the court of guard:²³⁰ first, I must tell thee this, Desdemona is
directly in love with him.
Roderigo.   With him! Why, 'tis not possible.

---

²²⁷ Loosen.   ²²⁸ Welcomed.   ²²⁹ Listen to.   ²³⁰ Guardhouse.

Iago. Lay thy finger thus, and let thy soul be instructed. Mark me with what violence she first loved the Moor but for bragging and telling her fantastical lies; and will she love him still for prating? let not thy discreet heart think it. Her eye must be fed; and what delight shall she have to look on the devil? When the blood is made dull with the act of sport, there should be, again to inflame it, and to give satiety a fresh appetite, loveliness in favour, sympathy in years, manners, and beauties; all which the Moor is defective in. Now, for want of these required conveniences, her delicate tenderness will find itself abused, begin to heave the gorge,[231] disrelish and abhor the Moor; very nature will instruct her in it, and compel her to some second choice. Now, sir, this granted, as it is a most pregnant[232] and unforced position, who stands so eminently in the degree of this fortune as Cassio does? a knave very voluble, no further conscionable[233] than in putting on the mere form of civil and humane seeming, for the better compassing of his salt[234] and most hidden loose affection? why, none; why, none: a slipper[235] and subtle knave, a finder-out of occasions, that has an eye can stamp and counterfeit advantages, though true advantage never present itself; a devilish knave! Besides, the knave is handsome, young, and hath all those requisites in him that folly and green minds look after; a pestilent complete knave! and the woman hath found him already.

Roderigo. I cannot believe that in her; she is full of most blessed condition.

Iago. Blessed fig's end! the wine she drinks is made of grapes;[236] if she had been blessed she would never have loved the Moor; blessed pudding! Didst thou not see her paddle with the palm of his hand? didst not mark that?

Roderigo. Yes, that I did; but that was but courtesy.

Iago. Lechery, by this hand! an index[237] and obscure prologue to the history of lust and foul thoughts. They met so near with their lips, that their breaths embraced together. Villanous thoughts, Roderigo! when these mutualities so marshal the way, hard at hand comes the master and main exercise, the incorporate[238] conclusion. Pish![239] But, sir, be you ruled by me: I have brought you from Venice. Watch you to-night; for the command, I'll lay 't upon you: Cassio knows you not. I'll not be far from you: do you find some occasion to anger Cassio, either by speaking too loud, or tainting[240] his discipline; or from what other course you please, which the time shall more favourably minister.

Roderigo. Well.

Iago. Sir, he is rash and very sudden in choler, and haply may strike at you: provoke him, that he may; for even out of that will I cause these of Cyprus to mutiny, whose qualification[241] shall come into no true taste again but by the displanting of Cassio. So shall you have a shorter journey to your desires by the means I shall then have to prefer[242] them; and the impediment most

---

[231] Vomit.   [232] Obvious.   [233] Conscientious.   [234] Lecherous.   [235] Slippery.
[236] I.e., she is only flesh and blood.   [237] Pointer.   [238] Carnal. [239] Exclamation of disgust.   [240] Disparaging.   [241] Appeasement.   [242] Advance.

profitably removed, without the which there were no expectation of our prosperity.

Roderigo.   I will do this, if I can bring it to any opportunity.

Iago.   I warrant thee. Meet me by and by at the citadel: I must fetch his necessaries ashore. Farewell.

Roderigo.   Adieu.   (*Exit.*)

Iago.   That Cassio loves her, I do well believe it;
That she loves him, 'tis apt,[243] and of great credit:[244]
The Moor, howbeit that I endure him not,
Is of a constant, loving, noble nature;
And I dare think he'll prove to Desdemona
A most dear[245] husband. Now, I do love her too;
Not out of absolute lust,—though peradventure[246]
I stand accountant[247] for as great a sin,—
But partly led to diet my revenge,
For that I do suspect the lusty Moor
Hath leap'd into my seat; the thought whereof
Doth like a poisonous mineral gnaw my inwards;
And nothing can or shall content my soul
Till I am even'd with him, wife for wife;
Or failing so, yet that I put the Moor
At least into a jealousy so strong
That judgment cannot cure. Which thing to do,
If this poor trash[248] of Venice, whom I trash[249]
For his quick hunting, stand the putting-on,[250]
I'll have our Michael Cassio on the hip;
Abuse him to the Moor in the rank garb,[251]
For I fear Cassio with my night-cap too,
Make the Moor thank me, love me, and reward me
For making him egregiously an ass
And practising upon his peace and quiet
Even to madness. 'Tis here, but yet confus'd:
Knavery's plain face is never seen till us'd.   (*Exit.*)

SCENE 2.   A Street.

(*Enter a Herald with a proclamation; people following.*)

Herald.   It is Othello's pleasure, our noble and valiant general, that, upon certain tidings now arrived, importing the mere[252] perdition of the Turkish

---

[243] Natural, probable.   [244] Easily believable.   [245] A pun on the word in the sense of expensive.   [246] Perchance, perhaps.   [247] Accountable.   [248] I.e., Roderigo.   [249] Check, control.   [250] Inciting.   [251] Gross manner.   [252] Utter.

fleet, every man put himself into triumph; some to dance, some to make bonfires, each man to what sport and revels his addiction leads him; for, besides these beneficial news, it is the celebration of his nuptial. So much was his pleasure should be proclaimed. All offices[253] are open, and there is full liberty of feasting from this present hour of five till the bell have told eleven. Heaven bless the isle of Cyprus and our noble general Othello!

(Exeunt.)

SCENE 3.   A Hall in the Castle.

(Enter Othello, Desdemona, Cassio, and Attendants.)

Othello.   Good Michael, look you to the guard to-night:
   Let's teach ourselves that honourable stop,[254]
   Not to outsport discretion.
Cassio.   Iago hath direction what to do:
   But, notwithstanding, with my personal[255] eye
   Will I look to 't.
Othello.   Iago is most honest.
   Michael, good-night; to-morrow with your earliest
   Let me have speech with you. *(To Desdemona.)* Come, my dear love,
   The purchase made, the fruits are to ensue;
   That profit's yet to come 'twixt me and you.   10
   Good-night.

(Exeunt Othello, Desdemona, and Attendants.)

(Enter Iago.)

Cassio.   Welcome, Iago; we must to the watch.
Iago.   Not this hour, lieutenant; 'tis not yet ten o' the clock. Our general casts us thus early for the love of his Desdemona, who let us not therefore blame; he hath not yet made wanton the night with her, and she is sport for Jove.
Cassio.   She's a most exquisite lady.
Iago.   And, I'll warrant her, full of game.
Cassio.   Indeed, she is a most fresh and delicate creature.
Iago.   What an eye she has! methinks it sounds a parley[256] of provocation.
Cassio.   An inviting eye: and yet methinks right modest.   20
Iago.   And when she speaks, is it not an alarum[257] to love?
Cassio.   She is indeed perfection.
Iago.   Well, happiness to their sheets! Come, lieutenant, I have a stoup of

---

[253] Kitchens and storehouses.   [254] Discipline.   [255] Own.   [256] Conference
[257] Call-to-arms.

wine, and here without are a brace[258] of Cyprus gallants that would fain have
a measure to the health of black Othello.

Cassio.   Not to-night, good Iago: I have very poor and unhappy brains for
drinking: I could well wish courtesy would invent some other custom of
entertainment.

Iago.   O! they are our friends; but one cup: I'll drink for you.

Cassio.   I have drunk but one cup to-night, and that was craftily qualified[259]
too, and, behold, what innovation[260] it makes here: I am unfortunate in the
infirmity, and dare not task my weakness with any more.

Iago.   What, man! 'tis a night of revels; the gallants desire it.

Cassio.   Where are they?

Iago.   Here at the door; I pray you, call them in.

Cassio.   I'll do 't; but it dislikes me.   (*Exit.*)

Iago.   If I can fasten but one cup upon him,
 With that which he hath drunk to-night already,
 He'll be as full of quarrel and offence
 As my young mistress' dog. Now, my sick fool Roderigo,   40
 Whom love has turn'd almost the wrong side out,
 To Desdemona hath to-night carous'd
 Potations pottle-deep;[261] and he's to watch.
 Three lads of Cyprus, noble swelling spirits,
 That hold their honours in a wary distance,[262]
 The very elements[263] of this warlike isle,
 Have I to-night fluster'd with flowing cups,
 And they watch too. Now, 'mongst this flock of drunkards,
 Am I to put our Cassio in some action
 That may offend the isle. But here they come.   50
 If consequence[264] do but approve my dream,
 My boat sails freely, both with wind and stream.

(*Re-enter Cassio, with him Montano, and Gentlemen. Servant following with
wine.*)

Cassio.   'Fore God, they have given me a rouse[265] already.

Montano.   Good faith, a little one; not past a pint, as I am a soldier.

Iago.   Some wine, ho!
 (*Sings.*) And let me the canakin[266] clink, clink;
    And let me the canakin clink:
    A soldier's a man;
    A life's but a span;
    Why then let a soldier drink.   60
 Some wine, boys!

---

[258] Pair. [259] Diluted. [260] Change, revolution. [261] Bottoms-up. [262] Take
offense easily. [263] Types. [264] Succeeding events. [265] Drink. [266] Small
cup.

Cassio.   'Fore God, an excellent song.

Iago.   I learned it in England, where indeed they are most potent in potting; your Dane, your German, and your swag-bellied[267] Hollander,—drink ho!— are nothing to your English.

Cassio.   Is your Englishman so expert in his drinking?

Iago.   Why, he drinks you[268] with facility your Dane dead drunk; he sweats not to overthrow your Almain;[269] he gives your Hollander a vomit ere the next pottle can be filled.

Cassio.   To the health of our general!   70

Montano.   I am for it, lieutenant; and I'll do you justice.

Iago.   O sweet England!

   (*Sings.*)   King Stephen was a worthy peer,
            His breeches cost him but a crown;
        He held them sixpence all too dear,
            With that he call'd the tailor lown.[270]
        He was a wight of high renown,
            And thou art but of low degree:
        'Tis pride that pulls the country down,
            Then take thine auld cloak about thee.   80

Some wine, ho!

Cassio.   Why, this is a more exquisite song than the other.

Iago.   Will you hear 't again?

Cassio.   No; for I hold him to be unworthy of his place that does those things. Well, God's above all; and there be souls must be saved, and there be souls must not be saved.

Iago.   It's true, good lieutenant.

Cassio.   For mine own part,—no offence to the general, nor any man of quality,—I hope to be saved.

Iago.   And so do I too, lieutenant.   90

Cassio.   Ay; but, by your leave, not before me; the lieutenant is to be saved before the ancient. Let's have no more of this; let's to our affairs. God forgive us our sins! Gentlemen, let's look to our business. Do not think, gentlemen, I am drunk: this is my ancient; this is my right hand, and this is my left hand. I am not drunk now; I can stand well enough, and speak well enough.

All.   Excellent well.

Cassio.   Why, very well, then; you must not think then that I am drunk.

                                                   (*Exit.*)

Montano.   To the platform, masters; come, let's set the watch.

Iago.   You see this fellow that is gone before;
He is a soldier fit to stand by Caesar   100
And give direction; and do but see his vice;
'Tis to his virtue a just equinox,[271]

---

[267] With a pendulous belly.
[269] German.   [270] Lout, rascal.
[268] The "ethical" dative, i.e., you'll see that he drinks.
[271] Equivalent.

The one as long as the other; 'tis pity of him.
I fear the trust Othello puts him in,
On some odd time of his infirmity,
Will shake this island.

Montano.   But is he often thus?

Iago.   'Tis evermore the prologue to his sleep;
He'll watch the horologe a double set,[272]
If drink rock not his cradle.

Montano.   It were well   110
The general were put in mind of it.
Perhaps he sees it not; or his good nature
Prizes the virtue that appears in Cassio,
And looks not on his evils. Is not this true?

(Enter Roderigo.)

Iago *(aside to him).*   How now, Roderigo!
I pray you, after the lieutenant; go.   *(Exit Roderigo.)*

Montano.   And 'tis great pity that the noble Moor
Should hazard such a place as his own second
With one of an ingraft[273] infirmity;
It were an honest action to say   120
So to the Moor.

Iago.   Not I, for this fair island:
I do love Cassio well, and would do much
To cure him of this evil. But hark! what noise?

(Cry within, 'Help! Help!' Re-enter Cassio, driving in Roderigo.)

Cassio.   You rogue! you rascal!

Montano.   What's the matter, lieutenant?

Cassio.   A knave teach me my duty!
I'll beat the knave into a twiggen[274] bottle.

Roderigo.   Beat me!

Cassio.   Dost thou prate, rogue?

(Striking Roderigo.)

Montano *(staying him).*   Nay, good lieutenant;
I pray you, sir, hold your hand.

Cassio.   Let me go, sir,
Or I'll knock you o'er the mazzard.[275]

---

[272] Stand watch twice twelve hours.   [273] Ingrained.   [274] Wicker.   [275] Head.

Montano.   Come, come; you're drunk.   130
Cassio.   Drunk!

(They fight.)

Iago *(aside to Roderigo)*.   Away, I say! go out, and cry a mutiny.

(Exit Roderigo.)

Nay, good lieutenant! God's will, gentlemen!
Help, ho! Lieutenant! sir! Montano! sir!
Help, masters! Here's a goodly watch indeed!

(Bell rings.)

Who's that that rings the bell? Diablo, ho!
The town will rise: God's will! lieutenant, hold!
You will be sham'd for ever.

(Re-enter Othello and Attendants.)

Othello.   What is the matter here?
Montano.   'Zounds! I bleed still; I am hurt to the death.

(He faints.)

Othello.   Hold, for your lives!
Iago.   Hold, ho, lieutenant! Sir! Montano! gentlemen!   140
Have you forgot all sense of place and duty?
Hold! the general speaks to you; hold for shame!
Othello.   Why, how now, ho! from whence ariseth this?
Are we turn'd Turks, and to ourselves do that
Which heaven hath forbid the Ottomites?
For Christian shame put by this barbarous brawl;
He that stirs next to carve for his own rage
Holds his soul light; he dies upon his motion.
Silence that dreadful bell! it frights the isle
From her propriety. What is the matter, masters?   150
Honest Iago, that look'st dead with grieving,
Speak, who began this? On thy love, I charge thee.
Iago.   I do not know; friends all but now, even now,
In quarter[276] and in terms like bride and groom
Devesting[277] them for bed; and then, but now,—
As if some planet had unwitted men,—
Swords out, and tilting one at other's breast,

---

[276] On duty.   [277] Undressing.

In opposition bloody. I cannot speak
Any beginning to this peevish odds,[278]
And would in action glorious I had lost   160
Those legs that brought me to a part of it!

Othello. How comes it, Michael, you are thus forgot?

Cassio. I pray you, pardon me; I cannot speak.

Othello. Worthy Montano, you were wont be civil;
The gravity and stillness of your youth
The world hath noted, and your name is great
In mouths of wisest censure:[279] what's the matter,
That you unlace[280] your reputation thus
And spend your rich opinion[281] for the name
Of a night-brawler? give me answer to it.   170

Montano. Worthy Othello, I am hurt to danger;
Your officer, Iago, can inform you,
While I spare speech, which something now offends[282] me,
Of all that I do know; nor know I aught
By me that 's said or done amiss this night,
Unless self-charity be sometimes a vice,
And to defend ourselves it be a sin
When violence assails us.

Othello.   Now, by heaven,
My blood begins my safer guides to rule,
And passion, having my best judgment collied,[283]   180
Assays to lead the way. If I once stir,
Or do but lift this arm, the best of you
Shall sink in my rebuke. Give me to know
How this foul rout began, who set it on;
And he that is approv'd[284] in this offence,
Though he had twinn'd with me—both at a birth—
Shall lose me. What! in a town of war,
Yet wild, the people's hearts brimful of fear,
To manage private and domestic quarrel,
In night, and on the court and guard of safety!   190
'Tis monstrous. Iago, who began 't?

Montano. If partially affin'd,[285] or leagu'd in office,
Thou dost deliver more or less than truth,
Thou art not soldier.

Iago.   Touch me not so near;
I had rather[286] have this tongue cut from my mouth
Than it should do offence to Michael Cassio;

---

[278] Silly quarrel.   [279] Judgment.   [280] Undo.   [281] High reputation.   [282] Pains, harms.   [283] Clouded.   [284] Proved (i.e., guilty).   [285] Favorably biased (by ties of friendship, or as Cassio's fellow officer).   [286] More quickly.

Yet, I persuade myself, to speak the truth
Shall nothing wrong him. Thus it is, general.
Montano and myself being in speech,
There comes a fellow crying out for help,   200
And Cassio following with determin'd sword
To execute upon him. Sir, this gentleman
Steps in to Cassio, and entreats his pause;
Myself the crying fellow did pursue,
Lest by his clamour, as it so fell out,
The town might fall in fright; he, swift of foot,
Outran my purpose, and I return'd the rather
For that I heard the clink and fall of swords,
And Cassio high in oath, which till to-night
I ne'er might say before. When I came back,—   210
For this was brief,—I found them close together,
At blow and thrust, even as again they were
When you yourself did part them.
More of this matter can I not report:
But men are men; the best sometimes forget:
Though Cassio did some little wrong to him,
As men in rage strike those that wish them best,
Yet, surely Cassio, I believe, receiv'd
From him that fled some strange indignity,
Which patience could not pass.
Othello.   I know, Iago.   220
Thy honesty and love doth mince[287] this matter,
Making it light to Cassio. Cassio, I love thee;
But never more be officer of mine.

(Enter Desdemona, attended.)

Look! if my gentle love be not rais'd up;
(To Cassio.) I'll make thee an example.
Desdemona.   What's the matter?
Othello.   All's well now, sweeting; come away to bed.
Sir, for your hurts, myself will be your surgeon.
Lead him off.   *(Montano is led off.)*
Iago, look with care about the town,
And silence those whom this vile brawl distracted.   230
Come, Desdemona; 'tis the soldier's life,
To have their balmy slumbers wak'd with strife.

(Exeunt all but Iago and Cassio.)

---

[287] Tone down.

Iago. What! are you hurt, lieutenant?

Cassio. Ay; past all surgery.

Iago. Marry, heaven forbid!

Cassio. Reputation, reputation, reputation! O! I have lost my reputation. I have lost the immortal part of myself, and what remains is bestial. My reputation, Iago, my reputation!

Iago. As I am an honest man, I thought you had received some bodily wound; there is more offence in that than in reputation. Reputation is an idle and most false imposition;[288] oft got without merit, and lost without deserving: you have lost no reputation at all, unless you repute yourself such a loser. What! man; there are ways to recover the general again; you are but now cast in his mood,[289] a punishment more in policy[290] than in malice; even so as one would beat his offenceless dog to affright an imperious lion. Sue to him again, and he is yours.

Cassio. I will rather sue to be despised than to deceive so good a commander with so slight, so drunken and so indiscreet an officer. Drunk! and speak parrot![291] and squabble, swagger, swear, and discourse fustian[292] with one's own shadow! O thou invisible spirit of wine! if thou hast no name to be known by, let us call thee devil!

Iago. What was he that you followed with your sword? What hath he done to you?

Cassio. I know not.

Iago. Is 't possible?

Cassio. I remember a mass of things, but nothing distinctly; a quarrel, but nothing wherefore. O God! that men should put an enemy in their mouths to steal away their brains; that we should, with joy, pleasance,[293] revel, and applause, transform ourselves into beasts.

Iago. Why, but you are now well enough; how came you thus recovered?

Cassio. It hath pleased the devil drunkenness to give place to the devil wrath; one unperfectness shows me another, to make me frankly despise myself.

Iago. Come, you are too severe a moraler. As the time, the place, and the condition of this country stands, I could heartily wish this had not befallen, but since it is as it is, mend it for your own good.

Cassio. I will ask him for my place again; he shall tell me I am a drunkard! Had I as many mouths as Hydra,[294] such an answer would stop them all. To be now a sensible man, by and by a fool, and presently a beast! O strange! Every inordinate cup is unblessed and the ingredient[295] is a devil.

Iago. Come, come; good wine is a good familiar creature if it be well used; exclaim no more against it. And, good lieutenant, I think you think I love you.

---

[288] Something external.   [289] Dismissed because he is angry.   [290] I.e., more for the sake of the example, or to show his fairness.   [291] I.e., without thinking.   [292] I.e., nonsense.   [293] Pleasure.   [294] Many-headed snake in Greek mythology.   [295] Contents.

Cassio.   I have well approved it, sir. I drunk!

Iago.   You or any man living may be drunk at some time, man. I'll tell you what you shall do. Our general's wife is now the general; I may say so in this respect, for that he hath devoted and given up himself to the contemplation, mark, and denotement of her parts and graces: confess yourself freely to her; importune her; she'll help to put you in your place again. She is of so free, so kind, so apt, so blessed a disposition, that she holds it a vice in her goodness not to do more than she is requested. This broken joint between you and her husband entreat her to splinter;[296] and, my fortunes against any lay[297] worth naming, this crack of your love shall grow stronger than it was before.

Cassio.   You advise me well.

Iago.   I protest, in the sincerity of love and honest kindness.

Cassio.   I think it freely; and betimes in the morning I will beseech the virtuous Desdemona to undertake for me. I am desperate of my fortunes if they check me here.

Iago.   You are in the right. Good-night, lieutenant; I must to the watch.

Cassio.   Good-night, honest Iago!   *(Exit.)*

Iago.   And what's he then that says I play the villain?   290
When this advice is free I give and honest,
Probal[298] to thinking and indeed the course
To win the Moor again? For 'tis most easy
The inclining Desdemona to subdue
In any honest suit; she's fram'd as fruitful[299]
As the free elements. And then for her
To win the Moor, were 't to renounce his baptism,
All seals and symbols of redeemed sin,
His soul is so enfetter'd to her love,
That she may make, unmake, do what she list,   300
Even as her appetite shall play the god
With his weak function.[300] How am I then a villain
To counsel Cassio to this parallel[301] course,
Directly to his good? Divinity of hell!
When devils will the blackest sins put on,
They do suggest at first with heavenly shows,
As I do now; for while this honest fool
Plies Desdemona to repair his fortunes,
And she for him pleads strongly to the Moor,
I'll pour this pestilence into his ear   310
That she repeals[302] him for her body's lust;
And, by how much she strives to do him good,
She shall undo her credit with the Moor.

---

[296] Bind up with splints.   [297] Wager.   [298] Provable.   [299] Generous.   [300] Faculties.
[301] Purposeful.   [302] I.e., seeks to recall.

So will I turn her virtue into pitch,
And out of her own goodness make the net
That shall enmesh them all.

(Re-enter Roderigo.)

How now, Roderigo!

Roderigo.   I do follow here in the chase, not like a hound that hunts, but one
    that fills up the cry.[303] My money is almost spent; I have been to-night
    exceedingly well cudgelled; and I think the issue will be, I shall have so much
    experience for my pains; and so, with no money at all and a little more wit,
    return again to Venice.

Iago.   How poor are they that have not patience!
    What wound did ever heal but by degrees?
    Thou know'st we work by wit and not by witchcraft,
    And wit depends on dilatory time.
    Does 't not go well? Cassio hath beaten thee,
    And thou by that small hurt hast cashiered Cassio.
    Though other things grow fair against the sun,
    Yet fruits that blossom first will first be ripe:
    Content thyself awhile. By the mass, 'tis morning;   330
    Pleasure and action make the hours seem short.
    Retire thee; go where thou art billeted:
    Away, I say; thou shalt know more hereafter:
    Nay, get thee gone. *(Exit Roderigo.)* Two things are to be done,
    My wife must move for Cassio to her mistress;
    I'll set her on;
    Myself the while to draw the Moor apart,
    And bring him jump[304] when he may Cassio find
    Soliciting his wife: ay, that's the way:
    Dull not device by coldness and delay.   *(Exit.)*

Act III

SCENE 1. Cyprus. Before the Castle.

(Enter Cassio, and some Musicians.)

Cassio.   Masters, play here, I will content your pains;[305]
    Something that's brief; and bid 'Good-morrow, general.'   *(Music.)*

(Enter Clown.)

---

[303] Pack (hunting term).   [304] At the exact moment.   [305] Reward your efforts.

Clown.   Why, masters, have your instruments been in Naples, that they speak
i' the nose[306] thus?
First Musician.   How, sir, how?
Clown.   Are these, I pray you, wind-instruments?
First Musician.   Ay, marry, are they, sir.
Clown.   O! thereby hangs a tale.
First Musician.   Whereby hangs a tale, sir?
Clown.   Marry, sir, by many a wind-instrument that I know. But, masters,
here's money for you; and the general so likes your music, that he desires
you, for love's sake, to make no more noise with it.
First Musician.   Well, sir, we will not.
Clown.   If you have any music that may not be heard, to 't again; but, as they
say, to hear music the general does not greatly care.
First Musician.   We have none such, sir.
Clown.   Then put up your pipes in your bag, for I'll away.
    Go; vanish into air; away!   *(Exeunt Musicians.)*
Cassio.   Dost thou hear, mine honest friend?
Clown.   No, I hear not your honest friend; I hear you.
Cassio.   Prithee, keep up thy quillets.[307] There's a poor piece of gold for thee.
If the gentlewoman that attends the general's wife be stirring, tell her there's
one Cassio entreats her a little favour of speech: wilt thou do this?
Clown.   She is stirring, sir: if she will stir hither, I shall seem to notify unto
her.
Cassio.   Do, good my friend.   *(Exit Clown.)*

(Enter Iago.)

                         In happy time, Iago.
Iago.   You have not been a-bed, then?
Cassio.   Why, no; the day had broke
Before we parted. I have made bold, Iago,
To send in to your wife; my suit to her
Is, that she will to virtuous Desdemona   30
Procure me some access.
Iago.   I'll send her to you presently;
And I'll devise a mean to draw the Moor
Out of the way, that your converse and business
May be more free.
Cassio.   I humbly thank you for 't.   *(Exit Iago.)*
                         I never knew
A Florentine more kind and honest.[308]

---

[306] Naples was notorious for venereal disease, and syphilis was believed to affect the nose.
[307] Quibbles.   [308] Cassio means that not even a fellow Florentine could behave to him in a
friendlier fashion than does Iago.

(Enter Emilia.)

Emilia.   Good-morrow, good lieutenant: I am sorry
 For your displeasure,[309] but all will soon be well.
 The general and his wife are talking of it,
 And she speaks for you stoutly: the Moor replies   40
 That he you hurt is of great fame in Cyprus
 And great affinity,[310] and that in wholesome wisdom
 He might not but refuse you; but he protests he loves you,
 And needs no other suitor but his likings
 To take the safest occasion by the front[311]
 To bring you in again.[312]
Cassio.   Yet, I beseech you,
 If you think fit, or that it may be done,
 Give me advantage of some brief discourse
 With Desdemona alone.
Emilia.   Pray you, come in:
 I will bestow you where you shall have time   50
 To speak your bosom[313] freely.
Cassio.   I am much bound to you.   *(Exeunt.)*

SCENE 2.   A Room in the Castle.

(Enter Othello, Iago, and Gentlemen.)

Othello.   These letters give, Iago, to the pilot,
 And by him do my duties to the senate;
 That done, I will be walking on the works;
 Repair there to me.
Iago.   Well, my good lord, I'll do 't.
Othello.   This fortification, gentlemen, shall we see 't?
Gentlemen.   We'll wait upon your lordship.   *(Exeunt.)*

SCENE 3.   Before the Castle.

(Enter Desdemona, Cassio, and Emilia.)

Desdemona.   Be thou assur'd, good Cassio, I will do
 All my abilities in thy behalf.
Emilia.   Good madam, do: I warrant it grieves my husband,
 As if the case were his.

---

[309] Disgrace.   [310] Family connection.   [311] Forelock.   [312] Restore you (to Othello's favor).   [313] Heart, inmost thoughts.

Desdemona.   O! that's an honest fellow. Do not doubt, Cassio,
But I will have my lord and you again
As friendly as you were.
Cassio.   Bounteous madam,
Whatever shall become of Michael Cassio,
He's never any thing but your true servant.
Desdemona.   I know 't; I thank you. You do love my lord;   10
You have known him long; and be you well assur'd
He shall in strangeness[314] stand no further off
Than in a politic[315] distance.
Cassio.   Ay, but, lady,
That policy may either last so long,
Or feed upon such nice[316] and waterish diet,
Or breed itself so out of circumstance,
That, I being absent and my place supplied,
My general will forget my love and service.
Desdemona.   Do not doubt[317] that; before Emilia here
I give thee warrant of thy place. Assure thee,   20
If I do vow a friendship, I'll perform it
To the last article; my lord shall never rest;
I'll watch him tame,[318] and talk him out of patience;
His bed shall seem a school, his board a shrift;[319]
I'll intermingle every thing he does
With Cassio's suit. Therefore be merry, Cassio;
For thy solicitor shall rather die
Than give thy cause away.[320]

(Enter Othello, and Iago at a distance.)

Emilia.   Madam, here comes my lord.
Cassio.   Madam, I'll take my leave.   30
Desdemona.   Why, stay, and hear me speak.
Cassio.   Madam, not now; I am very ill at ease,
Unfit for mine own purposes.
Desdemona.   Well, do your discretion.   *(Exit Cassio.)*
Iago.   Ha! I like not that.
Othello.   What dost thou say?
Iago.   Nothing, my lord: or if—I know not what.
Othello.   Was not that Cassio parted from my wife?
Iago.   Cassio, my lord? No, sure, I cannot think it,
That he would steal away so guilty-like,
Seeing you coming.

---

[314] Aloofness.   [315] I.e., dictated by policy.   [316] Slight, trivial.   [317] Fear.
[318] Outwatch him (i.e., keep him awake) till he submits.   [319] Confessional.   [320] Abandon
your cause.

Othello.   I do believe 'twas he.   40
Desdemona.   How now, my lord!
  I have been talking with a suitor here,
  A man that languishes in your displeasure.
Othello.   Who is 't you mean?
Desdemona.   Why, your lieutenant, Cassio. Good my lord,
  If I have any grace or power to move you,
  His present[321] reconciliation take;
  For if he be not one that truly loves you,
  That errs in ignorance and not in cunning,
  I have no judgment in an honest face.   50
  I prithee[322] call him back.
Othello.   Went he hence now?
Desdemona.   Ay, sooth; so humbled,
  That he hath left part of his grief with me,
  To suffer with him. Good love, call him back.
Othello.   Not now, sweet Desdemona; some other time.
Desdemona.   But shall 't be shortly?
Othello.   The sooner, sweet, for you.
Desdemona.   Shall 't be to-night at supper?
Othello.   No, not to-night.
Desdemona.   To-morrow dinner, then?
Othello.   I shall not dine at home;
  I meet the captains at the citadel.
Desdemona.   Why, then, to-morrow night; or Tuesday morn;
  Or Tuesday noon, or night; or Wednesday morn: 60
  I prithee name the time, but let it not
  Exceed three days: in faith, he's penitent;
  And yet his trespass, in our common reason,—
  Save that they say, the wars must make examples
  Out of their best,—is not almost[323] a fault
  To incur a private check.[324] When shall he come?
  Tell me, Othello: I wonder in my soul,
  What you could ask me, that I should deny,
  Or stand so mammering[325] on. What! Michael Cassio,   70
  That came a wooing with you, and so many a time,
  When I have spoke of you dispraisingly,
  Hath ta'en your part; to have so much to do
  To bring him in! Trust me, I could do much,—
Othello.   Prithee, no more; let him come when he will;
  I deny thee nothing.
Desdemona.   Why, this is not a boon;

---

[321] Immediate.   [322] Pray thee.   [323] Hardly.   [324] (Even) a private reprimand.
[325] Shilly-shallying.

'Tis as I should entreat you wear your gloves,
Or feed on nourishing dishes, or keep you warm,
Or sue to you to do a peculiar profit
To your own person: nay, when I have a suit   80
Wherein I mean to touch your love indeed,
It shall be full of poise[326] and difficult weight,
And fearful to be granted.

Othello.   I will deny thee nothing:
Whereon, I do beseech thee, grant me this,
To leave me but a little to myself.

Desdemona.   Shall I deny you? no: farewell, my lord.

Othello.   Farewell, my Desdemona: I'll come to thee straight.

Desdemona.   Emilia, come. Be as your fancies teach you;
Whate'er you be, I am obedient.   (*Exit, with Emilia.*)

Othello.   Excellent wretch![327] Perdition catch my soul,   90
But I do love thee! and when I love thee not,
Chaos is[328] come again.

Iago.   My noble lord,—

Othello.   What dost thou say, Iago?

Iago.   Did Michael Cassio, when you woo'd my lady,
Know of your love?

Othello.   He did, from first to last: why dost thou ask?

Iago.   But for a satisfaction of my thought;
No further harm.

Othello.   Why of thy thought, Iago?

Iago.   I did not think he had been acquainted with her.

Othello.   O! yes; and went between us very oft.   100

Iago.   Indeed!

Othello.   Indeed! ay, indeed; discern'st thou aught in that?
Is he not honest?

Iago.   Honest, my lord?

Othello.   Honest! ay, honest.

Iago.   My lord, for aught I know.

Othello.   What dost thou think?

Iago.   Think, my lord!

Othello.   Think, my lord!
By heaven, he echoes me,
As if there were some monster in his thought
Too hideous to be shown. Thou dost mean something:
I heard thee say but now, thou lik'dst not that,
When Cassio left my wife; what didst not like?   110
And when I told thee he was of my counsel
In my whole course of wooing, thou criedst, 'Indeed!'

---

[326] Weight.   [327] Here, a term of endearment.   [328] Will have.

And didst contract and purse thy brow together,
As if thou then hadst shut up in thy brain
Some horrible conceit.[329] If thou dost love me,
Show me thy thought.
Iago.   My lord, you know I love you.
Othello.   I think thou dost;
And, for[330] I know thou art full of love and honesty,
And weigh'st thy words before thou givest them breath,
Therefore these stops[331] of thine fright me the more;   120
For such things in a false disloyal knave
Are tricks of custom, but in a man that's just
They are close dilations,[332] working from the heart
That passion cannot rule.
Iago.   For Michael Cassio,
I dare be sworn I think that he is honest.
Othello.   I think so too.
Iago.   Men should be what they seem;
Or those that be not, would they might seem none!
Othello.   Certain men should be what they seem.
Iago.   Why then, I think Cassio's an honest man.
Othello.   Nay, yet there's more in this.   130
I pray thee, speak to me as to thy thinkings,
As thou dost ruminate, and give thy worst of thoughts
The worst of words.
Iago.   Good my lord, pardon me;
Though I am bound to every act of duty,
I am not bound to[333] that all slaves are free to.
Utter my thoughts? Why, say they are vile and false;
As where's that palace whereinto foul things
Sometimes intrude not? who has a breast so pure
But some uncleanly apprehensions[334]
Keep leets and law-days,[335] and in session sit   140
With meditations lawful?
Othello.   Thou dost conspire against thy friend, Iago,
If thou but think'st him wrong'd, and mak'st his ear
A stranger to thy thoughts.
Iago.   I do beseech you,
Though I perchance am vicious in my guess,—
As, I confess, it is my nature's plague
To spy into abuses, and oft my jealousy[336]
Shapes faults that are not,—that your wisdom yet,

---

[329] Fancy.   [330] Because.   [331] Interruptions, hesitations.   [332] Secret (i.e., involuntary, unconscious) revelations.   [333] Bound with regard to.   [334] Conceptions.
[335] Sittings of the local courts.   [336] Suspicion.

From one that so imperfectly conceits,
Would take no notice, nor build yourself a trouble   150
Out of his scattering and unsure observance.
It were not for your quiet nor your good,
Nor for my manhood, honesty, or wisdom,
To let you know my thoughts.
Othello.   What dost thou mean?
Iago.   Good name in man and woman, dear my lord,
Is the immediate jewel of[337] their souls:
Who steals my purse steals trash; 'tis something, nothing;
'Twas mine, 'tis his, and has been slave to thousands;
But he that filches from me my good name
Robs me of that which not enriches him,   160
And makes me poor indeed.
Othello.   By heaven, I'll know thy thoughts.
Iago.   You cannot, if my heart were in your hand;
Nor shall not, whilst 'tis in my custody.
Othello.   Ha!
Iago.   O! beware, my lord, of jealousy;
It is the green-ey'd monster which doth mock
The meat it feeds on: that cuckold[338] lives in bliss
Who, certain of his fate, loves not his wronger;
But, O! what damned minutes tells[339] he o'er
Who dotes, yet doubts; suspects, yet soundly loves!   170
Othello.   O misery!
Iago.   Poor and content is rich, and rich enough,
But riches fineless[340] is as poor as winter
To him that ever fears he shall be poor.
Good heaven, the souls of all my tribe defend
From jealousy!
Othello.   Why, why is this?
Think'st thou I'd make a life of jealousy,
To follow still the changes of the moon
With fresh suspicions? No; to be once in doubt
Is once to be resolved. Exchange me for a goat   180
When I shall turn the business of my soul
To such exsufflicate[341] and blown[342] surmises,
Matching thy inference. 'Tis not to make me jealous
To say my wife is fair, feeds well, loves company,
Is free of speech, sings, plays, and dances well;
Where virtue is, these are more virtuous:
Nor from mine own weak merits will I draw

---

[337] Jewel closest to.   [338] Husband of an adulterous woman.   [339] Counts.   [340] Boundless.
[341] Spat out (?).   [342] Fly-blown.

The smallest fear, or doubt of her revolt;
For she had eyes, and chose me. No, Iago;
I'll see before I doubt; when I doubt, prove;   190
And, on the proof, there is no more but this,
Away at once with love or jealousy!
Iago.   I am glad of it; for now I shall have reason
To show the love and duty that I bear you
With franker spirit; therefore, as I am bound,
Receive it from me; I speak not yet of proof.
Look to your wife; observe her well with Cassio;
Wear your eye thus, not jealous nor secure:
I would not have your free and noble nature
Out of self-bounty[343] be abus'd; look to 't: 200
I know our country disposition[344] well;
In Venice they do let heaven see the pranks
They dare not show their husbands; their best conscience
Is not to leave 't undone, but keep 't unknown.
Othello.   Dost thou say so?
Iago.   She did deceive her father, marrying you;
And when she seem'd to shake and fear your looks,
She lov'd them most.
Othello.   And so she did.
Iago.   Why, go to,[345] then;
She that so young could give out such a seeming,
To seel her father's eyes up close as oak,   210
He thought 'twas witchcraft; but I am much to blame;
I humbly do beseech you of your pardon
For too much loving you.
Othello.   I am bound to thee for ever.
Iago.   I see, this hath a little dash'd your spirits.
Othello.   Not a jot, not a jot.
Iago.   I' faith, I fear it has.
I hope you will consider what is spoke
Comes from my love. But I do see you're mov'd;
I am to pray you not to strain my speech
To grosser issues nor to larger reach
Than to suspicion.   220
Othello.   I will not.
Iago.   Should you do so, my lord,
My speech should fall into such vile success
As my thoughts aim not at. Cassio's my worthy friend—
My lord, I see you're mov'd.

---

[343] Innate generosity.   [344] I.e., that of Venice.   [345] Colloquialism; here, something like "all right."

Othello.   No, not much mov'd:
    I do not think but Desdemona's honest. [346]
Iago.   Long live she so! and long live you to think so!
Othello.   And yet, how nature erring from itself,—
Iago.   Ay, there's the point: as, to be bold with you,
    Not to affect many proposed matches
    Of her own clime, [347] complexion, and degree, [348]   230
    Whereto, we see, in all things nature tends;
    Foh! one may smell in such, a will most rank,
    Foul disproportion, thoughts unnatural.
    But pardon me; I do not in position[349]
    Distinctly[350] speak of her, though I may fear
    Her will, recoiling [351] to her better judgment,
    May fall to match you with her country forms
    And happily[352] repent.
Othello.   Farewell, farewell:
    If more thou dost perceive, let me know more;
    Set on thy wife to observe. Leave me, Iago.   240
Iago.   My lord, I take my leave.   *(Going.)*
Othello.   Why did I marry? This honest creature, doubtless,
    Sees and knows more, much more, than he unfolds.
Iago *(returning)*.   My lord, I would I might entreat your honour
    To scan this thing no further; leave it to time.
    Although 'tis fit that Cassio have his place,
    For, sure he fills it up with great ability,
    Yet, if you please to hold him off awhile,
    You shall by that perceive him and his means:
    Note if your lady strain his entertainment[353]   250
    With any strong or vehement importunity;
    Much will be seen in that. In the mean time,
    Let me be thought too busy[354] in my fears,
    As worthy cause I have to fear I am,
    And hold her free, I do beseech your honour.
Othello.   Fear not my government.
Iago.   I once more take my leave.   *(Exit.)*
Othello.   This fellow's of exceeding honesty,
    And knows all qualities, with a learned spirit,
    Of human dealings; if I do prove her haggard, [355]   260
    Though that her jesses[356] were my dear heart-strings,
    I'd whistle her off and let her down the wind, [357]

---

[346] Chaste.   [347] Country.   [348] Social rank.   [349] In definite assertion.
[350] Specifically.   [351] Reverting.   [352] Perhaps.   [353] Urge his re-welcome (i.e., to Othello's trust and favor).   [354] Meddlesome.   [355] Wild hawk.   [356] Leather thongs by which the hawk's legs were strapped to the trainer's wrist.   [357] I'd let her go and take care of herself.

To prey at fortune. Haply, for I am black,
And have not those soft parts of conversation
That chamberers[358] have, or, for I am declin'd
Into the vale of years—yet that's not much—
She's gone, I am abus'd;[359] and my relief
Must be to loathe her. O curse of marriage!
That we can call these delicate creatures ours,
And not their appetites. I had rather be a toad,   270
And live upon the vapour of a dungeon,
Than keep a corner in the thing I love
For others' uses. Yet, 'tis the plague of great ones;
Prerogativ'd[360] are they less than the base;
'Tis destiny unshunnable, like death:
Even then this forked plague[361] is fated to us
When we do quicken.[362]
                    Look! where she comes.
If she be false, O! then heaven mocks itself.
I'll not believe it.

(Re-enter Desdemona and Emilia.)

Desdemona.   How now, my dear Othello!
Your dinner and the generous[363] islanders   280
By you invited, do attend your presence.
Othello.   I am to blame.
Desdemona.   Why do you speak so faintly?
Are you not well?
Othello.   I have a pain upon my forehead here.[364]
Desdemona.   Faith, that's with watching; 'twill away again:
Let me but bind it hard, within this hour
It will be well.
Othello.   Your napkin[365] is too little:

(She drops her handkerchief.)

Let it alone. Come, I'll go in with you.
Desdemona.   I am very sorry that you are not well.

                    (Exeunt Othello and Desdemona.)

Emilia.   I am glad I have found this napkin;   290
This was her first remembrance from the Moor;

---

[358] Courtiers; or (more specifically): gallants, frequenters of bed chambers.   [359] Deceived.
[360] Privileged.   [361] I.e., the cuckold's proverbial horns.   [362] Are conceived, come
alive.   [363] Noble.   [364] Othello again refers to his cuckoldom.   [365] Handkerchief.

My wayward husband hath a hundred times
Woo'd me to steal it, but she so loves the token,
For he conjur'd her she should ever keep it,
That she reserves it evermore about her
To kiss and talk to. I'll have the work ta'en out,[366]
And giv 't Iago:
What he will do with it heaven knows, not I;
I nothing but[367] to please his fantasy.[368]

(Enter Iago.)

Iago.   How now! what do you here alone?   300
Emilia.   Do not you chide; I have a thing for you.
Iago.   A thing for me? It is a common thing—
Emilia.   Ha!
Iago.   To have a foolish wife.
Emilia.   O! is that all? What will you give me now
  For that same handkerchief?
Iago.   What handkerchief?
Emilia.   What handkerchief!
  Why, that the Moor first gave to Desdemona:
  That which so often you did bid me steal.
Iago.   Hath stol'n it from her?   310
Emilia.   No, faith; she let it drop by negligence,
  And, to the advantage, I, being there, took 't up.
  Look, here it is.
Iago.   A good wench; give it me.
Emilia.   What will you do with 't, that you have been so earnest
  To have me filch it?
Iago.   Why, what's that to you?   *(Snatches it.)*
Emilia.   If it be not for some purpose of import
  Give 't me again; poor lady! she'll run mad
  When she shall lack it.
Iago.   Be not acknown on 't;[369] I have use for it.
  Go, leave me.   *(Exit Emilia.)*
  I will in Cassio's lodging lose this napkin,   321
  And let him find it; trifles light as air
  Are to the jealous confirmations strong
  As proofs of holy writ; this may do something.
  The Moor already changes with my poison:
  Dangerous conceits are in their natures poisons,
  Which at the first are scarce found to distaste,[370]

---

[366] Pattern copied.   [367] I.e., only want.   [368] Whim.   [369] You know nothing about
it.   [370] Scarce can be tasted.

But with a little act upon the blood,
Burn like the mines of sulphur. I did say so:
Look! where he comes!

(Enter Othello.)

                                 Not poppy,[371] nor mandragora,[372]   330
Nor all the drowsy syrups[373] of the world,
Shall ever medicine thee to that sweet sleep
Which thou ow'dst yesterday.
Othello.   Ha! ha! false to me?
Iago.   Why, how now, general! no more of that.
Othello.   Avaunt! be gone! thou hast set me on the rack;
I swear 'tis better to be much abus'd
Than but to know 't a little.
Iago.   How now, my lord!
Othello.   What sense had I of her stol'n hours of lust?
I saw 't not, thought it not, it harm'd not me;
I slept the next night well, was free and merry;   340
I found not Cassio's kisses on her lips;
He that is robb'd, not wanting what is stol'n,
Let him not know 't, and he's not robb'd at all.
Iago.   I am sorry to hear this.
Othello.   I had been happy, if the general camp,[374]
Pioners[375] and all, had tasted her sweet body,
So[376] I had nothing known. O! now, for ever
Farewell the tranquil mind; farewell content!
Farewell the plumed troop and the big wars
That make ambition virtue! O, farewell!   350
Farewell the neighing steed, and the shrill trump,
The spirit-stirring drum, the ear-piercing fife,
The royal banner, and all quality,
Pride, pomp, and circumstance[377] of glorious war!
And, O you mortal engines,[378] whose rude throats
The immortal Jove's dread clamours counterfeit,
Farewell! Othello's occupation's gone!
Iago.   Is it possible, my lord?
Othello.   Villain, be sure thou prove my love a whore,
Be sure of it; give me the ocular proof;   360
Or, by the worth of mine eternal soul,
Thou hadst been better have been born a dog
Than answer my wak'd wrath.
Iago.   Is 't come to this?

---

[371] Opium.   [372] A soporific.   [373] I.e., soporifics.   [374] Whole army.   [375] Lowest
rank of manual laborers in the army.   [376] As long as.   [377] Pageantry.   [378] Deadly
artillery.

Othello.   Make me to see 't; or, at the least, so prove it,
That the probation[379] bear no hinge nor loop
To hang a doubt on; or woe upon thy life!
Iago.   My noble lord—
Othello.   If thou dost slander her and torture me,
Never pray more; abandon all remorse;
On horror's head horrors accumulate;   370
Do deeds to make heaven weep, all earth amaz'd;
For nothing canst thou to damnation add
Greater than that.
Iago.   O grace! O heaven forgive me!
Are you a man! have you a soul or sense?
God be wi' you; take mine office. O wretched fool!
That liv'st to make thine honesty a vice.
O monstrous world! Take note, take note, O world!
To be direct and honest is not safe.
I thank you for this profit,[380] and, from hence
I'll love no friend, sith[381] love breeds such offence.   380
Othello.   Nay, stay; thou shouldst be honest.
Iago.   I should be wise; for honesty's a fool,
And loses that it works for.
Othello.   By the world,
I think my wife be honest and think she is not;
I think that thou art just and think thou art not.
I'll have some proof. Her name, that was as fresh
As Dian's[382] visage, is now begrim'd and black
As mine own face. If there be cords or knives,
Poison or fire or suffocating streams,
I'll not endure it. Would I were satisfied!   390
Iago.   I see, sir, you are eaten up with passion.
I do repent me that I put it to you.
You would be satisfied?
Othello.   Would! nay, I will.
Iago.   And may; but how? how satisfied, my lord?
Would you, the supervisor,[383] grossly gape on;
Behold her tupp'd?
Othello.   Death and damnation! O!
Iago.   It were a tedious[384] difficulty, I think,
To bring them to that prospect; damn them then,
If ever mortal eyes do see them bolster[385]
More[386] than their own! What then? how then?   400
What shall I say? Where's satisfaction?
It is impossible you should see this,

---

[379] Proof.   [380] Lesson.   [381] Since.   [382] Diana's, the goddess of the moon.
[383] Observer. [384] Laborious.   [385] Lie together.   [386] Other.

Were they as prime[387] as goats, as hot as monkeys,
As salt as wolves in pride,[388] and fools as gross
As ignorance made drunk; but yet, I say,
If imputation, and strong circumstances,
Which lead directly to the door of truth,
Will give you satisfaction, you may have it.

Othello.   Give me a living reason she's disloyal.

Iago.   I do not like the office;   410
But, sith I am enter'd in this cause so far,
Prick'd to 't by foolish honesty and love,
I will go on. I lay with Cassio lately;
And, being troubled with a raging tooth,
I could not sleep.
There are a kind of men so loose of soul
That in their sleeps will mutter their affairs;
One of this kind is Cassio.
In sleep I heard him say, 'Sweet Desdemona,
Let us be wary, let us hide our loves!'   420
And then, sir, would he gripe[389] and wring my hand,
Cry, 'O, sweet creature!' and then kiss me hard,
As if he pluck'd up kisses by the roots,
That grew upon my lips; then laid his leg
Over my thigh, and sigh'd, and kiss'd; and then
Cried, 'Cursed fate, that gave thee to the Moor!'

Othello.   O monstrous! monstrous!

Iago.   Nay, this was but his dream.

Othello.   But this denoted a foregone conclusion:[390]
'Tis a shrewd doubt,[391] though it be but a dream.

Iago.   And this may help to thicken other proofs   430
That do demonstrate thinly.

Othello.   I'll tear her all to pieces.

Iago.   Nay, but be wise; yet we see nothing done;
She may be honest yet. Tell me but this:
Have you not sometimes seen a handkerchief
Spotted with strawberries in your wife's hand?

Othello.   I gave her such a one; 'twas my first gift.

Iago.   I know not that; but such a handkerchief—
I am sure it was your wife's—did I to-day
See Cassio wipe his beard with.

Othello.   If it be that,—

Iago.   If it be that, or any that was hers,   440
It speaks against her with the other proofs.

Othello.   O! that the slave had forty thousand lives;

---

[387] Lustful.   [388] Heat.   [389] Seize.   [390] Previous consummation.   [391] (1) Cursed,
(2) Acute, suspicion.

One is too poor, too weak for my revenge.
Now do I see 'tis true. Look here, Iago;
All my fond love thus do I blow to heaven:
'Tis gone.
Arise, black vengeance, from the hollow hell!
Yield up, O love! thy crown and hearted throne
To tyrannous hate. Swell, bosom, with thy fraught,[392]
For 'tis of aspics'[393] tongues!

Iago.   Yet be content.[394]   450
Othello.   O! blood, blood, blood!
Iago.   Patience, I say; your mind, perhaps, may change.
Othello.   Never, Iago. Like to the Pontic sea,[395]
Whose icy current and compulsive course
Ne'er feels retiring ebb, but keeps due on
To the Propontic and the Hellespont,[396]
Even so my bloody thoughts, with violent pace,
Shall ne'er look back, ne'er ebb to humble love,
Till that a capable[397] and wide revenge
Swallow them up.   (*Kneels.*)
                      Now, by yond marble heaven,   460
In the due reverence of a sacred vow
I here engage my words.
Iago.   Do not rise yet.   (*Kneels.*)
Witness, you ever-burning lights above!
You elements that clip[398] us round about!
Witness, that here Iago doth give up
The execution of his wit, hands, heart,
To wrong'd Othello's service! Let him command,
And to obey shall be in me remorse,[399]
What bloody business ever.[400]   (*They rise.*)
Othello.   I greet thy love,
Not with vain thanks, but with acceptance bounteous,   470
And will upon the instant put thee to 't:
Within these three days let me hear thee say
That Cassio 's not alive.
Iago.   My friend is dead; 'tis done at your request:
But let her live.
Othello.   Damn her, lewd minx! O, damn her!
Come, go with me apart; I will withdraw.
To furnish me with some swift means of death
For the fair devil. Now art thou my lieutenant.
Iago.   I am your own for ever.   (*Exeunt.*)

---

[392] Burden.   [393] Poisonous snakes.   [394] Patient.   [395] The Black Sea.   [396] The
Sea of Marmara, The Dardanelles.   [397] Comprehensive.   [398] Encompass.   [399] Probably
a corrupt line; the meaning appears to be: "to obey shall be my solemn obligation."   [400] Soever.

SCENE 4.   Before the Castle.

(Enter Desdemona, Emilia, and Clown.)

Desdemona.   Do you know, sirrah,[401] where Lieutenant Cassio lies?[402]
Clown.   I dare not say he lies any where.
Desdemona.   Why, man?
Clown.   He is a soldier; and for one to say a soldier lies, is stabbing.[403]
Desdemona.   Go to;[404] where lodges he?
Clown.   To tell you where he lodges is to tell you where I lie.
Desdemona.   Can anything be made of this?
Clown.   I know not where he lodges, and for me to devise[405] a lodging, and
   say he lies here or he lies there, were to lie in mine own throat.
Desdemona.   Can you inquire him out, and be edified by report?
Clown.   I will catechize the world for him; that is, make questions, and by
   them answer.
Desdemona.   Seek him, bid him come hither; tell him I have moved my lord
   in his behalf, and hope all will be well.
Clown.   To do this is within the compass of man's wit, and therefore I will
   attempt the doing it.   *(Exit.)*
Desdemona.   Where should I lose that handkerchief, Emilia?
Emilia.   I know not, madam.
Desdemona.   Believe me, I had rather have lost my purse
   Full of cruzadoes;[406] and, but my noble Moor   20
   Is true of mind, and made of no such baseness
   As jealous creatures are, it were enough
   To put him to ill thinking.
Emilia.   Is he not jealous?
Desdemona.   Who! he? I think the sun where he was born
   Drew all such humours from him.
Emilia.   Look! where he comes.
Desdemona.   I will not leave him now till Cassio
   Be call'd to him.

(Enter Othello.)

                      How is 't with you, my lord?
Othello.   Well, my good lady. *(Aside)* O! hardness to dissemble.
   How do you, Desdemona?
Desdemona.   Well, my good lord.
Othello.   Give me your hand. This hand is moist,[407] my lady.   30

---

[401] Common form of address to inferiors.   [402] Lives.   [403] I.e., is cause for stabbing.
[404] Here apparently: "Come on!"   [405] Invent.   [406] Portuguese gold coins.   [407] A
supposed symptom of a lustful nature.

Desdemona.   It yet has felt no age nor known no sorrow.
Othello.   This argues fruitfulness and liberal[408] heart;
  Hot, hot, and moist; this hand of yours requires
  A sequester[409] from liberty, fasting and prayer,
  Much castigation, exercise devout;
  For here 's a young and sweating devil here,
  That commonly rebels. 'Tis a good hand,
  A frank one.
Desdemona.   You may, indeed, say so;
  For 'twas that hand that gave away my heart.
Othello.   A liberal hand; the hearts of old gave hands,   40
  But our new heraldry[410] is hands not hearts.
Desdemona.   I cannot speak of this. Come now, your promise.
Othello.   What promise, chuck?[411]
Desdemona.   I have sent to bid Cassio come speak with you.
Othello.   I have a salt and sorry rheum offends me.
  Lend me thy handkerchief.
Desdemona.   Here, my lord.
Othello.   That which I gave you.
Desdemona.   I have it not about me.
Othello.   Not?
Desdemona.   No, indeed, my lord.
Othello.   That is a fault.
  That handkerchief
  Did an Egyptian[412] to my mother give;   50
  She was a charmer,[413] and could almost read
  The thoughts of people; she told her, while she kept it,
  'Twould make her amiable[414] and subdue my father
  Entirely to her love, but if she lost it
  Or made a gift of it, my father's eye
  Should hold her loathed, and his spirits should hunt
  After new fancies.[415] She dying gave it me;
  And bid me, when my fate would have me wive,
  To give it her. I did so; and take heed on 't;
  Make it a darling like your precious eye;   60
  To lose 't or give 't away, were such perdition
  As nothing else could match.
Desdemona.   Is 't possible?
Othello.   'Tis true; there 's magic in the web of it;
  A sibyl,[416] that had number'd in the world

---

[408] With overtones of: too free, loose.   [409] Separation.   [410] I.e., new heraldic symbolism
(Othello means that the new way is not to give the heart together with the hand).   [411] Common
term of endearment.   [412] Gypsy.   [413] Sorceress.   [414] Lovable, desirable.   [415] Loves.
[416] Prophetess.

The sun to course two hundred compasses,
In her prophetic fury sew'd the work;
The worms were hallow'd that did breed the silk,
And it was dy'd in mummy[417] which the skilful
Conserv'd of maidens' hearts.
Desdemona.   Indeed! is 't true?
Othello.   Most veritable; therefore look to 't well.   70
Desdemona.   Then would to heaven that I had never seen it!
Othello.   Ha! wherefore?
Desdemona.   Why do you speak so startingly and rash?
Othello.   Is 't lost? is 't gone? speak, is it out o' the way?
Desdemona.   Heaven bless us!
Othello.   Say you?
Desdemona.   It is not lost; but what an if[418] it were?
Othello.   How!
Desdemona.   I say, it is not lost.
Othello.   Fetch 't, let me see 't!
Desdemona.   Why, so I can, sir, but I will not now.
This is a trick to put me from my suit: 80
Pray you let Cassio be receiv'd again.
Othello.   Fetch me the handkerchief; my mind misgives.
Desdemona.   Come, come;
You'll never meet a more sufficient[419] man.
Othello.   The handkerchief!
Desdemona.   I pray, talk[420] me of Cassio.
Othello.   The handkerchief!
Desdemona.   A man that all his time
Hath founded his good fortunes on your love,
Shar'd dangers with you,—
Othello.   The handkerchief!
Desdemona.   In sooth, you are to blame.   90
Othello.   Away!   (*Exit.*)
Emilia.   Is not this man jealous?
Desdemona.   I ne'er saw this before.
Sure, there's some wonder in this handkerchief;
I am most unhappy in the loss of it.
Emilia.   'Tis not a year or two shows us a man;
They are all but[421] stomachs, and we all but[421] food;
They eat us hungerly, and when they are full
They belch us. Look you! Cassio and my husband.

(*Enter Iago and Cassio.*)

---

[417] Drug (medicinal or magic) derived from embalmed bodies.   [418] If.
[419] Adequate.   [420] Talk to.   [421] Only . . . only.

Iago.   There is no other way; 'tis she must do 't:
    And, lo! the happiness;[422] go and importune her.   100
Desdemona.   How now, good Cassio! what 's the news with you?
Cassio.   Madam, my former suit: I do beseech you
    That by your virtuous means I may again
    Exist, and be a member of his love
    Whom I with all the office[423] of my heart
    Entirely honour; I would not be delay'd.
    If my offence be of such mortal kind
    That nor my service past, nor present sorrows,
    Nor purpos'd merit in futurity,
    Can ransom me into his love again,   110
    But to know so must be my benefit;
    So shall I clothe me in a forc'd content,
    And shut myself up in some other course
    To fortune's alms.
Desdemona.   Alas! thrice-gentle Cassio!
    My advocation is not now in tune;
    My lord is not my lord, nor should I know him,
    Were he in favour[424] as in humour alter'd.
    So help me every spirit sanctified,
    As I have spoken for you all my best
    And stood within the blank of[425] his displeasure   120
    For my free speech. You must awhile be patient;
    What I can do I will, and more I will
    Than for myself I dare: let that suffice you.
Iago.   Is my lord angry?
Emilia.   He went hence but now,
    And certainly in strange unquietness.
Iago.   Can he be angry? I have seen the cannon,
    When it hath blown his ranks[426] into the air,
    And, like the devil, from his very arm
    Puff'd his own brother; and can he be angry?
    Something of moment[427] then; I will go meet him;   130
    There's matter in 't indeed, if he be angry.
Desdemona.   I prithee, do so. (*Exit Iago.*) Something, sure, of state,[428]
    Either from Venice, or some unhatch'd[429] practice
    Made demonstrable here in Cyprus to him,
    Hath puddled[430] his clear spirit; and, in such cases
    Men's natures wrangle with inferior things,
    Though great ones are their object. 'Tis even so;

---

[422] "What luck!"   [423] Duty.   [424] Appearance.   [425] As the target for.   [426] I.e.,
his soldiers.   [427] Important.   [428] Public affairs.   [429] Abortive or budding plot.
[430] Muddied.

For let our finger ache, and it indues[431]
Our other healthful members even to that sense
Of pain. Nay, we must think men are not gods,   140
Nor of them look for such observancy[432]
As fits the bridal.[433] Beshrew me much, Emilia,
I was—unhandsome warrior as I am—
Arraigning his unkindness with[434] my soul;
But now I find I had suborn'd the witness,[435]
And he 's indicted falsely.

Emilia.   Pray heaven it be state matters, as you think,
And no conception,[436] nor no jealous toy[437]
Concerning you.

Desdemona.   Alas the day! I never gave him cause.   150

Emilia.   But jealous souls will not be answer'd so;
They are not ever jealous for the cause,
But jealous for they are jealous; 'tis a monster
Begot upon itself, born on itself.

Desdemona.   Heaven keep that monster from Othello's mind!

Emilia.   Lady, amen.

Desdemona.   I will go seek him. Cassio, walk hereabout;
If I do find him fit, I'll move your suit
And seek to effect it to my uttermost.

Cassio.   I humbly thank your ladyship.   160

(Exeunt Desdemona and Emilia.)

(Enter Bianca.)

Bianca.   Save you, friend Cassio!

Cassio.   What make you from home?
How is it with you, my most fair Bianca?
I' faith, sweet love, I was coming to your house.

Bianca.   And I was going to your lodging, Cassio.
What! keep a week away? seven days and nights?
Eight score eight hours? and lovers' absent hours,
More tedious than the dial eight score times?
O weary reckoning!

Cassio.   Pardon me, Bianca,
I have this while with leaden thoughts been press'd;
But I shall, in a more continuate[438] time,   170
Strike off[439] this score of absence. Sweet Bianca,

(Giving her Desdemona's handkerchief.)

Take me this work out.

---

[431] Brings, leads.   [432] Attention.   [433] Wedding.   [434] To.   [435] I.e., caused
my soul to bring in wrong charges.   [436] Fancy, supposition.   [437] Fancy.
[438] Uninterrupted.   [439] Cancel (i.e., make up for).

Bianca.   O Cassio! whence came this?
  This is some token from a newer friend;
  To the felt absence now I feel a cause;
  Is 't come to this? Well, well.
Cassio.   Go to, woman!
  Throw your vile guesses in the devil's teeth,
  From whence you have them. You are jealous now
  That this is from some mistress, some remembrance:
  No, in good troth, Bianca.
Bianca.   Why, whose is it?   180
Cassio.   I know not, sweet; I found it in my chamber.
  I like the work well; ere it be demanded,—[440]
  As like enough it will,—I'd have it copied;
  Take it and do 't; and leave me for this time.
Bianca.   Leave you! wherefore?
Cassio.   I do attend here on[441] the general,
  And think it no addition,[442] nor my wish,
  To have him see me woman'd.
Bianca.   Why, I pray you?
Cassio.   Not that I love you not.
Bianca.   But that you do not love me.
  I pray you, bring me on the way a little   190
  And say if I shall see you soon at night.
Cassio.   'Tis but a little way that I can bring you,
  For I attend here; but I'll see you soon.
Bianca.   'Tis very good; I must be circumstanc'd.[443]   (*Exeunt.*)

Act IV

SCENE 1.   Cyprus. Before the Castle.

(*Enter Othello and Iago.*)

Iago.   Will you think so?
Othello.   Think so, Iago!
Iago.   What!
  To kiss in private?
Othello.   An unauthoriz'd kiss.
Iago.   Or to be naked with her friend a-bed
  An hour or more, not meaning any harm?
Othello.   Naked a-bed, Iago, and not mean harm?

---

[440] Asked for.   [441] Wait for.   [442] Advantage, credit.   [443] Governed by circumstances.

It is hypocrisy against the devil:[444]
They that mean virtuously, and yet do so,
The devil their virtue tempts, and they tempt heaven.
Iago.   If they do nothing, 'tis a venial slip;
But if I give my wife a handkerchief,—   10
Othello.   What then?
Iago.   Why, then, 'tis hers, my lord; and, being hers,
She may, I think, bestow 't on any man.
Othello.   She is protectress of her honour too;
May she give that?
Iago.   Her honour is an essence that 's not seen;
They have it very oft that have it not:[445]
But for the handkerchief,—
Othello.   By heaven, I would most gladly have forgot it:—
Thou said'st,—O! it comes o'er my memory,   20
As doth the raven[446] o'er the infected house,
Boding to all,—he had my handkerchief.
Iago.   Ay, what of that?
Othello.   That's not so good now.
Iago.   What,
If I had said I had seen him do you wrong?
Or heard him say, as knaves be such abroad,[447]
Who having, by their own importunate suit,
Or voluntary dotage[448] of some mistress,
Convinced or supplied them,[449] cannot choose
But they must blab.
Othello.   Hath he said any thing?
Iago.   He hath, my lord; but be you well assur'd,   30
No more than he'll unswear.
Othello.   What hath he said?
Iago.   Faith, that he did— I know not what he did.
Othello.   What? what?
Iago.   Lie—
Othello.   With her?
Iago.   With her, on her; what you will.
Othello.   Lie with her; lie on her! We say, lie on her, when they belie her.
Lie with her! that's fulsome. Handkerchief,—confessions,—handkerchief! To
confess, and be hanged for his labour. First, to be hanged, and then to
confess: I tremble at it. Nature would not invest herself in such shadowing
passion without some instruction.[450] It is not words that shake me thus. Pish!
Noses, ears, and lips. It is possible?—Confess!—Handkerchief!—O devil!

---

[444] I.e., by not committing the sin which the situation invites.   [445] I.e., some unchaste
women are thought chaste.   [446] (1) A bad omen, (2) A carrier of the plague.   [447] As
there are some such in the world.   [448] Foolish affection.   [449] Overcome (their reluc-
tance) or satisfied (their desires).   [450] I would not fall into such passion unless there were some
real grounds for it.

(Falls in a trance.)

Iago. Work on,
  My medicine, work! Thus credulous fools are caught;
  And many worthy and chaste dames even thus,
  All guiltless, meet reproach. What, ho! my lord!
  My lord, I say! Othello!

(Enter Cassio.)

                        How now, Cassio!
Cassio.   What's the matter?
Iago.   My lord is fallen into an epilepsy;[451]
  This is his second fit; he had one yesterday.
Cassio.   Rub him about the temples.
Iago.   No, forbear;
  The lethargy[452] must have his quiet course,   50
  If not, he foams at mouth, and by and by
  Breaks out to savage madness. Look! he stirs;
  Do you withdraw yourself a little while,
  He will recover straight; when he is gone,
  I would on great occasion[453] speak with you.   *(Exit Cassio.)*
  How is it, general? have you not hurt your head?
Othello.   Dost thou mock me?[454]
Iago.   I mock you! no, by heaven.
  Would you would bear your fortune like a man!
Othello.   A horned man's a monster and a beast.
Iago.   There's many a beast then, in a populous city,   60
  And many a civil[455] monster.
Othello.   Did he confess it?
Iago.   Good sir, be a man;
  Think every bearded fellow that's but yok'd
  May draw[456] with you; there's millions now alive
  That nightly lie in those unproper[457] beds
  Which they dare swear peculiar;[458] your case is better.
  O! 'tis the spite of hell, the fiend's arch-mock,
  To lip[459] a wanton in a secure[460] couch,
  And to suppose her chaste. No, let me know;
  And knowing what I am, I know what she shall be.   70
Othello.   O! thou art wise; 'tis certain.

---

[451] Seizure, fit.   [452] Coma.   [453] Important matter.   [454] Another allusion to the
cuckold's horns.   [455] Citizen.   [456] I.e., pull the burden of cuckoldom.   [457] Not
exclusively their own.   [458] Exclusively their own.   [459] Kiss.   [460] I.e., without
suspicion of having a rival.

Iago.   Stand you awhile apart;
    Confine yourself but in a patient list.[461]
    Whilst you were here o'erwhelmed with your grief,—
    A passion most unsuiting such a man,—
    Cassio came hither; I shifted him away,
    And laid good 'scuse upon your ecstasy;[462]
    Bade him anon return and here speak with me;
    The which he promis'd. Do but encave yourself,
    And mark the fleers, the gibes, and notable scorns,
    That dwell in every region of his face;   80
    For I will make him tell the tale anew,
    Where, how, how oft, how long ago, and when
    He hath, and is again to cope[463] your wife:
    I say, but mark his gesture. Marry, patience;
    Or I shall say you are all in all in spleen,[464]
    And nothing of a man.
Othello.   Dost thou hear, Iago?
    I will be found most cunning in my patience;
    But—dost thou hear?—most bloody.
Iago.   That's not amiss:
    But yet keep time[465] in all. Will you withdraw?   *(Othello goes apart.)*
    Now will I question Cassio of Bianca,   90
    A housewife[466] that by selling her desires
    Buys herself bread and clothes; it is a creature
    That dotes on Cassio; as 'tis the strumpet's plague
    To beguile many and be beguil'd by one.
    He, when he hears of her, cannot refrain
    From the excess of laughter. Here he comes:

(Re-enter Cassio.)

    As he shall smile, Othello shall go mad;
    And his unbookish[467] jealousy must construe
    Poor Cassio's smiles, gestures, and light behaviour
    Quite in the wrong. How do you now, lieutenant?   100
Cassio.   The worser that you give me the addition[468]
    Whose want[469] even kills me.
Iago.   Ply Desdemona well, and you are sure on 't.
    (Speaking lower.) Now, if this suit lay in Bianca's power,
    How quickly should you speed!
Cassio.   Alas! poor caitiff![470]
Othello.   Look! how he laughs already!

---

461 Bounds of patience.   462 Derangement, trance.   463 Close with.   464 Completely
overcome by passion.   465 Maintain control.   466 Hussy.   467 Unpracticed,
naive.   468 Title.   469 The want of which.   470 Wretch.

Iago.   I never knew woman love man so.

Cassio.   Alas! poor rogue, I think i' faith, she loves me.

Othello.   Now he denies it faintly, and laughs it out.

Iago.   Do you hear, Cassio?

Othello.   Now he importunes him   110
To tell it o'er: go to; well said, well said.

Iago.   She gives it out that you shall marry her;
Do you intend it?

Cassio.   Ha, ha, ha!

Othello.   Do you triumph, Roman?[471] do you triumph?

Cassio.   I marry her! what? a customer?[472] I prithee, bear some charity to my
wit;[473] do not think it so unwholesome. Ha, ha, ha!

Othello.   So, so, so, so. They laugh that win.[474]

Iago.   Faith, the cry goes that you shall marry her.

Cassio.   Prithee, say true.   120

Iago.   I am a very villain else.

Othello.   Have you scored me?[475] Well.

Cassio.   This is the monkey's own giving out: she is persuaded I will marry
her, out of her own love and flattery, not out of my promise.

Othello.   Iago beckons me;[476] now he begins the story.

Cassio.   She was here even now; she haunts me in every place. I was the other
day talking on the sea-bank with certain Venetians, and thither comes this
bauble,[477] and, by this hand, she falls me thus about my neck;—

Othello.   Crying, 'O dear Cassio!' as it were; his gesture imports it.

Cassio.   So hangs and lolls and weeps upon me; so hales[478] and pulls me; ha,
ha, ha!

Othello.   Now he tells how she plucked him to my chamber. O! I see that
nose of yours, but not the dog I shall throw it to.

Cassio.   Well, I must leave her company.

Iago.   Before me![479] look, where she comes.

Cassio.   'Tis such another fitchew![480] marry, a perfumed one.

(Enter Bianca.)

What do you mean by this haunting of me?

Bianca.   Let the devil and his dam haunt you! What did you mean by that
same handkerchief you gave me even now? I was a fine fool to take it. I must
take out the work! A likely piece of work, that you should find it in your
chamber, and not know who left it there! This is some minx's token, and I
must take out the work! There, give it your hobby-horse;[481] wheresoever you
had it I'll take out no work on 't.

---

[471] I.e., one who triumphs(?).   [472] Courtesan, prostitute.   [473] Give me credit for some
sense.   [474] "He who laughs last laughs longest"(?).   [475] Wounded, defaced(?); or: settled
my account(?).   [476] Signals.   [477] Plaything.   [478] Hauls.   [479] An exclamation
of surprise.   [480] Polecat, noted both for its strong smell and for its lechery.   [481] Harlot.

Cassio.   How now, my sweet Bianca! how now, how now!

Othello.   By heaven, that should be[482] my handkerchief!

Bianca.   An you'll come to supper to-night, you may; an you will not, come
when you are next prepared[483] for.   *(Exit.)*

Iago.   After her, after her.

Cassio.   Faith, I must; she'll rail in the street else.

Iago.   Will you sup there?

Cassio.   Faith, I intend so.

Iago.   Well, I may chance to see you, for I would very fain[484] speak with you.

Cassio.   Prithee come; will you?

Iago.   Go to; say no more.   *(Exit Cassio.)*

Othello *(advancing)*.   How shall I murder him, Iago?

Iago.   Did you perceive how he laughed at his vice?

Othello.   O! Iago!

Iago.   And did you see the handkerchief?

Othello.   Was that mine?

Iago.   Yours, by this hand; and to see how he prizes the foolish woman your
wife! she gave it him, and he hath given it his whore.

Othello.   I would have him nine years a-killing. A fine woman! a fair woman!
a sweet woman!

Iago.   Nay, you must forget that.

Othello.   Ay, let her rot, and perish, and be damned to-night; for she shall not
live. No, my heart is turned to stone; I strike it, and it hurts my hand. O! the
world hath not a sweeter creature; she might lie by an emperor's side and
command him tasks.

Iago.   Nay, that's not your way.[485]

Othello.   Hang her! I do but say what she is. So delicate with her needle! An
admirable musician! O, she will sing the savageness out of a bear. Of so high
and plenteous wit and invention!

Iago.   She's the worse for all this.

Othello.   O! a thousand, a thousand times. And then, of so gentle a condition![486]

Iago.   Ay, too gentle.[487]

Othello.   Nay, that's certain;—but yet the pity of it, Iago!
O! Iago, the pity of it, Iago!

Iago.   If you are so fond over her iniquity, give her patent to offend; for, if it
touch not you, it comes near nobody.

Othello.   I will chop her into messes.[488] Cuckold me!

Iago.   O! 'tis foul in her.

Othello.   With mine officer!

Iago.   That's fouler.

---

[482] I.e., I think that is.   [483] Expected (Bianca means that if he does not come that night, she
will never want to see him again).   [484] Gladly.   [485] Proper course.   [486] So much
the high-born lady.   [487] I.e., yielding.   [488] Bits.

Othello.   Get me some poison, Iago; this night: I'll not expostulate with her, lest her body and beauty unprovide my mind again.[489] This night, Iago.

Iago.   Do it not with poison, strangle her in her bed, even the bed she hath contaminated.

Othello.   Good, good; the justice of it pleases; very good.

Iago.   And for Cassio, let me be his undertaker;[490] you shall hear more by midnight.

Othello.   Excellent good. (*A trumpet within.*) What trumpet is that same?

Iago.   Something from Venice, sure. 'Tis Lodovico,
   Come from the duke; and see, your wife is with him.

(Enter Lodovico, Desdemona, and Attendants.)

Lodovico.   God save you, worthy general!

Othello.   With all my heart, sir.

Lodovico.   The duke and senators of Venice greet you.

(Gives him a packet.)

Othello.   I kiss the instrument of their pleasures.

(Opens the packet, and reads.)

Desdemona.   And what's the news, good cousin Lodovico?

Iago.   I am very glad to see you, signior;
   Welcome to Cyprus.

Lodovico.   I thank you. How does Lieutenant Cassio?

Iago.   Lives, sir.   200

Desdemona.   Cousin, there's fall'n between him and my lord
   An unkind[491] breach; but you shall make all well.

Othello.   Are you sure of that?

Desdemona.   My lord?

Othello (*reads*).   'This fail you not to do, as you will'—

Lodovico.   He did not call; he's busy in the paper.
   Is there division[492] twixt my lord and Cassio?

Desdemona.   A most unhappy one; I would do much
   To atone[493] them, for the love I bear to Cassio.

Othello.   Fire and brimstone!

Desdemona.   My lord?

Othello.   Are you wise?   210

Desdemona.   What! is he angry?

Lodovico.   May be the letter mov'd him;

---

[489] Unsettle my intention.   [490] Dispatcher.   [491] Unnatural.   [492] Estrangement.
[493] Reconcile.

For, as I think, they do command him home,
Deputing Cassio in his government.
Desdemona.   Trust me, I am glad on 't.
Othello.   Indeed!
Desdemona.   My lord?
Othello.   I am glad to see you mad.
Desdemona.   Why, sweet Othello?
Othello.   Devil!   *(Strikes her.)*
Desdemona.   I have not deserved this.
Lodovico.   My lord, this would not be believ'd in Venice,
    Though I should swear I saw 't; 'tis very much;
    Make her amends, she weeps.
Othello.   O devil, devil!
    If that the earth could teem with woman's tears,   240
    Each drop she falls[494] would prove a crocodile.[495]
    Out of my sight!
Desdemona.   I will not stay to offend you.   *(Going.)*
Lodovico.   Truly, an obedient lady;
    I do beseech your lordship, call her back.
Othello.   Mistress!
Desdemona.   My lord?
Othello.   What would you with her, sir?
Lodovico.   Why, I, my lord?
Othello.   Ay; you did wish that I would make her turn:
    Sir, she can turn, and turn, and yet go on,
    And turn again; and she can weep, sir, weep;
    And she's obedient, as you say, obedient,   230
    Very obedient. Proceed you in your tears.
    Concerning this, sir—O well-painted passion!—
    I am commanded home. Get you away;
    I'll send for you anon. Sir, I obey the mandate,
    And will return to Venice. Hence! avaunt![496]   *(Exit Desdemona.)*
    Cassio shall have my place. And, sir, to-night,
    I do entreat that we may sup together;
    You are welcome, sir, to Cyprus. Goats and monkeys!   *(Exit.)*
Lodovico.   Is this the noble Moor whom our full senate
    Call all-in-all sufficient? is this the noble nature   240
    Whom passion could not shake? whose solid virtue
    The shot of accident nor dart of chance
    Could neither graze nor pierce?
Iago.   He is much chang'd.
Lodovico.   Are his wits safe? is he not light of brain?
Iago.   He's that he is; I may not breathe my censure.

---

[494] Lets fall.   [495] The crocodile's tears were supposed to be hypocritical.   [496] Begone!

What he might be, if, what he might, he is not,
I would to heaven he were!⁴⁹⁷

Lodovico.   What! strike his wife!

Iago.   Faith, that was not so well; yet would I knew
That stroke would prove the worst!

Lodovico.   Is it his use?
Or did the letters work upon his blood,   250
And new-create this fault?

Iago.   Alas, alas!
It is not honesty in me to speak
What I have seen and known. You shall observe him,
And his own courses⁴⁹⁸ will denote him so
That I may save my speech. Do but go after
And mark how he continues.

Lodovico.   I am sorry that I am deceiv'd in him.   *(Exeunt.)*

SCENE 2.   A Room in the Castle.

(Enter Othello and Emilia.)

Othello.   You have seen nothing, then?

Emilia.   Nor ever heard, nor ever did suspect.

Othello.   Yes, you have seen Cassio and her together.

Emilia.   But then I saw no harm, and then I heard
Each syllable that breath made up between them.

Othello.   What! did they never whisper?

Emilia.   Never, my lord.

Othello.   Nor send you out o' the way?

Emilia.   Never.

Othello.   To fetch her fan, her gloves, her mask, nor nothing?⁴⁹⁹

Emilia.   Never, my lord.   10

Othello.   That's strange.

Emilia.   I durst, my lord, to wager she is honest,
Lay down my soul at stake: if you think other,
Remove your thought; it doth abuse your bosom.
If any wretch have put this in your head,
Let heaven requite it with the serpent's curse!
For, if she be not honest, chaste, and true,
There's no man happy; the purest of their wives
Is foul as slander.

---

⁴⁹⁷ Another of Iago's gnomic speeches; perhaps approximately: "If now he is not himself, I wish he would be what he could be!"   ⁴⁹⁸ Actions.   ⁴⁹⁹ Anything.

Othello.   Bid her come hither; go.   *(Exit Emilia.)*
 She says enough; yet she 's a simple⁵⁰⁰ bawd   20
 That cannot say as much. This is a subtle whore,
 A closet lock and key of villanous secrets;
 And yet she 'll kneel and pray; I have seen her do 't.

(Re-enter Emilia with Desdemona.)

Desdemona.   My lord, what is your will?
Othello.   Pray, chuck, come hither.
Desdemona.   What is your pleasure?
Othello.   Let me see your eyes;
 Look in my face.
Desdemona.   What horrible fancy 's this?
Othello *(to Emilia)*.   Some of your function,⁵⁰¹ mistress;
 Leave procreants alone and shut the door;
 Cough or cry 'hem' if any body come;
 Your mystery,⁵⁰² your mystery; nay, dispatch.   *(Exit Emilia.)*
Desdemona.   Upon my knees, what doth your speech import?   31
 I understand a fury in your words.
 But not the words.
Othello.   Why, what art thou?
Desdemona.   Your wife, my lord; your true
 And loyal wife.
Othello.   Come, swear it, damn thyself;
 Lest, being like one of heaven, the devils themselves
 Should fear to seize thee; therefore be double-damn'd;
 Swear thou art honest.
Desdemona.   Heaven doth truly know it.
Othello.   Heaven truly knows that thou art false as hell.
Desdemona.   To whom, my lord? with whom? how am I false?   40
Othello.   Ah! Desdemona; away, away, away!
Desdemona.   Alas, the heavy day!—Why do you weep?
 Am I the motive of these tears, my lord?
 If haply you my father do suspect
 An instrument of this your calling back,
 Lay not your blame on me; if you have lost him,
 Why, I have lost him too.
Othello.   Had it pleas'd heaven
 To try me with affliction, had he rain'd
 All kinds of sores and shames on my bare head,
 Steep'd me in poverty to the very lips,   50

---

⁵⁰⁰ Simpleminded.   ⁵⁰¹ To your duty, business.   ⁵⁰² Trade.

Given to captivity me and my utmost hopes,
I should have found in some part of my soul
A drop of patience; but, alas! to make me
The fixed figure for the time of scorn[503]
To point his slow and moving finger at;
Yet could I bear that too; well, very well:
But there, where I have garner'd[504] up my heart,
Where either I must live or bear no life,
The fountain from the which my current runs
Or else dries up; to be discarded thence!   60
Or keep it as a cistern for foul toads
To knot and gender in![505] Turn thy complexion there,[506]
Patience, thou young and rose-lipp'd cherubin;
Ay, there, look grim as hell!
Desdemona.   I hope my noble lord esteems me honest.
Othello.   O! ay; as summer flies are in the shambles,[507]
That quicken even with blowing. O thou weed!
Who art so lovely fair and smell'st so sweet
That the sense aches at thee, would thou hadst ne'er been born.
Desdemona.   Alas! what ignorant sin have I commited?   70
Othello.   Was this fair paper, this most goodly book,
Made to write 'whore' upon? What committed!
Committed! O thou public commoner![508]
I should make very forges of my cheeks,
That would to cinders burn up modesty,
Did I but speak thy deeds. What committed!
Heaven stops the nose at it and the moon winks,[509]
The bawdy wind that kisses all it meets
Is hush'd within the hollow mine of earth,
And will not hear it. What committed!   80
Impudent strumpet!
Desdemona.   By heaven, you do me wrong.
Othello.   Are not you a strumpet?
Desdemona.   No, as I am a Christian.
If to preserve this vessel for my lord
From any other foul unlawful touch
Be not to be a strumpet, I am none.
Othello.   What! not a whore?
Desdemona.   No, as I shall be sav'd.
Othello.   Is it possible?
Desdemona.   O! heaven forgive us.

---

[503] I.e., the scornful world.   [504] Stored.   [505] Bunch up and procreate.   [506] I.e.,
change your color to suit the "cistern for foul toads."   [507] Slaughterhouse.   [508] Harlot.
[509] Closes her eyes.

Othello.   I cry you mercy,[510] then;
I took you for that cunning whore of Venice
That married with Othello. You, mistress,   90
That have the office opposite to Saint Peter,
And keep the gate of hell!

(Re-enter Emilia.)

                                  You, you, ay, you!
We have done our course; there's money for your pains.
I pray you, turn the key and keep our counsel.   *(Exit.)*
Emilia.   Alas! what does this gentleman conceive?[511]
How do you, madam? how do you, my good lady?
Desdemona.   Faith, half asleep.
Emilia.   Good madam, what 's the matter with my lord?
Desdemona.   With who?
Emilia.   Why, with my lord, madam.   100
Desdemona.   Who is thy lord?
Emilia.   He that is yours, sweet lady.
Desdemona.   I have none; do not talk to me, Emilia;
I cannot weep, nor answer have I none,
But what should go by water.[512] Prithee, to-night
Lay on my bed my wedding sheets: remember:
And call thy husband hither.
Emilia.   Here is a change indeed!   *(Exit.)*
Desdemona.   'Tis meet I should be us'd so, very meet.
How have I been behav'd, that he might stick
The small'st opinion on my least misuse?[513]

(Re-enter Emilia, with Iago.)

Iago.   What is your pleasure, madam? How is it with you?   110
Desdemona.   I cannot tell. Those that do teach young babes
Do it with gentle means and easy tasks;
He might have chid me so; for, in good faith,
I am a child to chiding.
Iago.   What 's the matter, lady?
Emilia.   Alas, Iago, my lord hath so bewhor'd her,
Thrown such despite[514] and heavy terms upon her,
As true hearts cannot bear.
Desdemona.   Am I that name, Iago?
Iago.   What name, fair lady?
Desdemona.   Such as she says my lord did say I was.

---

[510] Beg your pardon.   [511] Imagine.   [512] Be conveyed by means of tears.   [513] The
least suspicion on my slightest misconduct.   [514] Abuse.

Emilia. He call'd her whore; a beggar in his drink   120
  Could not have laid such terms upon his callat.[515]
Iago. Why did he so?
Desdemona. I do not know; I am sure I am none such.
Iago. Do not weep, do not weep. Alas the day!
Emilia. Has she forsook so many noble matches,
  Her father and her country and her friends,
  To be call'd whore? would it not make one weep?
Desdemona. It is my wretched fortune.
Iago.   Beshrew[516] him for it!
  How comes this trick upon him?
Desdemona.   Nay, heaven doth know.
Emilia. I will be hang'd, if some eternal villain,   130
  Some busy and insinuating rogue,
  Some cogging[517] cozening slave, to get some office,
  Have not devis'd this slander; I 'll be hang'd else.
Iago. Fie! there is no such man; it is impossible.
Desdemona. If any such there be, heaven pardon him!
Emilia. A halter pardon him, and hell gnaw his bones!
  Why should he call her whore? who keeps her company?
  What place? what time? what form? what likelihood?
  The Moor 's abus'd by some most villanous knave,
  Some base notorious knave, some scurvy fellow.   140
  O heaven! that such companions[518] thou'dst unfold,
  And put in every honest hand a whip
  To lash the rascals naked through the world,
  Even from the east to west!
Iago.   Speak within door.
Emilia. O! fie upon them. Some such squire he was
  That turn'd your wit the seamy side without,[519]
  And made you to suspect me with the Moor.
Iago. You are a fool; go to.
Desdemona.   O good Iago,
  What shall I do to win my lord again?
  Good friend, go to him; for, by this light of heaven,   150
  I know not how I lost him. Here I kneel:
  If e'er my will did trespass 'gainst his love,
  Either in discourse of thought or actual deed,
  Or that mine eyes, mine ears, or any sense,
  Delighted them[520] in any other form;
  Or that I do not yet,[521] and ever did,
  And ever will, though he do shake me off
  To beggarly divorcement, love him dearly,

---

[515] Slut.   [516] Curse.   [517] Cheating.   [518] Fellows   (derogatory).
[519] Outward.   [520] Found delight.   [521] Still.

Comfort forswear me! Unkindness may do much;
And his unkindness may defeat[522] my life,   160
But never taint my love. I cannot say 'whore':
It does abhor me now I speak the word;
To do the act that might the addition earn
Not the world's mass of vanity could make me.
Iago.   I pray you be content, 'tis but his humour;
The business of the state does him offence,
And he does chide with you.
Desdemona.   If 'twere no other,—
Iago.   'Tis but so, I warrant.   *(Trumpets.)*
Hark! how these instruments summon to supper;
The messengers of Venice stay the meat: 170
Go in, and weep not; all things shall be well.

                              (Exeunt Desdemona and Emilia.)

(Enter Roderigo.)

How now, Roderigo!
Roderigo.   I do not find that thou dealest justly with me.
Iago.   What in the contrary?[523]
Roderigo.   Every day thou daffest me[524] with some device, Iago; and rather,
as it seems to me now, keepest from me all conveniency,[525] than suppliest
me with the least advantage of hope. I will indeed no longer endure it, nor
am I yet persuaded to put up[526] in peace what already I have foolishly suffered.
Iago.   Will you hear me, Roderigo?
Roderigo.   Faith, I have heard too much, for your words and performances are
no kin together.
Iago.   You charge me most unjustly.
Roderigo.   With nought but truth. I have wasted myself out of my means. The
jewels you have had from me to deliver to Desdemona would half have
corrupted a votarist;[527] you have told me she has received them, and returned
me expectations and comforts of sudden respect[528] and acquaintance, but I
find none.
Iago.   Well; go to; very well.
Roderigo.   Very well! go to! I cannot go to, man; nor 'tis not very well: by this
hand, I say, it is very scurvy, and begin to find myself fobbed[529] in it.
Iago.   Very well.
Roderigo.   I tell you 'tis not very well. I will make myself known to Desdemona;
if she will return me my jewels, I will give over my suit and repent my
unlawful solicitation; if not, assure yourself I will seek satisfaction of you.
Iago.   You have said now.[530]

---

[522] Destroy.   [523] I.e., what reason do you have for saying that.   [524] You put me
off.   [525] Favorable circumstances.   [526] Put up with.   [527] Nun.   [528] Immediate
consideration.   [529] Cheated.   [530] I.e, "I suppose you're through?" (?); or: "Now you're
talking" (?).

Roderigo. Ay, and said nothing, but what I protest intendment of doing.

Iago. Why, now I see there's mettle in thee, and even from this instant do build on thee a better opinion than ever before. Give me thy hand, Roderigo; thou hast taken against me a most just exception; but yet, I protest, I have dealt most directly in thy affair.

Roderigo. It hath not appeared.

Iago. I grant indeed it hath not appeared, and your suspicion is not without wit and judgment. But, Roderigo, if thou hast that in thee indeed, which I have greater reason to believe now than ever, I mean purpose, courage, and valour, this night show it: if thou the next night following enjoy not Desdemona, take me from this world with treachery and devise engines for[531] my life.

Roderigo. Well, what is it? is it within reason and compass?

Iago. Sir, there is especial commission come from Venice to depute Cassio in Othello's place.

Roderigo. Is that true? why, then Othello and Desdemona return again to Venice.

Iago. O, no! he goes into Mauritania, and takes away with him the fair Desdemona, unless his abode be lingered here by some accident; wherein none can be so determinate[532] as the removing of Cassio.

Roderigo. How do you mean, removing of him?

Iago. Why, by making him uncapable of Othello's place; knocking out his brains.

Roderigo. And that you would have me do?

Iago. Ay; if you dare do yourself a profit and a right. He sups to-night with a harlotry,[533] and thither will I go to him; he knows not yet of his honourable fortune. If you will watch his going thence,—which I will fashion to fall out between twelve and one,—you may take him at your pleasure; I will be near to second your attempt, and he shall fall between us. Come, stand not amazed at it, but go along with me; I will show you such a necessity in his death that you shall think yourself bound to put it on him. It is now high supper-time, and the night grows to waste; about it.

Roderigo. I will hear further reason for this.

Iago. And you shall be satisfied. *(Exeunt.)*

SCENE 3. Another Room in the Castle.

(Enter Othello, Lodovico, Desdemona, Emilia, and Attendants.)

Lodovico. I do beseech you, sir, trouble yourself no further.

Othello. O! pardon me; 'twill do me good to walk.

Lodovico. Madam, good-night; I humbly thank your ladyship.

---

[531] Devices against.   [532] Effective.   [533] Harlot.

Desdemona.   Your honour is most welcome.

Othello.   Will you walk, sir?
O! Desdemona,—

Desdemona.   My lord?

Othello.   Get you to bed on the instant; I will be returned forthwith; dismiss
your attendant there; look it be done.

Desdemona.   I will, my lord.   *(Exeunt Othello, Lodovico, and Attendants.)*

Emilia.   How goes it now? He looks gentler than he did.   240

Desdemona.   He says he will return incontinent;[534]
He hath commanded me to go to bed,
And bade me to dismiss you.

Emilia.   Dismiss me!

Desdemona.   It was his bidding; therefore, good Emilia,
Give me my nightly wearing, and adieu:
We must not now displease him.

Emilia.   I would you had never seen him.

Desdemona.   So would not I; my love doth so approve him,
That even his stubbornness,[535] his checks[536] and frowns,—
Prithee, unpin me,—have grace and favour in them.   250

Emilia.   I have laid those sheets you bade me on the bed.

Desdemona.   All's one.[537] Good faith! how foolish are our minds!
If I do die before thee, prithee, shroud me
In one of those same sheets.

Emilia.   Come, come, you talk.

Desdemona.   My mother had a maid call'd Barbara;
She was in love, and he she lov'd prov'd mad[538]
And did forsake her; she had a song of 'willow';
An old thing 'twas, but it express'd her fortune,
And she died singing it; that song to-night
Will not go from my mind; I have much to do   260
But to go hang my head all at one side,
And sing it like poor Barbara. Prithee, dispatch.

Emilia.   Shall I go fetch your night-gown?

Desdemona.   No, unpin me here.
This Lodovico is a proper man.

Emilia.   A very handsome man.

Desdemona.   He speaks well.

Emilia.   I know a lady in Venice would have walked barefoot to Palestine for
a touch of his nether lip.

Desdemona *(sings)*.
The poor soul sat sighing by a sycamore tree,
Sing all a green willow;   270

---

[534] At once.   [535] Roughness.   [536] Rebukes.   [537] I.e., it doesn't matter.
[538] Wild.

Her hand on her bosom, her head on her knee,
    Sing willow, willow, willow:
The fresh streams ran by her, and murmur'd her moans;
    Sing willow, willow, willow:
Her salt tears fell from her and soften'd the stones;—

Lay by these:—
    Sing willow, willow, willow:

Prithee, hie thee;[539] he 'll come anon.—

Sing all a green willow must be my garland.
    Let nobody blame him, his scorn I approve,—   280
Nay, that's not next. Hark! who is it that knocks?
Emilia.   It is the wind.
Desdemona.
    I call'd my love false love; but what said he then?
        Sing willow, willow, willow:
    If I court moe[540] women, you 'll couch with moe men.

So, get thee gone; good-night. Mine eyes do itch;
Doth that bode weeping?
Emilia.   'Tis neither here nor there.
Desdemona.   I have heard it said so. O! these men, these men!
    Dost thou in conscience think, tell me, Emilia,
    That there be women do abuse their husbands   290
    In such gross kind?
Emilia.   There be some such, no question.
Desdemona.   Wouldst thou do such a deed for all the world?
Emilia.   Why, would not you?
Desdemona.   No, by this heavenly light!
Emilia.   Nor I neither by this heavenly light;
    I might do 't as well i' the dark.
Desdemona.   Wouldst thou do such a deed for all the world?
Emilia.   The world is a huge thing; 'tis a great price
    For a small vice.
Desdemona.   In troth, I think thou wouldst not.
Emilia.   In troth, I think I should, and undo 't when I had done. Marry, I
    would not do such a thing for a joint-ring,[541] nor measures of lawn,[542] nor
    for gowns, petticoats, nor caps, nor any petty exhibition;[543] but for the whole
    world, who would not make her husband a cuckold to make him a monarch?
    I should venture purgatory for 't.

---

[539] Hurry.   [540] More.   [541] Ring made in separable halves.   [542] Fine linen.
[543] Offer, gift.

Desdemona.   Beshrew me, if I would do such a wrong
    For the whole world.
Emilia.   Why, the wrong is but a wrong i' the world; and having the world for
    your labour, 'tis a wrong in your own world, and you might quickly make it
    right.
Desdemona.   I do not think there is any such woman.
Emilia.   Yes, a dozen; and as many to the vantage,[544] as   310
    Would store[545] the world they played for.
    But I do think it is their husbands' faults
    If wives do fall. Say that they slack their duties,
    And pour our treasures into foreign laps,
    Or else break out in peevish jealousies,
    Throwing restraint upon us; or say they strike us,
    Or scant[546] our former having[547] in despite;
    Why, we have galls;[548] and though we have some grace,
    Yet have we some revenge. Let husbands know
    Their wives have sense like them; they see and smell,   320
    And have their palates both for sweet and sour,
    As husbands have. What is it that they do
    When they change us for others? Is it sport?[549]
    I think it is; and doth affection breed it?
    I think it doth; is 't frailty that thus errs?
    It is so too; and have not we affections,
    Desires for sport, and frailty, as men have?
    Then, let them use us well; else let them know,
    The ills we do, their ills instruct us so.
Desdemona.   Good-night, good night; heaven me such usage[550] send,   330
    Not to pick bad from bad, but by bad mend!   *(Exeunt.)*

Act V

SCENE 1.   Cyprus. A Street.

(Enter Iago and Roderigo.)

Iago.   Here, stand behind this bulk;[551] straight will he come:
    Wear thy good rapier bare, and put it home.
    Quick, quick; fear nothing; I 'll be at thy elbow.
    It makes us, or it mars us; think on that,
    And fix most firm thy resolution.

---

[544] Over and above.   [545] Populate.   [546] Reduce.   [547] Allowance.   [548] Spirits, temper.   [549] Lust, sexual enjoyment.   [550] Habits (?), treatment (?).   [551] Jutting part of a wall.

Roderigo.   Be near at hand; I may miscarry in 'i.
Iago.   Here, at thy hand: be bold, and take thy stand.   *(Retires.)*
Roderigo.   I have no great devotion to the deed;
    And yet he has given me satisfying reasons:
    'Tis but a man gone: forth, my sword; he dies.   10
Iago.   I have rubb'd this young quat[552] almost to the sense,[553]
    And he grows angry. Now, whether he kill Cassio,
    Or Cassio him, or each do kill the other,
    Every way makes my gain: live Roderigo,
    He calls me to a restitution large
    Of gold and jewels that I bobb'd[554] from him,
    As gifts to Desdemona;
    It must not be: if Cassio do remain,
    He hath a daily beauty in his life
    That makes me ugly: and, besides, the Moor   20
    May unfold me to him; there stand I in much peril.
    No, he must die. But so;[555] I hear him coming.

(Enter Cassio.)

Roderigo.   I know his gait; 'tis he. Villain, thou diest!

(Makes a pass at Cassio.)

Cassio.   That thrust had been mine enemy indeed
    But that my coat is better than thou know'st;
    I will make proof of thine.

(Draws, and wounds Roderigo.)

Roderigo.   O! I am slain.

(Iago from behind wounds Cassio in the leg, and exit.)

Cassio.   I am maim'd for ever. Help, ho! murder! murder!   *(Falls.)*

(Enter Othello, at a distance.)

Othello.   The voice of Cassio: Iago keeps his word.
Roderigo.   O! villain that I am!
Othello.   It is e'en so.
Cassio.   O, help, ho! light! a surgeon!   30

---

[552] Pimple.   [553] To the quick.   [554] Swindled.   [555] I.e., that's the only way.

Othello. 'Tis he: O brave Iago, honest and just!
That hast such noble sense of thy friend's wrong;
Thou teachest me. Minion,[556] your dear lies dead,
And your unblest fate hies; strumpet, I come!
Forth of my heart those charms, thine eyes, are blotted;
Thy bed lust-stain'd shall with lust's blood be spotted.   (*Exit.*)

(Enter Lodovico and Gratiano, at a distance.)

Cassio.   What ho! no watch? no passage?[557] murder! murder!
Gratiano.   'Tis some mischance; the cry is very direful.
Cassio.   O, help!
Lodovico.   Hark!
Roderigo.   O wretched villain!   40
Lodovico.   Two or three groans: it is a heavy[558] night;
    These may be counterfeits; let 's think 't unsafe
    To come in to the cry[559] without more help.
Roderigo.   Nobody come? then shall I bleed to death.
Lodovico.   Hark!

(Re-enter Iago, with a light.)

Gratiano.   Here 's one comes in his shirt, with light and weapons.
Iago.   Who 's there? whose noise is this that cries on murder?
Lodovico.   We do not know.
Iago.   Did not you hear a cry?
Cassio.   Here, here! for heaven's sake, help me.
Iago.   What's the matter?   50
Gratiano.   This is Othello's ancient, as I take it.
Lodovico.   The same indeed; a very valiant fellow.
Iago.   What are you here that cry so grievously?
Cassio.   Iago? O! I am spoil'd, undone by villains!
    Give me some help.
Iago.   O me, lieutenant! what villains have done this?
Cassio.   I think that one of them is hereabout,
    And cannot make away.
Iago.   O treacherous villains!
    (To Lodovico and Gratiano.) What are you there? come in, and
    give some help.
Roderigo.   O! help me here.   60

---

[556] (Cassio's) darling, i.e., Desdemona.   [557] Passer-by.   [558] Dark.   [559] Where the
cry comes from.

Cassio.   That's one of them.
Iago.   O murderous slave! O villain!

(Stabs Roderigo.)

Roderigo.   O damn'd Iago! O inhuman dog!
Iago.   Kill men i' the dark! Where be these bloody thieves?
How silent is this town! Ho! murder! murder!
What may you be? are you of good or evil?
Lodovico.   As you shall prove us, praise us.
Iago.   Signior Lodovico?
Lodovico.   He, sir.
Iago.   I cry you mercy. Here 's Cassio hurt by villains.
Gratiano.   Cassio!   70
Iago.   How is it, brother?
Cassio.   My leg is cut in two.
Iago.   Marry, heaven forbid.
Light, gentlemen; I 'll bind it with my shirt.

(Enter Bianca.)

Bianca.   What is the matter, ho? who is 't that cried?
Iago.   Who is 't that cried!
Bianca.   O my dear Cassio! my sweet Cassio!
O Cassio, Cassio, Cassio!
Iago.   O notable strumpet! Cassio, may you suspect
Who they should be that have thus mangled you?
Cassio.   No.   80
Gratiano.   I am sorry to find you thus; I have been to seek you.
Iago.   Lend me a garter. So. O! for a chair,
To bear him easily hence!
Bianca.   Alas; he faints! O Cassio, Cassio, Cassio!
Iago.   Gentlemen all, I do suspect this trash[560]
To be a party in this injury.
Patience awhile, good Cassio. Come, come.
Lend me a light. Know we this face, or no?
Alas! my friend and my dear countryman,
Roderigo? no: yes, sure, O heaven! Roderigo.   90
Gratiano.   What! of Venice?
Iago.   Even he, sir, did you know him?
Gratiano.   Know him! ay.

---

[560] I.e., Bianca.

Iago.   Signior Gratiano? I cry you gentle pardon;
  These bloody accidents must excuse my manners,
  That so neglected you.
Gratiano.   I am glad to see you.
Iago.   How do you, Cassio? O! a chair, a chair!
Gratiano.   Roderigo!

(*A chair brought in.*)

Iago.   He, he, 'tis he,—O! that 's well said; the chair:
  Some good men bear him carefully from hence;
  I 'll fetch the general's surgeon. (*To Bianca.*) For you, mistress,   100
  Save you your labour. He that lies slain here, Cassio,
  Was my dear friend. What malice was between you?
Cassio.   None in the world; nor do I know that man.
Iago (*to Bianca*).   What! look you pale? O! bear him out o' the air—

(*Cassio and Roderigo are borne off.*)

  Stay you, good gentlemen. Look you pale, mistress?—
  Do you perceive the gastness[561] of her eye?
  Nay, if you stare, we shall hear more anon.
  Behold her well; I pray you, look upon her.
  Do you see, gentlemen? nay, guiltiness will speak
  Though tongues were out of use.   110

(*Enter Emilia.*)

Emilia.   'Las! what 's the matter? what 's the matter, husband?
Iago.   Cassio hath here been set on in the dark
  By Roderigo and fellows that are 'scaped:
  He 's almost slain, and Roderigo dead.
Emilia.   Alas! good gentleman; alas! good Cassio!
Iago.   This is the fruit of whoring. Prithee, Emilia,
  Go know of Cassio where he supp'd to-night.
  (*To Bianca.*) What! do you shake at that?
Bianca.   He supp'd at my house; but I therefore shake not.
Iago.   O! did he so? I charge you, go with me.   120
Emilia.   Fie, fie, upon thee, strumpet!
Bianca.   I am no strumpet, but of life as honest
  As you that thus abuse me.
Emilia.   As I! foh! fie upon thee!

---

[561] Terror.

Iago.   Kind gentlemen, let 's go see poor Cassio dress'd.[562]
Come, mistress, you must tell 's another tale.
Emilia, run you to the citadel,
And tell my lord and lady what hath happ'd.
Will you go on afore? *(Aside.)* This is the night
That either makes me or fordoes[563] me quite.   *(Exeunt.)*

SCENE 2.   A Bedchamber in the Castle. Desdemona in bed asleep. A light burning.

(Enter Othello.)

Othello.   It is the cause,[564] it is the cause, my soul;
Let me not name it to you, you chaste stars!
It is the cause. Yet I 'll not shed her blood,
Nor scar that whiter skin of hers than snow,
And smooth as monumental alabaster.
Yet she must die, else she 'll betray more men.
Put out the light, and then put out the light:
If I quench thee, thou flaming minister,[565]
I can again thy former light restore,
Should I repent me; but once put out thy light,   10
Thou cunning'st[566] pattern of excelling nature,
I know not where is that Promethean[567] heat
That can thy light relume.[568] When I have pluck'd the rose,
I cannot give it vital growth again,
It needs must wither: I 'll smell it on the tree. *(Kisses her.)*
O balmy breath, that dost almost persuade
Justice to break her sword! One more, one more.
Be thus when thou art dead, and I will kill thee,
And love thee after. One more, and this the last:
So sweet was ne'er so fatal. I must weep,   20
But they are cruel tears; this sorrow 's heavenly,
It strikes where it doth love. She wakes.
Desdemona.   Who 's there? Othello?
Othello.   Ay, Desdemona.
Desdemona.   Will you come to bed, my lord?
Othello.   Have you pray'd to-night, Desdemona?
Desdemona.   Ay, my lord.

---

[562] Bandaged.   [563] Ruins.   [564] I.e., Desdemona's unchastity (Othello means that the severity of the punishment is required by the nature of her sin).   [565] I.e, the candle.
[566] Most intricately wrought.   [567] In Greek mythology the demi-god Prometheus stole fire from the gods and gave it to man.   [568] Relight.

Othello.   If you bethink yourself of any crime
    Unreconcil'd as yet to heaven and grace,
    Solicit for it straight.
Desdemona.   Alas! my lord, what may you mean by that?
Othello.   Well, do it, and be brief; I will walk by:[569]   30
    I would not kill thy unprepared spirit;
    No; heaven forfend![570] I would not kill thy soul.
Desdemona.   Talk you of killing?
Othello.   Ay, I do.
Desdemona.   Then heaven
    Have mercy on me!
Othello.   Amen! with all my heart.
Desdemona.   If you say so, I hope you will not kill me.
Othello.   Hum!
Desdemona.   And yet I fear you; for you are fatal then
    When your eyes roll so. Why I should fear I know not,
    Since guiltiness I know not; but yet I feel I fear.
Othello.   Think on thy sins.
Desdemona.   They are loves I bear to you.   40
Othello.   Ay, and for that thou diest.
Desdemona.   That death's unnatural that kills for loving.
    Alas! why gnaw you so your nether lip?
    Some bloody passion shakes your very frame;
    These are portents,[571] but yet, I hope, I hope
    They do not point on me.
Othello.   Peace, and be still!
Desdemona.   I will so. What 's the matter?
Othello.   That handkerchief which I so lov'd and gave thee
    Thou gav'st to Cassio.
Desdemona.   No, by my life and soul!
    Send for the man and ask him.
Othello.   Sweet soul, take heed,   50
    Take heed of perjury; thou 'rt on thy death-bed.
Desdemona.   Ay, but not yet to die.
Othello.   Yes, presently;[572]
    Therefore confess thee freely of thy sin;
    For to deny each article with oath
    Cannot remove nor choke the strong conception[573]
    That I do groan withal. Thou art to die.
Desdemona.   Then Lord have mercy on me!
Othello.   I say, amen.
Desdemona.   And have you mercy too! I never did
    Offend you in my life; never lov'd Cassio

---

[569] Nearby.   [570] Forbid.   [571] Omens.   [572] At once.   [573] Belief.

But with such general warranty[574] of heaven   60
    As I might love; I never gave him token.
Othello.   By heaven, I saw my handkerchief in 's hand.
    O perjur'd woman! thou dost stone[575] my heart,
    And mak'st me call what I intend to do
    A murder, which I thought a sacrifice:
    I saw the handkerchief.
Desdemona.   He found it then;
    I never gave it him. Send for him hither;
    Let him confess a truth.
Othello.   He had confessed.
Desdemona.   What, my lord?
Othello.   That he hath us'd thee.
Desdemona.   How? Unlawfully?
Othello.   Ay.   70
Desdemona.   He will not say so.
Othello.   No; his mouth is stopp'd:
    Honest Iago hath ta'en order for 't.[576]
Desdemona.   O! my fear interprets. What! is he dead?
Othello.   Had all his hairs been lives, my great revenge
    Had stomach[577] for them all.
Desdemona.   Alas! he is betray'd and I undone.
Othello.   Out, strumpet! Weep'st thou for him to my face?
Desdemona.   O! banish me, my lord, but kill me not!
Othello.   Down, strumpet!
Desdemona.   Kill me to-morrow; let me live to-night!   80
Othello.   Nay, if you strive,—
Desdemona.   But half an hour!
Othello.   Being done, there is no pause.
Desdemona.   But while I say one prayer!
Othello.   It is too late.   *(He smothers her.)*
Emilia *(within).*   My lord, my lord! what, ho! my lord, my lord!
Othello.   What noise is this? Not dead? Not yet quite dead?
    I that am cruel am yet merciful;
    I would not have thee linger in thy pain.
    So, so.
Emilia *(within).*   What, ho! my lord, my lord!
Othello.   Who's there?
Emilia *(within).*   O! good my lord, I would speak a word with you!   90
Othello.   Yes; 'tis Emilia: by and by.[578] She's dead.
    'Tis like[579] she comes to speak of Cassio's death;
    The noise was high. Ha! no more moving?

---

[574] Permission.   [575] Turn to stone.   [576] Taken steps.   [577] Appetite.   [578] I.e.,
"just a moment."   [579] Likely.

Still as the grave. Shall she come in? were 't good?[580]
I think she stirs again: no. What 's best to do?
If she come in she'll sure speak to my wife:
My wife! my wife! what wife? I have no wife;
O, insupportable! O heavy hour!
Methinks it should be now a huge eclipse
Of sun and moon, and that the affrighted globe   100
Should yawn[581] at alteration.
Emilia (*within.*)   I do beseech you
That I may speak with you, O! good my lord.
Othello.   I had forgot thee: O! come in, Emilia:
Soft, by and by: let me the curtains draw.
Where art thou?   (*Unlocks the door.*)

(*Enter Emilia*).

                    What 's the matter with thee now?
Emilia.   O! my good lord, yonder 's foul murder done.
Othello.   What! now?
Emilia.   But now, my lord.
Othello.   It is the very error[582] of the moon;
She comes more near the earth than she was wont,   110
And makes men mad.
Emilia.   Cassio, my lord, has kill'd a young Venetian
Call'd Roderigo.
Othello.   Roderigo kill'd!
And Cassio kill'd?
Emilia.   No, Cassio is not kill'd.
Othello.   Not Cassio kill'd! then murder 's out of tune,
And sweet revenge grows harsh.
Desdemona.   O! falsely, falsely murder'd.
Emilia.   Alas! what cry is that?
Othello.   That! what?
Emilia.   Out, and alas! that was my lady's voice:
Help! Help, ho! help! O lady, speak again!   120
Sweet Desdemona! O! sweet mistress, speak.
Desdemona.   A guiltless death I die.
Emilia.   O! who hath done this deed?
Desdemona.   Nobody; I myself; farewell:
Commend me to my kind lord. O! farewell!   (*Dies.*)
Othello.   Why, how should she be murder'd?
Emilia.   Alas! who knows?
Othello.   You heard her say herself it was not I.

---

[580] Would that be wise.   [581] Open up (as in an earthquake).   [582] Straying.

Emilia.   She said so; I must needs report the truth.

Othello.   She 's like a liar gone to burning hell;
    'Twas I that kill'd her.

Emilia.   O! the more angel she,   130
    And you the blacker devil.

Othello.   She turn'd to folly, and she was a whore.

Emilia.   Thou dost belie her, and thou art a devil.

Othello.   She was false as water.

Emilia.   Thou art rash as fire to say
    That she was false! O! she was heavenly true.

Othello.   Cassio did tup her; ask thy husband else.
    O! I were damn'd beneath all depth in hell
    But that I did proceed[583] upon just grounds
    To this extremity. Thy husband knew it all.

Emilia.   My husband!   140

Othello.   Thy husband.

Emilia.   That she was false to wedlock?

Othello.   Ay, with Cassio. Nay, had she been true,
    If heaven would make me such another world
    Of one entire and perfect chrysolite,[584]
    I'd not have sold her for it.

Emilia.   My husband!

Othello.   Ay, 'twas he that told me first:
    An honest man he is, and hates the slime
    That sticks on filthy deeds.

Emilia.   My husband!

Othello.   What needs this iterance,[585] woman? I say thy husband.   150

Emilia.   O mistress! villany hath made mocks with love.
    My husband say that she was false!

Othello.   He, woman;
    I say, thy husband: dost understand the word?
    My friend, thy husband, honest, honest Iago.

Emilia.   If he say so, may his pernicious soul
    Rot half a grain a day! he lies to the heart:
    She was too fond of her most filthy bargain.[586]

Othello.   Ha!

Emilia.   Do thy worst:
    This deed of thine is no more worthy heaven   160
    Than thou wast worthy her.

Othello.   Peace! you were best.[587]

Emilia.   Thou hast not half the power to do me harm
    As I have to be hurt. O gull! O dolt!

---

[583] Had I not proceeded.   [584] Topaz.   [585] Repetition.   [586] I.e., Othello.
[587] You'd better be quiet.

As ignorant as dirt! thou hast done a deed,—
I care not for thy sword; I'll make thee known,
Though I lost twenty lives. Help! help, ho! help!
The Moor has kill'd my mistress! murder! murder!

(Enter Montano, Gratiano, Iago, and others.)

Montano.   What is the matter? How now, general!
Emilia.   O! are you come, Iago? you have done well,
  That men must lay their murders on your neck.   170
Gratiano.   What is the matter?
Emilia.   Disprove this villain if thou be'st a man:
  He says thou told'st him that his wife was false.
  I know thou didst not, thou 'rt not such a villain.
  Speak, for my heart is full.
Iago.   I told him what I thought, and told no more
  Than what he found himself was apt and true.
Emilia.   But did you ever tell him she was false?
Iago.   I did.
Emilia.   You told a lie, an odious damned lie;
  Upon my soul, a lie, a wicked lie;   180
  She false with Cassio! Did you say with Cassio?
Iago.   With Cassio, mistress. Go to, charm[588] your tongue.
Emilia.   I will not charm my tongue; I am bound to speak.
  My mistress here lies murder'd in her bed.·
All.   O heavens forfend!
Emilia.   And your reports have set the murder on.
Othello.   Nay, stare not, masters; it is true, indeed.
Gratiano.   'Tis a strange truth.
Montano.   O monstrous act!
Emilia.   Villany! villany! villany!   190
  I think upon 't, I think, I smell 't; O villany!
  I thought so then;[589] I'll kill myself for grief.
  O! villany, villany!
Iago.   What! are you mad? I charge you, get you home.
Emilia.   Good gentlemen, let me have leave to speak:
  'Tis proper I obey him, but not now.
  Perchance, Iago, I will ne'er go home.
Othello.   O! O! O!   *(Falls on the bed.)*
Emilia.   Nay, lay thee down and roar,
  For thou hast kill'd the sweetest innocent
  That e'er did lift up eye.

---

[588] I.e., into silence.   [589] Cf. "I will be hang'd, if some eternal villain,/Some busy and
insinuating rogue,/Some cogging cozening slave, to get some office,/Have not devis'd this slander;
. . ." (IV, ii, 130 ff.). Emilia means, not that she guessed Iago's guilt, but that she rightly guessed
the slanderer's motive.

Othello.   O! she was foul.   (*Rises.*)

 I scarce did know you, uncle. There lies your niece,   201
 Whose breath, indeed, these hands have newly stopp'd:
 I know this act shows terrible and grim.

Gratiano.   Poor Desdemona! I am glad thy father's dead.
 Thy match was mortal to him, and pure grief
 Shore[590] his old thread in twain: did he live now,
 This sight would make him do a desperate turn,
 Yea, curse his better angel from his side,
 And fall to reprobation.[591]

Othello.   'Tis pitiful; but yet Iago knows   210
 That she with Cassio hath the act of shame
 A thousand times committed; Cassio confess'd it:
 And she did gratify[592] his amorous works
 With that recognizance and pledge of love
 Which I first gave her. I saw it in his hand:
 It was a handkerchief, an antique token
 My father gave my mother.

Emilia.   O heaven! O heavenly powers!

Iago.   Come, hold your peace.

Emilia.   'Twill out, 'twill out; I hold my peace, sir? no;
 No, I will speak as liberal as the north;[593]   220
 Let heaven and men and devils, let them all,
 All, all, cry shame against me, yet I'll speak.

Iago.   Be wise, and get you home.

Emilia.   I will not.

(Iago threatens to stab Emilia.)

Gratiano.   Fie!
 Your sword upon a woman!

Emilia.   O thou dull Moor! that handkerchief thou speak'st of
 I found by fortune and did give my husband;
 For often, with a solemn earnestness,
 More than, indeed, belong'd to such a trifle,
 He begg'd of me to steal it.

Iago.   Villainous whore!

Emilia.   She give it Cassio! no, alas! I found it,   230
 And I did give 't my husband.

Iago.   Filth, thou liest!

Emilia.   By heaven, I do not, I do not, gentlemen.
 O murderous coxcomb![594] what should such a fool
 Do with so good a wife?

---

[590] Cut.   [591] Damnation.   [592] Reward.   [593] I.e, the north wind (?), the supposedly free-spoken people of north England (?).   [594] Idiot.

Othello.   Are there no stones[595] in heaven
  But what serve for the thunder? Precious villain!

(He runs at Iago. Iago stabs Emilia.)

Gratiano.   The woman falls; sure, he has kill'd his wife.   *(Exit Iago.)*
Emilia.   Ay, ay; O! lay me by my mistress' side.
Gratiano.   He 's gone; but his wife 's kill'd.
Montano.   'Tis a notorious[596] villain. Take you this weapon,
  Which I have here recover'd from the Moor.   240
  Come, guard the door without; let him not pass,
  But kill him rather. I'll after that same villain,
  For 'tis a damned slave.   *(Exeunt Montano and Gratiano.)*
Othello.   I am not valiant neither,
  But every puny whipster[597] gets my sword.
  But why should honour outlive honesty?
  Let it go all.
Emilia.   What did thy song bode, lady?
  Hark, canst thou hear me? I will play the swan,
  And die in music:—
  (Sings.)   Willow, willow, willow.
  Moor, she was chaste; she lov'd thee, cruel Moor;
  So come my soul to bliss as I speak true;   250
  So speaking as I think, I die, I die.   *(Dies.)*
Othello.   I have another weapon in this chamber;
  It is a sword of Spain, the ice-brook's temper.[598]
  O! here it is. Uncle, I must come forth.
Gratiano *(within)*.   If thou attempt it, it will cost thee dear:
  Thou hast no weapon, and perforce must suffer.
Othello.   Look in upon me then, and speak with me,
  Or, naked[599] as I am, I will assault thee.

(Re-enter Gratiano.)

Gratiano.   What is the matter?
Othello.   Behold! I have a weapon;
  A better never did itself sustain   260
  Upon a soldier's thigh: I have seen the day,
  That with this little arm, and this good sword,
  I have made my way through more impediments
  Than twenty times your stop: but, O vain boast!

---

[595] I.e., thunderbolts (to strike Iago down).   [596] Notable.   [597] I.e., a small boy whipping a top.   [598] Tempered in icy water (or the reference may be to Innsbruck, famed for the quality of its steel, but this hardly fits "a sword of Spain").   [599] Unarmed.

Who can control his fate? 'tis not so now.
Be not afraid, though you do see me weapon'd;
Here is my journey's end, here is my butt,[600]
And very sea-mark of my utmost sail.[601]
Do you go back dismay'd? 'tis a lost fear;
Man but a rush[602] against Othello's breast,   270
And he retires. Where should Othello go?
Now how dost thou look now? O ill-starr'd wench!
Pale as thy smock! when we shall meet at compt,[603]
This look of thine will hurl my soul from heaven,
And fiends will snatch at it. Cold, cold, my girl!
Even like thy chastity.
O! cursed, cursed slave. Whip me, ye devils,
From the possession of this heavenly sight!
Blow me about in winds! roast me in sulphur!
Wash me in steep-down gulfs of liquid fire!   280
O Desdemona! Desdemona! dead!
Oh! Oh! Oh!

(Enter Lodovico, Montano, Cassio carried in a chair, and Officers with Iago, prisoner.)

Lodovico.   Where is this rash and most unfortunate man?
Othello.   That's he that was Othello; here I am.
Lodovico.   Where is that viper? bring the villain forth.
Othello.   I look down towards his feet;[604] but that's a fable.
If that thou be'st a devil, I cannot kill thee.   *(Wounds Iago.)*
Lodovico.   Wrench his sword from him.   *(Othello is disarmed.)*
Iago.   I bleed, sir; but not kill'd.
Othello.   I am not sorry neither; I'd have thee live;
For, in my sense,[605] 'tis happiness to die.   290
Lodovico.   O thou Othello! that wert once so good,
Fall'n in the practice[606] of a damned slave,[607]
What shall be said to thee?
Othello.   Why, any thing:
An honourable murderer, if you will;
For nought did I in hate, but all in honour.
Lodovico.   This wretch hath part confess'd his villany:
Did you and he consent in Cassio's death?
Othello.   Ay.
Cassio.   Dear general, I never gave you cause.

---

[600] Goal, end, limit.   [601] Destination of my farthest journey.   [602] Wield but a reed.
[603] On the day of judgment.   [604] I.e, for the Devil's cloven hoof.   [605] The way I
feel.   [606] Plot, machination.   [607] I.e., Iago.

Othello.   I do believe it, and I ask your pardon.   300
  Will you, I pray, demand that demi-devil
  Why he hath thus ensnar'd my soul and body?
Iago.   Demand me nothing: what you know, you know:
  From this time forth I never will speak word.
Lodovico.   What! not to pray?
Gratiano.   Torments will ope[608] your lips.
Othello.   Well, thou dost best.
Lodovico.   Sir, you shall understand what hath befall'n,
  Which, as I think, you know not. Here is a letter
  Found in the pocket of the slain Roderigo,
  And here another; the one of them imports   310
  The death of Cassio to be undertook
  By Roderigo.
Othello.   O villain!
Cassio.   Most heathenish and most gross!
Lodovico.   Now here's another discontented paper,
  Found in his pocket too; and this, it seems,
  Roderigo meant to have sent this damned villain,
  But that, belike,[609] Iago in the interim[610]
  Came in and satisfied him.
Othello.   O the pernicious caitiff!
  How came you, Cassio, by that handkerchief
  That was my wife's?
Cassio.   I found it in my chamber;   320
  And he himself confess'd but even now
  That there he dropp'd it for a special purpose
  Which wrought to his desire.
Othello.   O fool! fool! fool!
Cassio.   There is besides in Roderigo's letter
  How he upbraids Iago that he made him
  Brave me upon the watch; whereon it came
  That I was cast:[611] and even but now he spake,
  After long seeming dead, Iago hurt him,
  Iago set him on.
Lodovico.   You must forsake this room and go with us;   330
  Your power and your command is taken off,
  And Cassio rules in Cyprus. For this slave,
  If there be any cunning cruelty
  That can torment him much and hold him long,
  It shall be his. You shall close prisoner rest,

---

[608] Open.   [609] Most likely.   [610] In the meantime.   [611] Dismissed.

Till that the nature of your fault be known
To the Venetian state. Come, bring him away.
Othello.   Soft you; a word or two before you go.
I have done the state some service, and they know 't;
No more of that. I pray you, in your letters,   340
When you shall these unlucky deeds relate,
Speak of me as I am; nothing extenuate,
Nor set down aught[612] in malice: then, must you speak
Of one that lov'd not wisely but too well;
Of one not easily jealous, but, being wrought,
Perplex'd[613] in the extreme; of one whose hand
Like the base Indian,[614] threw a pearl away
Richer than all his tribe; of one whose subdu'd[615] eyes
Albeit unused to the melting mood,
Drop tears as fast as the Arabian trees   350
Their med'cinable gum. Set you down this;
And say besides, that in Aleppo once,
Where a malignant and a turban'd Turk
Beat a Venetian and traduc'd the state,
I took by the throat the circumcised dog,
And smote him, thus.   *(Stabs himself.)*
Lodovico.   O bloody period![616]
Gratiano.   All that's spoke is marr'd.
Othello.   I kiss'd thee ere I killed thee; no way but this.
    (Falling upon Desdemona.)
    (Dies.)
Killing myself to die upon a kiss.
Cassio.   This did I fear, but thought he had no weapon;
For he was great of heart.
Lodovico *(to Iago).*   O Spartan dog!
More fell[617] than anguish, hunger, or the sea.
Look on the tragic loading of this bed;
This is thy work; the object poisons sight;
Let it be hid. Gratiano, keep the house,
And seize upon the fortunes of the Moor,
For they succeed on you. To you, lord governor,
Remains the censure of this hellish villain,
The time, the place, the torture; O! enforce it.
Myself will straight aboard, and to the state   370
This heavy act with heavy heart relate.   *(Exeunt.)*

---

[612] Anything.   [613] Distracted.   [614] The Folio reads "ludean." Both readings denote the foolish infidel who fails to appreciate the treasure he possesses.   [615] Overcome (by grief).
[616] Ending.   [617] Grim, cruel.

QUESTIONS

1. In what sense might it be said that Othello is responsible for his own downfall? **2.** Compare the speeches of Cassio and Iago in Act II, Scene 1. What does the difference in language and style reveal about their characters? **3.** Carefully determine how much time elapses between the arrival at Cyprus and the end of the action. Can you find narrated events that could not possibly have occurred within that time? Do the chronological inconsistencies disturb you? Explain. **4.** The first part of Act IV, Scene 2 (until Othello exits), is sometimes called the "brothel" scene. What features of Othello's language and behavior justify that designation? **5.** Discuss the relationship between love and hate in this play.

WRITING TOPICS

1. Examine the reasons Iago gives for his actions. Do you find them consistent and convincing? Explain. **2.** Discuss the functions of the minor characters, such as Roderigo, Bianca, and Emilia, in the play. **3.** Othello crumbles in Act III, Scene 3, as Iago creates the jealousy that destroys Othello's self-confidence and peace of mind. Is the rapidity of Othello's emotional collapse justified? Does his being black have anything to do with his emotional turmoil?

LOVE
AND
HATE

Grosse Heidelberger Liederhandschrift "Codex Manesse" fol. 249ᵛ.

ESSAYS

Courtship through the Ages   1939

JAMES THURBER   [1894–1961]

Surely nothing in the astonishing scheme of life can have nonplussed Nature   1
so much as the fact that none of the females of any of the species she created
really cared very much for the male, as such. For the past ten million years
Nature has been busily inventing ways to make the male attractive to the female, but the whole business of courtship, from the marine annelids up to
man, still lumbers heavily along, like a complicated musical comedy. I have
been reading the sad and absorbing story in Volume 6 (Cole to Dama) of the
Encyclopaedia Britannica. In this volume you can learn all about cricket, cotton, costume designing, crocodiles, crown jewels, and Coleridge, but none of
these subjects is so interesting as the Courtship of Animals, which recounts the
sorrowful lengths to which all males must go to arouse the interest of a lady.

We all know, I think, that Nature gave man whiskers and a mustache with   2
the quaint idea in mind that these would prove attractive to the female. We
all know that, far from attracting her, whiskers and mustaches only made her
nervous and gloomy, so that man had to go in for somersaults, tilting with
lances, and performing feats of parlor magic to win her attention; he also had
to bring her candy, flowers, and the furs of animals. It is common knowledge
that in spite of all these "love displays" the male is constantly being turned
down, insulted, or thrown out of the house. It is rather comforting, then, to
discover that the peacock, for all his gorgeous plumage, does not have a particularly easy time in courtship; none of the males in the world do. The first
peahen, it turned out, was only faintly stirred by her suitor's beautiful train.
She would often go quietly to sleep while he was whisking it around. The
Britannica tells us that the peacock actually had to learn a certain little trick to
wake her up and revive her interest: he had to learn to vibrate his quills so as
to make a rustling sound. In ancient times man himself, observing the ways of
the peacock, probably tried vibrating his whiskers to make a rustling sound; if
so, it didn't get him anywhere. He had to go in for something else; so, among
other things, he went in for gifts. It is not unlikely that he got this idea from
certain flies and birds who were making no headway at all with rustling sounds.

One of the flies of the family Empidae, who had tried everything, finally hit   3
on something pretty special. He contrived to make a glistening transparent bal-

loon which was even larger than himself. Into this he would put sweetmeats and tidbits and he would carry the whole elaborate envelope through the air to the lady of his choice. This amused her for a time, but she finally got bored with it. She demanded silly little colorful presents, something that you couldn't eat but that would look nice around the house. So the male Empis had to go around gathering flower petals and pieces of bright paper to put into his balloon. On a courtship flight a male Empis cuts quite a figure now, but he can hardly be said to be happy. He never knows how soon the female will demand heavier presents, such as Roman coins and gold collar buttons. It seems probable that one day the courtship of the Empidae will fall down, as man's occasionally does, of its own weight.

The bowerbird is another creature that spends so much time courting the   4
female that he never gets any work done. If all the male bowerbirds became nervous wrecks within the next ten or fifteen years, it would not surprise me. The female bowerbird insists that a playground be built for her with a specially constructed bower at the entrance. This bower is much more elaborate than an ordinary nest and is harder to build; it costs a lot more, too. The female will not come to the playground until the male has filled it up with a great many gifts: silvery leaves, red leaves, rose petals, shells, beads, berries, bones, dice, buttons, cigar bands, Christmas seals, and the Lord knows what else. When the female finally condescends to visit the playground, she is in a coy and silly mood and has to be chased in and out of the bower and up and down the playground before she will quit giggling and stand still long enough even to shake hands. The male bird is, of course, pretty well done in before the chase starts, because he has worn himself out hunting for eyeglass lenses and begonia blossoms. I imagine that many a bowerbird, after chasing a female for two or three hours, says the hell with it and goes home to bed. Next day, of course, he telephones someone else and the same trying ritual is gone through with again. A male bowerbird is as exhausted as a night-club habitué before he is out of his twenties.

The male fiddler crab has a somewhat easier time, but it can hardly be said   5
that he is sitting pretty. He has one enormously large and powerful claw, usually brilliantly colored, and you might suppose that all he had to do was reach out and grab some passing cutie. The very earliest fiddler crabs may have tried this, but, if so, they got slapped for their pains. A female fiddler crab will not tolerate any caveman stuff; she never has and she doesn't intend to start now. To attract a female, a fiddler crab has to stand on tiptoe and brandish his claw in the air. If any female in the neighborhood is interested—and you'd be surprised how many are not—she comes over and engages him in light badinage, for which he is not in the mood. As many as a hundred females may pass the time of day with him and go on about their business. By nightfall of an average courting day, a fiddler crab who has been standing on tiptoe for eight or ten hours waving a heavy claw in the air is in pretty sad shape. As in the case of the male of all species, however, he gets out of bed next morning, dashes some water on his face, and tries again.

The next time you encounter a male web-spinning spider, stop and reflect   6
that he is too busy worrying about his love life to have any desire to bite you.
Male web-spinning spiders have a tougher life than any other males in the
animal kingdom. This is because the female web-spinning spiders have very
poor eyesight. If a male lands on a female's web, she kills him before he has
time to lay down his cane and gloves, mistaking him for a fly or a bumblebee
who has tumbled into her trap. Before the species figured out what to do about
this, millions of males were murdered by ladies they called on. It is the nature
of spiders to perform a little dance in front of the female, but before a male
spinner could get near enough for the female to see who he was and what he
was up to, she would lash out at him with a flat-iron or a pair of garden shears.
One night, nobody knows when, a very bright male spinner lay awake worrying
about calling on a lady who had been killing suitors right and left. It came to
him that this business of dancing as a love display wasn't getting anybody anywhere except the grave. He decided to go in for web-twitching, or strand-vi-
brating. The next day he tried it on one of the nearsighted girls. Instead of
dropping in on her suddenly, he stayed outside the web and began monkeying
with one of its strands. He twitched it up and down and in and out with such
a lilting rhythm that the female was charmed. The serenade worked beautifully;
the female let him live. The *Britannica*'s spider-watchers, however, report that
this system is not always successful. Once in a while, even now, a female will
fire three bullets into a suitor or run him through with a kitchen knife. She
keeps threatening him from the moment he strikes the first low notes on the
outside strings, but usually by the time he has got up to the high notes played
around the center of the web, he is going to town and she spares his life.

Even the butterfly, as handsome a fellow as he is, can't always win a mate   7
merely by fluttering around and showing off. Many butterflies have to have
scent scales on their wings. Hepialus carries a powder puff in a perfumed pouch.
He throws perfume at the ladies when they pass. The male tree cricket, Oecanthus, goes Hepialus one better by carrying a tiny bottle of wine with him
and giving drinks to such doxies as he has designs on. One of the male snails
throws darts to entertain the girls. So it goes, through the long list of animals,
from the bristle worm and his rudimentary dance steps to man and his gift of
diamonds and sapphires. The golden-eye drake raises a jet of water with his
feet as he flies over a lake; Hepialus has his powder puff, Oecanthus his wine
bottle, man his etchings. It is a bright and melancholy story, the age-old desire
of the male for the female, the age-old desire of the female to be amused and
entertained. Of all the creatures on earth, the only males who could be figured
as putting an irony into their courtship are the grebes and certain other diving
birds. Every now and then a courting grebe slips quietly down to the bottom
of a lake and then, with a mighty "Whoosh!" pops out suddenly a few feet
from his girl friend, splashing water all over. She seems to be persuaded that
this is a purely loving display, but I like to think that the grebe always has a
faint hope of drowning her or scaring her to death.

I will close this investigation into the mournful burdens of the male with   8

Britannica's story about a certain Argus pheasant. It appears that the Argus displays himself in front of a female who stands perfectly still without moving a feather. . . . The male Argus the *Britannica* tells about was confined in a cage with a female of another species, a female who kept moving around, emptying ashtrays and fussing with lampshades all the time the male was showing off his talents. Finally, in disgust, he stalked away and began displaying in front of his water trough. He reminds me of a certain male *(Homo sapiens)* of my acquaintance who one night after dinner asked his wife to put down her detective magazine so that he could read a poem of which he was very fond. She sat quietly enough until he was well into the middle of the thing, intoning with great ardor and intensity. Then suddenly there came a sharp, disconcerting *slap!* It turned out that all during the male's display, the female had been intent on a circling mosquito and had finally trapped it between the palms of her hands. The male in this case did not stalk away and display in front of a water trough; he went over to Tim's and had a flock of drinks and recited the poem to the fellas. I am sure they all told bitter stories of their own about how their displays had been interrupted by females. I am also sure that they all ended up singing "Honey, Honey, Bless Your Heart."

QUESTIONS
1. Here is a direct quote from the *Encyclopaedia Britannica* on the courtship of bowerbirds: "These birds clear playgrounds, in which special bowers (quite unlike nests) are constructed by some species. In the playground (if a bower is made opposite its entrance) is deposited a collection of bright objects. The objects differ with the species; they may include silvery leaves, flowers, shells, berries, bones, etc. When the female visits the playground, the male pursues her amorously round it (through the bower, when present). Here it appears that the bright objects collected serve instead of the brilliant plumage of the male birds to stimulate the female." Compare Thurber's account in the fourth paragraph. In what way does it differ from the description in the encyclopaedia?   **2.**   What devices does Thurber use to remind his readers that he is speaking of humans as well as animals and insects?   **3.**   What assumptions about the nature of the relationship between men and women is this essay based on? Explain.

WRITING TOPIC
What makes this essay funny?

The Iks
1974

LEWIS THOMAS   [b. 1913]

The small tribe of Iks, formerly nomadic hunters and gatherers in the moun- 1
tain valleys of northern Uganda, have become celebrities, literary symbols of
the ultimate fate of disheartened, heartless mankind at large. Two disastrously
conclusive things happened to them: the government decided to have a national park, so they were compelled by law to give up hunting in the valleys
and become farmers on poor hillside soil, and then they were visited for two
years by an anthropologist who detested them and wrote a book about them.

The message of the book is that the Iks have transformed themselves into an 2
irreversibly disagreeable collection of unattached, brutish creatures, totally selfish and loveless, in response to the dismantling of their traditional culture.
Moreover, this is what the rest of us are like in our inner selves, and we will
all turn into Iks when the structure of our society comes all unhinged.

The argument rests, of course, on certain assumptions about the core of 3
human beings, and is necessarily speculative. You have to agree in advance
that man is fundamentally a bad lot, out for himself alone, displaying such
graces as affection and compassion only as learned habits. If you take this view,
the story of the Iks can be used to confirm it. These people seem to be living
together, clustered in small, dense villages, but they are really solitary, unrelated individuals with no evident use for each other. They talk, but only to
make ill-tempered demands and cold refusals. They share nothing. They never
sing. They turn the children out to forage as soon as they can walk, and desert
the elders to starve whenever they can, and the foraging children snatch food
from the mouths of the helpless elders. It is a mean society.

They breed without love or even casual regard. They defecate on each oth- 4
er's doorsteps. They watch their neighbors for signs of misfortune, and only
then do they laugh. In the book they do a lot of laughing, having so much bad
luck. Several times they even laughed at the anthropologist, who found this
especially repellent (one senses, between the lines, that the scholar is not himself the world's luckiest man). Worse, they took him into the family, snatched
his food, defecated on his doorstep, and hooted dislike at him. They gave him
two bad years.

It is a depressing book. If, as he suggests, there is only Ikness at the center 5
of each of us, our sole hope for hanging onto the name of humanity will be in
endlessly mending the structure of our society, and it is changing so quickly
and completely that we may never find the threads in time. Meanwhile, left to
ourselves alone, solitary, we will become the same joyless, zestless, untouching
lone animals.

But this may be too narrow a view. For one thing, the Iks are extraordinary. 6
They are absolutely astonishing, in fact. The anthropologist has never seen

573

people like them anywhere, nor have I. You'd think, if they were simply examples of the common essence of mankind, they'd seem more recognizable. Instead, they are bizarre, anomalous. I have known my share of peculiar, difficult, nervous, grabby people, but I've never encountered any genuinely, consistently detestable human beings in all my life. The Iks sound more like abnormalities, maladies.

I cannot accept it. I do not believe that the Iks are representative of isolated, revealed man, unobscured by social habits. I believe their behavior is something extra, something laid on. This unremitting, compulsive repellence is a kind of complicated ritual. They must have learned to act this way; they copied it, somehow.   7

I have a theory, then. The Iks have gone crazy.   8

The solitary Ik, isolated in the ruins of an exploded culture, has built a new defense for himself. If you live in an unworkable society you can make up one of your own, and this is what the Iks have done. Each Ik has become a group, a one-man tribe on its own, a constituency.   9

Now everything falls into place. This is why they do seem, after all, vaguely familiar to all of us. We've seen them before. This is precisely the way groups of one size or another, ranging from committees to nations, behave. It is, of course, this aspect of humanity that has lagged behind the rest of evolution, and this is why the Ik seems so primitive. In his absolute selfishness, his incapacity to give anything away, no matter what, he is a successful committee. When he stands at the door of his hut, shouting insults at his neighbors in a loud harangue, he is a city addressing another city.   10

Cities have all the Ik characteristics. They defecate on doorsteps, in rivers and lakes, their own or anyone else's. They leave rubbish. They detest all neighboring cities, give nothing away. They even build institutions for deserting elders out of sight.   11

Nations are the most Iklike of all. No wonder the Iks seem familiar. For total greed, rapacity, heartlessness, and irresponsibility there is nothing to match a nation. Nations, by law, are solitary, self-centered, withdrawn into themselves. There is no such thing as affection between nations, and certainly no nation ever loved another. They bawl insults from their doorsteps, defecate into whole oceans, snatch all the food, survive by detestation, take joy in the bad luck of others, celebrate the death of others, live for the death of others.   12

That's it, and I shall stop worrying about the book. It does not signify that man is a sparse, inhuman thing at his center. He's all right. It only says what we've always known and never had enough time to worry about, that we haven't yet learned how to stay human when assembled in masses. The Ik, in his despair, is acting out this failure, and perhaps we should pay closer attention. Nations have themselves become too frightening to think about, but we might learn some things by watching these people.   13

QUESTIONS

1. To what, in the "civilized" world, do the Iks correspond? Is this essay about the Iks or about us? Explain.   **2.**   What is Thomas's view of human nature in this essay? How does it differ from the anthropologist's?

WRITING TOPIC
Analyze the sentence structure of the next to last paragraph. The paragraph defines *nation* with sentences of disparate length and forcefulness. Describe the relationship between the paragraph's rhetorical structure (i.e., sentence length, rhythm, balance, sequence of assertions) and the message it conveys.

Rage   (1955)

JAMES BALDWIN   [1924–1987]

. . . The year which preceded my father's death had made a great change in my   1
life. I had been living in New Jersey, working in defense plants, working and
living among southerners, white and black. I knew about the south, of course,
and about how southerners treated Negroes and how they expected them to
behave, but it had never entered my mind that anyone would look at me and
expect *me* to behave that way. I learned in New Jersey that to be a Negro meant,
precisely, that one was never looked at but was simply at the mercy of the reflexes
the color of one's skin caused in other people. I acted in New Jersey as I had
always acted, that is as though I thought a great deal of myself—I had to *act* that
way—with results that were, simply, unbelievable. I had scarcely arrived before
I had earned the enmity, which was extraordinarily ingenious, of all my superiors and nearly all my co-workers. In the beginning, to make matters worse, I
simply did not know what was happening. I did not know what I had done, and
I shortly began to wonder what *anyone* could possibly do, to bring about such
unanimous, active, and unbearably vocal hostility. I knew about jim-crow but I
had never experienced it. I went to the same self-service restaurant three times
and stood with all the Princeton boys before the counter, waiting for a hamburger and coffee; it was always an extraordinarily long time before anything was
set before me, but it was not until the fourth visit that I learned that, in fact,
nothing had ever been set before me: I had simply picked something up. Negroes
were not served there, I was told, and they had been waiting for me to realize that
I was always the only Negro present. Once I was told this, I determined to go
there all the time. But now they were ready for me and, though some dreadful
scenes were subsequently enacted in that restaurant, I never ate there again.

It was the same story all over New Jersey, in bars, bowling alleys, diners,   2
places to live. I was always being forced to leave, silently, or with mutual
imprecations. I very shortly became notorious and children giggled behind me
when I passed and their elders whispered or shouted—they really believed that I
was mad. And it did begin to work on my mind, of course; I began to be afraid
to go anywhere and to compensate for this I went places to which I really should
not have gone and where, God knows, I had no desire to be. My reputation in
town naturally enhanced my reputation at work and my working day became one
long series of acrobatics designed to keep me out of trouble. I cannot say that
these acrobatics succeeded. It began to seem that the machinery of the organization I worked for was turning over, day and night, with but one aim: to eject
me. I was fired once, and contrived, with the aid of a friend from New York, to
get back on the payroll; was fired again, and bounced back again. It took a while
to fire me for the third time, but the third time took. There were no loopholes
anywhere. There was not even any way of getting back inside the gates.

That year in New Jersey lives in my mind as though it were the year during   3 which, having an unsuspected predilection for it, I first contracted some dread, chronic disease, the unfailing symptom of which is a kind of blind fever, a pounding in the skull and fire in the bowels. Once this disease is contracted, one can never be really carefree again, for the fever, without an instant's warning, can recur at any moment. It can wreck more important things than race relations. There is not a Negro alive who does not have this rage in his blood—one has the choice, merely, of living with it consciously or surrendering to it. As for me, this fever has recurred in me, and does, and will until the day I die.

My last night in New Jersey, a white friend from New York took me to the nearest big town, Trenton, to go to the movies and have a few drinks. As it turned out, he also saved me from, at the very least, a violent whipping. Almost every detail of that night stands out very clearly in my memory. I even remember the name of the movie we saw because its title impressed me as being so patly ironical. It was a movie about the German occupation of France, starring Maureen O'Hara and Charles Laughton and called *This Land Is Mine*. I remember the name of the diner we walked into when the movie ended: it was the "American Diner." When we walked in the counterman asked what we wanted and I remember answering with the casual sharpness which had become my habit: "We want a hamburger and a cup of coffee, what do you think we want?" I do not know why, after a year of such rebuffs, I so completely failed to anticipate his answer, which was, of course, "We don't serve Negroes here." This reply failed to discompose me, at least for the moment. I made some sardonic comment about the name of the diner and we walked out into the streets.

This was the time of what was called the "brown-out," when the lights in all American cities were very dim. When we re-entered the streets something happened to me which had the force of an optical illusion, or a nightmare. The streets were very crowded and I was facing north. People were moving in every direction but it seemed to me, in that instant, that all of the people I could see, and many more than that, were moving toward me, against me, and that everyone was white. I remember how their faces gleamed. And I felt, like a physical sensation, a *click* at the nape of my neck as though some interior string connecting my head to my body had been cut. I began to walk. I heard my friend call after me, but I ignored him. Heaven only knows what was going on in his mind, but he had the good sense not to touch me—I don't know what would have happened if he had—and to keep me in sight. I don't know what was going on in my mind, either; I certainly had no conscious plan. I wanted to do something to crush these white faces, which were crushing me. I walked for perhaps a block or two until I came to an enormous, glittering, and fashionable restaurant in which I knew not even the intercession of the Virgin would cause me to be served. I pushed through the doors and took the first vacant seat I saw, at a table for two, and waited.

I do not know how long I waited and I rather wonder, until today, what I could possibly have looked like. Whatever I looked like, I frightened the waitress who shortly appeared, and the moment she appeared all of my fury flowed towards her. I hated her for her white face, and for her great, astounded, frightened eyes.

I felt that if she found a black man so frightening I would make her fright worthwhile.

She did not ask me what I wanted, but repeated, as though she had learned it somewhere, "We don't serve Negroes here." She did not say it with the blunt, derisive hostility to which I had grown so accustomed, but, rather, with a note of apology in her voice, and fear. This made me colder and more murderous than ever. I felt I had to do something with my hands. I wanted her to come close enough for me to get her neck between my hands.

So I pretended not to have understood her, hoping to draw her closer. And she did step a very short step closer, with her pencil poised incongruously over her pad, and repeated the formula: ". . . don't serve Negroes here."

Somehow, with the repetition of that phrase, which was already ringing in my head like a thousand bells of a nightmare, I realized that she would never come any closer and that I would have to strike from a distance. There was nothing on the table but an ordinary watermug half full of water, and I picked this up and hurled it with all my strength at her. She ducked and it missed her and shattered against the mirror behind the bar. And, with that sound, my frozen blood abruptly thawed, I returned from wherever I had been, I *saw*, for the first time, the restaurant, the people with their mouths open, already, as it seemed to me, rising as one man, and I realized what I had done, and where I was, and I was frightened. I rose and began running for the door. A round, potbellied man grabbed me by the nape of the neck just as I reached the doors and began to beat me about the face. I kicked him and got loose and ran into the streets. My friend whispered, *"Run!"* and I ran.

My friend stayed outside the restaurant long enough to misdirect my pursuers and the police, who arrived, he told me, at once. I do not know what I said to him when he came to my room that night. I could not have said much. I felt, in the oddest, most awful way, that I had somehow betrayed him. I lived it over and over and over again, the way one relives an automobile accident after it has happened and one finds oneself alone and safe. I could not get over two facts, both equally difficult for the imagination to grasp, and one was that I could have been murdered. But the other was that I had been ready to commit murder. I saw nothing very clearly but I did see this: that my life, my *real* life, was in danger, and not from anything other people might do but from the hatred I carried in my own heart.

QUESTIONS

1. What does Baldwin mean in the opening paragraph when he says, "I acted . . . as though I thought a great deal of myself—I had to *act* that way"? **2.** What are the various stages Baldwin passes through in his response to racism? **3.** Does Baldwin's powerful description of the rage he felt support his generalization at the end of paragraph 3: "There is not a Negro alive who does not have this rage in his blood . . ."? **4.** What does Baldwin mean by the final sentence of the essay?

WRITING TOPIC

Describe how hatred in you or someone you know became self-destructive.

Why We Crave Horror Movies (1982)

STEPHEN KING [b. 1947]

I think that we're all mentally ill; those of us outside the asylums only hide it a 1 little better—and maybe not all that much better, after all. We've all known people who talk to themselves, people who sometimes squinch their faces into horrible grimaces when they believe no one is watching, people who have some hysterical fear—of snakes, the dark, the tight place, the long drop . . . and, of course, those final worms and grubs that are waiting so patiently underground.

When we pay our four or five bucks and seat ourselves at tenth-row center in 2 a theater showing a horror movie, we are daring the nightmare.

Why? Some of the reasons are simple and obvious. To show that we can, that 3 we are not afraid, that we can ride this roller coaster. Which is not to say that a really good horror movie may not surprise a scream out of us at some point, the way we may scream when the roller coaster twists through a complete 360 or plows through a lake at the bottom of the drop. And horror movies, like roller coasters, have always been the special province of the young; by the time one turns 40 or 50, one's appetite for double twists or 360-degree loops may be considerably depleted.

We also go to re-establish our feelings of essential normality; the horror movie 4 is innately conservative, even reactionary. Freda Jackson as the horrible melting woman in *Die, Monster, Die!* confirms for us that no matter how far we may be removed from the beauty of a Robert Redford or a Diana Ross, we are still light-years from true ugliness.

And we go to have fun. 5

Ah, but this is where the ground starts to slope away, isn't it? Because this is 6 a very peculiar sort of fun, indeed. The fun comes from seeing others menaced— sometimes killed. One critic has suggested that if pro football has become the voyeur's version of combat, then the horror film has become the modern version of the public lynching.

It is true that the mythic, "fairy-tale" horror film intends to take away the 7 shades of gray. . . . It urges us to put away our more civilized and adult penchant for analysis and to become children again, seeing things in pure blacks and whites. It may be that horror movies provide psychic relief on this level because this invitation to lapse into simplicity, irrationality and even outright madness is extended so rarely. We are told we may allow our emotions a free rein . . . or no rein at all.

If we are all insane, then sanity becomes a matter of degree. If your insanity 8 leads you to carve up women like Jack the Ripper or the Cleveland Torso Murderer, we clap you away in the funny farm (but neither of those two amateur-night surgeons was ever caught, heh-heh-heh); if, on the other hand, your insanity leads you only to talk to yourself when you're under stress or to pick your nose on your morning bus, then you are left alone to go about your business . . . though it is doubtful that you will ever be invited to the best parties.

The potential lyncher is in almost all of us (excluding saints, past and present;   9
but then, most saints have been crazy in their own ways), and every now and
then, he has to be let loose to scream and roll around in the grass. Our emotions
and our fears form their own body, and we recognize that it demands its own
exercise to maintain proper muscle tone. Certain of these emotional muscles are
accepted—even exalted—in civilized society; they are, of course, the emotions
that tend to maintain the status quo of civilization itself. Love, friendship,
loyalty, kindness—these are all the emotions that we applaud, emotions that
have been immortalized in the couplets of Hallmark cards and in the verses (I
don't dare call it poetry) of Leonard Nimoy.

When we exhibit these emotions, society showers us with positive reinforce-   10
ment; we learn this even before we get out of diapers. When, as children, we hug
our rotten little puke of a sister and give her a kiss, all the aunts and uncles smile
and twit and cry, "Isn't he the sweetest little thing?" Such coveted treats as
chocolate-covered graham crackers often follow. But if we deliberately slam the
rotten little puke of a sister's fingers in the door, sanctions follow—angry remon-
strance from parents, aunts and uncles; instead of a chocolate-covered graham
cracker, a spanking.

But anticivilization emotions don't go away, and they demand periodic exer-   11
cise. We have such "sick" jokes as, "What's the difference between a truckload
of bowling balls and a truckload of dead babies?" (You can't unload a truckload
of bowling balls with a pitchfork . . . a joke, by the way, that I heard originally
from a ten-year-old). Such a joke may surprise a laugh or a grin out of us even
as we recoil, a possibility that confirms the thesis: If we share a brotherhood of
man, then we also share an insanity of man. None of which is intended as a
defense of either the sick joke or insanity but merely as an explanation of why the
best horror films, like the best fairy tales, manage to be reactionary, anarchistic,
and revolutionary all at the same time.

The mythic horror movie, like the sick joke, has a dirty job to do. It delib-   12
erately appeals to all that is worst in us. It is morbidity unchained, our most base
instincts let free, our nastiest fantasies realized . . . and it all happens, fittingly
enough, in the dark. For those reasons, good liberals often shy away from horror
films. For myself, I like to see the most aggressive of them— *Dawn of the Dead*,
for instance—as lifting a trap door in the civilized forebrain and throwing a
basket of raw meat to the hungry alligators swimming around in that subterranean river beneath.

Why bother? Because it keeps them from getting out, man. It keeps them   13
down there and me up here. It was Lennon and McCartney who said that all you
need is love, and I would agree with that.

As long as you keep the gators fed.   14

QUESTIONS

1. List the reasons King gives for viewing horror films. Do you agree? Explain. **2.** Do
you agree with King's assertion that "we're all mentally ill"? What, then, would it
mean to say that someone is mentally healthy? **3.** Does King successfully support his

view that we are all murderously aggressive? How do his comments about Hallmark cards and Leonard Nimoy's verses contribute to his argument? **4.** Explain what King means by "the hungry alligators."

WRITING TOPIC
Use the last two sentences of King's essay as the thesis for an essay on human nature.

Love and Hate

QUESTIONS AND WRITING TOPICS

1. Every story in this section incorporates some sexual element. Distinguish among the functions served by the sexual aspects of the stories. **Writing Topic:** Contrast the function of sexuality in Borges's "The Intruder" and Faulkner's "A Rose for Emily."

2. Examine the works in this section in terms of the support they provide for the contention that love and hate are closely related emotions. **Writing Topic:** Discuss the relationship among race, love, and hate in Shakespeare's *Othello* and Faulkner's "A Rose for Emily."

3. What images are characteristically associated with love in the prose and poetry of this section? What images are associated with hate? **Writing Topic:** Compare the image patterns in Shakespeare's sonnets 18 and 130 with the image patterns in Donne's "A Valediction: Forbidding Mourning."

4. The Greeks have three words that can be translated by the English word *love: eros, agape,* and *philia.* Discover the differences among these three manifestations of love. **Writing Topic:** For each of these three types of human love, find a story or poem that you think is representative. In analyzing each work, discuss the extent to which the primary notion of love being addressed or celebrated is tempered by the other two types.

5. Blake's "A Poison Tree," Dickinson's "Mine Enemy Is Growing Old," Plath's "Daddy," and Thomas's "The Iks" all deal with hatred. Distinguish among the sources of the hatred expressed in these works. **Writing Topic:** Compare and contrast the source of the hatred in two of these works.

6. Chopin's "The Storm" and Moravia's "The Chase" deal with infidelity. Distinguish between the attitudes toward infidelity developed by these stories. **Writing Topic:** Describe the effects of marital infidelity on the life of the major character in each story.

7. What are the sources of the hatred described in Thomas's "The Iks" and Baldwin's "Rage"? **Writing Topic:** Defend or refute the assertion that Baldwin's confrontation with an Ik-like society is responsible for his rage.

8. Moravia's "The Chase" and Shaw's "The Girls in Their Summer Dresses" deal with jealousy. Contrast both the sources of the jealousy and the resolution of the problems caused by jealousy in the stories. **Writing Topic:** Who in your opinion has the better reason for being jealous, the husband in "The Chase" or the wife in "The Girls in Their Summer Dresses"? Explain.

9. Define and discuss the differences in the description of love in such stories as Borges's "The Intruder" and Chopin's "The Storm." **Writing Topic:** Compare and contrast the attitudes toward love that emerge from these stories.

10. Which works in this section treat love or hate in a way that corresponds with your own experience or conception of those emotional states? Which contradict your experience? **Writing Topic:** Isolate, in each case, the elements in the work that provoke your response and discuss them in terms of their "truth" or "falsity."

The
Presence
of Death

Pandora's Box, 1951 by Rene Magritte

The inevitability of death is not implied in the biblical story of creation; it required an act of disobedience before an angry God passed sentence of hard labor and mortality on humankind: "In the sweat of your face you shall eat bread till you return to the ground, for out of it you were taken; you are dust and to dust you shall return." These words, written down some 2,800 years ago, preserve an ancient explanation for a condition of life that yet remains persistently enigmatic—the dissolution of the flesh and the personality as accident or age culminates in death, the "undiscovered country, from whose bourn / No traveller returns." Though we cannot know what death is like, from earliest times men and women have attempted to characterize death, to cultivate beliefs about it. The mystery of it and the certainty of it make death, in every age, an important theme for literary art.

Beliefs about the nature of death vary widely. The ancient Jews of the Pentateuch reveal no conception of immortality. Ancient Buddhist writings describe death as a mere transmigration from one painful life to another in an ongoing expiation that only the purest can avoid. The Christians came to conceive of a soul, separate from the body, which at the body's death is freed for a better (or worse) disembodied eternal life. More recently in the Western world, the history of the attitudes about death reflects the great ideological revolutions that affected all thought—the Copernican revolution, which displaced the earth from the center of the solar system; the Darwinian revolution, which exchanged for humans, the greatest glory of God's creation, an upright primate with an opposable thumb whose days, like the dinosaur's, are likely to be numbered by the flux between the fire and ice of geological history; and the Freudian revolution, which robbed men and women of their proudest certainty, the conviction that they possessed a dependable and controlling rational mind. All these ideological changes serve to diminish us, to mock our self-importance, and, inevitably, to alter our conception of death.

But despite the impact of intellectual history, death remains invested with a special awe—perhaps because it infallibly mediates between all human differences. For the religious, death, like birth and marriage, is the occasion for solemn ritual that reaffirms for the congregation its own communal life and the promise of a better life hereafter—though the belief in immortality does not eliminate sadness and regret. For those for whom there is no immortality, death is nonetheless a ceremonial affair, full of awe, for nothing human is so purely defined, so utterly important, as life ended. Furthermore, both the religious and the secular see death in moral terms. For both, the killer is hateful. For both, there are some deaths that are deserved, some deaths that human weakness makes inevitable, some deaths that are outrageously unfair. For both, there are courageous deaths, which exalt the community, and cowardly deaths too embarrassing to recognize.

Death sometimes comes, one feels, as a release from a dark and menacing world. And this conception of *release* from the prison of life animates much of the essentially optimistic religious poetry of death—John Donne's sonnet "Death, Be Not Proud" is an outstanding example. Another view that establishes death as the great leveler, brings kings and emperors to that selfsame dust, reassures the impoverished when they contrast their misery with the wealth of the mighty.

That leveling aspect of death, apparent in Shelley's "Ozymandias," leads easily and logically to the tradition wherein life itself is made absurd by the fact of death. You may remember that Macbeth finally declares that life is "a tale / Told by an idiot, full of sound and fury, / Signifying nothing." And the contemplation of suicide, which the pain and absurdity of life would seem to commend, provokes such diverse responses as Yukio Mishima's "Patriotism" and Edward Arlington Robinson's ironic "Richard Cory." Some rage against death—Dylan Thomas in "Do Not Go Gentle into That Good Night"; others caution a quiet resignation—Frost in "After Apple-Picking" and Catherine Davis in her answer to Thomas, "After a Time." Much writing about death is elegiac; it speaks the melancholy response of the living to the fact of death as in Donne's "Meditation XVII" and such poems as Housman's "To an Athlete Dying Young" and Roethke's "Elegy for Jane."

In short, literary treatments of death display immense diversity. Selzer's essay reveals the rage of a dying patient, while in Tolstoy's "The Death of Iván Ilých," dying leads to a redemptive awareness. In Malamud's tragicomic "Idiots First," the protagonist insists upon and wins fair treatment from death, and in Cummings's "nobody loses all the time," the comic lightens the weight of death. The inevitability of death and the way one confronts it, paradoxically, lend to life its meaning and its value.

FOR THINKING AND WRITING

As you read the selections in this section, consider the following questions. You may want to write out your thoughts informally in a journal or notebook as a way of preparing to respond to the selections, or you may wish to make one of these questions the basis for a formal essay.

1. Have you had a close relative or friend who died? Was the person young or old, vigorous or feeble? How did you feel? How might the circumstances of death alter one's feelings toward death, or toward the person who died?

2. Do you believe that some essential part of you will survive the death of your body? On what do you base the belief? How does it alter your feelings about the death of people close to you? How does it alter your own behavior?

3. Are there any circumstances that justify suicide? Explain. If you feel that some suicides are justifiable, would it also be justifiable to help someone end his or her life? Explain.

4. Are there any circumstances that justify killing someone? Explain.

5. Imagine as best you can and describe the circumstances of your own death.

THE
PRESENCE
OF DEATH

Funerary Head, Ghana, Ashanti Tribe, 19th–20th century

FICTION

The Death of Iván Ilých*   1886

LEO TOLSTOY [1828–1910]

CHAPTER I

During an interval in the Melvínski trial in the large building of the Law Courts the members and public prosecutor met in Iván Egorovich Shébek's private room, where the conversation turned on the celebrated Krasóvski case. Fëdor Vasílievich warmly maintained that it was not subject to their jurisdiction, Iván Egórovich maintained the contrary, while Peter Ivánovich, not having entered into the discussion at the start, took no part in it but looked through the *Gazette* which had just been handed in.

"Gentlemen," he said, "Iván Ilých has died!"

"You don't say so!"

"Here, read it yourself," replied Peter Ivánovich, handing Fëdor Vasílievich the paper still damp from the press. Surrounded by a black border were the words: "Praskóvya Fëdorovna Golbviná, with profound sorrow, informs relatives and friends of the demise of her beloved husband Iván Ilých Golovín, Member of the Court of Justice, which occurred on February the 4th of this year 1882. The funeral will take place on Friday at one o'clock in the afternoon."

Iván Ilých had been a colleague of the gentlemen present and was liked by them all. He had been ill for some weeks with an illness said to be incurable. His post had been kept open for him, but there had been conjectures that in case of his death Alexéev might receive his appointment, and that either Vínnikov or Shtábel would succeed Alexéev. So on receiving the news of Iván Ilých's death the first thought of each of the gentlemen in that private room was of the changes and promotions it might occasion among themselves or their acquaintances.

"I shall be sure to get Shtábel's place or Vínnikov's," thought Fëdor Vasílievich. "I was promised that long ago, and the promotion means an extra eight hundred rubles a year for me besides the allowance."

"Now I must apply for my brother-in-law's transfer from Kalúga," thought

---

* Translated by Aylmer Maude.

Peter Ivánovich. "My wife will be very glad, and then she won't be able to say that I never do anything for her relations."

"I thought he would never leave his bed again," said Peter Ivánovich aloud. "It's very sad."

"But what really was the matter with him?"

"The doctors couldn't say—at least they could, but each of them said something different. When last I saw him I thought he was getting better."

"And I haven't been to see him since the holidays. I always meant to go."

"Had he any property?"

"I think his wife had a little—but something quite trifling."

"We shall have to go to see her, but they live so terribly far away."

"Far away from you, you mean. Everything's far away from your place."

"You see, he never can forgive my living on the other side of the river," said Peter Ivánovich, smiling at Shébek. Then, still talking of the distances between different parts of the city, they returned to the Court.

Besides considerations as to the possible transfers and promotions likely to result from Iván Ilých's death, the mere fact of the death of a near acquaintance aroused, as usual, in all who heard of it the complacent feeling that "it is he who is dead and not I."

Each one thought or felt, "Well, he's dead but I'm alive!" But the more intimate of Iván Ilých's acquaintances, his so-called friends, could not help thinking also that they would now have to fulfill the very tiresome demands of propriety by attending the funeral service and paying a visit of condolence to the widow.

Fëdor Vasílievich and Peter Ivánovich had been his nearest acquaintances. Peter Ivánovich had studied law with Iván Ilých and had considered himself to be under obligations to him.

Having told his wife at dinner-time of Iván Ilých's death, and of his conjecture that it might be possible to get her brother transferred to their circuit, Peter Ivánovich sacrificed his usual nap, put on his evening clothes, and drove to Iván Ilých's house.

At the entrance stood a carriage and two cabs. Leaning against the wall in the hall downstairs near the cloak-stand was a coffin-lid covered with cloth of gold, ornamented with gold cord and tassels, that had been polished up with metal powder. Two ladies in black were taking off their fur cloaks. Peter Ivánovich recognized one of them as Iván Ilých's sister, but the other was a stranger to him. His colleague Schwartz was just coming downstairs, but on seeing Peter Ivánovich enter he stopped and winked at him, as if to say: "Iván Ilých has made a mess of things—not like you and me."

Schwartz's face with his Piccadilly whiskers, and his slim figure in evening dress, had as usual an air of elegant solemnity which contrasted with the playfulness of his character and had a special piquancy here, or so it seemed to Peter Ivánovich.

Peter Ivánovich allowed the ladies to precede him and slowly followed them upstairs. Schwartz did not come down but remained where he was, and Peter

Ivánovich understood that he wanted to arrange where they should play bridge that evening. The ladies went upstairs to the widow's room, and Schwartz with seriously compressed lips but a playful look in his eyes, indicated by a twist of his eye-brows the room to the right where the body lay.

Peter Ivánovich, like everyone else on such occasions, entered feeling uncertain what he would have to do. All he knew was that at such times it is always safe to cross oneself. But he was not quite sure whether one should make obeisances while doing so. He therefore adopted a middle course. On entering the room he began crossing himself and made a slight movement resembling a bow. At the same time, as far as the motion of his head and arm allowed, he surveyed the room. Two young men—apparently nephews, one of whom was a high school pupil—were leaving the room, crossing themselves as they did so. An old woman was standing motionless, and a lady with strangely arched eyebrows was saying something to her in a whisper. A vigorous, resolute Church Reader, in a frock-coat, was reading something in a loud voice with an expression that precluded any contradiction. The butler's assistant, Gerásim, stepping lightly in front of Peter Ivánovich, was strewing something on the floor. Noticing this, Peter Ivánovich was immediately aware of a faint odour of a decomposing body.

The last time he had called on Iván Ilých, Peter Ivánovich had seen Gerásim in the study. Iván Ilých had been particularly fond of him and he was performing the duty of a sick nurse.

Peter Ivánovich continued to make the sign of the cross slightly inclining his head in an intermediate direction between the coffin, the Reader, and the icons on the table in a corner of the room. Afterwards, when it seemed to him that this movement of his arm in crossing himself had gone on too long, he stopped and began to look at the corpse.

The dead man lay, as dead men always lie, in a specially heavy way, his rigid limbs sunk in the soft cushions of the coffin, with the head forever bowed on the pillow. His yellow waxen brow with bald patches over his sunken temples was thrust up in the way peculiar to the dead, the protruding nose seeming to press on the upper lip. He was much changed and had grown even thinner since Peter Ivánovich had last seen him, but, as is always the case with the dead, his face was handsomer and above all more dignified than when he was alive. The expression on the face said that what was necessary had been accomplished, and accomplished rightly. Besides this there was in that expression a reproach and a warning to the living. This warning seemed to Peter Ivánovich out of place, or at least not applicable to him. He felt a certain discomfort and so he hurriedly crossed himself once more and turned and went out of the door—too hurriedly and too regardless of propriety, as he himself was aware.

Schwartz was waiting for him in the adjoining room with legs spread wide apart and both hands toying with his top-hat behind his back. The mere sight of that playful, well-groomed, and elegant figure refreshed Peter Ivánovich. He felt that Schwartz was above all these happenings and would not surrender to any depressing influences. His very look said that this incident of a church service for Iván Ilých could not be a sufficient reason for infringing the order of the session—in other words, that it would certainly not prevent his unwrapping a new pack of cards and shuffling them that evening while a footman placed four fresh candles on the table: in fact, there was no reason for supposing that this incident would hinder their spending the evening agreeably. Indeed he said this in a whisper as Peter Ivánovich passed him, proposing that they should meet for a game at Fëdor Vasílievich's. But apparently Peter Ivánovich was not destined to play bridge that evening. Praskóvya Fëdorovna (a short, fat woman who despite all efforts to the contrary had continued to broaden steadily from her shoulders downwards and who had the same extraordinarily arched eyebrows as the lady who had been standing by the coffin), dressed all in black, her head covered with lace, came out of her own room with some other ladies, conducted them to the room where the dead body lay, and said: "The service will begin immediately. Please go in."

Schwartz, making an indefinite bow, stood still, evidently neither accepting nor declining this invitation. Praskóvya Fëdorovna recognizing Peter Ivánovich, sighed, went close up to him, took his hand, and said: "I know you were a true friend to Iván Ilých . . . " and looked at him awaiting some suitable response. And Peter Ivánovich knew that, just as it had been the right thing to cross himself in that room, so what he had to do here was to press her hand, sigh, and say, "Believe me . . . " So he did all this and as he did it felt that the desired result had been achieved: that both he and she were touched.

"Come with me. I want to speak to you before it begins," said the widow. "Give me your arm."

Peter Ivánovich gave her his arm and they went to the inner rooms, passing Schwartz who winked at Peter Ivánovich compassionately.

"That does for our bridge! Don't object if we find another player. Perhaps you can cut in when you do escape," said his playful look.

Peter Ivánovich sighed still more deeply and despondently, and Praskóvya Fëdorovna pressed his arm gratefully. When they reached the drawing-room, upholstered in pink cretonne and lighted by a dim lamp, they sat down at the table—she on a sofa and Peter Ivánovich on a low pouffe, the springs of which yielded spasmodically under his weight. Praskóvya Fëdorovna had been on the point of warning him to take another seat, but felt that such a warning was out of keeping with her present condition and so changed her mind. As he sat down on the pouffe Peter Ivánovich recalled how Iván Ilých had arranged this room and had consulted him regarding this pink cretonne with green leaves. The whole room was full of furniture and knick-knacks, and on her way to the sofa the lace of the widow's black shawl caught on the carved edge of the table. Peter Ivánovich rose to detach it, and the springs of the pouffe, relieved of his weight, rose also and gave him a push. The widow began detaching her shawl herself, and Peter Ivánovich again sat down, suppressing the rebellious springs of the pouffe under him. But the widow had not quite freed herself and Peter Ivánovich got up again, and again the pouffe rebelled and even creaked. When this was all over she took out a clean cambric handkerchief and began to weep. The

episode with the shawl and the struggle with the pouffe had cooled Peter Ivánovich's emotions and he sat there with a sullen look on his face. This awkward
situation was interrupted by Sokolóv, Iván Ilých's butler, who came to report
that the plot in the cemetery that Praskóvya Fëdorovna had chosen would cost
two hundred rubles. She stopped weeping and, looking at Peter Ivánovich with
the air of a victim, remarked in French that it was very hard for her. Peter
Ivánovich made a silent gesture signifying his full conviction that it must indeed
be so.

"Please smoke," she said in a magnanimous yet crushed voice, and turned
to discuss with Sokolóv the price of the plot for the grave.

Peter Ivánovich while lighting his cigarette heard her inquiring very circum-
stantially into the price of different plots in the cemetery and finally decide
which she would take. When that was done she gave instructions about engaging
the choir. Sokólov then left the room.

"I look after everything myself," she told Peter Ivánovich, shifting the albums
that lay on the table; and noticing that the table was endangered by his cigarette-
ash, she immediately passed him an ashtray, saying as she did so: "I consider
it an affectation to say that my grief prevents my attending to practical affairs.
On the contrary, if anything can—I won't say console me, but—distract me,
it is seeing to everything concerning him." She again took out her handkerchief
as if preparing to cry, but suddenly, as if mastering her feeling, she shook herself
and began to speak calmly. "But there is something I want to talk to you about."

Peter Ivánovich bowed, keeping control of the springs of the pouffe, which
immediately began quivering under him.

"He suffered terribly the last few days."

"Did he?" said Peter Ivánovich.

"Oh, terribly! He screamed unceasingly, not for minutes but for hours. For
the last three days he screamed incessantly. It was unendurable. I cannot understand how I bore it; you could hear him three rooms off. Oh, what I have
suffered!"

"Is it possible that he was conscious all that time?" asked Peter Ivánovich.

"Yes," she whispered. "To the last moment. He took leave of us a quarter of
an hour before he died, and asked us to take Volódya away."

The thought of the sufferings of this man he had known so intimately, first
as a merry little boy, then as a school-mate, and later as a grown-up colleague,
suddenly struck Peter Ivánovich with horror, despite an unpleasant consciousness of his own and this woman's dissimulation. He again saw that brow, and
that nose pressing down on the lip, and felt afraid for himself.

"Three days of frightful suffering and then death! Why, that might suddenly,
at any time, happen to me," he thought, and for a moment felt terrified. But—
he did not himself know how—the customary reflection at once occurred to
him that this had happened to Iván Ilých and not to him, and that it should
not and could not happen to him, and that to think that it could would be
yielding to depression which he ought not to do, as Schwartz's expression plainly
showed. After which reflection Peter Ivánovich felt reassured, and began to ask

with interest about the details of Iván Ilých's death, as though death was an accident natural to Iván Ilých but certainly not to himself.

After many details of the really dreadful physical sufferings Iván Ilých had endured (which details he learnt only from the effect those sufferings had produced on Praskóvya Fëdorovna's nerves) the widow apparently found it necessary to get to business.

"Oh, Peter Ivánovich, how hard it is! How terribly, terribly hard!" and she again began to weep.

Peter Ivánovich sighed and waited for her to finish blowing her nose. When she had done so he said, "Believe me . . ." and she again began talking and brought out what was evidently her chief concern with him—namely, to question him as to how she could obtain a grant of money from the government on the occasion of her husband's death. She made it appear that she was asking Peter Ivánovich's advice about her pension, but he soon saw that she already knew about that to the minutest detail, more even than he did himself. She knew how much could be got out of the government in consequence of her husband's death, but wanted to find out whether she could not possibly extract something more. Peter Ivánovich tried to think of some means of doing so, but after reflecting for a while and, out of propriety, condemning the government for its niggardliness, he said he thought that nothing more could be got. Then she sighed and evidently began to devise means of getting rid of her visitor. Noticing this, he put out his cigarette, rose, pressed her hand, and went out into the anteroom.

In the dining-room where the clock stood that Iván Ilých had liked so much and had bought at an antique shop, Peter Ivánovich met a priest and a few acquaintances who had come to attend the service, and he recognized Iván Ilých's daughter, a handsome young woman. She was in black and her slim figure appeared slimmer than ever. She had a gloomy, determined, almost angry expression, and bowed to Peter Ivánovich as though he were in some way to blame. Behind her, with the same offended look, stood a wealthy young man, an examining magistrate, whom Peter Ivánovich also knew and who was her fiancé, as he had heard. He bowed mournfully to them and was about to pass into the death-chamber, when from under the stairs appeared the figure of Iván Ilých's schoolboy son, who was extremely like his father. He seemed a little Iván Ilých, such as Peter Ivánovich remembered when they studied law together. His tear-stained eyes had in them the look that is seen in the eyes of boys of thirteen or fourteen who are not pure-minded. When he saw Peter Ivánovich he scowled morosely and shame-facedly. Peter Ivánovich nodded to him and entered the death-chamber. The service began: candles, groans, incense, tears, and sobs. Peter Ivánovich stood looking gloomily down at his feet. He did not look once at the dead man, did not yield to any depressing influence, and was one of the first to leave the room. There was no one in the anteroom, but Gerásim darted out of the dead man's room, rummaged with his strong hands among the fur coats to find Peter Ivánovich's and helped him on with it.

"Well, friend Gerásim," said Peter Ivánovich, so as to say something. "It's a sad affair, isn't it?"

"It's God's will. We shall all come to it some day," said Gerásim, displaying his teeth—the even, white teeth of a healthy peasant—and, like a man in the thick of urgent work, he briskly opened the front door, called the coachman, helped Peter Ivánovich into the sledge, and sprang back to the porch as if in readiness for what he had to do next.

Peter Ivánovich found the fresh air particularly pleasant after the smell of incense, the dead body, and carbolic acid.

"Where to, sir?" asked the coachman.

"It's not too late even now. . . . I'll call around on Fëdor Vasílievich."

He accordingly drove there and found them just finishing the first rubber, so that it was quite convenient for him to cut in.

CHAPTER II

Iván Ilých's life had been most simple and most ordinary and therefore most terrible.

He had been a member of the Court of Justice, and died at the age of forty-five. His father had been an official who after serving in various ministries and departments of Petersburg had made the sort of career which brings men to positions from which by reason of their long service they cannot be dismissed, though they are obviously unfit to hold any responsible position, and for whom therefore posts are specially created, which though fictitious carry salaries of from six to ten thousand rubles that are not fictitious, and in receipt of which they live on to a great age.

Such was the Privy Councillor and superfluous member of various superfluous institutions, Ilyá Epímovich Golovín.

He had three sons, of whom Iván Ilých was the second. The eldest son was following in his father's footsteps only in another department, and was already approaching that stage in the service at which a similar sinecure would be reached. The third son was a failure. He had ruined his prospects in a number of positions and was now serving in the railway department. His father and brothers, and still more their wives, not merely disliked meeting him, but avoided remembering his existence unless compelled to do so. His sister had married Baron Greff, a Petersburg official of her father's type. Iván Ilých was *le phénix de la famille*[1] as people said. He was neither as cold and formal as his elder brother nor as wild as the younger, but was a happy mean between them—an intelligent, polished, lively and agreeable man. He had studied with his younger brother at the School of Law, but the latter had failed to complete the course and was expelled when he was in the fifth class. Iván Ilých finished the course well. Even when he was at the School of Law he was just what he remained for the rest of his life: a capable, cheerful, good-natured, and sociable man, though strict in the fulfilment of what he considered to be his duty: and

---

[1] The phoenix of the family, here meaning "rare bird" or "prodigy."

he considered his duty to be what was so considered by those in authority. Neither as a boy nor as a man was he a toady, but from early youth was by nature attracted to people of high station as a fly is drawn to the light, assimilating their ways and views of life and establishing friendly relations with them. All the enthusiasms of childhood and youth passed without leaving much trace on him; he succumbed to sensuality, to vanity, and latterly among the highest classes to liberalism, but always within limits which his instinct unfailingly indicated to him as correct.

At school he had done things which had formerly seemed to him very horrid and made him feel disgusted with himself when he did them; but when later on he saw that such actions were done by people of good position and that they did not regard them as wrong, he was able not exactly to regard them as right, but to forget about them entirely or not be at all troubled at remembering them.

Having graduated from the School of Law and qualified for the tenth rank of the civil service, and having received money from his father for his equipment, Iván Ilých ordered himself clothes at Scharmer's, the fashionable tailor, hung a medallion inscribed *respice finen*[2] on his watch-chain, took leave of his professor and the prince who was patron of the school, had a farewell dinner with his comrades at Donon's first-class restaurant, and with his new and fashionable portmanteau, linen, clothes, shaving and other toilet appliances, and a travelling rug, all purchased at the best shops, he set off for one of the provinces where, through his father's influence, he had been attached to the Governor as an official for special service.

In the province Iván Ilých soon arranged as easy and agreeable a position for himself as he had had at the School of Law. He performed his official tasks, made his career, and at the same time amused himself pleasantly and decorously. Occasionally he paid official visits to country districts, where he behaved with dignity both to his superiors and inferiors, and performed the duties entrusted to him, which related chiefly to the sectarians,[3] with an exactness and incorruptible honesty of which he could not but feel proud.

In official matters, despite his youth and taste for frivolous gaiety, he was exceedingly reserved, punctilious, and even severe; but in society he was often amusing and witty, and always good-natured, correct in his manner, and *bon enfant*, as the governor and his wife—with whom he was like one of the family—used to say of him.

In the provinces he had an affair with a lady who made advances to the elegant young lawyer, and there was also a milliner; and there were carousals with aides-de-camp who visited the district, and after-supper visits to a certain outlying street of doubtful reputation; and there was too some obsequiousness to his chief and even to his chief's wife, but all this was done with such a tone of good breeding that no hard names could be applied to it. It all came under

---

[2] Regard the end.
[3] A large sect, whose members were placed under many legal restrictions, that broke away from the Russian Orthodox church in the seventeenth century.

the heading of the French saying: "Il faut que jeunesse se passe."[4] It was all done with clean hands, in clean linen, with French phrases, and above all among people of the best society and consequently with the approval of people of rank.

So Iván Ilých served for five years and then came a change in his official life. The new and reformed judicial institutions were introduced, and new men were needed. Iván Ilých became such a new man. He was offered the post of Examining Magistrate, and he accepted it though the post was in another province and obliged him to give up the connexions he had formed and to make new ones. His friends met to give him a send-off; they had a group-photograph taken and presented him with a silver cigarette-case, and he set off to his new post.

As examining magistrate Iván Ilých was just as *comme il faut*[5] and decorous a man, inspiring general respect and capable of separating his official duties from his private life, as he had been when acting as an official on special service. His duties now as examining magistrate were far more interesting and attractive than before. In his former position it had been pleasant to wear an undress uniform made by Scharmer, and to pass through the crowd of petitioners and officials who were timorously awaiting an audience with the governor, and who envied him as with free and easy gait he went straight into his chief's private room to have a cup of tea and a cigarette with him. But not many people had then been directly dependent on him—only police officials and the sectarians when he went on special missions—and he liked to treat them politely, almost as comrades, as if he were letting them feel that he who had the power to crush them was treating them in this simple, friendly way. There were then but few such people. But now, as an examining magistrate, Iván Ilých felt that everyone without exception, even the most important and self-satisfied, was in his power, and that he need only write a few words on a sheet of paper with a certain heading, and this or that important, self-satisfied person would be brought before him in the role of an accused person or a witness, and if he did not choose to allow him to sit down, would have to stand before him and answer his questions. Iván Ilých never abused his power; he tried on the contrary to soften its expression, but the consciousness of it and of the possibility of softening its effect, supplied the chief interest and attraction of his office. In his work itself, especially in his examinations, he very soon acquired a method of eliminating all considerations irrelevant to the legal aspect of the case, and reducing even the most complicated case to a form in which it would be presented on paper only in its externals, completely excluding his personal opinion of the matter, while above all observing every prescribed formality. The work was new and Iván Ilých was one of the first men to apply the new Code of 1864.[6]

On taking up the post of examining magistrate in a new town, he made new acquaintances and connexions, placed himself on a new footing, and assumed

---

[4] Youth must have its fling.
[5] Proper.
[6] Judicial procedures were thoroughly reformed after the emancipation of the serfs in 1861.

a somewhat different tone. He took up an attitude of rather dignified aloofness towards the provincial authorities, but picked out the best circle of legal gentlemen and wealthy gentry living in the town and assumed a tone of slight dissatisfaction with the government, of moderate liberalism, and of enlightened citizenship. At the same time, without at all altering the elegance of his toilet, he ceased shaving his chin and allowed his beard to grow as it pleased.

Iván Ilých settled down very pleasantly in this new town. The society there, which inclined towards opposition to the Governor, was friendly, his salary was larger, and he began to play *vint*,[7] which he found added not a little to the pleasure of life, for he had a capacity for cards, played good-humouredly, and calculated rapidly and astutely, so that he usually won.

After living there for two years he met his future wife, Praskóvya Fëdorovna Míkhel, who was the most attractive, clever, and brilliant girl of the set in which he moved, and among other amusements and relaxations from his labours as examining magistrate, Iván Ilých established light and playful relations with her.

While he had been an official on special service he had been accustomed to dance, but now as an examining magistrate it was exceptional for him to do so. If he danced now, he did it as if to show that though he served under the reformed order of things, and had reached the fifth official rank, yet when it came to dancing he could do it better than most people. So at the end of an evening he sometimes danced with Praskóvya Fëdorovna, and it was chiefly during these dances that he captivated her. She fell in love with him. Iván Ilých had at first no definite intention of marrying, but when the girl fell in love with him he said to himself: "Really, why shouldn't I marry?"

Praskóvya Fëdorovna came of a good family, was not bad looking and had some little property. Iván Ilých might have aspired to a more brilliant match, but even this was good. He had his salary, and she, he hoped, would have an equal income. She was well connected, and was a sweet, pretty, and thoroughly correct young woman. To say that Iván Ilých married because he fell in love with Praskóvya Fëdorovna and found that she sympathized with his views of life would be as incorrect as to say that he married because his social circle approved of the match. He was swayed by both these considerations: the marriage gave him personal satisfaction, and at the same time it was considered the right thing by the most highly placed of his associates.

So Iván Ilých got married.

The preparations for marriage and the beginning of married life, with its conjugal caresses, the new furniture, new crockery, and new linen, were very pleasant until his wife became pregnant—so that Iván Ilých had begun to think that marriage would not impair the easy, agreeable, gay and always decorous character of his life, approved of by society and regarded by himself as natural, but would even improve it. But from the first months of his wife's pregnancy, something new, unpleasant, depressing, and unseemly, and from which there was no way of escape, unexpectedly showed itself.

---

[7] A card game similar to bridge.

His wife, without any reason—*de gaieté de coeur* as Iván Ilých expressed it
to himself—began to disturb the pleasure and propriety of their life. She began
to be jealous without any cause, expected him to devote his whole attention to
her, found fault with everything, and made coarse and ill-mannered scenes.

At first Iván Ilých hoped to escape from the unpleasantness of this state of
affairs by the same easy and decorous relation to life that had served him here-
tofore: he tried to ignore his wife's disagreeable moods, continued to live in his
usual easy and pleasant way, invited friends to his house for a game of cards,
and also tried going out to his club or spending his evenings with friends. But
one day his wife began upbraiding him so vigorously, using such coarse words,
and continued to abuse him every time he did not fulfil her demands, so
resolutely and with such evident determination not to give way till he submitted—that is, till he stayed at home and was bored just as she was—that he
became alarmed. He now realized that matrimony—at any rate with Praskóvya
Fëdorovna—was not always conducive to the pleasures and amenities of life but
on the contrary often infringed both comfort and propriety, and that he must
therefore entrench himself against such infringement. And Iván Ilých began to
seek for means of doing so. His official duties were the one thing that imposed
upon Praskóvya Fëdorovna, and by means of his official work and the duties
attached to it he began struggling with his wife to secure his own independence.

With the birth of their child, the attempts to feed it and the various failures
in doing so, and with the real and imaginary illnesses of mother and child, in
which Iván Ilých's sympathy was demanded but about which he understood
nothing, the need of securing for himself an existence outside his family life
became still more imperative.

As his wife grew more irritable and exacting and Iván Ilých transferred the
centre of gravity of his life more and more to his official work, so did he grow
to like his work better and became more ambitious than before.

Very soon, within a year of his wedding, Iván Ilých had realized that marriage,
though it may add some comforts to life, is in fact a very intricate and difficult
affair towards which in order to perform one's duty, that is, to lead a decorous
life approved of by society, one must adopt a definite attitude just as towards
one's official duties.

And Iván Ilých evolved such an attitude towards married life. He only required of it those conveniences—dinner at home, housewife, and bed—which
it could give him, and above all that propriety of external forms required by
public opinion. For the rest he looked for light-hearted pleasure and propriety,
and was very thankful when he found them, but if he met with antagonism and
querulousness he at once retired into his separate fenced-off world of official
duties, where he found satisfaction.

Iván Ilých was esteemed a good official, and after three years was made
Assistant Public Prosecutor. His new duties, their importance, the possibility of
indicting and imprisoning anyone he chose, the publicity his speeches received,
and the success he had in all these things, made his work still more attractive.

More children came. His wife became more and more querulous and ill-tempered, but the attitude Iván Ilých had adopted towards his home life rendered him almost impervious to her grumbling.

After seven years' service in that town he was transferred to another province as Public Prosecutor. They moved, but were short of money and his wife did not like the place they moved to. Though the salary was higher the cost of living was greater, besides which two of their children died and family life became still more unpleasant for him.

Praskóvya Fëdorovna blamed her husband for every inconvenience they encountered in their new home. Most of the conversations between husband and wife, especially as to the children's education, led to topics which recalled former disputes, and those disputes were apt to flare up again at any moment. There remained only those rare periods of amorousness which still came to them at times but did not last long. These were islets at which they anchored for a while and then again set out upon that ocean of veiled hostility which showed itself in their aloofness from one another. This aloofness might have grieved Iván Ilých had he considered that it ought not to exist, but he now regarded the position as normal, and even made it the goal at which he aimed in family life. His aim was to free himself more and more from those unpleasantnesses and to give them a semblance of harmlessness and propriety. He attained this by spending less and less time with his family, and when obliged to be at home he tried to safeguard his position by the presence of outsiders. The chief thing however was that he had his official duties. The whole interest of his life now centered in the official world and that interest absorbed him. The consciousness of his power, being able to ruin anybody he wished to ruin, the importance, even the external dignity of his entry into court, or meetings with his subordinates, his success with superiors and inferiors, and above all his masterly handling of cases, of which he was conscious—all this gave him pleasure and filled his life, together with chats with his colleagues, dinners, and bridge. So that on the whole Iván Ilých's life continued to flow as he considered it should do—pleasantly and properly.

So things continued for another seven years. His eldest daughter was already sixteen, another child had died, and only one son was left, a schoolboy and a subject of dissension. Iván Ilých wanted to put him in the School of Law, but to spite him Praskóvya Fëdorovna entered him at the High School. The daughter had been educated at home and had turned out well: the boy did not learn badly either.

CHAPTER III

So Iván Ilých lived for seventeen years after his marriage. He was already a Public Prosecutor of long standing, and had declined several proposed transfers while awaiting a more desirable post, when an unanticipated and unpleasant occurrence quite upset the peaceful course of his life. He was expecting to be offered the post of presiding judge in a University town, but Happe somehow came to the front and obtained the appointment instead. Iván Ilých became irritable, reproached Happe, and quarrelled both with him and with his immediate superiors—who became colder to him and again passed him over when other appointments were made.

This was in 1880, the hardest year of Iván Ilých's life. It was then that it became evident on the one hand that his salary was insufficient for them to live on, and on the other that he had been forgotten, and not only this, but that what was for him the greatest and most cruel injustice appeared to others a quite ordinary occurrence. Even his father did not consider it his duty to help him. Iván Ilých felt himself abandoned by everyone, and that they regarded his position with a salary of 3,500 rubles as quite normal and even fortunate. He alone knew that with the consciousness of the injustices done him, with his wife's incessant nagging, and with the debts he had contracted by living beyond his means, his position was far from normal.

In order to save money that summer he obtained leave of absence and went with his wife to live in the country at her brother's place.

In the country, without his work, he experienced *ennui* for the first time in his life, and not only *ennui* but intolerable depression, and he decided that it was impossible to go on living like that, and that it was necessary to take energetic measures.

Having passed a sleepless night pacing up and down the veranda, he decided to go to Petersburg and bestir himself, in order to punish those who had failed to appreciate him and to get transferred to another ministry.

Next day, despite many protests from his wife and her brother, he started for Petersburg with the sole object of obtaining a post with a salary of five thousand rubles a year. He was no longer bent on any particular department, or tendency, or kind of activity. All he now wanted was an appointment to another post with a salary of five thousand rubles, either in the administration, in the banks, with the railways, in one of the Empress Márya's Institutions,[8] or even in the customs—but it had to carry with it a salary of five thousand rubles and be in a ministry other than that in which they had failed to appreciate him.

And this quest of Iván Ilých's was crowned with remarkable and unexpected success. At Kursk an acquaintance of his, F. I. Ilyín, got into the first-class carriage, sat down beside Iván Ilých, and told him of a telegram just received by the Governor of Kursk announcing that a change was about to take place in the ministry: Peter Ivánovich was to be superseded by Iván Semënovich.

The proposed change, apart from its significance for Russia, had a special significance for Iván Ilých, because by bringing forward a new man, Peter Petróvich, and consequently his friend Zachár Ivánovich, it was highly favourable for Iván Ilých, since Zachár Ivánovich was a friend and colleague of his.

In Moscow this news was confirmed, and on reaching Petersburg Iván Ilých found Zachár Ivánovich and received a definite promise of an appointment in his former Department of Justice.

---

[8] A charitable organization founded in the late eighteenth century by the Empress Márya.

A week later he telegraphed to his wife: "Zachár in Miller's place. I shall receive appointment on presentation of report."

Thanks to this change of personnel, Iván Ilých had unexpectedly obtained an appointment in his former ministry which placed him two stages above his former colleagues besides giving him five thousand rubles salary and three thousand five hundred rubles for expenses connected with his removal. All his ill humour towards his former enemies and the whole department vanished, and Iván Ilých was completely happy.

He returned to the country more cheerful and contented than he had been for a long time. Praskóvya Fëdorovna also cheered up and a truce was arranged between them. Iván Ilých told of how he had been fêted by everybody in Petersburg, how all those who had been his enemies were put to shame and now fawned on him, how envious they were of his appointment, and how much everybody in Petersburg had liked him.

Praskóvya Fëdorovna listened to all this and appeared to believe it. She did not contradict anything, but only made plans for their life in the town to which they were going. Iván Ilých saw with delight that these plans were his plans, that he and his wife agreed, and that, after a stumble, his life was regaining its due and natural character of pleasant lightheartedness and decorum.

Iván Ilých had come back for a short time only, for he had to take up his new duties on the 10th of September. Moreover, he needed time to settle into the new place, to move all his belongings from the province, and to buy and order many additional things: in a word, to make such arrangements as he had resolved on, which were almost exactly what Praskóvya Fëdorovna too had decided on.

Now that everything had happened so fortunately, and that he and his wife were at one in their aims and moreover saw so little of one another, they got on together better than they had done since the first years of marriage. Iván Ilých had thought of taking his family away with him at once, but the insistence of his wife's brother and her sister-in-law, who had suddenly become particularly amiable and friendly to him and his family, induced him to depart alone.

So he departed, and the cheerful state of mind induced by his success and by the harmony between his wife and himself, the one intensifying the other, did not leave him. He found a delightful house, just the thing both he and his wife had dreamt of. Spacious, lofty reception rooms in the old style, a convenient and dignified study, rooms for his wife and daughter, a study for his son— it might have been specially built for them. Iván Ilých himself superintended the arrangements, chose the wall-papers, supplemented the furniture (preferably with antiques which he considered particularly *comme il faut*), and supervised the upholstering. Everything progressed and progressed and approached the ideal he had set himself: even when things were only half completed they exceeded his expectations. He saw what a refined and elegant character, free from vulgarity, it would all have when it was ready. On falling asleep he pictured to himself how the reception-room would look. Looking at the yet unfinished drawing-room he could see the fireplace, the screen, the what-not, the little chairs dotted here and there, the dishes and plates on the walls, and the bronzes, as they would be when everything was in place. He was pleased by the thought of how his wife and daughter, who shared his taste in this matter, would be impressed by it. They were certainly not expecting as much. He had been particularly successful in finding, and buying cheaply, antiques which gave a particularly aristocratic character to the whole place. But in his letters he intentionally understated everything in order to be able to surprise them. All this so absorbed him that his new duties—though he liked his official work—interested him less than he had expected. Sometimes he even had moments of absent-mindedness during the Court Sessions, and would consider whether he should have straight or curved cornices for his curtains. He was so interested in it all that he often did things himself, rearranging the furniture, or rehanging the curtains. Once when mounting a step-ladder to show the upholsterer, who did not understand, how he wanted the hangings draped, he made a false step and slipped, but being a strong and agile man he clung on and only knocked his side against the knob of the window frame. The bruised place was painful but the pain soon passed, and he felt particularly bright and well just then. He wrote: "I feel fifteen years younger." He thought he would have everything ready by September, but it dragged on till mid-October. But the result was charming not only in his eyes but to everyone who saw it.

In reality it was just what is usually seen in the houses of people of moderate means who want to appear rich, and therefore succeed only in resembling others like themselves: there were damasks, dark wood, plants, rugs, and dull and polished bronzes—all the things people of a certain class have in order to resemble other people of that class. His house was so like the others that it would never have been noticed, but to him it all seemed to be quite exceptional. He was very happy when he met his family at the station and brought them to the newly furnished house all lit up, where a footman in a white tie opened the door into the hall decorated with plants, and when they went on into the drawing-room and the study uttering exclamations of delight. He conducted them everywhere, drank in their praises eagerly, and beamed with pleasure. At tea that evening, when Praskóvya Fëdorovna among other things asked him about his fall, he laughed, and showed them how he had gone flying and had frightened the upholsterer.

"It's a good thing I'm a bit of an athlete. Another man might have been killed, but I merely knocked myself, just here; it hurts when it's touched, but it's passing off already—it's only a bruise."

So they began living in their new home—in which, as always happens, when they got thoroughly settled in they found they were just one room short—and with the increased income, which as always was just a little (some five hundred rubles) too little, but it was all very nice.

Things went particularly well at first, before everything was finally arranged and while something had still to be done: this thing bought, that thing ordered, another thing moved, and something else adjusted. Though there were some disputes between husband and wife, they were both so well satisfied and had so much to do that it all passed off without any serious quarrels. When nothing was left to arrange it became rather dull and something seemed to be lacking, but they were then making acquaintances, forming habits, and life was growing fuller.

Iván Ilých spent his mornings at the law court and came home to dinner, and at first he was generally in a good humour, though he occasionally became irritable just on account of his house. (Every spot on the tablecloth or the upholstery, and every broken window-blind string, irritated him. He had devoted so much trouble to arranging it all that every disturbance of it distressed him.) But on the whole his life ran its course as he believed life should do: easily, pleasantly, and decorously.

He got up at nine, drank his coffee, read the paper, and then put on his undress uniform and went to the law courts. There the harness in which he worked had already been stretched to fit him and he donned it without a hitch: petitioners, inquiries at the chancery, the chancery itself, and the sittings public and administrative. In all this the thing was to exclude everything fresh and vital, which always disturbs the regular course of official business, and to admit only official relations with people, and then only on official grounds. A man would come, for instance, wanting some information. Iván Ilých, as one in whose sphere the matter did not lie, would have nothing to do with him: but if the man had some business with him in his official capacity, something that could be expressed on officially stamped paper, he would do everything, positively everything he could within the limits of such relations, and in doing so would maintain the semblance of friendly human relations, that is, would observe the courtesies of life. As soon as the official relations ended, so did everything else. Iván Ilých possessed this capacity to separate his real life from the official side of affairs and not mix the two, in the highest degree, and by long practice and natural aptitude had brought it to such a pitch that sometimes, in the manner of a virtuoso, he would even allow himself to let the human and official relations mingle. He let himself do this just because he felt that he could at any time he chose resume the strictly official attitude again and drop the human relation. And he did it all easily, pleasantly, correctly, and even artistically. In the intervals between the sessions he smoked, drank tea, chatted a little about politics, a little about general topics, a little about cards, but most of all about official appointments. Tired, but with the feelings of a virtuoso— one of the first violins who has played his part in an orchestra with precision— he would return home to find that his wife and daughter had been out paying calls, or had a visitor, and that his son had been to school, had done his homework with his tutor, and was duly learning what is taught at High Schools. Everything was as it should be. After dinner, if they had no visitors, Iván Ilých sometimes read a book that was being much discussed at the time, and in the evening settled down to work, that is, read official papers, compared the depositions of witnesses, and noted paragraphs of the Code applying to them. This was neither dull nor amusing. It was dull when he might have been playing bridge, but if no bridge was available it was at any rate better than doing nothing or sitting with his wife. Iván Ilých's chief pleasure was giving little dinners to which he invited men and women of good social position, and just as his drawing-room resembled all other drawing-rooms so did his enjoyable little parties resemble all other such parties.

Once they even gave a dance. Iván Ilých enjoyed it and everything went off well, except that it led to a violent quarrel with his wife about the cakes and sweets. Praskóvya Fëdorovna had made her own plans, but Iván Ilých insisted on getting everything from an expensive confectioner and ordered too many cakes, and the quarrel occurred because some of those cakes were left over and the confectioner's bill came to forty-five rubles. It was a great and disagreeable quarrel. Praskóvya Fëdorovna called him "a fool and an imbecile," and he clutched at his head and made angry allusions to divorce.

But the dance itself had been enjoyable. The best people were there, and Iván Ilých had danced with Princess Trúfonova, a sister of the distinguished founder of the Society "Bear my Burden."

The pleasures connected with his work were pleasures of ambition; his social pleasures were those of vanity; but Iván Ilých's greatest pleasure was playing bridge. He acknowledged that whatever disagreeable incident happened in his life, the pleasure that beamed like a ray of light above everything else was to sit down to bridge with good players, not noisy partners, and of course to four-handed bridge (with five players it was annoying to have to stand out, though one pretended not to mind), to play a clever and serious game (when the cards allowed it) and then to have supper and drink a glass of wine. After a game of bridge, especially if he had won a little (to win a large sum was unpleasant), Iván Ilých went to bed in specially good humour.

So they lived. They formed a circle of acquaintances among the best people and were visited by people of importance and by young folk. In their views as to their acquaintances, husband, wife and daughter were entirely agreed, and tacitly and unanimously kept at arm's length and shook off the various shabby friends and relations who, with much show of affection, gushed into the drawing-room with its Japanese plates on the walls. Soon these shabby friends ceased to obtrude themselves and only the best people remained in the Golovíns' set.

Young men made up to Lisa, and Petríshchev, an examining magistrate and Dmítri Ivanovich Petríshchev's son and sole heir, began to be so attentive to her that Iván Ilých had already spoken to Praskóvya Fëdorovna about it, and considered whether they should not arrange a party for them or get up some private theatricals.

So they lived, and all went well, without change, and life flowed pleasantly.

CHAPTER IV

They were all in good health. It could not be called ill health if Iván Ilých sometimes said that he had a queer taste in his mouth and felt some discomfort in his left side.

But this discomfort increased and, though not exactly painful, grew into a sense of pressure in his side accompanied by ill humour. And his irritability became worse and worse and began to mar the agreeable, easy, and correct life that had established itself in the Golovín family. Quarrels between husband and wife became more and more frequent, and soon the ease and amenity disappeared and even the decorum was barely maintained. Scenes again became frequent, and very few of those islets remained on which husband and wife could meet without an explosion. Praskóvya Fëdorovna now had good reason to say that her husband's temper was trying. With characteristic exaggeration she said he had always had a dreadful temper, and that it had needed all her good nature to put up with it for twenty years. It was true that now the quarrels were started by him. His bursts of temper always came just before dinner, often just as he began to eat his soup. Sometimes he noticed that a plate or dish was chipped, or the food was not right, or his son put his elbow on the table, or his daughter's hair was not done as he liked it, and for all this he blamed Praskóvya Fëdorovna. At first she retorted and said disagreeable things to him, but once or twice he fell into such a rage at the beginning of dinner that she realized it was due to some physical derangement brought on by taking food, and so she restrained herself and did not answer, but only hurried to get the dinner over. She regarded this self-restraint as highly praiseworthy. Having come to the conclusion that her husband had a dreadful temper and made her life miserable, she began to feel sorry for herself, and the more she pitied herself the more she hated her husband. She began to wish he would die; yet she did not want him to die because then his salary would cease. And this irritated her against him still more. She considered herself dreadfully unhappy just because not even his death could save her, and though she concealed her exasperation, that hidden exasperation of hers increased his irritation also.

After one scene in which Iván Ilých had been particularly unfair and after which he had said in explanation that he certainly was irritable but that it was due to his not being well, she said that if he was ill it should be attended to, and insisted on his going to see a celebrated doctor.

He went. Everything took place as he had expected and as it always does. There was the usual waiting and the important air assumed by the doctor, with which he was so familiar (resembling that which he himself assumed in court), and the sounding and listening, and the questions which called for answers that were forgone conclusions and were evidently unnecessary, and the look of importance which implied that "if only you put yourself in our hands we will arrange everything—we know indubitably how it has to be done, always in the same way for everybody alike." It was all just as it was in the law courts. The doctor put on just the same air towards him as he himself put on towards an accused person.

The doctor said that so-and-so indicated that there was so-and-so inside the patient, but if the investigation of so-and-so did not confirm this, then he must assume that and that. If he assumed that and that, then . . . and so on. To Iván Ilých only one question was important: was his case serious or not? But the doctor ignored that inappropriate question. From his point of view it was not the one under consideration, the real question was to decide between a floating kidney, chronic catarrh, or appendicitis. It was not a question of Iván Ilých's life or death, but one between a floating kidney and appendicitis. And that question the doctor solved brilliantly, as it seemed to Iván Ilých, in favour of the appendix, with the reservation that should an examination of the urine give fresh indications the matter would be reconsidered. All this was just what Iván Ilých had himself brilliantly accomplished a thousand times in dealing with men on trial. The doctor summed up just as brilliantly, looking over his spectacles triumphantly and even gaily at the accused. From the doctor's summing up Iván Ilých concluded that things were bad, but that for the doctor, and perhaps for everybody else, it was a matter of indifference, though for him it was bad. And this conclusion struck him painfully, arousing in him a great feeling of pity for himself and of bitterness towards the doctor's indifference to a matter of such importance.

He said nothing of this, but rose, placed the doctor's fee on the table, and remarked with a sigh: "We sick people probably often put inappropriate questions. But tell me, in general, is this complaint dangerous, or not? . . ."

The doctor looked at him sternly over his spectacles with one eye, as if to say: "Prisoner, if you will not keep to the questions put to you, I shall be obliged to have you removed from the court."

"I have already told you what I consider necessary and proper. The analysis may show something more." And the doctor bowed.

Iván Ilých went out slowly, seated himself disconsolately in his sledge, and drove home. All the way home he was going over what the doctor had said, trying to translate those complicated, obscure, scientific phrases into plain language and find in them an answer to the question: "Is my condition bad? Is it very bad? Or is there as yet nothing much wrong?" And it seemed to him that the meaning of what the doctor had said was that it was very bad. Everything in the streets seemed depressing. The cabmen, the houses, the passers-by, and the shops, were dismal. His ache, this dull gnawing ache that never ceased for a moment, seemed to have acquired a new and more serious significance from the doctor's dubious remarks. Iván Ilých now watched it with a new and oppressive feeling.

He reached home and began to tell his wife about it. She listened, but in the middle of his account his daughter came in with her hat on, ready to go out with her mother. She sat down reluctantly to listen to this tedious story, but could not stand it long, and her mother too did not hear him to the end.

"Well, I am very glad," she said. "Mind now to take your medicine regularly. Give me the prescription and I'll send Gerásim to the chemist's." And she went to get ready to go out.

While she was in the room Iván Ilých had hardly taken time to breathe, but he sighed deeply when she left it.

"Well," he thought, "perhaps it isn't so bad after all."

He began taking his medicine and following the doctor's directions, which had been altered after the examination of the urine. But then it happened that there was a contradiction between the indications drawn from the examination of the urine and the symptoms that showed themselves. It turned out that what was happening differed from what the doctor had told him, and that he had either forgotten, or blundered, or hidden something from him. He could not, however, be blamed for that, and Iván Ilých still obeyed his orders implicitly and at first derived some comfort from doing so.

From the time of his visit to the doctor, Iván Ilých's chief occupation was the exact fulfilment of the doctor's instructions regarding hygiene and the taking of medicine, and the observation of his pain and his excretions. His chief interests came to be people's ailments and people's health. When sickness, deaths, or recoveries, were mentioned in his presence, especially when the illness resembled his own, he listened with agitation which he tried to hide, asked questions, and applied what he heard to his own case.

The pain did not grow less, but Iván Ilých made efforts to force himself to think that he was better. And he could do this so long as nothing agitated him. But as soon as he had any unpleasantness with his wife, any lack of success in his official work, or held bad cards at bridge, he was at once acutely sensible of his disease. He had formerly borne such mischances, hoping soon to adjust what was wrong, to master it and attain success, or make a grand slam. But now every mischance upset him and plunged him into despair. He would say to himself: "There now, just as I was beginning to get better and the medicine had begun to take effect, comes this accursed misfortune, or unpleasantness . . . " And he was furious with the mishap, or with the people who were causing the unpleasantness and killing him, for he felt that this fury was killing him but could not restrain it. One would have thought that it should have been clear to him that this exasperation with circumstances and people aggravated his illness, and that he ought therefore to ignore unpleasant occurrences. But he drew the very opposite conclusion: he said that he needed peace, and he watched for everything that might disturb it and became irritable at the slightest infringement of it. His condition was rendered worse by the fact that he read medical books and consulted doctors. The progress of his disease was so gradual that he could deceive himself when comparing one day with another—the difference was so slight. But when he consulted the doctors it seemed to him that he was getting worse, and even very rapidly. Yet despite this he was continually consulting them.

That month he went to see another celebrity, who told him almost the same as the first had done but put his questions rather differently, and the interview with this celebrity only increased Iván Ilých's doubts and fears. A friend of a friend of his, a very good doctor, diagnosed his illness again quite differently from the others, and though he predicted recovery, his questions and suppositions bewildered Iván Ilých still more and increased his doubts. A homoeopathist diagnosed the disease in yet another way, and prescribed medicine which Iván Ilých took secretly for a week. But after a week, not feeling any improvement and having lost confidence both in the former doctor's treatment and in this one's, he became still more despondent. One day a lady acquaintance mentioned a cure effected by a wonder-working icon. Iván Ilých caught himself listening attentively and beginning to believe that it had occurred. This incident alarmed him. "Has my mind really weakened to such an extent?" he asked himself. "Nonsense! It's all rubbish. I mustn't give way to nervous fears but having chosen a doctor must keep strictly to his treatment. That is what I will do. Now it's all settled. I won't think about it, but will follow the treatment seriously till summer, and then we shall see. From now there must be no more of this wavering!" This was easy to say but impossible to carry out. The pain in his side oppressed him and seemed to grow worse and more incessant, while the taste in his mouth grew stranger and stranger. It seemed to him that his breath had a disgusting smell, and he was conscious of a loss of appetite and strength. There was no deceiving himself: something terrible, new, and more important than anything before in his life, was taking place within him of which he alone was aware. Those about him did not understand or would not understand it, but thought everything in the world was going on as usual. That tormented Iván Ilých more than anything. He saw that his household, especially his wife and daughter who were in a perfect whirl of visiting, did not understand anything of it and were annoyed that he was so depressed and so exacting, as if he were to blame for it. Though they tried to disguise it he saw that he was an obstacle in their path, and that his wife had adopted a definite line in regard to his illness and kept to it regardless of anything he said or did. Her attitude was this: "You know," she would say to her friends, "Iván Ilých can't do as other people do, and keep to the treatment prescribed for him. One day he'll take his drops and keep strictly to his diet and go to bed in good time, but the next day unless I watch him he'll suddenly forget his medicine, eat sturgeon—which is forbidden—and sit up playing cards till one o'clock in the morning."

"Oh, come, when was that?" Iván Ilých would ask in vexation. "Only once at Peter Ivánovich's."

"And yesterday with Shébek."

"Well, even if I hadn't stayed up, this pain would have kept me awake."

"Be that as it may you'll never get well like that, but will always make us wretched."

Praskóvya Fëdorovna's attitude to Iván Ilých's illness, as she expressed it both to others and to him, was that it was his own fault and was another of the annoyances he caused her. Iván Ilých felt that this opinion escaped her involuntarily—but that did not make it easier for him.

At the law courts too, Iván Ilých noticed, or thought he noticed, a strange attitude towards himself. It sometimes seemed to him that people were watching him inquisitively as a man whose place might soon be vacant. Then again, his friends would suddenly begin to chaff him in a friendly way about his low spirits, as if the awful, horrible, and unheard-of thing that was going on within him, incessantly gnawing at him and irresistibly drawing him away, was a very agreeable subject for jests. Schwartz in particular irritated him by his jocularity, vivacity, and *savoir-faire*, which reminded him of what he himself had been ten years ago.

Friends came to make up a set and they sat down to cards. They dealt, bending the new cards to soften them, and he sorted the diamonds in his hand and found he had seven. His partner said "No trumps" and supported him with two diamonds. What more could be wished for? It ought to be jolly and lively. They would make a grand slam. But suddenly Iván Ilých was conscious of that gnawing pain, that taste in his mouth, and it seemed ridiculous that in such circumstances he should be pleased to make a grand slam.

He looked at his partner Mikháil Mikháylovich, who rapped the table with his strong hand and instead of snatching up the tricks pushed the cards courteously and indulgently towards Iván Ilých that he might have the pleasure of gathering them up without the trouble of stretching out his hand for them. "Does he think I am too weak to stretch out my arm?" thought Iván Ilých, and forgetting what he was doing he over-trumped his partner, missing the grand slam by three tricks. And what was most awful of all was that he saw how upset Mikháil Mikháylovich was about it but did not himself care. And it was dreadful to realize why he did not care.

They all saw that he was suffering, and said: "We can stop if you are tired. Take a rest." Lie down? No, he was not at all tired, and he finished the rubber. All were gloomy and silent. Iván Ilých felt that he diffused this gloom over them and could not dispel it. They had supper and went away, and Iván Ilých was left alone with the consciousness that his life was poisoned and was poisoning the lives of others, and that this poison did not weaken but penetrated more and more deeply into his whole being.

With this consciousness, and with physical pain besides the terror, he must go to bed, often to lie awake the greater part of the night. Next morning he had to get up again, dress, go to the law courts, speak, and write; or if he did not go out, spend at home those twenty-four hours a day each of which was a torture. And he had to live thus all alone on the brink of an abyss, with no one who understood or pitied him.

CHAPTER V

So one month passed and then another. Just before the New Year his brother-in-law came to town and stayed at their house. Iván Ilých was at the law courts and Praskóvya Fëdorovna had gone shopping. When Iván Ilých came home and entered his study he found his brother-in-law there—a healthy, florid man—unpacking his portmanteau himself. He raised his head on hearing Iván Ilých's footsteps and looked up at him for a moment without a word. That stare told Iván Ilých everything. His brother-in-law opened his mouth to utter an exclamation of surprise but checked himself, and that action confirmed it all.

"I have changed, eh?"

"Yes, there is a change."

And after that, try as he would to get his brother-in-law to return to the subject of his looks, the latter would say nothing about it. Praskóvya Fëdorovna came home and her brother went out to her. Iván Ilých locked the door and began to examine himself in the glass, first full face, then in profile. He took up a portrait of himself taken with his wife, and compared it with what he saw in the glass. The change in him was immense. Then he bared his arms to the elbow, looked at them, drew the sleeves down again, sat down on an ottoman, and grew blacker than night.

"No, no, this won't do!" he said to himself, and jumped up, went to the table, took up some law papers and began to read them, but could not continue. He unlocked the door and went into the reception-room. The door leading to the drawing-room was shut. He approached it on tiptoe and listened.

"No, you are exaggerating!" Praskóvya Fëdorovna was saying.

"Exaggerating! Don't you see it? Why, he's a dead man! Look at his eyes—there's no light in them. But what is it that is wrong with him?"

"No one knows. Nikoláevich (that was another doctor) said something, but I don't know what. And Leshchetítsky (this was the celebrated specialist) said quite the contrary . . . "

Iván Ilých walked away, went to his own room, lay down, and began musing: "The kidney, a floating kidney." He recalled all the doctors had told him of how it detached itself and swayed about. And by an effort of imagination he tried to catch that kidney and arrest it and support it. So little was needed for this, it seemed to him. "No, I'll go to see Peter Ivánovich again." (That was the friend whose friend was a doctor.) He rang, ordered the carriage, and got ready to go.

"Where are you going, Jean?" asked his wife, with a specially sad and exceptionally kind look.

This exceptionally kind look irritated him. He looked morosely at her.

"I must go to see Peter Ivánovich."

He went to see Peter Ivánovich, and together they went to see his friend, the doctor. He was in, and Iván Ilých had a long talk with him.

Reviewing the anatomical and physiological details of what in the doctor's opinion was going on inside him, he understood it all.

There was something, a small thing, in the vermiform appendix. It might all come right. Only stimulate the energy of one organ and check the activity of another, then absorption would take place and everything would come right. He got home rather late for dinner, ate his dinner, and conversed cheerfully, but could not for a long time bring himself to go back to work in his room. At last, however, he went to his study and did what was necessary, but the consciousness that he had put something aside—an important, intimate matter which he would revert to when his work was done—never left him. When he had finished his work he remembered that this intimate matter was the thought of his vermiform appendix. But he did not give himself up to it, and went to the drawing-room for tea. There were callers there, including the examining magistrate who was a desirable match for his daughter, and they were conversing, playing the piano and singing. Iván Ilých, as Praskóvya Fëdorovna remarked, spent that evening more cheerfully than usual, but he never for a moment forgot that he had postponed the important matter of the appendix. At eleven o'clock he said good-night and went to his bedroom. Since his illness he had slept alone in a small room next to his study. He undressed and took up a novel by Zola, but instead of reading it he fell into thought, and in his imagination that desired improvement in the vermiform appendix occurred. There was the absorption and evacuation and the reestablishment of normal activity. "Yes, that's it!" he said to himself. "One need only assist nature, that's all." He remembered his medicine, rose, took it, and lay down on his back watching for the beneficent action of the medicine and for it to lessen the pain. "I need only take it regularly and avoid all injurious influences. I am already feeling better, much better." He began touching his side: it was not painful to the touch. "There, I really don't feel it. It's much better already." He put out the light and turned on his side . . . "The appendix is getting better, absorption is occurring." Suddenly he felt the old, familiar, dull, gnawing pain, stubborn and serious. There was the same familiar loathsome taste in his mouth. His heart sank and he felt dazed. "My God! My God!" he muttered. "Again, again! And it will never cease." And suddenly the matter presented itself in a quite different aspect. "Vermiform appendix! Kidney!" he said to himself. "It's not a question of appendix or kidney, but of life and . . . death. Yes, life was there and now it is going, going and I cannot stop it. Yes. Why deceive myself? Isn't it obvious to everyone but me that I'm dying, and that it's only a question of weeks, days . . . it may happen this moment. There was light and now there is darkness. I was here and now I'm going there! Where?" A chill came over him, his breathing ceased, and he felt only the throbbing of his heart.

"When I am not, what will there be? There will be nothing. Then where shall I be when I am no more? Can this be dying? No, I don't want to!" He jumped up and tried to light the candle, felt for it with trembling hands, dropped candle and candlestick on the floor, and fell back on his pillow.

"What's the use? It makes no difference," he said to himself, staring with wide-open eyes into the darkness. "Death. Yes, death. And none of them know or wish to know it, and they have no pity for me. Now they are playing." (He heard through the door the distant sound of a song and its accompaniment.) "It's all the same to them, but they will die too! Fools! I first, and they later, but it will be the same for them. And now they are merry . . . the beasts!"

Anger choked him and he was agonizingly, unbearably miserable. "It is impossible that all men have been doomed to suffer this awful horror!" He raised himself.

"Something must be wrong. I must calm myself—must think it all over from the beginning." And he again began thinking. "Yes, the beginning of my illness: I knocked my side, but I was still quite well that day and the next. It hurt a little, then rather more. I saw the doctors, then followed despondency and anguish, more doctors, and I drew nearer to the abyss. My strength grew less and I kept coming nearer and nearer, and now I have wasted away and there is no light in my eyes. I think of the appendix—but this is death! I think of mending the appendix, and all the while here is death! Can it really be death?" Again terror seized him and he gasped for breath. He leant down and began feeling for the matches, pressing with his elbow on the stand beside the bed. It was in his way and hurt him, he grew furious with it, pressed on it still harder, and upset it. Breathless and in despair he fell on his back, expecting death to come immediately.

Meanwhile the visitors were leaving. Praskóvya Fëdorovna was seeing them off. She heard something fall and came in.

"What has happened?"

"Nothing. I knocked it over accidentally."

She went out and returned with a candle. He lay there panting heavily, like a man who has run a thousand yards, and stared upwards at her with a fixed look.

"What is it, Jean?"

"No . . . o . . . thing. I upset it." ("Why speak of it? She won't understand," he thought.)

And in truth she did not understand. She picked up the stand, lit his candle, and hurried away to see another visitor off. When she came back he still lay on his back, looking upwards.

"What is it? Do you feel worse?"

"Yes."

She shook her head and sat down.

"Do you know, Jean, I think we must ask Leshchetítsky to come and see you here."

This meant calling in the famous specialist, regardless of expense. He smiled malignantly and said "No." She remained a little longer and then went up to him and kissed his forehead.

While she was kissing him he hated her from the bottom of his soul and with difficulty refrained from pushing her away.

"Good-night. Please God you'll sleep."

"Yes."

CHAPTER VI

Iván Ilých saw that he was dying, and he was in continual despair.

In the depth of his heart he knew he was dying, but not only was he not accustomed to the thought, he simply did not and could not grasp it.

The syllogism he had learnt from Kiezewetter's Logic:[9] "Caius is a man, men are mortal, therefore Caius is mortal," had always seemed to him correct as applied to Caius, but certainly not as applied to himself. That Caius—man in the abstract—was mortal, was perfectly correct, but he was not Caius, not an abstract man, but a creature quite, quite separate from all others. He had been little Ványa, with a mamma and a papa; with Mítya and Volódya, and the toys, a coachman and a nurse, afterwards with Kátenka and with all the joys, griefs, and delights of childhood, boyhood, and youth. What did Caius know of the

---

[9] Karl Kiezewetter (1766–1819), author of an outline of logic widely used in Russian schools at the time.

smell of that striped leather ball Ványa had been so fond of? Had Caius kissed his mother's hand like that, and did the silk of her dress rustle so for Caius? Had he rioted like that at school when the pastry was bad? Had Caius been in love like that? Could Caius preside at a session as he did? "Caius really was mortal, and it was right for him to die; but for me, little Ványa, Iván Ilých, with all my thoughts and emotions, it's altogether a different matter. It cannot be that I ought to die. That would be too terrible."

Such was his feeling.

"If I had to die like Caius I should have known it was so. An inner voice would have told me so, but there was nothing of the sort in me and I and all my friends felt that our case was quite different from that of Caius. And now here it is!" he said to himself. "It can't be. It's impossible! But here it is. How is this? How is one to understand it?"

He could not understand it, and tried to drive this false, incorrect, morbid thought away and to replace it by other proper and healthy thoughts. But that thought and not the thought only but the reality itself, seemed to come and confront him.

And to replace that thought he called up a succession of others, hoping to find in them some support. He tried to get back into the former current of thoughts that had once screened the thought of death from him. But strange to say, all that had formerly shut off, hidden, and destroyed, his consciousness of death, no longer had that effect. Iván Ilých now spent most of his time in attempting to re-establish that old current. He would say to himself: "I will take up my duties again—after all I used to live by them." And banishing all doubts he would go to the law courts, enter into conversation with his colleagues, and sit carelessly as was his wont, scanning the crowd with a thoughtful look and leaning both his emaciated arms on the arms of his oak chair; bending over as usual to a colleague and drawing his papers nearer he would interchange whispers with him, and then suddenly raising his eyes and sitting erect would pronounce certain words and open the proceedings. But suddenly in the midst of those proceedings the pain in his side, regardless of the stage the proceedings had reached, would begin its own gnawing work. Iván Ilých would turn his attention to it and try to drive the thought of it away, but without success. *It* would come and stand before him and look at him, and he would be petrified and the light would die out of his eyes, and he would again begin asking himself whether *It* alone was true. And his colleagues and subordinates would see with surprise and distress that he, the brilliant and subtle judge, was becoming confused and making mistakes. He would shake himself, try to pull himself together, manage somehow to bring the sitting to a close, and return home with the sorrowful consciousness that his judicial labours could not as formerly hide from him what he wanted them to hide, and could not deliver him from *It*. And what was worst of all was that *It* drew his attention to itself not in order to make him take some action but only that he should look at *It*, look it straight in the face: look at it and without doing anything, suffer inexpressibly.

And to save himself from this condition Iván Ilých looked for consolations—new screens—and new screens were found and for a while seemed to save him, but then they immediately fell to pieces or rather became transparent, as if *It* penetrated them and nothing could veil *It*.

In these latter days he would go into the drawing-room he had arranged—that drawing-room where he had fallen and for the sake of which (how bitterly ridiculous it seemed) he had sacrificed his life—for he knew that his illness originated with that knock. He would enter and see that something had scratched the polished table. He would look for the cause of this and find that it was the bronze ornamentation of an album, that had got bent. He would take up the expensive album which he had lovingly arranged, and feel vexed with his daughter and her friends for their untidiness—for the album was torn here and there and some of the photographs turned upside down. He would put it carefully in order and bend the ornamentation back into position. Then it would occur to him to place all those things in another corner of the room, near the plants. He could call the footman, but his daughter or wife would come to help him. They would not agree, and his wife would contradict him, and he would dispute and grow angry. But that was all right, for then he did not think about *It*. *It* was invisible.

But then, when he was moving something himself, his wife would say: "Let the servants do it. You will hurt yourself again." And suddenly *It* would flash through the screen and he would see it. It was just a flash, and he hoped it would disappear, but he would involuntarily pay attention to his side. "It sits there as before, gnawing just the same!" And he could no longer forget *It*, but could distinctly see it looking at him from behind the flowers. "What is it all for?"

"It really is so! I lost my life over that curtain as I might have done when storming a fort. Is that possible? How terrible and how stupid. It can't be true! It can't, but it is!"

He would go to his study, lie down, and again be alone with *It*: face to face with *It*. And nothing could be done with *It* except to look at it and shudder.

CHAPTER VII

How it happened it is impossible to say because it came about step by step, unnoticed, but in the third month of Iván Ilých's illness, his wife, his daughter, his son, his acquaintances, the doctors, the servants, and above all he himself, were aware that the whole interest he had for other people was whether he would soon vacate his place, and at last release the living from the discomfort caused by his presence and be himself released from his sufferings.

He slept less and less. He was given opium and hypodermic injections of morphine, but this did not relieve him. The dull depression he experienced in a somnolent condition at first gave him a little relief, but only as something new, afterwards it became as distressing as the pain itself or even more so.

Special foods were prepared for him by the doctors' orders, but all those foods became increasingly distasteful and disgusting to him.

For his excretions also special arrangements had to be made, and this was a torment to him every time—a torment from the uncleanliness, the unseemliness, and the smell, and from knowing that another person had to take part in it.

But just through this most unpleasant matter Iván Ilých obtained comfort. Gerásim, the butler's young assistant, always came in to carry the things out. Gerásim was a clean, fresh peasant lad, grown stout on town food and always cheerful and bright. At first the sight of him, in his clean Russian peasant costume, engaged on that disgusting task embarrassed Iván Ilých.

Once when he got up from the commode too weak to draw up his trousers, he dropped into a soft armchair and looked with horror at his bare, enfeebled thighs with the muscles so sharply marked on them.

Gerásim with a firm light tread, his heavy boots emitting a pleasant smell of tar and fresh winter air, came in wearing a clean Hessian apron, the sleeves of his print shirt tucked up over his strong bare young arms; and refraining from looking at his sick master out of consideration for his feelings, and restraining the joy of life that beamed from his face, went up to the commode.

"Gerásim!" said Iván Ilých in a weak voice.

Gerásim started, evidently afraid he might have committed some blunder, and with a rapid movement turned his fresh, kind, simple young face which just showed the first downy signs of a beard.

"Yes, sir?"

"That must be very unpleasant for you. You must forgive me. I am helpless."

"Oh, why, sir," and Gerásim's eyes beamed and he showed his glistening white teeth, "what's a little trouble? It's a case of illness with you, sir."

And his deft strong hands did their accustomed task, and he went out of the room stepping lightly. Five minutes later he as lightly returned.

Iván Ilých was still sitting in the same position in the armchair.

"Gerásim," he said when the latter had replaced the freshly-washed utensil. "Please come here and help me." Gerásim went up to him. "Lift me up. It is hard for me to get up, and I have sent Dmítri away."

Gerásim went up to him, grasped his master with his strong arms deftly but gently, in the same way that he stepped—lifted him, supported him with one hand, and with the other drew up his trousers and would have set him down again, but Iván Ilých asked to be led to the sofa. Gerásim, without an effort and without apparent pressure, led him, almost lifting him, to the sofa and placed him on it.

"Thank you. How easily and well you do it all!"

Gerásim smiled again and turned to leave the room. But Iván Ilých felt his presence such a comfort that he did not want to let him go.

"One thing more, please move up that chair. No, the other one—under my feet. It is easier for me when my feet are raised."

Gerásim brought the chair, set it down gently in place, and raised Iván Ilých's legs on to it. It seemed to Iván Ilých that he felt better while Gerásim was holding up his legs.

"It's better when my legs are higher," he said. "Place that cushion under them."

Gerásim did so. He again lifted the legs and placed them, and again Iván Ilých felt better while Gerásim held his legs. When he set them down Iván Ilých fancied he felt worse.

"Gerásim," he said. "Are you busy now?"

"Not at all, sir," said Gerásim, who had learnt from the townsfolk how to speak to gentlefolk.

"What have you still to do?"

"What have I to do? I've done everything except chopping the logs for to-morrow."

"Then hold my legs up a bit higher, can you?"

"Of course I can. Why not?" And Gerásim raised his master's legs higher and Iván Ilých thought that in that position he did not feel any pain at all.

"And how about the logs?"

"Don't trouble about that, sir. There's plenty of time."

Iván Ilých told Gerásim to sit down and hold his legs, and began to talk to him. And strange to say it seemed to him that he felt better while Gerásim held his legs up.

After that Iván Ilých would sometimes call Gerásim and get him to hold his legs on his shoulders, and he liked talking to him. Gerásim did it all easily, willingly, simply, and with a good nature that touched Iván Ilých. Health, strength, and vitality in other people were offensive to him, but Gerásim's strength and vitality did not mortify but soothed him.

What tormented Iván Ilých most was the deception, the lie, which for some reason they all accepted, that he was not dying but was simply ill, and that he only need keep quiet and undergo a treatment and then something very good would result. He however knew that do what they would nothing would come of it, only still more agonizing suffering and death. This deception tortured him—their not wishing to admit what they all knew and what he knew, but wanting to lie to him concerning his terrible condition, and wishing and forcing him to participate in that lie. Those lies—lies enacted over him on the eve of his death and destined to degrade this awful, solemn act to the level of their visitings, their curtains, their sturgeon for dinner—were a terrible agony for Iván Ilých. And strangely enough, many times when they were going through their antics over him he had been within a hairbreadth of calling out to them: "Stop lying! You know and I know that I am dying. Then at least stop lying about it!" But he had never had the spirit to do it. The awful, terrible act of his dying was, he could see, reduced by those about him to the level of a casual, un-pleasant, and almost indecorous incident (as if someone entered a drawing-room diffusing an unpleasant odour) and this was done by that very decorum which he had served all his life long. He saw that no one felt for him, because no one even wished to grasp his position. Only Gerásim recognized it and pitied him.

And so Iván Ilých felt at ease only with him. He felt comforted when Gerásim supported his legs (sometimes all night long) and refused to go to bed, saying: "Don't you worry, Iván Ilých. I'll get sleep enough later on," or when he suddenly became familiar and exclaimed: "If you weren't sick it would be another matter, but as it is, why should I grudge a little trouble?" Gerásim alone did not lie; everything showed that he alone understood the facts of the case and did not consider it necessary to disguise them, but simply felt sorry for his emaciated and enfeebled master. Once when Iván Ilých was sending him away he even said straight out: "We shall all of us die, so why should I grudge a little trouble?"—expressing the fact that he did not think his work burdensome, because he was doing it for a dying man and hoped someone would do the same for him when his time came.

Apart from this lying, or because of it, what most tormented Iván Ilých was that no one pitied him as he wished to be pitied. At certain moments after prolonged suffering he wished most of all (though he would have been ashamed to confess it) for someone to pity him as a sick child is pitied. He longed to be petted and comforted. He knew he was an important functionary, that he had a beard turning grey, and that therefore what he longed for was impossible, but still he longed for it. And in Gerásim's attitude towards him there was something akin to what he wished for, and so that attitude comforted him. Iván Ilých wanted to weep, wanted to be petted and cried over, and then his colleague Shébek would come, and instead of weeping and being petted, Iván Ilých would assume a serious, severe, and profound air, and by force of habit would express his opinion on a decision of the Court of Cassation and would stubbornly insist on that view. This falsity around him and within him did more than anything else to poison his last days.

CHAPTER VIII

It was morning. He knew it was morning because Gerásim had gone, and Peter the footman had come and put out the candles, drawn back one of the curtains, and begun quietly to tidy up. Whether it was morning or evening, Friday or Sunday, made no difference, it was all just the same: the gnawing, unmitigated, agonizing pain, never ceasing for an instant, the consciousness of life inexorably waning but not yet extinguished, that approach of that ever dreaded and hateful Death which was the only reality, and always the same falsity. What were days, weeks, hours, in such a case?

"Will you have some tea, sir?"

"He wants things to be regular, and wishes the gentlefolk to drink tea in the morning," thought Iván Ilých, and only said "No."

"Wouldn't you like to move onto the sofa, sir?"

"He wants to tidy up the room, and I'm in the way. I am uncleanliness and disorder," he thought, and said only:

"No, leave me alone."

The man went on bustling about. Iván Ilých stretched out his hand. Peter came up, ready to help.

"What is it, sir?"

"My watch."

Peter took the watch which was close at hand and gave it to his master.

"Half-past eight. Are they up?"

"No sir, except Vladímir Ivánich" (the son) "who has gone to school. Praskóvya Fëdorovna ordered me to wake her if you asked for her. Shall I do so?"

"No, there's no need to." "Perhaps I'd better have some tea," he thought, and added aloud: "Yes, bring me some tea."

Peter went to the door but Iván Ilých dreaded being left alone. "How can I keep him here? Oh yes, my medicine." "Peter, give me my medicine." "Why not? Perhaps it may still do me some good." He took a spoonful and swallowed it. "No, it won't help. It's all tomfoolery, all deception," he decided as soon as he became aware of the familiar, sickly, hopeless taste. "No, I can't believe in it any longer. But the pain, why this pain? If it would only cease just for a moment!" And he moaned. Peter turned towards him. "It's all right. Go and fetch me some tea."

Peter went out. Left alone Iván Ilých groaned not so much with pain, terrible though that was, as from mental anguish. Always and for ever the same, always these endless days and nights. If only it would come quicker! If only *what* would come quicker? Death, darkness? . . . No, no! Anything rather than death!

When Peter returned with the tea on a tray, Iván Ilých stared at him for a time in perplexity, not realizing who and what he was. Peter was disconcerted by that look and his embarrassment brought Iván Ilých to himself.

"Oh, tea! All right, put it down. Only help me to wash and put on a clean shirt."

And Iván Ilých began to wash. With pauses for rest, he washed his hands and then his face, cleaned his teeth, brushed his hair, and looked in the glass. He was terrified by what he saw, especially by the limp way in which his hair clung to his pallid forehead.

While his shirt was being changed he knew that he would be still more frightened at the sight of his body, so he avoided looking at it. Finally he was ready. He drew on a dressing-gown, wrapped himself in a plaid, and sat down in the armchair to take his tea. For a moment he felt refreshed, but as soon as he began to drink the tea he was again aware of the same taste, and the pain also returned. He finished it with an effort, and then lay down stretching out his legs, and dismissed Peter.

Always the same. Now a spark of hope flashes up, then a sea of despair rages, and always pain; always pain, always despair, and always the same. When alone he had a dreadful and distressing desire to call someone, but he knew beforehand that with others present it would be still worse. "Another dose of morphine—to lose consciousness. I will tell him, the doctor, that he must think of something else. It's impossible, impossible, to go on like this."

An hour and another pass like that. But now there is a ring at the door bell. Perhaps it's the doctor? It is. He comes in fresh, hearty, plump, and cheerful, with that look on his face that seems to say: "There now, you're in a panic about something, but we'll arrange it all for you directly!" The doctor knows this expression is out of place here, but he has put it on once for all and can't take it off—like a man who has put on a frock-coat in the morning to pay a round of calls.

The doctor rubs his hands vigorously and reassuringly.

"Brr! How cold it is! There's such a sharp frost; just let me warm myself!" he says, as if it were only a matter of waiting till he was warm, and then he would put everything right.

"Well now, how are you?"

Iván Ilých feels that the doctor would like to say: "Well, how are our affairs?" but that even he feels that this would not do, and says instead: "What sort of a night have you had?"

Iván Ilých looks at him as much as to say: "Are you really never ashamed of lying?" But the doctor does not wish to understand this question, and Iván Ilých says: "Just as terrible as ever. The pain never leaves me and never subsides. If only something . . . "

"Yes, you sick people are always like that. . . . There, now I think I am warm enough. Even Praskóvya Fëdorovna, who is so particular, could find no fault with my temperature. Well, now I can say good-morning," and the doctor presses his patient's hand.

Then, dropping his former playfulness, he begins with a most serious face to examine the patient, feeling his pulse and taking his temperature, and then begins the sounding and auscultation.

Iván Ilých knows quite well and definitely that all this is nonsense and pure deception, but when the doctor, getting down on his knee, leans over him, putting his ear first higher then lower, and performs various gymnastic movements over him with a significant expression on his face, Iván Ilých submits to it all as he used to submit to the speeches of the lawyers, though he knew very well that they were all lying and why they were lying.

The doctor, kneeling on the sofa, is still sounding him when Praskóvya Fëdorovna's silk dress rustles at the door and she is heard scolding Peter for not having let her know of the doctor's arrival.

She comes in, kisses her husband, and at once proceeds to prove that she has been up a long time already, and only owing to a misunderstanding failed to be there when the doctor arrived.

Iván Ilých looks at her, scans her all over, sets against her the whiteness and plumpness and cleanness of her hands and neck, the gloss of her hair, and the sparkle of her vivacious eyes. He hates her with his whole soul. And the thrill of hatred he feels for her makes him suffer from her touch.

Her attitude towards him and his disease is still the same. Just as the doctor had adopted a certain relation to his patient which he could not abandon, so had she formed one towards him—that he was not doing something he ought to do and was himself to blame, and that she reproached him lovingly for this—and she could not now change that attitude.

"You see he doesn't listen to me and doesn't take his medicine at the proper time. And above all he lies in a position that is no doubt bad for him—with his legs up."

She described how he made Gerásim hold his legs up.

The doctor smiled with a contemptuous affability that said: "What's to be done? These sick people do have foolish fancies of that kind, but we must forgive them."

When the examination was over the doctor looked at his watch, and then Praskóvya Fëdorovna announced to Iván Ilých that it was of course as he pleased, but she had sent to-day for a celebrated specialist who would examine him and have a consultation with Michael Danílovich (their regular doctor).

"Please don't raise any objections. I am doing this for my own sake," she said ironically, letting it be felt that she was doing it all for his sake and only said that to leave him no right to refuse. He remained silent, knitting his brows. He felt that he was so surrounded and involved in a mesh of falsity that it was hard to unravel anything.

Everything she did for him was entirely for her own sake, and she told him she was doing for herself what she actually was doing for herself, as if that was so incredible that he must understand the opposite.

At half-past eleven the celebrated specialist arrived. Again the sounding began and the significant conversations in his presence and in another room, about the kidneys and the appendix, and the questions and answers, with such an air of importance that again, instead of the real question of life and death which now alone confronted him, the question arose of the kidney and appendix which were not behaving as they ought to and would now be attacked by Michael Danílovich and the specialist and forced to amend their ways.

The celebrated specialist took leave of him with a serious though not hopeless look, and in reply to the timid question Iván Ilých, with eyes glistening with fear and hope, put to him as to whether there was a chance of recovery, said that he could not vouch for it but there was a possibility. The look of hope with which Iván Ilých watched the doctor out was so pathetic that Praskóvya Fëdorovna, seeing it, even wept as she left the room to hand the doctor his fee.

The gleam of hope kindled by the doctor's encouragement did not last long. The same room, the same pictures, curtains, wall-paper, medicine bottles, were all there, and the same aching suffering body, and Iván Ilých began to moan. They gave him a subcutaneous injection and he sank into oblivion.

It was twilight when he came to. They brought him his dinner and he swallowed some beef tea with difficulty, and then everything was the same again and night was coming on.

After dinner, at seven o'clock, Praskóvya Fëdorovna came into the room in evening dress, her full bosom pushed up by her corset, and with traces of powder on her face. She had reminded him in the morning that they were going to the theatre. Sarah Bernhardt was visiting the town and they had a box, which he had insisted on their taking. Now he had forgotten about it and her toilet offended him, but he concealed his vexation when he remembered that he had himself insisted on their securing a box and going because it would be an instructive and aesthetic pleasure for the children.

Praskóvya Fëdorovna came in, self-satisfied but yet with a rather guilty air. She sat down and asked how he was but, as he saw, only for the sake of asking and not in order to learn about it, knowing that there was nothing to learn—and then went on to what she really wanted to say: that she would not on any account have gone but that the box had been taken and Helen and their daughter were going, as well as Petríshchev (the examining magistrate, their daughter's fiancé) and that it was out of the question to let them go alone; but that she would have much preferred to sit with him for a while; and he must be sure to follow the doctor's orders while she was away.

"Oh, and Fëdor Petróvich" (the fiancé) "would like to come in. May he? And Lisa?"

"All right."

Their daughter came in in full evening dress, her fresh young flesh exposed (making a show of that very flesh which in his own case caused so much suffering), strong, healthy, evidently in love, and impatient with illness, suffering, and death, because they interfered with her happiness.

Fëdor Petróvich came in too, in evening dress, his hair curled *á la Capoul*, a tight stiff collar round his long sinewy neck, an enormous white shirt-front and narrow black trousers tightly stretched over his strong thighs. He had one white glove tightly drawn on, and was holding his opera hat in his hand.

Following him the schoolboy crept in unnoticed, in a new uniform, poor little fellow, and wearing gloves. Terribly dark shadows showed under his eyes, the meaning of which Iván Ilých knew well.

His son had always seemed pathetic to him, and now it was dreadful to see the boy's frightened look of pity. It seemed to Iván Ilých that Vásya was the only one besides Gerásim who understood and pitied him.

They all sat down and again asked how he was. A silence followed. Lisa asked her mother about the opera-glasses, and there was an altercation between mother and daughter as to who had taken them and where they had been put. This occasioned some unpleasantness.

Fëdor Petróvich inquired of Iván Ilých whether he had ever seen Sarah Bernhardt. Iván Ilých did not at first catch the question, but then replied: "No, have you seen her before?"

"Yes, In *Adrienne Lecouvreur*." [10]

Praskóvya Fëdorovna mentioned some roles in which Sarah Bernhardt was particularly good. Her daughter disagreed. Conversation sprang up as to the elegance and realism of her acting—the sort of conversation that is always repeated and is always the same.

---

[10] A play by the French dramatist Eugène Scribe (1791–1861).

In the midst of the conversation Fëdor Petróvich glanced at Iván Ilých and became silent. The others also looked at him and grew silent. Iván Ilých was staring with glittering eyes straight before him, evidently indignant with them. This had to be rectified, but it was impossible to do so. The silence had to be broken, but for a time no one dared to break it and they all became afraid that the conventional deception would suddenly become obvious and the truth become plain to all. Lisa was the first to pluck up courage and break that silence, but by trying to hide what everybody was feeling, she betrayed it.

"Well, if we are going it's time to start," she said, looking at her watch, a present from her father, and with a faint and significant smile at Fëdor Petróvich relating to something known only to them. She got up with a rustle of her dress.

They all rose, said good-night, and went away.

When they had gone it seemed to Iván Ilých that he felt better; the falsity had gone with them. But the pain remained—that same pain and that same fear that made everything monotonously alike, nothing harder and nothing easier. Everything was worse.

Again minute followed minute and hour followed hour. Everything remained the same and there was no cessation. And the inevitable end of it all became more and more terrible.

"Yes, send Gerásim here," he replied to a question Peter asked.

CHAPTER IX

His wife returned late at night. She came in on tiptoe, but he heard her, opened his eyes, and made haste to close them again. She wished to send Gerásim away and to sit with him herself, but he opened his eyes and said: "No, go away."

"Are you in great pain?"

"Always the same."

"Take some opium."

He agreed and took some. She went away.

Till about three in the morning he was in a state of stupefied misery. It seemed to him that he and his pain were being thrust into a narrow, deep black sack, but though they were pushed further and further in they could not be pushed to the bottom. And this, terrible enough in itself, was accompanied by suffering. He was frightened yet wanted to fall through the sack, he struggled but yet co-operated. And suddenly he broke through, fell, and regained consciousness. Gerásim was sitting at the foot of the bed dozing quietly and patiently, while he himself lay with his emaciated stockinged legs resting on Gerásim's shoulders; the same shaded candle was there and the same unceasing pain.

"Go away, Gerásim," he whispered.

"It's all right, sir. I'll stay a while."

"No. Go away."

He removed his legs from Gerásim's shoulders, turned sideways onto his arm, and felt sorry for himself. He only waited till Gerásim had gone into the next room and then restrained himself no longer but wept like a child. He wept on account of his helplessness, his terrible loneliness, the cruelty of man, the cruelty of God, and the absence of God.

"Why hast Thou done all this? Why hast Thou brought me here? Why, why dost Thou torment me so terribly?"

He did not expect an answer and yet wept because there was no answer and could be none. The pain again grew more acute, but he did not stir and did not call. He said to himself: "Go on! Strike me! But what is it for? What have I done to Thee? What is it for?"

Then he grew quiet and not only ceased weeping but even held his breath and became all attention. It was as though he were listening not to an audible voice but to the voice of his soul, to the current of thoughts arising within him.

"What is it you want?" was the first clear conception capable of expression in words, that he heard.

"What do you want? What do you want?" he repeated to himself.

"What do I want? To live and not to suffer," he answered.

And again he listened with such concentrated attention that even his pain did not distract him.

"To live? How?" asked his inner voice.

"Why, to live as I used to—well and pleasantly."

"As you lived before, well and pleasantly?" the voice repeated.

And in imagination he began to recall the best moments of his pleasant life. But strange to say none of these best moments of his pleasant life now seemed at all what they had then seemed—none of them except the first recollections of childhood. There, in childhood, there had been something really pleasant with which it would be possible to live if it could return. But the child who had experienced that happiness existed no longer, it was like a reminiscence of somebody else.

As soon as the period began which had produced the present Iván Ilých, all that had then seemed joys now melted before his sight and turned into something trivial and often nasty.

And the further he departed from childhood and the nearer he came to the present the more worthless and doubtful were the joys. This began with the School of Law. A little that was really good was still found there—there was light-heartedness, friendship, and hope. But in the upper classes there had already been fewer of such good moments. Then during the first years of his official career, when he was in the service of the Governor, some pleasant moments again occurred: they were the memories of love for a woman. Then all became confused and there was still less of what was good; later on again there was still less that was good, and the further he went the less there was. His marriage, a mere accident, then the disenchantment that followed it, his wife's bad breath and the sensuality and hypocrisy: then that deadly official life and those preoccupations about money, a year of it, and two, and ten, and twenty, and always the same thing. And the longer it lasted the more deadly it became. "It is as if I had been going downhill while I imagined I was going up.

And that is really what it was. I was going up in public opinion, but to the same extent life was ebbing away from me. And now it is all done and there is only death."

"Then what does it mean? Why? It can't be that life is so senseless and horrible. But if it really has been so horrible and senseless, why must I die and die in agony? There is something wrong!"

"Maybe I did not live as I ought to have done," it suddenly occurred to him. "But how could that be, when I did everything properly?" he replied, and immediately dismissed from his mind this, the sole solution of all the riddles of life and death, as something quite impossible.

"Then what do you want now? To live? Live how? Live as you lived in the law courts when the usher proclaimed 'The judge is coming!' " "The judge is coming, the judge!" he repeated to himself. "Here he is, the judge. But I am not guilty!" he exclaimed angrily. "What is it for?" And he ceased crying, but turning his face to the wall continued to ponder on the same question: Why, and for what purpose, is there all this horror? But however much he pondered he found no answer. And whenever the thought occurred to him, as it often did, that it all resulted from his not having lived as he ought to have done, he at once recalled the correctness of his whole life and dismissed so strange an idea.

CHAPTER X

Another fortnight passed. Iván Ilých now no longer left his sofa. He would not lie in bed but lay on the sofa, facing the wall nearly all the time. He suffered ever the same unceasing agonies and in his loneliness pondered always on the same insoluble question: "What is this? Can it be that it is Death?" And the inner voice answered: "Yes, it is Death."

"Why these sufferings?" And the voice answered, "For no reason—they just are so." Beyond and besides this there was nothing.

From the very beginning of his illness, ever since he had first been to see the doctor, Iván Ilých's life had been divided between two contrary and alternating moods: now it was despair and the expectation of this uncomprehended and terrible death, and now hope and an intently interested observation of the functioning of his organs. Now before his eyes there was only a kidney or an intestine that temporarily evaded its duty, and now only that incomprehensible and dreadful death from which it was impossible to escape.

These two states of mind had alternated from the very beginning of his illness, but the further it progressed the more doubtful and fantastic became the conception of the kidney, and the more real the sense of impending death.

He had but to call to mind what he had been three months before and what he was now, to call to mind with what regularity he had been going downhill, for every possibility of hope to be shattered.

Latterly during that loneliness in which he found himself as he lay facing the back of the sofa, a loneliness in the midst of a populous town and surrounded by numerous acquaintances and relations but that yet could not have been more complete anywhere—either at the bottom of the sea or under the earth—during that terrible loneliness Iván Ilých had lived only in memories of the past. Pictures of his past rose before him one after another. They always began with what was nearest in time and then went back to what was most remote—to his child-hood—and rested there. If he thought of the stewed prunes that had been offered him that day, his mind went back to the raw shrivelled French plums of his childhood, their peculiar flavour and the flow of saliva when he sucked their stones, and along with the memory of that taste came a whole series of memories of those days: his nurse, his brother, and their toys. "No, I mustn't think of that. . . . It is too painful," Iván Ilých said to himself, and brought himself back to the present—to the button on the back of the sofa and the creases in its morocco. "Morocco is expensive, but it does not wear well: There had been a quarrel about it. It was a different kind of quarrel and a different kind of morocco that time when we tore father's portfolio and were punished, and mamma brought us some tarts. . . ." And again his thoughts dwelt on his childhood, and again it was painful and he tried to banish them and fix his mind on something else.

Then again together with that chain of memories another series passed through his mind—of how his illness had progressed and grown worse. There also the further back he looked the more life there had been. There had been more of what was good in life and more of life itself. The two merged together. "Just as the pain went on getting worse and worse so my life grew worse and worse," he thought. "There is one bright spot there at the back, at the beginning of life, and afterwards all becomes blacker and blacker and proceeds more and more rapidly—in inverse ratio to the square of the distance from death," thought Iván Ilých. And the example of a stone falling downwards with increasing velocity entered his mind. Life, a series of increasing sufferings, flies, further and further towards its end—the most terrible suffering. "I am flying. . . ." He shuddered, shifted himself, and tried to resist, but was already aware that resistance was impossible, and again with eyes weary of gazing but unable to cease seeing what was before them, he stared at the back of the sofa and waited—awaiting that dreadful fall and shock and destruction.

"Resistance is impossible!" he said to himself. "If I could only understand what it is all for! But that too is impossible. An explanation would be possible if it could be said that I have not lived as I ought to. But it is impossible to say that," and he remembered all the legality, correctitude, and propriety of his life. "That at any rate can certainly not be admitted," he thought, and his lips smiled ironically as if someone could see that smile and be taken in by it. "There is no explanation! Agony, death. . . . What for?"

CHAPTER XI

Another two weeks went by in this way and during that fortnight an event occurred that Iván Ilých and his wife had desired. Petríshchev formally proposed. It happened in the evening. The next day Praskóvya Fëdorovna came into her husband's room considering how best to inform him of it, but that very night there had been a fresh change for the worse in his condition. She found him still lying on the sofa but in a different position. He lay on his back, groaning and staring fixedly straight in front of him.

She began to remind him of his medicines, but he turned his eyes towards her with such a look that she did not finish what she was saying; so great an animosity, to her in particular, did that look express.

"For Christ's sake, let me die in peace!" he said.

She would have gone away, but just then their daughter came in and went up to say good morning. He looked at her as he had done at his wife, and in reply to her inquiry about his health said dryly that he would soon free them all of himself. They were both silent and after sitting with him for a while went away.

"Is it our fault?" Lisa said to her mother. "It's as if we were to blame! I am sorry for papa, but why should we be tortured?"

The doctor came at his usual time. Iván Ilých answered "Yes" and "No," never taking his angry eyes from him, and at last said: "You know you can do nothing for me, so leave me alone."

"We can ease your sufferings."

"You can't even do that. Let me be."

The doctor went into the drawing-room and told Praskóvya Fëdorovna that the case was very serious and that the only resource left was opium to allay her husband's sufferings, which must be terrible.

It was true, as the doctor said, that Iván Ilých's physical sufferings were terrible, but worse than the physical sufferings were his mental sufferings which were his chief torture.

His mental sufferings were due to the fact that that night, as he looked at Gerásim's sleepy, good-natured face with its prominent cheek-bones, the question suddenly occurred to him: "What if my whole life has really been wrong?"

It occurred to him that what had appeared perfectly impossible before, namely that he had not spent his life as he should have done, might after all be true. It occurred to him that his scarcely perceptible attempts to struggle against what was considered good by the most highly placed people, those scarcely noticeable impulses which he had immediately suppressed, might have been the real thing, and all the rest false. And his professional duties and the whole arrangement of his life and of his family, and all his social and official interests, might all have been false. He tried to defend all those things to himself and suddenly felt the weakness of what he was defending. There was nothing to defend.

"But if that is so," he said to himself, "and I am leaving this life with the consciousness that I have lost all that was given me and it is impossible to rectify it—what then?"

He lay on his back and began to pass his life in review in quite a new way. In the morning when he saw first his footman, then his wife, then his daughter, and then the doctor, their every word and movement confirmed to him the awful truth that had been revealed to him during the night. In them he saw himself—all that for which he had lived—and saw clearly that it was not real at all, but a terrible and huge deception which had hidden both life and death. This consciousness intensified his physical suffering tenfold. He groaned and tossed about, and pulled at his clothing which choked and stifled him. And he hated them on that account.

He was given a large dose of opium and became unconscious, but at noon his sufferings began again. He drove everybody away and tossed from side to side.

His wife came to him and said:

"Jean my dear, do this for me. It can't do any harm and often helps. Healthy people often do it."

He opened his eyes wide.

"What? Take communion? Why? It's unnecessary! However. . . . "

She began to cry.

"Yes, do, my dear. I'll send for our priest. He is such a nice man."

"All right. Very well," he muttered.

When the priest came and heard his confession, Iván Ilých was softened and seemed to feel a relief from his doubts and consequently from his sufferings, and for a moment there came a ray of hope. He again began to think of the vermiform appendix and the possibility of correcting it. He received the sacrament with tears in his eyes.

When they laid him down again afterwards he felt a moment's ease, and the hope that he might live awoke in him again. He began to think of the operation that had been suggested to him. "To live! I want to live!" he said to himself.

His wife came in to congratulate him after his communion, and when uttering the usual conventional words she added:

"You feel better, don't you?"

Without looking at her he said "Yes."

Her dress, her figure, the expression of her face, the tone of her voice, all revealed the same thing. "This is wrong, it is not as it should be. All you have lived for and still live for is falsehood and deception, hiding life and death from you." And as soon as he admitted that thought, his hatred and his agonizing physical suffering again sprang up, and with that suffering a consciousness of the unavoidable, approaching end. And to this was added a new sensation of grinding shooting pain and a feeling of suffocation.

The expression of his face when he uttered that "yes" was dreadful. Having uttered it, he looked her straight in the eyes, turned on his face with a rapidity extraordinary in his weak state and shouted:

"Go away! Go away and leave me alone!"

CHAPTER XII

From that moment the screaming began that continued for three days, and was so terrible that one could not hear it through two closed doors without horror. At the moment he answered his wife he realized that he was lost, that there was no return, that the end had come, the very end, and his doubts were still unsolved and remained doubts.

"Oh! Oh! Oh!" he cried in various intonations. He had begun by screaming "I won't!" and continued screaming on the letter "o."

For three whole days, during which time did not exist for him, he struggled in that black sack into which he was being thrust by an invisible, resistless force. He struggled as a man condemned to death struggles in the hands of the executioner, knowing that he cannot save himself. And every moment he felt that despite all his efforts he was drawing nearer and nearer to what terrified him. He felt that his agony was due to his being thrust into that black hole and still more to his not being able to get right into it. He was hindered from getting into it by his conviction that his life had been a good one. That very justification of his life held him fast and prevented his moving forward, and it caused him most torment of all.

Suddenly some force struck him in the chest and side, making it still harder to breathe, and he fell through the hole and there at the bottom was a light. What had happened to him was like the sensation one sometimes experiences in a railway carriage when one thinks one is going backwards while one is really going forwards and suddenly becomes aware of the real direction.

"Yes, it was all not the right thing," he said to himself, "but that's no matter. It can be done. But what *is* the right thing?" he asked himself, and suddenly grew quiet.

This occurred at the end of the third day, two hours before his death. Just then his schoolboy son had crept softly in and gone up to the bedside. The dying man was still screaming desperately and waving his arms. His hand fell on the boy's head, and the boy caught it, pressed it to his lips, and began to cry.

At that very moment Iván Ilých fell through and caught sight of the light, and it was revealed to him that though his life had not been what it should have been, this could still be rectified. He asked himself, "What *is* the right thing?" and grew still, listening. Then he felt that someone was kissing his hand. He opened his eyes, looked at his son, and felt sorry for him. His wife came up to him and he glanced at her. She was gazing at him open-mouthed, with undried tears on her nose and cheek and a despairing look on her face. He felt sorry for her too.

"Yes, I am making them wretched," he thought. "They are sorry, but it will be better for them when I die." He wished to say this but had not the strength to utter it. "Besides, why speak? I must act," he thought. With a look at his wife he indicated his son and said: "Take him away . . . sorry for him . . . sorry for you too. . . ." He tried to add, "forgive me," but said "forego" and waved his hand, knowing that He whose understanding mattered would understand.

And suddenly it grew clear to him that what had been oppressing him and would not leave him was all dropping away at once from two sides, from ten sides, and from all sides. He was sorry for them, he must act so as not to hurt them: release them and free himself from these sufferings. "How good and how simple!" he thought. "And the pain?" he asked himself. "What has become of it? Where are you, pain?"

He turned his attention to it.

"Yes, here it is. Well, what of it? Let the pain be."

"And death . . . where is it?"

He sought his former accustomed fear of death and did not find it. "Where is it? What death?" There was no fear because there was no death.

In place of death there was light.

"So that's what it is!" he suddenly exclaimed aloud. "What joy!"

To him all this happened in a single instant, and the meaning of that instant did not change. For those present his agony continued for another two hours. Something rattled in his throat, his emaciated body twitched, then the gasping and rattle became less and less frequent.

"It is finished!" said someone near him.

He heard these words and repeated them in his soul.

"Death is finished," he said to himself. "It is no more!"

He drew in a breath, stopped in the midst of a sigh, stretched out, and died.

QUESTIONS

1. Why does Tolstoy begin the story immediately after Ilých's death and then move back to recount his life? **2.** Is there any evidence that Ilých's death is a moral judgment—that is, a punishment for his life? Explain. **3.** Why is Gerásim, Ilých's peasant servant, most sympathetic to his plight?

WRITING TOPIC

At the very end, Ilých achieves peace and understanding, and the questions that have been torturing him are resolved. He realizes that "though his life had not been what it should have been, this could still be rectified." What does this mean?

The Jilting
of Granny Weatherall   1930

KATHERINE ANNE PORTER [1890–1980]

She flicked her wrist neatly out of Doctor Harry's pudgy careful fingers and pulled the sheet up to her chin. The brat ought to be in knee breeches. Doctoring around the country with spectacles on his nose! "Get along now, take your schoolbooks and go. There's nothing wrong with me."

Doctor Harry spread a warm paw like a cushion on her forehead where the forked green vein danced and made her eyelids twitch. "Now, now, be a good girl, and we'll have you up in no time."

"That's no way to speak to a woman nearly eighty years old just because she's down. I'd have you respect your elders, young man."

"Well, Missy, excuse me." Doctor Harry patted her cheek. "But I've got to warn you, haven't I? You're a marvel, but you must be careful or you're going to be good and sorry."

"Don't tell me what I'm going to be. I'm on my feet now, morally speaking. It's Cornelia. I had to go to bed to get rid of her."

Her bones felt loose, and floated around in her skin, and Doctor Harry floated like a balloon around the foot of the bed. He floated and pulled down his waistcoat and swung his glasses on a cord. "Well, stay where you are, it certainly can't hurt you."

"Get along and doctor your sick," said Granny Weatherall. "Leave a well woman alone. I'll call for you when I want you. . . . Where were you forty years ago when I pulled through milk-leg and double pneumonia? You weren't even born. Don't let Cornelia lead you on," she shouted, because Doctor Harry appeared to float up to the ceiling and out. "I pay my own bills, and I don't throw my money away on nonsense!"

She meant to wave good-by, but it was too much trouble. Her eyes closed of themselves, it was like a dark curtain drawn around the bed. The pillow rose and floated under her, pleasant as a hammock in a light wind. She listened to the leaves rustling outside the window. No, somebody was swishing newspapers: no, Cornelia and Doctor Harry were whispering together. She leaped broad awake, thinking they whispered in her ear.

"She was never like this, *never* like this!" "Well, what can we expect?" "Yes, eighty years old. . . ."

Well, and what if she was? She still had ears. It was like Cornelia to whisper around doors. She always kept things secret in such a public way. She was always being tactful and kind. Cornelia was dutiful; that was the trouble with her. Dutiful and good: "So good and dutiful," said Granny, "that I'd like to spank her." She saw herself spanking Cornelia and making a fine job of it.

"What'd you say, Mother?"

Granny felt her face tying up in hard knots.

"Can't a body think, I'd like to know?"

"I thought you might want something."

"I do. I want a lot of things. First off, go away and don't whisper."

She lay and drowsed, hoping in her sleep that the children would keep out and let her rest a minute. It had been a long day. Not that she was tired. It was always pleasant to snatch a minute now and then. There was always so much to be done, let me see: tomorrow.

Tomorrow was far away and there was nothing to trouble about. Things were finished somehow when the time came; thank God there was always a little margin over for peace: then a person could spread out the plan of life and tuck in the edges orderly. It was good to have everything clean and folded away, with the hair brushes and tonic bottles sitting straight on the white embroidered linen: the day started without fuss and the pantry shelves laid out with rows of jelly glasses and brown jugs and white stone-china jars with blue whirligigs and words painted on them: coffee, tea, sugar, ginger, cinnamon, allspice: and the bronze clock with the lion on top nicely dusted off. The dust that lion could collect in twenty-four hours! The box in the attic with all those letters tied up, well she'd have to go through that tomorrow. All those letters—George's letters and John's letters and her letters to them both—lying around for the children to find afterwards made her uneasy. Yes, that would be tomorrow's business. No use to let them know how silly she had been once.

While she was rummaging around she found death in her mind and it felt clammy and unfamiliar. She had spent so much time preparing for death there was no need for bringing it up again. Let it take care of itself now. When she was sixty she had felt very old, finished, and went around making farewell trips to see her children and grandchildren, with a secret in her mind: This is the very last of your mother, children! Then she made her will and came down with a long fever. That was all just a notion like a lot of other things, but it was lucky too, for she had once for all got over the idea of dying for a long time. Now she couldn't be worried. She hoped she had better sense now. Her father had lived to be one hundred and two years old and had drunk a noggin of strong hot toddy on his last birthday. He told the reporters it was his daily habit, and he owed his long life to that. He had made quite a scandal and was very pleased about it. She believed she'd just plague Cornelia a little.

"Cornelia! Cornelia!" No footsteps, but a sudden hand on her cheek. "Bless you, where have you been?"

"Here, mother."

"Well, Cornelia, I want a noggin of hot toddy."

"Are you cold, darling?"

"I'm chilly, Cornelia. Lying in bed stops the circulation. I must have told you that a thousand times."

Well, she could just hear Cornelia telling her husband that Mother was getting childish and they'd have to humor her. The thing that most annoyed her was that Cornelia thought she was deaf, dumb, and blind. Little hasty glances and tiny gestures tossed around her and over her head saying, "Don't cross her, let her have her way, she's eighty years old," and she sitting there as if she lived in a thin glass cage. Sometimes Granny almost made up her mind to pack up and move back to her own house where nobody could remind her every minute that she was old. Wait, wait, Cornelia, till your own children whisper behind your back!

In her day she had kept a better house and had got more work done. She wasn't too old yet for Lydia to be driving eighty miles for advice when one of the children jumped the track, and Jimmy still dropped in and talked things over: "Now, Mammy, you've a good business head, I want to know what you think of this? . . ." Old Cornelia couldn't change the furniture around without asking. Little things, little things! They had been so sweet when they were little. Granny wished the old days were back again with the children young and everything to be done over. It had been a hard pull, but not too much for her. When she thought of all the food she had cooked, and all the clothes she had cut and sewed, and all the gardens she had made—well, the children showed it. There they were, made out of her, and they couldn't get away from that. Sometimes she wanted to see John again and point to them and say, Well, I didn't do so badly, did I? But that would have to wait. That was for tomorrow. She used to think of him as a man, but now all the children were older than their father, and he would be a child beside her if she saw him now. It seemed strange and there was something wrong in the idea. Why, he couldn't possibly recognize her. She had fenced in a hundred acres once, digging the post holes herself and clamping the wires with just a negro boy to help. That changed a woman. John would be looking for a young woman with the peaked Spanish comb in her hair and the painted fan. Digging post holes changed a woman. Riding country roads in the winter when women had their babies was another thing: sitting up nights with sick horses and sick negroes and sick children and hardly ever losing one. John, I hardly ever lost one of them! John would see that in a minute, that would be something he could understand, she wouldn't have to explain anything!

It made her feel like rolling up her sleeves and putting the whole place to rights again. No matter if Cornelia was determined to be everywhere at once, there were a great many things left undone on this place. She would start tomorrow and do them. It was good to be strong enough for everything, even if all you made melted and changed and slipped under your hands, so that by the time you finished you almost forgot what you were working for. What was it I set out to do? she asked herself intently, but she could not remember. A fog rose over the valley, she saw it marching across the creek swallowing the trees and moving up the hill like an army of ghosts. Soon it would be at the near edge of the orchard, and then it was time to go in and light the lamps. Come in, children, don't stay out in the night air.

Lighting the lamps had been beautiful. The children huddled up to her and breathed like little calves waiting at the bars in the twilight. Their eyes followed the match and watched the flame rise and settle in a blue curve, then they moved away from her. The lamp was lit, they didn't have to be scared and hang on to mother any more. Never, never, never more. God, for all my life I thank Thee. Without Thee, my God, I could never have done it. Hail, Mary, full of grace.

I want you to pick all the fruit this year and see that nothing is wasted. There's always someone who can use it. Don't let good things rot for want of using. You waste life when you waste good food. Don't let things get lost. It's bitter to lose things. Now, don't let me get to thinking, not when I am tired and taking a little nap before supper. . . .

The pillow rose about her shoulders and pressed against her heart and the memory was being squeezed out of it: oh, push down the pillow, somebody: it would smother her if she tried to hold it. Such a fresh breeze blowing and such a green day with no threats in it. But he had not come, just the same. What does a woman do when she has put on the white veil and set out the white cake for a man and he doesn't come? She tried to remember. No, I swear he never harmed me but in that. He never harmed me but in that . . . and what if he did? There was the day, the day, but a whirl of dark smoke rose and covered it, crept up and over into the bright field where everything was planted so carefully in orderly rows. That was hell, she knew hell when she saw it. For sixty years she had prayed against remembering him and against losing her soul in the deep pit of hell, and now the two things were mingled in one and the thought of him was a smoky cloud from hell that moved and crept in her head when she had just got rid of Doctor Harry and was trying to rest a minute. Wounded vanity, Ellen, said a sharp voice in the top of her mind. Don't let your wounded vanity get the upper hand of you. Plenty of girls get jilted. You were jilted, weren't you? Then stand up to it. Her eyelids wavered and let in streamers of blue-gray light like tissue paper over her eyes. She must get up and pull the shades down or she'd never sleep. She was in bed again and the shades were not down. How could that happen? Better turn over, hide from the light, sleeping in the light gave you nightmares. "Mother, how do you feel now?" and a stinging wetness on her forehead. But I don't like having my face washed in cold water!

Hapsy? George? Lydia? Jimmy? No, Cornelia, and her features were swollen and full of little puddles. "They're coming, darling, they'll all be here soon." Go wash your face, child, you look funny.

Instead of obeying, Cornelia knelt down and put her head on the pillow. She seemed to be talking but there was no sound. "Well, are you tongue-tied? Whose birthday is it? Are you going to give a party?"

Cornelia's mouth moved urgently in strange shapes. "Don't do that, you bother me, daughter."

"Oh, no, Mother, Oh, no. . . ."

Nonsense. It was strange about children. They disputed your every word. "No what, Cornelia?"

"Here's Doctor Harry."

"I won't see that boy again. He just left five minutes ago."

"That was this morning, Mother. It's night now. Here's the nurse."

"This is Doctor Harry, Mrs. Weatherall. I never saw you look so young and happy!"

"Ah, I'll never be young again—but I'd be happy if they'd let me lie in peace and get rested."

She thought she spoke up loudly, but no one answered. A warm weight on her forehead, a warm bracelet on her wrist, and a breeze went on whispering, trying to tell her something. A shuffle of leaves in the everlasting hand of God. He blew on them and they danced and rattled. "Mother, don't mind, we're going to give you a little hypodermic." "Look here, daughter, how do ants get in this bed? I saw sugar ants yesterday." Did you send for Hapsy too?

It was Hapsy she really wanted. She had to go a long way back through a great many rooms to find Hapsy standing with a baby on her arm. She seemed to herself to be Hapsy also, and the baby on Hapsy's arm was Hapsy and himself and herself, all at once, and there was no surprise in the meeting. Then Hapsy melted from within and turned flimsy as gray gauze and the baby was a gauzy shadow, and Hapsy came up close and said, "I thought you'd never come," and looked at her very searchingly and said, "You haven't changed a bit!" They leaned forward to kiss, when Cornelia began whispering from a long way off, "Oh, is there anything you want to tell me? Is there anything I can do for you?"

Yes, she had changed her mind after sixty years and she would like to see George. I want you to find George. Find him and be sure to tell him I forgot him. I want him to know I had my husband just the same and my children and my house like any other woman. A good house too and a good husband that I loved and fine children out of him. Better than I hoped for even. Tell him I was given back everything he took away and more. Oh, no, oh, God, no, there was something else besides the house and the man and the children. Oh, surely they were not all? What was it? Something not given back. . . . Her breath crowded down under her ribs and grew into a monstrous frightening shape with cutting edges; it bored up into her head, and the agony was unbelievable: Yes, John, get the doctor now, no more talk, my time has come.

When this one was born it should be the last. The last. It should have been born first, for it was the one she had truly wanted. Everything came in good time. Nothing left out, left over. She was strong, in three days she would be as well as ever. Better. A woman needed milk in her to have her full health.

"Mother, do you hear me?"

"I've been telling you—"

"Mother, Father Connolly's here."

"I went to Holy Communion only last week. Tell him I'm not so sinful as all that."

"Father just wants to speak to you."

He could speak as much as he pleased. It was like him to drop in and inquire about her soul as if it were a teething baby, and then stay on for a cup of tea and a round of cards and gossip. He always had a funny story of some sort, usually about an Irishman who made his little mistakes and confessed them, and the point lay in some absurd thing he would blurt out in the confessional showing his struggles between native piety and original sin. Granny felt easy about her soul. Cornelia, where are your manners? Give Father Connolly a chair. She had her secret comfortable understanding with a few favorite saints who cleared a straight road to God for her. All as surely signed and sealed as the papers for the new Forty Acres. Forever . . . heirs and assigns forever. Since the day the wedding cake was not cut, but thrown out and wasted. The whole bottom dropped out of the world, and there she was blind and sweating with nothing under her feet and the walls falling away. His hand had caught her under the breast, she had not fallen, there was the freshly polished floor with the green rug on it, just as before. He had cursed like a sailor's parrot and said, "I'll kill him for you." Don't lay a hand on him, for my sake leave something to God. "Now, Ellen, you must believe what I tell you. . . ."

So there was nothing, nothing to worry about any more, except sometimes in the night one of the children screamed in a nightmare, and they both hustled out shaking and hunting for the matches and calling, "There, wait a minute, here we are!" John, get the doctor now, Hapsy's time has come. But there was Hapsy standing by the bed in a white cap. "Cornelia, tell Hapsy to take off her cap. I can't see her plain."

Her eyes opened very wide and the room stood out like a picture she had seen somewhere. Dark colors with the shadows rising towards the ceiling in long angles. The tall black dresser gleamed with nothing on it but John's picture, enlarged from a little one, with John's eyes very black when they should have been blue. You never saw him, so how do you know how he looked? But the man insisted the copy was perfect, it was very rich and handsome. For a picture, yes, but it's not my husband. The table by the bed had a linen cover and a candle and a crucifix. The light was blue from Cornelia's silk lampshades. No sort of light at all, just frippery. You had to live forty years with kerosene lamps to appreciate honest electricity. She felt very strong and she saw Doctor Harry with a rosy nimbus around him.

"You look like a saint, Doctor Harry, and I vow that's as near as you'll ever come to it."

"She's saying something."

"I heard you, Cornelia. What's all this carrying-on?"

"Father Connolly's saying—"

Cornelia's voice staggered and bumped like a cart in a bad road. It rounded corners and turned back again and arrived nowhere. Granny stepped up in the cart very lightly and reached for the reins, but a man sat beside her and she knew him by his hands, driving the cart. She did not look in his face, for she knew without seeing, but looked instead down the road where the trees leaned over and bowed to each other and a thousand birds were singing a Mass. She felt like singing too, but she put her hand in the bosom of her dress and pulled out a rosary, and Father Connolly murmured Latin in a very solemn voice and tickled her feet. My God, will you stop that nonsense? I'm a married woman.

What if he did run away and leave me to face the priest by myself? I found another a whole world better. I wouldn't have exchanged my husband for anybody except St. Michael himself, and you may tell him that for me with a thank you in the bargain.

Light flashed on her closed eyelids, and a deep roaring shook her. Cornelia, is that lightning? I hear thunder. There's going to be a storm. Close all the windows. Call the children in. . . . "Mother, here we are, all of us." "Is that you, Hapsy?" "Oh, no, I'm Lydia. We drove as fast as we could." Their faces drifted above her, drifted away. The rosary fell out of her hands and Lydia put it back. Jimmy tried to help, their hands fumbled together, and Granny closed two fingers around Jimmy's thumb. Beads wouldn't do, it must be something alive. She was so amazed her thoughts ran round and round. So, my dear Lord, this is my death and I wasn't even thinking about it. My children have come to see me die. But I can't, it's not time. Oh, I always hated surprises. I wanted to give Cornelia the amethyst set—Cornelia, you're to have the amethyst set, but Hapsy's to wear it when she wants, and, Doctor Harry, do shut up. Nobody sent for you. Oh, my dear Lord, do wait a minute. I meant to do something about the Forty Acres, Jimmy doesn't need it and Lydia will later on, with that worthless husband of hers. I meant to finish the altar cloth and send six bottles of wine to Sister Borgia for her dyspepsia. I want to send six bottles of wine to Sister Borgia, Father Connolly, now don't let me forget.

Cornelia's voice made short turns and tilted over and crashed. "Oh, Mother, oh, Mother, oh, Mother. . . ."

"I'm not going, Cornelia. I'm taken by surprise. I can't go."

You'll see Hapsy again. What about her? "I thought you'd never come." Granny made a long journey outward, looking for Hapsy. What if I don't find her? What then? Her heart sank down and down, there was no bottom to death, she couldn't come to the end of it. The blue light from Cornelia's lampshade drew into a tiny point in the center of her brain, it flickered and winked like an eye, quietly it fluttered and dwindled. Granny lay curled down within herself, amazed and watchful, staring at the point of light that was herself; her body was now only a deeper mass of shadow in an endless darkness and this darkness would curl around the light and swallow it up. God, give a sign!

For the second time there was no sign. Again no bridegroom and the priest in the house. She could not remember any other sorrow because this grief wiped them all away. Oh, no, there's nothing more cruel than this—I'll never forgive it. She stretched herself with a deep breath and blew out the light.

QUESTIONS

1. Characterize Granny. What facts do we know about her life? 2. Why, after sixty full years, does the jilting by George loom so large in Granny's mind? Are we to accept her own strong statements that the pain of the jilting was more than

compensated for by the happiness she ultimately found with her husband John, her children, and her grandchildren? Explain.   **3.**   Why does the author not present us with Granny's final thoughts in an orderly and sequential pattern? **4.**   Granny is revealed to us not only through her direct thoughts but also through the many images that float through her mind—the fog, the blowing breeze, "a whirl of dark smoke," and others. What do these images reveal about Granny?

WRITING TOPIC
The final paragraph echoes Christ's parable of the bridegroom (Matthew 25:1–13). Why does Granny connect this final, deep religious grief with the grief she felt when George jilted her?

Idiots First

1963

BERNARD MALAMUD   [1914–1986]

The thick ticking of the tin clock stopped. Mendel, dozing in the dark, awoke in fright. The pain returned as he listened. He drew on his cold embittered clothing, and wasted minutes sitting at the edge of the bed.

"Isaac," he ultimately sighed.

In the kitchen, Isaac, his astonished mouth open, held six peanuts in his palm. He placed each on the table. "One . . . two . . . nine."

He gathered each peanut and appeared in the doorway. Mendel, in loose hat and long overcoat, still sat on the bed. Isaac watched with small eyes and ears, thick hair graying the sides of his head.

"Schlaf," he nasally said.

"No," muttered Mendel. As if stifling he rose. "Come, Isaac."

He wound his old watch though the sight of the stopped clock nauseated him.

Isaac wanted to hold it to his ear.

"No, it's late." Mendel put the watch carefully away. In the drawer he found the little paper bag of crumpled ones and fives and slipped it into his overcoat pocket. He helped Isaac on with his coat.

Isaac looked at one dark window, then at the other. Mendel stared at both blank windows.

They went slowly down the darkly lit stairs, Mendel first, Isaac watching the moving shadows on the wall. To one long shadow he offered a peanut.

"Hungrig."

In the vestibule the old man gazed through the thin glass. The November night was cold and bleak. Opening the door he cautiously thrust his head out. Though he saw nothing he quickly shut the door.

"Ginzburg, that he came to see me yesterday," he whispered in Isaac's ear.

Isaac sucked air.

"You know who I mean?"

Isaac combed his chin with his fingers.

"That's the one, with the black whiskers. Don't talk to him or go with him if he asks you."

Isaac moaned.

"Young people he don't bother so much," Mendel said in afterthought.

It was suppertime and the street was empty but the store windows dimly lit their way to the corner. They crossed the deserted street and went on. Isaac, with a happy cry, pointed to the three golden balls. Mendel smiled but was exhausted when they got to the pawnshop.

The pawnbroker, a red-bearded man with black horn-rimmed glasses, was eating a whitefish at the rear of the store. He craned his head, saw them, and settled back to sip his tea.

In five minutes he came forward, patting his shapeless lips with a large white handkerchief.

639

Mendel, breathing heavily, handed him the worn gold watch. The pawn-broker, raising his glasses, screwed in his eyepiece. He turned the watch over once. "Eight dollars."

The dying man wet his cracked lips. "I must have thirty-five."

"So go to Rothschild."

"Cost me myself sixty."

"In 1905." The pawnbroker handed back the watch. It had stopped ticking. Mendel wound it slowly. It ticked hollowly.

"Isaac must go to my uncle that he lives in California."

"It's a free country," said the pawnbroker.

Isaac, watching a banjo, snickered.

"What's the matter with him?" the pawnbroker asked.

"So let be eight dollars," muttered Mendel, "but where will I get the rest till tonight?"

"How much for my hat and coat?" he asked.

"No sale." The pawnbroker went behind the cage and wrote out a ticket. He locked the watch in a small drawer but Mendel still heard it ticking.

In the street he slipped the eight dollars into the paper bag, then searched in his pockets for a scrap of writing. Finding it, he strained to read the address by the light of the street lamp.

As they trudged to the subway, Mendel pointed to the sprinkled sky.

"Isaac, look how many stars are tonight."

"Eggs," said Isaac.

"First we will go to Mr. Fishbein, after we will eat."

They got off the train in upper Manhattan and had to walk several blocks before they located Fishbein's house.

"A regular palace," Mendel murmured, looking forward to a moment's warmth.

Isaac stared uneasily at the heavy door of the house.

Mendel rang. The servant, a man with long sideburns, came to the door and said Mr. and Mrs. Fishbein were dining and could see no one.

"He should eat in peace but we will wait till he finishes."

"Come back tomorrow morning. Tomorrow morning Mr. Fishbein will talk to you. He don't do business or charity at this time of the night."

"Charity I am not interested—"

"Come back tomorrow."

"Tell him it's life or death—"

"Whose life or death?"

"So if not his, then mine."

"Don't be such a big smart aleck."

"Look me in my face," said Mendel, "and tell me if I got time till tomorrow morning?"

The servant stared at him, then at Isaac, and reluctantly let them in.

The foyer was a vast high-ceilinged room with many oil paintings on the walls, voluminous silken draperies, a thick flowered rug at foot, and a marble staircase.

Mr. Fishbein, a paunchy bald-headed man with hairy nostrils and small patent leather feet, ran lightly down the stairs, a large napkin tucked under a tuxedo coat button. He stopped on the fifth step from the bottom and examined his visitors.

"Who comes on Friday night to a man that he has guests, to spoil him his supper?"

"Excuse me that I bother you, Mr. Fishbein," Mendel said. "If I didn't come now I couldn't come tomorrow."

"Without more preliminaries, please state your business. I'm a hungry man."

"Hungrig," wailed Isaac.

Fishbein adjusted his pince-nez. "What's the matter with him?"

"This is my son Isaac. He is like this all his life."

Isaac mewled.

"I am sending him to California."

"Mr. Fishbein don't contribute to personal pleasure trips."

"I am a sick man and he must go tonight on the train to my Uncle Leo."

"I never give to unorganized charity," Fishbein said, "but if you are hungry I will invite you downstairs in my kitchen. We having tonight chicken with stuffed derma."

"All I ask is thirty-five dollars for the train ticket to my uncle in California. I have already the rest."

"Who is your uncle? How old a man?"

"Eighty-one years, a long life to him."

Fishbein burst into laughter. "Eighty-one years and you are sending him this halfwit."

Mendel, flailing both arms, cried, "Please, without names."

Fishbein politely conceded.

"Where is open the door there we go in the house," the sick man said. "If you will kindly give me thirty-five dollars, God will bless you. What is thirty-five dollars to Mr. Fishbein? Nothing. To me, for my boy, is everything."

Fishbein drew himself up to his tallest height.

"Private contributions I don't make—only to institutions. This is my fixed policy."

Mendel sank to his creaking knees on the rug.

"Please, Mr. Fishbein, if not thirty-five, give maybe twenty."

"Levinson!" Fishbein angrily called.

The servant with the long sideburns appeared at the top of the stairs.

"Show this party where is the door—unless he wishes to partake food before leaving the premises."

"For what I got chicken won't cure it," Mendel said.

"This way if you please," said Levinson, descending.

Isaac assisted his father up.

"Take him to an institution," Fishbein advised over the marble balustrade. He ran quickly up the stairs and they were at once outside, buffeted by winds.

The walk to the subway was tedious. The wind blew mournfully. Mendel, breathless, glanced furtively at shadows. Isaac, clutching his peanuts in his frozen fist, clung to his father's side. They entered a small park to rest for a minute on a stone bench under a leafless two-branched tree. The thick right branch was raised, the thin left one hung down. A very pale moon rose slowly. So did a stranger as they approached the bench.

"Gut yuntif" [Happy holiday], he said hoarsely.

Mendel, drained of blood, waved his wasted arms. Isaac yowled sickly. Then a bell chimed and it was only ten. Mendel let out a piercing anguished cry as the bearded stranger disappeared into the bushes. A policeman came running, and though he beat the bushes with his nightstick, could turn up nothing. Mendel and Isaac hurried out of the little park. When Mendel glanced back the dead tree had its thin arm raised, the thick one down. He moaned.

They boarded a trolley, stopping at the home of a former friend, but he had died years ago. On the same block they went into a cafeteria and ordered two fried eggs for Isaac. The tables were crowded except where a heavy-set man sat eating soup with kasha. After one look at him they left in haste, although Isaac wept.

Mendel had another address on a slip of paper but the house was too far away, in Queens, so they stood in a doorway shivering.

What can I do, he frantically thought, in one short hour?

He remembered the furniture in the house. It was junk but might bring a few dollars. "Come, Isaac." They went once more to the pawnbroker's to talk to him, but the shop was dark and an iron gate—rings and gold watches glinting through it—was drawn tight across his place of business.

They huddled behind a telephone pole, both freezing. Isaac whimpered.

"See the big moon, Isaac. The whole sky is white."

He pointed but Isaac wouldn't look.

Mendel dreamed for a minute of the sky lit up, long sheets of light in all directions. Under the sky, in California, sat Uncle Leo drinking tea with lemon. Mendel felt warm but woke up cold.

Across the street stood an ancient brick synagogue.

He pounded on the huge door but no one appeared. He waited till he had breath and desperately knocked again. At last there were footsteps within, and the synagogue door creaked open on its massive brass hinges.

A darkly dressed sexton, holding a dripping candle, glared at them.

"Who knocks this time of night with so much noise on the synagogue door?"

Mendel told the sexton his troubles. "Please, I would like to speak to the rabbi."

"The rabbi is an old man. He sleeps now. His wife won't let you see him. Go home and come back tomorrow."

"To tomorrow I said goodbye already. I am a dying man."

Though the sexton seemed doubtful he pointed to an old wooden house next door. "In there he lives." He disappeared into the synagogue with his lit candle casting shadows around him.

Mendel, with Isaac clutching his sleeve, went up the wooden steps and rang the bell. After five minutes a big-faced, gray-haired bulky woman came out on the porch with a torn robe thrown over her nightdress. She emphatically said the rabbi was sleeping and could not be waked.

But as she was insisting, the rabbi himself tottered to the door. He listened a minute and said, "Who wants to see me let them come in."

They entered a cluttered room. The rabbi was an old skinny man with bent shoulders and a wisp of white beard. He wore a flannel nightgown and black skullcap; his feet were bare.

"Vey is mir" [Woe is me], his wife muttered. "Put on shoes or tomorrow comes sure pneumonia." She was a woman with a big belly, years younger than her husband. Staring at Isaac, she turned away.

Mendel apologetically related his errand. "All I need more is thirty-five dollars."

"Thirty-five?" said the rabbi's wife. "Why not thirty-five thousand? Who has so much money? My husband is a poor rabbi. The doctors take away every penny."

"Dear friend," said the rabbi, "if I had I would give you."

"I got already seventy," Mendel said, heavy-hearted. "All I need more is thirty-five."

"God will give you," said the rabbi.

"In the grave," said Mendel. "I need tonight. Come, Isaac."

"Wait," called the rabbi.

He hurried inside, came out with a fur-lined caftan, and handed it to Mendel.

"Yascha," shrieked his wife, "not your new coat!"

"I got my old one. Who needs two coats for one body?"

"Yascha, I am screaming—"

"Who can go among poor people, tell me, in a new coat?"

"Yascha," she cried, "what can this man do with your coat? He needs tonight the money. The pawnbrokers are asleep."

"So let him wake them up."

"No." She grabbed the coat from Mendel.

He held on to a sleeve, wrestling her for the coat. Her I know, Mendel thought. "Shylock," he muttered. Her eyes glittered.

The rabbi groaned and tottered dizzily. His wife cried out as Mendel yanked the coat from her hands.

"Run," cried the rabbi.

"Run, Isaac."

They ran out of the house and down the steps.

"Stop, you thief," called the rabbi's wife.

The rabbi pressed both hands to his temples and fell to the floor.

"Help!" his wife wept. "Heart attack! Help!"

But Mendel and Isaac ran through the streets with the rabbi's new fur-lined caftan. After them noiselessly ran Ginzburg.

It was very late when Mendel bought the train ticket in the only booth open.

There was no time to stop for a sandwich so Isaac ate his peanuts and they hurried to the train in the vast deserted station.

"So in the morning," Mendel gasped as they ran, "there comes a man that he sells sandwiches and coffee. Eat but get change. When reaches California the train, will be waiting for you on the station Uncle Leo. If you don't recognize him he will recognize you. Tell him I send best regards."

But when they arrived at the gate to the platform it was shut, the light out.

Mendel, groaning, beat on the gate with his fists.

"Too late," said the uniformed ticket collector, a bulky, bearded man with hairy nostrils and a fishy smell.

He pointed to the station clock. "Already past twelve."

"But I see standing there still the train," Mendel said, hopping in his grief.

"It just left—in one more minute."

"A minute is enough. Just open the gate."

"Too late I told you."

Mendel socked his bony chest with both hands. "With my whole heart I beg you this little favor."

"Favors you had enough already. For you the train is gone. You shoulda been dead already at midnight. I told you that yesterday. This is the best I can do."

"Ginzburg!" Mendel shrank from him.

"Who else?" The voice was metallic, eyes glittered, the expression amused.

"For myself," the old man begged, "I don't ask a thing. But what will happen to my boy?"

Ginzburg shrugged slightly. "What will happen happens. This isn't my responsibility. I got enough to think about without worrying about somebody on one cylinder."

"What then is your responsibility?"

"To create conditions. To make happen what happens. I ain't in the anthropomorphic business."

"Whatever business you in, where is your pity?"

"This ain't my commodity. The law is the law."

"Which law is this?"

"The cosmic universal law, goddamit, the one I got to follow myself."

"What kind of a law is it?" cried Mendel. "For God's sake, don't you understand what I went through in my life with this poor boy? Look at him. For thirty-nine years, since the day he was born, I wait for him to grow up, but he don't. Do you understand what this means in a father's heart? Why don't you let him go to his uncle?" His voice had risen and he was shouting.

Isaac mewled loudly.

"Better calm down or you'll hurt somebody's feelings," Ginzburg said with a wink toward Isaac.

"All my life," Mendel cried, his body trembling, "what did I have? I was poor. I suffered from my health. When I worked I worked too hard. When I didn't work was worse. My wife died a young woman. But I didn't ask from anybody nothing. Now I ask a small favor. Be so kind, Mr. Ginzburg."

The ticket collector was picking his teeth with a match stick.

"You ain't the only one, my friend, some got it worse than you. That's how it goes in this country."

"You dog you." Mendel lunged at Ginzburg's throat and began to choke. "You bastard, don't you understand what it means human?"

They struggled nose to nose, Ginzburg, though his astonished eyes bulged, began to laugh. "You pipsqueak nothing. I'll freeze you to pieces."

His eyes lit in rage and Mendel felt an unbearable cold like an icy dagger invading his body, all of his parts shriveling.

Now I die without helping Isaac.

A crowd gathered. Isaac yelped in fright.

Clinging to Ginzburg in his last agony, Mendel saw reflected in the ticket collector's eyes the depth of his terror. But he saw that Ginzburg, staring at himself in Mendel's eyes, saw mirrored in them the extent of his own awful wrath. He beheld a shimmering, starry, blinding light that produced darkness.

Ginzburg looked astounded. "Who me?"

His grip on the squirming old man slowly loosened, and Mendel, his heart barely beating, slumped to the ground.

"Go." Ginzburg muttered, "take him to the train."

"Let pass," he commanded a guard.

The crowd parted. Isaac helped his father up and they tottered down the steps to the platform where the train waited, lit and ready to go.

Mendel found Isaac a coach seat and hastily embraced him. "Help Uncle Leo, Isaakil. Also remember your father and mother."

"Be nice to him," he said to the conductor. "Show him where everything is."

He waited on the platform until the train began slowly to move. Isaac sat at the edge of his seat, his face strained in the direction of his journey. When the train was gone, Mendel ascended the stairs to see what had become of Ginzburg.

QUESTIONS

1. Can this story be read as a religious drama? In this connection, consider the rabbi, the only person who helps Mendel. His compassion and his indifference to material things reveal him as a man of God. What does the supernatural Ginzburg represent? **2.** What is the significance of the fact that Isaac, for whom Mendel is determined to provide before death claims him, is an idiot? **3.** Mendel wins his battle with Ginzburg. What does that victory signify?

WRITING TOPIC

How do the various episodes in this story establish Mendel's character and prepare the reader for the final, climactic confrontation between Mendel and Ginzburg?

Patriotism*

1966

YUKIO MISHIMA [1925–1970]

In the twenty-eighth of February, 1936 (on the third day, that is, of the February Incident[1]), Lieutenant Shinji Takeyama of the Konoe Transport Battalion—profoundly disturbed by the knowledge that his closest colleagues had been with the mutineers from the beginning, and indignant at the imminent prospect of Imperial troops attacking Imperial troops—took his officer's sword and ceremonially disemboweled himself in the eight-mat room of his private residence in the sixth block of Aoba-chō, in Yotsuya Ward. His wife, Reiko, followed him, stabbing herself to death. The lieutenant's farewell note consisted of one sentence: "Long live the Imperial Forces." His wife's, after apologies for her unfilial conduct in thus preceding her parents to the grave, concluded: "The day which, for a soldier's wife, had to come, has come. . . ." The last moments of this heroic and dedicated couple were such as to make the gods themselves weep. The lieutenant's age, it should be noted, was thirty-one, his wife's twenty-three; and it was not half a year since the celebration of their marriage.

2

Those who saw the bride and bridegroom in the commemorative photograph—perhaps no less than those actually present at the lieutenant's wedding—had exclaimed in wonder at the bearing of this handsome couple. The lieutenant, majestic in military uniform, stood protectively beside his bride, his right hand resting upon his sword, his officer's cap held at his left side. His expression was severe, and his dark brows and wide-gazing eyes well conveyed the clear integrity of youth. For the beauty of the bride in her white over-robe no comparisons were adequate. In the eyes, round beneath soft brows, in the slender, finely shaped nose, and in the full lips, there was both sensuousness and refinement. One hand, emerging shyly from a sleeve of the over-robe, held a fan, and the tips of the fingers, clustering delicately, were like the bud of a moonflower.

After the suicide, people would take out this photograph and examine it, and sadly reflect that too often there was a curse on these seemingly flawless unions. Perhaps it was no more than imagination, but looking at the picture after the tragedy it almost seemed as if the two young people before the gold-lacquered screen were gazing, each with equal clarity, at the deaths which lay before them.

Thanks to the good offices of their go-between, Lieutenant General Ozeki, they had been able to set themselves up in a new home at Aoba-chō in Yotsuya.

---

* Translated by Geoffrey W. Sargeant.

[1] On February 26, 1936, a long period of political turmoil culminated in an attempted coup led by young officers. Units commanded by the rebels seized and held central Tokyo for a number of days, and numerous high-ranking government officials, including Lord Privy Seal Saitō, were assassinated. The mutiny was crushed by loyal troops, and the leaders were executed.

"New home" is perhaps misleading. It was an old three-room rented house backing onto a small garden. As neither the six- nor the four-and-a-half-mat room downstairs was favored by the sun, they used the upstairs eight-mat room as both bedroom and guest room. There was no maid, so Reiko was left alone to guard the house in her husband's absence.

The honeymoon trip was dispensed with on the grounds that these were times of national emergency. The two of them had spent the first night of their marriage at this house. Before going to bed, Shinji, sitting erect on the floor with his sword laid before him, had bestowed upon his wife a soldierly lecture. A woman who had become the wife of a soldier should know and resolutely accept that her husband's death might come at any moment. It could be to-morrow. It could be the day after. But, no matter when it came—he asked—was she steadfast in her resolve to accept it? Reiko rose to her feet, pulled open a drawer of the cabinet, and took out what was the most prized of her new possessions, the dagger her mother had given her. Returning to her place, she laid the dagger without a word on the mat before her, just as her husband had laid his sword. A silent understanding was achieved at once and the lieutenant never again sought to test his wife's resolve.

In the first few months of her marriage Reiko's beauty grew daily more radiant, shining serene like the moon after rain.

As both were possessed of young, vigorous bodies, their relationship was passionate. Nor was this merely a matter of the night. On more than one occasion, returning home straight from maneuvers, and begrudging even the time it took to remove his mud-splashed uniform, the lieutenant had pushed his wife to the floor almost as soon as he had entered the house. Reiko was equally ardent in her response. For a little more or a little less than a month, from the first night of their marriage Reiko knew happiness, and the lieutenant, seeing this, was happy too.

Reiko's body was white and pure, and her swelling breasts conveyed a firm and chaste refusal; but, upon consent, those breasts were lavish with their in-timate, welcoming warmth. Even in bed these two were frighteningly and awe-somely serious. In the very midst of wild, intoxicating passions, their hearts were sober and serious.

By day the lieutenant would think of his wife in the brief rest periods between training; and all day long, at home, Reiko would recall the image of her hus-band. Even when apart, however, they had only to look at the wedding pho-tograph for their happiness to be once more confirmed. Reiko felt not the slightest surprise that a man who had been a complete stranger until a few months ago should now have become the sun about which her whole world revolved.

All these things had a moral basis, and were in accordance with the Education Rescript's[2] injunction that "husband and wife should be harmonious." Not once

---

[2] The Education Rescript was a code promulgated during the Meiji, the reign of Emperor Mutsuhito which lasted from 1867 to 1912. The period is regarded as an historic era in the development of Modern Japan.

did Reiko contradict her husband, nor did the lieutenant ever find reason to scold his wife. On the god shelf below the stairway, alongside the tablet from the Great Ise Shrine,[3] were set photographs of their Imperial Majesties, and regularly every morning, before leaving for duty, the lieutenant would stand with his wife at this hallowed place and together they would bow their heads low. The offering water was renewed each morning, and the sacred sprig of *sasaki* was always green and fresh. Their lives were lived beneath the solemn protection of the gods and were filled with an intense happiness which set every fiber in their bodies trembling.

3

Although Lord Privy Seal Saitō's house was in their neighborhood, neither of them heard any noise of gunfire on the morning of February 26. It was a bugle, sounding muster in the dim, snowy dawn, when the ten-minute tragedy had already ended, which first disrupted the lieutenant's slumbers. Leaping at once from his bed, and without speaking a word, the lieutenant donned his uniform, buckled on the sword held ready for him by his wife, and hurried swiftly out into the snow-covered streets of the still darkened morning. He did not return until the evening of the twenty-eighth.

Later, from the radio news, Reiko learned the full extent of this sudden eruption of violence. Her life throughout the subsequent two days was lived alone, in complete tranquility, and behind locked doors.

In the lieutenant's face, as he hurried silently out into the snowy morning, Reiko had read the determination to die. If her husband did not return, her own decision was made: she too would die. Quietly she attended to the disposition of her personal possessions. She chose her sets of visiting kimonos as keepsakes for friends of her schooldays, and she wrote a name and address on the stiff paper wrapping in which each was folded. Constantly admonished by her husband never to think of the morrow, Reiko had not even kept a diary and was now denied the pleasure of assiduously rereading her record of the happiness of the past few months and consigning each page to the fire as she did so. Ranged across the top of the radio were a small china dog, a rabbit, a squirrel, a bear, and a fox. There were also a small vase and a water pitcher. These comprised Reiko's one and only collection. But it would hardly do, she imagined. to give such things as keepsakes. Nor again would it be quite proper to ask specifically for them to be included in the coffin. It seemed to Reiko, as these thoughts passed through her mind, that the expressions on the small animals' faces grew even more lost and forlorn.

Reiko took the squirrel in her hand and looked at it. And then, her thoughts turning to a realm far beyond these childlike affections, she gazed up into the distance at the great sunlike principle which her husband embodied. She was ready, and happy, to be hurtled along to her destruction in that gleaming sun

---

[3] The Great Ise Shrine is the highest ranking shrine in Japan. The emperor's ancestors were buried there.

chariot—but now, for these few moments of solitude, she allowed herself to luxuriate in this innocent attachment to trifles. The time when she had genuinely loved these things, however, was long past. Now she merely loved the memory of having once loved them, and their place in her heart had been filled by more intense passions, by a more frenzied happiness. . . . For Reiko had never, even to herself, thought of those soaring joys of the flesh as a mere pleasure. The February cold, and the icy touch of the china squirrel, had numbed Reiko's slender fingers; yet, even so, in her lower limbs, beneath the ordered repetition of the pattern which crossed the skirt of her trim *meisen* kimono, she could feel now, as she thought of the lieutenant's powerful arms reaching out toward her, a hot moistness of the flesh which defied the snows.

She was not in the least afraid of the death hovering in her mind. Waiting alone at home, Reiko firmly believed that everything her husband was feeling or thinking now, his anguish and distress, was leading her—just as surely as the power in his flesh—to a welcome death. She felt as if her body could melt away with ease and be transformed to the merest fraction of her husband's thought.

Listening to the frequent announcements on the radio, she heard the names of several of her husband's colleagues mentioned among those of the insurgents. This was news of death. She followed the developments closely, wondering anxiously, as the situation became daily more irrevocable, why no Imperial ordinance was sent down, and watching what had at first been taken as a movement to restore the nation's honor come gradually to be branded with the infamous name of mutiny. There was no communication from the regiment. At any moment, it seemed, fighting might commence in the city streets where the remains of the snow still lay.

Toward sundown on the twenty-eighth Reiko was startled by a furious pounding on the front door. She hurried downstairs. As she pulled with fumbling fingers at the bolt, the shape dimly outlined beyond the frosted-glass panel made no sound, but she knew it was her husband. Reiko had never known the bolt on the sliding door to be so stiff. Still it resisted. The door just would not open.

In a moment, almost before she knew she had succeeded, the lieutenant was standing before her on the cement floor inside the porch, muffled in a khaki greatcoat, his top boots heavy with slush from the street. Closing the door behind him, he returned the bolt once more to its socket. With what significance, Reiko did not understand.

"Welcome home."

Reiko bowed deeply, but her husband made no response. As he had already unfastened his sword and was about to remove his greatcoat, Reiko moved around behind to assist. The coat, which was cold and damp and had lost the odor of horse dung it normally exuded when exposed to the sun, weighed heavily upon her arm. Draping it across a hanger, and cradling the sword and leather belt in her sleeves, she waited while her husband removed his top boots and then followed behind him into the "living room." This was the six-mat room downstairs.

Seen in the clear light from the lamp, her husband's face, covered with a heavy growth of bristle, was almost unrecognizably wasted and thin. The cheeks were hollow, their luster and resilience gone. In his normal good spirits he would have changed into old clothes as soon as he was home and have pressed her to get supper at once, but now he sat before the table still in his uniform, his head dropping dejectedly. Reiko refrained from asking whether she should prepare the supper.

After an interval the lieutenant spoke.

"I knew nothing. They hadn't asked me to join. Perhaps out of consideration, because I was newly married. Kano, and Homma too, and Yamaguchi."

Reiko recalled momentarily the faces of high-spirited young officers, friends of her husband, who had come to the house occasionally as guests.

"There may be an Imperial ordinance sent down tomorrow. They'll be posted as rebels, I imagine. I shall be in command of a unit with orders to attack them. . . . I can't do it. It's impossible to do a thing like that."

He spoke again.

"They've taken me off guard duty, and I have permission to return home for one night. Tomorrow morning, without question, I must leave to join the attack. I can't do it, Reiko."

Reiko sat erect with lowered eyes. She understood clearly that her husband had spoken of his death. The lieutenant was resolved. Each word, being rooted in death, emerged sharply and with powerful significance against this dark, unmovable background. Although the lieutenant was speaking of his dilemma, already there was no room in his mind for vacillation.

However, there was a clarity, like the clarity of a stream fed from melting snows, in the silence which rested between them. Sitting in his own home after the long two-day ordeal, and looking across at the face of his beautiful wife, the lieutenant was for the first time experiencing true peace of mind. For he had at once known, though she said nothing, that his wife divined the resolve which lay beneath his words.

"Well, then . . ." The lieutenant's eyes opened wide. Despite his exhaustion they were strong and clear, and now for the first time they looked straight into the eyes of his wife. "Tonight I shall cut my stomach."

Reiko did not flinch.

Her round eyes showed tension, as taut as the clang of a bell.

"I am ready," she said. "I ask permission to accompany you."

The lieutenant felt almost mesmerized by the strength in those eyes. His words flowed swiftly and easily, like the utterances of a man in delirium, and it was beyond his understanding how permission in a matter of such weight could be expressed so casually.

"Good. We'll go together. But I want you as a witness, first, for my own suicide. Agreed?"

When this was said a sudden release of abundant happiness welled up in both their hearts. Reiko was deeply affected by the greatness of her husband's trust in her. It was vital for the lieutenant, whatever else might happen, that there should be no irregularity in his death. For that reason there had to be a witness.

The fact that he had chosen his wife for this was the first mark of his trust. The second, and even greater mark, was that though he had pledged that they should die together he did not intend to kill his wife first—he had deferred her death to a time when he would no longer be there to verify it. If the lieutenant had been a suspicious husband, he would doubtless, as in the usual suicide pact, have chosen to kill his wife first.

When Reiko said, "I ask permission to accompany you," the lieutenant felt these words to be the final fruit of the education which he had himself given his wife, starting on the first night of their marriage, and which had schooled her, when the moment came, to say what had to be said without a shadow of hesitation. This flattered the lieutenant's opinion of himself as a self-reliant man. He was not so romantic or conceited as to imagine that the words were spoken spontaneously, out of love for her husband.

With happiness welling almost too abundantly in their hearts, they could not help smiling at each other. Reiko felt as if she had returned to her wedding night.

Before her eyes was neither pain nor death. She seemed to see only a free and limitless expanse opening out into vast distances.

"The water is hot. Will you take your bath now?"

"Ah yes, of course."

"And supper . . .?"

The words were delivered in such level, domestic tones that the lieutenant came near to thinking, for the fraction of a second, that everything had been a hallucination.

"I don't think we'll need supper. But perhaps you could warm some sake?"

"As you wish."

As Reiko rose and took a *tanzen* gown from the cabinet for after the bath, she purposely directed her husband's attention to the opened drawer. The lieutenant rose, crossed to the cabinet, and looked inside. From the ordered array of paper wrappings he read, one by one, the addresses of the keepsakes. There was no grief in the lieutenant's response to this demonstration of heroic resolve. His heart was filled with tenderness. Like a husband who is proudly shown the childish purchases of a young wife, the lieutenant, overwhelmed by affection, lovingly embraced his wife from behind and implanted a kiss upon her neck.

Reiko felt the roughness of the lieutenant's unshaven skin against her neck. This sensation, more than being just a thing of this world, was for Reiko almost the world itself, but now—with the feeling that it was soon to be lost forever—it had freshness beyond all her experience. Each moment had its own vital strength, and the senses in every corner of her body were reawakened. Accepting her husband's caresses from behind, Reiko raised herself on the tips of her toes, letting the vitality seep through her entire body.

"First the bath, and then, after some sake . . . lay out the bedding upstairs, will you?"

The lieutenant whispered the words into his wife's ear. Reiko silently nodded.

Flinging off his uniform, the lieutenant went to the bath. To faint background noises of slopping water Reiko tended the charcoal brazier in the living room and began the preparations for warming the sake.

Taking the *tanzen*, a sash, and some underclothes, she went to the bathroom to ask how the water was. In the midst of a coiling cloud of steam the lieutenant was sitting cross-legged on the floor, shaving, and she could dimly discern the rippling movements of the muscles on his damp, powerful back as they responded to the movement of his arms.

There was nothing to suggest a time of any special significance. Reiko, going busily about her tasks, was preparing side dishes from odds and ends in stock. Her hands did not tremble. If anything, she managed even more efficiently and smoothly than usual. From time to time, it is true, there was a strange throbbing deep within her breast. Like distant lightning, it had a moment of sharp intensity and then vanished without trace. Apart from that, nothing was in any way out of the ordinary.

The lieutenant, shaving in the bathroom, felt his warmed body miraculously healed at last of the desperate tiredness of the days of indecision and filled—in spite of the death which lay ahead—with pleasurable anticipation. The sound of his wife going about her work came to him faintly. A healthy physical craving, submerged for two days, reasserted itself.

The lieutenant was confident there had been no impurity in that joy they had experienced when resolving upon death. They had both sensed at that moment—though not, of course, in any clear and conscious way—that those permissible pleasures which they shared in private were once more beneath the protection of Righteousness and Divine Power, and of a complete and unassailable morality. On looking into each other's eyes and discovering there an honorable death, they had felt themselves safe once more behind steel walls which none could destroy, encased in an impenetrable armor of Beauty and Truth. Thus, so far from seeing any inconsistency or conflict between the urges of his flesh and the sincerity of his patriotism, the lieutenant was even able to regard the two as parts of the same thing.

Thrusting his face close to the dark, cracked, misted wall mirror, the lieutenant shaved himself with great care. This would be his death face. There must be no unsightly blemishes. The clean-shaven face gleamed once more with a youthful luster, seeming to brighten the darkness of the mirror. There was a certain elegance, he even felt, in the association of death with this radiantly healthy face.

Just as it looked now, this would become his death face! Already, in fact, it had half departed from the lieutenant's personal possession and had become the bust above a dead soldier's memorial. As an experiment he closed his eyes tight. Everything was wrapped in blackness, and he was no longer a living, seeing creature.

Returning from the bath, the traces of the shave glowing faintly blue beneath his smooth cheeks, he seated himself beside the now well-kindled charcoal brazier. Busy though Reiko was, he noticed, she had found time lightly to touch up her face. Her cheeks were gay and her lips moist. There was no shadow of sadness to be seen. Truly, the lieutenant felt, as he saw this mark of his young wife's passionate nature, he had chosen the wife he ought to have chosen.

As soon as the lieutenant had drained his sake cup he offered it to Reiko. Reiko had never before tasted sake, but she accepted without hesitation and sipped timidly.

"Come here," the lieutenant said.

Reiko moved to her husband's side and was embraced as she leaned backward across his lap. Her breast was in violent commotion, as if sadness, joy, and the potent sake were mingling and reacting within her. The lieutenant looked down into his wife's face. It was the last face he would see in this world, the last face he would see of his wife. The lieutenant scrutinized the face minutely, with the eyes of a traveler bidding farewell to splendid vistas which he will never revisit. It was a face he could not tire of looking at—the features regular yet not cold, the lips lightly closed with a soft strength. The lieutenant kissed those lips, unthinkingly. And suddenly, though there was not the slightest distortion of the face into the unsightliness of sobbing, he noticed that tears were welling slowly from beneath the long lashes of the closed eyes and brimming over into a glistening stream.

When, a little later, the lieutenant urged that they should move to the upstairs bedroom, his wife replied that she would follow after taking a bath. Climbing the stairs alone to the bedroom, where the air was already warmed by the gas heater, the lieutenant lay down on the bedding with arms outstretched and legs apart. Even the time at which he lay waiting for his wife to join him was no later and no earlier than usual.

He folded his hands beneath his head and gazed at the dark boards of the ceiling in the dimness beyond the range of the standard lamp. Was it death he was now waiting for? Or a wild ecstasy of the senses? The two seemed to overlap, almost as if the object of this bodily desire was death itself. But, however that might be, it was certain that never before had the lieutenant tasted such total freedom.

There was the sound of a car outside the window. He could hear the screech of its tires skidding in the snow piled at the side of the street. The sound of its horn re-echoed from near-by walls. . . . Listening to these noises he had the feeling that this house rose like a solitary island in the ocean of a society going as restlessly about its business as ever. All around, vastly and untidily, stretched the country for which he grieved. He was to give his life for it. But would that great country, with which he was prepared to remonstrate to the extent of destroying himself, take the slightest heed of his death? He did not know; and it did not matter. His was a battlefield without glory, a battlefield where none could display deeds of valor: it was the front line of the spirit.

Reiko's footsteps sounded on the stairway. The steep stairs in this old house creaked badly. There were fond memories in that creaking, and many a time, while waiting in bed, the lieutenant had listened to its welcome sound. At the thought that he would hear it no more he listened with intense concentration, striving for every corner of every moment of this precious time to be filled with the sound of those soft footfalls on the creaking stairway. The moments seemed transformed to jewels, sparkling with inner light.

Reiko wore a Nagoya sash about the waist of her *yukata*, but as the lieutenant reached toward it, its redness sobered by the dimness of the light, Reiko's hand moved to his assistance and the sash fell away, slithering swiftly to the floor. As she stood before him, still in her *yukata*, the lieutenant inserted his hands through the side slits beneath each sleeve, intending to embrace her as she was; but at the touch of his finger tips upon the warm naked flesh, and as the armpits closed gently about his hands, his whole body was suddenly aflame.

In a few moments the two lay naked before the glowing gas heater.

Neither spoke the thought, but their hearts, their bodies, and their pounding breasts blazed with the knowledge that this was the very last time. It was as if the words "The Last Time" were spelled out, in invisible brushstrokes, across every inch of their bodies.

The lieutenant drew his wife close and kissed her vehemently. As their tongues explored each other's mouths, reaching out into the smooth, moist interior, they felt as if the still unknown agonies of death had tempered their senses to the keenness of red-hot steel. The agonies they could not yet feel, the distant pains of death, had refined their awareness of pleasure.

"This is the last time I shall see your body," said the lieutenant. "Let me look at it closely." And, tilting the shade on the lampstand to one side, he directed the rays along the full length of Reiko's outstretched form.

Reiko lay still with her eyes closed. The light from the low lamp clearly revealed the majestic sweep of her white flesh. The lieutenant, not without a touch of egocentricity, rejoiced that he would never see this beauty crumble in death.

At his leisure, the lieutenant allowed the unforgettable spectacle to engrave itself upon his mind. With one hand he fondled the hair, with the other he softly stroked the magnificent face, implanting kisses here and there where his eyes lingered. The quiet coldness of the high, tapering forehead, the closed eyes with their long lashes beneath faintly etched brows, the set of the finely shaped nose, the gleam of teeth glimpsed between full, regular lips, the soft cheeks and the small, wise chin . . . these things conjured up in the lieutenant's mind the vision of a truly radiant death face, and again and again he pressed his lips tight against the white throat—where Reiko's own hand was soon to strike—and the throat reddened faintly beneath his kisses. Returning to the mouth he laid his lips against it with the gentlest of pressures, and moved them rhythmically over Reiko's with the light rolling motion of a small boat. If he closed his eyes, the world became a rocking cradle.

Wherever the lieutenant's eyes moved his lips faithfully followed. The high, swelling breasts, surmounted by nipples like the buds of a wild cherry, hardened as the lieutenant's lips closed about them. The arms flowed smoothly downward from each side of the breast, tapering toward the wrists, yet losing nothing of their roundness or symmetry, and at their tips were those delicate fingers which had held the fan at the wedding ceremony. One by one, as the lieutenant kissed them, the fingers withdrew behind their neighbor as if in shame. . . . The natural hollow curving between the bosom and the stomach carried in its lines a suggestion not only of softness but of resilient strength, and while it gave forewarning of the rich curves spreading outward from here to the hips it had, in itself, an appearance only of restraint and proper discipline. The whiteness and richness of the stomach and hips was like milk brimming in a great bowl, and the sharply shadowed dip of the navel could have been the fresh impress of a raindrop, fallen there that very moment. Where the shadows gathered more thickly, hair clustered, gentle and sensitive, and as the agitation mounted in the now no longer passive body there hung over this region a scent like the smoldering of fragrant blossoms, growing steadily more pervasive.

At length, in a tremulous voice, Reiko spoke.

"Show me. . . . Let me look too, for the last time."

Never before had he heard from his wife's lips so strong and unequivocal a request. It was as if something which her modesty had wished to keep hidden to the end had suddenly burst its bonds of constraint. The lieutenant obediently lay back and surrendered himself to his wife. Lithely she raised her white, trembling body, and—burning with an innocent desire to return to her husband what he had done for her—placed two white fingers on the lieutenant's eyes, which gazed fixedly up at her, and gently stroked them shut.

Suddenly overwhelmed by tenderness, her cheeks flushed by a dizzying uprush of emotion, Reiko threw her arms about the lieutenant's close-cropped head. The bristly hairs rubbed painfully against her breast, the prominent nose was cold as it dug into her flesh, and his breath was hot. Relaxing her embrace, she gazed down at her husband's masculine face. The severe brows, the closed eyes, the splendid bridge of the nose, the shapely lips drawn firmly together . . . the blue, cleanshaven cheeks reflecting the light and gleaming smoothly. Reiko kissed each of these. She kissed the broad nape of the neck, the strong, erect shoulders, the powerful chest with its twin circles like shields and its russet nipples. In the armpits, deeply shadowed by the ample flesh of the shoulders and chest, a sweet and melancholy odor emanated from the growth of hair, and in the sweetness of this odor was contained, somehow, the essence of young death. The lieutenant's naked skin glowed like a field of barley, and everywhere the muscles showed in sharp relief, converging on the lower abdomen about the small, unassuming navel. Gazing at the youthful, firm stomach, modestly covered by a vigorous growth of hair, Reiko thought of it as it was soon to be, cruelly cut by the sword, and she laid her head upon it, sobbing in pity, and bathed it with kisses.

At the touch of his wife's tears upon his stomach the lieutenant felt ready to endure with courage the cruelest agonies of his suicide.

What ecstasies they experienced after these tender exchanges may well be imagined. The lieutenant raised himself and enfolded his wife in a powerful embrace, her body now limp with exhaustion after her grief and tears. Passionately they held their faces close, rubbing cheek against cheek. Reiko's body was trembling. Their breasts, moist with sweat, were tightly joined, and every inch of the young and beautiful bodies had become so much one with the other that it seemed impossible there should ever again be a separation. Reiko cried out. From the heights they plunged into the abyss, and from the abyss they took wing and soared once more to dizzying heights. The lieutenant panted like the regimental standard-bearer on a route march. . . . As one cycle ended, almost immediately a new wave of passion would be generated, and together—with no trace of fatigue—they would climb again in a single breathless movement to the very summit.

4

When the lieutenant at last turned away, it was not from weariness. For one thing, he was anxious not to undermine the considerable strength he would need in carrying out his suicide. For another, he would have been sorry to mar the sweetness of these last memories by overindulgence.

Since the lieutenant had clearly desisted, Reiko too, with her usual compliance, followed his example. The two lay naked on their backs, with fingers interlaced, staring fixedly at the dark ceiling. The room was warm from the heater, and even when the sweat had ceased to pour from their bodies they felt no cold. Outside, in the hushed night, the sounds of passing traffic had ceased. Even the noises of the trains and streetcars around Yotsuya station did not penetrate this far. After echoing through the region bounded by the moat, they were lost in the heavily wooded park fronting the broad driveway before Akasaka Palace. It was hard to believe in the tension gripping this whole quarter, where the two factions of the bitterly divided Imperial Army now confronted each other, poised for battle.

Savoring the warmth glowing within themselves, they lay still and recalled the ecstasies they had just known. Each moment of the experience was relived. They remembered the taste of kisses which had never wearied, the touch of naked flesh, episode after episode of dizzying bliss. But already, from the dark boards of the ceiling, the face of death was peering down. These joys had been final, and their bodies would never know them again. Not that joy of this intensity—and the same thought had occurred to them both—was ever likely to be reexperienced, even if they should live on to old age.

The feel of their fingers intertwined—this too would soon be lost. Even the wood-grain patterns they now gazed at on the dark ceiling boards would be taken from them. They could feel death edging in, nearer and nearer. There could be no hesitation now. They must have the courage to reach out to death themselves, and to seize it.

"Well, let's make our preparations," said the lieutenant. The note of determination in the words was unmistakable, but at the same time Reiko had never heard her husband's voice so warm and tender.

After they had risen, a variety of tasks awaited them.

The lieutenant, who had never once before helped with the bedding, now cheerfully slid back the door of the closet, lifted the mattress across the room by himself, and stowed it away inside.

Reiko turned off the gas heater and put away the lamp standard. During the lieutenant's absence she had arranged this room carefully, sweeping and dusting it to a fresh cleanness, and now—if one overlooked the rosewood table drawn into one corner—the eight-mat room gave all the appearance of a reception room ready to welcome an important guest.

"We've seen some drinking here, haven't we? With Kanō and Homma and Noguchi. . . ."

"Yes, they were great drinkers, all of them."

"We'll be meeting them before long, in the other world. They'll tease us, I imagine, when they find I've brought you with me."

Descending the stairs, the lieutenant turned to look back into this calm clean room, now brightly illuminated by the ceiling lamp. There floated across his mind the faces of the young officers who had drunk there, and laughed, and innocently bragged. He had never dreamed then that he would one day cut open his stomach in this room.

In the two rooms downstairs husband and wife busied themselves smoothly and serenely with their respective preparations. The lieutenant went to the toilet, and then to the bathroom to wash. Meanwhile Reiko folded away her husband's padded robe, placed his uniform tunic, his trousers, and a newly cut bleached loincloth in the bathroom, and set out sheets of paper on the living-room table for the farewell notes. Then she removed the lid from the writing box and began rubbing ink from the ink tablet. She had already decided upon the wording of her own note.

Reiko's fingers pressed hard upon the cold gilt letters of the ink tablet, and the water in the shallow well at once darkened, as if a black cloud had spread across it. She stopped thinking that this repeated action, this pressure from her fingers, this rise and fall of faint sound, was all and solely for death. It was a routine domestic task, a simple paring away of time until death should finally stand before her. But somehow, in the increasingly smooth motion of the tablet rubbing on the stone, and in the scent from the thickening ink, there was unspeakable darkness.

Neat in his uniform, which he now wore next to his skin, the lieutenant emerged from the bathroom. Without a word he seated himself at the table, bolt upright, took a brush in his hand, and stared undecidedly at the paper before him.

Reiko took a white silk kimono with her and entered the bathroom. When she reappeared in the living room, clad in the white kimono and with her face lightly made up, the farewell note lay completed on the table beneath the lamp. The thick black brushstrokes said simply:

"Long Live the Imperial Forces—Army Lieutenant Takeyama Shinji."

While Reiko sat opposite him writing her own note, the lieutenant gazed in silence, intensely serious, at the controlled movement of his wife's pale fingers as they manipulated the brush.

With their respective notes in their hands—the lieutenant's sword strapped to his side, Reiko's small dagger thrust into the sash of her white kimono—the two of them stood before the god shelf and silently prayed. Then they put out all the downstairs lights. As he mounted the stairs the lieutenant turned his head and gazed back at the striking, white-clad figure of his wife, climbing behind him, with lowered eyes, from the darkness beneath.

The farewell notes were laid side by side in the alcove of the upstairs room. They wondered whether they ought not to remove the hanging scroll, but since it had been written by their go-between, Lieutenant General Ozeki, and consisted, moreover, of two Chinese characters signifying "Sincerity," they left it where it was. Even if it were to become stained with splashes of blood, they felt that the lieutenant general would understand.

The lieutenant sitting erect with his back to the alcove, laid his sword on the floor before him.

Reiko sat facing him, a mat's width away. With the rest of her so severely white the touch of rouge on her lips seemed remarkably seductive.

Across the dividing mat they gazed intently into each other's eyes. The lieutenant's sword lay before his knees. Seeing it, Reiko recalled their first night and was overwhelmed with sadness. The lieutenant spoke, in a hoarse voice:

"As I have no second to help me I shall cut deep. It may look unpleasant, but please do not panic. Death of any sort is a fearful thing to watch. You must not be discouraged by what you see. Is that all right?"

"Yes."

Reiko nodded deeply.

Looking at the slender white figure of his wife the lieutenant experienced a bizarre excitement. What he was about to perform was an act in his public capacity as a soldier, something he had never previously shown his wife. It called for a resolution equal to the courage to enter battle; it was a death of no less degree and quality than death in the front line. It was his conduct on the battlefield that he was now to display.

Momentarily the thought led the lieutenant to a strange fantasy. A lonely death on the battlefield, a death beneath the eyes of his beautiful wife . . . in the sensation that he was now to die in these two dimensions, realizing an impossible union of them both, there was sweetness beyond words. This must be the very pinnacle of good fortune, he thought. To have every moment of his death observed by those beautiful eyes—it was like being borne to death on a gentle, fragrant breeze. There was some special favor here. He did not understand precisely what it was, but it was a domain unknown to others: a dispensation granted to no one else had been permitted to himself. In the radiant, bridelike figure of his white-robed wife the lieutenant seemed to see a vision of all those things he had loved and for which he was to lay down his life—the Imperial Household, the Nation, the Army Flag. All these, no less than the wife who sat before him, were presences observing him closely with clear and never-faltering eyes.

Reiko too was gazing intently at her husband, so soon to die, and she thought that never in this world had she seen anything so beautiful. The lieutenant always looked well in uniform, but now, as he contemplated death with severe brows and firmly closed lips, he revealed what was perhaps masculine beauty as its most superb.

"It's time to go," the lieutenant said at last.

Reiko bent her body low to the mat in a deep bow. She could not raise her face. She did not wish to spoil her make-up with tears, but the tears could not be held back.

When at length she looked up she saw hazily through the tears that her husband had wound a white bandage around the blade of his now unsheathed sword, leaving five or six inches of naked steel showing at the point.

Resting the sword in its cloth wrapping on the mat before him, the lieutenant rose from his knees, resettled himself cross-legged, and unfastened the hooks of his uniform collar. His eyes no longer saw his wife. Slowly, one by one, he undid the flat brass buttons. The dusky brown chest was revealed, and then the stomach. He unclasped his belt and undid the buttons of his trousers. The pure whiteness of the thickly coiled loincloth showed itself. The lieutenant pushed the cloth down with both hands, further to ease his stomach, and then reached for the white-bandaged blade of his sword. With his left hand he massaged his abdomen, glancing downward as he did so.

To reassure himself on the sharpness of his sword's cutting edge the lieutenant folded back the left trouser flap, exposing a little of his thigh, and lightly drew the blade across the skin. Blood welled up in the wound at once, and several streaks of red trickled downward, glistening in the strong light.

It was the first time Reiko had ever seen her husband's blood, and she felt a violent throbbing in her chest. She looked at her husband's face. The lieutenant was looking at the blood with calm appraisal. For a moment—though thinking at the same time that it was hollow comfort—Reiko experienced a sense of relief.

The lieutenant's eyes fixed his wife with an intense, hawk-like stare. Moving the sword around to his front, he raised himself slightly on his hips and let the upper half of his body lean over the sword point. That he was mustering his whole strength was apparent from the angry tension of the uniform at his shoulders. The lieutenant aimed to strike deep into the left of his stomach. His sharp cry pierced the silence of the room.

Despite the effort he had himself put into the blow, the lieutenant had the impression that someone else had struck the side of his stomach agonizingly with a thick rod of iron. For a second or so his head reeled and he had no idea what had happened. The five or six inches of naked point had vanished completely into his flesh, and the white bandage, gripped in his clenched fist, pressed directly against his stomach.

He returned to consciousness. The blade had certainly pierced the wall of the stomach, he thought. His breathing was difficult, his chest thumped violently, and in some far deep region, which he could hardly believe was a part of himself, a fearful and excruciating pain came welling up as if the ground had split open to disgorge a boiling stream of molten rock. The pain came suddenly nearer, with terrifying speed. The lieutenant bit his lower lip and stifled an instinctive moan.

Was this *seppuku?*—he was thinking. It was a sensation of utter chaos, as if the sky had fallen on his head and the world was reeling drunkenly. His will power and courage, which had seemed so robust before he made the incision, had now dwindled to something like a single hairlike thread of steel, and he was assailed by the uneasy feeling that he must advance along this thread, clinging to it with desperation. His clenched fist had grown moist. Looking down, he saw that both his hand and the cloth were drenched in blood. His loincloth too was dyed a deep red. It struck him as incredible that, amidst this terrible agony, things which could be seen could still be seen, and existing things existed still.

The moment the lieutenant thrust the sword into his left side and she saw the deathly pallor fall across his face, like an abruptly lowered curtain, Reiko had to struggle to prevent herself from rushing to his side. Whatever happened, she must watch. She must be a witness. That was the duty her husband had lain upon her. Opposite her, a mat's space away, she could clearly see her husband biting his lip to stifle the pain. The pain was there, with absolute certainty, before her eyes. And Reiko had no means of rescuing him from it.

The sweat glistened on her husband's forehead. The lieutenant closed his eyes, and then opened them again, as if experimenting. The eyes had lost their luster, and seemed innocent and empty like the eyes of a small animal.

The agony before Reiko's eyes burned as strong as the summer sun, utterly remote from the grief which seemed to be tearing herself apart within. The pain grew steadily in stature, stretching upward. Reiko felt that her husband had already become a man in a separate world, a man whose whole being had been resolved into pain, a prisoner in a cage of pain where no hand could reach out to him. But Reiko felt no pain at all. Her grief was not pain. As she thought about this, Reiko began to feel as if someone had raised a cruel wall of glass high between herself and her husband.

Ever since her marriage her husband's existence had been her own existence, and every breath of his had been a breath drawn by herself. But now, while her husband's existence in pain was a vivid reality, Reiko could find in this grief of hers no certain proof at all of her own existence.

With only his right hand on the sword the lieutenant began to cut sideways across his stomach. But as the blade became entangled with the entrails it was pushed constantly outward by their soft resilience; and the lieutenant realized that it would be necessary, as he cut, to use both hands to keep the point pressed deep into his stomach. He pulled the blade across. It did not cut as easily as he had expected. He directed the strength of his whole body into his right hand and pulled again. There was a cut of three or four inches.

The pain spread slowly outward from the inner depths until the whole stomach reverberated. It was like the wild clanging of a bell. Or like a thousand bells which jangled simultaneously at every breath he breathed and every throb of his pulse, rocking his whole being. The lieutenant could no longer stop himself from moaning. But by now the blade had cut its way through to below the navel, and when he noticed this he felt a sense of satisfaction, and a renewal of courage.

The volume of blood had steadily increased, and now it spurted from the wound as if propelled by the beat of the pulse. The mat before the lieutenant was drenched red with splattered blood, and more blood overflowed onto it from pools which gathered in folds of the lieutenant's khaki trousers. A spot, like a bird, came flying across to Reiko and settled on the lap of her white silk kimono.

By the time the lieutenant had at last drawn the sword across to the right side of his stomach, the blade was already cutting shallow and had revealed its naked tip, slippery with blood and grease. But, suddenly stricken by a fit of vomiting, the lieutenant cried out hoarsely. The vomiting made the fierce pain fiercer still, and the stomach, which had thus far remained firm and compact, now abruptly heaved, opening wide its wound, and the entrails burst through, as if the wound too were vomiting. Seemingly ignorant of their master's suffering, the entrails gave an impression of robust health and almost disagreeable vitality as they slipped smoothly out and spilled over into the crotch. The lieutenant's head dropped, his shoulders heaved, his eyes opened to narrow slits, and a thin trickle of saliva dribbled from his mouth. The gold markings on his epaulettes caught the light and glinted.

Blood was scattered everywhere. The lieutenant was soaked in it to his knees, and he sat now in a crumpled and listless posture, one hand on the floor. A raw smell filled the room. The lieutenant, his head drooping, retched repeatedly, and the movement showed vividly in his shoulders. The blade of the sword, now pushed back by the entrails and exposed to its tip, was still in the lieutenant's right hand.

It would be difficult to imagine a more heroic sight than that of the lieutenant at this moment, as he mustered his strength and flung back his head. The movement was performed with sudden violence, and the back of his head struck with a sharp crack against the alcove pillar. Reiko had been sitting until now with her face lowered, gazing in fascination at the tide of blood advancing toward her knees, but the sound took her by surprise and she looked up.

The lieutenant's face was not the face of a living man. The eyes were hollow, the skin parched, the once so lustrous cheeks and lips the color of dried mud. The right hand alone was moving. Laboriously gripping the sword, it hovered shakily in the air like the hand of a marionette and strove to direct the point at the base of the lieutenant's throat. Reiko watched her husband make this last, most heart-rending, futile exertion. Glistening with blood and grease, the point was thrust at the throat again and again. And each time it missed its aim. The strength to guide it was no longer there. The straying point struck the collar and the collar badges. Although its hooks had been unfastened, the stiff military collar had closed together again and was protecting the throat.

Reiko could bear the sight no longer. She tried to go to her husband's help, but she could not stand. She moved through the blood on her knees, and her white skirts grew deep red. Moving to the rear of her husband, she helped no more than by loosening the collar. The quivering blade at last contacted the naked flesh of the throat. At that moment Reiko's impression was that she herself had propelled her husband forward; but that was not the case. It was a movement planned by the lieutenant himself, his last exertion of strength. Abruptly he threw his body at the blade, and the blade pierced his neck, emerging at the nape. There was a tremendous spurt of blood and the lieutenant lay still, cold blue-tinged steel protruding from his neck at the back.

5

Slowly, her socks slippery with blood, Reiko descended the stairway. The upstairs room was now completely still.

   Switching on the ground-floor lights, she checked the gas jet and the main gas plug and poured water over the smoldering, half-buried charcoal in the brazier. She stood before the upright mirror in the four-and-a-half-mat room and held up her skirts. The bloodstains made it seem as if a bold, vivid pattern was printed across the lower half of her white kimono. When she sat down before the mirror, she was conscious of the dampness and coldness of her husband's blood in the region of her thighs, and she shivered. Then, for a long while, she lingered over her toilet preparations. She applied the rouge generously to her cheeks, and her lips too she painted heavily. This was no longer make-up to please her husband. It was make-up for the world which she would leave behind, and there was a touch of the magnificent and the spectacular in her brushwork. When she rose, the mat before the mirror was wet with blood. Reiko was not concerned about this.

   Returning from the toilet, Reiko stood finally on the cement floor of the porchway. When her husband had bolted the door here last night it had been in preparation for death. For a while she stood immersed in the consideration of a simple problem. Should she now leave the bolt drawn? If she were to lock the door, it could be that the neighbors might not notice their suicide for several days. Reiko did not relish the thought of their two corpses putrifying before discovery. After all, it seemed, it would be best to leave it open. . . . She released the bolt, and also drew open the frosted-glass door a fraction. . . . At once a chill wind blew in. There was no sign of anyone in the midnight streets and stars glittered ice-cold through the trees in the large house opposite.

   Leaving the door as it was, Reiko mounted the stairs. She had walked here and there for some time and her socks were no longer slippery. About halfway up, her nostrils were already assailed by a peculiar smell.

   The lieutenant was lying on his face in a sea of blood. The point protruding from his neck seemed to have grown even more prominent than before. Reiko walked heedlessly across the blood. Sitting beside the lieutenant's corpse, she stared intently at the face, which lay on one cheek on the mat. The eyes were opened wide, as if the lieutenant's attention had been attracted by something. She raised the head, folding it in her sleeve, wiped the blood from the lips, and bestowed a last kiss.

   Then she rose and took from the closet a new white blanket and a waist cord. To prevent any derangement of her skirts, she wrapped the blanket about her waist and bound it firmly with the cord.

   Reiko sat herself on a spot about one foot distant from the lieutenant's body.

Drawing the dagger from her sash, she examined its dully gleaming blade intently, and held it to her tongue. The taste of the polished steel was slightly sweet.

Reiko did not linger. When she thought how the pain which had previously opened such a gulf between herself and her dying husband was now to become a part of her own experience, she saw before her only the joy of herself entering a realm her husband had already made his own. In her husband's agonized face there had been something inexplicable which she was seeing for the first time. Now she would solve that riddle. Reiko sensed that at last she too would be able to taste the true bitterness and sweetness of that great moral principle in which her husband believed. What had until now been tasted only faintly through her husband's example she was about to savor directly with her own tongue.

Reiko rested the point of the blade against the base of her throat. She thrust hard. The wound was only shallow. Her head blazed, and her hands shook uncontrollably. She gave the blade a strong pull sideways. A warm substance flooded into her mouth, and everything before her eyes reddened, in a vision of spouting blood. She gathered her strength and plunged the point of the blade deep into her throat.

QUESTIONS

1. Despite the title and the political event that sets the plot in motion, this story focuses almost exclusively on the relationship between the hero and heroine, their lovemaking, and their ritual suicides. In what ways do the intensely psychological explorations of the story define and clarify the meaning of patriotism for Lieutenant Takeyama? **2.** In the West, we tend to view the family—the relationship between husband and wife—as a private and personal matter that has little to do with public, political life. How do Lieutenant Takeyama and his wife view their relationship? **3.** Lieutenant Takeyama views "the urges of his flesh and the sincerity of his patriotism" as "two parts of the same thing." What does he mean by this? **4.** What does Mishima achieve by the opening paragraph? Why does he sacrifice suspense by recounting at the outset the major events and the story's outcome? **5.** What is the significance of Reiko's deliberations as to whether or not she should leave the door bolt drawn?

WRITING TOPIC

What connections does the story establish between love, marriage, and death?

The Man to Send Rain Clouds 1981

LESLIE SILKO [b. 1948]

They found him under a big cottonwood tree. His Levi jacket and pants were faded light blue so that he had been easy to find. The big cottonwood tree stood apart from a small grove of winterbare cottonwoods which grew in the wide, sandy arroyo. He had been dead for a day or more, and the sheep had wandered and scattered up and down the arroyo. Leon and his brother-in-law, Ken, gathered the sheep and left them in the pen at the sheep camp before they returned to the cottonwood tree. Leon waited under the tree while Ken drove the truck through the deep sand to the edge of the arroyo. He squinted up at the sun and unzipped his jacket—it sure was hot for this time of year. But high and northwest the blue mountains were still in snow. Ken came sliding down the low, crumbling bank about fifty yards down, and he was bringing the red blanket.

Before they wrapped the old man, Leon took a piece of string out of his pocket and tied a small gray feather in the old man's long white hair. Ken gave him the paint. Across the brown wrinkled forehead he drew a streak of white and along the high cheekbones he drew a strip of blue paint. He paused and watched Ken throw pinches of corn meal and pollen into the wind that fluttered the small gray feather. Then Leon painted with yellow under the old man's broad nose, and finally, when he had painted green across the chin, he smiled.

"Send us rain clouds, Grandfather." They laid the bundle in the back of the pickup and covered it with a heavy tarp before they started back to the pueblo.

They turned off the highway onto the sandy pueblo road. Not long after they passed the store and post office they saw Father Paul's car coming toward them. When he recognized their faces he slowed his car and waved for them to stop. The young priest rolled down the car window.

"Did you find old Teofilo?" he asked loudly.

Leon stopped the truck. "Good morning, Father. We were just out to the sheep camp. Everything is O.K. now."

"Thank God for that. Teofilo is a very old man. You really shouldn't allow him to stay at the sheep camp alone."

"No, he won't do that any more now."

"Well, I'm glad you understand. I hope I'll be seeing you at Mass this week—we missed you last Sunday. See if you can get old Teofilo to come with you." The priest smiled and waved at them as they drove away.

Louise and Teresa were waiting. The table was set for lunch, and the coffee was boiling on the black iron stove. Leon looked at Louise and then at Teresa.

"We found him under a cottonwood tree in the big arroyo near sheep camp. I guess he sat down to rest in the shade and never got up again." Leon walked toward the old man's bed. The red plaid shawl had been shaken and spread carefully over the bed, and a new brown flannel shirt and pair of stiff new Levi's were arranged neatly beside the pillow. Louise held the screen door open while Leon and Ken carried in the red blanket. He looked small and shriveled, and after they dressed him in the new shirt and pants he seemed more shrunken.

It was noontime now because the church bells rang the Angelus. They ate the beans with hot bread, and nobody said anything until after Teresa poured the coffee.

Ken stood up and put on his jacket. "I'll see about the gravediggers. Only the top layer of soil is frozen. I think it can be ready before dark."

Leon nodded his head and finished his coffee. After Ken had been gone for a while, the neighbors and clanspeople came quietly to embrace Teofilo's family and to leave food on the table because the gravediggers would come to eat when they were finished.

The sky in the west was full of pale yellow light. Louise stood outside with her hands in the pockets of Leon's green army jacket that was too big for her. The funeral was over, and the old men had taken their candles and medicine bags and were gone. She waited until the body was laid into the pickup before she said anything to Leon. She touched his arm, and he noticed that her hands were still dusty from the corn meal that she had sprinkled around the old man. When she spoke, Leon could not hear her.

"What did you say? I didn't hear you."

"I said that I had been thinking about something."

"About what?"

"About the priest sprinkling holy water for Grandpa. So he won't be thirsty."

Leon stared at the new moccasins that Teofilo had made for the ceremonial dances in the summer. They were nearly hidden by the red blanket. It was getting colder, and the wind pushed gray dust down the narrow pueblo road. The sun was approaching the long mesa where it disappeared during the winter. Louise stood there shivering and watching his face. Then he zipped up his jacket and opened the truck door. "I'll see if he's there."

Ken stopped the pickup at the church, and Leon got out; and then Ken drove down the hill to the graveyard where people were waiting. Leon knocked at the old carved door with its symbols of the Lamb. While he waited he looked up at the twin bells from the king of Spain with the last sunlight pouring around them in their tower.

The priest opened the door and smiled when he saw who it was. "Come in! What brings you here this evening?"

The priest walked toward the kitchen, and Leon stood with his cap in his hand, playing with the earflaps and examining the living room—the brown sofa, the green armchair, and the brass lamp that hung down from the ceiling by links of chain. The priest dragged a chair out of the kitchen and offered it to Leon.

"No thank you, Father. I only came to ask you if you would bring your holy water to the graveyard."

The priest turned away from Leon and looked out the window at the patio full of shadows and the dining-room windows of the nuns' cloister across the patio. The curtains were heavy, and the light from within faintly penetrated; it was impossible to see the nuns inside eating supper. "Why didn't you tell me he was dead? I could have brought the Last Rites anyway."

Leon smiled. "It wasn't necessary, Father."

The priest stared down at his scuffed brown loafers and the worn hem of his cassock. "For a Christian burial it was necessary."

His voice was distant, and Leon thought that his blue eyes looked tired.

"It's O.K. Father, we just want him to have plenty of water."

The priest sank down into the green chair and picked up a glossy missionary magazine. He turned the colored pages full of lepers and pagans without looking at them.

"You know I can't do that, Leon. There should have been the Last Rites and a funeral Mass at the very least."

Leon put on his green cap and pulled the flaps down over his ears. "It's getting late, Father. I've got to go."

When Leon opened the door Father Paul stood up and said, "Wait." He left the room and came back wearing a long brown overcoat. He followed Leon out the door and across the dim churchyard to the adobe steps in front of the church. They both stooped to fit through the low adobe entrance. And when they started down the hill to the graveyard only half of the sun was visible above the mesa.

The priest approached the grave slowly, wondering how they had managed to dig into the frozen ground; and then he remembered that this was New Mexico, and saw the pile of cold loose sand beside the hole. The people stood close to each other with little clouds of steam puffing from their faces. The priest looked at them and saw a pile of jackets, gloves, and scarves in the yellow, dry tumbleweeds that grew in the graveyard. He looked at the red blanket, not sure that Teofilo was so small, wondering if it wasn't some perverse Indian trick—something they did in March to ensure a good harvest—wondering if maybe old Teofilo was actually at sheep camp corraling the sheep for the night. But there he was, facing into a cold dry wind and squinting at the last sunlight, ready to bury a red wool blanket while the faces of his parishioners were in shadow with the last warmth of the sun on their backs.

His fingers were stiff, and it took him a long time to twist the lid off the holy water. Drops of water fell on the red blanket and soaked into dark icy spots. He sprinkled the grave and the water disappeared almost before it touched the dim, cold sand; it reminded him of something—he tried to remember what it was, because he thought if he could remember he might understand this. He sprinkled more water; he shook the container until it was empty, and the water fell through the light from sundown like August rain that fell while the sun was still shining, almost evaporating before it touched the wilted squash flowers.

The wind pulled at the priest's brown Franciscan robe and swirled away the corn meal and pollen that had been sprinkled on the blanket. They lowered the bundle into the ground, and they didn't bother to untie the stiff pieces of new rope that were tied around the ends of the blanket. The sun was gone, and over on the highway the eastbound lane was full of headlights. The priest walked away slowly. Leon watched him climb the hill, and when he had disappeared within the tall, thick walls, Leon turned to look up at the high blue mountains in the deep snow that reflected a faint red light from the west. He felt good because it was finished, and he was happy about the sprinkling of the holy water; now the old man could send them big thunderclouds for sure.

THE
PRESENCE
OF DEATH

Orderly Retreat, 1943 by Philip Evergood

POETRY

Edward

ANONYMOUS

1

"Why does your brand° sae° drap wi' bluid,   sword/so
　　　Edward, Edward,
Why does your brand sae drap wi' bluid,
　And why sae sad gang° ye, O?"   go
"O I ha'e killed my hawk sae guid,
　　　Mither, mither,
O I ha'e killed my hawk sae guid,
　And I had nae mair but he, O."

2

"Your hawke's bluid was never sae reid,°   red
　　　Edward, Edward,   10
Your hawke's bluid was never sae reid,
　My dear son I tell thee, O."
"O I ha'e killed my reid-roan steed,
　　　Mither, mither,
O I ha'e killed my reid-roan steed,
　That erst was sae fair and free, O."

3

"Your steed was auld, and ye ha'e gat mair,
　　　Edward, Edward,
Your steed was auld, and ye ha'e gat mair,
　Some other dule° ye drie,° O."   grief/suffer
"O I ha'e killed my fader dear,   21
　　　Mither, mither,
O I ha'e killed my fader dear,
　Alas, and wae° is me, O!"

4

"And whatten penance wul ye drie for that,
            Edward, Edward?
And whatten penance wul ye drie for that,
    My dear son, now tell me O?"
"I'll set my feet in yonder boat,
            Mither, mither,   30
I'll set my feet in yonder boat,
    And I'll fare over the sea, O."

5

"And what wul ye do wi' your towers and your ha',
            Edward, Edward?
And what wul ye do wi' your towers and your ha',
    That were sae fair to see, O?"
"I'll let them stand tul they down fa',
            Mither, mither,
I'll let them stand tul they down fa',   39
    For here never mair maun° I be, O."   must

6

"And what wul ye leave to your bairns° and your wife,   children
            Edward, Edward?
And what wul ye leave to your bairns and your wife,
    Whan ye gang over the sea, O?"
"The warlde's° room, let them beg thrae° life,   world's/through
            Mither, mither,
The warlde's room, let them beg thrae life,
    For them never mair wul I see, O."

7

"And what wul ye leave to your ain mither dear,
            Edward, Edward?   50
And what wul ye leave to your ain mither dear,
    My dear son, now tell me, O?"
"The curse of hell frae° me sall° ye bear,   from/shall
            Mither, mither,
The curse of hell frae me sall ye bear,
    Sic° counsels ye gave to me, O."   such

QUESTIONS

1. Why does the mother reject Edward's answers to her first two questions? **2.** Does the poem provide any clues as to the motive of the murder? **3.** Edward has murdered his father and then bitterly turns away from his mother, wife, and children. What basis is there in the poem for nevertheless sympathizing with Edward?

WRITING TOPIC

What effects are achieved through the question-and-answer technique and the repetition of lines?

Sonnet   1609

WILLIAM SHAKESPEARE [1564–1616]

73

That time of year thou mayst in me behold
When yellow leaves, or none, or few, do hang
Upon those boughs which shake against the cold,
Bare ruined choirs, where late the sweet birds sang.
In me thou see'st the twilight of such day
As after sunset fadeth in the west;
Which by and by black night doth take away,
Death's second self, that seals up all in rest.
In me thou see'st the glowing of such fire,
That on the ashes of his youth doth lie,   10
As the deathbed whereon it must expire,
Consumed with that which it was nourished by.
This thou perceiv'st, which makes thy love more strong,
To love that well which thou must leave ere long.

A Litany in Time of Plague   1600

THOMAS NASHE [1567–1601]

Adieu, farewell, earth's bliss;
This world uncertain is;
Fond° are life's lustful joys;   foolish
Death proves them all but toys;
None from his darts can fly;
I am sick, I must die.
    Lord, have mercy on us!

Rich men, trust not in wealth,
Gold cannot buy you health;
Physic himself must fade.   10
All things to end are made,
The plague full swift goes by;
I am sick, I must die.
    Lord, have mercy on us!

Beauty is but a flower
Which wrinkles will devour;
Brightness falls from the air;
Queens have died young and fair;
Dust hath closed Helen's[1] eye.
I am sick, I must die.   20
    Lord, have mercy on us!

Strength stoops unto the grave,
Worms feed on Hector[2] brave;
Swords may not fight with fate,
Earth still holds ope her gate.
"Come, come!" the bells do cry.
I am sick, I must die.
    Lord, have mercy on us.

Wit with his wantonness
Tasteth death's bitterness;   30
Hell's executioner
Hath no ears for to hear
What vain art can reply.
I am sick, I must die.
    Lord, have mercy on us.

Haste, therefore, each degree,
To welcome destiny;
Heaven is our heritage,
Earth but a player's stage;
Mount we unto the sky.   40
I am sick, I must die.
    Lord, have mercy on us.

A *Litany in Time of Plague*
  [1] Helen of Troy, a fabled beauty.
  [2] Commander of the Trojan forces in the Trojan War.

Death, Be Not Proud   1633

JOHN DONNE   [1572–1631]   *Italian Sonnet*

Death, be not proud, though some have calléd thee A
Mighty and dreadful, for thou art not so; b
For those whom thou think'st thou dost overthrow b
Die not, poor Death, nor yet canst thou kill me. A   } *Octave*
From rest and sleep, which but thy pictures be, A
Much pleasure; then from thee much more must flow, b
And soonest our best men with thee do go, b
Rest of their bones, and soul's delivery. A
Thou art slave to fate, chance, kings, and desperate men c
And dost with poison, war, and sickness dwell, d   10
And poppy or charms can make us sleep as well d x   } *Sestet*
And better than thy stroke; why swell'st thou then? c
One short sleep past, we wake eternally e
And death shall be no more; Death, thou shalt die. f x

The Destruction
of Sennacherib[1]   1815

GEORGE GORDON, LORD BYRON   [1788–1824]

The Assyrian came down like the wolf on the fold,
And his cohorts were gleaming in purple and gold;
And the sheen of their spears was like stars on the sea,
When the blue wave rolls nightly on deep Galilee.

Like the leaves of the forest when summer is green,
That host with their banners at sunset were seen:
Like the leaves of the forest when autumn hath blown,
That host on the morrow lay withered and strown.

For the Angel of Death spread his wings on the blast,
And breathed in the face of the foe as he passed;   10
And the eyes of the sleepers waxed deadly and chill,
And their hearts but once heaved—and for ever grew still!

The Destruction of Sennacherib
  [1] Byron retells the account of the Assyrian siege of Jerusalem, found in 2 Kings 19, which culminates in the death of 185,000 Assyrian troops at the hand of the angel of the Lord.

And there lay the steed with his nostril all wide,
But through it there rolled not the breath of his pride;
And the foam of his gasping lay white on the turf,
And cold as the spray of the rock-beating surf.

And there lay the rider distorted and pale,
With the dew on his brow, and the rust on his mail;
And the tents were all silent, the banners alone,
The lances unlifted, the trumpet unblown.   20

And the widows of Ashur² are loud in their wail,
And the idols are broke in the temple of Baal;³
And the might of the Gentile,⁴ unsmote by the sword,
Hath melted like snow in the glance of the Lord!

Ozymandias¹   1818

PERCY BYSSHE SHELLEY   [1792–1822]

I met a traveller from an antique land
Who said: Two vast and trunkless legs of stone
Stand in the desert . . . Near them, on the sand,
Half sunk, a shattered visage lies, whose frown,
And wrinkled lip, and sneer of cold command,
Tell that its sculptor well those passions read
Which yet survive, stamped on these lifeless things,
The hand that mocked them, and the heart that fed:
And on the pedestal these words appear:
"My name is Ozymandias, king of kings: 10
Look on my works, ye Mighty, and despair!"
Nothing beside remains. Round the decay
Of that colossal wreck, boundless and bare
The lone and level sands stretch far away.

---

² Another name for Assyria.
³ A Canaanite deity.
⁴ A non-Hebrew, in this case Sennacherib, the King of Assyria.

Ozymandias
¹ Egyptian monarch of the thirteenth century B.C., said to have erected a huge statue of himself.

Ode on a Grecian Urn   1820

JOHN KEATS [1795–1821]

I

Thou still unravished bride of quietness,
   Thou foster child of silence and slow time,
Sylvan historian, who canst thus express
   A flowery tale more sweetly than our rhyme:
What leaf-fringed legend haunts about thy shape
   Of deities or mortals, or of both,
      In Tempe or the dales of Arcady?[1]
   What men or gods are these? What maidens loath?
What mad pursuit? What struggle to escape?
      What pipes and timbrels? What wild ecstasy?   10

II

Heard melodies are sweet, but those unheard
   Are sweeter; therefore, ye soft pipes, play on;
Not to the sensual ear, but, more endeared,
   Pipe to the spirit ditties of no tone:
Fair youth, beneath the trees, thou canst not leave
   Thy song, nor ever can those trees be bare;
      Bold Lover, never, never canst thou kiss,
Though winning near the goal—yet, do not grieve;
      She cannot fade, though thou hast not thy bliss,
   Forever wilt thou love, and she be fair!   20

III

Ah, happy, happy boughs! that cannot shed
   Your leaves, nor ever bid the Spring adieu;
And, happy melodist, unwearièd,
   Forever piping songs forever new;
More happy love! more happy, happy love!
   Forever warm and still to be enjoyed,
      Forever panting, and forever young;
All breathing human passion far above,[2]

Ode on a Grecian Urn
  [1] Tempe and Arcady are valleys in Greece famous for their beauty. In ancient times, Tempe was regarded as sacred to Apollo.
  [2] I.e., far above all breathing human passion.

That leaves a heart high-sorrowful and cloyed,
   A burning forehead, and a parching tongue.   30

IV

Who are these coming to the sacrifice?
   To what green altar, O mysterious priest,
Lead'st thou that heifer lowing at the skies,
   And all her silken flanks with garlands dressed?
What little town by river or sea shore,
   Or mountain-built with peaceful citadel,
      Is emptied of this folk, this pious morn?
And, little town, thy streets forevermore
   Will silent be; and not a soul to tell
      Why thou art desolate, can e'er return.   40

V

O Attic³ shape! Fair attitude! with brede
   Of marble men and maidens overwrought,
With forest branches and the trodden weed;
   Thou, silent form, dost tease us out of thought
As doth eternity: Cold Pastoral!
   When old age shall this generation waste,
      Thou shalt remain, in midst of other woe
Than ours, a friend to man, to whom thou say'st,
   "Beauty is truth, truth beauty,—that is all
      Ye know on earth, and all ye need to know."   50

QUESTIONS
1. Describe the scene the poet sees depicted on the urn. Describe the scene the poet imagines as a consequence of the scene on the urn. **2.** Why are the boughs, the piper, and the lovers happy in stanza 3? **3.** Explain the assertion of stanza 2 that "Heard melodies are sweet, but those unheard / Are sweeter." **4.** Does the poem support the assertion of the last two lines? What does that assertion mean?

WRITING TOPIC
In what sense might it be argued that this poem is about mortality and immortality? In this connection, consider the meaning of the phrase "Cold Pastoral!" (l. 45).

After Great Pain, a Formal Feeling Comes   (ca. 1862)

EMILY DICKINSON   [1830–1886]

After great pain, a formal feeling comes—
The Nerves sit ceremonious, like Tombs—
The stiff Heart questions was it He, that bore,
And Yesterday, or Centuries before?

The Feet, mechanical, go round—
Of Ground, or Air, or Ought—
A Wooden way
Regardless grown,
A Quartz contentment, like a stone—

This is the Hour of Lead—   10
Remembered, if outlived,
As Freezing persons, recollect the Snow—
First—Chill—then Stupor—then the letting go—

QUESTION
1. Is this poem about physical or psychic pain? Explain.

WRITING TOPIC
What is the meaning of "stiff Heart" (l. 3) and "Quartz contentment" (l. 9)? What part do they play in the larger pattern of images?

I Heard a Fly Buzz— When I Died   (ca. 1862)

EMILY DICKINSON   [1830–1886]

I heard a Fly buzz—when I died—
The Stillness in the Room
Was like the Stillness in the Air—
Between the Heaves of Storm—

The Eyes around—had wrung them dry—
And Breaths were gathering firm

For that last Onset—when the King
Be witnessed—in the Room—

I willed my Keepsakes—Signed away
What portion of me be   10
Assignable—and then it was
There interposed a Fly—

With Blue—uncertain stumbling Buzz—
Between the light—and me—
And then the Windows failed—and then
I could not see to see—

Apparently with No Surprise (ca. 1884)

EMILY DICKINSON [1830–1886]

Apparently with no surprise
To any happy flower,
The frost beheads it at its play
In accidental power.
The blond assassin passes on,
The sun proceeds unmoved
To measure off another day
For an approving God.

To an Athlete Dying Young   1896

A. E. HOUSMAN [1859–1936]

The time you won your town the race
We chaired you through the market place;
Man and boy stood cheering by,
And home we brought you shoulder-high.

Today, the road all runners come,
Shoulder-high we bring you home,
And set you at your threshold down,
Townsman of a stiller town.

Smart lad, to slip betimes away
From fields where glory does not stay   10
And early though the laurel grows
It withers quicker than the rose.

Eyes the shady night has shut
Cannot see the record cut,
And silence sounds no worse than cheers
After earth has stopped the ears:

Now you will not swell the rout
Of lads that wore their honors out,
Runners whom renown outran
And the name died before the man.   20

So set, before its echoes fade,
The fleet foot on the sill of shade,
And hold to the low lintel up
The still defended challenge cup.

And round that early laureled head
Will flock to gaze the strengthless dead
And find unwithered on its curls
The garland briefer than a girl's.

Sailing to Byzantium[1]   1927

WILLIAM BUTLER YEATS   [1865–1939]

1

That is no country for old men. The young
In one another's arms, birds in the trees
—Those dying generations—at their song,
The salmon-falls, the mackerel-crowded seas,

Sailing to Byzantium
   [1] Capital of the ancient Eastern Roman Empire, Byzantium (modern Istanbul) is celebrated for its great art, including mosaics (in ll. 17–18, Yeats addresses the figures in one of these mosaics). In *A Vision*, Yeats cites Byzantium as possibly the only civilization which had achieved what he called "Unity of Being," a state where "religious, aesthetic and practical life were one. . . ."

Fish, flesh, or fowl, commend all summer long
Whatever is begotten, born, and dies.
Caught in that sensual music all neglect
Monuments of unaging intellect.

2

An aged man is but a paltry thing,
A tattered coat upon a stick, unless   10
Soul clap its hands and sing, and louder sing
For every tatter in its mortal dress,
Nor is there singing school but studying
Monuments of its own magnificence;
And therefore I have sailed the seas and come
To the holy city of Byzantium.

3

O sages standing in God's holy fire
As in the gold mosaic of a wall,
Come from the holy fire, perne in a gyre,[2]
And be the singing-masters of my soul.
Consume my heart away; sick with desire   20
And fastened to a dying animal
It knows not what it is; and gather me
Into the artifice of eternity.

4

Once out of nature I shall never take
My bodily form from any natural thing,
But such a form as Grecian goldsmiths make
Of hammered gold and gold enameling
To keep a drowsy Emperor awake;[3]
Or set upon a golden bough to sing   30
To lords and ladies of Byzantium
Of what is past, or passing, or to come.

---

[2] I.e., whirl in a spiral motion. Yeats associated this motion with the cycles of history and the fate of the individual. Here he entreats the sages represented in the mosaic to take him out of the natural world described in the first stanza and into the eternal world of art.

[3] "I have read somewhere," Yeats wrote, "that in the Emperor's palace at Byzantium was a tree made of gold and silver, and artificial birds that sang." The poet wishes to become an artificial bird (a work of art) in contrast to the real birds of the first stanza.

QUESTIONS
1. This poem incorporates a series of contrasts, among them "That" country and Byzantium, the real birds of the first stanza and the artificial bird of the final stanza. What others do you find?   **2.** What are the meanings of "generations" (l. 3)?   **3.** For what is the poet "sick with desire" (l. 21):   **4.** In what sense is eternity an "artifice" (l. 24)?

WRITING TOPIC
In what ways are the images of bird and song used throughout this poem?

Richard Cory   1897

EDWIN ARLINGTON ROBINSON   [1869–1935]

Whenever Richard Cory went down town,
We people on the pavement looked at him:
He was a gentleman from sole to crown,
Clean favored, and imperially slim.

And he was always quietly arrayed,
And he was always human when he talked;
But still he fluttered pulses when he said,
"Good-morning," and he glittered when he walked.

And he was rich—yes, richer than a king—
And admirably schooled in every grace: 10
In fine, we thought that he was everything
To make us wish that we were in his place.

So on we worked, and waited for the light,
And went without the meat, and cursed the bread;
And Richard Cory, one calm summer night,
Went home and put a bullet through his head.

Mr. Flood's Party   1921

EDWIN ARLINGTON ROBINSON   [1869–1935]

Old Eben Flood, climbing alone one night
Over the hill between the town below
And the forsaken upland hermitage
That held as much as he should ever know
On earth again of home, paused warily.

The road was his with not a native near;
And Eben, having leisure, said aloud,
For no man else in Tilbury Town to hear:

"Well, Mr. Flood, we have the harvest moon
Again, and we may not have many more;   10
The bird is on the wing, the poet says,
And you and I have said it here before.
Drink to the bird." He raised up to the light
The jug that he had gone so far to fill,
And answered huskily: "Well, Mr. Flood,
Since you propose it, I believe I will."

Alone, as if enduring to the end
A valiant armor of scarred hopes outworn,
He stood there in the middle of the road
Like Roland's ghost winding a silent horn.   20
Below him, in the town among the trees,
Where friends of other days had honored him,
A phantom salutation of the dead
Rang thinly till old Eben's eyes were dim.

Then, as a mother lays her sleeping child
Down tenderly, fearing it may awake,
He set the jug down slowly at his feet
With trembling care, knowing that most things break;
And only when assured that on firm earth
It stood, as the uncertain lives of men   30
Assuredly did not, he paced away,
And with his hand extended paused again:

"Well, Mr. Flood, we have not met like this
In a long time; and many a change has come
To both of us, I fear, since last it was
We had a drop together. Welcome home!"
Convivially returning with himself,
Again he raised the jug up to the light;
And with an acquiescent quaver said:
"Well, Mr. Flood, if you insist, I might.   40

"Only a very little, Mr. Flood—
For auld lang syne. No more, sir; that will do."
So, for the time, apparently it did,
And Eben evidently thought so too;
For soon amid the silver loneliness

Of night he lifted up his voice and sang,
Secure, with only two moons listening,
Until the whole harmonious landscape rang—

"For auld lang syne." The weary throat gave out,
The last word wavered; and the song being done,   50
He raised again the jug regretfully
And shook his head, and was again alone.
There was not much that was ahead of him,
And there was nothing in the town below—
Where strangers would have shut the many doors
That many friends had opened long ago.

After Apple-Picking   1914

ROBERT FROST [1874–1963]

My long two-pointed ladder's sticking through a tree
Toward heaven still,
And there's a barrel that I didn't fill
Beside it, and there may be two or three
Apples I didn't pick upon some bough.
But I am done with apple-picking now.
Essence of winter sleep is on the night,
The scent of apples: I am drowsing off.
I cannot rub the strangeness from my sight
I got from looking through a pane of glass   10
I skimmed this morning from the drinking trough
And held against the world of hoary grass.
It melted, and I let it fall and break.
But I was well
Upon my way to sleep before it fell,
And I could tell
What form my dreaming was about to take.
Magnified apples appear and disappear,
Stem end and blossom end,
And every fleck of russet showing clear.   20
My instep arch not only keeps the ache,
It keeps the pressure of a ladder-round.
I feel the ladder sway as the boughs bend.
And I keep hearing from the cellar bin
The rumbling sound
Of load on load of apples coming in.

For I have had too much
Of apple-picking: I am overtired
Of the great harvest I myself desired.
There were ten thousand thousand fruit to touch,   30
Cherish in hand, lift down, and not let fall.
For all
That struck the earth,
No matter if not bruised or spiked with stubble,
Went surely to the cider-apple heap
As of no worth.
One can see what will trouble
This sleep of mine, whatever sleep it is.
Were he not gone,
The woodchuck could say whether it's like his   40
Long sleep, as I describe its coming on,
Or just some human sleep.

QUESTIONS
1. What does apple-picking symbolize? **2.** At the end of the poem, why is the speaker uncertain about what kind of sleep is coming on him?

Nothing Gold Can Stay   1923

ROBERT FROST [1874-1963]

Nature's first green is gold,
Her hardest hue to hold.
Her early leaf's a flower;
But only so an hour.
Then leaf subsides to leaf.
So Eden sank to grief,
So dawn goes down to day.
Nothing gold can stay.

QUESTIONS
1. Does this poem protest or accept the transitoriness of things? **2.** Why does Frost use the word "subsides" in line 5 rather than a word like "expands" or "grows"? **3.** How are "Nature's first green" (l. 1), "Eden" (l. 6), and "dawn" (l. 7) linked together?

'Out, Out—'[1]   1916

ROBERT FROST   [1874–1963]

The buzz-saw snarled and rattled in the yard
And made dust and dropped stove-length sticks of wood,
Sweet-scented stuff when the breeze drew across it.
And from there those that lifted eyes could count
Five mountain ranges one behind the other
Under the sunset far into Vermont.
And the saw snarled and rattled, snarled and rattled,
As it ran light, or had to bear a load.
And nothing happened: day was all but done.
Call it a day, I wish they might have said   10
To please the boy by giving him the half hour
That a boy counts so much when saved from work.
His sister stood beside them in her apron
To tell them 'Supper.' At the word, the saw,
As if to prove saws knew what supper meant,
Leaped out at the boy's hand, or seemed to leap—
He must have given the hand. However it was,
Neither refused the meeting. But the hand!
The boy's first outcry was a rueful laugh,
As he swung toward them holding up the hand   20
Half in appeal, but half as if to keep
The life from spilling. Then the boy saw all—
Since he was old enough to know, big boy
Doing a man's work, though a child at heart—
He saw all spoiled. 'Don't let him cut my hand off—
The doctor, when he comes. Don't let him, sister!'
So. But the hand was gone already.
The doctor put him in the dark of ether.
He lay and puffed his lips out with his breath.
And then—the watcher at his pulse took fright.   30
No one believed. They listened at his heart.
Little—less—nothing!—and that ended it.
No more to build on there. And they, since they
Were not the one dead, turned to their affairs.

'Out, Out—'
    [1] The title is taken from the famous speech of Macbeth upon hearing that his wife has died
(*Macbeth*, Act V, Scene 5).

Stopping by Woods on a Snowy Evening 1923

ROBERT FROST [1874–1963]

Whose woods these are I think I know.
His house is in the village though;
He will not see me stopping here
To watch his woods fill up with snow.

My little horse must think it queer
To stop without a farmhouse near
Between the woods and frozen lake
The darkest evening of the year.

He gives his harness bells a shake
To ask if there is some mistake.   10
The only other sound's the sweep
Of easy wind and downy flake.

The woods are lovely, dark and deep.
But I have promises to keep,
And miles to go before I sleep,
And miles to go before I sleep.

QUESTIONS
1. What does the description of the horse tell us about the speaker? **2.** What function does the repetition in the last two lines of the poem serve? **3.** Why does the speaker refer to the owner of the woods in the opening stanza?

Design 1936

ROBERT FROST [1874–1963]

I found a dimpled spider, fat and white,
On a white heal-all, holding up a moth
Like a white piece of rigid satin cloth—
Assorted characters of death and blight
Mixed ready to begin the morning right,
Like the ingredients of a witches' broth—
A snow-drop spider, a flower like a froth,
And dead wings carried like a paper kite.

What had that flower to do with being white,
The wayside blue and innocent heal-all?   10
What brought the kindred spider to that height,
Then steered the white moth thither in the night?
What but design of darkness to appall?—
If design govern in a thing so small.

WRITING TOPIC

Compare this poem with Emily Dickinson's "Apparently with No Surprise" (p. 678).

Tract   1917

WILLIAM CARLOS WILLIAMS [1883–1963]

I will teach you my townspeople
how to perform a funeral—
for you have it over a troop
of artists—
unless one should scour the world—
you have the ground sense necessary.
See! the hearse leads.
I begin with a design for a hearse.
For Christ's sake not black—
nor white either—and not polished!   10
Let it be weathered—like a farm wagon—
with gilt wheels (this could be
applied fresh at small expense)
or no wheels at all:
a rough dray to drag over the ground.

Knock the glass out!
My God—glass, my townspeople!
For what purpose? Is it for the dead
to look out or for us to see
how well he is housed or to see   20
the flowers or the lack of them—
or what?
To keep the rain and snow from him?
He will have a heavier rain soon:
pebbles and dirt and what not.
Let there be no glass—

and no upholstery! phew!
and no little brass rollers
and small easy wheels on the bottom—
my townspeople what are you thinking of!   30

A rough plain hearse then
with gilt wheels and no top at all.
On this the coffin lies
by its own weight.
                    No wreaths please—
especially no hot-house flowers.
Some common memento is better,
something he prized and is known by:
his old clothes—a few books perhaps—
God knows what! You realize   40
how we are about these things,
my townspeople—
something will be found—anything—
even flowers if he had come to that.
So much for the hearse.

For heaven's sake though see to the driver!
Take off the silk hat! In fact
that's no place at all for him
up there unceremoniously
dragging our friend out of his own dignity!   50
Bring him down—bring him down!
Low and inconspicuous! I'd not have him ride
on the wagon at all—damn him—
the undertaker's understrapper!
Let him hold the reins
and walk at the side
and inconspicuously too!

Then briefly as to yourselves:
Walk behind—as they do in France,
seventh class, or if you ride   60
Hell take curtains! Go with some show
of inconvenience; sit openly—
to the weather as to grief.
Or do you think you can shut grief in?
What—from us? We who have perhaps
nothing to lose? Share with us
share with us—it will be money
in your pockets.
                    Go now
I think you are ready.   70

Hurt Hawks   1928

ROBINSON JEFFERS   [1887–1962]

1

The broken pillar of the wing jags from the clotted shoulder,
The wing trails like a banner in defeat,
No more to use the sky forever but live with famine
And pain a few days: cat nor coyote
Will shorten the week of waiting for death, there is game without talons.
He stands under the oak-bush and waits
The lame feet of salvation; at night he remembers freedom
And flies in a dream, the dawns ruin it.
He is strong and pain is worse to the strong, incapacity is worse.
The curs of the day come and torment him   10
At distance, no one but death the redeemer will humble that head,
The intrepid readiness, the terrible eyes.
The wild God of the world is sometimes merciful to those
That ask mercy, not often to the arrogant.
You do not know him, you communal people, or you have forgotten him;
Intemperate and savage, the hawk remembers him;
Beautiful and wild, the hawks, and men that are dying, remember him.

2

I'd sooner, except the penalties, kill a man than a hawk; but the great
   redtail[1]
Had nothing left but unable misery
From the bone too shattered for mending, the wing that trailed under his
   talons when he moved.   20
We had fed him six weeks, I gave him freedom,
He wandered over the foreland hill and returned in the evening, asking
   for death,
Not like a beggar, still eyed with the old
Implacable arrogance. I gave him the lead gift in the twilight. What fell
   was relaxed,
Owl-downy, soft feminine feathers; but what
Soared: the fierce rush: the night-herons by the flooded river cried fear at
   its rising
Before it was quite unsheathed from reality.

Hurt Hawks
   [1] I. e., red-tailed hawk.

Dulce et Decorum Est 1920

WILFRED OWEN [1893–1918]

Bent double, like old beggars under sacks,
Knock-kneed, coughing like hags, we cursed through sludge,
Till on the haunting flares we turned our backs,
And towards our distant rest began to trudge.
Men marched asleep. Many had lost their boots,
But limped on, blood-shod. All went lame, all blind;
Drunk with fatigue; deaf even to the hoots
Of gas-shells dropping softly behind.

Gas! GAS! Quick, boys!—An ecstasy of fumbling,
Fitting the clumsy helmets just in time,   10
But someone still was yelling out and stumbling
And flound'ring like a man in fire or lime.—
Dim through the misty panes and thick green light,
As under a green sea, I saw him drowning.
In all my dreams before my helpless sight
He plunges at me, guttering, choking, drowning.

If in some smothering dreams, you too could pace
Behind the wagon that we flung him in,
And watch the white eyes writhing in his face,
His hanging face, like a devil's sick of sin,   20
If you could hear, at every jolt, the blood
Come gargling from the froth-corrupted lungs
Bitter as the cud
Of vile, incurable sores on innocent tongues,—
My friend, you would not tell with such high zest
To children ardent for some desperate glory,
The old lie: *Dulce et decorum est*
Pro patria mori. [1]

nobody loses all the time 1926

E. E. CUMMINGS [1894–1962]

nobody loses all the time

Dulce et Decorum Est
[1] A quotation from the Roman poet Horace, "It is sweet and fitting to die for one's country."

i had an uncle named
Sol who was a born failure and
nearly everybody said he should have gone
into vaudeville perhaps because my Uncle Sol could
sing McCann He Was A Diver on Xmas Eve like Hell Itself which
may or may not account for the fact that my Uncle

Sol indulged in that possibly most inexcusable
of all to use a highfalootin phrase
luxuries that is or to   10
wit farming and be
it needlessly
added

my Uncle Sol's farm
failed because the chickens
ate the vegetables so
my Uncle Sol had a
chicken farm till the
skunks ate the chickens when

my Uncle Sol   20
had a skunk farm but
the skunks caught cold and
died and so
my Uncle Sol imitated the
skunks in a subtle manner

or by drowning himself in the watertank
but somebody who'd given my Uncle Sol a Victor
Victrola and records while he lived presented to
him upon the auspicious occasion of his decease a
scrumptious not to mention splendiferous funeral with   30
tall boys in black gloves and flowers and everything and

i remember we all cried like the Missouri
when my Uncle Sol's coffin lurched because
somebody pressed a button
(and down went
my Uncle
Sol

and started a worm farm)

QUESTIONS
1. Explain the title. **2.** What is the speaker's attitude toward Uncle Sol?

In Memory of W. B. Yeats   1940
(D. JAN. 1939)

W. H. AUDEN   [1907–1973]

1

He disappeared in the dead of winter:
The brooks were frozen, the airports almost deserted,
And snow disfigured the public statues;
The mercury sank in the mouth of the dying day.
O all the instruments agree
The day of his death was a dark cold day.

Far from his illness
The wolves ran on through the evergreen forests,
The peasant river was untempted by the fashionable quays;
By mourning tongues   10
The death of the poet was kept from his poems.

But for him it was his last afternoon as himself,
An afternoon of nurses and rumors;
The provinces of his body revolted,
The squares of his mind were empty,
Silence invaded the suburbs,
The current of his feeling failed: he became his admirers.

Now he is scattered among a hundred cities
And wholly given over to unfamiliar affections;
To find his happiness in another kind of wood   20
And be punished under a foreign code of conscience.
The words of a dead man
Are modified in the guts of the living.

But in the importance and noise of tomorrow
When the brokers are roaring like beasts on the floor of the Bourse,[1]
And the poor have the sufferings to which they are fairly accustomed,
And each in the cell of himself is almost convinced of his freedom;
A few thousand will think of this day
As one thinks of a day when one did something slightly unusual.
O all the instruments agree   30
The day of his death was a dark cold day.

In Memory of W. B. Yeats
 [1] A European stock exchange, especially that in Paris.

2

You were silly like us: your gift survived it all;
The parish of rich women, physical decay,
Yourself; mad Ireland hurt you into poetry.
Now Ireland has her madness and her weather still,
For poetry makes nothing happen: it survives
In the valley of its saying where executives
Would never want to tamper; it flows south
From ranches of isolation and the busy griefs,
Raw towns that we believe and die in; it survives,
A way of happening, a mouth.

3

Earth, receive an honored guest;
William Yeats is laid to rest:
Let the Irish vessel lie
Emptied of its poetry.

In the nightmare of the dark
All the dogs of Europe bark,
And the living nations wait,
Each sequestered in its hate;

Intellectual disgrace   50
Stares from every human face,
And the seas of pity lie
Locked and frozen in each eye.

Follow, poet, follow right
To the bottom of the night,
With your unconstraining voice
Still persuade us to rejoice;

With the farming of a verse
Make a vineyard of the curse,
Sing of human unsuccess   60
In a rapture of distress;

In the deserts of the heart
Let the healing fountain start,
In the prison of his days
Teach the free man how to praise.

QUESTIONS

1. In what sense does a dead poet become "his admirers" (l. 17)? **2.** Is Auden's statement that "poetry makes nothing happen" (l. 36) consistent with the attitudes expressed in the final three stanzas?

WRITING TOPIC

Why does Auden view the death of Yeats as a significant event?

Landscape with the Fall of Icarus, c. 1560 by Pieter Brueghel the Elder

Musée des Beaux Arts   1940

W. H. AUDEN [1907–1973]

About suffering they were never wrong,
The Old Masters: how well they understood
Its human position; how it takes place
While someone else is eating or opening a window or just walking dully
    along;
How, when the aged are reverently, passionately waiting
For the miraculous birth, there always must be

Children who did not specially want it to happen, skating
On a pond at the edge of the wood:
They never forgot
That even the dreadful martyrdom must run its course   10
Anyhow in a corner, some untidy spot
Where the dogs go on with their doggy life and the torturer's horse
Scratches its innocent behind on a tree.
In Brueghel's *Icarus*,[1] for instance: how everything turns away
Quite leisurely from the disaster; the ploughman may
Have heard the splash, the forsaken cry,
But for him it was not an important failure; the sun shone
As it had to on the white legs disappearing into the green
Water; and the expensive delicate ship that must have seen
Something amazing, a boy falling out of the sky,   20
Had somewhere to get to and sailed calmly on.

Elegy for Jane   1958

MY STUDENT, THROWN BY A HORSE

THEODORE ROETHKE   [1908–1963]

I remember the neckcurls, limp and damp as tendrils;
And her quick look, a sidelong pickerel smile;
And how, once startled into talk, the light syllables leaped for her,
And she balanced in the delight of her thought,
A wren, happy, tail into the wind,
Her song trembling the twigs and small branches.
The shade sang with her;
The leaves, their whispers turned to kissing;
And the mold sang in the bleached valleys under the rose.

Oh, when she was sad, she cast herself down into such a pure depth,   10
Even a father could not find her:
Scraping her cheek against straw;
Stirring the clearest water.

My sparrow, you are not here,
Waiting like a fern, making a spiny shadow.

Musée des Beaux Arts
[1]This poem describes and comments on Pieter Brueghel's painting *Landscape with the Fall of Icarus*. (See p. 694). According to myth, Daedalus and his son Icarus made wings, whose feathers they attached with wax, to escape Crete. Icarus flew so near the sun that the wax melted and he fell.

The sides of wet stones cannot console me,
Nor the moss, wound with the last light.

If only I could nudge you from this sleep,
My maimed darling, my skittery pigeon.

Over this damp grave I speak the words of my love: 20
I, with no rights in this matter,
Neither father nor lover.

Between the World and Me   1935

RICHARD WRIGHT   [1908–1960]

And one morning while in the woods I stumbled suddenly upon the
    thing,
Stumbled upon it in a grassy clearing guarded by scaly oaks and elms.
And the sooty details of the scene rose, thrusting themselves between the
    world and me. . . .
There was a design of white bones slumbering forgottenly upon a cushion
    of ashes.
There was a charred stump of a sapling pointing a blunt finger accusingly
    at the sky.
There were torn tree limbs, tiny veins of burnt leaves, and a scorched coil
    of greasy hemp;
A vacant shoe, an empty tie, a ripped shirt, a lonely hat, and a pair of
    trousers stiff with black blood.
And upon the trampled grass were buttons, dead matches, butt-ends of
    cigars and cigarettes, peanut shells, a drained gin-flask, and a whore's
    lipstick;
Scattered traces of tar, restless arrays of feathers, and the lingering smell of
    gasoline.
And through the morning air the sun poured yellow surprise into the eye
    sockets of a stony skull. . . .   10
And while I stood my mind was frozen with a cold pity for the life that
    was gone.
The ground gripped my feet and my heart was circled by icy walls of
    fear—
The sun died in the sky; a night wind muttered in the grass and fumbled
    the leaves in the trees; the woods poured forth the hungry yelping of
    hounds; the darkness screamed with thirsty voices; and the witnesses
    rose and lived: The dry bones stirred, rattled, lifted, melting themselves
    into my bones.

The grey ashes formed flesh firm and black, entering into my flesh.
The gin-flask passed from mouth to mouth; cigars and cigarettes glowed,
   the whore smeared the lipstick red upon her lips,
And a thousand faces swirled around me, clamoring that my life be
   burned. . . .
And then they had me, stripped me, battering my teeth into my throat till
   I swallowed my own blood.
My voice was drowned in the roar of their voices, and my black wet body
   slipped and rolled in their hands as they bound me to the sapling.
And my skin clung to the bubbling hot tar, falling from me in limp
   patches.   20
And the down and quills of the white feathers sank into my raw flesh, and
   I moaned in my agony.
Then my blood was cooled mercifully, cooled by a baptism of gasoline.
And in a blaze of red I leaped to the sky as pain rose like water, boiling
   my limbs.
Panting, begging I clutched childlike, clutched to the hot sides of death.
Now I am dry bones and my face a stony skull staring in my yellow
   surprise at the sun. . . .

Do Not Go Gentle
into That Good Night   1952

DYLAN THOMAS   [1914–1953]

Do not go gentle into that good night,
Old age should burn and rave at close of day;
Rage, rage against the dying of the light.

Though wise men at their end know dark is right,
Because their words had forked no lightning they
Do not go gentle into that good night.

Good men, the last wave by, crying how bright
Their frail deeds might have danced in a green bay,
Rage, rage against the dying of the light.

Wild men who caught and sang the sun in flight,   10
And learn, too late, they grieved it on its way,
Do not go gentle into that good night.

Grave men, near death, who see with blinding sight
Blind eyes could blaze like meteors and be gay,
Rage, rage against the dying of the light.

And you, my father, there on the sad height,
Curse, bless, me now with your fierce tears, I pray.
Do not go gentle into that good night.
Rage, rage against the dying of the light.

QUESTIONS
1. What do wise, good, wild, and grave men have in common? **2.** Why does the poet use the adjective "gentle" rather than the adverb "gently"? **3.** What is the "sad height" (l.16)?

The Death of the Ball Turret Gunner   1945

RANDALL JARRELL   [1914–1965]

From my mother's sleep I fell into the State,
And I hunched in its belly till my wet fur froze.
Six miles from earth, loosed from its dream of life,
I woke to black flak and the nightmare fighters.
When I died they washed me out of the turret with a hose.

QUESTIONS
1. To what do "its" (ll. 2 and 3) and "they" (l. 5) refer? **2.** Why is the mother described as asleep?

The Pardon   1950

RICHARD WILBUR   [b. 1921]

My dog lay dead five days without a grave
In the thick of summer, hid in a clump of pine
And a jungle of grass and honeysuckle-vine.
I who had loved him while he kept alive

Went only close enough to where he was
To sniff the heavy honeysuckle-smell
Twined with another odor heavier still
And hear the flies' intolerable buzz.

Well, I was ten and very much afraid.   10
In my kind world the dead were out of range
And I could not forgive the sad or strange
In beast or man. My father took the spade

And buried him. Last night I saw the grass
Slowly divide (it was the same scene
But now it glowed a fierce and mortal green)
And saw the dog emerging. I confess

I felt afraid again, but still he came
In the carnal sun, clothed in a hymn of flies,
And death was breeding in his lively eyes.
I started in to cry and call his name,   20

Asking forgiveness of his tongueless head.
. . . I dreamt the past was never past redeeming:
But whether this was false or honest dreaming
I beg death's pardon now. And mourn the dead.

Aubade [1]   1977

PHILIP LARKIN   [1922–1985]

I work all day, and get half drunk at night.
Waking at four to soundless dark, I stare.
In time the curtain-edges will grow light.
Till then I see what's really always there:
Unresting death, a whole day nearer now,
Making all thought impossible but how
And where and when I shall myself die.
Arid interrogation: yet the dread
Of dying, and being dead,
Flashes afresh to hold and horrify.   10

Aubade.
   [1] Morning song.

The mind blanks at the glare. Not in remorse
—The good not done, the love not given, time
Torn off unused—nor wretchedly because
An only life can take so long to climb
Clear of its wrong beginnings, and may never;
But at the total emptiness for ever,
The sure extinction that we travel to
And shall be lost in always. Not to be here,
Not to be anywhere,
And soon; nothing more terrible, nothing more true.   20

This is a special way of being afraid
No trick dispels. Religion used to try,
That vast moth-eaten musical brocade
Created to pretend we never die,
And specious stuff that says *No rational being*
Can fear a thing it will not feel, not seeing
That this is what we fear—no sight, no sound.
No touch or taste to smell, nothing to think with.
Nothing to love or link with,
The anaesthetic from which none come round.   30

And so it stays just on the edge of vision,
A small unfocused blur, a standing chill
That slows each impulse down to indecision.
Most things may never happen: this one will.
And realisation of it rages out
In furnace-fear when we are caught without
People or drink. Courage is no good:
It means not scaring others. Being brave
Lets no one off the grave.
Death is no different whined at than withstood.   40

Slowly light strengthens, and the room takes shape.
It stands plain as a wardrobe, what we know,
Have always known, know that we can't escape,
Yet can't accept. One side will have to go.
Meanwhile telephones crouch, getting ready to ring
In locked-up offices, and all the uncaring
Intricate rented world begins to rouse.
The sky is white as clay, with no sun.
Work has to be done.
Postmen like doctors go from house to house.   50

Watching *Dark Circle*[1]   1984

DENISE LEVERTOV   [b. 1923]

"*Why, this is hell, nor am I out of it*" Marlowe, Dr. Faustus

Men are willing to observe
the writhing, the bubbling flesh and
swift but protracted charring of bone
while the subject pigs, placed in cages designed for this,
don't pass out but continue to scream as they turn to cinder.
The Pentagon wants to know
something a child could tell it:
it hurts to burn, and even a match
can make you scream, pigs or people,
even the smallest common flame can kill you.   10
This plutonic calefaction is redundant.

Men are willing
to call the roasting of live pigs
a simulation of certain conditions. It is
not a simulation. The pigs (with their high-rated intelligence,
their uncanny precognition of disaster) are real,
their agony real agony, the smell
is not archetypal breakfast nor ancient feasting
but a foul miasma irremovable from the nostrils,
and the simulation of hell these men   20
have carefully set up
is hell itself,
            and they in it, dead in their lives,
and what can redeem them? What can redeem them?

After a Time   (1961?)

CATHERINE DAVIS   [b. 1924]

After a time, all losses are the same.
One more thing lost is one thing less to lose;
And we go stripped at last the way we came.

Watching Dark Circle
   [1] *Dark Circle* is a 1982 documentary film dealing with nuclear power and atomic warfare.

Though we shall probe, time and again, our shame,
Who lack the wit to keep or to refuse,
After a time, all losses are the same.

No wit, no luck can beat a losing game;
Good fortune is a reassuring ruse:
And we go stripped at last the way we came.

Rage as we will for what we think to claim,   10
Nothing so much as this bare thought subdues:
After a time, all losses are the same.

The sense of treachery—the want, the blame—
Goes in the end, whether or not we choose,
And we go stripped at last the way we came.

So we, who would go raging, will go tame
When what we have we can no longer use:
After a time, all losses are the same;
And we go stripped at last the way we came.

QUESTIONS

1. What difference in effect would occur if the refrain "After a time" were changed to "When life is done"? **2.** What are the various meanings of "stripped" in line 3 and line 19? **3.** Explain the meaning of "The sense of treachery" (l. 13). **4.** Does this poem say that life is meaningless? Explain.

WRITING TOPIC

Compare this poem with Dylan Thomas's "Do Not Go Gentle into That Good Night" (p. 697).

Casual Wear   1984

JAMES MERRILL [b. 1926]

Your average tourist: Fifty. 2.3
Times married. Dressed, this year, in Ferdi Plinthbower
Originals. Odds 1 to 9^{10}
Against her strolling past the Embassy

Today at noon. Your average terrorist:
Twenty-five. Celibate. No use for trends,
At least in clothing. Mark, though, where it ends.
People have come forth made of colored mist

Unsmiling on one hundred million screens
To tell of his prompt phone call to the station,   10
"Claiming responsibility"—devastation
Signed with a flourish, like the dead wife's jeans.

Five Ways to Kill a Man   1963

EDWIN BROCK   [b. 1927]

There are many cumbersome ways to kill a man:
you can make him carry a plank of wood
to the top of a hill and nail him to it. To do this
properly you require a crowd of people
wearing sandals, a cock that crows, a cloak
to dissect, a sponge, some vinegar and one
man to hammer the nails home.

Or you can take a length of steel,
shaped and chased° in a traditional way,   ornamented
and attempt to pierce the metal cage he wears.   10
But for this you need white horses,
English trees, men with bows and arrows,
at least two flags, a prince and a
castle to hold your banquet in.

Dispensing with nobility, you may, if the wind
allows, blow gas at him. But then you need
a mile of mud sliced through with ditches,
not to mention black boots, bomb craters,
more mud, a plague of rats, a dozen songs
and some round hats made of steel.   20

In an age of aeroplanes, you may fly
miles above your victim and dispose of him by
pressing one small switch. All you then
require is an ocean to separate you, two
systems of government, a nation's scientists,
several factories, a psychopath and
land that no one needs for several years.

These are, as I began, cumbersome ways
to kill a man. Simpler, direct, and much more neat
is to see that he is living somewhere in the middle   30
of the twentieth century, and leave him there.

Relic

1960

TED HUGHES   [b. 1930]

I found this jawbone at the sea's edge:
There, crabs, dogfish, broken by the breakers or tossed
To flap for half an hour and turn to a crust
Continue the beginning. The deeps are cold:
In that darkness camaraderie does not hold:
Nothing touches but, clutching, devours. And the jaws,
Before they are satisfied or their stretched purpose
Slacken, go down jaws; go gnawn bare. Jaws
Eat and are finished and the jawbone comes to the beach:
This is the sea's achievement; with shells,   10
Vertebrae, claws, carapaces, skulls.

Time in the sea eats its tail, thrives, casts these
Indigestibles, the spars of purposes
That failed far from the surface. None grow rich
In the sea. This curved jawbone did not laugh
But gripped, gripped and is now a cenotaph.°   empty tomb

QUESTIONS
1.   What is the "relic" of the title? What characteristic of nature does it symbolize?   **2.**   What does "Continue the beginning" (l. 4) signify?   **3.**   This poem is
metrically quite irregular and thus difficult to scan. Further, there are only two pair
of perfect rhymes (ll. 4-5 and 15-16). Yet the poem is richly musical. Identify the
poetic devices that generate the music.

People*

(trans. 1962)

YEVGENY YEVTUSHENKO   [b. 1933]

No people are uninteresting.
Their fate is like the chronicle of planets.

Nothing in them is not particular,
and planet is dissimilar from planet.

People
  * Translated by Robin Milner-Gulland and Peter Levi.

And if a man lived in obscurity
making his friends in that obscurity
obscurity is not uninteresting.

To each his world is private,
and in that world one excellent minute.

And in that world one tragic minute.   10
These are private.

In any man who dies there dies with him
his first snow and kiss and fight.
It goes with him.

They are left books and bridges
and painted canvas and machinery.

Whose fate is to survive.
But what has gone is also not nothing:

by the rule of the game something has gone.
Not people die but worlds die in them.   20

Whom we knew as faulty, the earth's creatures.
Of whom, essentially, what did we know?

Brother of a brother? Friend of friends?
Lover of lover?

We who knew our fathers
in everything, in nothing.

They perish. They cannot be brought back.
The secret worlds are not regenerated.

And every time again and again
I make my lament against destruction.   30

Cambridge Elegy   1987

(For Henry Averell Gerry, 1941–60)

SHARON OLDS   [b. 1942]

I hardly know how to speak to you now,
you are so young now, closer to my daughter's age
than mine—but I have been there and seen it, and must
tell you, as the seeing and hearing
spell the world into the deaf-mute's hand.
The tiny dormer windows like the ears of a fox, like the
long row of teats on a pig, still
perk up over the Square, though they're digging up the
street now, as if digging a grave,
the shovels shrieking on stone like your car   10
sliding along on its roof after the crash.
How I wanted everyone to die if you had to die,
how sealed into my own world I was,
deaf and blind. What can I tell you now,
now that I know so much and you are a
freshman still, drinking a quart of orange juice and
playing three sets of tennis to cure a hangover, such an
ardent student of the grown-ups! I can tell you
we were right, our bodies were right, life was
really going to be that good, that   20
pleasurable in every cell.
Suddenly I remember the exact look of your body, but
better than the bright corners of your eyes, or the
light of your face, the rich Long Island
puppy-fat of your thighs, or the slick
chino of your pants bright in the corners of my eyes, I
remember your extraordinary act of courage in
loving me, something no one but the
blind and halt had done before. You were
fearless, you could drive after a sleepless night   30
just like a grown-up, and not be afraid, you could
fall asleep at the wheel easily and
never know it, each blond hair of your head—and they were
thickly laid—put out like a filament of light,
twenty years ago. The Charles still
slides by with that ease that made me bitter when I
wanted all things hard as your death was hard;
wanted all things broken and rigid as the

bricks in the sidewalk or your love for me
stopped cell by cell in your young body.   40
Ave—I went ahead and had the children,
the life of ease and faithfulness, the
palm and the breast, every millimeter of delight in the body,
I took the road we stood on at the start together, I
took it all without you as if
in taking it after all I could most
honor you.

Metamorphosis   1985

LOUISE GLÜCK   [b. 1943]

1. NIGHT

The angel of death flies
low over my father's bed.
Only my mother sees. She and my father
are alone in the room.

She bends over him to touch
his hand, his forehead. She is
so used to mothering
that now she strokes his body
as she would the other children's,
first gently, then   10
inured to suffering.

Nothing is any different.
Even the spot on the lung
was always there.

2. METAMORPHOSIS

My father has forgotten me
in the excitement of dying.
Like a child who will not eat,
he takes no notice of anything.

I sit at the end of his bed
while the living circle us   20
like so many tree stumps.

Once, for the smallest
fraction of an instant, I thought
he was alive in the present again;
then he looked at me
as a blind man stares
straight into the sun, since
whatever it could do to him
is done already.

Then his flushed face   30
turned away from the contract.

3. FOR MY FATHER

I'm going to live without you
as I learned once
to live without my mother.
You think I don't remember that?
I've spent my whole life trying to remember.

Now, after so much solitude,
death doesn't frighten me,
not yours, not mine either.
And those words, *the last time,*   40
have no power over me. I know
intense love always leads to mourning.

For once, your body doesn't frighten me.
From time to time, I run my hand over your face
lightly, like a dustcloth.
What can shock me now? I feel
no coldness that can't be explained.
Against your cheek, my hand is warm
and full of tenderness.

QUESTIONS

1. Explain the title of the poem.   **2.** What is the relationship among the three parts of the poem?   **3.** Describe the speaker's feelings toward her father.

THE
PRESENCE
OF DEATH

Tombstones, 1942 by Jacob Lawrence

DRAMA

Steambath[*] 1970

BRUCE JAY FRIEDMAN   [b. 1930]

SETTING: A Steambath
TIME: The Present

Act One

A steamroom. Benches or slabs and a single overhead shower. Effect of steam is achieved by either steam or light or both. People speak, disappear in the haze, reappear. Characters are costumed in sheets or cloths or something in between. At the beginning of the action, a young man (thirty-five to forty-five) enters and sits down next to an Oldtimer. He is ever so slightly puzzled by his surroundings but does his best to conceal this mild concern. He has a great deal of trouble when he makes contact with the hot seat.

Oldtimer.   That's really something, isn't it, when you sit down?
Tandy.   It's a bitch.
Oldtimer.   It don't bother me. When you're a young fellow, it bothers you, but then you develop a tough ass.
Tandy.   I knew your beard got tough, but I didn't realize the other thing . . .
Oldtimer.   It's true.

(They sit awhile)

I've had some wonderful sweats in my time.
Tandy.   That right?
Oldtimer.   Oh yeah. When the Polish came in, the union gave them a steambath down on Fulton Street . . . Nobody sweats like the Polish . . . What you're doing now . . .
Tandy (*Feeling himself*).   Yes?
Oldtimer.   That's garbage. You're not sweatin' . . . I never exercised much, though. You see this area here. (*Pulls flesh in his lower back region*) I always wanted to keep that nice and soft in case I got some spinal trouble. So the

---

* Edited for television version.

needle could go right in. I know guys, athletes, they're so hard you can't stick a needle into them . . . I figure it's a good idea to keep it soft back there.

(They sit awhile longer)

How do you feel about heart attacks?

Tandy.   I'm against them.

Oldtimer.   Lot of people are. I'll say this for them, though. They don't mark you on the outside. They leave you clean as a whistle. That's more than you can say for a gall bladder.

Tandy.   I agree with you there.

Oldtimer.   I seen guys get cut up for ulcers they got bellies look like the map of downtown Newark, New Jersey . . . People have always been a little too rough on heart attacks. The heart attack's always gotten a raw deal.

(Bieberman, an unattractive fellow, concealed behind a pillar, clears his throat and then spits on the floor)

Hey, I saw that.

Bieberman.   What?

Oldtimer.   You know what. What you did. Expectorating like that. It's disgusting.

Bieberman.   What's wrong? It's a natural fluid.

Oldtimer.   You're a disgrace. *(To Tandy)* You got to watch him like a hawk. Probably farting back there, too. Who the hell would ever know in a steambath.

Bieberman *(Still concealed)*.   I heard that. I'm not farting.

Oldtimer.   Congratulations . . .

Bieberman.   My generation doesn't do that.

Oldtimer.   Your generation can kiss my tail. *(To Tandy)* What's your line, young fella?

Tandy.   I just quit my job. I was teaching art appreciation over at the Police Academy.

Oldtimer.   That right. What the hell . . . I guess you got to do something. Police, eh? Ever notice how you never get any trouble from the good people?

Tandy.   Well, that's for sure.

Oldtimer.   It's the bad ones you got to watch. You run the bad ones off the street that'll be the end of your crime. You got a son?

Tandy.   No, I've got a little girl.

Oldtimer.   You got a son, I hope he's a drunk. That'll keep him off drugs. He starts in on that dope stuff you can bid him a fond farewell. *(In reference to Bieberman)* What's that guy doing now?

Tandy *(Checking behind pillar)*.   Looks like he's eating an orange.

Oldtimer.   Yeah, but what's he *doing*?

Tandy *(Checks again, gets hit by a shower of seeds)*.   He's spitting out the pits.

Oldtimer.   Stupid mother. *(Shouting to Bieberman)* Hey, knock it off, will you?

Bieberman.   Well, what am I supposed to do with them?

Oldtimer.   Hold them in your hand. Swallow them. Stick 'em up your nose, what do I care. Just don't spit them out. Didn't you ever hear of a person tripping on pits? (*To Tandy*) They get some crowd in here. He's probably a fag, too.

Two Young Men (*Invisible, speaking in unison*).   No, we're the fags.

Oldtimer.   I beg your pardon. (*More or less to himself*) I knew there were fags in here. (*To Tandy*) You broke a sweat yet, son?

Tandy.   I can feel one coming.

Oldtimer.   You know what would go down really well now? A nice cool brew.

(*A Bar Boy enters with two cold beers and glasses. In later appearances, he is referred to as Gottlieb. Tandy and the Oldtimer each take a beer and begin to sip at it.*)

I drank a lot of beer in my time. One thing I'll say for myself is that I never gained weight. I gained bloat. The trouble is—bloat weighs a lot too. Most people don't realize that. Bloat can kill you.

Tandy.   What do you do?

Oldtimer.   I done a lot of things. In my late years I took to hackin' a cab. I was terrific once I got my daily icebreaker. But until then I wasn't fit to live with. That's how I had my crash—worried sick about getting my icebreaker. I come on the job at eight in the morning, it's twelve o'clock noon I still hadn't nailed a fare. I'm so upset I drive right through a furrier's window. Into the beaver pelts, I wound up with a car radio in my stomach. And I mean in my stomach, too. I had folk music coming out of my butt. So that was it.

Tandy.   That was it?

Oldtimer.   That was it.

(*A beautiful young girl comes forth, wearing a sheet, humming a tune. She is very blonde. Matter-of-factly She drops the sheet, steps beneath the shower and pulls the shower chain. Little cry of alarm when the water hits her, but She enjoys it. She puts the sheet back on and disappears in the haze.*)

Tandy.   She come in here often?

Oldtimer.   Can't say. Nice set of maracas on her, though.

Tandy.   Damn right.

Oldtimer.   You know, a lot of guys let the little old frankfurter rule their heads. I always say, let your head rule the little old frankfurter. You go along with that?

Tandy (*After thinking it over*).   Yeah! Well . . .

Oldtimer.   I never forget this rich bitch on Long Island had her eye on me. I said, madame, that little old weenie you're so interested in don't run the show. I'm the one that runs the show. She didn't like that.

Tandy (*Distracted*).   That was unusual.

Oldtimer.   What's that?

Tandy.   That girl. Taking a shower that way.

Oldtimer.   Nah, they got everything today.

(The Two Young Men come down and do a dancing and singing musical number from a popular Broadway musical comedy, complete with intricate steps, high kicks—in perfect unison. They have a little Panasonic-type player, of the cheap 42nd Street variety. This is the source of the music. They are quite good, semi-professional. They finish up big and then go back to their seats)

Tandy.   This is some place.
Oldtimer.   Lucky they didn't slip on the pits.

(Hoarse, guttural sounds in the back, suspiciously from Bieberman's direction)

Oldtimer.   What are you doing now?
Bieberman.   Gargling. I have a rough throat.
Oldtimer.   That's what I was afraid of. You watch your step, meathead. *(To Tandy)* He starts blowing his nose, I'm going after him . . .
Tandy.   They were very good. The dancers.
Oldtimer.   They do some good work. I never could enjoy a show much. I was always more interested in what was going on in the wings. I figured the real show, the good stuff, was going on back there. I'd rather sit and watch the wings than your top show on Broadway.
Tandy.   I'd rather watch a show. I've never been that interested in the wings. But I see what you mean.

(Blonde Girl approaches)

Meredith.   Are you all right?
Tandy.   I'm fine. How was your shower?
Meredith.   It was wonderful. Some day I'd like to meet the man who invented the needle-point showerhead and thank him for all the pleasure he's given me.
Tandy.   Do you come here often?
Meredith.   I don't know. All I can remember is that I was buying this little skirt at Bloomingdale's . . . it couldn't have been this big and they were . . .
Bieberman *(Appearing for the first time, on a ledge above Tandy and Meredith. He speaks with a certain stopped-up anger).*   You have no idea what those skirts have meant to members of my generation. What a skirt like that means to a fellow who could sit through the same movie seven times, willing to sell himself into bondage on a farm in Mississippi if he could see just an eighth of an inch of Ann Rutherford's inner thigh. And then there they are, out of the blue, those pitzel cocker skirts. And the girls wearing them, more beautiful than Ann Rutherford herself, are handing out massive looks at their thighs and crotches. No one has properly realized the effect of all that exposed and quivering flesh on the national character. And my generation is condemned to watch this country, representing one of the greatest social experiments in Western civilization, choke itself to death on an easy diet of boobs and tushes.
Tandy.   Look, do you mind? We were having a private conversation . . .
Bieberman.   As you wish.

(He drops his sheet, and, in his jockey shorts, begins to do a vigorous exercise, disgustingly close to Tandy and Meredith)

Tandy.   Do you have to do that here?

Oldtimer.   He's just getting warmed up.

Bieberman.   It's just till I work up a good healthy sweat.

Tandy.   Do it somewhere else, will you.

Bieberman (*Under his breath, as he moves off*).   Putz.[1]

Tandy (*Starting to chase Bieberman*).   Hey! (*To Oldtimer*) He *is* disgusting. I never saw it until just now.

Meredith.   You were a little hard on him.

Tandy.   Was I? I didn't realize it. I was with the cops for a while. In the cultural section. I still have a little of the cop style left.

Meredith.   Listen, if you were with the cops, could you tell me exactly where to kick someone so that he's temporarily paralyzed and can't rape you—yet at the same time doesn't feel you're an insensitive person . . .

Tandy.   We stayed away from that stuff in the art department. . . .

Meredith.   Well, I have to move out of the city anyway. All the men you meet here insist on dressing you up in something before they make love to you—garter belts, stiletto heels (*Demonstrates*), earmuffs, Luftwaffe[2] costumes. Right in the middle of this cultural wonderland, I spend all my time dressing up for weirdos, I don't need that. I could've gotten that in St. Louis. . . .

Tandy.   What really puzzles me is that I am able to talk to you so easily.

Meredith.   What do you mean?

Tandy.   Well, until recently, I had a great deal of trouble talking to yellow-haired girls. I felt I had to talk to them in verse or something . . . maybe wear special gloves. But apparently I've gotten over that.

Meredith.   You're so nice. I love meeting a nice new person like you. But look, I don't want to get involved.

Tandy.   Involved?

Meredith.   I just can't go through with that again . . . I've had that this year . . . the phone calls . . . My skin . . . For what it does to my skin alone, it's not worth it . . . Look, I just don't have the strength for another affair . . . Maybe around Labor Day . . . If it's worth anything, it'll be good then, too . . . Will you call me then?

Tandy (*Thinks awhile*).   I'll give you a ring.

Meredith.   You're not angry, are you?

Tandy.   I'm not angry.

Meredith.   It's got nothing to do with you personally . . . you seem like a very sensual person.

Oldtimer.   There is a terrible stink in here. And I got a pretty good idea who's responsible for it.

---

[1] Yiddish, a slang expression for the male organ.

[2] The German air force during World War II.

Bieberman.   I haven't done a thing recently.

Oldtimer.   You'll never convince me of that. Whatever you're doing, cut it out—for my sake, for the sake of this steambath, and for the sake of America.

Bieberman.   I'm just sitting here, being natural, being myself . . .

Oldtimer.   That's what it is? Natural? . . . That's what you've got to stop.

Tandy (*To Meredith*).   Listen, what do you think of this place?

Meredith.   I like it.

Tandy.   Notice anything peculiar about it?

Meredith.   It smells a little funny.

Oldtimer.   It sure as hell does.

Bieberman.   I haven't done a thing. I've been doing a crossword puzzle. (*To Tandy*) What's a six-letter word that means little red spikes of corn?

Oldtimer.   How about "giggie"? Used in a sentence, it goes: "Up your giggie."

Bieberman.   Lovely.

(*Lights darken. A screen drops. Stock quotations flash across the screen as they do in a brokerage office. A fellow appears with a chair, sits down opposite the screen, and watches the quotations*)

Broker (*Taking notes*).   They put that in for me.

Tandy.   How's the market?

Broker.   Lousy. If you own good stocks. When I went into this business, I had one piece of advice for every one of my customers: "Put your money in good stuff. Stay away from garbage. That's what you want, find yourself another broker. I don't touch it." So what happens in the last five years? The good stuff lays there, garbage goes right through the roof. Some of my customers, they went to other brokers, they bought garbage, they made fortunes . . .

Meredith (*Very trusting*).   Maybe the good stuff will improve. If it's really and truly good.

Broker.   Nah . . . It's too late for that . . .

(*Screen disappears. He picks up chair, recedes into the haze*)

Tandy.   That's the kind of thing I was talking about . . .

Meredith.   What do you mean?

Tandy.   A guy like that . . . in here . . . watching stocks . . . it's strange.

Meredith.   I just wish the numbers wouldn't go by so fast. You hardly have any time to enjoy them. Am I wrong or have you been doing pretty well lately?

Tandy.   I'm doing fine. I got a divorce. I quit the Police Academy. I'm writing a novel about Charlemagne.[3] And I just got involved in a charity. Helping brain-damaged welders. I was looking for a charity and that's the one I picked. They send out a terrific brochure. There are an awful lot of them . . . welders . . . with brain damage . . . and they're really grateful when you help them.

---

[3] A king who ruled the European kingdom of the Franks (768–814).

You should see the looks on some of those welders' faces. Could break your heart . . . I've been doing pretty well . . . I'm real close to my ten-year-old daughter.

Meredith.   You have a ten-year-old daughter?

Tandy.   Oh yeah, we just got back from Vegas.

Meredith.   How did she like it?

Tandy.   We got very close on that trip. So I've been doing pretty well lately . . .

Meredith.   Listen, you don't think . . .

Tandy.   What? What?

Meredith.   All I can remember is that Sheila and I were buying skirts at Bloomingdale's. Then we went back to our high-rise apartment on 84th Street and, oh, yes, the supermarket delivery boy was waiting behind the drapes, with a crazy look on his face, holding a blunt instrument . . .

Tandy.   I was in my favorite restaurant, eating some Chinese food. I was just about to knock off a double order of won shih pancakes . . .

Meredith.   You don't think?

Tandy.   . . . We're dead? Is that what you were going to say? That's what I was going to say. That's what we are. The second I said it, I knew it. Bam! Dead! Just like that! Christ!

Meredith.   I had it pictured an entirely different way.

Tandy.   What's that?

Meredith.   Being dead. I thought dying meant that you'd have to spend every day of your life at a different Holiday Inn. Then I decided it was seeing *So Proudly We Hail* with Veronica Lake[4] over and over for the rest of time. In a place where there were no Mounds bars.

(*Voice is heard: "Cold drinks, popcorn, Raisinettes, Goobers. And no Mounds bars"*)

Tandy.   Don't pay any attention. Somebody's kidding around.

Meredith (*With real loss*).   No Mounds bars . . .

Tandy.   I don't know about you, but I'm not accepting this.

Meredith.   What do you mean?

Tandy.   I don't like the whole way it was done. Bam. Dead. Just like that. Just like you're a schmuck[5] or something.

Meredith.   What are you going to do?

Tandy.   I'll do something. Don't worry. I'm a doer. If you had any idea of the agony I went through to change my life around you'd see why I'm so roped off. To be picked off like this when I haven't even started to enjoy the good stuff.

Meredith.   Well, how about me? I just had my first orgasm.

Tandy.   Just now?

Meredith.   No. While I was watching the Dick Cavett Show. I was all alone, eating some peach yogurt and I got this funny feeling.

---

[4] A Hollywood actress popular in films of the 1940s.

[5] Yiddish, a slang expression for the male organ.

Tandy. I'll tell you right now, I'm not going along with it. Not now. Not when I'm just getting off the ground. Another time, later on, they want me to be dead, fine. Not now. Uh-uh.

Meredith. I feel exactly the same way. How can I die? I haven't even bought any of those chunky platform shoes. And I've got to get my thighs down. Everything I eat has a little sign on it that says, "Do not pass go. Move directly to thighs." No, I absolutely can't die. Is there something you can do?

Tandy. I'll check around, see if I can find out something.

(Disappears in haze)

Oldtimer (*Reading newspaper*). Says here they got a new gas, one gallon of it'll wipe out an entire enemy country . . .

Broker. They got more than that. They got another one—just one drop in the water supply and the whole continent starts vomiting.

Oldtimer (*Sniffing*). They could bottle the smell around here, they don't need any gas. You hear that back there?

Bieberman. I'm not doing anything. I'm working on my toes.

Oldtimer. I knew it, the sonofabitch. What are you doing to them?

Bieberman. Trimming down the nails.

Oldtimer. In here? This is where you picked? Cut it out will you, you slob, you're trying my patience.

Tandy (*Taking aside Oldtimer*). Can I see you a second, Oldtimer?

Oldtimer. What's on your mind, fella? Havin' trouble breathin'? (*Demonstrating*) Suck it in through your mouth awhile.

Tandy. I was sitting over there with this girl . . .

Oldtimer (*Lasciviously*). The one with them chitty-chitty bang-bangs?

Tandy. That's the one.

Oldtimer. Don't let her get hold of your liverwurst. They get an armlock on that they never let go.

Tandy. I got the idea that we were dead. And she agrees with me. Now I can take the dead part. That doesn't scare me. I get older, a little tired, fine. I even thought maybe later on, things go smoothly, maybe I'll knock myself off. Make it simple. But the timing's all wrong now. I'm just getting off the ground. I'm in the middle of writing an historical novel. Right in the goddamn middle. (I don't talk this way in the book.) It's about Charlemagne. I've got a great new girl friend cooks me shish kebab. Bryn Mawr[6] girl. And she still cooks shish kebab. Doesn't bother her a bit. And I never think about Wendy.

Oldtimer. Wendy?

Tandy. My ex-wife. Wendy Tandy. Jesus, I just realized, she was Wendy Hilton, I turned her into Wendy Tandy. I probably blew the whole marriage right there. She never went for that name. Can't say that I blame her. Anyway, I don't think about her anymore. Weeks at a time. She could be out

---

[6] A women's college in Pennsylvania.

balling the whole Royal Canadian Mounties I don't give it a thought. I forgive her. She's a little weak. It's got nothing to do with me. So, you see, I'm really just starting a wonderful new chapter of my life. And along comes this death number—I thought maybe you could help me . . .

Oldtimer.   I hardly know what to say to you, fella. You come at me like a ten-foot wave.

Tandy.   Is there a guy in charge? Somebody I can talk to. E. G. Marshall? Raymond Burr?

Oldtimer.   There's a guy comes around. I see him I'll point him out.

Tandy.   Thanks. You're a good guy. When we get out of this, maybe we can pal around together.

Oldtimer.   You probably smell the sea on me. Before I took up hackin' I worked the China coast for seventeen years. Me and my friend Ollie were the most widely respected duo west of Macao. We'd get ourselves a couple of juki-juki girls, take 'em up on deck and do a little missionary work with 'em anchored in front of Bruce Wong's Monkey Meat Shop in Hong Kong Harbor. They arrested Ollie for abusing himself into the holy water fountain at the Merchant Seaman's Chapel. He died in irons and I lost the best friend I ever had . . .

(Fades off, a bit overcome with emotion)

Meredith.   What did that old man say?

Tandy.   He said there's a fellow around who seems to be in charge. That he'd point him out to me. Listen, how do you feel?

Meredith.   I don't mind being nude, if that's what you mean. I just don't attribute that much importance to it.

Tandy.   I know that. I can tell.

Meredith.   I wouldn't want to get out there and do splits or anything.

Tandy.   Who asked you to do splits? Is that what you think I want—splits?

Meredith.   I just like to be nude sometimes. It's very tranquil.

(A Puerto Rican Attendant has been mopping up the steambath for awhile. He comes clearly into view now. He sings "Sorrento." Lah lah lah lah sentimento . . . lah lah lah lah sentirinco . . . lah lah lah lah ladimento . . . lah lah lah lah lah lah lah. Stops mopping to do the bridge, really performing now . . . lah lah lah lah lah lah . . . etc. After a big finish, He says, "Thank you, music lovers" as though to a nightclub audience . . .)

Oldtimer *(Signaling to Tandy).*   Psssst.

Tandy *(Gesturing toward Attendant).*   Him?

(Oldtimer acknowledges correctness with a wink)

You sure?

Oldtimer. Yup . . .
Tandy (*To Meredith*).   He says that's the fellow in charge.
Meredith. He's cute.
Attendant. Hiya, baby.

(*Attendant now wheels out what appears to be a console with a screen. It is a very tacky-looking affair. The screen is visible to the attendant but not to the audience. The console, from time to time, answers the Attendant with little blipping noises as though taking note of his instructions. In between sections of his monologue, the Puerto Rican does little snatches of "Sorrento" again*)

(*Leaning over console*)   San Diego Freeway . . . All right, first thing, I want that Pontiac moving south past Hermosa Beach to crash into the light blue Eldorado coming the other way. Make it a head-on collision . . . the guy in the Chevy—his wife's got her behind out the window—it's the only way they get their kicks—they're going to jump the rail into the oncoming lane, and screw up a liquor salesman in a tan Cougar. No survivors . . .

All right, what's-his-name, Perez, the Puerto Rican schmuck from the Bronx. The one who says, "My wife and I—we are married forty years. We are born on the same hill. There can be no trouble." He comes home tonight, I want her in bed with her brother. Perez walks in, goes crazy, starts foaming at the mouth, the other tenants in the building have to tie him to a radiator . . .

All right, the guy from St. Louis . . . bedspread salesman . . . adopted all those Korean kids. Him they pick up in the men's room of the Greyhound Bus Terminal, grabbing some truckdriver's schvontz.[7] They ask around, find out he's been doing it for years . . . The kids get shipped back to Korea.

Now, here's one I like . . . The screenwriter flying out to Beverly Hills. Coming on with the broads. Here's what happens. Over Denver, a stewardess throws a dart in his eye. No doctor on board. He has to go all the way to Los Angeles like that. Give Debbie Reynolds an ear infection.

Now, the producer up in New Haven. Never had a hit. Doing a $750,000 musical . . . the whole show depends on the female star. All right. A police dog gets loose in the theatre and bites her tits off. The understudy is scared to death, but she goes on anyway. Bombsville. Next day, the guy gets out of the business . . .

(*Starts to leave, returns*)

Wait a minute, I got an idea. Back to the Freeway. That guy whose radiator boiled over . . . on the side of the road, saw the whole thing. Thought he got away clean. He gets knocked unconscious by the broad with her behind out the window. Never knew what hit him. That's all for now.

---

[7] Yiddish, a slang expression for the male organ.

(He picks up mop and continues to mop the steambath floor. He sings "Sorrento." And he disappears for the moment in the haze)

Tandy.   You sure that's the fellow in charge?
Oldtimer.   That's him all right. He runs the show.
Tandy.   What's his name?
Oldtimer.   Morty.
Tandy.   A Puerto Rican guy? Morty?
Oldtimer.   It's Spanish. *(Pronouncing name with Spanish inflection)* Mawwrrr-teee.
Tandy *(To Meredith)*.   He's sure that's the fellow in charge.
Meredith.   Well if he isn't, he certainly has a rich imagination.
Tandy.   You say he hangs around here.
Oldtimer.   All the time. He comes and goes.

(Attendant returns, singing softly, sweeping, goes to console again. His voice is much softer now)

Attendant.   Okay, the other side of the coin. The kid in a hospital in Trenton, beautiful kid, works for Kentucky Fried Chicken. Got his foot shot off in a stick-up. The night nurse comes in, jerks him off under the covers. Lovely broad, little old, but she really knows what she's doing . . .
   Give Canada a little more rain . . .
   That Indian tribe outside of Caracas. Sick little guys, they ain't got a hundred bucks between 'em . . . Government doesn't give a damn. CBS moves in, shoots a jungle series there, throws a lot of money around . . .
   The old lady with the parakeet, flies out the window, flies back in . . .
   Wellesley[8] girl, parents got a lot of dough—she's sitting on a ledge—35th floor of the Edison Hotel. A cop crawls out after her, tells her she's full of hot air. They go back in, watch a hockey game on TV . . . And clean up that garbage in the lobby . . . It's disgusting . . . All right, that's enough good stuff.
Voice.   You need one more.
Attendant.   Christ, I'm exhausted. Uhh . . . Put bigger bath towels in all the rooms at the Tel Aviv Hilton Hotel.
Voice.   Terrific!
Attendant.   You kidding, buddy . . .

(Exits)

Meredith.   I liked him much more the second time.
Tandy.   He's got some style. Who's he think he is?
Oldtimer.   God.
Tandy.   You believe that?

---

[8] A women's college in Massachusetts.

Oldtimer. I'm not saying yes and I'm not saying no. I been around and I seen a lot of strange things in my time. I once stood in an Algerian pissoir urinal and watched the head of a good friend of mine come rolling up against my size 12 moccasins like a bowling ball. Cut right off at the neck. He'd gotten into a little scuffle with some Gurkhas. May have called one of them a fag. Didn't know there aren't any fag Gurkhas.

Two Young Men. That's what you think.

Tandy. Well, what the hell are we supposed to do, just stay here?

Broker. There's nothing that great out there. The market stinks. You don't make a quarter unless you're in pork bellies. That ain't investing.

Tandy. I'm not going along with this. For Christ's sakes, I'm in the middle of writing an historical novel. About Charlemagne. I got all that research to do. So far I've been going on instinct. What the hell do I know about Charlemagne. But the book feels good . . .

Meredith. And I've got an appointment at the beauty parlor. To get a Joan of Arc haircut. And my roommate Sheila and I are going to make little plastic surrealistic doodads and sell them to boutiques.

Tandy. I'll get us out of this. Did you try the door?

Meredith. No, why?

Tandy. Don't try it. I'm pretty sure it doesn't open. If I find out for sure I'll get claustrophobia . . . Is there another way out? What's this door? (*Referring to second door at opposite side of the stage*)

Oldtimer. You go through there.

Tandy. When's that?

Oldtimer. Hard to say . . . We had a guy, a baker, he put him in there.

Tandy. What did he do?

Oldtimer. Not much. Beat the Puerto Rican in arm-wrestling.

Broker. Had a little trouble with his baking though. Everything used to burn up on him. Pastries, cupcakes . . . meat pies . . .

Tandy. Don't tell me about cupcakes now . . . no cupcakes. When he puts you in there, does he let you out?

(*Oldtimer chuckles, as if to say, "Are you kidding?"*)

And that's it, the two doors?

Oldtimer. That's it. That's the whole cheesecake.

(*Tandy very casually sidles up to entrance door, tries it. It doesn't open. Tries a little harder. Still won't*)

Tandy. About the way I figured. I'll get us out of here, don't worry. You with me?

Meredith. Are you serious? Of course. But you haven't said how.

Tandy. I'll get us out. You'll find I do most things well. Of course, I have never been able to get out to Kennedy Airport. On my own. I can get near it, but never really in it. The Van Wyck Expressway scene really throws me.

Meredith.   You're sort of inconsistent, aren't you?

Tandy.   You noticed that, eh. I admit it. I've got wonderful qualities, but getting out to airports is not one of them. Don't worry, though, I'll get us out of here. By sheer strength of will and determination. I believe I can do anything if I really put my mind to it. I've always felt that even if I had a fatal illness, with an army of diseased phagocytes coursing through my body in triumph, if I really decided to, I could reverse the course of those phagocytes and push them the hell back where they belong . . .

Meredith.   The world admires that kind of determination.

Tandy.   You're damned right.

Meredith.   What if we really are dead, though?

Tandy.   I know. I've been trying not to think about it. No more toast. No more clams. Clams oregano . . . *Newsweek* . . . Jesus, no more *Newsweek*. Wait a minute, I'll get this straightened out right now . . . (*He approaches Attendant, who has come mopping into view*) Say, fella . . .

Attendant.   You addressing I?

Tandy.   That's right. What's the deal around here? The Oldtimer says you're God.

Attendant.   Some people call me that.

Tandy.   But that's ridiculous . . . a Puerto Rican . . .

Attendant.   The Puerto Ricans go back hundreds of years. Millions. There were Puerto Ricans in Greece, Rome. Diogenes—very big, very strong Puerto Rican. Too many people make fun of the Puerto Ricans. Very fine people. Lots of class. We got Herman Badillo[9] Mario Puzo.[10]

Tandy.   All right, I'll go along with you for a second. You're God. Why would you be sweeping up, a lowly job like that?

Attendant.   It's therapeutic. I like it. It's easy on the nerves.

Tandy.   God . . . A Puerto Rican steambath attendant. That'll be the day.

Attendant.   Look, I'll tell you what, fella. You say I'm not God. All right. You got it. I'm not God. Fabulous. You got what you want. (*Pointing to Bieberman*) He's God.

Oldtimer.   He ain't God. He's a slob.

Bieberman.   Everything doesn't pay off in cleanliness. There are other virtues.

Oldtimer.   You stink to the high heavens.

Two Young Men.   We've reached the conclusion that you're being much too tough on him.

Oldtimer.   Don't you two ever split up?

Two Young Men (*Seductively*).   Make us an offer.

Attendant.   Mister, just don't bug me. All right? I got a lot on my mind.

Tandy.   There's another one. God talking slang. How can I go along with that?

---

[9] A Puerto Rican novelist and politician.
[10] American novelist and screenwriter.

Attendant.   I talk any way I want, man. The Lord speaks in funny ways. Remember that. You want to discuss the relativity of mass, the Lorentz Transformation, galactic intelligence, I'll give you that, too. Just don't bug me. All right? Don't be no wise ass.

Tandy.   That was more like it. You had me going there for a second. I respect anyone who really knows something, my work being as transitory as it is. It's when you talk dirty . . .

Attendant.   The way I talk, the way I talk . . . Don't you see that's just a little blink of an eye in terms of the universe, the job I got to do? The diameter of an electron is one ten-trillionth of an inch. And you're telling me I shouldn't talk dirty. Let me talk the way I want. Let me relax a little.

(Approaches console screen again)

All right, give that girl on the bus a run on her body stocking. I want to close up that branch of Schrafft's . . . And send up a bacon-and-lettuce-and-tomato sandwich, hold the mayo. You burn the toast, I'll smite you down with my terrible swift sword.

(Leaves the console)

Tandy.   I still don't buy it. That could be an ordinary TV screen. You could have been watching *All in the Family.*

Attendant   *All in the Family? (Goes over to console)* Cancel *All in the Family.* You still want to fool around?

Tandy.   I don't watch *All in the Family.* Only thing I watch on TV is pro football. Gets better every year. Look, you're asking me to buy a whole helluva lot. You're challenging every one of my beliefs.

Attendant.   You think I care about your beliefs? With the job I got on my mind?

Tandy.   You care. I may be one man, but there exists within me the seed of all mankind.

Attendant.   Very good. I'm going to give you a ninety on that.

Tandy.   I used to tell that to my art-appreciation students over at the Police Academy.

Attendant.   Nice bunch of boys.

Tandy.   You mean to tell me that you control every action on earth by means of that monitor over there? Every sneeze, every headache, every time a guy cuts himself? How can you possibly do so much?

Attendant.   I go very fast. You got to move like crazy. You can't stop and talk to every schmuck who comes along . . .

(Gottlieb, Attendant's assistant, comes in with a tray)

Gottlieb.   Your BLT down, sir.

Attendant.   Thank you. What do I owe you for that?

Gottlieb.   Are you kidding, sire?

Attendant.   Just thought I'd ask. You don't have to get snotty about it.

(Gottlieb goes off. Attendant eats)

Tandy.   I don't know. It's awfully hard to accept. I've heard of having your faith tested, but this is ridiculous.

Attendant (*Chewing BLT*).   And who said you could speak while I was eating?

Tandy.   All right. I'm sorry. I beg your pardon. One minute you're casual, the next you're formal. How can I keep up with you?

Attendant.   Changeable, mysterious, infinite, unfathomable. That's my style . . .

Tandy.   Yeah—except that you're not God.

Attendant.   That's the conclusion you reached after all the time I spent with you? I'll tell you right now you're getting me roped off. I get roped off, watch out. Then you're really in trouble. (*Pulling himself together*) All right. I'll tell you what. You say I'm not God, right?

Tandy.   Right.

Attendant (*Pulling out deck of cards, and spreading them, like fan*).   All right. Pick a card, any card.

Tandy.   What's that gonna prove?

Attendant.   Go ahead, just do what I'm tellin' you. You'll see.

(Tandy picks card)

You look at it?

Tandy.   Yes.

Attendant (*Squinting eyes*).   Okay . . . you got the . . . King of Hearts . . . Right?

(Broker, most nervous of all characters, applauds)

Tandy.   All right. You did it. So what?

Attendant.   So there y'are.

Tandy.   There I am what? You do a simple card trick that any kid can do—a retarded kid can do—and I'm supposed to think you're God.

Attendant.   Can you do it?

Tandy.   No, I can't do it. I can't even deal a hand of blackjack. But there are hundreds of guys who can do that trick. In every village and hamlet in the country. What the hell does that prove?

Attendant.   Not in the hamlets. It's not that easy. In the villages, maybe, but not in the hamlets. All right, I show you a trick that's not as easy as it seems, you won't buy it. Fair enough. You're pushing me to the wall. I'm not saying a word. Now, check my pants. And easy on the corporeal contact.

(Tandy begrudgingly does so)

Anything in there?

Tandy.   There's nothing in there.

Attendant *(With a flourish).*   Now . . . *(Pulls out a long multi-colored scarf)* How's that? *(Drapes it over Meredith as a shawl)*

Tandy.   I've seen it about a dozen times.

Attendant.   Where?

Tandy.   On the Sullivan Show.[11] These Slavic guys come over here and do that trick. On a bicycle. Look, I'm sorry. I don't know quite how to say this, but you are not even putting a *dent* in me. What kind of second-rate crap is this?

Attendant *(Gesturing as though he is pulling a knife out of his chest).*   Madre de Dios. You hurt my feelings just now, you know that, don't you?

Tandy.   There's a perfect example. God with his feelings hurt. Ridiculous.

Attendant.   My feelings are not supposed to get hurt? Once in a while? All right. Now I'm really going to give you one. *(Calling into the wings)* Gottlieb.

(Assistant runs out with a footlocker kept shut by a huge padlock. Sets it down)

Thanks, Gottlieb, I won't forget this. *(To Tandy)* All right. Check the lock.

Tandy *(Following instructions).*   I checked it.

Attendant.   Is it strong?

Tandy.   Very strong, very powerful. Big deal.

Attendant.   All right. Observez-vous.

(Gottlieb ties his hands behind him. He kneels down and, with his teeth, sawing away like a bulldog, chews and chews and finally springs the lock. Gottlieb has been doing an accompanying song-and-dance routine, neatly timed, as though they have been through this many times before. With lock in his teeth, arms upraised, like a trapeze man, Attendant acknowledges applause. Gottlieb throws a few ribbons of confetti over his head)

Voilà!

Tandy.   It was okay, I admit. It was a little better than the others. At least you're showing me a little something. Look, I don't know how to get this across to you, but you are not reaching me with this stuff. Maybe I'm crazy. If you had made one interesting intellectual assault on my mind, maybe that would do it.

Attendant.   De gustibus non est disputandum.[12]

Tandy.   That's it? That's the intellectual assault? Freshman English?

Attendant.   Have you ever really pondered it? Savored it? Rolled it around on your tongue and really tasted of its fruit?

---

[11] A popular television show, hosted by Ed Sullivan, that aired from 1955 to 1971.

[12] Latin, meaning "There is no disputing about taste."

Tandy.   That's right. I have. And it's nothing. It's garbage. It's not the kind of insight to make the senses reel.

Attendant (*Gathering others about him*).   Consider the mind, an independent substance implanted within the soul and incapable of being destroyed . . . The City of Satan, whatever its artifices in art, war, or philosophy, was essentially corrupt and impious, its joy but a comic mask and its beauty the whitening of a sepulchre. It stood condemned before man's better conscience by its vanity, cruelty, and secret misery, by its ignorance of all that it truly behooved a man to know who was destined to immortality . . . Or how about this one: "A little philosophy inclineth man's mind to atheism, but depth in philosophy bringeth men's minds about to religion."

Tandy.   Much better. Maybe I could even chew on some of that. But you still haven't got me. All I can see is a fairly interesting guy. For a Puerto Rican. If I ran into you at a bar—a Puerto Rican bar—maybe we could kick around a few ideas. All I'm saying is I don't see God yet. Where's God?

Attendant.   You don't see God, huh? Boy, you're some pistol. All right, here comes a little number that is going to make your head swim. You happen to be in luck, fella, because you caught me at cocktail time and I'm dry as a bone. Gottlieb . . . Now you watch this carefully . . .

(*Gottlieb emerges with tray of drinks*)

How many drinks you estimate are on that tray?

Tandy.   Ten . . .

(*Attendant begins to knock them off, one at a time*)

. . . and you don't even have to bother drinking them, because I can name you two lushes out there on Eighth Avenue who can do the same thing . . . I mean, what is this . . . it's not even as good as the trunk. You might have snapped off a few teeth on that one . . . but this cheap, trivial, broken-down, ninth-rate . . .

(*As He speaks, Gottlieb returns, struggling to bring in an enormous whiskey sour, one that towers above Tandy's head. Tandy is thunderstruck*)

Are you mad?

Attendant.   Un momento.

(*He leaps to top tier of column, sits opposite rim of glass, pulls out a straw and takes a sip*)

Delicious. That sonofabitch makes some drink.

(*Attendant finishes up with a flourish, leaps down*)

All right, what have you got to say to that, baby? Incidentally, you like the cherry, go ahead, don't be embarrassed . . .

Tandy.   It was pretty good. All right. I take that back. Fair is fair. It was great. My hat goes off to you. It was really remarkable. I figure the odds were about fifty to one against. I hardly know how to say this next thing, but I'm still not buying it. The God routine.

Attendant.   You're still not buying it?

Tandy.   No sir. The fact that I just said "sir" will give you an indication that I'm really impressed. You got a lot going for you. But I'm not really there yet. If I said I bought the whole thing you'd know I wasn't being straight. It would be an injustice of a kind. A real sell-out.

Attendant.   So then you still don't buy it?

Tandy.   No sir.

Attendant.   You really making me work, boy. All right. I have but one choice, my son. (*Gestures*) Shazam . . .

(*Stage, theatre, suddenly fill with deafening organ music, churchlike, ancient, soaring, almost unbearable. Theatre then fills with angels or other miraculous and heavenly effects. Attendant stands majestically, his head crowned with celestial light. He ascends to highest tier in steambath. Music is deafening in its churchlike call to the divinity. Voice of Attendant, magnified a hundred-fold, booms out*)

Attendant's Voice.   ASCRIBE UNTO THE LORD YE KINDREDS OF THE PEOPLES . . .
ASCRIBE UNTO THE LORD
GLORY AND STRENGTH . . .
ASCRIBE UNTO THE LORD
THE GLORY DUE UNTO HIS NAME
BRING AN OFFERING
AND COME UNTO HIS COURTS
OH, WORSHIP THE LORD
IN THE BEAUTY OF HOLINESS
TREMBLE BEFORE HIM
ALL THE EARTH . . .

(*One by one, the Steambath People drop to their knees. Tandy looks around, observes that He is the only one standing. He shrugs, goes to one knee*)

Curtain

Act Two

People are all lying around, exhausted, as though after a heavy night-long bacchanal

(Broker comes skipping in with a rope)

Broker *(To Tandy)*.   You ought to try this . . . Really gets the weight off you . . . Look in the mirror sometime while you're doing it. Everything moves. The stuff way inside—where you have the real weight—that's moving too . . . *(Stops jumping)* How much do you weigh? . . .

Tandy.   Me? Around 190 . . . 195 . . . somewhere in there . . .

Broker.   I'm 179 myself. I'd like to lose around ten, twelve pounds. Twelve pounds I'd feel like a tiger . . . *(Grabbing some flesh about his waist)* I got to lose it around here—that's where it's rough . . . 'specially when you get around my age . . .

Tandy.   That's right . . .

Broker.   One hundred sixty-eight. That's my perfect weight. You should see me at 168. Never seen anything like it . . .

Tandy.   I bet you look great . . .

Broker.   I do. I get up in the middle, high seventies, forget it. It's all gone . . . You want to hear something else . . .

Tandy.   Shoot.

Broker.   When I'm 168, I get a beautiful bowel movement . . . How about you. You pretty regular?

Tandy.   I don't want to hurt your feelings or anything, but I'm really not that interested in your bowel movements . . .

Broker.   I can see that . . . Sorry if I was presumptuous . . .

Tandy.   Perfectly all right . . .

Broker.   I once bought a stock at 168—my exact weight . . . Fellow who recommended it said this is a stock you don't worry about. It goes off, for argument's sake, ten, twenty, fifty points, I don't care if it goes off a hundred points . . . you don't worry about this stock. So I hold it. And it *does* go off ten, twenty, over a hundred points. The stock is now selling at a fast ten points. So I call the guy. It's down to ten, I say. When do I start worrying? "Never," he says. He just wasn't a worrier. I lost every penny . . . Shows you . . . go trust people . . . I should've stuck to ferns . . .

Tandy.   Ferns?

Broker.   That's right. I was in the fern game for a while. A lot of people go in for ferns, you'd be surprised. I was cleaning up. But I couldn't take the social pressure . . . Guy at a party'd ask me what do you do, I'd say I'm in ferns . . . How do you think that made me feel?

Oldtimer.   Turn off that TV set . . .

Broker.   I had to get out . . .

Bieberman.   I'm watching a wonderful forties' movie. And it's down very low.

Oldtimer.   Turn it off, I tell you. I'm trying to catch a quick snooze. Turn it off or I'll come up there and kick you in the bazanzas . . .

Bieberman.   What are they?

Oldtimer.   Never mind. You'll find out fast enough if I kick you there.

Bieberman.   Anti-Semite.

Oldtimer.   I'm an anti-stinkite. That's what *you* got to worry about. Now turn it off, I tell you . . .

Bieberman (*Always a little bitter, angry when He speaks, spitting the words out deliberately*).   I suppose it never occurred to you that every smile, every whisper, every puff of a cigarette taken by my generation was inspired by the forties' movie. That my generation wouldn't know how to mix a drink, drive a car, kiss a girl, straighten a tie—if it weren't for Linda Darnell[13] and George Brent . . . That the sole reason for my generation's awkward floundering in the darkness is that Zachary Scott is gone . . . and I assure you that Mick Jagger is no substitute . . .

Oldtimer.   I'll tell you what your generation needs. A movie that instructs you on how to smell like a human being. You can star in it. (*To Tandy*) How can he even see the screen with all this steam . . .

Bieberman.   When it gets too dense I smear it off with a corner of my jockey shorts . . .

Oldtimer.   I spent four years in the Philippines I never ran into a slob like that. (*Suddenly clutches at his chest, as though having a heart attack, then realizes this is impossible and gestures as if to say "The hell with it"*)

Tandy.   C'mon, you guys, knock it off. You're supposed to be dead. Act like it.

Meredith.   It's wonderful the way they listen to you.

Tandy.   It's probably that time I spent with the cops. It really changes you. Even when you're in the art department.

Meredith.   Oh, my God . . .

Tandy.   What's wrong?

Meredith.   I just remembered. I haven't paid my Bloomingdale's bill.

Tandy.   When was it due?

Meredith.   Last Monday . . . now they'll probably send me one of those thin gray envelopes . . . You have no idea how much I hate those envelopes . . .

Tandy.   But it's ridiculous. You can't pay your bills now. The store will understand.

Meredith.   Bloomingdale's!

Tandy.   Look, obviously none of this has sunk in. We're in big trouble. We could be stuck in this lousy steambath forever. You're sitting around talking Bloomingdale's. You saw that Puerto Rican guy . . . He wasn't kidding around . . .

Meredith.   That was fun.

---

[13] Hollywood actress popular in films of the 1940s. George Brent and Zachary Scott were actors during the same era.

Tandy.   What do you mean?

Meredith.   The part where we got down on our knees. We used to do that at Marymount every morning, first thing, and it was freezing. It was fun getting down on a nice warm floor for a change . . .

Tandy.   It wasn't any fun for me. I got to get out of here. I got all this Charlemagne research to do. There's going to be a whole Charlemagne revival, I can tell. Books, movies, musical comedies. Dolls—that's right. Little Charlemagne dolls. And I'll be left out of it. Where is that guy? I'm going to take another shot at him.

(Disappears for the moment in haze)

Bieberman.   Anyone have some pimple lotion?

Oldtimer.   There he goes again, the meathead.

Bieberman.   Well, can I control my complexion, can I?

Oldtimer.   Of course you can. Ever hear of cutting down on malteds?

Bieberman.   I'll never cut down on malteds, never.

Oldtimer.   Well, then, don't come to me with your pimples, you stupid bastard.

Bieberman.   Malteds are the marijuana of my generation.

Oldtimer.   Your generation . . . what the hell generation is that?

Bieberman.   It went by very quickly . . . It was Dolf Camilli, Dane Clark, Uncle Don, Ducky Medwick and out . . .

Oldtimer.   Sounds like a bunch of winners.

Bieberman.   We produced Norman Podhoretz.

Oldtimer.   Congratulations . . . *(To the Broker)* Who the hell is Norman Podhoretz?

Broker.   Probably some wealthy guy who made it when you could keep it.

Tandy *(Entering)*.   We're all set.

Meredith.   What's up?

Tandy.   I've got a whole bunch of carpet tacks.

Meredith.   Wow. Where did you get them?

Tandy.   They got an old carpet rolled up back there.

Meredith.   What good'll they do?

Tandy.   Plenty. Don't undersell them. I once saw a guy with only a handful of carpet tacks get the best of two armed cops.

Meredith.   That's remarkable, overpowering two policemen that way.

Tandy.   That's right. Where is that guy. Listen, we get out, I'd like you to see my apartment. I've got big steel bars on the windows—I had a few robberies—but I've got the bars painted in psychedelic colors. I've got huge double security locks—they're painted in psychedelic colors, too. Burglar alarm—same deal.

Meredith.   I'd love to see your apartment.

Tandy.   I'd like you to see it. It's not a horny thing. I won't jump on you or anything.

Meredith.   Oh, I know that.

Tandy.   Well, as a matter of fact, it *is* a partially horny thing. You're a very good-looking girl . . . but I'm also proud of the apartment.

Meredith.   Don't you have a girl friend?

Tandy.   Oh yes, I've got an ex-wife, a mistress, a mother . . . I'm covered on all sides. Now I just need a girl . . .

Meredith.   I understand. You just want someone totally uncomplicated.

Tandy.   That's right.

Meredith.   It's only fair to tell you that I can only sleep with one man at a time. If I slept with you I might reach across in the middle of the night and think I was stroking Raymondo.

Tandy.   Raymondo? Listen, don't worry about it. I just want you to see my place sometime . . . Listen, you and your roommate don't . . . I mean . . . together.

Meredith.   Make scenes? . . . Oh no . . . we don't do that.

Tandy.   I hope you don't take offense . . . I was just checking.

Meredith.   We don't any more, that is. We did take a mescaline trip recently with one of my stockbroker friends. It didn't work out. It turned into a sort of business trip.

Tandy.   Well, look, I don't need that right now. I got my hands full the way it is . . . It's just that when you work with the cops you see a lot of crazy things, you get ideas. You should go out on a few homicides. You should see what incensed Mexicans do to their common-law wives when they step out of line. Believe me, you'd never want to be a Mexican common-law wife.

Meredith.   Oh, I don't know. I hear Cuernavaca's beautiful.

Oldtimer (*To Broker*).   Toughest sonofabitch I ever knew used to dress up like Carmen Miranda.[14] They found him floating five kilometers outside Hamburg Harbor . . . all those bananas bobbing in the water.

(*Attendant enters, Gottlieb along with him*)

Attendant.   All right, everybody, campfire time. Gottlieb, give out the Mounds bars.

(*Gottlieb distributes candy bars to Steambath Inhabitants, who gather round an improvised campfire site*)

Meredith (*Accepting a candy bar*).   Oh, I love these . . .

Tandy (*Calling Attendant aside*).   Listen, I want to talk to you about getting out of here. I got a lot of deals going on the outside, a lot of things to clear up. I don't know if you know anything about Charlemagne . . .

Attendant.   The Puerto Rican?

---

[14] Portuguese-born actress who appeared in popular Hollywood films of the 1940s set in Latin America. In these films, she often danced in elaborate costumes.

Tandy.   Cute. Listen, I haven't mentioned it yet, but I want you to know that was very impressive stuff you did, drinking all that stuff, those lights . . . very good . . .

Attendant.   I saw you on your knees.

Tandy.   One knee. I just went down on one knee . . . Maybe that's half-assed, I don't know. Maybe a straight solid guy—a Henry Kissinger—would have either given you both knees or said the hell with it . . . I don't know. I figured you run the place I'll throw you one knee. A little respect. Meanwhile, I got to talk to you about getting out of here. I don't belong here, I don't need this.

Attendant.   You know what I don't need? Right now? Aggravation.

Tandy.   God, aggravated. There's another hot one.

Attendant.   Listen, if you're God, the name of the game is aggravation. Anyway, I don't want to hear anymore. You say another word, baby, I'll become wrathful and vengeance-seeking.

(Gestures to Broker to begin)

Broker.   For twenty years I was mad at my partner.

Attendant.   Once upon a time . . .

Broker.   Excuse me . . . Once upon a time for twenty years I was mad at my partner.

Attendant.   Hold it a second. Any broads in this story?

Broker.   No.

Attendant.   Gottlieb, you want to stay?

(Gottlieb shrugs)

He likes serious stuff, too, otherwise I wouldn't keep him around. But once in a while he likes to hear about broads. Go ahead . . .

Broker.   We were partners for twenty years. Somehow he had everything—a glass house, schnauzer dogs, cuff links you should have seen the size of them . . . And I'm living in three rooms in Washington Heights. It was eating at me. I figure we're partners. How come I don't have a glass house and schnauzer dogs. So one day I went to visit him in his house and I put it to him. He listens to my complaints, goes inside, and comes out with a check for eight hundred dollars. Well, I couldn't figure out that check. How did he come up with that figure? But amazingly, I wasn't angry. After all, eight hundred was eight hundred. So I went outside and sat on the golf course. I never liked to play, but I do like to sit on a golf course. And that's how they found me, sitting on a director's chair, right near the fourth hole, with the eight-hundred-dollar check in my lap and my head thrown back like this (*He demonstrates, throwing back his head, opening his mouth wide and baring his teeth grotesquely*) They all came back and when they saw me, they all made that face too, that same face. They all threw back their heads and opened their mouths and made the same dead face I had. (*He demonstrates again*)

Attendant.   It's going to be hard to give you a ninety on that one.

Meredith.   I thought it was fascinating. I wonder why they wanted to make that face. (*She tries it*)

Oldtimer.   That's easy. They wanted to taste a little death without really being dead.

Meredith.   Oh, I see. Gee, this is good. It's just like Camp Aurora. Who's next?

Two Young Men.   We both hung ourselves for love of the same boy—a swing dancer in the national company of *Zorba*.[15]

We never realized we could love someone that . . . indifferent . . . we loved the way he moved . . . the rough carving of his arms . . . the way the veins were printed on them.

We'd go to the all-night skating rinks . . . And then, unaccountably, he simply left the show—and went back to school in North Carolina.

Totally unmarked by us—as though we'd been a slight change in the direction of the wind.

Neither of us meant a thing to him . . .

. . . We were no more than a pair of cats that crossed his path in a strange village and slowed his walk for a moment.

He was beautiful.

Attendant.   To tell you the truth, I never went in very much for fag stories.

Meredith.   I thought it was very touching.

Attendant.   I'm a sympathizer . . . but they don't really satisfy me.

Two Young Men: Well, you wrote it.

Attendant.   That's true. But you know how it is when you're a writer. You write some stuff you don't like. Who's got a good one?

Tandy.   This is very unjust. You've obviously set this thing up for your own amusement.

Attendant.   And you don't like that. I'm not allowed to have a few laughs. Listen, you been giving me a hard time ever since you come in here . . . You show up . . . you don't like it . . . you hand me this Charlemagne routine . . . I'm going to do a bad thing to you now.

Tandy (*Alarmed*).   What's that? I admit I'm frightened. What are you going to do? (*Looks at second door*) You're not going to put me in there, are you?

Attendant.   No. (*Points to Oldtimer*) I'm putting him in there. (*To Tandy*) You come in here . . . you're looking for fair, reasonable . . . Where'd you get that from? Old man . . .

Oldtimer (*Rising*).   My time, eh?

Attendant.   That's right, baby.

Oldtimer.   Well, that's okay. I done everything. I once had a pair of perfectly matched wooden-legged frauleins powder me up from head to toe and dress me up in silk drawers. I run up against a Greek sailor walking around for thirty

---

[15] A musical based on Greek writer Nikos Kazantzakis's novel *Zorba the Greek*.

years with a lump on his chest he took to be a natural growth. Turned out to be the unborn fetus of a twin brother he'd spent all his life hankering for. I seen most everything. I dipped my beak in Madrid, Spain; Calcutta, India; Leningrad, Russia, and I never once worried about them poisoning the water. I had myself the fifth-richest woman in Sydney, Australia, genuine duchess she was, all dressed up in a tiger suit; by the time I finished with her I had them stripes going the wrong way. I played a pretty good trumpet. I had to face the fact that I was no Harry James, but then again, Sir Harry couldn't go in there and break up a Polish wedding the way I could. I talked back to the biggest guys. Didn't bother me. I didn't care if it was me way down in the valley, hollering up at Mount Zion. I'd holler up some terrific retorts. You're not going to show me anything I haven't seen. I paid my dues. (*Starts to go*) And I'll tell you something else. If there's anything in there kicks me, you watch and see if I don't bite.

(*He hitches himself up with great dignity and does a sailor's dance, then a proud oldman's walk into the grated room*)

Attendant.   Old man had a lot of balls.

Tandy.   Damn right. (*To Attendant*) Listen, I was the wise guy. Why didn't you send me in there?

Attendant.   That's direct. I don't work that way. I always put a little spin on the ball. Okay. This is the last one. I want live actors this time.

(*A cheap lower-class bar is set up—or at least the skeletal representation of one. Two Men stand on opposite sides of the bar. One is a Longshoreman; the other is Gottlieb, who plays the part of a bartender for this scene*)

Longshoreman (*Setting the scene for the Attendant*).   A longshoreman's bar in Astoria, Queens.

(*Attendant gestures for him to proceed*)

Longshoreman.   We ought to take our six toughest guys—and the Russians—they take their six toughest guys. Send 'em into a forest—they can have it over there if they want. And the guys that walk out of that forest—that's it.

Gottlieb (*Tending bar*).   Those Commies would have to shut up.

Longshoreman.   Oh, the Russians are all right. If you ask me, they can build a machine as good as America. But fortunately for us, they lack the human people to operate that machine.

Gottlieb.   You better believe it.

(*A couple enters the bar. The Man is in a wheelchair; his legs, braced, are apparently useless. He wears steel-rimmed glasses and his neck, too, is coiled in a brace, as though he has been in a whiplash accident. Very eerie. He is with a young, pretty girl in a short skirt. The Girl puts a quarter in the jukebox—some rock music begins. The Girl starts to dance—in the modern style—quite seductively, in front of the wheelchaired fellow. The Fellow in the chair snaps his fingers and responds to the music to the best of his abilities)*

Gottlieb *(Referring to couple)*.   Hey . . .
Longshoreman.   Yeah . . .
Gottlieb.   Ever seen anything like that?
Longshoreman.   No, I never have.

(They watch the couple awhile)

Longshoreman.   Watch this. *(He approaches Couple, speaks to Girl)* Say, miss . . .
Girl Dancer.   Yes . . .
Longshoreman *(Referring to fellow in chair)*.   All systems are not go . . .
Girl Dancer *(Still dancing)*.   I don't follow you . . .
Longshoreman.   You know . . . astronauts . . . all systems are not go. Wouldn't you rather move around with a guy whose systems are all à go-go?
Wheelchaired Man *(Talking through a throat box, as though the victim of a laryngectomy)*.   Why are you harassing us? We were behaving peaceably.
Longshoreman.   I hadn't noticed. *(He grabs Girl)* C'mon, baby, let's move around a little . . . *(Girl moves halfheartedly)*
Wheelchaired Man.   You just made a serious mistake, fella.
Longshoreman.   That right?
Wheelchaired Man.   That's right. First of all . . . *(He switches off throat box and speaks in a normal tone)* I don't really speak that way. *(Twirls off whiplash collar)* Second of all, I don't wear this . . . Third of all . . . *(Getting to his feet and kicking off braces)* I don't need these. Last but not least . . . *(Whipping off his shirt to show a well-muscled frame and huge championship belt)* . . . silver-belt karate, the highest karate level of all . . . *(With three quick moves, He wipes out Longshoreman, who falls to the floor. At a certain point in the Wheelchaired Man's metamorphosis, it has become apparent that He is Bieberman)*
Bieberman.   That's right.
Attendant.   How many times you get away with that stunt?
Bieberman.   Twenty-five times. Sarah and I started to do it every Friday night, as a form of social involvement, a means of smoking out society's predators . . .
Attendant.   But you kept getting away with it. I forget, what are you doing here?
Bieberman.   An Arab at the 92nd Street YMHA[16] dropped a 200-pound barbell on my neck.

---

[16] Young Men's Hebrew Association.

Attendant.   That's right. And don't you forget it. . . . All right, everybody, that
does it . . . You told some pretty good stuff, but we got to make room for the
next crowd. (*Gesturing toward second door*) . . . Everybody in there . . . We
enjoyed having you, sincerely.

Broker.   All this exercise—the steam—what good did it do?

Attendant.   What are you complaining about—you're in the best shape of your
life . . .

Broker.   That's true. Well, I'll go first. I been finished for a long time.
(*Hesitates*) Years ago, when you wound up your steambath, there'd be a man
outside selling pumpernickel and pickled fish . . .

Attendant.   I'll send some in . . . don't worry . . . Now let's go . . . chop-
chop . . .

(Broker goes through the door)

1st Young Man.   Do I look all right?

2nd Young Man.   You look great. It'll be a relief to get out of all that steam.

1st Young Man.   It's destroyed your hair. Maybe Ralph will be in there.

2nd Young Man.   Ralph? From Amagansett?

1st Young Man.   He *was* tacky.

(They go through the door)

Bieberman (*To Meredith*).   Goodbye. My generation's out of style—I know
that—but you'll never know the thrill of having belonged to it. (*Starting
through grated door*) John Hodiak[17]—hold on, I'll be right with you . . .

(He goes through)

Attendant (*Hollering after departed group*).   And if I find any candy wrappers
I'll send Gottlieb in there to kick your ass.

(Only Tandy and Meredith remain)

Tandy.   Kick your ass, kick your ass . . . I'm supposed to respect that? . . .
Where's the grandeur? . . . the majesty? . . .

Attendant.   I'm saving that for the next group that's coming in. I hear they got
some terrific broads. They're single. Bunch of nurses. They fell from a cable
car . . . I'm going to hit them with all this grandeur and majesty . . .

(Goes over to console, which appears in the mist)

Start a new rock and roll group called Grandeur and Majesty . . .

---

[17] An actor popular in films of the 1940s.

(Console blips back its response. To Meredith)

You goin', lady?

Meredith *(Hesitating)*.   Well, as I was telling Mr. Tandy, I've only recently had my first orgasm . . . and I haven't paid my Bloomingdale's bill. I've never been to Nassau in the Bahamas . . .

Attendant.   First orgasm . . . good-looking girl like you . . . Must have been a slip-up. Maybe you been having them all along and didn't realize it . . . All right, let's go, you two . . . I got a lot of cleaning up to do . . .

Tandy.   I told you I'm not accepting this.

Attendant.   You want me to get rough?

Tandy.   How would you like it if you were in the middle of a great Chinese restaurant . . . you've had your spare-ribs, a little soup—you're working up a terrific appetite and bam! You're thrown out of the restaurant. You never get to enjoy the won shih pancakes.

Attendant.   I can get any kind of food I want up here . . . except lox. The lox is lousy, pre-sliced . . . the kind you get in those German delicatessens . . . I can't get any fresh lox . . . I don't know why that is . . .

Tandy.   It's like a guy about to have some terrific operation. The odds against him surviving are ridiculous, Newton High School against the Miami Dolphins. They're working on his eyes, ears, nose, throat, and brains. A whole squadron of doctors is flown in from the Caucasus where they have all these new Caucasus techniques. He's hanging by a hair—and miracle of miracles, he makes it. Gets back on his feet, says goodbye to the doctors, goes home, and gets killed by a junkie in front of the Automat . . . That's the kind of thing you want me to accept.

Attendant.   That's a pretty good one. *(Takes a note on it)* I'm gonna use that . . . Yes, come to think of it, that is the kind of thing I want you to accept.

Tandy.   Well, I can't. I worked too hard to get where I am . . . You know about Wendy Tandy, my ex-wife . . .

Attendant.   Good-looking broad, I know about her . . .

Tandy.   That stunt she pulled?

Attendant.   That was a good one . . . Gottlieb, you got to hear this . . .

(Gottlieb comes over)

Tandy *(More to Meredith than anyone)*.   She's an unfaithful wife. Fine. You put up with it, you don't. I did. Fair and square. So then we meet a retired hairdresser who has become an underground film-maker. He shoots his film through those filters of teased hair . . . it's a new technique. This is the guy Wendy falls madly in love with. And she moves out—to live with him. Fair and square. She prefers him, she's got him. Swingin'. I'm getting along fine—got a few deals of my own cooking—and all of a sudden I get an invitation to go see a film that this hairdresser has put Wendy in—down on Charles Street. And I find out—in one of the Village papers—that what he's done is make a huge blow-up—in one of the scenes—I don't know how to say this—of her private parts. It's very artistic, don't get me wrong . . . The audience thinks it's a Soviet train station . . .

Meredith.   God, I'd never do that. How did he get her to do that. She must have really loved him.

Attendant.   Hey, Gottlieb, what did I tell you?

(Gottlieb hangs his head. He's shy)

Tandy.   Well, that makes me the supreme schmuck, cuckold, whatever you want to call it, everybody agreed? Half the city sitting in a theater, looking at my wife's gazoo for Christ's sakes . . .

Meredith.   For heaven's sake, what did you do?

Tandy.   That's what I'm getting at. The old me would have come in with guns. I'm a very good shot—at under seven feet. There's a technique I learned over at the Academy. You run into a little room after this cornered guy and as you shoot you're supposed to start screaming *(Demonstrates)* YI, YI, YI, YI, YI, YI. That's in case you miss, you scare the hell out of him. But I finally figured, what the hell, it's nothing to do with me. She's that kind of a girl. I knock off this guy, the next one'll be Xeroxing her ass all over Times Square. So I said the hell with it and I went to the movie.

Meredith.   How was it?

Tandy.   Not bad. As a director, the guy had some pretty good moves. It fell apart in the middle, but it was worth seeing. I sat in the balcony . . . But you see, I got past all that baloney. Out in the clear, after ten years . . . and I started getting straight in other areas, too. I got a wonderful, calm girl friend . . . We could be sitting at McGinnis' restaurant and Fidel Castro could walk in, she'd stay calm, low, even, maybe give him a little smile. I love that. I never had it . . . And then I forgave my mother . . .

Meredith.   For what?

Tandy.   I never liked the work she was doing. She ran a chain of dancing schools in Appalachia. She'd talk these starving families into taking mambo lessons . . . very bitter woman. Anyway, I took her out of Appalachia, got her an apartment in White Plains, and I like her now. She's seventy, and all that iron has dropped out of her.

Gottlieb *(To Attendant).*   Any more sex parts?

Attendant.   Shut up, Gottlieb. I think that's wonderful the boy's nice to his mother. I didn't know that . . . *(To Tandy).* What else you got? . . .

Tandy.   I just kept ironing out all the wrinkles in my life. The toughest thing, believe it or not, was leaving my art-appreciation job over at the Police Academy. I really thought those cops would kill me if I left. They didn't. They gave me a wonderful send-off party. They hired a little combo—four convicted forgers—and they ran some Danish art films they'd confiscated at a Bar Mitzvah in Great Neck.[18] And then at the end my art students gave me

---

[18] A town on Long Island, New York.

a replica of Michelangelo's *David*—seventy-five bucks over at Brentano's . . .
Only one fellow gave me any trouble, detective named Flanders, said if I left
he'd trail me all over the world, any place I tried to hide—and hunt me down
like a dog.

(Detective Flanders appears, gun in hand)

Flanders.   Tandy . . .
Tandy (*Running*).   Jesus . . .
Attendant.   You kidding? Don't worry about this guy.

(Gestures and Flanders' gun turns to a milkshake)

All right now, get in there.

(Flanders goes through the door)

Tandy.   That was close.
Meredith.   I'm glad he's on our side.
Attendant.   You see, I told you. And you said nasty things about me. You
    called me a bad guy . . .
Tandy.   Anyway, you get the idea. I've gotten my whole life on the right track
    for the first time. I don't hate Wendy. I'm doing this wonderful work for
    brain-damaged welders. You ask the welders what they think of me. And
    I've got a marvelous new girl who's got this surprising body. You look at her
    face you just don't expect all that voluptuousness. You say to yourself, she's a
    little girl, a quiet little girl, comes from a nice family, where did these tits
    come from . . .
Attendant.   Hey, hey, there's a lady . . .
Meredith.   Oh, that's all right. I don't mind tits. Knockers is the one I don't
    care for.
Tandy.   All right, excuse me, but do you get the idea? I got everything bad
    swept out of the room. I'm closer than ever to my daughter. That trip to Vegas
    really brought us together. I'm doing work that I love. Warner Brothers saw
    the first hundred pages of my Charlemagne book and I understood they like it
    for Steve McQueen . . .
Attendant.   Twentieth is going to buy it . . . for Charlton Heston . . .
Tandy.   Then you admit . . . you admit I'm getting out of here.
Attendant.   They're going to buy it from your estate . . .
Tandy.   I'm at the goddamned starting line. I'm ready to breathe clean air. I
    tore myself inside out to get where I am—and I'm not taking up anybody's
    space. I'm ready to cook a little. Swing. What kind of fellow is that to snuff
    out?
Attendant.   A good fellow. But I'm snuffing him out anyway.
Tandy.   Where's your compassion?

Attendant.   I do plenty of good things. Half the things I do are good, maybe even a little more, that's right, maybe even a little more. Nobody notices them. I never get any credit, but I do plenty of good things. I make trees, forests, soccer fields. I let hernias get better . . .

Tandy.   But you'll wipe out a guy like me . . . and a lovely blonde girl like that . . .

Meredith.   Oh, listen, the blonde part shouldn't enter into it, I can see that.

Attendant.   I let you go, I got to let the next guy go. Pretty soon nobody's dead. You'd have people coming out of your ears. Have you seen Istanbul lately? Downtown Istanbul? Los Angeles?

Meredith.   I'd never live in L.A. I don't think there's one sincere person in the whole city.

Attendant.   Let me ask you something. While you were doing all those things, unloading your old lady, you know, straightening out your head, how did you feel?

Tandy.   Good. Excited . . . it was like being in a whirlpool bath. An emotional whirlpool bath. It even made my body feel good; it got springy and toughened up . . .

Attendant.   There y'are. You felt good, you had a whirlpool bath . . . a springy body . . . Need I say more?

Tandy.   You don't understand something. I probably never made it clear. This is very important to me. We're talking about my life. I'm not asking you for seats to a hockey game.

Attendant (*Mocking*).   It's very important to him. Nobody else is alive.

Tandy.   Is there anything I can do for you?

Attendant.   You got to be kidding. *You* do something for *me?* What in the world would God want?

Tandy.   A sacrifice? . . . burnt offering?[19]

Attendant (*As though He is finished with Tandy*).   I got no time to fool around. I got a whole new crowd coming in.

Tandy.   That's it. You're going through with this? Well, I'll tell you right now, if you're capable of wiping out a once-confused fellow who's now a completely straight and sweet guy, then I got no choice but to call you a putz. (*To Meredith*) I'm sorry.

Meredith.   Oh, that's all right. You can say putz. Schvontz is the one I don't care for.

Attendant (*Astonished*).   God? . . . Did I hear you correctly? . . . Can I believe my ears? . . . Blasphemy? . . .

Tandy.   That's right. If you're capable of doing something like that. Taking a fellow to the very threshold of marvelous things, teasing him along and then aceing him out just when he's ready to scoop up one lousy drop of gravy—that is bad news, I'm sorry . . .

---

[19] An animal, food, or other substance burned upon an altar as a sacrifice or offering to a god.

Attendant. I'll tell you right now nobody ever called me that. That's bad, boy, that *is* low. Wowee . . . That's what I call sinning, baby. You're in real trouble now. You have put your foot in it this time, fella . . . You going to stick to what you called me? . . . that dirty name? . . . talking that way to God?

Tandy. Yeah, I'm going to stick to it . . . and you know why . . . because when I was in that Chinese restaurant . . . and I lost my breath, and I had no feelings, and I was numb and white, as white as a piece of typing paper, and I said over and over and over I don't want to die, I don't want to die, I don't want to die . . . and told you, in my way, how much I treasured every drop of life—you weren't impressed, you didn't hear a whisper of it . . .

Attendant. That right, Gottlieb? Did he do that?

(Gottlieb nods)

Tandy. I thought you knew everything.

Attendant. Almost everything. Once in a while there's an administrative error. Anyway, I did hear you. You came over a little weak, a little static thrown in there, but I heard you. That's why you're here. Otherwise . . . (*Pointing to grated door*) . . . you'd have gone straight in there . . .

Tandy. Then not everybody comes here . . .

Attendant. Neurotics, freaks . . . (*contemptuously*) . . . those with stories to tell.

Tandy. How was mine?

Attendant. Not bad. I heard worse.

Tandy. You were touched . . . You just won't admit it. (*He advances, threateningly*) Now let me out of here.

Attendant. You come near me, I'll send you back with cancer, then you'll know real trouble.

(Tandy grabs Gottlieb, wrestles him to the floor, holding him around the neck, threatening him with his other hand)

Tandy. All right, talk, and be quick about it. Otherwise, you get these carpet tacks right in your face. How do we get out of here?

Attendant. You talk, Gottlieb, and I'll see to it that you never work again. What can he do with a lousy bunch of carpet tacks?

Gottlieb. I don't know. But I'm not taking any chances . . . Get a mirror.

Meredith (*Reaching into a purse*). I've got one here.

Gottlieb. Shine it in his face. He can't stand that.

(She hesitates, then does)

Attendant (*Cringing, trying to hide*). Take that away. I don't want to see myself. A homely guy, with pockmarks.

Tandy (*Releasing Gottlieb, deflecting Meredith's mirror*).   All right, wait a
minute, I can't go through with this . . . Leave him alone . . .
Attendant (*Gets himself together—then, as though feelings are really hurt*).   Et
tu,[20] Gottlieb . . . (*Makes a move to Meredith, indicating it is her turn*)
Meredith: Au revoir, Mr. Tandy. Did I do all right with the mirror?
Tandy.   You did fine, kid.

(*Meredith goes through the door*)

Attendant (*To Tandy*).   You couldn't stand that, right, to see God get wiped out
. . . It gave you a funny feeling.
Tandy.   I don't like to see anybody get wiped out . . . I'm notorious for
breaking up fights . . . I once threw a guy through the window of a furniture
store because somebody was picking on him and I didn't want him to get hurt.
Attendant.   You got a lot of nice qualities . . . Too bad I'm filled up. I'd let you
work around here for a while . . . Listen, what are you giving yourself such a
hard time for . . . Suppose, for a second, I let you out of here . . . What
would you do? . . .
Tandy.   What would I do? . . . Are you kidding? . . . What is this, a put-on?
. . . You didn't hear me go on about my new life? My new style? The exciting
world that's out there waiting for me? . . . This terrific new quiet girl friend
who practically brings me the newspaper in her teeth—who watches me like
a hawk for the slightest sign of sexual tension—and then *whop*—she's in there
like a shot to drain it off and make me feel comfortable again . . . And if I feel
like going out at four in the morning to get some eggs—she's right there at my
side—because she comes from a tradition where the man is like a gypsy king
and the woman is someone who drags mutton to him on her back, all the way
up a hill. And all she ever hopes for is that he'll throw her a lousy mutton bone
while she's sleeping in the dirt at his feet . . . And this is an intelligent girl,
too . . . a Bryn Mawr girl . . . When I'm alone with her . . .
Attendant.   You like this girl . . .
Tandy.   Like her? . . . Oh, I see what you mean . . . Yeah . . . if I'm so crazy
about her, how come I'm constantly chasing chicks all over the place . . . All
right, I'll admit to you that she's a little on the quiet side—that sometimes all
that quiet drives me nuts . . . All right, let's face it, she's basically a dull girl.
Terrific kid, loyal, faithful, brings you mutton, but the sparks don't fly . . .
And it did cross my mind that maybe I'll find another girl who's got a little
more pizazz . . . I'll give you that . . .
Attendant.   Another girl . . .
Tandy.   Yeah. Another girl. Oh, I got ya', I got ya'—a new one isn't going to
be the answer either . . . As delicious as she looks now, in two months I'm a
little restless again . . . And that's the way it's got to be if I live to be a hundred

---

[20] Latin, meaning "Thou also." The famous line from Shakespeare's *Julius Caesar* is uttered by
Julius Caesar on seeing his friend Brutus among his assassins.

. . . (*Trails off*) . . . I got friends, terrific friends. We hang around this bar called The Quonset Hut, run by a dyke, a rich retired dyke. We hang around there, sometimes till five in the morning, talking about Milton[21] and the Brontë sisters.[22] These friends of mine are terrific people—they're a little screwed up in their personal lives—most of them have been divorced three or four times—but very often those are the best people, the ones who get divorced over and over . . . Anyway, I want to do a lot more of that, hanging around this dyke bar till five in the morning with my divorced friends, talking about Milton and the Brontë sisters . . .

And I have to get back to my book. Now I know what you're going to say and I'm way ahead of you—that I have no real visceral interest in Charlemagne—that I just picked that subject because it has a prestige sound to it. Well, you're wrong. To me it's just a loosening-up process, a way of warming up the writing muscles so I can be ready for the real book I want to write on—Vasco da Gama and the Straits of Magellan. (*Weak little laugh as though aware He's told a joke. No response from Attendant*) No, seriously . . . you have to get the muscles limber . . . What you're saying is if I really wanted to write I'd stop crapping around with Charlemagne . . . I see what you mean . . . You get more prestige from a truly observed book about . . . cheeseburgers than you can from a schlock Charlemagne book . . . Boy, you really nailed that one down . . .

I'll tell you what, let me smoke a cigar, all right?

(*Takes one out; Attendant has sat down and begun to arrange the cards for a game of solitaire*)

I get these from Switzerland from a guy who brings them in from Cuba. It costs you a little extra, but it's really worth it. They say you're supposed to stop smoking these when you get about half way down, but I don't know. Sometimes I think the last half of the cigar is the best part.

I can tell a Havana cigar in one puff. It's not the tobacco so much as the rolling process they use. They have a secret rolling process that nobody's ever been able to pry away from the Cubans . . .

If it kills me I got to get back and have some more weekends with my daughter. Those weekends are the most beautiful part of my life now. I mean there's no more hassle . . . no more crazy marriage in the background . . . It all gets telescoped down to just me and her, hanging around together.

(*Looks at Attendant for response, doesn't get one*)

. . . So you're asking me how come I'm always going crazy thinking up places to take her . . . How come I'm always dragging her to puppet shows . . . Well,

---

[21] John Milton (1608–1674), an English poet.
[22] Charlotte (1816–1855), Emily (1818–1848), and Anne (1820–1849) Brontë, English novelists.

all I can say is that it's the city's fault . . . Where the hell are you supposed to take a kid in the city . . . If we were out on a farm, it'd be a different story . . .

But I do see what you mean—Jesus, you really know how to zing it in there . . . what you're driving at is that I have to keep taking her places because I actually have nothing to say to her . . . Maybe I don't even like kids . . . She'd be better off staying home and hanging around with a pack of little girls . . . (*Handling cigar*) A guy once told me the reason for the special flavor of these Havana cigars is that the tobacco is supposed to be rolled on the thighs of Cuban women . . . Jesus, wouldn't that be something . . .

I got to get out of here . . . I got to get out of here . . . I got things to do . . .

(*Attendant continues his game of solitaire—the last sound heard is the flicking of the cards . . .*)

Curtain

QUESTIONS
1. Why is Tandy outraged by his situation? Are his reasons convincing? Do you admire him? **2.** Does the play ridicule homosexuals? Explain. **3.** What is Meredith's role in the play? Are we meant to respect her? Explain. **4.** Compare the Oldtimer's justification for his life just before he passes through the door with Tandy's final monologue. How do the passages define the characters? Which character, if either, do you find admirable? Explain.

WRITING TOPICS
1. What effect does the author achieve by making God a Puerto Rican steambath attendant? Do you find the God in this play believable? **2.** Discuss the theme of the play, particularly with respect to what the playwright is saying about the values we should cultivate.

THE PRESENCE OF DEATH

St. George and the Dragon, late fifteenth-century painting

ESSAYS

Meditation XVII, from *Devotions upon Emergent Occasions*

1623

JOHN DONNE [1572–1631]

Nunc lento sonitu dicunt morieris.
Now this bell tolling softly for another says to me, Thou must die.

Perchance he for whom this bell tolls may be so ill as that he knows not it tolls 1
for him; and perchance I may think myself so much better than I am, as that
they who are about me and see my state may have caused it to toll for me, and
I know not that. The church is catholic, universal, so are all her actions; all
that she does belongs to all. When she baptizes a child, that action concerns
me; for that child is thereby connected to that head which is my head too, and
ingrafted into that body whereof I am a member. And when she buries a man,
that action concerns me: all mankind is of one author and is one volume; when
one man dies, one chapter is not torn out of the book, but translated into a
better language; and every chapter must be so translated. God employs several
translators; some pieces are translated by age, some by sickness, some by war,
some by justice; but God's hand is in every translation, and his hand shall bind
up all our scattered leaves again for that library where every book shall lie open
to one another. As therefore the bell that rings to a sermon calls not upon the
preacher only, but upon the congregation to come, so this bell calls us all; but
how much more me, who am brought so near the door by this sickness. There
was a contention as far as a suit[1] (in which piety and dignity, religion and
estimation, were mingled) which of the religious orders should ring to prayers
first in the morning; and it was determined that they should ring first that rose
earliest. If we understand aright the dignity of this bell that tolls for our evening
prayer, we would be glad to make it ours by rising early, in that application,
that it might be ours as well as his whose indeed it is. The bell doth toll for

---

[1] An argument settled by a lawsuit.

him that thinks it doth, and though it intermit again, yet from that minute that that occasion wrought upon him, he is united to God. Who casts not up his eye to the sun when it rises? but who takes off his eye from a comet when that breaks out? Who bends not his ear to any bell which upon any occasion rings? but who can remove it from that bell which is passing a piece of himself out of this world? No man is an island, entire of itself; every man is a piece of the continent, a part of the main. If a clod be washed away by the sea, Europe is the less, as well as if a promontory were, as well as if a manor of thy friend's or of thine own were. Any man's death diminishes me, because I am involved in mankind; and therefore never send to know for whom the bell tolls; it tolls for thee. Neither can we call this a begging of misery or a borrowing of misery, as though we were not miserable enough of ourselves but must fetch in more from the next house, in taking upon us the misery of our neighbors. Truly it were an excusable convetousness if we did; for affliction is a treasure, and scarce any man hath enough of it. No man hath affliction enough that is not matured and ripened by it, and made fit for God by that affliction. If a man carry treasure in bullion, or in a wedge of gold, and have none coined into current moneys, his treasure will not defray him as he travels. Tribulation is treasure in the nature of it, but it is not current money in the use of it, except we get nearer and nearer our home, heaven, by it. Another man may be sick too, and sick to death, and this affliction may lie in his bowels as gold in a mine and be of no use to him; but this bell that tells me of his affliction digs out and applies that gold to me, if by this consideration of another's danger I take mine own into contemplation and so secure myself by making my recourse to my God, who is our only security.

QUESTIONS

1. John Donne is justly admired for his use of figurative language. What extended metaphors does he use to characterize humankind and death? **2.** What does Donne mean when he asserts that the death bell "tolls for thee"? **3.** Toward the end of his meditation, Donne states that "tribulation is treasure." What does he mean? What will that treasure purchase?

WRITING TOPIC

In what sense is "No man is an island, entire of itself" an accurate description of the human condition? In what sense is it inaccurate?

Lost in the Snow[1]

1872

MARK TWAIN   [1835–1910]

Plainly the situation was desperate. We were cold and stiff and the horses were   1
tired. We decided to build a sage-brush fire and camp out till morning. This was
wise, because if we were wandering from the right road and the snow-storm
continued another day our case would be the next thing to hopeless if we kept
on.

All agreed that a camp fire was what would come nearest to saving us, now,   2
and so we set about building it. We could find no matches, and so we tried to
make shift with the pistols. Not a man in the party had ever tried to do such a
thing before, but not a man in the party doubted that it *could* be done, and
without any trouble—because every man in the party had read about it in books
many a time and had naturally come to believe it, with trusting simplicity, just
as he had long ago accepted and believed *that other* common book-fraud about
Indians and lost hunters making a fire by rubbing two dry sticks together.

We huddled together on our knees in the deep snow, and the horses put their   3
noses together and bowed their patient heads over us; and while the feathery
flakes eddied down and turned us into a group of white statuary, we proceeded
with the momentous experiment. We broke twigs from a sage bush and piled
them on a little cleared space in the shelter of our bodies. In the course of ten
or fifteen minutes all was ready, and then, while conversation ceased and our
pulses beat low with anxious suspense, Ollendorff applied his revolver, pulled the
trigger and blew the pile clear out of the county! It was the flattest failure that ever
was.

This was distressing, but it paled before a greater horror—the horses were   4
gone! I had been appointed to hold the bridles, but in my absorbing anxiety over
the pistol experiment I had unconsciously dropped them and the released animals had walked off in the storm. It was useless to try to follow them, for their
footfalls could make no sound, and one could pass within two yards of the
creatures and never see them. We gave them up without an effort at recovering
them, and cursed the lying books that said horses would stay by their masters for
protection and companionship in a distressful time like ours.

We were miserable enough, before; we felt still more forlorn, now. Patiently,   5
but with blighted hope, we broke more sticks and piled them, and once more the
Prussian shot them into annihilation. Plainly, to light a fire with a pistol was an
art requiring practice and experience, and the middle of a desert at midnight in
a snow-storm was not a good place or time for the acquiring of the accomplish-
ment. We gave it up and tried the other. Each man took a couple of sticks and

---

[1] Mark Twain's *Roughing It* (1872) recounts his experiences in California and Nevada prospecting for silver. In this episode, Twain and his friends are caught in a snowstorm while returning to
Carson City, Nevada, from the Humboldt mining district in California.

fell to chafing them together. At the end of half an hour we were thoroughly chilled, and so were the sticks. We bitterly execrated the Indians, the hunters and the books that had betrayed us with the silly device, and wondered dismally what was next to be done. At this critical moment Mr. Ballou fished out four matches from the rubbish of an overlooked pocket. To have found four gold bars would have seemed poor and cheap good luck compared to this. One cannot think how good a match looks under such circumstances—or how lovable and precious, and sacredly beautiful to the eye. This time we gathered sticks with high hopes; and when Mr. Ballou prepared to light the first match, there was an amount of interest centered upon him that pages of writing could not describe. The match burned hopefully a moment, and then went out. It could not have carried more regret with it if it had been a human life. The next match simply flashed and died. The wind puffed the third one out just as it was on the imminent verge of success. We gathered together closer than ever, and developed a solicitude that was rapt and painful, as Mr. Ballou scratched our last hope on his leg. It lit, burned blue and sickly, and then budded into a robust flame. Shading it with his hands, the old gentleman bent gradually down and every heart went with him—everybody, too, for that matter—and blood and breath stood still. The flame touched the sticks at last, took gradual hold upon them—hesitated—took a stronger hold—hesitated again—held its breath five heart-breaking seconds, then gave a sort of human gasp and went out.

Nobody said a word for several minutes. It was a solemn sort of silence; even the wind put on a stealthy, sinister quiet and made no more noise than the falling flakes of snow. Finally a sad-voiced conversation began, and it was soon apparent that in each of our hearts lay the conviction that this was our last night with the living. I had so hoped that I was the only one who felt so. When the others calmly acknowledged their conviction, it sounded like the summons itself. Ollendorff said:

"Brothers, let us die together. And let us go without one hard feeling towards each other. Let us forget and forgive bygones. I know that you have felt hard towards me for turning over the canoe, and for knowing too much and leading you round and round in the snow—but I meant well; forgive me. I acknowledge freely that I have had hard feelings against Mr. Ballou for abusing me and calling me a logarythm, which is a thing I do not know what, but no doubt a thing considered disgraceful and unbecoming in America, and it has scarcely been out of my mind and has hurt me a great deal—but let it go; I forgive Mr. Ballou with all my heart and—"

Poor Ollendorff broke down and the tears came. He was not alone, for I was crying too, and so was Mr. Ballou. Ollendorff got his voice again and forgave me for things I had done and said. Then he got out his bottle of whisky and said that whether he lived or died he would never touch another drop. He said he had given up all hope of life, and although ill-prepared, was ready to submit humbly to his fate; that he wished he could be spared a little longer, not for any selfish reason, but to make a thorough reform in his character, and by devoting himself to helping the poor, nursing the sick, and pleading with the people to guard themselves against the evils of intemperance, make his life a beneficent example to the young, and lay it down at last with the precious reflection that it had not been lived in vain. He ended by saying that his reform should begin at this moment, even here in the presence of death, since no longer time was to be vouchsafed wherein to prosecute it to men's help and benefit—and with that he threw away the bottle of whisky.

Mr. Ballou made remarks of similar purport, and began the reform he could not live to continue, by throwing away the ancient pack of cards that had solaced our captivity during the flood[2] and made it bearable. He said he never gambled, but still was satisfied that the meddling with cards in any way was immoral and injurious, and no man could be wholly pure and blemishless without eschewing them. "And therefore," continued he, "in doing this act I already feel more in sympathy with that spiritual saturnalia necessary to entire and obsolete reform." These rolling syllables touched him as no intelligible eloquence could have done, and the old man sobbed with a mournfulness not unmingled with satisfaction.

My own remarks were of the same tenor as those of my comrades, and I know that the feelings that prompted them were heartfelt and sincere. We were all sincere, and all deeply moved and earnest, for we were in the presence of death and without hope. I threw away my pipe, and in doing it felt that at last I was free of a hated vice and one that had ridden me like a tyrant all my days. While I yet talked, the thought of the good I might have done in the world and the still greater good I might *now* do, with these new incentives and higher and better aims to guide me if I could only be spared a few years longer, overcame me and the tears came again. We put our arms about each other's necks and awaited the warning drowsiness that precedes death by freezing.

It came stealing over us presently, and then we bade each other a last farewell. A delicious dreaminess wrought its web about my yielding senses, while the snow-flakes wove a winding sheet about my conquered body. Oblivion came. The battle of life was done.

I do not know how long I was in a state of forgetfulness, but it seemed an age. A vague consciousness grew upon me by degrees, and then came a gathering anguish of pain in my limbs and through all my body. I shuddered. The thought flitted through my brain, "this is death—this is the hereafter."

Then came a white upheaval at my side, and a voice said, with bitterness: "Will some gentleman be so good as to kick me behind?"

It was Ballou—at least it was a towzled snow image in a sitting posture, with Ballou's voice.

I rose up, and there in the gray dawn, not fifteen steps from us, were the frame buildings of a stage station, and under a shed stood our still saddled and bridled horses!

An arched snow-drift broke up, now, and Ollendorff emerged from it, and the three of us sat and stared at the houses without speaking a word. We really had nothing to say. We were like the profane man who could not "do the subject

9

10

11

12

13

14

15

16

17

---

[2] Earlier in the narrative, Twain and his friends had been trapped in a cabin during a flash flood.

justice," the whole situation was so painfully ridiculous and humiliating that words were tame and we did not know where to commence anyhow.

The joy in our hearts at our deliverance was poisoned; well-nigh dissipated, indeed. We presently began to grow pettish by degrees, and sullen; and then, angry at each other, angry at ourselves, angry at everything in general, we moodily dusted the snow from our clothing and in unsociable single file plowed our way to the horses, unsaddled them, and sought shelter in the station.   18

I have scarcely exaggerated a detail of this curious and absurd adventure. It occurred almost exactly as I have stated it. We actually went into camp in a snowdrift in a desert, at midnight in a storm, forlorn and hopeless, within fifteen steps of a comfortable inn.   19

For two hours we sat apart in the station and ruminated in disgust. The mystery was gone, now, and it was plain enough why the horses had deserted us. Without a doubt they were under that shed a quarter of a minute after they had left us, and they must have overheard and enjoyed all our confessions and lamentations.   20

After breakfast we felt better, and the zest of life soon came back. The world looked bright again, and existence was as dear to us as ever. Presently an uneasiness came over me—grew upon me—assailed me without ceasing. Alas, my regeneration was not complete—I wanted to smoke! I resisted with all my strength, but the flesh was weak. I wandered away alone and wrestled with myself an hour. I recalled my promises of reform and preached to myself persuasively, upbraidingly, exhaustively. But it was all vain, I shortly found myself sneaking among the snow-drifts hunting for my pipe. I discovered it after a considerable search, and crept away to hide myself and enjoy it. I remained behind the barn a good while, asking myself how I would feel if my braver, stronger, truer comrades should catch me in my degradation. At last I lit the pipe, and no human being can feel meaner and baser than I did then. I was ashamed of being in my own pitiful company. Still dreading discovery, I felt that perhaps the further side of the barn would be somewhat safer, and so I turned the corner. As I turned the one corner, smoking, Ollendorff turned the other with his bottle to his lips, and between us sat unconscious Ballou deep in a game of "solitaire" with the old greasy cards!   21

Absurdity could go no further. We shook hands and agreed to say no more about "reform" and "examples to the rising generation."   22

QUESTIONS
1. What is the first indication that Twain's piece is humorous? **2.** In the end, Twain and his friends are disgusted with themselves for backsliding, the author even going so far as to say, "I was ashamed of being in my own pitiful company." Is this a serious judgment the reader is expected to share? Explain.

WRITING TOPIC
Analyze the ways in which Twain achieves humor by examining both the situations he creates and the language he uses.

The American Way of Death   1963

JESSICA MITFORD   [b. 1917]

O Death, where is thy sting? O grave, where is thy victory?[1] Where, indeed.
Many a badly stung survivor, faced with the aftermath of some relative's funeral, has ruefully concluded that the victory has been won hands down by a
funeral establishment—in disastrously unequal battle.

Much has been written of late about the affluent society in which we live,
and much fun poked at some of the irrational "status symbols" set out like
golden snares to trap the unwary consumer at every turn. Until recently, little
has been said about the most irrational and wierdest of the lot, lying in ambush
for all of us at the end of the road—the modern American funeral.

If the Dismal Traders (as an eighteenth-century English writer calls them)
have traditionally been cast in a comic role in literature, a universally recognized symbol of humor from Shakespeare to Dickens to Evelyn Waugh, they
have successfully turned the tables in recent years to perpetrate a huge, macabre and expensive practical joke on the American public. It is not consciously conceived of as a joke, of course; on the contrary, it is hedged with
admirably contrived rationalizations.

Gradually, almost imperceptibly, over the years the funeral men have constructed their own grotesque cloud-cuckooland where the trappings of Gracious
Living are transformed, as in a nightmare, into the trappings of Gracious Dying.
The same familiar Madison Avenue language, with its peculiar adjectival range
designed to anesthetize sales resistance to all sorts of products, has seeped into
the funeral industry in a new and bizarre guise. The emphasis is on the same
desirable qualities that we have all been schooled to look for in our daily search
for excellence: comfort, durability, beauty, craftsmanship. The attuned ear will
recognize too the convincing quasi-scientific language, so reassuring even if
unintelligible.

So that this too, too solid flesh might not melt, we are offered "solid copper—a quality casket which offers superb value to the client seeking long-last-
ing protection," or "the Colonial Classic Beauty—18 gauge lead coated steel,
seamless top, lap-jointed welded body construction." Some are equipped with
foam rubber, some with innerspring mattresses. Elgin offers "the revolutionary
'Perfect-Posture' bed." Not every casket need have a silver lining, for one may
choose between "more than 60 color matched shades, magnificent and unique
masterpieces" by the Cheney casket-lining people. Shrouds no longer exist.
Instead, you may patronize a grave-wear couturière who promises "handmade
original fashions—styles from the best in life for the last memory—dresses,
men's suits, negligees, accessories." For the final, perfect grooming: "Nature-

---

[1] See 1 Corinthians 15:55.

Glo—the ultimate in cosmetic embalming." And, where have we heard the phrase "peace of mind protection" before? No matter. In funeral advertising, it is applied to the Wilbert Burial Vault, with its 3/8-inch precast asphalt inner liner plus extra-thick, reinforced concrete—all this "guaranteed by Good Housekeeping." Here again the Cadillac, status symbol par excellence, appears in all its gleaming glory, this time transformed into a pastel-colored funeral hearse.

You, the potential customer for all this luxury, are unlikely to read the lyri-cal descriptions quoted above, for they are culled from *Mortuary Management* and *Casket and Sunnyside*, two of the industry's eleven trade magazines. For you there are ads in your daily newspaper, generally found on the obituary page, stressing dignity, refinement, high-caliber professional service and that intangible quality, *sincerity*. The trade advertisements are, however, instruc-tive, because they furnish an important clue to the frame of mind into which the funeral industry has hypnotized itself. 6

A new mythology, essential to the twentieth-century American funeral rite, has grown up—or rather has been built up step by step—to justify the peculiar customs surrounding the disposal of our dead. And, just as the witch doctor must be convinced of his own infallibility in order to maintain a hold over his clientele, so the funeral industry has had to "sell itself" on its articles of faith in the course of passing them along to the public. 7

The first of these is the tenet that today's funeral procedures are founded in "American tradition." The story comes to mind of a sign on the freshly sown lawn of a brand-new Midwest college: "There is a tradition on this campus that students never walk on this strip of grass. This tradition goes into effect next Tuesday." The most cursory look at American funerals of past times will estab-lish the parallel. Simplicity to the point of starkness, the plain pine box, the laying out of the dead by friends and family who also bore the coffin to the grave—these were the hallmarks of the traditional funeral until the end of the nineteenth century. 8

Secondly, there is the myth that the American public is only being given what it wants—an opportunity to keep up with the Joneses to the end. "In keeping with our high standard of living, there should be an equally high stan-dard of dying," says the past president of the Funeral Directors of San Fran-cisco. "The cost of a funeral varies according to individual taste and the nice-ties of living the family has been accustomed to." Actually, choice doesn't enter the picture for the average individual, faced, generally for the first time, with the necessity of buying a product of which he is totally ignorant, at a moment when he is least in a position to quibble. In point of fact the cost of a funeral almost always varies, not "according to individual taste" but according to what the traffic will bear. 9

Thirdly, there is an assortment of myths based on half-digested psychiatric theories. The importance of the "memory picture" is stressed—meaning the last glimpse of the deceased in open casket, done up with the latest in embalm-ing techniques and finished off with a dusting of makeup. A newer one, im- 10 pressively authentic-sounding, is the need for "grief therapy," which is beginning to go over big in mortuary circles. A historian of American funeral directing hints at the grief-therapist idea when speaking of the new role of the undertaker—"the dramaturgic role, in which the undertaker becomes a stage manager to create an appropriate atmosphere and to move the funeral party through a drama in which social relationships are stressed and an emotional catharsis or release is provided through ceremony."

Lastly, a whole new terminology, as ornately shoddy as the satin rayon casket   11
liner, has been invented by the funeral industry to replace the direct and serviceable vocabulary of former times. Undertaker has been supplanted by "funeral director" or "mortician." (Even the classified section of the telephone directory gives recognition to this; in its pages you will find "Undertakers—see Funeral Directors.") Coffins are "caskets"; hearses are "coaches," or "professional cars"; flowers are "floral tributes"; corpses generally are "loved ones," but mortuary etiquette dictates that a specific corpse be referred to by name only—as, "Mr. Jones"; cremated ashes are "cremains." Euphemisms such as "slumber room," "reposing room," and "calcination—the *kindlier* heat" abound in the funeral business.

If the undertaker is the stage manager of the fabulous production that is the   12
modern American funeral, the stellar role is reserved for the occupant of the open casket. The decor, the stagehands, the supporting cast are all arranged for the most advantageous display of the deceased, without which the rest of the paraphernalia would lose its point—*Hamlet* without the Prince of Denmark. It is to this end that a fantastic array of costly merchandise and services is pyramided to dazzle the mourners and facilitate the plunder of the next of kin.

Grief therapy, anyone? But it's going to come high. According to the funeral   13
industry's own figures, the *average* undertaker's bill in 1961 was $708 for casket and "services," to which must be added the cost of a burial vault, flowers, clothing, clergy and musician's honorarium, and cemetery charges. When these costs are added to the undertaker's bill, the total average cost for an adult's funeral is, as we shall see, closer to $1,450.

The question naturally arises, *is* this what most people want for themselves   14
and their families? For several reasons, this has been a hard one to answer until recently. It is a subject seldom discussed. Those who have never had to arrange for a funeral frequently shy away from its implications, preferring to take comfort in the thought that sufficient unto the day is the evil thereof. Those who have acquired personal and painful knowledge of the subject would often rather forget about it. Pioneering "Funeral Societies" or "Memorial Associations," dedicated to the principle of dignified funerals at reasonable cost, have existed in a number of communities throughout the country, but their membership has been limited for the most part to the more sophisticated element in the population—university people, liberal intellectuals—and those who, like doctors and lawyers, come up against problems in arranging funerals for their clients.

Some indication of the pent-up resentment felt by vast numbers of people   15 against the funeral interests was furnished by the astonishing response to an article by Roul Tunley, titled "Can You Afford to Die?" in *The Saturday Evening Post* of June 17, 1961. As though a dike had burst, letters poured in from every part of the country to the *Post*, to the funeral societies, to local newspapers. They came from clergymen, professional people, old-age pensioners, trade unionists. Three months after the article appeared, an estimated six thousand had taken pen in hand to comment on some phase of the high cost of dying. Many recounted their own bitter experiences at the hands of funeral directors; hundreds asked for advice on how to establish a consumer organization in communities where none exists; others sought information about pre-need plans. The membership of the funeral societies skyrocketed. The funeral industry, finding itself in the glare of public spotlight, has begun to engage in serious debate about its own future course—as well it might.

Is the funeral inflation bubble ripe for bursting? A few years ago, the United States public suddenly rebelled against the trend in the auto industry towards ever more showy cars, with their ostentatious and nonfunctional fins, and a demand was created for compact cars patterned after European models. The all-powerful auto industry, accustomed to *telling* the customer what sort of car he wanted, was suddenly forced to *listen* for a change. Overnight, the little cars became for millions a new kind of status symbol. Could it be that the same cycle is working itself out in the attitude towards the final return of dust to dust, that the American public is becoming sickened by ever more ornate and costly funerals, and that a status symbol of the future may indeed be the simplest kind of "funeral without fins"?

16

QUESTIONS

1. What four "articles of faith" does Mitford attribute to the funeral industry? **2.** In the final three paragraphs, Mitford speculates about what most people want. What assumptions does she put forward? Do you agree with her? Explain.

WRITING TOPIC

What other "costly and ornate" cultural customs would you consider open to ridicule? Imitating Mitford's approach and style, write an essay critical of "The American Way of ___." (Examples might include high school proms, weddings, football half-time shows, etc.)

The Discus Thrower   1977

RICHARD SELZER   [b.1928]

I spy on my patients. Ought not a doctor to observe his patients by any means   1
and from any stance, that he might the more fully assemble evidence? So I
stand in the doorways of hospital rooms and gaze. Oh, it is not all that furtive
an act. Those in bed need only look up to discover me. But they never do.

From the doorway of Room 542 the man in the bed seems deeply tanned.   2
Blue eyes and close-cropped white hair give him the appearance of vigor and
good health. But I know that his skin is not brown from the sun. It is rusted,
rather, in the last stage of containing the vile repose within. And the blue eyes
are frosted, looking inward like the windows of a snowbound cottage. This man
is blind. This man is also legless—the right leg missing from midthigh down,
the left from just below the knee. It gives him the look of a bonsai, roots and
branches pruned into the dwarfed facsimile of a great tree.

Propped on pillows, he cups his right thigh in both hands. Now and then   3
he shakes his head as though acknowledging the intensity of his suffering. In
all of this he makes no sound. Is he mute as well as blind?

The room in which he dwells is empty of all possessions—no get-well cards,   4
small, private caches of food, day-old flowers, slippers, all the usual kickshaws
of the sickroom. There is only the bed, a chair, a nightstand, and a tray on
wheels that can be swung across his lap for meals.

"What time is it?" he asks.   5
"Three o'clock."
"Morning or afternoon?"
"Afternoon."
He is silent. There is nothing else he wants to know.
"How are you?" I say.   10
"Who is it?" he asks.
"It's the doctor. How do you feel?"
He does not answer right away.
"Feel?" he says.
"I hope you feel better," I say.   15
I press the button at the side of the bed.
"Down you go," I say.
"Yes, down," he says.
He falls back upon the bed awkwardly. His stumps, unweighted by legs and
feet, rise in the air, presenting themselves. I unwrap the bandages from the
stumps, and begin to cut away the black scabs and the dead, glazed fat with
scissors and forceps. A shard of white bone comes loose. I pick it away. I wash
the wounds with disinfectant and redress the stumps. All this while, he does

not speak. What is he thinking behind those lids that do not blink? Is he remembering a time when he was whole? Does he dream of feet? Of when his body was not a rotting log?

He lies solid and inert. In spite of everything, he remains impressive, as   20
though he were a sailor standing athwart a slanting deck.

"Anything more I can do for you?" I ask.

For a long moment he is silent.

"Yes," he says at last and without the least irony. "You can bring me a pair of shoes."

In the corridor, the head nurse is waiting for me.

"We have to do something about him," she says. "Every morning he orders   25
scrambled eggs for breakfast, and, instead of eating them, he picks up the plate and throws it against the wall."

"Throws his plate?"

"Nasty. That's what he is. No wonder his family doesn't come to visit. They probably can't stand him any more than we can."

She is waiting for me to do something.

"Well?"

"We'll see," I say.   30

The next morning I am waiting in the corridor when the kitchen delivers his breakfast. I watch the aide place the tray on the stand and swing it across his lap. She presses the button to raise the head of the bed. Then she leaves.

In time the man reaches to find the rim of the tray, then on to find the dome of the covered dish. He lifts off the cover and places it on the stand. He fingers across the plate until he probes the eggs. He lifts the plate in both hands, sets it on the palm of his right hand, centers it, balances it. He hefts it up and down slightly, getting the feel of it. Abruptly, he draws back his right arm as far as he can.

There is the crack of the plate breaking against the wall at the foot of his bed and the small wet sound of the scrambled eggs dropping to the floor.

And then he laughs. It is a sound you have never heard. It is something new under the sun. It could cure cancer.

Out in the corridor, the eyes of the head nurse narrow.   35

"Laughed, did he?"

She writes something down on her clipboard.

A second aide arrives, brings a second breakfast tray, puts it on the night-stand, out of his reach. She looks over at me shaking her head and making her mouth go. I see that we are to be accomplices.

"I've got to feed you," she says to the man.

"Oh, no you don't," the man says.   40

"Oh, yes I do," the aide says, "after the way you just did. Nurse says so."

"Get me my shoes," the man says.

"Here's oatmeal," the aide says. "Open." And she touches the spoon to his lower lip.

"I ordered scrambled eggs," says the man.

"That's right," the aide says.   45

I step forward.

"Is there anything I can do?" I say.

"Who are you?" the man asks.

In the evening I go once more to that ward to make my rounds. The head nurse reports to me that Room 542 is deceased. She has discovered this quite by accident, she says. No, there had been no sound. Nothing. It's a blessing, she says.

I go into his room, a spy looking for secrets. He is still there in his bed. His   50 face is relaxed, grave, dignified. After a while, I turn to leave. My gaze sweeps the wall at the foot of the bed, and I see the place where it has been repeatedly washed, where the wall looks very clean and very white.

QUESTIONS

1. Why does the patient in Room 542 hurl his scrambled eggs against the wall? **2.** What unstated assumptions govern the nurse's attitude towards the dying man?

WRITING TOPICS

1. Compare the characterization of this dying man with the characterization of Iván Ilých in Tolstoy's story (p. 589). **2.** Analyze the essay's rhetorical devices with special attention to sentence structure, images, and understatement. How does Selzer's rhetoric contribute to this account of a patient's death?

The Presence of Death

QUESTIONS AND WRITING TOPICS

1. Although Housman's "To an Athlete Dying Young," Auden's "In Memory of W. B. Yeats," and Roethke's "Elegy for Jane" employ different poetic forms, they all embody a poetic mode called *elegy*. Define *elegy* in terms of the characteristic tone of these poems. **Writing Topic:** Compare the elegiac tone of one of these poems with the tone of Owen's "Dulce et Decorum Est" or Thomas's "Do Not Go Gentle into That Good Night."

2. What figurative language in the prose and poetry of this section is commonly associated with death itself? Contrast the characteristic imagery of this section with the characteristic imagery of love poetry. **Writing Topic:** Compare the imagery in Shakespeare's Sonnet 18 (p. 000) with the imagery in sonnet 73 (p. 000).

3. In Tolstoy's "The Death of Iván Ilých" and Donne's "Meditation XVII," death and dying are considered from a religious viewpoint. **Writing Topic:** Discuss whether these works develop a similar attitude toward death, or whether the attitudes they develop differ crucially.

4. State the argument against resignation to death made in Thomas's "Do Not Go Gentle into That Good Night." State the argument of Catherine Davis's reply, "After a Time." **Writing Topic:** Using these positions as the basis of your discussion, select for analysis two works that support Thomas's argument and two works that support Davis's.

5. Yevtushenko, in his poem "People," writes, "Not people die but worlds die in them." **Writing Topic:** Illustrate the meaning of this line with a discussion of Katherine Anne Porter's "The Jilting of Granny Weatherall."

6. Discuss the attitude toward death developed in Larkin's poem "Aubade." **Writing Topic:** Contrast the treatment of death in "Aubade" with the treatment of death developed in any other work in this section.

7. Malamud's "Idiots First" and Friedman's *Steambath* both present a grim picture of the human condition, yet they are often funny. What function does humor serve in each work? **Writing Topic:** Which work embodies a more hopeful vision of the human condition? Explain.

8. Contrast the attitudes toward death revealed in Donne's "Meditation XVII" and Selzer's "The Discus Thrower." **Writing Topic:** Analyze the figurative language and other stylistic elements in each essay. How does style account for the contrasting attitudes toward death expressed in these essays?

9. Which works in this section treat death and dying in a way that corresponds most closely with your own attitudes toward mortality? Which contradict your attitudes? **Writing Topic:** Isolate, in each case, the elements in the work responsible for your response and discuss them in terms of their "truth" or "falsity."

APPENDICES

A Lady Writing, c. 1665 by Jan Verme

APPENDICES

Poems about Poetry

Most of us would probably define poetry as a form of writing that employs rhyme and metrical regularity and deals with serious and "heavy" subjects (unless, of course, it's light verse). But you don't have to go further than the poems in this anthology to see that many poems do not use rhyme, have no metrical regularity, and deal with ordinary subjects in prosaic language. Maybe we can best define poetry (someone once did) as the kind of writing where the lines don't end at the same place on the right-hand side of the page. Here are a few poems about poetry, in which poets attempt to describe what it is, how it works, what it does, and why it does it.

Pitcher   1960

ROBERT FRANCIS   [1901–1987]

His art is eccentricity, his aim
How not to hit the mark he seems to aim at,

His passion how to avoid the obvious,
His technique how to vary the avoidance.

The others throw to be comprehended. He
Throws to be a moment misunderstood.

Yet not too much. Not errant, arrant, wild,
But every seeming aberration willed.

Not to, yet still, still to communicate
Making the batter understand too late.   10

QUESTIONS
1. The poem describes the art of the baseball pitcher. But the description is an extended metaphor for the art of the poet. Is the pitcher described accurately? **2.** Is the analogy between pitcher and poet apt? Explain.

Very Like a Whale   1945

OGDEN NASH   [1902–1971]

One thing that literature would be greatly the better for
Would be a more restricted employment by authors of simile and metaphor.
Authors of all races, be they Greeks, Romans, Teutons or Celts,
Can't seem just to say that anything is the thing it is but have to go out of
    their way to say that it is like something else.
What does it mean when we are told
That the Assyrian came down like a wolf on the fold?[1]
In the first place, George Gordon Byron had had enough experience
To know that it probably wasn't just one Assyrian, it was a lot of Assyrians.
However, as too many arguments are apt to induce apoplexy and thus
    hinder longevity,
We'll let it pass as one Assyrian for the sake of brevity.   10
Now then, this particular Assyrian, the one whose cohorts were gleam-
    ing in purple and gold,
Just what does the poet mean when he says he came down like a wolf on
    the fold?
In heaven and earth more than is dreamed of in our philosophy there are
    a great many things,
But I don't imagine that among them there is a wolf with purple and gold
    cohorts or purple and gold anythings.

No, no, Lord Byron, before I'll believe that this Assyrian was actually
    like a wolf I must have some kind of proof;
Did he run on all fours and did he have a hairy tail and a big red mouth
    and big white teeth and did he say Woof woof?
Frankly I think it very unlikely, and all you were entitled to say, at the
    very most,
Was that the Assyrian cohorts came down like a lot of Assyrian cohorts
    about to destroy the Hebrew host.
But that wasn't fancy enough for Lord Byron, oh dear me no, he had to
    invent a lot of figures of speech and then interpolate them,
With the result that whenever you mention Old Testament soldiers to
    people they say Oh yes, they're the ones that a lot of wolves dressed
    up in gold and purple ate them.   20
That's the kind of thing that's being done all the time by poets, from
    Homer to Tennyson;
They're always comparing ladies to lilies and veal to venison,
And they always say things like that the snow is a white blanket after a
    winter storm.

Very Like a Whale
  [1] Nash is responding to Lord Byron's "The Destruction of Sennacherib," a poetic account of the event in 2 Kings 19. Byron's poem appears on p. 673.

Oh it is, is it, all right then, you sleep under a six-inch blanket of snow
and I'll sleep under a half-inch blanket of unpoetical blanket material
and we'll see which one keeps warm,
And after that maybe you'll begin to comprehend dimly
What I mean by too much metaphor and simile.

Constantly Risking Absurdity   1958

LAWRENCE FERLINGHETTI   [b. 1919]

Constantly risking absurdity
                  and death
      whenever he performs
             above the heads
                   of his audience
  the poet like an acrobat
           climbs on rime
              to a high wire of his own making
and balancing on eyebeams
              above a sea of faces   10
    paces his way
            to the other side of day
  performing entrechats
           and sleight-of-foot tricks
and other high theatrics
           and all without mistaking
      any thing
         for what it may not be

  For he's the super realist
              who must perforce perceive   20
     taut truth
           before the taking of each stance or step
in his supposed advance
           toward that still higher perch
where Beauty stands and waits
          with gravity
            to start her death-defying leap

  And he
      a little charleychaplin man
           who may or may not catch   30
    her fair eternal form
         spreadeagled in the empty air
   of existence

The Writer   1976

RICHARD WILBUR [b. 1921]

In her room at the prow of the house
Where light breaks, and the windows are tossed with linden,
My daughter is writing a story.

I pause in the stairwell, hearing
From her shut door a commotion of typewriter-keys
Like a chain hauled over a gunwale.

Young as she is, the stuff
Of her life is a great cargo, and some of it heavy:
I wish her a lucky passage.

But now it is she who pauses,   10
As if to reject my thought and its easy figure.
A stillness greatens, in which

The whole house seems to be thinking.
And then she is at it again with a bunched clamor
Of strokes, and again is silent.

I remember the dazed starling
Which was trapped in that very room, two years ago;
How we stole in, lifted a sash

And retreated, not to affright it;
And how for a helpless hour, through the crack of the door,   20
We watched the sleek, wild, dark

And iridescent creature
Batter against the brilliance, drop like a glove
To the hard floor, or the desk-top,

And wait then, humped and bloody,
For the wits to try it again; and how our spirits
Rose when, suddenly sure,

It lifted off from a chair-back,
Beating a smooth course for the right window
And clearing the sill of the world.

It is always a matter, my darling,
Of life or death, as I had forgotten. I wish
What I wished you before, but harder.

QUESTIONS
1. What is the relationship between the "dazed starling" and the young writer? **2.** What is the significance of the alternate clamor of the typewriter and silence? **3.** What does the speaker wish for his daughter?

WRITING TOPIC
How do the central metaphors of the poem, the ship (stanzas 1–3) and the bird (6–10), convey the theme?

A Poet's Progress   1950

MICHAEL HAMBURGER   [b. 1924]

Like snooker balls thrown on the table's faded green,
Rare ivory and weighted with his best ambitions,
At first his words are launched: not certain what they mean,
He loves to see them roll, rebound, assume positions
Which—since not he—some power beyond him has assigned.

But now the game begins: dead players, living critics
Are watching him—and suddenly one eye goes blind,
The hand that holds the cue shakes like a paralytic's,
Till every thudding, every clinking sound portends
New failure, new defeat. Amazed, he finds that still   10
It is not he who guides his missiles to their ends
But an unkind geometry that mocks his will.

If he persists, for years he'll practise patiently,
Lock all the doors, learn all the tricks, keep noises out,
Though he may pick a ghost or two for company
Or pierce the room's inhuman silence with a shout.
More often silence wins; then soon the green felt seems
An evil playground, lawless, lost to time, forsaken,
And he a fool caught in the water weeds of dreams
Whom only death or frantic effort can awaken.   20

At last, a master player, he can face applause,
Looks for a fit opponent, former friends, emerges;
But no one knows him now. He questions his own cause,
And has forgotten why he yielded to those urges,

Took up a wooden cue to strike a coloured ball.
Wise now, he goes on playing; both his house and heart
Unguarded solitudes, hospitable to all
Who can endure the cold intensity of art.

For Saundra   1968

NIKKI GIOVANNI   [b. 1943]

i wanted to write
a poem
that rhymes
but revolution doesn't lend
itself to be-bopping

then my neighbor
who thinks i hate
asked—do you ever write
tree poems—i like trees
so i thought   10

i'll write a beautiful green tree poem
peeked from my window
to check the image
noticed the school yard was covered
with asphalt
no green—no trees grow
in manhattan

then, well, i thought the sky
i'll do a big blue sky poem

but all the clouds have winged   20
low since no-Dick[1] was elected

so i thought again
and it occurred to me
maybe i shouldn't write
at all

For Saundra
    [1] A derogatory reference to Richard Nixon.

but clean my gun
and check my kerosene supply

perhaps these are not poetic
times
at all   30

Today Is a Day of Great Joy   1968
VICTOR HERNÁNDEZ CRUZ   [b.1949]

when they stop poems
in the mail & clap
their hands & dance to
them
when women become pregnant
by the side of poems
the strongest sounds making
the river go along

it is a great day

as poems fall down to   10

movie crowds in restaurants
in bars

when poems start to
knock down walls to
choke politicians
when poems scream &
begin to break the air

that is the time of
true poets that is
the time of greatness   20

a true poet aiming
poems & watching things
fall to the ground

it is a great day.

Reading Fiction

An author is a god, creator of the world he or she describes. That world has a limited and very special landscape. It is peopled with men and women of a particular complexion, of particular gifts and failings. Its history, almost always, is determined by the interaction of its people within its narrow geography. Everything that occurs in a work of fiction—every figure, every tree, every furnished room and crescent moon and dreary fog—has been *purposely* put there by its creator. When a story pleases, when it moves its reader, he or she has responded to that carefully created world. The pleasure, the emotional commitment, the human response are not results of analysis. The reader has not registered in some mental adding machine the several details that establish character, the particular appropriateness of the weather to the events in the story, the marvelous rightness of the furnishings, the manipulation of the point of view, the plot, the theme, the style. The reader has recognized and accepted the world of the author and has been delighted (or saddened or angered) by what happens in it.

But how does it come about that readers recognize the artificial worlds, often quite different from their own, that authors create? And why is it that readers who recognize some fictional worlds effortlessly are bewildered and lost in other fictional worlds? Is it possible to extend the boundaries of readers' recognition? Can more and more of the landscapes and societies of fiction be made available to that onlooking audience?

The answer to the first of these questions is easy. Readers are comfortable in literary worlds that, however exotic the landscapes and the personalities that people them, incorporate moral imperatives that reflect the value system in the readers' world. Put another way, much fiction ends with its virtuous characters rewarded and its villains punished. This we speak of as poetic justice, and *poetic* seems to suggest that somehow such endings are ideal rather than "real." Not much experience of life is required to recognize that injustice, pain, frustration, and downright villainy often prevail, that the beautiful young heroine and the strong, handsome hero do not always overcome all obstacles, marry, and live happily ever after, that not every man is strong and handsome nor every woman beautiful. But readers, knowing that, respond to tragic fiction as well—where virtue is defeated, where obstacles prove too much for the men and women, where ponderous forces result in defeat, even death. Unhappy outcomes are painful to contemplate, but it is not difficult to recognize the world in which they occur. That world is much like our own. And unhappy outcomes serve to emphasize the very ideals that we have established in this world as the aims and goals of human activity. Consequently, both the "romantic" comedies that gladden with justice and success and the "realistic" stories that end in defeat provide readers with recognizable and available emotional worlds, however exotic the settings and the characters in those stories might be.

If we look at fiction this way, the answer to the question "Why is it that some readers are bewildered and lost in some fictional worlds?" is clearly implied. Some fictional worlds *seem* to incorporate a strange set of moral imperatives. Readers are not altogether certain who are the virtuous characters and who are the villains or even what constitutes virtue and evil. Sometimes tragic oppositions in a fictional world that brooks no compromise puzzle readers who live in a world where compromise has become almost a virtue. Sometimes, particularly in more recent fiction that reflects the ever-widening influence of psychoanalytic theory, the landscape and the behavior of characters is designed to represent deep interiors, the less-than-rational hearts and minds of characters. Those weird interiors are not part of the common awareness of readers; the moral questions raised there are not the same moral questions that occupy most of our waking hours. Such fictional worlds are difficult to map, and bewildered readers may well reject these underworlds for the sunshine of the surfaces they know more immediately.

Fiction and Reality

Why do people read fiction (or go to movies)? The question is not so easy to answer as one might suppose. The first response is likely to have something to do with "amusement" or "entertainment." But you have doubtless read stories and novels (or seen movies) that end tragically. Is it accurate to say that they were amusing or entertaining? Is it entertaining to be saddened or to be angered by the defeat of "good" people? Or does the emotional impact of such stories somehow enlarge our own humanity? Fiction teaches its readers by providing them a vast range of experience that they could not acquire otherwise. Especially for the relatively young, conceptions of love, of success in life, of war, of malignant evil and cleansing virtue are learned from fiction—not from life. And herein lies a great danger, for literary artists are notorious liars, and their lies frequently become the source of people's convictions about human nature and human society.

To illustrate, a huge number of television series based on the exploits of the FBI, or the Miami police force, or the dedicated surgeons at the general hospital, or the young lawyers always end with a capture, with a successful (though dangerous) operation, with justice triumphant. But, in the real world, police are able to resolve only about 10 percent of reported crime, disease ravages, and economic and political power often extends into the courtroom. The very existence of such television drama bespeaks a yearning that things should be different; their heroes are heroic in that they regularly overcome those obstacles that we all experience but that, alas, we do not overcome.

Some writers, beginning about the middle of the nineteenth century, were particularly incensed at the real damage that a lying literature promotes, and they devoted their energies to exposing and counteracting the lies of the novelists, particularly those lies that formed attitudes about what constituted human success and happiness. Yet that popular fiction, loosely called *escapist*, is still most widely read for reasons that would probably fill several studies in social psychology. It needs no advocate. The fiction in this book, on the other hand, has been chosen largely because it does not lie about life—at least it does not lie about life in the ordinary way. And the various authors employ a large variety of literary methods and modes in an effort to illuminate the deepest wells of human experience. Consequently, many of these stories do not retail high adventure (though some do), since an adventurous inner life does not depend on an incident-filled outer life. Some stories, like Toomer's "Theater" and Porter's "The Jilting of Granny Weatherall," might almost be said to be about what does *not* happen rather than what does—not-happening being as much incident, after all, as happening.

All fiction attempts to be interesting, to involve readers in situations, to force some aesthetic response from them—most simply put, in the widest sense of the word, to entertain. Some fiction aspires to nothing more. Other fiction seeks, as well, to establish some truth about the nature of humankind—Hemingway's "A Clean, Well-Lighted Place" and Tolstoy's "The Death of Iván Ilých" ask readers to perceive the inner life of a central figure. Some fiction seeks to explore the relationships among people—Faulkner's "A Rose for Emily" and Toomer's "Theater" depend for their force on the powerful interaction of one character with another. Still other fiction seeks to explore the connection between people and society—Ellison's " 'Repent, Harlequin!' Said the Ticktockman" acquires its force from the implied struggle between people seeking a free and rich emotional life and the tyrannically ordering society that would sacrifice their humanity to some ideal of social efficiency.

We have been talking about that aspect of fiction that literary theorists identify as *theme*. Theorists also talk about plot, characterization, setting, point of view, and conflict—all terms naming aspects of fiction that generally have to do with the author's technique. Let us here deal with one story—James Joyce's "Araby" (p. 29). Read it. Then compare your private responses to the story with what we hope will be helpful and suggestive remarks about the methods of fiction.

The Methods of Fiction

One can perceive only a few things simultaneously and can hardly respond to everything contained in a well-wrought story all at once. After reading the story, the reader likely thinks back, makes adjustments, and reflects on the significance of things before reaching that set of emotional and intellectual experiences that we refer to as *response*. Most readers of short stories respond first to what may be called the *tone* of the opening lines. Now tone is an aspect of literature about which it is particularly difficult to talk, because it is an aura—a shimmering and shifting atmosphere that depends for its substance on rather delicate emotional responses to language and situation. Surely, before readers know anything at all about the plot of "Araby," they have experienced the tone.

> North Richmond Street, being blind, was a quiet street except at the hour when the Christian Brothers' School set the boys free. An uninhabited house of two storeys stood at the blind end, detached from its neighbors in a square ground. The other houses of the street, conscious of decent lives within them, gazed at one another with brown imperturbable faces.

Is the scene cheerful? Vital and active? Is this opening appropriate for a story that goes on to celebrate joyous affirmations about life and living? You will probably answer these questions negatively. Why? Because the dead-end street is described as "blind," because the Christian Brothers' School sounds much like a prison (it "sets the boys free"), because a vacant house fronts the dead end, because the other houses, personified, are "conscious of decent lives within" (a mildly ironic description—*decent* suggesting ordinary, thin-lipped respectability rather than passion or heroism), because those houses gaze at one another with "brown imperturbable faces"—*brown* being nondescript, as opposed, say, to scarlet, gold, bright blue, and *imperturbable faces* reinforcing the priggish decency within.

Short stories, of course, are short, but this fact implies some serious considerations. In some ways, a large class of good short fiction deals with events that may be compared to the tip of the proverbial iceberg. The events animating the story represent only a tiny fraction of the characters' lives and experiences; yet, that fraction is terribly important because it provides the basis for wide understanding both to the characters within the story and to its readers. In "Araby," the *plot*—the connected sequence of events—may be simply stated. A young boy who lives in a rather drab, respectable neighborhood develops a crush on the sister of one of his playmates. She asks him if he intends to go to a charity fair that she cannot attend. He resolves to go and purchase a gift for her. He is tormented by the late and drunken arrival of his uncle who has promised him the money he needs. When the boy finally arrives at the bazaar, he is disappointed by the difference between his expectation and the actuality of the almost deserted fair. He perceives some minor events, overhears some minor conversation, and finally sees himself "as a creature driven and derided by vanity." Yet this tiny stretch of experience out of the life of the boy introduces him to an awareness about the differences between imagination and reality, between his romantic infatuation and the vulgar reality all about him. We are talking now about what is called the *theme* of the story. Emerging from the mundane events that constitute the story's plot is a general statement about intensely idealized childish "love," the shattering recognition of the false sentimentality that occasions it, and the enveloping vulgarity of adult life. The few pages of the story, by detailing a few events out of a short period of the protagonist's life, illuminate one aspect of the loss of innocence that we all endure and that is always painful. In much of the literature in the section on innocence and experience, the protagonists learn painfully the moral complexities of a world that had once seemed uncomplicated and predictable. That education does not always occur, as in "Araby," at an early age, either in literature or life.

Certainly theme is a centrally important aspect of prose fiction, but "good" themes do not necessarily ensure good stories. One may write a wretched story with the same theme as "Araby." What, then, independent of theme, is the difference between good stories and bad stories? Instinctively you know how to answer this question. Good stories, to begin with, are interesting; they present characters you care about; however fantastic, they are yet somehow plausible; they project a moral world you recognize. One of the obvious differences between short stories and novels is that story writers develop characters rapidly and limit the number of developed characters. Many stories have only one fleshed character; the other characters are frequently two-dimensional projections or even stereotypes. We see their surface only, not their souls. Rarely does a short story have more than three developed characters. Again, unlike novels, short stories usually work themselves out in a restricted geographical setting, in a single place, and within a rather short period of time.

We often speak of character, setting, plot, theme, and style as separate aspects of a story in order to break down a complex narrative into more manageable parts. But it is important to understand that this analytic process of separating various elements is something we have done to the story—the story (if it is a good one) is an integrated whole. The more closely we examine the separate elements, the clearer it becomes that each is integrally related to the others.

It is part of the boy's character that he lives in a brown imperturbable house in North Richmond Street, that he does the things he does (which is, after all, the plot), that he learns what he does (which is the theme), and that all of this characterization emerges from Joyce's rich and suggestive style. Consider this paragraph:

> Her image accompanied me even in places the most hostile to romance. On Saturday evenings when my aunt went marketing I had to go to carry some of the parcels. We walked through the flaring streets, jostled by drunken men and bargaining women, amid the curses of labourers, the shrill litanies of shop-boys who stood on guard by the barrels of pigs' cheeks, the nasal chanting of street-singers, who sang a *come-all-you* about O'Donovan Rossa, or a ballad about the troubles in our native land. These noises converged in a single sensation of life for me: I imagined that I bore my chalice safely through a throng of foes. Her name sprang to my lips at moments in strange prayers and praises which I myself did not understand. My eyes were often full of tears (I could not tell why) and at times a flood from my heart seemed to pour itself out into my bosom. I thought little of the future. I did not know whether I would

ever speak to her or not or, if I spoke to her, how I could tell her of my confused adoration. But my body was like a harp and her words and gestures were like fingers running upon the wires.

This paragraph furthers the plot. But it suggests much more. The boy thinks of his friend's sister even when he carries parcels for his aunt during the shopping trips through a crowded and coarse part of town. In those coarse market streets the shop-boys cry shrill "litanies," the girl's name springs to his lips in strange "prayers and praises," and the boy confesses a confused "adoration." Further, he bears "his chalice safely through a throng of foes." Now the words *litanies, prayers, praises, adoration* all come from a special vocabulary that is easy to identify. It is the vocabulary of the Roman Catholic Church. The *chalice* and the *throng of foes* come from the vocabulary of chivalric romance, which is alluded to in the first line of the quoted paragraph. Joyce's diction evokes a sort of holy chivalry that characterizes the boy on this otherwise altogether ordinary shopping trip. This paragraph suggests to the careful reader that the boy has cast his awakening sexuality in a mold that mixes the disparate shapes of the heroic knight, winning his lady by force of arms, and the ascetic penitent, adoring the Blessed Virgin, Mother of God.

Playing the word game, of course, can be dangerous. But from the beginning of this story to its end, a certain religious quality shimmers. That now-dead priest of the story's second paragraph had three books (at least). One is a romantic chivalric novel by Sir Walter Scott; one is a sensational account of the adventures of a famous criminal-turned-detective; one is what a priest might be expected to have at hand—an Easter week devotional guide. That priest who read Scott novels might have understood the boy's response—that mixture of religious devotion and romance. Shortly after the shopping trip, the boy finally speaks to the girl, and it is instructive to see her as he does. He stands at the *railings* and looks up (presumably) at her, she bowing her head towards him. "The light from the lamp opposite our door caught the white curve of her neck, lit up her hair that rested there and, falling, lit up the hand upon the railing. It fell over one side of her dress and caught the white border of a petticoat, just visible as she stood at ease." Skip the petticoat, for a moment. Might the description of Mangan's sister remind the careful reader of quite common sculptured representations of the Virgin Mary? But the petticoat! And the white curve of her neck! This erotic overlay characterizes the boy's response. The sexuality is his own; the chivalry, the religious adoration, come from the culture in which he is immersed—come from Scott, the ballads sung in the market place, the "Arab's Farewell to his Steed" that the boy's uncle threatens to recite, and from his Catholic background. And it is the culture that so romanticizes and elevates the boy's yearning.

He finally gets to Araby—"the syllables of the word . . . were called to [him] through the silence in which [his] soul luxuriated and cast an Eastern enchantment over [him]." His purpose is to serve his lady—to bring her something from that exotic place. What he finds is a weary-looking man guarding a turnstile, the silence that pervades a church after a service, and two men counting money on a salver (that tray is called a *salver* by design). **And in** this setting he overhears a young woman flirting with two gentlemen:

"O, I never said such a thing!"
"O, but you did!"
"O, but I didn't!"
"Didn't she say that?"
"Yes, I heard her."
"O, there's a . . . fib!"

This is Araby, this is love in a darkened hall where money is counted. Is it any wonder that the boy, in the moment of personal illumination that Joyce calls an epiphany, sees himself as a creature driven and derided by vanity?

"Araby" is a careful, even a delicate story. Nothing much happens—what does occurs largely in the boy's perception and imagination. The story focuses on the boy's confusion of sexual attraction with the lofty sentiments of chivalry and religion. The climax occurs when he confronts the darkened, money-grubbing fair and the banal expression of the sexual attraction between the gentlemen and the young woman. The result is a sudden deflation of the boy's ego, his sense of self, as he recognizes his own delusions about the nature of love and the relationship between men, women, heroism, God, and money.

We would like to conclude with a discussion of one feature of fiction that sometimes proves troublesome to many readers. Often the events of a story, upon which much depends, puzzle or annoy readers. Why does that fool do that? Why doesn't X simply tell Y the way he or she feels and then the tragedy would be averted? In a sense, such responses reflect the intrusion of a reader into the world of the story. The reader, a sensible and sensitive person, understands some things about life after all and is oppressed by the characters' inability to understand at least as much. Characters choose to die when they might with a slight adjustment live. They risk danger when with a slight adjustment they might proceed safely. They suffer the pain of an unfortunate marriage when with a little trouble they might be free to live joyously. If the "whys" issuing from the reader are too insistent, too sensible, then the story must fail, at least for that reader. But many "whys" are not legitimate. Many are intrusions of the reader's hindsight, the reader's altogether different cultural and emotional fix. Henry James urged that the author must be allowed his or her *donnée*, his or her "given." The author creates the society and the rules by which it operates within his or her own fictional world. Sometimes this creation is so close to the reader's own world that it is hardly possible to object. Readers who have grown up in a southern town will recognize the atmosphere of Faulkner's "A Rose for Emily." But few readers of this book know 1895 Dublin and Irish middle-class society, which play a brooding role in "Araby" (as it does in almost all of Joyce's work). None know the futuristic world of Harlan Ellison's Harlequin. In every case, we must finally imagine those worlds, even where setting is familiar. If we cannot, the events that take place in them will be of no consequence. If those worlds are unimaginable, then the stories must fail. If they too much strain belief or remain too foreign to the reader's heart, they must likewise fail. But all response to fiction depends on the reader's acquiescence to the world of the author and his or her perceptions of the moral consequences of acts and attitudes in that world. At best, that acquiescence will provide much pleasure as well as emotional insight into his or her own existence.

Reading Poetry

For many people, the question "What is poetry?" is irrelevant if not irreverent. The attempt to answer such a question leads to abstract intellectual analysis, the very opposite of the emotional pleasure one seeks in a good poem. Why does it matter what poetry is so long as readers enjoy poems? Doesn't the attempt to define the nature of poetry lead to technical analysis of poetic devices so that study, finally, destroys pleasure?

These are valid issues that touch on very real dangers. If the study of poetry bogs down in theoretical or historical issues and the study of a poem becomes a mere exercise in the identification and discussion of poetic devices, the reader may well find that reading a poem is more effort than pleasure. He or she may begin to feel like the many nineteenth-century poets who complained that science, in laying bare the laws of nature, robbed the universe of its ancient awe and mystery. Walt Whitman, for example, describes such a feeling in his poem "When I Heard the Learn'd Astronomer."

> When I heard the learn'd astronomer,
> When the proofs, the figures, were ranged in columns before me,
> When I was shown the charts and diagrams, to add, divide, and measure them,
> When I sitting heard the astronomer where he lectured with much applause in the
>   lecture-room,
> How soon unaccountable I became tired and sick,
> Till rising and gliding out I wander'd off by myself,
> In the mystical moist night-air, and from time to time,
> Look'd up in perfect silence at the stars.

The distinction implicit in Whitman's poem between the mind (intellectual knowledge) and the heart (emotion and feelings) is very old, but still a useful one. All of us have no doubt felt at some time that the overexercise of the mind interfered with our capacity to feel. Compelled to analyze, dissect, categorize, and classify, we finally yearn for the simple and "mindless" pleasure of unanalytical enjoyment, the pleasure of sensuous experience. The distinction between the mind and the heart is, however, a fiction that cannot be pushed too far before it breaks down. Readers may very well enjoy Dylan Thomas's "Fern Hill" without understanding Thomas's use of symbolism or color or religious imagery. But understanding that symbolism and imagery will certainly deepen the pleasure derived from the poem.

We don't mean to suggest by all this that every poem needs to be studied in detail or that it is possible to say in the abstract what kind and amount of study will be rewarding. Some poems are straightforward, requiring little by way of analysis; others, dense and complex, seem to yield little without some study. But study of even the simplest poems can be rewarding. (Consider the effect of the special vocabulary implied by such words as "arrayed," "imperially," "crown," and "glittered" in Edwin Arlington Robinson's "Richard Cory.") On the other hand, it is possible to be moved on first reading by the tone and quality of such complex poems as Wallace Stevens's "Sunday Morning" and T. S. Eliot's "The Love Song of J. Alfred Prufrock" even though they are difficult to understand immediately.

As to our original question—What is poetry?—we cannot offer anything like a definitive and comprehensive answer. Poetry is a form of writing that often employs rhyme, a regular rhythm, unusual word order, and an intense or heightened language. This formal definition will serve about as well as any although it is by no means comprehensive, as any collection of poems will readily demonstrate. Up to about a century ago, poetry was governed by rather precise and often elaborate rules and conventions; if a poem did not use rhyme, it certainly was characterized by rhythmic regularity, or meter. Further, there existed a long tradition of poetic types (epic, elegiac, odic, etc.), each with quite specific rules and characteristics. While these traditions still retain some force, the old notion that these forms are part of the natural scheme of things has been largely abandoned. No one insists that the form of writing we call poetry must exhibit a combination of fixed characteristics.

Consider poetry from a different angle and ask not what poetry is but rather what functions it serves. Poetry fulfills some deep and abiding human need, for no culture we know of has been without it. We know also that in ancient societies, the arts were not divided by types or differentiated from science. In ancient tribal societies, poetry, dance, sculpture, and painting might all be parts of a tribal ceremony designed to propitiate the gods and thereby ensure a full harvest or a successful hunt. Poetry, then, was part of a primitive (we would now label it "superstitious") science that defined and helped control the external world. Though one can only guess in these matters, it is probably safe to assume that in such a primitive society the inner emotional world of the individual was not sharply distinguished from the outer world of nature. Nature and the gods who controlled it might be harsh and unpredictable, and the function of ritual was to control and appease these gods (to ensure rain, for example). But ritual also nurtured and strengthened the individual's communal spirit and conditioned his or her feelings about the arduous work that the life of the tribe required.

The conditions of our lives are, of course, vastly different. We operate within an enormous industrialized society that developed over centuries as societies abandoned primitive explanations of the universe and sought others. One result of that development was a continuing differentiation and specialization of human endeavors, as science broke away from art and both divided into separate if related disciplines. Science became astronomy, biology, physics, and the like, while art branched into various types of aesthetic creation. And it was modern science, not poetry or the other arts, that produced profound and measurable changes in people's lives. Poetry might movingly and memorably remind us of the sorrow of unrequited love or the ravages of growing old, but science created a technology that produced undreamed of material wealth and power.

Is the very persistence of poetry evidence that it serves some important function, however obscure? On the other hand, maybe poetry is merely a vestigial organ of evolution that, like the appendix, continues to exist even though it has outlived its usefulness. Certainly, the historical process we have sketched here seems to involve a gradual diminution in the importance we attach to poetry.

It would be misleading, of course, to suggest that the scientist and the poet exist in separate worlds. But the differences between them are important. The truth that science seeks is the truth of physical reality. Social sciences such as psychology, sociology, and economics have attempted to demonstrate that human behavior can be understood in terms of a set of definite and quantifiable mechanisms. And, though no one would assert that science has achieved final answers, it is clear that the spectacular discoveries of science have left many, Walt Whitman among them, with the feeling that our importance in the universe has diminished.

Science may describe and educate us about the outer world and its inexorable laws with as rigorous an objectivity and neutrality as it can achieve. It may explain to us that in a naturalistic world death comes to all living creatures or that sunsets result from certain physical phenomena; but it is silent on the terror of death and its human emotional meaning or on the beauty of a sunset. To understand those emotions, to give them form and meaning, we turn to poetry—we read it and, perhaps, even write it. For poetry, so to speak, educates our emotions and our feelings, allows us to learn who we are and to articulate what we feel.

We might wonder whether such an assertion makes sense. What we feel, we feel. We don't need a poem to tell us that. Not so. Often we don't know what we feel except in a vague and inarticulate way. A powerful poem articulates and thereby clarifies. Further, a poem may even deepen feelings. Although the literary historian might observe that it is an academic exercise in wit, Andrew Marvell's poem "To His Coy Mistress" may well help readers understand their own feelings about physical love and mortality. The outrageous absurdity of death cutting down a person whose life has barely begun is articulated in Robert Frost's " 'Out, Out—' " and Theodore Roethke's "Elegy for Jane."

Poetry at its highest and most general level is a form of communication, a means of defining, affirming, and deepening our humanity. This is not to say that we should approach poetry solemnly, expecting always to be loftily enlightened. We may, for instance, look upon a poem as a kind of game in which the poet skillfully works within a set of self-imposed rules—rhyme, meter, and stanzaic pattern—and delights in clever rhymes, as when Lord Byron rhymes "intellectual" with "henpecked you all" or "maxim" with "tax 'em." Anyone familiar with Plato's theory that everything in our world is an imperfect replica of an ideal heavenly form will appreciate the beauty and condensed brilliance of William Butler Yeats's lines from "Among School Children":

> Plato thought nature but a spume that plays
> Upon a ghostly paradigm of things.

Some will discover in poetry, as children often do in nursery rhymes, the pleasure of rhythm, meter, and sound—the musical aspects of poetry. The pleasures of poetry range from the loftiest insights and discoveries to memorable lines and clever rhymes.

A discussion of the major techniques and devices of poetry will provide some suggestions about how to approach poems and also furnish tools and a vocabulary for analyzing and discussing them.

The Words of Poetry

It is not unusual to hear an original philosopher, sociologist, or economist referred to as a mediocre writer. Yet, even while judging the writing poor, one may at the same time recognize and honor the originality and significance of the idea conveyed. Such a distinction cannot be made in poetry. If a poem is written poorly, it is a poor poem. "In reading prose," Ralph Waldo Emerson said, "I am sensitive as soon as a sentence drags; but in poetry, as soon as one word drags." *Where* a poem arrives is inseparable from *how* it arrives. Everything must be right in a poem, every word. "The correction of prose," said Yeats, "is endless, a poem comes right with a click like a closing box."

"Poetry is heightened language" means, among other things, that the poet strives for precision and richness in the words he or she uses, and "precision" and "richness" are not contradictory for the poet. Words have dictionary or denotative meanings as well as associative or connotative meanings; they also have histories and relationships with other words. The English language is rich in synonyms, groups of words whose denotative meanings are roughly the same but whose connotations vary widely (portly, stout, fat; horse, steed, courser). Many words are identical in sound and often in spelling but different in meaning (forepaws, four paws; lie [recline], lie [fib]). The meanings of words have changed in the course of time, and the poet may consciously select a word whose older meaning adds a dimension to the poem. There are, of course, no rules that can be given to a reader for judging a poet's effectiveness and skill in the handling of words (or anything else, for that matter). All we can do is look at particular works for examples of how a good poet manipulates words.

In a moving and passionate poem on his dying father, "Do Not Go Gentle into That Good Night," Dylan Thomas pleads with his father not to accept death passively but rather to "Rage, rage against the dying of the light." He declares that neither "wise men" nor "good men" nor "wild men" accept death quietly. And neither, Thomas says, do "grave men," punning on *grave* in its meaning of both "serious" and "burial place." William Blake's poem about the inhumane jobs children were forced into in eighteenth-century England, "The Chimney Sweeper" begins:

> When my mother died I was very young.
> And my Father sold me while yet my tongue
> Could scarcely cry " 'weep! 'weep! 'weep! 'weep!"
> So your chimneys I sweep, and in soot I sleep.

" 'Weep," a clipped form of "sweep," is what the boy cries as he walks a street looking for work, but *weep* clearly evokes the tears and sorrow of the mother's death and the sadness of the small boy's cruel life. And this is only part of Blake's skillful handling of words. "Cry" is also an effective pun, the precise word to describe how the boy seeks work while simultaneously reinforcing the emotional meaning of *weep*.

Henry Reed's "Naming of Parts" develops a contrast between the instructions a group of soldiers are receiving on how to operate a rifle (in order to cause death) and the lovely world of nature (which represents life and beauty). In the fourth stanza, bees are described as "assaulting and fumbling the flowers." "Fumbling," with its meaning of awkwardness and nervous uncertainty, may strike us as an arresting and perhaps puzzling word at first. Yet anyone who has watched a bee pollinating a flower will find the word extremely effective. In addition, of course, *fumbling* describes the actions of human beings caught up in sexual passion—a connotation appropriate to the poet's purposes, since pollination is, in a sense, a sexual process. Furthermore, these various interpretations of *fumbling* contrast powerfully with the cold, mechanical precision of the death-dealing instruments the recruits are learning to use. The next line of Reed's poem exhibits yet another resource of words: "They call it easing the Spring." The line is an exact repetition of a phrase used two lines earlier except *Spring* is now capitalized. While *Spring* retains its first meaning as part of the bolt action of the rifle, the capitalization makes it the season of the year when flowers are pollinated and the world of nature is reborn. With a mere typographical device, Reed has charged a single word with the theme of his poem.

Sometimes meanings are not inherent in the isolated words but created in the poet's use of the word. A tree is a tree and a rose is a rose. A tree is also the apple tree in Frost's "After Apple-Picking" and something quite different in William Blake's "A Poison Tree"; a rose is specially defined in Robert Burns's "A Red, Red Rose" and Edmund Waller's "Go, Lovely Rose!" In these poems, because *tree* and *rose* are given such rich and varied meaning, they exceed mere connotation and become images that, finally, are symbolic.

Imagery

The world is revealed to us through our senses—sight, sound, taste, touch, and smell. And while some philosophers and psychologists might challenge the statement, it seems pretty clear that much, if not all, of our knowledge is linked to sensory experience. *Imagery* is the representation in poetry of sensory experience, one of the means by which the poet creates a world that we all know and share. Or, put another way, imagery allows the poet to create a recognizable world by drawing upon a fund of common experiences. Bad poetry is often bad because the imagery is stale ("golden sunset," "the smiling sun," "the rolling sea") or so skimpy that the poem dissolves into vague and meaningless abstractions.

A good poet never loses touch with the sensory world. The invisible, the intangible, the abstract, are anchored to the visible, the tangible, the concrete. Andrew Marvell begins his poem "To His Coy Mistress" with an elaborate statement of how he would court his beloved if their lives were measured in centuries rather than years. In the second stanza, he describes the reality:

> But at my back I always hear
> Time's wingéd chariot hurrying near;
> And yonder all before us lie
> Deserts of vast eternity.
> Thy beauty shall no more be found,
> Nor, in thy marble vault, shall sound
> My echoing song; then worms shall try
> That long-preserved virginity,
> And your quaint honor turn to dust,
> And into ashes all my lust:
> The grave's a fine and private place,
> But none, I think, do there embrace.

Time, eternity, honor, and *lust* are all abstractions, vague and diffuse as abstractions always are. To persuade his coy mistress, Marvell needs to impart a sense of passionate urgency, to make her (and the reader) *see* these abstractions by linking them with the concrete. He does this by making time a *chariot,* eternity endless *deserts,* having honor turn to *dust* and lust dwindle into *ashes.*

Any analysis of the imagery of a poem will soon reveal that our definition of imagery as the representation of sensory experience needs to be qualified. One of the primary functions of language is to bring meaning and order into our lives, and poetry uses language most intensely. We will find, therefore, that the images in poetry tend to be charged with meanings. A rose may be only a rose, but it becomes much more in Burns's and Waller's poems. Imagery, then, is closely related to *figurative language* (which we will discuss in more detail shortly), the language that *says* one thing and *means* another.

The difference between good and bad poetry often turns on the skill with which imagery (or figurative language) is used. When Robert Frost in his poem "Birches" compares life to "a pathless wood," the image strikes us as natural and appropriate (the comparison of life to a path or road is a common one, as is a wood or forest to a state of moral bewilderment). However, when John Donne in "A Valediction: Forbidding Mourning" describes his relationship with his beloved in terms of a drawing compass, the image may seem jarring or even ludicrous; how can such a prosaic object help the poet define the nature of love, especially a love based upon spiritual affinities? In using such a *conceit* (see Glossary of Literary Terms), Donne startles the reader into attention, maybe even hoping to create resistance or doubt that such an image is appropriate to the theme of love. It is a daring strategy. And, as Donne elaborates the comparison through various stages, concluding it with the brilliantly appropriate image of the completed circle, our resistance and doubt give way to admiration for what Donne has done.

Figurative Language

Figurative language is the general phrase we use to describe the many devices of language that allow us to speak nonliterally, to say one thing and mean another. Any attempt to communicate an emotion will very quickly utilize figurative language. When Robert Burns compares his love to a red rose, he does so not because he is unable to find the literal language he needs but because what he wants to say can only be expressed in figurative language. (Literal language might be used by a scientist to describe the physiological state of someone in love, but that is not what interests Burns.) The world of emotions, feelings, attitudes remains shadowy and insubstantial until figurative language gives it form and substance.

Consider, for example, these familiar old sayings: "The grass is always greener on the other side of the fence"; "A rolling stone gathers no moss"; "A bird in the hand is worth two in the bush"; "The early bird catches the worm." While these sayings unquestionably make sense in literal terms (the grass you see from a distance looks greener than the grass under your feet), the meaning of these phrases to a native speaker of English is clearly nonliteral. When we use them we are not speaking about grass or rolling stones or birds; we are making general and highly abstract observations about human attitudes and behavior. Yet, strangely, these generalizations and abstractions are embodied in concrete and sensuous imagery. Try to explain what any one of these expressions means and you will quickly discover that you are using many more words and much vaguer language than the expression itself. Indeed, this is precisely what happens when you attempt to paraphrase—that is, put into your own words—the meaning of a poem. Like poetry, these sayings rely on the figurative use of language.

Since poetry is an intense and heightened use of language that explores the world of feeling, it uses more varied figurative devices than does ordinary language. One of the most common figurative devices, *metaphor,* where one thing is called something else, occurs frequently in ordinary speech. "School is a rat race," we say, or "She's a bundle of nerves," and the meaning is perfectly clear—too clear, perhaps, because these metaphors are by now so common and unoriginal they have lost whatever vividness they may once have had. But when Thomas Nashe declares that "Beauty is but a flower / Which wrinkles will devour" or W. H. Auden, commenting on the death of William Butler Yeats, says, "Let the Irish vessel lie / Emptied of its poetry," we have metaphors that compel readers to confront certain painful aspects of life.

Simile is closely related to metaphor. But whereas metaphor says that one thing *is* another, simile says that one thing is *like* another, as in Burns's "O My Luve's like a red, red rose" and Frost's "life is too much like a pathless wood." The distinction between simile and metaphor, while easy enough to make technically, is often difficult to distinguish in terms of effects. Frost establishes a comparison between life and a pathless wood and keeps the two even more fully separated by adding the qualifiers, "too much." Burns's simile maintains the same separation and, in addition, because it occurs in the opening line of the poem, eliminates any possible confusion the reader might momentarily experience about the subject of the poem if the line read, "O My Luve is a red, red rose." The reader can test the difference in effect between simile and metaphor by changing a metaphor into a simile or a simile into a metaphor to see if the meaning of the poem is thereby altered.

The critical vocabulary useful in discussions of poetry includes several additional terms, all of which name particular figures of speech: *metonymy, synecdoche, personification, hyperbole, understatement, paradox.* (These terms are defined and illustrated in the Glossary of Literary Terms.) But, though there may be a certain academic pleasure in recognizing the figures a poet uses, naming a figure of speech will never explain its effectiveness.

Symbol

A *symbol* is anything that stands for or suggests something else. In this sense, most words are symbolic: the word *tree* stands for an object in the real world. When we speak of a symbol in poetry, however, we usually mean something more precise. In poetry, a symbol is an object or event that suggests more than itself. It is one of the most common and most powerful devices available to the poet, for it allows him or her to convey economically and simply a wide range of meanings.

It is useful to distinguish between two kinds of symbols, *public symbols* and *contextual symbols*. Public symbols are those objects or events that history has invested with rich meanings and associations. In a sense, then, a public symbol is a ready-made symbol. Yeats utilizes such a symbol in his poem "Leda and the Swan," assuming that his readers will be familiar with the myths that tell of the erotic affairs of Zeus and the consequences of those affairs—in this case, the birth of Clytemnestra, the wife of Agamemnon, and Helen, the most beautiful woman of antiquity, whose abduction precipitated the Trojan War. In "The Conscientious Objector," Karl Shapiro uses Noah's Ark and the Mayflower as symbols of a political prison whose inmates refuse to conform.

When poets use a public symbol, they are drawing from what they assume is a common and shared fund of knowledge and tradition. If Yeats's readers are unaware of the symbolic meaning with which history has invested the Trojan War, it is doubtful that the poem will have much meaning for them. Nor will Shapiro's poem be clear unless readers understand that Noah's Ark and the Mayflower evoke unique virtue and daring and heroic nonconformity.

In contrast to public symbols, contextual symbols are objects or events that are symbolic by virtue of the poet's handling of them in a particular poem—that is, by virtue of the context. Consider for example, the opening lines of Robert Frost's "After Apple-Picking":

> My long two-pointed ladder's sticking through a tree
> Toward heaven still,
> And there's a barrel that I didn't fill
> Beside it, and there may be two or three
> Apples I didn't pick upon some bough.

The apple tree is a literal tree, but as one reads through the poem, it becomes clear that the apple tree also symbolizes the speaker's life with a wide range of possible meanings (do the few apples he hasn't picked symbolize the hopes, dreams, aspirations that even the fullest life cannot satisfy?).

Amy Lowell's "Patterns" is rich in symbols. The speaker is an aristocratic woman whose life and most vital emotions are kept in rigid control by a series of patterns that the society she lives in has imposed on her. She describes herself as walking in her elegant gown down the garden paths laid out in precise patterns. Her gown is real; the path is a real path. But it very quickly becomes apparent that the patterned paths and her elegant gown are symbolic of the narrowly restricted and oppressive life her deepest feelings are at war with. They are the visible manifestation, the symbols, of the trap in which she is caught. She weeps when she notices "The daffodils and squills / Flutter in the breeze / As they please" because the flowers symbolize a freedom she knows she will never have.

The paths and flowers in Amy Lowell's poem are clear and easily recognizable examples of contextual symbols. However, contextual symbols by their very nature tend to present more difficulties than public symbols, because recognizing them depends on a sensitivity to everything else in the poem. In T. S. Eliot's dense and difficult poem "The Love Song of J. Alfred Prufrock," the speaker twice says, "In the room the women come and go / Talking of Michelangelo," a couplet that is baffling at first because it seems to have no clear relationship to what precedes and follows it. But as one reads through the poem, one begins to see that Prufrock is a man, like the young woman in Amy Lowell's poem, trapped in a life of upper-class superficialities and meaninglessness. The women discussing Michelangelo symbolize this dilettantish and arid life from which Prufrock desperately wishes to escape. Prufrock reminds himself that he will have time "To prepare a face to meet the faces that you meet," and Eleanor Rigby, in John Lennon and Paul McCartney's song, is described as "wearing the face that she keeps in a jar by the door." In both poems, the face symbolizes a lonely existence in a society where people play elaborate games in order to conceal from others their real emotions.

A final word on symbols. The reader who fails to recognize a symbol misses an important part of the poem's meaning. On the other hand, one of the pitfalls of reading poetry is that some readers become so intent on finding symbols they tend to forget than an object must first have a literal meaning before it can function as a symbol. Or, put in terms of our earlier definition, an object or event is itself before it is something else.

The setting of "After Apple-Picking" is an orchard, and the setting of "Patterns" the paths of a manorial garden. As we begin to understand the theme of each poem, we come to recognize the symbolic meanings these objects gradually take on. But there are rules that will allow a reader to identify symbols. If you do not know what Troy symbolizes and have never heard of Helen of Troy, you will not discover the meanings of these public symbols by repeated and intensive readings of the poem; like unfamiliar words, you must look up (or be told of) their significance. On the other hand, the recognition of contextual symbols often depends on careful and sensitive reading. Readers may very well disagree on whether or not something should be taken as a symbol. When this occurs, one can only consider whether the symbolic reading adds meanings that are consistent with other elements in the poem. Is the fly in Emily Dickinson's "I Heard a Fly Buzz—When I Died" a symbol or merely an insect? Your answer will depend on what you see as the theme of the poem.

Archibald MacLeish (1892–1982) renders the modern critical attitude toward symbolism in poetry and, at the same time, argues for the view that poems do not "mean" in the ordinary sense of that word. The various elements of a poem—imagery, figurative language, symbol—coalesce to form an *object*, something characterized not by its truth but by its objective correlation to some human experience. And most remarkably, MacLeish renders these rather complex critical positions in a poem rich in contextual symbols:

ARS POETICA   1926

A poem should be palpable and mute
As a globed fruit,

Dumb
As old medallions to the thumb,

Silent as the sleeve-worn stone
Of casement ledges where the moss has grown—

A poem should be wordless
As the flight of birds.

A poem should be motionless in time
As the moon climbs,

Leaving, as the moon releases
Twig by twig the night-entangled trees,

Leaving, as the moon behind the winter leaves,
Memory by memory the mind—

A poem should be motionless in time
As the moon climbs.

A poem should be equal to:
Not true.

For all the history of grief
An empty doorway and a maple leaf.

For love
The leaning grasses and two lights above the sea—

A poem should not mean
But be.

Music

The *music* of poetry, by which we mean the poetic use of all the devices of sound and rhythm inherent in language, is at once central to the poetic effect and yet the most difficult to account for. We can discuss the ways in which figurative language works with some clarity because we are using words to explain words. Any listener who has ever tried to explain the effect a piece of music (or who has read music criticism) will be familiar with the problem of describing a nonverbal medium with words.

The possible musical effects of language are complex. The terms we have to describe various musical devices deal only with the most obvious and easily recognizable patterns. *Alliteration, assonance, consonance, caesura, meter, onomatopoeia, rhythm,* and *rhyme* (all of them defined in the Glossary of Literary Terms) are the key traditional terms for discussing the music of poetry. Along with the other terms already introduced, they are an indispensable part of the vocabulary one needs to discuss poetry. But the relationship between sound and sense is illustrated nicely in a celebrated passage from Alexander Pope's "An Essay on Criticism," in which his definitions of bad verse and then of well-managed verse are ingeniously supported by the music of the lines:

> These[1] equal syllables alone require,
> Though oft the ear the open vowels tire;
> While expletives their feeble aid do join;
> And ten low words oft creep in one dull line:
> While they ring round the same unvaried chimes,
> With sure returns of still expected rhymes;

---

[1] Bad poets.

Where 'er you find "the cooling western breeze,"
In the next line, it "whispers through the trees";
If crystal streams "with pleasing murmurs creep,"
The reader's threatened (not in vain) with "sleep";
Then, at the last and only couplet fraught
With some unmeaning thing they call a thought,
A needless Alexandrine[2] ends the song
That, like a wounded snake, drags its slow length along.

    . . . . .

True ease in writing comes from art, not chance,
As those move easiest who have learned to dance.
'Tis not enough no harshness gives offense,
The sound must seem an echo to the sense:
Soft is the strain when Zephyr gently blows,
And the smooth stream in smoother numbers flows;
But when loud surges lash the sounding shore,
The hoarse, rough verse should like the torrent roar:
When Ajax[3] strives some rock's vast weight to throw,
The line too labors, and the words move slow;
Not so, when swift Camilla[4] scours the plain,
Flies o'er the unbending corn, and skims along the main.

When Pope speaks of open vowels, the line is loaded with open vowels. When Pope condemns the use of ten monosyllables, the line contains ten monosyllables. When Pope urges that the sound should echo the sense and speaks of the wind, the line is rich in sibilants that hiss, like the wind. When he speaks of Ajax striving, the combination of final consonants and initial sounds slow the line; when he speaks of Camilla's swiftness, the final consonants and initial sounds form liaisons that are swiftly pronounceable.

Or, consider the opening lines of Wilfred Owen's poem "Dulce et Decorum Est," describing a company of battle-weary World War I soldiers trudging toward their camp and rest:

Bent double, like old beggars under sacks,
Knock-kneed, coughing like hags, we cursed through sludge.

These lines are dominated by a series of harsh, explosive consonant sounds (*b*, *d*, *k*, *g*) that reinforce the meaning of the lines. More specifically, the first two syllables of each line are heavily stressed, which serves to slow the reading. And, finally, while the poem ultimately develops a prevailing meter, the meter is only faintly suggested in these opening lines, through the irregular rhythms used to describe a weary, stumbling march.

Let us remember, then, that analysis of musical (or for that matter any other)

---

[2] Twelve-syllable line.
[3] A Greek warrior celebrated for his strength.
[4] A swift-footed queen in Virgil's *Aeneid*.

devices can illuminate and enrich our understanding of poetry. But let us also remember that analysis has its limitations. Dylan Thomas once remarked:

> You can tear a poem apart to see what makes it technically tick and say to yourself when the works are laid out before you—the vowels, the consonants, the rhymes, and rhythms—"Yes, this is it. This is why the poem moves me so. It is because of the craftsmanship." But you're back where you began. The best craftsmanship always leaves holes and gaps in the works of the poem so that something that is not in the poem can creep, crawl, flash, or thunder in.

Another writer, X. J. Kennedy, doubtless with MacLeish's observations in mind, puts the same idea with less reverence:

ARS POETICA   1985

The goose that laid the golden egg
Died looking up its crotch
To find out how its sphincter worked.
Would you lay well? Don't watch.

Reading Drama

Plays are fundamentally different from other literary forms. Unlike stories and poems, almost all plays are designed to be performed, not to be read. Consequently, the aural and the visual aspects of the drama, which should be at least as important as its dialogue, are left altogether to the imagination of the reader (with the aid of some meager stage directions). Great effort is invested in such matters as costuming, set design, lighting effects, and stage movement by the director and his staff; all of that effort is lost to the reader who must somehow contrive to supply imaginatively some of those dramatic features not contained on the printed page.

As much as possible, the way to read a play is to imagine that you are its director. Hence you will concern yourself with creating the set and the lighting. You will see people dressed so that their clothes give support to their words. You will think about timing—how long between events and speeches—and blocking—how the characters move as they interact on stage. Perhaps the best way to confront the literature of the stage, to respond most fully to what is there, is to attempt to produce some scenes in class or after class. If possible, attend the rehearsals of plays in production on the campus. Nothing will provide better insight into the complexities of the theater than attending a rehearsal where the problems are encountered and solved.

As an exercise, read the opening speeches of any of the plays here and make decisions. How should the lines be spoken (quietly, angrily, haltingly)? What should the characters do as they speak (remain stationary, look in some direction, traverse the stage)? How should the stage be lit (partially, brightly, in some color that contributes to the mood of the dialogue and action)? What should the characters who are not speaking do? What possibilities exist for conveying appropriate signals solely through gesture and facial expression—signals not contained in the words you read?

Staging

Since plays are written to be staged, the particular kind of theater available to the dramatist is often crucial to the structure of the play. The Greek theater of Dionysius in Athens, for which Sophocles wrote, was an open-air amphitheater seating about 14,000 people. The skene, or stage house, from which actors entered, was fixed, though it might have had painted panels to suggest the scene. Consequently, there is no scene shifting in *Oedipus Rex*. All the dialogue and action take place in the same location before the skene building, which represents the Palace of Oedipus. Important things happen elsewhere, but the audience is informed of these events by messenger. A death occurs, but not in sight of the audience, partly as a matter of taste and partly because the conditions of the Greek stage prevented the playwright from moving the action inside the palace. Later dramatists, writing for a more flexible stage and a more intimate theater, were able to profit from the intensely dramatic nature of murder and suicide, but the Greeks, almost invariably, chose to tell, rather than show, the most gripping physical events in their stories.

Further, an outdoor theater of vast dimensions implies obvious restrictions on acting style. Facial expression can play no important role in such a theater, and, in fact, the actors of Sophoclean tragedy wore masks, larger than life and probably equipped with some sort of megaphone device to aid in voice projection. Those voices were denied the possibility of subtle variety in tone and expression, and the speeches were probably delivered in rather formal declamatory style. The characters wore special built-up footwear which made them larger than life. In addition to these limitations, Sophocles had as well to write within the formal limitations imposed by the Athenian government, which made available only three principal actors, all male, as the cast (exclusive of the chorus) for each play. Consequently, there are never more than three players on stage at once, and the roles are designed so that each actor takes several parts—signified by different masks. Yet, despite the austerity of production values, the unavoidable clumsiness of fortuitous messengers appearing at all the right moments, and the sharply restricted dramatis personae, among the few Greek plays that have survived are some still universally regarded as superlatively fine dramatic representations of tragic humanity.

Until recently we thought we had a clear conception of what Shakespeare's stage looked like. Scholarship has raised some doubts about this conception, but though we no longer accept the accuracy of the reconstruction shown here, we still have a good enough understanding of the shape of the playing area to recreate roughly the staging of a Shakespearean play. That staging was altogether different from the Greek. Though both theaters were open air, the enclosure around the Elizabethan stage was much smaller and the audience capacity limited to something between 2,000 and 3,000. As in classical drama, men played all the roles, but they no longer wore masks, and a stage that protruded into the audience made for great intimacy. Hence the actors' art expanded to matters of facial expression, and the style of speech and movement was certainly closer than was Greek style to what we might loosely call realism. Shakespeare has Hamlet caution the actors: "Suit the action to the word, the word to the action, with this special observance, that you o'erstep not the modesty of nature: for anything so overdone is from the purpose of playing, whose end, both at first and now, was and is, to hold as 't were, the mirror up to nature. . . ." But the characteristic matter of Shakespearean tragedy certainly did not lend itself to a modern realistic style. Those great speeches are written

The Globe Theatre

Interior of the Swan Theatre, London, 1596

Hypothetical reconstruction of the interior of the Globe Theatre in the days of Shakespeare

A seventeenth-century French box stage

The ancient theater at Epidaurus, Greece

in verse; they frequently are meant to augment the rather meager set design by providing verbal pictures to set the stage; they are much denser in texture, image, and import than is ordinary speech. These characteristics all serve to distinguish the Shakespearean stage from the familiar realism of most recent theater and film.

The Elizabethan stage made possible a tremendous versatility for the dramatist and the acting company. Most of the important action was played out on the uncurtained main platform, jutting into the audience and surrounded on three sides by spectators. The swiftly moving scenes followed each other without interruption, doubtless using different areas of the stage to signify different locations. There was some sort of terrace or balcony one story above the main stage, and there was an area at the back of the main protruding stage that could be curtained off when not in use. Although Shakespeare's plays are usually divided into five separate acts in printed versions, they were played straight through, without intermission, much like a modern motion picture.

Though more versatile and intimate than the Greek stage, the Elizabethan stage had limitations which clearly influenced the playwright. Those critical imperatives of time, place, and action (i.e., the time represented should not exceed one day, the location should be fixed in one place, and the action should be limited to one cohesive story line—one plot), the so-called unities that Aristotle discovered in the drama of Sophocles, may well reflect the physical conditions of the Greek theater. Elizabethan dramatists largely ignored them, and in *Othello* we move from Venice to Cyprus, from the fortifications of the island to the city streets to Desdemona's bedchamber. Certainly some props were used to suggest these locations, but nothing comparable to the furniture of Ibsen's stage. Instead, the playwright often wove a sort of literary scenery into the speeches of the characters. For example, in *Othello*, Roderigo has occasion to say to Iago, "Here is her father's house; I'll call aloud." The second act of *Othello* opens with some gentlemen at "an open place near the Quay." Notice the dialogue:

> **Montano.**   What from the cape can you discern at sea?
> **First Gentleman.**   Nothing at all: it is a high-wrought flood;
>   I cannot 'twixt the heaven and the main
>   Descry a sail.
> **Montano.**   Methinks the wind hath spoke aloud at land;
>   A fuller blast ne'er shook our battlements;
>   If it hath ruffian'd so upon the sea,
>   What ribs of oak, when mountains melt on them,
>   Can hold the mortise?

There is no sea, of course, and Elizabethan technology was not up to a wind machine. The men are, doubtless, looking off stage and creating the stormy setting through language. An open-air theater which played in daylight had few techniques for controlling lighting, and speeches had to be written to supply the effect:

> But look, the morn, in russet mantle clad,
> Walks o'er the dew of yon high eastern hill.

Further, the company had not the resources to place armies on the stage; hence, a speaker in *King Henry* V boldly invites the audience to profit from imagination:

> Piece out our imperfections with your thoughts;
> Into a thousand parts divide one man,
> And make imaginary puissance;
> Think, when we talk of horses, that you see them
> Printing their proud hoofs i' the receiving earth.
> For 'tis your thoughts that now must deck our kings.

The theater in the Petit-Bourbon Palace, built about twenty-five years after Shakespeare's death, was a forerunner of the common "box stage" on which so much recent drama is acted. Essentially, this stage is a box with one wall removed so that the audience can see into the playing area. Such a stage lends itself to realistic settings. Since the stage is essentially a room, it can easily be furnished to look like one. If street scenes are required, painted backdrops provide perspective and an accompanying sense of distance. Sets at an angle to the edge of the stage might be constructed. The possibilities for scenic design allowed by such a stage soon produced great set designers, and the structure of such a stage led to the development of increasingly sophisticated stage machinery, which in turn freed the dramatist from the physical limitations imposed by earlier stages. By Ibsen's time the versatility of the box stage enabled him to write elaborately detailed stage settings for the various locations in which the drama unfolds. Further, the furnishing of the stage in Ibsen's plays sometimes functions symbolically to convey visually the choking quality of certain bourgeois life-styles.

None of the historical stages has passed into mere history. The modern theater still uses Greek amphitheaters such as that at Epidaurus, constructs approximations of the Elizabethan stage for Shakespeare festivals, and employs the box stage with ever-increasing inventiveness. Early in the twentieth century, some plays were produced in the "round," the action taking place on a stage in the center of the theater with the audience on all sides. A number of theaters were built that incorporated a permanent in-the-round arrangement. But versatility has become so important to the modern production designer that some feel the very best theater is simply a large empty room (with provisions for technical flexibility in the matter of lighting) that can be rearranged to suit the requirements of specific productions. This ideal of a "theater space" that can be freely manipulated has become increasingly attractive—some have been constructed—since it frees the dramatist and the performance from limitations built into permanent stage design.

Drama and Society

The history of dramatic literature (like the history of literature in general) provides evidence for another kind of history as well—the history of changing attitudes, changing values, and even changing taste. In ancient Greece, in Elizabethan England when Shakespeare wrote his enduring tragedies, right up to the end of the eighteenth century, certain expectations controlled the nature of tragedy. Those expectations were discussed by Aristotle as early as 335 B.C.; they involved the fall of a noble figure from a high place. Such tragedy reflects important cultural attitudes. It flourished in conjunction with a certain sort of politics and certain notions about human nature. The largest part of an audience of several thousand Athenians in the fifth century B.C. was certainly not itself noble. Neither was Shakespeare's audience at the Globe Theatre in London. That audience, much as a modern audience, was composed of tradesmen, artisans, and petty officials. In Greece, even slaves attended the tragedy festivals. Why then were there no tragedies in which the central figure was a storekeeper, a baker, or a butcher?

There have been many attempts to answer this difficult question, and those answers tend to make assumptions about the way individuals see themselves and their society. If the butcher down the street dies, well, that is sad, but after all rather unimportant to society. If the king falls, however, society itself is touched, and a general grief prevails that makes possible sweeping observations about the chancy conditions of life. A culture always elevates some of its members to the status of heroes—often by virtue of the office they hold. Even now, societies are collectively moved, and moved profoundly, by the death of a president, a prime minister—a Kennedy, a de Gaulle, a Churchill—when they are not nearly so moved by immense disasters such as killing storms or earthquakes or civil wars. But things have changed, and most rapidly within the last 150 years or so.

Simply stated, new cultural values—new attitudes about human nature—have developed, especially since the advent of industrialism and since Freud began publishing his systematic observations about the way men's minds interact with their bodies. The result has been an increasing humanization of those who used to be heroes and an increasing realization of the capacity for heroism in those who are merely bakers and butchers. Thus Henrik Ibsen, frequently referred to as "the father of modern drama," can compel a serious emotional response from his audience over the tribulations of a middle-class lawyer's wife in A Doll's House. Realistic plays succeed in spite of their commonplace heroes because, as a society, we can now accept the experiences of ordinary people as emblems of our own. Perhaps we can because political institutions in the modern republics and in the socialist countries have, theoretically, exalted common men and women and rejected political aristocracy. Certainly the reasons for the change are complex. But it remains true that neither Sophocles nor Shakespeare could have written A Doll's House.

Dramatic Irony

Dramatic irony allows the audience to know more than the characters do about their own circumstances. Consequently, that audience hears more (the ironic component) than do the characters who speak. Shakespeare's *Othello* provides an excellent illustration of the uses of dramatic irony. At the end of Act II, Cassio, who has lost his position as Othello's lieutenant, asks Iago for advice on how to regain favor. Iago, who, unknown to Cassio, had engineered Cassio's disgrace, advises him to ask Desdemona, Othello's adored wife, to intervene. Actually this is good advice; ordinarily the tactic would succeed, so much does Othello love his wife and wish to please her. But Iago explains, in a soliloquy to the audience, that he is laying groundwork for the ruin of all the objects of his envy and hatred—Cassio, Desdemona, and Othello:

> . . . for while this honest fool
> Plies Desdemona to repair his fortunes,
> And she for him pleads strongly to the Moor,
> I'll pour this pestilence into his ear
> That she repeals him for her body's lust;
> And, by how much she strives to do him good,
> She shall undo her credit with the Moor.
> So will I turn her virtue into pitch,
> And out of her own goodness make the net
> That shall enmesh them all.

Of course Desdemona, Cassio, and Othello are ignorant of Iago's enmity. Worse, all of them consider Iago a loyal friend. But the audience knows Iago's design, and that knowledge provides the chilling dramatic irony of Act III, scene 3.

When Cassio asks for Desdemona's help, she immediately consents, declaring, "I'll intermingle every thing he does / With Cassio's suit." At this, the audience, knowing what it does, grows a little uneasy—that audience, after all, rather likes Desdemona and doesn't want her injured. As Iago and Othello come on stage, Cassio, understandably ill as ease, leaves at the approach of the commander who has stripped him of his rank, thus providing Iago with a magnificent tactical advantage. And as Cassio leaves, Iago utters an exclamation and four simple words that may rank among the most electrifying in all of English drama:

> Ha! I like not that.

They are certainly not very poetic words; they do not conjure up any telling images; they do not mean much either to Othello or Desdemona. But they are for the audience the intensely anticipated first drop of poison. Othello hasn't heard clearly:

> What dost thou say?

Maybe it all will pass, and Iago's clever design will fail. But what a hiss of held breath the audience expels when Iago replies:

> Nothing, my lord: or if—I know not what.

And Othello is hooked:

> Was not that Cassio parted from my wife?

The bait taken, Iago begins to play his line:

> Cassio, my lord? No, sure, I cannot think it,
> That he would steal away so guilty-like,
> Seeing you coming.

And from this point on in the scene, Iago cleverly and cautiously leads Othel-lo. He assumes the role of Cassio's great friend—reluctant to say anything that might cast suspicion on him. But he is also the "friend" of Othello and cannot keep silent his suspicions. So honest Iago (he is often called "honest" by the others in the play), apparently full of sympathy and kindness, skillfully brings the trusting Othello to emotional chaos. And every word they exchange is dou-bly meaningful to the audience, which perceives Othello led on the descent into a horrible jealousy by his "friend." The scene ends with Othello visibly shaken and convinced of Desdemona's faithlessness and Cassio's perfidy:

> Damn her, lewd minx! O, damn her!
> Come, go with me apart; I will withdraw,
> To furnish me with some swift means of death
> For the fair devil. Now art thou my lieutenant.

To which Iago replies:

> I am your own for ever.

Now, all of Iago's speeches in this scene operate on the audience through dramatic irony. The tension, the horror, the urge to cry out, to save Cassio, Desdemona, and Othello from the devilish Iago—all the emotional tautness in the audience results from irony, from knowing what the victims do not know. The play would have much less force if the audience did not know Iago's intentions from the outset and did not anticipate as he bends so many innocent events to his own increasingly evil ends. Note that dramatic irony is not limited to the drama; poetry, sometimes (as in Robert Browning's "My Last Duchess"), and fiction, often (as in Frank O'Connor's "My Oedipus Complex"), make use of this technique. But dramatic irony is the special tool of the dramatist, well suited to produce an electric tension in a live audience that overhears the in-teraction of people on stage.

Drama and Its Audience

Scholarly ordering that identifies the parts of drama and discusses the perceptive distinctions made by Aristotle among its parts can help you confront a play and understand how your responses were triggered by the playwright, the designers of the play, and the performers. But such analysis cannot substitute for the emo-tional experience produced by successful drama—your deepest responses have to do with states of mind, not with the three dramatic unities. Plays, perhaps more than other art forms, address themselves to the complex mélange of belief, attitude, intellect, and awareness that constitutes a human psyche. A lyric poem may simply meditate on the transience of life or express the pain of love unrequited. Plays, however, set characters within demanding social and cultural settings. Those cultural imperatives create dissatisfaction and conflict that may lead to a heightened awareness of or a tragic insight into one's own limitations. For example, many of the plays in this anthology embody beliefs and assumptions about fundamental issues. What happens when the viewer's (or reader's) assumptions and beliefs conflict with those embodied in the play? If we do not believe that the world is ruled by the gods or a God, can we appreciate *Oedipus Rex?* If we believe that a woman's place is in the home and that, above all, nothing can justify a mother's abandoning her children, can we get anything out of *A Doll's House?* These are questions that cannot be answered easily. We can say, however, that one of the functions of art is to force us to reexamine our most cherished abstract beliefs in the revealing light of the artist's work. Thus, despite our abstract beliefs about motherhood, Ibsen's skill in creating character and social structure in *A Doll's House* may compel our sympathy for Nora and force us to rethink our position.

Reading Essays

Essays differ from fiction in that they generally do not create imaginary worlds inhabited by fictional characters. We know, for example, through media accounts and the testimony of his friends, that Martin Luther King, Jr., was indeed jailed in Birmingham, Alabama, where he wrote his famous argument for social justice, "Letter from Birmingham Jail." And, although we cannot independently verify that George Orwell actually shot an elephant, or that Richard Selzer is describing a real patient, their works exhibit the formal nonfictional qualities of the essay rather than the imagined world of the short story.

Writers turn to the essay form when they wish to confront their readers directly with an idea, a problem (often with a proposed solution), an illuminating experience, an important definition, some flaw (or virtue) in the social system. Usually, the essay is relatively short, and almost always it embodies the writer's personal viewpoint. And although the essay may share many elements with other literary forms, it generally speaks with the voice of a real person about the real world. The term *essay* derives from the French verb *essayer*, "try," "attempt." That verb, in turn, derives from the Latin verb *exigere*, "weigh out," "examine."

While the French term calls attention to the personal perspective that characterizes the essay, the Latin verb suggests another dimension. The essay not only examines personal experiences but also explores and clarifies ideas, argues for or against a position. Thus, "My First Encounter with Death" is obviously the title of an essay. So is "The American Way of Death." The titles, however, suggest that the first essay will be intensely personal and the second will be less personal and more analytical, perhaps even argumentative.

As you read an essay, you need to ask yourself, "What is the central argument or idea?" Sometimes the answer is obvious. One essay attacks extravagant funerals fostered by the undertaker industry, another justifies feminism by revealing the miserable position of women in Elizabethan society. In either case, these essays, if successful, will change—or, perhaps, reinforce—the reader's attitudes toward death rituals and the status of women.

Some essays address the inner lives of their readers. John Donne's "Meditation XVII," for example, does not attack or justify anything. Rather, it insists that we be aware of our mortality; that awareness might well alter our behavior, our interaction with or perception of the people around us. Such essays often investigate the nature of love, of courage, of what it means to be human.

Types of Essays

In freshman composition, you probably read and were required to write narrative, descriptive, expository, and argumentative essays. Let us recall the characteristics of each of these types, while keeping in mind that in the real world, essays, more interested in effectiveness than in purity of form, frequently combine features of different formal types.

Narrative Essays

Narrative essays recount a sequence of related events and are often autobiographical. But those events are chosen because they suggest or illustrate some truth or insight. In "Shooting an Elephant," for example, George Orwell narrates an episode from his life that led him to an important insight about imperialism. In "Rage," James Baldwin uses an episode from his life to show how a frustrating powerlessness can lead to self-destructive behavior. In these narrative essays, the writers discover in their own experiences the evidence for generalizations about themselves and their societies.

Descriptive Essays

Descriptive essays depict in words sensory observations—they evoke in the reader's imagination the sights and sounds, perhaps even the smells, that transport him or her to such places as Joan Didion's Las Vegas or E. M. Forster's little patch of woodland. Sometimes, the writer is satisfied simply to create a lifelike evocation of some engaging object or landscape; but Didion and Forster use their descriptions as vehicles for expressing ideas about the debasement of marriage and the corrupting power of property ownership. The descriptive essay, like the narrative essay, often addresses complex issues that trouble our lives—but it does so by appealing primarily to sensory awareness—sight, sound, touch, taste, smell—rather than to intellect. The power of description is so great that narrative and expository essays often use lengthy descriptive passages to communicate forcefully.

Expository Essays

Expository essays attempt to explain and elucidate, to organize and provide information. Often they embody an extended definition of a complex conception such as love or patriotism. Or expository essays may describe a process—how to do something. This essay, for example, is clearly not narrative, because it doesn't depend for its form on a chronological sequence of meaningful events. It is not descriptive in the pure sense of that type, because it does not depend on conveying sensory impressions of anything. It is, in fact, expository. It acquaints its readers with the techniques and types of essays and provides some tips to help students read essays both analytically and pleasurably. To that end, we have made use of a number of rhetorical strategies that you will remember from your freshman writing course. We *classify* essays by type; we *compare and contrast* them; we use *definition*; we give *examples* to make a point; we imply that there is a *cause and effect* relationship between what readers bring to an essay and the pleasure they derive from it. Similarly, the essayists represented in this book use a variety of such rhetorical strategies to achieve their aims.

Argumentative Essays

Although we described Orwell's "Shooting an Elephant" as a narrative essay, we might reasonably assert that it is also argumentative, because it is designed to convince readers that imperialism is as destructive to the oppressors as to the oppressed. The argumentative essay wishes to persuade its readers. Thus, it usually deals with controversial ideas; it marshals arguments and evidence to support a view; it anticipates and answers opposing arguments. Martin Luther King, Jr., accomplishes all these ends in his "Letter from Birmingham Jail." So does Jonathan Swift in "A Modest Proposal," although his approach is more complicated in that he relies on irony and satire.

Analyzing the Essay

The Thesis

The best way to begin analyzing an essay is to ask "What is the point of this piece of writing; what is the author trying to show, attack, defend or prove?" If you can answer that question satisfactorily and succinctly, then the analysis of the essay's elements (that is, its rhetorical strategies, its structure, style, tone, and language) becomes easier. Lewis Thomas's "The Iks" is a very short and relatively simple essay, and the author clearly states the thesis when he says, "Nations have themselves become too frightening to think about, but we might learn some things by watching [the Iks]." On the other hand, a much more complex and ambitious essay such as Virginia Woolf's "What If Shakespeare Had Had a Sister" does not yield up its thesis quite so easily. We might say that Woolf's examination of the historical record leads her to argue that women did not write during the Elizabethan period because literary talent could not flourish in a social system that made women the ill-educated property of men. This defensible formulation of the essay's thesis, as you will see when you read the essay, leaves a good deal out—notably the exhortation to action with which Woolf concludes the piece.

Structure and Detail

Read carefully the first and last paragraphs of a number of essays. Attend to the writers' strategy for engaging you at the outset with an irresistible proposition.

> In Moulmein, in Lower Burma, I was hated by large numbers of people—the only time in my life that I have been important enough for this to happen to me.

> Surely nothing in the astonishing scheme of life can have nonplussed Nature so much as the fact that none of the females of any of the species she created really cared very much for the male, as such.

> I spy on my patients.

These randomly chosen opening sentences are startling, and most readers will eagerly read on to find out what it was that made the writer so hated in Burma, why females naturally do not care for males, why the doctor spies on his patients. You will find that the opening lines of all well-wrought essays instantly capture your attention.

Endings, too, are critical. And if you examine the concluding lines of any of the essays in this collection, you will find forceful assertions that focus the matter that precedes them to sharp intensity. Essayists, unsurprisingly, systematically use gripping beginnings and forceful endings.

Let us turn to what comes between those beginnings and endings.

Essays often deal with abstract issues—the nature of love, the inevitability of death, the evils of imperialism. Though such abstractions do significantly influence our lives, they tend to remain impersonal and distant. Reading about great ideas becomes a sort of academic task—we may record the ideas in notebooks, but we tend to relegate them to some intellectual sphere, separate from the pain and passion of our own humanity. The accomplished essay writer, however, forces us to confront such issues by converting abstract ideas into concrete and illustrative detail.

For example, George Orwell points out early in "Shooting an Elephant" that the "anti-European feeling was very bitter" in British-controlled Burma. But he immediately moves from the abstraction of "anti-European feeling" to "if a European woman went through the bazaars alone somebody would probably spit betel juice over her dress" and "when a nimble Burman tripped me up on the football field and the referee (another Burman) looked the other way, the crowd yelled with hideous laughter." The tiny bits of hateful experience, because they are physical and concrete, powerfully reinforce the abstract assertion about "anti-European feeling" that lies at the center of Orwell's essay, and the narrative account of the speaker's behavior in front of the mob culminates in a specific statement—"I perceived in this moment that when the white man turns tyrant it is his own freedom that he destroys." The large generality emerges from deeply felt personal experience.

In another essay, Richard Selzer spies on his terminally ill patient who has become a "discus thrower." How, after all, can a writer, trying to deal with the inevitability of death, convey the intense pain and emotional agony of a dying person? Selzer's patient concretizes that pain and agony in a simple repetitive act:

> In time the man reaches to find the rim of the tray, then on to find the dome of the covered dish. He lifts off the cover and places it on the stand. He fingers across the plate until he probes the eggs. He lifts the plate in both hands, sets it on the palm of his right hand, centers it, balances it. He hefts it up and down slightly, getting the feel of it. Abruptly, he draws back his right arm as far as he can.
>
> There is the crack of the plate breaking against the wall at the foot of his bed and the small wet sound of the scrambled eggs dropping to the floor.
>
> And then he laughs. It is a sound you have never heard.

Can you imagine any objective and clinical description of the anguish and rage of a dying person that would convey the feeling more effectively than the concrete details of this understated anecdote?

Style and Tone

The word *style* refers to all the writing skills that contribute to the effect of any piece of literature. And *tone*—the attitude conveyed by the language a writer chooses—is a particularly significant aspect of writing style. As an illustration of the effect of tone, consider these opening lines of two essays—Margaret Sanger's "The Turbid Ebb and Flow of Misery" and Stephen King's "Why We Crave Horror Movies."

> During these years in New York, trained nurses were in great demand. Few people wanted to enter hospitals; they were afraid they might be "practiced" upon, and consented to go only in desperate emergencies. Sentiment was especially vehement in the matter of having babies. A woman's own bedroom, no matter how inconveniently arranged, was the usual place for her lying-in. I was not sufficiently free from domestic duties to be a general nurse, but I could ordinarily manage obstetrical cases because I was notified far enough ahead to plan my schedule. And after serving my two weeks I could get home again.

> I think that we're all mentally ill; those of us outside the asylums only hide it a little better—and maybe not all that much better, after all. We've all known people who talk to themselves, people who sometimes squinch their faces into horrible grimaces when they believe no one is watching, people who have some hysterical fear—of snakes, the dark, the tight place, the long drop . . . and, of course, those final worms and grubs that are waiting so patiently underground.

The tonal differences between these two excerpts produce differing voices. Although both are first-person accounts, Sanger's essay has a rather formal tone—in every sentence but the last, she uses some form of the verb *be*, and she often employs the passive voice: "they might be 'practiced' upon," "I was notified." As well, Sanger marshals a host of rather weighty Latinate words: *practiced, consented, desperate, sentiment, vehement, inconveniently, sufficiently, notified.*

King's tone, in contrast, is personal and informal. He prefers active verbs and uses contractions and slang expressions *(squinch, the tight place, the long drop)*. When he says "we've all known people . . . ," he seems to invite the reader to share personal confidences. And the phrase "final worms and grubs that are waiting so patiently underground" is quite unimaginable in the first excerpt.

The tone a writer creates contributes substantially to the message he or she conveys. Jonathan Swift might have written a sound, academic essay about the economic diseases of Ireland and how to cure them—but his invention of the speaker of "A Modest Proposal," who ironically and sardonically proposes the establishment of a human-baby meat-exporting industry, jars the reader in ways no scholarly essay could. The outraged tone of Jessica Mitford's "The American Way of Death" comically reinforces her attack on greedy undertakers. The high seriousness of Donne's tone in "Meditation XVII" perfectly suits his contemplation of the relationship among the living, the dying, and the dead.

Style is a more difficult quality to define than tone. Dictionaries will tell you that style is both "a manner of expression in language" and "excellence in expression." Certainly it is easier to distinguish between various *manners* of expression than it is to describe just what constitutes *excellence* in expression. For example, the manners of expression of John Donne in "Meditation XVII," of Richard Selzer in "The Discus Thrower," of Jessica Mitford in "The American Way of Death" clearly differ. The first muses about death in a style characterized by formality and complex extended images. The second achieves informality with a style characterized by short direct sentences and understatement. The essay's figurative language describes the dying patient rather than the nature of death. The third uses the breezy style of a muckraking journalist, replete with contemptuous asides and sardonic exclamations.

Nonetheless, we can describe the excellence of each style. Donne, an Anglican priest, meditates on the community of all living humans and the promise of eternal life in the face of physical death. He creates a remarkable image when he argues that "all mankind is of one author." Not so remarkable, you might argue; God is often called the "author of mankind." But Donne insists on the figurative quality of God as author and the intimate relationship among all people when he adds that all humankind "is one volume." Then he extends this metaphor by arguing that "when one man dies, one chapter is not torn out of the book, but translated into a better language." The daring image is further extended. "God," Donne tells us, "employs several translators; some pieces are translated by age, some by sickness, some by war, some by justice." By alluding to the actual making of a book by the bookbinder, Donne elaborates on the central image and reestablishes the idea of community—"God's hand is in every translation, and his hand shall bind up all our scattered leaves again for that library where every book shall lie open to one another." Surely, this magnificent figurative characterization of death (regardless of your personal beliefs) exhibits stylistic excellence.

Richard Selzer also deals with death.

> From the doorway of Room 542 the man in the bed seems deeply tanned. Blue eyes and close-cropped white hair give him the appearance of vigor and good health. But I know that his skin is not brown from the sun. It is rusted, rather, in the last stage of containing the vile repose within. And the blue eyes are frosted, looking inward like the windows of a snowbound cottage. This man is blind.

Here you see a very different style. Whereas Donne's sentences are long and move with the rolling cadence of oratory, Selzer's are terse and direct. Selzer's metaphors and similes characterize the ugliness of dying. The man's skin is not tanned by the sun; it is "rusted." His sightless eyes are frosted "like the windows of a snowbound cottage." These images, together with the artful simplicity of Selzer's short, halting sentences, powerfully convey the degradation and the impotence of the dying. Here again, style plays a significant role.

Jessica Mitford's attack on the American funeral industry begins:

> O Death, where is thy sting? O grave, where is thy victory? Where indeed? Many a badly stung survivor, faced with the aftermath of some relative's funeral, has ruefully concluded that the victory has been won hands down by a funeral establishment—in disastrously unequal battle.

This essay opens with a quote from St. Paul's Epistle to the Corinthians—certainly a sober and exalted allusion. But immediately, the tone turns sardonic with the question "Where indeed?" And the writer compounds the sarcasm by extending the biblical metaphor that compares death with a painful bee-sting to the equally painful experience of the "stung" survivor who has been conned into enormous expenditure by a funeral establishment. Her breezy style juxtaposes the ancient biblical promise of a spiritual victory over death with the crass modern reality—the only victor, nowadays, is the greedy funeral director. The perception is "rueful," and the victory "has been won hands down" in an encounter characterized as a "disastrously unequal battle." Mitford's language, playing off the high seriousness of the biblical quotation, stylistically advances her purpose by introducing a note of mockery. Certainly her argument gains force from the pervasive sardonic tone that characterizes her style.

Three different writers, all discussing some aspect of death, exhibit three distinctive manners of expression and three distinctive varieties of excellence—in short, three distinctive styles.

Your principal concern, when reading an essay, must always be to discover the essay's central thesis. What does the writer wish you to understand about his or her experience, the world, or yourself? Once you have understood the essay's thesis, you can increase your pleasure by examining the means the author used to convey it and, perhaps, recognize techniques that will enhance the quality of your own writing. To that end, you ought to examine the essay's structure and the rhetorical strategies that shape it. How does it begin and end? What type is it—narrative, descriptive, expository, argumentative? How do rhetorical strategies—definition, cause and effect, classification, exemplification, comparison and contrast—function to serve the author's purposes? Then, discover the sources of reading pleasure by closely analyzing the language of the essay. Watch writers energize abstract ideas with detailed and moving experience; consider the uses of figurative language—the metaphors and similes that create both physical and emotional landscapes in the prose; respond to the tone of voice and the stylistic choices that create it. When you have done all this successfully, when you have discovered not only *what* the author has said, but also *how* the author moved you to his or her point of view—then you will have understood the essay.

Three Critical Approaches: Formalist, Sociological, Psychoanalytic

Literary criticism has to do with the *value* of literature, its goodness or badness, not with the history of literature. Because value judgments tend to be highly subjective, lively, and sometimes even acrimonious, debates among literary critics accompany their diverse responses to and judgments of the same work. The judgment a literary critic makes about a story or poem is bound to reflect his or her own cherished values. The truth of a work of art is, obviously, very different from the truth of a mathematical formula. Certainly one's attitudes toward war, religion, sex, and politics are irrelevant to the truth of a formula but quite relevant to one's judgment of a literary work.

Yet, any examination of the broad range of literary criticism reveals that groups of critics (and all readers, ultimately, are critics) share certain assumptions about literature. These shared assumptions govern the way critics approach a work, the elements they tend to look for and emphasize, the details they find significant or insignificant, and, finally, the overall judgment of the value of the work. In order to illustrate diverse critical methodologies, we have examined two of the works in this anthology—Matthew Arnold's poem, "Dover Beach" (p. 446), and Nathaniel Hawthorne's short story, "My Kinsman, Major Molineux" (p. 7)—from three different critical positions: the formalist, the sociological, and the psychoanalytic. We have selected these three critical positions not because they are the only ones (there are others), but because they represent three major and distinctive approaches that may help readers formulate their own responses to a work of literature.

We do not suggest that one approach is more valid than the others or that the lines dividing the approaches are always clear and distinct. Readers will, perhaps, discover one approach more congenial to their temperament, more "true" to their sense of the world, than another. Again, they may find that some works seem to lend themselves to one approach, other works to a different approach. More likely, they will find themselves utilizing more than one approach in dealing with a single work. What readers will discover in reading the three analyses of the Arnold poem and the Hawthorne story is not that they contradict one another, but that, taken together, they complement and enrich one another.

Formalist Criticism

While the formalist critic would not deny the relevance of sociological, biographical, and historical information to a work of art, he or she insists that the function of criticism is to focus on the work itself as a verbal structure and to discover the ways in which the work achieves (or does not achieve) unity. The job of criticism is to show how the various parts of the work are wedded together into an organic whole. That is to say, we must examine the *form* of the work, for it is the form that is its meaning. Put somewhat oversimply, the formalist critic views a work as a timeless aesthetic object; we may find whatever we wish in the work as long as what we find is demonstrably in the work itself.

Dover Beach

From the perspective of the formalist critic, the fact that Matthew Arnold was deeply concerned with how to enjoy a civilized life under the pressures of modern industrialization or that Arnold appears to have suffered in his youth an intense conflict between sexual and spiritual love may be interesting but ought not to be the focal point in an analysis of his poetry. After all, the historian is best equipped to reconstruct and illuminate Matthew Arnold's Victorian England, and it is the biographer's and psychologist's job to tell us about his personal life. A critic of "Dover Beach" who speculates on these matters is doing many things, perhaps quite interesting things, but he or she is not giving us a description of the work itself.

"Dover Beach" is a dramatic monologue, a poem in which a speaker addresses another person at a particular time and place. In the opening lines, Arnold skillfully sets the scene, introduces the image of the sea that is to dominate the poem, and establishes a moment of tranquility and moon-bathed loveliness appropriate to a poem in which a man addresses his beloved. The beauty of the scene is established through visual images that give way, beginning with line 9, to a series of auditory images that undermine or bring into serious question the atmosphere established by the opening eight lines. In this contrast between visual and auditory imagery, a contrast developed through the entire poem, Arnold embodies one of the poem's major themes: appearance differs from reality.

In the second stanza, the "eternal note of sadness" struck in the final line of the first stanza is given an historical and universal dimension by the allusion to Sophocles, the Greek tragedian of fifth-century B.C. Athens. We become aware that the sadness and misery the speaker refers to are not the consequences of some momentary despair or particular historical event but are rather perennial, universal human conditions of mortal life. Indeed, the allusion to Sophocles and the Aegean Sea extends the feeling not only over centuries of time but over an immense geographical area, from the Aegean Sea to the English Channel.

The third stanza develops further the dominant sea imagery. But the literal seas of the earlier stanzas now become a metaphor for faith, perhaps religious faith, which once gave unity and meaning to life but now has ebbed away and left humankind stranded, bereft of virtually any defenses against sadness and misery. The "bright girdle furled," suggesting a happy and universal state, turns into a "roar" down the "naked shingles [i.e., pebble beaches] of the world."

The poet, therefore, turns, in the final stanza, to his beloved, to their love for each other as the only possible hope, meaning, and happiness in such a world. And his words to her echo the imagery of the opening lines with the important difference that the controlling verb *is* of the opening lines, denoting the actual and the real, is now replaced by the verb *seems*. The beautiful world is an illusion concealing the bleak truth that the world provides no relief for human misery. This grim realization leads to the powerful final image which compares life to a battle of armies at night. We have moved from the calm, serene, moon-bathed loveliness of the opening scene to an image of violence in a dark world where it is impossible to distinguish friend from foe or indeed even to understand what is happening.

"Dover Beach," then, is a meditation upon the irremediable pain and anguish of human existence, in the face of which the only possibility for joy and love and beauty is to be found in an intimate relationship between two human beings. The depth of the speaker's sadness is emphasized by his powerful evocation in the opening lines of the beauty of the scene. The first eight lines move with a quiet ease and flow with liquids and nasals, a movement enhanced by the balancing effect of the caesuras. In lines 9 to 14 the sounds also echo the sense, for now the sounds are much harsher as the plosive *b*s intrude and most of the lines are irregular, broken up by more than one caesura.

We have already noted that the dominant image of the poem, the key to the poem's structure, is the sea. It is the real sea the speaker describes in the opening stanza, but when it sounds the "eternal note of sadness," the sea becomes symbolic. In the second stanza, the speaker is reminded of another real sea, the Aegean, which he associates with Sophocles, and the developing unity is achieved, not only at the literal level (Sophocles listening to the Aegean parallels the speaker's listening to the northern sea) but at the symbolic level (Sophocles perceived the ebb and flow of human misery as the speaker perceives the eternal note of sadness). The third stanza further develops the sea image but presents something of a problem, for it is not altogether clear what the speaker means by "Faith." If he means religious faith, and that seems most likely, we face the problem of determining what period of history Arnold is alluding to. "Dover Beach" establishes two reference points in time—the present (1867) and fifth-century B.C. Athens—that are related to each other by negative auditory images. Since the function of the lines about the Sea of Faith is to provide a sharp contrast between the poem's present and fifth-century Athens (the visual image of "a bright girdle furled" associates the Sea of Faith with the opening eight lines), the time when the Sea of Faith was full must lie somewhere between these two points or earlier than the fifth century. Since a formalist critic deals only with the work *itself* and since there appears to be nothing elsewhere in the poem that will allow us to make a choice, we might conclude that these lines weaken the poem.

For the formalist critic, however, the final stanza presents the most serious problem. Most critics of whatever persuasion agree that they are moving and memorable lines, poignant in the speaker's desperate turning to his beloved in the face of a world whose beauty is a deception, and powerful in their description of that world, especially in the final image. But what, the formalist critic will ask, has become of the sea image? Is it not strange that the image which had dominated the poem throughout, has given it its unity, is in the climactic stanza simply dropped? On the face of it, at least, a formalist critic would have to conclude that the abandonment of the unifying image in the concluding stanza is a serious structural weakness, lessened perhaps by the power of the images that replace it, but a structural weakness nonetheless. On the other hand, a formalist critic might commend Arnold for his effective alternation of visual and auditory imagery throughout the poem. The first four lines of the final stanza return to visual images of an illusory "good" world (controlled by *seems*, as we have already noted) and concludes with a simile that fuses a somber vision of darkness and night, with the harsh auditory images of *alarms* and *clashes*.

My Kinsman, Major Molineux

This story by Hawthorne may be summarized easily. After an opening paragraph in which Hawthorne comments on the harsh treatment of the British colonial governors at the hands of the people of the Massachusetts Bay Colony, we meet an eighteen-year-old boy named Robin who crosses the ferry one night into an unnamed town. He is the second son of a country minister and has been sent to town to seek out his powerful kinsman, Major Molineux, who, presumably, will use his influence to help the boy make his way in the world. Strangely, the boy is unsuccessful in locating the residence of his kinsman. Worse, he is mocked and threatened by the several people he accosts and is almost seduced by a pretty harlot. Finally, he is told to wait in a certain spot, and shortly a boisterous procession passes, led by a man with a face painted half red and half black. The procession conducts an open cart in which his kinsman, Major Molineux, tarred and feathered, is being run out of town. The boy joins in the laughter at the plight of his once powerful relative but soon decides (his prospects blasted) to return home. A kindly bystander urges him to stay and make his way in the world without the help of his kinsman.

The formalist critic would note that the story is about a young man's initiation into the rude adult world where he must make his own way unprotected by a sheltering family. That world is at best morally ambiguous and at worst menacingly hostile. The transformation in Robin from a self-confident but ignorant grown child to a self-doubting but aware young adult is conveyed through a series of events culminating in a violent climax. Those events, and the atmosphere surrounding them, make for a story that creates, through irony, a mounting suspense released for Robin and the reader with explosive suddenness. Hawthorne's skill in creating that suspense and his method for releasing it are fundamental to the successful embodiment of the *theme*. Naive Robin, a "good child," becomes experienced Robin, more sober and more aware of evil.

The story opens with an apparently superfluous preface in which Hawthorne tells his readers that royal governors in Massachusetts Bay (that is, governors appointed by the British Crown rather than elected by the people) were treated roughly, even if they were fair and lenient. The discussion is to serve as "a preface to the following adventures, which chanced upon a summer night, not far from a hundred years ago [approximately 1732]." Hawthorne concludes that opening paragraph: "The reader, in order to avoid a long and dry detail of colonial affairs, is requested to dispense with an account of the train of circumstances that had caused much temporary inflammation of the popular mind." Now it is an article of faith for the formalist critic that no part of a literary work is superfluous. Art is *organic*. All its parts are essential to the whole. The reader may remain ignorant of some particular events that caused some particular social inflammation, but he or she cannot go on to the adventures of that summer night without some expectation that they will have something to do with the politics of colonial Massachusetts. If this prefatory paragraph is really superfluous, then it constitutes a flaw in the work. If it is not, we shall have, finally, to understand its function in the story.

The narrative begins with an account of the arrival of an eighteen-year-old country-bred youth on his first visit to town, at nine o'clock of a moonlit evening. All of the details provided in this second paragraph are significant and repay close reading. The young man from the country, on his first visit to town, dressed humbly but serviceably, with brown curly hair, well-shaped features, and bright cheerful eyes, presents an agreeable character. He is doubtless innocent (being country-bred and on his first visit to town). But he arrives at night and remains hidden in darkness until illuminated by some light-giving source. The moonlight alone doesn't suffice, and we require the help of the boatman's lantern to see him.

The manipulation of light and darkness in the story is crucial. As Robin walks about the town looking for the lodging of his kinsman, Major Molineux, he encounters six different people. The first, a rather dignified old man, is stopped by Robin "just when the light from the open door and windows of a barber's shop fell upon both their figures." The second encounter is within the inn, where there is light. The third encounter is with the harlot, who is discerned by Robin as "a strip of scarlet petticoat, and the occasional sparkle of an eye, as if the moonbeams were trembling on some bright thing." We will see those moonbeams trembling on something altogether different later on. The fourth encounter, like the first two, ends with a threat from the sleepy watchman who carries a lantern. The fifth encounter is with the demonic man with the parti-colored face who "stepped back into the moonlight" when he unmuffled to Robin.

Now for all the local illumination that surrounds the threats, the temptation, and the final promise to Robin that his kinsman would soon pass by, Robin remains in the dark. He does not understand why his questions generate such fierce threats from the elderly gentleman, the innkeeper, the watchman, and the demonic man. He sees the harlot in her parlor but doubts (quite rightly) her words and, finally, frightened a bit by the watchman, resists her seduction. The sixth encounter differs from the rest. The kindly stranger dimly sees Robin in the darkness—a literal and metaphorical darkness—and joins him. What of all this?

When the climactic moment occurs, when the procession arrives, it is lit by a dense multitude of torches "concealing, by their glare, whatever object they illuminated." Paradoxically, when there is at last adequate light, the very glare conceals—and conceals what Robin must discover. Yet again, when the demonic leader of the procession fixes his eyes on Robin, "the unsteady brightness of the [torches] formed a veil which he could not penetrate." Finally, as the cart stops before Robin, "the torches blazed the brightest, there the moon shone out like day, and there, in tar-and-feathery dignity, sat his kinsman, Major Molineux!"

The orchestration of the light and darkness in the story becomes a metaphor for Robin's condition. Throughout, he is blind, despite the light. Rebuffs and laughter repeatedly greet his simple question, and in every case Robin—being, as he says, a "shrewd" youth—rationalizes the responses so that he can accept them without loss of self-esteem. The old man who threatens him is a "country representative" who simply doesn't know how powerful his kinsman is. The innkeeper who expels him is responding to Robin's poverty. The grinning demonic man with face painted half red, half black generates the ejaculation "Strange things we travellers see!" And Robin engages in some philosophical speculations upon the weird sight, which "settled this point shrewdly, rationally, and satisfactorily." In every case, however, Robin's rationalizations are wrong. As "shrewd" as he is, he constantly misunderstands because he is optimistic and self-confident. The reality would shatter both his optimism and his confidence. Despite the lighted places, he remains in the dark. At the climax, as the light becomes brighter and brighter, it does not illuminate but rather conceals by glare, forming an impenetrable veil. Finally, when the torches blaze the brightest and the moon shines out like day, Robin sees! Presumably, now, he understands correctly the events of that long night.

But what is it that Robin understands? The question might be put another way. What is it that from the outset Robin doesn't understand? A good-looking, "shrewd" lad with a powerful relative, he expects the people he meets to behave with kindness and civility. A country youth, a minister's son, his experience of the world is limited. As the night wears on, the reader perceives Robin doggedly refusing to recognize that some sinister, evil action is afoot. Robin doesn't accept the existence of evil—everything can be explained in some rational way. With the temptation by the lovely harlot, Robin discovers within himself a sinfulness he might indignantly deny—and he does, after all, resist the temptation. But his weakness might be the beginning of wisdom, because Robin must discover that the human condition is not simple—it is complex. As he waits by the church, he peers into the window and notices the "awful radiance" within; he notices that a solitary ray of moonlight dares to rest upon the open page of the Bible. He wonders whether "that heavenly light" was "visible because no earthly and impure feet were within the walls?" And the thought makes him shiver with a strong loneliness. The implication that humans are inevitably impure grows strong.

This notion is driven home by the cryptic exchange between Robin and the kindly stranger when a great shout comes up from the still distant crowd. Robin is astonished by the numerous voices which constitute that one shout, and the stranger replies, "May not a man have several voices, Robin, as well as two complexions?" The notion that an individual may have several voices has never occurred to Robin. In his attempt to deal with the strange sight of the man with two complexions, Robin rationalizes. But he does not learn from the evidence of his senses that humans are complex, have different, even conflicting aspects. The stranger tries to teach him this truth—"a man" has "many voices." Robin, taking the stranger's words literally, and thinking of the pretty harlot, responds: "Perhaps a man may; but Heaven forbid that a woman should!" What does he mean? Doubtless he wishes to believe that the harlot was indeed the major's housekeeper, that she told the truth, spoke with one voice, and was not the embodiment of evil attempting to entrap him. All in all, Robin's view of the world from the outset is simplistic. And that view encourages him in his optimistic confidence. The stranger tells him that the world is not simple—that each person speaks with many voices, that the human condition comprises many aspects. The heavenly radiance enters only an empty church, unsoiled by impure human feet. But Robin still does not understand.

The procession approaches. Grotesque sounds announce the rout. Laughter dominates, and the light grows brighter and brighter. But still Robin does not understand. There sits his kinsman in tar-and-feathery dignity. Their eyes meet in an anguished and humiliating recognition. And Robin laughs.

That laughter is the outward symbol of his understanding. He has learned of human complexity. He has learned that he too contains a satanic aspect. His innocent optimism, based on an unrealistic conception of people, is altered to experienced doubt by his new understanding of the complexity and universality of that evil aspect of humanity that is symbolized by the behavior of the mob and the wild abiding laughter that infects even Robin.

The story is based on colonial history. The opening paragraph serves to remind us of the literal level on which the story operates. Mobs did roam the streets of Boston, did disguise themselves as "Indians," did tar and feather and expel Crown officers. But our attention is directed to a young, inexperienced boy. Finally, we must ask: how is Robin changed by his experiences? The images of darkness and light, the temptation scene, the moonlit church, the mob, and Robin's response to it all weave together into a single cord, the strands of which guide him to a new awareness both of himself and of his world.

Sociological Criticism

In contrast to the formalist critic, who maintains that the proper job of criticism is to approach each work of art as a self-contained aesthetic object and to attempt to illuminate its inherent structure and unity, the sociological critic asserts that since all humans are the products of a particular time and place, we can never fully understand a work without some understanding of the social forces that molded the author and all that he or she did and thought. The sociological critic feels that the formalist critic's attempt to view a work as timeless denies the fundamental and self-evident fact that authors do not (and cannot) divest themselves of all the shaping forces of their history and environment. Consequently, the critic must look to those forces if he or she is to understand an author's works.

Dover Beach

To understand "Dover Beach," we must, according to the sociological critic, know something about the major intellectual and social currents of Victorian England and the way in which Arnold responded to them. By the time Arnold was born in 1822, the rapid advances in technology that had begun with the Industrial Revolution of the eighteenth century were producing severe strains on the social and intellectual fabric of society. An agrarian economy was giving way to an industrial economy, and the transition was long and painful. The new economy was creating a merchant middle class whose growing wealth and power made it increasingly difficult for the upper classes to maintain exclusive political power. The passage of the celebrated Reform Bill of 1832, extending suffrage to any man (women were not enfranchised until 1928) who owned property worth at least ten pounds in annual rent, shifted political power to the middle class and gave cities a greater political voice. It was not until 1867 that the franchise was extended to men of the lower classes. The intervening years were marked by severe social crises: depression, unemployment, rioting. Indeed, during these critical years when England was attempting to cope with the new problems of urban industrialism, the agitation and rioting of the lower classes created genuine fears of revolution (many remembered very clearly the French Revolution of 1789).

The ferment was no less intense and disruptive in the more rarefied world of intellectual and theoretical debate. While it would be erroneous to assume that pre-industrial England was a world of idyllic stability, there can be little doubt that the pace of change had been much slower than during the nineteenth century. Despite sectarian strife, perhaps the greatest stabilizing force in pre-industrial England was religion. It offered answers to the ultimate questions of human existence and, on the basis of those answers, justification and authority for the temporal order—monarchy (or political control by a small aristocracy), sharp class distinctions, and the like. The technology that made industrialism possible grew out of the scientific discoveries and methodologies that challenged some fundamental assumptions and articles of faith. Scientific discoveries seemed to undermine the old religious faith (for example, Darwin's *On the Origin of Species*, published in 1859); the scientific approach of skepticism and empirical investigation, in addition to critical scholarship, led to numerous studies of the Bible not as a sacred text of infallible truth but as a historical text that arose out of a particular historical time and place. Close examination of the Bible itself resulted in discoveries of inconsistencies and contradictions as well as demonstrable evidence of its temporal rather than supernatural origin.

Matthew Arnold, born into a substantial middle-class family and educated at England's finest schools, established himself early as an important poet and as one of the leading social critics of the period. In much of his poetry and his voluminous prose writings, Arnold addressed critical questions of his time. The old values, particularly religious, were crumbling under the onslaught of new ideas; Arnold recognized that a simple reactionary defense of the old values was not possible (even if one still believed in them). Unless some new system of values could be formulated, society was likely to, at worst, fall into anarchy or, at best, offer the prospect of an arid and narrow life to individuals. And since the destiny of the nation was clearly devolving into the hands of the middle class, Arnold spent much of his career attempting to show the middle class the way to a richer and fuller life.

For an understanding of "Dover Beach," however, Arnold's attempt to define and advance cultural values is less important than his confrontation with the pain and dilemma of his age. Caught in what he called in one of his poems "this strange disease of modern life," Arnold found that modern discoveries made religious faith impossible, and yet he yearned for the security and certainty of his childhood faith. In his darker and more despairing moments, it seemed to him that with the destruction of old values the world was dissolving into chaos and meaninglessness. In these moments, he saw himself as "wandering between two worlds, one dead, / The other powerless to be born."

"Dover Beach" expresses one of those dark moments in Arnold's life—a moment shared by many of Arnold's contemporaries and modern readers as well, who, in many ways, instinctively understand the mood and meaning of the poem because the realities to which it responds are still very much with us. Simply stated, it is a poem in which the speaker declares that even in a setting of the utmost loveliness and tranquility (a sociological critic might very well here discuss the opening lines in much the same way a formalist critic does) the uncertainty and chaos of modern life cannot for long be forgotten or ignored. For uncertainty and chaos so permeate the life and consciousness of the speaker that everything he sees, everything he meditates upon, is infected. The scene of silent loveliness described in the opening lines turns into a grating roar that sounds the eternal note of sadness.

In the second stanza, the speaker turns to ancient Greece and its greatest tragic playwright in an effort to generalize and thereby lessen and defend against the overwhelming despair he feels. If the confusion and chaos of modern life are part of the eternal human condition, then perhaps it can be borne with resignation. Yet the third stanza seems to deny this possibility, for it suggests that at some other time in Western history Christian faith gave meaning and direction to life but now that faith is no longer available.

Trapped in a world where faith is no longer possible, the speaker turns in the final stanza—turns with a kind of desperation because no other possibilities seem to exist—to his beloved and their relationship as the only chance of securing from a meaningless and grim life some fragment of meaning and joy. Everything else, he tells her, everything positive in which humans might place their faith, is a mere "seeming." The real world, he concludes, in a powerful and strikingly modern image, is like two armies battling in darkness. Whether or not the final image is an allusion to a particular historical battle (as many critics have suggested), it is a graphic image to describe what modern life seemed to a sensitive Victorian who could see no way out of the dilemma.

For the sociological critic, then, an understanding of "Dover Beach" requires some knowledge of the major stresses and intellectual issues of Victorian England, because the poem is a response to and comment upon those issues by one of the great Victorian poets and social critics. Our description of those issues and Arnold's ideas is extremely sketchy and selective; it merely illustrates the approach a sociological critic might take in dealing with the poem. Nevertheless, the sketchiness of the presentation raises important questions about sociological criticism: Where does the sociological critic stop? How deep and detailed an understanding of the times and the writer's relationship to the period is necessary to understand the work? Formalist critics might charge that sociological critics are in constant danger of becoming so immersed in sociological matters (and even biography) that they lose sight of the work they set out to investigate. The danger, of course, is a real one, and sociological critics must be mindful, always, that their primary focus is art, not sociology, history, or biography; the extent of their sociological investigations will be controlled and limited by the work they are attempting to illuminate. To this charge, sociological critics might very well respond that formalist critics become so preoccupied with matters of structure and unity that their criticism becomes arid and apparently divorced from all the human concerns that make people want to read poems in the first place. Sociological critics would agree with the comment made by Leon Trotsky, the Russian Marxist revolutionary, in his book *Literature and Revolution*:

> The methods of formal analysis are necessary, but insufficient. You may count up the alliterations in popular proverbs, classify metaphors, count up the number of vowels and consonants in a wedding song. It will undoubtedly enrich our knowledge of folk art, in one way or another; but if you don't know the peasant system of sowing, and the life that is based on it, if you don't know the part the scythe plays, and if you have not mastered the meaning of the church calendar to the peasant, of the time when the peasant marries, or when the peasant women give birth, you will have only understood the outer shell of folk art, but the kernel will not have been reached.

As a final note, a few remarks need to be made on a special form of socio-logical criticism, namely, *ideological* (i.e., Marxist, Christian, etc.) criticism. While the sociological critic differs from the formalistic critic in his or her approach to literature, the sociological critic tends to share with the formalist critic the view that works of art are important in their own right and do not need to be justified in terms of any other human activity or interest. The Marxist critic, on the other hand, while sharing many of the assumptions and the approaches of the sociological critic, carries the approach an important step further. The Marxist critic sees literature as one activity among many that are to be studied and judged in terms of a larger and all-encompassing ideology. He or she holds that one cannot understand the literature of the past unless one understands how it reflects the relationship between economic production and social class. And since the Marxist sees his or her duty—indeed, the duty of all responsible and humane people—as not merely to describe the world but to change it in such a way as to free the oppressed masses of the world, he or she will not be content merely to illuminate a work, as does the sociological critic, or to demonstrate its aesthetic unity and beauty, as does the formalist critic. The Marxist critic will judge contemporary literature by the contribution it makes to bringing about revolution or in some way making the masses of workers (the proletariat) more conscious of their oppression and, therefore, more equipped to struggle against the oppressors.

The Marxist critic might describe "Dover Beach" very much as the sociological critic, but he or she would go on to point out that the emotion Arnold expresses in the poem is predictable, the inevitable end product of a dehumanizing, capitalist economy in which a small class of oligarchs is willing, at whatever cost, to protect and increase its wealth and power. Moreover, the Marxist critic, as a materialist who believes that humankind makes its own history, would find Arnold's reference to "the eternal note of sadness" a mystic evasion of the real sources of his alienation and pain; Arnold's misery can be clearly and unmystically explained by the socioeconomic conditions of his time. It is Arnold's refusal to face this fact which leads him to the conclusion typical of a bourgeois artist-intellectual who refuses to face the truth; the cure for Arnold's pain cannot be found in a love relationship, because relationships between people, like everything else, are determined by socioeconomic conditions. The cure for the pain which he describes so well will be found in the world of action, in the struggle to create a socioeconomic system that is just and humane. "Dover Beach," then, is both a brilliant evocation of the alienation and misery caused by a capitalist economy and a testimony to the inability of a bourgeois intellectual to understand what is responsible for his feelings.

My Kinsman, Major Molineux

"My Kinsman, Major Molineux" presents a nocturnal world, viewed largely from the point of view of its young hero, where nothing makes sense to him. It appears to be an allegoric or symbolic world, a dreamlike world where everything seems to mean something else. Robin searches for the meaning to the strange behavior of townspeople he accosts, for some key which will unlock the mystery. The sociological critic also searches for the key, and finds it in the opening paragraph of the story, the paragraph that in most short stories is crucial in setting the stage for the action about to unfold.

That paragraph, the sociological critic would note, is not a part of the narrative itself but is rather a summary of the historical situation in the American colonies prior to the Revolutionary War. We are given this summary, Hawthorne tells us, "as a preface to the following adventures." No critic, of whatever persuasion, can ignore that paragraph. In contrast to the actual story, the opening paragraph is clear and straightforward: on the eve of the Revolution, the bitterness and hostility of the colonists toward England had become so intense that no colonial administrators, even those who were kindest in exercising their power, were safe from the wrath of the people. It is in the context of this moment of American history, when there occurred a "temporary inflammation of the popular mind," that the story of Robin's search for his kinsman must be read and interpreted. For "My Kinsman, Major Molineux" is an examination of and comment upon the American colonies as they prepared to achieve, by violence if necessary, independence from the increasingly intolerable domination of England.

We are introduced to Robin as he arrives in town, an energetic, likable, and innocent young man who has left the secure comfort of his rural family to commence a career. He is on the verge of adulthood and independence, filled with anticipation and promise, as well as apprehension, as he confronts an uncertain future. But Robin, unlike most young men in his position, has the advantage of a wealthy cousin who has offered to help him. The story narrates Robin's polite and reasonable inquiries as to where Major Molineux resides and the bafflingly rude and hostile responses of the townspeople.

The mystery is Major Molineux, or, rather, the hostility his name evokes. For readers, at least, the mystery begins to dispel when they learn that the major, an aristocratic and commanding figure, represents inherited wealth and civil and military rank—in short, the authority and values of England. To Robin, fresh from the simple and nonpolitical world of his pastoral home, Major Molineux is a real person, his cousin, whose aid he seeks. To the townspeople, on the other hand, Molineux is a symbol of the hated England in a political struggle that is turning increasingly ugly.

This difference between what Major Molineux means to Robin and what he means to the townspeople is implied at the very outset of the narrative. Robin has left the morally simplistic and nonpolitical world of his country home and come to a town that is seething with revolutionary fervor. The countryside is the past, America's past; the town is the present, the place where America's future will be decided. As Robin wends his way through the metropolis vainly searching for his kinsman, Hawthorne skillfully weaves into the narrative details suggestive of the political theme. Robin, we are told, enters the town "with as eager an eye as if he were entering London city." Before entering the tavern, "he beheld the broad countenance of a British hero swinging before the door." Once in the tavern, he observes a group of men who look like sailors drinking punch, which, Hawthorne tells us, "the West India trade had long since made a familiar drink in the colony." More significantly, this episode ends when the innkeeper, in response to Robin's inquiry about his cousin, merely points to a poster offering a reward for a runaway "bounden servant" and ominously advises Robin to leave. The suggestion is clear—anyone seeking Major Molineux must be a willing bond servant (bond servitude being a form of limited slavery used by England to help populate the American colonies) and, therefore, an enemy of the revolutionaries.

Robin continues his wanderings, his confusion deepening, until a stranger he accosts tells him that Major Molineux will soon pass by the very spot where they are standing. As Robin waits, his thoughts drift to his country home and family. In a dreamlike state, he dwells upon the warmth and security of the life he has left, the sturdy simplicity of a happy family bound together by a gentle and loving minister father. The dream ends abruptly, however, when Robin, attempting to follow his family into their home, finds the door locked. After an evening of "ambiguity and weariness," it is natural that Robin's thoughts should turn back to his home. It is just as natural that his dream should end as it does, for Robin has begun the journey to adulthood and independence from which there is no turning back. Although he is not fully aware of the fact, he shares a good deal with the townspeople who have so baffled and angered him. The adult world of independence is the complex and ambiguous world where political battles are fought, and Robin, like America itself, is set upon a course of action from which there is no turning back. The simplicities of an older, rural America, where authority is vested in a gentle parent and the Scriptures or figures of authority like Major Molineux, must inevitably yield to the ambiguities of the metropolis, where the future will be decided.

That future, Robin's and the nation's, is dramatically embodied in the climactic episode, when Robin finally finds his kinsman. Tarred and feathered, Major Molineux sits in the midst of a garish and riotous procession, led by a man whose face is half red and half black. This man, Hawthorne tells us, is the personification of war and its consequences:

> The single horseman, clad in a military dress, and bearing a drawn sword, rode onward as the leader, and, by his fierce and variegated countenance, appeared like war personified; the red of one cheek an emblem of fire and sword; the blackness of the other betokened the mourning that attends them.

The "Indian" masquerade of those in the procession is a clear allusion to the disguise of the rebellious participants in the Boston tea party. The incomprehensible words addressed to Robin earlier by various townspeople are clearly passwords arranged to identify the conspirators.

The meaning of the night's events begins to dawn on Robin as he joins in the laughter of the throng as it wildly celebrates the demise of Major Molineux, whom Hawthorne compares to "some dead potentate, mighty no more, but majestic still in his agony." The entire scene, the entire story which this scene brings to a climax, gives Robin's laughter a crucial meaning. In joining in the laughter of the throng, Robin identifies himself with the political goals of the revolutionaries. But more than that, in so doing he begins, finally, to see that his personal relationship, to both his home and his cousin, is parallel with and inseparable from the relationship of the colonies to its past and to England. Robin's joy in seeing his dignified and powerful cousin a scorned captive of the townspeople is intensely personal, the joy a youth feels, ambivalent though it may be, when released from the bonds of an authority figure. But the meaning of that authority figure, as the story makes clear, cannot be separated from the political theme, as Robin himself now recognizes.

Such a reading is not meant to imply that "My Kinsman, Major Molineux" is a simple story, a kind of allegory, that embodies a straightforward set of abstract ideas. It is, rather, a story revealing how complex a particular historical event is. That Hawthorne himself had equivocal feelings about the event is made clear by his description of the major, whose dignity and majestic bearing the utmost humiliation cannot altogether extinguish. This fact, together with the unflattering way the townspeople are presented throughout, suggests that Hawthorne viewed the event itself, at least in part, as the victory of mob rule over dignified and settled authority.

At any rate, the procession past, the tension released, Robin turns to the friendly citizen and asks directions back to the ferry. Defeated in his purpose, shaken by and perhaps not yet fully comprehending the extraordinary events of the evening, he decides to return to his family. But the kindly stranger urges Robin to stay. "Perhaps," he says, "as you are a shrewd youth, you may rise in the world without the help of your kinsman, Major Molineux." The stranger's comment is an appropriate conclusion to the story, for it appeals to Robin as an adult, as an American who must achieve independence through his own efforts, however difficult and ambiguous the struggle. Robin must make his way without the aid of his wealthy and powerful kinsman, just as America must make its way without the aid of England. However problematical that freedom is, however dangerous and frightening, it is the inescapable price that real independence exacts.

Psychoanalytic Criticism

Psychoanalytic criticism always proceeds from a set of principles which describes the inner life of *all* men and women. Though there is great diversity of conviction about the nature of inner life and how to deal with it, certainly all analysts, and all psychoanalytic critics, assume that the development of the psyche in humans is analogous to the development of the body. Doctors can provide charts indicating physical growth stages, and analysts can supply similar charts, based on generations of case history, indicating stages in the growth of the psyche. Obviously the best psychoanalytic critic is a trained analyst, but few analysts engage in literary criticism. Most of that criticism is performed by more or less knowledgeable amateurs, and much of that criticism is based on a relatively few principles set down by Sigmund Freud that describe the dominating human drives and the confusions they produce. We must examine those principles.

First among them is the universality of the Oedipus complex. Freud contends that everyone moves through a psychic history which at one point, in early childhood, involves an erotic attachment to the parent of the opposite sex and an accompanying hostility and aggression against the parent of the same sex, who is seen as a rival. Such feelings, part of the natural biography of the psyche, pass or are effectively controlled in most cases. But sometimes, the child grown to adulthood is still strongly gripped by that Oedipal mode, which then may result in neurotic or even psychotic behavior. A famous analysis of Shakespeare's *Hamlet* argues that Hamlet is best understood as gripped by Oedipal feelings which account for his difficulties and his inability to act decisively, and the Laurence Olivier film of *Hamlet* presents such an interpretation. But how could Shakespeare create an Oedipal Hamlet when Freud was not to be born for some two and a half centuries? Freud did not invent the Oedipus complex—he simply described it. It was always there, especially noticeable in the work of great literary artists who in every era demonstrate a special insight into the human condition. At one point in Sophocles' *Oedipus Rex*, written about 429 B.C., Iocastê the queen says to her son-husband, "Have no more fear of sleeping with your mother: / How many men, in dreams, have lain with their mothers / No reasonable man is troubled by such things." And the situation of Oedipus, and the awareness of Iocastê, provide for Freud the very name for the psychic phase he detects.

Paralleling the Oedipal phase in the natural history of the psyche is the aggressive phase, the urge to attack those who exercise authority, that is, those in a position to control and to deny our primal desires. For the young, the authority figure is frequently a parent. For the more mature, that authority figure may be the police officer, the government official, the office manager. As far back as the Hebrew Bible story of the Tower of Babel and the old Greek myths in which the giant Titans, led by Cronus, overthrow their father Uranus, and Zeus and the Olympians subsequently overthrow Cronus, there appears evidence of the rebellion against the parent-authority figure. Freud views that aggressive hostility as another ever-present component of the developing psyche. But, in the interest of civilization and the advantages which organized society provides, that aggressiveness must be controlled. The mechanisms of control are various. Early on comes the command to honor one's father and mother. The culture demands of its members that they love and revere their parents. What, then, of the frequent hostility children feel toward those parents who punish them and deny them the freedom they seek? That hostility often results in guilt—one is supposed to love not hate one's parents—and the guilt can be severe as the child (or adult) senses the contradiction between his or her desires and his or her "duty." Such guilt feelings sometimes generate behavior that effectively punishes. The punishment may be internal—may take the form of psychotic withdrawal or psychosomatic illness. Or the guilt may generate external behavior that requires punishment at the hands of society. In any case, the psychoanalytic critic is constantly aware that authors and/or their characters suffer and resuffer a primal tension that results from the conflict between psychic aggressions and social obligations.

Dover Beach

"Dover Beach" is richly suggestive of the fundamental psychic dilemma of people in civilization. And since people in civilization are, by definition, discontent because social duties require them to repress their primal urges, it is not surprising that the opening visual images which create a lovely and tranquil scene—calm sea, glimmering cliffs, a tranquil bay, sweet night air—are quickly modified by the ominous "only" that begins the seventh line of the poem. That *only*, in the sense of "in contrast," is addressed to a woman who has been called to the window to see the quiet and reassuring scene. No reassurance, finally, remains, as the images shift to an auditory mode:

> Listen! you hear the grating roar
> Of pebbles which the waves draw back, and fling

The tone is strangely changed, the emotional impact of "roar" suggesting something quite different from the serenity of the opening image, and the second stanza closes with the sounds of the surf bringing "the eternal note of sadness in."

Why should sadness be an *eternal* note? And why is the visual imagery largely pleasing while the auditory imagery is largely ominous? The answers to these two questions provide the focus for a psychoanalytic reading of the poem.

The "eternal note of sadness" (an auditory image) represents Arnold's recognition that, however sweet the night air and calm the sea, the central human experience is sadness. At the point in the poem where that sadness is recognized, the poet recalls the Greek tragedian Sophocles, who heard that same note of sadness over 2,000 years ago. (It is, after all, an eternal sadness.) For Sophocles, the sadness brings to mind the "turbid ebb and flow of human misery." Now Sophocles' *Oedipus Rex* ends with the chorus pointing out that no one should count himself or herself happy until at the moment of death he or she can look back over a life without pain. Fate, as it afflicted Oedipus, afflicts us all. As we mentioned, the fate of Oedipus provided Freud with the name of that psychic mode through which we all pass. We might all be guilty of parental murder and incest were it not necessary to repress those urges in order to construct a viable society. The unacceptable passions are controlled by guilt. We may not commit murder or incest on pain of punishment. We may not even desire to commit murder or incest on pain of possible psychic punishment. The dilemma, the guarantee of guilt or the guarantee of discontent, defines that eternal note of sadness which the poet hears.

We might go further. In infancy and very early childhood the tactile and the visual senses are most important. Somewhat later the auditory sense increases in importance. Consequently, the child recognizes security—certitude, peace, help for pain—tactilely and visually, in the warmth and the form of the omnipresent and succoring parent. Later, through the child's ears comes the angry "no!" When discipline and painful interaction with others begin, the child experiences the auditory admonition which frustrates his or her desires. It is significant to the psychoanalytic critic that in "Dover Beach" the tranquilities are visual but the ominous sadness is auditory—the "roar" which brings in the "note" of sadness, the "roar" of the sea of faith retreating to the breath of the night-wind, the "alarms," and the "clash" of ignorant armies by night.

We need to look at the opening lines of the final stanza. Certainly the principal agency developed by society to enforce the morality it required was religion. Ancient religious teaching recognized those primal urges that Freud systematically described and made them offenses against God. Faith, then, became the condition that made society possible; religious injunction and religious duty served as a sort of cultural superego, a mass conscience, that not only controlled human aggression but substituted for it a set of ideal behavior patterns that could guarantee a set of gratifying rewards. Hence the poet recalls:

> The Sea of Faith
> Was once, too, at the full, and round earth's shore
> Lay like the folds of a bright girdle furled.

This is a strange image. Surely the emotional tone of "the folds of a bright girdle furled" is positive—that bright girdle is a '"good" thing, not an ominous thing. Yet, that girdle (i.e., a sash or belt worn round the waist) is restrictive. It is furled (i.e., rolled up, bound) around the land. In short, the Sea of Faith contains, limits, strictly controls the land. In the context of the poem, that containment is a good thing, for without the restricting Sea of Faith the world, despite appearances,

> Hath really neither joy, nor love, nor light,
> Nor certitude, nor peace, nor help for pain.

Without strong religious faith, acting as a cultural superego, the primal aspects of the psyche are released—aggression comes to dominate human activity:

> And we are here as on a darkling plain
> Swept with confused alarms of struggle and flight,
> Where ignorant armies clash by night.

A certain confusion persists. On the one hand, the Sea of Faith serves a useful function as an emblem of the *superego* (loosely, the conscience), the name Freud gives to the guilt-inducing mechanism that incessantly "watches" the *ego*, or self, to punish it for certain kinds of behavior. When it is at the full, ignorant armies, presumably, do not clash by night. On the other hand, the superego as associated with auditory imagery is ominous. It reverberates with the painful experience of frustration. Finally, however, the usefulness of the Sea of Faith is illusory. The note of sadness is eternal. Sophocles, long before the foundation of Christianity, heard it. What emerges from the poem's images, understood psychoanalytically, is a progression from a mild note of sadness (frustrated desires) to alarms and clashes (threatening, uncontrolled, aggressive desires). The calm sea and the fair moon suggest a land of dreams—illusory and without substance. Sadness, struggle, and flight are real.

We need to deal with the woman to whom the poet speaks; we need to understand his relationship to her. The quest for that understanding involves another psychoanalytic principle, another set of images, and a reconsideration of the image of the Sea of Faith.

In earliest infancy, the *ego* (the sense of self), is not yet formed. The infant child considers the mother, particularly the mother's breast, as part of himself or herself. A gradual and a painful recognition must occur in which the child is dissociated from the mother. The process begins with the birth trauma. In the womb, the child is utterly safe, never hungry, never cold. Although there are discomforts for a time after birth, the mother and her nourishing breast are so much present that the infant does not distinguish where he or she ends and the other, the mother, begins. But this state of affairs does not continue, and the infant becomes increasingly dissociated. Slowly the infant learns what is "him" or "her" and what is not, what he or she can control by will (moving an arm, say) and what he or she cannot (the mother's availability). In short, the infant learns the borders of his or her being, the edges of his or her existence.

Images of borders and edges constantly recur in the poem. Such images may be taken as emblems of dissociation—that is, symbols of the separation between the warm, nourishing mother and the child. Consequently, they are symbols of painful dissatisfaction. The Sea of Faith that

> . . . round earth's shore
> Lay like the folds of a bright girdle furled

seems, on the other hand, much like that warm, encompassing mother who, to the infant, was a part of the infant. But dissociation occurs, and the distressed speaker perceives that comforting entity withdrawing, retreating "down the vast edges drear / And naked shingles of the world." He has an edge and can no longer reside safely in close association with the source of comfort and security.

Instantly the speaker turns to the woman and says

> Ah, love, let us be true
> To one another!

He perceives his companion not erotically but as the source of security, as a replacement for the withdrawing emblematic mother. He offers his "love" a mutual fidelity not to reassure her of his commitment but to assure himself of hers. He wishes to dissolve the edges of his ego and associate, as in infancy, with his "mother." Such an association will protect him from a world in which "ignorant armies clash by night."

My Kinsman, Major Molineux

The story opens with Robin crossing a river into an unnamed town after dark. If one takes a psychoanalytic stance, the mysterious opening symbolizes a sort of spiritual journey into mysterious realms. More specifically, the opening suggests an inward journey into the dark recesses of the human spirit. Robin has to confront the psychic confusion resulting from the conflict between the civilized and the psychological response to (in Robin's case, paternal) authority. Robin takes his journey to find the paternal figure that is identified in his mind with safety and security, his powerful kinsman, Major Molineux. From a psychoanalytic point of view, it is reasonable to point out that Robin has at least two fathers, since his kinsman, if Robin ever finds him, will serve a paternal function. Some critics suggest that every male Robin encounters serves as a surrogate father. Note that the men Robin meets, with one exception, all act threateningly, all offer to punish him, all assume a position of authority, and, hence, all in some respect are paternalistic. The one exception, the kindly stranger who joins Robin in his watch and who urges him to make his own way without the aid of a paternalistic power is in some ways himself a kind of unreal, idealized father figure, who, though kindly and helpful, requires no price for his help.

From the psychoanalytic point of view, the story is precisely about the price required of young men by their fathers. The price, of course, is not coin. It is behavior. Robin must behave as authority wishes, not as Robin wishes. In return, he will be secure—but almost certainly discontent. Perhaps, deeper than consciousness, Robin feels the pinch of such an economy and unwittingly seeks to avoid payment. After all, the story runs its course as Robin seeks directions to the house of his kinsman. But a kind of haunting inefficiency constantly disrupts his search. Early on he realizes that he should have asked the ferryman to take him to Major Molineux. But he didn't. He stops an old gentleman by seizing hold of his coat—rather curious behavior to an elderly stranger. And the stranger's response to the youth's behavior is an angry threat. That threat provokes the first round of recurrent laughter from the loungers in the barber shop. And the threat frightens Robin. Next he becomes "entangled in a succession of crooked and narrow streets," a set of literal streets near the waterfront (but also a lovely metaphor for the human psyche), where he is attracted to an inn. There he receives his second rebuff from the innkeeper, another threat, and is followed out into the street by more laughter.

Robin responds to this rebuff with considerable anger, thinks violent thoughts, but continues to pursue his quest in a most curious way. He walks up and down the main street of the town hoping to run into his kinsman. Actually he is thrilled by the rich and exotic shop windows and strollers. Robin, it seems, is not seeking his kinsman at all. He is, for once, doing what he wishes to do. He is enjoying himself, free from any paternal interference. Remarkably, as he gawks along the exotic street, he hears the distinctive cough of the old gentleman he first encountered, the gentleman who threatened him with the stocks, the gentleman who proclaimed, "I have—hem, hem—authority." Robin responds by declaring "Mercy on us!" and ducking around a corner to avoid meeting him. Strange as this evasion of authority might seem, stranger still is the half-opened door through which Robin discerns "a strip of scarlet petticoat, and the occasional sparkle of an eye."

This encounter is quite different from the others which occur both before and after. That red petticoat and sparkling eye belong to a vivacious and attractive harlot. She tells Robin, in response to his standard question, that Major Molineux is asleep within (an outrageous lie that Robin can't help but doubt), and she takes him by the hand "and the touch was light, and the force was gentleness, and though Robin read in her eyes what he did not hear in her words, yet the slender-waisted woman in the scarlet petticoat proved stronger than the athletic country youth. She had drawn his half-willing footsteps nearly to the threshold" when the watchman appears. The woman hastily withdraws, and Robin is once again warned by authority of punishment for bad behavior.

The frightened youth does not realize until the watchman has turned the corner that *he* would certainly know the whereabouts of his kinsman, Major Molineux, but his tardy shouted request to the vanished watchman is answered only by more vague laughter. Why didn't Robin ask for directions immediately? Well, he was about to sin against the paternal authority which generally represses and most particularly represses the sexual instincts of sons. The psychoanalytic critic might go even further here in explaining the sources of Robin's guilty demeanor before the watchman whose appearance is fantastically coincidental. (Is he the ever-present psychic "watchman" who cries "guilty" at even our ego-gratifying *thoughts* when they violate the "law?") The desirable woman in the scarlet petticoat says that Major Molineux cohabits with her. Her eyes and her behavior invite Robin to a sexual encounter which he, however nervously, welcomes. If Major Molineux is a surrogate father for Robin, is not the woman in scarlet a surrogate mother? And is not an Oedipal situation developed? For students not familiar with principles of psychoanalytic criticism, this will seem a rather wild reading. But reserve judgment. Consider how the story ends. Then, perhaps, the Oedipal feature will not seem bizarre.

Now events move rapidly. Robin, brought to his "senses" by the intrusion of the watchman, remembers that he is a "good" boy and rejects the lovely beckoning arm. But he is upset and feeling violent. He intends to succeed in his quest, even if it means clubbing someone with his stout oak cudgel. The next man he meets, mysteriously muffled, is forced to answer—and answer he does. The muffling, dropped, reveals a hideous, satanic face painted half red and half black. Certainly that painting is a disguise. But this man, we later discover, is the leader of the mob that destroys Major Molineux's power and dignity and, as such, represents a certain aspect first of the community but also of each person in it, particularly of Robin. An old-fashioned Freudian would have no trouble identifying him as Robin's embodied *id*, the name given by Freud to the insistent selfish, lustful, and aggressive aspect of a person's psyche, just as such a critic would have no trouble earlier identifying the intrusive watchman as Robin's *superego*. The demonic parti-colored citizen tells Robin to wait where he is and within a few moments he will surely meet his kinsman, Major Molineux.

Robin waits and experiences some dreams that are almost hallucinations. He is standing by a church and notices the graves. Perhaps the major is already dead and will appear to haunt him. Wouldn't it be nice to be at home, safe in his family circle? And he is there, but when he seeks to follow his family into the house, the door is closed in his face and locked. It is a normal dream for a frightened young man away from home for the first time. But in the context of the story, this dream acts as a metaphor for Robin's expulsion from the safety of home. Even if he would submit again to the "father" in return for security, the opportunity is denied. One father only remains for him—his kinsman, Major Molineux (who may be dead). It is home that Robin must seek if he wishes shelter from all the perils of independence. But the price is the same—

submission and repression. The rioters draw near, the tumult grows loud, the torches cast a great light into the darkness—some revelation is at hand. And the light reveals the demonic man on horseback with a drawn sword leading a riotous procession around a cart in which the powerful, gray, dignified, upright, fatherly Major Molineux sits trembling and humiliated. All the figures Robin encountered during the night return—old "hem-hem," the laughing innkeeper, the saucy harlot. And all laugh. But Robin's laugh is louder than all the rest. For the psychoanalytic critic, that laugh cannot be interpreted other than as the laugh of exultant release from the tyranny of the father, of established authority, and the prospect of independent activity free of stifling guilt.

The psychoanalytic critic might go further. He or she might call attention to the drawn sword held by the embodied id and remark on the relationship between that phallic symbol and the thwarted desire of Robin in the encounter with the harlot. Certain figures that recur throughout the history of literature (and in dreams) are accepted by Freudian critics as symbols of the sexual and aggressive aspects of the human condition. Such deep reading, like all deep reading, is perilous. Yet to the reader versed in the premises of psychoanalysis and the universal symbols behind which the mind conceals its primal nature, the bold analysis enriches the literary art.

Did Hawthorne deliberately design the psychoanalytic structure of "My Kinsman, Major Molineux"? A difficult question. He certainly did not incorporate an embodied superego and id. He never heard of those psychic abstractions. He certainly did not incorporate by design a phallic sword suggesting that Robin's sexual freedom is obtained through Major Molineux's exile. But, the psychoanalytic critic responds, Hawthorne, as a sensitive artist, perceives the deep struggle between desire and duty, between primal urge and social restraint. And that struggle he dramatizes. As for the drawn sword, he probably had no conscious idea of its psychic significance. He would be appalled by the modern psychoanalytic response. But, for the analyst, that does not in the least contradict the modern conviction that universal symbols, however unconscious, struggle to the surface in all art. That psychoanalytic critic would admire Hawthorne's "My Kinsman, Major Molineux" for effectively and accurately portraying the rite of passage of young Robin from innocence to experience, from repressed childhood to independent adulthood.

Writing about Literature*

Writing about literature compels the student to discover and come to terms with his or her response to an author's work. Every element in a literary work has been deliberately incorporated by the author—the description of the setting, the events that constitute the plot, the dialogue, the imagery. A rather mysterious intellectual and emotional event occurs within the reader as a result of the writer's purposeful manipulation of language. An essay about literature inevitably attempts some description of the author's purposes and techniques and some discussion of the reader's response.

As an illustration of the relationship between author's purpose and reader's response, consider these opening lines of a poem by W. H. Auden (the poem appears on p. 455):

> That night when joy began
> Our narrowest veins to flush,
> We waited for the flash
> Of morning's levelled gun.

The stanza tells of a new joy, probably erotic, that the speaker and his companion experience one night. But the reader must see that the speaker is apprehensive about that joy. The writer has created that mood of apprehension by using a violent image—the flash of morning's gun—to characterize the speaker's fears about the consequences of possible discovery. The images in the subsequent stanzas of the poem suggest that the lovers are trespassers and that the leveled gun they fear belongs to the keeper of the forbidden fields they enjoyed. Thus, the reader responds to the poem with an awareness that the lovers have risked danger for the sake of joy.

Though the correspondence between "writer's purpose" and "reader's response" is by no means exact, any attempt to write about literature is, in one way or another, an attempt to discover and describe that correspondence. In other words, whatever the assignment, your fundamental task is to provide the answers to two questions: "How do I respond to this piece? How has the author brought about my response?"

The Journal

Many instructors will require you to keep a journal, a day-by-day account of your reactions to and reflections about what you've been reading. Even if a journal is

---

* See, as well, the appendices "Reading Fiction," "Reading Poetry," "Reading Drama," and "Three Critical Approaches." Those discussions may well suggest useful approaches to writing assignments.

not required, you might want to keep one for a variety of reasons. From a purely practical perspective, a journal provides valuable mental exercise: forcing yourself to write in a journal regularly is an excellent way to limber up your writing abilities and overcome the fear of facing a blank page. Because journals are like diaries in the sense that they are not meant to be seen by anyone else, you need not worry about whether you are constructing grammatical sentences, whether you are writing cohesive paragraphs and developing your ideas, or even whether you are always making sense. You are free to comment on some aspect of a work or set down a highly personal recollection that something in the work triggered. What is important is that you are recording your reactions, ideas, feelings, questions. If you are conscientious about keeping your journal, you may come to find the act of writing a challenging and—who knows?—even a pleasant activity.

A journal's usefulness extends beyond personal pleasure. When the time comes to write a formal essay for your class, the journal can provide you with a large range of possible topics. Suppose while you were reading Alastair Reid's poem "Curiosity" you confided to your journal your own curiosity about the reasons the poet selected cats and dogs to carry the theme. You might write an interesting essay on this topic, based on the thesis that, although both are domestic animals, the cat is a far wilder creature than the more docile and domestic dog.

You can also use a journal to record unfamiliar words that you encounter in your reading and plan to look up later. In reading Stevie Smith's "To Carry the Child," for example, you might wonder what *carapace* means. You enter the word in your journal, and when you look it up, you find that *carapace* means a bony shell, such as a turtle's. With this knowledge you can return to the poem and appreciate the image, which might suggest the topic of an essay.

Some of your journal entries will probably be confessions of bafflement and confusion. Why does Tolstoy begin "The Death of Iván Ilých" at the end? Why does Crane in "The Bride Comes to Yellow Sky" open part III with a reference to a character's shirt and the place where it was made as well as the ethnic origin of the people who made it? Working out an answer to either of these questions could lead to an interesting essay.

Anything you want to enter in your journal is relevant, including the most personal feelings and recollections triggered by a work. Dylan Thomas's "Fern Hill" might remind you of feelings you experienced during a particular period of your childhood. Exploring your own childhood feelings and comparing them with those expressed in Thomas's poem could lead in any number of ways to a fascinating essay (for example, how poets give memorable and vivid expression to experiences we've all had). Or you might jot down, after reading Kate Chopin's "The Storm," your moral disapproval of the story's central event—marital infidelity. You might then reread the story to discover whether it seems to disapprove of infidelity or whether you have imposed on it your own personal moral values. Sorting out such feelings could result in an essay on the interaction between the moral values of a reader and those embodied in a particular work.

Finally, remember that (unless your instructor has specific guidelines for your journal keeping) your journal will be the one place where you can write as much or as little as you please, as often or infrequently as you wish, with care and deliberation or careless speed. Its only purpose is to serve your needs. But if you write fairly regularly, you will probably be surprised not only at how much easier the act of writing becomes but also at how many ideas suddenly pop into your head in the act of writing. Henry Adams was surely right when he observed, "The habit of expression leads to the search for something to express."

Essays

Your journal will allow you to struggle privately with your reading. It may produce wonders of understanding; it should, as well, reveal to you lapses in understanding. The journal, while a useful tool for recording thoughts, responses, and impressions, remains, after all, a set of rough notes. Most instructors will demand some organization of those notes—they will ask you to write formal essays that provide evidence of your talent for critical response. Formal essays in introduction-to-literature courses characteristically fall into one of three modes: explication, analysis, and comparison and contrast.

Explication

In explication, you examine a work in as much detail as possible, line by line, stanza by stanza, scene by scene, explaining each part as fully as you can and showing how the author's techniques produce your response. An explication is essentially a demonstration of your thorough understanding of the poem, the story, or the play.

Here is a sample essay that explicates a relatively difficult poem, Dylan Thomas's "Do Not Go Gentle into That Good Night." (The poem appears on p. 697).

    Dylan Thomas's villanelle "Do Not Go Gentle into That
    Good Night" is addressed to his aged father. The poem is
    remarkable in a number of ways, most notably in that contrary
    to the most common poetic treatments of the inevitability of
    death, which argue for serenity or celebrate the peace that
    death provides, this poem urges resistance and rage in the
    face of death. It justifies that unusual attitude by
    describing the rage and resistance to death of four kinds of
    men, all of whom can summon up the image of a complete and
    satisfying life that is denied to them by death.

    The first tercet of the intricately rhymed villanelle
    opens with an arresting line. The adjective <u>gentle</u> appears
    where we would expect the adverb <u>gently</u>. The strange diction

suggests that <u>gentle</u> may describe both the going (i.e., gently dying) and the person (i.e., gentleman) who confronts death. Further, the speaker characterizes "night," here clearly a figure for death, as "good." Yet in the next line, the speaker urges that the aged should violently resist death, characterized as the "close of day" and "the dying of the light." In effect, the first three lines argue that however good death may be, the aged should refuse to die gently, should passionately rave and rage against death.

In the second tercet, the speaker turns to a description of the way the first of four types of men confronts death (which is figuratively defined throughout the poem as "that good night" and "the dying of the light"). These are the "wise men," the scholars, the philosophers, those who understand the inevitability of death, men who "know dark is right." But they do not acquiesce in death "because their words had forked no lightning," because their published wisdom failed to bring them to that sense of completeness and fulfillment that can accept death. Therefore, wise as they are, they reject the theoretical "rightness" of death and refuse to "go gentle."

The second sort of men——"good men," the moralists, the social reformers, those who attempt to better the world through action as the wise men attempt to better it through "words"——also rage against death. Their deeds are, after all, "frail." With sea imagery, the speaker suggests that these men might have accomplished fine and fertile things—— their deeds "might have danced in a green bay." But with the "last wave" gone, they see only the frailty, the impermanence of their acts, and so they, too, rage against the death that deprives them of the opportunity to leave a meaningful legacy.

So, too, the "wild men," the poets who "sang" the loveliness and vitality of nature, learn, as they approach death, that the sensuous joys of human existence wane. As the life-giving sun moves toward dusk, as death approaches, their singing turns to grieving, and they refuse to surrender gently, to leave willingly the warmth and pleasure and beauty that life can give.

And finally, with a pun suggestive of death, the "grave men," those who go through life with such high seriousness as never to experience gaiety and pleasure, see, as death ap-

proaches, all the joyous possibilities that they were blind
to in life. And they, too, rage against the dying of a light
that they had never properly seen before.

The speaker then calls upon his aged father to join
these men raging against death. Only in this final stanza do
we discover that the entire poem is addressed to the speaker's father and that, despite the generalized statements
about old age and the focus upon types of men, the poem is a
personal lyric. The edge of death becomes a "sad height,"
the summit of wisdom and experience old age attains includes
the sad knowledge of life's failure to satisfy the vision we
all pursue. The depth and complexity of the speaker's sadness
is startlingly given in the second line when he calls upon
his father to both curse and bless him. These opposites
richly suggest several related possibilities. Curse me for
not living up to your expectations. Curse me for remaining
alive as you die. Bless me with forgiveness for my failings.
Bless me for teaching you to rage against death. And the
curses and blessings are contained in the "fierce tears"—
fierce because you will burn and rave and rage against death.
As the poem closes by bringing together the two powerful refrains, we may reasonably feel that the speaker himself,
while not facing imminent death, rages because his father's
death will cut off a relationship that is incomplete.

The explication, as you can see, deals with the entire poem by coming to grips
with each element in it. This same mode can be used to write about the drama
as well, but the length of plays will probably require that you focus on a single
segment—a scene, for example—rather than the entire play.

You can learn a great deal about the technique of drama by selecting a short
self-contained scene and writing a careful description of it. This method, a
variety of explication, will force you to confront every speech and stage direction
and to come to some conclusion regarding its function. Why is the set furnished
as it is? Why does a character speak the words he or she does or remain silent?
What do we learn of characters from the interchanges among them? Assume that
everything that occurs in the play, whether on the printed page or on the stage,
is put there for a purpose. Seek to discover the purpose, and you will, at the same
time, discover the peculiar nature of dramatic art.

Fiction, too, can be treated effectively in a formal explication. As with drama,
it will be necessary to limit the text—you will not be able to explicate a 10-page
story in a 1,000-word essay. Choose a key passage—a half page that reflects the
form and content of the overall story, if possible. Often the first half page of a
story, where the author, like the playwright, must supply information to the

reader, will make a fine text for an explication. Although the explication will deal principally with only an excerpt, feel free to range across the story and show how the introductory material foreshadows what is to come. Or, perhaps, you can explicate the climax of the story—the half page that most pointedly establishes the story's theme—and subject it to a close line-by-line reading that illuminates the whole story.

Analysis

Analyzing literature is not the same kind of exercise as analyzing a chemical compound: breaking a literary work down into its elements is only the first step in literary analysis. When you are assigned an analysis essay, you are expected to focus on one of the elements that contribute to the complex compound that is the substance of any work of literary merit. This process requires that you extricate the element you plan to explore from the other elements that you can identify, study this element—not only in isolation but also in relation to the other elements and the work as a whole—and, using the insights you have gained from your special perspective, make an informed statement about it.

This process may sound complicated, but if you approach it methodically, each stage follows naturally from the stage that precedes it. If, for example, an instructor assigns an analysis essay on some aspect of characterization in *Othello*, you would begin by thinking about each character in the play. You would then select the character whose development you would like to explore and reread carefully those speeches that help to establish his or her substance. Exploring a character's development in this way involves a good deal of explication: in order to identify the "building blocks" that Shakespeare uses to create a three-dimensional role, you must comb very carefully through that character's speeches and actions. You must also be sensitive to the ways in which other characters respond to these speeches and actions. When you have completed this investigation, you will probably have a good understanding of why you intuitively responded to the character as you did when you first read the play. You will also probably be prepared to make a statement about the character's development: "From a realistic perspective, it is hard to believe that a man of Othello's position could be so gullible; however, Shakespeare develops the role with such craft that we accept the Moor as flesh and blood." At this point, you have moved from the broad *subject* "characterization in *Othello*" to a *thesis*, a statement that you must prove. As you formulate your thesis, think of it as a position that you intend to *argue* for with a reader who is not easy to persuade. This approach is useful in any essay that requires a thesis—in other words, in any essay in which you move beyond simple explication and commit yourself to a stand. Note that "From a realistic perspective, it is hard to believe that a man of Othello's position could be so gullible; however, Shakespeare develops the role with such craft that we accept him as flesh and blood" is *argumentative* on two counts. "Characterization in *Othello*" is not remotely argumentative. Further, you have more than enough material to write a well-documented essay of 1,000 words supporting your proposition; you cannot write a well-documented 1,000-word essay on the general subject of characterization in *Othello* without being superficial.

You may be one among the many students who find it difficult to find a starting point. For example, you have been assigned an analysis essay on a very broad subject, such as "imagery in love poetry." A few poems come to mind, but you don't know where to begin. You read these poems and underline all the images that you can find. You look at these images over and over, finding no relation among them. You read some more poems, again underlining the images, but you still do not have even the germ of a thesis.

The technique of freewriting might help to overcome your block. You have read and reread the works you intend to write about. Now, put the assignment temporarily out of your mind and start writing about one or two of the poems without organizing your ideas, without trying to reach a point. Write down what you like about a poem, what you dislike about it, what sort of person the speaker is, which images seemed striking to you—anything at all about the work. If you do this for perhaps ten minutes, you will probably discover that you are voicing opinions. Pick one that interests you or seems the most promising to explore.

There are a few variations on the basic form of the analysis assignment. Occasionally, an instructor will narrow the subject to a specific assignment: analyze the development of Othello's character in Act I. This sort of assignment saves you the trouble of selecting a character on whom to focus and also limits the amount of text that you will have to study. However, the process from this point on is no different from the process that you would employ addressing a broader subject. Sometimes instructors will supply you with a thesis, and you will have to work backward from the thesis to find supporting material. Again, careful analysis of the text is required.

The problem you will have to address when writing an analytical essay remains the same regardless of the literary genre you are asked to discuss. You still must find an arguable thesis that deals with the literary sources of your response to the work. For instance, an analysis of a poem might show how a particular pattern of imagery contributes to the meaning of the poem. Or it might argue, from clues within the poem, that the speaker of the poem is a certain kind of character. Or it might demonstrate how the connotations of certain words in a poem help to create a particular mood. An analysis may also go outside the poem to throw light on it (see the discussion of sociological criticism, p. 814). For instance, a poem might be analyzed as an embodiment of (or departure from) a particular religious, social, political, or scientific doctrine; as an example of traditional poetic form such as the ballad or the pastoral elegy; or as a new expression of an ancient myth. These are but a few examples; the possibilities are almost endless.

Though plays can be analyzed, like stories and poems, in terms of theme, image patterns, and the like, the playwright must solve problems that are unique to drama as a literary form meant to be acted on a stage before an audience. For example, the mechanics of staging a play limit the extent to which the playwright can shift the locations and times of the action, whereas the writer of fiction can make such shifts readily. Similarly, the writer of fiction can, if he or she wishes, tell the story through a narrator who not only can comment on the meaning of events but can describe the thoughts and motives of the characters. In a play, on the other hand, the curtain rises and the characters must convey information through their own words or behavior. The audience does not generally know what the characters think unless they speak their thoughts aloud. As *readers* of a play, we may read the stage directions and any other information the author has provided for the director and actors (and perhaps for readers). We must bear in mind that the audience viewing the play can only know such things as the time of year, the location of the setting, the relationships among characters, or the events that have led up to the action with which the play begins if they are stated in the program or if someone or something on the stage conveys that information.

Playwrights have developed many techniques for solving their special problems, and you may wish to focus on one of these in your analysis of some aspect of a play. For example, you might explain the role of the chorus or the dramatic function of the messenger in Sophocles' *Oedipus Rex*. Or you might argue that the passage of time is distorted for dramatic purposes in Shakespeare's *Othello*. All of these subjects would involve the consideration of problems that are peculiar to the drama as a literary form that is meant to be acted on a stage.

When you confront the assignment to write about a play, ask yourself some fundamental questions. For instance, what sort of person is the protagonist? Is he or she admirable? If so, in what respects? Generous? Wise? Courageous? Fair-minded? What evidence do you find to support your judgment? Does it come from his or her own speeches and behavior or from what other characters say about him or her? If the latter, are we meant to take the opinions of those characters as the truth? Is the tragic conclusion of the play brought about by some flaw or weakness in the character or merely by the malice of others?

Of course, these questions represent only a very few of those you might ask as you think about a play and search for a thesis. If you do choose to deal with some aspect of characterization, you may find that a minor character interests you more as a subject than a major one. And, as we have suggested, you can also ask questions about imagery, about theme, or about various formal or structural aspects of a play. If you ask yourself enough questions, you will discover some thesis that you can argue.

Suppose your instructor has made the following assignment: write an analysis of Harlan Ellison's story, " 'Repent, Harlequin!' Said the Ticktockman" (p. 238), in which you discuss the theme of the story in terms of the characters and the setting. Now consider the following opening (taken from a student paper):

```
" 'Repent, Harlequin!' Said the Ticktockman" is a story
depicting a society in which time governs one's life. The
setting is the United States, the time approximately A.D.
2400 somewhere in the heart of the country. Business deals,
work shifts, and school lessons are started and finished with
exacting precision. Tardiness is intolerable as this would
```

```
hinder the system. In a society of order, precision, and
punctuality, there is no room for likes, dislikes, scruples,
or morals. Thus, personalities in people no longer exist. As
these "personless" people know no good or bad, they very
happily follow in the course of activities which their
society has dictated.
```

At the outset, can you locate a thesis statement? The only sentences that would seem to qualify are the last three in the paragraph. But notice that, although those sentences are not unreasonable responses to the story, they do not establish a thesis that is *responsive to the assignment*. Because the assignment calls for a discussion of theme in terms of character and setting, there should be a thesis statement about the way in which character and setting embody the theme. Here is another opening paragraph on the same assignment (also taken from a student paper):

```
    Harlan Ellison's " 'Repent, Harlequin!' Said the
Ticktockman" opens with a quotation from Thoreau's essay
"Civil Disobedience," which establishes the story's theme.
Thoreau's observations about three varieties of men, those
who serve the state as machines, those who serve it with
their heads, and those who serve it with their consciences,
are dramatized in Ellison's story, which takes place about
400 years in the future in a setting characterized by
machinelike order. The interaction among the three char-
acters, each of whom represents one of Thoreau's types,
results in a telling restatement of his observation that
"heroes, patriots, martyrs, reformers in the great sense, and
men . . . necessarily resist [the state] and . . . are
commonly treated as enemies by it."
```

Compare the two opening paragraphs sentence by sentence for their responsiveness to the assignment. The first sentence of the first opening does not refer to the theme of the story (or to its setting or characterization). In the second sentence, the discussion of the setting ignores the most important aspect—that the story is set in a machine- and time-dominated future. The last three sentences deal obliquely with character, but they are imprecise and do not establish a thesis. The second opening, on the other hand, immediately states the theme of the story. It goes on to emphasize the relevant aspects of the futuristic setting and then refers to the three characters that animate the story in terms of their reactions to the setting. The last sentence addresses the assignment directly and also serves as a thesis statement for the paper. It states the proposition that will be developed and supported in the rest of the paper. The reader of the second opening will expect the next paragraph of the paper to discuss the setting of the story and subsequent paragraphs to discuss the response to the setting of the three principal characters.

The middles of essays are largely determined by their opening paragraphs. However long the middle of any essay may be, each of its paragraphs ought to be responsive to some explicit statement made at the beginning of the essay. Note that it is practically impossible to predict what the paragraph following the first opening will address. Here is the first half of that next paragraph as the first student wrote it.

> The Harlequin is a man in the society with no sense of time. His having a personality enables him to have a sense of moral values and a mind of his own. The Harlequin thinks that it is obscene and wrong to let time totally govern the lives of people. So, he sets out to disrupt the time schedule with ridiculous antics such as showering people with jelly beans in order to try to break up the military fashion in which they are used to doing things.

The paragraph then goes on to discuss the Ticktockman, the capture and brainwashing of the Harlequin, and the resulting lateness of the Ticktockman.

Note that nothing in the opening of this student's paper prepared readers for the introduction of the Harlequin. In fact, the opening concluded rather inaccurately that the people within the story "happily follow in the course of activities which their society has dictated." Hence, the description of the Harlequin in the second paragraph is wholly unexpected. Further, because the student has not dealt with the theme of the story (remember the assignment explicitly asked for a discussion of *theme* in terms of character and setting), the comments about the Harlequin's antics remain disconnected from any clear purpose. They are essentially devoted to what teachers constantly warn against: a mere plot summary. The student has obviously begun to write before she has analyzed the story sufficiently to understand its theme. With further thought, the student would have perceived that the central thematic issue is resistance to an oppressive state—the issue stated in the epigraph from Thoreau. On the other hand, because the second opening makes that thematic point clearly, we can expect it to be followed by a discussion of the environment (that is, the setting) in which the action occurs. Here is such a paragraph taken from the second student's paper:

> Ellison creates a society that reflects one possible future development of the modern American passion for productivity and efficiency. The setting is in perfect keeping with the time-conscious people who inhabit the city. It is pictured as a neat, colorless, and mechanized city. No mention is made of nature: grass, flowers, trees, and birds do not appear. The buildings are in a "Mondrian arrangement,"

```
stark and geometrical. The cold steel slidewalks, slowstrips,
and expresstrips move with precision. Like a chorus line,
people move in unison to board the movers without a wasted
motion. Doors close silently and lock themselves auto-
matically. An ideal efficiency so dominates the social system
that any "wasted time" is deducted from the life of an
inefficient citizen.
```

Once the setting has been established, as in the paragraph just quoted, writers attentive to the assignment will turn to the characters. But they will insistently link those characters to thematic considerations. It might be well to proceed with a short transitional paragraph that shapes the remainder of the middle of the essay:

```
Into this smoothly functioning but coldly mechanized
society, Ellison introduces three characters: Pretty Alice,
one of Thoreau's machinelike creatures; the Ticktockman, one
of those who "serve the state chiefly with their heads, and,
as they rarely make any moral distinctions, they are as
likely to serve the Devil without intending it, as God"; and
Everett C. Marm, the Harlequin, whose conscience forces him
to resist the oppressive state.
```

The reader will now expect a paragraph devoted to each of the three characters:

```
     Pretty Alice is, probably, very pretty. (Everett didn't
fall in love with her brains.) In the brief section in which
we meet her, we find her hopelessly ordinary in her attitudes.
She is upset that Marm finds it necessary to go about "annoy-
ing people." She finds him ridiculous and wishes only that he
would stay home, as other people do. Clearly, she has no
understanding of what Everett is struggling against. Though
her anger finally leads her to betray him, Everett himself
can't believe that she has done so. His own loyal and
understanding nature colors his view of her so thoroughly
that he cannot imagine the treachery that must have been so
simple and satisfying for Pretty Alice, whose only desire is
to be like everybody else.
     The Ticktockman is more complex. He sees himself as a
servant of the state, and he performs his duties with resolu-
tion and competence. He skillfully supports a System he has
never questioned. The System exists; it must be good. His
conscience is simply not involved in the performance of his
```

duty. He is one of those who follows orders and expects others to follow orders. As a result, the behavior of the Harlequin is more than just an irritant or a rebellion against
authority. It is unnerving. The Ticktockman wishes to understand that behavior, and with Everett's time-card in his
hand, he muses that he has the name of "<u>what</u> he is . . . not
<u>who</u> he is. . . . Before I can exercise proper revocation, I
have to know who this what is." And when he confronts Everett, he does not just liquidate him. He insists that Everett
repent. He tries to convince Everett that the System is
sound, and when he cannot win the argument, he dutifully re-
conditions Everett, since he is, after all, more interested
in justifying the System than in destroying its enemies. It
is easy to see this man as a competent servant of the devil
who thinks he is serving God.

But only Everett C. Marm truly serves the state, because
his conscience requires him to resist. He is certainly not
physically heroic. His very name suggests weak conformity.
Though he loves his Pretty Alice, he cannot resign from the
rebellious campaign on which his conscience insists. So,
without violence, and mainly with the weapon of laughter, he
attacks the mechanical precision of the System and succeeds
in breaking it down simply by making people late. He is himself, as Pretty Alice points out, always late, and the delays
that his antics produce seriously threaten the well-being of
the smooth but mindless System he hates. He is, of course,
captured. He refuses, even then, to submit and has his personality destroyed by the authorities that fear him. The
Ticktockman is too strong for him.

An appropriate ending emerges naturally from this student's treatment of the
assignment. Having established that the story presents characters who deal in
different ways with the oppressive quality of life in a time- and machine-obsessed
society, the student concludes with a comment on the author's criticisms of such
a society:

Harlequin is defeated, but Ellison, finally, leaves us
with an optimistic note. The idea of rebellion against the
System will linger in the minds of others. There will be more
Harlequins and more disruption of this System. Many rebels
will be defeated, but any System that suppresses individualism will give birth to resistance. And Harlequin's
defeat is by no means total. The story ends with the
Ticktockman himself arriving for work three minutes late.

Comparison and Contrast

An essay in comparison and contrast, showing how two works are similar to and different from one another, almost always starts with a recognition of similarities, most likely similarities of subject matter. While it is possible to compare *any* two works, the best comparison and contrast essays emerge from the analysis of two works similar enough to illuminate each other (most comparison and contrast assignments involve two works of the same genre). Two works about love, or death, or conformity, or innocence, or discovery give you something to begin with. But these are very large categories; two random poems about the same subject may be so dissimilar that a comparison and contrast essay about them would be very difficult. Both Shelley's "Ozymandias" and Randall Jarrell's "The Death of the Ball Turret Gunner" are about death; but they deal with the subject so differently that they would probably not yield a very interesting essay. On the other hand, not only are Dickinson's "Apparently with No Surprise" and Frost's "Design" both about death, but they both use remarkably similar events as the occasion for the poem. And starting with these similarities, you would soon find yourself noting the contrasts (in tone, for example, and theme) between nineteenth-century and twentieth-century views of the nature of God.

Before you begin writing your paper, you ought to have clearly in mind the points of comparison and contrast you wish to discuss and the order in which you can most effectively discuss them. You will need to give careful thought to the best way to organize your paper. As a general rule, it is best to avoid dividing the paper into separate discussions of each work. That method tends to produce two separate, loosely joined analysis essays. The successful comparison and contrast essay treats some point of similarity or contrast between the two works, then moves on to succeeding points, and ends with an evaluation of the comparative merits of the works.

Like analysis essays—indeed like any essay that goes beyond simple explication—comparison and contrast essays require theses. However, a comparison and contrast thesis is generally not difficult to formulate: you must identify the works under consideration and summarize briefly your reasons for making the comparison.

Here is a student paper that compares and contrasts a Dylan Thomas poem ("Do Not Go Gentle into That Good Night," explicated earlier in this discussion) with the poetic response it triggered from a poet with different views.

>   Dylan Thomas's "Do Not Go Gentle into That Good Night"
> and Catherine Davis's "After a Time" demand comparison:
> Davis's poem was written in deliberate response to Thomas's.
> Davis assumes the reader's familiarity with "Do Not Go
> Gentle," which she uses to articulate her contrasting ideas.
> "After a Time," although it is a literary work in its own
> right, might even be thought of as serious parody—perhaps
> the greatest compliment one writer can pay another.
>
>   "Do Not Go Gentle into That Good Night" was written by

a young man of thirty-eight who addresses it to his old and ailing father. It's interesting to note that the author himself had very little of his own self-destructive life left as he was composing this piece. Perhaps that is why he seems to have more insight into the subject of death than most people of his age. He advocates raging and fighting against it, not giving in and accepting it.

"After a Time" was written by a woman of about the same age and is addressed to no one in particular. Davis has a different philosophy about death. She "answers" Thomas's poem and presents her differing views using the same poetic form--a villanelle. Evidently, she felt it necessary to present a contrasting point of view eight years after Thomas's death.

While "Do Not Go Gentle" protests and rages against death, Davis's poem suggests a quiet resignation and acquiescence. She seems to feel that raging against death is useless and profitless. She argues that we will eventually become tame, anyway, after the raging is done. At the risk of sounding sexist, I think it interesting that the man rages and the woman submits, as if the traditionally perceived differences between the behavior of men and women are reflected in the poems.

Thomas talks about different types of men and why they rage against death. "Wise men" desire immortality. They rage against death occurring before they've made their mark on history. "Good men" lament the frailty of their deeds. Given more time, they might have accomplished great things. "Wild men" regret their constant hedonistic pursuits. With more time they could prove their worth. "Grave men" are quite the opposite and regret they never took time for the pleasures in life. Now it is too late. They rage against death because they are not ready for it.

His father's death is painful to Thomas because he sees himself lying in that bed; his father's dying reminds him of his own inevitable death. The passion of the last stanza, in which the poet asks his father to bless and curse him, suggests that he has doubts about his relationship with his father. He may feel that he has not been enough of a son. He put off doing things with and for his father because he always felt there would be time later. Now time has run out and he feels cheated. He's raging for his father now. He'll rage for himself later.

Catherine Davis advocates a calm submission, a peaceful acquiescence. She feels raging is useless and says that those of us who rage will finally "go tame / When what we have we can no longer use." When she says "One more thing lost is one thing less to lose," the reader can understand and come to terms with the loss of different aspects of the mind and body, such as strength, eyesight, hearing, and intellect. Once we've lost one of these, it's one thing less to worry about losing. After a time, everything will be lost, and we'll accept that, too, because we'll be ready for it.

In a contest of imagery, Thomas would certainly win the day. His various men not only rage and rave, they <u>burn</u>. Their words "forked no lightning," their deeds might have "danced in a green bay," they "sang the sun in flight," and they see that "blind eyes could blaze like meteors." Davis's images are quiet—generally abstract and without much sensory suggestiveness. She gives us "things lost," a "reassuring ruse," and "all losses are the same." Her most powerful image—"And we go stripped at last the way we came"—makes its point with none of the excitement of Thomas's rage. And yet, I prefer the quiet intelligence of Davis to the high energy of Thomas.

"And we go stripped at last the way we came" can give strange comfort and solace to those of us who always envied those in high places. Death is a great leveler. People are not all created equal at birth, not by a long shot. But we will bloody well all be equal when we make our final exit. Kings, popes, and heads of state will go just as "stripped" as the rest of us. They won't get to take anything with them. All wealth, power, and trappings will be left behind. We will all finally and ultimately be equal. So why rage? It won't do us any good.

Writing the Essay

If you have thought about an assignment sufficiently and reread the work you intend to write about with enough care to formulate a thesis, then you have already accomplished a major part of the task. You have, however loosely, constructed an argument and marshaled some of the evidence to support it. Now you must begin to be rigorous. Take notes. The most efficient method is to use three-by-five-inch index cards. Take one note per card, and use some key words at the top to identify the subject of the note. This procedure allows you to arrange your note cards in the most workable order when you are drafting your paper.

As you take your notes and then arrange the cards, you will begin to get some sense of the number of paragraphs you will need to support the thesis you have announced in the opening paragraph. Generally, each paragraph will focus on one major point (perhaps with its own mini-thesis), and bring together the evidence necessary to support that point.

As you write and rewrite, you should make sure that the progression of ideas from paragraph to paragraph is clear. To accomplish this, link each paragraph to the preceding one with a transitional word or phrase. Even the most carefully organized essay may seem abrupt or disjointed to the reader if you neglect to provide bridges between the paragraphs. A simple *however, nevertheless, further-more,* or *on the other hand* will often be adequate. Sometimes the entire opening sentence of a paragraph may provide the transition (and avoid the monotony of the standard words and phrases). Let us assume, for example, that you are writing an essay in which you argue that in Dylan Thomas's poem "Fern Hill" the mature speaker, now keenly aware of mortality, perceives the innocence of his childhood as a state of religious grace. In one or more paragraphs, you have analyzed the religious imagery of the poem, and you now begin a new paragraph with the sentence, "While the religious imagery dominates the poem, it is supported by a well-developed pattern of color imagery." Such a transitional sentence signals the reader that you will now consider another pattern of imagery that provides further evidence to support the thesis, because, as you will show, the color imagery is in fact a subpattern of the religious imagery.

Simply stated, in a tightly organized essay there ought to be a reason why one paragraph follows rather than precedes another. In fact, you can test the organization of your essay by asking yourself whether the paragraphs can be rearranged without significant effect. If they can be, chances are that your organization is weak, your ideas unclarified.

Having worked out an opening paragraph with a thesis and worked through the body of your essay to support the thesis, you now must confront the problem of how to conclude. Your conclusion should be brief, rarely more than three or four sentences. Ideally, it should leave the reader with a sense of both complete-ness and significance. For a short paper, it is unnecessary to restate or summarize your main points, because your reader will not have trouble remembering them. If your essay has been primarily appreciative and impressionistic, a general statement about the value of the work to you might bring the essay nicely to rest. Or you might conclude with a statement about the relevance of the work to the world in which we live. When you have said all you have to say, you have finished. Avoid the common error of turning the conclusion into a beginning by taking up new evidence or ideas in the final paragraph.

Exploring Fiction, Poetry, Drama, and the Essay

Here are a number of pertinent questions you might ask yourself when you are faced with the task of writing about literature. Your answers to these questions can help you overcome the awful whiteness of the empty page.

Fiction

1. From what point of view is the story told? Can you speculate on the appropriateness of that point of view? If a story is told from the point of view of a first-person narrator who participates in the action, what significant changes would occur if it were told from the point of view of an omniscient author? And, of course, vice versa. Note that first-person narrators do not know what other characters think. On the other hand, omniscient narrators know everything about the lives of the characters. How would the story you are writing about be changed if the viewpoint were changed?
2. What is the tone of the story? The first several paragraphs of the story establish that tone. Does the tone change with events, or remain fixed? How does the tone contribute to the effect of the story?
3. Who are the principal characters in the story? (There will rarely be more than three in a short story—the other characters will often be portrayed sketchily; sometimes they are even stereotypes.) What functions do the minor characters serve? Do any of the characters change during the course of the story? How, and why?
4. What is the plot of the story? Do the events that constitute the plot emerge logically from the nature of the characters and circumstances, or are the plot elements coincidental and arbitrary?
5. What is the setting of the story? Does the setting play an important role in the story, or is it simply the place where things happen? You might ask yourself what the consequences of some other setting might be for the effectiveness of the story.
6. What is the theme of the story? This, finally, is the most significant question to answer. All of the elements of fiction—point of view, tone, character, plot, setting—have been marshaled to project a theme—the moral proposition the author wishes to advance. When you write about fiction, or any literary form, you must resist the tendency to do the easiest thing—retell the plot, incident by incident. You must, instead, come to understand the artful devices the author uses to convey his or her theme, and, in your paper, reveal that understanding.

Poetry

1. Who is the speaker? What does the poem reveal about the speaker's character? In some poems the speaker may be nothing more than a voice meditating on a theme, while in others the speaker takes on a specific personality. For example, the speaker in Shelley's "Ozymandias" is a voice meditating on the transitoriness of all things; except for the views expressed in the poem, we know nothing about the speaker's character. The same might be said of the speaker in Hopkins's "Spring and Fall" but with this important exception: we know that he is older than Margaret and therefore has a wisdom she does not.
2. Is the speaker addressing a particular person? If so, who is that person, and why is the speaker interested in him or her? Many poems, like "Ozyman-

dias," are addressed to no one in particular and therefore to anyone, any reader. Others, such as Donne's "A Valediction: Forbidding Mourning," while addressed to a specific person, reveal nothing about that person because the focus of the poem is on the speaker's feelings and attitudes. In a *dramatic monologue* (see Glossary of Literary Terms), the speaker usually addresses a silent auditor. The identity of the auditor will be important to the poem.

3. Does the poem have a setting? Is the poem occasioned by a particular event? The answer to these questions will often be "no" for lyric poems, such as Frost's "Fire and Ice." It will always be "yes" if the poem is a dramatic monologue or a poem that tells or implies a story, such as Tennyson's "Ulysses" and Lowell's "Patterns."

4. Is the theme of the poem stated directly or indirectly? Some poems, such as Frost's "Provide, Provide" and Owen's "Dulce et Decorum Est," use language in a fairly straightforward and literal way and state the theme, often in the final lines. Others may conclude with a statement of the theme that is more difficult to apprehend because it is made with figurative language and symbols. This difference will be readily apparent if you compare the final lines of these Frost and Owen poems with, say, the final stanzas of Stevens's "Sunday Morning."

5. If the speaker is describing specific events, from what perspective (roughly similar to point of view in fiction) is he or she doing so? Is the speaker recounting events of the past or events that are occurring in the present? If past events are being recalled, what present meaning do they have for the speaker? These questions are particularly appropriate to the works in the section "Innocence and Experience," many of which contrast an early innocence with adult experience.

6. Does a close examination of the *figurative language* (see Glossary of Literary Terms) of the poem reveal any patterns? Yeats's "Sailing to Byzantium" may begin to open up to you once you recognize the pattern of bird imagery. Likewise, Thomas's attitude toward his childhood in "Fern Hill" will be clearer if you detect the pattern of biblical imagery that associates childhood with Adam and Eve before the fall.

7. What is the structure of the poem? Because narrative poems, those that tell stories, reveal a high degree of selectivity, it is useful to ask why the poet has focused on particular details and left out others. Analyzing the structure of a nonnarrative or lyric poem can be more difficult because it does not contain an obvious series of chronologically related events. The structure of Thomas's "Fern Hill," for example, is based in part on a description of perhaps a day and a half in the speaker's life as a child. But more significant in terms of its structure is the speaker's present realization that the immortality he felt as a child was merely a stage in the inexorable movement of life toward death. The structure of the poem, therefore, will be revealed through an analysis of patterns of images (biblical, color, day and night, dark and light) that embody the theme. To take another example, Marvell's "To His Coy Mistress" is divided into three verse paragraphs, the opening words of each ("Had

we . . . ," "But . . . ," "Now therefore . . . ,") suggesting a logically constructed argument.

8. What do sound and *meter* (see Glossary of Literary Terms) contribute to the poem? Alexander Pope said that in good poetry "the sound must seem an echo to the sense," a statement that is sometimes easier to agree with than to demonstrate. For sample analyses of the music of poetry, see the section on music in the appendix "Reading Poetry" (p. 778) and the discussion of "Dover Beach" under formalist criticism (p. 809) in "Three Critical Approaches."

9. What was your response to the poem on first reading? Did your response change after rereadings and study of the poem?

Drama

1. How does the play begin? Is the exposition presented dramatically through the interaction among characters, or novelistically through long, unrealistic, and unwieldy speeches that convey a lot of information, or through some device such as the reading of long letters or lengthy reports delivered by a messenger?

2. How does the information conveyed in exposition (which may occur at various moments throughout the play) establish the basis for dramatic irony— that is, the ironic response generated in an audience when it knows more than do the characters? For example, because we know that Iago is a villain in Shakespeare's *Othello*, we hear an ironic dimension in his speeches that the characters do not hear, and that irony is the source of much tension in the audience. An assessment of dramatic irony in a play makes an interesting and instructive writing assignment.

3. Who are the principal characters, and how are the distinctive qualities of each dramatically conveyed? Inevitably, there will be minor characters in a play. What function do they serve? A paper that thoughtfully assesses the role of minor characters can often succeed better than the attempt to analyze the major figures who may embody too much complexity to deal with in 1,000 words.

4. Where is the play set? Does it matter that it is set there? Why? Does the setting play some significant role in the drama, or is it merely a place, anyplace?

5. What is the central conflict in the play? How is it resolved? Do you need to know something of the historical circumstances out of which the play emerged, or something of the life of the author in order fully to appreciate the play? If so, how does that information enhance your understanding?

6. Since plays are usually written to be performed rather than read, what visual and auditory elements of the play are significant to your response? Obviously, if you are writing from a reading text, you will have to place yourself in the position of the director and the actors in order to respond to this aspect of drama.

7. What is the play's theme? How does the dramatic action embody that theme?

Note that any one of these questions might provoke an effective paper—one could do a thousand words on the settings of *Othello*, or the minor characters of *A Doll's House*, or the methods of exposition in *Oedipus Rex*. But each of those papers, to be successful, needs to relate the issues it deals with to the thematic force of the play. Plot summaries (except as a variety of note-taking) are unsatisfactory.

Essays

1. What is the author's thesis (or unifying idea)? What evidence or arguments does the author advance to support the thesis? Is the thesis convincing? If not, why not? Does the author rely on any basic but unstated assumptions?
2. What is the author's tone? Select for analysis a passage you consider illustrative of the author's tone. Does the author maintain that tone consistently throughout the essay?
3. How would you characterize the author's style? For example, are the syntax, length of sentences, and diction elevated and formal or familiar and informal?
4. What rhetorical strategies does the author use? For example, can you identify the effective use of classification, comparison and contrast, analogy, cause and effect, or definition? Note that one of these rhetorical strategies may constitute the unifying idea of the essay and the means of structuring it. Jessica Mitford's "The American Way of Death" is an essay in definition that effectively uses comparison and contrast and analogy.
5. What are the major divisions in the essay and how are they set off? Are the transitions between the divisions effective and easy to follow?
6. Analyze the author's opening paragraph. Is it effective in gaining the reader's attention? Does it clearly state the essay's thesis? If it does not, at what point does the author's thesis and purpose become clear?

A Final Word

Many questions may be asked about literature. Your assignment may require you to compare and contrast literary works, to analyze the language of a work, to discuss the interaction of parts of a work, to discuss the theme of a work. Sometimes the instructor may give you free choice and ask simply that you write an essay on one of the pieces you have read. This liberty will require that you create your own feasible boundaries—you will have to find a specific focus that suits the piece you choose and is manageable within a paper of the assigned length. But be sure that you do create boundaries—that, as we urged at the outset, you have a clear thesis.

Give yourself time. If you attempt to write your paper the night before it is due, you are unlikely to write a paper that is worth reading. Even professional writers rarely accomplish serious and thoughtful writing overnight. You must give yourself time to think before you write a draft. Let the draft age a bit before rewriting a final draft. If you do not allow yourself a reasonable time period, you will convert an assignment that has the potential to enlarge your understanding and to produce real pleasure into an obstacle that will surely trip you.

Consider also that, finally, you have to feel something, know something, bring something of yourself to the assignment. We can discuss formal methods for dealing with the problem of writing essays—but if you bring neither awareness, nor information, nor genuine interest to the task, the essay will remain an empty form.

Suggestions for Writing

Fiction

1. Explicate the opening paragraph or page of a story in order to demonstrate how it sets the tone and anticipates what is to follow.
2. Select a story that uses a central symbol or symbolic event and analyze its function. Some suggestions:
   A. The tree in White's "The Second Tree from the Corner."
   B. Iván's fall from the ladder in Tolstoy's "The Death of Iván Ilých."
   C. The quilt in Walker's "Everyday Use."
3. Select a story in which the narrative does not unfold chronologically and explain why.
4. Here are some suggestions for essays in comparison and contrast:
   A. Compare and contrast the idea of "the hero" in Crane's "The Bride Comes to Yellow Sky" and Thurber's "The Greatest Man in the World."
   B. Compare and contrast the significance of the religious experience of the central characters in the final paragraphs of Tolstoy's "The Death of Iván Ilých" and Porter's "The Jilting of Granny Weatherall."
   C. Compare and contrast the attitude toward sexuality in Chopin's "The Storm" and Shaw's "The Girls in Their Summer Dresses."
   D. Compare and contrast the marriages in Shaw's "The Girls in Their Summer Dresses" and Mason's "Shiloh."
5. Write an essay on an interesting story title.
6. Did the ending of any story you read violate your expectations? What led you to those expectations? Do you find the author's ending more satisfactory than the one you had anticipated?
7. Select a story you feel is weak, and explain why you feel so. You might consider the credibility of the plot or of a character's behavior.

Poetry

1. Select a short lyric poem you found difficult, and explicate it line by line. Conclude with a paragraph or two describing how the process of explication helped you to clarify the meaning of the poem.

2. Here is a list of poems about poets and poetry. Select two and compare and contrast their treatment of the subject.
Auden, "In Memory of W. B. Yeats"
Housman, "Terence, This Is Stupid Stuff"
MacLeish, "Ars Poetica"
Kennedy, "Ars Poetica"
Francis, "Pitcher"
Hamburger, "A Poet's Progress"
Wallace, "In a Spring Still Not Written Of"
Giovanni, "For Saundra"
Cruz, "Today Is a Day of Great Joy"

3. The poems listed below tell or imply a story. Select one, and write out the story in your own words. Use your imagination to fill in details.
Anonymous, "Bonny Barbara Allen"
Anonymous, "Edward"
Tennyson, "Ulysses"
Browning, "My Last Duchess"
Hardy, "The Ruined Maid"
Lowell, "Patterns"
Eliot, "The Love Song of J. Alfred Prufrock"
Owen, "Dulce et Decorum Est"
Wright, "Between the World and Me"

4. Analyze a poem in which the author uses a particular kind of diction. Identify the pattern, and explain how it functions in the poem. Some suggestions:
   A. The language of bureaucracy in Auden's "The Unknown Citizen" or Baker's "Formal Application."
   B. Contrasting patterns of diction in Reed's "Naming of Parts."
   C. Colloquial and formal diction in Hughes's "Same in Blues."
   D. Prosaic diction in Forchés "The Colonel" or Locklin's, "the best year of her life."
   E. Colloquial diction in Kizer's "Bitch."

5. As an exercise to illuminate the importance of connotation, select a poem that you like, identify some of its key words, and then consult a dictionary or thesaurus for synonyms of those key words. Reread the poem, substituting the synonyms for the words the poet used (for purposes of this exercise, ignore the fact that the synonyms may have more or fewer syllables and thus alter the rhythm). Write an essay analyzing the effects of your substitutions. Provide a sample of the rewritten poem.

6. Select one of the following titles for an essay in comparison and contrast.
   A. The Cost of Conformity: Dickinson's "What Soft—Cherubic Creatures" and Cummings's "the Cambridge ladies who live in furnished souls."
   B. The Psychology of Hate: Blake's "A Poison Tree" and Dickinson's "Mine Enemy Is Growing Old."
   C. The Meaning of Love: Marvell's "To His Coy Mistress" and Donne's "A Valediction: Forbidding Mourning."

   D. The Images of Love: Shakespeare's Sonnet 130 and Millay's "Love Is Not All."
   E. In Praise of a Beloved: Shakespeare's Sonnet 130 and Roethke's "I Knew a Woman."
   F. Remembering Childhood: Frost's "Birches" and Thomas's "Fern Hill."
   G. What the Young Can Never Understand: Hopkins's "Spring and Fall" and Wallace's "In a Spring Still Not Written Of."
   H. The Meaning of Nature: Dickinson's "Apparently with No Surprise" and Frost's "Design."
   I. The Meaning of Old Age: Housman's "To an Athlete Dying Young" and Yeats's "Sailing to Byzantium."
   J. Untimely Death: Housman's "To an Athlete Dying Young" and Roethke's "Elegy for Jane."
   K. The Attitude toward Death: Stevens's "Sunday Morning" and Thomas's "Do Not Go Gentle into That Good Night."
7. Analyze the allusions in a poem. Include in your discussion an explanation of the allusion and what it contributes to the poem. Some suggestions:
   Eliot's "The Love Song of J. Alfred Prufrock"
   Auden's "The Unknown Citizen"
   Frost's "Provide, Provide"
   Reid's "Curiosity"
   Wordsworth's "The World Is Too Much with Us"
   Cummings's "the Cambridge ladies who live in furnished souls"
   Arnold's "Dover Beach"
   Plath's "Daddy"
   Yeats's "Sailing to Byzantium"
   Frost's " 'Out, Out—' "
8. Analyze the use of irony in a poem. Some suggestions:
   Blake's "The Chimney Sweeper"
   Browning's "My Last Duchess"
   Hardy's "The Ruined Maid"
   Robinson's "Richard Cory"
   Frost's " 'Out, Out—' "
   Swenson's "Women"
   Bishop's "One Art"
9. Analyze the use of one form of figurative language in a poem. Some suggestions:
   A. Hyperbole in Burns's "A Red, Red Rose" or Marvell's "To His Coy Mistress."
   B. Simile and metaphor in Donne's "A Valediction: Forbidding Mourning," Marvell's "To His Coy Mistress," Burns's "A Red, Red Rose," Keats's "On First Looking into Chapman's Homer," Shakespeare's Sonnets 18 and 130, or MacLeish's "Ars Poetica."
   C. Symbols in Waller's "Go Lovely Rose!" Blake's "The Tyger," Frost's "Fire and Ice," Lowell's "Patterns," Reid's "Curiosity," or Meinke's "Advice to My Son."

   D. Paradox in Wallace's "In a Spring Still Not Written Of," Meinke's "Advice to My Son," Yeats's "Easter 1916," Blake's "The Tyger," Stevens's "Sunday Morning," or Donne's "Death, Be Not Proud."
10. Look carefully at the reproduction of Brueghel's painting *The Fall of Icarus* (p. 694) and jot down your impression of it. Include a sentence or two on the "statement" you think Brueghel is making. Now read Auden's poem "Musée des Beaux Arts." In an essay, compare your impressions of the painting with those of the poet. If the poem taught you something about the painting, include that in your essay.

Drama

1. Explicate the opening scene of a play in order to demonstrate how the dramatist lays the groundwork for what is to follow. Some questions you might consider: What information necessary to understanding the action are we given? What do we learn about the characters and their relationships? Do settings and costumes contribute to the exposition?
2. Analyze a play in order to show how nonverbal elements, such as costumes and stage sets, contribute to the theme.
3. Select a minor character in a play and analyze that character's function. Some possibilities: Roderigo in *Othello*; Dr. Rank in *A Doll's House*; Bieberman in *Steambath*.
4. Analyze the language of a play for patterns of imagery that contribute to the development of character, mood, or theme. Some suggestions: images of bestial sexuality in Shakespeare's *Othello*; images of blindness and seeing in Sophocles' *Oedipus Rex*; images used by Helmer to express his affection for Nora in Ibsen's *A Doll's House*.
5. Assume you are the director of one of the plays in this anthology. For one of the major characters, write a set of director's notes intended for the actor playing the role, in which you describe your conception of how the role should be played.
6. In an essay, describe the playwright's method for achieving dramatic irony in one of the plays you have read.
7. When you attend a performance of a play, you are usually given a program indicating, among other things, the number of acts, the elapsed time between acts, the time and place of the action. It will not include the stage directions of the printed version of the play. Examine the stage directions of a play and suggest how a director might convey in a performance what the dramatist describes in the stage directions.
8. If you have the opportunity to see the film version of any of the works in this anthology, write an essay evaluating the success or failure of the film adaptation. Some suggestions:
   A. What did the film adaptation omit? Can you suggest why?
   B. What did the film adaptation add? Can you suggest why?

C. Melville's "Bartleby the Scrivener" is a first-person narration. How does the film director deal with the problem of the narrative voice?
D. Write an essay on the general problems of transposing a story into a film.

Essays

1. Carefully analyze the first paragraph or two of an essay in order to demonstrate how it sets the tone and attracts the reader's attention. Look for unusual language, imagery, prose rhythm, and notable sentence structure as evidence to support your assertions.
2. Select an essay that uses a central symbol or symbolic event and analyze its function. Some suggestions:
   A. Shooting the elephant in Orwell's essay.
   B. The Iks in Thomas's essay.
   C. The tolling bell in Donne's "Meditation XVII."
   D. Las Vegas wedding chapels in Didion's "Marrying Absurd."
   E. The plate in Selzer's "The Discus Thrower."
3. Here are some suggestions for studies in comparison and contrast:
   A. Compare and contrast the attitude toward political power in Orwell's "Shooting an Elephant" and Rich's "What Does a Woman Need to Know?"
   B. Compare and contrast the experience of minorities as revealed in Baldwin's "Rage" and King's "Letter from Birmingham Jail."
   C. Compare and contrast the satirical methods of Swift in "A Modest Proposal" and Thomas in "The Iks."
   D. Compare and contrast the prose style of Didion's "Marrying Absurd" and Woolf's "What If Shakespeare Had Had a Sister?"
4. Select an essay you particularly like and create a set of notes in which you systematically convert the original to brief study aids. After a few days, try to recreate the essay, or a portion of it, from your notes. Compare your effort with the original and write an analysis of the differences.
5. Discover, describe, and analyze the unspoken assumptions on which an author depends. Some suggestions:
   A. The sacredness of life in Swift's "A Modest Proposal."
   B. The solemnity of marriage in Didion's "Marrying Absurd."
   C. The survival of the soul in Donne's "Meditation XVII."
   D. The nature of power in Orwell's "Shooting an Elephant."
   E. The right to equal justice in King's "Letter from Birmingham Jail."
   F. Deathbed promises in Twain's "Lost in the Snow."
   G. Tension between the sexes in Thurber's "Courtship among the Animals."
   H. The proper response to death in Mitford's "The American Way of Death."
   I. The rights of animals in Goodall's "A Plea for the Chimps."

And one final general question: One of the commonly accepted notions of art is that it helps us to clarify our own feelings, to give us in vivid and memorable form what we had perhaps felt or thought only vaguely. Select a work (one that you found especially relevant to your own life), and describe how it clarified your own feelings.

Some Matters of Form

Titles

The first word and all main words of titles are capitalized. Ordinarily (unless they are the first or last word), articles (*a, an,* and *the*), prepositions (*in, on, of, with, about,* etc.), and conjunctions (*and, but, or,* etc.) are not capitalized.

The titles of parts of larger collections, short stories, poems, articles, essays, and songs are enclosed in quotation marks.

The titles of plays, books, movies, periodicals, operas, paintings, and newspapers are italicized. In typed and handwritten manuscripts, italics are represented by underlining.

The title you give your own essay is neither placed in quotation marks nor underlined. However, a quotation used as a part of your title would be enclosed in quotation marks (see the following section on quotations). Similarly, the title of a literary work used as a part of your title would be either placed in quotation marks or underlined, depending on the type of work it is.

Quotations

Quotation marks indicate you are transcribing someone else's words; those words must, therefore, be *exactly* as they appear in your source. (See the next section, "Documentation," for guidelines on identifying the source of a quotation.)

As a general rule, quotations of not more than four lines of prose or two lines of poetry are placed between quotation marks and incorporated in your own text:

```
At the climactic moment, Robin observes "an uncovered cart.
There the torches blazed the brightest, there the moon shone
out like day, and there, in tar-and-feathery dignity, sat his
kinsman, Major Molineux!"
```

If you are quoting two lines of verse in your text, indicate the division between lines with a slash. Leave a space before and after the slash:

```
Prufrock hears the dilletantish talk in a room where "the
women come and go / Talking of Michelangelo."
```

Longer quotations are indented ten typewriter spaces and are double-spaced. They are not enclosed in quotation marks, since the indentation signals a quotation.

As noted above, anything quoted, whether enclosed in quotation marks or indented, must be reproduced exactly. If you insert anything—even a word—the inserted material must be placed within brackets. If you wish to omit some material from a passage in quotation marks, the omission (ellipsis) must be indicated by three spaced periods: . . . (an ellipsis mark). When an ellipsis occurs between complete sentences or at the end of a sentence, a fourth period, indicating the end of the sentence, should be inserted. No space precedes the first period.

Full quotation from original:

```
As one critic puts it, "Richard Wright, like Dostoevsky
before him, sends his hero underground to discover the truth
about the upper world, a world that has forced him to confess
to a crime he has not committed."
```

With insertion and omissions:

```
As one critic puts it, "Richard Wright . . . sends his hero
[Fred Daniels] underground to discover the truth about the
upper world. . . ."
```

Use a line of spaced periods the length of the longest line of the poem to indicate the omission of a line or more of poetry:

```
For I have known them all already, known them all—
Have known the evenings, mornings, afternoons,
I have measured out my life with coffee spoons;
.  .  .  .  .  .  .  .  .  .  .  .  .  .  .  .  .  .  .  .  .  .  .
And I have known the eyes already, known them all—
The eyes that fix you in a formulated phrase.
```

Periods and commas are placed *inside* quotation marks:

```
In "My Oedipus Complex," the narrator says, "The war was the
most peaceful period of my life."
```

Other punctuation marks go outside the quotation marks unless they are part of the material being quoted.

For poetry quotations, provide the line number or numbers in parentheses immediately following the quotation:

```
With ironic detachment, Prufrock declares that he is "no
prophet" (1. 83).
```

Documentation

You must acknowledge the source of ideas you paraphrase and material you quote. Such acknowledgments are extremely important, for even an unintentional failure to give formal credit to others for their words or ideas can leave you open to an accusation of plagiarism—that is, the presentation of someone else's ideas as your own.

If you use published works as you prepare your paper, you should list those sources as the last page of your essay. Then, in the body of your essay, you will use parenthetical citations that refer to the works you quote or paraphrase. Here is a sample list of works cited that illustrates the mechanical form for different kinds of sources. These samples will probably satisfy your needs, but if you use kinds of sources not listed here, you should consult Joseph Gibaldi and Walter S. Achtert, *MLA Handbook for Writers of Research Papers*, 3rd ed. (New York: Modern Language Association, 1988). That handbook provides sample entries for every imaginable source.

Works Cited

Abcarian, Richard, and Marvin Klotz, eds. Literature: The Human Experience. 5th ed. New York: St. Martin's, 1989.

Cooper, Wendy. Hair, Sex, Society, Symbolism. New York: Stein, 1971.

Fiedler, Leslie. "Come Back to the Raft Ag'in, Huck Honey." Partisan Review 15 (1948): 664:71.

Joyce, James. "Araby." Literature: The Human Experience. 5th ed. Ed. Richard Abcarian and Marvin Klotz. New York: St. Martin's, 1989. 51–55.

———. Dubliners. Ed. Robert Scholes and A. Walton Litz. New York: Penguin, 1976.

The first of these citations is this book. You would use it if you used materials from the editors' introduction or critical appendices. The entry illustrates the form for citing a book with two editors. Note that the first editor's name is presented surname first, but the second is presented with the surname last.

The second entry illustrates the form for citing a book with one author. The third gives the form for an article published in a journal (note that the title of the article is in quotes and the title of the journal is underlined). The fourth entry shows how to cite a work included in an anthology. The fifth citation, because it is by the same author as the fourth, begins with three hyphens in place of the author's name.

The following paragraph demonstrates the use of parenthetical citations.

Leslie Fiedler's controversial view of the relationship between Jim and Huck (669–70) uses a method often discussed by other critics (Abcarian and Klotz 1264–65). Cooper's 1971

study (180) raises similar issues, but such methods are not
useful when one deals with such a line as "North Richmond
Street, being blind, was a quiet street except at the hour
when the Christian Brothers' School set the boys free"
(Joyce, "Araby" 51). But when Joyce refers to the weather
(Dubliners 224), the issue becomes clouded.

This rather whimsical paragraph illustrates the form your parenthetical citations should take. The first citation gives only the page reference, which is all
that is necessary because the author's name is given in the text and only one work
by that author appears in the list of works cited.

The second citation gives the editors' names and thus identifies the work being
cited. It then indicates the appropriate pages.

The third citation, because the author's name is mentioned in the text, gives
only a page reference.

The fourth citation must provide the author's name *and* the work cited,
because two works by the same author appear in the bibliography.

The last citation, because it refers to an author with two works in the list of
works cited, gives the name of the work and the page where the reference can be
found.

In short, your parenthetical acknowledgment should contain (1) the *minimum*
information required to lead the reader to the appropriate work in the list of
works cited and (2) the location within the work to which you refer.

Rather than parenthetical references, some instructors may prefer notes (end-
notes, which appear in a list of *Notes* at the end of the paper, or footnotes, which
appear on the same text page as the references they identify). Here is the same
paragraph documented with notes, followed by the corresponding list of end-
notes.

Leslie Fiedler's controversial view of the relationship
between Jim and Huck[1] uses a method often discussed by other
critics.[2] Cooper's 1971 study[3] raises similar issues, but
such methods are not useful when one deals with such a line
as "North Richmond Street, being blind, was a quiet street
except at the hour when the Christian Brothers' School set
the boys free."[4] But when Joyce refers to the weather,[5] the
issue becomes clouded.

Notes

[1] Leslie Fiedler, "Come back to the Raft Ag'in, Huck Honey," *Partisan Review* 15 (1948): 664–71.

[2] Richard Abcarian and Marvin Klotz, eds., *Literature:
The Human Experience*, 5th ed. (New York: St. Martin's, 1989)
1264–65.

³ Wendy Cooper, *Hair, Sex, Society, Symbolism* (New York: Stein, 1971) 180.

⁴ James Joyce, "Araby," *Literature: The Human Experience,* 5th ed., ed. Richard Abcarian and Marvin Klotz (New York: St. Martin's, 1989) 67.

⁵ James Joyce, *Dubliners,* ed. Robert Scholes and A. Walton Litz (New York: Penguin, 1976) 224.

Note that complete information for a source is given the first time it appears in a note. Subsequent references to a work generally require only the surname of the author (or authors, editor, or editors), short title if more than one work by an author is cited, and the page number; thus:

⁶ Cooper 175.

⁷ Joyce, "Araby" 52.

If you need to find a model for a different kind of source, don't despair. Simply refer to the *MLA Handbook* (1988).

The main thing to remember about citations is that the object is to give credit to others wherever it is due and to enable your reader to go directly to your sources, if he or she wishes to do so, as quickly and easily as possible.

Summing Up: A Checklist

1. Start early. You're going to need time for thinking, time for reading and taking notes, time for writing, and (very important) time for breaks between steps.

2. Read the work carefully, and more than once.

3. If you are allowed to choose a topic, choose one that interests you and that you can explore in some depth in a paper of the assigned length. If you have trouble finding a topic, ask yourself as many questions as you can about the work: *What* is it about? *Who* is it about? *Why* do I respond to it as I do? And so forth. Many kinds of questions have been suggested in the preceding pages, and there are numerous questions following the selections and at the ends of the four main sections in this anthology.

4. Convert your topic into a clearly defined thesis, a proposition you intend to argue for and support with evidence from the work. If you have trouble shaping a thesis, try the technique of freewriting—forget about form and just scribble down all your thoughts and opinions: what you like, what you don't like, anything at all. Then ask yourself what made you think or feel as you do.

5. Once you have a thesis, reread the work and take careful notes on three-by-five-inch cards, one note to a card, with a page (or, for poetry, line) reference and a short descriptive heading to remind you of the note's significance. Then arrange the cards in the order that seems appropriate to follow in your essay.

6. Start writing, and keep going. This is a rough draft—essentially a blueprint—and is for your eyes only, so don't worry about formalities and polishing. The point is to get your ideas down on paper in approximately the right order. If making a rough outline first will help you, do it. If spontaneous writing works better, do that. But do get a clear statement of your thesis into your first paragraph; it will guide you as you write, since everything you write will (or should) be related to it.

7. Take a break. Let the rough draft cool for at least a few hours, preferably overnight. When you come back to it, you'll be refreshed and you'll think more clearly. You may find that you want to do some reorganizing or add or delete material. You may also want to go back and reread or at least take another look at the work you're writing about.

8. Now, more carefully, working from your rough draft, write a second draft. This will be fuller, clearer, more polished. You'll have a chance to revise (assuming you followed step 1, above), so don't get unnecessarily bogged down; but write this version *as if* it were the version your reader will see. This version, when finished, should be logically and clearly organized. The point of each paragraph should be clear—well expressed and well supported by details or examples—and its relationship to the thesis should be apparent. Transitions between paragraphs should be supplied wherever necessary to make the argument progress smoothly. Quotations should be in place and accurately transcribed.

9. Take a break. This time allow the draft to age for two or three days. At the moment, you're too close to the draft to read it objectively.

10. Pick up the draft as if you were the reader and had never seen it before. Now you will make your final revisions. More than polishing is involved here. This is the time to cut out, mercilessly, things that are not pertinent to your discussion, no matter how interesting or well written they may be. Putting yourself in your reader's place, clarify anything that is vague or ambiguous. Make sure each word is the most precise one you could have chosen for your purpose. Watch, too, for overkill—points that are driven into the ground by too much discussion or detail. Finally, no matter how careful you think you have been, check all your quotations and citations for accuracy. Instructors—rightly—take these things seriously.

11. Type or neatly write out in ink the final copy for submission to your instructor, taking care to follow any special instructions about format that you have been given. Don't rush; be meticulous. When you have finished,

proofread the final copy very carefully, keeping an eye out for errors in spelling or punctuation, omitted words, disagreement between subjects and verbs or between pronouns and antecedents, and other flaws (such as typographical errors) that will detract from what you have worked so hard to write.

Biographical Notes on the Authors

Samuel Allen (b. 1917)   Born in Columbus, Ohio, the son of a member of the clergy, Allen attended Fisk University and graduated from Harvard Law School in 1941. He spent a year as deputy assistant district attorney in New York City, had his own private law practice, and held an assortment of posts including assistant deputy counsel for the U.S. Information Agency (1961–1964). Previously a professor of law (Texas Southern University) and humanities (Tuskegee Institute), Allen joined the English department of Boston University in 1971, the same year he won the National Endowment for the Arts award for poetry. Allen's translations, essays, and poems have appeared in scores of anthologies and journals, including *Presence Africaine* and *Journal of Afro-American Studies*, often under the pen name Paul Vesey.

Matthew Arnold (1822–1888)   Born in Middlesex, England, Arnold attended Rugby School (where his father was headmaster) and studied classics at Oxford. Following his graduation in 1844, he became a fellow at Oxford and a master at Rugby School. In 1851, he was appointed inspector of schools in England and was sent by the government to observe educational systems in Europe. He remained in that post for some thirty-five years. As a poet, Arnold took inspiration from Greek tragedies, Keats, and Wordsworth. His collections include *Empedocles on Etna and Other Poems* (1852). An eminent social and literary critic in his later years, Arnold lectured in the United States in 1883 and 1886. His essay "The Function of Criticism" sheds light on his transition from poet to critic. Much of his work is collected in *Complete Prose Works* (11 volumes, 1960–1977).

W. H. Auden (1907–1973)   A poet, playwright, translator, librettist, critic, and editor, Wystan Hugh Auden was born in York, son of a medical officer and a nurse. He attended Oxford from 1925 to 1928, then taught, traveled, and moved from faculty to faculty of several universities in the United States (where he became a naturalized citizen in 1946). He won the Pulitzer Prize in 1948 for his collection *The Age of Anxiety: A Baroque Eclogue*, an expression he coined to describe the 1930s. While his early writing exhibited Marxist sympathies and reflected the excitement of new Freudian psychoanalytic thought, he later embraced Christianity and produced sharply honed verse in the rhyme and meter of traditional forms.

Donald W. Baker (b. 1923)   Born in Boston, son of a cabdriver, Baker earned a Ph.D. in 1955 from Brown University, where he taught English from 1948 to 1953. He joined the faculty of Wabash College in Crawfordsville, Indiana, in 1953, served six years as the director of drama, and was named poet-in-residence in 1964. Married in 1945 and the father of two, Baker has enjoyed giving readings and workshops. However, he is no stranger to writer's block and wryly admits: "I'm not prolific and have a lot of trouble producing anything at all."

James Baldwin (1924–1987)   Born in New York City, the son of a Harlem minister, Baldwin began preaching as a young teenager. Some years later, he experienced a religious crisis, left the church, and moved to New York City's bohemian Greenwich Village, where he began his career as a writer, supporting himself with menial jobs and publishing occasional articles in journals such as the *Nation* and *Commentary*.By the end of the 1940s, Baldwin's anger over the treatment of African-Americans led him into exile in France. There, Baldwin completed his acclaimed first novel, *Go Tell It on the Mountain* (1953), a work in which he drew heavily on his own childhood to depict the lives of members of a Harlem church, focusing on a minister's son. His next work, *Notes of a Native Son* (1955), a collection of personal, literary, and social essays, secured Baldwin's reputation as a major American writer. Two later collections of essays, *Nobody Knows My Name* (1961) and *The Fire Next Time* (1963), established Baldwin as one of the most powerful voices of the turbulent civil rights movement of the 1960s. But as riots, bombings, and other violence grew more frequent, Baldwin grew increasingly pessimistic over the prospect that white America could ever overcome its racism. That pessimism was deepened by two traumatic events: the 1964 bombing of the Sixteenth Avenue Baptist Church in Birmingham, Alabama, that killed four young girls attending a Sunday school class and the assassination of the Reverend Martin Luther King, Jr., in 1968. Baldwin began making periodic trips to France, settling there permanently in 1974.

Toni Cade Bambara (b. 1939)   Born in New York City, Bambara was educated there and in Italy and Paris. Early in her career she worked as an investigator for the New York State Department of Social Welfare but has devoted herself for many years to teaching and writing. One of the best representatives of a group of African-American writers who emerged in the 1960s, Bambara has been a consistent civil rights activist, both politically and culturally involved in African-American life. Much of her writing focuses on African-American women, particularly as they confront experiences that force them to new awareness. She is the author of three collections of short stories, *Gorilla, My Love* (1972), *Tales and Stories for Black Folks* (1971), and *The Sea Birds Are Still Alive: Collected Stories* (1977), and two novels, *The Salt Eaters* (1980) and *If Blessing Comes* (1987). She is also editor of *The Black Woman: An Anthology* (1970).

Donald Barthelme (1931–1989)   Born in Philadelphia and raised in Texas, Barthelme wrote poetry, essays, and reviews for his high school and college papers before turning to short fiction. His first stories appeared in the *New Yorker*, where he continued to publish. His first collection of stories, *Come Back, Doctor Caligari* (1964) brought him immediate critical fame; popular fame followed with his novel *Snow White* (1967). Barthelme's early reputation as an experimentalist and technical innovator was enhanced by *City Life* (1970), a collection of short stories. Although some Barthelme detractors have called his fiction "nonsensical," "absurd," and "deranged," the publication of *Sixty Stories* (1981) led to a surge of critical interest that secured his reputation as a major writer. He was the recipient of a Guggenheim Fellowship (1966), and *The Slightly Irregular Fire Engine* won the 1971 National Book Award for Children's Literature.

Elizabeth Bishop (1911–1979)   Bishop was born in Worcester, Massachusetts. Her father died before she was a year old; four years later, when her mother suffered a mental breakdown, Bishop was taken to live with her grandmother in Nova Scotia. Although her mother lived until 1934, Bishop saw her for the last time in 1916, a visit recalled in one of her rare autobiographical stories, "In the Village." Bishop planned to enter Cornell Medical School after graduating from Vassar, but was persuaded by poet Marianne Moore to become a writer. For the next fifteen years, she was a virtual nomad, traveling in Canada, Europe, and North and South America. In 1951, she finally settled in Rio de Janeiro, where she lived for almost twenty years. During the final decade of her life, Bishop continued to travel, but she resumed living in the United States and taught frequently at Harvard. She was an austere writer, publishing only four slim volumes of poetry: *North and South* (1946); *A Cold Spring* (1955), which won the Pulitzer Prize; *Questions of Travel* (1965), and *Geography III* (1976), which won the National Book Critics' Circle Award. *The Complete Poems 1927–1979* was published after her death, as was a collection of her prose. Despite her modest output, she has earned an enduring place of respect among twentieth-century poets.

William Blake (1757–1827)   Born in London to an obscure family, Blake was educated at home until he was ten, then enrolled in a drawing school, advancing ultimately to a formal apprenticeship as an engraver. At an early age, Blake exhibited talent as both an artist and a poet, and throughout his life read widely among modern philosophers and poets. During most of his life, he experienced mystical visions that provided him with the inspiration for many of his poems. Blake devised a process he called illuminated printing, which involved the preparation of drawings and decorative frames to complement his poems. He published *Songs of Innocence* (1789) and *Songs of Experience* (1794) in this fashion. These books, as well as the many subsequent works he wrote and illustrated, earned him a reputation as one of the most important artists of his day. Many of Blake's works assert his conviction that the established church and state hinder rather than nurture human freedom and the sense of divine love.

Louise Bogan (1897–1970)   Bogan was born in Livermore Falls, Maine, attended Girls' Latin School in Boston (1910–1915), and spent one year at Boston University. After her husband's death in 1920, she spent time in Vienna and published her first collection of poems, *Body of This Death* (1923). She was visiting professor at the University of Washington (1948) and Brandeis University (1964–1965), as well as a frequent contributor to the *New Yorker* (1931–1968). Bogan's concise and emotionally restrained poems resemble Emily Dickinson's. Her poems are collected in *The Blue Estuaries* (1968). Her sharp wit is revealed in a 1973 collection of correspondence, *What the Woman Lived: Selected Letters 1920–1970*, and in her collection of critical essays, *A Poet's Alphabet: Reflections on the Literary Art and Vocation* (1970). Bogan's honors include two Guggenheim Fellowships and the 1955 Bollingen Prize.

Jorge Luis Borges (1899–1986)   Borges was born in Buenos Aires, Argentina, to a middle-class family that spoke both Spanish and English at home. His love of literature began early, encouraged by a father who had himself aspired to a writing career. As a young man, Borges traveled and studied in Europe, where he published reviews, essays, and poetry. When he returned to Buenos Aires in 1921, he became a well-known exponent of experimental writing. However, he remained relatively unknown outside Argentina until he received an important international literary prize in 1961, the Prix Formentor. The fame that came with the prize led to the simultaneous publication in six countries of a collection of short stories, *Fictions* (1945), and to the first of his many lecture tours in the United States. Borges created much of his best-known fiction during his later years, when failing eyesight (eventually resulting in blindness) and poor health made him a semi-invalid. By the time of his death, his prolific and innovative writing had earned him a reputation and influence that extended far beyond his native Argentina.

Edwin Brock (b. 1927)   Born in London, Brock served two years in the Royal Navy. He was a police officer when he completed his first poetry collection, *An Attempt at Exorcism* (1959). Influenced by American confessional poets, Brock writes about family relationships, childhood memories, and sometimes shifts into the linguistic mode of an advertising copywriter (which he became in 1959). Suggesting that all poetry is to some extent autobiographical, Brock argues "that most activity is an attempt to define oneself in one way or another: for me poetry, and only poetry, has provided this self-defining act." His works include over a dozen poetry collections; a novel, *The Little White God* (1962); and an autobiography, *Here. Now. Always.* (1977).

Gwendolyn Brooks (b. 1917)   Brooks was born in Topeka, Kansas, attended public schools in Chicago, and graduated from Wilson Junior College in 1936. Her poetic talent was recognized when she attended a poetry workshop at Chicago's Southside Community Art Center. Shortly after, she published her first book of poems, *A Street in Bronzeville* (1945). She soon established her reputation as a major poet and won many honors, including the Pulitzer Prize for poetry in 1950. No African-American woman before her had ever achieved such critical acclaim as a poet. While her poetry has always focused on the hardships and joys of being poor and black in America, she steadily moved away from the apolitical integrationist views of her early years until, by the 1960s, she had become a passionate advocate of African-American consciousness and activism. Besides reworking traditional forms such as the ballad and sonnet, Brooks achieves great power in many of her poems by juxtaposing formal speech with black vernacular. Among her other works are *Annie Allen* (1949), *The Bean Eaters* (1960), *In the Mecca* (1968), and *To Disembark* (1981).

Robert Browning (1812–1889)   Born in London, Browning attended a private school and was later tutored at home. After one year as a student of Greek at the University of London, he moved with his family to Hatcham, where he studied, wrote poetry, and practiced writing for the theater. In 1845, he began exchanging poems and letters with the already famous poet Elizabeth Barrett; they eloped in 1846. They moved to Italy, where Browning completed most of his work. When Elizabeth died in 1861, he returned to England and began to establish his own reputation. He is noted especially for his fine dramatic monologues in which a wide range of characters reveals the complexity of human belief and passion. His many volumes of poetry include *Dramatis Personae* (1864) and *The Ring and the Book* (1868–1869).

Robert Burns (1759–1796)   Born in Scotland to a family of poor tenant farmers, Burns was working in the fields with his father by age twelve. During these early years, the family moved often in fruitless attempts to improve its lot. Although Burns received formal education only intermittently, he read widely on his own. After the death of his father, Burns and his brother worked vainly to make their farm pay, an effort Burns was able to abandon when his first volume of poetry, *Poems, Chiefly in the Scottish Dialect* (1786) brought him overnight fame. One result of this fame was his appointment as an excise officer, a position that gave him some financial security while he continued to write poetry. Burns's humble origins instilled in him a lifelong sympathy for the poor and downtrodden, the rebels and iconoclasts, as well as a disdain for religion, particularly Calvinism and what he considered the hypocrisy of its "devout" ministers.

George Gordon, Lord Byron (1788–1824)   Born in London of an aristocratic family, Byron was educated at the best grammar schools and at Cambridge. He early became a public figure, as much for the notoriety of his personal life as for the popularity of his irreverent, satiric poetry. Among his scandalous affairs, the one he was rumored to have had with his half-sister forced him into European exile in 1816. His political life was equally flamboyant: he began his career in the House of Lords with a speech defending the working classes, and he met his death in Greece as the result of a fever he contracted while fighting for Greek independence. Byron published a volume of poetry while at Cambridge, but fame and popularity came with later volumes of poems, notably *Childe Harold's Pilgrimage* (1812–1818) and *Don Juan* (1819–1824). Despite Byron's acknowledged literary greatness and popularity, he was deemed morally unfit for burial in Westminster Abbey.

Thomas Campion (1567–1620)   Campion spent his early childhood in London, studied at Cambridge, then returned to London in 1586 to study law. It appears that Campion served, for a short time, as a soldier in France. In 1595, he published a collection of Latin poems, *Poemata*. After the publication of this volume, he apparently went abroad to study medicine and, later, music (though it is not known when or where). His first volume of English poems, *A Book of Ayres*, appeared in 1601; the other three volumes appeared between 1601 and 1617. Campion also wrote masques for presentation at court, often composing the music for his own lyrics. Toward the end of his life, he wrote a treatise on music that became a standard text.

Kate Chopin (1851–1904)   Born Kate O'Flaherty in St. Louis, Missouri, Chopin was raised by her mother, grandmother, and great-grandmother, all widows, after her father's death when she was four. In 1870, following her graduation from Sacred Heart Convent, she married Oscar Chopin and moved to New Orleans, where she became a housewife and mother (she had six children). Upon her husband's death in 1882, she returned to her mother's home in St. Louis and began her career as a writer. Her first novel, *At Fault* (1890), and her stories, collected in *Bayou Folk* (1894) and *A Night in Acadie* (1897), gained her a reputation as a vivid chronicler of the lives of Creoles and Acadians ("Cajuns") in Louisiana. Many of these stories explore a female protagonist's attempts to achieve self-fulfillment. Her novel *The Awakening* (1899) is probably her most ambitious exploration of this theme. It is the story of a woman whose awakening to her passion and inner self leads her to adultery and suicide. The storm of controversy with which this work was met virtually ended Chopin's literary career.

Michael Cleary (b. 1945)   Cleary grew up in Glen Falls, a small town in the Adirondack Mountains region of New York. He was an all-county athlete in football and basketball. A part-time job driving a beer truck enabled him to become the first in his family to attend college. He earned a Ph.D. and now teaches English at Broward Community College in Fort Lauderdale, Florida, where he lives with his wife and two children. For Cleary, a poem is successful "when the music of the language carries it toward observations which are both surprising and inevitable."

Lucille Clifton (b. 1936)   Born in Depew, New York, Clifton attended Howard University (1953–1955) and Fredonia State Teachers College. She worked as a claims clerk in the New York State Division of Employment, Buffalo (1958–1960), and as literature assistant in the Office of Education in Washington, D.C. (1960–1971). In 1969, she received the YM-YWHA Poetry Center Discovery Award, and her first collection, *Good Times*, was selected as one of the ten best books of 1969 by the *New York Times*. From 1971 to 1974, she was poet-in-residence at Coppin State College in Baltimore, and in 1979, she was named poet laureate of the state of Maryland. She has written many collections for children and a free-verse chronicle of five generations of her family, *Genera-tions: A Memoir* (1976). Noted for celebrating everyday people and things, Clifton has said "I am a black woman poet, and I sound like one."

Stephen Crane (1871–1900)   Born in Newark, New Jersey, the fourteenth and youngest child of a Methodist minister who died when Stephen was nine years old, Crane was raised by his strong-minded mother. His brief college career, first at Lafayette College and then at Syracuse University, was dominated by his interest in baseball; he left college after two semesters and moved on to a bohe-mian life in New York City. There he wandered through the slums, observing and developing a strong sympathy for the underclass of boozers and prostitutes that inhabited the Bowery. His first novel, *Maggie: A Girl of the Streets* (1893), describes the inevitable consequences of grinding poverty—but no publisher would take a chance on Crane's bleak and biting vision. He published it at his own expense, but it found no audience. Without any military experience, and at the age of twenty-four, Crane produced *The Red Badge of Courage* (1895), a novel that made him famous and became an American classic. For the remain-der of his life, he traveled about the world as a writer and war correspondent. He died of a tubercular infection in Badenweiler, Germany. Despite the brevity of his writing career, Crane left behind a substantial volume of work that includes a number of brilliant short stories and innovative poems.

Victor Hernández Cruz (b. 1949)   Cruz was born in Aguas Buenas, Puerto Rico, and came with his family to New York City in 1954. He recalls, "My family life was full of music, guitars and conga drums, maracas and songs. . . . Even when it was five below zero in New York [my mother] sang warm tropical ballads." By 1966, he had already completed a collection of verse, *Papo Got His Gun*, and in 1969 published *Snaps*. He has edited *Umbra* magazine in New York, lectured at the University of California, Berkeley, and taught at San Francisco State University. Cruz says he writes in three languages: Spanish, English, and Bilingual. "From the mixture a totally new language emerges, an intense collision, not just of words, but of attitudes." His other works include *Mainland* (1973) and *Tropicalizations* (1976).

Countee Cullen (1903–1946) Born Countee L. Porter in New York City, Cullen was adopted by the Reverend and Mrs. Cullen in 1918 and raised in Harlem. He was extraordinarily precocious, and by 1920, his poems had been published in *Poetry*, the *Nation*, and *Harper's*. He published his famous poem "Heritage" in 1925, the year he graduated from New York University. After earning an M.A. in English from Harvard in 1926, he taught French in a junior high school and was assistant editor of the National Urban League's *Opportu-nity: Journal of Negro Life*. Cullen, along with Langston Hughes and Jean Toomer, was a central figure in the Harlem Renaissance of the 1920s. He received a Guggenheim Fellowship in 1929. In addition to five volumes of poetry, he published a novel, *One Way to Heaven* (1932), which deals with the interaction between upper- and lower-class African-Americans in Harlem in the 1920s.

E. E. Cummings (1894–1962)   Born in Cambridge, Massachusetts, Edward Estlin Cummings attended Harvard (B.A., 1915; M.A., 1916), served as a volunteer ambulance driver in France during World War I, was imprisoned for three months in a French detention camp, served in the United States Army (1918–1919), then studied art and painting in Paris (1920–1924). His prose narrative *The Enormous Room* (1922), a recollection of his imprisonment, brought instant acclaim. Several volumes of poetry followed. His experiments with punctuation, line division, and capitalization make his work immediately recognizable. In a letter to young poets published in a high school newspaper, cummings said, "Nothing is quite so easy as using words like somebody else. We all of us do exactly this nearly all the time—and whenever we do it, we're not poets."

Emily Dickinson (1830–1886)   Dickinson, one of three children, was born in Amherst, Massachusetts. Her father was a prominent lawyer. Except for one year away at a nearby college and a trip with her sister to Washington, D.C., to visit her father when he was serving in Congress, she lived out her life, unmarried, in her parents' home. During her trip to Washington, she met the Reverend Charles Wadsworth, a married man, whom she came to characterize as her "dearest earthly friend." Little is known of this relationship except that Dickinson's feelings for Wadsworth were strong. In 1862 Wadsworth moved to San Francisco, an event that coincided with a period of Dickinson's intense poetic creativity. Also in that year, she initiated a literary correspondence with the critic T. W. Higginson, to whom she sent some of her poems for his reactions. Higginson, although he recognized her talent, was puzzled by her startling originality and urged her to write more conventionally. Unable to do so, she concluded, we may surmise, that she would never see her poems through the press. In fact, only seven of her poems were published while she was alive, none of them with her consent. After her death, the extraordinary richness of her imaginative life came to light with the discovery of her more than one thousand lyrics.

Joan Didion (b. 1934)   A fifth-generation Californian, Didion was born in Sacramento and raised in the great central plain of California, an area she often describes nostalgically in her work. As an undergraduate English major at the University of California, Berkeley, she won an essay prize sponsored by *Vogue* magazine. As a result, *Vogue* hired her, and for eight years, she lived in New York City while she rose to associate features editor. She published her first novel, *Run River*, in 1963 and in the same year, married the writer John Gregory Dunne. In 1964 the couple returned to California, where they remained for twenty-five years. Although Didion wrote three more novels, her reputation rests on her essays collected as *Slouching toward Bethlehem* (1968) and *The White*

Album (1979). In addition to her work as a columnist, essayist, and fiction writer, she has collaborated with her husband on a number of screenplays. She has focused her trenchant powers of observation in two documentary, book-length studies: *Salvador* (1983) and *Miami* (1987). Her reputation as a prose stylist is reflected in a comment by one critic who asserts that "nobody writes better English prose than Joan Didion. Try to rearrange one of her sentences, and you've realized that the sentence was inevitable, a hologram." Didion characterizes herself as uneasy with abstractions: "I would try to think about the Great Dialectic and I would find myself thinking instead about how the light was falling through the window in an apartment I had on the North Side. How it was hitting the floor."

John Donne (1572–1631)   Born in London into a prosperous Roman Catholic family of tradespeople, at a time when England was staunchly anti-Catholic, Donne was forced to leave Oxford without a degree because of his religion. He studied law and, at the same time, read widely in theology in an attempt to decide whether the Roman or the Anglican church was the true Catholic church, a decision he was not able to make for many years. In the meantime, he became known as a witty man of the world and the author of original, often dense, erotic poems. Donne left his law studies, participated in two naval expeditions, and then became secretary to a powerful noble, a job he lost when he was briefly sent to prison for secretly marrying his patron's niece. In 1615, at the age of forty-two, Donne accepted ordination in the Anglican church. He quickly earned a reputation as one of the greatest preachers of his time. He was dean of St. Paul's from 1621 until his death. In his later years, Donne rejected the poetry of his youth.

Paul Laurence Dunbar (1872–1906)   The son of former slaves, Dunbar was born in Dayton, Ohio, where he graduated from Dayton High School (1891) and worked for two years as an elevator operator. In 1894, he worked in Chicago at the World's Columbian Exhibition. His first verse collection, *Oak and Ivy*, was published in 1893. William Dean Howells, an eminent editor, author, and critic, encouraged him to write and had him join a Lecture Bureau in 1896. Dunbar read his own works in the United States and traveled to England in 1897. While Dunbar maintained that black poetry was not much different from white (and wrote many poems in standard English), he often wrote poems in black dialect that seemed to cater to the racial stereotypes of his white audience. He died of tuberculosis in 1906. His complete works appear in *The Dunbar Reader* (1975).

T. S. Eliot (1888–1965)   Thomas Stearns Eliot was born in St. Louis, Missouri. His father was president of the Hydraulic Press Brick Company, his mother a teacher, social worker, and writer. Educated in private academies, Eliot earned two philosophy degrees at Harvard (B.A., 1909; M.A., 1910). After graduate study in Paris and England, he worked for eight years as a clerk in Lloyd's Bank in London and became a naturalized British citizen in 1927. He was editor, then director of Faber & Gwyer Publishers (later Faber & Faber) from 1925 to 1965 and spent time in the United States as a visiting lecturer and scholar. Admirers and detractors agree that Eliot was the most imposing and influential poet writing between the world wars. His poems "The Love Song of J. Alfred Prufrock" (1917) and *The Waste Land* (1922) are among his earliest and most famous. Acknowledging his dependence on preexisting cultural tradition, Eliot explained: "The existing order is complete before the new work arrives; for order to persist after the supervention of novelty, the whole existing order must be altered." Eliot also wrote plays, including *Murder in the Cathedral* (1935) and *The Cocktail Party* (1950). The long-running Broadway musical *Cats* is based on his 1939 verse collection, *Old Possum's Book of Practical Cats*. He won the Nobel Prize for literature in 1948.

Harlan Ellison (b. 1934)   Born in Cleveland, Ohio, Ellison published his first story when he was thirteen and founded a science-fiction society when he was sixteen. After two years at Ohio State University, he worked at a variety of odd jobs while establishing himself as a writer. In a career spanning nearly thirty-five years, he has won numerous awards for his books, stories, essays, newspaper articles and columns, teleplays, and motion pictures. Ellison, who calls himself a "fantasist," is best known as an innovative and boldly experimental writer of science-fiction, but he is also widely respected as a critic of popular culture and as the editor of the anthology *Dangerous Visions* (1967). *The Essential Ellison* (1987) offers a thirty-year retrospective of his work; *Angry Candy* and *Harlan Ellison's Watching* (both 1988) are compilations of his film criticism.

William Faulkner (1897–1962)   Faulkner was born in New Albany, Mississippi, and lived most of his life in Oxford, the seat of the University of Mississippi. Although he did not graduate from high school, he did attend the university as a special student from 1919 to 1921. During this period, he also worked as a janitor, a bank clerk, and a postmaster. His southern forebears had held slaves, served during the Civil War, endured the indignities of Reconstruction, fought duels, even wrote the occasional romance of the old South. Faulkner mined these generous layers of history in his work. He created the mythical Yoknapatawpha County in northern Mississippi and traced the destinies of its inhabitants from the colonial era to the middle of the twentieth century in such novels as *The Sound and the Fury* (1929), *Light in August* (1932), and *Absalom, Absalom!* (1936). Further, Faulkner described the decline of the pre–Civil War aristocratic families and the rise of mean-spirited money grubbers in a trilogy: *The Hamlet* (1940), *The Town* (1957), and *The Mansion* (1959). Recognition came late, and Faulkner fought a constant battle to keep afloat financially. During the 1940s, he wrote screenplays in Hollywood. But, finally, his achievement brought him the Nobel Prize in 1950.

Lawrence Ferlinghetti (b. 1919)   Born Lawrence Ferling, this irreverent writer restored his original family name in 1954. He earned a B.A. in journalism from the University of North Carolina in 1941, became lieutenant commander in the U.S. Naval Reserve during World War II, then received graduate degrees from Columbia and the Sorbonne. He worked as a translator of French before rising to prominence in the "beat" poetry movement of the 1950s, which sought to rejuvenate and popularize poetry. His controversial work drew raves from many critics, even though one critic called it "real jivy, real groovy, all that—but ultimately kind of stupid." Known chiefly for his poetry, he has written a novel, *Her* (1960), and some unsympathetically reviewed plays. As a successful publisher (he cofounded a San Francisco bookstore, City Lights, and two publishing enterprises, City Lights Books and the Pocket Poets Series), Ferlinghetti appreciates the irony of his ascendance in a system he has repudiated. His early work, *A Coney Island of the Mind* (1958), remains a best-selling poetry collection.

Carolyn Forché (b. 1950)   Born in Detroit, Forché earned a B.A. in International Relations and Creative Writing at Michigan State University in 1972. After graduate study at Bowling Green State University in 1975, she taught at the University of Virginia, the University of Arkansas, New York University, Vassar, and Columbia. She won the Yale Series of Younger Poets Award in 1976 for her first collection, *Gathering the Tribes*. Other honors include a Guggenheim Fellowship and the Lamont Award (1981). Forché was a journalist for Amnesty International in El Salvador in 1983 and Beirut correspondent for the National Public Radio program "All Things Considered." Her collection *The Country between Us* (1981) embodies an unusual combination of political passion and technical proficiency.

E. M. Forster (1879–1970)   Edward Morgan Forster was born in London. He attended Tonbridge School and moved on to King's College, Cambridge, where he found the friends and the intellectual companionship that would shape the rest of his life. His early travels to Greece and Italy (1901) and later stays in India (1912 and 1922) introduced him to societies markedly different from his own, and he found the vitality of European peasant life more attractive than the decorous, even stuffy, quality of the English. He was a member of the famous Bloomsbury Group (named for the district in London where some of the members lived), a remarkable coterie of intellectuals and artists including (among others) the writer Virginia Woolf, art historians Clive Bell and Roger Fry, and influential economist John Maynard Keynes. Forster's own vigorous intelligence caused him to question the slogans and conventional wisdom of the day in "My Wood," reprinted here, and an essay collection, *Two Cheers for Democracy* (1951). *A Passage to India* (1924) is the best of his six novels, and *Aspects of the Novel* (1927) is still cited by literary theorists.

Robert Francis (1901–1987)   Born in Upland, Pennsylvania, Francis studied at

Harvard (A.B., 1923; Ed.M. 1926). He taught at summer workshops and conferences and lectured at universities across the United States. His works include *Stand with Me Here* (1936); *Like Ghosts of Eagles: Poems 1966–1974* (1974); a novel, *We Fly Away* (1948); and an autobiography, *The Trouble with Francis* (1971). He won the Shelley Memorial Award in 1939.

Bruce Jay Friedman (b. 1930)   Friedman began writing while in high school in the Bronx, New York, where he was born. He attended the University of Missouri, earning a degree in journalism in 1951. Friedman's novels, stories, and plays have earned him critical acclaim for his mordantly comic portrayal of (mostly) Jewish protagonists who, alienated from both their Jewish heritage and the wasteland of urban America, are unable to live authentic lives. Friedman is usually labeled a black humorist, a term he himself used to describe his writings, which include four novels, *Stern* (1962), *A Mother's Kisses* (1964), *The Dick* (1970), and *About Harry Towns* (1974); two plays, *Scuba Duba: A Tense Comedy* (1968) and *Steambath* (1971); and two collections of short stories, *Far from the City of Class* (1963) and *Black Angels* (1966).

Robert Frost (1874–1963)   Frost was born in San Francisco but from the age of ten lived in New England. He attended Dartmouth College briefly, then became a teacher, but soon decided to resume his formal training and enrolled in Harvard. He left Harvard after two years without a degree and for several years supported himself and his growing family by tending a farm his grandfather bought for him. When he was not farming, he read and wrote intensively, though he received little recognition. Discouraged by his lack of success, he sold the farm and moved his family to England, where he published his first volumes of poetry. *A Boy's Will* (1913) and *North of Boston* (1914). After three years in England, Frost returned to the United States a recognized poet. Later volumes, notably *Mountain Interval* (1916), *New Hampshire* (1923), *West-Running Brook* (1928), and *A Further Range* (1936), won Frost numerous awards, including two Pulitzer Prizes, and a wide popularity. By the time he delivered his poem "The Gift Outright" at the inauguration of President John F. Kennedy in 1962, Frost had achieved the status of unofficial poet laureate of America, widely revered and beloved for his folksy manner and seemingly artless, accessible poems.

Nikki Giovanni (b. 1943)   Born Yolande Cornelia Giovanni, Jr., in Knoxville, Tennessee, daughter of a probation officer and a social worker, Giovanni graduated with honors from Fisk University in 1967. She attended the University of Pennsylvania School of Social Work and Columbia School of the Arts, was assistant professor of black studies at Queens College (1968), associate professor of English at Rutgers University (1968–1970), and founded a publishing firm, Niktom, in 1970. Giovanni's early work reflected her social activism as an African-American college student in the 1960s. Later, she fell outside the mainstream of African-American poetry, concentrating on the individual struggle for fulfillment rather than the collective struggle for black empowerment. Her books include *Black Feeling, Black Talk* (1970), *My House (1972)*, and *The Women and the Men* (1975).

Louise Glück (b. 1943)   Born in New York City, Glück (pronounced "Glick") attended Sarah Lawrence College and Columbia. Her first poetry collection, *Firstborn*, was published in 1968. She has been visiting instructor at Province-town Fine Arts Work Center, lecturer at many universities, artist-in-residence at Goddard College (1970–1971), and instructor at Williams College. Her honors include a National Endowment for the Arts grant, a Rockefeller Foundation grant, and a Guggenheim Fellowship. Her other books include *The House on Marshland* (1976) and *The Triumph of Achilles* (1985). Glück has observed wryly that "the impulse to write is usually spent in a brief lyric."

Jane Goodall (b. 1934)   Born in London, Goodall received a Ph.D. in zoology from Cambridge University in 1965, only the eighth person in the history of that university to have received a Ph.D. without first earning a baccalaureate. In 1960, Goodall's interest in chimpanzees led her to what is now Gombe National Park in Tanzania, Africa. Through patient and protracted daily contact, she won the trust of many chimpanzees and was able to observe them at close range. These observations (her Ph.D. was based on this early work), which continued over many years, provided the basis for her pioneering studies that proved many scientific beliefs about chimpanzees wrong. Her most significant discovery was that chimpanzees use tools more than any other animal except human beings. A television special, "Miss Goodall and the Wild Chimpanzees," filmed for the National Geographic Society, was aired by CBS in 1965 (it is available on video under the title "Among the Wild Chimpanzees"). Her books include *My Friends, the Wild Chimpanzees* (1967), *In the Shadow of Man* (1971), and *The Chimpanzees of Gombe* (1986).

Michael Hamburger (b. 1924)   Hamburger was born in Berlin. His father, a physician and professor, took the family to England in 1933 at Hitler's rise to power. After serving four years in the British army, Hamburger graduated from Oxford (B.A., M.A., 1948), then worked as a free-lance writer until 1952. From 1952 to 1964, he lectured in German at the Universities of London and Reading. Hamburger has held visiting professorships at many universities in the United States. He is most renowned for his superb translation of the German poet Hölderlin. Translator of over thirty-five works, he won the Institute of Linguists' Gold Medal in 1977. His poems are compiled in *Collected Poems 1941–1983* (1984).

Thomas Hardy (1840–1928)   Hardy was born near Dorchester, in southeastern England (on which he based the "Wessex" of many of his novels and poems). Hardy worked for the ecclesiastical architect John Hicks from 1856–1861. He then moved to London to practice architecture and took evening classes at King's

College for six years. In 1867, he gave up architecture to become a full-time writer, and after writing short stories and poems, found success as a novelist. *The Mayor of Casterbridge* (1886) and *Tess of the d'Urbervilles* (1891) reveal Hardy's concern for victims of circumstance and his appeal to humanitarian sympathy in readers. After his novel *Jude the Obscure* (1896) was strongly criticized, Hardy set aside prose fiction and returned to poetry—a genre in which he was most prolific and successful after he reached the age of seventy.

Nathaniel Hawthorne (1804–1864)   The son of a merchant sea-captain who died in a distant port when Nathaniel was four, Hawthorne grew up in genteel poverty in Massachusetts and Maine. His earliest American ancestor, the magistrate William Hathorne, ordered the whipping of a Quaker woman in Salem. William's son John was one of the three judges at the Salem witch trials of 1692. Aware of his family's role in colonial America, Hawthorne returned to Salem after graduating from Bowdoin College (where future president Franklin Pierce was a friend and classmate), determined to be a writer. He recalled and destroyed copies of his first novel, the mediocre *Fanshawe* (1828). His short stories, often set in Puritan America, reveal a moral complexity that had not troubled his righteous ancestors William and John. His success as an author allowed him to marry Sophia Peabody in 1842 (after a four-year engagement). Although his stories were critically praised, they did not earn much money, and in 1846, he used his political connections with the Democratic party to obtain a job at the Salem custom house. His dismissal in 1849 (when the Democrats lost) produced both anger and resolve. The result was a great American novel, *The Scarlet Letter* (1850), which made him famous and improved his fortune. Although he was friendly with Emerson and his circle of optimistic transcendentalists (some of whom established the utopian socialist community at Brook Farm), Hawthorne's vision of the human condition was considerably darker. Herman Melville dedicated *Moby Dick* to Hawthorne and characterized him as a man who could say "No" in thunder.

Robert Hayden (1913–1980)   Born in Detroit, Hayden studied at Wayne State University and the University of Michigan (M.A., 1944). In 1946, he joined the faculty of Fisk University. He left Fisk in 1968 for a professorship at the University of Michigan, where he remained until his death. He produced some ten volumes of poetry but did not receive the acclaim many thought he deserved until late in life, with the publication of *Words in the Mourning Time: Poems* (1971). In the 1960s, he aroused some hostility from African-Americans who wanted him to express more militancy. But Hayden did not want to be part of what he called a "kind of literary ghetto." He considered his own work "a form of prayer—a prayer for illumination, perfection."

Anthony Hecht (b. 1923)   Born in New York City, Hecht attended Bard College (B.A., 1944). After three years in the U.S. Army, serving in Europe and Japan with temporary duty in the Counter-Intelligence Corps, he continued his education at Columbia (M.A., 1950). Hecht taught at several universities and was named professor of poetry and rhetoric in 1967 at the University of Rochester. Acclaimed for his technical expertise, Hecht was first devoted to traditional forms, and his work was sometimes described as "baroque" and "courtly." More recently, his work has become less decorative. He has published several poetry collections and won the Pulitzer Prize in 1968 for *The Hard Hours*. His other awards include the 1951 Prix de Rome, and Guggenheim, Rockefeller, and Ford Foundation Fellowships.

Ernest Hemingway (1898–1961)   Born in Oak Park, Illinois, Hemingway became a cub reporter after high school. He was seriously wounded while serving as an ambulance driver in World War I. After the war, he lived in Paris, a member of a lively and productive expatriate community characterized by Gertrude Stein as "a lost generation." He lived an active life, not only as a writer, but as a war correspondent, big game hunter, and fisherman. In such novels as *The Sun Also Rises* (1926), *A Farewell to Arms* (1929), and *For Whom the Bell Tolls* (1940), his fictional characters exhibit a passion for courage and integrity, for grace under pressure. Hemingway's spare, unembellished style reinforced his central theme that one must confront danger and live honorably. He won the Nobel Prize in 1954. In 1961, unable to write because treatment for mental instability affected his memory, he killed himself with the shotgun he had so often used as a hunter.

Gerard Manley Hopkins (1844–1889)   Raised in London, Hopkins won a scholarship to Balliol College, Oxford, where he studied classical literature. He converted to Roman Catholicism in 1866 and two years later entered the Jesuit Novitiate. In 1877, he was ordained as a Jesuit priest and served in missions in London, Liverpool, Oxford, and Glasgow until 1882. From 1884 to his death in 1889, he was professor of Greek at University College, Dublin. A technically innovative poet, Hopkins saw only three of his poems published during his lifetime but gained posthumous recognition in 1918 when a friend (the Poet Laureate Robert Bridges) published his complete works. His early poems celebrate the beauty of God's world, but later works reflect his poor health and depression.

A. E. Housman (1859–1936)   Born in Fockbury, England, and an outstanding student, Alfred Edward Housman nonetheless failed his final examinations at Oxford in 1881. Working as a clerk in the Patent Office in London, he pursued classical studies on his own, earned an M.A., and was appointed to the chair of Latin at University College, London. In 1910, he became professor of Latin at Cambridge, where he remained until his death in 1936. As a poet, Housman was concerned primarily with the fleetingness of love and the decay of youth. After his first collection, *A Shropshire Lad*, was rejected by several publishers, Housman published it at his own expense in 1896. It gained popularity during World War I, and his 1922 collection, *Last Poems*, was well received. In his lecture "The Name and Nature of Poetry" (1933), Housman argued that poetry should appeal to emotions rather than intellect. *More Poems* (1936) was published posthumously.

Langston Hughes (1902–1967) Hughes was born in Joplin, Missouri. His father was a businessperson and lawyer, his mother a teacher. Hughes attended Columbia, graduated from Lincoln University in 1929, traveled throughout the world, and held many odd jobs as a young man. While Hughes had a long and prolific career as a writer in all genres, he is still remembered as the central figure of the Harlem Renaissance of the 1920s, a movement that committed itself to the examination and celebration of black life in the United States and its African heritage. He was the Madrid correspondent for the Baltimore *Afro-American* (1937) and a columnist for the Chicago *Defender* (1943–1967) and the New York *Post* (1962–1967). His poems of racial affirmation and protest are often infused with the rhythms of blues and jazz music. He wrote over two dozen plays (many musicalized) and founded the Suitcase Theater (Harlem, 1938), the New Negro Theater (Los Angeles, 1939), and the Skyloft Players (Chicago, 1941). His works include *The Weary Blues* (1926), *Montage of a Dream Deferred* (1951), and *The Panther and the Lash: Poems of Our Times* (1969).

Ted Hughes (b. 1930) Born in Yorkshire, Hughes served two years in the Royal Air Force and attended Pembroke College, Cambridge (B.A. in archaeology and anthropology, 1954; M.A., 1959). His first wife was poet Sylvia Plath, who committed suicide in 1963. A full-time writer of plays, essays, children's verse, and editor of many anthologies, Hughes created a poetry of animals, full of primitive passion and violence. The most famous of these is the title character of his 1970 volume, *Crow*. One critic calls Hughes a "20th-century Aesop whose fables lack an explicit moral." Many have found in his animal subjects a telling portrayal of the human condition.

Henrik Ibsen (1828–1906) Ibsen was born in Skien, Norway (a seaport about a hundred miles south of Oslo), the son of a wealthy merchant. When Ibsen was eight, his father's business failed, and at fifteen he was apprenticed to an apothecary in the tiny town of Grimstad. He hated this profession. To solace himself, he read poetry and theology and began to write. When he was twenty-two, he became a student in Christiania and published his first play. In 1851, his diligent, though unremarkable, writing earned him an appointment as "theater-poet" to a new theater in Bergen, where he remained until 1857, learning both the business and the art of drama. He wrote several plays based on Scandinavian folklore, held positions at two theaters in Christiania, and married. When he was thirty-six, he applied to the government for a poet's pension—a stipend that would have permitted him to devote himself to writing. The stipend was refused. Enraged, he left Norway and though he was granted the stipend two years later, spent the next twenty-seven years in Italy and Germany, where he wrote the realistic social dramas that established his reputation as the founder of modern theater. Such plays as *Ghosts* (1881), *An Enemy of the People* (1882), and *A Doll's House* (1878) inevitably generated controversy as Ibsen explored venereal disease, the stupidity and greed of the "compact majority," and the position of women in society. In 1891, he returned to live in Christiania where he was recognized and honored as one of Norway's (and Europe's) finest writers.

Randall Jarrell (1914–1965)   Called by Robert Lowell "the most heartbreaking English poet of his generation," Jarrell was born in Nashville, Tennessee, and studied at Vanderbilt University (B.S. in psychology, 1936; M.A. in English, 1939). During World War II, he served as a navigation tower operator in the air corps. He taught at Sarah Lawrence College, Kenyon College, and was visiting fellow, lecturer, and professor at other colleges and universities across the country. In 1947, he joined the faculty at the Women's College of the University of North Carolina (now U.N.C. at Greensboro) where he remained until his death. In his poetry, Jarrell explored loneliness and lost childhood; in his influential criticism, he encouraged other writers and helped determine the course of contemporary poetry. His works include three volumes of poetry, *Little Friend, Little Friend* (1945), *Losses* (1948), and *The Lost World* (1965), and a novel, *Pictures from an Institution*, (1954). Jarrell was struck and killed by an automobile in 1965.

Robinson Jeffers (1887–1962)   Born in Pittsburgh, Pennsylvania, Jeffers was tutored by his father and educated in Switzerland and Germany. He attended the University of Western Pennsylvania and graduated from Occidental College in 1905. He studied medicine at the University of Southern California and forestry at the University of Washington. In 1912, he inherited an income and in 1924 settled in an isolated house he built on the Pacific coast near Carmel, California. Influenced by Greek myths, his early work includes the long poem *Roan Stallion* and the collection *Tamar, and Other Poems* (both 1924). With a later collection, *The Women at Point Sur* (1972), he alienated many readers by handling such controversial themes as bestiality and incest. In *Themes in My Poems* (1956), Jeffers justifies his preoccupation with violence and his pessimism. He won the Shelley Memorial Award in 1961.

James Joyce (1882–1941)   Although educated in Jesuit schools, Joyce came to reject Catholicism; although an expatriate living in Paris, Trieste, and Zurich for most of his adult life, he wrote almost exclusively about his native Dublin. Joyce's rebelliousness, which surfaced during his university career, generated a revolution in modern literature. His novels *Ulysses* (1922) and *Finnegans Wake* (1939) introduced radically new narrative techniques. "Araby," from his first collection of short stories, *Dubliners* (1914), is one of a series of sharply realized vignettes based on Joyce's experience in Ireland, the homeland he later characterized as "a sow that eats its own farrow." Joyce lived precariously on earnings as a language teacher and modest contributions from wealthy patrons. That support Joyce justified—he is certainly one of the most influential novelists of the twentieth century. Because *Ulysses* dealt frankly with sexuality and used coarse language, the U.S. Post Office charged that the novel was obscene, and forbade its importation. A celebrated 1933 court decision lifted the ban in the United States.

John Keats (1795–1821)   Keats was born in London, the eldest son of a stablekeeper who died in an accident in 1804. His mother died of tuberculosis shortly after remarrying, and the grandmother who raised Keats and his siblings died in 1814. At eighteen, Keats wrote his first poem, "Imitation of Spenser," inspired by Edmund Spenser's long narrative poem, *The Faerie Queene*. The thirty-three poems he wrote while training to be a surgeon were published in 1817, and Keats then gave up medicine for writing. After more traumatic losses in 1818, including the departure of one brother for America and the death of his other brother of tuberculosis, Keats wrote his second collection, *Lamia, Isabella, The Eve of St. Agnes, and Other Poems* (1820). Ill with tuberculosis himself, Keats was sent to Rome to recover. He died at twenty-six, but despite his short career, he is a major figure of the romantic period.

X. J. Kennedy (b. 1929)   Born Joseph Charles Kennedy in Dover, New Jersey, Kennedy published his own science-fiction magazine, *Terrifying Test-Tube Tales*, at age twelve. He honed his writing skills at Seton Hall University and earned an M.A. from Columbia in 1951. From 1951 to 1955, he served in the U.S. Navy, at one time generating a daily newssheet for the entertainment-starved crew of a destroyer at sea. Kennedy notes: "Nothing I have ever written since has been received so avidly." After further study at the Sorbonne and the University of Michigan, Kennedy taught English at the University of North Carolina and moved to Tufts University in 1963. His first poetry collection, *Nude Descending a Staircase* (1961), won the 1961 Lamont Award. A free-lance writer since 1979, Kennedy has preferred writing within the constraints of established rhyme and metrical patterns, claiming to discover more linguistic challenges when he suppresses his ego.

Martin Luther King, Jr. (1929–1968)   King was born in Atlanta, Georgia, where his father was pastor of the Ebenezer Baptist Church. He attended public schools (skipping the ninth and twelfth grades) and entered Morehouse College in Atlanta. He was ordained as a Baptist minister just before his graduation in 1948. He then enrolled in Crozer Theological Seminary in Pennsylvania and after earning a divinity degree there, attended graduate school at Boston University, where he earned a Ph.D. in theology in 1955. At Boston University, he met Coretta Scott; they were married in 1953. King's rise to national and international prominence began in Montgomery, Alabama, in 1955. In that year, Rosa Parks, an African-American passenger, was arrested for refusing to obey a city ordinance that required African-Americans to sit or stand at the back of municipal buses. The African-American citizens of the city (one of the most thoroughly segregated in the South) organized a bus boycott in protest and asked

King to serve as their leader. Thousands boycotted the buses for more than a year, and despite segregationist violence against them, King grounded their protests on his deeply held belief in nonviolence. In 1956, the U.S. Supreme Court ordered Montgomery to provide integrated seating on public buses. In the following year, King and other African-American ministers founded the Southern Christian Leadership Conference (SCLC) to carry forward the nonviolent struggle against segregation and legal discrimination. As protests grew, so did the unhappiness of King and his associates with the unwillingness of the president and Congress to support civil rights. The SCLC, therefore, organized massive demonstrations in Montgomery (King wrote "Letter from Birmingham Jail" during these demonstrations). With the civil rights movement now in the headlines almost every day, President Kennedy proposed to Congress a far-reaching civil rights bill. On August 28, 1963, over 200,000 blacks and whites gathered at the Lincoln Memorial in Washington, D.C., where King delivered his now famous speech, "I Have a Dream." In the following year, Congress passed the Civil Rights Act of 1964, prohibiting racial discrimination in public places and calling for equal opportunity in education and employment. In that year, King received the Nobel Peace Prize. In 1965, King and others organized a march to protest the blatant denial of African-Americans' voting rights in Selma, Alabama, where the march began. Before the protesters were able to reach Birmingham, the state capital, they were attacked by police with tear gas and clubs. This outrage, viewed live on national television, led President Johnson to ask Congress for a bill that would eliminate all barriers to voting rights. Congress responded by passing the landmark Voting Rights Act of 1965. King remained committed to nonviolence, but his conviction that economic inequality—not just race—was one of the root causes of injustice led him to begin organizing a Poor People's Campaign that would unite all poor people in the struggle for justice. These views also led him to criticize the role played by the United States in the Vietnam War. The Poor People's Campaign took King to Memphis, Tennessee, to support a strike of African-American sanitation workers, where on April 4, 1968, he was shot and killed while standing on the balcony of his hotel room. Riots immediately erupted in scores of cities across the nation. A few months later, Congress enacted the Civil Rights Act of 1968, banning discrimination in the sale and rental of housing. King is the author of *Stride toward Freedom* (1958), dealing with the Montgomery bus boycott; *Strength to Love* (1953), a collection of sermons; and *Why We Can't Wait* (1964), a discussion of his general views on civil rights.

Stephen King (b. 1947)   The son of a sailor, Stephen King was born in Portland, Maine. He graduated from the University of Maine in 1970 and worked in a laundry, a knitting mill, and as a janitor before becoming a high school English teacher. He had the satisfaction of returning to his alma mater as a writer-in-residence and is probably the best-known and most popular writer of horror fiction in the world. In *Carrie*, an early novel, King tapped the feelings of humiliation and isolation he had suffered as an unathletic child when he created a character who could use her psychic powers to take vengeance on her tormenters. Hollywood has made several of his many novels—notably, *Carrie*, *The Shining*, and *Pet Sematary*—into successful movies.

Carolyn Kizer (b. 1925)   Kizer was born in Spokane, Washington. Her father was a lawyer, her mother a biologist and professor. After graduating from Sarah Lawrence College in 1945, Kizer pursued graduate study at Columbia and the University of Washington. From 1959 to 1965, she was editor of *Poetry Northwest* (which she founded in 1959 in Seattle) and spent 1964 and 1965 as a State Department specialist in Pakistan, where she taught at a women's college and translated poems from Urdu into English. She chose to leave after the U.S. decision to bomb North Vietnam in 1965. Later, she joined archaeological tours in Afghanistan and Iran. She has worked as director of literary programs for the National Endowment for the Arts in Washington, D.C., has taught at several universities, and was poet-in-residence at the University of North Carolina and Ohio University. Her works include *Poems* (1959) and *Mermaids in the Basement: Poems for Women* (1984).

Etheridge Knight (1933–1991)   Knight was born in Corinth, Mississippi, attended two years of public school in Kentucky, and served in the U.S. Army from 1948 to 1951. Convicted on a robbery charge and sentenced in 1960 to twenty years in Indiana State Prison, he discovered poetry; his first collection is entitled *Poems from Prison* (1968). Knight was paroled after eight years. From 1968 to 1971 he was poet-in-residence at several universities. An important African-American voice in the 1960s and 1970s, Knight rejected the American and European esthetic tradition, arguing that "the red of this esthetic rose got its color from the blood of black slaves, exterminated Indians, napalmed Vietnamese children." His collection *Belly Song and Other Poems* was nominated for the National Book Award and the Pulitzer Prize in 1973. His last collection of poems, *Born of a Woman: New and Selected Poems*, was published in 1980. His awards include National Endowment for the Arts and Guggenheim grants, and the 1987 American Book Award for *The Essential Etheridge Knight* (1986). On March 10, 1991, in his home in Indianapolis, he died of lung cancer.

Philip Larkin (1922–1985)   Born in Coventry, Larkin attended St. John's College, Oxford (B.A., 1943; M.A., 1947). He was appointed librarian at the University of Hull in 1955, wrote jazz feature articles for the London *Daily Telegraph* from 1961 to 1971, and won numerous poetry awards, including the Queen's Gold Medal (1965) and the Benson Medal (1975). His first collection, *The North Ship* (1945), was not well received, but he gained recognition after publication of *The Less Deceived* (1960). Larkin once said, "Form holds little interest for me. Content is everything."

Ursula K. LeGuin (b. 1929)   The daughter of distinguished University of California, Berkeley, anthropologists, LeGuin graduated from Radcliffe and earned an M.A. from Columbia. She enjoyed early success writing for science-fiction and fantasy magazines (a genre often stigmatized as subliterary popular fiction). But she quickly established a reputation that places her alongside such modern writers as Kurt Vonnegut, Jr., and in the tradition of older writers who used fantastic circumstances to shape their understanding of the human condition, such as Jonathan Swift, Edgar Allan Poe, and H. G. Wells. In addition to speculative fiction, she has written poetry and children's books.

John Lennon (1940–1980) and Paul McCartney (b. 1942)   Lennon and Mc-Cartney met at a church fete in 1957 where they were both performing. Later that year, they formed a duo called the Nurk Twins. By 1962, after various incarnations and personnel changes, Lennon, McCartney, George Harrison, and Ringo Starr emerged as the Beatles and were launched on their successful career by their new manager, Brian Epstein. Lennon and McCartney wrote most of the Beatles's songs. "Love Me Do," their first recording with E.M.I., sold 100,000 copies in 1962. Exhausted by obsessed fans at sold-out concerts around the world, the foursome became a studio band in 1966. Epstein's death in 1967 and Lennon's marriage to Yoko Ono in 1969 contributed to the group's demise. Ego problems plagued their 1971 movie *Let It Be*, and the group officially disbanded a month after its release. Lennon and McCartney continued their songwriting careers separately. Lennon died of gunshot wounds inflicted by a deranged fan on December 8, 1980.

Denise Levertov (b. 1923)   Born in Ilford, England, Levertov was raised in a literary household (her father was an Anglican priest) and educated privately. She was a nurse at a British Hospital in Paris during World War II; after the war, she worked in an antique store and bookstore in London. Married to an American writer, she came to the United States in 1948, became a naturalized citizen in 1956, and taught at several universities, including M.I.T. and Tufts. Levertov began as what she called a "British romantic with almost Victorian background" and has become more politically active and feminist with time. She protested U.S. involvement in the Vietnam War and has also been involved in the anti-nuclear movement. Regarding angst-filled confessional poetry, Levertov once said, "I do not believe that a violent imitation of the horrors of our times is the concern of poetry. . . . I long for poems of an inner harmony in utter contrast to the chaos in which they exist." Her works include *The Double Image* (1946) and *Relearning the Alphabet* (1970).

C. Day Lewis (1904–1972)   Born in Ireland, son of a minister, Cecil Day Lewis began writing poetry at age six. He attended Oxford, taught for seven years, served as editor for the Ministry of Information (1941–1946), was professor of poetry at Oxford (1951–1956), and visiting professor at Harvard (1964–1965). His early works *From Feathers to Iron* (1931) and *The Magnetic Mountain* (1933) reflect a politically radical ideology, but Lewis mellowed enough to be named poet laureate in 1968. From 1935 to 1964 he wrote nearly two dozen detective novels under the pseudonym Nicholas Blake. He commented, "In my young days, words were my antennae, my touch-stones, my causeway over a quaking bog of mistrust."

Gerald Locklin (b. 1941)   Born in Rochester, New York, Locklin attended McQuaid Jesuit High School, where he was cocaptain of the football, basketball, and track teams. He entered the College of the Holy Cross on a football scholarship, "found himself a boy playing a man's game, and, before all his brains could be kicked out," transferred to St. John Fisher College in Rochester and received a B.A. in English (1961). He earned a Ph.D. (1964) from the University of Arizona and has been teaching English at California State University, Long Beach, since 1965. Encouraged by an aunt, Locklin began dictating poems almost as soon as he could talk and has published over thirty-five volumes of poetry and fiction. Three of his books have been translated and published in West Germany. He has been married three times, has seven children and one grandchild, swims for survival, and remains an avid fan of the Lakers, the Raiders, the Yankees, and since the acquisition of Wayne Gretzky, the Kings.

Audre Lorde (b. 1934)   Lorde was born in New York City, where she attended Hunter College (B.A., 1959) and Columbia (M.L.S., 1961). She was on the staff of the Mount Vernon Public Library (1961–1963), served as a head librarian for a New York City school (1966–1968), then spent a year as poet-in-residence at Tougaloo College. After teaching at the City College of New York and Lehman College, she joined the English department of John Jay College of Criminal Justice in 1970. Her first collection, *The First Cities* (1968), chronicles the overwhelming effect of racism on African-Americans. A voice of black pride, Lorde also fought a feminist struggle within the Black Power movement. Addressing sexism among African-Americans, Lorde wrote, "I do not believe / our wants have made all our lies / holy."

Amy Lowell (1874–1925)   Born to a prominent family in Brookline, Massachusetts, Lowell was privately educated. After the death of her parents, she inherited the family's ten-acre estate, including a staff of servants and a well-stocked library. Lowell wrote a great deal of undistinguished poetry that, unfortunately, prejudiced critics and readers against her better work. While traveling abroad, she became associated with the Imagists, a group of English and American poets in London who felt that sharply realized images gave poetry its power, and she gained recognition promoting their work in the Unites States after 1913. Her first collection of poems, *A Dome of Many-Coloured Glass*, appeared in 1912. Though her poetry never reached a wide audience, her criticism helped shape American poetic tastes of the time.

Archibald MacLeish (1892–1982)   Born in Glencoe, Illinois, MacLeish earned a B.A. from Yale (1915), then went on to Harvard, where he earned a law degree (1919) and taught constitutional and international law for one year. After three years with a law firm, MacLeish gave up law in 1923, moved to France, and began his career as a writer. The works of this expatriate period, many of them verse dramas, express the despair and alienation found in many post–World War I writings. The works following MacLeish's return in 1928 to the depression-era United States reflect his growing interest in his national and cultural heritage. *Frescoes for Mr. Rockefeller's City* (1933) celebrates the American dream, while his Pulitzer Prize–winning epic poem *Conquistador* (1932) tells the story of the conquest of Mexico. MacLeish's later works include *Collected Poems, 1917–1952* (1952; which won the Pulitzer Prize, Bollingen Prize, Shelley Memorial Award, and National Book Award), *New and Collected Poems* (1976), as well as verse dramas and essays. His distinguished career as a person of letters was recognized by his appointments as librarian of Congress (1939–1944), assistant secretary of state (1944–1945), and Boylston Professor of Rhetoric and Oratory at Harvard (1948–1962).

Bernard Malamud (1914–1986)   Born in Brooklyn, New York, and educated at the City College of New York and Columbia, Malamud is one of a number of post–World War II writers whose works have drawn heavily on their urban New York, Jewish backgrounds. Malamud's works often dramatize the tension arising out of the clash between Jewish conscience and American energy and materialism or the difficulty of keeping alive the Jewish sense of community and humanism in American society. *A New Life* (1961), *The Fixer* (1966; winner of both a National Book Award and a Pulitzer Prize), and *Pictures of Fidelman* (1969) all have protagonists who struggle with these problems. Some of his other novels are *The Natural* (1952), *The Assistant* (1957), *The Tenants* (1971), and *God's Grace* (1982). His short stories are collected in *The Magic Barrel* (1958; winner of the National Book Award in 1959), *Idiots First* (1963), and *Rembrandt's Hat* (1973).

Thomas Mann (1875–1955)   Son of a merchant and senator in northern Germany, Mann moved to Munich at nineteen and worked in an insurance office while he learned the craft of writing. After some time at the university and a sojourn in Italy, Mann published his first novel, *Buddenbrooks, Decline of a Family* (1901). In this chronicle, Mann explored themes he would return to throughout his literary career—civilization in decay and the conflict between art and life. This theme appears in his classic short novel, *Death in Venice* (1925). His masterpiece, *The Magic Mountain* (1924), explored the forces that disrupted European society. He was awarded the Nobel Prize in 1929. His political liberalism made life in Hitler's Germany impossible, and Mann left in 1933. Deprived of his citizenship in 1936, he became an American citizen in 1944 and in 1954, moved to Zurich, Switzerland, where he died the following year.

Christopher Marlowe (1564–1593)   Born in Canterbury, Marlowe was educated at Cambridge, where he embarked on a career of writing and political activity, eventually giving up his original intention of entering the priesthood.

He was arrested in 1593 on a charge of atheism, but before he could be brought to trial, he was murdered in a brawl apparently involving a wealthy family that had reason to want him silenced. Marlowe's literary reputation rests primarily on his plays, powerful in their own right and the most significant precursors of Shakespeare's poetic dramas. The most important are *Tamburlaine, Parts I and II* (c. 1587–1588; published 1590), *The Jew of Malta* (1589; published 1633), and *The Tragical History of the Life and Death of Dr. Faustus* (1592; published 1604).

Andrew Marvell (1621–1678)   Born in Yorkshire and educated at Cambridge, an inheritance upon his father's death allowed him to spend four years traveling the Continent. Although not a Puritan himself, Marvell supported the Puritans' cause during the civil war and held a number of posts during the Puritan regime, including that of assistant to the blind John Milton, Cromwell's Latin secretary. In 1659, a year before the Restoration, Marvell was elected to Parliament, where he served until his death. Soon after the Restoration, Marvell expressed strong disagreements with the government in a series of outspoken and anonymously printed satires. It was for these satires, rather than for his many love poems, that he was primarily known in his own day.

Bobbie Ann Mason (b. 1940)   Born in Mayfield, Kentucky, Mason was educated at the University of Kentucky, the State University of New York at Binghampton, and the University of Connecticut, where she received a Ph.D. in 1972. Following publication of a number of nonfiction books, including *The Girl Sleuth: A Feminist Guide to the Bobbsey Twins, Nancy Drew, and Their Sisters* (1975), as well as short stories in numerous magazines, she published her first volume of short fiction, *Shiloh and Other Stories* (1982). The collection, which established her reputation as an important southern voice in American literature, won the 1982 Hemingway Foundation Award and was widely praised for its vivid evocation of what one critic called "a region's physical and social geography" and Mason's ability to create a world of ordinary people valiantly striving to give meaning and order to their lives. While *Shiloh* remains thus far her only collection, she has continued to publish short stories, and in 1985, her first novel, *In Country*, was published to general acclaim.

Claude McKay (1890–1948)   Born in Sunny Ville, Jamaica, McKay had already completed two volumes of poetry before coming to the United States in 1912 at the age of twenty-three (the two volumes earned him awards, which paid his way). The racism he encountered as a black immigrant brought a militant tone to his writing. His popular poem "If We Must Die" (1919) helped to initiate the Harlem Renaissance of the 1920s. Between 1922 and 1934 he lived in Great Britain, Russia, Germany, France, Spain, and Morocco. His writings include four volumes of poems; many essays; an autobiography, *A Long Way from Home* (1937); a novel, *Home to Harlem* (1928); and a sociological study, *Harlem: Negro Metropolis* (1940). His conversion to Roman Catholicism in the 1940s struck his audience as an ideological retreat. McKay wrote in a letter to a friend: "To have a religion is very much like falling in love with a woman. You love her for her . . . beauty, which cannot be defined."

Peter Meinke (b. 1932)   Born in Brooklyn, New York, son of a salesperson, Meinke served in the U.S. army from 1955 to 1957, attended Hamilton College (B.A., 1955), the University of Michigan (M.A., 1961), and the University of Minnesota (Ph.D., 1965). He taught English at a New Jersey high school, Hamline University, and Presbyterian College (now Eckerd College) in Florida, where he began directing the writing workshop in 1972. His reviews, poems, and stories have appeared in periodicals such as the *Atlantic*, the *New Yorker*, and the *New Republic*. The latest of his three books in the Pitt Poetry Series is *Nightwatch on the Chesapeake* (1987). His collection of stories, *The Piano Tuner*, won the 1986 Flannery O'Connor Award. Also, he has been the recipient of a National Endowment for the Arts Fellowship in Poetry.

Herman Melville (1819–1891)   The death of his merchant father when Melville was twelve shattered the economic security of his family. The financial panic of 1837 reduced the Melvilles to the edge of poverty, and at age nineteen, Melville went to sea. Economic conditions upon his return were still grim, and after a frustrating stint as a country school teacher, he again went to sea—this time on a four-year whaling voyage. He deserted the whaler in the South Pacific, lived some time with cannibals, made his way to Tahiti and Hawaii, and finally joined the navy for a return voyage. He mined his experiences for two successful South Sea–adventure books, *Typee* (1846) and *Omoo* (1847). On the strength of these successes he married, but his next novel, *Mardi* (1849), was too heavy-handed an allegory to succeed. Driven by the obligation to support his growing family, Melville returned to sea-adventure stories, with moderate success. But neither his masterpiece, *Moby Dick* (1851), nor his subsequent short stories and novels found much of an audience, and in 1886, he accepted an appointment as customs inspector in Manhattan, a job he held until retirement. He continued to write, mostly poetry, and lived to see himself forgotten as an author. *Billy Budd*, found among his papers after his death and published in 1924, led to a revival of interest in Melville, now recognized as one of America's greatest writers.

James Merrill (b. 1926)   Born into a wealthy New York family (his father cofounded the Merrill Lynch stockbrokerage firm), Merrill was educated at Amherst College, where he received a B.A. in 1947. His first volume of commercially published poems, *First Poems* (1951), established his reputation as a writer of technical virtuosity, urbane eloquence, and wit. With the more personal and passionate poems of *Nights and Days* (1966) and *Mirabell: Books of Number* (1978), both recipients of the National Book Award, Merrill gained a wider and more enthusiastic audience. Merrill is probably most widely known as "the Ouija poet" for his narrative poems that record the Ouija board sessions he and a friend conducted with "spirits from another world." Merrill has also written plays, *The Immortal Husband* (1956) and *The Bait* (1960), and novels, *The Seraglio* (1957) and *The (Diblos) Notebook* (1965).

Robert Mezey (b. 1935)   Born in Philadelphia, Mezey attended Kenyon College and served a troubled hitch in the U.S. Army before earning his B.A. from the University of Iowa in 1959. He worked as a probation officer, advertising copywriter, and social worker, did graduate study at Stanford, and began teaching English at Case Western Reserve University in 1963. After a year as poet-in-residence at Franklin and Marshall College, he joined the English department of California State University, Fresno, spent three years at the University of Utah, and settled in 1976 at Pomoma College in Claremont, California. Winner in 1960 of the Lamont Award for *The Lovemaker*, he has published many poetry collections, coedited *Naked Poetry* (1969), and was one of several translators for *Poems from the Hebrew* (1973).

Edna St. Vincent Millay (1892–1950)   Millay was born in Maine and educated at Vassar. By the time she graduated in 1917, she had already achieved considerable fame as a poet; in the same year, she moved to Greenwich Village in New York City and published her first volume of poetry, *Renascence and Other Poems*. In Greenwich Village, she established her reputation as a poet and became notorious for her bohemian life and passionate love affairs. In 1923, she received a Pulitzer Prize for a collection of sonnets, *The Harp-Weaver*, that dealt wittily and flippantly with love. Her later works exhibit a more subdued and contemplative tone as well as a growing preoccupation with social and political affairs. Nevertheless, her best and most memorable verse deals with the bittersweet emotions of love and the brevity of life.

John Milton (1608–1674)   Born in London to an affluent and artistic family, Milton was educated privately as a child and later attended Cambridge, where he wrote both Latin and English poems. After leaving Cambridge, he was supported for five years by his family while he read the classics, wrote, and traveled. When civil war broke out in 1642, Milton actively supported the Puritans against the Crown. The Puritan victory in 1649 led to his appointment as Latin secretary to Oliver Cromwell, his main duty being to translate foreign diplomatic correspondence. He voluntarily wrote many pamphlets defending the new regime, including a justification of the execution of Charles I in 1649. Doctors warned him that continued writing would damage his eyesight, but Milton ignored their advice and at age forty-three became totally blind. Thereafter, Andrew Marvell assisted him in his secretarial duties. With the Restoration of Charles II in 1660, Milton went into retirement and was able to devote himself to composing the epic work he had long contemplated. This project reached fruition in 1667 with the publication of *Paradise Lost*, a blank-verse epic in which Milton announced that he would "justify the ways of God to men." One of Milton's last works, often seen as autobiographical, is *Samson Agonistes* (1671), a poetic drama about the blind Samson triumphing over the treachery of those around him.

Yukio Mishima (1925–1970)   Born Kimitake Hiroaka in Tokyo, Japan, Mishima (his pen name) established his reputation in 1949 with the publication of his first novel, *Confessions of a Mask*, a fictional account of the author's own awareness that he would have to conceal his homosexuality. Mishima's life, and much of his writings, were devoted to extolling the virtues of the *Samurai* tradition—honor, obedience to the emperor, and military discipline. The clash between Japanese traditional values and the modern world is explored in his novel *The Temple of the Golden Pavilion* (1959). Mishima's career ended with his dramatic suicide—a ritual act of *seppuku*—following his failed attempt to spark a military revolt that he hoped would be the first step in rescuing Japan from what he saw as the corruptions of Western industrialism. It appears that Mishima recognized, long before his suicide, that his efforts to revive the old values were doomed to failure; one critic reports, "Mishima said that he worked so hard on body building because he intended to die before he was fifty and wanted to have a good-looking corpse."

Jessica Mitford (b. 1917)   One of six sisters, Mitford was born in Gloucestershire, England, into an aristocratic and rather eccentric family. She was educated at home and early adopted political views that contrasted violently with those of her sister Diana, who married Sir Oswald Mosley, the pre–World War II leader of the British fascist movement. Jessica, on the other hand, traveled to Loyalist Spain during its civil war, where she met her first husband. He was killed in action during World War II, and she later married a labor lawyer. They moved to California and joined the Communist party. They left the party in 1958, and Jessica embarked on a successful career as a muckraking journalist and writer. Her first work, *Lifeitselfmanship*, was privately published in 1956, but her attack on undertakers in *The American Way of Death* (1963) established her reputation as an incisive and witty enemy of social and economic pretentiousness. Her many books include *Kind and Usual Punishment: The Prison Business* (1973), the autobiographical *A Fine Old Conflict* (1979), and a collection of articles, *Poison Penmanship: The Gentle Art of Muckraking* (1979).

Alberto Moravia (1907–1990)   Born in Rome, Moravia contracted tuberculosis as a child and was educated privately at home. Following the publication of his first novel, *A Time of Indifference* (1929), he traveled widely in Europe and America, supporting himself by writing articles for Italian newspapers. Moravia's writings brought him to conflict with the Fascist regime, and he was forced to flee Italy when the Germans occupied Rome. Moravia's international fame was established in the postwar period with the publication of such novels as *The Woman of Rome* (1947), *Conjugal Love* (1949), and *The Conformist* (1951). Many of his short stories appear in *Roman Tales* (1954) and *More Roman Tales* (1969).

Ogden Nash (1902–1971)   Frederick Ogden Nash was born in Rye, New York, and attended Harvard. He worked as a teacher, a bond salesperson, and then in the editorial and publicity departments of Doubleday Doran, Publishers, in New

York City. For a time he moved to a rival publishing house but soon joined the editorial staff of the *New Yorker*. Nash enjoyed immense popularity as a writer of light verse, choosing simple subjects and relying heavily on rhyme. His poems are collected in *I Wouldn't Have Missed It* (1975). Author of many children's books, Nash also cowrote the 1943 Broadway musical *One Touch of Venus* (music by Kurt Weill).

Thomas Nashe (1567–1601) Born in Lowestoft, England, the son of a minister, Nashe graduated from Cambridge, made a tour of France and Italy, and by 1588 was establishing himself in London as a professional writer. His hatred of Puritanism led him to join a group of pamphleteers who were defending the Anglican church and its bishops against Puritan attacks. Nashe also wrote several plays and a picaresque prose narrative, *The Unfortunate Traveler* (1954), that inaugurated the novel of adventure in English literature.

Flannery O'Connor (1925–1964) Afflicted with lupus erythematosus, O'Connor spent most of her tragically short life in Milledgeville, Georgia. She began writing while a student at Georgia State College for Women in her hometown and in 1947 earned an M.F.A. degree from the University of Iowa. Back in Milledgeville, she lived on a farm with her mother, raised peacocks, and endured the indignity of constant treatment for her progressive and incurable disease. She traveled and lectured when she could. She wrote two novels, *Wise Blood* (1952) and *The Violent Bear It Away* (1960), and two collections of stories, *A Good Man Is Hard to Find* (1955) and *Everything That Rises Must Converge* (1965). She was deeply religious, and wrote numerous book reviews for Catholic newspapers. Her southern gothic tales often force readers to confront physical deformity, spiritual depravity, and the violence they often engender.

Frank O'Connor (1903–1966) Born Michael O'Donovan in Cork, Ireland, O'Connor later adopted his pen name to separate his civil-service career from his writing career. His family's poverty forced him to leave school at age fourteen. During the Irish struggle for independence, O'Connor served in the Irish Republican Army and after the establishment of the Irish Free State, worked as a librarian. Despite his lack of formal education, he became director of the Abbey Theatre in Dublin. He moved to the United States in the 1950s and taught at Harvard and Northwestern. A storyteller in the great Gaelic oral tradition, he appeared for a time on Sunday morning television. A perfectionist, O'Connor constantly polished and reworked his stories. He added to his stature with fine critical studies of the novel, *The Mirror in the Roadway* (1956), and of the short story, *The Lonely Voice* (1963), and introduced Gaelic poetry to a wide audience through his English translations.

Sharon Olds (b. 1942) Born in San Francisco, Olds attended Stanford (B.A., 1964), and Columbia (Ph.D., 1972). She joined the faculty of the Theodor Herzl Institute in 1976 and has given readings at many colleges. She won the

Madeline Sadin Award from the *New York Quarterly* in 1978 for "The Death of Marilyn Monroe." Often compared to confessional poets Sylvia Plath and Anne Sexton, Olds published her first collection, *Satan Says*, in 1980 and won both the National Book Critics' Circle Award and the Lamont Award for *The Dead and the Living* in 1983. Her most recent book of poems, *The Gold Cell*, was published in 1987.

George Orwell (1903–1950)   Born Eric Blair in India, the son of a minor British colonial officer, Orwell was raised in England. His education at good grammar schools, culminating with a stay at Eton, introduced him to what he later called the snobbish world of England's middle and upper classes. Denied a university scholarship, he joined the Indian Imperial Police in 1922 and served in Burma until he resigned in 1927, disgusted with the injustice of British imperialism in India and Burma. He was determined to be a writer and living at the edge of poverty, deliberately mingled with social outcasts and impoverished laborers. These experiences produced *Down and Out in Paris and London* (1933). Although he was a socialist, his experiences while fighting with the leftists during the Spanish Civil War disillusioned him, and he embodied his distaste for any totalitarian system in *Animal Farm* (1945), a satirical attack on the leadership of the Soviet Union. In his pessimistic novel *1984* (1949), he imagined a social order shaped by a propagandistic perversion of language, in which the government, an extension of "Big Brother," uses two-way television to control the citizenry. Orwell succumbed to tuberculosis at the age of forty-seven, but not before he produced six novels, three documentary works, over seven hundred newspaper articles and reviews, and a volume of essays.

Wilfred Owen (1893–1918)   Born in the Shropshire countryside of England, Owen had begun writing verse before he matriculated at London University, where he was known as a quiet and contemplative student. After some years of teaching English in France, Owen returned to England and joined the army. He was wounded in 1917 and killed in action leading an attack a few days before the armistice was declared in 1918. Owen's poems, published only after his death, along with his letters from the front to his mother, are perhaps the most powerful and vivid accounts of the horror of war to emerge from the First World War.

Sylvia Plath (1932–1963)   Plath was born in Boston, Massachusetts, where her parents taught at Boston University. She graduated summa cum laude in English from Smith College (1955), earned an M.A. as a Fulbright scholar at Newnham College, Cambridge (1955–1957), and married British poet Ted Hughes (1956). Plath's poetry reveals the anger and anxiety that would eventually lead to her suicide. Her view that all relationships were in some way destructive and predatory surely darkened her life. Yet in 1963, during the month between the publication of her only novel, *The Bell Jar* (about a suicidal college student), and her death, Plath was extraordinarily productive; she produced finished poems every day. One critic suggests that for Plath, suicide was a positive act, a "refusal to collaborate" in a world she could not accept. Her *Collected Poems* was published in 1981.

Katherine Anne Porter (1890–1980)   Born in Texas and educated mostly at small convent schools, Porter traveled widely in her early years, living for some time in Mexico and, more briefly, in Germany. She gained a reputation primarily as a writer of finely crafted stories, gathered in *The Collected Stories of Katherine Anne Porter* (1965). She published one novel, *Ship of Fools*, in 1962. Porter's output of fiction was small, and she earned her livelihood mostly as a reporter, lecturer, scriptwriter, speaker, and writer-in-residence. Her achievement in fiction was recognized by a National Book Award and a Pulitzer Prize for fiction, both in 1966. Her final work, *The Never-Ending Wrong* (1977), is a memoir about her involvement in the celebrated Sacco-Vanzetti case.

Sir Walter Ralegh (1552?–1618)   Born in Devonshire, England, into the landed gentry, Ralegh attended Oxford but dropped out after a year in order to fight for the Huguenot cause in France. He returned to England, began the study of law, but again was drawn to a life of adventure and exploration. Through the influence of friends he came to the attention of Queen Elizabeth, and thenceforth his career flourished: he was knighted, given a number of lucrative commercial monopolies, made a member of Parliament, and in 1587, named captain of the Yeoman of the Guard. During these years, he invested in various colonies in North America, but all his settlements failed. He was briefly imprisoned in the Tower of London for offending the queen but was soon back in favor and in command of an unsuccessful expedition to Guiana (now Venezuela) in 1595. In 1603, he was again imprisoned in the Tower, this time on a probably trumped-up charge of treason, where he remained until 1616, spending part of his time writing *A History of the World* (1614). After his release, he undertook still another expedition to Guiana but again returned empty-handed. As a consequence of more political intrigue, James I ordered him executed. Although Ralegh epitomized the great merchant adventurers of Elizabethan England, he was also a gifted poet.

Dudley Randall (b. 1914)   Born in Washington, D.C., Randall worked during the depression in the foundry of the Ford Motor Company in Dearborn, Michigan, and then as a carrier and clerk for the U.S. Post Office in Detroit. He served in the U.S. Army Signal Corps (1942–1946) and graduated from Wayne State University (B.A., 1949) and the University of Michigan (M.A.L.S., 1951). He was a librarian at several universities and in 1965, founded the Broadside Press, "so black people could speak to and for their people." Randall told *Negro Digest*, "Precision and accuracy are necessary for both white and black writers. . . . 'A black aesthetic' should not be an excuse for sloppy writing." He urges African-American writers to reject what was false in "white" poetry but not to forsake universal concerns in favor of a racial agenda. His works include *On Getting a Natural* (1969) and *A Litany of Friends: New and Selected Poems* (1981).

Henry Reed (b. 1914)   Reed was born in Birmingham, England, earned a B.A. from the University of Birmingham (1937), worked as a teacher and free-lance writer (1937–1941), and served in the British army (1941–1942). His early poetry dealt with political events before and during World War II. "Naming of Parts" and "Judging Distances" were based on his frustrating experience in cadet training. His only collection of poetry, A *Map of Verona* (1946), revealed a formal, reverent, but also humorous and ironic voice. Reed began writing radio plays in 1947 and has generated as many as four scripts a year. His best-known satirical work is the "Hilda Tablet" series, a 1960s BBC-Radio production that parodied British society of the 1930s.

Alastair Reid (b. 1926)   Born in Scotland, son of a minister, Reid graduated with honors from St. Andrews University after serving in the Royal Navy. He taught at Sarah Lawrence College (1951–1955) and after his appointment as staff writer on the *New Yorker* in 1959, occasionally enjoyed visiting professorships across the United States and in England, teaching Latin American studies and literature. Acclaimed for his light, engaging style, Reid has been enthusiastically received as a poet, translator, essayist, and author of children's books, moving between genres as easily as he has moved between countries. Reid has lived in Spain, Latin America, Greece, and Morocco (to name a few places) and rejects the label *Scottish* writer. His deliberate rootlessness shows in his poetry, which is characterized by, in one critic's words, "natural irregularity."

Adrienne Rich (b. 1929)   Born to a middle-class family, Rich was educated by her parents until she entered public school in the fourth grade. She graduated Phi Beta Kappa from Radcliffe College in 1951, the same year her first book of poems, A *Change of World*, appeared. That volume, chosen by W. H. Auden for the Yale Series of Younger Poets Award, and her next, *The Diamond Cutters and Other Poems* (1955), earned her a reputation as an elegant, controlled stylist. In the 1960s, however, Rich began a dramatic shift away from her earlier mode as she took up political and feminist themes and stylistic experimentation in such works as *Snapshots of a Daughter-in-Law: Poems 1954–1962* (1963), *The Necessities of Life: Poems 1962–1965* (1966), *Leaflets: Poems 1965–1968* (1969), and *The Will to Change: Poems 1968–1970* (1971). In *Diving into the Wreck: Poems 1971–1972* (1973) and *The Dream of a Common Language: Poems 1974–1977* (1978), she continues to experiment with form and to deal with the experiences and aspirations of women from a feminist perspective. In addition to her poetry, Rich has published many essays on poetry, feminism, motherhood, and lesbianism.

Edwin Arlington Robinson (1869–1935)   Robinson grew up in Gardiner, Maine, attended Harvard, returned to Gardiner as a free-lance writer, then settled in New York City in 1896. His various odd jobs included a one-year stint as subway-construction inspector. President Theodore Roosevelt, a fan of his poetry, had him appointed to the United States Customs House in New York, where he worked from 1905 to 1909. Robinson wrote about people, rather than nature, particularly New England characters remembered from his early years. Describing his first volume of poems, *The Torrent and the Night Before* (1896), he told a friend there was not "a single red-breasted robin in the whole collection." Popular throughout his career, Robinson won three Pulitzer Prizes (1921, 1924, 1927).

Theodore Roethke (1908–1963)   Born in Saginaw, Michigan, Roethke was the son of a greenhouse owner; greenhouses figure prominently in the imagery of his poems. He graduated magna cum laude from the University of Michigan in 1929, where he also earned an M.A. in 1936 after graduate study at Harvard. He taught at several universities, coached two varsity tennis teams, and settled at the University of Washington in 1947. Intensely introspective and demanding of himself, Roethke was renowned as a great teacher, though sometimes incapacitated by an on-going manic-depressive condition. His collection *The Waking: Poems 1933–1953* won the Pulitzer Prize in 1954. Other awards include Guggenheim Fellowships in 1945 and 1950, and a National Book Award and the Bollingen Prize in 1959 for *Words for the Wind* (1958).

Muriel Rukeyser (1913–1980)   Born in New York City, Rukeyser attended Vassar and Columbia, then spent a short time at Roosevelt Aviation School, which no doubt helped shape her first published volume of poetry, *Theory of Flight* (1935). In the early 1930s, she joined Elizabeth Bishop, Mary McCarthy, and Eleanor Clark in founding a literary magazine that challenged the policies of the *Vassar Review*. (The two magazines later merged.) A social activist, Rukeyser witnessed the Scottsboro trials (where she was one of the reporters arrested by authorities) in 1933. She visited suffering tunnel workers in West Virginia (1936) and went to Hanoi to protest U.S. involvement in the Vietnam War. She gave poetry readings across the United States and received several awards, including a Guggenheim Fellowship and the Copernicus Award. *Waterlily Fire: Poems 1935–1962* appeared in 1962, and later work was collected in *29 Poems* (1970). *The Collected Poems of Muriel Rukeyser* appeared in 1978. Her only novel, *The Orgy*, appeared in 1965.

Margaret Sanger (1883–1966)   The sixth of eleven children, Margaret Higgins Sanger was born in Corning, New York. She chose nursing as a career, and the tragic events that determined the course of her life occurred while she worked as an obstetrical nurse in the impoverished Lower East Side of Manhattan. Her experiences with the poor and desperate women she nursed compelled her to action; she decided to educate women about birth control (an expression she invented) and help them avoid pregnancy. She founded the National Birth Control League in 1914 under the slogan "No gods; no masters!," and began publishing a magazine, *Woman Rebel*. In 1915, she was indicted for sending birth-control information through the mail, and in 1916, she was arrested and jailed for operating a birth-control clinic in Brooklyn, New York. While in prison, she founded and edited *Birth Control Review*. Her personal integrity and her prodigious energy finally triumphed, and legislative changes allowed doctors to provide sex education and prescribe contraceptives. Her work culminated in 1952, in Bombay, India, when the International Planned Parenthood Federation was established and made her its first president.

Richard Selzer (b. 1928)   The son of a family doctor, Selzer was born in Troy, New York. He attended Union College in Schenectady, New York, and earned an M.D. at Albany Medical College in 1953. He wrote *Rituals of Surgery* (1974), a collection of short stories, and he subsequently published numerous essays and stories in such magazines as *Redbook*, *Esquire*, and *Harper's*. These he collected in two volumes of essays, *Mortal Lessons* (1977) and *Confessions of a Knife* (1979), and a volume of essays and fiction, *Letters to a Young Doctor* (1982). In his writing, he draws upon his experience as a surgeon, and as one critic points out, he "forces physicians to think about the morality of medicine."

William Shakespeare (1564–1616)   Shakespeare was born at Stratford-on-Avon in April 1564. His father became an important public figure, rising to the position of high bailiff (equivalent to mayor) of Stratford. Although we know practically nothing of his personal life, we may assume that Shakespeare received a decent grammar school education in literature, logic, and Latin (though not in mathematics or natural science). When he was eighteen, he married Anne Hathaway, eight years his senior; six months later their son was born. Two years later, Anne bore twins. We do not know how the young Shakespeare supported his family, and we do not hear of him again until 1592, when a rival London playwright sarcastically refers to him as an "upstart crow." Shakespeare seems to have prospered in the London theater world. He probably began as an actor and earned enough as author and part owner of his company's theaters to acquire property. His sonnets, which were written during the 1590s, reveal rich and varied interests. Some are addressed to an attractive young man (whom the poet urges to marry); others to the mysterious dark lady; still others suggest a love triangle of two men and a woman. His dramas include historical plays based on English dynastic struggles; comedies, both festive and dark; romances such as *Pericles* (1608) and *Cymbeline* (1611) that cover decades in the lives of their characters; and the great tragedies: *Hamlet* (1602), *Othello* (1604), *King Lear* (1605), and *Macbeth* (1606). About 1611 (at age forty-seven), he retired to the second largest house in Stratford. He died in 1616, leaving behind a body of work that still stands as a pinnacle in world literature.

Karl Shapiro (b. 1913)   Born in Baltimore, Maryland, Shapiro attended the University of Virginia, Johns Hopkins University, and Pratt Library School. He gained early recognition with his first poetry collection, *Person, Place and Thing*, published in 1942 while he served in the U.S. Army. This collection won a Pulitzer Prize in 1945. After several visiting professorships, Shapiro taught for ten years at the University of Nebraska and then at the University of California, Davis, from 1968 to 1984. He eventually rejected the traditionalism that characterized his early work and wrote free-form poetry. *Poems of a Jew* (1958) traces his search for identity and a "Jewish consciousness."

Irwin Shaw (1913–1984)   Born and educated in New York City, where he received a B.A. from Brooklyn College in 1934, Shaw began his career as a scriptwriter for popular radio programs of the 1930s, then went to Hollywood to write for the movies. Disillusioned with the film industry, Shaw returned to New York. His first piece of serious writing, an antiwar play entitled *Bury the Dead*, was produced on Broadway in 1936. About this time, Shaw began contributing short stories to such magazines as the *New Yorker* and *Esquire*. His first collection of stories, *Sailor off the Bremen and Other Stories* (1939), earned him an immediate and lasting reputation as a writer of fiction. While continuing to write plays and stories, Shaw turned to the novel and published in 1948 *The Young Lions*, which won high critical praise as one of the most important novels to come out of World War II. The commercial success of the book and the movie adaptation brought Shaw financial independence and allowed him to devote the rest of his career to writing novels, among them *The Troubled Air* (1951), *Lucy Crown* (1956), *Rich Man, Poor Man* (1970), and *Acceptable Losses* (1982). Shaw's stories are collected in *Short Stories: Five Decades* (1978).

Percy Bysshe Shelley (1792–1822)   Born near Horsham, England, Shelley was the son of a wealthy landowner who sat in Parliament. At University College, Oxford, he befriended Thomas Jefferson Hogg. Both became interested in radical philosophy and quickly became inseparable. After one year at Oxford, they were expelled together for writing and circulating a pamphlet entitled "The Necessity of Atheism." Shelley married Harriet Westbrook soon after leaving Oxford. Although they had two children, the marriage was unsuccessful, and in 1814, Shelley left Harriet for Mary Wollstonecraft Godwin (author of *Frankenstein* [1818]). After Harriet's death (an apparent suicide), Shelley and Godwin were married. Escaping legal problems in England, he settled in Pisa, Italy, in 1820 and died in a sailing accident before his thirtieth birthday. A playwright and essayist as well as a romantic poet, Shelley is admired for his dramatic poem "Prometheus Unbound" (1820).

Leslie Silko (b. 1948)   Born in Albuquerque, New Mexico, Silko grew up on the Laguna Pueblo Reservation. She was educated in Bureau of Indian Affairs schools and at the University of New Mexico, where she graduated with highest honors. After three semesters in the American Indian Law program, Silko decided to devote her talents to writing about native Americans. Her short stories quickly earned her a reputation; in 1974, she published a volume of poems, *Laguna Woman*. Her novel, *Ceremony* (1977), was widely acclaimed and revived interest in her earlier short stories. *Storyteller* (1981) is a semiautobiographical collection of stories and poems. Silko has taught at the University of Arizona and the University of New Mexico but, with a $176,000 award from the prestigious MacArthur Foundation she has been, in her words, "a little less beholden to the everyday world."

Stevie Smith (1902–1971)   Born Florence Margaret Smith in Hull, England, Stevie Smith was a secretary at Newnes Publishing Company in London from 1923 to 1953 and occasionally worked as a writer and broadcaster for the BBC. Although she began publishing verse, which she often illustrated herself, in the 1930s, Smith did not reach a wide audience until 1962—with the publication of *Selected Poems* and her appearance in the Penguin Modern Poets Series. She is noted for her eccentricity and mischievous humor, often involving an acerbic twist on nursery rhymes, common songs, or hymns. Force-fed with what she considered the lifeless language of the *New English Bible*, she often aimed satirical barbs at religion. Smith won the Queen's Gold Medal for poetry in 1969, two years before her death. She published three novels in addition to her eight volumes of poetry.

Sophocles (496?–406 B.C.)   Born into a wealthy family at Colonus, a village just outside Athens, Sophocles distinguished himself early in life as a performer, musician, and athlete. Our knowledge of him is based on a very few ancient laudatory notices, but he certainly had a brilliant career as one of the three great Greek classical tragedians (the other two are Aeschylus, an older contemporary, and Euripides, a younger contemporary). He won the drama competition associated with the Dionysian festival (entries consisted of a tragic trilogy and a farce) at least twenty times (far more often than his two principal rivals). However, *Oedipus Rex*, his most famous tragedy, and the three other plays it was grouped with, took second place (ca. 429 B.C.). He lived during the golden age of Athens, when architecture, philosophy, and the arts flourished under Pericles. In 440 B.C., Sophocles was elected as one of the ten *strategoi* (military commanders), an indication of his stature in Athens. But his long life ended in sadder times—when the Peloponnesian War (431–404 B.C.), between the Athenian empire and an alliance led by Sparta, darkened the region. Although Sophocles wrote some 123 plays, only 7 have survived; nonetheless, these few works establish him as the greatest of the ancient Western tragedians.

Helen Sorrells (b. 1908)   Born in Stafford, Kansas, the daughter of farmers, Sorrells earned a B.S. from Kansas State University in 1931. She married a technical writer, had two children and was approaching her seventh decade when she won the Borestone Award for her poem "Cry Summer." In 1968, she won the *Arizona Quarterly* Award for poetry and in 1973 received a creative writing grant from the National Endowment for the Arts, as well as the Poetry Society of America's Cecil Hemley Award for the poem "Tunnels." She has contributed to *Esquire* and *Reporter*, among others, and published a collection of poems, *Seeds as They Fall* (1971).

Wallace Stevens (1879–1955)   Born in Reading, Pennsylvania, Stevens graduated from Harvard in 1900, worked for a year as a reporter for the New York *Herald Tribune*, graduated from New York University Law School in 1903, and practiced law in New York for twelve years. From 1916 to 1955, Stevens worked for the Hartford Accident and Indemnity Company, where he was appointed vice president in 1934. He was in his forties when he published his first book of poetry, *Harmonium* (1923). Stevens argued that poetry is a "supreme fiction" that shapes chaos and provides order to both nature and human relationships. He illuminates his philosophy in *Ideas of Order* (1935) and *Notes toward a Supreme Fiction* (1942). His *Collected Poems* (1954) won the Pulitzer Prize and established him as a major American poet.

May Swenson (1919–1989)   Raised in Utah, Swenson earned a B.A. from Utah State University in 1939, and later settled in New York City. She has lectured and given readings at over thirty colleges and was poet-in-residence at Purdue University (1966–1967), University of North Carolina (1968–1969 and 1975), and Letheridge University in Alberta, Canada (1970). Described as an accessible yet challenging poet, Swenson is noted for her experimentalism; sometimes she arranges the words of a poem to create a pictorial shape. She has won numerous honors including a Guggenheim Fellowship (1959) and Shelley Memorial Award (1968). Her poetry collections include *Another Animal* (1954), *Iconographs* (1970), and a volume for children, *Poems to Solve* (1966). She is also known for the many journals she has published.

Johnathan Swift (1667–1745)   Born in Dublin, Ireland, of English parents, Swift moved to England following his graduation from Trinity College, Dublin. In 1695, he was ordained minister of the Anglican church of Ireland and five years later became a parish priest in Laracor, Ireland. The conduct of church business took Swift to England frequently, where his wit and skill in defense of Tory politics made him many influential friends. He was rewarded for his efforts in 1713, when Queen Anne appointed him dean of St. Patrick's Cathedral in Dublin. The accession of George I to the throne in the following year, followed by the Tory's loss of the government to Whig control, ended the political power of Swift and his friends. He spent the rest of his life as dean of St. Patrick's, writing during this period his most celebrated satirical narrative, *Gulliver's Travels* (1726), and his most savage essay, "A Modest Proposal" (1729). Among his many other works are *A Tale of a Tub* and *The Battle of the Books* (both 1704), and many poems.

Alfred, Lord Tennyson (1809–1892)   Tennyson was born in Lincolnshire and attended Trinity College, Cambridge (1828–1831), where he won the Chancellor's Medal for Poetry in 1829. His 1842 collection, *Poems*, was not well received, but he gained prominence and the queen's favor with the 1850 publication of *In Memoriam*, an elegy written over seventeen years and inspired by the untimely death of his friend Arthur Hallam in 1833. That same year he finally married Emily Sellwood (after a fourteen-year engagement). In 1850, he was named poet laureate of England after Wordsworth's death. His works include *Maud and Other Poems* (1855) and *Idylls of the King* (1859), based on the legendary exploits of King Arthur and the knights of the Round Table.

Dylan Thomas (1914–1953)   Born in Swansea, Wales, Thomas decided to pursue a writing career directly after grammar school. At age twenty, he published his first collection, *Eighteen Poems* (1934), but his lack of a university degree deprived him of most opportunities to earn a living as a writer in Great Britain. Consequently, his early life (as well as the lives of his wife and children) was darkened by a poverty compounded by his free spending and heavy drinking. A self-proclaimed romanticist, Thomas called his poetry a "record of [his] struggle from darkness towards some measure of light." *The Map of Love* appeared in 1939 and *Deaths and Entrances* in 1946. Later, as a radio playwright and screenwriter, Thomas delighted in the sounds of words, sometimes at the expense of sense. *Under Milk Wood* (produced in 1953) is filled with his private, onomatopoetic language. He suffered from alcoholism and lung ailments and died in a New York hospital in 1953. Earlier that year, he noted in his *Collected Poems*: "These poems, with all their crudities, doubts and confusions are written for the love of man and in Praise of God, and I'd be a damn fool if they weren't."

Lewis Thomas (b. 1913)   Thomas was born in Flushing, New York. The son of a surgeon, he graduated from Princeton University and in 1937 earned an M.D. from Harvard. In his distinguished medical career, he combines an active practice with teaching and administration. He served as dean of the medical schools of Yale and New York universities and is currently chief executive officer of the Sloan-Kettering Institute in New York City. His many scientific papers earned him membership in the National Academy of Sciences. But even as a medical student, Thomas displayed literary ambition and published a number of poems. In 1971, he began contributing a regular column, "Notes of a Biology Watcher," to the prestigious *New England Journal of Medicine*. Some of these essays he collected and published in 1974 as *The Lives of a Cell: Notes of a Biology Watcher*. These graceful essays found a sizable audience and won the National Book Award. Subsequent essay collections include *The Medusa and the Snail* (1979) and *Late Night Thoughts on Listening to Mahler's Ninth Symphony* (1983). *The Youngest Science: Notes of a Medicine Watcher* (1983) describes the making of a doctor.

James Thurber (1894–1961)   Born in Columbus, Ohio, Thurber went through the local public schools and graduated from Ohio State University. He began his writing career as a reporter, first for an Ohio newspaper and later in Paris and New York City, before he became a staff member of the *New Yorker*. There he wrote the humorous satirical essays and fables (often illustrated with his whimsical drawings of people and animals) upon which his reputation rests—the most famous being "The Secret Life of Walter Mitty." In 1929, he and another *New Yorker* staffer, E. B. White, wrote *Is Sex Necessary? or, Why You Feel the Way You Do*, a spoof of the increasingly popular new psychological theories. In 1933, he published his humorous autobiography, *My Life and Hard Times*. With Elliott Nugent, he wrote *The Male Animal* (1940), a comic play that pleads for academic freedom, and in 1959, he memorialized his associates at the *New Yorker* in *The Years with Ross*.

Leo Tolstoy (1828–1910)   Born in Russia into a family of aristocratic land-owners, Tolstoy cut short his university education and joined the army, serving among the primitive Cossacks, who became the subject of his first novel, *The Cossacks* (1863). Tolstoy left the army and traveled abroad but was disappointed by Western materialism and returned home. After a brief period in St. Petersburg (now Leningrad), he became bored with the life of literary celebrity and returned to his family estate. There he wrote his two greatest novels, *War and Peace* (1869) and *Anna Karenina* (1877). Around 1876, Tolstoy experienced a kind of spiritual crisis that ultimately led him to reject his former beliefs, way of life, and literary works. Henceforth, he adopted the simple life of the Russian peasants and rejected orthodoxy in favor of a rational Christianity that disavowed private property, class divisions, secular and institutional religious authority, as well as all art (including his own) that failed to teach the simple principles he espoused.

Jean Toomer (1894–1967)   Descended from Pinckney Benton Stewart Pinchback, a Reconstruction governor of Louisiana whose mother had been a slave, Jean Toomer became one of the leaders in the literary world of the Harlem Renaissance and produced one of that movement's most distinguished works, *Cane* (1923). He also worked in the mainstream white New York literary scene. Although his best work illuminates the African-American experience of the Georgia sugarcane fields, he once wrote, "I would consider it libelous for anyone to refer to me as a colored man, for I have not lived as one." Born in Washington, D.C., he graduated from public school and, aiming for a law degree, enrolled briefly at the University of Wisconsin and the City College of New York. But college life proved ungratifying, and he wandered, living among a variety of social and racial groups. He married twice—first a novelist, who died in childbirth, then the daughter of a wealthy New York broker. Both his wives were white. He said of himself: "I am of no particular race, I am of the human race, a man at large in the human world, preparing a new race."

Mark Twain (1835–1910)   Born Samuel L. Clemens in Florida, Missouri, Twain grew up in Hannibal, Missouri, on the banks of the Mississippi River (*mark twain*, a phrase meaning "two fathoms deep," was used by Mississippi riverboat pilots in making soundings). Sometime after his father's death in 1847, Twain left school to become a printer's apprentice, worked as a journeyman printer and newspaper reporter in the East and Middle West, and became a steamboat pilot on the Mississippi River until the outbreak of the Civil War. In 1861, he departed for Nevada with his brother, spent a year prospecting for silver, then returned to newspaper work as a reporter. In 1867, a San Francisco newspaper sent him as correspondent on a cruise ship to Europe and the Holy Land. He used the dispatches he wrote about this voyage as the basis for his first, highly successful book, *The Innocents Abroad* (1869). His second book, *Roughing It* (1872), described his western years and added to his already considerable reputation as an irreverent humorist. No longer explicitly autobiographical but still drawing on his own life, Twain published his masterpieces, the novels *The Adventures of Tom Sawyer* (1876) and *The Adventures of Huckleberry Finn* (1884). Twain remained a prolific and important writer and by the time of his death had become something of a national institution, although he never again quite matched the achievements of these early works. Financial problems and personal tragedies contributed to his increasingly bleak view of the human condition, expressed most powerfully in such works as *A Connecticut Yankee in King Arthur's Court* (1889), *Pudd'nhead Wilson* (1894), *The Man That Corrupted Hadleyburg* (1900), and the posthumously published *The Mysterious Stranger* (1916).

Rosmarie Waldrop (b. 1935)   Born in Germany, she holds a Ph.D. in Comparative Literature from the University of Michigan and is a National Endowment for the Arts Fellow as well as a recipient of a Columbia Translation Center Award. She has written six books of poetry, including *The Aggressive Ways of the Casual Stranger* (1972), *Streets Enough to Welcome Snow* (1986), *Reproduction of the Profiles* (1987), and *Lawn of the Excluded Middle* (1991). She has also written two novels and many articles and reviews, and her translations include Edmond Jabes's *The Book of Questions*. With Keith Waldrop she is the editor and publisher of Burning Deck Press.

Alice Walker (b. 1944)   Born in Eatonton, Georgia, the eighth child of sharecroppers, Walker was educated at Spelman College and Sarah Lawrence College. She has been deeply involved in the civil rights movement, working to register voters in Georgia and on behalf of welfare rights and Head Start in Mississippi. She also worked for the New York City Department of Welfare. She has taught at Wellesley and Yale and been an editor of *Ms.* Her nonfiction works include a biography for children, *Langston Hughes: American Poet* (1973); numerous contributions to anthologies about African-American writers; and a collection of essays, *In Search of Our Mothers' Gardens: Womanist Prose* (1983). She has published four novels, all dealing with the African-American experience: *The Third Life of Grange Copeland* (1973), *Meridian* (1976), *The Color Purple* (1982), which won the Pulitzer Prize and established her as a major writer, and *The Temple of My Familiar* (1989). Her short stories are collected in two volumes, *In Love and Trouble: Stories of Black Women* (1973) and *You Can't Keep a Good Woman Down* (1981). Her five collections of poetry include *Good Night, Willie Lee, I'll See You in the Morning* (1979) and *Horses Make a Landscape Look More Beautiful* (1984).

Robert Wallace (b. 1932)   Born in Springfield, Missouri, Wallace graduated summa cum laude from Harvard in 1953. After serving in the U.S. Army, he earned an M.A. (with honors) from Cambridge in 1959. He taught English at Bryn Mawr, Sweet Briar College, and Vassar, and in 1965 joined the English department of Case Western Reserve University in Cleveland. There Wallace directs Bits Press, which publishes the work of contemporary poets. An award-winning poet himself, Wallace has contributed poems to many periodicals, including the *New Yorker*, the *Atlantic, Harper's,* and the *New Republic.* In addition to his several collections of poems, he has published a book of children's poems, *Critters* (1978), and a textbook, *Writing Poems* (1982).

Edmund Waller (1606–1687) Born in Hertfordshire, England, Waller was privately instructed as a young child, then sent to Eton and Cambridge. He served for several years as a member of Parliament, first as an opponent of the Crown and later as a Royalist. His advocacy of the Royalist cause and his attempts to moderate between the Crown and the Puritans in an increasingly revolutionary period led to his imprisonment and exile. He made his peace with Cromwell and returned to England in 1651. When the monarchy was restored in 1660, Waller regained his seat in Parliament. Waller was one of the earliest poets to use the heroic couplet, a form that was to dominate English poetry for over a century.

E. B. White (1899–1985) Born in Mount Vernon, New York, Elwyn Brooks White was educated at Cornell and began his career as a journalist, but he soon abandoned journalism in favor of essay writing. His graceful and witty style led to his appointment to the staff of the *New Yorker*, where over the years his personal, informal essays earned him a reputation as one of America's finest writers. From 1938 to 1943 he wrote a regular column for *Harper's*, pieces that were collected in *One Man's Meat* (1944). Other essays, as well as short stories, are collected in *The Second Tree from the Corner* (1954). If, as one critic has observed, White is known among writers as "an essayist's essayist," he is more widely known to the general public as the author of two classic works of children's literature, *Stuart Little* (1945) and *Charlotte's Web* (1952). Among his many other works, White wrote, with James Thurber, *Is Sex Necessary? or, Why You Feel the Way You Do* (1929).

Walt Whitman (1819–1892) One of nine children, Whitman was born in Huntington, Long Island, in New York, and grew up in Brooklyn, where his father worked as a carpenter. At age eleven, after five years of public school, Whitman took a job as a printer's assistant. He learned the printing trade and, before his twentieth birthday, became editor of the *Long Islander*, a Huntington newspaper. He edited several newspapers in the New York area and one in New Orleans before leaving the newspaper business in 1848. He then lived with his parents, worked as a part-time carpenter, and began writing *Leaves of Grass*, which he first published at his own expense in 1855. After the Civil War (during which he was a devoted volunteer, ministering to the wounded), Whitman was fired from his job in the Department of the Interior by Secretary James Harlan, who considered *Leaves of Grass* obscene. Soon, however, he was rehired in the attorney general's office, where he remained until 1874. In 1881, after many editions, *Leaves of Grass* finally found a publisher willing to print it uncensored. Translations were enthusiastically received in Europe, but Whitman remained relatively unappreciated in America, where it was only after his death that a large audience would come to admire his original and innovative expression of American individualism.

Richard Wilbur (b. 1921)   Son of a portrait artist, Wilbur was born in New York City, graduated from Amherst College in 1942, became staff sergeant in the U.S. Army during World War II, then earned an M.A. from Harvard in 1947. He taught English at Harvard, Wellesley, and Wesleyan University, and was named writer-in-residence at Smith College in 1977. Winner of the Pulitzer Prize, National Book Award, and Bollingen Prize, Wilbur has distinguished himself in his several volumes of poetry. Though he uses established poetic forms and meters, he mines new insights from common, tangible images. A translator of French plays by Molière and Racine, Wilbur was colyricist (with Lillian Hellman) of *Candide*, the 1957 Broadway musical based on Voltaire's satirical novel.

William Carlos Williams (1883–1963)   Born in Rutherford, New Jersey, Williams graduated from the University of Pennsylvania (M.D., 1906), interned at hospitals in New York City for two years, studied pediatrics in Leipzig, then returned to practice medicine in his hometown. As a general practitioner, Williams found ample poetic inspiration in his patients and scribbled down lines between appointments and on the way to house calls. His early collections include *The Tempers* (1913), *Kora in Hell: Improvisations* (1920), and *Sour Grapes* (1921). A stroke in the mid-1950s forced him to retire from his medical practice but gave him more time to write. His many honors include the National Book Award (1950) and the Pulitzer Prize (1963). *The Williams Reader* was published in 1965.

Virginia Woolf (1882–1941)   Born in London, where she spent most of her life, Woolf, because of her frail health and her father's Victorian attitudes about the proper role of women, received little formal education (none at the university level). Nevertheless, the advantages of an upper-class family (her father, Sir James Stephens, was a distinguished scholar and man of letters who hired tutors for her) and an extraordinarily powerful and inquiring mind allowed Woolf to educate herself. She began keeping a regular diary in her early teens. After moderate success with her first novels, the publication of *To the Lighthouse* (1927) and *Orlando* (1929) established her as a major novelist. While Woolf's reputation rests primarily on her novels, which helped revolutionize fictional technique, she was also a distinguished literary and social critic. A strong supporter of women's rights, she expressed her views on the subject in a series of lectures published as *A Room of One's Own* (1929) and in a collection of essays, *Three Guineas* (1938). Her reputation grew with the publication of her letters and diaries following her suicide by drowning.

William Wordsworth (1770–1850)   Born in Cockermouth, in the Lake District of England, Wordsworth was educated at Cambridge. During a summer tour in France in 1790, Wordsworth had an affair with Annette Vallon that resulted in the birth of a daughter. The tour also made of Wordsworth an ardent defender of the French Revolution of 1789 and kindled his sympathies for the plight of the common person. Wordsworth's acquaintance with Samuel Taylor Coleridge in 1795 began a close friendship that led to the collaborative publication of *Lyrical Ballads* in 1798. Wordsworth supplied a celebrated preface to the second edition in 1800, in which he announced himself a nature poet of pantheistic leanings, committed to democratic equality and the language of common people. He finished *The Prelude* in 1805, but it was not published until after his death. As he grew older, Wordsworth grew increasingly conservative, and while he continued to write prolifically, little that he wrote during the last decades of his life attained the heights of his earlier work. In 1843, he was appointed poet laureate.

Richard Wright (1908–1960)   Wright grew up in Memphis, Tennessee, where his sharecropper father moved the family after he was forced off the farm near Natchez, Mississippi, where Wright was born. When Wright was six, his father abandoned the family, leaving his mother to support Wright and his younger brother with whatever jobs she could find. While their mother worked, the boys shifted for themselves. When he was eight, Wright's mother enrolled him in grammar school, but she fell ill and was unable to work. Consequently, Wright and his brother were placed in an orphanage; reunited, the family lived with relatives, and Wright was able to resume his education, graduating from high school as valedictorian in 1925. Wright left the South for Chicago in 1927, hoping, as he said, that "gradually and slowly I might learn who I was, what I might be." After working at odd jobs, his efforts at writing paid off when he received a job as publicity agent for the Federal Negro Theater. Wright joined the Communist party in 1932 and was a member of the Federal Writers' Project from 1935 to 1937. He published his first collection, *Uncle Tom's Children*, in 1938. About the same time, he began a novel about a poor and angry inner-city youth who accidentally murders the daughter of his white, millionaire employer. The novel, *Native Son* (1940), was published to much critical and popular acclaim and remains his best-known work. Unable to accept party discipline, Wright quit the Communist party in 1944 and in the following year published *Black Boy*, an autobiography of his early years. Discouraged with the racism of America, Wright soon moved his family to France, where he spent the remainder of his life writing and supporting the cause of African independence. His later works include the novels *The Outsider* (1953) and *The Long Dream* (1958) and the nonfiction works *Black Power* (1954) and *White Man, Listen!* (1957).

William Butler Yeats (1865–1939)   Yeats was born in Ireland and educated in both Ireland and London. Much of his poetry and many of his plays reflect his fascination with the history of Ireland, particularly the myths and legends of its ancient, pagan past, as well as his interest in the occult. As Yeats matured, he turned increasingly to contemporary subjects, expressing his nationalism in poems about the Irish struggle for independence from England. In 1891, he became one of the founders of an Irish literary society in London (the Rhymers' Club) and of another in Dublin the following year. Already a recognized poet, Yeats helped to establish the Irish National Theater in 1899; its first production was his play *The Countess Cathleen* (written in 1892). His contribution to Irish cultural and political nationalism led to his appointment as a senator when the Irish Free State was formed in 1922. Yeats's preeminence as a poet was recognized in 1923 when he received the Nobel Prize for Literature. Among his works are *The Wanderings of Oisin and Other Poems* (1889), *The Wind among the Reeds* (1899), *The Green Helmet and Other Poems* (1910), *Responsibilities: Poems and a Play* (1914), *The Tower* (1928), *Last Poems and Two Plays* (1939).

Yevgeney Yevtushenko (b. 1933)   Son of two geologists, Yevtushenko was born in Siberia. He attended Gorky Literary Institute from 1951 to 1954 and worked on a geological expedition, at the same time establishing himself as an influential Soviet poet. During the 1950s, his books were published regularly and he was allowed to travel abroad. In 1960, he gave readings in Europe and the United States, but was criticized by Soviets for linking them with anti-Semitism in his poem "Babi Yar," the name of a ravine near Kiev where 96,000 Jews were killed by Nazis during World War II. Although considering himself a "loyal revolutionary Soviet citizen," he elicited official disapproval by opposing the 1968 occupation of Czechoslovakia (a performance of his play *Bratsk Power Station* [1967] was cancelled as a result) and for sending a telegram to then-Premier Brezhnev expressing concern for Aleksandr Solzhenitsyn after Solzhenitsyn's arrest in 1974. His works include *A Precocious Autobiography* (1963) and *From Desire to Desire* (1976).

Glossary of Literary Terms

Abstract Language Language that describes ideas, concepts, or qualities, rather than particular or specific persons, places, or things. *Beauty, courage, love* are abstract terms, as opposed to such concrete terms as *man, stone, woman.* George Washington, the Rosetta Stone, and Helen of Troy are particular concrete terms. Characteristically, literature uses *concrete* language to animate *abstract* ideas and principles. When Robert Frost, in "Provide, Provide" (p. 89), describes the pain of impoverished and lonely old age, he doesn't speak of an old, no longer beautiful female. He writes:
> The witch that came (the withered hag)
> To wash the steps with pail and rag,
> Was once the beauty Abishag.

Alexandrine In poetry, a line containing six iambic feet (iambic hexameter). Alexander Pope, in "An Essay on Criticism" (p. 789), reveals his distaste for the form in a couplet: "A needless Alexandrine ends the song, / That like a wounded snake, drags its slow length along." *See* Meter.

Allegory A narrative in verse or prose, in which abstract qualities (*death, pride, greed,* for example) are personified as characters. In Bernard Malamud's story "Idiots First" (p. 639), Ginzburg is the personification of death.

Alliteration The repetition of the same initial consonant (or any initial vowel) sounds in close proximity. The W sounds in these lines from Robert Frost's "Provide, Provide" (p. 89) alliterate: "The witch that came (the withered hag) / To wash the steps with pail and rag, / was once the beauty Abishag."

Allusion A reference in a literary work to something outside the work. The reference is usually to some famous person, event, or other literary work.

Ambiguity A phrase, statement, or situation that may be understood in two or more ways. In literature, ambiguity is used to enrich meaning or achieve irony by forcing readers to consider alternative possibilities. When the duke in Robert Browning's "My Last Duchess" (p. 74) says that he "gave commands; / Then all smiles stopped together. There she stands / As if alive," the reader cannot know exactly what those commands were or whether the last words refer to the commands (as a result of which she is no longer alive) or merely refer to the skill of the painter (the painting is extraordinarily lifelike).

Anapest A three-syllable metrical foot consisting of two unaccented syllables followed by an accented syllable. *See* Meter.

Antagonist A character in a story, play, or narrative poem who stands in opposition to the hero (*see* Protagonist). The conflict between antagonist and protagonist often generates the action or plot of the story.

Antistrophe *See* Strophe.

Apostrophe A direct address to a person who is absent, or to an abstract or inanimate entity. In one of his Holy Sonnets (p. 673), John Donne admonishes: "Death, be not proud!" And Wordsworth speaks to a river in Wales: "How oft, in spirit, have I turned to thee, / O sylvan Wye! thou wanderer through the woods."

Archaism   The literary use of obsolete language. When Keats, in "Ode on a Grecian Urn" (p. 675), writes: "with brede / Of marble men and maidens overwrought," he uses an archaic word for *braid* and intends an obsolete definition, "worked all over" (that is, "ornamented"), for *overwrought*.

Archetype   Themes, images, and narrative patterns that are universal and thus embody some enduring aspects of human experience. Some of these themes are the death and rebirth of the hero, the underground journey, and the search for the father.

Assonance   The repetition of vowel sounds in a line, stanza, or sentence. For example, Gwendolyn Brooks, in "The Children of the Poor" (p. 278), describes a character whose "lesions are legion." By using assonance that occurs at the end of words—*my*, *pie*—or a combination of assonance and consonance (that is, the repetition of final consonant sounds)—*fish, wish*—poets create rhyme. But some poets, particularly modern poets, often use assonantial and consonantial off rhymes (*see* Near Rhyme). W. H. Auden, in "Five Songs" (p. 455), writes:

> That night when joy began
> Our narrowest veins to flush,
> We waited for the flash
> Of morning's levelled gun.

Flush and *gun* are assonantial, *flush* and *flash* are consonantial (and, of course, alliterative).

Atmosphere   *See* Tone.

Aubade   A love song or lyric to be performed at sunrise. Richard Wilbur's comic "A Late Aubade" (p. 459) is a modern example. Philip Larkin's "Aubade" (p. 699) uses the form ironically in a somber contemplation of mortality.

Ballad   A narrative poem, originally of folk origin, usually focussing upon a climactic episode and told without comment. The most common ballad form consists of quatrains of alternating four- and three-stress iambic lines, with the second and fourth lines rhyming. Often, the ballad will employ a *refrain*—that is, the last line of each stanza will be identical or similar. "Edward" (p. 669) and "Bonny Barbara Allan" (p. 435) are traditional ballads. Dudley Randall's "Ballad of Birmingham" (p. 276) is a twentieth-century example of the ballad tradition.

Blank Verse   Lines of unrhymed iambic pentameter. Shakespeare's dramatic poetry and Milton's *Paradise Lost* (p. 255) are written principally in blank verse. *See* Meter.

Cacophony   Language that sounds harsh and discordant, sometimes used to reinforce the sense of the words. Consider the plosive *b*, *p*, and *t* sounds in the following lines from Shakespeare's Sonnet 129 (p. 439): " . . . and till action, lust / Is perjured, murderous, bloody, full of blame, / Savage, extreme, rude, cruel, not to trust." *Compare* Euphony.

Caesura   A strong pause within a line of poetry. Note the caesuras in these lines from Robert Browning's "My Last Duchess" (p. 74):

> That's my last Duchess painted on the wall,
> Looking as if she were alive. ‖ I call
> That piece a wonder, now: ‖ Frà Pandolf's hands
> Worked busily a day, ‖ and there she stands.

Carpe Diem   Latin, meaning "seize the day." A work, usually a lyric poem, in which the speaker calls the attention of the auditor (often a young woman) to the shortness of youth, and life, and then urges the auditor to enjoy life while there is time. Andrew

Marvell's "To His Coy Mistress" (p. 443) is among the best of the *carpe diem* tradition in English. The opening stanza of a famous Robert Herrick poem nicely illustrates *carpe diem* principles.

> Gather ye rosebuds while ye may,
> Old Time is still a-flying
> And this same flower that smiles today,
> Tomorrow will be dying.

Catharsis   A key concept in the *Poetics* of Aristotle that attempts to explain why representations of suffering and death in drama paradoxically leave the audience feeling relieved rather than depressed. According to Aristotle, the fall of a tragic hero arouses in the viewer feelings of "pity" and "terror"—pity because the hero is an individual of great moral worth, and terror because the viewer identifies with and, consequently, feels vulnerable to the hero's tragic fate. Ideally, the circumstances within the drama allow viewers to experience a catharsis that purges those feelings of pity and terror and leaves them emotionally purified.

Central Intelligence   *See* Point of View.

Chorus   Originally, a group of masked dancers who chanted lyric hymns at religious festivals in ancient Greece. In the plays of Sophocles, the chorus, while circling around the alter to Dionysius, chants the odes that separate the episodes. These odes, in some respects, represented an audience's reaction to, and comment on, the action in the episodes. In Elizabethan drama, and even, on occasion, in modern drama, the chorus appears, usually as a single person who comments on the action.

Comedy   In drama, the representation of situations that are designed to delight and amuse, and which end happily. Comedy often deals with ordinary people in their human condition, while tragedy deals with the ideal and heroic and, until recently, embodied only the high born as tragic heroes. *Compare* Tragedy.

Conceit   A figure of speech that establishes an elaborate parallel between unlike things. The *Petrarchan conceit* (named for the fourteenth-century Italian writer of love lyrics) was often imitated by Elizabethan sonneteers until the device became so hackneyed that Shakespeare mocked the tendency in Sonnet 130 (p. 440):

> My mistress' eyes are nothing like the sun;
> Coral is far more red than her lips' red;
> If snow be white, why then her breasts are dun;
> If hairs be wires, black wires grow on her head.

The *metaphysical conceit*, as used by John Donne for example, employs strange, even bizarre, comparisons to heighten the wit of the poem. Perhaps the most famous metaphysical conceit is Donne's elaborate and extended parallel of a drawing compass to the souls of the couple in "A Valediction: Forbidding Mourning" (p. 441).

Concrete Language   *See* Abstract Language.

Conflict   The struggle of a protagonist, or main character, with forces that threaten to destroy him or her. The struggle creates suspense and is usually resolved at the end of the narrative. The force opposing the main character may be either another person— the antagonist—(as in Frank O'Connor's "My Oedipus Complex," p. 39), or society (as in Harlan Ellison's " 'Repent Harlequin!' Said the Ticktockman," p. 238), or natural forces (as in Bernard Malamud's "Idiots First," p. 639). A fourth type of conflict reflects the struggle of opposing tendencies within an individual (as in Tolstoy's "The Death of Iván Ilých," p. 589).

Connotation   The associative and suggestive meanings of a word, in contrast to its literal or *denotative* meaning. One might speak of an *elected official*, a relatively neutral term without connatative implications. Others might call the same person a *politician*, a more negative term; still others might call him or her a *statesman*, a more laudatory term. *Compare* Denotation.

Consonance   Repetition of the final consonant sounds in stressed syllables. In the following verse from W. H. Auden's "Fire Songs" (p. 455), lines one and four illustrate consonance, as do lines two and three.

> That night when joy began
> Our narrowest veins to flush,
> We waited for the flash
> Of morning's levelled gun.

Couplet   A pair of rhymed lines—for example, these from A. E. Housman's "Terence, This is Stupid Stuff" (p. 85):

> Why, if 'tis dancing you would be,
> There's brisker pipes than poetry.

Dactyl   A three-syllable metrical foot consisting of an accented syllable followed by two unaccented syllables. *See* Meter.

Denotation   The literal dictionary definition of a word, without associative and suggestive meanings. *See* Connotation.

Denouement   The final revelations that occur after the main conflict is resolved; literally, the "untying" of the plot following the climax.

Deus ex Machina   Latin for "god from a machine." Difficulties were sometimes resolved in ancient Greek and Roman plays by a god, who was lowered to the stage by means of machinery. The term is now used to indicate the use of unconvincing or improbable coincidences to advance or resolve a plot.

Diction   The choice of words in a work of literature, and hence, an element of style crucial to the work's effectiveness. The diction of a story told from the point of view of an inner-city child (as in Toni Cade Bambara's "The Lesson," p. 64) will differ markedly from a similar story told from the point of view of a jaded professional (as in E. B. White's "The Second Tree from the Corner," p. 223).

Didactic   A term applied to works with the primary and avowed purpose of teaching the reader that some philosophical, religious, or moral doctrine is true. Hence, although some didactic works are nonetheless successful works of art, the emphasis on moral purposes usually occurs at the expense of aesthetic considerations and produces preachy narratives.

Dimeter   A line of poetry consisting of two metrical feet. *See* Meter.

Distance   The property that separates an author or a narrator from the actions of the characters he or she creates, thus allowing a disinterested, or aloof, narration of events. Similarly, distance allows the reader or audience to view the characters and events in a narrative dispassionately.

Dramatic Irony   *See* Irony.

Dramatic Monologue   A type of poem in which the speaker addresses another person (or persons) whose presence is known only from the speaker's words. During the course of the monologue, the speaker (often unintentionally) reveals his or her own character. Such poems are dramatic because the speaker interacts with another character at a specific time and place; they are monologues because the entire poem is uttered by the speaker. Robert Browning's "My Last Duchess" (p. 74), Matthew Arnold's "Dover Beach" (p. 446), and T. S. Eliot's "The Love Song of J. Alfred Prufrock" (p. 448) are dramatic monologues.

Elegy   Usually, a poem lamenting the death of a particular person, but often used to describe meditative poems on the subject of human mortality. A. E. Houseman's "To an Athlete Dying Young" (p. 678) and W. H. Auden's "In Memory of W. B. Yeats" (p. 692) are elegies.

End-rhyme   *See* Rhyme.

End-stopped Line   A line of verse that embodies a complete logical and grammatical unit. A line of verse that does not constitute a complete syntactic unit is called *run-on*. For example, in the opening lines of Robert Browning's "My Last Duchess" (p. 74): "That's my last Duchess painted on the wall, / Looking as if she were alive. I call / That piece a wonder, now: . . . ," The opening line is end-stopped, while the second line is run-on because the direct object of *call* runs on to the third line.

English Sonnet   Also called *Shakespearean sonnet*. *See* Sonnet.

Enjambment   The use of run-on lines. *See* End-stopped Line.

Epigraph   In literature, a short quotation or observation related to the theme and placed at the head of the work. T. S. Eliot's "The Love Song of J. Alfred Prufrock" (p. 448) has an epigraph, as does Donald W. Baker's "Formal Application" (p. 282).

Epiphany   In literature, a showing forth, or sudden manifestation. James Joyce used the term to indicate a sudden illumination that enables a character (and, presumably, the reader) to understand his situation. The narrator of Joyce's "Araby" (p. 30) experiences an epiphany toward the end of the story, as does Iván Ilých in Tolstoy's "The Death of Iván Ilých" (p. 589).

Epode   *See* Strophe.

Euphony   Language embodying sounds pleasing to the ear. *Compare* Cacophony.

Exposition   Information supplied to readers and audiences that enables them to understand narrative action. Often, exposition establishes what has occurred before the narrative begins or informs the audience about relationships among principal characters. The absence of exposition from some modern literature, particularly modern drama, contributes to the unsettling feelings sometimes experienced by the audience.

Farce   A type of comedy, usually satiric, that relies on exaggerated character types, ridiculous situations, and, often, horseplay.

Feminine Rhyme   A two-syllable rhyme in which the second syllable is unstressed, as in the second and fourth lines of these verses from Edward Arlington Robinson's "Miniver Cheevy" (p. 262):

> Miniver Cheevy, child of scorn,
> Grew lean while he assailed the seasons;
> He wept that he was ever born,
> And he had reasons.

Figurative Language   A general term covering the many ways in which language is used nonliterally. *See* Hyperbole, Irony, Metaphor, Metonymy, Paradox, Simile, Symbol, Synecdoche, Understatement.

First-person Narrator   *See* Point of View.

Foot   *See* Meter.

Free Verse   Poetry, usually unrhymed, that does not adhere to the metrical regularity of traditional verse. Walt Whitman's "Out of the Cradle Endlessly Rocking" (p. 76) is an early example, and many modern poets use this form. Although free verse is not metrically regular, it is nonetheless clearly more rhythmic than prose and makes use of other aspects of poetic discourse to achieve its effects.

Heroic Couplet   Iambic pentameter lines that rhyme *aa*, *bb*, *cc*, and so on. Usually, heroic couplets are *closed*—that is, the couplet's end coincides with a major syntactic unit so that the line is end-stopped. These lines from Alexander Pope's "Essay on Man" illustrate the form: "And, spite of pride, in erring reason's spite, / One truth is clear; Whatever IS, is RIGHT."

Hexameter   A line of verse consisting of six metrical feet. *See* Meter.

Hubris   In Greek tragedy, arrogance resulting from excessive pride. Oedipus, in Sophocles' *Oedipus Rex* (p. 107), is guilty of hubris.

Hyperbole   Figurative language that embodies overstatement or exaggeration. The boast of the speaker in Robert Burns's "A Red, Red Rose" (p. 445) is hyperbolic: "And I will luve thee still, my dear, / Till a' the seas gang dry."

Iamb   A metrical foot consisting of an unstressed syllable followed by a stressed syllable. *See* Meter.

Imagery   Language that embodies an appeal to a physical sense, usually sight, although the words may invoke sound, smell, taste, and touch as well. The term is often applied to all figurative language.

Internal Rhyme   *See* Rhyme.

Irony   Figurative language in which the intended meaning differs from the literal meaning. *Verbal irony* includes overstatement (hyperbole), understatement, and opposite statement. The following lines from Robert Burns's "A Red, Red Rose" (p. 445) embody overstatement:

> As fair as thou, my bonnie lass,
> So deep in luve am I;
> And I will luve thee still, my dear,
> Till a' the seas gang dry.

These lines from Andrew Marvell's "To His Coy Mistress" (p. 443) understate: "The grave's a fine and private place, / but none, I think, do there embrace." W. H. Auden's ironic conclusion to "The Unknown Citizen" (p. 273) reveals opposite statement: "Was he free? Was he happy? The question is absurd: / Had anything been wrong, we should certainly have heard." *Dramatic irony* occurs when a reader or audience knowns things a character does not and, consequently, hears things differently. For example, in Shakespeare's *Othello* (p. 475), the audience knows that Iago is Othello's enemy, but Othello doesn't. Hence, the audience's understanding of Iago's speeches to Othello differs markedly from Othello's.

Italian Sonnet   Also called *Petrarchan sonnet*. *See* Sonnet.

Lyric   Originally, a song accompanied by lyre music. Now, a relatively short poem expressing the thought or feeling of a single speaker. Almost all the nondramatic poetry in this anthology is lyric poetry.

Metaphor   A figurative expression consisting of two elements in which one element is provided with special attributes by being equated with a second, unlike element. In Theodore Roethke's "Elegy for Jane" (p. 695), for example, the speaker addresses his dead student: "If only I could nudge you from this sleep, / My maimed darling, my skittery pigeon." Here, Jane is characterized metaphorically as a "skittery pigeon," and all the reader's experience of nervous pigeon's movement becomes attached to Jane. *See* Simile.

Meter Refers to recurrent patterns of accented and unaccented syllables in verse. A metrical unit is called a *foot*, and there are four basic accented patterns. An *iamb*, or *iambic foot*, consists of an unaccented syllable followed by an accented syllable (bĕfóre, tŏdáy). A *trocee*, or *trochaic foot*, consists of an accented syllable followed by an unaccented syllable (fúnnȳ, phántŏm). An *anapest*, or *anapestic foot*, consists of two unaccented syllables followed by an accented syllable (in the line "If eV̆ ‖ erȳthīng há ‖ pēns thāt cán't ‖ bē dóne," the second and third metrical feet are anapests). A *dactyl*, or *dactyllic foot*, consists of a stressed syllable followed by two unstressed syllables (sýllăblĕ, métrīcăl). One common variant, consisting of two stressed syllables, is called a *spondee*, or *spondaic foot* (dáybrĕak, moónshíne).

Lines are classified according to the number of metrical feet they contain.

one foot	monometer
two feet	dimeter
three feet	trimeter
four feet	tetrameter
five feet	pentameter
six feet	hexameter (An iambic hexameter line is an *Alexandrine*.)

Here are some examples of various metrical patterns:

Tŏ eách ‖ hĭs súff ‖ erīngs: áll ‖ āre mén,	*iambic tetrameter*
Cŏndemńed ‖ āliké ‖ tŏ groán;	*iambic trimeter*

Ońce ŭp ‖ oń ă ‖ mídnīght ‖ dréarȳ, ‖ whĭle I ‖ póndered ‖ wéak ānd ‖ wéarȳ	*trochaic octameter*
Thĕ Āssýr ‖ iăn came doẃn ‖ lĭke ă wólf ‖ ŏn the fóld	*anapestic tetrameter*
Ĭs thís ‖ thĕ rég ‖ iŏn, thís ‖ thĕ soíl, ‖ thĕ clíme,	*iambic pentameter*
Fóllŏw ĭt ‖ úttĕrlȳ,	*dactyllic dimeter*
Hópe bĕ ‖ yońd hópe:	*dimeter line—trochee and spondee*

Metonymy A figure of speech in which a word stands for a closely related idea. In the expression "The pen is mightier than the sword," *pen* and *sword* are metonyms for written ideas and physical force.

Muses Nine goddesses, the daughters of Zeus and Mnemosyne (memory), who preside over various humanities. Although there are some variations, generally they may be assigned as follows: Calliope, epic poetry; Clio, history; Erato, lyric poetry; Euterpe, music; Melpomene, tragedy; Polyhymnia, sacred poetry; Tersichore, dance; Thalia, comedy; and Urania, astronomy.

Near Rhyme Also called *off rhyme*, *slant rhyme*, or *oblique rhyme*. Usually the occurrence of consonance where rhyme is expected, as in *pearl, alcohol* or *heaven, given. See* Rhyme.

Octave An eight-line stanza. More often, the opening eight-line section of an Italian sonnet, rhymed *abbaabba*, followed by the sestet that concludes the poem. *See* Sonnet.

Ode Usually, a long, serious poem on exalted subjects, often in the form of an address. Keats's "Ode on a Grecian Urn" (p. 675) is representative. In Greek dramatic poetry, odes consisting of three parts, the *strophe*, the *antistrophe*, and the *epode*, were sung by the chorus between the episodes of the play. *See* Strophe.

Off Rhyme *See* Near Rhyme.

Omniscient Point of View *See* Point of View.

Onomatopoeia Language that sounds like what it means. Words like *buzz, bark,* and *hiss* are onomatopoetic. Also, sound patterns that reinforce the meaning may be designated onomatopoetic. Alexander Pope illustrates such onomatopoeia in a passage from "An Essay on Criticism" (p. 788):

> 'Tis not enough no harshness gives offense,
> The sound must seem an echo to the sense:
> Soft is the strain when Zephyr gently blows,
> And the smooth stream in smoother numbers flows;
> But when loud surges lash the sounding shore,
> The hoarse, rough verse should like the torrent roar:
> When Ajax strives some rock's vast weight to throw,
> The line too labors, and the words move slow;
> Not so, when swift Camilla scours the plain,
> Flies o'er th'unbending corn, and skims along the main.

Opposite Statement   *See* Irony.

Ottava Rima   An eight-line, iambic pentameter stanza rhymed *ababab̄cc*. Originating with the Italian poet Boccaccio, the form was made popular in English poetry by Milton, Keats, and Byron, among others.

Oxymoron   Literally, "acutely silly." A figure of speech in which contradictory ideas are combined to create a condensed paradox: *thunderous silence, sweet sorrow, wise fool.*

Paean   In classical Greek drama, a hymn of praise, usually honoring Apollo. Now, any lyric that joyously celebrates its subject.

Paradox   A statement that seems self-contradictory or absurd but is, somehow, valid. The conclusion of Donne's "Death, Be Not Proud" (p. 673) illustrates: "One short sleep past, we wake eternally / And death shall be no more; Death, thou shalt die." In Holy Sonnet 14, Donne, speaking of his relationship with God, writes: "Take me to You, imprison me, for I, / Except You enthrall me, never shall be free, / Nor ever chaste, except You ravish me."

Pastoral   *Pastor* is Latin for "shepherd," and the pastoral is a poetic form invented by ancient Roman writers that deals with the complexities of the human condition as if they exist in a world peopled by idealized rustic shepherds. Pastoral poetry suggests that country life is superior to urban life. In the hands of such English poets as Marlowe and Milton, the pastoral embodies highly conventionalized and artificial language and situations. Christopher Marlowe's "The Passionate Shepherd to His Love" (436) is a famous example, as is Sir Walter Ralegh's mocking response, "The Nymph's Reply to the Shepherd" (437).

Pentameter   A line containing five metrical feet. *See* Meter.

Persona   Literally, "actor's mask." The term is applied to a first-person narrator in fiction or poetry. The persona's views may differ from the author's.

Personification   The attribution of human qualities to nonhuman things, such as animals, aspects of nature, or even ideas and processes. When Donne exclaims in "Death, Be Not Proud" (p. 673), "Death, thou shalt die," he uses personification, as does Edmund Waller when the persona of "Go, Lovely Rose!" (p. 443) says:

> Go, lovely rose!
> Tell her that wastes her time and me
>   That now she knows,
> When I resemble her to thee,
> How sweet and fair she seems to be.

Petrarchan Sonnet   Also called *Italian sonnet. See* Sonnet.

Plot   A series of actions in a story or drama that bear a significant relationship to each other. E. M. Forster illuminates the definition: " 'The King died, and then the Queen died,' is a story. 'The King died, and then the Queen died of grief,' is a plot."

Poetic License   Variation from standard word order to satisfy the demands of rhyme and meter.

• Point of View   The person or intelligence a writer of fiction creates to tell the story to the reader. The major techniques are:

First person, where the story is told by someone, often, though not necessarily, the principal character, who identifies himself or herself as "I" (as in James Joyce's "Araby") (p. 30).

Third person, where the story is told by someone (not identified as "I") who is not a participant in the action and who refers to the characters by name or as "he," "she," and "they" (as in Harlan Ellison's " 'Repent, Harlequin!' Said the Ticktockman") (p. 238).

Omniscient, a variation on the third person, where the narrator knows everything about the characters and events, can move about in time and place as well as from character to character at will, and can, whenever he or she wishes, enter the mind of any character as in Tolstoy's "The Death of Iván Ilých") (p. 589).

Central intelligence, another variation on the third person, where narrative elements are limited to what a single character sees, thinks, and hears.

Prosody   The study of the various elements that contribute to the *poetic* qualities of a verse, such as *rhyme, meter, stanza,* and so on.

Protagonist   Originally, the first actor in a Greek drama. In Greek, *agon* means "contest." Hence, the protagonist is the hero, the main character in a narrative, in conflict either with his or her situation or with another character. *See* Antagonist

Quatrain   A four-line stanza.

Refrain   The repetition within a poem of a group of words, often at the end of ballad stanzas.

Rhyme   The repetition of the final stressed vowel sound and any sounds following (*cat, rat; debate, relate; pelican, belly can*) produces perfect rhyme. When the last stressed syllable rhymes, the rhyme is called masculine (*cat, rat*). Two-syllable rhymes with unstressed last syllables are called feminine (*ending, bending*). When rhyming words appear at the end of lines, the poem is *end-rhymed*. When rhyming words appear within one line, the line contains *internal rhyme*. When the correspondence in sounds is imperfect (*heaven, given; began, gun*) *off rhyme, slant rhyme,* or *near rhyme* is produced.

Rhythm   The quality created by the relationship between stressed and unstressed syllables. A regular pattern of alternation between stressed and unstressed syllables produces *meter*. Irregular alternation of stressed and unstressed syllables produces *free verse*. Compare the rhythm of the following verses from Robert Frost's "Stopping by Woods on a Snowy Evening" (p. 686) and Walt Whitman's "Out of the Cradle Endlessly Rocking" (p. 76):

Whose woods these are I think I know.
His house is in the village though;
He will not see me stopping here
To watch his woods fill up with snow.

> Out of the cradle endlessly rocking,
> Out of the mocking-bird's throat, the musical shuttle,
> Out of the Ninth-month midnight,
> Over the sterile sands and the fields beyond, where the child leaving his bed
>   wander'd alone, bareheaded, barefoot,
> Down from the shower'd halo,

Run-on Line   *See* End-stopped Line.

Satire   Writing in a comic mode that holds a subject up to scorn and ridicule, often with the purpose of correcting human vice and folly. Harlan Ellison's " 'Repent Harlequin!' Said the Ticktockman" (p. 238) satirizes a society obsessed with time and order.

Scansion   The analysis of patterns of stressed and unstressed syllables in order to establish the metrical or rhythmical pattern of a poem.

Sestet   The six-line resolution of a Petrarchan sonnet. *See* Sonnet.

Setting   The place where a story occurs. Often the setting contributes significantly to the story; for example, the radiance of Munich in Thomas Mann's "Gladius Dei" (p. 207) highlights the gloom of the religious zealot Hieronymus.

Shakespearean Sonnet   Also called *English sonnet*. *See* Sonnet.

Simile   Similar to metaphor, the simile is a comparison of unlike things introduced by the words *like* or *as*. Robert Burns, in "A Red, Red Rose" (p. 445) for example, exclaims, "O My Luve's like a red, red rose," and Shakespeare mocks extravagant similes when he admits in Sonnet 130, "My mistress' eyes are nothing like the sun" (p. 440).

Slant Rhyme   *See* Rhyme.

Soliloquy   A dramatic convention in which an actor, alone on the stage, speaks his or her thoughts aloud. Iago's speech that closes Act I of Shakespeare's *Othello* (p. 475) is a soliloquy, as is Othello's speech in Act III, Scene 3, lines 258–78.

Sonnet   A lyric poem of fourteen lines, usually of iambic pentameter. The two major types are the Petrarchan (or Italian) and Shakespearean (or English). The Petrarchan sonnet is divided into an octave (the first eight lines, rhymed *abbaabba*) and sestet (the final six lines, usually rhymed *cdecde* or *cdcdcd*). The Shakespearean sonnet consists of three quatrains and a concluding couplet, rhymed *abab cdcd efef gg*. In general, the sonnet establishes some issue in the octave or three quatrains and then resolves it in the sestet or final couplet. Robert Frost's "Design" (p. 686) is an Italian sonnet; several Shakespearean sonnets appear in the text.

Spondee   A metrical foot consisting of two stressed syllables, usually a variation within a metrical line. *See* Meter.

Stanza   The grouping of a fixed number of verse lines in a recurring metrical and rhyme pattern. Keats's "Ode on a Grecian Urn," (p. 675) for example, employs ten-line stanzas rhymed *ababcdecde*.

Stream of Consciousness   The narrative technique that attempts to reproduce the full and uninterrupted flow of a character's mental process, in which ideas, memories, and sense impressions may intermingle without logical transitions (as in Katherine Anne Porter's "The Jilting of Granny Weatherall," p. 631). Writers using this technique sometimes abandon conventional rules of syntax and punctuation.

Strophe   In Greek tragedy, the unit of verse the chorus chanted as it moved to the left in a dance rhythm. The chorus sang the *antistrophe* as it moved to the right and the *epode* while standing still.

Style   The way an author expresses his or her matter. Style embodies, and depends upon, all the choices an author makes—the diction, syntax, figurative language, and sound patterns of the piece.

Subplot   A second plot, usually involving minor characters. The subplot is subordinate to the principal plot, but often is resolved by events that figure in the main plot. For example, Iago's manipulation of Roderigo in Shakespeare's *Othello* (p. 475) is a subplot that enters the main plot and figures prominently in the play's climax.

Symbol   An object, an action, or a person that represents more than itself. In Stephen Crane's "The Bride Comes to Yellow Sky" (p. 21), Scratchy represents the old mythic West made obsolete by the encroachment of eastern values. The entire action of Nathaniel Hawthorne's "My Kinsman, Major Molineux" (p. 7) symbolizes Robin's transition from innocent childhood to adult maturity. The urn in Keats's "Ode on a Grecian Urn" (p. 675) symbolizes the cold immortality of art. In all these, the symbolism arises from the *context*. *Public* symbols, in contrast to these *contextual* symbols, are objects, actions, or persons that history, myth, or legend has invested with meaning—the cross, Helen of Troy, a national flag.

Synecdoche   A figure of speech in which a part is used to signify the whole. In "Elegy Written in a Country Churchyard," Gray writes of "Some heart once pregnant with celestial fire; / Hands that the rod of empire might have swayed." That heart, and those hands, of course, refer to whole persons who are figuratively represented by significant parts.

Synesthesia   An image that uses a second sensory impression to modify the primary sense impression. When one speaks of a "cool green," for example, the primary *visual* evocation of green is combined with the *tactile* sensation of coolness. Keats, in "Ode to a Nightingale," asks for a drink of wine "Tasting of Flora and the country green, / Dance, and Provençal song, and sunburnt mirth!" Here, the *taste* of wine is synesthetically extended to the sight of flowers and meadows, the movement of dance, the sound of song, and the heat of the sun.

Tetrameter   A verse line containing four metrical feet. *See* Meter.

Theme   The abstract moral proposition that a literary work advances through the concrete elements of character, action, and setting. The theme of Harlan Ellison's " 'Repent Harlequin!' Said the Ticktockman" (p. 238), in which an ordinary person defies an oppressive system, might be that to struggle against dehumanizing authority is obligatory.

Third-person Narrator   A voice telling a story that refers to characters by name or as "he," "she," "they." *See* Point of View.

Tone   The attitude embodied in the language a writer chooses. The tone of a work might be sad, joyful, ironic, solemn, playful. Compare, for example, the somber tone of Matthew Arnold's "Dover Beach" (p. 446) with the comic tone of Anthony Hecht's "The Dover Bitch" (p. 460).

Tragedy   The dramatic representation of serious and important actions that culminate in catastrophe for the protagonist, or chief actor, in the play. Aristotle saw tragedy as the fall of a noble figure from a high position and happiness to defeat and misery as a result of *hamartia*, some misjudgment or frailty of character. *Compare* Comedy.

Trimeter   A verse line consisting of three metrical feet. *See* Meter.

Triplet   A sequence of three verse lines that rhyme.

Trochee   A metrical foot consisting of a stressed syllable followed by an unstressed syllable. *See* Meter.

Understatement   A figure of speech that represents something as less important than it really is, hence, a form of irony. When in Robert Browning's "My Last Duchess" (p. 74) the duke asserts ". . . This grew; I gave commands; / Then all smiles stopped together . . . ," the words ironically understate what was likely an order for his wife's execution.

Villanelle   A French verse form of nineteen lines (of any length) divided into six stanzas—five tercets and a final quatrain—employing two rhymes and two refrains. The refrains consist of lines one (repeated as lines six, twelve, and eighteen) and three (repeated as lines nine, fifteen, and nineteen). Dylan Thomas's "Do Not Go Gentle into That Good Night" (p. 697) and Catherine Davis's response "After a Time" (p. 701) are villanelles.

Acknowledgments   (continued from p. iv)

JOAN DAVES: "My Oedipus Complex" by Frank O'Connor. From *Collected Stories* by Frank O'Connor. Reprinted with permission of Joan Daves Agency as indicated by Alfred A. Knopf, Inc. who control U.S. rights to this material.

CATHERINE DAVIS: "After a Time" by Catherine Davis. Reprinted by permission of the author.

DOUBLEDAY: "My Papa's Waltz" copyright 1942 by Hearst Magazines, Inc. "Elegy for Jane" and "I Knew a Woman" copyright 1950, 1954 by Theodore Roethke. From *The Collected Poems of Theodore Roethke*. Reprinted by permission of Doubleday, a division of Bantam, Doubleday, Dell Publishing Group, Inc.

THE ECCO PRESS: "Metamorphosis" by Louise Glück. Copyright © 1985 by Louise Glück from *The Triumph of Achilles*, first published by The Ecco Press in 1985. Reprinted by permission.

FABER AND FABER LIMITED: "In Memory of W. B. Yeats," "That Night When Joy Began," "The Unknown Citizen" and "Musée des Beaux Arts" by W. H. Auden. Reprinted by permission of Faber and Faber Ltd. from *Collected Poems* by W. H. Auden.

"The Love Song of J. Alfred Prufrock" by T. S. Eliot. Reprinted by permission of Faber and Faber Ltd. from *Collected Poems 1909–1962* by T. S. Eliot.

"Relic" by Ted Hughes. Reprinted by permission of Faber and Faber Ltd. from *Lupercal* by Ted Hughes.

"Crow's First Lesson" by Ted Hughes. Reprinted by permission of Faber and Faber Ltd. from *Crow* by Ted Hughes.

FABBRI, BOMPAIANI: "The Chase" by Alberto Moravia. From *Command and I Will Obey You*. English translation copyright © 1969 by Martin Secker and Warburg Limited. Reprinted by permission of Gruppo Editoriale, Fabbri, Bompaiani, Sonzongno, ETAS S.P.A.

FARRAR, STRAUS AND GIROUX, INC.: "One Art" from *The Complete Poems*, 1927–1979 by Elizabeth Bishop. Copyright © 1976 by Elizabeth Bishop. Copyright © 1979, 1983 by Alice Helen Methfessel. Reprinted by permission of Farrar, Straus and Giroux, Inc.

"The Dream" from *The Blue Estuaries* by Louise Bogan. Copyright © 1938, 1968 by Louise Bogan. Reprinted by permission of Farrar, Straus and Giroux, Inc.

"Marrying Absurd" from *Slouching Towards Bethlehem* by Joan Didion. Copyright © 1967, 1968 by Joan Didion. Reprinted by permission of Farrar, Straus and Giroux, Inc.

"The Death of the Ball Turret Gunner" from *The Complete Poems* by Randall Jarrell. Copyright © 1945 by Mrs. Randall Jarrell. Renewal copyright © 1972 by Mrs. Randall Jarrell. Reprinted by permission of Farrar, Straus and Giroux, Inc.

"Idiots First" from *Idiots First* by Bernard Malamud. Copyright © 1961, 1963 by Bernard Malamud. Reprinted by permission of Farrar, Straus and Giroux, Inc.

THE UNIVERSITY OF GEORGIA PRESS: "First Confession" and "Ars Poetica" by X. J. Kennedy. Reprinted from *Cross Ties*, © 1985 X. J. Kennedy. Reprinted by permission of the University of Georgia Press.

G. K. HALL & CO.: "If We Must Die" by Claude McKay. Copyright 1981 and reprinted by permission of Twayne Publishers, a division of G. K. Hall & Co., Boston.

RENEE WAYNE GOLDEN: "The American Way of Death" by Jessica Mitford. Copyright © 1988 by Jessica Mitford. Reprinted by permission of the author.

GRM ASSOCIATES: "Incident" by Countee Cullen. Reprinted by permission of GRM Associates, agents for the Estate of Ida M. Cullen. From the book *On These I Stand* by Countee Cullen. Copyright © 1925 by Harper & Brothers; copyright renewed 1953 by Ida M. Cullen.

MICHAEL HAMBURGER: "A Poet's Progress" by Michael Hamburger from *Collected Poems*, Carcanet Press, Manchester & New York, 1984. 1985, 1988. Reprinted by permission of the author.

HARCOURT BRACE JOVANOVICH: "The Love Song of J. Alfred Prufrock" from *Collected Poems 1909–1962* by T. S. Eliot, copyright 1936 by Harcourt Brace Jovanovich, Inc.; copyright © 1963, 1964 by T. S. Eliot. Reprinted by permission of the publisher.

"Good Country People" from *A Good Man is Hard to Find and Other Stories*, copyright 1955 by Flannery O'Connor and renewed 1983 by Regina O'Connor, reprinted by permission of Harcourt Brace Jovanovich, Inc.

"The Jilting of Granny Weatherall" copyright 1930, 1958 by Katherine Anne Porter, reprinted from her volume *Flowering Judas and Other Stories* by permission of Harcourt Brace Jovanovich, Inc.

The Antigone of Sophocles: An English Version by Dudley Fitts and Robert Fitzgerald, copyright 1939 by Harcourt Brace Jovanovich, Inc. 1967 by Dudley Fitts and Robert Fitzgerald, reprinted by permission of the publisher.

Caution: All rights, including professional, amateur, motion picture, recitation, lecturing, public reading, and radio broadcasting, and television are strictly reserved. Inquiries on all rights should be addressed to Harcourt Brace Jovanovich, Inc.

E. M. Forster, "My Wood" from *Abinger Harvest*, copyright 1936, 1964 by Edward Morgan Foster. Reprinted by permission of Harcourt Brace Jovanovich, Inc.

Virginia Woolf, "What If Shakespeare Had Had a Sister?" from *A Room of One's Own* by Virginia Woolf, copyright 1929 by Harcourt Brace Jovanovich, Inc.; renewed 1957 by Leonard Woolf. Reprinted by permission of the publisher.

The Oedipux Rex of Sophocles: An English Version by Dudley Fitts and Robert Fitzgerald, copyright 1949 by Harcourt Brace Jovanovich, Inc. and renewed 1977 by Cornelia Fitts and Robert Fitzgerald, reprinted by permission of the publisher.

Caution: All rights, including professional, amateur, motion picture, recitation, lecturing, public reading, radio broadcasting, and television are strictly reserved. Inquiries on all rights should be addressed to Harcourt Brace Jovanovich, Inc.

"Everyday Use," copyright 1973 by Alice Walker, reprinted from her volume *In Love & Trouble* by permission of Harcourt Brace Jovanovich, Inc.

"A Late Aubade," copyright © 1968 by Richard Wilbur, reprinted from his volume *Walking to Sleep* by permission of Harcourt Brace Jovanovich, Inc.

"The Pardon" from *Ceremony and Other Poems*, copyright 1950, 1978 by Richard Wilbur, reprinted by permission of Harcourt Brace Jovanovich, Inc.

"The Writer," copyright © 1975 by Richard Wilbur, reprinted from his volume *The Mind Reader* by permission of Harcourt Brace Jovanovich, Inc.

HARPER & ROW: "The Colonel" copyright © 1982 by Carolyn Forche from *The Country Between Us* by Carolyn Forche.

"Crow's First Lesson" copyright © 1982 by Ted Hughes from *New Selected Poems* by Ted Hughes.

"Shiloh" from *Shiloh and Other Stories* by Bobbie Ann Mason. Copyright © 1982 by Bobbie Ann Mason. Reprinted by permission of Harper & Row, Publishers, Inc.

"The Second Tree from the Corner" copyright 1947 by E. B. White from *The Second Tree from the Corner* by E. B. White.

Martin Luther King, Jr., "Letter from Birmingham Jail, April 16, 1963" from *Why We Can't Wait* by Martin Luther King, Jr. Copyright © 1963 by Martin Luther King, Jr. Reprinted by permission of Harper & Row, Publishers, Inc.

HARVARD UNIVERSITY PRESS: Poems no. 465, "I Heard a Fly Buzz"; no. 1509, "Mine Enemy Is Growing Old"; no. 341, "After Great Pain"; no. 435, "Much Madness"; no. 280, "I Felt a Funeral"; no. 401, "What Soft—Cherubic Creatures"; no. 162, "Apparently with No Surprise," by Emily Dickinson. Reprinted by permission of the Publishers and the Trustees of Amherst College from *The Poems of Emily Dickinson*, edited by Thomas H. Johnson, Cambridge, Mass.: The Belknap Press of Harvard University Press, Copyright 1951, © 1955, 1979, 1983 by the President and Fellows of Harvard College.

A. M. HEATH: "Shooting an Elephant" by George Orwell. Copyright © 1950 by Sonia Brownell Orwell, renewed 1978 by Sonia Pitt-Rivers. Reprinted by permission of A. M. Heath.

DAVID HIGHAM ASSOCIATES LIMITED: "Fern Hill" and "Do Not Go Gentle into that Good Night" by Dylan Thomas from *The Poems*, published by J M Dent. Reprinted by permission of David Higham Associates Limited.

HENRY HOLT AND COMPANY, INC.: "After Apple-Picking"; "Birches"; "Provide, Provide"; "The Silken Tent"; "Fire and Ice"; "Departmental"; "Design"; "Stopping by Woods on a Snowy Evening," by Robert Frost. From *The Poetry of Robert Frost* edited by Edward Connery Lathem. Copyright © 1916, 1923, 1930, 1939, 1969 by Holt, Rinehart and Winston, Inc. Copyright © 1936, 1944, 1951, 1958 by Robert Frost. Copyright © 1964, 1967 by Lesley Frost Ballantine. Reprinted by permission of Henry Holt and Company, Inc.

"When I Was One-and-Twenty," "To an Athlete Dying Young," and "Terence, This Is Stupid Stuff" by A. E. Housman. Reprinted from "A Shropshire Lad"—Authorised Edition—from the *The Collected Poems of A. E. Housman*. Copyright © 1967 by Robert E. Symons. Reprinted by permission of Henry Holt and Company, Inc.

VIRGINIA KIDD AGENCY: "The Ones Who Walk Away from Omelas" by Ursula K. Le Guin; first appeared in *New Dimensions 3*; reprinted by permission of the author and the author's agent.

THE KILIMANJARO CORPORATION: " 'Repent, Harlequin!' Said the Ticktockman" by Harlan Ellison. Copyright © 1966 by Harlan Ellison. Reprinted by arrangement with, and permission of, the Author and the Author's agent, Richard Curtis Associates, Inc., New York. All rights reserved.

STEPHEN KING: "Why We Crave Horror Movies" by Stephen King; first appeared in *Playboy* 12/81. Copyright © 1981, 1988 by Stephen King. Reprinted by permission of the author.

ALFRED A. KNOPF, INC.: *Steambath* by Bruce Jay Friedman. Copyright © 1971 by Bruce Jay Friedman. Reprinted by permission of Alfred A. Knopf, Inc.

"Harlem" by Langston Hughes. Copyright 1951 by Langston Hughes. Reprinted from *Selected Poems of Langston Hughes*, by permission of Alfred A. Knopf, Inc.

"Gladius Dei" by Thomas Mann. Copyright 1936 and renewed 1964 by Alfred A. Knopf, Inc. Reprinted from *Stories of Three Decades*, by Thomas Mann, by permission of Alfred A. Knopf, Inc.

"My Oedipus Complex" by Frank O'Connor. Copyright 1950 by Frank O'Connor. Reprinted from *Collected*

NEW DIRECTIONS PUBLISHING CORPORATION: "Constantly Risking Absurdity" and "In Goya's Greatest Scenes" by Lawrence Ferlinghetti. Lawrence Ferlinghetti, *A Coney Island of the Mind*. Copyright © 1958 by Lawrence Ferlinghetti. Reprinted by permission of New Directions Publishing Corporation.

"The Mutes" by Denise Levertov. Denise Levertov, *Poems 1960–1967*. Copyright © 1964, 1966 by Denise Levertov Goodman. Reprinted by permission of New Directions Publishing Corporation.

"Thinking About El Salvador" and "Watching 'Dark Circle' " by Denise Levertov. Denise Levertov. *Oblique Prayers*. Copyright © 1984 by Denise Levertov. Reprinted by permission of New Directions Publishing Corporation.

"Patriotism" by Yukio Mishima. Yukio Mishima, *Death in Midsummer*. Copyright © 1966 by New Directions Publishing Corporation. Reprinted by permission of New Directions Publishing Corporation.

"To Carry the Child" by Stevie Smith. Stevie Smith, *Collected Poems*. Copyright © 1972 by Stevie Smith. Reprinted by permission of New Directions Publishing Corporation.

"Fern Hill" and "Do not go gentle into that good night" by Dylan Thomas. Dylan Thomas, *The Poems of Dylan Thomas*. Copyright 1946 by New Directions Publishing Corporation; 1952 by Dylan Thomas. Reprinted by permission of New Directions Publishing Corporation.

"Tract" by William Carlos Williams. William Carlos Williams, *Collected Poems, Volume I: 1909-1939*. Copyright 1938 by New Directions Publishing Corporation. Reprinted by permission of New Directions Publishing Corporation.

UNIVERSITY PRESS OF NEW ENGLAND: "Pitcher" by Robert Francis; from *The Orb Weaver*. Copyright © 1960 by Robert Francis. Reprinted by permission of Wesleyan University Press and University Press of New England.

THE NEW YORKER: "Curiosity" by Alastair Reid. From *Weathering* (Dutton). © 1959 Alastair Reid. Originally in *The New Yorker*.

THE NEW YORK TIMES: "A Plea for the Chimps" by Jane Goodall, May 17, 1987. (Mag) Copyright © 1987 by The New York Times Company. Reprinted by permission of The New York Times.

W. W. NORTON & COMPANY, INC.: "Hanging Fire" is reprinted from *The Black Unicorn*. Poems by Audre Lorde, by permission of W. W. Norton & Company, Inc. Copyright © 1978 by Audre Lorde.

"The Middle-aged" and "Living in Sin" are reprinted from *The Fact of a Doorframe, Poems Selected and New, 1950-1984*, by Adrienne Rich, by permission of W. W. Norton & Company, Inc. Copyright © 1984 by Adrienne Rich. Copyright © 1975, 1978 by W. W. Norton & Company, Inc. Copyright © 1981 by Adrienne Rich.

HAROLD OBER ASSOCIATES: "Same in Blues" from *Montage of a Dream Deferred* by Langston Hughes. Reprinted by permission of Harold Ober Associates Incorporated. Copyright 1951 by Langston Hughes. Copyright renewed 1979 by George Houston Bass.

OXFORD UNIVERSITY PRESS: "The Death of Iván Ilých" is reprinted from *The Death of Iván Ilých and Other Stories* by Leo Tolstoy translated by Louise and Aylmer Maude (1935) by permission of Oxford University Press.

OXFORD UNIVERSITY PRESS, INC.: "Tilth" by Robert Graves. From *Collected Poems 1975* by Robert Graves. Copyright © 1975 by Robert Graves. Reprinted by permission of Oxford University Press, Inc.

PENGUIN BOOKS LTD.: "People" from *Selected Poems of Yevgeny Yevtushenko* translated by Robin Milner-Gulland and Peter Levi (Penguin Modern European Poets, 1962), copyright © Robin Milner-Gulland and Peter Levi, 1962.

PENGUIN USA: "The Intruder" from *The Aleph And Other Stories* by Jorge Luis Borges, translated by Norman Thomas di Giovanni, Translation copyright © 1968, 1969, 1970 by Emece Editores, S. A. and Norman Thomas di Giovanni. Used by permission of the publisher, Dutton, an imprint of New American Library, a division of Penguin Books USA Inc.

PETERS FRASER & DUNLOP: "Naming of Parts" from *A Map of Verona* by Henry Reed. Reprinted with permission of Peters Fraser & Dunlop Group Ltd.

"Come live with me and be my love" from *Collected Poems 1954*, by C. Day Lewis. Reprinted with permission of the Executors of the Estate of C. Day Lewis, the source, Peters Fraser & Dunlop, and Jonathon Cape as publishers.

UNIVERSITY OF PITTSBURGH PRESS: "The ABC of Aerobics" by Peter Meinke is reprinted frrom *Night Watch on the Chesapeake* by Peter Meinke by permission of the University of Pittsburgh Press © 1987 by Peter Meinke.

RANDOM HOUSE, INC.: "The Unknown Citizen" Copyright 1940 and renewed 1968 by W. H. Auden. Stanza II from "Five Songs" Copyright 1937 and renewed 1965 by W. H. Auden. "In Memory of W. B. Yeats" Copyright 1940 and renewed 1968 by W. H Auden. "Musée des Beaux Arts" Copyright 1940 and renewed 1968 by W. H. Auden. Reprinted from *W. H. Auden: Collected Poems*, edited by Edward Mendelson, by permission of Random House, Inc.

"The Lesson" from *Gorilla, My Love*, by Toni Cade Bambara. Copyright © 1972 by Toni Cade Bambara. Reprinted by permission of Random House, Inc.

"Today Is a Day of Great Joy" from *Snaps*, by Victor Hernández Cruz. Copyright © 1969 by Victor Hernández Cruz. Reprinted by permission of Random House, Inc.

"A Rose for Emily" by William Faulkner. Copyright 1930 and renewed 1958 by William Faulkner. Reprinted from *Collected Stories of William Faulkner*, by permission of Random House, Inc.

"Hurt Hawks" by Robinson Jeffers. Copyright 1928 and renewed 1956 by Robinson Jeffers. Reprinted from *The Selected Poetry of Robinson Jeffers*, by permission of Random House, Inc.

OTTO REINERT: "Othello" notes by Otto Reinert. Copyright 1964. Reprinted by permission of the author.

WILLIAM L. RUKEYSER: "Myth" by Muriel Rukeyser. Copyright by Muriel Rukeyser; reprinted by permission of William L. Rukeyser.

GRANT SANGER: "The Turbid Ebb and Flow of Misery" by Margaret Sanger. Reprinted by permission of Grant Sanger.

SCOTT, FORESMAN/LITTLE, BROWN: "A Doll's House" by Henrik Ibsen, translated by Otto Reinert. Copyright © 1977 by Otto Reinert. Reprinted from *Twenty-Three Plays: An Introductory Anthology*, edited by Otto Reinert and Peter Arnott, by permission of Scott, Foresman and Company.

ADAM SHAW: "The Girls in Their Summer Dresses" by Irwin Shaw. Reprinted with permission of Adam Shaw.

THE IRWIN SHAW LITERARY ESTATE: "The Girls in Their Summer Dresses" by Irwin Shaw. Reprinted by permission of The Irwin Shaw Literary Estate.

CHARLOTTE SHEEDY LITERARY AGENTS: "Power" by Audre Lorde. Reprinted with permission of Charlotte Sheedy Literary Agency.

LESLIE MARMON SILKO: "The Man to Send Rain Clouds" by Leslie Marmon Silko from *Storyteller*. Reprinted by permission of author.

SIMON & SCHUSTER, INC.: "To Room Nineteen" by Doris Lessing. From *A Man and Two Women* by Doris Lessing. Copyright © 1958, 1962, 1963 by Doris Lessing. Reprinted by permission of Simon & Schuster, Inc.

THE SOCIETY OF AUTHORS: "My Wood" from *Abinger Harvest* by E. M. Forster. Reprinted with the permission of King's College, Cambridge and The Society of Authors as the literary representatives of E. M. Forster Estate.

THE LITERARY ESTATE OF MAY SWENSON: "Women" by May Swenson. Copyright © 1968 by May Swenson and used with the permission of The Literary Estate of May Swenson.

ROSEMARY A. THURBER: "The Greatest Man in the World" by James Thurber. Copyright © 1935 James Thurber. Copyright © 1963 Helen W. Thurber and Rosemary A. Thurber. From *The Middle-Aged Man on The Flying Trapeze*, published by Harper & Row.

"Courtship Through the Ages" by James Thurber. Copyright © 1970 Helen Thurber and Rosemary A. Thurber. From *My World–and Welcome to It*, published by Harcourt Brace Jovanovich, Inc.

VANDERBILT UNIVERSITY PRESS: "From a Correct Address in a Suburb of a Major City" and "To a Child Born in Time of Small War" from *Seeds As They Fall* by Helen Sorrells. Reprinted by permission of Vanderbilt University Press.

VIKING PENGUIN INC.: "Araby," *Dubliners* by James Joyce. Copyright 1916 by B. W. Huebsch, Inc. Definitive Text Copyright © 1967 by the Estate of James Joyce. All rights reserved. Reprinted by permission of Viking Penguin, a division of Penguin Books USA, Inc.

Lewis Thomas, "The Iks" from *The Lives of a Cell* by Lewis Thomas. Copyright © 1973 by the Massachusetts Medical Society. Reprinted by permission of Viking Penguin Inc.

ROSMARIE WALDROP: "Confession to Settle a Curse" from *The Aggressive Ways of The Casual Stranger*, by Rosmarie Waldrop. Copyright (1972) by Rosmarie Waldrop. Reprinted by permission of the author.

WIESER AND WIESER: "The Conscientious Objector" by Karl Shapiro; from *Collected Poems: 1940–1978*. Reprinted by permission of Wieser and Wieser.

WYLIE, AITKEN & STONE: "The Sandman" by Donald Barthelme. Originally published in *The Atlantic*, included in *Sadness*. Copyright © 1979, 1971, 1972 by Donald Barthelme, reprinted with the permission of Wylie, Aitken & Stone.

PICTURE CREDITS

INNOCENCE AND EXPERIENCE *Part opener, p. 2: The Garden of Peaceful Arts (Allegory of the Court of Isabelle d'Este)*, c. 1530 by Lorenzo Costa. The Louvre, Paris. Photograph Bridgeman/Art Resource, NY. *Fiction, p. 6: Woman and Child on a Beach*, c. 1901 by Pablo Picasso. Private collection. Photograph, Bridgeman/Art Resource, NY. © 1989 ARS NY / SPADEM. *Poetry, p. 70: The Mysterious Rose Garden*, c. 1894–1895 by Aubrey Beardsley. Black ink over graphite on white paper, 224 × 125 mm. Courtesy of the Fogg Art Museum, Harvard

University. Bequest of Grenville L. Winthrop. *Drama, p. 106: The Merry-go-round*, 1916 by Mark Gertler, The Tate Gallery, London. Photograph, Art Resource, NY. *Essays, p. 150: Child in a Straw Hat*, 1886 by Mary Cassatt. National Gallery of Art, Washington; Collection of Mr. and Mrs. Paul Mellon.

CONFORMITY AND REBELLION *Part opener, p. 174: The Closing of Whittier Boulevard*, 1984 by Frank Romero. Photograph, © 1989 Douglas M. Parker Studio, Los Angeles, CA. *Fiction, p. 178: The Trial*, 1950 by Keith Vaughan. Worthing Museum and Art Gallery, England. *Poetry, p. 254: Eve and the Serpent*, 1989 by Robert Freeman. Oil on canvas, 60 × 46″. Courtesy of the June Kelly Gallery. *Drama, p. 290: Self Portrait*, c. 1900–1905 by Gwen John. National Portrait Gallery, London. *Essays, p. 348: The Accused*, 1886 by Odilon Redon. Charcoal, sheet: 21 × 14 ⅝″. Collection, The Museum of Modern Art, New York. Acquired through the Lillie P. Bliss Bequest.

LOVE AND HATE *Part opener, p. 388: Untitled.* c. 1770 by Buncho. Chuban color print, c. 9¾ × 7½″ (25 × 19 cm). From *Japanese Erotic Art* by Richard Illing. © 1978 John Calmann and King, Ltd., London. *Fiction, p. 392: A Husband Parting from His Wife and Child*, 1799 by William Blake. Pen and watercolor on paper, 11⅞ × 8⅞″. '64-110-3, Philadelphia Museum of Art: Given by Mrs. William T. Tonner. *Poetry, p. 434: Equestrian*, 1931 by Marc Chagall. Collection, Stedelijk Museum, Amsterdam. *Drama, p. 474: Judith and Her Maidservant with the Head of Holofernes*, c. 1625 by Artemisia Gentileschi. Oil on canvas, 72½ × 55¾″ (185.2 × 141.6 cm). © The Detroit Institute of the Arts, gift of Mr. Leslie H. Green. *Essays, p. 568: Grosse Heidelberger Liederhandschrift "Codex Manesse" fol 249ᵛ*. Universitätsbibliothek, Heidelberg.

THE PRESENCE OF DEATH *Part opener, p. 584: Pandora's Box, 1951* by Rene Magritte. Yale University Art Gallery, Gift of Dr. and Mrs. John A. Cook. *Fiction, p. 588: Funerary Head*, Ghana, Ashanti Tribe, 19th–20th century. The Metropolitan Museum of Art, The Michael C. Rockefeller Memorial Collection, Gift of Nelson A. Rockefeller, 1964. (1978.412.352) *Poetry, p. 668: Orderly Retreat*, 1943 by Philip Evergood. Oil, 40 × 25″. From the Carleton College Collection. Gift of the Encyclopedia Britannica. *p. 694: Landscape with the Fall of Icarus*, c. 1560 by Pieter Brueghel the Elder. Museum of Fine Arts, Brussels. Photograph, Art Resource, New York. *Drama, p. 711: Tombstones*, 1942 by Jacob Lawrence. Gouache, 29 × 20¾″. Collection of Whitney Museum of American Art. *Essays, p. 746: St. George and the Dragon*, late fifteen-century painting. Photograph, courtesy of the Bettmann Archive.

APPENDICES *Opening, p. 762: A Lady Writing*, c. 1665 by Jan Vermeer. National Gallery of Art, Washington, Gift of Harry Waldron Havemeyer and Horace Havemeyer, Jr., in memory of their father, Horace Havemeyer. *pp. 793–794: The Globe Theatre; Interior of the Globe Theatre in the days of Shakespeare; and a French theater during Molier's management*: Courtesy of the Bettmann Archive, Inc. *Interior of the Swan Theatre*, London: Courtesy of Culver Pictures. *The Greek theater at Epidaurus*: Courtesy of the Greek National Tourist Office.

Index of Authors and Titles